Principles of Enterprise Law

Major enterprises shape our lives in countless ways: big tech and 'surveillance media' that affect democratic debate; algorithms that influence online shopping; transport to work and home; energy and agriculture corporations that drive climate damage; and public services that provide our education, health, water and housing. The twentieth century experienced swings between private and public ownership, between capitalism and socialism, without any settled, principled outcome and without settling major questions of how enterprises should be financed, governed and the rights we have in them. This book's main questions 'are there principles of enterprise law', and, if they are missing, 'what principles of enterprise law should there be'?

Principles of Enterprise Law gives a functional account of the 'general' enterprise laws of companies, investment, labour, competition and insolvency, before moving into specific enterprises, from universities to the military. It is an original guide to our economic constitution and human rights.

Ewan McGaughey is a Reader at the School of Law, King's College, London, and a Research Associate at the Centre for Business Research, University of Cambridge. He has taught corporate law, insolvency law, contracts, property, labour law and economic regulation at UCL, the Paris and London School of Economics, and has worked as a visiting researcher at the University of California, Berkeley and the University of Sydney. He has also published *A Casebook on Labour Law* (2019) and is a volunteer advocate at the Free Representation Unit.

Law in Context

Since 1970, the Law in Context series has been at the forefront of a movement to broaden the study of law. The series is a vehicle for the publication of innovative monographs and texts that treat law and legal phenomena critically in their cultural, social, political, technological, environmental and economic contexts. A contextual approach involves treating legal subjects broadly, using materials from other humanities and social sciences, and from any other discipline that helps to explain the operation in practice of the particular legal field or legal phenomena under investigation. It is intended that this orientation is at once more stimulating and more revealing than the bare exposition of legal rules. The series includes original research monographs, coursebooks and textbooks that foreground contextual approaches and methods. The series includes and welcomes books on the study of law in all its contexts, including domestic legal systems, European and international law, transnational and global legal processes, and comparative law.

Books in the Series

Acosta: *The National versus the Foreigner in South America: 200 Years of Migration and Citizenship Law*
Ali: *Modern Challenges to Islamic Law*
Alyagon Darr: *Plausible Crime Stories: The Legal History of Sexual Offences in Mandate Palestine*
Anderson, Schum & Twining: *Analysis of Evidence, 2nd Edition*
Ashworth: *Sentencing and Criminal Justice, 6th Edition*
Barton & Douglas: *Law and Parenthood*
Baxi, McCrudden & Paliwala: *Law's Ethical, Global and Theoretical Contexts: Essays in Honour of William Twining*
Beecher-Monas: *Evaluating Scientific Evidence: An Interdisciplinary Framework for Intellectual Due Process*
Bell: *French Legal Cultures*

Bercusson: *European Labour Law, 2nd Edition*
Birkinshaw: *European Public Law*
Birkinshaw: *Freedom of Information: The Law, the Practice and the Ideal, 4th Edition*
Blick: *Electrified Democracy: The Internet and the United Kingdom Parliament in History*
Broderick & Ferri: *International and European Disability Law and Policy: Text, Cases and Materials*
Brownsword & Goodwin: *Law and the Technologies of the Twenty-First Century: Text and Materials*
Cane & Goudkamp: *Atiyah's Accidents, Compensation and the Law, 9th Edition*
Clarke: *Principles of Property Law*
Clarke & Kohler: *Property Law: Commentary and Materials*
Collins: *The Law of Contract, 4th Edition*
Collins, Ewing & McColgan: *Labour Law, 2nd Edition*
Cowan: *Housing Law and Policy*
Cranston: *Commercial Law from the Nineteenth Century: Law as Backcloth*
Cranston: *Legal Foundations of the Welfare State*
Darian-Smith: *Laws and Societies in Global Contexts: Contemporary Approaches*
Dauvergne: *Making People Illegal: What Globalisation Means for Immigration and Law*
David: *Kinship, Law and Politics: An Anatomy of Belonging*
Davies: *Perspectives on Labour Law, 2nd Edition*
Dembour: *Who Believes in Human Rights?: Reflections on the European Convention*
de Sousa Santos: *Toward a New Legal Common Sense: Law, Globalization, and Emancipation*
Diduck: *Law's Families*
Dupret: *Positive Law from the Muslim World*
Emon: *Jurisdictional Exceptionalisms: Islamic Law, International Law, and Parental Child Abduction*
Estella: *Legal Foundations of EU Economic Governance*
Fortin: *Children's Rights and the Developing Law, 3rd Edition*
Garnsey: *The Justice of Visual Art: Creative State-Building in Times of Political Transition*
Garton, Probert & Bean: *Moffat's Trusts Law: Text and Materials, 7th Edition*
Ghai & Woodman: *Practising Self-Government: A Comparative Study of Autonomous Regions*
Glover-Thomas: *Reconstructing Mental Health Law and Policy*
Gobert & Punch: *Rethinking Corporate Crime*
Goldman: *Globalisation and the Western Legal Tradition: Recurring Patterns of Law and Authority*
Haack: *Evidence Matters: Science, Proof, and Truth in the Law*
Harlow & Rawlings: *Law and Administration, 4th Edition*
Harris: *An Introduction to Law, 8th Edition*
Harris, Campbell & Halson: *Remedies in Contract and Tort, 2nd Edition*
Harvey: *Seeking Asylum in the UK: Problems and Prospects*
Herring: *Law and the Relational Self*
Hervey & McHale: *European Union Health Law: Themes and Implications*
Hervey & McHale: *Health Law and the European Union*

Holder & Lee: *Environmental Protection, Law and Policy: Text and Materials, 2nd Edition*
Jackson & Summers: *The Internationalisation of Criminal Evidence: Beyond the Common Law and Civil Law Traditions*
Kostakopoulou: *The Future Governance of Citizenship*
Kreiczer-Levy: *Destabilized Property: Property Law in the Sharing Economy*
Kubal: *Immigration and Refugee Law in Russia: Socio-Legal Perspectives*
Lewis: *Choice and the Legal Order: Rising above Politics*
Likosky: *Law, Infrastructure and Human Rights*
Likosky: *Transnational Legal Processes: Globalisation and Power Disparities*
Lixinski: *Legalized Identities*
Loughnan: *Self, Others and the State: Relations of Criminal Responsibility*
Lunney: *A History of Australian Tort Law 1901–1945: England's Obedient Servant?*
Maughan & Webb: *Lawyering Skills and the Legal Process, 2nd Edition*
McGlynn: *Families and the European Union: Law, Politics and Pluralism*
Mertens: *A Philosophical Introduction to Human Rights*
Moffat: *Trusts Law: Text and Materials*
Monti: *EC Competition Law*
Morgan: *Contract Law Minimalism: A Formalist Restatement of Commercial Contract Law*
Morgan & Yeung: *An Introduction to Law and Regulation: Text and Materials*
Nash: *British Islam and English Law: A Classical Pluralist Perspective*
Nicola & Davies: *EU Law Stories: Contextual and Critical Histories of European Jurisprudence*
Norrie: *Crime, Reason and History: A Critical Introduction to Criminal Law, 3rd Edition*
O'Dair: *Legal Ethics: Text and Materials*
Oliver: *Common Values and the Public–Private Divide*
Oliver & Drewry: *The Law and Parliament*
Palmer & Roberts: *Dispute Processes: ADR and the Primary Forms of Decision-Making, 1st Edition*
Palmer & Roberts: *Dispute Processes: ADR and the Primary Forms of Decision-Making, 3rd Edition*
Picciotto: *International Business Taxation*
Probert: *The Changing Legal Regulation of Cohabitation, 1600–2010: From Fornicators to Family, 1600–2010*
Radi: *Rules and Practices of International Investment Law and Arbitration*
Reed: *Internet Law: Text and Materials*
Richardson: *Law, Process and Custody*
Roberts & Palmer: *Dispute Processes: ADR and the Primary Forms of Decision-Making, 2nd Edition*
Rowbottom: *Democracy Distorted: Wealth, Influence and Democratic Politics*
Sauter: *Public Services in EU Law*
Scott & Black: *Cranston's Consumers and the Law*
Seneviratne: *Ombudsmen: Public Services and Administrative Justice*
Seppänen: *Ideological Conflict and the Rule of Law in Contemporary China: Useful Paradoxes*
Siems: *Comparative Law, 3rd Edition*

Stapleton: *Product Liability*
Stewart: *Gender, Law and Justice in a Global Market*
Tamanaha: *Law as a Means to an End: Threat to the Rule of Law*
Tuori: *Properties of Law: Modern Law and After*
Turpin & Tomkins: *British Government and the Constitution: Text and Materials, 7th Edition*
Twining: *General Jurisprudence: Understanding Law from a Global Perspective*
Twining: *Globalisation and Legal Theory*
Twining: *Human Rights, Southern Voices: Francis Deng, Abdullahi An-Na'im, Yash Ghai and Upendra Baxi*
Twining: *Jurist in Context: A Memoir*
Twining: *Karl Llewellyn and the Realist Movement, 2nd Edition*
Twining: *Rethinking Evidence: Exploratory Essays, 2nd Edition*
Twining & Miers: *How to Do Things with Rules, 5th Edition*
Wan: *Film and Constitutional Controversy*
Ward: *A Critical Introduction to European Law, 3rd Edition*
Ward: *Law, Text, Terror*
Ward: *Shakespeare and Legal Imagination*
Wells & Quick: *Lacey, Wells and Quick: Reconstructing Criminal Law: Text and Materials, 4th Edition*
Zander: *Cases and Materials on the English Legal System, 10th Edition*
Zander: *The Law-Making Process, 6th Edition*

International Journal of Law in Context: A Global Forum for Interdisciplinary Legal Studies

The *International Journal of Law in Context* is the companion journal to the Law in Context book series and provides a forum for interdisciplinary legal studies and offers intellectual space for ground-breaking critical research. It publishes contextual work about law and its relationship with other disciplines including but not limited to science, literature, humanities, philosophy, sociology, psychology, ethics, history and geography. More information about the journal and how to submit an article can be found at http://journals.cambridge.org/ijc

Principles of Enterprise Law

The Economic Constitution and Human Rights

EWAN MCGAUGHEY

School of Law, King's College London

Centre for Business Research, University of Cambridge

CAMBRIDGE
UNIVERSITY PRESS

CAMBRIDGE
UNIVERSITY PRESS

University Printing House, Cambridge CB2 8BS, United Kingdom

One Liberty Plaza, 20th Floor, New York, NY 10006, USA

477 Williamstown Road, Port Melbourne, VIC 3207, Australia

314–321, 3rd Floor, Plot 3, Splendor Forum, Jasola District Centre, New Delhi – 110025, India

103 Penang Road, #05–06/07, Visioncrest Commercial, Singapore 238467

Cambridge University Press is part of the University of Cambridge.

It furthers the University's mission by disseminating knowledge in the pursuit of education, learning, and research at the highest international levels of excellence.

www.cambridge.org
Information on this title: www.cambridge.org/9781316517642
DOI: 10.1017/9781009042802

First published 2022

A catalogue record for this publication is available from the British Library.

ISBN 978-1-316-51764-2 Hardback
ISBN 978-1-009-04573-5 Paperback

For Mum and Gavin

Brief Contents

Contents

Figures

Tables

Table of cases

UK cases

EU cases

ECHR cases

US cases

German cases

International cases

European Patent cases

UK statutes

US statutes

Statutory Instruments

EU sources

EU treaties

EU legislation

International and comparative sources

International instruments

International Labour Organization Instruments

Australian law

Dutch law

Italian law

New Zealand law

Russian law

South African law

Switzerland

Roman law

Babylonian law

Abbreviations

AG	Aktiengesellschaft
AHA	Agricultural Holdings Act
AMNT	Association of Member Nominated Trustees
ARPA	Advanced Research Projects Agency
AT&T	American Telephone & Telegraph Co.
ATA	Agricultural Tenancies Act
BA	British Airways
BEA	Bank of England Act
BTC	British Transport Commission
BV	Besloten Vennootschap
CA	2003 Communications Act 2003
CA	2006 Companies Act 2006
CAC	Central Arbitration Committee
CAP	Common Agricultural Policy
CAR	Current Annuity Rate
CAT	Competition Appeal Tribunal
CCG	Clinical Commissioning Group
CDDA	Company Directors Disqualification Act
CEARA	Consumers, Estate Agents and Redress Act
CEB	Central Electricity Board
CEGB	Central Electricity Generating Board
CFREU	Charter of Fundamental Rights of the European Union
CJEU	Court of Justice of the European Union
CMA	Competition and Markets Authority
CMAR	Companies (Model Articles) Regulations
CPA	Consumer Protection Act
CPI	Consumer Price Index
CQC	Care Quality Commission
CRA	Consumer Rights Act
DB	Defined Benefit
DBEIS	Department for Business, Energy and Industrial Strategy
DC	Defined Contribution
DCMS	Department of Digital, Culture, Media & Sport

DECC	Department of Energy and Climate Change
DfT	Department for Transport
DoJ	Department of Justice
DPA	Data Protection Act
DPR	Direct Payments Regulation
DUKES	Digest of United Kingdom Energy Statistics
DWP	Department for Work and Pensions
EA	Education Act
EAFRD	European Agricultural Fund for Rural Development
EAGF	European Agricultural Guarantee Fund
ECB	European Central Bank
ECHR	European Convention on Human Rights
EPA	Environmental Protection Agency
EPR	Environmental Permitting (England and Wales) Regulations
ERA	Employment Rights Act
ESA	Electricity (Supply) Act
EU	European Union
FAO	Food and Agriculture Organization
FCA	Financial Conduct Authority
FRC	Financial Reporting Council
FSMA	Financial Services and Markets Act
FTC	Federal Trade Commission
GAR	guaranteed annuity rates
GBER	General Block Exemption Regulation
GBR	Great British Railways
GDP	Gross Domestic Product
GDPR	General Data Protection Regulation
GEMA	Gas and Electricity Markets Authority
GLA	Greater London Authority
GLAA	Greater London Authority Act
GP	General Practitioner/General Practice
GPO	General Post Office
HA	Housing Act
HEGSA	Higher Education Governance (Scotland) Act
HERA	Higher Education and Research Act
HSCA	Health and Social Care Act
IA	Insolvency Act
IATA	International Air Transport Association
IB	International Baccalaureate
IBRD	International Bank for Reconstruction and Development
ICANN	Internet Corporation for Assigned Names and Numbers
ICB	Integrated Care Board
ICC	Interstate Commerce Commission
ICCPR	International Covenant on Civil and Political Rights

ICER	Information and Consultation of Employees Regulations
ICESCR	International Covenant on Economic, Social and Cultural Rights
ICO	Information Commissioner's Office
IEA	International Energy Agency
ILO	International Labour Organization
IMF	International Monetary Fund
IPCC	Intergovernmental Panel on Climate Change
IPO	initial public offering
IR	Implementation Regulation
ISP	Internet Service Provider
ISS	Information Society Service
ITU	International Telecommunication Union
LCCC	Low Carbon Contracts Company Ltd
LGOC	London General Omnibus Company
LLATLA	London Local Authorities and Transport for London Act
LSE	London School of Economics
Mbps	Megabits per Second
MHCLG	Ministry of Housing, Communities and Local Government
NHS	National Health Service
NICE	National Institute for Health and Care Excellence
NICs	National Insurance Contributions
NMWA	National Minimum Wage Act
NMWR	National Minimum Wage Regulations
NSA	National Security Agency
NTC	National Telephone Company
OCA	Office of Communications Act
ODPM	Office of the Deputy Prime Minister
OECD	Organisation for Economic Co-operation and Development
Ofcom	Office of Communications
Ofgem	Office of Gas and Electricity Markets
OfStu	Office for Students
OFT	Office of Fair Trading
OGA	Oil and Gas Authority
OIA	Office of the Independent Adjudicator
OMO	Open Market Operations
OPEC	Organization of Petroleum Exporting Countries
ORR	Office of Rail and Road
OS	Operating System
OTA	Oil Taxation Act
PA	Petroleum Act 1998
PCT	Primary Care Trust
PFI	Private Finance Initiative
PLD	Product Liability Directive
PMSC	Private Military Security Contractor

PPA	Petroleum (Production) Act
PPP	Public Private Partnerships
PRA	Prudential Regulation Authority
PSA	Postal Services Act
RED	Renewable Energy Directive
REIT	Real Estate Investment Trust
ROC	Renewable Obligation Certificate
RPI	Retail Price Index
RSC	Regional Schools Commissioner
SA	Société anonym
SEC	Securities and Exchange Commission
SFO	Serious Fraud Office
SMEs	Small and Medium-Sized Enterprises
SSCBA	Social Security Contributions and Benefits Act
TA	2000 Trustee Act 2000
TA	1984 Telecommunications Act 1984
TCPA	Town and Country Planning Act
TEU	Treaty on European Union
TFEU	Treaty on the Functioning of the European Union
TfL	Transport for London
TRIPS	Trade-Related Aspects of Intellectual Property Rights
TULRCA	Trade Union and Labour Relations (Consolidation) Act
UCITSD	Undertakings for Collective Investment in Transferable Securities Directive
UCTA	Unfair Contract Terms Act
UDHR	Universal Declaration of Human Rights
UKRI	UK Research and Innovation
UN	United Nations
UNESCO	United Nations Educational, Scientific and Cultural Organization
UTCCD	Unfair Terms in Consumer Contracts Directive
VAT	Value Added Tax
WFP	World Food Programme
WHO	World Health Organization
WIA	Water Industry Act
WTA	Wireless Telegraphy Act
WTD	Working Time Directive
WTO	World Trade Organization
WTR	Working Time Regulations

Introduction
What Is Enterprise Law?

Enterprise law is the regulation of the finance, governance and rights in economic life. It includes everything from global tech corporations, to universities, to oil cartels, to arms-makers, to the health service. Enterprise law is probably the dominant cause of the most basic threats that we must resolve in the twenty-first century, namely escalating inequality, climate damage and war, because the enterprise is the primary type of association that stands between polities and families. In its literal sense, enterprise means 'doing' or 'undertaking', after the French word *entreprende*. The ideas of the 'entrepreneur', the 'state-owned enterprise', the 'multinational enterprise' or the 'enterprise state', are powerful psychological and social concepts as well as legal ones, and they are constantly changing. However, across time and space, most enterprises fulfil three main functions. They:

(1) accumulate resources, particularly capital used for production:[1] a finance function
(2) coordinate production, especially by sharing voting power: a governance function
(3) distribute resources, such as goods, services, income or wealth: a rights function.

These three functions of enterprise – of finance, governance and rights – account for the incredible growth, welfare and prosperity of humankind since the Industrial Revolution. Modern enterprise, most often organised in corporations and by the state, gives us the ability to live a life of splendour and holds the promise of a future when poverty may be forgotten. Yet when out of balance, enterprise law also accounts for inhuman levels of squander, abuse of power and exploitation that we constantly witness. Enterprises may allocate resources for everyone's benefit, or they help hoard capital to enrich a few. They may organise efficient, dynamic business and public service, or be a vessel for abuse of power. They may deliver a good livelihood and all universal

[1] A. Smith, *An Inquiry into the Nature and Causes of the Wealth of Nations* (1776) Book II, ch. 1, distinguishing property used to make 'revenue' (i.e. capital) from property used for 'immediate consumption'. Also A. A. Berle, 'Property, Production and Revolution' (1965) 65 *Columbia L Rev* 1; H. Sinzheimer, *Grundzüge des Arbeitsrechts* (1926) ch. 2, 22–7.

human rights, or they may exploit us and evaporate our common wealth. The functions of enterprise law, in a very real sense, shape human destiny.

The notion that we have an 'enterprise law', or that we might even have *Principles of Enterprise Law*, depends upon shifting social views about what is important in life, and where we should place our efforts. Of course, there is no such thing as an *objective* idea of 'enterprise law' that we can reach out, touch and describe, any more than there is some objective concept of 'law' itself. All words have meaning from the context in which we use them,[2] not from some underlying atomic-like fact,[3] and different people can mean different things with the same words. As ideas spread, like language, they often seem to take on a life of their own, but always one in which everybody who thinks and discusses can take part.[4]

So, this book is about the most important enterprises that shape our lives or, as the subtitle says, *The Economic Constitution and Human Rights*. Probably the first time 'enterprise' was defined in law was in the US Fair Labor Standards Act of 1938, to say who is responsible for rights such as the minimum wage. An 'enterprise' was said to mean activities for a 'common business purpose ... whether performed in one or more establishments or by one or more corporate or other organizational units'.[5] Similarly, in the European Union (EU) General Data Protection Regulation 2016, an 'enterprise' means 'a natural or legal person engaged in an economic activity, irrespective of its legal form'.[6] The UK has passed various 'Enterprise Acts',[7] which include laws on competition, the public interest, insolvency, consumers, regulators, labour rights, education, company law, banking and equality, though none have felt the need to say what an 'enterprise' is. But make no mistake: enterprise law is almost entirely about corporations and states, and their use or abuse of power. The sheer scope of enterprise law is one of its challenges, and the fluidity of its concepts means it has lacked structure. This book's central goal is to answer this question: are there principles of enterprise law, ones that we can use in a practical way to understand our economic constitution today?[8]

This book is organised into four lopsided parts. Part I is history and theory. Throughout modern history, the notion of enterprise law has recurred in legal discourse. In 1947, the great New Deal architect, A. A. Berle wrote in 'The

[2] L. Wittgenstein, *Philosophical Investigations* (1953) §§23, 43, 199–203. Q. Skinner, *Visions of Politics* (2002) vol. I.

[3] E.g. B. Russell, 'The Philosophy of Logical Atomism' (1919) 29(3) *Monist* 345; L. Wittgenstein, *Tractatus Logico-Philosophicus* (1922); H. L. A. Hart, *The Concept of Law* (1961).

[4] Cf. O. Gierke, *The Social Role of Private Law* (1889) 4, trans. E. McGaughey (2018) 19(4) *German LJ* 1017.

[5] Fair Labor Standards Act of 1938, 29 USC, §203(r)(1).

[6] General Data Protection Regulation (EU) 2016/679, art. 4(18).

[7] E.g. Enterprise Act 2002; Companies (Audit, Investigations and Community Enterprise) Act 2004; Enterprise and Regulatory Reform Act 2013; Small Business, Enterprise and Employment Act 2015; Enterprise Act 2016. Also the Oil and Gas (Enterprise) Act 1982 and Enterprise and New Towns (Scotland) Act 1990.

[8] See Ch. 2(5) and this book's Conclusion.

Theory of Enterprise Entity' that legal forms, like the corporation, take their 'being from the reality of the underlying enterprise', and this was important because more 'often than not, a single large-scale business is conducted, not by a single corporation, but by a constellation of corporations controlled by a central holding'.[9] Berle's thinking reflected the norms of the Fair Labor Standards Act of 1938. Thinking of economic institutions laterally, beyond existing strictures of legal form, was and remains a crucial part of reforming competition, tax, accounting, tort and labour regulation. In 1988, writing in a similar tradition from Germany, Thomas Raiser, explained that 'the social purpose of [constitutional] rights and the principle of the social state are of utmost importance in enterprise law'. Nineteenth-century or pre-World War Two views of commercial or company law tended to exclude the public and employee interests, so enterprise law reflected a 'new macro-economic and legal environment' including 'anti-trust law', 'certain elements of central planning' or 'state-owned production and service enterprises (including banks)'. Enterprise law is 'aware of the fact that the governance of an enterprise includes the exercise of power, and therefore requires legal mechanisms for its control'.[10] In the UK, Simon Deakin has argued that to understand 'business enterprise or firm' behaviour, company law explains just a 'fraction' of reality. We must 'bring in insolvency law, employment law, tort law and, arguably competition and tax law, to get the full picture'.[11]

This is far from the first text on enterprise law,[12] but it adopts a new structure that will be familiar to contract lawyers: with the general and specific. After Part I on history and theory, Part II is 'General Enterprise Law'. Like the four edges of a pyramid, company and investment, labour, competition and insolvency law support most enterprises (see Figure 0.1). Chapter 3 explains the corporate constitution. Company law, at its heart, concerns 'member' rights against a company, its board of directors and reciprocal duties. Chapter 4 concerns shareholders and the real investors, usually beneficiaries of pension or other funds. Chapter 5 explores labour law and the relations of management, workers and unions. Chapter 6 concerns consumers and competition law. Chapter 7 covers rights of creditors near or after insolvency.

These general enterprise laws are basic building blocks of any modern economy, but they are often insufficient to protect the public interest. Part III examines 'Specific Enterprise Law', which aims for just this. Chapters 8–19

[9] A. A. Berle, 'The Theory of Enterprise Entity' (1947) 47(3) *Columbia L Rev* 343, 344.

[10] T. Raiser, 'The Theory of Enterprise Law in the Federal Republic of Germany' (1988) 36(1) *Am J Comp L* 111, 113–14. Also T. Raiser, *Das Unternehmen als Organisation* (1969).

[11] S. Deakin, 'The Corporation as Commons: Rethinking Property Rights, Governance and Sustainability in the Business Enterprise' (2012) 37(2) *Queen's LJ* 339, 365.

[12] E.g. P. T. Muchlinski, *Multinational Enterprises & the Law* (3rd ed. 2021); B. Means and J. W. Yockey (eds.), *The Cambridge Handbook of Social Enterprise Law* (2019); D. Milman (ed.), *Regulating Enterprise: Law and Business Organisation in the UK* (1999).

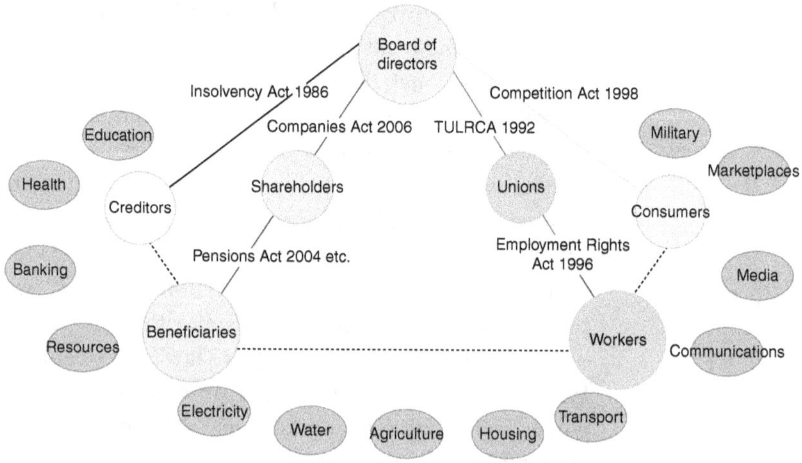

Figure 0.1 The pyramid of general enterprise law and specific enterprise law in the UK

cover the major enterprises in life: in education, health, banking, natural resources, electricity, food and water, housing, transport, communications, media, marketplaces and the military. These enterprises often start with the 'general enterprise law' basics, but specific regulation makes them unique. Think of a furniture shop, and then of a bank. Both are enterprises, but there are no special Furniture Shop Acts. We expect general enterprise law, especially on fair competition, to ensure furniture enterprises follow the consumer or public interest. Not so with banks, where the Bank of England Act 1946 makes the central bank publicly owned; the Bank of England Act 1998 controls monetary policy; the Financial Services and Markets Act 2000 subjects all private banks to licensing and standards; and the Banking Act 2009 created a special bank-bankruptcy system after the global bank crash. For similar reasons we have the Education Act 1996, National Health Service Act 2006, Petroleum Act 1998, Electricity Act 1989, Agriculture Act 2020, Water Act 1989, Housing Act 1985, Railways Act 1993, Communications Act 2003 and Armed Forces Act 2006, to name just a few, and not to mention the array of EU Directives or Regulations, and international treaties, Declarations, Covenants or Conventions that underpin our global economic constitution. Often, general enterprise law is enough to protect the public interest. But most of the time it is not, so we enact specific enterprise laws, and we do it (ideally) based on experience, data and reason.

What enterprises are not in this book? Aside from furniture shops (though they are indeed fascinating[13]) this book also leaves out many enterprises mostly regulated under the general law: manufactured goods, electronics,

[13] E.g. R. B. Handfield, S. V. Walton, L. K. Seegers and S. A. Melnyk, '"Green" Value Chain Practices in the Furniture Industry' (1998) 15(4) *J Operations Management* 293.

Table 0.1 FTSE and S&P 500 enterprise classifications

FTSE, ICB	Ch.	GISC	Ch.
Oil & gas	11	Oil & gas	11
Chemicals, Forestry, Mining	11	Chemicals, Mining, Forestry	11
Construction, industrials, transport	15	Industrials, transport	15
Auto, food, household goods	15, 13	Auto, consumer, retail	15
Healthcare	9	Consumer staples	13
Retail, media, leisure	17	Healthcare	9
Telecoms	16	Financials	10
Electricity, gas, water	12, 13	IT	16
Banks, insurance, real estate, finance	10, 14	Telecoms, media	17
Computers, software, Internet	17	Electricity, gas, water	12, 13
		Real estate	14

chemicals, restaurants and music, art and entertainment. Yet even in these instances, there are many specifics to be found, particularly in safety or environmental standards. Because of space, there are also no chapters on vitally important specific enterprises, including religious bodies, policing, sports clubs, pubs and breweries, and clothing.[14] However, looking at the standard classifications of industry used in the stock markets, this book succeeds in covering a majority of our economic constitution (see Table 0.1).[15]

Enterprise law is equally concerned with public services and human rights. Indeed, this book covers every major public service and economic and social right (see Ch. 2(4)).

Finally, private finance may work in some enterprises, but public finance proves better elsewhere. This book focuses on those where public finance has become an important part of the law, although it may not always be desirable. Part IV and Chapter 20 concentrates on fiscal and social policy, and takes a macro-legal and macro-economic perspective on enterprise finance, tax and spending, and how budgeting decisions are made. Ultimately this depends on the goals we choose as a polity and the theories of justice we seek to uphold.

***

A question underlying the whole book is whether 'enterprise law' can hold together. This meets a basic challenge from 'Chicago School' theories. In the words of Frank Easterbrook, our law 'courses should be limited to subjects that illuminate the entire law', and not include 'courses suited to dilettantes' like the 'law of the horse' or 'cyberspace'. We should only 'study general rules', such as

[14] These enterprises also engage universal human rights: UDHR 1948, arts. 2–3, 18 and 24–25. Chapters are possible additions for future years. The author has had several brilliant master's dissertations on these very topics.

[15] FTSE Russell, *Industry Classification Benchmark (Equity)* (February 2019) v2.6; S&P Global and MSCI, *Global Industry Classification Standard* (2018).

'property, torts, commercial transactions',[16] and even corporations should be seen as a contract that ideally avoids 'some form of public control'.[17] But if we must, the Chicago School thinking suggested that other legal subjects should be regarded as having singular purposes: corporate law was for shareholder profit,[18] labour law was for the individual employee, competition law or antitrust for the consumer[19] and insolvency law for the creditor.[20] Absent was any notion of the public interest, or social goals that might combine the interests of the individual investor, worker, consumer or creditor. Yet the majority of this book *is* made up of the so-called 'dilettantes' subjects, and it even includes laws of 'the horse' and 'cyberspace' (Chs. 15 and 16). A central thesis is that a coherent enterprise law does and can exist, and this is superior to the Chicago School thinking. Can that be right? Can enterprise law be a coherent subject?

There are at least four good reasons both to reject the Chicago School theses and be persuaded that enterprise law can be a coherent subject. First, it 'illuminates the entire law' to a far greater extent than systems of legal thinking which attempt to exclude public law from the dimensions of corporate, labour, competition or insolvency law. Doing that makes us less informed about the real world, not more, because in reality that legislation develops inseparably from a web of constitutional and administrative laws. Second, concentrating on 'specific enterprises' matches how modern government works – like, for instance, the departments or ministries that nearly every country sets up for education, health, finance, energy, agriculture, housing, transport, media or defence. Third, and better than debating whether a corporation is like a 'contract' or not, understanding the real world's context helps us to solve real world problems, particularly inequality, climate damage and war. It is fair to say that some people (and Chicago School authors may or may not be included in this) do not want to address these problems. This book is for those who do.

Fourth, enterprise law can have a coherent taxonomy: a grammar that may find common issues across seemingly disparate fields. After giving historical background, each chapter on specific enterprises follows the pattern of examining (1) finance, (2) governance and (3) rights of each stakeholder. As well as each fulfilling an important function (namely accumulating resources, coordinating production and distributing goods, services or wealth), each includes a mechanism of accountability, and this resembles Albert Hirschman's

[16] F. H. Easterbrook, 'Cyberspace and the Law of the Horse' [1996] *U Chicago L Forum* 207, 208.

[17] F. H. Easterbrook and D. R. Fischel, 'The Corporate Contract' (1989) 89(7) *Columbia L Rev* 1416.

[18] M. Friedman, 'The Social Responsibility of Business Is to Increase Its Profits', *New York Times* (13 September 1970).

[19] R. Bork, *The Antitrust Paradox: A Policy at War with Itself* (1978) 426–9.

[20] D. G. Baird and T. H. Jackson, 'Corporate Reorganizations and the Treatment of Diverse Ownership Interests: A Comment on Adequate Protection of Secured Creditors in Bankruptcy' (1984) 51(1) *U Chicago L Rev* 97.

distinctions between 'exit, voice and loyalty'.[21] 'Exit' is the language of economics, and here it is enlarged to how enterprises are financed, either through markets, prices, regulatory subsidies[22] or taxes. 'Voice' is the language of political science, and here this becomes a broader question of governance, centred upon the right to vote and participation in decisions. 'Loyalty' to Hirschman involved notions of belonging and social influence within organisations, familiar to sociologists, which here are broadened to rights of individuals within an enterprise. This is how human rights, such as to education, health, food, natural resouces, housing or other rights, are enforceable in court, beyond an enterprise's finance and governance. It has been remarked that 'judicial review always has a tendency to fragment into disparate branches of law' like education or housing but 'general principles have emerged'.[23] The same can be said for contract and corporate law principles, which routinely intermingle with administrative law as they each touch enterprise. The goal of a good taxonomy is to give a clear guide to understand a subject's anatomy. How is an enterprise financed? Who governs it? What rights do people have in it? These questions are the grammar and life of enterprise law.

If there is an enterprise law, which unifies our economic constitution, and it does have a conceptual structure, the question then becomes, what principles does it have? The thesis that this book puts forward is that principles of enterprise law, based on the public interest, can be found. Those principles may be contested. They are certainly not always fulfilled. But principles of enterprise law are there. This thesis is taken up at the end of Chapter 2, on theory; it underlies every other chapter and is returned to in the book's conclusion.

[21] A. O. Hirschman, *Exit, Voice and Loyalty* (1970).

[22] A 'regulatory subsidy' is one that exists where costs are externalised by an enterprise onto third parties, and the law fails to make those responsible pay: Ch. 2(2)(c), e.g. D. Coady, I. Parry, N.-P. Le and B. Shang, 'Global Fossil Fuel Subsidies Remain Large: An Update Based on Country-Level Estimates', IMF Working Paper No. 19/89 (May 2019).

[23] A. W. Bradley, K. D. Ewing and C. J. S. Knight, *Constitutional and Administrative Law* (2019) ch. 24, 641.

Part I
History and Theory

1

History: State and Corporate Power

Contents

The history of enterprise law, the evolution of state and corporate power, is essential to know in order to understand why our economic constitution is as we see it today. Why is enterprise financed by a mix of taxes, savings in the stock market or banks, prices and regulatory subsidies, but without any clear consensus on what should be public or privately owned? Why are the votes in our economy partially spread among investors, workers and the public, yet decisively influenced by asset managers and banks? Why are social, economic and political rights enshrined in international law, yet their realisation in national law is so uncertain? Why has enterprise law changed, and where should it go? History does not let us see into the future, but when we learn from the past, we understand our options better for deciding what to change. Change is both a dangerous and marvellous truth: like the serpent said to Eve, some people 'see things' as they are and 'say "Why?"' but we may also 'dream things that never were' and 'say "Why not?"'[1] Knowing our past fortifies our thinking and our imaginations.

Yet there is no shortage of attempts to shut down imagination. When the Iron Curtain fell, a political theorist named Francis Fukuyama argued we had reached 'The End of History', since 'liberal democracy' had (not surprisingly) proved superior to the Soviet dictatorship.[2] Two corporate lawyers soon added we had also reached an 'end of history for corporate law', because the 'force of

[1] Cf. G. B. Shaw, *Back to Methuselah* (1921) Act I, §i; the serpent is incorrect that we dream things that 'never' were.

[2] F. Fukuyama, *The End of History and the Last Man* (1992).

logic', 'example' and 'competition' showed that 'shareholder primacy' was superior to all other forms of corporate governance, whether director-dominated, labour or state-oriented models.[3] Ironically, the same game was played by Hegel and Marx.[4] Hegel argued a 'dialectic' process between 'the state' and 'civil society' had led to the peak of human freedom, apparently, under the Prussian monarchy, in 1820.[5] In 1848, Marx argued, no, a dialectical process was still under way, as the world had moved from slavery, to feudalism, to an age of capital, and from this the communist revolution would inevitably follow. Capital's power structure would collapse under the weight of its internal contradictions.[6] Of course, claiming something is 'inevitable' may have a persuasive force, but reality usually defeats rhetoric in time. In 2021, the post-cold war certainties of a liberal, shareholding democracy, appear as fanciful as the 'end' of history, given our state of escalating inequality, the global-warming catastrophe and ongoing armed conflict. History is chaotic and long, but also rich with ideas, and can show remarkable patterns. This chapter charts the broad changes between state and corporate power from the ancient, medieval and mercantile worlds, to the industrial, the corporate and the global revolutions of today.

(1) Ancient and Medieval Enterprise

The modern law of enterprise emerged over the industrial, corporate and global revolutions, and yet all basic questions of our economic constitution – who should finance, govern or have rights in enterprise – are as old as recorded law. History is often only visible to us through fragments, but we know, for example, that Ancient Egypt had a vast slave population for constructing the pyramids, and that the first recorded strike appears around 1150 BC. Workers building the Royal Necropolis for Pharaoh Rameses III (who was later murdered in a coup) downed their tools because they were not being paid their wages.[7] Even earlier, the first recorded insolvency law was in the *Codex Hammurabi*, from Ancient Babylon (today, Baghdad), where merchants who failed to pay their debts could be imprisoned by their creditors and, with their wives and children, be enslaved for three years.[8]

[3] H. Hansmann and R. Kraakman, 'The End of History for Corporate Law' (2000) 89 *Georgetown LJ* 439.

[4] Cf. H. Butterfield, *The Whig Interpretation of History* (1931); Voltaire, *Candide, ou l'optimisme* (1759).

[5] G. W. F. Hegel, *Grundlinien der Philosophie des Rechts or Elements of the Philosophy of Right* (1820); G. W. F. Hegel, *Vorlesungen über die Philosophie der Weltgeschichte or Lectures on the Philosophy of History*, trans. J. Sibree (1857).

[6] K. Marx and F. Engels, *The Communist Manifesto* (1848); K. Marx, *Capital: A Critique of Political Economy* (1867) vol. I, ch. 32. See G. Kitching, *Marxism and Science: Analysis of an Obsession* (1994).

[7] W. F. Edgerton, 'The Strikes in Ramses III's Twenty-Ninth Year' (1951) 10(3) *J Near Eastern Studies* 137. Cf. Genesis 11:9 and Exodus 5:7, recording labour disputes.

[8] *Codex Hammurabi* (1754 BC) cll. 115–19.

In these brutal, ancient worlds, large enterprises were entirely associated with the rulers, and laws defined many aspects of individual economic relations. In the time of Darius the Great (550–486 BC) in the Achaemenid Empire, a 2,700-km network of roads stretched out from Babylon to India and to the Mediterranean, and was so fast that there was 'nothing mortal which accomplishes a journey with more speed' than the messengers that used them.[9] In the Roman Republic, the Twelve Tables (*c.* 450 BC) required that the width of certain roads was standard, and damaged waterways repaired on private property. Debtors were treated particularly harshly, so that, if an insolvent trader had several creditors, they could cut his body into several pieces as 'satisfaction'.[10] Thus, the basic relations then were of the individual to the state, and private, small group enterprises were juxtaposed to the large-scale public enterprise. As incorporations only came later, there was not yet a 'social law' body of major organisations standing between 'public' and 'private'. Indeed, persons of wealth, commanding any major enterprise, would directly threaten a ruling establishment.

The political and economic relationships of the ruler and the ruled appear to be first discussed extensively in Ancient Athens. The teacher, Socrates, was sentenced to death by the city, and he refused to escape because he said he undertook a 'social contract' to obey the law.[11] After this his student, Plato, wrote *The Republic* (*c.* 380 BC). Plato argued that most systems of government were doomed to spiral towards tyranny,[12] a tyranny like that which killed Socrates. When a typical government broke down, it would slide into 'timocracy' dominated by a military, whose ruling class would accumulate wealth and so become an oligarchy. An oligarchy, controlled by property owners, would impel discontent among the lower classes, who would stage a revolution committed to equality. But then people with greater merit, with equality thrust upon them, would support a tyrant. The tyrant, who promised stability, would then enslave the people and launch war. So instead of going down this (ostensibly inevitable) path, Plato argued that in a just society the philosophers (presumably like Plato) would become the kings. They would renounce private property, which might otherwise corrupt them, and take a subsistence allowance.[13]

In *The Laws*, Plato went even further. He argued that 'the ideal society and state, and the best code of laws, where the old saying [is followed that] "friends' property is genuinely shared"', are ones where 'the notion of "private property" will have been by hook or crook completely eliminated from life . . . the laws in force impose the greatest possible unity on the state – and you'll never produce a better or truer criterion of an absolutely perfect law than that'.[14] In this world,

[9] Herodotus, *The History of Herodotus* (440 BC) Book VIII, §98.

[10] L. Levinthal, 'The Early History of Bankruptcy Law' (1918) 66(5) *U Penn L Rev* 223, 230.

[11] Plato, *Crito* (*c.* 380 BC) trans. B. Jowett (1892); *Phaedo* (*c.* 380 BC) trans. B Jowett (1892).

[12] Plato, *The Republic* (*c.* 380 BC) Book VIII.

[13] Plato, *The Republic*, Book III.

[14] Plato, *The Laws* (350 BC) Book 5, trans. T. J. Saunders (1970) 207–8.

the rulers would rule based on an apparently fixed and natural-born merit. When each person stuck, said Plato, to their 'own job and minds [their] own business, that is justice and makes our state just'. Indeed, 'the worst of evils' that 'spells destruction to our state' was 'interchange of jobs'.[15] As it appeared to Plato, people were born for a certain condition (worker, soldier, philosopher-king) and there would be no movement. And *everything* including 'wives, children and all property', even 'eyes and ears and hands', would be owned by the 'community'.[16] On the other hand, Plato thought land should be worked individually, saying farmers 'must not farm in common, which is a practice too demanding for those born and bred and educated as ours . . . [but] each man who receives a portion of land should regard it as the common possession of the entire state'.[17]

Plato's pupil, Aristotle, also supported an 'aristocratic' style of government, supposedly based upon rule by merit. However, he defended the notion of private property. 'Property should be in a certain sense common, but,' wrote Aristotle 'as a general rule, private; for, when everyone has a distinct interest, men will not complain of one another, and they will make more progress, because every one will be attending to his own business.' In his view, people would be more likely to share if they had property, and the 'business of the legislator is to create in men this benevolent disposition'. 'These advantages are lost', he argued, 'by excessive unification of the state.'[18] This view also appeared consistent with some basic divisions in the concept of 'justice' that Aristotle introduced.[19] 'Distributive' justice was to follow 'merit in some sense', in 'geometric' proportions. Democrats might equate merit 'with the status of freeman, supporters of oligarchy with wealth . . . and supporters of aristocracy with excellence'. By contrast 'corrective justice' was suited for 'justice in transactions between man and man' and supposedly following a logic of 'arithmetic' proportion. Thus, Aristotle argued a different kind of justice applied to the affairs of the state, while justice among individuals and property was simply about 'correcting' imbalances.

Aristotle's most famous pupil was not another philosopher, but Alexander the Great (356–323 BC). With the wisdom passed down from Socrates, to Plato, to Aristotle, after Alexander's accession to the crown he launched a military campaign that overran Egypt and all Persia to India, and then he was killed, and his Macedonian Empire soon splintered. Meanwhile the new Roman Republic was growing. From 338 to 218 BC it took over the Italian peninsula, and by 50 BC it had conquered the Mediterranean, the Nile, Anatolia, Iberia, Gaul, and invaded Britain. Rome was a military entity (see Ch. 19), and the Twelve Tables continued to invest in public roads that aided rapid troop movement (see Ch. 15). The Mediterranean was its nexus of trade and supplied

[15] Plato, *The Republic*, Book IV, Part V, 139. [16] Plato, *The Laws*, 207–8.
[17] Plato, *The Laws*, 208. [18] Aristotle, *Politics* (*c.* 340 BC) Book II, V.
[19] Aristotle, *Nicomachean Ethics* (*c.* 340 BC) Book V, Parts III and IV, trans. D. P. Chase (1930).

the materials of war. To make grain prices stable Roman law punished anyone who deliberately and insidiously stopped supply ships.[20] Rome and its cities were hydraulic powered, agriculture was seen as the noble pursuit and labour was servile or enslaved (see Ch. 13). Cities were planned, and public buildings, streets and theatres were seen as part of a science of civilisation.[21] When Julius Caesar was assassinated and as the Republic fell, public works were seen as reflecting the august emperors' power (see Ch. 14).

Over the Roman Empire, the divide was entrenched and eventually codified in the *Corpus Juris Civilis* around 535 AD, that public law concerns the administration of the state, while private law relates to the interests of individuals.[22] However, it was clear that a multitude of 'corporate bodies' had emerged in the law of 'persons'. They organised everything from establishments in the 'City of Alexandria [that had a] duty of taking care of the river', and corporate bodies organised advocates, farmers and pork butchers.[23] In matters of competition, the law 'prohibited monopolies and forb[ade] ... agreements of corporate bodies'.[24] Yet slavery remained the basis for labour throughout the ancient period. Enslavement shifted those people from the law of 'persons' to the law of property,[25] where people could not own property because they were property, nor make obligations except on their masters' behalf.[26] Thus Roman enterprise was powered by wood and water, transported by horses, roads and triremes, and financed by military conquest and slaves: other human beings were the dominant source of wealth, the 'machines of the ancient world'.[27]

Over the Dark and Middle Ages, slavery in Europe gradually gave way to serfdom, where people were owned less, but still tied to land and lord. In medieval England the enslaved and feudal ties gave way more quickly. In 1086 when Domesday Book was compiled by William the Conqueror for levying taxes, 12% of people were free, 30% were serfs, 35% were subservient bordars and cottars, and 9% were slaves.[28] Power in Europe still centred upon Rome, but the king of England was more remote from the pope and God-given authority. So, when the third crusade was launched, costing huge sums in tax, King John was forced in the Barons' Revolt to agree Magna Carta in 1215.

20 *Lex Julia de Annona* (*c.* 50 BC).
21 Vitruvius Pollio, *De architectura* (*c.* 20 BC) trans. M. H. Morgan (1914).
22 *Institutes* 1.1.4; *Digest* 1.1.2. Of the two great jurists whose work most informed the *Corpus Juris Civilis*, Gaius lived *c.* 130–80 AD, and Ulpian lived *c.* 170–223 AD.
23 E.g. *Codex*, Book XI, Titles XVI, XVII and XXVIII, trans. S. P. Scott (1932).
24 *Codex*, Book IV, Title LIX. Diocletian in 301 AD also passed an edict on maximum price, backed by the death penalty.
25 E.g. *Institutes* 1.3.2: 'Slavery is a provision of the Law of Nations by means of which one person is subjected to the authority of another, contrary to nature.'
26 E.g. *Institutes* 2.9.3: 'a slave who is under the control of another can have nothing of his own'; *Institutes* 3.17.1: 'the stipulation of slaves' allowed them to make personal obligations according as masters' agents.
27 B. Nicholas, *An Introduction to Roman Law* (1962) II.1, 70.
28 D. D. McGarry, *Medieval History and Civilization* (1976) 242.

Far from the Roman public–private divisions, this stood as a first true charter of rights against a ruler, as opposed to laws that the ruler ordained. The most significant were rights to common land to hunt, gather plants and sustain life (see Ch. 13);[29] to trial by law and one's peers; to no tax without 'common counsel'; and to the liberties of the City of London and merchant enterprise.[30] The City grew into part of a much wider European union of towns in the Hanseatic League, whose members stretched from London to Boston, to Hamburg and Lübeck, Stockholm and Novgorod, and whose organisation of trade was more important than local kings.[31]

In this time the City itself was one of a growing number of corporations that included Oxford and Cambridge Universities (see Ch. 8). Then there were business groups such as the 'Worshipful Company of Fishmongers', incorporated by royal charter in 1272, the 'Merchant Taylors' in 1326 and the 'Company of Merchant Adventurers of London' chartered in 1407. Often these companies had monopolies or certain privileges in trade, but also regulated their affairs. For example, the 'Girdlers' (that is, beltmakers) were incorporated in 1449, but already in 1344 their guild had passed a resolution for a two-day weekend and holidays, 'that no man of the trade shall work on Saturday, or on the Eve of a Double Feast'.[32] As people traded from markets to fairs (see Ch. 18), the seismic event that shook the medieval world was plague, reaching from Mongol armies in Crimea (see Ch. 19) to the banks of the Thames in 1348. It killed up to half the population of Europe, and 60 per cent of Londoners. Italians who traded in London's Lombard Street began to flee (see also Ch. 9), and a panic about evading debts led to a statute in 1350 declaring that if one member of the companies of Lombards left, all others would be liable.[33]

With so many lords dead, many indentured people were simply now free.[34] But then the Statute of Labourers 1351 targeted the 'malice of servants, who were idle and refused to serve after the pestilence',[35] fixing their wages through

[29] Magna Carta 1215, cl. 47 (disafforesting common land) and cl. 48 (abolishing 'evil customs' banning land use) and then recast as Charter of the Forest 1217, cl. 1 (right of herbage in forests, gathering plants), cl. 9 (agistment and pannage, right of grazing including pigs) and cl. 10 (right to farm).

[30] Magna Carta 1215, cll. 12–13, 39. Cf. F. Pollock and F. W. Maitland, *History of English Law*, vol. I, 173: 'the nearest approach to an irrepealable "fundamental statute" that England has ever had'.

[31] P. Dollinger, *The German Hansa* (1967) (trans. and ed. D. S. Ault and S. H. Steinberg), ch. 1, in M. Casson (ed.), *The Emergence of International Business 1200–1800* (1999) vol. I.

[32] H. T. Riley, *Memorials of London and London Life* (1868) 216–20, 1344 AD.

[33] I. Treiman, 'Escaping the Creditor in the Middle Ages' (1927) 43 *LQR* 230, 232; Statute of Edward III (1350).

[34] E. P. Cheyney, 'The Disappearance of English Serfdom' (1900) 15(57) *English Historical Rev* 20; and later see A. Fitzherbert, *Surueyenge* (1546) 31: servitude 'the greatest inconvenience that nowe is suffred by the lawe'.

[35] Statute of Labourers 1351, which also fixed food prices. Also Ordinance of Labourers 1349.

force.[36] As life ground on, in 1377, the king introduced a poll tax, triggering the Peasants' Revolt of 1381. One of the leaders, John Ball, preached to the followers that they should go to the king and 'by fairness or otherwise' win their freedom. As he said, 'matters goeth not well to pass in England, nor shall not do till everything be common', when 'there be no villains nor gentlemen, but that we may be all unied [*sic*] together, and that the lords be no greater masters than we be'.[37] The revolt was thwarted, and repression followed banning free movement,[38] yet people could still undertake pilgrimages, like those in the famous cross-section of professions in *The Canterbury Tales*. There was a merchant, a physician, a franklin, a miller, a clerk, a pardoner and a knight, all telling their tales. But the one who represented the vast majority of people was the person for whom Chaucer never wrote a tale, the ever silent ploughman,[39] who lived on fixed subsistence wages.[40] Most of Chaucer's pilgrims would have been outside the Statute of Labourers, although there was price fixing across goods and services, including bans on co-operation.[41] Statutes for fair competition,[42] and laws for 'just prices', were now seen across Europe,[43] and medieval enterprise was ever more sophisticated, well-financed, international and gradually breaking free from the strictures of servitude (see Table 1.1).

[36] L. R. Poos, 'The Social Context of the Statute of Labourers Enforcement' (1983) 1(1) *L & History Rev* 27, 31–3.

[37] J. Froissart, *The Chronicles of Froissart* (1385) trans. G. C. Macaulay (1895) 250–2.

[38] Statute of Cambridge 1388.

[39] G. Chaucer, *The Canterbury Tales* (1387) General Prologue, saying of the 'Plowman', 'God loved he best with al his hole herte.'

[40] 'Wages' may not be correct, as most people were paid in kind: D. Graeber, *Debt: The First 5,000 Years* (2011) ch. 11, 312, 352.

[41] E.g. Ordinance of the Staples 1353 (27 Edw. III, Stat. 2, c. 25), regulating ports ('staples') for trade into the kingdom, and saying 'no merchant or other shall make Confederacy, Conspiracy, Coin, Imagination, or Murmur, or Evil Device'. Statute of Diet and Apparel 1363 (37 Edw. III, Stat. 1, c. 5): 'Merchants shall not engross merchandise to enhance the prices of them, nor use but one sort of merchandise.' Cf. *Dyer's case* (1414) 2 Hen V, 5 Pl 26. Ordinances of Corporations Act 1503 (19 Hen. VII, c. 7) s. I. 'Corporations shall not make or enforce any Ordinances, without the Approbation of the Chancellor, & c.' Price of Victuals Act 1533 (25 Hen. VIII, c. 2): 'prices of such victuals [food] be many times enhanced and raised by the Greedy Covetousness and Appetites of the Owners . . . to the great damage and impoverishing of the King's subjects'. Wines Act 1542 (34 & 35 Hen. VIII, c. 7).

[42] E.g. Municipal Statutes of Florence in 1322 and 1325 banned monopolies, and Emperor Charles V made a law 'to prevent losses resulting from monopolies and improper contracts which many merchants and artisans made in the Netherlands'. Wenceslas II of Bohemia between 1283 and 1305 passed the *Constitutiones juris metallici*, which condemned combinations of ore traders increasing prices. See R. Wilberforce, *The Law of Restrictive Practices and Monopolies* (1966) ch. 1.

[43] See also T. Aquinas, *Summa Theologica* (1265–74) II–II, question 77, art. 4. Also question 78, art. 2, reply to objection 3, on a person's right to 'receive the reward for his labor'.

Table 1.1 Snapshots of enterprise law history

	Public enterprise	Companies	Labour	Competition	Insolvency
1150 BC, Egypt	Pyramids, army	-	Slavery	-	-
400 BC, Athens	Temples, markets, army	-	Slavery and free	Part fixed, and free	Enslaved
160 AD, Rome	Temples, water, roads, markets, army	*Societas*	Slavery and free	Part fixed, and free	Punished, enslaved
1381, England	Common lands, roads, markets, army	Companies, guilds	Slaves, serfs, free, wage fixing	Wage and price fixing, privileges	Punished, possibly killed
1615, England	Roads, post, markets, military	Guilds, corporations	Most indebted, some free	Wage fixing, privileges	Debt prison
1780, Britain	Roads, post, markets, military	Corporations, partnerships	Most indebted, some free Restraint of trade laws	Statutory monopolies, restraint of trade rules	Debt prison
1880, Britain	Bank regulation, roads, rail regulation, post, telegraph, military, colonialism	Free incorporation, partnerships, trusts	Most indebted, some free, union freedom	Statutory monopolies, laissez-faire	Basic bankruptcy and insolvency rights
1980, Britain	Education, health, banking, coal, oil, gas, electricity, land planning, water, homes, roads, rail, post, telecoms, BBC, military	Free incorporation, basic shareholder rights, joint pension trustees, some worker directors	Union freedom, fair wage scales, basic equal treatment, basic job security, free movement	Monopoly control, cartel controls, consumer rights	Bankruptcy and insolvency rights, minimal enterprise rescue

(2) Mercantilism, 1492–1765

As a plague from the east changed Europe forever in the 1300s, in the 1400s European merchants and soldiers brought their own plagues from their east to the Americas. The capture of Constantinople in 1453 by the Ottomans nailed the eastern Roman Empire's end, leading Christopher Columbus to voyage to find a new route to China (see Ch. 19). But instead, the New World's 'discovery' inaugurated a new mercantile age, and revived and reshaped old ideas. In an ironic recasting of Plato's *Republic* in 1516, Sir Thomas More wrote of a fictitious voyager who had discovered a new island, *Utopia* ('no place' in Greek). While Book II was devoted to the voyager, Raphael 'Nonsenso', explaining Utopia's land and its laws (which continually seem absurd), Book I was a real critique of England at the time, and probably reflects what Lord Chancellor More thought. Sheep farming, said Nonsenso, had blighted the countryside, turning farm labourers to vagrants. Instead of creating this 'great army of unemployed', the state should 'Stop the rich from cornering markets and establishing virtual monopolies . . . Revive agriculture and the wool industry, so that there is plenty of honest, useful work.'[44] 'I don't see how you can ever get any real justice or prosperity', said Nonsenso, 'so long as there's private property, and everything's judged in terms of money.'[45] In the same year and modelled on those in the Holy Roman Empire, Henry VIII established the public role of the Master of the Posts (see Ch. 16). The following year in Wittenberg, Martin Luther launched the Reformation. Luther was driven in reaction to bankers taking over the papacy, their pardons and indulgences (see Ch. 10), but in England reformation came from Henry VIII's penchant for executing those near to him, including two of his wives and More.

The Elizabethan age, under the child of a murdered mother, represented a period of relative domestic peace and reform, including to bankruptcy,[46] labour and social security laws,[47] yet it ended with the establishment of ever more corporations to exploit and colonise the opening world. Even if 'London streets were paved with gold' much less than grime,[48] 'every promoter with a new scheme gravitated toward' the City, its dwellers 'ready to invest' in every new corporate promotion.[49] There was the Muscovy Company chartered in

44 T. More, *Utopia* (1516) Book I, trans. P. Turner (2004). 45 More, *Utopia*, 44.

46 Fraudulent Conveyances Act 1571 (13 Eliz., c. 5) and Statute of Bankrupts Act 1542 (34 & 35 Hen. VIII, c. 4) introducing the *pari passu* standard.

47 Statute of Artificers 1562 (5 Eliz., c. 4), fixing workers' wages, enforced by justices of the peace. Poor Relief Act 1601 (43 Eliz., c. 2). S. Deakin and F. Wilkinson, *The Law of the Labour Market: Industrialization, Employment and Legal Evolution* (2005) ch. 2, noting that wage fixing ceased to be much enforced over time.

48 By legend, this was the call for Dick Whittington and his cat to go to London, from rags to riches, and then Lord Mayor. The real-life Lord Mayor, Richard Whittington (1354–1423), was an aristocrat and cloth merchant, and probably had no cat. Cf. R. Dahl, *Rhyme Stew* (1989) 'Dick Whittington and His Cat'.

49 T. K. Rabb, 'Enterprise and Empire: Merchant and Gentry Investment in the Expansion of England, 1575–1630' (1967) in M. Casson (ed.), *The Emergence of International Business 1200–1800* (1999) vol. III, 19–22

1555 to trade with Russia, the Levant Company in 1592 to trade with the Ottomans, and the Virginia Company in 1606 for the colonies in North America. However, there was real opposition to companies and this growing system in general. Elizabeth I's Chief Justice, Sir Edward Coke, believed that 'all monopolies' were against Magna Carta 'because they are against the liberty and freedome of the subject'.[50] He held the tailors' guild could not reserve half the work on cloth to be finished by guild members.[51] He reported that a playing-card patent held by a royal official was void.[52] The College of Physicians had no power to imprison those practising medicine without approval,[53] and the tailors' guild (again) could not prevent someone working without having been an apprentice. The 'common law abhors all monopolies', raged Coke, 'which prohibit any from working in any lawful trade'.[54] As his attack on guilds continued, the Crown's revenue from taxing guilds declined.[55] This led James I to grant yet more trade monopolies abroad. Parliament reacted in the Statute of Monopolies 1623 (a law still in force[56]) saying any new monopoly 'shalbe utterlie void and of none effecte', except patents for the 'true and first inventors', grants in an Act of Parliament, for the City, boroughs or town corporations.

The best-known mercantile corporation, the East India Company, was chartered in 1600 with a monopoly on trade east of the Cape of Good Hope, and west of the Straits of Magellan, now the southern tip of Chile. With this, and grants from Mughals to trade and set up factories, it built posts in Surat in 1619, Madras in 1639, Bombay in 1668 and Calcutta in 1690. Though a monopoly and without an Act, the East India Company's existence was justified by the courts as necessary to undertake foreign trade.[57] While England passed through the Civil War in 1640, and the Glorious Revolution in 1688, it built up its own private military. First, they manned the forts, then they fought wars and gradually offered security 'services' to the Mughal

[50] E. Coke, *Institutes* (1797) vol. II, 47, based on Magna Carta 1215, ch. 29: 'No Freeman shall be taken or imprisoned, or be disseised of his Freehold, or Liberties . . . but by lawful judgment of his Peers, or by the Law of the land.' Also at 62–3, Coke argued the right against monopoly is implicit in ch. 30, for freedom of merchants for 'buying and selling by the ancient and right customs'.

[51] *Davenant v Hurdis* (1599) Moore 576: 'by-laws that establish monopolies are against common law and void'.

[52] *Darcy v Allin*, or the *Case of Monopolies* (1602) 11 Co Rep 84b, saying monopoly 'tends to the impoverishment of divers artificers and others, who before, by the labor of their hands in their art or trade, had maintained themselves and their families, who now will be constrained to live in idleness and beggary'.

[53] *Dr Bonham's Case* (1610) 77 Eng Rep 646.

[54] *Case of the Tailors of Ipswich* (1614) 11 Co Rep 53a, 77 ER 1218.

[55] T. B. Nachbar, 'Monopoly, Mercantilism, and the Politics of Regulation' (2005) 91(6) *Virginia L Rev* 1313, 1322 and 1346.

[56] Statute of Monopolies 1623 (c. 3) ss. I and VI–IX.

[57] *East India Company v Sandys* (1683) 90 ER 103: 'if it happen to be of advantage to the publick as this trade is, then it ceases also to be against the politique part of the law'. Sandys's ship was arrested before sailing to trade to the East Indies at customs' house: (1682) 90 ER 43.

princes. Control of the East India Company was vested in its major shareholders with smaller investors excluded from votes,[58] and yet the Court of Directors and its agents in the field were the real ones making the decisions. Robert Clive, a clerk who rose to be Governor of Bengal, a 'violent, utterly ruthless and intermittently mentally unstable corporate predator',[59] oversaw the key change. Following a battle in 1757 led by Clive against the hereditary Nawab in Bengal, in 1765 the Mughal Emperor Shah Alam II replaced his own tax officials with the Company's in Bengal, Bihar and Orissa, and increasingly relied on Company military support. With these keys to power, monetary and military, the independence of Indian rulers was not just a shell. The Company grew and expanded, raising more taxes and transferring more and more wealth away from India and back to Britain.[60]

The other vast corporations established in this age were the Royal African Company, chartered in 1660;[61] the Bank of England from 1694; and the South Sea Company from 1711. The Royal African Company was primarily responsible for kidnapping and enslaving people from the Gambia to Ghana, its monopoly spanning the West African coast. Its original object was to trade or steal gold, but slavery proved more lucrative, as it tortured and transported terrified men, women and children to South America, the Caribbean islands and Britain's North American colonies. 'DoY' (for Duke of York) was burned into their skin, after the man who became King James II, before he was dethroned by Parliament in 1688. Although the Trade with Africa Act 1697 removed the company's coastal monopoly, the transatlantic slave trade continued. The South Sea Company also sought to take part when, after the Treaty of Utrecht 1713, Britain secured an *asiento* to sell slaves to Spanish colonies, and Queen Anne conferred that right on it (see Ch. 10(1)). This company was backed as a financial rival to the Bank of England, itself incorporated as a Whig venture with the Bank of England Act 1694.[62] But slaving seemed not to be enough, so it was decided that the South Sea Company should assume the national debt of Britain. Speculation on South Sea Company shares soared, as did its share price, until it was realised that it was doing little business, leading everyone to sell, and thus the world's first stock market and bank crash in 1720. Originally to protect the South Sea Company's monopoly, but then as a symbol of its downfall and public disgust, Parliament prohibited any further corporations without an Act, a measure that primarily targeted trust-based

[58] S. Williston, 'History of the Law of Business Corporations before 1800. II. (Concluded)' (1898) 2(4) *Harvard L Rev* 149, 156. NB: Voting limits were eventually put in place in the East India Company, and the usual voting practice was a show of hands.

[59] W. Dalrymple, *The Anarchy: The Relentless Rise of the East India Company* (2019) xxxi.

[60] S. Tharoor, *Inglorious Empire: What the British Did to India* (2016) ch. 1.

[61] K. G. Davies, 'The Royal African Company' (1957) in M. Casson (ed.), *The Emergence of International Business 1200–1800* (1999) vol. V, ch. 1, though the company was bankrupted and rechartered in 1672.

[62] Bank of England Act 1694 (5 & 6 Will. & Mar., c. 20). £500 of stock bought one vote.

companies that 'presume to act as a Corporate Body'.[63] Because they enabled a powerful few to act without answering to anyone else, major corporations, in their inception, were the very essence of colonialism, slavery, debt and ruin.

While large corporations excluded small investors from having a voice,[64] and exploited everyone else that they could, after the 'South Sea Bubble' and bust, the common law of company governance became much more accountable.[65] Already in the 1600s it was recognised that corporations had independent personhood, were able to hold property and make obligations, and that they are 'invisible, immortal, & resteth only in intendment and consideration of the Law'.[66] Investors had a kind of limited liability if a company went insolvent, since creditors could only recover debts if there was a power in a company charter to make calls on members.[67] But also, a major consequence of the Bubble was the ousting of the corrupt Lord Chancellor Macclesfield, who had taken bribes and lost investors' money in South Sea speculation. He had previously held that fiduciaries (such as company directors) were allowed to take money from a trust without consent, invest it, profit and only restore losses.[68] This precedent was eradicated when his successor, Lord King LC, held in *Keech v Sandford* that anyone in position of a trustee (and so also a company director) may have no possibility of a conflict of interest, and, if there is, give a full account of profits.[69]

But that was not all. It was held that a company director could be dismissed as a default right of members, since 'a power of amotion is incident to the corporation'.[70] By default, incorporators as of 'common right . . . all are upon an equal foot'.[71] And 'wherever a certain number are incorporated, a major part of them may do any corporate act'.[72] Directors were duty bound to act with care, judged not by hindsight, but objectively.[73] As a core democratic

63 Royal Exchange and London Assurance Corporation Act 1719 (6 Geo., c. 18) s. XVIII. An 'undertaking' was 'illegal and void' without an Act. See also Bubble Schemes, Colonies Act 1740 (14 Geo. II, c. 37).

64 Another example is the Greenland Trade Act 1692 (4 Will. & Mar., c. 17) s. 17. £500 of stock bought one vote, £1,000 bought two. Also M. Freeman, R. Pearson and J. Taylor, *Shareholder Democracies? Corporate Governance in Britain and Ireland Before 1850* (2012) 151–3: 'In every sector except railways, larger companies were more likely to exclude their smallest shareholders from voting.'

65 J. Taylor, *Creating Capitalism: Joint-Stock Enterprise in British Politics and Culture 1800-1870* (2006) 5–6 noting the Bubble Act was almost never enforced. Freeman et al., *Shareholder Democracies?*, 23 found 224 of 514 companies operating in their sample between 1720 and 1844 were unincorporated.

66 *Case of Sutton's Hospital* (1612) 77 ER 960.

67 *Salmon v The Hamborough Co.* (1671) 1 Ch Cas 204, 22 ER 763; *Edmunds v Brown and Tillard* (1668) 1 Lev 237, 83 ER 385–7, debts of the Company of Woodmongers.

68 *Bromfield v Wytherley* (1718) Prec Ch 505.

69 *Keech v Sandford* [1726] EWHC J76, on a lease on a market in Romford. See also Ch. 18.

70 *Lord Bruce's Case* (1728) 93 ER 870.

71 *Stoughton v Reynolds* (1735) 93 ER 1023, Lord Hardwicke CJ, a church corporation.

72 *Attorney General v Davy* (1741) 26 ER 531, Lord Hardwicke LC, a parish.

73 *The Charitable Corporation v Sutton* (1742) 26 ER 642, Lord Hardwicke, set up to give loans to the poor.

principle, the members of the company themselves, not the courts, were the ultimate judges of good governance.[74] Similar values were reflected in the Public Companies Act 1767, passed to protect company rules that put a ceiling on the votes large shareholders could exercise, and to ban vote splitting. As Parliament said, it would not tolerate companies being 'sacrificed to the partial and interested views of a few, and those perhaps temporary Proprietors'.[75] Yet the treatment of insolvency remained punishing, with debts equated to fraud,[76] and bankruptcy 'considered a crime',[77] and it was widely seen as unjustifiable for a non-trader to 'encumber himself with debts of any considerable value'.[78] Creditors were strongly protected against fraudulent transactions of an insolvent,[79] but only rarely by the Lord Chancellor could bankrupts be discharged.[80] For labour, any combination of workers for better wages was still regarded as an illegal 'conspiracy',[81] and the slave trade went on.

(3) Industrial Revolution, 1765–1855

In 1765, the same year that the East India Company took over the tax and treasury of the Mughal princes, a weaver and carpenter from Lancashire, James Hargreaves, perfected the 'spinning jenny' to make cloth from cotton. Before long, it was adapted for power from a water wheel. Then in 1774 James Watt invented and patented the steam engine, initially used to lift coal from mines, which itself fuelled engines for mines of iron or coal (see Ch. 15). Then the first 'power loom' was patented in 1785. Mechanised production meant that for the first time in human history, we could produce far more than we needed to simply subsist (Figure 1.1). As inventions continued, all indicators of production started to go off the charts. The first locomotive began working in 1814, and the pace of invention also went exponential (see Table 1.2). The Industrial Revolution was born.

Seeing the vast changes in enterprise around him at the University of Glasgow, a professor of moral philosophy[82] and law,[83] and friend of James Watt, Adam Smith, began to ask, what was it that created the wealth of nations?[84] Published in 1776, Smith argued that mercantilism and corporate monopolies were evils that should remain repressed, castigating the East India,

[74] *R v Richardson* (1758) 1 Burr 517, 97 Eng Rep 426, Lord Mansfield, Corporation of Ipswich.
[75] Public Companies Act 1767 (7 Geo. III, c. 48).
[76] *Pinnel's case* (1602) 5 Co Rep 117a, stating there could be no 'consideration' for an agreement to reduce debt.
[77] *Fowler v Padget* (1798) 101 ER 1103: 'and a bankrupt in the old laws is called an offender'.
[78] W. Blackstone, *Commentaries on the Lawes of England* (1766) Book II, ch. 31, 473.
[79] *Alderson v Temple* (1768) 96 ER 384. [80] Bankruptcy Act 1705 (4 & 5 Anne, c. 17).
[81] *R v Journeymen-Taylors of Cambridge* (1721) 88 ER 9; J. V. Orth, *Combination and Conspiracy: A Legal History of Trade Unionism, 1721–1906* (1991).
[82] A. Smith, *The Theory of Moral Sentiments* (1759).
[83] A. Smith, *Lectures on Justice, Police, Revenue and Arms* (1763). These are still excellent.
[84] A. Smith, *An Inquiry into the Nature and Causes of the Wealth of Nations* (1776).

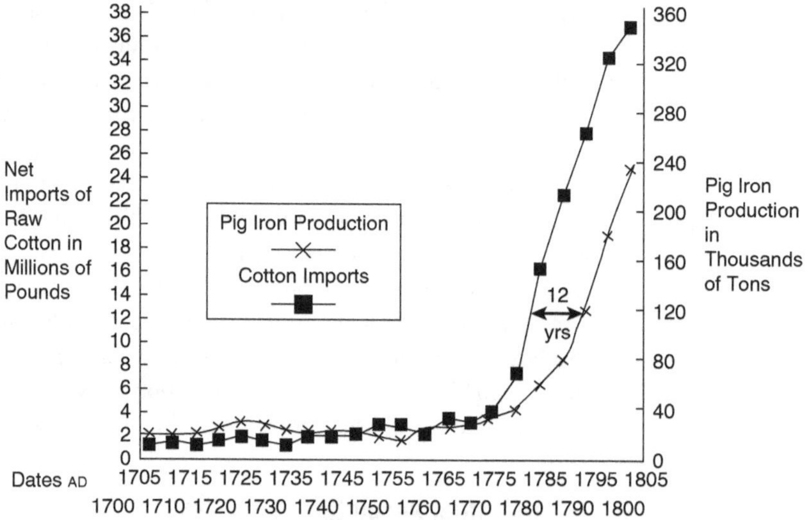

Figure 1.1 Cotton imports and iron production, 1700–1805

Royal African and South Sea Companies the most. 'Negligence and profusion must always prevail', he said, when directors are in charge of 'other people's money' and unaccountable. Small competitive partnerships, like 'the butcher, the baker and the brewer', were the basis of sustainable wealth. Yet a broad role for public corporate activity, if it could be reduced to 'routine', was desirable, namely in banking, insurance, canals and water. He also endorsed all public works 'necessary for facilitating Commerce in general', including roads, harbours, the post and defence.[85] Far from the caricatures of today, the 'invisible hand' was Smith's metaphor for the working of *this* world. He envisaged that a just system of law, as if guided by an invisible hand, would lead to an equal distribution of wealth at home, and raise the wealth of all nations abroad (see Ch. 2(1)(a)).

So why did the Industrial Revolution take place in Britain first? The answer to this popular historical question has usually centred on economic factors such as the relative mobility of British labour, the transfer of riches from Britain's colonial empire, and the scarcity of wood that drove inventors to coal: Britain's energy was cheaper.[86] An additional factor, most obvious to writers like Smith at the time, is clearly the legal structures of enterprise, facilitating both accountable small-scale production and global monopolies, the benevolent and the brutal. The same year as *The Wealth of Nations* was published, the USA declared independence. This was driven by a combination of northern colonies protesting about taxes without votes in Parliament, and

85 Smith, *Wealth of Nations* Book V, ch. 1, part III.

86 E.g. R. C. Allen, *The British Industrial Revolution in Global Perspective* (2009).

Table 1.2 Major inventions and discoveries

Year	Invention	People	Ch.
BC	Fire	?	12
BC	Irrigation	?	13
BC	Water wheel	?	12
BC	Horseback riding	?	15
BC	Roads	?	15
500 BC	Military tactics	Sun Tzu	19
50 AD	Wind turbines	Hero of Alexandria	12
1450	Printing	Johannes Gutenburg	18
1543	Astronomy	Copernicus	15
1765	Spinning jenny (textiles)	James Hargreaves	–
1774	Steam engine	James Watt	15
1824	Concrete	William Aspdin	14
1837	Telegraphs, Morse code	Cooke and Wheatstone	16
1848	Oil refining	James Young	11
1851	Flushing toilet	Thomas Crapper	13
1856	Steel	Henry Bessemer	14
1859	Nursing	Seacole and Nightingale	9
1859	Sewers for London	Joseph Bazalgette	13
1876	Telephone	Alexander Graham Bell	16
1880	Electric light	Thomas Edison	12
1881	Electric car	Gustave Trouvé	15
1884	Machine gun	Sir Hiram Stevens Maxim	19
1886	Combustion engine	Daimler and Benz	15
1893	Film	Edison Studios	17
1897	Radio	Guglielmo Marconi	16, 19
1903	Flight	Wright Brothers	15
1927	Seed genetics	Vavilov	13
1928	Penicillin	Fleming	9
1936	Television	Various	17
1936	Computers	Alan Turing	16
1939	Solar cells	Russell Ohl	12
1945	Nuclear energy	J. Robert Oppenheimer	12, 19
1989	Internet	US Dept of Defense	16

southern colonies opposed to Lord Mansfield's landmark judgment in *Somerset v Stewart*, in 1772, that slavery was 'so odious, that nothing can be suffered to support it, but positive law', and that it was illegal by the 'law of nations'.[87] In 1781, the French Revolution was launched, and in 1789 both the US Bill of Rights and the French Declaration of the Rights of Man were issued,

[87] *Somerset v Stewart* (1772) 98 ER 499; and see A. W. Blumrosen, 'The Profound Influence in America of Lord Mansfield's Decision in Somerset v Stuart' (2007) 13 *Texas Wesleyan L Rev* 645.

in part modelled after the British Bill of Rights 1689, but also declaring that rights were 'self-evident',[88] or 'natural, inalienable, and sacred'.[89] These rights were primarily directed towards property-owning men, not for women or people still enslaved, or people whose incomes and wealth excluded them from property-based voting qualifications. This 'Age of Revolution' therefore involved both the economic and the political, each with deep contradictions.[90] By contrast, in *A Vindication of the Rights of Woman*, possibly the most brilliant thinker of her time, Mary Wollstonecraft argued that 'rights and duties' come from 'reason, virtue, and knowledge'. Moreover, she wrote, from the 'respect paid to property flow, as from a poisoned fountain, most of the evils and vices which render this world such a dreary scene to the contemplative mind'.[91]

The dreary scene of industrialisation, represented by William Blake in 1808 as 'dark Satanic Mills',[92] brought untold misery to masses of people, who toiled in the expanding factories, bled in the mines and choked in the toxic air. The booming production in textiles, iron, steam engines, coal and, above all, after 1825 the railway companies did nothing to improve people's real standards of living. All the benefits of science and technology, all the new enterprises, were either worthless for people's lives or an active source of repression without changes in social regulation. This is graphically illustrated by changes in real wages.

Figure 1.2 shows the wild fluctuations, but total stagnation in real wages until about 1830, sixty-five years after the spinning jenny. The Master and Servant Act 1747 suppressed wages and extended punishments for leaving employment,[93] and the 'Speenhamland' system of poor-law magistrates determined that working people should receive poor-law relief, as well as the unemployed,[94] but rejected any kind of minimum wage.[95] This basic income fashioned a system of 'universal pauperism'.[96] Each change was the cue for punitive cuts to people's living standards, as employers reduced wages thinking workers got parish relief. Even worse, in the Poor Law Amendment Act 1834, Parliament removed wage subsidies but added a system of workhouses for the unemployed *intended* to be humiliating and inhumane. Throughout this time there was also the repression of workers organising to collectively bargain for fair pay, through Acts against 'combinations', 'unlawful oaths' and 'unlawful

88 US Declaration of Independence (1776).
89 *Déclaration des droits de l'homme et du citoyen* (1789).
90 E. Hobsbawm, *The Age of Revolution: 1789–1848* (1962).
91 M. Wollstonecraft, *A Vindication of the Rights of Woman* (1792) chs. I and IX.
92 W. Blake, 'Jerusalem' (1808): 'And was Jerusalem builded here, / Among these dark Satanic Mills? / . . . I will not cease from Mental Fight, / Nor shall my Sword sleep in my hand: / Till we have built Jerusalem, / In England's green & pleasant Land.'
93 Deakin and Wilkinson, *The Law of the Labour Market*, 63–7.
94 K. Polayni, *The Great Transformation* (1944) chs. 7–9, especially 82.
95 Deakin and Wilkinson, *The Law of the Labour Market*, ch. 3, 125–7.
96 E. Hobsbawm and G. Rudé, *Captain Swing* (1969) 50–1.

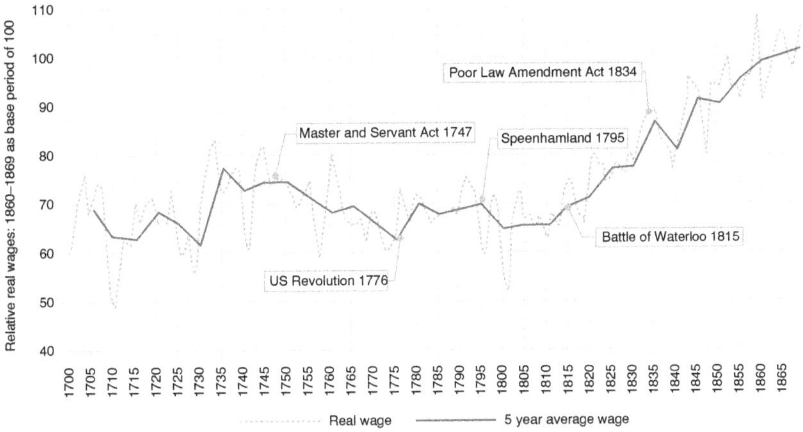

Figure 1.2 Real wages in England, 1700–1869
Source: G. Clark, 'The Long March of History', UC Davis Working Paper No. 05-40 (2005)

societies'.[97] The beginning of the end only came in the 1830s, with the persecution of six farm workers from Tolpuddle, Dorset. They formed a union, and were sentenced to be transported to Australia for their 'crimes'.[98] In response a workers' movement in London and its surrounds launched massive demonstrations that eventually led to the sentences being commuted.[99] Even though organising or breaking a work contract was criminal,[100] this relentless pressure edged up wages. At the same time abroad, Britain finally committed to end slavery within its growing empire, by paying off the slave owners.[101]

As production in enterprise boomed, so did the production of laws, since most new corporations had to have a new Act,[102] peaking with '119 railway Acts in 1845, 263 in 1846, and 187 in 1847'.[103] There was equally a boom in gas and lighting corporations (see Ch. 12) and companies supplying running water and sewerage (see Ch. 13).[104] A parallel movement was an increase in public accountability. First, in 1810, in *Allnutt v Inglis*, Lord Ellenborough declared

[97] Combination of Workmen Act 1796 (c. 111), Unlawful Oaths Act 1797 (c. 123), Unlawful Societies Act 1799 (c. 79), Unlawful Combinations of Workmen Act 1799 (c. 81), Unlawful Combinations of Workmen Act 1800 (c. 106), Combinations of Workmen Act 1801 (c. 38), Unlawful Oaths Act 1812 (c. 104). The Combination of Workmen Act 1824 (c. 95) lifted the 1799 and 1800 Acts, but after strikes the Combinations of Workmen Act 1825 (c. 129) reimposed bans on collective and criminalised persuading people to not work.

[98] *R v Lovelass* (1834) 172 ER 1380.

[99] S. Webb and B. Webb, *The History of Trade Unionism* (1894) ch. 3, 144–8.

[100] Master and Servant Act 1823, and strikes were an aggravated breach of contract.

[101] Slavery Abolition Act 1833, abolished slavery everywhere in the empire, except areas dealt with in the Indian Slavery Act 1843. The Slave Trade Act 1807 abolished only the *trade* within the empire.

[102] Cf. Bubble Companies, etc. Act 1825 (c. 91).

[103] M. Casson, *The World's First Railway System: Enterprise, Competition, and Regulation on the Railway Network in Victorian Britain* (2009) ch. 2, 44–6.

[104] J. Foreman-Peck and R. Millward, *Public and Private Ownership of British Industry 1820–1990* (1994) 30–7.

that though 'the general principle' is that 'every man may fix what price he pleases upon his own property', if 'the public have a right to resort to his premises . . . and he have a monopoly in them . . . he must, as an equivalent, perform the duty attached to it on reasonable terms'.[105] Whatever the defects of enforcement in nineteenth-century courts, this was a remarkable statement of principle on economic fairness. Second, there was an increasing number of public duties within Acts themselves, such as price rise limits for water companies,[106] and dividend controls for gas companies.[107] Third, after a report into the corruption of existing town corporations, the Municipal Corporations (England) Act 1835 required ratepayers to elect new local governments, which would gradually set up their own public services. A growing number of public duties on local authorities, particularly for public health (see Ch. 8), then arose. Yet the system of incorporation was unwieldy. Parliament first decided to standardise a process for registering corporate status without an Act,[108] and then consolidated model company constitutions.[109] Companies could still be established and regulated by an Act, and they were. The most remarkable example is that after mounting discontent at universities, and a complaint at Oxford about 'successive interventions by which the government of the University was reduced to a narrow oligarchy',[110] the Oxford University Act 1854 guaranteed the right of staff to elect its governing Council,[111] and Cambridge won the same right (see Ch. 8).[112]

And yet despite these stunning developments, with increasing public rights, with democratic voice in local government and in universities, the industrial company system was rotten and brutal to the core. Charles Dickens relentlessly castigated its central institutions, the Court of Chancery that oversaw – or refused to oversee[113] – corporate functioning,[114] the sham promoters of

105 *Allnutt v Inglis* (1810) 104 ER 206, regarding a warehouse. Also *Bolt v Stennett* (1800) 101 ER 1572.

106 Waterworks Clauses Act 1847 (c. 17) codified the standard provisions, followed by Acts in 1852 and 1863. Statutory water companies were mainly created in the mid-nineteenth century following these model clauses.

107 Gasworks Clauses Act 1847, ss. XXIX (dividend caps) and XX (pollution penalties). Foreman-Peck and Millward *Public and Private Ownership*, 32, referring to price and dividend controls for Nottingham, Oxford, Worcester and Bristol.

108 Joint Stock Companies Act 1844 and Joint Stock Companies Winding-Up Act 1844.

109 Companies Clauses Consolidation Act 1845.

110 Oxford University Commission, Report of Her Majesty's Commissioners appointed to inquire into State, Discipline, Studies and Revenues of University and Colleges of Oxford (1852) 8. See also P. Searby, *A History of the University of Cambridge*, III: *1750–1870* (1997) 518–23 and 530–3, on the parallel report aiming to end the 'contradictory elements of democracy, anarchy, and oligarchic centralism'.

111 Oxford University Act 1854, ss. 16 and 21.

112 Cambridge University Act 1856, ss. 5 and 12.

113 E.g. *Carlen v Drury* (1812) 35 ER 61, per Lord Eldon scoffing: 'This Court is not to be required on every Occasion to take the Management of every Playhouse and Brewhouse in the Kingdom.'

114 E.g. C. Dickens, *Bleak House* (1853).

whizz-bang-puff ventures that spirited investors' money away[115] and, most of all, the inhuman debtors' prisons that robbed his father's freedom, and forced Dickens as a child to work in a boot-blacking factory.[116] The laws on imprisoning people for debt were especially perilous for people doing any kind of trade, and potentially investing.[117] In short, if people had unlimited liability for debts, they risked losing their liberty.

The momentous shifts in the Industrial Revolution reshaped all understandings of political economy, and probably the two most important were those of John Stuart Mill and Karl Marx. Mill, the child prodigy who grew up and broke down on a Benthamite education and found solace in poetry,[118] published *Principles of Political Economy* in 1848, the very year that on the Continent a wave of revolutions erupted against the suppression of political liberty and lack of food. Mill's principles argued that while laissez-faire should be the basic rule, there should be major exceptions for all economic organisation. Anything which 'can only be done by joint-stock associations, will often be as well, and sometimes better done . . . by the state' which gave 'greater publicity and more active discussion and comment'.[119] Mill's argument was even more curious given that he worked for the East India Company from 1823 to 1858 and publicly defended its rule.[120] Mill also argued that labour rights should be passed into law to overcome the collective action problems faced by labour (see Ch. 2(1)(a)). Then there was Karl Marx, who with Friedrich Engels wrote the *Communist Manifesto* in 1848 calling for a proletarian revolution in response to the bourgeoisie class despots. After living in Berlin, Paris, Brussels and Cologne, Marx was forced to leave mainland Europe; he arrived in London in 1849 and began writing *Capital: A Critique of Political Economy* in the British Museum Reading Room. The basic critique was that the commodification of labour, the buying and selling of human beings' work, led to such exploitation and alienation, and led capital to accumulate and concentrate so much, that it would become ever easier for 'expropriation of a few usurpers by the mass of the people'.[121] Though there is no evidence they ever met, Mill and Marx's theories were together profoundly influential in the next century of revolution.

[115] E.g. C. Dickens, *Martin Chuzzlewit* (1843) ch. 27, Anglo–Bengalee Disinterested Loan and Life Assurance Co.

[116] E.g. C. Dickens, *David Copperfield* (1850), *Hard Times* (1854) and *Little Dorrit* (1857).

[117] M. Lester, *Victorian Insolvency: Bankruptcy, Imprisonment for Debt, and Company Winding-up in Nineteenth-Century England* (1995) on this being one of the most important social issues of the century.

[118] J. S. Mill, *Autobiography* (3rd ed. 1874).

[119] J. S. Mill, *Principles of Political Economy* (1848) Book V, ch. 11, §11.

[120] 'Memorandum of the improvements in the administration of India during the last thirty years, and the petition of the East-India Company to Parliament' (1858).

[121] Marx, *Capital*, vol. I, ch. 32.

(4) Corporate Revolution, 1855–1945

The 'corporate revolution' is the name given to the rise of the modern corporation by A. A. Berle, the corporate lawyer, New Deal architect and writer of President Franklin D. Roosevelt's speech extolling an 'economic declaration of rights, an economic constitutional order' (see Ch. 2(1)(a)).[122] That revolution began with the Companies Acts passed in Britain from the 1840s to 1860s and, above all, the Limited Liability Act 1855. According to the 'father of modern company law',[123] an MP, later Chancellor of the Exchequer, Robert Lowe, the right of property owners to incorporate a company, with liability limited to investments if the venture went insolvent, was a part of 'human liberty'.[124] There appears to be no mention of the effect that free incorporation with limited liability was to have on debtor prison during the debates on the Companies Acts. But having lost the biggest source of their 'clients' – bankrupt traders – the debtor prisons were soon abolished.[125] The company laws were recast in 1856 and 1862,[126] and ever since the limited corporation was a basic unit of enterprise. While the name 'company' originally reflected the need for twenty and then seven people to incorporate (not run as a smaller partnership), in practice any single person could register a company with a few other nominal members, and have limited liability.[127] Yet the real significance was for the mass enterprise. After the UK, there was the proliferation of similar laws from the USA to Germany, giving rise to corporations of unprecedented size and scope.

There was also an unprecedented expansion of and demand for public regulation. Whether it was because of Mill's *Principles*, or Marx's *Manifesto*, or neither, or both, public enterprise grew. There was already the post and parish roads, and the Bank of England was no doubt intertwined with the state, as it had gained exclusive privileges in issuing notes.[128] Further, the Railway Regulation Act 1844 had given the option to government to purchase railway companies within twenty-five years (though it was not used).[129] By far the most dramatic was the nationalisation of the East India Company's functions

122 F. D. Roosevelt, Campaign Address on Progressive Government at the Commonwealth Club in San Francisco, California (1932); A. A. Berle and G. C. Means, *The Modern Corporation and Private Property* (1933).

123 J. Micklethwait and A. Wooldridge, *The Company: A Short History of a Revolutionary Idea* (2003) 57.

124 Hansard HC Debs. (1 February 1856) vol. 140, col. 131.

125 Debtors Act 1869, after the Bankruptcy Act 1861 abolished the distinction between traders and non-traders who could both apply for bankruptcy. The Bankruptcy Act 1869, s. 32 established the first preferential debt system.

126 Joint Stock Companies Acts 1856 and 1862.

127 See Ch. 3(1)(b) and *Salomon v A Salomon & Co. Ltd* [1896] UKHL 1.

128 Bank Charter Act 1844, while the Bank Restriction Act 1797 had removed any duty to convert notes to gold on demand.

129 Railway Regulation Act 1844, ss. 2–6. Also the Railway and Canal Traffic Act 1888, inaugurated the Railway and Canal Commission.

themselves, formally establishing the British Empire.[130] Though it had been subject to an increasing volume of Acts overseeing its conduct, after the Indian 'Mutiny' of 1857 – a liberation uprising against British rule where a million people perished – Parliament resolved to end this corporate kleptocracy, and replace it with a new one: the British state. If the essence of political control was taxation and the military, new communications were, like the post, quickly seen as also a vital public and probably a security interest. The Telegraph Act 1869 nationalised the lines for Morse code, which had rapidly become a monopoly, and when the telephone was invented, in 1880 the courts extended the Act to the telephone enterprises *by a court judgment* (see Ch. 16).[131] The Public Health Acts, particularly from 1848, gave responsibility to local governments to create water facilities and build the sewers (see Ch. 9), and the Elementary Education Act 1870 created the first comprehensive system of public schools (see Ch. 8). Thus, the corporate revolution was not just a rise of private and public enterprise, but a new social order in place of both.

The choice to create public responsibility for education was profoundly political. In the Second Reform Act 1867, Parliament had lowered the property qualification to vote, and thereby enfranchised more people. The leading opponent was none other than Robert Lowe MP, the founder of modern company law, who railed against the 'elite of the working classes', and said that if the 'principle of equality' was followed it would empower trade unions that were 'founded on principles of the most grinding tyranny'. Giving people the vote would 'make those trades unions the most dangerous political agencies that could be conceived'.[132] Fortunately for democracy, Lowe's arguments did not win, and subsequent Acts in 1884, 1918 and 1928 eventually scrapped the property qualifications and ended the exclusion of women.[133] There was also major reform in the Trade Union Act 1871 to let workers freely unionise, organise their internal affairs, collectively bargain including for all-union workplaces and strike, including in solidarity with workers at other companies.[134] Lowe pleaded that if democracy must unfold, it was imperative that Parliament took steps to 'educate our masters' and create 'the most universal measures of education that can be devised'. This was heeded, and well.[135]

[130] Government of India Act 1858 (c. 106).

[131] *Attorney General v Edison Telephone Company of London Ltd* (1880) 6 QBD 244.

[132] Hansard HC Debs. (15 July 1867) vol. 188, col. 1546.

[133] Representation of the People Act 1884 (18% of population enfranchised), Representation of the People Act 1918 (male suffrage over 21), Representation of the People (Equal Franchise) Act 1928 (women's suffrage).

[134] Trade Union Act 1871; Conspiracy and Protection of Property Act 1875; *Allen v Flood* [1898] AC 1.

[135] Hansard HC Debs. (15 July 1867) vol. 188, col. 1549; A. J. Marcham, 'Educating Our Masters: Political Parties and Elementary Education 1867 to 1870' (1973) 21(2) *Brit J Educational Studies* 180.

Ironically, none other than Karl Marx probably agreed with Robert Lowe, writing in his later life that if the English working classes won universal suffrage, this would be tantamount to a revolution. In the third and final volume of *Capital*, published after his death in 1883, Marx also said the corporation was 'the abolition of capital as private property within the boundaries of capitalist production itself'. It remained as 'a whole system of swindling and cheating' and 'private production without the control of private property'.[136] And with free incorporation, nowhere grew the corporations as fast, and as many, as in the USA, even as the rights of real people were held back. Its population had just surpassed the UK's on the eve of the US Civil War, which erupted as Abraham Lincoln, a well-known opponent of slavery, was elected president. Lincoln, like all Republicans, read the *New York Daily Tribune*, to which Marx was a 'prolific contributor',[137] and it appears no coincidence that in his first annual message, Lincoln proclaimed that 'Labor is the superior of capital, and deserves much the higher consideration.'[138] As the southern confederacy seceded, Lincoln issued the Emancipation Proclamation 1862, freeing all slaves in rebellion states, with no compensation for slave owners. After the tragedy of Lincoln's assassination, the reconstruction brought the Thirteenth and Fourteenth Amendments, which guaranteed everyone due process and equal protection of the law. Implementing this, the Civil Rights Act of 1875 guaranteed people the right to equal treatment in access to housing, transport and entertainment regardless of skin colour or prior status of servitude. Then, in *Munn v Illinois*, the Supreme Court held that 'when private property is devoted to a public use, it is subject to public regulation'.[139] But just seven years later, the logic was inverted and perverted in the *Civil Rights Cases*, to hold that the 1875 Act was 'unconstitutional' because the due process clause in the Fourteenth Amendment ostensibly prevented imposing any duties of equal treatment upon 'private' property owners. Harlan J dissented, arguing that this left people 'practically at the mercy of corporations and individuals wielding power under public authority'.[140] As segregation and 'Jim Crow' laws festered, this racist legal legacy was not reversed until the Civil Rights Act of 1964.

There was also a lack of effective public accountability for corporate monopolies until the Clayton Act of 1914. As the USA approached fifty states, with fifty corporate laws, their courts' enforcement of the restraint of trade doctrine was not enough, and so the Sherman Act of 1890 was passed to 'extend the common law principles, which protected fair competition in trade in old times in England, to international and interstate commerce in the United States'.[141]

[136] K. Marx, *Capital* (1894) vol. III, ch. 27.

[137] R. Blackburn, 'Lincoln and Marx', *Jacobin* (28 August 2012) https://jacobinmag.com/2012/08/lincoln-and-marx.

[138] A. Lincoln, First Annual Message (3 December 1861).

[139] *Munn v Illinois*, 94 US 113 (1876). [140] *Civil Rights Cases*, 109 US 3 (1883).

[141] Senator Hoar, 21 Congressional Record 3146, 3151–2 (1890).

The original goal was to target the big business 'trusts' that had built up,[142] particularly the Standard Oil network of corporations, created by J. D. Rockefeller, where votes on shares were transferred to trusts controlled by Rockefeller and his confidantes.[143] But instead, the courts' first use of the Act's restraint of trade offence was against workers' unions on the railways, not large corporations.[144] By contrast, and at the same time, the UK's House of Lords decided that small enterprise co-operatives were legal, just as worker organisation was, and not an unlawful conspiracy or cartel.[145] Yet the US Supreme Court went further in *Lochner v New York*, declaring that laws for a fair working day, and then nearly all social rights (pensions, bans on child labour and minimum wages[146]), would be 'unconstitutional' since they interfered (ostensibly) with 'liberty of contract'.[147] The Sherman Act of 1890 also set off a massive merger wave, as businesses realised that they would be sued for being a cartel, but they would not for merging and having the same effect as a cartel. After twenty-one years, and a renewed Department of Justice, the Supreme Court did approve the break-up of Standard Oil in 1911,[148] and the Clayton Act of 1914 added controls on mergers that substantially lessened competition. It also exempted labour from antitrust actions on the ground that 'labor is not a commodity or article of commerce'.[149] The same year, World War One broke out (see Ch. 19). That horrendous conflict ended in the defective Versailles Treaty, based on perpetual debt, not perpetual peace.[150] However, the Treaty did create the International Labour Organization, which recalled that 'peace can be established only if it is based upon social justice',[151] proclaimed that 'labour is not a commodity' and set about fashioning global standards for labour rights.

Karl Marx had believed that the most advanced capitalist nations would be the first to undergo a communist revolution, and that this was a matter of

[142] J. J. Flynn, 'The Reagan Administration's Antitrust Policy, "Original Intent" and the Legislative History of the Sherman Act' (1988) 33 *Antitrust Bulletin* 259.

[143] See generally, E. B. Andrews, 'Trusts According to Official Investigations' (1889) 3(2) *QJ Economics* 117, 119–20, referred to in H. Hovenkamp, 'Antitrust Policy, Federalism and the Theory of the Firm: An Historical Perspective' (1990) 59(1) *Antitrust LJ* 75 and H. Hovenkamp, *Enterprise and American Law, 1836–1937* (1991) ch. 20, 250–1.

[144] *In re Debs*, 158 US 564 (1895). See later, *Loewe v Lawlor*, 208 US 274 (1908) on Danbury hatmakers.

[145] *Mogul Steamship Co. Ltd v McGregor, Gow & Co.* [1892] AC 25 (association to limit ships); *Nordenfelt v Maxim, Nordenfelt Gun Co.* [1894] AC 535.

[146] E.g. *Railroad Retirement Board v Alton Railroad Co.*, 295 US 330 (1935) (railway pension); *State Board of Control v Buckstegge*, 158 Pac 837, 842 (1916) (state pension law); *Hammer v Dagenhart*, 247 US 251 (1918) (child labour); *Adkins v Children's Hospital*, 261 US 525 (1923) (minimum wages).

[147] *Lochner v New York*, 198 US 45 (1905).

[148] *Standard Oil of New Jersey v United States*, 221 US 1 (1911).

[149] Clayton Antitrust Act of 1914, §6; 15 USC, §17.

[150] J. M. Keynes, *The Economic Consequences of the Peace* (1919); I. Kant, *Perpetual Peace: A Philosophical Essay* (1795) trans. M. C. Smith (1903), also *Zum Ewigen Frieden* (1795).

[151] Treaty of Versailles 1919, Part XIII.

historical inevitability, driven by the internal contradictions of labour commodification, exploitation, alienation and capital accumulation. However, the Marxists that first seized power were not in Britain, Germany or America (if Lincoln is excepted), but in agrarian Russia, upon the October Revolution of 1917. Vladimir Lenin had been put on a train to Russia by the German military, and sure enough he took advantage of the ruinous tsarist state and seized power. Because he personally believed that a period of bloodbath like the French Revolution was a necessary step to reconstruct Russia, Lenin's Bolsheviks conducted massacres throughout the civil war and, to take just one example, decreed that criminal punishments should not inflict injury or needless suffering, but only for non-political offences.[152] Transfers to public ownership occurred mainly through force, and without compensation, encouraged during the state of civil war that lasted until 1923. This started with banks, and then all factories, and industry. While some private enterprise lasted until 1928, from then a series of five-year plans replaced market exchange and collectivised land.[153] After Lenin, who died in 1924, the leading theorist of Soviet law was Evgeny Pashukanis, who argued that a transition to communism meant the 'withering away of the bourgeois form of law'.[154] In 1930, according to Stalin, the bank robber who took over, this was taken further to 'the withering away of the state' and 'the strengthening of the dictatorship of the proletariat',[155] by which he meant the dictatorship of himself. In 1936, Stalin announced that 'the complete victory of the socialist system in all spheres of national economy is now a fact' and 'socialist ownership' was 'the unshakeable foundation of our socialist society'.[156] From Leon Trotsky's view in exile, before he and Pashukanis and millions of others were murdered, the state had not withered away but had 'grown into a hitherto unheard of apparatus of compulsion'.[157] Every enterprise was covered. The Soviet economy grew faster, and lifted more from poverty than under the tsar, but not compared to any democratic country, and at a terrible price of freedom and lives.

After World War One, and with reform, Germany, Britain and the USA were becoming less undemocratic in politics,[158] and all had plans for an 'industrial democracy' in the language inspired by Sidney and Beatrice

[152] J. Hamilton and S. Deakin, 'Russia's Legal Transitions: Marxist Theory, Neoclassical Economics and the Rule of Law' (2015) 7 *Hague J Rule of Law* 283, 289, citing J. Hostettler, *Law and Terror in Stalin's Russia* (2003) 30.

[153] Hamilton and Deakin, 'Russia's Legal Transitions', 289–90.

[154] E. Pashukanis, *The General Theory of Law and Marxism* (1924) 63.

[155] Stalin, Speech to the Sixteenth Party Congress (1930).

[156] Stalin, Report on the draft 1936 Constitution (1936) in M. Head, *Evgeny Pashukanis: A Critical Reappraisal* (2008) 149.

[157] Head, *Evgeny Pashukanis: A Critical Reappraisal*, 109.

[158] In Germany the Weimar Constitution 1919 guaranteed universal adult suffrage. In Britain, the Representation of the People Act 1918 had male suffrage over 21, but required women to be over 30 and hold property until 1928, and in much of the empire, particularly India and Africa, there was violent suppression. The US Nineteenth Amendment prohibited denial of the right

Webb.[159] But each adopted very different models. In Germany, following a collective agreement among unions and business, the Weimar Constitution 1919, article 165 said that workers and employers would 'cooperate . . . on an equal footing . . . in the entire field of the economic development of the forces of production'.[160] Written by Hugo Sinzheimer, this was implemented in a Work Council Act 1920, giving elected work councils rights to co-operate in setting work conditions, to manage pensions and to veto unjustified dismissals. A Supervisory Board Act 1922 then gave workers minority representation on company boards. However, the Social Democratic government referred the question of which enterprises should be in public ownership to a commission.[161] One of the 'cruel ironies' was that this socialist government (unlike the Bolsheviks), that was in 'complete possession of the political power', did 'nothing more . . . than to set up a commission'.[162] It did nationalise coal in 1919, but then lost power in 1920.[163] A member of the commission, Karl Kautsky, would write in 1924 that strategic enterprises should be in public ownership, and that the worker, the consumer and the state were the three basic groups to represent.[164] But there was no government to do it.

In the UK, the primary model of 'industrial democracy', rather than votes at work or in public institutions, was institutionalised, sectoral collective bargaining, promoted by the Ministry of Labour.[165] A series of social rights had been enacted before the war to guarantee a minimum floor of welfare,[166] and the Trade Disputes Act 1906 had protected collective bargaining for workers in unions to get fair standards beyond the minimum.[167] But after the war it was understood that active government was needed to ensure fair pay scales across major sectors of industry. The ministry ensured that 'joint industrial councils'

to vote based on sex, but it was not until the Voting Rights Act of 1965 that widespread suppression of black people voting was ended in the southern states.

159 S. Webb and B. Webb, *Industrial Democracy* (1897) and see especially vol. II, part III, ch. 4.

160 Weimar Constitution 1919, art. 165, following the *Stinnes-Legien Abkommen*; see E. McGaughey, 'The Codetermination Bargains: The History of German Corporate and Labour Law' (2016) 23(1) *Columbia J Eur L* 135, 154–8.

161 *Kommission zur Vorbereitung der Sozialisierung der Industrie* (November 1918) whose members included Dr Josef Schumpter and Dr Karl Kautsky.

162 E. Frankel, 'The Status of "Socialization" in Germany' (1924) 32(1) *J Political Economy* 68, 69.

163 The Socialization Act 1919 or *Gesetz über Sozialisierung* (23 March 1919) enabled purchase of industry with compensation, and the Coal Socialization Act 1919 or *Gesetz über die Regelung der Kohlenwirtschaft* (23 March 1919) placed coal under a National Coal Council. Also *Gesetz über die Regelung der Kaliwirtschaft* (24 April 1919). A planned electricity Act never took effect.

164 K. Kautsky, *The Labour Revolution* (1924) ch. 3, part VIII(e).

165 New Ministries and Secretaries Act 1916; Trade Boards Act 1918.

166 Old Age Pensions Act 1908 (pensions), Trade Boards Act 1909 (minimum wages), National Insurance Act 1911 (unemployment protection and limited healthcare). Previously also the Preferential Payments in Bankruptcy Amendment Act 1897 created preferential status for employees' claims in insolvency.

167 This reversed three cases where the House of Lords imposed liability on striking workers for economic loss to employers: *Taff Vale Railway Co. v ASRS* [1901] UKHL 1, *Quinn v Leathem* [1901] UKHL 2 and *South Wales Miners' Federation v Glamorgan Coal Co.* [1905] AC 239.

were established by voluntary agreement among unions and employer groups, and if they failed it had power to fix wages.[168] This system, however, was partly aborted after just four years between 1918 and 1922 and only revived after 1934. Aside from collective bargaining, it was only in the universities, a number of gas companies and the Port of London that workers had rights to elect company board representatives.[169] In fact, the Conservative Minister for Transport had proposed that workers elect a third of railway boards, but the plan did not pass against management opposition, and unions who were focused on nationalisation. Although the unions, along with the Webbs and the Labour Party, had called for 'common ownership of the means of production, distribution and exchange',[170] there was merely a reorganisation of rail and a new rates tribunal.[171] Not only were calls for public mine ownership ignored,[172] swingeing wage cuts against coal miners led to the General Strike of 1926. On the other hand, the Petroleum Act 1918 cemented the UK government's ownership in what became British Petroleum and control over oil reserves. The Forestry Act 1919 established the Forestry Commission to restore Britain's trees, felled for war trench beams. The Housing of the Working Classes Act 1919 started a large home-building programme. The British Broadcasting Corporation was founded in 1926. The London Passenger Transport Act 1933 enabled public bus networks. And the British Overseas Airways Act 1939 created the forerunner to British Airways. The public was working.

In the USA, a short-lived attempt at industrial democracy focused on arbitration overseen by the War Labor Board, with five employee, five employer and two public representatives to hear labour dispute appeals.[173] However this was shut down with political change in 1919,[174] while the *Lochner*-era Supreme Court continued to strike down all attempts by states and federal government to create social rights. Since this included any public pension, such as those that existed in Germany or Britain, people put their savings in the stock market. The soaring fortunes of Wall Street from so many workers' capital combined with an absence of duties of disclosure and prudence in securities trade. So, companies and stocks were systematically overvalued. This led to the Wall Street Crash of 1929, only worsened as President

[168] K. D. Ewing, 'The State and Industrial Relations' (1998) 5 *Historical Studies in Industrial Relations* 1.

[169] See South Metropolitan Gas Act 1896; Port of London Act 1908, s. 1(6); E. McGaughey, 'Votes at Work in Britain: Shareholder Monopolisation and the "Single Channel"' (2018) 47(1) *Industrial LJ* 76.

[170] Labour Party Constitution 1918, cl. IV and see S. Webb and B. Webb, *A Constitution for the Socialist Commonwealth of Great Britain* (1920).

[171] Railways Act 1921.

[172] Coal Industry Commission, *Reports and Minutes of Evidence on the Second Stage of Inquiry*, Cmd 360, vol. II (1919).

[173] R. B. Gregg, 'The National War Labor Board' (1919) 33(1) *Harvard L Rev* 39, 40.

[174] E. McGaughey, 'Democracy in America at Work: The History of Labor's Vote in Corporate Governance' (2019) 42 *Seattle UL Rev* 697, 717–18.

Hoover shut off international trade with the Smoot-Hawley Tariff Act of 1930. As unemployment soared to a quarter of the US workforce, Franklin D. Roosevelt was elected in 1932, promising a 'New Deal'. A. A. Berle and the other members of his 'brains trust' set about creating a new economic constitution, including labour rights,[175] social security,[176] bank reform, securities and exchange regulation,[177] fair competition rules,[178] agricultural reform, public production of energy, rural electrification, new standards for telecommunications and education funding.[179] This brought the USA back out of the Great Depression slowly, but not entirely, before the eve of World War Two. In 1944, President Roosevelt argued they must create a 'Second Bill of Rights' by legislation, including fair wages, fair competition, housing, social security, health and education.

World War Two erupted because of the conditions for reparations in the Versailles Treaty; the economic depredation that Germany faced; the impact of the Great Depression; the resulting psychological susceptibility to Adolf Hitler's delusional, racist conspiracies and lies (see Ch. 10); and the financial backing of banks and major industry for Hitler's election campaign.[180] As President Roosevelt later put it, 'people who are hungry and out of a job are the stuff of which dictatorships are made'. According to Otto Kahn-Freund, a Berlin judge who fled to London, fascism was also enabled through an unconscious culture in the judiciary, which dismantled labour rights in favour of business.[181] Hitler made the implicit very explicit. Once Hitler took control of the police, it was irrelevant that the conservatives in his coalition held onto the Ministry of Finance, because the use of terror and the state of emergency enabled the abolition of unions and political parties. The Nazi economy first destroyed free trade unions, then abolished the right of workers to co-determine company boards, then created the concept of 'reprivatisation' of enterprise,[182] entrenched monopolies and cartels that funded the Nazis,[183] concentrated shareholder votes in companies into the hands of banks and

[175] National Labor Relations Act of 1935, Fair Labor Standards Act of 1938 and Employment Act of 1946.

[176] Social Security Act of 1935.

[177] Securities Act of 1933 and Securities and Exchange Act of 1934.

[178] National Industrial Recovery Act of 1933, but this was struck down as unconstitutional, so the more limited Robinson-Patman Act of 1936 including bans on price discrimination.

[179] Servicemen's Readjustment Act of 1944.

[180] A. Schweitzer, *Big Business in the Third Reich* (1964) 104–5; McGaughey, 'The Codetermination Bargains', 140–1.

[181] O. Kahn-Freund, 'Autobiographische Errinerungen an die Weimarer Republik. Ein Gesprach mit Wolfgang Luthardt' [1978] *Kritische Justiz* 183, trans. (2016) KCL Law School Research Paper No. 2016-34.

[182] S. Merlin, 'Trends in German Economic Control since 1933' (1943) 57(2) *QJ Economics* 169.

[183] *Gesetz uber Errichtung von Zwangskartellen* (15 July 1933) RGBl, Part I, 487–8, or the Compulsory Cartel Act 1933, forced cartel membership across business, and gave the Ministry of Economic Affairs power to organise: total Nazi economic control. See I. E. Schwartz, 'Antitrust Legislation and Policy in Germany – a Comparative Study' (1957) 105(5) *U Penn L Rev* 617, 641–2. Cf. F. Neumann, *Behemoth* (1944) 23.

made company boards irremovable by their investors or workforce. As one crazed Nazi lawyer put it: 'Democracy of capital will vanish just as it did in politics.'[184] The only thing left was the 'leader'. And then the 'leader' went too.

(5) Global Revolution, 1945–2021

Out of the tragedy and bestiality of war, a 'global revolution' is the best way to explain the times we have come to live in since, for three main reasons. First, a new constitution of humanity was proclaimed, enshrined in the Charter of the United Nations 1945, and the Universal Declaration of Human Rights (UDHR) 1948. These two documents were written 'to save succeeding generations from the scourge of war, which twice in our lifetime has brought untold sorrow to mankind' and to recognise that 'equal and inalienable rights of all members of the human family is the foundation of freedom, justice and peace in the world'. The British and French Empires were rapidly dissolved,[185] and the new European Economic Community, and then the European Union (EU), led as an example of regional integration. Second, there was an increasingly integrated global economy, supported by dozens of new United Nations (UN) organisations, such as the United Nations Educational, Scientific and Cultural Organization, the World Health Organization, the World Bank, International Monetary Fund (IMF) and the World Trade Organization from 1994 that freed-up trade. Third, there was an increasingly global culture and social integration, particularly with the creation of the Internet, and the end of distance as a barrier to communication. Cities like London, New York, Los Angeles, Paris, Amsterdam, Berlin, Sydney, Singapore and Toronto each came to contain people from *every* part of the world within them, something never seen in human history. The Covid-19 pandemic of 2020–21, though it shut off borders to halt the virus, simply underlined the globe's integration. It brought people together even more by video, and created a yearning for an open world again. Equally, the continued use of coal, oil and gas had created a climate emergency that required both collective action by the UN, and unilateral action by every country, to end all fossil fuels, for the sake of the very planet.

Yet in this global revolution there was not yet a global consensus on the nature and shape of enterprise law. The defining feature of the post-war era has been swings, like a pendulum, between poles of nationalisation and privatisation, and back to an uncertain end. Despite the human rights enshrined in international law for education, health, housing, food, freedom of expression and the benefits of science (see Ch. 2(4)), the finance, governance and legal structures for realising rights were contested. After World War Two, the most

[184] J. C. D. Zahn, *Wirtschaftsführertum und Vertragsethik im Neuen Aktienrecht* [*Economic Leadership and Contractual Ethics in the New Corporate Law*] (1934); and see F. Kessler, 'Book Review' (1935) 83 *U Penn L Rev* 393.

[185] E.g. Indian Independence Act 1947, Ghana Independence Act 1957, Trinidad and Tobago Independence Act 1962 and Singapore Act 1966.

Table 1.3 Major steps in public ownership of enterprise

	Enterprise	Laws
1	Common land	Magna Carta 1215, Charter of the Forest 1217
2	Post	Master of the Post, 1516
3	Local services	Municipal Corporations (England) Act 1835
4	East India Co.	Government of India Act 1858
5	Telegraphs	Telegraph Act 1869
6	Schools	Elementary Education Act 1870
7	Telephones	*Attorney General v Edison* (1880)
8	Oil and gas	Petroleum Act 1918
9	Housing	Housing of the Working Classes Act 1919
10	Radio, TV	BBC Charter 1926
11	Buses in London	London Passenger Transport Act 1933
12	Air	British Overseas Airways Act 1939
13	University (grants)	Education Act 1944 and 1962
14	Water	Water Act 1945
15	Coal	Coal Industry Nationalisation Act 1946
16	Central bank	Bank of England Act 1946
17	Health	National Health Service Act 1946
18	Rail, buses	Transport Act 1947
19	Electricity	Electricity Act 1947
20	Land planning	Town and Country Planning Act 1947
21	Gas	Gas Act 1948
22	Iron and steel	Iron and Steel Act 1949
23	Agriculture	European Communities Act 1972

comprehensive plan of public ownership was created by the UK Labour Party under Prime Minister Clement Attlee, elected in 1945 on a platform to 'win the peace'. Together with the wartime coalition, Labour passed ten major pieces of legislation to extend public ownership of industry (see Table 1.3).

The theories of what should be publicly owned were less based on an overarching, or even articulated, concept, and more a tendency to test what worked.[186] In 1948, a Labour Party document on *Public Ownership: The Next Step* contended that industries should be nationalised if they fell within one or more of five categories – namely, if they (1) were 'basic' to other industries, for human life, health or defence; (2) were monopolised; (3) were inefficient without capital development; (4) were large enough to affect overall employment; or (5) suffered from poor industrial relations.[187] While this was an admirable attempt to collect reasons, such open and interpretable criteria did not command lasting support. In other countries, the attempts to codify principles were not decisive either. For example, in the Italian Constitution

[186] Cf. W. A. Robson, 'The Public Corporation in Britain Today' (1950) 63(8) *Harvard L Rev* 1321.
[187] Labour Party, *Public Ownership: The Next Step* (1948).

1947, article 43 stated that 'specific enterprises' could be put into public ownership when they 'relate to essential public services or sources of energy or monopolistic situations and which have the nature of primary general interest'. But what was 'essential'? What counted as 'monopolistic'? And what was of 'general interest'? Coupled to these questions was an absence of principle behind who would participate in enterprise governance. While a 1934 Labour document had called for employees to always have 'an effective share in the control and direction of the industry',[188] the dominant model became that proposed by Herbert Morrison, who originally set up a public bus network in London. This was simply that a minister (like Morrison) appointed 'experts', perhaps in consultation with unions or consumer groups, but not giving them any votes.[189] It was ever more clear, as nationalisation went on, that consumers or the public did not significantly 'influence the style of economic thinking and administration of the public corporations'.[190]

By contrast, in the general laws of enterprise, post-war reform was wide reaching, more principled and informed by the experience of the Great Depression. Following A. A. Berle and Gardiner Means theories of the New Deal, the Companies Act 1947 enacted the principle that company directors could be dismissed by a simple majority of members,[191] while stock exchange regulation pressured companies to hold to a principle of 'one share, one vote'.[192] Labour rights reform was achieved through the protection of collective bargaining, and the Wages Councils Act 1945 ensuring default fair pay scales for each sector. Gradually the scope of competition law expanded to control the abuse of big business power over competitors, consumers and the public.[193] In Germany, the post-fascist occupying forces,[194] and then a new constitutional West German government, restored the right to collectively bargain, and unions restored the right to elect work councils and be represented on boards.[195] This revived system of 'co-determination' was seen as essential to bring democracy to the economy. In fact, having *themselves* been 'nationalised' by the Nazis, German unions were focused on 'socializing power

[188] Labour Party, *For Socialism and Peace* (1934).

[189] H. Morrison, *Socialisation and Transport: Organisation of Socialised Industries with the Particular Reference to the London Passenger Transport Bill* (1933).

[190] A. M. Neuman, 'Some Economic Aspects of Nationalization' (1951) 16(4) *L & Cont Probs* 702, 711.

[191] Lord Cohen, *Report of the Committee on Company Law Amendment*, Cmd 6659 (1945).

[192] E. McGaughey, *Participation in Corporate Governance* (2014) ch. 5.

[193] Monopoly and Restrictive Practices (Inquiry and Control) Act 1948, Restrictive Practices Act 1956, Resale Prices Act 1964, Fair Trading Act 1973. Cf. at common law, *Esso Petroleum Co. Ltd v Harper's Garage (Stourport) Ltd* [1968] AC 269 (21-year agreement to exclusively buy petrol invalid, but 5 years valid. Lord Reid could find no 'dividing line'); *Schroeder Music Publishing Co. Ltd v Macaulay* [1974] 1 WLR 1308 (exclusive copyright invalid); *Alec Lobb (Garages) Ltd v Total Oil (Great Britain) Ltd* [1985] 1 WLR 173 (exclusive purchase valid).

[194] Control Council Law No. 22 (10 April 1946) Works Councils.

[195] Mining Codetermination Act 1951, Work Constitution Act 1972 and Codetermination Act 1976.

without socializing ownership', and '[d]istribution of power to the people, rather than [a] concentration of ownership in the state'.[196] Trade unions and the Social Democratic Party of Germany did still support public ownership of 'key industries',[197] but similar to Kautsky's theory this came to favour local over national management, and placed an emphasis (albeit far from complete either) on direct voting rights of workers, and consumers or the public, in its administration.[198] In the UK, attempts were made in the 1970s to introduce board co-determination more widely than at universities, and steps were made to increase public participation particularly in education and health institutions, but not yet on a widespread basis. No general Act succeeded.[199]

Crucially, nation state practice was now embedded in international law. The forming of the European Economic Community (EEC) in 1957, which became the EU in 1992, sought to create 'not merely an economic union', but aimed 'to ensure social progress and seek the constant improvement of the living and working conditions'.[200] First, the EEC's foundations took after the post-war Marshall Plan in providing large agricultural subsidies to guarantee food security and support fair incomes at a time when much of the labour force still farmed (see Ch. 13). Second, it aimed to break down barriers to trade in goods and services, but also was clear that the 'Treaties shall in no way prejudice the rules in Member States governing the system of property ownership.'[201] In the midst of the cold war, this meant agnosticism about either pole of capitalism or communism, at least on paper. Third, the treaties steadily built up, through the theory of integrating a common market, a body of standards for companies, investment, competition, consumer protection and labour rights, excepting that direct regulation of wages, collective bargaining and strike action were reserved for member states.[202] The development of EU law was consistent with the two treaties that recast the UDHR, namely the International Covenant on Civil and Political Rights (ICCPR) and the International Covenant on Economic, Social and Cultural Rights 1966 (ICESCR), not to mention the burgeoning number of International Labour Organization Conventions that served as a model for all countries' laws. Steadily, the number of countries that adopted public ownership, an extended democratic voice for labour in enterprise and more stringent standards against monopoly in private enterprise grew.

However, a much more extreme picture evolved at either pole of the 'cold war' between the Soviet Union and the USA. The USSR held to its repression of

[196] C. Kerr, 'The Trade Union Movement and the Redistribution of Power in Postwar Germany' (1954) 68 *QJ Economics* 535, 544–5, quoting Viktor Agartz of the DGB, German Union Federation.

[197] *Protokoll Gründungskongress des Deutschen Gewerkschaftsbundes, 12-14 Oktober 1949* (1950) 318–32.

[198] E.g. *Gemeindeordnung Nordrhein-Westfalen* [Community Ordinance North Rhine Westphalia] 1994, §§107–14 at Ch. 12(3)(d).

[199] McGaughey, 'Votes at Work in Britain'.

[200] *Defrenne v Sabena (No. 2)* (1976) Case 43/75.

[201] Now TFEU, art. 345.

[202] Now TFEU, art. 153.

all political parties, and to free trade unions, until it crumbled under the weight of dissent in 1991. Although the 'Communist' Party, with its rigid anti-community command of enterprise, promised that they would 'bury' the West through its superior economic performance, it was all a lie. When Stalin died, his successor Khrushchev exposed the mass murder, the purges and the crimes perpetrated through collectivisation, but maintained all elements of the police state. In the USA, after President Roosevelt passed away, a renewed Republican Party won a majority in the Congress in 1946. With southern Democrat support, they charged through the Taft-Hartley Act of 1947, removing from unions the right to collectively bargain, to take action against more than one employer, to bargain for all-union workplaces and to control their own pension funds, and they created rights for employers to sue unions for 'unfair labor practices'. While unions grew in Europe, this Act levelled off growth in unions in the USA. The movement for gender and racial equality succeeded in winning the Equal Pay Act of 1963 and the Civil Rights Act of 1964, which quickly served as models for European equality laws. A. A. Berle wrote at this point that this was part of the larger system of rights in the economic constitution, a fact which amounted to a 'revolution' in property relations. Yet he also noted the growth of pension, insurance and mutual funds that invested money in corporate shares and that this growth of institutional intermediation separated the true investor even further from control over their capital.[203] In 1976, the US Supreme Court decided that the First Amendment ostensibly protected the right of people to spend unlimited money in political campaigns as an act of 'free speech',[204] and this was soon extended to corporate spending too.[205] From this very point, American people lost meaningful influence over the political process, and growth in real wages stagnated entirely for the next four decades. There were no significant developments in labour rights, consumer rights[206] nor in public enterprise, excepting the fallout from the global financial crisis in 2007–8. With a total 'ossification' of democratic society,[207] the US political process was simply dominated by money, where public opinion did less and less to shape policy and law.[208]

The shifts in politics were at each stage accompanied by theories supporting shareholder control of corporations,[209] and more generally deregulation,

[203] A. A. Berle, 'Property, Production and Revolution' (1965) 65 *Columbia L Rev* 1.

[204] *Buckley v Valeo*, 424 US 1 (1976) after L. F. Powell Jr, 'Attack on American Free Enterprise System', Confidential Memo to US Chamber of Commerce (1971).

[205] *First National Bank of Boston v Bellotti*, 435 US 765 (1978); *Citizens United v Federal Election Commission*, 558 US 310 (2010).

[206] L. Khan and S. Vaheesan, 'Market Power and Inequality: The Antitrust Counterrevolution and Its Discontents' (2017) 11 *Harvard L & Policy Rev* 235.

[207] C. L. Estlund, 'The Ossification of American Labor Law' (2002) 102 *Columbia L Rev* 1527.

[208] M. Gilens and B. I. Page, 'Testing Theories of American Politics: Elites, Interest Groups, and Average Citizens' (2014) 12(3) *Perspectives on Politics* 564.

[209] E.g. M. Friedman, 'The Social Responsibility of Business Is to Increase Its Profits', *New York Times Magazine* (13 September 1970).

Table 1.4 Major reprivatisations in UK enterprise

	Enterprise	Laws
1	Military hardware	British Aerospace Act 1980
2	Oil and gas	BP sale, Oil and Gas (Enterprise) Act 1982
3	Telecoms	British Telecommunications Act 1981, Telecommunications Act 1984
4	Air	Civil Aviation Act 1980
5	Housing	Housing Act 1980
6	Nuclear	Atomic Energy (Miscellaneous Provisions) Act 1981
7	Buses	Transport Act 1985
8	Gas	Gas Act 1986
9	Water	Water Act 1986
10	Car-makers	Jaguar 1984, Rolls Royce 1986, Rover 1988, etc.
11	Banking	Trustee Savings Bank Act 1986
12	Electricity	Electricity Act 1989
13	Rail	Railways Act 1993
14	Coal	Coal Industry Act 1994
15	Nuclear fuels	Atomic Energy Authority Act 1995
16	Universities	Higher Education Acts 1998, 2004, 2010
17	Air traffic control	Transport Act 2000
18	Post	Postal Services Act 2011
19	Health	Health and Social Care Act 2012

reprivatisation and removal of taxation.[210] As well as the Reagan administration from 1980 in the US, in the UK the election of Margaret Thatcher in 1979 set this chain in motion. Under Thatcher, there were twelve major pieces of legislation, along with administrative acts, to reprivatise enterprises that by post-war consensus had been held in the public sector (see Table 1.4). The mechanisms varied, but usually involved initial public offerings of shares to the public, such as in British Telecom, or the transfer of shares to employees, such as in the Transport Act 1985.

In addition, there were ten major Acts to break down the voice of people at work through trade unions,[211] and a retrenchment of the worker directors that existed at the Post Office. This loss of labour voice was a primary driver of increasing income inequality (see Ch. 5(1)(d)). On the other hand, the strength of protection for minority shareholders was improved in the Companies Act 1985 and for creditors in the Insolvency Act 1986.[212] But what started as measures for accountability of directors ended by primarily benefiting asset managers and banks (see Chs. 4 and 7). The same basic patterns continued

[210] E.g. M Friedman, *Capitalism and Freedom* (1962); F. A. Hayek, *The Constitution of Liberty* (1960).

[211] Now recast in the Trade Union and Labour Relations (Consolidation) Act 1992, the Employment Rights Act 1996 and the National Minimum Wage Act 1998.

[212] After Kenneth Cork, *Report of the Review Committee on Insolvency Law and Practice*, Cmnd 8558 (1982) and the Bankruptcy Reform Act 1978.

under the Blair and Brown administrations with minor adjustments, and the pace of privatisation (of whatever was left) picked up again under the Cameron-led coalition of Conservatives and Liberal Democrats. Privatisation did not mean, however, a complete return to unregulated private enterprise since it was recognised that a new regulator was needed for every sector, with powers ranging from price controls to determination of contract standards with consumers: new 'Offices of' enterprise, including Oftel and then Ofcom, Ofgem, Ofwat, the Office of Rail and Road, and most recently Ofstu. This regulation limited the detrimental welfare impact of selling off public assets,[213] and an unexpected 'offspring' was this new public service law.[214]

Globally, the policies of Thatcher and Reagan had an extreme influence through the development of the 'Washington consensus', a set of policies adopted by the World Bank and IMF to require that countries in need of loans privatise and deregulate enterprise. After the fall of the Berlin Wall, and as the Communist Party leader Mikhail Gorbachev was ejected from power, the IMF advised that the new Russian Federation privatise its assets primarily by giving its workers company shares.[215] As production seized up, and people plunged into poverty, they sold their shares in droves for food to the men that emerged as the new Russian oligarchs – people who were successful in buying up more cheap, ex-state assets than anyone. The oligarch establishment supported Gorbachev's replacement, Yeltsin, and integrated with the police-state establishment under Vladimir Putin. Putin's thesis was that he could make Russia great again by exploiting and exporting Russia's vast reserves of metals, and primarily coal, oil and gas – the fossil fuels that were driving climate damage.[216] Like the economies of Saudi Arabia, Australia, Canada, the UK and the USA, this created an intense lobby group vested in denying the catastrophic climate damage taking place, and backing of deniers of scientific fact.

Yet eclipsing the 'first' and 'second' worlds, from the turn of the twenty-first century, there was an exponential rise of developing countries, and particularly China and India. In terms of population, these countries were dwarfing the USA, the ex-USSR and the EU (see Figure 1.3). In terms of production, they looked set to do so too. By 1999, just over a year after the UK returned Hong Kong to Chinese control, China's gross domestic product had surpassed the UK's and, by 2020, India's had done so as well. The central difference between China and India was that, despite the reforms of Deng Xiaoping to open Chinese enterprise to private investment, China's politics remained authoritarian, suppressing other political parties and free trade unions. India's political system was open and democratic but thoroughly corrupt

[213] M. Florio, *The Great Divestiture: Evaluating the Welfare Impact of the British Privatizations, 1979–1997* (2004) ch. 1.

[214] T. Prosser, 'Public Service Law: Privatization's Unexpected Offspring' (2000) 63(4) *L & Cont Probs* 63.

[215] B. Black, R. Kraakman and A. Tarassova, 'Russian Privatization and Corporate Governance: What Went Wrong?' (2000) 52(6) *Stanford L Rev* 1731.

[216] H. Balzer, 'The Putin Thesis and Russian Energy Policy' (2005) 21 *Post-Soviet Affairs* 210.

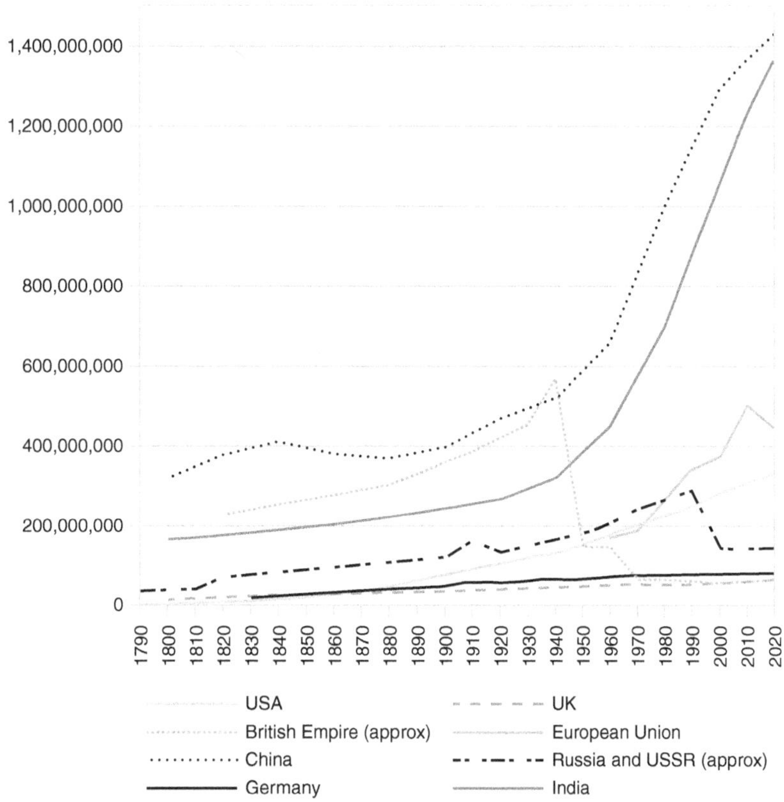

Figure 1.3 Populations of the USA, UK, Germany, EU, Russia, India and China
Sources: Worldometer and R. Johnson, *Historical World Population Data* (2015)

and, under Prime Minister Modi from 2014, was turning increasingly authoritarian. The UN Sustainable Development Goals in 2015 were promising targets by 2030 for the realisation of human rights – from ending poverty, to universal education and health, clean energy and transport, and free communication. But the vast divergences of political and economic structures to achieve those goals appeared to stand in the way.

The turn in the climate of politics towards authoritarianism was acutely felt in the 'global north' from 2015, as the US presidential election saw Donald Trump go from TV to the White House, backed with 'active measures' by Russian intelligence exploiting social media. A similar rise of far-right parties was being supported around Europe, and in Brazil, through weaponisation of the Internet to spread disinformation (see Ch. 17). While the 2020 US presidential election ejected Trump in favour of Joe Biden, it was not clear whether basic changes would be made to the structure of enterprise law. There were proposals in the USA for changes to tax and labour rights, but essentially remaining weaker than what already existed in Europe or the Commonwealth.

Figure 1.4 Cola-Cola advertisement, around 1992, from the Richards Group

There were, however, very significant plans for spending money to end climate damage and to institute a global system of corporate tax. But the essential functioning of private and global enterprise was unchanged, so far. Of all the people who came and went over the course of history, privatised enterprise, with a precarious attachment to human rights, with all its social, economic and environmental costs, was still dominant (see Figure 1.4).

(6) Conclusion

The reasons that we see enterprise law today as we do depend primarily on changes in ideas. The limited yet significant role for public enterprise, the limited yet growing governance voice for people who create enterprise and the precarious but mounting realisation of universal human rights are a result of how people think, where we perceive our interests to lie and the political and economic power that people have to achieve their aims. Over the grand course of history, humanity had moved from ancient societies based on water and wood, horses and post, to industrial societies based on coal and oil, combustion motors and telecoms, and we are now moving to a modern society based on sun and wind, electric vehicles and the Internet. Underlying all of these shifts is vast change in education, health and political practice. The transitions of enterprise, the speed and adoption of technological and scientific change were always dependent on social institutions and, ultimately, the laws. These in turn were guided by the theories behind them, to which Chapter 2 now turns.

2

Modern Theory

Contents

Theories of enterprise law go to the heart of economics, politics and a just society. First, there are 'positive' theories that explain how the world works. For example, a positive theory might argue that labour rights raise employment and productivity, and reduce inequality (see Ch. 5), or that public healthcare gives longer life than privatised or insurance health systems (see Ch. 9). As in natural science, social science frames hypotheses, develops methods for testing the hypotheses, finds results and draws conclusions.[1] However, natural science differs from social science, where we participate in our own experiments.[2] People often draw conclusions that suit their own interests or prejudices and, unlike the natural world, people's belief in a social phenomenon may actually make it true. No matter how many people believe the world is flat, it is a sphere. But if many people believe a stock market will crash or an economy will depress, that prophecy may self-fulfil. Second, there are 'normative' theories about what we should do. They are usually based either on consequences or principles. For example, a consequentialist theory may say that because public healthcare systems outperform others, we *should* have a fully public health service. By contrast a principle-based theory may argue that regardless of the consequences, the right to 'liberty' implies the government should provide free healthcare. In politics, we often use all forms of argument to persuade people, though principles or reasons based on shared values are more persuasive among voters.[3]

[1] Cf. M. Friedman, 'The Methodology of Positive Economics' in *Essays in Positive Economics* (1953) 4.

[2] Q. Skinner, *Visions of Politics* (2002) vol. I, ch. 2.

[3] T. Nelson and J. Garst, 'Values-Based Political Messages and Persuasion' (2005) 26(4) *Political Psychology* 489.

This chapter focuses on the modern theories of enterprise law: on its finance, governance and rights. How should we construct markets? When should we use prices or taxes to fund the production of goods and services? Which enterprises should be publicly and which privately owned? Who should participate in enterprise governance? What economic and social rights should we have? And what is the best way to realise these human rights? Answers to these questions ideally depend on reasons and evidence. Fortunately, in the twenty-first century, our access to history, knowledge of experiments in countries across the globe and data computing make finding answers ever more possible. Unfortunately, and particularly since 2015, we have also witnessed a decline in the integrity of democratic politics, and open contempt for truth and facts.[4] These problems are connected to theories of enterprise, because our economic and political systems affect one another. Problems include the regulation of corporate money in politics (see Ch. 3(2)), financial capital (Ch. 10), the ongoing use of fossil fuels (Ch. 11), unaccountable control of media (Ch. 17) and the problems of inequality and climate damage that recur throughout this book. Theory is the prelude of change, and it matters because dominant narratives set people's psychological starting points.[5] This chapter explores (1) theories of economics and law on enterprise, (2) categories of 'market failures' and conditions for markets to work, (3) methods of empirical evidence and politics, and (4) basic theories of human rights and justice.

(1) Economic Theory

(a) Historical Theories

While Chapter 1 covered historical theories in a bare outline, it makes sense to elaborate the main points of the leading authors, so as to set the context of modern economic theory. Despite their political differences – as liberals, socialists, conservatives or with elements of all – among classical political economists, there was a remarkable unity of analysis in a distrust of free markets, particularly for labour or land, and a fierce opposition to corporations. Adam Smith's *Theory of Moral Sentiments* in 1759 and *Wealth of Nations* in 1776 painted an ideal world where trade was freed from corporate power and monopoly. Among small business partnerships, the 'butcher, the baker, or the brewer',[6] free markets, as if guided by 'an invisible hand', were supposed to 'make nearly the same distribution' as if 'the earth had been divided into equal portions among all its inhabitants'.[7] However, even without

[4] See T. Snyder, *The Road to Unfreedom: Russia, Europe, America* (2018).

[5] Cf. D. Kahneman, *Thinking, Fast and Slow* (2011) on 'system 1' thinking.

[6] A. Smith, *An Inquiry into the Nature and Causes of the Wealth of Nations* (1776) Book I, ch. 2, §12.

[7] A. Smith, *The Theory of Moral Sentiments* (1759) Part IV, ch. 1, §10. This is based on an evidential assumption that wealthier people have a propensity to consume all their income, which seems now mistaken. Smith, *Wealth of Nations*, Book I, ch. 2, §9 also uses the metaphor of

corporations as a way to organise capital, Smith said workers are not as free as employers. In all 'disputes the masters can hold out much longer' because property is unequally distributed. Workers, from fear of hunger, submit to the employer's contract terms.[8] As well as inequality from the distribution of property,[9] the law suppressed labour combinations while encouraging capital combinations, the most corrosive being the joint stock company (i.e. a corporation). Because company directors manage 'other people's money', wrote Smith, they were prone to 'negligence and profusion', and this was why joint stock companies were often less efficient than 'private adventurers'.[10] Smith thought corporations with monopolies from the state should be banned, lambasting those like the South Sea Company or Royal Africa Company. However, there were six main types of enterprise where corporate production was more efficient, because 'all the operations are capable of being reduced to what is called a routine, or to such a uniformity of method as admits of little or no variation'.[11] For Smith, corporate production was synonymous with the state,[12] and it could specifically handle banking, insurance, canals, water or public works 'necessary for facilitating Commerce in general', including roads, harbours, the post and defence.[13] Thus public ownership or control was justified, for Smith, in whole or part for most enterprises in this book.[14]

In 1848, John Stuart Mill's *Principles of Political Economy* took an even more explicit view, arguing that government constitutes markets, by deciding the terms on which contracts are enforced or property is held.[15] Mill argued that '*laisser faire* . . . should be the general principle', but with at least five major exceptions.[16] First, in education 'the intervention of government is justifiable' and similarly so in cases where people cannot easily judge their interests: the 'consumer' in a market can do so only with 'numerous abatements and exceptions'. A second exception was in any long-term contract, where people

an 'invisible hand' for an unintended consequence that people working in their own interest, and preferring domestic over foreign goods, contribute to growth and the public good.

8 Smith, *Wealth of Nations*, Book I, ch. 8, §12.

9 Cf. M. Wollstonecraft, *A Vindication of the Rights of Woman: With Strictures on Political and Moral Subjects* (1792) ch. 9.

10 Smith, *Wealth of Nations*, Book V, ch. 1, §107.

11 Smith, *Wealth of Nations*, Book V, ch. 1, §121.

12 Smith, *Wealth of Nations*, Book V, ch. 1: 'Of the Expences of the Sovereign or Commonwealth'.

13 Smith, *Wealth of Nations*, Book V, ch. 1, part III.

14 See banking (Ch. 10), water (Ch. 13), transport (Ch. 15), communications (Ch. 16), markets (Ch. 18) and military (Ch. 19). In Smith's time, recall that the modern technology and enterprises of healthcare, electricity, housing and media had not yet been invented. In education, Smith perhaps lost objectivity somewhat, appearing to favour student fees over endowments that supported his lazy colleagues! Smith, *Wealth of Nations*, Book V, ch. 1, §§130–4. At this time, of course, students often paid lecturers personally at each lecture. That would be nice (*joke*).

15 J. S. Mill, *Principles of Political Economy* (1848) Book V, ch. 1, §2: 'when once it is admitted that there are any engagements which for reasons of expediency the law ought not to enforce, the same question is necessarily opened with respect to all engagements'.

16 Mill, *Principles of Political Economy*, Book V, ch. 11, §§7–13.

decide what they will be bound to 'at some future and distant time', such as marriage. Third, there was an exception when 'individuals can only manage [a] concern by delegated agency'. This included companies[17] and, according to Mill, whatever 'can only be done by joint-stock associations, will often be as well, and sometimes better done, as far as the actual work is concerned, by the state'. This was because shareholders had such 'difficulty of exercising' a power of removal over directors to establish accountability, and because government may achieve 'greater publicity and more active discussion and comment'.[18] Furthermore in many cases (and without companies having legal monopoly) 'a practical monopoly, with all the power it confers of taxing the community, cannot be prevented from existing', including in cases of 'gas and water companies', 'paving and cleansing of the streets' and 'a road, a canal, or a railway'. Fourth, there are cases where people cannot easily 'give effect' to their own interest, even by acting in 'concert', such as workers in a union. Here pressures on 'every individual would lie in violating' attempts to maintain solidarity, for instance to demand fair working time. For Mill, this justified labour rights in law.[19] Fifth, government intervention was justified for social security, at the time in managing the 'poor law'.[20] Mill summed this up in *On Liberty*, saying that regulation of all trade was justified to prevent harm, because 'trade is a social act', not a private one.[21] Like Smith, Mill's exceptions to laissez-faire cover all enterprises in this book.[22] Ultimately, Mill said he was 'not charmed' by a human future based on ceaseless competition, 'that the trampling, crushing, elbowing, and treading on each other's heels, which form the existing type of social life, are the most desirable lot of human kind, or anything but the disagreeable symptoms of one of the phases of industrial progress'.[23] We should, he suggested, aim for a 'stationary state', one of peace, with a 'democratic constitution … supported by democratic institutions in detail'.[24]

[17] Recall, when Mill's first edition was published in 1848, companies were still prohibited without an Act, though free incorporation was permitted by 1856 and subsequent editions of Mill's book.

[18] Mill, *Principles of Political Economy*, Book V, ch. 11, §11. Curiously, Mill also penned a 'Memorandum of the improvements in the administration of India during the last thirty years, and the petition of the East-India Company to Parliament' (1858) before Crown rule replaced company rule: Government of India Act 1858 (c. 106).

[19] Mill, *Principles of Political Economy*, Book V, ch. 11, §12.

[20] Mill, *Principles of Political Economy*, Book V, ch. 11, §13. Mill also refers to colonisation for the supposedly 'unoccupied parts of the earth's surface'. This, of course, reflects the imperialist, deeply racist culture of which Mill was a part. The forcible clearance of indigenous people is genocide and mass human rights law violation.

[21] J. S. Mill, *On Liberty* (1859) ch. 5.

[22] Curiously, many contemporary libertarians fail to understand both Smith's and Mill's views, and think their theories lend support to a privatisation or 'deregulation' agenda, e.g. the so-called 'Adam Smith Institute'.

[23] Mill, *Principles of Political Economy*, Book IV, ch. 4, §2.

[24] Mill, *Principles of Political Economy*, Book V, ch. 11, §6.

Karl Marx and Friedrich Engels's *Communist Manifesto* was published the same year as Mill's *Principles*, while Marx's three-volume *Capital: A Critique of Political Economy* was published between 1867 and 1894. Most of Marx's work was critique, not proposals, except that the ten points of the *Communist Manifesto* included in highly general terms (2) a progressive income tax, (5) a national bank that controlled money, (6) state responsibility for communication and transport, (7) state cultivation and improvement of land and (10) free education for children and abolition of child labour. Today these policies are found as a bare minimum in every democratic country, or are part of international human rights law.[25] In the midst of the industrial revolution, Marx viewed the system of capital as inherently exploitative and alienating, because it treated human beings as commodities.[26] People at work were exploited by having the surplus value of their labour appropriated by the employer, and they were alienated both from the fruits of production, and from their peers in their work.[27] In the competition between labour and capital, Marx (like Smith and Mill) argued that labour was always at a disadvantage.[28] As the capitalist contradictions increased, Marx thought a proletarian revolution would inevitably be triggered. For Marx, communism would replace what people later came to call 'capitalism', just as the capital class replaced feudalism, and feudalism replaced slavery.[29] In Marx's later life, as corporations grew phenomenally, he wrote that they amounted to 'the abolition of capital as private property within the boundaries of capitalist production itself'.[30] In 'companies the function [of managing] is separated from the ownership of capital, and labour, of course, is entirely separated from the ownership of means of production and of surplus-labour'. It was creating a 'new aristocracy of finance', 'a whole system of swindling and cheating' and 'private production without the control of private property'. Capital also drove colonisation, pushing 'by force' into other countries, in the pursuit of profits

[25] K. Marx and F. Engels, *Communist Manifesto* (1848) II. Other communist demands, which are not widespread or are incompatible with human rights, included (1) 'Abolition of property in land' – though everywhere planning is now publicly regulated; (3) 'Abolition of all right of inheritance' – though there is now inheritance tax; (4) confiscation of emigrant and rebel property – this is a human rights violation if applied to real people; (7) extension of state factories – this occurred in many countries, but is less common now; (8) equal liability of all to labour – today there is rather a 'right to work' and social security, not a duty, which may amount to a human rights violation of forced labour; and (9) 'a more equable distribution of population' over the country – a policy which was followed by American settlers, Stalin, South African apartheid, Pol Pot and numerous colonisers against native populations. These involved massive human rights violations by forced resettlement.

[26] See also F. Engels, *The Condition of the Working Class in England* (1844) ch. 9: 'The children and young people who are employed in transporting coal and iron-stone . . . lie down on the way home, and are found by their parents late at night asleep on the road.'

[27] K. Marx, *Capital: A Critique of Political Economy* (1867) vol. I, ch. 13; K. Marx, *Economic & Philosophic Manuscripts* (1844) on alienation.

[28] K. Marx, *Wage Labour and Capital* (1847).

[29] Marx and Engels, *Communist Manifesto*, I.

[30] K. Marx, *Capital* (1894) vol. III, ch. 27.

and new markets.[31] Marx believed that a proletarian government should replace private with public ownership of the means of production, and favoured a system of property that 'rests on the producers' own labor' being owned by the workers themselves.[32] He also thought that, if the working classes in England ever got the vote in Parliament, this would probably go much of the way to those goals.[33]

By the turn of the twentieth century, and in contrast to revolutionary communists, there was mass growth of socialist, labour and social democratic parties rooted in trade unions, who sought peaceful, progressive reform. In the UK, Beatrice and Sidney Webb, who founded the London School of Economics (LSE) and the Fabian Society, argued in *Industrial Democracy* that an economy based on private ownership was shaped by systemic inequality of bargaining power. In the 'higgling of the market', a stream of pressure was exerted through the pyramid of production. At the top was a consumer, 'free as air' to buy or not buy goods or services, pressuring retailers to price lower, which pressured suppliers, which pressured manufacturers. This pressure 'finally crushes the isolated workman at the base of the pyramid'.[34] Everyone was pressured, and nobody was free, the opposite of the Webbs' goal of liberty and 'the utmost possible development of faculty in the individual human being'.[35] The Webbs said the economy involved three functions of production: there were decisions about *what* to produce, *how* to produce and the *conditions* of production. In their initial writing, they argued for a 'separation of powers', so that the consumer decided what is produced; managers decided how; and a full system of collective bargaining, supported by a national minimum of labour rights, would decide the conditions.[36] This was the basis of industrial democracy. They believed that shareholder-owned companies were inherently reckless and exploitative, and that managers should instead be appointed by the government, as it progressively created 'common ownership of the means of production, distribution and exchange'. This is what Sidney Webb wrote into the original 'clause IV' of the British Labour Party constitution.[37] In 1920, the Webbs adjusted their view on the strict separation of powers, and said it was a 'real social gain' if labour could also participate in appointing

31 K. Marx, *Capital*, vol. I, ch. 33. Cf. V. I. Lenin, *Imperialism, the Highest Stage of Capitalism* (1917).

32 Marx, *Capital*, vol. I, ch. 33. Note the opposite conception in V. I. Lenin, *Role and Functions of the Trade Unions under the New Economic Policy* (1922) where free trade unions were banned, unnecessary in the Soviet Union.

33 The Representation of the People Act 1884, the year after Marx died, gave the vote in the UK to just 18% of the population, all male and with property. People who lived in the colonies of the vast British Empire had no representation at all.

34 S. Webb and B. Webb, *Industrial Democracy* (1897) Part III, ch. 2, 671.

35 Webb and Webb, *Industrial Democracy* Part III, ch. 4.

36 Webb and Webb, *Industrial Democracy* Part III, ch. 4, 818–22.

37 Constitution of the Labour Party 1918, clause IV. See S. Webb, *The New Constitution of the Labour Party* (1918) 3.

management – as well as bargaining collectively – especially in companies taken under public ownership.[38]

In Germany, at the end of World War One, the suppression of the social democrats could no longer hold, and they took power in the 1918 revolution that deposed the kaiser. Hugo Sinzheimer was the co-author of the parts on economic regulation in the Weimar Constitution 1919. In his *Fundamentals of Labour Law*, Sinzheimer followed the view of Smith that inequality of bargaining power is caused at root by unequal distribution of property.[39] He saw a system of social rights as a constitutional matter[40] and, following the post-war collective agreement among unions and business, the Weimar Constitution read that 'employees shall be called upon to cooperate with employers, and on an equal footing, in the regulation of salaries and working conditions, as well as in the entire field of the economic development of the forces of production'.[41] This became the basis of legislation on the right to vote at work, both in work councils and in representation on company boards. The other principle written by Sinzheimer was that 'Property carries responsibility.'[42] While this alluded to the social democratic goal of socialising key industries, there was in 1918 not yet a plan about how this should be done. A 'Socialisation Commission' was set up, but it took longer to deliberate than social democrats held power. A member, Karl Kautsky, later wrote in *The Labour Revolution* in 1924 that the composition of enterprises should be based upon the three key constituents: workers, consumers and the community represented by the state in socialised industry. It was better that 'consumers and producers would be brought together in every branch of production' to avoid 'always quarrelling and only coming together before the supreme court'.[43] Socialisation was to 'proceed gradually' rather than extending over everything immediately, and public ownership at municipal level was often preferable to nationalisation in many cases such as water, gas, electricity and roads. As in the UK, where the Webbs wanted 'progressive' public ownership, what counts as the 'key' industry, and why, would become a central theoretical question of enterprise.

In the USA, A. A. Berle was a leading architect of the concepts behind the New Deal. In 1919, he had attended the Versailles Peace Conference but despite the advances in creating the International Labour Organization, he had left disillusioned. Returning to America, he wrote about 'How Labor Could Control' by acquiring votes as shareholders,[44] but over the 1920s, as

[38] S. Webb and B. Webb, *A History of Trade Unionism* (1920) Appendix VIII, 760.

[39] H. Sinzheimer, *Grundzüge des Arbeitsrechts* (1926) ch. 2, 22.

[40] R. Dukes, 'Constitutionalizing Employment Relations: Sinzheimer, Kahn-Freund, and the Role of Labour Law' (2008) 35(3) *JL & Society* 341.

[41] Weimar Constitution 1919, art. 165.

[42] Weimar Constitution 1919, art. 153, or *Eigentum verpflichtet* now in Grundgesetz 1949, art. 14(2).

[43] K. Kautsy, *The Labour Revolution* (1924) ch. 3, part VIII(e).

[44] A. A. Berle, 'How Labor Could Control', *New Republic* (7 September 1921) 37, 38.

Berle wrote more about corporate finance, he altered this idea, realising the risks of workers holding undiversified share portfolios, and instead advocating diversified holdings by larger worker funds including pensions.[45] After the Wall Street Crash hit in 1929, Berle went to work for the US presidential candidate Franklin D. Roosevelt, and wrote one of Roosevelt's most famous speeches in 1932. This said America needed a new 'economic declaration of rights, an economic constitutional order', that went beyond the civil and political nature of the original Bill of Rights.[46] In *The Modern Corporation and Private Property*, Berle and his co-author Gardiner Means argued that the Wall Street Crash was caused by the growing unaccountability of company managers. Property used for *consumption* was fundamentally different from property used for *production*. Productive property, above all in corporations, should be subject to a constitution of rights, particularly among 'passive' owners of shares, whose primary function had become the circulation and distribution of wealth.[47] The 'separation of ownership and control' between directors and investors (who, ultimately, were mostly workers saving for retirement) had grown, because the law on director elections, shareholder voting and market disclosure had been eroded.[48] 'With the corporate revolution', wrote Berle and Means, any voice 'has been lost to the property owner much as it has been lost to the worker through the industrial revolution.'[49] Berle and Means argued a company is a 'social institution' and should fulfil the public interest, not director, and not shareholder interests.[50] A system of corporate law that followed shareholder interests was merely the 'lesser of two evils', because corporations should 'serve . . . all society'.[51]

45 See A. A. Berle, *Studies in the Law of Corporate Finance* (1928) 39 and ' Property, Production and Revolution' (1965) 65(1) *Columbia L Rev* 1, 17, on using tax to 'encourage pension trust or social security trust entry into [the] stockholder position'.

46 F. D. Roosevelt, Campaign Address on Progressive Government at the Commonwealth Club in San Francisco, California (1932).

47 A. A. Berle and G. C. Means, *The Modern Corporation and Private Property* (1932) Book I, ch. 1 and ch. 3, 25–6, fully articulated in Berle, 'Property, Production and Revolution', 4–5.

48 Berle and Means, *The Modern Corporation and Private Property*, Book I, ch. 5. G. C. Means, 'The Separation of Ownership and Control in American Industry' (1931) 46(1) *QJ Economics* 68 identified the period between 1916 and 1919 as the start of increasing stock dispersion.

49 Berle and Means, *The Modern Corporation and Private Property*, Book I, ch. 4, 67.

50 Berle and Means, *The Modern Corporation and Private Property*, Book I, ch. 1, 1; Book IV, ch. 3, 351.

51 Berle and Means, *The Modern Corporation and Private Property*, Book IV, ch. 4, 355–6. A common myth is that Berle was a pro-shareholder advocate. This is wrong. In a commonly misunderstood debate with Merrick Dodd, Berle argued that it was better that there was shareholder control of companies than pure director control. He originally argued that corporate powers should be used 'only for the ratable benefit of all the shareholders' (when most shareholders were workers saving for retirement, as social security was still held illegal by the US Supreme Court) as opposed to being left to director discretion: (1931) 44(7) *Harvard L Rev* 1049. But he quickly clarified, after a challenge by Dodd (1932) 45(7) *Harvard L Rev* 1145, that this was merely a historical theory 'as a matter of law', and the task was to change it. The 'shareholder . . . may ultimately be conceived of as having an equal participation with a number of other claimants' or be 'subordinated to a number of claims by labor, by customers and

Towards the end of his life in 1965, with the New Deal's success, Berle argued the growing system of legislative rights, from labour to consumer to equality rights, was building this new economic constitution. Progressive taxes also made the public an 'equal partner' in the revenue corporations raised, and Berle hoped corporate regulation could lead to a rational system of wealth distribution.[52] 'Justification for the stockholder's existence thus depends on increasing distribution within the American population' so that 'every American family has its fragment . . . of the wealth by which the opportunity to develop individuality becomes fully actualized'.[53] Berle also pointed to the state being both 'an administrator' and 'a direct distributor of certain products', namely education, research, roads, housing and 'probably' soon healthcare, because 'these noncommercial functions are . . . essential to the continued life, stability and growth of the non-statist corporate enterprise'.[54]

Like Berle, John Maynard Keynes attended and left the Versailles Peace Conference, deeply disillusioned by the post-World War One settlement. He predicted an economic collapse and a second world war.[55] Until Keynes' book in 1936, *The General Theory of Employment, Interest and Money*, economists had conceived production through a lens of supply and demand among individuals, unions and businesses, but not at the aggregate level that a state could influence. With notable exceptions like Sidney Webb,[56] mass unemployment in the Great Depression was generally seen as voluntary.[57] Keynes argued the crash decreased investment, leading to people being fired and having less money to spend. This meant a fall in 'aggregate demand', and it would not self-correct.[58] People with lower incomes have a higher 'propensity to consume' all their income, while richer people tend to save or invest capital in the financial sector.[59] The loss of confidence to invest, to bring back jobs, could not be rectified without the state providing certainty. To increase demand, and restore the economy with a higher 'velocity of money', there needed to be government spending.[60] Underinvestment was also affected by 'social practices and . . . a distribution of wealth which result in a propensity to consume which is unduly low'.[61] For Keynes, this was not merely another exception to laissez-faire to add to Mill's list, but an argument that ultimately government underwrote all social prosperity and the viability of all enterprises. For this

patrons, by the community' but this needed to be worked out in enforceable laws, not just by giving managers power 'on trust' (1932) 45(8) *Harvard L Rev* 1365 fn. 3, 1372.

52 Berle, 'Property, Production and Revolution', 17.

53 Berle, 'Property, Production and Revolution', 17.

54 Berle, 'Property, Production and Revolution', 19. By 'non-statist', Berle means 'not state owned'.

55 J. M. Keynes, *The Economic Consequences of the Peace* (1919).

56 S. Webb, *How the Government Can Prevent Unemployment* (1912).

57 E.g. A. C. Pigou, *The Theory of Unemployment* (1933).

58 J. M. Keynes, *The General Theory of Employment, Interest and Money* (1936) chs. 2–3.

59 Keynes, *The General Theory of Employment, Interest and* Money, ch. 9.

60 Keynes, *The General Theory of Employment, Interest and* Money, chs. 15 and 21.

61 Keynes, *The General Theory of Employment, Interest and* Money, ch. 22.

reason, Keynes argued for a general social responsibility for full employment and economic management.

Together, as we saw in Chapter 1, the ideas of the Webbs, Sinzheimer, Kautsky, Berle and Keynes were reflected in the Universal Declaration of Human Rights (UDHR), enshrining economic and social rights as a constitutive duty of all members of the United Nations (UN).[62] In the post-World War Two years, these ideas also influenced the decisions of governments to guarantee a growing set of rights for labour, investors and consumers in all enterprises, the taking of major industries into public ownership, particularly in Europe, and setting up specific industry regulators, particularly in the USA.

(b) Chicago School Theory

While the theories of political economy, and the economic constitution, have shaped enterprise law today in fundamental ways, beginning at the University of Chicago another body of thinking arose in reaction. It found growing political support, first in the US Supreme Court, and then with the Ronald Reagan and Margaret Thatcher governments. Friedrich von Hayek, who had spent his early career at the LSE, debating Keynes, argued that increased state power would lead society down *The Road to Serfdom*.[63] For Hayek, there was an inherent tendency of government to assume more and more control over society if Keynesian or socialist economic policies were adopted. Unemployment was natural because some people's skills were worthless and unemployable, and if government tried to spend or use monetary policy to get to full employment, it would lead to 'major inflationary effects', driving government 'to control ever increasing parts of the economy'.[64] (There is no credible evidence to support this claim.[65]) In *Law, Legislation and Liberty*, Hayek argued that markets were a 'spontaneous order', and it was a category error to expect distributive justice in them.[66] Because nobody directs markets, and there is no decision-maker, there is nobody responsible that could make market outcomes distributively unjust. People who sought 'social justice' (like Mill, the Webbs and Berle) were really seeking an 'outlet for moral emotion'.[67] Worker unions were cartels that should be broken up. All labour rights should be abolished. State-owned enterprises should be all but eliminated to protect 'liberty'.[68]

62 UDHR 1948, arts. 20–9, a resolution of the UN General Assembly.
63 F. A. Hayek, *The Road to Serfdom* (1944).
64 F. A. Hayek, 'Full Employment, Planning and Inflation' (1950) 4(6) *Institute Public Affairs Rev* 174.
65 E. McGaughey, 'Will Robots Automate Your Job Away? Full Employment, Basic Income and Economic Democracy' (2021) *Industrial LJ*.
66 F. A. Hayek, *Law, Legislation and Liberty* (1973) vol. II, ch. 9, 230–2.
67 Hayek, *Law, Legislation and Liberty*, vol. II, ch. 9, 227.
68 E.g. F. A. Hayek, *The Constitution of Liberty* (1960) ch. 8, 109.

Another leading figure of the Chicago School was Milton Friedman, who in 1967 became president of the American Economic Association. The son of a textile factory owner, Friedman followed Hayek's assertion that unemployment was natural and that all labour rights such as the minimum wage, collective bargaining or pro-union government procurement harmed workers and excluded the most vulnerable from the labour force.[69] All rights raised the costs of labour, so employers would be more reluctant to hire workers, leading to a drop in demand, hence unemployment. Government had in fact been responsible for the Great Depression (not poor corporate governance, absence of social security or growing inequality, as Keynes, Berle and Means had explained) because the US Federal Reserve (its central bank) allowed the supply of money to shrink unduly.[70] All attempts to reach full employment, and secure a right to work at fair wages, would trigger uncontrollable inflation. During the OPEC crisis, and the inflation in the 1970s that resulted (see Ch. 11), Friedman pushed this argument strongly.[71] He also argued against all government intervention, including creating public schools (to be replaced with vouchers), healthcare (there should be private insurance) or in any other sector.[72] Corporations should have a social responsibility to increase profits, because shareholders 'own' corporations, and executives should act as their 'agents'. (This is wrong in law, as shareholders own their shares, not the company: Ch. 3.) For Friedman, if corporations were 'providing employment, eliminating discrimination, avoiding pollution' any more than the law required, this was 'preaching pure and unadulterated socialism', 'undermining the basis of a free society'. Being 'socially responsible' really meant spending shareholders', customers' and apparently workers' money, like a tax without getting political approval.[73]

While the fields had diverged in the early twentieth century, economics and law began to remerge at the University of Chicago. This merger is often credited to Ronald Coase, who while studying undergraduate economics at the LSE took a course titled Commercial and Industrial Law that inspired much of his later writing.[74] Of course, Smith, Mill and Marx had all studied or

[69] M. Friedman, 'The Role of Monetary Policy' (1968) 58(1) *Am. Economic Rev* 1, 10; Friedman, 'The Methodology of Positive Economics', 4–7.

[70] M. Friedman and A. J. Schwarz, *A Monetary History of the United States, 1867–1960* (1963).

[71] M. Friedman, 'Inflation and Unemployment' (1977) 85 *J Political Economy* 451, 458. Note that at 462–3, Friedman's charts show the exact opposite of what he claimed: inflation falling in 5 of 7 countries.

[72] E.g. M. Friedman, *Capitalism and Freedom* (1962) ch. 6, 89 and 95 fn. 2. There was never a credible evidential basis for Friedman's empty assertions. On the application of Friedman's ideas under General Pinochet in Chile, see N. Klein, *The Shock Doctrine: The Rise of Disaster Capitalism* (2007) ch. 2.

[73] M. Friedman, 'The Social Responsibility of Business is to Increase its Profits', *New York Times Magazine* (13 September 1970). This argument is backward in law, because shareholders own their shares, not a company.

[74] The author's first job was teaching this course, from 2008 to 2015, and it was the oldest course at the LSE: *Calendar for the London School of Economics and Political Science at London University*

taught law, but as economics had become more specialised, more economists had disengaged from legal detail. Coase argued that firms (e.g. a company, or created in any employment contract) exist, as opposed to markets (with independent contractors), as a way to reduce transaction costs. Firms will keep growing, by taking workers or suppliers in house, unless the transaction costs are cheaper by continuing to operate on the open market. Crucially, Coase's theory excluded any mention of bargaining power as a reason that might influence the extent to which firms grow.[75] Similarly, in 1960, Coase argued that if property rights are certain, and if we imagined that transaction costs did not exist, any allocation of liability in tort or its absence would be equally efficient and 'maximises the value of production' because people would rationally contract to fully utilise resources.[76] For Coase, the distribution of liability, property or wealth, and the differences in bargaining power that these create, had no impact on productive efficiency – only the existence of transaction costs did. (This is evidentially false, because different distributions affect people's motivation to work, and therefore productive efficiency.[77]) So, Coase argued, the idea of taxing polluting companies or imposing liability is only justified from an efficiency perspective if transaction costs raise a barrier to the parties deciding on rules themselves. Extra costs were often created by excessive government intervention,[78] and were not inherent in markets.

For most of the Chicago School, 'government failure', not market failure, was the true evil of our society. In its most strident expression, George Stigler argued that all attempts of governments to regulate markets harm consumers. When regulators are established, for instance, to fix fair prices for energy or transport, the businesses involved would lobby the agencies to get friendly supporters, and regulators would end up being used to maintain anticompetitive profits through subsidies, licensing, tariffs, standards or price controls. In fact, 'as a rule, regulation is acquired by the industry and is designed and operated primarily for its benefit'.[79] Regulation fails, thought Stigler, because democracy is inferior to property rights: 'The expressions of preferences in voting will be less precise', said Stigler, 'than the expressions of preferences in

(1895–1896) LSE Archives, LSE/Unregistered/27/5. Sadly, the course (LL209) was suspended in 2017, a short-sighted decision.

75 R. Coase, 'The Nature of the Firm' (1937) 4 *Economica* 386. Cf. J. R. Commons, 'Institutional Economics' (1931) 21 *Am Economic Rev* 648, on the original concept of transaction costs, and note J. R. Commons and J. B. Andrews, *Principles of Labor Legislation* (1916) ch. 1, 9 on bargaining power.

76 R. Coase, 'The Problem of Social Cost' (1960) 3 *JL & Economics* 1, 8.

77 See E. McGaughey, 'Behavioural Economics and Labour Law', LSE Legal Studies Working Paper No. 20/2014 (2015), shorter version published as 'Behavioural Psychology and Labour Law' in A. Ludlow and A. Blackham (eds.), *New Frontiers in Empirical Labour Law Research* (2015) ch. 6.

78 R. Coase, 'The Lighthouse in Economics' (1974) 17(2) *JL & Economics* 357.

79 G. J. Stigler, 'The Theory of Economic Regulation' (1971) 2(1) *Bell J Economics and Management Science* 3.

the marketplace because many uninformed people will be voting and affecting the decision.'[80]

In the early 1970s and 1980s, the Chicago School theory also began to construct an account of the functions of different parts of enterprise law: the roles of corporate, labour, competition (or antitrust) and insolvency (or bankruptcy) law. First, according to the Chicago consensus, corporate law's single goal should be to maximise value for shareholders. Like Friedman, Jensen and Meckling argued a corporation is merely legal 'fiction', and is better understood as a 'nexus of contracts' between different actors, particularly directors and shareholders.[81] Corporate law should simply reduce 'agency costs' for the benefit of shareholders. These are the costs of monitoring or bonding directors to shareholders, or in their language aligning the interests of the 'agent' with those of the 'principal'. Markets would not automatically correct rules of internal governance, because if 'my competitors all incur agency costs equal to or greater than mine I will not be eliminated from the market by their competition'.[82] However, for Jensen and Meckling most problems could be solved in contracts, without other regulation. They believed that workers should have no governance rights in firms, claiming laws creating worker-elected directors like the German Codetermination Act 1976 could only result from the 'fiat' of law. Because it did not result from the process of market competition, for them this meant co-determination was inefficient. The worker's voice in companies would lead to economic decline, as in Marshall Tito's Yugoslavia.[83] (Both claims are historically false: workers first gained votes in companies through collective agreements, not laws, and Germany's economy did not become like Yugoslavia's after its 1976 reforms.[84])

Second, it was argued that labour law's single goal should be to protect the interests of the individual worker. This apparently meant dismantling most labour laws, particularly collective rights that support trade unions, all of which were argued to cause unemployment.[85] The most important objective instead was to reduce barriers to labour market flexibility and mobility. Third, competition or antitrust law's single goal should be maximising consumer welfare. It should take no account of wider industrial strategy or the interests of the broader community or environment.[86] Fourth, insolvency or bankruptcy

[80] Stigler, 'The Theory of Economic Regulation', 10–11.

[81] The 'nexus of contracts' view appears to have first been developed in Nazi corporate law theory. See F. Kessler (1934) 83 *U Penn L Rev* 393, 394. Also E. McGaughey (2015) 78(6) *MLR* 1057.

[82] M. Jensen and T. Meckling, 'Theory of the Firm: Managerial Behavior, Agency Costs and Ownership Structure' (1976) 3 *J Financial Economics* 305, 330.

[83] M. C. Jensen and W. H. Meckling, 'Rights and Production Functions: An Application to Labor-Managed Firms and Codetermination' (1979) 52(4) *J Business* 469, 473, 503–4.

[84] E. McGaughey, 'The Codetermination Bargains: The History of German Corporate and Labour Law' (2016) 23(1) *Columbia J Eur L* 135.

[85] Friedman, 'The Methodology of Positive Economics', 6.

[86] E.g. R. Bork, *The Antitrust Paradox: A Policy at War with Itself* (1978) 426–9. Cf. L. Khan and S. Vaheesan, 'Market Power and Inequality: The Antitrust Counterrevolution and Its Discontents' (2017) 11 *Harvard L & Policy Rev* 235.

law's single goal should be maximising creditor wealth. It should not be distracted by the interests of the broader community, or the maintenance and rescue of failed business, but solely focused on realising as much value from a liquidation as possible,[87] especially for the benefit of secured creditors.

Chicago School theory assigns one legal actor as the exclusive object of concern in each legal subject: the shareholder for corporate law, the isolated worker for labour law, the consumer for competition law and the creditor for insolvency law. In the later writing of Easterbrook and Fischel, it was added that none of these subjects had any 'unity of concept or event', compared to traditional subjects of contract, tort, property or constitutional law. They were merely 'contextual' legal subjects, not conceptual, at best an appendage, but not the substance of a proper legal education.[88] In other words, all the components of enterprise law, all thinking about the great questions that preoccupied political economy since the industrial revolution, were to this school of law and economics random and unwelcome. This approach to law is untenable, because the same people are invariably the beneficiaries of shareholders, workers, consumers, creditors, citizens and human beings. Attempts to divide these capacities from one another serve to inhibit solidarity among investors, workers, consumers and citizens, and ultimately obstruct the coherence of the public interest. In other words, the final achievement of Chicago theory, though often eloquent, has been little more than an extended excuse for unaccountable corporate power.

(c) Corporate Law and Theories of the Firm

Since the 1980s, and in contrast to the hard-line views of the Chicago School, there have been two main directions in the theories about the distribution of power within private enterprise. The first group of theories sought to defend shareholder control with more sophisticated arguments than Friedman (shareholders should control because they 'own' companies) or Jensen and Meckling (shareholders should control because this just happens naturally without the 'fiat' of law).[89] In *The Economic Institutions of Capitalism*, Oliver Williamson argued shareholders hold exclusive voting rights in firms because they make the only 'asset specific investments' – that is investments that could not be transferred on insolvency – that could not otherwise be protected without controlling the whole company board.[90] Employee interests could, Williamson

87 E.g. D. G. Baird and T. H. Jackson, 'Corporate Reorganizations and the Treatment of Diverse Ownership Interests: A Comment on Adequate Protection of Secured Creditors in Bankruptcy' (1984) 51(1) *U Chicago L Rev* 97.

88 F. H. Easterbrook, 'Cyberspace and the Law of the Horse' [1996] *U Chicago L Forum* 207, 208.

89 Cf. B. R. Cheffins, *Corporate Governance: Theory, Structure and Operation* (1997).

90 O. E. Williamson, *The Economic Institutions of Capitalism* (1985) 304, 306, asserting without evidence, or even a remote reference to history, that shareholder control 'arises endogenously'. Cf. E. McGaughey, 'Democracy in America at Work: The History of Labor's Vote in Corporate Governance' (2019) 42 *Seattle UL Rev* 697.

said, be adequately protected with job security, but upon insolvency the capital investments shareholders make are 'always at hazard'.[91] Similarly, Frank Easterbrook and Daniel Fischel claimed that because shareholders bear the residual risk of insolvency (they are paid last behind other creditors), they would more keenly and efficiently monitor the board than any other stakeholder. Ostensibly, the right of 'voting flows with the residual interest in the firm', which they believed is the shareholder.[92] (These views are based on a factually mistaken premise: asset managers hold most voting rights, but beneficiaries of pension and other funds invest and bear risks of insolvency: Ch. 4.) To complete the picture, Henry Hansmann contended that representation of other stakeholders, particularly employees, would create conflicts of interest and decrease the efficiency of operation of the board.[93] In 1999, Hansmann and Reiner Kraakman claimed that society had reached 'The End of History for Corporate Law', and that meant shareholder primacy, which had (ostensibly) outcompeted rival models of worker-oriented, public-oriented or director-dominated systems of corporate law.[94]

The second group of theories sought to defend the growing number of systems with broader stakeholder rights in companies, particularly worker representation on company boards. Kochan and Rubinstein said a 'stakeholder' is someone who contributes something of value to production, and is at risk if a firm fails.[95] Stakeholder theorists contended it was a mistake to suggest only investors of capital are more at risk if a firm goes into insolvency, because the job risk to workers is far more severe for most people's livelihoods.[96] Moreover, they pointed out that registered shareholders are invariably asset management institutions, which pool investments from multiple beneficiaries. The asset managers and banks that control votes invariably bear no risk, and so the central arguments for shareholder primacy (that votes follow risk) are based on an entirely false premise.[97] According to Thomas Raiser, a fuller concept of 'enterprise law' is needed that combines company, labour, competition and public law. This recognises 'the fact that the governance of an enterprise includes the exercise of power, and therefore requires

[91] Williamson, *The Economic Institutions of Capitalism*, 241.

[92] F. Easterbrook and D Fischel, 'Voting in Corporate Law' (1983) 26 *JL & Economics* 395, 409.

[93] H. Hansmann, *The Ownership of Enterprise* (1996).

[94] H. Hansmann and R. Kraakman, 'The End of History for Corporate Law' (2000) 89 *Georgetown LJ* 439.

[95] T. A. Kochan and S. A. Rubinstein, 'Toward a Stakeholder Theory of the Firm: The Saturn Partnership' (2000) 11(4) *Organizational Science* 367, 369. Cf. R. E. Freeman, *Strategic Management: A Stakeholder Approach* (1984) saying more loosely that a stakeholder is someone that is 'affected' by a firm.

[96] E. Warren, 'Bankruptcy Policy' (1987) 54 *U Chicago L Rev* 775; G. Kelly and J. Parkinson, 'The Conceptual Foundations of the Company: A Pluralist Approach' in A. Gamble et al. (eds.), *The Political Economy of the Company* (2000).

[97] E. McGaughey, *Participation in Corporate Governance* (2014) ch. 3(2)(a).

legal mechanisms for its control'.[98] An enterprise is not just an 'association of the shareholders' but 'a transaction and communication system' among social groups, and it has constitutional significance.[99]

Meanwhile, in economics, Elinor Ostrom pioneered empirical research showing that communities tended to develop governance mechanisms to ensure common property is not depleted or mismanaged.[100] This debunked a theory of the 'tragedy of the commons', which had argued that only private property rights could stop the squandering of resources, because when property is held in common people overuse and mismanage it.[101] Ostrom's work showed this theory was factually inaccurate: people usually overcome this tendency by setting up representative and voting structures. In 2012, Simon Deakin extended Ostrom's work by analogy to the corporation, and argued that viewing the 'corporation as commons' was more empirically accurate than the shareholder primacy view, depending on theories of agency or property rights. According to Deakin, 'empirical grounding is more important than elegance in a model'.[102] A corporation was not merely a legal fiction, but it was created by socially relevant laws that had an impact on its behaviour. To understand firm or enterprise behaviour it is necessary to include 'insolvency law, employment law, tort law and, arguably competition and tax law, to get the full picture'.[103] Understanding the firm as a commons could in turn help 'in generating the conditions for social and environmental sustainability'. By contrast, 'shareholder value' is a 'cultural norm', not a legal norm.[104] Understanding the corporation as a commons would imply strengthening models of law based on 'multi-stakeholder governance' rather than shareholder primacy, 'autonomy for rule-making processes' against capital market pressures and 'respect for local and national democratic choices' over regulatory competition between different countries.[105]

(d) Public and Private Ownership

While theories of corporate law and the firm conceptualised internal enterprise governance, mostly focused on the private sector, a parallel debate focused on

[98] T. Raiser, 'The Theory of Enterprise Law in the Federal Republic of Germany' (1988) 36(1) *Am J Comp L* 111, 113–14.

[99] Raiser, 'The Theory of Enterprise Law in the Federal Republic of Germany', 113, 119.

[100] E. Ostrom, *Governing the Commons: The Evolution of Institutions for Collective Action* (1990).

[101] Cf. G. Hardin, 'The Tragedy of the Commons' (1968) 162(3859) *Science* 1243, which provided no evidence.

[102] S. Deakin, 'The Corporation as Commons: Rethinking Property Rights, Governance and Sustainability in the Business Enterprise' (2012) 37(2) *Queen's LJ* 339, 341.

[103] Deakin, 'The Corporation as Commons', 365.

[104] S. Deakin, 'The Coming Transformation of Shareholder Value' (2005) 13(1) *Corporate Governance* 11.

[105] Deakin, 'The Corporation as Commons', 379.

the finance of enterprise, by either public or private means. When should enterprises be funded by private investors on the equity or debt markets, and when should enterprises be publicly owned? And if an enterprise is public, how should it be governed?

On these huge questions, of privatisation, nationalisation or socialisation, legal literature has been relatively mute since World War Two. Legal scholars on the whole have not yet formulated clear, applicable principles, or isolated the terms of a debate, on which enterprises should be public or private.[106] Instead it has been common to read that no conclusions can be reached, or the questions are not ones for the law. Similarly, while there have been economic and social rights enshrined in international law since 1919 or 1948,[107] human rights law has not yet engaged with issues of private or public ownership, but it is impossible to maintain 'the path of agnosticism' when these issues impact the expediency with which human rights claims are realised.[108] Among constitutional and administrative lawyers, a concept has developed that an enterprise may have the inherent character of a 'public service',[109] and in EU law there is a concept of a 'service of general economic interest'.[110] This character is retained whether or not the enterprise is in fact privatised or publicly owned (see Ch. 6(4)).[111] However, there are not yet clear criteria to determine what is such a service of 'general economic interest', beyond it exhibiting 'special characteristics' as decided by ad hoc case law. Thus, the Court of Justice of the EU (CJEU) has largely left the definition to member states. Finally, in legal literature there is no developed debate or agreement on principles of governance that should follow once a 'public service' is identified. There is a thread of literature that rests on an assumption of the 'inefficiencies of state ownership', and suggests that a state's corporate governance functions should be separated from its control of shares, to avoid its apparent conflicts of interest in being both regulator and regulated.[112] There is also a thread of literature that starts from the premise that the private profit motive is inherently suspect and

[106] But contrast I. Galnoor, 'Privatisation Policy: The Burden of Proof' in A. Paz-Fuchs et al. (eds.), *The Privatization of Israel* (2018) ch. 2.

[107] See the ILO and its programme of developing labour rights in the Versailles Treaty 1919, art. 427, and the UDHR 1948, arts. 20–9.

[108] P. Alston, 'Extreme Poverty and Human Rights' (26 September 2018) Report of the Special Rapporteur on extreme poverty and human rights. At 5, human rights lawyers 'have chosen the path of agnosticism' but should begin to engage. Alston's criticism is equally directed at himself, as a leading author in human rights, but see P. Alston and R. Goodman, *International Human Rights Law* (2012) ch. 16.

[109] T. Prosser, 'Public Service Law: Privatization's Unexpected Offspring' (2000) 63(4) *L & Cont Probs* 63.

[110] TFEU, arts. 14 and 106(2); Charter of Fundamental Rights of the EU 2000, art. 36.

[111] E.g. *Griffin v South West Water Services* [1995] IRLR 15.

[112] See M. Pargendler, 'State Ownership and Corporate Governance' (2012) 80(6) *Fordham L Rev* 2917; C. J. Milhaupt and M. Pargendler, 'Governance Challenges of Listed State-Owned Enterprises around the World: National Experiences and a Framework for Reform' (2017) 50 *Cornell Int'l LJ* 473.

corrosive,[113] but this has not yet suggested exactly which enterprises (if any) should not be put into public ownership.

In economic literature, principles are also difficult to discover. As we saw above, Adam Smith briskly stated that the public sector (or in his time corporations) could better run enterprises where tasks are 'routine, or to such a uniformity of method as admits of little or no variation'.[114] If we were to develop this idea into a theory, one might draw a conclusion that where there is high technological innovation (i.e. not 'uniformity of method'), the enterprise is best left to the private sector. Where there is less technological innovation, such a theory could go, an enterprise is best placed in the public sector. However, experience in the twentieth century has shown that most technological innovation is funded by the state, including most medicines, the Internet, mobile-phone hardware, and solar and wind technology.[115] Moreover, many services where there has been no real technological development for millennia, for instance restaurants, work well when privately owned.

By contrast, John Stuart Mill elaborated five exceptions to laissez-faire, and his largest exception was that anything a corporation could do, a government might do better. He also named gas, water, road and rail as 'practical monopolies'. Yet in Mill's time, modern company law was in its infancy and had limited experience with the variety of stakeholder regulation models we know today. Mill cautioned against the state being 'overcharged' with duties, as cabinet government might have limited capacity to apply full attention or care to all issues.[116] Yet, Mill explicitly favoured democratic government being 'supported by democratic institutions in detail',[117] suggesting municipal or worker ownership is often beneficial. Marx, Engels and the Webbs did not articulate any real limits to public ownership,[118] while at the opposite end of the spectrum in 1992 a World Bank economist wrote there 'are virtually no limits on what can be privatized'.[119] Clear principles to decide the division between public and private ownership – if any – have not yet emerged. Empirical literature on the effects of privatisation or state ownership is plentiful, but the principles are scarce. Instead, the dominant theoretical frame of economics is 'market failure'.

(2) Market Failures and Market Conditions

'Market failure' is the most common frame in economics to decide whether to 'regulate' markets, and if there should be public ownership. On this view,

[113] E.g. W. A. Robson, 'The Public Corporation in Britain Today' (1950) 63(8) *Harvard L Rev* 1321, 1329–30; P. Ireland, 'Company Law and the Myth of Shareholder Ownership' (1999) 62(1) *MLR* 32; J. Bakan, *The Corporation* (2003).

[114] Smith, *Wealth of Nations*, Book V, ch. 1, §121.

[115] M. Mazzucato, *The Entrepreneurial State: Debunking Public vs Private Sector Myths* (2011).

[116] Mill, *Principles of Political Economy*, Book V, ch. 11, §§4–5.

[117] Mill, *Principles of Political Economy*, Book V, ch. 11, §6. [118] See Ch. 2(1)(a).

[119] M. M. Shirley, 'The What, Why and How of Privatization: A World Bank Perspective' (1992) 60(6) *Fordham L Rev* S23, S24.

markets 'fail' if they do not reach a state of productive efficiency, where supply satisfies demand and resources are fully utilised.[120] This abstract condition is unlikely to ever be fulfilled in any market. Instead, most frameworks adopt categories of failure. This resembles John Stuart Mill's exceptions to laissez-faire, but before elaborating, two caveats must be highlighted. First, unlike Mill, today's discourse of market failure unhelpfully presumes there is something called 'the market' that law 'regulates'. By a 'market', many people think of freedom of contract, private property, liability for negligent harm (but less liability for economic loss by competition), limited liability of investors and separate personhood of companies. But of course, there are infinite arrangements of these rules alone (e.g. duties of good faith, anti-discrimination laws, strict liability, unfair competition laws, veil piercing, governance duties, etc.). As an objective fact, there is no such thing as 'the market'.[121] There are only laws and the society that upholds them, in infinite variety. Second, once one identifies a market failure, this does not in itself explain the right legal response, except to depart from 'the market' paradigm. It does not explain the proper scope of justiciable social rights, regulatory enforcement, ownership, governance or finance structures. It is often also argued that there is 'government failure' when 'intervention' produces worse outcomes than a 'free market', but this likewise presumes, quite falsely, that government is not creating markets by upholding certain rules of property, contract, tort or persons. Nevertheless, the framework of market failure is an important starting point for analysis, and dominated by the late twentieth century.

In *The Economics of the Public Sector*, a leading economics text, Joseph Stiglitz and Jay Rosengard set out five main categories of market failure,[122] which are generally accepted even if the details are heavily contested. These are (a) the failure of competition and natural monopoly, (b) public goods, (c) externalities, (d) information failure and incomplete markets and (e) unemployment, inflation and disequilibrium. To these can be added two more: the central concern of classical economics and modern law with (f) unequal bargaining power, flowing from unequal distribution of property, and (g) irrational decision-making, as understood in behavioural economics and psychology. The next section goes through each of these categories, and concludes by turning the logic around to suit a legal perspective and discussing (h) what conditions we need for markets to work. The greater the market failure, the greater the subsidies and unjustified finance for enterprise.

[120] V. Pareto, *Manual of Political Economy* (1906) ch. 6; N. Kaldor, 'Welfare Propositions in Economics and Interpersonal Comparisons of Utility' (1939) 49(195) *Economic J* 549; J. Hicks, 'The Foundations of Welfare Economics' (1939) 49(196) *Economic J* 696.

[121] There are, however, physical and virtual 'marketplaces', which have a rich tradition of regulation. See Ch. 18.

[122] J. E. Stiglitz and J. K. Rosengard, *The Economics of the Public Sector* (3rd ed. 2015) chs. 1 and 4.

(a) Failure of Competition and Natural Monopoly

According to Stiglitz and Rosengard, the first market failure is 'failure of competition', including 'natural monopoly'.[123] At its most basic, a market is thought to 'work' if the competing firms that supply a good (e.g. grain businesses selling corn) satisfy demand (e.g. by consumers who want to eat). This idea of an 'equilibrium' in supply and demand, and a hypothetically efficient market price, was first expressed in a chart in 1887 by Fleeming Jenkin (see Figure 2.1).[124]

In this example, if many grain businesses sell to many grain consumers, the competition among them is thought to reduce prices to the costs of production plus a reasonable return.[125] Few businesses can set a higher price than the market competition allows (although some could be lucky in ripping off the

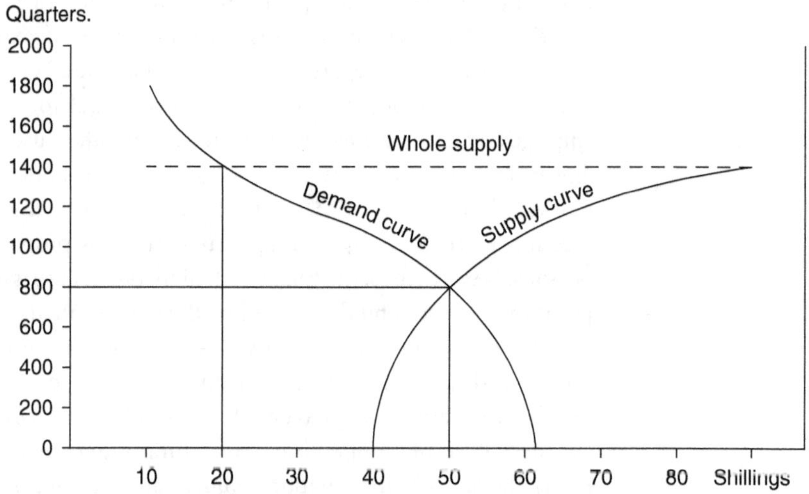

Whole supply for sale at any price, 1,400 quarters of wheat.
Price at which whole supply would be sold, 90*s*.
Price at which whole supply would be bought, 20*s*.
Market price, 50*s*.
Price below which no sale could take place, 40*s*.
Price above which no sale could take place, 62*s*.
Quantity which will be sold, 800 quarters.

Figure 2.1 Graphical representation of a corn market, according to Fleeming Jenkin

[123] Stiglitz and Rosengard, *The Economics of the Public Sector*, ch. 4, 83–4.

[124] F. Jenkin, *The Graphic Representation of the Laws of Supply and Demand and other Essays on Political Economy* (1887). Note that 'corn' in the nineteenth century referred to all kinds of grain, such as wheat, oats, barley or maize.

[125] Smith, *The Wealth of Nations*, Book I, ch. 7, §27 (a competitive price is 'the lowest which the sellers can commonly afford to take, and at the same time continue their business').

occasional, unwitting customer). Suppose that a business called Corn Ltd attempted to raise its prices. Consumers (perhaps just a marginal group) will instead buy from Barley Ltd or Oats Ltd, and so force Corn Ltd to quickly drop its price back to the 'equilibrium'.[126] The consumer is sovereign.

So what causes a 'failure of competition'? First, Adam Smith observed that business people often have a tendency, if they meet, to quickly start talking about halting competition, in a 'conspiracy against the public, or in some contrivance to raise prices'.[127] This is why competition law prohibits unjustified collusion and places a duty on undertakings to behave independently on the market (see Ch. 6(3) and (1)(b)). Otherwise, on this view, the 'market' would 'fail'. If all corn businesses colluded, corn prices would be raised artificially above the market equilibrium price. This would transfer wealth from consumers to producers, but it would also mean some consumers could no longer afford corn. Total supply is reduced through raised prices. The number of buyers would reduce. This would mean a loss of total economic output, harming social welfare, for the enrichment of a few.

Second, classical economic theory always held that a monopoly was 'a great enemy to good management',[128] and that it perpetuates an unjust distribution of wealth.[129] This is why abuse of a dominant position is controlled by law (see Ch. 6(2)). It was also agreed in classical economics that monopolies can result either from laws granting monopolies over industries or trade, or simply from the use of property rights,[130] including takeovers, mergers, exploiting a new technology and very occasionally beating competitors 'on the merits'. However, a significant change in economic theory took place from 1935 when John Hicks argued a monopoly had a narrower meaning: monopoly exists when, and is also inefficient because, it has declining marginal revenues compared to a competitive state.[131] The logic here, and depicted in the chart (see Figure 2.2), is that a monopoly has to sell at the same price to everyone (it cannot, supposedly, have different prices for different consumers). It follows that to increase the quantity it sells, it must incrementally reduce its prices for everyone, bringing marginal revenue (the extra revenue from each additional sale) below the competitive revenue (if the market involved many businesses). Thus, the problem of monopoly is this type of deadweight loss to total production.

126 M. J. Trebilcock, 'An Economic Approach to the Doctrine of Unconscionability' in B. J. Reiter and J. Swan (eds.) *Studies in Contract* (1980) 412–13.

127 Smith, *The Wealth of Nations*, Book I, ch. 10.

128 Smith, *The Wealth of Nations*, Book I, ch. 11.

129 Smith, *The Wealth of Nations*, Book I, ch. 11, on a landlord demanding prices 'not at all proportioned' to improvement, but based on 'what the farmer can afford to give'. A. Marshall, *Principles of Economics* (1890) Book IV, ch. 14, §7 (the monopolist's aim is to fix prices so that the benefit to itself is 'as large as possible').

130 Smith, *The Wealth of Nations*, Book I, ch. 11 (rent from land 'is naturally a monopoly price').

131 J. R. Hicks, 'Annual Survey of Economic Theory: The Theory of Monopoly' (1935) 3(1) *Econometrica* 1, 17.

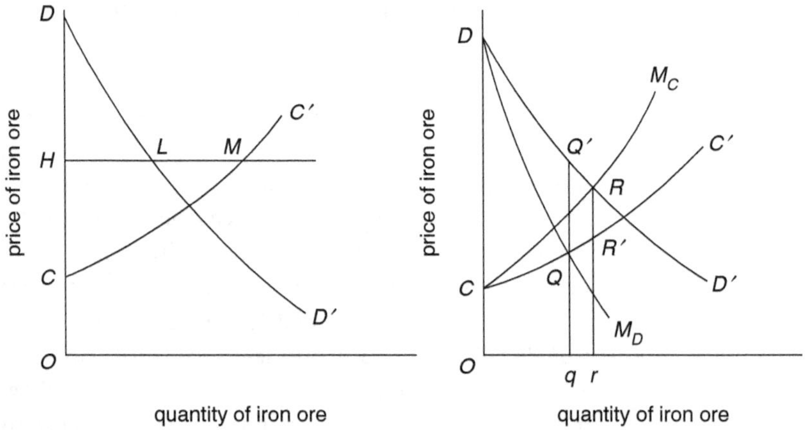

Figure 2.2 Graphical representation of competitive and monopoly pricing, according to John Hicks[i]

[i] In the chart, the monopolist is said to produce at the level of the curve C-MC, instead of C-C1 (i.e. less quantity for a higher price) because the monopolist has to charge the same prices for customers, or cannot optimally discriminate among customers in the prices it charges.

Hicks's definition of monopoly implied that the company did not (or legally could not) discriminate in prices among customers (e.g. the Royal Mail with a uniform price for stamps). Yet companies systematically *do* aim to price discriminate (and therefore not be subject to declining marginal revenues with increased output). In 1969, Richard Posner argued that price discrimination is never perfect, so monopoly always has an irreducible cost.[132] (As an empirical assertion, this is doubtful.) Yet most dominant firms should be left alone, not broken up, unless a rare merger is unlawful, said Posner, because the costs of break-up are greater.[133] This definition of monopoly is widely adopted in economic texts as the basis for market failure,[134] but is not the meaning of monopoly used in law (see Ch. 6(2)(a)). It is also far removed from the original concerns of political economy with power and distribution. There is no good reason to limit the perceived evils of monopoly to marginal revenue curves. The better view is that monopoly is an extreme type of unequal bargaining power (see Ch. 2(2)(f)).

The specific idea of 'natural monopoly', today, is 'a situation in which it is cheaper for a single firm to produce the entire output than for each of several firms to produce part of it'.[135] This differs from the broader, original use of the term by Mill, who referred to 'a natural monopoly in favour of skilled labourers

[132] R. A. Posner, 'Natural Monopoly and Its Regulation' (1969) 21(3) *Stanford L Rev* 548, 557–8; also R. A. Posner, *Economic Analysis of Law* (2011) ch. 9, 351 fn. 1.

[133] E.g. R. A. Posner, *Antitrust: An Economic Perspective* (1976) ch. 4.

[134] Stiglitz and Rosengard, *The Economics of the Public Sector*, 85; A. Manning, *Monopsony in Motion: Imperfect Competition in Labour Markets* (2003) ch. 2, 31.

[135] Stiglitz and Rosengard, *The Economics of the Public Sector*, 84.

against the unskilled'.[136] For Mill, if people had rare skills, they could unfairly charge more than others for their services (examples might be doctors, professors or footballers). This also appears to contribute to unequal bargaining power (see Ch. 2(2)(f)). By contrast, Mill's 'practical monopoly' (giving examples of gas, water, road and rail) matches the use of 'natural monopoly' today.[137] The difficulty is that there is no agreement among economists about the enterprises where a monopoly is in fact 'natural' (or practical), and what to do if there is one. For instance, during British privatisations of the 1980s, it was argued that because there could be competitive tendering for licences to run local monopolies (in telecoms, electricity, rail or water), this sidestepped any concern about natural monopoly: even if water was 'the natural monopoly par excellence' (because it makes no sense to lay competing pipes and sewers), competition could supposedly still be constructed in the capital markets with 'the benefits of this competition . . . passed on to consumers in . . . lower prices' (contrast reality: Ch. 13).[138] Others argued that competitive tendering does not work, and public ownership is the appropriate solution.[139] There are also network enterprises, where the value to everyone in the network increases when all users join the same, and average costs decrease as more people are served (e.g. Facebook, WhatsApp, telephones). There is no agreement about whether network effects constitute a natural monopoly, or if they are problematic.

(b) Public Goods

The second main category of market failure is 'public goods'. Despite the inclusive name, economists refer to a narrow idea, with common examples being lighthouses, the military and defence, public health (e.g. vaccinations for a pandemic) and fire brigades. Public goods are those that 'will be supplied in insufficient quantity' by 'the market', because suppliers cannot easily prevent people who do not pay from using the good (it is 'non-excludable') and many people can enjoy the benefits at the same time (it is 'non-rivalrous').[140] With these two conditions, goes the logic, private businesses will be unable to charge fees on an open market to cover the costs of production, and they will therefore not provide enough. This undersupply is the market failure, and 'a rationale for many government activities'.[141] While in a 'natural monopoly' less is supplied

[136] Mill, *Principles of Political Economy*, Book II, ch. 14, §14.

[137] Mill, *Principles of Political Economy*, Book V, ch. 11, §12.

[138] E.g. S. C. Littlechild, 'Economic Regulation of Privatised Water Authorities' (25 January 1986) 2.8 and 2.22.

[139] Cf. G. A. Boyne, 'Competitive Tendering in Local Government: A Review of Theory and Evidence' (1998) 76(4) *Public Admin* 695.

[140] Stiglitz and Rosengard, *The Economics of the Public Sector*, 86 and ch. 5.

[141] Stiglitz and Rosengard, *The Economics of the Public Sector*, 86. Further J. E. Stiglitz, 'Theory of Local Public Goods' in M. S. Feldstein and R. P. Inman (eds.), *The Economics of Public Services*

because a business has power to charge too much, for a 'public good' less is supplied because businesses do not have power to charge enough.

In economics texts, the idea of public goods is said to rationalise many government activities. However, there are three problems with this view. First, enforcing property and contract rules is a government activity.[142] This fits the definition of a public good, because people are not excluded from the benefits of these laws (at least formally), and they are non-rivalrous. From this come all private enterprises and markets, including those which exclude rivals in access to resources. The idea of a 'public good' cannot be very useful in distinguishing where markets fail or not: what matters is the legal rules. Second, the idea of 'non-excludable' and 'non-rivalrous' goods has rarely (if ever) been used historically in justifying government-run lighthouses, the military, public health or fire brigades. People do not think in such abstract, counterintuitive ways, and instead think about how to get things done. Third, again, it is unclear what kind of 'activities' government should undertake even if something is a public good. In 'The Lighthouse in Economics', Ronald Coase pointed out that lighthouses in Britain have historically been provided by quasi-private companies (Trinity House and others) so a lighthouse was not 'a service which could only be provided by the government'.[143] Yet interestingly, Coase's own history highlighted that private shipping groups lobbied Parliament for lighthouse companies to be set up, and given the right to charge tolls on shipping lanes. The governance of lighthouse corporations gave the key stakeholders – 'representing Shipowners, Underwriters, and Shippers' – voting rights in the management of services.[144] Although not funded by general tax, this was certainly not normal private enterprise.[145] It therefore does plainly fit within Stiglitz and Rosengard's economic definition of public goods and regulation. But equally, the lighthouse system can hardly be transposed to the military, public health or fire: each enterprise differs, and so must the rules.[146]

(c) Externalities

The third main category of market failure is 'externalities'.[147] This is where an enterprise 'imposes a cost on other[s] but does not compensate them' (a negative externality) or creates a benefit when it cannot 'reap a reward for

(1977); P. A. Samuelson, 'The Pure Theory of Public Expenditure' (1954) 34(6) *Rev Economics and Statistics* 387.

142 It would appear that the law itself – defining rights and duties – is a public good, assuming there is access to justice. See *R (Unison) v Lord Chancellor* [2017] UKSC 51, [66]–[75].

143 Coase, 'The Lighthouse in Economics'.

144 Coase, 'The Lighthouse in Economics', 357, 363–4, 373.

145 Thus overcoming the condition of an ordinary market where people cannot be excluded, and many may use the service at the same time.

146 On the military, see Ch. 19. On public health, see Ch. 9(2)(e).

147 Stiglitz and Rosengard, *The Economics of the Public Sector*, 86–7 and ch. 6.

providing it' (a positive externality[148]). If a factory pollutes a river, but does not pay for the clean-up, it can sell its goods more cheaply or profit more than otherwise. The transcendent 'externality' (on these terms) is climate damage, as coal, oil and gas companies; auto manufacturers; plane or ship companies; or any businesses that emit greenhouse gases fail to pay for the destruction of the ecosphere through global warming. In classical economics, it was said that a government's preferred response should be to tax externalities, so as to 'internalise' the costs.[149] Taxes enable people with the ability to pay to continue the harm, but are supposed to provide a financial incentive against the harm. The most common response of the law, by contrast, is to require damages and injunctions in tort, or criminal penalties under a statute, for harm that is caused.[150] Strict liability or insurance is the most common response for major harms (in product liability, workplace accidents, motor accidents and environmental law).[151] Most legal systems have default liability for negligence.[152] Intentional harm tends to be criminal.[153]

Sadly, there is not yet consensus in economics that externalities require a legal response, or what. In 'The Problem of Social Cost', Ronald Coase argued that if we imagine a transaction-cost-free world, whatever kind of property or liability rule the law creates, businesses may contract around it to reach a productively efficient result.[154] Using examples of railway sparks or cows damaging crops, and a sweet-maker's machinery disturbing a doctor, Coase argued that if there were no transaction costs in reaching a deal about property use (e.g. the time in negotiation), the parties would always choose a result that maximised production. For instance, if the sweet-maker has the right to continue using the machinery, and has no liability for nuisance, the doctor could pay off the sweet-maker, if the doctor's practice is more profitable. According to Coase, without the obstacle of transaction costs, the result that maximises production would *always* be reached. This suggested that the distribution of property rights was irrelevant for productive efficiency or, more bluntly, that inequality was not an economic problem, only transaction costs were. As a pure theory, it had no empirical evidence to support it, and evidently it is wrong. If one party has property rights (or no liability for pollution) this gives them more bargaining power to demand more out of any deal, and bargaining power affects distribution of gains (as Coase admitted). But distribution of gains also affects the motivation to work, because we know that fairness matters in how people act (which Coase did not admit).

148 Thus a 'positive externality' is logically indistinguishable from the first condition of a 'public good', above.

149 C. Pigou, *The Economics of Welfare* (1952) Part II, ch. 2: 'costs are thrown upon people not directly concerned'.

150 Cf. Mill, *On Liberty* and the 'harm principle'.

151 E.g. Environmental Protection Act 1990, s. 33; *R (Green Environmental Industries Ltd) v Hertfordshire CC* [2001] UKHL 11.

152 E.g. *Donoghue v Stevenson* [1932] UKHL 3.

153 E.g. Criminal Damage Act 1971, ss. 1 and 4–5.

154 Coase, 'The Problem of Social Cost'.

This means distribution does change productive efficiency.[155] Thus, the idea that there is no economic reason to be concerned with climate damage, pollution or externalities – absent transaction costs – was fundamentally wrong.

(d) Information Failure and Incomplete Markets

According to Stiglitz and Rosengard the next two categories of market failure, which it makes sense to treat together, are 'information failure' and 'incomplete markets'. An 'information failure' or 'asymmetry' arises where one party to a bargain is more informed than another, and there are high costs to find information. Uninformed people are likely to overpay or undersell goods and services, or potentially not contract at all: this is the market failure.[156] In law, the simplest rules of contract law prohibit fraudulent misrepresentation, and from the late nineteenth century the law also admitted liability for negligent misrepresentation.[157] In parallel, a slowly growing set of duties of utmost good faith, and positive disclosure, were acknowledged, starting with insurance and securities markets wherever there was speculation.[158] Positive disclosure has gradually become the norm in most markets, including for consumers, in finance and in employment.[159] This includes food nutrition and ingredient labelling, accounting information in annual reports, requirements for written contracts, property registers and so on. In economics, information is itself a 'public good', and it can be disseminated at very low cost. Intellectual property rights do the opposite: they restrict the sharing of information.

An 'incomplete market' refers to a special category of information failure. A key example is the so-called 'market for lemons', where a 'lemon' is American slang for a shoddy used car. If buyers in the second-hand car market know that a number of second-hand cars will probably soon break down, but they do not know which ones, they tend to discount the amount they will pay for *all* vehicles (whether or not the car in front of them is good), to account for that risk and uncertainty.[160] The market failure is that prices systematically do not match the value of goods or services, and may result in fewer sales. The same phenomenon – which begins with lack of perfect information – is argued

[155] McGaughey, 'Behavioural Economics and Labour Law'.

[156] Stiglitz and Rosengard, *The Economics of the Public Sector*, 91–2. B. Greenwald and J. E. Stiglitz, 'Externalities in Economies with Imperfect Information and Incomplete Markets' (1986) 105 *QJ Economics* 229.

[157] E.g. *Derry v Peek* [1889] UKHL 1 (fraud); *Redgrave v Hurd* (1881) 20 Ch D 1 (misrepresentation); *Hedley Byrne & Co. Ltd v Heller & Partners Ltd* [1963] UKHL 4 (negligence); Misrepresentation Act 1967, s. 2(1).

[158] E.g. *Carter v Boehm* (1766) 3 Burr 1905, per Lord Mansfield.

[159] E.g. Ch. 6(1)(a) for consumers.

[160] G. Akerlof, 'The Market for Lemons: Qualitative Uncertainty and the Market Mechanism' (1970) 84 *QJ Economics* 488.

to apply to markets for insurance, securities and lending markets.[161] Again, this is said to justify regulation of information, disclosure, or prices, but it is not clear which solution should follow where.

(e) Unemployment, Inflation and Disequilibrium

Stiglitz and Rosengard's last category of market failure is 'unemployment, inflation and disequilibrium'. It can be seen immediately that this category differs from the others, as these are effects, not causes. They are 'widely recognized symptoms of market failure', not explanations for why the symptoms happen. It is 'evidence that *something* is not working well in the market' but it is said this is 'complicated' (i.e. there is no consensus in economics) and may 'warrant a separate course in macroeconomics'.[162]

From a legal viewpoint, what are the causes of these 'market failures'? Regarding unemployment, first, the most credible view is that owners of capital and employers have an incentive and often legal rights to make people unemployed, if there is poor job security (see Ch. 5(4)). Without the threat of poverty from unemployment following dismissal, 'workers would "get out of hand" and the "captains of industry" would be anxious to "teach them a lesson"'.[163] If unemployment is maintained at a steady level, employers as a group have few reasons to do anything to reduce it because they may (however irrationally) perceive short term profits from lower wages.[164] In other words, unemployment reduces worker bargaining power, and owners of capital have an interest in keeping it low (see Ch. 2(2)(f)). Second, there can be unemployment from stock market crashes brought about by 'irrational exuberance' or other irrational decision-making (see Ch. 2(2)(g)). Third, it is generally accepted that unemployment results from lack of investment to create jobs, whether from the public or the private sector.[165] This means those with assets, or borrowing capacity, withhold property from investment. It follows that unemployment is caused by poor job security, unrestricted private property rights and their enforcement by the state (see Ch. 2(2)(h).[166]

What about the causes of inflation? This is a general rise in prices, and is particularly a concern if people's wages are not rising as well. If prices go up but pay stays the same, real pay is actually being cut. Again, there is no consensus in economics about the causes or the policy solutions for inflation, except that the central bank and the government have a role in administering monetary

161 Stiglitz and Rosengard, *The Economics of the Public Sector*, 89–91.
162 Stiglitz and Rosengard, *The Economics of the Public Sector*, 93 and ch. 28.
163 M. Kalecki, 'Political Aspects of Full Employment' (1943) 14(4) *Political Q* 322.
164 C. Shapiro and J. E. Stiglitz, 'Equilibrium Unemployment as a Worker Discipline Device' (1984) 74(3) *Am Economic Rev* 433.
165 White Paper, *Employment Policy*, Cmd 6527 (1944) [43]–[45], [57]–[63]; also summarised by M. Kalecki (1944) 6(8) *Oxford Bulletin of Economics and Statistics* 131.
166 A. A. Berle, 'A New Look at Management Responsibility' (1962) 2 *Human Resource Management* 3. Webb, *How the Government Can Prevent Unemployment*, 6–9.

policy and fiscal policy. If there is more credit from banks, more lending or more spending from government, but not on productive investment that expands the supply of goods and services, then the scarcity of resources will mean price rises, and vice versa. Overall, this may be called 'disequilibrium'. The legal foundations of unemployment and inflation are further discussed in Chapters 10 and 20.

(f) Unequal Bargaining Power

The salient omission in modern economic texts on market failure is the most familiar to classical economists, and to legal policy: unequal bargaining power. This pervades all markets, but is systemic in employment, consumer, tenancy and investment relations. It has three main causes. First, it flows from an unequal distribution of property or resources.[167] As Smith explained, this enables the person with more to 'hold out' longer in any negotiation,[168] and appropriate an unjust share of the benefits in any transaction's terms. Second, unequal bargaining power derives from greater collective organisation. As Mill explained, those with obstacles to taking collective action will be at a disadvantage in bargaining.[169] When individuals bargain with a corporation, there is likely to be unequal bargaining power. Third, unequal power is exacerbated by imbalances in information.[170] These factors create a greater 'probability that one actor within a social relationship will be in a position to carry out his own will, despite resistance'.[171]

It follows that unequal bargaining power must be seen as a super-category that contains failures of competition (a) and information failure (d), and is at the root of unemployment (f). Recently, Thomas Piketty has written that overall return to capital (or labour) 'depends on the relative bargaining power of the various parties involved'.[172] Under our current institutional and ideological framework, returns to capital (r) have persistently exceeded growth (g) – that is, $r > g$ – leading to escalating income inequality and concentration of wealth. Every system of inequality relies on an ideology to produce a dominant narrative and justify its laws.[173] Ideologies shape the laws

[167] Sinzheimer, *Grundzüge des Arbeitsrechts*, ch. 2, 22.

[168] Smith, *Wealth of Nations*, Book I, ch. 8.

[169] Mill, *Principles of Political Economy*, Book V, ch. 11, §12. Cf. M. Olson, *The Logic of Collective Action* (1957) which describes collective action problems mostly without reference to Mill, problems of power or the governance of corporate forms.

[170] W. S. Jevons, *Theory of Political Economy* (3rd ed. 1888) ch. 4, 124: 'The power of reading another man's thoughts is of high importance in business.'

[171] M. Weber, *Economy and Society* (1915) ch. 1, §16. Other factors may also augment 'power', such as psychology.

[172] T. Piketty, *Capital in the Twenty-First Century* (2014) ch. 6, 212 (capital), ch. 9, 312 (labour) and 331 (executives).

[173] T. Piketty, *Capital and Ideology* (2020) Introduction and chs. 5 and 11.

of property, contract, corporations, competition and human rights – the bases of the law of enterprise.

Unequal bargaining power is also a major determinant of prices, that may depart from an equilibrium, or fair and just price, within the limits set by supply and demand. In contrast to the standard chart from Jenkin (see Ch. 2(2)(a)), most prices of goods and services are decided within a range or a band, depending on the parties' bargaining positions. There is not a single line of alternatives, because there is often room for higher or lower prices or wages, such as a 'consumer surplus'. For instance, Asda plc might pay £15 an hour to staff if it reduced dividends on each share from 15 pence to 14 pence, or the CEO could raise his salary from £4.5 to £5 million a year if worker wages were cut from £10 to £9 an hour. Thus, the accurate way to depict most markets, with bargaining power, is as set out in Figure 2.3.

It also follows that if the law fixes dividends, wages or prices at a given level within the range (the diamond square in the middle), it will have no necessary effect on total output. This depiction eclipses Hicks's or Posner's monopoly revenue curves. The better view is the classic one: the monopolist with more bargaining power insists on the highest price at lowest output possible – in the chart at the top corner of the diamond, not the bottom.

It has been claimed that 'unequal bargaining power is not a standard market failure, because even powerful [businesses] have a profit-maximizing motive to provide benefits'.[174] This view was encouraged by Coase's theory (see Ch. 2(2)(c)) that, in a world without transaction costs, any clear allocation of property rights,

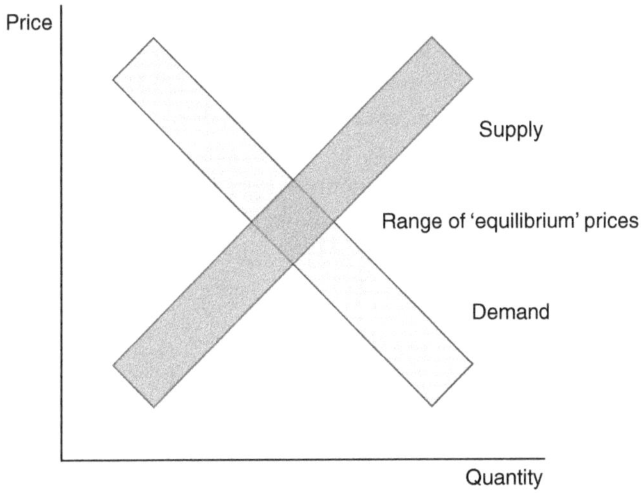

Figure 2.3 Prices with bargaining power: a band in space, not a single line

[174] S. J. Schwab, 'Law-and-Economics Approaches to Labour and Employment Law' (2017) 33 *Int'l J Comparative Labour L* 115, 139–42.

no matter how arbitrary, will enable the maximisation of production and no cost to efficiency.[175] Thus Coase claimed that unequal bargaining power affects distribution, but not efficiency. This is evidently false because different distributions of property, when they are seen as unfair, affect the motivation to work and produce.[176] Those who are underpaid are undermotivated. Also, those who are overpaid become undermotivated if they can profit from their office and not from working, again harming productive efficiency.[177] Coase's arguments stand as an evidence-free interlude in economic theory.[178] Unequal bargaining power is a market failure.

(g) Irrational Decision-Making

A final category of market failure, which is not directly articulated by Stiglitz and Rosengard, but is well understood, is irrational decision-making. In 1848, Mill's exceptions to laissez-faire included lack of foresight, and recently economics has drawn heavily upon psychological experiments to show that, even with full information, as human beings we are predictably irrational. Irrational behaviour leads markets to fail both through a misallocation of resources and widespread damage to production.

According to Daniel Kahneman, our thinking processes can be understood as having two main 'systems'.[179] Our 'system 1' is used for quick, everyday judgements, such as whether to buy a 'two-for-one' deal on a supermarket shelf. We tend to apply a rule of thumb, from experience. We can also be conditioned. For instance, if people choose a ball with a number on it from a hat (e.g. the ball says '12' or '39'), and then are asked separately, 'how much do you think this bottle of champagne is worth?' people typically pick a number close to the random ball (e.g. £15 or £40). This is the 'anchoring effect'.[180] Our 'system 2' is our slow, deliberative thought process, used in long discussions, seminars, in writing and critical thinking. This can change our 'system 1' over time, but our system 1 remains inherently irrational. The many other examples of our irrationality include valuing something we create more highly than others would,[181] valuing things we possess more highly than promises of money or future rewards (the 'endowment effect' and 'loss

175 Coase, 'The Problem of Social Cost', 5–8.

176 A. Cohn, E. Fehr, B. Herrmann and F. Schneider, 'Social Comparison in the Workplace: Evidence from a Field Experiment' (2014) 12(4) *J Eur Economic Assoc* 877.

177 Berle and Means, *The Modern Corporation and Private Property*, 114.

178 E.g. Marshall, *Principles of Economics* (3rd ed. 1895) Book VI, ch. 4, 649: 'the effects of the laborer's disadvantage in bargaining are therefore cumulative in two ways. It lowers his wages; and, as we have seen, this lowers his efficiency as a worker, and thereby lowers the normal value of his labor.'

179 Kahneman, *Thinking, Fast and Slow*.

180 E.g. A. Tversky and D. Kahneman, 'Judgment under Uncertainty: Heuristics and Biases' (1974) 185(4157) *Science* 1124.

181 D. Ariely et al., 'Man's Search for Meaning: The Case of Legos' (2008) 67 *J Economic Behavior & Organization* 671–7.

aversion'), or preferring things as they are even if it is bad for us (the 'status quo bias').[182]

The market implications of irrational decisions, or 'irrational exuberance', are seen most acutely in stock, bond, real estate or other market bubbles and in booms and busts.[183] From speculation on tulips, to the South Sea Bubble, to the Wall Street Crash, the dot-com bubble, or the sub-prime mortgage and global financial crisis, there have been repeated examples (particularly in the USA) of irrational market speculation, over-inflation of asset prices, a crash and worldwide fallout. Economists such as John Maynard Keynes[184] and Robert Shiller have tended to analyse mass irrationality based upon perspectives from 'psychology, demography, sociology, and history',[185] but less so the law. Depending on emphasis, the law could be seen as the sole causative factor, by enabling people to be misled, exploited, confused or our institutions destabilised. Legal reformers have consistently viewed the problem not so much as how human beings behave – there is not much we can do about the biological and psychological structure of our brains for now – but how our social institutions behave. Law can make the 'choice architecture' of individuals rational, to improve outcomes.[186] Thus the differences in regulation explain, entirely, why the USA has fostered repeated financial crashes, while Canada, the UK and other European countries have not to the same degree.

(h) Market Conditions

An alternative to market failures is to set out the conditions for markets to work. Again, 'the market' is not one thing, not a single operation that may fail or succeed, but an infinite variety of constituent rules, of property, contract, corporations, human rights, tax or any other law. From this perspective 'failures of competition' occur because the law empowers unjust infliction of economic loss, or holding productive property without responsibility. 'Public goods' are undersupplied if people have rights to goods and services without an adequate duty to contribute. 'Externalities' persist only if tort, criminal or tax law allow them. 'Information failures' occur with gaps in duties of good faith disclosure. 'Unequal bargaining power' results from property or contract rights without responsibility. 'Irrational decisions' are only exploited in absence of rights. In a sense, there is only 'legal failure', and at best 'market failure' is a misleading euphemism for it. This fact focuses negative attention

182 D. Kahneman, J. L. Knetsch and R. H. Thaler, 'Anomalies: The Endowment Effect, Loss Aversion, and Status Quo Bias' (1991) 5(1) *J Economic Perspectives* 193.

183 R. Shiller, *Irrational Exuberance* (3rd ed. 2015) chs. 1–3.

184 Keynes, *The General Theory of Employment, Interest and Money*, ch. 12, VI.

185 Shiller, *Irrational Exuberance*, xxvi.

186 Cf. R. Thaler and C. Sunstein, *Nudge: Improving Decisions about Health, Wealth and Happiness* (2008).

on what should be changed, but equally positive conditions for productive, efficient markets can be set out. Seven main conditions appear to be these:

(1) in all transactions, good faith disclosure of material information
(2) in all transactions, relative equality of bargaining power among the parties
(3) in any situation, effective compensation for harm, or restitution for loss of rights
(4) for all enterprises, broadly equal distribution of assets or finance for production
(5) within enterprises, enforceable duties of careful, conflict-free conduct, bound by law
(6) within enterprises, a symmetry between people's contribution and their voting rights
(7) if enterprises fail, a fair priority and social insurance for distribution of losses.

The first two conditions are determined by contract and commercial law,[187] infused with the investor, employment, consumer, creditor or other rights that emerged in the twentieth century.[188] The third condition, as the corollary of 'externalities', depends on tort, criminal and public law. The fourth condition depends on the distribution of property rights used for production, and engages the whole of enterprise law, including monetary and fiscal policy.[189] The finance of enterprise also constitutes a key principle of enterprise law (see Ch. 2(5)). The fifth and sixth conditions engage classic corporate governance, in which duties are owed by directors (Ch. 3) and stakeholders vote (Chs. 4 and 5). A dominant theme of this book is that rights to participate in governance, and other rights of service, broaden in scope to also include members of the public in specific enterprises. The seventh, and last, condition concerns social security and insolvency law (Chs. 5 and 7), as well as the ultimate guarantee of economic security set by government fiscal policy (Ch. 20).

If these market conditions are not present, enterprises will fail under private ownership: in a crash, by maldistribution of wealth, or through inefficient production and waste of resources. It will lead the rate of returns to capital to far outpace the rate of growth, increasing economic inequality and influencing

[187] See R. Goode and E. McKendrick, *Goode and McKendrick on Commercial Law* (6th ed. 2020) ch. 3.74–5 on good faith and disclosure. Lord Mansfield in *Pawson v Watson* (1778) 2 Cowp 786, 788: 'by the law of merchants, all dealings must be fair and honest, fraud infects and vitiates every mercantile contract'; *Carter v Boehm* (1766) 3 Burr 1905: 'Good faith forbids either party by concealing what he privately knows, to draw the other into a bargain from his ignorance of that fact, and his believing the contrary.' Though Lord Mansfield's efforts were confined to insurance contracts, after the Wall Street Crash, duties of disclosure were spread to securities law, consumer law, employment and most other contract forms. The approach in *Smith v Hughes* (1871) LR 6 QB 597 became the exception, and arguably should be scrapped as it was in Canada with *Bhasin v Hrynew* (2014) SCC 71.

[188] See Chs. 3–7 on investor, employment, consumer and creditor rights. Chapters 8–19 on most others.

[189] Cf. Berle, 'Property, Production and Revolution'.

political power.[190] Conditions 1, 3, 5 and 6 are also applicable to public or regulated enterprises, but of course the very problems of radically unequal bargaining power (2), infeasibility of broadly distributed productive property (4) and the undesirability of allowing specific enterprises to fail (7) mean that these rules must be altered. Here, altered conditions for public or regulated enterprises must turn on broader theories of human rights, development and justice (see Ch. 2(4)).

(3) Evidence and Politics

Positive theories are all very well, but they should be built on evidence, and theories should be abandoned if they contradict the evidence. In natural science, the role of evidence is certain: if one example does not fit a theory, the theory is wrong, and it must be changed. In social science the same principle is not so easy to follow. First, because people's behaviour is conscious, yet follows patterns and culture, economic and social theories tend to have many exceptions. It may, for example, be generally true that higher prices lead to lower demand in most places, but if advertisements succeed in telling people that only a *more* expensive perfume or scarf is socially desirable, higher prices may create more demand. Second, social phenomena are always multi-causal, and it is harder to isolate the dominant causes of any effect. The next sections summarise three main approaches to gathering empirical evidence, and how evidence is overshadowed by politics and ideology.

(a) Quantitative Studies

First, empirical evidence may be gathered through quantitative studies. We may not easily agree, given one instance in one country, on why unemployment rises or falls, why inequality increases or decreases or why stock market crashes occur. But when we see similar patterns repeated across many countries, and we see corresponding patterns in legal regulation, convincing explanations may begin to emerge. Quantitative studies correlate data to see whether close relationships exist between two or more phenomena, such as between laws and economic effects. This was made possible by the organised collection of statistics by governments and modern computing power.[191] Relationships between unemployment and wage regulation,[192] social security

[190] Piketty, *Capital in the Twenty-First Century* and *Capital and Ideology*.

[191] E.g. Census Act 1800, Bureau of Labor Act 1884, ILO Labour Statistics Convention (1985) C 160.

[192] E.g. D. E. Card and A. B. Krueger, *Myth and Measurement: The New Economics of the Minimum Wage* (1995); S. Machin and A. Manning, 'Minimum Wages and Economic Outcomes in Europe' (1997) 41 *Eur Economic Rev* 733.

and innovation,[193] shareholder rights and banking crises[194] or potentially privatisation and damage to human rights,[195] can all be tracked.

The most important quantitative studies in enterprise law began with efforts by financial economists at the World Bank to show that the US system of corporate governance was superior to all others. These studies initially examined how strong protection was for minority shareholders in corporate laws (such as in derivative claims or unfair prejudice petitions: see Ch. 3(4)(e)), and then argued that this explained whether stock markets were dispersed or concentrated (i.e. that companies had many small shareholders, or more large block shareholders). It was argued that better minority shareholder protection caused more dispersion, on the theory that block-holders would be encouraged to sell their shares if they knew their cash-flow rights would be protected if they became a minority.[196] A similar method was then applied to labour laws, in an attempt to justify deregulation.[197]

After serious flaws in the World Bank's methods were found (i.e. simply misunderstanding the laws),[198] modern 'leximetric' studies have drawn on researchers across law, economics and sociology to evaluate the strength of protectiveness in company, labour and insolvency laws.[199] For instance, how strong are shareholder rights to bring derivative claims? How many holidays are workers guaranteed each year? How far are creditors protected by directors' duties?[200] Different laws are assigned a value (e.g. 0 is no rights, 1 is the most protective, 0.5 is in between) and traced over time. Once a quantitative change from 0 to 1 in laws is established, these can be correlated through 'regression analysis' to economic variables. For instance, how has worker productivity changed? How has the concentration of shareholder ownership in companies changed? Econometricians use software, such as STATA, to compute the data.[201] When they 'run the regression', this shows whether the relations between two variables (i.e. the laws and economic outcomes) are

193 E.g. V. V. Acharya, R. P. Baghai and K. V. Subramanian, 'Labor Laws and Innovation' (2013) 56(4) *JL & Economics* 997; S. K. Bhaumik and R. Dimova, 'Good and Bad Institutions: Is the Debate Over? Cross-Country Firm-Level Evidence from the Textile Industry' (2014) 38(1) *Cambridge J Economics* 109–26.

194 E.g. D. Ferreira, D. Kershaw, T. Kirchmaier and E. P. Schuster, 'Shareholder Empowerment and Bank Bailouts', Finance Working Paper No. 345/2013 (2013).

195 Cf. Alston, 'Extreme Poverty and Human Rights', calling for this.

196 R. La Porta, F. Lopez-de-Silanes, A. Shleifer and R. W. Vishny, 'Law and Finance' (1998) 106 *J Political Economy* 1113, 1130, 1145.

197 J. C. Botero, S. Djankov, R. La Porta, F. Lopez-de-Silanes and A. Shleifer, 'The Regulation of Labor' (2004) 119(4) *QJ Economics* 1139.

198 H. Spaman, 'On the Insignificance and/or Endogeneity of La Porta et al's "Anti-Director Rights" Index Under Consistent Coding', Harvard JMOCLEB Discussion Paper No. 7 (2006) 61–2.

199 E.g. J. Armour, S. Deakin, P. Lele and M. Siems, 'How Do Legal Rules Evolve? Evidence from a Cross-Country Comparison of Shareholder, Creditor, and Worker Protection' (2009) 57(3) *Am J Comp L* 579.

200 J. Armour et al., *CBR Extended Creditor Protection Index* (August 2009).

201 See R. Pedace, *Econometrics for Dummies* (2013). This is an excellent introduction.

repeated. This may show a correlation is statistically significant or there is no more than a random relationship.

Quantitative methods can be powerfully persuasive, but can never *prove* causation, just as a theory of natural science can never be *proven* right. We might always discover an exception in the future. Yet quantitative methods can show that bad theories are wrong (e.g. that job security creates unemployment: see Ch. 5(4)), and can suggest with sound logic and reason that another theory is better.

(b) Qualitative Studies

Second, empirical evidence can be gathered through qualitative studies. Interviewers or surveyors ask people what they think about an issue, why they do what they do or their assessments of how social institutions work.[202] Qualitative work is done by economists, and also widely by sociologists, anthropologists, lawyers, political scientists and historians. It also tends to reveal that there are many different types of rational behaviour, rather than one model.[203] When placed in different contexts, people's behaviour and perception of what is rational or morally acceptable changes.[204]

In some cases, there is a risk that people who are interviewed or surveyed may change their answers when presented with an 'outsider' interviewer. So 'ethnographic research' goes even further, as the interviewer attempts to embed themselves in an environment, and to understand how people think and act from the same perspective: they live or work in the institutions and with people they seek to understand.[205]

(c) Behavioural Economics

Third, empirical evidence may come from behavioural economics or psychology. Unlike collecting data or interviewing, behavioural psychologists set up experiments, with many test subjects, and observe how people react to incentives.[206] To give an example, in one study, pairs of people were hired to give out vouchers to get into night clubs, and gather customer information, on

[202] P. M. Cawthorne, 'Identity, Values and Method: Taking Interview Research Seriously in Political Economy' (2001) 1(1) *Qualitative Research* 65. Examples are T. Schuller and J. Hyman, 'Pensions: The Voluntary Growth of Participation' (1983) 14(1) *Industrial Relations J* 70; E. Batstone, A. Ferner and M. Terry, *Unions on the Board: An Experiment in Industrial Democracy* (1983) ch. 5.

[203] M. Granovetter, 'Economic Action and Social Structure: The Problem of Embeddedness' (1985) 91(3) *Am J Sociology* 481.

[204] This is also confirmed in behavioural economics research: R. H. Frank, T. Gilovich and D. T. Regan, 'Does Studying Economics Inhibit Cooperation?' (1993) 7(2) *J Economic Perspectives* 159 (people were less likely to co-operate after studying economics, in the 1990s).

[205] E.g. A. Ludlow and A. Blackham (eds.), *New Frontiers in Empirical Labour Law Research* (2015) ch. 7.

[206] McGaughey, 'Behavioural Economics and Labour Law'.

a German high street. The test was that among different pairs, the observer cut the pay of both, then neither in the pair, then just one in the pair, and watched how their productivity (handing out vouchers, getting customer information) changed. This showed a drop in productivity when both people's pay was cut, but an *even worse* drop when just one person's pay was cut, than for both combined. The conclusion is that fairness affects the motivation to work.[207]

Another famous study tested how many people would join pension plans.[208] In an American company, before 1999, employees could get an occupational pension if they paid money from their salary, with additional employer contributions, if they took the step of opting in. New employees opted in at a rate of 49%, rising to 77% for employees who stayed five to ten years, and 83% for those over twenty years. After 1999 this was changed. Employees were automatically enrolled in the pension, with a right to opt out: 86% of people participated from the start.[209] This means that even though people were giving up substantial amounts of money, 34% of people lost years of savings: a status quo bias.

(d) Politics and Ideology

There are strengths and weaknesses to all kinds of empirical research. Quantitative studies have opaque methods, which are not easy to verify without considerable training. Qualitative studies may show results that are easily cast as anecdotal, or liable to change. Behavioural studies give examples of how people behave, but may also show biases that are not replicated when studying people in other cultures or societies. Yet evidence is preferable by far to the alternative of unthinking ideology. Ideology is a set of beliefs, often contradictory, that usually serve an individual or sectional interest, not the universal good. Ideology has a psychological function, in that it aims to dictate quick 'system 1' thinking, and banishes uncomfortable reasoning that may question authority. Evidence matters most in a political democracy where deliberative discourse can ensure that good ideas are adopted. In declining or damaged democracies, or under authoritarian governments, reasons and evidence are typically selected according to a dominant ideology to serve the interests of the ruling group.

While empirical understanding of enterprise law and social institutions has improved dramatically in recent decades, since 2015 there has also been a dramatic degradation in political discourse. The Russian and (until 2021) US presidents display open contempt for facts, and sow distrust through a narrative of 'fake news',[210] while senior UK ministers have argued we should

207 Cohn et al., 'Social Comparison in the Workplace'.

208 B. C. Madrian and D. F. Shea, 'The Power of Suggestion: Inertia in 401(k) Participation and Savings Behavior' (2001) 116(4) *QJ Economics* 1149, 1151.

209 Madrian and Shea, 'The Power of Suggestion', 1158.

210 Snyder, *The Road to Unfreedom*.

distrust 'experts', and ignore 'doomsters and gloomsters'. Corporations, particularly in fossil fuels, have long denied scientific evidence exists if this conflicts with their profits, and have funded think tanks to produce faux-academic propaganda, or recruited vulnerable and sympathetic researchers to publish journal articles, with or without disclosing conflicts of interest. Academic research plainly involves heavy disagreements over reason, evidence and values. Yet having a commitment to truth is very different from motivated reasoning, to reach a result, for the promise of financial or political gain or fame.

(4) Principles, Rights and Justice

So far, this chapter has concentrated on economic theories of enterprise. These tend to focus on consequentialist reasoning and assume that values like maximum production, growth or 'utility' are desirable. In *Utilitarianism*, Mill defended the idea that the ultimate goal of society should be to make as many people as happy as possible: for Mill this was 'utility'. It was the 'highest abstract standard of social and distributive justice towards which all institutions, and the efforts of all virtuous citizens, should be made in the utmost possible degree to converge'.[211] Some types of happiness were plainly better than others (e.g. from reading poetry over playing push-pin), and this could be judged by people who knew both.[212]

In contrast, over the twentieth century, international law developed universal human rights that, it was argued, should not be traded off or sacrificed for the general good.[213] The idea of rights has roots in natural law and justice,[214] and in 'reason, knowledge and virtue'.[215] In modern international law the basis for human rights appeals to experience of humanitarian tragedy in World War Two,[216] an appeal to evidence and consequences. Utility and rights, experience and principle, empiricism and deontology, are frequently seen as opposites.[217] But in practice they are mutually reinforcing. The law develops constantly through a process of 'reflexive equilibrium', where societies constantly update the balance of rights they value, in line with their histories and experiences. The difference between principles, such as these, and ideology is that, though

211 J. S. Mill, *Utilitarianism* (1863) ch. 5.

212 Mill, *Utilitarianism*, ch. 2. Cf. J. Bentham, *The Rationale of Reward* (1830).

213 Cf. B. Franklin, *Objections to Barclay's Draft Articles of February 16* (1775): 'They who can give up essential Liberty to obtain a little temporary Safety, deserve neither Liberty nor Safety.'

214 F. Kessler, 'Natural Law, Justice and Democracy – Some Reflections on Three Types of Thinking about Law and Justice' (1944) 19 *Tulane L Rev* 32, 54–5.

215 Wollstonecraft, *A Vindication of the Rights of Woman*, chs. 1 and 9.

216 UDHR 1948, Preamble: 'Whereas disregard and contempt for human rights have resulted in barbarous acts which have outraged the conscience of mankind . . .'. Charter of the United Nations 1945, Preamble: 'We the Peoples of the United Nations determined to save succeeding generations from the scourge of war, which twice in our lifetime has brought untold sorrow to mankind, and to reaffirm faith in fundamental human rights . . .'

217 H. L. A. Hart, 'Between Utility and Rights' (1979) 79(5) *Columbia L Rev* 828.

both involve rules that do not change for individual cases, principles are constantly revised, and ideologies resist change. This section summarises (a) the sociopolitical nature of rights; (b) the relation between international human rights, domestic law and enforcement; and (c) the modern concepts of justice, as they relate to enterprise law.

(a) The Sociopolitical Nature of Rights

As we saw in Chapter 1, the genesis of human rights has a long history, including Magna Carta 1215, the Bill of Rights 1688, the US Declaration of Independence 1776 and Bill of Rights 1789, and the French Declaration of the Rights of Man and of the Citizen 1789. While Magna Carta contained civil, political, economic, social and environmental rights, the rights of the Glorious, American and French Revolutions focused on civil and political rights. In the USA, President Roosevelt called for a 'Second Bill of Rights' in 1944, including fair wages, fair competition, housing, social security, health and education. These were ultimately reflected in the UDHR 1948, and the twin Covenants of 1966. In 1977, the claim was made that rights followed three 'generations'. The first generation of human rights was civil and political, the second generation was economic and social, and the third generation was environmental or collective.[218] This may have sounded neat, but it was historically mistaken, both in domestic legal systems and in international law. Social, economic, environmental, political and civil rights always evolved hand in hand.[219] In the UK, trade union freedoms were won in tandem with rights to democracy. In the USA, the right to charge income tax was won in constitutional amendments alongside representation in the Senate, and before votes for women. In international law, labour rights were in the Versailles Treaty before the UDHR's codification of civil and political rights. Rights have always been mutually supportive. They are indivisible.

Various other theoretical claims are made that 'civil and political rights' should be treated as superior to 'economic, social or environmental' rights. First, it is asserted that civil and political rights are less costly to enforce as they simply articulate a 'freedom from' state interference, while economic and social rights involve 'rights to' get something.[220] But this is a baseless assertion, since a judicial system, courts, bailiffs and/or police all require positive social expenditure and resources. At best there is a difference of degree, and at worst this argument is a shady accountant's trick, illegitimately focusing on government fiscal outlays, and ignoring the cost of *not* providing social and economic rights, including unemployment, poverty, crime, lower life expectancy or early death. Second, in philosophy, it was asserted by John Rawls that any civil or

[218] K. Vašák, 'Human Rights: A Thirty-Year Struggle: The Sustained Efforts to Give Force of Law to the Universal Declaration of Human Rights' (1977) 11 *UNESCO Courier* 29–32.

[219] See also C. Gearty, *Civil Liberties* (2007).

[220] I. Berlin, 'Two Concepts of Liberty' (1958) in *Four Essays on Liberty* (1969).

political 'right' should be prior to the social and economic 'good'.[221] But without economic and social rights most civil and political rights become empty, and vice versa. Social rights are themselves civil, and are political, particularly where they confront power. Corporations, which are constituted by social rights, may undermine civil and political rights as much as the state (suppressing rights to privacy, expression or association). Third, in some judicial decisions, a method to denigrate social rights has been to declare that they are merely 'programmatic', to be implemented by legislation, not case law.[222] This fails to see that providing no judicial remedy is itself a programme. In most modern constitutions, economic and social rights have proliferated, and reject the idea of secondary status.[223] In international law, and in the UDHR in particular, any division among rights is unfounded.[224]

(b) International Rights and National Law

While this book is not the place to elaborate the full practice of human rights law,[225] one of its central concerns is human rights. The most important international human rights norms are the UDHR 1948, the International Covenant on Economic, Social and Cultural Rights 1966 (ICESCR) and the International Covenant on Civil and Political Rights 1966 (ICCPR). The Universal Declaration is not a treaty, rather a declaration of the UN General Assembly, and was directly inspired by the experience of the war and the USA in the Great Depression. As a principal drafter, Eleanor Roosevelt said it would become the 'Magna Carta of all' people.[226] While the Versailles Treaty 1919 included labour rights in the constitution of the International Labour Organization, it was believed that a commitment to all rights was needed to prevent the conditions that led to the atrocities of world war.[227] The ICESCR and ICCPR are treaties, signed by almost every country in the world, and they repeat and extend the provisions of the Universal Declaration. They share three social rights: the right to resources, the right to equal treatment and the right to freedom of association.

[221] J. Rawls, *A Theory of Justice* (1971) 302 and 396: 'the concept of right is prior to that of the good'.

[222] An argument used by the Empire Labour Court in the Weimar Republic, to not enforce the right of workers to participate in economic management, 107 RGZ 245 (25 September 1923) and contrast the opinion of the author of the constitutional provisions, H. Sinzheimer, *Grundzuge des Arbeitsrechts* (2nd ed. 1927) 73.

[223] O. De Schutter, *International Human Rights Law* (2019) ch. 8.1.2.

[224] NB: The ICESCR 1966 entered into force (3 January 1976) before the ICCPR 1966 (23 March 1976).

[225] A. W. Bradley, K. D. Ewing and C. J. S. Knight, *Constitutional and Administrative Law* (2018) chs. 14–20; Alston and Goodman, *International Human Rights*, chs. 3–4 and 16–17.

[226] UDHR 1948, Preamble, on the 'conscience of mankind'.

[227] F. D. Roosevelt, 'Eleventh State of the Union Address' (1944): 'people who are hungry and out of a job are the stuff of which dictatorships are made'.

Within Europe, the European Convention on Human Rights 1950 (ECHR) is mainly a civil and political rights document, yet article 11 enshrines freedom of association, and Protocol 1 includes a right to peaceful enjoyment of possessions and to education. The European Social Charter 1961 (ESC), revised in 1996, enshrines further economic and social rights. Both are ratified by most members of the Council of Europe, but only the Convention is interpreted with an enforcement process by the European Court of Human Rights in Strasbourg.[228] In addition, the Charter of Fundamental Rights of the European Union (CFREU) is a declaration of human rights for European Union (EU) member states, enforced by the CJEU in member states.[229] Despite 'Brexit', when UK laws follow EU law, the CJEU's Charter case law is relevant to the domestic legal order. Table 2.1 sets out the rights key to this book.

How do international or other human rights operate in domestic legal systems? It is commonly said there are two methods. In a 'dualist' system, the signing of a treaty or its ratification does not have direct legal effect without implementation in an Act of Parliament or other legislative instrument. In a 'monist' system (for example in the Netherlands where the International Court of Justice is based),

Table 2.1 Human rights and enterprise law

Human rights	UDHR	ICESCR	ECHR	ESC	This book
Democracy	art. 21	*ICCPR art. 25*	Prot. 1, art. 3	-	Ch. 3, and all
Social security	art. 22	art. 9	-	arts. 12, 24	Chs. 4, 5, 10
Property	art. 17	-	Prot. 1, art. 1	-	Chs. 4, 7, 10
Free association	art. 20	*ICCPR art. 22*	art. 11	arts. 5–6	Ch. 5, and all
Fair work	arts. 23, 24	arts. 6–8	-	arts. 1–4	Ch. 5
Democracy at work	-	-	-	arts. 21–22	Ch. 5
Equal treatment	arts. 1, 7, 23	art. 2(2)	art. 14	art. 20	Ch. 5, and all
Business	-	-	*CFREU art. 16*	-	Chs. 6, 7, 17, 18
Education	art. 26	art. 13	Prot. 1, art. 2	arts. 7, 10	Ch. 8
Healthcare	art. 25	art. 12	-	arts. 13–14	Ch. 9
Life	art. 3	*ICCPR art. 6*	art. 2	-	Ch. 9, 11–15, 19
Natural resources	-	arts. 1(2), 25	-	-	Chs. 11, 12
Food and water	art. 25(1)	art. 11	-	-	Ch. 13
Housing	art. 25(1)	art. 11	art. 8	art. 31	Ch. 14
Benefits of science	art. 27	art. 15(1)(b)	-	-	Chs. 12, 15, 16
Free expression	art. 19	*ICCPR art. 19*	art. 10	-	Chs. 16, 17
Privacy	art. 12	*ICCPR art. 17*	art. 8	-	Chs. 16, 17
Security	art. 3	*ICCPR art. 9*	art. 5	-	Ch. 19
Social justice	art. 29(1)	Preamble	-	-	All chapters

[228] ECHR enforcement, and contrast the European Social Charter 1996, art. 1.
[229] CFREU 2000 recasts most rights in the ECHR 1950 and ESC 1996.

signing a treaty will automatically make its terms enforceable by domestic courts. Yet a third method, and the one that most countries follow in practice, is that courts may commit to interpret domestic law in light of international law (with greater or lesser enthusiasm). Of course, every legal system contains many legislative rights, whether or not they have also codified these as 'human rights' that rank above other laws. In this way, the generality of human rights often guides the purpose of highly specific legislative provisions, to make rights effective.

In the UK, the Supreme Court has indicated a shift towards giving indirect effect to international treaties,[230] yet has not adopted a full monist position.[231] The Human Rights Act 1998 requires UK national courts to interpret domestic law so far as possible in line with the ECHR. If that is not possible, by bending or adding words up to the point of complete contradiction, courts must make a declaration of incompatibility so that Parliament can amend the law.[232] Other countries' positions depend on their constitution. In Germany, the Basic Law (Grundgesetz) contains civil, political, social and economic rights, and is directly interpreted and applied by its Constitutional Courts and others. In the USA, the Amendments to the Constitution (the Bill of Rights) are also given direct effect by the Supreme Court. In both cases, priority is given to the domestic legal order, although the German Courts are explicit in stating they will attempt to reconcile conflicts of domestic and international law, so long as international law upholds essential principles of democracy, the rule of law and the social state.[233]

To what extent are human rights effective in reality? Much depends on the judiciary, its culture and commitment to values that transcend politics. As it was put by Otto Kahn-Freund, 'the power to interpret . . . is the power to destroy'.[234] Since 1976, the US Supreme Court has systematically assaulted human rights, particularly labour rights, equal treatment, freedom of speech and the democratic process, in the same way that it did from 1883 to 1937.[235] The Supreme Court's political hostility to human rights was one of the reasons that the Roosevelt government wanted a 'Second Bill of Rights' built into legislation, not constitutional norms that judges could redefine. There is

[230] *Hounga v Allen* [2014] UKSC 47.

[231] Cf. *R (SG) v Secretary of State for Work and Pensions* [2015] UKSC 16, [247]–[257] per Lord Kerr.

[232] Human Rights Act 1998, ss. 3–4. Also s. 6 requires that all public bodies uphold human rights.

[233] E.g. *Re Wünsche Handelsgesellschaft* (22 October 1986) BVerfGE 73, 339; *Grundgesetz* 1949, art. 20.

[234] O. Kahn-Freund, 'The Impact of Constitutions on Labour Law' (1976) 35(2) *Cambridge LJ* 240, 244, himself paraphrasing Marshall CJ in *M'Culloch v Maryland* (1819) 4 Wheat 316, 431: 'The power to tax involves the power to destroy.'

[235] See *Civil Rights Cases*, 109 US 3 (1883) striking down a post-Civil War equality Act; *Lochner v New York*, 198 US 45 (1905) finding 'freedom of contract' in the constitution and striking down most social rights; and *West Coast Hotel Co. v Parrish*, 300 US 379 (1937) upholding the minimum wage. For modern history, E. McGaughey, 'Fascism-lite in America or the Social Ideal of Donald Trump' (2018) 7(2) *Brit J Am L Studies* 291.

scant international guidance, since the International Court of Justice rarely rules upon the meaning of economic and social human rights,[236] an unsurprising fact since only states, not real people, have the standing to bring claims. Moreover, it is unclear that having more human rights on paper results in social progress.[237] Rights only create minimum standards or processes. A country's governance and political structure is necessary to realise fair standards beyond the minimum. This gap is particularly seen in the UN Sustainable Development Goals 2015, adopted by all UN members, which set seventeen targets by 2030 for all countries. The 'targets' are in fact the realisation of human rights, such as to food, universal education, housing or healthcare,[238] rights yet to be made real in law, despite being universally declared in 1948.

(c) Justice

Ultimately, any system of rights will produce conflicts. What if a business owner asserts the right to property against a worker's right to equal treatment? What if a right to use natural resources, such as coal, damages the right to life through global heating? What should prevail when one person's right to privacy meets another person's freedom of expression? There is no way to resolve such conflicts without a larger, and overriding aim, a dominant purpose or ethic that decides how rights go together. There must be a theory of justice.

Justice is the most important value of any true legal system, but there is not yet agreement on what justice should mean. At its most reductive, justice is about what people are 'due'.[239] But then what are we due? In *Economic Analysis of Law*, Richard Posner argued that 'perhaps the most common' meaning of 'justice' is 'efficiency' because 'in a world of scarce resources waste should be regarded as immoral'.[240] But why does having more resources, more property and less waste matter in itself? This can only be a means to another end. In Ancient Athens, Aristotle distinguished two main types of justice. Corrective justice, or 'justice in transactions between man and man', was where people had to be compensated if they suffered a loss, or restitution made for an unjust gain, like 'arithmetic'. Then there was distributive justice,

[236] Cf. M. Ssenyonjo, *Economic, Social and Cultural Rights in International Law* (2016).

[237] E.g. O. Ferraz, 'The Right to Health in the Courts of Brazil: Worsening Health Inequities?' (2009) 11(2) *Health and Human Rights* 33.

[238] Sustainable Development Goals (2015). The goals are: No Poverty; Zero Hunger; Good Health and Wellbeing; Quality Education; Gender Equality; Clean Water and Sanitation; Affordable and Clean Energy; Decent Work and Economic Growth; Industry, Innovation and Infrastructure; Reducing Inequality; Sustainable Cities and Communities; Responsible Consumption and Production; Climate Action; Life Below Water; Life on Land; Peace, Justice and Strong Institutions; and Partnerships for the Goals.

[239] Plato, *The Republic* (*c.* 380 BC) Book IV; *Institutes* 1.1; *Digest* 1.1.10.

[240] Posner, *Economic Analysis of Law*, 37.

which should follow 'merit in some sense', in 'geometric' proportions. Democrats, wrote Aristotle, might equate merit 'with the status of freeman, supporters of oligarchy with wealth ... and supporters of aristocracy with excellence'.[241] It seems clear that Aristotle's 'corrective justice' is best understood as a subcategory of distributive justice, while Posner's notion of justice-as-efficiency seems to be related to concerns about distribution. However, all these conceptions presume a static state of human relations,[242] and encompass no sense of human or social progress.

A larger ideal of justice recurs in the modern history of philosophy, and throughout the literature behind enterprise law: this is social justice. Social justice is a creative justice. It does not only correct or redistribute what is already there.[243] In a just society, human capacity expands through education, better health and sustainable prosperity. Human creativity is freed when people have a voice in political and economic power, security to plan their lives and material resources to fulfil their potential. The ethical philosophy of social justice is that our highest duty is to improve the content of our 'character' and 'to lend a helping hand' to others.[244] A just society should expand people's 'capacity'.[245] It should enable the 'utmost development of faculty in the individual human being'.[246] It should create 'direct available opportunity', so that 'the opportunity to develop individuality becomes fully actualized'.[247]

[241] Aristotle, *Nicomachean Ethics* (*c.* 340 BC) Book V, Parts III and IV, trans. D. P. Chase.

[242] Cf. Plato, *The Republic*, Book IV, Part V, 139, trans. D. Lee: 'the worst of evils' that 'spells destruction to our state' is 'interchange of jobs'. When each class 'does its own job and minds its own business, that is justice and makes our state just'.

[243] Cf. Aristotle, *Nicomachean Ethics*, Book V.

[244] B. Spinoza, *On the Improvement of the Understanding* (1677) §§13–14: 'man conceives a human character much more stable than his own, and sees that there is no reason why he should not himself acquire such a character ... This, then, is the end for which I strive, to attain to such a character myself, and to endeavor that many should attain to it with me. In other words, it is part of my happiness to lend a helping hand ... .'

[245] E.g. T. Paine, *The Rights of Man* (1792) Part II, ch. 3: 'There is existing in man, a mass of sense lying in a dormant state ... As it is to the advantage of society that the whole of its faculties should be employed, the construction of government ought to be such as to bring forward, by a quiet and regular operation, all that extent of capacity which never fails to appear in revolutions.'

[246] S. Webb and B. Webb, *Industrial Democracy* (9th ed. 1926) Part IV, ch. 4, 847–9: 'We ourselves understand by the words "Liberty" or "Freedom," not any quantum of natural or inalienable rights, but such conditions of existence in the community as do, in practice, result in the utmost possible development of faculty in the individual human being ... When the conditions of employment are deliberately regulated so as to secure adequate food, education, and leisure to every capable citizen, the great mass of the population will, for the first time, have any real chance of expanding in friendship and family affection, and of satisfying the instinct for knowledge or beauty. It is an even more unique attribute of democracy that it is always taking the mind of the individual off his own narrow interests and immediate concerns, and forcing him to give his thought and leisure, not to satisfying his own desires, but to considering the needs and desires of his fellows.'

[247] A. A. Berle, *Power without Property: A New Development in American Political Economy* (1959) 133: 'the economic system shall give direct available opportunity – which is the real meaning of social justice – to all individuals. Averages and statistical aggregates are no longer enough'; Berle, 'Property, Production and Revolution', 17.

The idea of justice follows the people 'with one voice', and yet rules may 'bend in season' where this is necessary to act equitably.[248]

This concept is directly expressed at the end of the Universal Declaration itself, in article 29(1). 'Everyone has duties to the community in which alone the free and full development of his personality is possible.'[249] Social justice includes, but eclipses, efficiency and distributive or corrective justice. Modern concepts of human development pursue the same goals, and are increasingly well measured by methods such as the inequality-adjusted human development index.[250] It does not command complete agreement. For Friedrich von Hayek, social justice was merely an 'outlet for moral emotion'.[251] However, the better view is that social justice has a consistent meaning over 400 years of modern philosophy, and sits at the heart of human rights. It should be regarded as the first goal of a living law,[252] and the basis for geopolitical harmony in international law, because 'peace can be established only if it is based upon social justice'.[253] Accordingly, social justice will be treated as the goal of enterprise law in this book: to build a society where every human being fulfils their potential, and that we help each other to do so.

(5) Conclusion: The Principles of Enterprise Law

The theory of enterprise law is a rich and fiercely contested field, yet it is in a deeply inadequate state. It seems obvious that some enterprises work best with private ownership, such as clothing, restaurants or making electrical goods. There is innovation where businesses adapt to changing tastes in consumer demand, while also trying to lead new fashions and trends. Government could run those enterprises (for instance, many countries have public canteens) but if there is sound credit, reasonable rent, good faith contracting and labour rights, private enterprise may be expected to thrive. Other enterprises, it seems equally obvious, work best in public ownership such as schools, healthcare or road building. This is true whether or not the issue is politically contested (as health is in the USA). For every enterprise we can answer empirically, and increasingly well, isolated questions of what works best. But are there any principles of enterprise law that can be found to guide us?

The thesis of this book is that principles of enterprise law can be found. This is very different, of course, from saying principles are presently realised in the law. A sceptical view might say that enterprise law in the UK, EU or worldwide

248 Sophocles, *Antigone* (441 BC) trans. R. C. Jebb (1917) in the words of Haemon to King Creon. Cf. Aristotle, *Nicomachean Ethics*, Book V.

249 UDHR 1948, art. 29 and art. 28, on right to a 'social and international order' where rights are 'fully realized'.

250 See UN Development Programme, *Human Development Report 2010, 20th Anniversary Edition. The Real Wealth of Nations: Pathways to Human Development* (2010).

251 Hayek, *Law, Legislation and Liberty*, vol. II, ch. 9, 230.

252 See L. Brandeis, 'The Living Law' (1916) 10(7) *Illinois L Rev* 461.

253 Versailles Treaty 1919, Part XIII.

is at best a work in progress, with often incoherent justifications behind its norms, a lack of consensus on basic facts and primitive or experimental models of governance. If enterprise law exists as a coherent subject at all, it is deeply unprincipled, and the task to establish it will be long. But a more optimistic view can also be defended. There is evidently, in law, a set of clear patterns of finance, governance and rights which – if they do not realise principles consistently – do see and often meet an underlying social need. The historically fragmented nature of our economic constitution reflects fierce political disagreements, over values, goals and process, and yet our access to data and evidence today can reduce these conflicts. While some political groups do reject evidence, data and science (especially when it affects their privilege), such a strategy is not likely to last, because more people are educated today than ever.

With this said, ten principles of enterprise law can be identified: these are normative claims about what the law should do, but are also based on tendencies that we can already identify in the law as it has been emerging by the twenty-first century. They will come out over the course of the book, though all are open to amendment and change. Each of these principles is rooted in the theory of enterprise and universal human rights discussed over this chapter. They involve the finance, governance and rights that recur throughout (principles 1–3); the purposive divide between competition in 'general' enterprises and 'specific' enterprises (principle 4); the social security basis for innovative enterprises (principle 5); the interplay of science, the environment and technology that particularly arise in Chapters 11 to 18 (principles 6–8); the macro-relationship of prices and taxes (principle 9); and the greater goal of enterprise law (principle 10).

Principles of Enterprise Law

(1) The finance of enterprise should realise human rights as expediently as possible.[254]

(2) Governance power should mirror people's investments of labour, savings and custom.[255]

(3) Human rights should be made effective in legislation, courts and all social institutions.[256]

(4) Private enterprise should follow broad distribution of productive property and finance.[257]

[254] P. Alston, 'Extreme Poverty and Human Rights', A/73/396 (26 September 2018).

[255] Deakin, 'The Corporation as Commons'; Kautsky, *The Labour Revolution*, ch. 8; Webb and Webb, *A History of Trade Unionism*, Appendix VIII.

[256] F. D. Roosevelt, Campaign Address on Progressive Government at the Commonwealth Club in San Francisco (1932).

[257] Berle, 'Property, Production and Revolution'.

(5) An enterprise state upholds social security, placing risks onto the broadest shoulders.[258]
(6) An enterprise state educates, and distributes the benefits of science rapidly and equally.[259]
(7) Environmental and human health should be improved, and no harm allowed.[260]
(8) Communication privacy and deliberative media should strengthen democratic politics.[261]
(9) Prices and taxes should be charged transparently, efficiently and by the ability to pay.[262]
(10) Enterprise law should enable every member of society to realise their full potential.[263]

In this book's conclusion, we will return to these principles, to evaluate the extent to which they are fulfilled in enterprise law today.

258 Warren, 'Bankruptcy Policy', 775. Acharya et al., 'Labor Laws and Innovation'.
259 UDHR 1948, arts. 26–27(1); M. Mazzucato, *The Entrepreneurial State: Debunking Public vs Private Sector Myths* (2013).
260 Paris Agreement 2015. Mill, *On Liberty*.
261 UDHR 1948, arts. 12 and 19–21.
262 Smith, *Wealth of Nations*, Book V, ch. 2.
263 UDHR 1948, arts. 28 and 29.

Part II
General Enterprise Law

3

Corporate Constitutions and Directors

Contents

With nation states and international organisations, the corporation is probably the most significant 'social institution' in modern history.[1] But what exactly is it? How are corporations created? Who runs them? And to what extent are they accountable in their exercise of power? Leading company law textbooks engage all of these questions.[2] They mostly analyse the relationships among company directors, shareholders, often creditors, sometimes workers and occasionally the beneficiaries of shareholding institutions. Modern company law texts do not analyse the public dimensions in which most major companies work. This is problematic because a glance at the FTSE 100 or a list of the largest global corporations (see Tables 3.1 and 3.2 below) reveals that most operate as specifically regulated enterprises, such as health, finance, natural resources, energy, transport, communications, media or military (see Chs. 9–19). In these enterprises, the general rules of competitive private enterprise are not seen as enough to protect the consumer or public interest. The paradoxical fact is we cannot grasp the true nature of most major companies – who runs them, and to whom they account – from company law alone. While Part III of this book

[1] Cf. A. A. Berle and G. C. Means, *The Modern Corporation and Private Property* (1932) ch. 1, 1: 'a major social institution'. Every good corporate or securities lawyer has this book.

[2] D. Kershaw, *Company Law in Context: Text, Cases and Materials* (2nd ed. 2012); L. Sealy and S. Worthington, *Cases and Materials in Company Law* (11th ed. 2016); P. Davies, S. Worthington and E. Micheler, *Gower and Davies Principles of Modern Company Law* (10th ed. 2016); P. Davies, *Introduction to Company Law* (3rd ed. 2020); A. Dignam and J. Lowry, *Company Law* (10th ed. 2018); J. Armour, 'Companies and Other Associations' in A. Burrows (ed.), *English Private Law* (3rd ed. 2013).

Table 3.1 Top 50 public companies on the FTSE 100, September 2018[i]

	Name	Capitalisation £m	Enterprise	Share price p.
1	Royal Dutch Shell	221919.6	Natural resources	2689
2	HSBC Holdings	134140.4	Finance	669.8
3	BP	117556.3	Natural resources	589.3
4	British American Tobacco	82217.9	Agriculture	3584.5
5	GlaxoSmithKline	76217.9	Health	1536.8
6	AstraZeneca	75530.2	Health	5963
7	Diageo	66910.2	Food distribution	2719
8	Unilever	51931.3	Consumer goods	4216
9	Rio Tinto	51622.3	Natural resources	3880
10	Reckitt Benckiser Group	49538.6	Consumer goods	7016
11	Glencore	47846.9	Natural resources	331.7
12	Prudential	45603.8	Finance	1759.5
13	Vodafone Group	43882.9	Communications	164.5
14	Lloyds Banking Group	42702.5	Finance	59.27
15	Shire	42257.2	Health	4623.5
16	BHP Billiton	35296.9	Natural resources	1671.2
17	RELX	31905.7	Publishing	1616
18	Royal Bank of Scotland Group	30068.3	Finance	250
19	Sky	29721.8	Media	1729
20	Barclays	29389	Finance	171.78
21	Compass Group	27017.5	Food distribution	1706
22	National Grid	26563.9	Energy	791.4
23	Imperial Brands	25474.3	Agriculture	2671
24	Anglo American	24204.2	Natural resources	1723
25	Tesco	23465.8	Marketplace	239.8
26	BT Group	22354	Communications	225.3
27	CRH	21081.1	Building materials	2512
28	Standard Chartered	21025.8	Finance	636.4
29	BAE Systems	20109.7	Military	629.8
30	Aviva	19536.2	Banking	489.5
31	Rolls-Royce Group	18364.2	Engineering	987.4
32	Associated British Foods	18129.3	Food distribution	2290
33	Experian	18093	Travel	1970.5
34	London Stock Exchange Group	15958.7	Marketplace	4586
35	Legal & General Group	15624.1	Finance	262.2
36	Ferguson	15101.7	Plumbing, heating	6515
37	WPP Group	14188.2	Advertising	1124.5
38	Int. Consol. Airlines Group SA	13447.5	Transport	660.2
39	Smith & Nephew	12238.3	Health	1399.5
40	Ashtead Group	11932.2	Equipment rental	2437
41	SSE	11634	Energy	1146
42	Hargreaves Lansdown	10601	Finance	2235
43	Carnival	9961.2	Transport	4764
44	Melrose Industries	9682.1	Engineering	199.9

Table 3.1 (cont.)

	Name	Capitalisation £m	Enterprise	Share price p.
45	Coca-Cola HBC AG	9619.2	Food distribution	2613
46	Informa	9539.2	Publishing	762.2
47	3i Group	9157	Finance	941.2
48	Standard Life Aberdeen	9114.1	Finance	305.9
49	InterContinental Hotels Group	9114	Hotels	4780
50	Centrica	8689.5	Energy	154.9

[i] See the current FTSE 100 Index at markets.ft.com/data/indices/tearsheet/constituents?s=FTSE:FSI. NB: enterprises subject to specific laws in Part III are highlighted. This does not mean food distribution, publishing or advertising involve no sector-specific regulation (such as health & safety, environmental or advert laws), but those rules apply to everyone.

Table 3.2 Top 50 public companies globally, March 2018[i]

	Name	Capitalisation $bn	Enterprise	Location
1	Apple	851	Technology	US
2	Alphabet	719	Marketplace, etc.	US
3	Microsoft	703	Technology	US
4	Amazon.com	701	Marketplace, etc.	US
5	Tencent	496	Marketplace, etc.	China
6	Berkshire Hathaway	492	Finance	US
7	Alibaba	470	Marketplace, etc.	China
8	Facebook	464	Marketplace, etc.	US
9	JPMorgan Chase	375	Finance	US
10	Johnson & Johnson	344	Health	US
11	ICBC	336	Finance	China
12	Exxon Mobil	316	Natural resources	US
13	Bank of America	307	Finance	US
14	Samsung Electronics	298	Consumer goods	S. Korea
15	Royal Dutch Shell	263	Natural resources	UK
16	Walmart	264	Marketplace, etc.	US
17	China Construction Bank	259	Finance	China
18	Wells Fargo	256	Finance	US
19	Nestle	246	Consumer goods	Switzerland
20	Visa	246	Finance	US
21	Intel	243	Technology	US
22	Anheuser-Busch In Bev	222	Consumer goods	Belgium
23	Taiwan Semiconductor	220	Technology	Taiwan
24	AT&T	219	Communications	US
25	Chevron	218	Natural resources	US

Table 3.2 (cont.)

	Name	Capitalisation $bn	Enterprise	Location
26	PetroChina	212	Natural resources	China
27	Novartis	211	Health	Switzerland
28	Pfizer	211	Health	US
29	Toyota	210	Consumer goods	Japan
30	UnitedHealth Group	207	Health	US
31	Cisco Systems	207	Technology	US
32	Home Depot	206	Consumer goods	US
33	Agricultural Bank of China	202	Finance	China
34	Procter & Gamble	200	Consumer goods	US
35	Roche	198	Health	Switzerland
36	Verizon Communications	197	Communications	US
37	Boeing	193	Engineering	US
38	Ping An Insurance	190	Finance	China
39	China Mobile	188	Communications	Hong Kong
40	HSBC	187	Finance	UK
41	Oracle	187	Technology	US
42	Coca-Cola	185	Consumer goods	US
43	Mastercard	184	Finance	US
44	Bank of China	178	Finance	China
45	Citigroup	173	Finance	US
46	Unilever	165	Consumer goods	Netherlands
47	Comcast	159	Media	US
48	LVMH	156	Consumer goods	France
49	PepsiCo	155	Food	US
50	Philip Morris Int.	155	Agriculture	US

[i] PWC, *Global Top 100 Companies by Market Capitalisation* (31 March 2018).
NB: from FTSE 100 companies, just Shell (15) and HSBC (40) reach the global top 50. The ranking is by 'market capitalisation', multiplying the traded share price by the number of shares. Total prices diverge from actual value, influenced by changes in regulation and tax.

explores the laws of specific enterprises that modify the general law, Part II outlines the general laws of enterprise.

This chapter explains how law constitutes the corporation, and how directors are both empowered by and accountable under law. The UK Companies Act 2006 says less than one might expect about how power and rights should be shared among directors, investors, workers, creditors, consumers or the public. A company only needs 'members', who in some way contribute to the collective enterprise, and a board of directors which acquires authority to act for them. Members could be anyone in law. In reality shareholders, who handle other people's money, dominate the membership of business corporations and ultimately control the board. Employees, consumers, other creditors and members of the public typically lack the bargaining power to have a voice, as do the true investors of capital behind the shareholders (see Ch. 2(2)(f)). Three central mechanisms of accountability for the board are voting rights, duties that may be vindicated in court and the capacity to exit relations with the company.[3] This chapter concerns the first two. In principle these mechanisms of accountability could be exercised by members whoever they are, but law and reality restrain that capacity. Accountability in markets, and the structural rights of investors, workers, consumers and creditors, follow in Chapters 4–7.

(1) Nature and Formation of Companies

Every corporation,[4] from a one-person 'company' to a multinational corporation, exists because of recognition by law.[5] 'There is in fact no such thing', wrote Lord Hoffmann in 1995, 'as the company as such, no *Ding an sich*, only the applicable rules.'[6] A company exists because law recognises the acts of people as having legal effect. Practically, the simplest way to register a company in the UK is to log onto the Companies House website, pay a £12 fee, and fill in an online form. This is how you, with state recognition, create a company. Once you have done so, you can use it to run anything from a business, to a charity, to a football club. There are at least five major choices to be made about the company, which partly mirror what have been described as five main features of major corporations: (a) separate legal personality, (b) limited liability, (c) delegated agency, (d) transferability of shares[7] and (e) a company's self-ownership, though this is contested.[8] Each will be taken in turn below.

Although corporations are the most common, they are not the only legal vehicles to run an enterprise.[9] First, people can begin a business as individuals

[3] Cf. R. C. Clark, *Corporate Law* (1986) 93: 'The important powers of shareholders can be put under three headings: voting rights, rights to sue, and rights to information'; A. O. Hirschman, *Exit, Voice and Loyalty: Responses to Decline in Firms, Organizations and States* (1970) chs. 1–3; R. Kraakman et al., *The Anatomy of Corporate Law* (2nd ed. 2009) 37–9, setting out ten strategies against agency problems.

[4] NB: The term 'corporation' and 'company' are interchangeable. In the UK, the word 'company' is often preferred (originally it represented that more than one person was in it), while the USA prefers 'corporation'.

[5] *Case of Sutton's Hospital* (1612) 77 ER 960, 973, per Sir Edward Coke: 'a Corporation aggregate of many is invisible, immortal, & resteth only in intendment and consideration of the Law'. This held the Charterhouse School and Hospital was validly incorporated as a charity, and could therefore receive Sutton's inheritance.

[6] *Meridian Global Funds Management Asia Ltd v Securities Commission* [1995] UKPC 5, [9] (upper case added to *Ding*).

[7] Clark, *Corporate Law*, 2, defined modern public corporations by four features of separate legal personality, limited liability, centralised management and freely transferable shares.

[8] A supposed fifth element of 'shareholder ownership' of companies was argued for by Kraakman et al., *The Anatomy of Corporate Law* (2004) ch. 1.2.5, shifting in (3rd ed. 2017) ch. 1.2.5 to the even less accurate 'investor ownership'. Discussed below at Ch. 3(2)(e).

[9] See Armour, 'Companies and Other Associations' for an overview.

or 'sole traders', using their rights of property, and rights to contract, to start up. Second, people can work with each other. If any person or group is holding assets on behalf of others, there will be a trust. If they are also acting for profit, the Partnership Act 1890, section 1 deems that they are partners. Partnerships may register for all or some partners to limit their liability upon insolvency.[10] Most law and accounting firms are partnerships, and increasingly 'LLPs'. Third, there are at least three minor organisational forms under special statutes, including 'community interest companies',[11] 'charitable companies'[12] and 'provident' societies.[13] These do nothing worthwhile that an ordinary company cannot do, and reflect that at various times Parliament has been lobbied into creating a new legal form with a new name. They may get tax breaks. Fourth, an enterprise could be created by a statute, deeming an organisation to exist, often also called a corporation. Examples include universities, National Health Service (NHS) foundations, the Bank of England and more, explored in Chapters 8–19. But by far the most important legal form of enterprise is the ordinary company, formed under the Companies Act 2006.

(a) Separate Legal Personality

The first main feature of a company is that, once registered, it is deemed to be a 'separate legal person'. In law, it is separate from the real human beings that invest their money, labour or custom into the enterprise. 'To be a legal person is to be the subject of rights and duties',[14] and this mainly means the capacity to make contracts, own property, be liable for torts or to sue or be sued.[15]

The use of the word 'person', as an analogy or metaphor for human beings, does not mean that corporations do or should have the same rights as real people. Nation states also have legal personality, but are generally thought of as entities which exist to serve people, not the other way around.[16] The rights of these persons differ, not least because nation states are expected to uphold 'human rights'. So too with companies. It is generally accepted that human rights extend only in a limited fashion to corporations,[17] but that corporations

[10] Limited Liability Partnership Act 2000, ss. 1–14; Limited Partnership Act 1907, s. 6 (non-active partners).

[11] Companies (Audit, Investigations and Community Enterprise) Act 2004, s. 35(2) if activity benefits community.

[12] Charities Act 2011, ss. 204–50, on charitable incorporated organisations.

[13] Co-operative and Community Benefit Societies Act 2014, ss. 1ff.

[14] B. Smith, 'Legal Personality' (1928) 37(3) *Yale LJ* 283.

[15] Cf. *Arab Monetary Fund v Hashim (No. 3)* [1991] 2 AC 114, referring to 'the right to own, contract and litigate'. Here fundholders incorporated in the United Arab Emirates claimed successfully they had legal capacity.

[16] E.g. Aristotle, *Politics* (330 BC) Book III: 'the state exists for the sake of a good life'. T. Aquinas, *Summa Theologica* (1274) I-II, Q90, A2 and Q92, A1.

[17] Cf. M. Emberland, *The Human Rights of Companies: Exploring the Structure of ECHR Protection* (2006) 4, acknowledging protection under the Convention is not 'plain sailing'; A. Kulick, 'Corporate Human Rights?' (2021) *Eur J Int'l L*.

are themselves bound to uphold human rights such as labour rights, privacy rights and environmental rights.[18] When a 'corporation' does have rights in law, this will inevitably benefit the people who actually have financial interests or governance power in it.

This view (that corporations are not and should not be treated like real people) is not yet accepted in the US Supreme Court. A narrow majority of judicial appointees maintain that corporations have, for example, an unlimited right to exercise 'freedom of speech', and 'speech' supposedly includes spending money in politics.[19] Corporations also, apparently, have religious freedom to deny their employees healthcare.[20] This is why in the USA, unlike countries which have maintained a democratic political system and a functioning judiciary, there is unlimited corporate spending in elections, and politics is divorced from people's preferences.[21] The better view is that while separate legal personhood, by its nature, means having rights and duties, not all persons must have unlimited legal capacity. Legal capacity is 'the gateway to involvement in the operations of a market economy',[22] as well as participation in political life. Companies may be limited by law in the rights they have, by their own constitutions, and practically by use of internal governance structures.

If a corporation is a separate legal person, how does an 'enterprise' differ? 'Enterprise' literally means a 'doing' or an 'undertaking', and usually refers to any 'economic activity, irrespective of its legal form'.[23] If a single human being runs an incorporated business without any network or close affiliation, then the company is the same as the enterprise. But more widely, 'enterprise' can be the name for a 'constellation of corporations controlled by a central holding company' through share ownership, or perhaps through contractual networks.[24] The law may recognise enterprises, regardless of legal form, for tax, competition, accounting, labour law or any public purpose. Usually, the goal of focusing on the 'enterprise' is to prevent the law being evaded. Although companies may be primarily responsible for rights and duties, the enterprise as a whole can be made ultimately responsible for duties owed by companies within it, because the enterprise benefits and so should bear the

[18] See further P. Alston and R. Goodman, *International Human Rights* (2012) ch. 16.

[19] *Buckley v Valeo*, 424 US 1 (1976); *First National Bank of Boston v Bellotti*, 435 US 765 (1978); *Citizens United v Federal Election Commission*, 558 US 310 (2010).

[20] *Burwell v Hobby Lobby*, 573 US _ (2014).

[21] M. Gilens and B. I. Page, 'Testing Theories of American Politics: Elites, Interest Groups, and Average Citizens' (2014) 12(3) *Perspectives on Politics* 564 (policy preferences of most US citizens ceased to have any relation to legislation in a data period from 1981 to 2002).

[22] S. Deakin, '"Capacitas": Contract Law and the Institutional Preconditions of a Market Economy' (2006) 2(3) *Eur Rev Contract L* 317, pointing out restriction on capacity 'both protects the incapable from exploitation, but, equally importantly, protects the market against the incapable'.

[23] General Data Protection Regulation (EU) 2016/679, art. 4(11) adopts this view.

[24] A. A. Berle, 'The Theory of Enterprise Entity' (1947) 47(3) *Columbia L Rev* 343, suggesting law can attribute responsibility by the 'actual existence and extent and operations of the underlying enterprise'.

burdens.[25] The law may say that one corporate person is responsible for another, just as real people can be. Practically, this matters because of limited liability.

(b) Limited Liability

The second main feature in major corporations (but not all) is that most people who register companies opt for 'limited liability' of the real people who create them. During registration, Companies House will ask you a series of questions in its online or posted 'IN01' form. These include whether you choose an 'unlimited' or a 'limited' company.[26] If the company goes insolvent, if it cannot pay its debts as they fall due,[27] the company will usually be put into administration (and perhaps rescued) or liquidation (to sell off the assets: see Ch. 7). If your company is 'unlimited' this means that you, as a member or perhaps as a director, will have to pay the outstanding debts.[28] But if your company is 'limited', this means that *your* liability (as member, shareholder, etc.) is limited to the amount of your investment.

Companies House will also ask whether you wish a company to be registered as a company 'limited by guarantee' or one 'limited by shares'.[29] Relatively few companies are limited by guarantee: here, people who incorporate guarantee to pay up (usually small sums of) money if a company goes insolvent. This limits the ability of companies to raise credit, because relatively little money is being invested and lenders want to ensure borrowers can repay. Most companies limited by guarantee are charitable or fulfil quasi-public functions, such as Oxfam, the London School of Economics or the insurance firm, Bupa.[30]

A company could incorporate outside the UK, but be recognised as having legal personality and limited liability in the UK. Under the principle of 'freedom of establishment' in European Union (EU) law and recognised in the UK–EU Withdrawal Agreement,[31] a company incorporated in one member state has to be accorded legal capacity (to contract, holding property, have rights and duties) unless there is an objective justification.[32] In practice, this

[25] Cf. *Turberville v Stampe* (1697) 91 ER 1072, per Holt CJ, finding an employer's vicarious liability for a worker: 'it shall be intended, that the servant had authority from his master, it being for the master's benefit'.

[26] Companies Act (CA) 2006, s. 9(2) asking for the name, nation of office and type of company.

[27] Insolvency Act (IA) 1986, s. 123(1)(e) uses this definition of insolvency, most of the time.

[28] CA 2006, s. 3(4). [29] CA 2006, s. 3(3).

[30] It is worth pointing out, that although such entities may state accurately that they are 'not for profit', in the sense that they have no shareholders, in practice large sums of money they generate may go to management.

[31] TFEU, art. 49.

[32] *Centros Ltd v Erhvervs- og Selskabsstyrelsen* (1999) C-212/97, [36]–[38], holding that Danish minimum capital rules were a disproportionate restriction on freedom of establishment in the supposed aim of creditor protection. France abolished its private company minimum capital requirement in 2003. Germany created a private limited company form without minimum capital in 2008: GmbHG, §5a.

means that a German AG (*Aktiengesellschaft*) or GmbH, a French SA (*Société anonym*) or a Dutch BV (*Besloten Vennootschap*) may all trade in the UK, as a UK plc or Ltd may abroad. These different forms in principle operate subject to justified, mandatory protective rules – for instance, those in favour of investors, employees, consumers, creditors or the environment.[33]

Most people register companies 'limited by shares'. Under the Insolvency Act 1986, section 74(2)(d) this means 'no contribution is required from any member exceeding the amount (if any) unpaid on the shares'. If the company goes bust, you lose your investment. But the default position is that you lose no more. This obviously shifts substantial risk of corporate failure onto creditors, who have unpaid debts when the company goes bust. So, the law requires that limited companies publicise their nature by affixing 'Ltd' to their names (or 'plc' for a public company, below).[34] Of course, shareholders or directors who set up limited companies may contract away their limited liability. People often give personal guarantees, mortgage their homes or give other security to get a bank loan.[35] A central justification for limited liability is that creditors know they are transacting with a limited company, and they voluntarily agree to the risk of not being paid on insolvency.[36] Thus, limited liability is deeply problematic if it is allowed to operate against creditors who do not have the knowledge or bargaining power to contract around it.

Although the idea of limited liability has been recognised since the Renaissance,[37] it only became widely available by simple registration from the Limited Liability Act 1855 (see Ch. 1(4)). This required at least twenty people, and after the 1862 Act seven people, to be a 'company'. Although statute remained this way until the twentieth century, in 1896 company law's most famous case, *Salomon v A. Salomon & Co. Ltd*, effectively extended limited liability to one-person companies, by very literal statutory interpretation. The company liquidator (a person appointed by creditors to replace directors and recover unpaid debts) sued Mr Salomon personally for the outstanding debts to creditors. Mr Salomon's boot-making business in Whitechapel had gone insolvent after he lost an order from the British military in an 1890s economic slump. Mr Salomon had run the business alone and held 20,001 of its shares. But when he registered the company, Mr Salomon had asked his wife and children to each subscribe for one share, to meet the (then) statutory minimum threshold of seven shareholders. Mr Salomon also gave the

[33] *Überseering BV v Nordic Construction Company Baumanagement GmbH* (2002) C-208/00, [92]: 'overriding requirements relating to the general interest, such as the protection of the interests of creditors, minority shareholders, employees and even the taxation authorities . . . justify restrictions on freedom of establishment'.

[34] CA 2006, ss. 58–9. [35] E.g. *Royal Bank of Scotland v Etridge (No. 2)* [2001] UKHL 44.

[36] Davies, *An Introduction to Company Law* (3rd ed. 2010) ch. 4.

[37] E.g. *Edmunds v Brown and Tillard* (1668) 1 Lev 237, 83 ER 385, holding that Brown and Tillard, who were principals of the dissolved Company of Woodmongers, were not liable for a £500 debt, because the plaintiff, Edmunds, had dealt with the company in its name, not Brown and Tillard.

new company a loan, by selling his boot-making business to the new company for £39,000, but not yet taking payment. Mr Salomon and the new company (which, of course, Mr Salomon was controlling) made a debenture contract (like an 'IOU' note) that entitled Mr Salomon to have a 'floating charge' over the company's assets. This meant, if it went insolvent, Mr Salomon would have a proprietary right over the company's assets, to get paid before other creditors who were only owed contractual debts (see Ch. 7(2)). After the company could no longer pay its debts, other creditors appointed the liquidator to take control. The liquidator (acting in the name of the company) A. Salomon & Co. Ltd, sued Mr Salomon, arguing he should pay the debts because he had 'abused' the corporate form and 'evaded' the statutory requirement for seven people by giving his wife and children shares when they actually played no real role in the business.

Although the liquidator and creditors were successful in the High Court and Court of Appeal,[38] the House of Lords held that Mr Salomon had not abused the corporate form. He had complied to the letter with the registration requirements. So, he had limited liability. It was true that Mr Salomon had been able through the debenture's security interest to elevate payment of debts owed to himself over other creditors. But in Lord Macnaghten's view, the 'unsecured creditors of A. Salomon and Company, Limited, may be entitled to sympathy, but they have only themselves to blame for their misfortunes'. For 'such a catastrophe' of their bad debts, he continued, 'some would blame the law that allows the creation of a floating charge'. He argued 'the ordinary trade creditors of a trading company ought to have a preferential claim on the assets in liquidation in respect of debts ... Everybody knows that when there is a winding-up debenture-holders generally step in and sweep off everything; and a great scandal it is.' Lord Macnaghten knew proposals in Parliament were coming: these soon said employees and the tax authorities (but not trade creditors) had to be paid ahead of floating-charge holders.[39] But, at common law, creditors could not sue Salomon directly. 'There was no fraud or misrepresentation, and there was nobody deceived.'[40]

Although *Salomon* has been described as a 'calamitous' decision,[41] from a policy viewpoint it was in line with regulation today: one-person companies can have limited liability. Trade creditors are not able to sue those behind a company unless they have been defrauded,[42] and arguably should not be able to if they have the bargaining power to contract for security or could choose not to deal with a company at all. Arguably, *Salomon* illustrates a legitimate

38 [1895] 2 Ch 323. Lindley LJ held Salomon liable, in a principled and informed judgment. See N. Lindley, *The Law of Companies Considered as a Branch of the Law of Partnership* (5th ed. 1889) Book II, ch. 4, 253.

39 Preferential Payments in Bankruptcy Amendment Act 1897; and see Ch. 7(1)(a).

40 [1896] UKHL 1, [1897] AC 22.

41 O. Kahn-Freund, 'Some Reflections on Company Law Reform' [1944] 7 *MLR* 54.

42 See *Petrodel Resources Ltd v Prest* [2013] UKSC 34.

protective function of limited liability: shielding a small entrepreneur from destitution through impossible debt to wealthy creditors. Mr Salomon had already lost a great deal. The economic slump caused the business failure, and it was not Mr Salomon's fault.

This said, in some jurisdictions, such as New York, the view developed (which may be calamitous) that limited liability should also shield parent companies in large groups from the debts of insolvent subsidiaries. Solvent parent companies and their owners running otherwise healthy businesses, in taxis or trams, could get away when subsidiaries went insolvent without paying their debts to injured claimants.[43] The better approach is to say that parent companies are liable for a subsidiary's debts when they may exercise significant control.[44] This is done in competition law,[45] tax law[46] and corporate accounting.[47] Limited liability's central protective function is arguably to shift risks onto those who can best bear them: protecting small human persons, not large corporate persons. While the general assumption among UK corporate lawyers may be that parent companies can escape liability for insolvent subsidiaries, there is no case definitively deciding this. On the contrary, as explored in Chapter 7(4), recent case law suggests the opposite.

Another highly problematic view is that creditors who lack any bargaining power, including tort victims who never contract, should lose rights against the real people who cause them loss or harm even though they never have any chance to contract for security interests. Lord Macnaghten's reasoning, and the facts of *Salomon*, did not extend to such propositions. With one exception,[48] there seems to be no case in UK law where it has been accepted that tort victims of an insolvent company have no recourse against the shareholders or directors that profit from activities that result in damage. The lack of litigation in the UK, particularly compared to the USA, probably reflects the fact that the NHS eliminates people's medical costs (see Ch. 9), and compulsory workplace

[43] E.g. *Walkovszky v Carlton*, 223 NE 2d 6 (NY 1966) holding a pedestrian run down by a cab, owned by a deliberately undercapitalised subsidiary, could not sue the parent. Also *Berkey v Third Avenue Railway*, 244 NY 602 (1927) per Cardozo J (complete domination of a parent over subsidiary was needed for liability).

[44] E.g. *Davis v Alexander*, 269 US 114 (1925) per Brandeis J: if a 'company actually controls another and operates both as a single system, the dominant company will be liable for injuries due to the negligence of the subsidiary company'. A variation in *United States v Bestfoods*, 524 US 51 (1998) is that a parent should be liable for a subsidiary's debts where it 'actively participated in, and exercised control over, the operations'.

[45] *Viho Europe BV v Commission* [1996] ECR I-5457 (on group liability, as a single economic unit) or *Akzo Nobel BV v Commission* (2009) C-97/08P, [60] on joint liability with decisive influence. See Ch. 6(1)(b).

[46] E.g. Corporation Tax Act 2010, s. 141, reduced tax liability when other companies in the group make losses.

[47] CA 2006, ss. 399–408, based ultimately on 'dominant influence', from the Seventh Company Law Directive 83/349/EEC.

[48] *Adams v Cape Industries plc* [1990] Ch 433, of which Lord Neuberger remarked in *VTB Capital plc v Nutritek International Corp.* [2013] UKSC 5, included '*obiter* observations and [is] anyway not binding in this court'.

insurance ensures compensation regardless of corporate legal structure.[49] This reduces the need for tort lawsuits, or to challenge corporate personality. There have, however, been conflicting judgments from the Court of Appeal, as will be explored in Chapter 7(4).[50]

Another justification for limited liability, together with separate legal personality, is that it makes stock markets possible, where millions of shares are transferred every day (see Ch. 3(1)(d)). It is said that separate legal personality and limited liability serve an 'asset partitioning' or 'entity shielding' function.[51] If companies go insolvent, creditors cannot demand payment from shareholders: shareholder assets are 'partitioned', and other corporate entities' assets are 'shielded' from such claims. This is said to reduce the costs of monitoring companies: if you invested in a company, but knew that creditors could chase you for outstanding debts on insolvency, you would have to intensively monitor the company to ensure you were making a safe investment. You would probably want to invest in fewer companies, if any, because your monitoring costs would increase arithmetically with every new company in which you bought shares. This would deter you from having a very diversified share portfolio. And if, like you, fewer people diversified, this would concentrate systemic risk. Therefore, limited liability is good to reduce systemic risk.

The limits of this justification are that creditors also have monitoring costs and risks. Some creditors and shareholders (banks and asset managers) have greater capacity than others (consumers or pension beneficiaries) to perform monitoring. These justifications for limited liability (which are based in theory, as opposed to empirical evidence about actual monitoring costs) seem incapable of extending to any rule that protects those creditors with bargaining power over those without,[52] or any creditor that cannot bargain to adjust their security in response to the risk of insolvency that a contracting partner poses.[53]

(c) Delegated Agency

A third feature of major companies is that agents are delegated power to run the company. When filling out the form at Companies House, you have to say who will be the company's directors. In small companies, like Mr Salomon's,

[49] Employers' Liability (Compulsory Insurance) Act 1969, s. 1, referring to 'every employer'.

[50] I.e. *Chandler v Cape plc* [2012] EWCA Civ 525 and *Thompson v Renwick Group plc* [2014] EWCA Civ 635.

[51] H. Hansmann and R. Kraakman, 'The Essential Role of Organizational Law' (2000) 110(3) *Yale LJ* 387.

[52] Cf. H. Hansmann and R. Kraakman, 'Toward Unlimited Shareholder Liability for Corporate Torts' (1991) 100(7) *Yale LJ* 1879.

[53] L. A. Bebchuk and J. M. Fried, 'The Uneasy Case for the Priority of Secured Claims in Bankruptcy' (1996) 105 *Yale LJ* 857, 881–90, identifying tort victims, employees, consumers and, potentially, small businesses as non-adjusting creditors, whereas a bank would typify an adjusting creditor.

the same people who own shares are often the directors. There is no separation of ownership of shares and control on the board. But as companies grow, and there are more investors, a 'division of labour' usually emerges.[54] Ideally, investors will delegate to expert agents on the board to promote the company's success. Every company must have a board with at least one director (whether different from the members or not), while a public company (below) must have at least two directors.[55]

The efficiency of delegated agency has long been controversial. As we saw in Chapter 2(1) the great lawyer and economist, Adam Smith, argued that in any company, if some people are in charge of 'other people's money' then 'Negligence and profusion ... must always prevail.'[56] The liberal philosopher John Stuart Mill argued that, for the same reason, in any organisation where there are delegated agents, the justifications for laissez-faire or contractual freedom drop away, and the enterprise may be run more effectively in the public sector.[57] The communist philosopher, Karl Marx, also argued that in ever-larger corporations where 'the person of the manager is divorced from ownership of capital', just like 'labour is entirely divorced from ownership of means of production', this produces a new 'financial aristocracy, a new variety of parasites ... promoters, speculators and simply nominal directors; a whole system of swindling and cheating ... It is private production without the control of private property.'[58] Together, these views of Smith, Mill and Marx were echoed after the Wall Street Crash, when A. A. Berle and G. C. Means wrote that the unregulated 'separation of ownership and control' in large corporations was responsible for the descent into the Great Depression. In response, modern corporate law did not eliminate the corporation (as Smith favoured), or nationalise every one (as Mill and Marx preferred). But it has sought to ensure that in private enterprise, as Berle and Means advocated,[59] there is a charter of legal rights by which corporate directors can be held to account. If directors are managing other people's labour, money or other assets, they should as 'delegated agents' be accountable (see Ch. 3(2)–(4)).

(d) Transferable Shares

A fourth choice at Companies House will be whether a company (if it is limited by shares) is registered as 'private' or 'public'. The central difference is that only 'public' companies (plc) can offer their shares to the public for sale.[60] Shares in private companies (Ltd) are not easily transferable. Typically, existing

[54] A. Smith, *An Inquiry into the Nature and Causes of the Wealth of Nations* (1776) Book I, ch. 1.
[55] CA 2006, s. 154. [56] Smith, *Wealth of Nations*, Book V, ch. 1, §107.
[57] J. S. Mill, *Principles of Political Economy* (1848) Book V, ch. 11, §11.
[58] K. Marx, *Capital* (1883) vol. III, ch. 27.
[59] Berle and Means, *The Modern Corporation and Private Property* (2nd ed. 1991) Book II, ch. 1, 129–31.
[60] CA 2006, s. 755.

shareholders will have a 'pre-emption' right, to buy shares first from any shareholder who wants to sell theirs.[61] Private companies may not offer shares to the public, or make an offer that is 'calculated to result' in the shares 'becoming available to persons other than those receiving the offer'.[62] If initially registered as private, companies can always reregister as public, especially as they grow and seek more capital. The first occasion is called an 'initial public offering' (or IPO). The reverse can happen: a 'take-private' transaction, for instance, through a 'management buyout' (or MBO).[63] Companies may switch back and forth as corporate actors seek to reduce or augment their control.

Public companies must have a secretary, must attach 'plc' to their name, have at least two directors who are individually voted upon, and maintain a minimum capital fund of £50,000.[64] Perhaps the most important additional rules for public companies surround information: accounting[65] and auditing[66] before annual general meetings.[67] Largely inspired by the New Deal reforms of the 1930s in the USA,[68] the purpose of the law is to give full and material information to investors, to enable them to make the best choices possible about where they invest. If a company's business is stumbling or failing, accounting information will reveal this and enable investors to cut through marketing and promotion noise to accurately assess the company's fundamentals.

Most, but not all, UK public companies are 'listed' on the London Stock Exchange, or the Alternative Investment Market in the UK. Major companies may also be listed abroad. For instance, HSBC bank (second on the FTSE 100 in 2018) is also listed on the Euronext market in Amsterdam, the New York Stock Exchange, the Hong Kong Stock Exchange and the Bermuda Stock Exchange. Global corporations seek multiple listings to spread the volume of investment they receive, though there are few limits to foreign capital investing in the London Stock Exchange directly.[69] Further duties apply to listed (or 'quoted' and 'traded') companies. These include the duty to include business on the agenda at an annual general meeting that members request,[70] to publish

[61] See CA 2006, ss. 564–7.

[62] CA 2006, s. 756(3). If offerees are connected by family, employment, debenture-holding, or through a trust, the offer is presumed to be private.

[63] CA 2006, ss. 89–111, also setting out reregistration rules to and from unlimited company form.

[64] Respectively CA 2006, ss. 12(1)(c), 271–3, 58, 154, 160 and 761–3.

[65] CA 2006, ss. 437–8, laying accounts before AGM.

[66] CA 2006, ss. 489–91, where s. 490 also includes a power of the Secretary of State to appoint an auditor.

[67] CA 2006, ss. 336–40B

[68] Berle and Means, *The Modern Corporation and Private Property*, Book III led directly to the Securities Act of 1933 and the Securities and Exchange Act of 1934.

[69] The world's largest stock exchanges in 2018 were (1) NYSE, (2) NASDAQ, (3) Japan Exchange Group, (4) Shanghai Stock Exchange, (5) Euronext, (6) LSE, (7) HKSE, (8) Shenzhen Stock Exchange, (9) Deutsche Börse, (10) Bombay Stock Exchange.

[70] See CA 2006, ss. 336–40B.

the results of polls at meetings[71] and put accounts on a public website.[72] Another body of rules for listed companies is contained in the UK Corporate Governance Code (see Ch. 3(3)). Information enables shareholders both to make decisions about buying or transferring shares, and to engage in governance by voting.

(e) Ownership

A fifth essential feature of major companies is self-ownership. A company's stakeholders share in the benefits it produces. As a 'legal person' nobody owns a company, but investors, employees, consumers and creditors may all have legitimate claims upon its revenue or assets. By contrast it has been argued in an influential book, *The Anatomy of Corporate Law*, that large corporations are defined by 'investor ownership'.[73] This minority view has less support outside the USA, and it is descriptively wrong. Most investors own a beneficial title to shares, not the company. Shareholders with legal title likewise own shares, not the company. Ownership of shares usually brings with it governance and cash-flow rights, under the law and a company's constitution, similar to other stakeholders. But owning shares, and getting rights with them, is not owning the company. Shareholders do not own a company's assets either, even if assets were purchased with their investments. For example, in *Macaura v Northern Assurance Co. Ltd* a shareholder claimed that an insurance policy, which he took out in his name, covered timber that was owned by his company: Irish Canadian Sawmills Ltd, in County Tyrone, Northern Ireland. Mr Macaura owned all the shares, either directly or through nominees (to meet the then seven-person requirement). Sadly, the timber was destroyed in a fire. When Mr Macaura claimed to Northern Assurance for the cost of the timber, he was refused. The insurer said it had only contracted with him, not the company. The House of Lords agreed, because it was 'clear that the appellant had no insurable interest in the timber described. It was not his.'[74]

The governance and cash-flow rights that usually attach to shares can be (and often are) allocated among multiple stakeholders. First, governance rights are guaranteed for workers in a majority of Organisation for Economic Co-operation and Development (OECD) countries. The most common model is reserving a third of seats on the board of directors for worker representatives, although a legal system could also allocate a percentage of votes in the general meeting (see Ch. 5(3)(a)). Often consumers have voting rights in an enterprise's governance structure, although words more agreeable than 'consumer' are usually used to connote membership, rather than the passive receipt of services. Thus 'students', 'patients', 'passengers' or 'ratepayers', in universities,

[71] CA 2006, s. 341. [72] CA 2006, s. 430.
[73] Kraakman et al., *The Anatomy of Corporate Law* (3rd ed. 2017) 1.2.5 on 'Investor ownership'.
[74] [1925] AC 619, 630.

healthcare, water, energy or transport often have voice (see Chs. 8–9 and 12–15). This pattern is particularly evident where important social and economic rights are in play. Occasionally, major creditors also seek board representation, to safeguard their lending. It was argued in 1999 that we reached an 'End of History for Corporate Law', and that 'shareholder primacy' had beaten all other models of enterprise governance.[75] But the reality since has proved to be that many models of public participation in enterprise governance have thrived and spread.

Second, cash flows from company production are not only paid out to shareholders, through dividends or share buy-backs (see Ch. 4(2)). Workers receive wages. Directors receive their pay. Creditors receive interest, money, or pay in kind. Consumers receive goods and services, at prices that may be higher or lower. Governments receive tax. A company's cash-flow may also be reinvested, to research, innovate or expand production. Multiple stakeholders (not just shareholders) share the bundle of rights that make up a corporation.

UK statute is neutral about who becomes a company member, and who gets governance or cash-flow rights. But the reality is that shareholders do dominate corporate governance in the UK, USA and most other countries. Shareholders often monopolise the membership of companies, because as providers of capital they have more bargaining power than other stakeholders to get a voice. Shareholders, therefore, usually hold all of the votes for a company board. Together, they can change the constitution, call meetings, circulate proposals and potentially pass resolutions to pay money out or even finish and liquidate the company. This amounts to considerable power, which has driven a culture of pursuing 'shareholder value', often at the expense of sustainable enterprise, economic efficiency and social prosperity. Shareholder value and the rhetoric of shareholder ownership are cultural norms, not legal norms.[76] But they have been enabled by the law. This is expressed in the patterns of constitutions and rights in most UK companies, to which we now turn.

(2) Company Constitutions and Members' Rights

Like any nation state or organisation, companies have constitutions, also called 'articles of association'. These contain the company's rules, its procedures and the rights and duties of the actors. Historically, a corporation was conceptualised as a contract. Like a contract, the people who form a company agree to the terms of its content. Like a contract, it can only be changed by agreement among the parties (but a contract itself can have majority decisions).[77] And like a contract, its terms

[75] H. Hansmann and R. Kraakman, 'The End of History for Corporate Law' (1999) 89 *Georgetown LJ* 439.

[76] S. Deakin, 'The Coming Transformation of Shareholder Value' (2005) 13(1) *Corporate Governance: An Int'l Rev* 11.

[77] As we see below, company constitutions are typically amendable by a 75% majority, whereas a normal contract is only amendable, by default, by consensus. Nevertheless, all investors agree to this variation rule when they invest.

depend on recognition of the law and enforcement in court, either by members or whoever the law gives standing. The Companies Act 2006, section 33 contains this analogy, saying the 'provisions of a company's constitution bind the company and its members ... as if there were covenants' among all of them. This gives each member the right to enforce the constitution, in a claim for an injunction or damages, against any director who has failed to follow the constitution.[78] The three main mechanisms of accountability for directors are votes (see Ch. 3(2)–(3)), duties (Ch. 3(4)) and markets (Ch. 4). This section sets out (a) the concept of membership and the vote, (b) members' governance rights and (c) how constitutions are constructed.

(a) Membership and the Vote

Who is a member of a company? Section 112 says members are 'subscribers of a company's memorandum' at registration, and after that everyone else who agrees 'and whose name is entered in its register of members'. Members do not need to hold shares.[79] Shares are presumed to be transferable to other people, but like other rights including membership, the right to trade can be limited by the constitution.[80] If a company constitution allows it, workers, customers, creditors or anyone else could be registered as members.[81] There is, however, a statutory presumption that each member has one vote per share, unless the constitution says otherwise. Members can hire 'proxies' to vote for them.[82] The common law presumption is that members take part in 'the common right, which is in the whole assembly, where all are upon an equal foot'.[83] Notably, the Treaty on the Functioning of the European Union (TFEU) also understands companies as having 'members', not shareholders, by enabling company law measures 'for the protection of the interests of members and others'.[84]

The right to vote has long been seen as 'a most transcendent thing',[85] and no less in company law. But as voting in nineteenth-century politics depended on holding land, company law conceptions of voting rights used to be wedded to shareholding: property in land or money was assumed to be the main gateway to votes. In *Pender v Lushington*, Lord Jessel MR stressed that each member 'has a right to say, "Whether I vote in the majority or minority, you shall record my vote, as that is a right of property belonging to my interest in this company, and if you refuse to record my vote I will institute legal proceedings against you to compel you."'[86] This statement remains good law on the power of remedies

[78] See Ch. 3(4)(a); CA 2006, s. 171.
[79] CA 2006, ss. 112–13. Cf. CA 2006, s. 779, a warrant may entitle a holder to shares on delivery, or an allotment letter of allotment without already being on the member register.
[80] CA 2006, s. 544. [81] See further G. Morse (ed.), *Palmer's Company Law* (2016) 7.002, 7.004.
[82] CA 2006, ss. 284–5. [83] *Stoughton v Reynolds* (1735) 93 ER 1023, per Hardwicke CJ.
[84] TFEU, art. 50(2)(g). [85] *Ashby v White* (1703) 92 ER 126, per Holt CJ.
[86] *Pender v Lushington* (1877) 6 Ch D 70.

for breach of a member's personal rights (see Ch. 3(4)(e)). In that case, John Pender, a wealthy telecoms cable investor, wanted to evade the articles that capped the number of his voting rights. The Direct United States Cable Company Ltd's constitution said no member would be allowed to vote on more than 100 shares. Pender had 1,000, but appointed nominees (proxies) to cast votes in support of a resolution. He wanted the company to co-operate with a competitor where he also held shares, the Anglo-American Telegraph Co. The board's chair, Lushington, opposed the motion and refused to count the nominees' votes. The Court of Appeal held Lushington had to record Pender's votes: it was a right of 'property'. It is hard to see the same outcome being reached today, because the purpose was plainly to limit one person holding too much power. More broadly, although one's vote should be recorded (subject to the constitution's rules), it seems unnecessary to wed votes to property, rather than seeing it as an essential governance right, and 'transcendent' of legal form.

In UK law, the right to vote is not guaranteed to shareholders in the Companies Act 2006. But through regulatory pressure the norm became 'one share, one vote'.[87] In most countries this standard is written into legislation,[88] and it followed the disastrous experiences of the pre-Wall Street Crash era in the USA and the concentration of corporate power before and in Nazi Germany.[89] However, during the 1980s, after years of maintaining a 'one share, one vote' norm the US Securities and Exchange Commission (SEC) permitted stock exchanges to list shares with multiple votes. This was driven by competition between the NYSE and the new Amex and Nasdaq exchanges.[90] Many American companies, including Google, Facebook, Snap and Uber, have boldly issued vast swathes of multiple voting shares to their founders, and shares without any votes at all. Moreover, the IPO of the Chinese marketplace company, Alibaba, pressured the Hong Kong and Singapore stock exchanges to decrease their standards and enable voteless share listing, after Alibaba instead listed in the USA. A similar effort by the oil monopoly Saudi Aramco (now controlled by a 'Crown Prince' who oversees political executions[91]) led the London Stock Exchange to consider diluting its requirement for minority shareholders to have board seats if under 25 per cent of shares were listed.[92] All multiple and non-voting shares concentrate power in the hands of founders and directors, unaccountable no matter what.

87 E. McGaughey, *Participation in Corporate Governance* (2014) ch. 5(1).

88 ISS, Shearman & Sterling and ECGI, *Report on the Proportionality Principle in the European Union* (12 June 2007) 81.

89 McGaughey, *Participation in Corporate Governance*, ch. 5(2)–(3).

90 Securities and Exchange Act 1934, §19(c); 15 USC, §78s(c) on the power of the SEC to amend exchange rules.

91 UN Special Rapporteur, 'Investigation into the Unlawful Death of Mr. Jamal Khashoggi', HRC (19 June 2019).

92 D. Afanasieva and M. Price, 'London Tries to Lure Saudi Aramco', *Reuters* (3 May 2017).

(b) Members' Governance Rights

What can members do with the right to vote? The most important uses of voting rights are appointment or removal of the board, and altering the constitution (below). Short of that, sections 303–5 enable members who have 'at least 5% of such of the paid-up capital of the company as carries the right of voting' to require directors to call a general meeting within twenty-one days. After the call, the meeting should be held within twenty-eight days, at the company's expense.[93] Members in public companies 'representing at least 5% of the total voting rights', but also any 100 members with at least £100 in share capital each, can require an item is placed on the agenda before an annual general meeting if they do so six weeks in advance,[94] and can also circulate a statement at the meeting making any proposal they like.[95] In private companies, members have a right to circulate written resolutions.[96] This does not mean that shareholders can generally instruct the board to do anything with a majority vote: usually a 75 per cent vote is required (a 'special resolution', below) to do that. To count votes at a meeting, a show of hands is usually taken, but a poll recording actual shares can usually be demanded by a director, two or more members or a 10 per cent vote-holder.[97]

Members have extra control over three main types of transaction. First, any director's contract over two years requires member approval.[98] Second, substantial property transactions, over 10 per cent of the company's value or £100,000, must be approved.[99] Third, and most important for the health of democracy, members must approve any 'political donations' or 'expenditure' over £5,000 in the space of twelve months, by a majority resolution that can last up to four years.[100] These rules have the effect of making political expenditure by companies much less likely, because it is unlikely that members have unified political beliefs, and therefore wish corporate money to fund a particular party or cause. The definition in section 365 of 'expenditure' covers publicity material or 'activities' intended to affect public support or influence voters. This is a wide definition, and though not explicit it probably requires that companies do not spend money on lobbyists without authorisation. Lobbyists talking to MPs to get favours for a corporation will inevitably 'affect public support for [that] political party', and will usually involve 'publicity material' whether fliers, papers or slides. The control of political expenditure is all the more important because of the conflicts of interest among directors and investors, and diverse political views of investors.

[93] CA 2006, ss. 303–5. The Companies (Shareholders' Rights) Regulations 2009/1632 Pt 2, reg. 4 reduced the threshold to 5% from 10%.

[94] CA 2006, s. 338. [95] CA 2006, s. 314. [96] CA 2006, ss. 288–300.

[97] Companies (Model Articles) Regulations (CMAR) 2008, Sch. 3, para. 34.

[98] CA 2006, ss. 188–9. [99] CA 2006, ss. 190–6. [100] CA 2006, ss. 362–79.

(c) Constitutional Models and Construction

In principle, a company can put any rules it wants in its constitution, so long as it complies with the compulsory rules of the Companies Act 2006 or other legislation. In practice, most companies adopt the 'Model Articles' (short for 'articles of association'), a template of rules for private companies limited by shares, companies limited by guarantee and public companies.[101] These are deemed to apply if incorporators do not write and submit their own constitution.[102] There is a mild incentive to adopt the Model Articles, and to not write one's own, because Companies House charges £40, instead of £12, to submit one's own rules. Large companies on the FTSE 100 invariably hire solicitors to write their own constitutions, occasionally instilled with some public-relations eloquence. But the meaningful differences are small because central aspects of governance are covered by statute. The Model Articles contain five main parts on (1) definitions; (2) directors' rights and duties; (3) member decision-making; (4) share payments and dividends; and (5) communications, administration and directors' indemnity and insurance. All of these rules have to be interpreted and construed by a court.

Probably the most important feature that a company's articles may change is the balance of power between the board and the members. In the Model Articles for Public Companies, paragraph 3 says that a company's 'directors are responsible for the management of the company's business' and so 'may exercise all the powers of the company'. Under paragraph 4, members have a 'reserve power' to instruct directors by a 75 per cent vote, a 'special resolution'.[103] These rules are only a default, and may be changed. But since 1947, the law has required that directors are removable by a simple majority vote, an 'ordinary resolution'. This is now in the Companies Act 2006, section 168, and cannot be changed. It was seen historically as a fundamental mechanism for democratic accountability within companies.[104] Because of its strength it has been called a 'statutory shotgun'.[105] This is the basic balance of power: ultimately members can control the board. Whether they do is another issue (see Ch. 4).

Once the constitution is set, it cannot be circumvented. So, for example, in *Automatic Self-Cleansing Filter Syndicate Co. Ltd v Cuninghame*, a shareholder called Mr McDiarmid claimed that the directors of this liquid purification company should sell off assets because a majority resolution supported this.[106] McDiarmid had 1,202 of the company's 2,700 shares. He got support to pass a resolution to make the company sell assets, but only with 1,502 shares

[101] CMAR 2008, Sch. 3. [102] CA 2006, s. 20. [103] CA 2006, s. 283.

[104] Sir Stafford Cripps, Hansard HC Debs. (6 June 1947) vol. 438, cols. 585–8. This has clear echoes of Berle and Means, *The Modern Corporation and Private Property* (rev. ed. 1933) Book II, ch. 1, 139–41.

[105] M. Moore, *Corporate Governance in the Shadow of the State* (2013) 210ff., on the 'statutory shotgun'.

[106] *Automatic Self-Cleansing Filter Syndicate Co. Ltd v Cuninghame* [1906] 2 Ch 34.

(55.6 per cent). The board of directors, led by Cuninghame, was opposed. At that time, before 1947, directors could only be removed by a 75 per cent majority. But like paragraph 4 today, directors had the general power of management only subject to a 75 per cent majority vote.[107] The Court of Appeal held that the majority resolution did not bind the directors, because that would undermine the requirement for a three-quarters vote in the constitution. As Cozens-Hardy LJ said, this must be the case, because members like McDiarmid had 'by their express contract mutually stipulated that their common affairs should be managed' under the constitution's rules.

How do you construe what a constitution really does or should mean? In *Attorney General of Belize v Belize Telecom Ltd*, the Privy Council took the view that the exercise follows the same principles, whether 'a contract, a statute or articles of association'. Here, the Attorney General of Belize, in the small Central American state, claimed the government should be able to remove two directors from Belize Telecom Ltd, even though it did not clearly have such a right under the constitution. Belize Telecom had been privatised by an eager ex-government, run by the conservative People's United Party, in 2004. To hurry through the sale, the government gave a loan to the buyers, Belize Telecom Ltd, which was secured upon the shares it was selling. This meant, if the loan went unpaid, the government could repossess those shares. There were three classes: class 'C' shares, which the government was selling; class 'B' shares, held by private investors; and a 'special share'. Together, class C shareholders could appoint four directors; B shareholders, two; and the 'special' shareholder, two. But if the same person owned the special share and over 37.5 per cent of the C shares, that person could appoint two out of the C shareholders' four directors. Belize Telecom Ltd bought the C shares and the special share with the government loan.

Sadly, Belize Telecom Ltd's venture was not a financial success, and it defaulted on repaying the government loan. This caused the government to repossess the C shares. But they soon realised that nobody had remembered to write anything about repossessing the special share into the loan document. This meant two directors, who had been appointed by the 'C' and the special shareholder, now were apparently subject to nobody's votes, because nobody held the 'C' and special share at the same time. The constitution, in article 90(E), said those directors would hold office 'subject only to article 112', and article 112 said directors would have to vacate 'only' if they became conflicted, bankrupt or a lunatic. The Attorney General submitted that it was absurd that they could not be removed, and the Privy Council agreed. In Lord Hoffmann's view, a term had to be implied to reflect the 'reasonable expectations of the parties'.[108] This 'would plainly be necessary' to ensure the 'overriding purpose'

[107] Under the old Table A, the predecessor to the Model Articles, art. 96 read 'subject to such regulations as might from time to time be made by extraordinary resolution'.

[108] [2009] UKPC 11, [23].

that the board continued 'reflecting the appropriate shareholder interests'.[109] Although a literal reading of the constitution said otherwise, Lord Hoffmann said those provisions 'cannot in the Board's opinion be construed as contradicting the proposed implied term, to which the draftsman plainly did not address his mind'. In effect, the Privy Council scrapped the conflicting terms ('only'), with the implied term overriding the express terms, to uphold the reasonable expectation of good governance.

Cases like *Belize*, though rare, are an important reminder of the need to construe all legal documents according to the background of social expectations, not by mechanistic adherence to syntax divorced from design or purpose.[110] Part of the problem, however, is that UK company law (and jurisdictions like Belize's) do make it hard for companies to alter their constitutions. Under section 21, a three-quarters majority of votes (a 'special' resolution) is needed. A constitution may also choose a higher (but not lower) threshold.[111] If some shares have been given special or class rights (unlike in the Model Articles), then those rights can only be changed when those shareholders agree by a three-quarters majority, or by another procedure (if any) in the constitution.[112]

(3) Board Removal, Appointment and Pay

The simplest way to reduce the 'agency costs' of directors, where they (as agents) may act against the interests of a company (as a principal), is the use of votes over their position and pay. This can be seen in rules on (a) removal, (b) appointment and (c) setting of pay.

(a) Removal

Real power in corporate governance comes with removing the board. Before 1947, most companies gravitated towards the maximum level of entrenchment for directors. In practice, this was 75 per cent of voting rights, because that was the statutory threshold in the Companies Acts by which members could change the constitution. Earlier common law was very different. Smaller companies were more democratic, enabling removal of directors through a simple majority vote.[113] Larger companies were oligarchical, entrenching

[109] [2009] UKPC 11, [30]–[32].

[110] The idea that express terms always override implied terms is going out of fashion, unless a contract is negotiated between parties of equal bargaining power: *Marks and Spencer plc v BNP Paribas Ltd* [2015] UKSC 72. For companies, construction should uphold principles of good enterprise governance.

[111] CA 2006, ss. 21–7. [112] CA 2006, s. 630.

[113] *Attorney General v Davy* (1741) 26 ER 531, Lord Hardwicke LC: 'wherever a certain number are incorporated, a major part of them may do any corporate act'. *R v Richardson* (1758) 1 Burr 517, 539, Lord Mansfield: 'where the offence is merely against his duty as a corporator, he can only be tried for it by the corporation'.

boards and usually disenfranchising small investors altogether.[114] The experience of the Wall Street Crash led company lawyers to argue that removal by simple majority was essential.[115] To reverse the trend where 'the relationship between management and ownership' had 'tended progressively to be more and more shadowy',[116] the Companies Act 1947 required that every company general meeting have the right to remove directors with a simple majority.[117] The Companies Act 2006, section 168 contains this rule. Directors have the right to twenty-eight days' notice, and to circulate a statement in their own support. But subject to this right to a fair hearing, they cannot challenge a decision to remove them. They are ejected from office.

Directors can, however, claim that they have been dismissed in breach of contract. In *Southern Foundries (1926) Ltd v Shirlaw*, a director named Shirlaw claimed he should have an injunction against being removed from the board.[118] He had a ten-year contract to be the managing director, until a new shareholder took over the iron-casting company and changed the constitution to enable any director to be removed. The House of Lords held that Shirlaw could claim damages for being removed before his contract had expired, but was not entitled to an injunction to remain in office. There was no implied term that the company should not alter its articles, nor would it be right to prevent a company's members exercising their inherent governance rights. But this did not mean that using those rights could not be a breach of contract. Obviously, this decision meant that it could be costly to remove directors: for this reason, long-term service contracts are limited today (see Ch. 3(3)(c)).

For smaller companies, it has been debated whether section 168 is in fact a compulsory rule. It is clear that the core problem driving reform was unaccountable directors in large companies, where investors were separated and management was prone to 'negligence and profusion'. It is less clear that the same rationale should apply to companies that are small quasi-partnerships. In *Bushell v Faith*, two sisters and a brother were the three equal shareholders, and three directors of their company.[119] After falling out, the brother claimed that the two sisters were not able to remove him from the board, because an article stated that, should a director be facing removal, this director's votes would be tripled. The House of Lords, by a majority, held that

[114] E.g. Bank of England Act 1694 (5 & 6 Will. & Mar., c. 20). £500 of stock bought one vote. S. Williston, 'History of the Law of Business Corporations before 1800. II. (Concluded)' (1898) 2(4) *Harvard L Rev* 149, 156 (vote limits were put in place in the East India Company, and the usual voting practice was a show of hands).

[115] Berle and Means, *The Modern Corporation and Private Property* (rev. ed. 1933) Book II, ch. 1, 139–41.

[116] Companies Bill, Second Reading, Hansard HC Debs. (6 June 1947) vol. 438, col. 585, Sir Stafford Cripps.

[117] Companies Act 1947, s. 29; re-enacted by Companies Act 1948, s. 184; then Companies Act 1985, s. 303; now CA 2006, s. 168.

[118] [1940] AC 701. [119] [1970] AC 1099.

the vote-tripling article was valid, even though it appeared to plainly undermine the majority removal right. According to Lord Morris of Borth-y-Gest, who dissented, 'to sanction this would be to make a mockery of the law'. Lord Donovan's reasoning, however, stressed its potential legitimacy in 'small companies ... particularly family companies running a family business'. It seems doubtful that attempts to undermine section 168 in any other context, and in any larger company, would work.

(b) Appointment

If members can remove directors, how are directors appointed? The answer is that directors usually appoint themselves. This unsatisfactory state of affairs reflects what is still a closed and cosy culture among boards and asset managers in the City of London. As late as 2003, the Higgs Report on corporate governance found that nearly half of non-executive directors were hired 'through personal contacts', just 4 per cent did an interview, and 99 per cent of posts were not even advertised.[120] There is nothing in the Companies Act 2006 about rules for appointment. The Model Articles in paragraph 20 state that anyone can be appointed as a director 'by ordinary resolution' or 'by a decision of the directors'.[121] So, members with at least 5 per cent of votes could (if organised) propose any nominee, and attempt to garner support at a general meeting. For instance, pension funds, trade unions and investors could field candidates that will demand long-term investment strategies, fair wage scales within the firm or decarbonisation. Tremendous battles have been fought to simply get such a right in the USA.[122] These rights are well established in UK law, but shareholders have not been active. This is mainly because shareholders are mostly asset managers holding 'other people's money', and are themselves separated from accountability to the real investors: Ch. 4(1).

The standard appointments procedure is seen in the UK Corporate Governance Code. This is written by the Financial Reporting Council (FRC), a quasi-autonomous non-government organisation, which is delegated power to regulate listed companies under the Financial Services and Markets Act 2000.[123] After a series of scandals in the early 1990s, the FRC began drafting codes, with which listed companies must 'comply or explain'. If investors think the explanations for not following the Code's rules are inadequate, they may sell their shares, so putting pressure on companies to comply. First, the Code suggests companies split the roles of executive directors who carry out day-to-day

[120] Higgs Committee, *Review of the Role and Effectiveness of Non-executive Directors* (2003) 10.5, 'Almost half of the non-executive directors surveyed for the Review were recruited to their role through personal contacts or friendships. Only four per cent had had a formal interview, and one per cent had obtained their job through answering an advertisement.'

[121] CMAR 2008, Sch. 3, para. 20.

[122] E.g. *Business Roundtable v Securities and Exchange Commission*, 647 F.3d 1144 (DC Cir 2011); SEC Rule 14a-11.

[123] Financial Services and Markets Act 2000, s. 1B(6)(a); FCA Handbook, Listing Rule 9.8.6(6).

functions, and non-executive directors who are meant to supervise the executives. These non-executives are meant to be 'independent'. The Code's criteria for 'independence' include not having worked for the company for over five years and not being a significant shareholder.[124] Second, a company should split the role of the chief executive who manages day-to-day affairs, from the chair who focuses on long-term strategy. Third, a company board is expected to have an appointment committee, with a majority of 'independent' members.

It is doubtful that these 'independence' criteria for 'independent' directors on the appointments committee achieve any real goal. The fact remains that independent directors (as defined by the Code) work with the other board members. They will be friendly and partial to one another's preferences. They hire one another. Presumably the goal should be, not to make directors 'independent' from scrutiny by anyone, but to make them dependent on the preferences of the people who invest their capital, labour or custom into the company. The Code suggests there should be 'annual re-election'. In practice any vote from the general meeting is a rubber-stamping exercise. The vast majority of votes are controlled by a tiny handful of asset managers who want no surprises. The only exception is that since January 2019, listed companies have had to comply with or explain non-compliance with a rule that they should have a mechanism of employee involvement that could include 'a director appointed from the workforce'.[125] It appears few companies took this option up in a meaningful way (see Ch. 5).

(c) Pay

Like their appointments, director pay is almost entirely determined by directors themselves. The Model Articles, paragraph 23, in an almost self-ridiculing turn of phrase states: 'Directors are entitled to such remuneration as the directors determine.'[126] It is difficult to think of a more conflicted sentence in the law of the UK. The law was not always this way: before 1985, the predecessor to the Model Articles, known as Table A, stated that director pay would be either set by a company's articles, or by a vote among shareholders. As a default rule, directors could replace this. Increasingly they did. By 2006, a reluctant draftsperson appears to have simply decided to reflect the standard practice of directors paying and enriching themselves. Whatever the justifications proffered by a dwindling minority for this, executive pay has inflated out of all proportion. As Figure 3.1 shows, and against the background of rising income inequality, chief executive pay relative to employees has soared.

[124] UK Corporate Governance Code (July 2018) §10; also a 'material business relationship' in the last 3 years, receiving extra pay, bonus or pensions, family ties with senior company staff, holding cross-directorships, being a significant shareholder or being on the board for over 9 years.

[125] UK Corporate Governance Code (July 2018) §5.

[126] CMAR 2008, Sch. 3, para. 20.

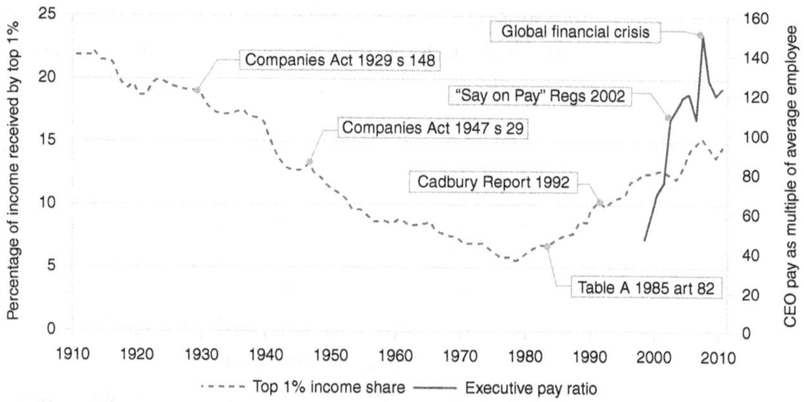

Figure 3.1 UK inequality and executive pay ratios, 1910–2010
Sources: T. Piketty, *Capital in the Twenty-First Century* (2014) and Manifest and MM&K, 'Total Remuneration Survey' (2011)

The fact that directors pay themselves is supposed to be tempered by the UK Corporate Governance Code's requirement for a 'remuneration committee'.[127] Like with appointments, a supposedly 'independent' majority of directors should sit on this committee, independence again defined in terms of not working with the company too long, and other factors. This nominal independence can hardly conceal that directors will look favourably upon their colleagues. They progressively ratchet up each other's pay, especially when directors of other enterprises do too, in what seems to be a competition of ever-inflating egos.

Public opinion consistently opposes escalating inequality and executive pay,[128] and does so even though people vastly underestimate the scale of inequality.[129] Yet legislative reform has been cosmetic. In 2004, a 'say on pay' was introduced, so that members acquired the right to cast a non-binding resolution on a director's pay package. This did not affect the soaring pay of most executives. At any time, shareholders could pass a binding 75 per cent resolution, or could simply vote to sack the board (s. 168). But shareholder voting rights are controlled by asset managers who are also highly

[127] UK Corporate Governance Code (July 2018) §§32–41.

[128] E.g. British Social Attitudes (BSA) 30, 'Government Spending and Welfare' (2013) 40, Figure 2.2, showing in 2012, over 80% thought income inequality was too high and 40% thought government should redistribute more income. Cf. BSA 36 (2019) 152. *Americans and CEO Pay: 2016 Public Perception Survey on CEO Compensation* (2016). Also S. Svallfors, 'Dimensions of Inequality: A Comparison of Attitudes in Sweden and Britain' (1993) 9(3) *Eur Sociological Rev* 267.

[129] E.g. M. I. Norton and D. Ariely, 'Building a Better America – One Wealth Quintile at a Time' (2011) 6 *Perspectives on Psychological Science* 9, 11, finding that among 5,522 people it was thought, ideally, the top 20% should own 32% of total wealth, was estimated to own 58%, and in fact they owned 84%.

Table 3.3 Worst 10 UK companies for excessive pay

	Company	Chief executive	Pay	Ratio	Enterprise
1	Persimmon	Jeff Fairburn	47087000	1,130:1	Construction
2	Melrose Industries	Simon Peckham	42764000	1,134:1	Management
3	Berkeley Group	Rob Perrins	27963000	273:1	Construction
5	Sky	Jeremy Darroch	16343000	312:1	Media
6	WPP	Martin Sorrell	13930000	295:1	Advertising
7	Coca-Cola HBC AG	Zoran Bogdanovic	13783000	563:1	Food
8	Reckitt Benckiser	Rakesh Kapoor	12480000	362:1	Consumer goods
9	Intertek	Andre Lacroix	11683000	458:1	Consumer goods
10	British American Tobacco	Nicandro Durante	11423000	424:1	Food
11	BP	Bob Dudley	10486000	106:1	Oil and gas

paid.[130] In 2012, a new amendment was passed so that shareholders have a binding say on directors' pay policies, but not the actual amount.[131] The results have again been irrelevant. Consultants are still hired to make ever more elaborate calculations on bonuses, 'long-term incentive plans' and extensive hypothetical discussion of linking pay to 'performance'. The top ten most highly paid chief executives in UK companies, who happen to all be men, are as set out in Table 3.3.[132]

As Table 3.3 shows, the top ten CEO pay is astronomically higher than that of the average earner: number ten, BP plc's Bob Dudley, earning £10.4 million, is 106 times the average BP plc worker. The fact that Persimmon plc's Jeff Fairburn earned 1,130 times the salary of his workers, yet was paid four times as much, is explained by the low pay in the construction industry.[133] Most CEOs work hard and deserve some reward. But such disproportionate rewards result from legal power, not worth: the scales today have no moral basis, or economic function. They are the product of irrational, systemic greed.

(4) Directors' Duties and Litigation

Second to voting rights, legal duties are essential to ensure directors promote the company's success before their own. Directors' duties, however, are limited

[130] E.g. R. Gribben, 'Investors Champion Boardroom Pay Rises', *The Daily Telegraph* (19 July 1999) 27 (asset managers surveyed in 1999 'indicated that they supported bigger salary increases for UK executives'). Referred to in B. Cheffins, 'The Metamorphosis of "Germany Inc.": The Case of Executive Pay' (2001) 49(3) *Am J Comp L* 497, 510.

[131] CA 2006, ss. 420–2A and 439A.

[132] D. Hellier, S. Ring and A. Morales, 'British CEOs Will Earn as Much as a Typical Worker Makes in a Year by Lunchtime', *Bloomberg* (4 January 2019).

[133] For original research, see High Pay Centre, *Executive Pay: Review of FTSE 100 Executive Pay* (August 2018) and, for the next year's update, *Executive Pay in the FTSE 100: Is Everyone Getting a Fair Slice of the Cake?* (August 2019).

in practical effect. Voting rights can impel directors to actively, consciously, even passionately pursue the interests of the people who vote them in or out. If you owe your job to someone, you will usually try to please them. The same might also be said about the need to respond to market demand. Legal duties can hardly do more than instil minimum standards of good conduct, and sanction egregious conduct. Duties cannot create the sort of 'positive motivational environment' that voting, and perhaps the operation of markets, will.[134] This said, directors' duties have always been essential to reflect principles of integrity, competence and honesty in the economy. The central duties are to follow the constitution,[135] use reasonable care[136] and avoid any possibility of a conflict of interest.[137]

Who counts as a director? Obviously, those who are appointed to the board count as *de jure* directors, regardless of their title (e.g. the CEO, chair, etc.).[138] The Companies Act 2006, section 251 also recognises 'shadow' directors. If the real directors are in the habit of acting in accordance with someone else's instructions, that person is deemed a 'shadow director'. Professional advisers are excepted, so 'shadow directors' will often be parent companies, banks or other major shareholders or creditors that interfere in the company's affairs. This reflects a basic principle that responsibility must follow power, whatever its form.

To whom do directors owe duties? Under the Companies Act 2006, section 170(1), directors owe their duties to the 'company'. Of course, the 'company' is only a legal, not a real, person, and so this means that real people must ultimately be capable of bringing claims on its behalf. Every true duty has a correlative right, and every true right entails a duty.[139] If a 'duty' gives nobody a right to enforce it, it is not worth the paper it is written on: it becomes more political distraction than law.[140] Under company constitutions, directors hold the power of day-to-day management, including the power to litigate.[141] Occasionally, a board of directors may decide to bring legal action against one of their own number. They may wish to distance themselves from that

[134] Cf. J. E. Parkinson, *Corporate Power and Responsibility* (1993) 134, directors' duties 'cannot, unlike the market and market-linked devices, create a more positive motivational environment'. The operation of markets, discussed in Chs. 4–7, may be more like voting, but markets are subject to constraints on bargaining power.

[135] CA 2006, s. 171. An early analogy in trust law is *Page v Lane* (1754) Amb 233.

[136] CA 2006, s. 174. *Charitable Corporation v Sutton* (1742) 26 ER 642 remains a leading case on the standard of care.

[137] CA 2006, ss. 175 and 177. This traces back to the post-South Sea case *Keech v Sandford* (1726) 25 ER 223.

[138] CA 2006, s. 250.

[139] W. Hohfeld, 'Some Fundamental Legal Conceptions as Applied in Judicial Reasoning' (1913) 23 *Yale LJ* 16.

[140] E.g. Proclamation of Queen Victoria (1858). The British Empire had an 'earnest desire to stimulate the peaceful industry of India, to promote works of public utility and improvement, and to administer the government for the benefit of all our subjects resident therein'. See S. Tharoor, *Inglorious Empire: What the British Did to India* (2018) ch. 2.

[141] E.g. CMAR 2008, Sch. 3, art. 3.

director if the culprit has already departed, or if a new board is in place. But most of the time, directors are not going to sue one another, even on a bad day, and even if a wrong has been done, because they are colleagues and friends.

So, because directors are unlikely to sue each other, the law gives company members (and some non-members) standing to litigate. First, there is a 'derivative claim'. The claim to sue 'derives' from the company, and standing depends on case law. Second, members can sue through a statutory unfair prejudice petition, though this is mostly used in small companies. Third, if a company has gone insolvent, the administrator or liquidator takes charge of the board and may sue, but in practice insolvency practitioners are reluctant (see Ch. 7(3)). Whoever brings the case, the duties that directors owe are codified in the Companies Act 2006, sections 171–7. These are meant to both reflect, and develop with, principles of common law and equity.[142] This means any developments in the law of trustees' duties, fiduciary duties, or the duty of care determine company law.[143] The next sections set out four principal duties and then the central procedures to vindicate them in litigation.

(a) Following the Constitution: Section 171

The first duty of a director, under section 171, is to (a) 'act in accordance with the company's constitution' and (b) 'only exercise powers for the purposes for which they are conferred'. This deceptively simple passage mirrors the idea of following 'express' provisions of a company's constitution, and what the court may say is 'implied' according to its view of a constitution's purpose. As we saw at Chapter 3(2)(c), and the *Belize Telecom* case, courts have moved towards construing constitutions consistently with statutory norms, and generally accepted standards of good governance. Ideally, the meaning of a constitution, and what counts as a 'proper' purpose, should be consistent with a coherent vision of successful enterprise from Companies Act policy.[144] The difficulty lies in deciding what that should be.

Cases on acting outside the express terms of the constitution (s. 171(a)) are straightforward. In *Guinness plc v Saunders*, the directors of Guinness plc unusually turned upon one of their former colleagues, and sued for paying himself too much.[145] A committee of the board, composed of three directors named Saunders, Roux and Ward, decided that for completing a takeover of a Scottish whisky company (Distillers) Ward would be paid £5.2 million. The trouble was, the company's article 91 vested the power to pay 'remuneration of

[142] CA 2006, s. 170(4).

[143] E.g. *AIB Group (UK) plc v Mark Redler & Co. Solicitors* [2014] UKSC 58, [51] per Lord Toulson, highlighting duties of custody, management and loyalty (correlating to CA 2006, ss. 171, 174 and 175).

[144] E.g. *Attorney General of Belize* [2009] UKPC 10, [32]: 'to ensure that the board reflects the appropriate shareholder interests'.

[145] [1990] 2 AC 663.

directors' or 'special remuneration' in the board, not a committee. Although article 2 enabled the board to appoint a committee to 'act on its behalf', this was held not to override the specific rule in article 91. The House of Lords held article 91 'authorises the board, and only the board, to grant special remuneration to a director who serves on a committee'. Ward had to give the £5.2 million back. It was not paid out in accordance with the company constitution.[146]

Cases on acting for an improper purpose (s. 171(b)) are varied. They concern directors acting within the letter, but not the spirit, of their powers. They depend upon a judicial understanding of what the purpose of directors' power actually is. If it is clear that directors have certain powers under the constitution (for instance, to make contracts, sell property, litigate and so on) it does not always follow that they may use these for any reason. The use may conflict with important principles of governance, such as directors' accountability to the general meeting, procedural integrity, or not furthering one's own interests with no benefit and considerable cost to everyone else.[147] In one of many cases arising after former *Daily Mirror* owner, Robert Maxwell, fell off a yacht and died, the son Ian Maxwell was held to have been unauthorised to transfer shares from an investment company to the Maxwell Group plc for nothing.[148] These shares were meant to have funded the newspaper employees' pension scheme. After Robert died it was revealed that the pensions had been raided to bail out the business and the owners' lavish lifestyle. Hoffmann LJ held that the cause of action against Ian was simply 'the improper transfer of the shares'. Because 'he gave away the company's assets for no consideration to a private family company of which he was a director', Maxwell used 'his powers as a director for an improper purpose'. He had the burden 'to demonstrate the propriety of the transaction'. He could not. This reasoning appears similar to a proportionality test: one should ask if there is a legitimate aim, and then if the director's conduct was appropriate, necessary and reasonable.

Leading improper-purpose cases often involve directors trying to frustrate takeovers. When companies are taken over, existing directors are often made redundant because bidders want to change the company's direction and management to make more profit. But directors do not want to be dismissed, so they often do not want takeovers.[149] In *Howard Smith Ltd v Ampol Petroleum Ltd* the Privy Council advised that the directors of R. W. Miller

[146] Saunders, the chair, was then convicted for conspiracy, false accounting and theft, though he won a challenge under the ECHR, art. 6 on incriminating evidence being used against him: *Saunders v United Kingdom* (1996) 23 EHRR 313.

[147] Analogous principles in constitutional law include parliamentary sovereignty (e.g. *R (Miller) v Prime Minister* [2019] UKSC 41) and the rule of law (e.g. *R (Unison) v Lord Chancellor* [2017] UKSC 51).

[148] *Bishopsgate Investment Management Ltd (in liq.) v Maxwell (No. 2)* [1993] BCLC 814.

[149] See also *Hogg v Cramphorn Ltd* [1967] Ch 254. Colonel Cramphorn acted improperly by issuing shares with ten votes each to the employee pension fund, controlled by the board, to block a takeover bid from a Mr Baxter.

(Holdings) Ltd improperly issued $10 million in new shares to a friendly company, Howard Smith Ltd. The directors said they had done this to finance the purchase of two new tankers for the business, but it was done when Ampol Ltd, a rival petrol firm, was bidding to take over R. W. Miller Ltd. Lord Wilberforce advised that the power was exercised for an improper purpose, to block the takeover bid. 'To define in advance exact limits beyond which directors must not pass' was, he said, 'impossible'. But it had to be done 'in light of modern conditions'.[150] It could not be used 'purely for the purpose of destroying an existing majority' among shareholders 'or creating a new majority which did not previously exist'.[151] That was, evidently, the ulterior purpose here: it did not need to be the dominant one. Any issue of a 'poison pill' (the colloquial name for rights attached to securities that would frustrate a takeover bidder's control) will probably be improper (see further, Ch. 4(3)).[152]

Another example is *Eclairs Group Ltd v JKX Oil & Gas plc*, where Eclairs Group Ltd aimed to take over JKX plc, an oil and gas firm with most assets in Ukraine and Russia. Eclairs Ltd claimed that their voting rights as shareholders were unlawfully suspended by the directors, before a meeting where it was asking other shareholders to vote against re-electing the board. The directors' pretext was that under article 42 of the constitution, it could suspend voting rights if a shareholder was issued with a statutory notice to disclose agreements among shareholders about co-ordinating use of their rights.[153] The trouble was, the Companies Act 2006 does not enable rights to be suspended without a court order. The disclosure notice was promptly complied with, but the directors suspected there was more to it, and suspended voting rights anyway. The Supreme Court held this was unlawful, and done for an improper purpose of affecting the vote, rather than securing disclosure.[154]

(b) The Company's Success: Sections 172 and 173

The second duty of a director, in section 172, is to 'act in the way [she or] he considers, in good faith, would be most likely to promote the success of the company for the benefit of its members as a whole, and in doing so have regard' to a list of matters. These include 'long term' consequences, the interests of employees, relations with suppliers and customers, 'the community and the environment', maintaining 'high standards of business conduct' and acting fairly between members. The only stakeholders not mentioned at all are the directors themselves. Section 172's general norm is overridden by the company constitution, and all rules requiring action in creditors' interests (see Ch. 7). This duty provoked the most debate in Parliament, sadly becoming an

[150] [1974] AC 832, 835. [151] [1974] AC 832, 837.

[152] See also *Criterion Properties plc v Stratford UK Properties LLC* [2004] UKHL 28. NB: The UK Takeover Code, rule 21 voids any measure, without shareholder approval, with the effect of frustrating a takeover bid. This is reflected in the Takeover Directive 2004/25/EC, art. 9(2).

[153] CA 2006, ss. 793 and 820–5. [154] [2015] UKSC 71.

unhelpfully abstract discussion about the purposes of the company, removed from the realities of practical legal and economic power.

Section 172 is often said to have followed a model of 'enlightened shareholder value',[155] in contrast to a 'shareholder primacy' or a fully stakeholder-oriented model. This is wrong for two clear reasons. First, the word 'shareholder' is not in section 172.[156] This essential fact is often ignored. UK law uses the term 'member'. Although shareholders are usually the members, anyone can be on the members' register. Many companies (e.g. those limited by guarantee) do not have shareholders at all. Thus, the idea that UK company law promotes 'shareholder value', enlightened or otherwise, is wrong, even as a descriptive legal matter. 'Shareholder value', where it exists, is a cultural norm, not a legal norm.[157]

Second, the case law refutes directly any enlightened shareholder primacy in UK law. The 'Enlightened Shareholder Value' view argues (without any credible support) that directors should pay regard to stakeholders, other than shareholders, if such an 'enlightened' approach is consistent with maximising shareholder value, but if there is a conflict shareholders come first. Yet in *Shepherd v Williamson* a company director, Mr Shepherd, was alleged to have breached section 172 by telling a client that his own company was being investigated by the competition authority, then the Office of Fair Trading, for being in a cartel (see Ch. 6(2)). After this the company went into insolvent administration (see Ch. 7(2)). Insolvency is not good for shareholders. Tipping off clients about a cartel investigation is not good for business. However, under section 172 abiding by competition law (and in this case, a director distancing himself from illegal conduct) was consistent with considering the impact on 'the community' and maintaining 'high standards of business conduct'. Proudman J held there was no breach of section 172, as Mr Shepherd had acted in good faith and 'was balancing the deleterious consequences . . . against the Company's reputation as a whole . . . in the light of the OFT investigation'. Thus, in law, a director is entitled to subordinate shareholder profit to the interests of the community, or any other stakeholder, at any time. These legal facts, however, do nothing to change the powerful critiques of the culture of so-called 'shareholder value'.

So, if directors can place the interests of any stakeholder above any other, including shareholders, what does section 172 actually do? First, it operates more as a defence than a duty,[158] and particularly as a defence to shareholders

155 E.g. R. Williams, 'Enlightened Shareholder Value in UK Company Law' (2012) 35 *U New South Wales LJ* 360; A. Keay, *The Enlightened Shareholder Value Principle and Corporate Governance* (2014).

156 Cf. Companies Act 1985, s. 309(1) previously read: 'The matters to which the directors of a company are to have regard in the performance of their functions include the interests of the company's employees in general, as well as the interests of its members.' This was never litigated.

157 Deakin, 'The Coming Transformation of Shareholder Value'.

158 Sealy and Worthington, *Cases and Materials in Company Law* (10th ed. 2013) 341.

claiming that directors should seek solely to maximise profit. Past cases did allow shareholders to sue for failing to put their interests first, and they have been reversed both in case law and legislation in the UK[159] and in the USA.[160] Section 172 makes clear that directors can act in the way *they* consider, in good faith, will promote the company's success. This is all the more important because, since the late twentieth century, shareholders mostly became asset managers handling other people's money (see Ch. 4). This means there is no credible, moral or economic defence for any system of company law acting in the 'shareholder' interest, as opposed to the interests of real investors, employees, customers and the public. The legitimacy of shareholder primacy is a myth.[161]

Second, section 172 and its criteria are of concrete relevance for the derivative claim. Under sections 260–3, factors to which directors *may* have regard are the factors to which a court *must* have regard in deciding whether to allow members or others to bring a claim (see Ch. 3(4)(e)). Third, section 172's criteria guide the annual Director's Report, where companies have to explain how they have complied with duties in relation to stakeholders.[162] Part of the idea behind reporting is to 'mainstream' pro-stakeholder values into the consciousness of company management. The limit is that much reporting of this kind risks turning into a public relations exercise that produces fancy brochures and PDFs, but alters little of substance.

A broader conceptual problem underlying the debates and content of section 172 is that duties are functionally inept at ensuring directors act in anyone's interests. Directors will respond most to the interests of those who give them jobs and pay. Duties, at best, set outer boundaries. This is even more clear through experience in the USA, where most states have enacted 'constituency statutes' since the 1980s, exhorting boards to balance the interests of multiple stakeholders, including employees, customers, etc.[163] A rudimentary understanding of comparative law quickly reveals that American directors have always responded to shareholder interests most: asset managers and banks. That is because shareholders monopolise voting rights. Duties matter, but not as much as voting power.

159 See *Hutton v West Cork Railway Co.* (1883) 23 Ch D 654 and *Parke v Daily News Ltd* [1962] Ch 927 suggesting directors of insolvent companies could not make provision for employees, though this was reversed by statute: IA 1986, s. 187 and CA 2006, s. 247.

160 *Dodge v Ford Motor*, 170 NW 668 (Mich 1919) reversed in multiple cases, e.g. *A. P. Smith Manufacturing Co. v Barlow*, 13 NJ 145, 98 A.2d 581 (1953) (donation to Princeton University) and *Shlensky v Wrigley*, 237 NE 2d 776 (Ill App 1968) (no baseball lights, for local residents). Also see C. Hansen, 'Other Constituency Statutes: A Search for Perspective' (1991) 46(4) *Business Lawyer* 1355.

161 See E. McGaughey, 'Democracy in America at Work: The History of Labor's Vote in Corporate Governance' (2019) 42 *Seattle UL Rev* 697, 746.

162 CA 2006, s. 419.

163 E.g. New York Business Corporations Law, §717(b). For a list, see Hansen, 'Other Constituency Statutes: A Search for Perspective', Appendix A.

Section 173 adds that directors 'must exercise independent judgment'. This repeats what is already in section 172, as the director must act in the way she or 'he considers' will promote the success of the company, and not fetter their judgment to other parties.[164]

(c) Duty of Care: Section 174

Section 174(1) contains the duty to 'exercise reasonable care, skill and diligence'. Functionally equivalent to the tort law duty to not be negligent, this was partly necessary because directors were originally exempt from the general duty of care on all service providers.[165] Now, however, there is a higher standard, as section 174(2) says directors must both show an objective minimum level of 'knowledge, skill and experience' commensurate for that director's job, plus the 'knowledge, skill and experience that the director has'. This 'objective plus subjective' standard means that, first, executive directors in large companies will be expected to show greater care than non-executives or directors in smaller companies. But second, if a director has special skills, such as an accounting or engineering degree, and something on their watch goes wrong in accounts or explodes, they will have a more difficult time explaining that they took care.[166] Losses flowing from negligence must be compensated. However, under section 1157 directors may be relieved from paying compensation if they have acted 'honestly and reasonably' and in the court's view 'ought fairly to be excused'.

Before statutory codification, this standard was introduced in *Re D'Jan of London Ltd* by analogy to the Insolvency Act 1986, section 214, on wrongful trading (see Ch. 7(4)(b)).[167] The liquidator of Mr D'Jan's insolvent company claimed compensation (for the creditors) after it transpired that D'Jan failed to fill out an insurance form correctly. D'Jan ticked 'no' to the question of whether he had ever been a director of an insolvent company. This 'mistake' (as it was politely assumed to be) invalidated his insurance policy after the company's Cornwall warehouse burned down. Hoffmann LJ held that D'Jan was negligent but relieved D'Jan from liability under section 1157 (as it is now) because D'Jan was the 99 per cent shareholder. 'It may be reasonable to take a risk', said Hoffmann LJ, 'in relation to your own money which would be unreasonable in relation to someone else's.' From this principle it seems courts

[164] Cf. *Fulham Football Club Ltd v Cabra Estates plc* [1994] 1 BCLC 363.

[165] Supply of Goods and Services Act 1982, s. 13 (duty of care); but Supply of Services (Exclusion of Implied Terms) Order 1982/1771, reg. 2(2) exempted directors. Reg. 2(1) still exempts barristers!

[166] For the discredited subjective standard, see *Re Cardiff Savings Bank* [1892] 2 Ch 100, *In re Brazilian Rubber Plantations and Estates Ltd* [1911] 1 Ch 425 and *Re City Equitable Fire Insurance Co.* [1925] Ch 407. These cases, in essence, enabled directors to argue that the stupider they were, the less liable they must be. Cf. *Report on the Investigation into Russian Interference in the 2016 Presidential Election* (2019) vol. I, 187, on 'willfulness'.

[167] [1994] 1 BCLC 561.

are unlikely to relieve negligent directors where there is any separation of ownership and control.

If a company has gone insolvent, the same negligence standard justifies disqualifying directors under the Company Director Disqualification Act 1986 (see Ch. 7(3)(c)). This means case law on disqualifications is to be used to interpret section 174. In *Re Barings plc (No. 5)* the Secretary of State applied to disqualify the ex-directors of Barings plc, the world's second oldest merchant bank (established 1762). Barings plc had gone insolvent after a 'rogue trader' employee called Nick Leeson was revealed to have been falsifying records of his trading in foreign exchange contracts at the Singapore office. Leeson accumulated massive losses from trading (in the 'front' office), but he had signed off on his own trades (in the 'back' office). His fraud was exposed after an earthquake in Kobe, Japan, sent global markets into free fall and the losses became too large to conceal. This mattered for the directors in London, because they had been presented with an audit report before the crash saying that the Singapore front and back offices were not separate and this was a risk. The directors ignored the report. Upheld by the Court of Appeal, Jonathan Parker J held that the directors were negligent and had breached their duty of care. They had to be declared 'unfit' for office and disqualified. Directors could 'delegate particular functions to those below them in the management chain' and 'trust their competence and integrity to a reasonable extent' but this would 'not absolve a director from the duty to supervise' those functions.[168]

(d) Duty to Avoid Conflicts of Interest: Sections 175–7

Section 175 is probably the most important prohibitive norm in all governance: to avoid any possibility of a conflict of interest. This duty evolved as a direct consequence of the South Sea Bubble (see Ch. 1(2)), and in opposition to the view of the disgraced Lord Chancellor Macclesfield (who was impeached, and imprisoned in the Tower of London) that it was lawful to profit from one's office, if one restored any loss.[169] His successor, Lord Chancellor King, held in *Keech v Sandford* that any inquiry into wrongdoing was to be avoided: there was a positive duty to avoid any possibility of conflicting interests. It was not enough to say there was no actual conflict on the facts of a case.[170] Through the eighteenth and nineteenth centuries, the rule was continually reaffirmed, and said even to be necessary for the 'safety of mankind'.[171] In view of the economic and political collapse that came with the

168 [1999] 1 BCLC 433, 489, approved by the Court of Appeal, [2001] BCC 273, 283.

169 *Bromfield v Wytherley* (1718) Prec Ch 505.

170 *Keech v Sandford* (1726) Sel Cas Ch 61, a trustee bought the lease on Romford market for himself instead of for the trust. It was no answer to say the seller would not have renewed the lease for the infant beneficiary.

171 *Parker v McKenna* (1874) LR 10 Ch App 96, 124–5, per James LJ. See also *Whelpdale v Cookson* (1747) 1 Ves Sen 9, 27 ER 856; *Ex parte James* [1803–13] All ER Rep 7; and *Bray v Ford* [1896] AC 44.

South Sea Company's corruption this is best seen, not as hyperbole, but as a measured and sensible statement.

Section 175 states that directors 'must avoid a situation' where their 'direct or indirect' interests do conflict or 'possibly may conflict, with the interests of the company'. Although this is strict, liability can easily be neutralised under section 175(4)–(6) if authorised by disinterested directors before an act. After an act the general meeting may resolve by a majority to approve the conflicted act, excluding any interested voters, under section 239.[172] The company may also act by consensus to approve breaches.[173]

What counts as a conflict? A central example is a director taking an opportunity that *could* interest the company. In *Cook v Deeks*, a director of the Toronto Construction Co., Mr Cook, claimed that three co-directors wrongfully took in their own names a contract to build railways, instead of offering it to the whole company. Each director was a 25 per cent shareholder. When Cook found out and complained, the three directors passed a majority resolution approving their actions. The Privy Council advised that the opportunity belonged to the company, and the attempt of the three to 'ratify' their own wrongs was ineffective.[174] Unlike the duty of care where the remedy is compensation for loss, breach of the duty to avoid any possibility of conflict leads to a remedy of restitution of all profits from the wrong.

The rule remains very strict. In *Regal (Hastings) Ltd v Gulliver* the directors and solicitor of a cinema business were sued by the shareholder after a takeover for profiting from the leases on two cinemas. Before selling the cinema business in Hastings, the landlord asked the company to give personal guarantees, or raise the subsidiary company's share capital by £5,000 (to ensure the rent would be paid). The company itself put in £2,000. But instead of getting the company to take out a loan for the other £3,000 (which would mean the company would recoup any profit), the four directors and the chair (Mr Gulliver) invested £500 each, and found other subscribers for the rest. There were twenty shareholders in the company, who were therefore excluded from the profits of this deal upon the takeover. Although the Court of Appeal held there was no wrong, the House of Lords found that the directors had to give up their profits to the company (i.e. the shareholder who subsequently bought it). According to Lord Wright, the Court of Appeal's conclusion was 'dead in the teeth of the wise and salutary rule so stringently enforced' of no possibility of conflict since *Keech v Sandford*.[175] Today, a court might use its power under section 1157 to absolve directors in a similar situation, but presumably only if (after the principle in *D'Jan*) the directors and shareholders were identical.

To what extent can a company claim it was interested in an opportunity? Section 175 clarifies that something will be deemed to 'possibly . . . conflict' if it

[172] CA 2006, s. 239.

[173] *Multinational Gas & Petrochemical Co. v Multinational Gas and Petrochemical Services Ltd* [1983] Ch 258.

[174] [1916] 1 AC 554, [1916] UKPC 10.

[175] [1942] 1 All ER 378 and [1967] 2 AC 134, 157.

can 'reasonably be regarded' as possibly giving rise to a conflict.[176] This depends on the company's line of business. In *Bhullar v Bhullar* two sides of a family business had fallen out. In an unfair prejudice petition (below), Mohan sued his brother, Sohan, when Sohan's son, Inderjit, bought a car park on sale near a company property. Inderjit set up a separate company to buy the car park without telling the family members of the company. Jonathan Parker LJ held there was a breach of duty to avoid conflicts because the company could have benefited from the opportunity to buy the property. The very anxiety that Inderjit had to keep the car park opportunity secret was 'eloquent of the existence of a possible conflict of duty and interest'.[177] From this, it seems to follow that some opportunities (e.g. buying a sandwich) will not reasonably be regarded as a conflicting opportunity, but if it is anywhere close to the line of company business it will.

The duty to avoid conflicts continues after a director resigns.[178] In *CMS Dolphin Ltd v Simonet* it was held to be unlawful for Mr Simonet to resign as managing director of his advertising company, set up a new company, and take staff and major clients with him. Lawrence Collins J held there had to be 'some reasonable connection between the breach of duty and the profits for which the fiduciary is accountable'. Here there was.[179]

A subcategory of the no-conflict principle is that under section 176 directors 'must not accept a benefit from a third party' for being a director. This underlines that directors should only profit from doing good work, and not profit from any influence their office holds.

Section 177, a further prohibitive rule, requires that directors must not engage in any self-dealing transaction (when a director is on both sides of a deal) without full disclosure to the board. If a director 'is in any way . . . interested in a proposed transaction' with the company they must disclose it. This disclosure must be made in a meeting or in writing, but either way should therefore be publicised in minutes so that company members can also evaluate the conflict. For example, in *Aberdeen Railway Co. v Blaikie Brothers*, the managing director of Blaikie Brothers, Mr Blaikie, had also been the chairman of Aberdeen Railway Co., and had arranged a contract to sell iron chairs to the railway company. When he sued to enforce the contract, the Aberdeen Railway Co. argued it was not bound, because of the conflict of interest. Mr Blaikie tried to argue the price was fair. According to Lord Cranworth LC, 'no question is allowed to be raised as to the fairness or unfairness of a contract so entered into' and 'so inflexible is the rule that no inquiry on that subject is permitted'.[180]

[176] This standard follows *Boardman v Phipps* [1966] UKHL 2, per Lord Upjohn.

[177] [2003] EWCA Civ 424. [178] CA 2006, s. 170(2).

[179] [2001] 2 BCLC 704. See also *Industrial Development Consultants v Cooley* [1972] 1 WLR 443, *In Plus Group Ltd v Pyke* [2002] EWCA Civ 370, and *Foster Bryant Surveying Ltd v Bryant* [2007] EWCA Civ 200.

[180] (1854) 1 Paterson 394.

Today if there is a failure to disclose, then the transaction is void and restitution of all profits must be made, unless it is positively approved. The company's articles may always raise these requirements, for instance, to member approval before a transaction.[181] If such a transaction has taken place, there remains a duty to disclose and failure becomes a criminal offence, subject to a £5,000 fine.[182] The larger the transaction, the more stringent the requirements. Member approval is needed for transactions with directors or connected persons if the money involved is over 10 per cent of a company's value, and over £5,000, or is over £100,000 in any company.[183] Loans to directors also require approval.[184] The strictness of these rules stands in striking contrast to the ease with which directors can pay themselves eye-watering sums of money in salaries and bonuses (see Ch. 3(3)(c)). It is unsatisfactory that where conflicts of interest are most naked and severe, the law drops its standards.

(e) Litigation: Derivative Claims and Alternatives

Duties are one thing, but rights to vindicate them are another. Historically, the law was reluctant to endorse corporate litigation. If directors can be dismissed according to the constitution, and now by a simple majority of members (s. 168), should internal problems not be resolved internally? If a minority wish to litigate for an alleged breach of director's duty, but a majority do not, why should the minority be able to waste company time and resources in court? Of course, if members have personal rights by virtue of the constitution, like the right to vote (see Ch. 3(2)(a)), they can apply to the court to enforce their rights. Any single member may apply to enforce a provision in the constitution, such as a special procedure (now s. 171).[185] If people are conferred benefits under a company constitution they may bring personal claims, notwithstanding the arcane defects of 'privity of contract'.[186] But for other duties where there could be disagreement about the virtues of litigation – even if a wrong is admittedly committed – should votes, not courts, be used to resolve differences?

181 See CA 2006, s. 180(1)(b); *Imperial Mercantile Credit Association v Coleman* (1871) LR 6 Ch App 558; *Costa Rica Railway Company v Forwood* [1901] 1 Ch 746; *Motivex v Bulfield Ltd* [1988] BCLC 104, 117; *Boulting v ACTAT* [1963] 2 QB 606, 636.

182 CA 2006, ss. 182–3.

183 Under CA 2006, ss. 252–4, a 'connected person' includes family members, and companies, partnerships and trusts where the director has a large stake.

184 CA 2006, ss. 197–214.

185 *Edwards v Halliwell* [1950] 2 All ER 1064 (a member of the National Union of Vehicle Builders could require the constitution was followed, to have a two-third vote before the union increased fees).

186 Although the Contracts (Rights of Third Parties) Act 1999, s. 6(2) exempts companies from the right to claim benefits, *Gamlestaden Fastigheter AB v Baltic Partners Ltd* [2007] UKPC 26 held a member could claim losses in unfair prejudice as a creditor, even without having any loss as a member. This probably overrules *Eley v Positive Government Security Life Assurance Co. Ltd* (1876) 1 Ex D 88, where Lord Cairns LC held Mr Eley, named company solicitor in art. 118, could not enforce a right to be solicitor. He did not sue as a member.

These sentiments were expressed in 1812 by Lord Eldon in *Carlen v Drury*, when he scoffed that this 'Court is not required on every Occasion to take the Management of every Playhouse and Brewhouse in the Kingdom'.[187] In 1843, it was further held in *Foss v Harbottle* that the company was the proper claimant for wrongs done to the company. So, if directors were thought to have been negligent, the majority of members were entitled to sue, but as a starting point the minority should not be allowed to do it for them.[188] This restrictive approach gradually gave way to more and more exceptions, until the Companies Act 2006 fully liberalised the right to vindicate wrongs. Now, any single company member – and anyone that a court says has a sufficient interest – can apply to sue for breach of directors' duties in a derivative claim, if they pass the test of their claim being in the 'interests of the company'. Moreover, members (but only members) have a right to bring unfair prejudice claims, based both on derivative claims, and on a wider set of 'equitable considerations', such as promises or assurances that are relied on.

(i) Derivative Claims

A 'derivative' claim is one where the right to sue derives from the company's right to sue. This is now partially codified, although the common law may add rights. Section 260(3) states derivative claims concern vindicating breaches of directors' duty owed to the company. Section 261 states that a member must apply to court for permission and show there is a good prima facie case to be made. This is like the strike-out application stage in a tort claim. So long as there is a good legal case, section 263 then requires the court to evaluate:[189]

- whether the claimant is acting in good faith
- whether it should go ahead in the interests of the company with regard to the criteria in section 172 (see Ch. 3(4)(b))
- whether the directors' conduct was or is likely to be duly authorised or ratified[190]
- whether the company has already decided against pursuing the claim
- whether members could sue based on a personal right[191]
- the views of the disinterested majority of members.[192]

187 (1812) 1 Ves & B 154, 158.

188 (1843) 67 ER 189. See also *Alexander Ward v Samyang* [1975] 2 All ER 424 and *Breckland Group Holdings Ltd v London & Suffolk Properties Ltd* [1989] BCLC 100. This follows the default principle that 'wherever a certain number are incorporated, a major part of them may do any corporate act': *Attorney General v Davy* (1741) 26 ER 531.

189 CA 2006, s. 263(3)–(4).

190 Recall *Cook v Deeks* [1916] 1 AC 554, where interested directors could not ratify their own wrongs.

191 Recall *Pender v Lushington* (1877) 6 Ch D 70, above on the right to vote.

192 CA 2006, s. 263(4); and see *Smith v Croft (No. 2)* [1988] Ch 114, where claimants held 14% of shares, defendants held 63%, but others, who did not want litigation, had 21%. Knox J refused the claim.

Among these criteria, the court must refuse permission if the conduct was authorised or ratified, and if it would not be in the company's interests under section 172.[193] Also, if a personal right could be available,[194] a shareholder cannot sue in a personal action for losses that are reflected in fall in share value. This principle against reflective loss (which only affects shareholders) means only a derivative claim may be brought.[195] This may be problematic where a majority of a company's shareholders have chosen not to sue and settled at an undervalue, but this will never bar claims by beneficiaries of shareholders (that is, the true investors), or employees or creditors.[196] If claims are approved to proceed, since *Wallersteiner v Moir (No. 2)* members have a right to be indemnified by the company for the cost of the claim, even if it fails.[197]

Interestingly, although the derivative claim was codified, in *Re Fort Gilkicker Ltd*, Briggs J (from 2017, Lord Briggs) held that it remained open at common law to bring derivative claims outside the statutory procedure. A shareholder in the parent company of Fort Gilkicker Ltd applied to bring a derivative claim against a director. As a shareholder of a shareholder, the claimant was not a member. Nevertheless, Briggs J held the Companies Act 2006 only codified the manner in which members could bring claims, not non-members. Allowing the claim was 'the consequence of the law's search for a suitably interested representative, or champion, of the wronged company'.[198]

Fort Gilkicker raises a key question of principle: if shareholders of shareholders can bring a claim, why not any other stakeholder? For public bodies, the rule is that anyone with a 'sufficient interest' may bring claims in judicial review.[199] In Canada, the Supreme Court has held that a bondholder of a telecommunications company could bring an equivalent action for breach of directors' duties.[200] In India, employees were acknowledged to have standing to bring derivative claims.[201] Reasons favouring such an approach in the UK include the fact that shareholders may have interests conflicting with the company as a whole, or that they are merely apathetic about vindicating a breach of duty. Investors, bondholders and employees are inherently closely

[193] CA 2006, s. 263(2). Early illustrations of the claim procedure include *Mission Capital plc v Sinclair* [2008] EWHC 1339 and *Franbar Holdings Ltd v Patel* [2008] EWHC 1534.

[194] See *Prudential Assurance v Newman Industries Ltd* [1982] Ch 204, right not to be misled by company circulars. The duty to not mislead arises from the law of tort and negligent misstatement.

[195] *Sevilleja v Marex Financial Ltd* [2020] UKSC 31, holding creditors of an insolvent company could sue shareholders who asset stripped a company. Cf. *Johnson v Gore Wood & Co.* [2002] 2 AC 1 (Lord Millett's comments on employees are now disapproved).

[196] [2020] UKSC 31, [55] and [89] per Lord Reed. Lord Sales, Lady Hale and Lord Kitchin support abolishing the rule against reflective loss, as issues of double recovery could be dealt with in case management, at [194].

[197] [1975] QB 373. [198] [2013] EWHC 348 (Ch). [199] Senior Courts Act 1981, s. 31(3).

[200] *BCE Inc. v 1976 Debenture Holders* [2008] 3 SCR 560.

[201] J. Cottrell, 'Indian Judicial Activism, the Company and the Worker' (1990) 39(2) *Int'l and Comparative LQ* 433.

connected to the company's affairs. For other groups the concept of 'sufficient interest' in judicial review is a workable and familiar tool to set limits.

(ii) Unfair Prejudice Petitions

With derivative claims, another statutory litigation procedure is the 'unfair prejudice' petition. Since introduction in 1985, they have come to fill up a large part of the Chancery Courts' time. Before then, first, there were derivative actions but, as explained above, the rules were much more restrictive. There is also a common law right to claim that a company's articles were amended in directly discriminatory fashion without objective justification, or as the older cases put it, not 'bona fide for the benefit of the company as a whole'.[202] However, this failed to ensure protection against indirect discrimination, even where calculated.[203] Second, from the Companies Act 1948, there was also an 'oppression' petition, but the need to show 'oppressive' conduct was also seen as unduly restrictive.[204] Third, there was a drastic remedy, now in the Insolvency Act 1986, section 122(1), of presenting a winding-up petition on 'just and equitable' grounds. In 1985 it was felt that remedies should be capable of being granted more freely, and without winding up companies, and so the unfair prejudice petition was introduced. Now that the derivative claim procedure has been liberalised, there is considerable overlap. Functionally, both are procedures that enable minority members to vindicate their rights. But three main differences are that unfair prejudice petitions: (1) can be brought for breaches of private assurances as well as directors' duties; (2) because of this are probably not available in public companies;[205] and (3) are only for members, not non-members. Thus, the crucial addition of unfair prejudice petitions is a claim for not fulfilling estoppel-like assurances.

A leading case on 'just and equitable' winding-up petitions also illustrates how unfair prejudice claims work. In *Ebrahimi v Westbourne Galleries Ltd*,[206] Mr Ebrahimi claimed that his former co-director and co-shareholder, Mr Nazar, had acted inequitably. Ebrahimi and Nazar had started their small business together. Later Nazar's son was invited on the board and had become a shareholder. Sadly, they then fell out. Ebrahimi was removed, and the Nazars began paying out all profits in director fees, not dividends. This made Ebrahimi's shares worthless. Lord Wilberforce held that the court would wind up the company, because the Nazars' conduct undercut the expectations

[202] *Allen v Gold Reefs of West Africa Ltd* [1900] 1 Ch 656. Also, *Brown v British Abrasive Wheel Co.* [1919] 1 Ch 290; *Sidebottom v Kershaw, Leese & Co. Ltd* [1920] 1 Ch 154; *Dafen Tinplate Co. Ltd v Llanelly Steel Co. (1907) Ltd* [1920] 2 Ch 124; *Shuttleworth v Cox Bros. and Co. (Maidenhead)* [1927] 1 Ch 154; *Southern Foundries (1926) Ltd v Shirlaw* [1940] AC 701; and *Citco Banking Corporation NV v Pusser's Ltd* [2007] UKPC 13.

[203] *Greenhalgh v Arderne Cinemas Ltd* [1951] Ch 286, removing shareholder pre-emption rights affecting only one shareholder, with a disparate impact on one shareholder: this was held to be lawful.

[204] Cf. *Scottish Cooperative Wholesale Society v Meyer* [1959] AC 324.

[205] *Re Blue Arrow plc* [1987] BCLC 585. [206] [1973] AC 360.

on which the company was founded. Three factors were that the company was a small 'quasi-partnership' founded on mutual confidence, that the shareholders participated in the business and there were restrictions on free transfer of shares. Now, under the Companies Act 2006, section 994, Mr Ebrahimi could have brought an unfair prejudice petition, and under section 996 probably would have been awarded the right to have his shares bought out at a fair value.

Any breach of director's duty will count as unfair prejudice (as in *Bhullar v Bhullar*, above). But also, a broken assurance that is relied upon, that was inequitable to go back on, would be grounds for claiming unfair prejudice. By contrast, in *O'Neill v Phillips*, Mr O'Neill claimed that he should have been given a 50 per cent stake in an asbestos stripping company owned by Mr Phillips. O'Neill had been a prodigious trainee, and had worked for many years. But when the business hit poor economic conditions, O'Neill fell out with Phillips and was demoted. He sued because he had expected to become an equal partner. Lord Hoffmann held that an aspiration that O'Neill might have been given shares was not enough: there was no promise or concrete assurance.[207] There could not, therefore, be any unfair prejudice.[208]

The remedy for unfair prejudice, while at the court's discretion, is most commonly being bought out at a fair value. This raises the question of the appropriate date for valuation. In *Profinance Trust SA v Gladstone*, Profinance won an action to be bought out by Gladstone, who disputed the proper date. Robert Walker LJ held that the value of the company at the hearing date is the proper starting point, but an earlier date could be appropriate if the company is deprived of business, or is reconstructed and has a new identity, or if there is a market fall, all depending on the parties' conduct.[209] The court also does not discount the price of shares just because a shareholder lacks control, and generally takes a *pro rata* valuation to be proper.[210]

(5) Conclusion

The basic elements of a corporate constitution have been settled in the UK for nearly eight decades. Members have binding rights to vote, can choose or dismiss the board, change the constitution and enforce directors' duties. Around the world, these rights have become increasingly strong, as shown

[207] [1999] 1 WLR 1092.

[208] See also *Re Macro (Ipswich) Ltd* [1994] BCLC 959, per Arden J, unfair prejudice for mismanagement. A director, elderly and autocratic, Mr Thompson, had badly managed the business, including self- dealing, leading to heavy losses.

[209] [2001] EWCA Civ 1031.

[210] *Re Bird Precision Bellows Ltd* [1984] Ch 658, per Oliver LJ, majority ordered to buy out a 26% shareholder on a *pro rata* basis. There could be an exception for shares acquired at a discount as an investment.

by empirical data on the development of corporate laws.[211] However, these rights usually benefit shareholders if shareholders are the members. In UK law, any stakeholder can be a company 'member' by agreement, yet shareholders typically monopolise power. As Chapter 4 explains, shareholders are not usually the investors of capital: they are instead intermediary asset managers or banks holding other people's money. In practice, they have not exercised shareholder rights to make directors accountable for long-term, sustainable enterprise. Boardroom power has concentrated, executive pay has unjustifiably escalated and directors' duties are frequently unenforced to the detriment of society, the environment, consumers, staff as well as the true investors in capital.

[211] P. P. Lele and M. M. Siems, 'Shareholder Protection: A Leximetric Approach' (2007) 7(1) *J Corporate L Studies* 17; M. M. Siems, 'Shareholder Protection around the World (Leximetric II)' (2008) 33 *Delaware J Corporate L* 111. This measures 10 core variables on members' (1) control over major asset sales, (2) agenda-setting power, (3) member proxy voting rights, (4) ban on super-voting rights, (5) independent board members, (6) director dismissal power, (7) derivative claim strength, (8) minority litigation rights, (9) mandatory bids over 30% of takeover and (10) disclosure of major ownership. See Centre for Business Research, *Index* (February 2009).

4

Investment and Shareholding

Contents

As Chapter 3 explored, corporate governance centres upon the accountability of directors through votes and duties to members. Membership is mainly monopolised by shareholders. So, who are shareholders, and what influence do they exert in financial markets? For many years, real people held shares directly. Characters like Mr Salomon with his boots, Mr Macaura and his (company's) smouldering timber, and Mr Pender in his telecoms empire helped write the script, and still animate the world imagined in company law texts. But individuals today own under 10 per cent of UK shares (see Figure 4.1) and even those shares are mostly owned indirectly, through High Street banks. Registered shareholders are financial institutions: asset managers and banks, usually corporations as well. They hold shares with 'other people's money',[1] and the 'other people' are usually workers saving for retirement, in pension, life insurance or mutual funds. If modern company law is about making directors accountable, how are financial institutions accountable to the real investors?[2] The 'separation of ownership and control' was corporate law's key issue from the eighteenth century. But from the late twentieth century the 'separation of ownership and ownership', of legal owners from the beneficial owners of capital, has become a titanic problem that today's law must navigate.[3]

[1] A. Smith, *An Inquiry into the Nature and Causes of the Wealth of Nations* (1776) Book V, ch. 1, §107. L. D. Brandeis, *Other People's Money* (1914).

[2] P. L. Davies, 'Institutional Investors: A U.K. View' (1991) 57 *Brooklyn L Rev* 129, 141: 'should there not also be a mechanism for making [intermediaries] accountable to the people who have contributed the investment monies?' See also E. McGaughey, *Participation in Corporate Governance* (2014) ch. 6.

[3] Cf. L. Strine, 'Toward Common Sense and Common Ground-Reflections on the Shared Interests of Managers and Labor in a More Rational System of Corporate Governance' (2007) 33(1)

Shareholders' identity matters because they influence the use of scarce resources, and ultimately the finances of enterprises to realise social and economic rights. They have three key functions. First, shareholders *accumulate* capital, aggregating money from millions of people, enabling investment at global scale, funding enterprises as large as nation states. Second, shareholders decide how to *allocate* investment between companies. Using votes, they also allocate resources within companies, influencing dividend and wage policy, retaining profit for future company use and paying or evading tax. Third, shareholders *diversify* investments across global markets, limiting risk to the ultimate investors. If one company in a share portfolio goes insolvent, the loss is minimal (or there could even be a profit) if the investor invests in competitors. Shareholding institutions that handle other people's money profit from fees, and so typically they bear no risk on portfolio insolvencies. The risk is borne by the ultimate investors in capital. So, in exercising their accumulation, allocation and diversification functions shareholders' interests systematically conflict with the ultimate investors. But unlike company law's rules for directors, the mechanisms for shareholder accountability are based upon an uncodified web of contract, trust or corporate law, interacting with legislation for investment and securities markets. This chapter navigates (1) the constitution of shareholding, (2) equity finance, (3) takeovers and (4) tax.

(1) Finance and Governance of Shareholding

Shareholding is financed and governed through a chain of investments built on contracts, trusts and corporations. The chain usually starts with ordinary people saving for retirement. At the end is a company or some other asset. This is the standard UK investment chain:

Beneficiary → Pension/Life insurance/Mutual fund → Asset manager → CREST → Company

↗

Individual saver → High Street Bank

In this chain, asset managers (or banks) mostly appear as the shareholders on the company register in major listed companies. They hold shares through CREST, the 'Certificateless Registry for Electronic Share Transfer' which is an organisation for logging whose shares are traded, much like the Land Registry. But asset managers invariably accumulate and invest other people's money. The main sources of capital are pensions, life insurance or mutual funds, which all have their own beneficiaries. Alternatively, in about 10 per cent of cases of share ownership, individual savers may also buy shares through banks, who act as an agent. The next sections look at (a) the regulator of securities markets, the

J Corporation L 1, 6; R. J. Gilson and J. N. Gordon, 'The Agency Costs of Agency Capitalism: Activist Investors and the Revaluation of Governance Rights' (2013) 113(4) *Columbia L Rev* 863.

Financial Conduct Authority (FCA), (b) asset managers and custodians, (c) pension funds, (d) life insurance, (e) mutual funds and (f) retail shareholders.

(a) Financial Conduct Authority

UK securities markets are supervised by the FCA, based in Stratford. Like the US Securities and Exchange Commission (SEC),[4] or the German BaFin,[5] the FCA has duties to supervise and ultimately underpin the stability of financial markets. It should pre-empt crashes like the global financial crisis, or mitigate the impact of shocks like Covid-19. Its governing body is appointed by HM Treasury, and therefore the Secretary of State, except that the Bank of England's deputy governor also sits on the board (see Ch. 10).[6] Its 'operational objectives' are protecting consumers of financial services to 'an appropriate degree', ensuring the 'integrity' of the 'UK financial system' and 'promoting effective competition'.[7] Its so-called 'strategic objective' is to ensure 'relevant markets . . . function well'.

Of course, these general duties do not mean much compared to the detailed rules, which the FCA has broad discretion to write for 'regulated activities'.[8] The key document is the FCA Handbook, an extensive set of general principles and duties. Many of these follow and extend duties of constitutionality, care and no conflicts, that apply to directors (see Ch. 3(4)).[9] The basic norm is that no 'person may carry on a regulated activity' unless they are authorised or exempted by the FCA, and this means any business that 'relates to an investment' of a kind specified by Treasury order.[10] So anyone selling or promoting shares, bonds, options, futures or other derivatives has to apply for permission. The FCA then decides whether the applicant has appropriate resources for the riskiness of their activity, if they are 'fit and proper', if they have a suitable 'business model' and are capable of being effectively supervised in the UK.[11] In theory these powers are strong: any breach of rules can lead to withdrawal of permission to operate. In practice, enforcement is haphazard, depending on the people in charge, their activism and their relations to business – a problem worldwide.[12]

4 Securities and Exchange Act of 1934, 15 USC, §78d.

5 This is *Bundesanstalt für Finanzdienstleistungsaufsicht* (Federal Financial Supervisory Authority), established by the *Gesetz über die Bundesanstalt für Finanzdienstleistungsaufsicht* 2002 (BGBl. S. 1633).

6 Financial Services and Markets Act (FSMA) 2000, Sch. 1ZA, para. 2.

7 FSMA 2000, ss. 1C–G.

8 FSMA 2000, s. 137A.

9 See www.handbook.fca.org.uk/handbook. After 'High Level Standards', the most important provisions are found in 'Business Standards', which includes sourcebooks on 'Conduct of Business' (COBS), Insurance, Mortgages (MCOB), Banking, Claims Management, Client Assets, Market Conduct and Product Intervention.

10 FSMA 2000, ss. 19–22.

11 FSMA 2000, Sch. 6, paras. 2B–2F.

12 E.g. see a remarkable exchange between US Senator Warren and SEC Chair White on YouTube in 2016.

(b) Asset Managers

(i) Financing

The first and most important actor in modern financial markets is the asset manager. The Companies Act 2006, section 112 requires every company to have a register of members. Major shareholders are disclosed by regulations abroad, like the USA, revealed when companies cross-list.[13] In UK company law disclosure is required only if there is 'significant control' such as by holding 25 per cent of shares, a threshold that has limited value.[14] As it can be seen, the 'major holders' in large companies are invariably asset managers, or banks. Table 4.1 shows the top ten shareholders in six major FTSE 100 companies in 2018.[15]

In the UK, these examples show that top ten shareholders have combined stakes of between (at least) 15 and 35 per cent of companies, and the same firms repeat. BlackRock, Vanguard, State Street (SSgA) and Invesco are major US firms. Legal & General, Aberdeen Asset Management, Abbey National, Standard Life, M&G and Schroders are major UK firms. Norges Bank is the Norwegian sovereign wealth and pension fund, deriving from its socialised oil wealth (see Ch. 11). UBS is a Swiss bank, BNP Paribas is a French bank, and so on. These global financial institutions serve very similar functions, channelling savings into investment. Of course, not all investments go into corporate shares. Savings will usually also be allocated to corporate bonds (see Ch. 7(1)), commodities, real estate and cash. Either way, collectively, the top ten firms invest other people's money. Little or nothing is their own money, yet they can exercise decisive influence across virtually all governance decisions.

Asset managers also hold shares through intermediaries. First, CREST is like HM Land Registry, but for shares. It is a 'central securities depositary'.[16] Everyone's shares in listed companies are registered there.[17] Registration is the conclusive record of ownership. When shares are traded, changes in ownership are made on this register. CREST is currently owned by Euroclear plc, part of the Euroclear group with headquarters in Brussels. The largest institutions buy membership in CREST. Second, CREST members may act as 'custodians' when they hold and trade shares for smaller institutions other than

[13] E.g. International Disclosure Standards, *Securities Act Release No. 33-7745* (28 September 1999) (64 Federal Register 53900) Item 7. Also Regulation S-K, Item 403, issued under the Securities Act of 1933.

[14] Companies Act (CA) 2006, ss. 790M–O, 1136 and Sch. 1A. These rules are scattered and long-winded.

[15] Source: www.MarketScreener.com as stated on 30 October 2018. In terms of size, see Table 3.1. In the top 50 they are placed (2) HSBC, (3) BP, (13) Vodafone, (19) Sky, (25) Tesco and (41) SSE.

[16] Companies Act 1985 (Electronic Communications) Order 2000 (SI 2000/3373) and Uncertificated Securities Regulations 2001 (SI 2001/3755). E Micheler, 'English and German Securities Law: A Thesis in Doctrinal Path Dependence' (2007) 123 *LQR* 251, 267–71, explaining its origins.

[17] NB: Shareholders in non-listed companies still get paper certificates from each company.

Table 4.1 Major shareholders in UK blue chip companies

HSBC plc (see Ch. 10)			BP plc (see Ch. 11)		
Major holders	Shares	%	Major holders	Shares	%
Ping An Asset Mgt Co., Ltd	1253254972	6.29%	BlackRock Inv. Mgt (UK) Ltd	746987626	3.72%
BlackRock Inv. Mgt (UK) Ltd	704654217	3.54%	Norges Bank Inv. Mgt	457621000	2.28%
The Vanguard Group Inc.	483732164	2.43%	The Vanguard Group Inc.	448483622	2.24%
Legal & General Inv. Mgt Ltd	435107189	2.18%	Legal & General Inv. Mgt Ltd	417030805	2.08%
Norges Bank Inv. Mgt	368994000	1.85%	Invesco Asset Mgt Ltd	276578037	1.38%
SSgA Funds Mgt Inc.	195820030	0.98%	M&G Inv. Mgt Ltd	265052750	1.32%
BlackRock Advs. (UK) Ltd	195473551	0.98%	SAFE Inv. Co. Ltd	252479000	1.26%
Aberdeen Asset Invs. Ltd	189329417	0.95%	Aberdeen Asset Invs. Ltd	223937497	1.12%
Standard Life Invs. Ltd	164914930	0.83%	Capital Research & Mgt Co.	214534898	1.07%
Aviva Investors Global Serv Ltd	149252357	0.75%	Standard Life Invs. Ltd	186963323	0.93%
		20.78%			**17.40%**
SSE plc (see Ch. 12)			Vodafone Group plc (see Ch. 16)		
Major holders	Shares	%	Major holders	Shares	%
Capital Research & Mgt Co.	93517080	9.11%	BlackRock Inv. Mgt (UK) Ltd	715704102	2.68%
Causeway Capital Mgt LLC	46731000	4.55%	Norges Bank Inv. Mgt	628914000	2.35%
UBS Ltd (Market Maker)	36287337	3.54%	Legal & General Inv. Mgt Ltd	606412021	2.27%
Mondrian Inv. Partners Ltd	32673000	3.18%	The Vanguard Group Inc.	605753058	2.27%
Invesco Asset Mgt Ltd	28896231	2.82%	Standard Life Invs. Ltd	402897432	1.51%
The Vanguard Group Inc.	25490000	2.48%	Capital Research & Mgt Co.	383878719	1.44%
Legal & General Inv. Mgt Ltd	24919000	2.43%	Aberdeen Asset Invs. Ltd	329316448	1.23%
Norges Bank Inv. Mgt	24737000	2.41%	SSgA Funds Mgt Inc.	316533091	1.18%
BlackRock Inv. Mgt (UK) Ltd	21066596	2.05%	BlackRock Advs. (UK) Ltd	286601262	1.07%
SSgA Funds Mgt Inc.	15249000	1.49%	State St Global Advs Ltd	272803261	1.02%
		34.06%			**17.02%**
Sky plc (see Ch. 17)			Tesco plc (see Ch. 18)		
Major holders	Shares	%	Major holders	Shares	%
UBS AG (Inv. Mgt)	51416557	2.99%	Norges Bank Inv. Mgt	391473927	4.00%
HSBC Global Asset Mgt (UK) Ltd	51398615	2.99%	Artisan Partners LP	379897335	3.88%
BlackRock Inv. Mgt (UK) Ltd	37977139	2.21%	Mondrian Inv. Partners Ltd	346145881	3.53%
The Vanguard Group Inc.	32886502	1.91%	Schroder Inv. Mgt Ltd	337925490	3.45%
Norges Bank Inv. Mgt	23411457	1.36%	Majedie Asset Mgt Ltd	317668216	3.24%
Legal & General Inv. Mgt Ltd	17923940	1.04%	GIC Pte Ltd (Inv. Mgt)	291715568	2.98%
BNP Paribas Asset Mgt France SAS	17632490	1.03%	The Vanguard Group Inc.	282909714	2.89%
1832 Asset Mgt LP	17073217	0.99%	Magellan Asset Mgt Ltd	278707559	2.85%
Abbey National Treasury Serv plc	16204787	0.94%	BlackRock Inv. Mgt (UK) Ltd	270022857	2.76%
After Sept. 2018 takeover	1691252644		State St Global Advs Ltd	226090808	2.31%
Comcast Corp.		**15.46%**			**31.89%**
		98.40%			

themselves who do not buy membership. When CREST members act in this capacity they are called 'sub-custodians'.[18]

The accessible figures of 'major holders' in large UK companies do not always give a full picture, because big mutual funds separate their holdings into different funds (e.g. BlackRock's two funds in HSBC). The funds have different names, but they can still exercise shareholder rights, by a common policy in all of them. In the last three decades there has been an astonishing level of concentration. In the USA, if one combines the shares held by the three biggest mutual funds – BlackRock, Vanguard and State Street – they would together be the largest shareholder in 438 of the 500 largest companies, and 40 per cent of all companies.[19] The largest five shareholders (mostly mutuals) owned an average 20.8 per cent of the top twenty corporations.[20] This concentration of shareholding correlates with reductions in price competition (see Ch. 6(3)).[21] We do not yet have adequate UK data, but matters seem similar because UK investment markets are open and global. We also do not have a clear picture of asset manager size, except from surveys by investment advisers who rely on self-reporting (see Table 4.2).[22]

Self-reported numbers are not strictly reliable, but they are a guide. The figures are measured in millions of US dollars. So, the top asset manager, BlackRock, holds over $5 trillion. For perspective, in the same year the UK government budget was $1 trillion (£800 billion, see Ch. 20) and its nominal gross domestic product for one year was $2.6 trillion. That of the European Union (EU) was $17.27 trillion.[23] Again, almost all of BlackRock's holdings, and voting power with it, is from employees and beneficiaries of other funds saving for retirement. It is other people's money.

(ii) Legal Basis

What is the legal basis of asset managers? First, the top asset managers are disproportionately incorporated under US, UK and Canadian law. German, French, Swiss and Italian institutions are mainly life insurers (like Allianz, AXA, Generali) and banks (like Deutsche, UBS or Credit Suisse). These are corporations, listed or private, incorporated under the national law of their home country (see Ch. 3(1)(b)).

[18] Cf. A. Hainsworth, 'The Shareholder Rights Directive and the Challenge of Re-enfranchising Beneficial Shareholders' [2007] *L & Financial Markets Rev* 11.

[19] E. A. Posner, F. S. Morton and E. G. Weyl, 'Proposal to Limit the Anti-Competitive Power of Institutional Investors' (2017) 81 *Antitrust LJ* 1, 2.

[20] L. A. Bebchuk, A. Cohen and S. Hirst, 'The Agency Problems of Institutional Investors' (2017) 31(3) *J Economic Perspectives* 89, 92, showing figures in Table 1.

[21] J. Azar, M. C. Schmalz and I. Tecu, 'Anti-Competitive Effects of Common Ownership', Ross School of Business Paper No. 1235 (2016); Posner et al., 'Proposal to Limit the Anti-Competitive Power of Institutional Investors' 1, 2, describing this as 'the major new antitrust challenge of our time'.

[22] P&I and Willis, Towers, Watson, *The World's 500 Largest Asset Managers* (October 2017).

[23] World Bank, *World Development Indicators: GDP (current US$)* (2017).

Table 4.2 Top 50 asset managers in the world by assets under management

	Name	Assets (m)	Country		Name	Assets (m)	Country
1	BlackRock	$5,147,852	US	26	Aegon Group	$783,927	Netherlands
2	Vanguard Group	$3,965,018	US	27	Morgan Stanley	$778,003	US
3	State Street Global	$2,468,456	US	28	Prudential	$736,866	UK
4	Fidelity Investments	$2,130,798	US	29	Franklin Templeton	$719,989	US
5	Allianz Group	$1,971,211	Germany	30	Legg Mason	$710,387	US
6	J. P. Morgan Chase	$1,770,867	US	31	Sumitomo Mitsui Trust	$699,484	Japan
7	Bank of New York Mellon	$1,647,990	US	32	Affiliated Managers Group	$688,700	US
8	AXA Group	$1,505,537	France	33	MassMutual Financial	$675,000	US
9	Capital Group	$1,478,523	US	34	Sun Life Financial	$670,600	Canada
10	Goldman Sachs Group	$1,379,000	US	35	Manulife Financial Corp.	$660,437	Canada
11	Prudential Financial	$1,263,765	US	36	Nippon Life Insurance	$647,484	Japan
12	BNP Paribas	$1,215,482	France	37	Ameriprise Financial	$629,600	US
13	UBS	$1,208,275	Switzerland	38	Principal Financial	$591,600	US
14	Deutsche Bank	$1,190,523	Germany	39	Mitsubishi UFJ Financial	$584,765	Japan
15	Amundi	$1,141,000	France	40	New York Life Investments	$504,649	US
16	Legal & General Group	$1,099,919	UK	41	Great-West Lifeco	$489,342	Canada
17	Northern Trust Asset Mgt	$979,210	US	42	Old Mutual	$485,790	UK
18	Wellington Mgt	$942,452	US	43	Generali Group	$479,370	Italy
19	Wells Fargo	$936,900	US	44	Schroder Investment Mgt	$476,976	UK
20	Nuveen	$881,748	US	45	Advisers	$460,010	US
21	Nat Xis Global Asset Mgt	$877,108	France	46	Royal Bank of Canada	$433,054	Canada
22	HSBC Holdings	$831,000	UK	47	Aviva	$423,813	UK
23	Invesco	$812,918	US	48	DZ Bank	$413,282	Germany
24	T. Rowe Price	$810,800	US	49	Credit Suisse	$396,707	Switzerland
25	MetLife	$800,806	US	50	Blackstone Group	$366,553	US

Second, what laws determine the money that they accumulate? The answer is each country's retirement system. The UK, USA, Canada and most English-speaking countries developed their state pensions to provide a minimum safety net in retirement, or a floor through which nobody could fall (see Ch. 5(2)(b)).[24] By contrast, continental European countries and Japan have income-linked state pensions. When you retire, the state's insurance system replaces a percentage of

[24] In the UK, the Social Security, Contributions and Benefits Act 1992. In the USA, the Social Security Act of 1935.

your income.[25] This means, in the UK, etc., people need occupational pension funds, or private savings, to make up the difference between the minimum state benefit and one's pre-retirement income. This has led to more money in the stock market, and a massive asset management industry to handle that money. Because stock markets are bigger, shareholding in companies is much more dispersed. In Germany, France or Italy (as in the UK's state pension, etc.), the state guarantees retirement savings but there is no fund of money that is invested. There is simply less money saved and invested. This shows in the nearly linear correlation between the amount of spending on a country's state pension and share ownership dispersion (measured by the prevalence of large block shareholders in companies). See Figure 4.1.

Figure 4.1 shows that the less an Organisation for Economic Co-operation and Development (OECD) country spends on its public pension (i.e. the pension is not linked to an employee's final salary) the more dispersed shareholding is (i.e. the fewer 20 per cent block shareholders there are). The countries clustered around the middle have hybrid state pensions, part income-linked up to a low cap. The outliers are emerging economies (Chile, Mexico) while Japan has unique cross-shareholding culture.

The link between the pension system and stocks went largely unnoticed in corporate law literature until 2014.[26] The best-known, but much criticised, theory in corporate finance has been that dispersed shareholding is caused by

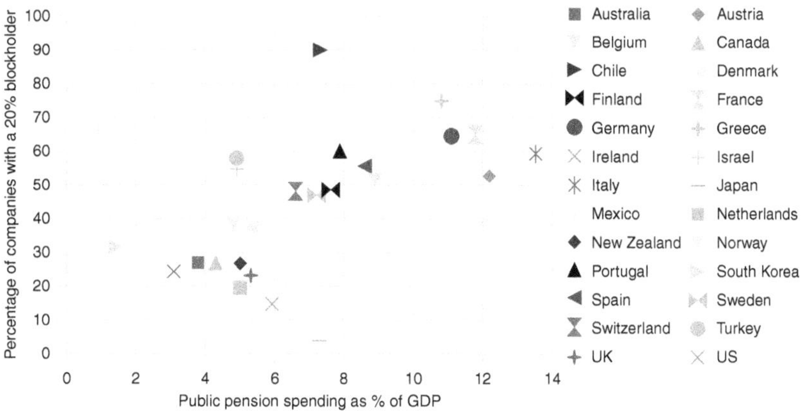

Figure 4.1 Share ownership dispersion and public pension spending
Sources: A. Gourevetich and J. Shinn, *Political Power and Corporate Control: The New Global Politics of Corporate Governance* (2005) 18; and OECD, Pensions at a Glance 2013: OECD and G20 Indicators (2013) 171

[25] In Germany, the *Sozialgesetzbuch* 1992, Book VI (the Social Code 1992).

[26] A notable exception is M. Hauck, 'The Equity Market in Germany and Its Dependency on the System of Old Age Provisions' in T. Baums et al. (eds.), *Institutional Investors and Corporate Governance* (1994) ch. 19, 555, 556.

better protections for minority shareholders.[27] This theory said shareholders are less likely to invest in a company where they are a minority, against a big block shareholder, and minority shareholder protection rights are weaker (see Ch. 3(4)(e)). Another theory was that block shareholding was capital's response, building up financial power as a counterweight, to overly social democratic governments.[28] Though popular, there was never any credible legal basis or empirical evidence for these theories, since they were based on the World Bank's flawed understanding of company law, or the OECD's defective understanding of employment laws.[29] The reason for large stock markets (and dispersed shareholders) is the system and funding of a large non-state retirement system. More occupational pensions mean more assets under management. More assets under management means larger stock markets. Larger stock markets mean more dispersed shares. But in every system, asset managers and banks end up controlling votes.

(iii) Trustee and Fiduciary Duties

Like most persons or entities that manage other people's money (cf. Ch. 10), asset managers are trustees, owing fiduciary and other duties to their clients. The 'assets and moneys' they have 'are trust moneys held on trust for all or some of [their] investors'.[30] Unlike directors' duties, trustee duties are mainly not codified, but three main duties mirror those in company law (see Ch. 3(4)).[31]

First, there are duties to act within the terms of the trust, typically set out by a contract or trust deed, and only to act for proper purposes. If a trust document says a fund should invest ethically, it must. Trustees may also choose or limit investments (e.g. divesting from fossil fuels, or other morally repugnant investments such as tobacco and arms) if this accords with the purpose of their fund, or their beneficiaries' views.[32] In *Harries v The Church Commissioners for England*, Donald Nicholls VC (as he then was) held the Church of England pension could divest from South Africa, during apartheid,

[27] E.g. R. La Porta, F. Lopez-de-Silanes, A. Shleifer and R. W. Vishny, 'Law and Finance' (1998) 106 *J Political Economy* 1113 and 'Corporate Ownership around the World' (1999) 54 *J Finance* 471.

[28] M. J. Roe, *Political Determinants of Corporate Governance* (2003).

[29] E. McGaughey, 'OECD Employment Protection Legislation Indicators and Reform' (27 June 2019).

[30] *Barlow Clowes International Ltd v Vaughan* [1991] EWCA Civ 11, per Dillon LJ: 'it is accepted that . . . the assets and moneys in question are trust moneys held on trust for all or some of the would-be investors . . . who paid moneys to BCI or associated bodies for investment, and are not general assets of BCI'. In *F&C Alternative Investments (Holdings) Ltd v Barthelemy (No. 2)* [2011] EWHC 1731 (Ch), [223]–[225] Sales J (now Lord Sales) helpfully recounts general principles.

[31] *AIB Group (UK) plc v Mark Redler & Co. Solicitors* [2014] UKSC 58, [51] per Lord Toulson, describing the following as 'custodial', 'management' and 'loyalty' duties (cf. CA 2006, ss. 171, 174 and 175).

[32] Law Commission, *Fiduciary Duties of Investment Intermediaries*, No. 350 (2014) ch. 6.

since race discrimination and human rights violations conflict with Christian values.[33] If a fund is silent or purposes are not clear (e.g. the fund is not a religious or trade union entity), the only requirement today according to the Law Commission is that investments lead to no 'risk of significant financial detriment' – there may be some detriment, but not too much.[34] Standard financial literature shows that investing in just 20 different companies equals 95 per cent of the (risk reduction) value of investing in a full stock market index, and investing in just 100 companies achieves a 99 per cent reduction.[35] This means even large divestment policies may not be successfully challenged, as there are so many investment choices. Since most funds invest for the long term, divesting from fossil fuels is always lawful, because burning coal, oil and gas destroys the future. Arguably, it is a breach of duty for trustees to *not* divest from fossil-fuel investments, which now consistently underperform others, are destined to be worthless and so are a 'significant detriment' to the beneficiaries' long-term financial interests (see Ch. 11).[36]

The Supreme Court has further held in *R (Palestine Solidarity Campaign Ltd) v Secretary of State for Housing, Communities and Local Government*, endorsing the Law Commission's approach, that a fund's trustees may clearly take into account ethical concerns, of any kind, in choosing its investment so long as it 'would not involve risk of significant financial detriment'.[37] In that case, members of the Local Government Pension Fund made an application that government guidance, which said it could not divest from or boycott investments in Israel, be declared unlawful. The campaign group in the action opposed the military occupation of the West Bank by the incumbent Israeli government (which at the time, was run by a well-known liar[38]), and its policy to build settlements in Palestine in violation of international law.[39] The whole Supreme Court was agreed on the principles set out by the Law Commission,

33 *Harries v The Church Commissioners for England* [1992] 1 WLR 1241, per Nicholls VC, later Lord Nicholls; and see Lord Nicholls, *Trustees and Their Broader Community: Where Duty, Morality and Ethics Converge* (1996) 70 *Australian LJ* 206. The notorious earlier case, *Cowan v Scargill* [1985] Ch 270, where a legally untrained union leader made submissions to the court, was inconsistent, wrong and now overruled: [2020] UKSC 16, [43], per Lord Wilson (there was no dissent on this point). That High Court judgment followed the motivated reasoning of J. Langbein and R. Posner, 'Social Investing and the Law of Trusts' (1980) 79 *Michigan L Rev* 72, an attempt to justify decoupling Wall Street investment practice from the interests of investors. It is not UK law.

34 Law Commission, *Fiduciary Duties of Investment Intermediaries*, para. 6.34.

35 E.g. R. A. Brealey and S. C. Myers, *Principles of Corporate Finance* (3rd ed. 1988) 156.

36 E.g. '2019 Stock Index Results Show Fossil Companies as Worst-Performing Segment', *Energy Mix* (14 January 2020); B. Nauman, 'Sharp Rise in Number of Investors Dumping Fossil Fuel Stocks', *Financial Times* (9 September 2019).

37 *R (Palestine Solidarity Campaign Ltd) v Secretary of State for Housing, Communities and Local Government* [2020] UKSC 16, [43].

38 E.g. 'Sarkozy, Obama Bemoan Netanyahu over Open Mic', CNN (8 November 2011): '"I can't stand him any more, he's a liar," Mr Sarkozy said in French. "You may be sick of him, but me, I have to deal with him every day," Mr Obama replied.'

39 E.g. *Legal Consequences of the Construction of a Wall in the Occupied Palestinian Territory* [2004] ICJ 3.

and the majority held that government guidance against divestment and boycotts of Israel was ultra vires. Lady Arden and Lord Sales dissented on the specific point of the government's discretion in issuing guidance, and held that it was not beyond its powers to define the funds' non-financial criteria.[40] Plainly many people, including judges, have deeply held views on the long and desperately sad Israeli–Palestinian conflict, which are difficult to ignore. However, a key legal discrepancy between the majority and minority appears to be that the minority viewed pension funds as something belonging to the employer (or in this case, strangely, central government), but the majority explicitly stated that the funds represent the employees' money, paid for by their work, so the guidance against divesting by the employer was ultra vires.[41]

Second, the Trustee Act 2000 codifies duties of 'care and skill as is reasonable in the circumstance', a standard which rises for professional asset managers.[42] These duties are also a core principle of asset management in the FCA Handbook.[43] The primary purpose of a modern asset manager, of course, is to invest savings in shares, bonds or other securities.[44] It must have regard to 'standard investment criteria', which means diversifying the asset portfolio.[45]

Third, there are duties to avoid any possibility of a conflict of interest. This is the core fiduciary duty, tracing back to the South Sea Bubble (see Ch. 1(2)).[46] It ultimately underpins financial stability. As a starting point, this duty is strict and absolute, but at the same time flexible: a fiduciary must simply secure fully informed and true consent to approve what would otherwise be conflicted action.[47] The rule ensures that those managing other people's money put the beneficiaries' interests first, despite the profit-making nature of their business.

(iv) Governance Rights

What rights do the clients or the beneficiaries of asset managers have in governance? This depends on the asset manager's legal system. In the UK, the Companies Act 2006 eschews involvement. Section 126 states that no 'notice of any trust' should be entered on the register of members.[48] However, companies can require people to disclose their beneficial interest or voting arrangements in shares (see *Eclairs v JKX Oil*; Ch. 3(4)(a)), and

[40] [2020] UKSC 16, [62] and [80]. [41] [2020] UKSC 16, [30].

[42] Trustee Act (TA) 2000, s. 1 and Sch. 1, para. 7 suggests this can be excluded, but this is limited in relation to large asset management corporations (as opposed to family trustees, etc.) by the Unfair Contract Terms Act (UCTA) 1977, s. 3 and Sch. 2, depending on the parties' bargaining power. See also the suggestion in *Armitage v Nurse* [1998] Ch 241, per Millett LJ, that the duty to avoid conflicts may not be excluded, and also (1998) 114 LQR 214 suggesting gross negligence should not be excludable at all. Pensions Act 1995, ss. 33(1) and 34 (exclusions prohibited in regulated pensions); FSMA 2000, s. 253 (unit trusts); CA 2006, s. 750 (debenture trusts).

[43] FCA Handbook, PRIN 2.1.2: 'A firm must conduct its business with due skill, care and diligence.'

[44] TA 2000, s. 3, as if 'absolutely entitled'. Also Pensions Act 1995, s. 34 for pension trustees.

[45] TA 2000, s. 4. [46] *Keech v Sandford* [1726] EWHC Ch J76; *Bray v Ford* [1896] AC 44.

[47] See *Boardman v Phipps* [1966] UKHL 2. [48] CA 2006, s. 126.

companies can voluntarily recognise non-members as bearers of rights.[49] The original reason for section 126 was to ensure that companies are not embroiled in conflicts over rights behind those on the share register.[50] This leaves the duties to contract and trust law. Asset manager clients are often pension funds, but they may also directly sell pensions or life insurance policies to individuals or employers, or sell mutual fund products.

What duties do asset managers owe their clients? The Hampel Committee in 1998, which informed the UK Corporate Governance Code (see Ch. 3(3)), stated that 'an institution has a responsibility to the client to make considered use' of voting rights and recommended 'institutional investors of all kinds, wherever practicable, to vote all the shares under their control, according to their own best judgement, unless a client has given contrary instructions'.[51] Since 2012, the Stewardship Code from the Financial Reporting Council (FRC) has set out a list of 'comply or explain' duties that should create 'long-term value for clients and beneficiaries leading to sustainable benefits for the economy, the environment and society'.[52] It requires that asset managers disclose and report their policy on voting and stewardship, have guidelines on escalating stewardship activity and explain 'how they have sought and received clients views' or at least 'what they have communicated to clients about their stewardship'.[53] But this fails to articulate clear standards for following instructions from people who ultimately own assets, and arguably falls below the standards of equity (see below).

Since 2016 a group of pension fund trustees, called the Association of Member Nominated Trustees (AMNT), has organised a voting policy and sought to give asset managers instructions for how to vote on the shares their money buys. This policy sought minimum standards on environmental, social and governance issues. For instance, pension trustees wanted asset managers to use their money to vote against a company board if it did not have an environmental committee, did not comply with the Paris Agreement, did not ensure gender or ethnic balance on the board, paid the chief executive over 100 times the average employee, used zero-hour contracts or did not recognise an independent union for collective bargaining.[54] So far, UK asset managers have uniformly refused to follow instructions, leaving no market options.[55] Some large asset managers acknowledge a 'fiduciary duty to clients to exercise its voting rights responsibly',[56] but an express statutory duty to follow instructions is lacking. This means that case law matters.

49 CA 2006, ss. 145–6.

50 R. C. Nolan, 'Indirect Investors: A Greater Say in the Company?' (2003) 3(1) *J Corporate L Studies* 73.

51 Hampel Committee, *Committee on Corporate Governance: Final Report* (1998) para. 5.7.

52 Stewardship Code 2020, Principle 1.

53 Stewardship Code 2020, Principle 6.

54 AMNT, *Red Line Voting* (April 2016).

55 AMNT, *AMNT Review into Fund Managers' Voting Policies and Practices* (May 2019).

56 Legal & General Investment Management, *UK Stewardship Code* (2014). Updates have dropped this sentence.

The principles of equity were first set out in 1929, in *Kirby v Wilkins*. This held that where 'a shareholder holds shares as a bare trustee for a third person, he is no doubt obliged to exercise his voting power in the way that the *cestui que* trust desires', but can vote on the beneficiary's behalf until the beneficiary 'has indicated his wish'.[57] This was approved by the Court of Appeal in *Butt v Kelson*. According to Romer LJ, 'The right of a beneficiary, or of the beneficiaries if they are united, is to compel the trustees to use their voting power in the best interests of the trust estate.'[58] It follows that whenever a contract between the client and the asset manager is silent upon the use of voting rights, the asset manager should, according to these established principles, follow all instructions.[59]

Could asset managers exclude the duty to follow voting instructions on shares? This seems unlikely. First, the FCA Handbook for regulated financial institutions makes fiduciary duties mandatory. A firm must act 'in accordance with the best interests of its client'.[60] This 'imposes positive obligations on investment firms . . . [to] assess their clients' objectives so that their clients' best interests can be ascertained and achieved'.[61] This duty cannot be excluded or restricted, and a firm must not 'accept any fee or commission' which could 'impair compliance with the firm's duty to act in the best interests of the client'.[62] Second, the duty to act in the beneficiary's interests is part of the 'irreducible core of obligations' that in principle cannot be excluded.[63] Third, the Unfair Contract Terms Act 1977 applies to an asset management contract like any other.[64] It invalidates terms that limit implied contractual duties if they are unreasonable, by being imposed through bargaining power, by lacking transparency or when there is no market choice.[65]

A central problem is that asset managers concentrate astonishing levels of power into very few hands. The fund managers set the norms for shareholder voting. These norms will be carried out by each asset manager's corporate governance department, with three, five, or twenty people.[66] The corporate

[57] *Kirby v Wilkins* [1929] 2 Ch 444, 454, per Romer J.

[58] [1952] Ch 197, 205, per Romer LJ. Birkett LJ and Evershed MR agreed. The case is cited with approval in *Schmidt v Rosewood Trust Ltd* [2003] 2 AC 709, 734, highlighting a lack of distinction between the principles applicable in trusts and companies.

[59] E. McGaughey, 'Does Corporate Governance Exclude the Ultimate Investor?' (2016) 16(1) *J Corporate L Studies* 221, further explaining why it is irrelevant that money is held in pooled funds.

[60] FCA Handbook, COBS 2.1.1. [61] A. Hudson, *The Law of Finance* (2009) 230.

[62] FCA Handbook, COBS 2.12R and 2.3.1R.

[63] *Armitage v Nurse* [1997] EWCA Civ 1279. Cf. *Spread Trustee Co. Ltd v Hutcheson* [2011] UKPC 13.

[64] UCTA 1977, Sch. 1. The exception for contracts for 'creation or transfer of securities' does not apply since a voting right subsists in securities. *Baker v J. E. Clark & Co. (Transport) UK Ltd* [2006] EWCA Civ 464, [19] suggested UCTA 1977 did not apply to a trust, 'because a trust is not a contract'. It is unclear why this matters for the application of the statute, particularly in cases where contract and trusts are mixed.

[65] UCTA 1977, s. 3 and Sch. 2.

[66] S. Krouse, D. Benoit and T. McGinty, 'Meet the New Corporate Power Brokers: Passive Investors', *Wall Street Journal* (24 October 2016). Vanguard employed fifteen people for

governance department may take positions on selected voting topics, but they delegate much of the technical work of casting votes to a proxy adviser, invariably either ISS or GlassLewis. These advisers give standard recommendations tailored to the asset managers' preferences.[67] Another company called Broadridge largely monopolises the mechanics of voting. Fundamentally, however, it is fund managers who set vote patterns. Thus, a few dozen people control most of the votes in the UK, US and EU economies.

Asset managers have mass conflicts of interest. They cast votes in companies, but also sell financial products to those same companies, especially pensions for company workers.[68] This is self-dealing. Their business practice has been to inflate the fees they earn by encouraging collective pension funds to close, in favour of individual accounts with less bargaining power: 'smashing and scattering' pensions.[69] Asset managers support company directors 90 per cent of the time.[70] They oppose attempts to restrain spiralling executive pay, advance employment rights, control corporate political spending or stop climate damage.[71] They support mergers and takeovers, which leads to a concentration of industry and rising consumer prices.[72] This has been described as 'the major new antitrust challenge of our time' (see Ch. 6).[73] It is also a major challenge to economic, social and human rights.

(c) Pension Funds

The second main actor in investment is occupational pension funds. The 'three pillars' of pensions are (1) the state pension, which is a flat payment to everyone of £134.25 a week in 2020, from government (see Ch. 5(2)(b)); (2) occupational pensions, which aim to be proportionate to people's pre-retirement income; and

engagement and voting in 13,000 companies, BlackRock twenty people for 14,000 companies, and State Street under ten people for 9,000 companies.

67 See M. C. Schouten, 'Do Institutional Investors Follow Proxy Advice Blindly' (2012) https://papers.ssrn.com/sol3/papers.cfm?abstract_id=1978343; S. Choi, J. Fisch and M. Kahan, 'The Power of Proxy Advisors: Myth or Reality?' (2010) 59 *Emory LJ* 869.

68 This goes far back, e.g. J. Rifkin and R. Barber, *The North Will Rise Again: Pensions, Politics and Power in the 1980s* (1978) 114–16, explaining how Chase Manhattan managed a $423m pension for the tyre company, Firestone, and at the same time held 950,000 shares in Firestone. The former Chase president sat on Firestone's board. J. S. Taub, 'Able but Not Willing: The Failure of Mutual Fund Advisers to Advocate for Shareholders' Rights' (2009) 34(3) *J Corporation L* 843, 847: 'the greater the dependency of the Adviser upon the DC channel for asset management business, the less likely the fund family will be to support shareholder-sponsored governance resolutions'.

69 D. Webber, 'The Real Reason the Investor Class Hates Pensions', *New York Times* (5 March 2018).

70 D. S. Lund, 'The Case Against Passive Shareholder Voting' (2018) 43(3) *J Corporation L* 101, 124. Vanguard, BlackRock and State Street have almost identical voting guidelines.

71 S. Hirst, 'Social Responsibility Resolutions' (2018) 43 *J Corporation L* 217, 224–7.

72 J. Azar, M. C. Schmalz and I. Tecu, 'Anticompetitive Effects of Common Ownership' (2018) 73(4) *J Finance* 1513.

73 Posner et al., 'Proposal to Limit the Anti-Competitive Power of Institutional Investors', 2.

(3) private pensions that people buy into outside their workplace, such as in life insurance or mutual funds (see Ch. 4(1)(d)–(e)).

Occupational pension funds, unlike the state pension, build up a savings fund from a worker's contributions. Savings will be pooled with other workers in an enterprise, because collective investment means more money to buy more shares, or other securities, to diversify and spread risk. 'Workers' capital' was once the largest share of the stock market,[74] but since 1979 as wage inequality has grown, and labour rights were attacked, the wealth in pensions fell. So did pensions relative to other forms of investor in the stock market (see Figure 4.2).

What is the legal basis of pension funds? In UK law, many pensions are trusts, but they may also be corporations. A trust is typically established through a contract or a trust deed, that shows the 'three certainties' of the intention to create a trust, for certain beneficiaries and a certain property.[75] A trust corporation is incorporated like any other company. Many asset managers have also marketed so-called pure 'contract pensions', where the apparent goal is to evade trustee or fiduciary duties. This is not possible in law, whatever the market practice. If one person manages another's money, there is a trust, and it is highly doubtful that fiduciary duties can be evaded if a saver or investor lacks bargaining power.[76]

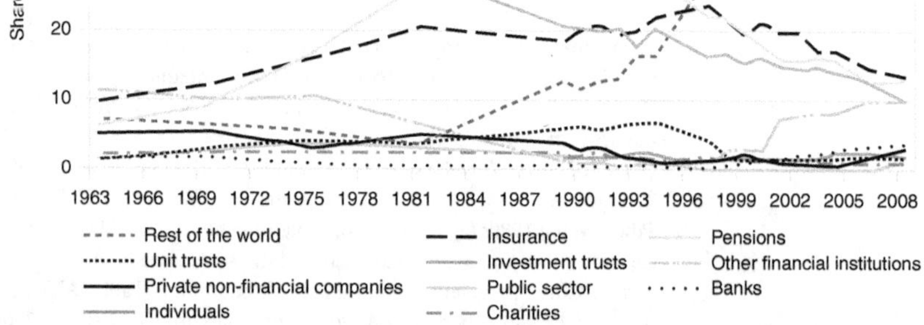

Figure 4.2 UK share ownership, 1963–2008
Source: Office for National Statistics, 'Share Ownership Survey' (2008) Table A

[74] D. Webber, *The Rise of the Working-Class Shareholder* (2018) chs. 1, 7 and 8.

[75] *Repington v Roberts-Gawen* (1881–2) LR 19 Ch D 520, per Lord Jessel MR: 'the modern doctrine is not to hold a will void for uncertainty unless it is utterly impossible to put a meaning upon it. The duty of the Court is to put a fair meaning on the terms used, and not, as was said in one case, to repose on the easy pillow of saying that the whole is void for uncertainty.'

[76] UCTA 1977, s. 3 and Sch. 2.

What are the governance rights of beneficiaries? According to the Pensions Act 2004, sections 241–3, at least one-third of the trustees or directors have to be 'member-nominated'. This may be raised to one-half by statutory instrument, but the government has not chosen to do it yet.[77] Either an election must take place among beneficiaries, or the independent trade union that bargained for the pension will codetermine the trustees. The legal requirement for member-nominated trustees was introduced after the Robert Maxwell scandal, stealing his employees' pension money from the *Daily Mirror*, before falling off a yacht and drowning.[78] After this, it was thought that employers should no longer have 'undue influence' over pension trustees, and the original recommendation from the report by Professor Roy Goode was for defined contribution schemes to require two-third member-nominated trustees.[79]

There are notable exceptions to the right to member-nominated pension trustees, which the Secretary of State may make by order. First, the National Employment Savings Trust (NEST) was established as a 'public option' asset manager, that could serve as a default fund for people who were automatically enrolled under the Pensions Act 2008.[80] It is also a trust corporation. All of its trustees are appointed by the Secretary of State. It is unclear why, now that it is running, it should be exempt. Second, older, collectively negotiated pension trusts have continued operating without any clear exception being made in law: notably the Universities Superannuation Scheme, which has three union-appointed, four employer-appointed and five 'co-opted' trustees. Co-opted trustees are supposedly agreed upon by both sides, but in practice seem to represent the asset management industry. Third, so-called 'contract pensions' are purporting to not be 'trusts' or 'trustee corporations' so as to evade the right to member nominated trustees. This practice appears wrong in law: all pension trusts start in contract, but it does not matter whether one means to create a trust in form, if there is the intention to do so in substance.[81] The right to member-nominated trustees serves a protective function, like fiduciary duties, and cannot be contracted out of by employers.

All pension trustees have duties to act within the trust terms, take care by investing prudently and diversifying, and avoid conflicts.[82] These duties mirror directors' duties (see Ch. 3(4)). In practice, most trustees delegate the task

[77] Pensions Act 2004, ss. 241–3.

[78] See Ch. 3(5)(a) and *Bishopsgate Investment Management Ltd (in liq.) v Maxwell (No. 2)* [1993] BCLC 814.

[79] R. Goode, *Pension Law Reform*, Cm. 2342 (1993) para. 4.5.40.

[80] Pensions Act 2008, Sch. 1, para. 1(1).

[81] Cf. *Twinsectra Ltd v Yardley* [2002] UKHL 12, [71]: if someone 'enters into arrangements which have the effect of creating a trust, it is not necessary that [they] should appreciate that they do so'.

[82] Pensions Act 1995, ss. 33–6. This essentially runs parallel to the TA 2000, ss. 3–5, except that unlike under TA 2000, s. 6, under Pensions Act 1995, s. 33(1) there can be no exclusion of the duty.

of investment to asset managers.[83] As explained earlier, BlackRock, Legal & General, J. P. Morgan, etc., will provide their services under a contract, and charge a fee, such as 0.5 per cent of earnings. Asset managers also give the 'service' (or realistically have taken the power) to vote on shares.[84] Usually there is nothing explicit about this in the contract, but the practice is pervasive. In the USA, many public and union-run pension funds perform their investment and voting tasks in-house, and express very different priorities from the mutual funds who dominate stock exchanges.[85] But in the UK, pension trustees have not yet taken the voting agenda back into their own hands.

Pension funds' share of the stock market has stagnated and declined since 1980 compared to other classes of shareholder (see Figure 4.2). While individual share ownership was in terminal decline over the late twentieth century, the relative rise of pensions up to 1980 coincided with growing wages through collective bargaining. Had this rate continued, pension funds would have accounted for a majority of share ownership by around 1997. The plateau from 1980 to 1993 coincides with the Thatcher government's attacks on collective bargaining. Even then, had pension fund beneficiaries been able to voice their preferences in governance, they could have commanded majority influence in every large company. From 1993, there was a rapid increase in ownership by the 'rest of the world'. But also life insurance plans and 'other financial institutions' (i.e. managed funds) partially displaced pension funds, as retirement schemes were closed or reduced (see Figure 4.2). Overall, the share of pension funds in the stock market has declined, a reflection of growing inequality and concentration of wealth since 1980.

(d) Life Insurance

A third main actor is life insurance funds. These are invariably also run by general asset management firms. Life insurance policies are different in legal form to pension trusts or corporations, but serve virtually identical functions. Over the mid-twentieth century, many people bought into life insurance policies as an alternative to pensions. This was encouraged by American businesses seeking to break into the UK markets.[86] Despite the name, life insurance will normally pay out an annuity (an annual payment for the rest of your life) when one reaches retirement age. If you are unlucky and die before retirement, your family would typically receive a lump-sum payment: the same is usually true in an occupational pension scheme. Just like a pension, one

[83] Pensions Act 1995, s. 33(1)(b) envisages that the same duties apply.

[84] E. McGaughey, 'Member Nominated Trustees and Corporate Governance', King's College London Law School Research Paper No. 2015-26 (2013).

[85] Hirst, 'Social Responsibility Resolutions', 224–7, shows tables of resolutions and voting records of support on political spending disclosure and carbon emission disclosure.

[86] L. Hannah, *Inventing Retirement* (1986) ch. 3, 'The Insurance Challenge (1927–1956)'.

makes regular contributions. The insurance company will accumulate assets, and invest them in order to generate a return.

What is the legal basis of a life insurance policy? While functionally indistinguishable from pensions, it is a contract, not a trust. However, duties are similar, and perhaps identical. Classically an insurance contract is one of utmost good faith, which entails open and fair dealing.[87] It has historically been denied that fiduciary duties are owed by one contracting party to the other. But it is not clear whether this distinction does, or ought to, remain meaningful, given the ongoing willingness of the courts to control abuse of contractual power. For example, in *Equitable Life Assurance Society v Hyman*, a group of life insurance policyholders, who had bought 'guaranteed annuity rates' (GAR), claimed that the directors of Equitable Life should pay compensation for reducing their insurance benefits.[88] Their 'guaranteed' rate was meant to be safe from market fluctuations, although they also received an end of year bonus. By contrast, 'current annuity rate' (CAR) policyholders received fluctuating annuities, depending on what the markets did. Sadly, the markets were performing poorly. Under the constitution, the directors used their discretion to reduce the bonuses for the GAR policyholders, to prop up payments to CAR policyholders. Strictly they had the power to vary bonuses under Equitable Life's Articles of Association, article 65, but the GAR policyholders argued the point of guaranteed rates was to protect against market fluctuations. The House of Lords held the directors' bonus-cutting breached an implied term to not vary the bonuses in a way that defeated the policyholders' 'reasonable expectations'. Lord Steyn said 'an implication precluding the use of the directors' discretion in this way is strictly necessary' or 'essential to give effect to the reasonable expectations of the parties'.[89]

The language of 'reasonable expectations' in *Hyman* dates back to Adam Smith's conception of the 'foundation of contract'.[90] It may be seen as equivalent to the duty not to act outside of the purpose of the contractual terms: like a director's duty under the Companies Act 2006, section 171(2).[91] Although the directors had a power to vary bonuses, their purpose was not consistent with the terms of the contract. But also, the directors of Equitable Life were concerned about the insurer's solvency, and therefore their own jobs. Because of their mistakes, Equitable Life had moved into a ruinous position. In seeking to preserve their own jobs by cutting one group of policyholder benefits, they were acting upon a conflict of interest, direct or indirect. This problem is covered in the duty in section 175(1). Conceptually, the construction of the proper 'purpose' of a person's power often entails a normative view about the

87 *Carter v Boehm* (1766) 3 Burr 1905.

88 [2000] UKHL 39, [2002] 1 AC 408.

89 [2002] 1 AC 408, 459.

90 A. Smith, *Lectures on Justice, Police, Revenue and Arms* (1763) Part I, Introduction; F. Kessler, 'Contracts of Adhesion – Some Thoughts about Freedom of Contract' (1943) 43(5) *Columbia L Rev* 629.

91 See Ch. 3(4)(a).

legitimate interests a director may pursue. In any event, the implied 'contract' terms begin to look very similar to the functions that fiduciary duties perform in equity. This may be why fiduciary duties have themselves been explained as implied terms.[92] Had those contractual duties been clearly articulated from the outset, the disaster of Equitable Life's insolvency, which did unfold,[93] could have been averted.

In many continental European countries, notably Germany, life insurance markets are much larger than in the UK. In the 1950s and 1960s in Germany, insurance-based pensions were held (based on vapid reasoning) to exclude rights of worker co-determination, analogous to member-nominated trustees.[94] This was a good reason for employers to offer insurance-based pensions. Related to this, there are significant cross-holdings between German banks and insurance companies, particularly Allianz, and banks' own ability to influence the voting on company shares. Insurance companies were traditionally heavily regulated in Germany, including minimum capital requirements. This has influenced the model behind the Institutions for Occupational Retirement Plan Directives.[95]

(e) Mutual Funds

A fourth main actor is mutual funds, also called 'managed funds'. Like life insurance, asset management firms often run mutual funds. At the back of the *Financial Times* are thousands of fund listings, in which people may invest. The legal form of most of these will be an 'open-ended investment company', or OEIC, pronounced as 'oik' for short. These function like any company, but have special Regulations.[96] The investment company is 'open-ended' because anyone can buy in and get shares, and redeem them. This adds to or subtracts from the invested capital. A 'closed-end' fund has a fixed number of shares that are traded.

What is the legal basis of a mutual fund? In EU law terminology, oiks are classified as one type of 'collective investment' fund, in the Undertakings for Collective Investment in Transferable Securities Directive 2009 (UCITSD). This requires that collective investment schemes are authorised by a member-state

[92] J. Edelman, 'When Do Fiduciary Duties Arise?' (2010) 126 *LQR* 302; cf. M. Conaglen, 'Fiduciary Duties and Voluntary Undertakings' (2013) 7 *J Equity* 105.

[93] See Lord Penrose, Report of the Equitable Life Inquiry (2004) vol. I, ch. 19 [86]–[88], [135], [137], noting the board committees' preoccupation with its own pay and appointments rather than risk management, and executives' failure to get reinsurance.

[94] The Federal Labour Court Decisions, BAGE 27, 194 (12 June 1975) 3 ABR 13/74, DB 1975, 1559 = AP Nr 1 zu §87. A. Hueck and H. C. Nipperdey, *Lehrbuch des Arbeitsrechts* (2nd ed. 1930) Bd II, §66 Nr 9. Cf. G. Flatow and O. Kahn-Freund, *Betriebsrätegesetz* (1931) 348, explaining the better view that the law was designed to constrain the one-sided power of employers.

[95] Institutions for Occupational Retirement Provision Directive (EU) 2016/2341.

[96] Open-Ended Investment Companies Regulations 2001/1228 (amended by SI 2005/923, etc.).

regulator.[97] In the UK, this is the FCA. They must also, for example, hold a minimum capital, have a separate depositary and disclose financial and performance information to clients.[98] The UCITSD says little on governance and voting rights,[99] except that article 19(3)(o) presumes member states will have rules on 'the exercise of unit-holders' voting rights and other unit-holders' rights'. The common framework of standards ensures that collective investment schemes can operate across borders.[100] Equivalents to oiks include Ireland's common contractual fund,[101] France's *société d'investissement à capital variable*, and Germany's *Investmentaktiengesellschaft*.[102]

How are the oiks governed? The answer is that they are subject to the Companies Act 2006 like any other company, but with a number of special rules that may displace the Model Articles. The members are those who buy into the fund. Under the Regulations, 10 per cent of members can call an extraordinary general meeting.[103] At this, like any company, directors might be removed, but also a simple majority may bind the company,[104] and therefore be used to instruct the company directors on how to conduct a voting policy. This could, in theory, be used to determine any mutual fund's policy to a greater degree than in companies where instructions require 75 per cent of the vote.

One of the central problems, however, in mutual, managed or oik funds is that even assuming policyholders wish to organise, information may not be readily accessible to enable them to do so. If policyholders are mostly individuals saving for retirement on their own account, a 'rational apathy' or 'collective action' problem arises. The costs of any activism by one person outweigh any personal gains, even if it would benefit the group (see Ch. 2(1)). On the other hand, in many mutual funds the investors may themselves be pension funds who have no such problem. If policyholders are willing and able to access information about their fellow policyholders, in law they have the right to control the fund's governance.

The asset manager who sets up the oik, and appoints its directors, is a trustee and owes fiduciary duties to clients. This was accepted by the Court of Appeal in *Barlow Clowes International Ltd v Vaughan*.[105] Here the asset manager,

97 UCITSD 2009/65/EC, art. 5. 98 UCITSD, arts. 5, 25, etc.

99 Cf. Shareholder Rights Directive 2007/36/EC, amended by 2017/828, arts. 6–8 (agenda, resolutions, voting), 9a (binding vote on pay policy), 9c (member control of self-dealing) and 10 (proxy voting).

100 UCITSD 2009, art. 16.

101 European Communities (Undertakings for Collective Investment in Transferable Securities) Regulations 2003 (SI 211/2003) regs. 20(c) and 66.

102 *Kapitalanlagegesetzbuch* 2013, §119. 103 OEICR 2001, reg. 34A.

104 OEICR 2001, reg. 39(1)(b): 'the power of such a company in general meeting to bind the company . . . [is] deemed to be free of any limitation under the company's constitution'. Such a phrase presumably refers to the majority, because according to the general law 'wherever a certain number are incorporated, a major part of them may do any corporate act'. *Attorney General v Davy* (1741) 26 ER 531, per Lord Hardwicke LC.

105 [1991] EWCA Civ 11.

Barlow Clowes, had gone insolvent after the accounting fraud of its founder, Peter Clowes, had been revealed in an investigation by the Department of Trade and Industry. Vaughan and other investors, who had invested first in the fund, were claiming that everyone should share in the losses proportionally, or *pari passu*, from their pooled fund. The court should not apply a 'first in, first out' rule to determine who lost money from the fraud.[106] Dillon LJ emphasised that 'the assets and moneys in question are trust moneys held on trust for all or some of the would-be investors ... who paid moneys to BCI or associated bodies for investment, and are not general assets of BCI'. It was further the 'presumed intention' of the parties that a proportional rule for sharing losses should apply (perhaps obvious, since everyone would share proportionally in the pooled fund's investment gains).[107] More broadly, this means that, as well as duties of care, duties to avoid conflicts of interest apply to asset managers.

(f) Retail Shareholders

A final group are 'retail shareholders'. Though the number of such individual shareholders has been in terminal decline, they remain important. Most High Street banks, like HSBC, Lloyds, Barclays or NatWest, will have a service enabling customers to buy shares for a fee. Individuals can tell the bank which shares they want to buy, and the bank will buy them on their behalf. They ought to count, therefore, as the registered shareholder.

In practice, however, banks have standard terms and conditions in their brokerage contracts, which may purport to limit shareholder rights. For example, the Barclays Bank brokerage service contract states: 'If you ask us to vote as proxy for you, we may refuse or agree on payment of a fee.'[108] As explained above in the case of pension fund voting, the demand of a fee for performing a duty violates equity and the FCA Handbook.[109] Major UK banks have not taken a serious interest in appropriating votes and exercising them, as asset managers have done. However, in the US broker-dealers (who are in the same position as UK retail banks) had become a significant problem.[110] This led to the Dodd-Frank Act of 2010, §957 abolishing the right of brokers to vote without instructions.[111] It was proposed in the US presidential campaigns of 2020 to extend this ban to all asset managers, unless they are following instructions on how to vote by their clients, and further ensure

[106] Cf. *Clayton's Case* [1814–23] All ER Rep 1. [107] [1991] EWCA Civ 11, per Woolf LJ.

[108] Barclays Wealth Management and Investment, *Barclays Terms: Your Agreement with Us* (June 2015) Section B, Part 5, 7.15; Part 7, 3.2.

[109] FCA Handbook, COBS 2.3.1R, duties to be performed without charging fees.

[110] Securities and Exchange Act of 1934, §14b and New York Stock Exchange's Rule 452, from the Great Depression prevented brokers voting without instructions on mergers or if it might 'affect substantially the rights or privileges of such stock'.

[111] Securities and Exchange Act of 1934, §6(b)(10).

that beneficiaries have the right to vote for representatives on how votes are cast.[112] The same principle was enacted into law in Switzerland after a 2013 people's initiative.[113]

(2) Equity Finance and Profit Distribution

The main goal of shareholding funds is a long-term, stable return from equity investments, just like funds investing in corporate bonds (see Ch. 7) or banks giving loans (see Ch. 10). But generally speaking, equity finance differs from debt finance in three ways. First, most shares carry the right to vote, and most debt does not. Second, equity investments have uncertain profits, while debts often carry a fixed rate of interest. Third, investments in shares rank last in the creditor queue if a company goes insolvent. These generalisations depend on law to guard the equity–debt boundary. If regulation breaks down, non-voting and multiple-voting shares proliferate (see Ch. 3(2)(a)). Shareholders may demand stable 8 per cent per annum returns by forcing directors to cut wages and jobs, or raise consumer prices, whatever the long-term harm. Shareholders may even create rights to rank over other creditors in insolvency (see Ch. 7(1)). Without rights in law, rights follow arbitrary patterns of contractual power.[114]

How much freedom do shareholders have to take corporate profits? The answer today is 'a lot', a fact entrenched as shareholders tend to monopolise votes in company general meetings. The default rule is that if directors recommend it, shareholders can pass a majority resolution to pay out dividends.[115] The key limits are that dividends may only be paid out of 'distributable profits', and from funds above a company's called-up share capital (what shareholders initially paid into the company).[116] These rules are designed to prevent asset stripping that would erase creditor security, though they amount to little if shareholders still monopolise governance. There are also rules to ensure fair treatment among shareholders, particularly those not in control. This section examines (a) share allotments and issues, (b) public offerings, (c) pre-emption rights, (d) the maintenance of minimum

[112] See Bernie Sanders, 'Shareholder Democracy' (2019) https://berniesanders.com/issues/corporate-accountability-and-democracy/ berniesanders.com.

[113] *Verordnung gegen übermässige Vergütungen bei börsenkotierten Aktiengesellschaften 2013* (Regulation against Excessive Compensation at Listed Companies 2013).

[114] Another way of putting this is that, absent prudent regulation, 'equity and debt are labels for different types of financial contracts': D. Kershaw, *Company Law in Context* (2012) 645. Cf. *Borland's Trustee v Steel Brothers & Co. Ltd* [1901] 1 Ch 279, per Farwell J: 'The contract contained in the articles of association is one of the original incidents of the share.' This makes clear that the contract is underpinned by the Companies Acts.

[115] Companies (Model Articles) Regulations (CMAR) 2008, Sch. 3, para. 70. Shareholders can instruct directors with a 75% vote. Dividend declarations create an enforceable claim in debt in favour of the registered shareholder at the declaration date: *Re Accrington Corporation Steam Tramways Company* [1909] 2 Ch 40.

[116] CA 2006, ss. 830–1.

and legal capital and (e) the extent of bans on leveraged buyouts or financial assistance to buy shares.

(a) Share Allotments and Issues

The power of a company to create shares is based on its constitution. A share reflects a 'proportionate part in the capital of the company' (i.e. the money and assets it holds).[117] First, if registering a company limited by shares, the incorporators who subscribe to the memorandum must make a 'statement of capital'. That is the number of shares, their 'nominal value', how much is paid and the rights the shares have attached to them.[118] For example, some shares may be 'preferential' and have rights to more dividends than 'ordinary' shares. All rights are a question of construction.[119] A share's 'nominal value' or 'par value' is simply a figure selected for a share (e.g. 10 pence). Its actual sale price could be above this (e.g. £2). The difference is the share 'premium' (i.e. £1.90). Shares cannot be sold without a nominal value being paid.[120] This rule is meant to ensure a company gets some money for its shares to create security for creditors,[121] but in practice it just leads companies to set low nominal values. Because it is so easy to evade, it is widely seen as 'an anachronism'.[122]

Second, once a share capital is created, shares must be 'allotted' by directors in accordance with the constitution (i.e. 'when a person acquires the unconditional right to be included in the company's register of members').[123] Shares are considered to be 'issued' to a person with the entry of their name on the register,[124] and share certificates may be given as evidence of title.[125] Directors are authorised to allot shares according to the constitution, but in public companies only for up to five years, before authority must be

117 *Birch v Cropper* (1889) 14 App Cas 525, per Lord Macnaghten; CA 2006, s. 540(1).

118 CA 2006, ss. 9(4)(a) and 10(2).

119 See *Attorney General of Belize* (Ch. 3(2)(c)). Also *Scottish Insurance Corp. Ltd v Wilsons & Clyde Coal Co. Ltd* [1949] UKHL 3, holding preferential shareholders, with higher dividend rights, had no greater claim to compensation from compulsory asset purchase after the Coal Industry Nationalisation Act 1946 (c. 59). Shareholders are presumed equal unless expressed to be otherwise: *Birch v Cropper* (1889) 14 App Cas 525. Cf. *Alliance Perpetual Building Society v Clifton* [1962] 1 WLR 1270, on whether shares are ordinary or preference shares.

120 CA 2006, s. 542 and Directive 2012/30/EU, art. 8. CA 2006, ss. 588–9: later shareholders are liable jointly with a prior shareholder for breaches of the Act unless they are a bona fide purchaser. CA 2006, ss. 584–7 enables a court to grant relief, if just and equitable, taking into account what is actually paid.

121 *Ooregum Gold Mining Co. of India v Roper* [1892] AC 125, common law rule against shares being issued at a discount below nominal value. *Mosely v Koffontein Mines Ltd* [1904] 2 Ch 108, applied rule to bonds that are convertible into shares. Cf. *Hilder v Dexter* [1902] AC 474, on options attached to shares.

122 See Company Law Review Steering Group, *The Strategic Framework* (1999): 'the requirement that shares should have a nominal value has become an anachronism'. Gedge Committee, *Report of the Committee on Shares of No Par Value*, Cmd 9112 (1954).

123 CA 2006, s. 558. 124 CA 2006, s. 554.

125 CA 2006, ss. 768–9 (certificate is issued unless conditions of shares state otherwise).

renewed.[126] The price of shares from initial subscribers to the memorandum in a public company 'must be paid up in cash'.[127] After this, in private companies shares can be paid for in kind. No public company can issue shares in return for a promise of services,[128] and if assets are promised, they must be given an independent valuation.[129] These rules, such as they are, are meant to protect creditors by ensuring some value is put into the company.[130]

(b) Public Offers, Accounts and Market Abuse

Public companies have special rules for disclosure, no conflicts and enforcement, from their 'initial public offering' (IPO) of shares, onwards. These rules are critical for systematic stability, as disasters from the South Sea Bubble, to the Wall Street Crash, to the Global Financial Crisis testify.[131] They persist despite evidence-free economic theories that capital markets are naturally 'efficient' and tend to reflect all available information, with or without rules of good faith and fair dealing.[132] First, when offering shares to the public, a company must publish listing particulars with 'all such information as investors and their professional advisers would reasonably require', or expect, to make 'an informed assessment' of the company's assets, liabilities, profits, losses and prospects, and the rights the securities have.[133] This general duty is overseen by the FCA.[134] Nobody can sell securities to the public without authorisation.[135]

Second, public companies must produce public accounts, subject to an independent audit, that show a 'true and fair' view of the financial position both in individual companies and company groups.[136] A significant practical problem is that accounting firms (usually PWC, KPMG, Deloitte or EY) are paid by the companies they audit. This is a direct conflict of interest,

[126] CA 2006, ss. 549–51. Unless constrained, share allotment is part of management: CMAR 2008, Sch. 3, para. 3.

[127] CA 2006, s. 584. [128] CA 2006, s. 585; Directive 2012/30/EU, art. 7.

[129] CA 2006, ss. 593–7; Directive 2012/30/EU, art. 10.

[130] But in private companies, see *In re Wragg Ltd* [1897] 1 Ch 796, per Lindley LJ, allowing any consideration to be given that is 'honestly and not colourably' agreed to. 'We must not allow ourselves to be misled by talking of value. The value paid to the company is measured by the price at which the company agrees to buy what it thinks it worth its while to acquire. Whilst the transaction is unimpeached, this is the only value to be considered.' If both parties know that what is given is insufficient this will be 'colourable': *In re White Star Line Ltd* [1938] Ch 458 and *Pilmer v Duke Group Ltd* [2001] 2 BCLC 773. This is an extremist laissez-faire view.

[131] On the beginning of modern standards and their need, see A. A. Berle and G. C. Means, *The Modern Corporation and Private Property* (1932) Book III. This was the blueprint for the US Securities Act of 1933 and Securities and Exchange Act of 1934, on which the FSMA 2000 and FCA are ultimately modelled..

[132] E.g. E. F. Fama, 'Efficient Capital Markets: A Review of Theory and Empirical Work' (1970) 25(2) *J Finance* 383, asserting without irony that his own 'efficient markets model stands up well'. No. It never did.

[133] FSMA 2000, s. 80(1). [134] FSMA 2000, s. 79. [135] FSMA 2000, ss. 21–6.

[136] CA 2006, ss. 393, 399 and 403–7 follow International Accounting Standards Regulation.

systematically compromising auditor independence. The law has not yet squarely confronted this basic problem.[137] One post-financial crisis, post-Eurozone crisis reform was to require rotation of auditors, but the maximum duration was set at ten years, from 2023, a period of time that would seem pointless.[138] However any duration where the auditor is still paid by the people they audit makes 'independence' somewhat difficult to achieve.

Third, the law prohibits all forms of 'market abuse' that create unfair advantages or disadvantages among investors. This includes 'insider dealing' (or insider trading), where directors, shareholders or other officers buy and sell securities based on 'inside information' unknown to the public. This is a criminal offence,[139] and any contract to do it will be void.[140] The market abuse rules also prohibit disseminating information that gives 'misleading signals' to others.[141] A central reason why this is a problem is that directors or managers are often shareholders in the companies they are meant to serve, and this has been encouraged for executives.[142] This is based on the theory that giving directors more shares or options supposedly aligns their interest with the long-term prosperity of enterprise.[143] The opposite is true: as major investors, directors attempt to inflate dividends and game share prices whether or not this is good long-term enterprise strategy.[144] They also have a greater incentive to commit crimes, including market abuse. Excessive pay and bonuses are a symptom of agency costs, not its solution. The law has not yet confronted the conflict that directors having large numbers of shares creates and required that directors limit or end investments in the enterprises they serve.

(c) Pre-emption Rights

New share issues increase the total assets of the company, raising money to expand or invest, potentially benefiting everyone. However, new share issues may dilute the relative proportion of total votes and cash-flow rights of existing shareholders.[145] To give the option to maintain their relative stakes, the

[137] Contrast extensive literature on how this basic conflict can be mitigated: e.g. J. C. Coffee, 'Gatekeeper Failure and Reform: The Challenge of Fashioning Relevant Reforms' (2004) 84 *Boston UL Rev* 301.

[138] Public Interest Audit Regulation (EU) No. 5372014, arts. 17 and 41.

[139] Criminal Justice Act 1993, s. 52.

[140] Cf. *Patel v Mirza* [2016] UKSC 42, a claim in unjust enrichment to recover £620,000 paid in an insider dealing.

[141] Market Abuse Regulation (EU) No. 596/2014, arts. 7–17.

[142] Cf. UK Corporate Governance Code 2018, 5.34, which now states pay for 'non-executive directors should not include share options or other performance-related elements'.

[143] E.g. M. C. Jensen and K. J. Murphy, 'Performance Pay and Top-Management Incentives' (1990) 98(2) *J Political Economy* 225.

[144] See the evidential and psychological basis for this, and the incentives to cheat, discussed in D. Ariely, *The Upside of Irrationality: The Unexpected Benefits of Defying Logic* (2011) ch. 1.

[145] E.g. if Adam and Brenda each have one share, they hold 50% of the company. If they issue one share to Chris, all now have 33% of the company.

Companies Act 2006, section 561 creates the right of current shareholders to be offered new shares first, in proportion to their existing holding. They have a right to buy shares before others, or 'pre-empt' purchase, within fourteen days.[146] Pre-emption rights do not apply if a company is issuing bonus shares, partly paid-up shares or those for employee share schemes, and private companies can remove pre-emption rights.[147] Pre-emption rights can also be annulled if the company passes a special resolution, with 75 per cent of the votes.[148] Larger companies often reserve rights to disapply pre-emption rights to company directors, a practice endorsed by the asset management industry. Major UK shareholders suggest the general practice is to allow directors to disapply pre-emption rights for no more than 5 per cent of total share capital each year, or 7.5 per cent over three years.[149]

(d) Profits, Dividends, Buy-Backs and Capital Maintenance

Ultimately shareholders want money from the company, but the law says they may only take 'distributable profits' beyond the 'legal capital'. First, profit means 'accumulated, realised profits, so far as not previously utilised by distribution or capitalisation, less its accumulated, realised losses'.[150] This is calculated by the company's accountants following 'Generally Accepted Accounting Principles' in the UK. It is not an objective, scientific process, but one based on political and social choices. For example, current practice requires companies to take account of foreseeable liabilities to tort victims (e.g. for asbestos injuries), but it does not yet require companies to take account of foreseeable risks and liabilities for climate damage, and the cost of decarbonisation.[151] If accountants do not write down liabilities, it increases what companies can call 'profit'.

Second, public companies may not distribute profits below 'the aggregate of its called-up share capital and undistributable reserves'.[152] This mainly means the amount that shareholders initially paid for their shares. For example, if a new public company held an IPO selling 100,000 shares at £1 each, its legal capital will be £100,000. If the company is successful – and it can be expected to declare consistently high dividends, or profits are reinvested – then the share prices will rise to, say, £3, £5 or £50 per share. The legal capital, however, remains the fixed level that was originally contributed. Public companies must also have at least a minimum capital of £50,000, a figure that has now been reduced in EU member states to €25,000.[153] The only reason for these rules on

146 CA 2006, s. 562(5). 147 CA 2006, ss. 564–7. 148 CA 2006, ss. 570–1.

149 Pre-emption Group, *Disapplying Pre-emption Rights: A Statement of Principles* (2015) following P. Myners, *Pre-Emption Rights: Final Report*, DTI (2005).

150 CA 2006, s. 830.

151 See proposals in R. Murphy, 'Sustainable Cost Accounting: The Case for Building Climate Reporting into Financial Accounting', Corporate Accountability Network (November 2019).

152 CA 2006, s. 831(1); Company Law Directive 2017/1132, art. 56.

153 CA 2006, ss. 761–3; Company Law Directive 2017, art. 45.

capital maintenance is to keep money aside if the company goes insolvent, in the faintly ridiculous hope that something is left for creditors, such as employees, customers, suppliers or tax authorities. The problem is that capital requirements do not rise with the company's riskiness or size, as they have been made to in banks (see Ch. 10). The drawback of any capital requirement is that it removes assets from the circular flow of income: it is a deadweight subtraction from economic investment, like hoarding cash under a mattress or in a Bermuda trust. There is widespread consensus that legal capital requirements are insufficient to protect creditors.[154] But there are sharp disagreements on what to do instead or as well. Some suggest abandoning all rules because the whole exercise is pointless. Others agree with the creditor protection aim, but instead of abandoning capital rules, workers and consumers or the public in specific enterprise should also have governance voice to prevent wanton profiteering before disaster unfolds.[155]

If companies have no more money than the legal capital, but still want to give shareholders a return, they may conduct a 'reduction of capital' and then pay out dividends. This means reducing on paper the recorded sum of what counts as undistributable capital. Private companies may do this with a 75 per cent vote of shareholders, and directors warranting that the company will stay solvent and pay its debts.[156] Directors may be held liable for a negligent statement, but it is unlikely that money can be taken back from shareholders even if the statement was wrong. Public companies require a 75 per cent vote and a court order.[157] The court may add conditions, for instance that creditors are protected with a security interest.[158] Shareholders of the same class must be treated equally in making capital reductions,[159] but preferential shares can be cancelled before other shares, taking into account 'the position of the company itself as an economic entity'.[160]

Share buy-backs are another way to give shareholders money: if a company buys 5 per cent of every shareholder's shares, this is like a dividend of 5 per cent of the company's value. However, buy-backs reduce a company's capital (e.g. from £100,000 to £95,000), and also tend to increase the price of each share.[161] The main reason companies do this is if taxation of income on dividends is

154 E.g. J. Armour, 'Legal Capital: An Outdated Concept?' (2006) 7 *Eur Business Org L Rev* 5.

155 Examples of major corporate collapses, firing staff, taking pensions or leaving the public huge bills include Carillion, BHS, Royal Bank of Scotland and the Mirror Group, etc. In all cases an extremely wealthy old man escaped responsibility and continued to live in excessive luxury while others suffered: Richard Howson, 'Sir' Phillip Green and 'Sir' Fred Goodwin. The exception is Maxwell, who fell off his yacht and died (see Ch. 3(4)).

156 CA 2006, ss. 641–4. A court may decide if directors are not unanimous.

157 CA 2006, ss. 645–53.

158 CA 2006, s. 646(4).

159 Second Company Law Directive 2012/30/EU, art. 46.

160 *Re Chatterley-Whitfield Collieries Ltd* [1948] 2 All ER 593, per Lord Greene MR. Also *Re Saltdean Estate Co. Ltd* [1968] 3 All ER 829; cf. *Re Northern Engineering Industries plc* [1994] 2 BCLC 704.

161 This is true if there are fewer shares, but the money paid to buy back shares is less than value in the company.

higher than capital gains tax: shareholders can game the revenue.[162] However, proposals to completely prohibit share buy-backs have not yet been enacted.[163] The original common law approach was to prohibit buy-backs,[164] but statute since made two exceptions if (like dividends) money comes from distributable profits.[165] First, shares can be bought back if they are expressly issued as redeemable shares under the company constitution.[166] Second, shares can be bought back if directors make a statement that they will be able to pay all debts, and this is approved by a special resolution.[167] The FCA Listing Rules require that shareholders in public companies all receive the same buy-back offer, and shares are bought back *pro rata*.[168] Once shares are repurchased, they can be retained by the company treasury, or cancelled: this must be reported to Companies House.[169]

While share buy-backs are not fully banned, 'disguised' distributions are. For instance, a salary payment to a director's wife who had done no work was a disguised distribution, and had to be returned.[170] A transfer of a property at half its market value to another company in the group was a disguised distribution, and the value had to be returned.[171] In *Progress Property Co. Ltd v Moorgarth Group Ltd*, the Supreme Court held that if a transaction is negotiated at arm's length and in good faith it may not be unwound.[172] However, it seems likely that if a transaction is at a significant undervalue this will be strong evidence that it was not a good faith, arm's length deal.[173] Recipients of unlawful, disguised distributions are constructive trustees.[174] For example, in *It's A Wrap (UK) Ltd v Gula* an insolvent company's directors asserted they were unaware that dividends they paid themselves were unlawful, because there were no profits, on the basis that their tax advisers had said it was permissible. The Court of Appeal held that ignorance was no defence, and the directors were liable because they should have known the dividends contravened the law.[175] If directors fail to take reasonable care, they will be liable to restore the money wrongfully paid out.[176]

[162] E.g. M. Jacob and M. Jacob, 'Taxation, Dividends, and Share Repurchases: Taking Evidence Global' (2013) 48(4) *J Financial and Quantitative Analysis* 1241.

[163] E.g. in the USA, Reward Work Act of 2018 (S. 2605).

[164] *Trevor v Whitworth* (1887) 12 App Cas 409.

[165] CA 2006, s. 658 reenacts the default illegality of buy-backs.

[166] CA 2006, ss. 684–90 and 735. See *Culross Global SPC Ltd v Strategic Turnaround Master Partnership Ltd* [2010] UKPC 33 (a Cayman Islands mutual fund could suspend share redemptions under its articles, but not suspend payment of redemption proceeds after giving a valid redemption notice).

[167] CA 2006, ss. 714–17. [168] Listing Rule 12.4.2–3. [169] CA 2006, s. 707.

[170] *Re Halt Garage* [1982] 3 All ER 1016, Oliver J.

[171] *Aveling Barford Ltd v Period Ltd* [1989] BCLC 626, Hoffmann J. [172] [2010] UKSC 55.

[173] See also Ch. 7(3)(b).

[174] CA 2006, s. 847; see J. Payne, 'Unjust Enrichment, Trusts and Recipient Liability for Unlawful Dividends' (2003) 119 *LQR* 583.

[175] [2006] EWCA Civ 544.

[176] *In re Exchange Banking Company* or *Flitcroft's Case* (1882) LR 21 Ch D 519 and *Bairstow v Queen's Moat Houses plc* [2001] EWCA Civ 712.

(e) Prohibition on Financial Assistance

One of the most important rules against asset stripping is the prohibition on companies financing other people purchasing their own shares.[177] In a 'leveraged buyout', a takeover bidder asks a bank for a loan, to be secured on the assets of the company they want to buy (but have not yet bought). Thus, a leveraged buyout is similar to buying a house with a mortgage secured on the house you want. However, unlike a home mortgage, in a company there are other stakeholders, including employees, consumers, taxpayers or trade creditors, who face consequences if a company is loaded with debt without their consent, and who will rank behind a bank's secured loan. To prevent risky loans, this kind of 'financial assistance' (i.e. the company's assets being used as security) for share purchase is prohibited for public companies.[178] But since 1981, 'take private' transactions became lawful: leveraged buyouts are allowed if the company ceases to be public.[179] This has fuelled the UK 'private equity' industry,[180] and added to the general problems of corporate takeovers.

(3) Takeovers and Transfers

Takeovers and transfers of companies, including asset sales, mergers and acquisitions, present acute problems for investor rights, labour rights (see Ch. 5(4)(c)) and competition policy (Ch. 6(2)(c)). On one view the 'market for corporate control', where people compete to buy up shares, is said to create accountability of directors. According to this story, if directors fail to perform well, the company share price will drop, and this raises the threat of a takeover bid (i.e. an outsider promising to pay a higher price to existing shareholders), and then removal of the board by the new shareholders. The potential for a takeover battle disciplines management to perform better. So, takeovers should be welcomed.[181] The contrary view is that this theory is 'wholly imaginary'.[182] Takeovers usually involve directors in their twilight years building an empire to aggrandise their self-image. They typically reduce returns for shareholders, but if they do succeed it is by reducing competition, and

[177] See Greene Committee, *Company Law Amendment Committee Report*, Cmd 2657 (1925–6) §30 and Jenkins Committee, *Report of the Company Law Committee*, Cmnd 6707 (1962) §173.

[178] CA 2006, ss. 677–8; cf. Company Law Directive 2017/1132 arts. 64–7. Formerly Companies Act 1929, s. 45.

[179] CA 2006, s. 678, after the Companies Act 1981, s. 43.

[180] J. Armour, 'Share Capital and Creditor Protection: Efficient Rules for a Modern Company Law' (2000) 63(3) *MLR* 355, 374, noting 'LBOs do have the capacity to harm creditors' and some are motivated by 'asset stripping', though the benefits to shareholders may be high.

[181] H. G. Manne, 'Mergers and the Market for Corporate Control' (1965) 73 *J Political Economy* 110.

[182] A. A. Berle, 'Modern Functions of the Corporate System' (1962) 62(3) *Columbia L Rev* 433, noting Manne 'did not live through World War I and the decade of the twenties, and the crash of 1929, culminating in the breakdown of the American economic system in 1933'.

redistributing wealth from consumers and worker wages to inflate short-term profit.[183] The social costs usually outweigh any private gains.

Of course, most recognise that neither absolute is true: some takeovers improve productive efficiency, for instance, by increasing economies of scale. Indeed, before World War Two, democrats and socialists encouraged merger activity to consolidate industry as a prelude to public ownership.[184] The possibility of enterprise being taken over by the public sector itself (as opposed to another private company) may be an important discipline device for private enterprise.[185] However, companies which could benefit from new management are often not taken over,[186] because improvement will take as much effort for new shareholders or directors as for the existing ones. Ultimately the impact of takeovers depends on who writes the rules,[187] and crucially which stakeholders control the process. Legal systems with stronger labour, consumer and investor (as opposed to shareholder) rights see fewer takeovers. Those dominated by directors, shareholders or financiers see more.[188]

In the USA, where the debate is most developed (and takeovers are most hostile) a first camp argues that directors should be able to block takeovers, to protect workers, consumers and others.[189] There should not be a metaphorical 'for sale' sign permanently on every company's lawn.[190] A second camp argues that directors usually just want to hold onto their jobs, and if they can frustrate takeover bids, they will enrich themselves.[191] They should not be able to influence takeover bids. If these were the only two choices, the second is clearly preferable: experience in the USA suggests that executives put themselves first, whether a few pay lip service to jobs and customers or not. But there is clearly a third choice: to increase worker and consumer rights, so all the people affected have a say.

[183] E.g. S. Deakin and G. Slinger, 'Hostile Takeovers, Corporate Law, and the Theory of the Firm' (1997) 24(1) *JL & Society* 124.

[184] E.g. F. Neumann, *Behemoth* (1944) 23.

[185] Contrast the position in UK bus and rail transport in Ch. 15.

[186] Company Law Review Steering Group, *Developing the Framework* (2000) para. 3.164.

[187] D. Kershaw, *Principles of Takeover Regulation* (2016) chs. 3–4 (on merchant bankers writing takeover rules in the City of London). Cf. J. Armour and D. A. Skeel Jr, 'Who Writes the Rules for Hostile Takeovers, and Why? – The Peculiar Divergence of US and UK Takeover Regulation' (2007) 95 *Georgetown LJ* 1727.

[188] J. Rudden, 'Largest Acquiring Countries for Mergers and Acquisitions (M&A) Worldwide in 2018, by Number of Deals', *Statista* (8 February 2021).

[189] E.g. M. Lipton and W. Savitt, 'The Many Myths of Lucian Bebchuk' (2007) 93(3) *Virginia L Rev* 733.

[190] See J. C. Coffee, 'Regulating the Market for Corporate Control: A Critical Assessment of the Tender Offer's Role in Corporate Governance' (1984) 84 *Columbia L Rev* 1145.

[191] See W. Cary, 'Corporate Devices Used to Insulate Management from Attack' (1970) 39 *Antitrust LJ* 318, listing six strategies, such as classifying boards, just cause removal of directors, requiring high merger approval, and suggesting 'if there were ever any traumatic economic turmoil in this country again, federal incorporation would be the next step'. See the Accountable Capitalism Act of 2018, §4 (S. 3348).

The basic principle of UK law, reflected in the Takeover Directive 2004,[192] is that the board of directors should remain neutral and do nothing that would have the effect of unduly frustrating a takeover bid. The Takeover Code, rule 21, states that 'the board must not, without the approval of the shareholders in general meeting, take any action which may result in any offer ... being frustrated'.[193] This includes any form of frustrating measure, other than attempting to persuade shareholders through reasoned argument, or attempting to find different buyers, if a bidder appears to the incumbent directors to be unattractive. In essence the non-frustration rule recasts directors' duties (see Ch. 3(4)) as a specific, effects-based norm.

Which frustrating measures are prohibited? A 'poison pill' means an amendment to the company's constitution to create options enabling directors to issue more shares once any bidder buys enough shares to approach a controlling interest (e.g. 30 per cent).[194] If that threshold is reached, every shareholder (except the bidder) gets more shares. This will impossibly raise the cost of a bid. This practice is widespread in the USA, but banned in the UK due to the duty on directors to exercise powers for a proper purpose,[195] the principle of equal treatment of shareholders as well as rule 21. 'Greenmail' means simply bribing the bidder to go away.[196] A 'crown jewels' strategy is where a company purports to sell a key asset to a friendly party, without which the bidder cannot run the business even if they gain control of shares.[197] Another strategy could be issuing a large block of shares to a friendly or controlled party.[198] All such measures are unlawful in UK and EU law. By contrast, in US law, centred on Delaware, directors can frustrate takeovers if they act in 'good faith' with measures that are 'proportionate' to the 'threat' posed to the company and its stakeholders.[199] In addition, directors are often entrenched in office, incapable of being removed by a majority of shareholders

[192] Takeover Directive 2004/25/EC, art. 9(2), but art. 12(1) allows member states to opt out of the rule requiring 'prior authorisation of the general meeting of shareholders' before frustrating measures. This was a condition for countries, such as Germany, that were unwilling to let shareholders monopolise takeover control.

[193] The Takeover Code (2018) rule 21.

[194] See M. Lipton, 'Takeover Bids in the Target's Boardroom' (1979) 35(1) *The Business Lawyer* 101; M. Lipton and A. R. Brownstein, 'Takeover Responses and Directors' Responsibilities—An Update' (1985) 40(4) *The Business Lawyer* 1403, 1422 referring to the 'Share Purchase Rights Plan' that Lipton devised.

[195] See Ch. 3(4)(a) and *Criterion Properties plc v Stratford UK Properties LLC* [2004] UKHL 28.

[196] Cf. *Cheff v Mathes*, 199 A2d 548 (1964) a director of a door-to-door furnace seller bought up the bidder's shares at an inflated price. The Delaware Supreme Court held this was a good faith, lawful use of company funds.

[197] See Ch. 3(4)(a) and *Howard Smith Ltd v Ampol Petroleum Ltd* [1974] AC 821.

[198] *Hogg v Cramphorn Ltd* [1967] Ch 254. The director, Colonel Cramphorn, issued shares to a supposed employee trust (which the board controlled) to defeat a bidder who apparently wanted to make large numbers of staff redundant. Buckley J held this was an improper purpose, as it was not to raise capital. Now CA 2006, s. 171(b).

[199] *Unocal Corp. v Mesa Petroleum Co.*, 493 A 2d 946 (Del 1985); *Paramount Communications Inc. v Time Incorporated*, 571 A2d 1140 (Del 1989).

unless there is a 'just cause'.[200] This inevitably leads to vast pay-outs or 'golden parachutes' to eject unwanted executives, to avoid even more costly litigation.

Underlying the non-frustration rule, there are six main principles in the Takeover Code.[201] First, shareholders of the same class should be treated equally. Second, there must be time for shareholders 'to reach a properly informed decision', including about the 'effects . . . of the bid on employment'. Directors should give shareholders information on the bid,[202] and not simply recommend the highest offer.[203] Third, the board 'must act in the interests of the company as a whole' (not in its own). Fourth, false markets must not be created in company securities, that distort share prices. Fifth, bidders should announce their intentions only when they have secured 'in full any cash consideration'. Sixth, a bid should not hinder the conduct of business longer than reasonable.

The limit of the Takeover Code is that it is written to protect shareholders. This mirrors the priorities of the Takeover Panel that administers and enforces it. Since 2006, the Takeover Panel's functions have been authorised by statute,[204] but it was originally created in 1968 as a club of shareholding institutions. Its decisions are subject to judicial review,[205] but its current governance, which is not transparent (nor remotely 'independent' as the website asserts), is dominated by City asset managers, such as the Association of British Insurers, Association of Investment Companies, the Pensions and Lifetime Savings Association, the Confederation of British Industry and the Institute of Chartered Accountants.[206] These bodies have no democratic structure to represent the ultimate investors in shares, through the vote, nor employees or other stakeholders.

Shareholders write the takeover rules, and they are unaccountable institutions, controlling other people's money. This is why the UK has faced a serious problem with takeovers that strip assets to the detriment of the workforce, and potentially against the public interest. In a notorious case, the American food and 'cheese' corporation, Kraft, took over the beloved English chocolate company, Cadbury. This happened after the global financial crisis, when asset prices were low. Kraft publicly promised it would not sack 500 workers at Cadbury's Somerdale plant. Then it bought the shares, and it sacked 500 workers at Cadbury's Somerdale plant. It threatened pay cuts, and destroyed its

[200] Delaware General Corporation Law, §141(k) enables companies to opt for 'just cause' removal if the board is classified, i.e. only one-third can be removed in any given year.

[201] The Takeover Code (2018) B1. [202] *Gething v Kilner* [1972] 1 All ER 1166.

[203] *Re a Company No. 008699 of 1985* [1986] BCLC 383.

[204] CA 2006, s. 942. The Takeover Directive 2004/25/EC, art. 4 required a designated 'supervisory authority'.

[205] *R (Datafin plc) v Takeover Panel* [1987] QB 815 held it was subject to judicial review because it exercised public power in practice, even before it was recognised in statute. No actions succeeded, but cf. *Ex parte Guinness plc* [1990] 1 QB 146 (Panel found 'insensitive and unwise'). See also, *Ex parte Fayed* [1992] BCLC 938.

[206] See 'The Takeover Panel: Panel Membership' at www.thetakeoverpanel.org.uk.

defined benefit pension claiming it to be 'unaffordable' (the present CEO of Kraft-Heinz is paid $27 million a year).[207] The Takeover Panel 'criticised' Kraft.[208] By contrast, the Competition and Markets Authority can block takeovers, or subject bidders to binding conditions, whenever it could significantly impede competition (see Ch. 6(2)(c)). This stands in stark contrast to the weakness of the Takeover Panel in combating abuse towards employees and other stakeholders, even though it could write rules to stop such practice at any time.[209] Rules 24 and 25 of the Takeover Code require the bidder to 'make the offer document readily available' to employee representatives, unions, pension trustees or employees themselves, explaining its 'intentions' and 'strategic plans', and for employee representatives to give their 'opinion'.[210] This does not address the issue, because it fails to give employees votes and a voice to participate in approving a bid and its terms. Staff are left only with minimal job security (see Ch. 5(4)).

The remaining rules on takeovers protect both minority shareholders and the bidder against exploitation. If a takeover bidder acquires 90 per cent of a company's shares, minority shareholders may require that their stakes are bought out at a fair value.[211] Conversely, the bidder may compulsorily purchase or 'squeeze out' the minority at the same price paid to other shareholders.[212] A shareholder may only challenge this if the price is held to be 'manifestly unfair',[213] if the scheme is designed to unjustly expropriate a minority,[214] or if other shareholders were not given enough information to properly evaluate the offer.[215]

A final point is that the Companies Act 2006 and the Listing Rules separately regulate major asset sales. As opposed to a sale of shares to effect a change of control, a 'transfer of undertakings' means selling the business, or parts, as a going concern. Large asset sales over 10 per cent of value or £100,000 must be approved by shareholders.[216] As we will see, this presents similar problems for a workforce, as it is largely deprived of a voice (see Ch. 5(4)).

(4) Corporation, Dividend Income and Capital Gains Tax

One of the most important reasons for investment and shareholding is to secure a stable and fair return, consistent with the public interest. Since the mid-twentieth century, albeit to varying degrees, it has been understood that shareholders are not entitled to simply maximise 'value', whatever the social

207 E. Rigby and N. Cohen, 'Cadbury Staff Issued with Pension Ultimatum', *Financial Times* (2 April 2010).
208 L. Lucas and A. Rappeport, 'Mergers and Acquisitions: A Bitter Taste', *Financial Times* (23 May 2011).
209 CA 2006, ss. 943(2), 945–6 and 952.
210 The Takeover Code (2018) rules 24.1, 24.2 and 25.9.
211 CA 2006, s. 983.
212 CA 2006, s. 979.
213 *Re Grierson Oldham and Adams Ltd* [1968] Ch 17.
214 *Re Bugle Press Ltd* [1961] Ch 270.
215 *Fiske Nominees Ltd v Dwyka Diamond Ltd* [2002] EWHC 770.
216 CA 2006, ss. 190–6.

cost, even though this had increasingly become a cultural norm since the 1970s.[217] Corporation, income and capital gains taxes together ensured that the public is 'an equal partner as far as profits are concerned' because while corporations 'derive their profits indeed from their own operations' they also do so 'from their market position and increasingly from techniques resulting from state expenditures of taxpayers' money'. Thus, the 'state is an investor in practically every substantial enterprise'.[218] On this view, the gains of investment should be fairly shared, though this depends on what tax rates actually are.

While tax statutes are vast, and each merit books in themselves,[219] it is essential to note three basic points of structure. First, corporation tax 'is charged on profits of companies',[220] which they report in their accounts,[221] as opposed to the whole 'income', revenue or turnover of the company.[222] This is what real people usually have to pay in 'employment income tax' (see Ch. 5(2)(a)). Set to rise to 25 per cent by 2023 in the UK, corporation tax is already at an historic low point, after a previous high of 52 per cent. The structure of both the Corporation Tax Act 2009 and 2010 is such that substantially their whole content concerns the exceptions to the duty to pay tax, and narrowing of the definition of profits or income on which tax is charged. So, for example, while section 5 states that a UK resident company is 'chargeable to corporation tax on income on all its profits wherever arising', sections 18A to 18S create exemptions for profits or losses of foreign permanent establishments.

Second, investors pay tax on dividend income, when companies declare profits. Under the Income Tax Act 2007, section 8, and at the levels in 2021, there is a dividend income rate of 0% for up to £2,000 of dividends, 7.5% when people's total income (including employment) is between £12,571 and £50,270, 32.5% when total income is between £50,271 and £150,000, and 38.1% over £150,000.[223] This means tax on dividends – that is, for doing no work but simply investing money in companies where other people work – is lower than the 20%, 40% and 45% taxes on employment income (see Ch. 5(2)(a)). This makes no sense.

Third, when investors buy shares or other securities, and later sell them at a profit (say, if a share price increases) the Taxation of Chargeable Gains Act 1992, section 1 requires that tax is paid on 'chargeable gains computed in accordance with this Act'.[224] This is generally 20 per cent on investment gains, a lower sum of money than dividend income. This may encourage companies to engage in share buy-backs, rather than declaring dividends. This makes no sense.

[217] S. Deakin, 'The Coming Transformation of Shareholder Value' (2005) 13(1) *Corporate Governance* 11.

[218] A. A. Berle, 'Property, Production and Revolution' (1965) 65 *Columbia L Rev* 1, 9.

[219] G. Loutzenhiser, *Tiley's Revenue Law* (2019) chs. 32–43, 59–68 and 73–4.

[220] Corporation Tax Act 2009, s. 2(1). [221] Corporation Tax Act 2009, s. 8.

[222] Corporation Tax Act 2009, s. 3.

[223] Income Tax Act 2007, s. 8 and see www.gov.uk/tax-on-dividends.

[224] Taxation of Chargeable Gains Act 1992, s. 1.

In addition to these rules, the UK government allows people to pay no tax on investments if they hold money in an 'Individual Savings Account', with deposits of up to £20,000 a year.[225] Thus, if someone invests £20,000 every year into shares through an ISA, they pay no tax on dividends or capital gains, and continue to do so as long as they wish, without limit. Again, this contrasts with the higher rates of tax on employment income.

(5) Conclusion

Unlike for company members, the rights of the true investors in capital are uncodified and unprincipled. This is a problem because corporate power is deprived of legitimacy when people who contribute to enterprise have no vote or voice. No credible theory justifies directors or shareholders monopolising votes with 'other people's money', though reform is slowly occurring. This includes the US ban in 2010 on bank-brokers voting on other people's shares without instructions, and the Swiss law after 2013 banning banks voting except on instructions from pension funds. Through statutory instrument, the UK could ensure a majority of trustees are elected in pensions or other funds, that all asset managers and banks vote on instructions, and that voting only follows instructions or policy decided by representatives of beneficiaries.[226] The present state of unaccountable governance drives the central problems in corporate finance, takeovers, falling tax receipts and the falling number of people who share in the prosperity of enterprise. The real investors who lack a vote and a voice are also often the same people as the workforce, consumers and creditors of enterprise, to which we now turn.

[225] Individual Savings Account Regulations 1998, as amended.

[226] Pensions Act 2004, s. 243, and FCA using its rule-making and enforcement powers.

5

Labour Rights

Contents

Even 'if your aim is not to understand all of law's effects on corporate activities but only to grasp the basic legal "constitution" or make-up of the modern corporation', wrote the former Dean of Harvard Law School, 'you must, at the very least, also gain a working knowledge of labor law'.[1] While many enterprises need capital and investment to start up, all need labour. Even in automated or capital-intensive industry, labour ultimately directs everything, and as US President Abraham Lincoln said in 1861, capital 'could never have existed if labor had not first existed'.[2] Labour rights shape the relations between workers, unions and employers (usually organised in corporate form). Without rights people are left 'at the mercy of corporations',[3] so modern labour law pursued two main aims: a floor of rights that nobody can fall through, and voice at work to get fair standards above the floor.[4] Rights replace primitive property and contract rules, because people with nothing to sell but their labour lack the bargaining power to 'hold out' in negotiations.[5] Unequal bargaining power begins with an unequal distribution of wealth, so rights replace these arbitrary patterns. As the Universal Declaration of Human Rights (UDHR) 1948 says, everyone 'as a member of society, has the right to social security', 'to work', to equal treatment, to 'just and favourable

1 R. C. Clark, *Corporate Law* (1986) 32.

2 A. Lincoln, First Annual Message (1861): 'Labor is prior to and independent of capital . . .'.

3 *Civil Rights Cases*, 109 US 3 (1883) per Harlan J, dissenting, that post-Civil War equality law was constitutional.

4 S. Webb and B. Webb, *Industrial Democracy* (1920).

5 A. Smith, *An Inquiry into the Nature and Causes of the Wealth of Nations* (1776) Book I, ch. 8, §12.

remuneration', 'to form and to join trade unions' and to 'periodic holidays with pay'.[6] Each right is equal to property and affects the quality of everybody's lives.

Labour rights are human rights, yet they have been consistently attacked in economic theory, particularly at the Chicago School (see Ch. 2(1)(b)). All labour rights, it was said, have the unintended 'consequence' of hurting the people they are meant to help, by raising costs to employers, who refuse to hire. The minimum wage, it was asserted, prices women and minorities out of a job.[7] Discrimination laws do the same, and unions are a price-fixing cartel that entrench unemployment.[8] Fair dismissal rights deter employers from hiring.[9] Even government's attempts to secure full employment by law through fiscal or monetary policy, it was asserted, will cause runaway inflation and therefore harm workers the most.[10] The problem is, none of these assertions ever had credible empirical evidence behind them. On the contrary, in a study of 117 countries, looking at forty types of labour laws since 1970, it appears that rights protection, job security, unions and votes at work improve labour's share of income, reduce unemployment and lead to greater productivity and innovation.[11]

(1) Management, Employment, Unionisation

Co-ordination of labour in enterprise today begins with a contract of employment. Employment contracts are currently the main 'gateway' into work, and to rights,[12] although there is no reason why rights in the future could not be based on a broader concept akin to membership or citizenship in the economic constitution.[13] The movement of society has generally 'been a movement from status to contract' in the past,[14] and today there is a movement towards the

[6] UDHR 1948, arts. 17 and 20–4.

[7] M. Friedman, 'The Methodology of Positive Economics' in *Essays in Positive Economics* (1953) ch. 1.

[8] G. Becker, *The Economics of Discrimination* (1957); R. A. Posner, *Economic Analysis of Law* (1973) ch. 11.

[9] R. Epstein, 'In Defense of the Contract at Will' (1984) 51(4) *University of Chicago L Rev* 947.

[10] M. Friedman, 'The Role of Monetary Policy' (1968) 58(1) *Am Economic Rev* 1.

[11] Z. Adams, L. Bishop, S. Deakin, C. Fenwick, S. Martinsson and G. Rusconi, 'The Economic Significance of Laws Relating to Employment Protection and Different Forms of Employment: Analysis of a Panel of 117 Countries, 1990–2013' (2019) 158(1) *Int'l Labour Rev* 1.

[12] J. Prassl, *The Concept of the Employer* (2016).

[13] E. McGaughey, 'The Future of Democracy and Work: The Vote in Our Economic Constitution', Sefton-Williams Lecture 2021, University of Toronto (2021). Membership, including in companies, does not fit the contract model of offer and acceptance. At best it is stretched, and probably broken, since it is fictitious to say that every existing member of a group 'agrees' to entry of a new member, illustrated by *The Satanita* [1897] AC 59, and see A. Burrows, *A Casebook on Contract Law* (2020) ch. 1. The consent-based element of a contract will always be necessary, but the terms are set not by contract but by law and members' votes.

[14] H. S. Maine, *Ancient Law* (1861) ch. V.

transcendence of 'rights' over contract.[15] Statuses fixed and often suppressed people's entitlements. Contracts are shaped by economic power. By contrast, rights are minimums that people build upon. Rights must, however, be made effective and properly enforced, either in court, through workplace institutions, or united action.

Employment contracts invariably subject people to the direction of management. In law, the contract is often with a company or other legal entity. But real people – directors, managers, supervisors – will fulfil management functions on that entity's behalf. Contracts also set the terms of employment and, where workers have joined unions, they will be shaped by collective agreements. The scope of labour rights, which override any contract term, depends primarily on who the law counts as an 'employee' or 'worker'. Independent contractors are outside this scope, but still have rights against the state or another party, and the practical boundaries are blurred. The next sections take (a) management, (b) the scope of rights, (c) the employment contract and (d) unions and their governance, in turn.

(a) Management and Delegated Agency

As we saw in Chapter 3(2), all companies have constitutions. Under the Model Articles, which companies follow by default, 'directors are responsible for the management of the company's business, for which purpose they may exercise all the powers of the company'.[16] Directors are themselves employees under a contract (below),[17] separate to their capacity as officeholders on the board under the constitution.[18] The Model Articles say that 'directors may delegate any of the powers which are conferred on them' by the constitution.[19] Delegation produces a chain of command, from directors, to managers, to supervisors down to shop floor employees or workers. A company itself may be part of a larger hierarchy, with parents instructing a subsidiary company's board members. Company groups are already treated as a single enterprise in accounting, tax, competition law and consultation laws.[20]

15 O. Kahn-Freund, 'A Note on Status and Contract in British Labour Law' (1967) 30(6) *MLR* 635.

16 Companies (Model Articles) Regulations (CMAR) 2008, Sch. 3, para. 3.

17 *Secretary of State for Trade and Industry v Bottrill* [1999] EWCA Civ 781, claiming insolvency protection. Cf. *Asscher v Staatssecretaris van Financiën* (1996) C-107/94, the Court of Justice holding a director and sole shareholder of a company was not a 'worker' with 'a relationship of subordination' in EU law. Also *Boulting v Association of Cinematograph, Television and Allied Technicians* [1963] 2 QB 606, Lord Denning MR, dissenting, suggested that in English law directors should not be employees.

18 *Southern Foundries (1926) Ltd v Shirlaw* [1940] AC 701 (see Ch. 3(3)(a)).

19 CMAR 2008, Sch. 3, para. 5, limited by duties in the Companies Act (CA) 2006, s. 171.

20 E.g. CA 2006, ss. 339–408 (accounts); Corporation Tax Act 2010, ss. 141ff. (group tax liability relief); *Akzo Nobel v Commission* (2009) C-97/08P (group liability for competition infringement); European Works Council Directive, 2009/38/EC, art. 2(1)(c) (duty to consult employees in transnational enterprises).

Who acts on behalf of the company or enterprise? To the outside world, real people perform the functions of making contracts, buying property or commissioning wrongs. Enterprises also have websites, apps, vending machines, computers and robots that are programmed to do their work. Apps and websites may even fulfil management functions, directing workers according to an algorithm.[21] But as a starting point, the Companies Act 2006, section 40 ensures that directors, almost always, are empowered to act on behalf of the company. The company is responsible for what they do. Previously this was more complex, as companies had objects of business in their constitutions (e.g. 'Apple Ltd shall only sell apples'). Actions outside the objects were held to be ultra vires, and void, leaving third parties (like a supplier or customer) with an unenforceable obligation.[22] Now, by default, companies are deemed to have unlimited objects. If directors' step beyond their constitutional limits, directors are liable for breach of section 171 to the company (see Ch. 3(4)(a)).[23] But towards a third party, directors are 'deemed to be free of any limitation under the company's constitution' unless the third party is acting in bad faith,[24] for instance by taking advantage of a company in collusion with a director in a self-dealing contract.

Generally, agency law determines who acts for the company. First, an agent (e.g. an employee) may have 'express actual authority' to enter obligations or transfer property under their contract or the constitution. Second, an agent may have 'implied actual authority'. For example, *Hely-Hutchinson v Brayhead Ltd* held that Mr Richards, the managing director of Brayhead Ltd, had implied actual authority to make a contract to indemnify Mr Hely-Hutchinson, who bought another company that later made losses. Brayhead Ltd claimed it had no liability for Mr Richards' deal. It argued the board had not approved it, and the power to make such contracts was not expressed anywhere. But Lord Denning MR held the power was implied, because the board 'over many months had acquiesced' in Mr Richards making 'contracts without the necessity of sanction from the board'.[25] Third, an agent may have 'apparent authority'. If there is no express or implied authority, a company can still be bound if a reasonable person would rely on the agent's representations that they have authority. In *Freeman & Lockyer v Buckhurst Park Properties (Mangal) Ltd* the company argued it should not be bound to a contract made by its director, Mr Kapoor, with an architect firm, Freeman & Lockyer, because its constitution required the whole board to consent expressly. Authority could not be implied.

[21] J. Prassl, *Humans as a Service: The Problems and Perils of Work in the Gig Economy* (2018).

[22] *Ashbury Railway Carriage and Iron Co. Ltd v Riche* (1875) LR 7 HL 653: a company with objects of making railway carriages could not give loans to build railways. Cf. *Hazell v Hammersmith and Fulham LBC* [1992] 2 AC 1, holding councils had no power to enter interest rate swap contracts.

[23] CA 2006, ss. 31 and 39.

[24] CA 2006, s. 40(2)(iii) has an effect similar to *Hartog v Colin & Shields* [1939] 3 All ER 566, snapping up an offer.

[25] [1968] 1 QB 549.

The Court of Appeal held the contract was valid (though the company could sue the director) because like 'an estoppel' Freeman and Lockyer reasonably relied on the director's representation that he had authority.[26] Of course, it is less reasonable to think agents have wide authority if they are lower down the chain.

How far are enterprises responsible for their employees or agents? Companies will often want to escape bad contracts, and will want to escape responsibility for torts and crimes even more. *Panorama Developments Ltd v Fidelis Furnishing Fabrics Ltd* held that a company was bound to pay £570 in debt after Fidelis Ltd's secretary, Mr Bayne, hired Jaguar and Rolls Royce cars from Panorama Ltd to go joyriding. He fraudulently stated they were for the director. Even though the company was defrauded, Mr Bayne had apparent authority, and his contract bound the company.

Can enterprises be responsible for people whom they do not directly contract with? The answer is 'yes', but the scope is uncertain because the law has not yet adopted a functional test for the scope of who is an 'employer'.[27] In tort law, it has long been established that employers must take the burdens of agents' wrongs because they take the benefits.[28] A 'business enterprise necessarily involves risks' and if 'those risks ripen into loss, it is just that the business should be responsible for compensating the person who has been wronged'.[29] This principle extends to subcontracted workers, even without a direct employment contract from a company. In *Viasystems Ltd v Thermal Transfer Ltd* a young man, Darren, clambered through an air conditioning vent; it collapsed, causing a flood on a building site. He was the mate of an employee of CAT Metalwork Services, a subcontractor of S&P Darwell Ltd, itself a subcontractor of Thermal Transfer Ltd, which was meant to fix Viasystems Ltd's air conditioning. That was a chain of six parties. The Court of Appeal held that CAT and S&P had 'dual vicarious liability' for Darren because both exercised equal control.[30] Civil liability for crime is the same. If an employee's action is either in the 'course of employment', or with a 'close connection between the torts' and employment,[31] or within the scope of 'enterprise risk',[32] then the employer is liable even if the wrong is the last thing the employer would authorise.

[26] [1964] 2 QB 480.

[27] Cf. S. Deakin, 'The Changing Concept of the "Employer" in Labour Law' (2001) 30(1) *Industrial LJ* 72.

[28] *Turberville v Stampe* (1697) 91 ER 1072, Lord Holt CJ holding a master responsible for a servant causing a fire: 'it shall be intended, that the servant had authority from his master, it being for the master's benefit'.

[29] *Dubai Aluminium Co. Ltd v Salaam* [2002] UKHL 48, [21].

[30] [2005] EWCA Civ 1151.

[31] *Lister v Hesley Hall Ltd* [2001] UKHL 22, [20] critiqued by S. Deakin, '"Enterprise-Risk": The Juridical Nature of the Firm Revisited' (2003) 32(2) *Industrial LJ* 97.

[32] *Catholic Child Welfare Society v Institute of the Brothers of the Christian Schools* [2012] UKSC 56, [65].

Criminal liability of a company for crimes of employees raises the issue of a company's non-existent *mens rea*, or otherwise the construction of any criminal statute. In *Tesco Supermarkets Ltd v Nattrass*, the House of Lords held that guilty knowledge should be attributed to a company only if someone with the 'directing mind and will' of the company had knowledge of a crime. This meant Tesco Ltd was not liable under the Trade Descriptions Act 1968 after a store manager failed to remove prices for washing powder that were higher than advertised. The store manager was not a 'directing mind'.[33] By contrast, in *Meridian Global Funds Management Asia Ltd v Securities Commission*, the Privy Council advised that Meridian Ltd was liable for two employees failing to notify the Securities Commission that they had bought a substantial stake in a company. This was because the statutory offence simply depended on when a person 'knows or ought to know' of buying a stake. Although the employees were acting covertly, their knowledge was automatically attributable to the company.[34] The Corporate Manslaughter and Corporate Homicide Act 2007, section 1 makes it an offence if a company is 'managed or organised' in a way that causes death and 'amount[s] to a gross breach of' what can reasonably be expected. This leads to fines.[35] Such sanctions against companies, however, are unlikely to motivate managers compared to personal liability (see Ch. 15(3)(b)). There is currently some confusion over whether the illegality principle (that one cannot have a cause of action out of one's own wrong) precludes a company suing one of its own directors. This matters particularly after a company is insolvent and a liquidator has taken over in the name of creditors. One case held that a company's liquidator is precluded from suing a director when the company was just one person.[36] Another case has not followed this,[37] and it would seem that this view is correct given a company's separate legal personality.[38]

(b) Scope of Employment Rights

Enterprise *responsibility* for its agents to the outside world is one thing, but to whom must an enterprise guarantee *rights*? The answers are not identical. This matters because while human rights in international law, including labour rights, are for 'everyone', UK statute draws a line between the 'employee' and the 'self-employed'. The genuinely self-employed cannot claim rights against an employer. They must rely on the state to frame a system of enterprise law that guarantees the universal 'right to work', to 'just and favourable

[33] [1971] UKHL 1, [1972] AC 153. [34] [1995] UKPC 5, [1995] 2 AC 500.

[35] *R v Cotswold Geotechnical Holdings Ltd* [2011] EWCA Crim 1337, a first conviction. An employee was killed in an unsupported pit. A £385k penalty, just enough to avoid making the business go bankrupt.

[36] *Stone & Rolls Ltd v Moore Stephens* [2009] UKHL 39.

[37] *Jetivia SA v Bilta (UK) Ltd* [2015] UKSC 23.

[38] *Singularis Holdings Ltd v Daiwa Capital Markets Europe Ltd* [2019] UKSC 50, [29]–[35].

remuneration', no discrimination, the right to unionise and job or social security. The employed/self-employed distinction is used for collecting income tax and for National Insurance Contributions (NICs) that fund social security.[39] But also rights have historically been guaranteed to 'employees' because they would not be able to bargain as it may be thought that the self-employed can. Thus, labour law is seen as 'an attempt to infuse law into a relation of command and subordination' – that is, between employer and employee.[40]

However, UK law has at least five statuses for the purpose of employment rights: employee, worker, jobholder, employment relationship and occupation. Of these, the first two are the most significant, and the most contested. Employees have all workers' rights, and workers have a more minimal set of rights (explained in Ch. 5(2)–(4) and see Table 5.1).

Who is an employee? Statute unhelpfully defines 'employee' as someone with a 'contract of service', but fails to define it. This points us to case law.[41] This matters because rights are at stake. If the definition of 'employee' or 'worker' depends on a contract's content, which an employer dictates, rights become illusory. So, the consensus has become that it must solely be based on objective factors, not the contract, in order to uphold the law's purpose.[42]

In the leading case, *Autoclenz Ltd v Belcher*, the Supreme Court held that a group of car valets were 'employees', even though their contracts stated they were 'independent contractors'. Mr Belcher and his co-workers claimed that they should be paid the minimum wage and get paid holidays. They cleaned and drove cars for Autoclenz Ltd, which was subcontracted by British Car Auctions (now BCA Marketplace plc). Lord Clarke stated three factors should

Table 5.1 Employee and worker rights

Employee	Statute	Worker	Statute
All worker rights	→→→	Minimum wage	NMWA 1998, s. 1
Dismissal protection	ERA 1996, ss. 86, 94, 135	No unjust wage cuts	ERA 1996, s. 13
		Working time rights	WTR 1998
Time off for childcare	ERA 1996, ss. 72ff.	Union organising	TULRCA 1992
Undertaking transfers	TUPER 2006	Equal treatment	Equality Act 2010
Insolvency protection	ERA 1996, s. 182	Whistleblowing	ERA 1996, ss. 43A–L
National Insurance	SSCBA 1992	Health and safety	HSWA 1974, s. 2
		Work pension[i]	Pensions Act 2008, s. 1

[i] Only for workers aged 16–75.

[39] S. Deakin and F. Wilkinson, *The Law of the Labour Market* (2005) ch. 3.
[40] O. Kahn-Freund, *Labour and the Law*, Hamlyn Lectures (1972) 7.
[41] Employment Rights Act (ERA) 1996, s. 230.
[42] *Uber BV v Aslam* [2021] UKSC 5, [75]–[78].

be considered: whether the staff (1) perform work for a wage, (2) are subject to the employer's control and (3) personally perform work.[43] Underlying this was a key principle that the 'relative bargaining power of the parties must be taken into account in deciding whether the terms of any written agreement in truth represent what was agreed'.[44] The claimants only needed to be classed as workers for wage and holiday claims, but they were also held to be employees. Later Court of Appeal decisions have sometimes failed to follow this,[45] which is regrettable since relations generated by contract should be 'of no consequence'.[46] The key principle is economic reality trumps legal drafting, to uphold rights.

Who is a worker? The Employment Rights Act 1996, section 230(2) says a 'worker' includes an employee or any other person who 'undertakes to personally perform work', or services that are not for a 'client or a customer'. Because employers have to make NICs for 'employees', there is a strong incentive to try and draft contracts to deny 'employee' status. But also from the staff member's viewpoint, self-employed contributions are 3 per cent less for non-employee workers too (see Ch. 5(2)(a)). This leads to cases where a workers' union attempts to establish 'worker' status for their members, but aims to leave the 'employee' question unanswered. In *Aslam v Uber BV* the Supreme Court held that drivers for the app-based transport company (see Ch. 15(3)(d)) were at least 'workers' and so entitled to the minimum wage and holiday pay. The drivers were providing work, minutely controlled and disciplined through the Uber app, and they personally performed work.[47] It upheld the Tribunal which stated that Uber was an 'excellent illustration of "armies of lawyers" contriving documents in their clients' interests which simply misrepresent the true rights and obligations on both sides'.[48] But the courts have not been asked to answer whether drivers are *also* employees. It seems they should be, as they are in most other countries.[49]

The vast majority of people at work are and should in law be treated as employees. Most workers are too. So, the critical dividing issue is: who is a 'non-employee worker'? The first leading case is *Clyde & Co. LLP v Bates van Winkelhof*, where the Supreme Court held that a law-firm partner was not an employee, but was a worker, and therefore had protection for whistleblowing on bribes paid by the firm in Tanzania to win court cases and get work. She personally performed work for the firm, not for clients and customers directly. Lady Hale also alluded to the need to interpret Ms Bates van Winkelhof's status

43 [2011] UKSC 41, [18]–[19]. See also *City of Montreal v Montreal Locomotive Works Ltd* [1946] UKPC 44.

44 [2011] UKSC 41, [35].

45 E.g. *Quashie v Stringfellow Restaurants Ltd* [2012] EWCA Civ 1735.

46 *Allonby v Accrington and Rossendale College* (2004) C-256/01, [72].

47 *Uber BV v Aslam* [2021] UKSC 5.

48 *Aslam and Farrar v Uber BV* (2016) 2202550/2015, [96].

49 E. McGaughey, 'Uber, the Taylor Review, Mutuality and the Duty Not to Misrepresent Employment Status' (2019) 48(2) *Industrial LJ* 180.

in light of the right to freedom of expression in the European Convention on Human Rights (ECHR), article 10.[50] A second Supreme Court case, *Pimlico Plumbers Ltd v Smith*, held that a highly paid plumber was a non-employee worker. Mr Smith did not have a right to go to Tribunal over the fairness of his dismissal (though this may not exclude a common law or equitable claim: Ch. 5(4)(b)) but had the right to holiday pay, sick pay and against wage deductions and discrimination. A significant group of cases concern judges, arbitrators and ministers: the proper position now appears to be that these people are to be regarded as workers, particularly where the rights at stake are human rights.[51]

By contrast, at the time of writing in *Independent Workers Union of Great Britain v Central Arbitration Committee* the Court of Appeal decided cyclists for Deliveroo were not even 'workers' (and not entitled to statutory recognition of their union) because their contracts allowed them to substitute other staff. It was said this meant (ostensibly) that the person no longer 'undertakes to personally perform work'.[52] This result is impossible to square with the *Uber* case or with *Autoclenz*; it is wrong, and contrary to principle. Most substitution clauses (drafted by the employer) should be irrelevant. If a worker substitutes another for one or more shifts, then logically the employer has two employment relationships. If the worker does in fact run a firm with their own workers substituted, this is a different matter. In sum, the better side of the cases say non-employee workers are those with higher bargaining power and pay: people who do not need core employee rights because they have the bargaining power to protect themselves. Only rarely are the genuinely self-employed not workers at all.

If it is agreed that someone is an employee or worker, who is the employer? Often enterprises function through groups of companies, subcontracting or looser networks. All labour rights imply a correlative duty that real people fulfil,[53] but there seems no reason why multiple parties cannot bear those duties, as in *Viasystems* (see Ch. 5(1)(a)).[54] In the context of employment agencies, where a firm subcontracts labour, there have been broadly conflicting judgments. However, the Court of Appeal has held that both an end-user[55] and an agency[56] may be considered employers. Arguably the correct principle is

[50] [2014] UKSC 32, [41]–[45], not deciding the point, as it was possible by interpreting the meaning of 'worker', despite the Limited Liability Partnerships Act 2000, s. 4(4) saying a partner is not 'employed'.

[51] *Gilham v Ministry of Justice* [2019] UKSC 44. Cf. *Jivraj v Hashwani* [2011] UKSC 40 (commercial arbitrator not employed for a discrimination claim); *President of the Methodist Conference v Preston* [2013] UKSC 29 (minister not an employee for an unfair dismissal claim).

[52] [2021] EWCA Civ 952, [2019] EWHC 728 (Admin).

[53] Cf. W. N. Hohfeld, 'Some Fundamental Legal Conceptions as Applied in Judicial Reasoning' (1913) 23 *Yale LJ* 16, 42–5.

[54] See also Ch. 7(5)(b) and *Chandler v Cape plc* [2012] EWCA Civ 525.

[55] *Dacas v Brook Street Bureau (UK) Ltd* [2004] EWCA Civ 217.

[56] *Cable & Wireless plc v Muscat* [2006] EWCA Civ 220; *McMeechan v Secretary of State for Employment* [1996] EWCA Civ 1166.

that the agency should be primarily liable for wages and all employment rights because that is what they are contracted for, but the end-user is jointly liable. This principle matters most if the agency or end-user is insolvent, or the wrong to the worker is motivated by bad faith.[57]

There are three other statuses for labour rights. First, a 'jobholder' under the Pensions Act 2008, section 1 is the same as a worker but is within pensionable age, from 16 to 75 years old. Second, an 'occupation' is a term used in European Union (EU) law, and in one unfortunate decision became relevant for who is protected against discrimination: the Supreme Court held that a volunteer is ostensibly not in an 'occupation'.[58] This decision must be regarded as wrong because it was made without reference to case law of the Court of Justice which has found volunteers to be workers (and therefore with an occupation).[59] It would further seem unacceptable that anyone can be outside of the scope of discrimination protection, since equal treatment is a universal right of 'everyone' (see Ch. 5(2)(d)).[60] Third, the 'worker' in EU law, confusingly, is probably the same as an 'employee' in UK law. It is used for free movement rights, and many other labour rights in EU law, although the scope is also frequently left to member-state definition. The UK, however, is unique in having such a disorganised system of labour protection, with three instead of two main statuses. Statutory reform is desirable. As in international law, 'everyone' who works personally should be guaranteed all rights.

(c) Contract of Employment

While everyone who works or gives services has a contract, only employees have a 'contract of employment'. In its basic elements it functions like other contracts. Rules of formation, terms, cancellation and remedies are often similar. But where any rights are at stake, the basic contract rules change to ensure the effectiveness of rights and to be more favourable to the employee who has less bargaining power.[61] As Lord Kerr said in *Gisda Cyf v Barratt*, the 'need to segregate intellectually common law principles relating to contract law, even in the field of employment, from statutorily conferred rights is fundamental'.[62]

All employment contracts can be formed by simple verbal agreement, but employees have a right to have them written down by employers within two months.[63] As employment lasts over a period of time, and both parties make an exchange of work for wages, new terms may be added to the contract without

[57] Cf. *Harrods Ltd v Remmick* [1998] ICR 156.
[58] *X v Mid Sussex Citizens Advice Bureau* [2012] UKSC 59.
[59] *Steymann v Staatssecretaris van Justitie* (1988) Case 196/87. [60] UDHR 1948, art. 7.
[61] Cf. Lady Hale in *Braganza v BP Shipping Ltd* [2015] UKSC 17, [18].
[62] [2010] UKSC 41, [39].
[63] ERA 1996, s. 1. *Stefanko v Maritime Hotel Ltd* [2019] IRLR 322 makes clear the right applies whether or not the employees are dismissed.

the need for strict 'consideration': if an employer assures employees they will receive a benefit, such an assurance will be binding.[64] All terms that conflict with statutory rights will be void,[65] but also terms will be voidable if they are an unreasonable and unfair term that undermines the employee's reasonable expectations,[66] or operate as an unreasonable restraint on trade.[67] If an employment contract or its terms are illegal, this does not prevent an employee claiming protection from statutory rights, since the purpose of rights is to protect the weaker party.[68]

The content of a contract in the UK today is mainly written by employers, and issued on a 'take it or leave it' basis.[69] This is because workers' collective power has declined with the loss of strong unions (see Ch. 5(3)). Employees rarely negotiate anything except trivial elements. Even highly paid professionals who hold out for more money have little input on other terms. The staff handbook is typically incorporated as a term into a contract, often by reference to a written and signed agreement. This can be useful to employees if it contains any rights, such as a right to take loans.[70] The contract will also incorporate any collective agreements. The result of bargaining by a union, collective agreements are the best method for contracts to not be unilaterally imposed regardless of the workforce's will. Important norms will include pay rates in collectively agreed wage scales, disciplinary and dismissal procedures or policies on intellectual property and privacy. However, UK statute has long stated that collective agreements are not themselves to be considered legally binding, unless expressly stated.[71] This old, unsatisfactory rule has led to problems as courts try to distinguish rules in collective agreements that create individual rights (and are incorporated) from those of an ostensibly collective nature that are not 'apt' for incorporation.[72]

[64] *CSC Computer Sciences Ltd v McAlinden* [2013] EWCA Civ 1435. It seems time for the general law of contract to follow the same path; there is dwindling support for estoppel never being used as a 'sword'.

[65] ERA 1996, s. 203.

[66] Unfair Contract Terms Act 1977, ss. 2, 3, 11 and Sch. 2; *Johnstone v Bloomsbury Health Authority* [1992] QB 333.

[67] E.g. *Herbert Morris Ltd v Saxelby* [1916] 1 AC 688.

[68] *Hounga v Allen* [2014] UKSC 47, finding a claimant could sue for race discrimination. Obiter, she could also have brought claims for unlawful wage deductions as a *quantum meruit*.

[69] See F. Kessler, 'Contracts of Adhesion – Some Thoughts about Freedom of Contract' (1943) 43 *Columbia L Rev* 629.

[70] *French v Barclays Bank plc* [1998] EWCA Civ 1092, loan could not be withdrawn without employee's consent.

[71] Trade Union and Labour Relations (Consolidation) Act (TULRCA) 1992, s. 179. Tracing back to *Young v Canadian National Railway* [1930] UKPC 94, 5. See B. Hepple, 'Intention to Create Legal Relations' (1970) 28(1) *Cambridge LJ* 122.

[72] E.g. *Kaur v MG Rover Group Ltd* [2004] EWCA 1507 (promise of no compulsory redundancies was not binding). In *Malone v British Airways plc* [2010] EWCA Civ 1225, a promise on cabin crew numbers not binding. Arguably no coherent division exists because collective rights improve individual circumstances, and individual rights affect resources that are collectively available. Arguably the proper meaning of the TULRCA 1992, s. 179 is that employers may not

Where terms are not expressed, or incorporated by reference, the law construes the gaps to be filled with implied terms. Traditionally, contract law has distinguished terms implied 'in fact' and those implied 'in law',[73] a distinction resting on a (sometimes chimerical) difference between reasonable expectations of the parties in particular circumstances, and standard expectations in contracts of different categories (employment, sales, tenancies, consumer, insurance, etc.). The parties' 'reasonable expectations' are at the foundation of contract,[74] and in employment the most important expectations of workers and enterprise are surely that statutory and human rights will be upheld. Arguably this means all rules of common law and equity should be construed in a consistent way.[75] But because the UK does not yet have a Labour Code (or, for that matter, an Enterprise Code) the implied terms of employment contracts are constantly evolving.

The two main implied terms that tend to favour the enterprise, by co-ordinating labour, are that the employer directs labour and appropriates the benefits. First, the right to direct, although it flows from management functions (see Ch. 5(1)(a)), need not be expressed in the contract to exist.[76] It means that within the law and express contract terms, employers have residual discretion to direct employees on how to do their work. Courts used to call this a 'master–servant' term, but it was recognised in the landmark case of *Wilson v Racher* that the distinct limit lies in the employer's 'duty of mutual respect'.[77] Here the employer, a landed aristocrat named Mr Racher, hectored his gardener employee, Mr Wilson about leaving string on a lawn, after he ran for shelter from the rain. Racher also falsely accused Wilson of avoiding work. According to the Court of Appeal, Wilson responded 'regrettably' by telling his employer to 'get stuffed, go and sh** yourself', and then walking off. But Wilson won his claim for unfair dismissal. That is, although the employer has a right to direct employees, the 'duty of mutual respect' means they must treat employees fairly and with courtesy. Racher's brazen contempt amounted to a constructive unfair dismissal (see Ch. 5(4)(b)).

Second, the right to appropriate the benefits of labour has been an embedded assumption of employment since the Industrial Revolution.[78] If employees work on the employer's property, or create intellectual property in the 'course of employment', it has been implied that the employer will have property over the things employees create.[79] On the other hand, a course of dealing can vest

enforce collective agreements against unions, and vice versa, but workers may individually enforce all rights.

[73] *Liverpool City Council v Irwin* [1977] AC 239.

[74] A. Smith, *Lectures on Jurisprudence* (1763); *Equitable Life Assurance Society v Hyman* [2002] 1 AC 408, 459; *Attorney General of Belize v Belize Telecom Ltd* [2009] UKPC 10.

[75] Support in *Gilham v Ministry of Justice* [2019] UKSC 44; *R (Unison) v Lord Chancellor* [2017] UKSC 51, [68].

[76] Cf. *Lister v Romford Ice & Cold Storage Co. Ltd* [1956] UKHL 6.

[77] [1974] ICR 428, per Edmund Davies LJ. [78] Cf. *Hutton v Warren* [1836] EWHC Exch J61.

[79] E.g. *Stevenson, Jordan & Harrison Ltd v MacDonald & Evans* [1952] 1 TLR 101.

property in workers. This is significant when combined with the right to direct, because it means that by telling employees what to do (e.g. work faster) the employer can unilaterally alter the consideration in the contract. A third, limited implied term favouring the enterprise is that an employee may owe a duty of loyalty if they are put in special positions of trust and confidence.[80] Because these implied terms deviate from the general law (that people have the right to liberty and own what their labour creates[81]), they should be restrictively construed.[82]

Numerous terms are implied in favour of employees, reflecting the courts' attempt to construe the law consistently with statutory rights. First, there is a right to mutual trust and confidence, the flip-side of the employer's duty of mutual respect. In *Malik v BCCI SA* a bank breached this duty by running a criminal operation, and so owed compensation to its (unaware) employees for their loss of future job prospects, resulting from the stigma of working for the bank.[83] Mutual trust and confidence is also called 'good faith' and is adaptable to many situations.[84] Second, there is a duty to pay wages whenever an employee is ready and able to work, even if no work exists or an employer is proposing to dismiss its workers.[85] Third, employers owe a duty to provide a safe system of work. While there are also statutory health and safety duties (see Ch. 5(2)(e)), the implied term meant that an employer could not require an employee to work overtime until he became sick, even though a discretion to do so was expressed in the contract.[86] In this way, implied rights can cut down or even override express contract terms.[87] Fourth, the Supreme Court has held, confirming *Wilson v Racher*, that employees have an implied right to a fair process before any dismissal.[88]

What if an employer wants to change the terms of the contract of employment? The basic principle, since *Rigby v Ferodo Ltd*, is that there can be no change without the consent of all parties.[89] Even if a contract contains 'flexibility' clauses that purport to allow the employer to unilaterally vary terms, the courts have stated that they will not allow a variation that is unreasonable.[90]

80 *Attorney General v Blake* [2000] UKHL 45; but contrast *Nottingham University v Fishel* [2000] IRLR 471.
81 E.g. ECHR 1950, arts. 5 and 10 and Prot. 1, art. 1; *Hutton v Warren* [1836] EWHC J61.
82 Cf. *Pfeiffer v Deutsches Rotes Kreuz* (2005) C-397/01, [82] and [116] and *contra proferentem*.
83 *Malik and Mahmud v Bank of Credit and Commerce International SA* [1997] UKHL 23.
84 *Eastwood v Magnox Electric plc* [2004] UKHL 35.
85 *Devonald v Rosser & Sons* [1906] 2 KB 728. See also E. McGaughey, 'Are Zero Hours Contracts Lawful?', SSRN Paper (2014).
86 *Johnstone v Bloomsbury HA* [1992] QB 333, Browne-Wilkinson LJ.
87 See also *Attorney General of Belize v Belize Telecom Ltd* [2009] UKPC 10, at Ch. 3(3)(a).
88 *West London Mental Health NHS Trust v Chhabra* [2013] UKSC 80, [37].
89 *Rigby v Ferodo Ltd* [1988] ICR 29, a lathe operator could refuse to accept a 5% wage cut, keep working and claim the money back later as an unlawful deduction.
90 *Wandsworth LBC v D'Silva* [1998] IRLR 193, per Lord Woolf MR. Cf. *Bateman v ASDA Stores Ltd* [2010] IRLR 370.

This is best seen as an extension of the principle that terms are construed to reflect the parties' reasonable expectations: no power in a contract, express or implied, should be used to undermine an employee's expectations or rights.

(d) Unions

Acting alone, employees and workers will be largely subject to the authority and discretion of their employers, so people form unions. The five main functions of unions are to provide services to their members such as insurance or legal advice;[91] to represent them in negotiations with management, particularly to improve pay; to regulate the workplace by upholding rights; to give political representation; and to take part in public administration.[92] Without unions, employees typically lack the resources to 'hold out' in negotiations.[93] Employers will be in a position to take most of the gains from production.[94] Over time this has left most UK employees with wages ever closer to the minimum (see Ch. 5(2)(a)). Also, as union membership in the UK was attacked and has fallen since 1979, inequality has risen as a virtual mirror image (see Figure 5.1).

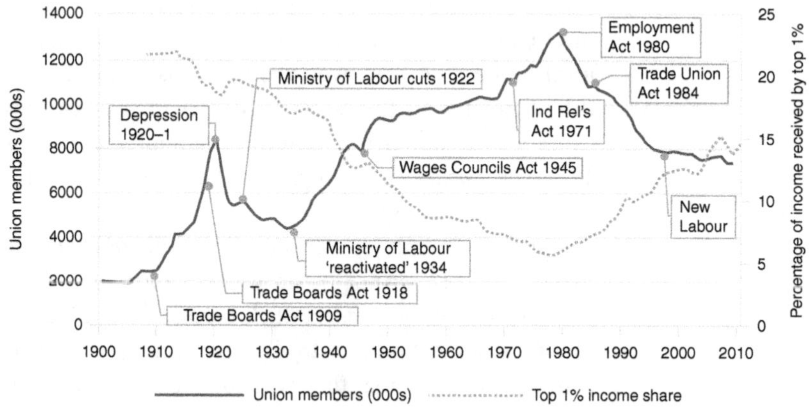

Figure 5.1 UK union membership and income inequality, 1900–2010
Source: N. Brownlie, *Trade Union Membership 2011* (2012) 22–3; T. Piketty, *Capital in the Twenty-First Century* (2014) Tech. Appendices, Table S9.2

91 Cf. E. McGaughey, 'Unions' Freedom to Establish and Provide Services' in T. Papadopoulos (ed.), *Cross-Border Mergers: EU Perspectives and National Experiences* (2019) 171, on union protection in EU law.

92 K. D. Ewing, 'The Function of Trade Unions' (2005) 34 *Industrial LJ* 1.

93 Smith, *Wealth of Nations*, Book I, ch. 8; and see Ch. 2(2)(f).

94 This is an empirically verifiable fact. Notably Epstein, 'In Defense of the Contract at Will', argued (disingenuously) that if bargaining power really existed, then workers' wages would depress. They did.

The same pattern holds true in all countries where unions are the main channel for voice, but not in countries with the strongest worker voting rights for boards (see Ch. 5(3)(a)). Full employment may raise all workers' bargaining power individually. But full employment has not existed in the UK, or other EU and Commonwealth countries since 1973 (see Ch. 5(4)(a)). Full employment resulted partly from unions' greater political influence. Unions' role in human development is the reason that 'freedom of association' is a fundamental human right, for instance under the ECHR, article 11. This includes the right to organise unions, collectively bargain and strike.[95] In the UK, the Human Rights Act 1998, section 3 requires all statutes, common law and equity to be interpreted in line with European Convention rights, including trade union freedom in article 11. Section 4 requires courts to declare legislation incompatible if they cannot interpret statute compatibly (common law and equity *always* can be). Section 6 requires public bodies, including courts, to act compatibly with the Convention.[96]

How are unions constituted? Like companies, union rules have been heavily regulated, now in the Trade Union and Labour Relations (Consolidation) Act 1992. Section 1 says an association is a 'trade union' if its 'principal purpose includes the regulation of relations between workers' and employers or other unions. The UK Certification Officer may give a union a certificate of independence, that warrants it is not unduly influenced by an employer.[97] Unions have freedom to draw up their own rules,[98] subject to the duties of democratic governance in the Act. However, the law does not provide a model constitution.

Three main groups of union member rights are to vote, to fair standards of treatment and of entry and exit from the union. First, a union executive body must be directly elected by its members, at least every five years, as must its general secretary or president.[99] A member's right to vote is guaranteed by law, and they may bring a claim if they are unreasonably excluded.[100] Second, the constitution binds everyone unless it is validly changed. Any member may bring a claim for enforcement of the union rule book. For instance, in *Edwards v Halliwell*, a National Union of Vehicle Builders member claimed that a union fee rise was ultra vires. His union's rule 19 required a two-third majority ballot. There was no ballot, so he won.[101] Union members also have a right to not be unjustifiably disciplined.[102] For instance, a union member who fell behind

[95] ECHR 1950, art. 11; Charter of Fundamental Rights of the EU 2000, arts. 12 and 28; UDHR 1948, arts. 20 and 23(4); ICCPR 1966, art. 22(1); ICESCR 1966, art. 8.

[96] Human Rights Act 1998, ss. 3, 4 and 6. [97] TULRCA 1992, ss. 5–8.

[98] ILO Freedom of Association and Protection of the Right to Organise Convention 1948 (c. 87) art. 3(1), reflecting the idea of 'freedom of contract' in English law.

[99] TULRCA 1992, ss. 46 and 50.

[100] *Breen v Amalgamated Engineering Union* [1971] 2 QB 175. [101] [1950] 2 All ER 1064.

[102] TULRCA 1992, ss. 64–7.

in membership fees was held to have been unjustly excluded: they should have been allowed to make up arrears.[103]

Third, people have the right to enter and exit the union. Unions, of course will usually be happy to welcome members with common goals. But they need not admit members whose values are opposed, for instance fascist, sexist or racist activists.[104] More importantly, employers may wish to deter workers from joining unions. In *Wilson v United Kingdom*, the European Court of Human Rights held that the UK had failed to sufficiently protect an employee at the *Daily Mail* from being subject to detriment. Everyone was offered a pay rise if they agreed to leave a collective agreement negotiated by the union. Mr Wilson refused. He got no rise. The UK legislation at the time did not explicitly prevent this, and so the UK stood in violation of Mr Wilson's right to freedom of association under article 11.[105]

Workers may also exit unions. Since 1980 it has been unlawful in the UK,[106] and shortly after it was held incompatible with the European Convention,[107] to have a 'closed shop', where unions signed collective agreements with employers to require that all employees are union members.[108] There are important historical reasons for not compelling people to belong to an association. For example, the Nazi-controlled German Labour Front compelled everyone to join.[109] But it is not entirely clear that it is a human right to not be in an association when one voluntarily undertakes a job, if the employer makes clear that the two go hand in hand. There is a right to negatively associate by taking another job.[110] Lawyers in the UK, of course, have no right to not associate with the Law Society or the Bar Council. This said, there is no clamour for a return to the closed shop. By contrast, there are very strong arguments in favour of employees being automatically enrolled in a union, with the right to opt out, when they start a job. Many want to join unions for the security it affords, but the status quo bias leads many to not join, irrationally lowering participation rates. Auto-enrolment is compatible with freedom of association, and is found in student unions.[111]

103 *Bonsor v Musicians' Union* [1956] AC 104. This was especially important as there used to be a closed shop.

104 *ASLEF v United Kingdom* [2007] ECHR 184 held the union was entitled to exclude a BNP activist. Contrary to ECHR, art. 11, the UK had failed to properly protect the union's autonomy with a blanket ban on unions discriminating against members on grounds of political affiliation. TULRCA 1992, s. 174 is now updated.

105 [2002] ECHR 552. TULRCA 1992, ss. 146–8 updated the prohibition on detriment to employees. Cf. ILO Right to Organise Convention 1949 (c. 98) art. 1 and Workers' Representatives Convention 1971 (c. 135) art. 1.

106 TULRCA 1992, s. 146(1)(c) first introduced in the Employment Act 1980.

107 *Young, James and Webster v United Kingdom* [1981] ECHR 4 held that it was unlawful for the British Railways Board to dismiss 57 workers who were not members of the three main unions.

108 Famous old cases revolving around the closed shop include *Crofter Hand Woven Harris Tweed Co. Ltd v Veitch* [1942] AC 435 and *Morgan v Fry* [1968] 2 QB 710.

109 F. Neumann, *Behemoth* (1944) 340.

110 Cf. UDHR 1948, art. 20(2).

111 Education Act 1994, s. 22(2)(c).

(2) The Minimum Floor of Rights

Labour law mainly concerns relations between managements, workers and unions, but the state plays two overarching roles. It sets a minimum floor of rights, and it guarantees voice and votes at work to achieve fair standards beyond that minimum. The three main functions of these rights are to ensure justice and fairness at work; to ensure that businesses compete 'on the merits',[112] not by wage cutting; and to guarantee the material security for people to participate in political and social life. This section discusses the rights to (a) wages and taxes on income; (b) the state pension and occupational pensions; (c) fair working time, including paid holidays and childcare; (d) equal treatment, regardless of gender, race, belief and other characteristics; (e) health and safety; and (f) civil liberties, such as privacy and expression.

(a) Wages and Income Tax

International law enshrines the right to 'just and favourable remuneration', and 'fair wages',[113] but modern UK statute does not yet uphold more than a minimum wage. Historically, a statutory system of fair wage scales, not just a minimum, was achieved by active government.[114] It was cross-party policy to encourage employers and unions to reach a collective agreement,[115] but if they failed to do so, the Secretary of State could fix terms and conditions of work through wages councils.[116] In effect, the democratic process set fair wage scales as a default, instead of the market imposing arbitrary wages upon staff with 'deficient bargaining power'.[117] Fair wage scales supported the systems of bargaining and voice at work.

The fair wage system was abolished by Prime Minister Thatcher, and in its place Prime Minister Blair restored only the National Minimum Wage Act 1998. Section 1 creates a right for every 'worker' to receive the minimum wage, which in 2021 was £8.91 an hour for people over 23 years old.[118] This is typically measured by how many hours people are working or must be available for work, including being on call.[119] However (and inconsistently

[112] *Intel v Commission* (2017) C-413/14 P, [133]–[134].

[113] UDHR 1948, art. 23(3); ICESCR 1966, art. 7(a).

[114] English common law failed to articulate any coherent sense of fair wages, but in Australia, *Ex parte HV McKay* (1907) 2 CAR 1, Higgins J held a 'fair and reasonable' wage was one that a hypothetical collective agreement would reach, reflecting the needs of 'a human being in a civilised community'.

[115] K. D. Ewing, 'The State and Industrial Relations: "Collective Laissez-Faire" Revisited' (1998) 5 *Historical Studies in Industrial Relations* 1, extracted in E. McGaughey, *A Casebook on Labour Law* (2019) ch. 1.

[116] See Trade Boards Act 1918, Wages Councils Act 1945 and the Wages Councils Act 1979, s. 14 and Sch. 2.

[117] *France v James Coombes & Co.* [1929] AC 496, per Lord Blanesburgh, read by Lord Atkin.

[118] National Minimum Wage Act (NMWA) 1998, ss. 1 and 54.

[119] National Minimum Wage Regulations (NMWR) 2015, regs. 21–44. See *Walton v Independent Living Organisation* [2003] EWCA Civ 199 (agreement may set actual hours worked, if contract leaves unmeasured).

with working time rules), people who are allowed to sleep are not paid while sleeping, even if they must be at a workplace and on call.[120] The minimum or 'living' wage (as it was rebranded in 2015) is, however, riddled with exceptions.[121] Based on the evidence-free assertion that higher wages lead to unemployment, the minimum living wage is lower for younger people: £8.36 for under 23-year-olds, £6.56 under 21, £4.62 under 18 and £4.30 for those classed as 'apprentices'. Meanwhile, youth unemployment is persistently 10 per cent higher than average. This demonstrates the economic failure of the age exception, on top of the simple injustice of a 20-year-old being told they are worth £2.35 an hour less than a 23-year-old who does the same work, by an employer who keeps the difference. There are also inexplicable exceptions for domestic workers,[122] people in immigration detention centres,[123] people working in prison[124] and even members of Her Majesty's armed forces.[125] These exceptions have an indirectly discriminatory impact on multiple grounds, particularly class, race and gender. Paying less to people in detention also depresses wages of people who are *not* detained, whenever employers choose to use incarcerated labour instead of employing free people. Arguably, a minimum wage should be a minimum for everyone, without arbitrary loopholes.

All wages, including the minimum wage, should in principle be paid in money, not in kind. There can be deductions of £6 a day if an employer provides accommodation.[126] But there can be no other deductions for other perks or payment in kind, for instance food. International law is strict on the no-deduction principle.[127] But by contrast the Employment Rights Act 1996, section 13 entitles a 'worker' to bring a claim for any deduction where the worker has not 'previously signified in writing [their] agreement or consent'.[128] This does allow deductions for 'cash shortage' or 'stock deficiency' up to 10 per day,[129] but only the most ineffective employers should have to resort to this. Deductions may also be made for strikes but this must be strictly

[120] NMWR 2015, regs. 27 and 32; *Royal Mencap Society v Tomlinson-Blake* [2021] UKSC 8.

[121] In addition to those in statute, the Court of Appeal created another exception in *Edmonds v Lawson QC* [2000] EWCA Civ 69, asserting pupil barristers were not workers but were 'conscientious in receiving the instruction given'. This should be considered as wrong. The Bar Council required higher wages afterwards.

[122] NMWR 2015, reg. 57(3)(b); *Nambalat v Taher* [2012] EWCA Civ 1249.

[123] NMWA 1998, s. 45B.

[124] NMWA 1998, s. 45 and Prisoners' Earnings Act 1996, s. 2(1)(b), to pay for prison. Whatever the empirical impact on rehabilitation, this cannot justify employers unjustly profiting by undercutting wages of free people.

[125] NMWA 1998, s. 37, and see Ch. 19.

[126] NMWR 2015, regs. 11–16. See *Leisure Employment Services Ltd v HM Revenue & Customs* [2007] EWCA Civ 92.

[127] See the ILO Protection of Wages Convention No. 1949 (c. 95), but this was denounced by the UK in 1983.

[128] ERA 1996, ss. 13 and 23–4, on process for claims.

[129] ERA 1996, ss. 14–17.

proportionate to time not lost,[130] and arguably no deductions may be allowed when the trade dispute is the employer's fault.[131] Finally, employers have no right to steal worker tips: this money belongs in UK law to workers.[132]

Without a statutory system for fair wages, including collective bargaining and votes at work (see Ch. 5(3)), more and more people have been pressed down to the minimum wage.[133] Inequality has increased. High earners are increasingly divided from low earners. The median earner earns ever less than the average. This tendency is exacerbated by changes in income tax and NICs. Growing inequality primarily flows from voice at work (recall Figure 5.1). Yet tax has not only ceased to correct the inequality produced by the maldistribution of corporate power, it has exacerbated this trend. Income tax covers income from employment, trade or dividends. The effective top rate has been cut from over 90 per cent in 1979 to 45 per cent in 2020. This means the highest earners contribute less to pay for public services, even though they have benefited the most from the education, health, transport and corporate infrastructure that society has provided to them and workers or renters who make them money. The counter-argument rests on the view that all income is earned fairly, so they should get to keep it. Progressive income tax is 'graduated robbery'. But this counter-argument rests on a fiction, and clearly so because we should not be looking at individuals (who we can always argue merit what they have) and perceive long-term systemic changes. Wages are a direct product of the legal framework, including the corporate 'command structure'.[134] If I have votes as a shareholder, or powers as a director, I will likely use them to take more.

In 2020, the three income tax bands were 45% on earnings over £150,000 a year, 40% over £50,000 and 20% over £12,000.[135] The tax free 'personal allowance' under £12,000 is currently being raised to match the minimum wage for someone who works thirty hours a week, or about four days with a 7.5-hour day.[136] Average working time is far higher (see Ch. 5(2)(c)).

NICs are also deducted from income at a rate of 12% for 'employees' and 9% for the 'self-employed' (see Ch. 5(1)(c)).[137] While these contributions notionally pay for the state pension, unemployment insurance and insolvency protection, in fact they are mixed with all other government funds, and are in

130 ERA 1996, s. 14(5) and *Hartley v King Edward VI College* [2017] UKSC 39, in effect overturning *Miles v Wakefield MDC* [1987] UKHL 15.

131 On this view, suspension of performance by workers, in response to an employer's breach, will not justify an employer's further breach in non-payment of wages. Cf. *Kingston v Preston* (1773) 2 Doug KB 689, per Lord Mansfield.

132 Theft Act 1968, s. 1; SI 2009/1902; cf. *Nerva v United Kingdom* (2003) 36 EHRR 4. See also Gordon Ramsay, YouTube (17 February 2016).

133 E. McGaughey, '"All in It Together". Worker Wages without Worker Votes' (2016) 27(1) *King's LJ* 1.

134 J. Pen, *Income Distribution* (1971) 361.

135 Finance Act 2017, s. 2; the Income Tax Act 2007, ss. 10, 12 and 35.

136 Income Tax Act 2007, s. 57A.

137 Social Security Contributions and Benefits Act (SSCBA) 1992, ss. 1, 8–9 and 15.

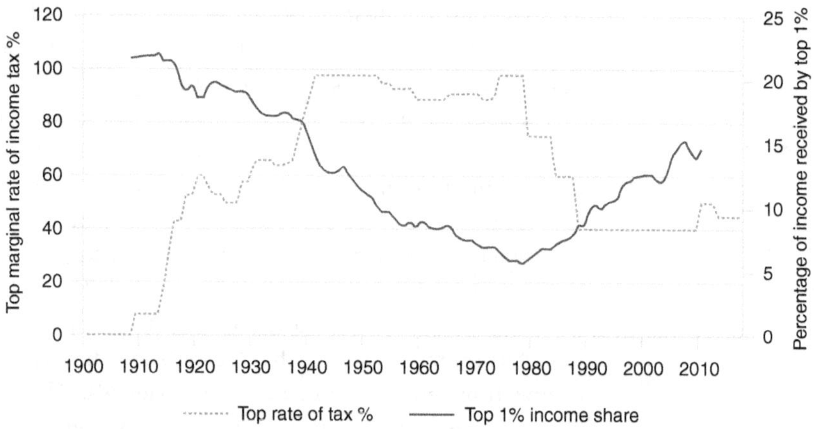

Figure 5.2 UK top rate of income tax and inequality, 1900–2017
Source: T. Piketty, *Capital in the Twenty-First Century* (2014) Tech. Appendices, Tables S9.2 and S14.1

effect another income tax. Unlike income tax, NICs begin at £6,240. Employers also pay 13.8% on the employee's wages, but this begins at £8,784.[138] As it ceases to be paid on income over £50,004, National Insurance operates as a regressive flat tax. It has consistently risen, while income tax was cut.[139] It is only levied on work-based income, so people who get income from capital, shares, interest or rents pay less tax. UK tax is welfare for the rich. People who do not work, but live off workers or renters, contribute less to society than they take.

(b) State and Occupational Pensions

As mentioned in Chapter 4(1)(c), the three pillars of the pension system are (1) the state pension, (2) occupational pensions and (3) pension savings people buy privately, like mutual funds.[140] The state pension is paid from NICs in theory, but in practice the Treasury rolls its plans from this and the Consolidated Fund from tax into one (see Ch. 20). In 2020, the basic state pension was £134.25 a week for someone who met the minimum qualification.[141] This is a bare minimum floor of social security in old age, so people need occupational pensions to match their income in retirement.

138 SSCBA 1992, s. 9.

139 National Insurance rates rose from 6.5% in 1978, see www.taxhistory.co.uk/National%20Insurance%20rates.htm.

140 See Ch. 4(1)(e) for discussion of mutual funds. Another alternative is private life insurance: Ch. 4(1)(d).

141 SSCBA 1992, ss. 43–55C and Sch. 3, para. 5.

Occupational pensions are financed by the employee's work. It is part of their pay,[142] and no part of it belongs to the employer, even though in accounting both the employer and worker make contributions to a fund.[143] First, there are 'defined contribution' (DC) pensions where contributions are usually put in a collective savings account with other beneficiaries', and this money is invested.[144] If the fund performs well, they will get more, but this depends on the market. The Pensions Act 2008, section 3 gives every 'jobholder' (i.e. worker aged 16 to 75[145]) the right to a DC pension. This was introduced because the UK has very low rates of adequate pension coverage.[146] From 2019, everyone enrolled has the right to at least 8% of earnings to be contributed, with at least 3% from the employer.[147] Jobholders can opt out of contributions,[148] but few should do this, because it is free money from the employer, and the state pension may not be enough in retirement. Employers can always contribute more than the minimum, and many do so in employment contracts and in collective agreements. Employers may appoint trustees for a separate fund, but most vest auto-enrolled money with the National Employment Savings Trust (NEST), a cheap public option fund (see Ch. 4(1)(c)).

Second, there are 'defined benefit' (DB) pensions, where contributions are pooled and the employer uses life expectancy (actuarial) tables to calculate how long the workforce will live, and promise the benefit as a percentage of workers' salary accordingly. Since 1979, as unions have been attacked (see Ch. 5(4)), these DB pensions have been closed. The employer may find that a fund accumulates more money than needed, or it may find that the markets perform less well, but the risk stays with it. To shift risk back onto workers, employers have shut DB schemes and opened DC schemes instead. But with a DC scheme, if a worker lives longer than expected they may run out of money. Often people with DC schemes pay extra fees to an asset manager on retirement to buy an annuity for life, for very high fees. This takes away the risk, as a DB scheme would, but reduces people's retirement income. For instance, a 1.5% annual fee can subtract 35.7% in forty years, and a 0.5% annual fee takes 13.7% over the same time.[149]

[142] *R (Palestine Solidarity Campaign Ltd) v Secretary of State for Housing, Communities and Local Government* [2020] UKSC 16.

[143] Cf. *Air Jamaica Ltd v Charlton* [1999] UKPC 20, [54], Lord Millett advising contributions are held on resulting trust for employer and employee, as both make contributions. This is inconsistent with *Palestinian Solidarity*.

[144] Cf. Pension Schemes Act 1993, s. 181 calls these 'money purchase' schemes. On the meaning of this, *Houldsworth v Bridge Trustees Ltd* [2011] UKSC 42.

[145] Pensions Act 2008, ss. 1 and 88; see Ch. 5(2) on the 'worker' meaning.

[146] OECD, *Pensions at a Glance 2013: OECD and G20 Indicators* (2013) ch. 8, 189, shows the UK had a private pension coverage rate of 43.3%; the USA, 47.1%; and Germany, 71.3% (with an income linked state pension).

[147] Pensions Act 2008, s. 20.

[148] Pensions Act 2008, s. 8; Occupational and Personal Pension Schemes (Automatic Enrolment) Regulations 2010/772.

[149] Imagine the worker's fund gets a stable 8% a year return. If there are no fees, the fund will accumulate £800,173 after 40 years. If there is a 1.5% fee on the fund each year, the result will be

To ensure that DB schemes are fully funded, the Pensions Act 2004 says each scheme has a statutory funding objective of 'sufficient and appropriate assets' to meet its obligations.[150] The fund trustees must prepare a 'statement of funding principles' that include the 'methods and assumptions' behind pension evaluation, and get yearly actuarial valuations on funding.[151] If actuarial valuations show that funding is not adequate, there must be a 'recovery plan', which potentially means changing the schedule of contributions from the employer and workers.[152] For all of these issues, the trustees must obtain the agreement of the employer, which gives the latter a high level of influence.[153] One of the most significant problems, which has led to employers closing DB schemes, is where funding valuations are conducted as share prices are down, revealing a supposed pension deficit, but in fact when investments go back up there is no problem. 'Mark to market' accounting, which changes with the market, encourages this. A better alternative is that actuarial valuations are based on 'smoothed market accounting', where averages are calculated to smooth out natural volatility.

(c) Working Time and Child Care

Before retirement, within people's working lives, among the most important rules is paid time off work. Paid holidays and fair limits to the working day are universal rights,[154] while the European Social Charter 1996, article 2(1) requires the 'working week to be progressively reduced to the extent that the increase of productivity and other relevant factors permit'.[155] The 'long hours culture' in many workplaces is a result in the low standards, and this affects productivity. The Working Time Regulations 1998 require at least twenty-eight days of holidays,[156] with a right to take these in weekly blocks if the worker chooses.[157] Time spent sick cannot be designated as 'holiday' by an employer. The worker must receive the same pay they would have received when not working, including wages and bonuses, but not expenses or other reimbursements for costs when not working.[158] Holiday cannot be rolled up into wages, because the purpose of the law is that people actually take time

£518,297. That is, 35.3% vanishes into the City of London (multiply that by every worker who is saving money). If the fee is 0.5%, 13.7% of the fund will be eliminated.

150 Pensions Act 2004, s. 222. Institutions for Occupational Retirement Provision Directive 2016/2341, arts. 13–14.

151 Pensions Act 2004, ss. 223–4.

152 Pensions Act 2004, ss. 226–7.

153 Pensions Act 2004, s. 229. The Pensions Regulator also has power under s. 231(2), if trustees fail to comply with the relevant rules, to (a) modify future accrual of benefits; (b) direct calculations, including methods and assumptions, or the period to meet the funding objective; or (c) impose a schedule of contributions. This may not affect subsisting rights of members.

154 UDHR 1948, art. 24; ICESCR 1966, art. 7(d).

155 European Social Charter 1996, art. 2(1).

156 Working Time Regulations (WTR) 1998, regs. 13–16. Working Time Directive (WTD) 2003/88/EC, art. 7.

157 *Russell v Transocean International Resources Ltd* [2011] UKSC 57.

158 *Williams v British Airways plc* (2011) C-155/10.

off.[159] However, if a worker's job terminates and they have not yet used up holidays, they must be given pay for those holidays.[160] There are not yet statutory minimum hours, but the common law creates a right to not have hours varied arbitrarily as so-called 'zero hours' contracts purport to.[161] Everyone has the right to work no more than forty-eight hours a week, though people may individually opt out. Time spent on call, even if given sleeping facilities, is work time.[162] Every worker has the right to at least twenty minutes of paid, uninterrupted, breaks per six hours' work, twenty-four hours of rest each week and limits on night work.[163] There is also a right to request flexible working time, such as moving from full time to part time work.[164]

In people's lives, some of the most important time off will be to care for children. Unfortunately, UK law is founded on the sexist assumptions of mothers caring for children, while fathers work.[165] Instead of a single right to 'parental leave' for each parent, regardless of gender, there is maternity, paternity, adoption, parental leave with extra rules for trading leave between parents and modifications for same-sex couples. This baffling complexity impelled one judge to say the best way to understand the law was with a 'wet towel' wrapped around the head. Paid maternity leave is two weeks compulsory, six weeks at 90 per cent of pay, a further thirty-three weeks on statutory pay of £151.20 and the remainder of a year unpaid. Paternity leave is two weeks, unpaid. Parental leave is four weeks. Parents may trade time-off rights if they fill out a tiresome set of forms between both of their employers. In practice, with any trading, and on current law, women end up taking more time off for childcare. This has the effect of entrenching gender stereotypes, putting women workers back in promotion on average compared to men and so entrenching the gender pay gap.

(d) Equality

One of the most important rights at work, like access to education, housing and any services offered to the public, is equal treatment. 'Equality' is a referential right, not self-standing, and so to have importance it needs to be coupled with independent notions of fairness and justice. Yet it also fulfils a crucial function of solidarity: without it, employers and politicians may aim to divide people by race, gender, sexuality, beliefs or anything to distract the focus from their own responsibility for injustice. Equal treatment is a right at common law, and treatment that is 'partial and unequal in their operation as

159 *Robinson-Steele v RD Retail Services Ltd* (2006) C-131/04.
160 WTR 1998, reg. 13(9); WTD 2003, art. 7(2).
161 *Borrer v Cardinal Security Ltd* [2013] UKEAT 0416_12_1607.
162 *Sindicato de Medicos de Asistencia Publica v Conselleria de Sanidad y Consumo de la Generalidad Valenciana* (2000) C-303/98; *Landeshauptstadt Kiel v Jaegar* (2003) C-151/02.
163 WTR 1998, regs. 10–12 and 24; WTD 2003, arts. 3–5.
164 ERA 1996, s. 80F; *Commotion Ltd v Rutty* [2006] IRLR 171.
165 A. C. L. Davies, *Perspectives on Labour Law* (2004) 111.

between different classes' may be remedied in judicial review of public bodies, in companies and in tort.[166] Unjustified unequal treatment will also violate the implied term of mutual trust and confidence.[167] This may be seen as akin to the general principle of equality in EU law.[168]

The Equality Act 2010 is a partial codification of the general principles of equality for eight specific 'protected characteristics'. These are race, sex, sexual orientation, a deeply held belief or religion, age, disability, gender reassignment and marriage or civil partnership. To this can be added three slightly weaker duties of equal treatment relating to contractual statuses of fixed-term contracts, part-time work or agency work.[169] There are also the rights against any detriment for union activities.[170] The general tendency of the case law has been to construe the meaning of protected characteristics expansively,[171] an approach which surely matches the general principle that people should be treated according to their conduct and merit, the 'content of their character', not according to arbitrary considerations.[172] Similarly, people are entitled to claim for discrimination if they do not themselves have the perceived attribute but are treated less favourably anyway,[173] and suffer unfavourable treatment because of a related party's protected characteristic.[174]

The three main types of unlawful conduct are 'direct' discrimination, 'indirect' discrimination and failing to take positive action where needed, particularly to accommodate disabled or pregnant people and remedy historical disadvantage. First, 'direct' discrimination means treating someone less favourably because of a protected characteristic.[175] This requires imagining a hypothetical comparator with all the attributes of the claimant, except for the relevant characteristic, and asking whether treatment was less favourable due

[166] *Kruse v Johnson* [1898] 2 QB 91, per Lord Russell of Killowen CJ (an interesting question arises about the manner of review of companies); *Constantine v Imperial Hotels Ltd* [1944] KB 693, per Birkett J.

[167] E.g. *Transco plc v O'Brien* [2002] EWCA Civ 379, on arbitrary singling out of an agency worker.

[168] *Kücükdeveci v Swedex GmbH & Co. KG* (2010) C-555/07; *Mangold v Helm* (2005) C-144/04.

[169] Part-time Work (Prevention of Less Favourable Treatment) Regulations 2000 (applying to workers); Part-time Work Directive 97/81/EC; Fixed-Term Employees (Prevention of Less Favourable Treatment) Regulations 2002 (only applying to employees, and creating a right to a permanent contract after four years unless there is an objective justification); Fixed-Term Work Directive 1999/70/EC; Agency Workers Regulations 2010 (right to at least equal pay and working time as a direct worker, agency is the employer); Temporary Agency Work Directive 2008/104/EC.

[170] TULRCA 1992, ss. 146–8; and see Ch. 5(1)(d).

[171] *Mandla v Dowell Lee* [1983] 2 AC 548 (construing the meaning of 'ethnicity' to include Sikhs).

[172] Cf. Martin Luther King Jr (28 August 1963): 'I have a dream that my four little children will one day live in a nation where they will not be judged by the color of their skin but by the content of their character.'

[173] *English v Sanderson Blinds Ltd* [2008] EWCA Civ 1421 (a man who was not gay harassed as if he were gay).

[174] *Coleman v Attridge Law* (2008) C-303/06 (a mother vilified at work because of her disabled child).

[175] Equality Act 2010, s. 13.

to that characteristic.[176] Because evidence of racist, sexist or bigoted intent is rarely, if ever, going to be revealed, but instead kept covert or subconscious, the burden of proof requires simply that a claimant shows facts from which it could be inferred that there was discrimination.[177] It is then up to the defendant to prove the conduct was not discrimination. So for example, where a hotel employer told a staff member to 'f*** off back to Poland' after the 2016 Brexit poll, this was prima facie evidence of discrimination on grounds of race (including nationality), and the employer failed to prove there was no discrimination.[178] Direct discrimination can only be justified if differential treatment reflects a 'genuine occupational requirement'.[179] For example, a woman actor may be needed for a woman's part in a play, although evolution in social attitudes may mean that fewer of these exceptions are to be made. Age is an exceptional characteristic. Here broader justifications based on business needs or other objectives can be brought, since it is thought that practices such as retirement ages, or reward for experience (which are directly related to age) are socially justified.[180]

Second, 'indirect' discrimination occurs when an employer has a neutral practice, but this disproportionately affects some groups more than others. If a particular disadvantage is created (often evident in statistical outcomes[181]), it must be objectively justified by the needs of a business or other legitimate policy, or the practice will be unlawful. For example, the instruction of British Airways to not wear a crucifix necklace, as part of a policy against jewellery, was held to be unlawful. It applied to everyone, but put Christians (more likely to wear crosses) at a particular disadvantage, and it was unjustified since BA had only recently changed its uniform to require lower-cut tops (revealing the necklace). It easily changed back.[182] An employer's objective justification for disparate impact could include following an equality policy,[183] or having a transitionary period towards equalising terms and conditions,[184] but cannot include saving costs.[185] An objective justification starts with showing a 'legitimate aim' – saving money at the cost of equality is not legitimate – and the employer must then explain how measures they took were appropriate, necessary and reasonable towards that aim. Unfortunately, cases have conflicted on whether paying a 'market rate' is legitimate, even where

[176] *Shamoon v Chief Constable of the Royal Ulster Constabulary* [2003] UKHL 11, a real male comparator inappropriate since that person did not have negative complaints made about his performance.

[177] Equality Act 2010, s. 136. [178] *Stefanko v Maritime Hotel Ltd* [2019] IRLR 322.

[179] Equality Act 2010, Sch. 9, paras. 1–4.

[180] E.g. *Seldon v Clarkson Wright & Jakes* [2012] UKSC 16.

[181] *R (Seymour-Smith) v Secretary of State for Employment* [2000] UKHL 12.

[182] *Eweida v United Kingdom* [2013] ECHR 37.

[183] *Ladele v London Borough of Islington* [2009] EWCA Civ 1357, affirmed in [2013] ECHR 37.

[184] *Naeem v Secretary of State for Justice* [2017] UKSC 27.

[185] *Kutz-Bauer v Freie und Hansestadt Hamburg* (2003) C-187/00.

(as is common) so-called market pay is shaped by unconscious bias.[186] The big exception to this structure is for equal pay between men and women. For indefensible historical reasons, it is harder to bring equal pay claims for gender alone, because there is a non-extendable six-month time limit (as opposed to an *extendable* three-month limit for other claims),[187] and there must be a real comparator (not also a hypothetical comparator).[188] However, claims may be brought in the High Court as well as a Tribunal. It is unclear why the same, and higher, standards are not available for all claims: the likely answer is that these details were simply not appreciated in the drafting of the Equality Act 2010.

Third, there are duties of affirmative action. First, there is a duty to make reasonable adjustments for disabled people, to ensure that everyone is included at work.[189] For example, in *Archibald v Fife Council*, a council worker was entitled after a workplace accident to not have to undergo competitive interviews as a reasonable adjustment.[190] The duty, therefore, is a powerful one. In the post-war period, enterprises with over twenty staff had express duties to hire a proportion of disabled veterans.[191] Today, it would appear that if an enterprise does not already have a proportion of people with disabilities that reflects society, and they fail to make adjustments to accommodate those applicants, they should be regarded as having acted unlawfully. Second, there are express duties to accommodate pregnant women, particularly for the safety of the mother and child.[192] Third, there is an option for employers to undertake voluntary 'positive action'. Usually discrimination is unlawful whether 'positive' or not, in the sense that it is directed at correcting historical or social disadvantage, but the law makes several exceptions. Enterprises may reserve quotas for representative jobs (such as company directors, where the function is representation). For non-representative jobs enterprise may take softer measures such as ensuring equal places in interviews or training, and choose people from an underrepresented group in 'tie-breaker' cases where two candidates' qualifications are equal (but quotas are not allowed).[193]

(e) Health and Safety

The right to life and health (see Ch. 9) is vitally affected by workplace safety, stress and balance with time off work. Under the Health and Safety at Work, etc. Act 1974, section 2 places a strict, general duty of care on employers 'to ensure, so far as is reasonably practicable, the health, safety and welfare at work

[186] Cf. *Clay Cross (Quarry Services) Ltd v Fletcher* [1978] IRLR 361 but see *Enderby v Frenchay Health Authority* (1993) C-127/92, [26]. This appears inconsistent with *Kutz-Bauer* above, and should not now be followed.

[187] Equality Act 2010, s. 123.

[188] Equality Act 2010, ss. 64–79; Equal Treatment Directive 2006/54/EC.

[189] Equality Act 2010, ss. 13(3), 15, 20–1, 60 and Sch. 8. [190] [2004] UKHL 32.

[191] Disabled Persons (Employment) Act 1944.

[192] Pregnant Workers Directive 92/85/EEC; *Parviainen v Finnair Oyj* (2010) C-471/08.

[193] Equality Act 2010, ss. 158–9; *Re Badeck's application* (2001) C-158/97.

of all his employees'. This includes 'a working environment . . . that is, so far as is reasonably practicable, safe, *without* risks to health' (emphasis added). A good illustration, during the Covid-19 pandemic, is that online work including teaching is 'without risks' and wherever reasonably practicable had to be done, regardless of whether people found it inconvenient, or less exciting than classes in person.[194] This was necessary to prevent people dying, but tragically was not followed in full.[195] There is a further right of staff to suffer no 'detriment' for refusing to work in any situation where danger to safety or health is 'serious and imminent'.[196] This is backed with a 'duty of every employer, if requested to do so by [workplace or union] safety representatives' to set up 'a safety committee' that will 'co-operate effectively' in improving health and safety.[197]

(f) Privacy and Expression

The human rights to privacy and freedom of expression are ever more an issue as information technology and social media becomes part of work and life. While the right to privacy focuses on one's 'home' and 'correspondence',[198] both of these things are affected by modern work practices as more people work from home, and use emails with servers controlled by employers or multinational corporations (particularly Microsoft). In *Copland v United Kingdom*, the European Court of Human Rights held that Ms Copland had been 'given no warning that her calls would be liable to being monitored, therefore she had a reasonable expectation to privacy of calls made from her workplace telephone'.[199] It follows that where employers provide email, call or web browsing services they have no implicit right to put the personal messages and activities of their staff under surveillance, as if staff were potential criminals. Indeed, an employer's policies cannot ban private use of email or messaging because it would be wrong to 'reduce private social life in the workplace to zero'.[200]

The right to freedom of expression is also broad. For example, posts on a Facebook account,[201] or taking part in political activities even if unpalatable,[202] will not be grounds for dismissal where they concern the

[194] Health and Safety at Work, etc. Act 1974, s. 2.

[195] E. McGaughey, 'A Social Recovery, Workplace Democracy and Security: COVID-19 and Labour Law' (2021) 32(1) *King's LJ* 122.

[196] ERA 1996, s. 44. [197] Health and Safety at Work, etc. Act 1974, s. 2(6).

[198] ECHR, art. 8(1).

[199] *Copland v United Kingdom* [2007] ECHR 253, [42]; but cf. *Fosh v Cardiff University* [2009] EWCA Civ 38, a defective decision where a staff member was subjected to detriment for assisting a student in a race discrimination claim, where her emails were searched and the staff member was dismissed. This is wrong.

[200] *Barbulescu v Romania* [2017] ECHR 754.

[201] *Smith v Trafford Housing Trust* [2012] EWHC 3221.

[202] *Redfearn v Serco Ltd* [2012] ECHR 1878.

right to freely express views and one's conscience. There is particular backing for 'protected disclosures' including revealing that a criminal offence has been committed, that health and safety is endangered or the environment is being or may be damaged.[203] Non-disclosure agreements or 'gagging clauses' are void wherever they try to suppress protected disclosures.[204] Expression, however, was limited in a case of a probation worker for child sex offences, who was found online to have been involved in sado-masochistic sex acts, and this was deemed inappropriate: it was within the state's margin of appreciation to allow an employer to dismiss the employee.[205]

(3) Participation and Fair Standards

To have fair standards beyond the minimum rights guaranteed in law, people must be able to participate in their workplace's governance. The gulf between democracy in politics and the economy, 'the contrast between our political liberty and our industrial absolutism',[206] remains a striking reality. Rights to vote at work have spread worldwide, but in the UK this is patchy at best.[207] This section covers (a) worker participation in governance, such as on a board of directors, and election of work councils with binding participation rights. Unlike other countries, the UK has participation rights only in pension governance, and limited information and consultation rights in other fields. This means the primary channel of participation is (b) through unions collectively bargaining and, ultimately (c) unions taking collective action, including using the right to strike.

(a) Worker Participation in Corporate Governance

As Chapter 3(2)(a) explored, anyone can be registered as a company 'member' and have the right to vote for the board of directors.[208] In practice shareholders monopolise membership, because capital investors have historically had greater bargaining power than labour. There are rules to encourage employee share schemes, disapplying pre-emption rights to issue employee shares.[209] But share schemes are unlikely to be more than a tokenistic mechanism of voice, and concentrate undiversified risk in one company in a way that no

[203] ERA 1996, s. 43B and see *Clyde & Co. LLP v Bates van Winkelhof* [2014] UKSC 32.
[204] ERA 1996, s. 43J.
[205] *Pay v United Kingdom* [2008] ECHR 1007; for criticism at an earlier instance see H. Collins, 'The Protection of Civil Liberties in the Workplace' (2006) 69(4) *MLR* 619, 623.
[206] L. D. Brandeis, *Testimony to Commission on Industrial Relations* (1916) vol. VIII, 7659–60.
[207] For history, see E. McGaughey, 'Votes at Work in Britain: Shareholder Monopolisation and the "Single Channel"' (2018) 47(1) *Industrial LJ* 76; S. Webb and B. Webb, *The History of Trade Unionism* (1920) Appendix VIII; Alan Bullock, *Report of the Committee of Inquiry on Industrial Democracy*, Cmnd 6706 (1977).
[208] CA 2006, ss. 112 and 284; Model Articles, Sch. 3, para. 34 (members' register and voting).
[209] Cf. Ch. 4(2)(a) and see CA 2006, ss. 1166, 549, 566 and 586 (employee share schemes).

prudent investor would.[210] In 2018, the UK Corporate Governance Code was amended to include for the first time a duty on listed companies to comply or explain with one of three employee involvement options.[211] These are to have a director appointed from the workforce, a formal workforce advisory panel or a designated non-executive director.[212] None of these options explicitly suggest that employees actually may vote for directors. Company boards have in practice simply appointed their own chosen employees, if doing anything at all.

The changes in the Code were taken partly because of the post-Brexit poll leadership campaign of Theresa May and due to opposition Labour Party proposals. The Labour policy required at least one-third of boards in companies with over 250 workers to be elected, a standard that is widely found in the Organisation for Economic Co-operation and Development (OECD) (see Figure 5.3). It also endorsed *The Manifesto for Labour Law*, a document for a new labour rights system by labour law academics and QCs. This recommended making all workers 'members' of companies, with at least 20 per cent of the votes in each general meeting reserved on a 'one person, one vote' basis, and at least two directors on each board, amendable by statutory instrument.[213] Currently few enterprises, outside universities, ensure workers have voting rights. The best universities have a majority elected governing body (see Ch. 8(3)(b)). Students or alumni usually have representation as well.

A majority of EU and OECD countries now have laws for worker representation on company boards, while the European Social Charter 1996, also signed by the UK, states that workers have a right 'to the determination and the improvement of the working conditions, work organisation and working environment'.[214] The most common model is for workers to elect around a third of board seats, as is the case in Sweden.[215] Usually, as in the UK, countries have a single board of directors. By contrast the best-known system, with a very developed history, is Germany.[216] German companies have two-tier boards. An executive board runs the company's day-to-day affairs. It is appointed by a supervisory board that sets strategy.[217] The Codetermination Act 1976 says that in companies with over 2,000 staff, half the supervisory board must be elected by employees, although the chair has a casting vote and is elected by

210 P. J. Purcell, 'The Enron Bankruptcy and Employer Stock in Retirement Plans' CRS Report for Congress (11 March 2002), on Enron employees losing around two-thirds of their pensions from a share scheme.

211 The result of a leadership-bid promise by Theresa May in July 2016.

212 UK Corporate Governance Code 2018, ch. 1.5.

213 *Manifesto for Labour Law* (2016) endorsed at 2016 conference. *Rolling out the Manifesto for Labour Law* (2018) ch. 5.

214 ESC 1996, arts. 21–2.

215 Board Representation (Private Sector Employees) Act 1987 (SFS 1987: 1245).

216 E. McGaughey, 'The Codetermination Bargains: The History of German Corporate and Labour Law' (2016) 23(1) *Columbia J Eur L* 135.

217 *Aktiengesetz* 1965, §§76, 84, 87, 95–6, 101–5 and 111 (best translated as the Public Companies Act 1965, but often also the Stock Corporations Act 1965).

shareholders.[218] In practice, as Chapter 4 explained, shareholder votes are cast by banks. Workers may delegate their votes to their union and, in companies with over 8,000 staff, votes are delegated by default (but may always be cast by staff).[219] In companies with over 500 staff, there is a right to elect one-third of the board.[220] This is generally seen as one of the strongest co-determination systems.

In the USA, two leading candidates for the 2020 presidential election support one-third workers on boards for listed companies,[221] and either 40 per cent on boards of companies with over $1 billion in revenue,[222] or 45 per cent on boards of companies with over £100 million in revenue.[223] These proposals are

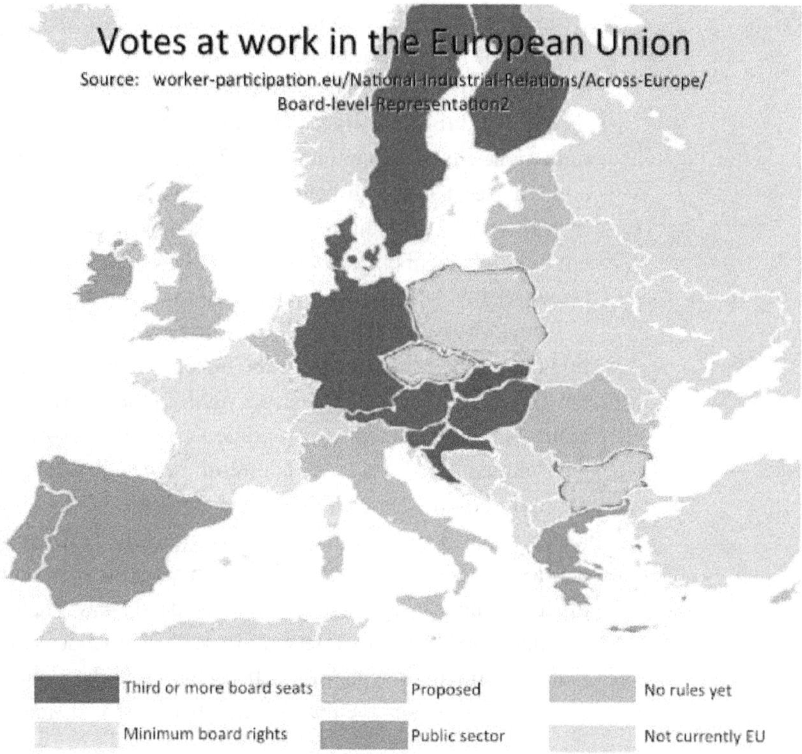

Figure 5.3 Votes at work in the European Union
Source: www.worker-participation.eu/National-Industrial-Relations/Across-Europe/Board-level-Representation2

[218] *Mitbestimmungsgesetz* 1976, §§1, 5–9. [219] *Mitbestimmungsgesetz* 1976, §§9 and 18.
[220] *Drittelbeteiligungsgesetz* 2004, §§4–5.
[221] Reward Work Act of 2018 (S. 2605 and HR 6096).
[222] Accountable Capitalism Act, 115th Congress (2017–18) S. 3348 proposed by Elizabeth Warren.
[223] Bernie Sanders, *Corporate Accountability and Democracy* (2019).

the first at federal level, though the USA also has a remarkable history of experiment and unions collectively bargaining for board seats.[224]

Below board level, many countries have work council laws with binding rights over specific issues of workplace management. The German Work Constitution Act 1972, §87 requires rights of participation or co-determination on thirteen issues, including working time and holidays, methods of pay, any devices for monitoring employees, safety, pension management and suggestion systems.[225] If agreement cannot be reached, a conciliation committee must make a decision. Under §76, this is 'appointed in equal number by the employer and the works council and of an independent chair accepted by both sides'. If there is no agreement on the chair, a court makes the appointment. Employers must have the work council's agreement before changes in these fields take effect. On the issue of dismissals for redundancy, an employer may ultimately push through job cuts, but this is subject to a social plan set by a court, which aims to internalise social costs of redundancy.[226]

By contrast, the UK has very developed rights for co-determination in pension funds, but nothing more than information and consultation in other fields. Under the Pensions Act 2004, any pension trust or trust corporation must have at least one-third 'member nominated trustees' on its board.[227] This means elections by employees and beneficiaries of the pension, or appointment through the recognised trade union. This norm arguably applies to any fund where money is saved on behalf of workers or beneficiaries, because this will automatically be a trust regardless of legal drafting or form.[228] Nevertheless, many so-called 'contract pensions' usually administered by a large asset manager fail to have member-nominated trustees. The Secretary of State may raise the threshold to one-half by statutory instrument, but has as yet failed to do so. Exemptions may also be made, as has been done for the National Employment Savings Trust.[229] Before 2004, unions had collectively bargained most pensions and representation on their boards.[230] It is also open to unions to collectively bargain for work councils on any issue. Indeed, the UK government helped to write a law expressly enabling German unions to re-establish work councils during the post-World War Two occupation, but is yet to do the same for workers at home.[231]

Short of binding participation rights, the Information and Consultation of Employees Regulations (ICER) 2004 give employees in workplaces with over fifty staff rights to be informed and consulted if there are major changes

224 E. McGaughey, 'Democracy in America at Work: The History of Labor's Vote in Corporate Governance' (2019) 42 *Seattle UL Rev* 697.

225 *Betriebsverfassungsgesetz* 1972, §87. 226 *Betriebsverfassungsgesetz* 1972, §§111–12.

227 Pensions Act 2004, ss. 241–3. 228 See Ch. 4(1)(c).

229 Pensions Act 2008, Sch. 1 for board structure.

230 E. McGaughey, *Participation in Corporate Governance* (2014) ch. 6(1).

231 Control Council Law No. 22 (10 April 1946) Works Councils.

proposed in workplace organisation or contract relations.[232] This has to include consultation on the 'probable development of employment', any 'threat' to employment and substantial changes in work organisation or contracts. Any 2 per cent of employees can require that a consultation begins. More unions are taking up statutory consultation, because a £75,000 penalty is payable by employers who refuse to inform and negotiate with their staff.[233] The Transnational Information and Consultation of Employees Regulations 1999 give employees in multinational corporations with over 1,000 employees in different EU member states the right to combined cross-border consultation for the whole affected workforce. The idea of 'consultation' is that it 'imposes an obligation to negotiate' on the employer.[234] This gives considerable strength when engaging in collective bargaining.

(b) Right to Collectively Bargain

The right to collectively bargain is a key element of freedom of association, because people can get better terms at work if they bargain together with one voice.[235] Although a corporation is a separate 'person' in law, in reality it is a social institution, combining investors of capital and labour, represented by a board. But because corporations and enterprises tend to be dominated by capital interests, collective agreements about workplace terms are often not made without considerable struggle and support by law.

UK law's support for collective bargaining is basic, and unnecessarily complex. Since 1999, there has been a right for unions to go through a 'statutory recognition procedure', to be officially recognised by the union in order to bargain. Before this, unions ultimately went on strike if an employer refused to bargain, an option still open without recourse to the procedure. Does the procedure add anything useful, or just result in delay? Under the Trade Union and Labour Relations (Consolidation) Act (TULRCA) 1992, Schedule A1, an independent union can apply to the Central Arbitration Committee (CAC) for statutory recognition in workplaces with twenty-one or more workers.[236] No collective agreement must already exist for a union's application to succeed: if it does then the applicant union will have to apply for the other union to be de-recognised.[237] The CAC will determine what is the appropriate bargaining unit, and whether in that unit the union has majority support.[238] The smaller the unit, the greater the likelihood the union has

[232] After the Information and Consultation of Employees Directive 2002/14.

[233] ICER 2004, regs. 22–3; see *Amicus v Macmillan Publishers Ltd* [2007] IRLR 378, Elias J imposing a £55,000 penalty on an employer who failed to set up an election for employee representatives.

[234] *Junk v Kühnel* (2005) C-188/03.

[235] *Demir and Baykara v Turkey* [2008] ECHR 1345 (right to collectively bargain).

[236] TULRCA 1992, Sch. A1, paras. 4–7.

[237] TULRCA 1992, Sch. A1, para. 35.

[238] TULRCA 1992, Sch. A1, paras. 11–19.

support, but the union's efforts cover fewer workers.[239] If it is not clear that the union has a majority of supporters in the unit, a ballot must be conducted with fair procedures to show there is a majority.[240] In 2017, the average time for this procedure was twenty-three weeks if there is a ballot,[241] while workers may be suffering pay cuts or redundancies.

If employers litigate, the procedure may take years because there are many loopholes. *Pharmacists' Defence Association Union v Secretary of State for Business, Innovation and Skills* held that to become recognised the Union had to first apply to de-recognise a sham union called the 'Boots Pharmacists Association' (BPA). Boots Ltd recognised the BPA purely so that it could exploit paragraph 35. This says a collective agreement 'already in force' blocks an application unless that union is formally de-recognised. The Court of Appeal declined to interpret paragraph 35 so that the word 'union' did not include an employer-dominated organisation, as BPA was.[242] As explained in Chapter 5(1)(b), employers have also challenged whether their staff are even workers, and one case still in appeal held that bicycle delivery staff are not even workers because they could substitute others.[243] Experience suggests that the greater volume of detail in the law, the more chances there are for determined or hostile employers to not collectively bargain.

(c) Right to Strike

The right to take collective action, including a strike, is fundamental to international law,[244] though in the UK it has been under considerable pressure. Strikes – the right to just say 'no' – are the vanguard of democracy, and brought the fall of the kaiser, Indian Independence and the end of Apartheid.

[239] Cf. *Lidl Ltd v Central Arbitration Committee* [2017] EWCA Civ 328. Lidl Ltd challenged a finding that an appropriate bargaining unit was a single warehouse in Bridgend, around 1.2% of the company's total workforce, arguing Sch. A1, para. 19B(3)(c) prevented this because it refers to 'the desirability of avoiding small fragmented bargaining units'. It held that if there was only one proposed bargaining unit, it could not be 'fragmented' (even if small). *R (Kwik-Fit (GB) Ltd) v Central Arbitration Committee* [2002] EWCA Civ 512 held that the CAC's determination of a bargaining unit for the M25 could not be challenged.

[240] TULRCA 1992, Sch. A1, paras. 22–6 and 36. [241] CAC, *Annual Report 2016/17* (2017) 9.

[242] [2017] EWCA Civ 66. The better approach would have been to ensure that the court interpreted the word 'union' in a way that fully realised the right to freedom of association in the ECHR, art. 11. See also *R (National Union of Journalists) v Central Arbitration Committee* [2005] EWCA Civ 1309 (holding that a one-person union could block an application of a union with widespread support).

[243] *R (Independent Workers Union of Great Britain) v Central Arbitration Committee* [2018] EWHC 3342 (Admin).

[244] UDHR 1948, art. 23(4). Under ICESCR 1966, art. 8(1)(d) member states must guarantee the 'right to strike, provided that it is exercised in conformity with the laws of the particular country'. ILO Freedom of Association and Protection of the Right to Organise Convention 1948 (c. 87) art. 3(1): worker organisations 'shall have the right . . . to organise their administration and activities and to formulate their programmes'. This includes the right to strike: B. Gernigon, A. Odero and H. Guido, 'ILO Principles Concerning the Right to Strike' (1998) 137 *Int'l Labour Rev* 441.

The dominant view of the courts is that the right to strike is 'a right which was first conferred by Parliament in 1906, which has been enjoyed by trade unions ever since and which is today recognised as encompassing a fundamental human right'.[245] In *Morgan v Fry*, Lord Denning MR said it 'ha[d] been held for over 60 years that workmen have a right to strike'.[246] Other judges have doubted this, arguing that the 'common law confers no right to strike in this country'.[247] Yet Parliament has expressly legislated that any 'terms of a collective agreement which prohibit or restrict the right of workers to engage in a strike or other industrial action, or have the effect of prohibiting or restricting that right, shall not form part of any contract' unless contained in an express collective agreement.[248] This means that Parliament recognised 'the right of workers to engage in a strike' at common law, international law or both, and so all legal norms must be construed consistently.

This said, UK statute has no elaboration on the right to strike. The common law long assumed that if workers take collective action, which causes economic loss to an employer, unions are liable in tort.[249] However, since the Trade Disputes Act 1906,[250] and now in TULRCA 1992, section 219, it has been said that unions have immunity from being sued in tort if they take action 'in contemplation or furtherance of a trade dispute'. Section 219 alludes to three main torts: (1) a union inducing workers to breach their contracts of employment, (2) a conspiracy to injure the employer's economic interests and (3) a union causing loss by unlawful means. It is very debatable whether these old torts can be said to exist anymore, especially since in *OBG Ltd v Allan* Lord Hoffmann stressed that the 'common law has traditionally been reluctant to become involved in devising rules of fair competition',[251] and endorsed an influential dictum of Lord Bramwell in *Mogul Steamship Co. Ltd v McGregor*, which says that 'a combination of workmen, an agreement among them to cease work except for higher wages, and a strike in consequence, [is] lawful at common law'.[252] The current structure of TULRCA 1992 proceeds on the basis that unions *could* be liable in tort (it does not say they *are*) if a strike is not 'in contemplation or furtherance of a trade dispute', or does not fulfil the Act's other requirements. If immunity is withdrawn, employers invariably apply for an injunction – a court order – to stop a strike occurring.

What is a 'trade dispute'? TULRCA 1992, section 244 defines a trade dispute as something wholly or mainly relating to terms and conditions of employment, dismissal of workers and similar workplace issues. What is not in the

245 *London Underground Ltd v RMT* [1996] ICR 170, per Millett LJ, approved again in *British Airways plc v Unite the Union* [2010] EWCA Civ 669.

246 [1968] 2 QB 710, referring to the Trade Disputes Act 1906.

247 *RMT v Serco Ltd* [2011] EWCA Civ 226, [2] per Elias LJ.

248 TULRCA 1992, s. 180.

249 *Rookes v Barnard* [1964] AC 1129.

250 Also before the Conspiracy and Protection of Property Act 1875 and *Eleventh and Final Report of the Royal Commissioners Appointed to Inquire into the Organization and Rules of Trades Unions and Other Associations* (1868–69).

251 [2007] UKHL 21, [56].

252 [1892] AC 25, 47.

list? The most notable silence is for strikes that relate to political disputes. In *BBC v Hearn*, the BBC successfully applied for an injunction against the Association of Broadcasting Staff, who had announced a strike to stop broadcasting the FA Cup Final to South Africa. The union, ABS, aimed to stop the broadcast to oppose the far-right Apartheid regime that held power up to 1994. However, the Court of Appeal held that this did not relate to the workers' terms and conditions. Lord Denning MR suggested that, to be allowed, the union could have asked for a new term in their contracts to say that they were not required to broadcast to South Africa, but as it stood the strike was purely political.[253] In *Universe Tankships Inc. of Monrovia v International Transport Workers Federation*, Lord Cross of Chelsea doubted that this would work (i.e. he did not like it).[254] This illustrates once more the widely diverging political views of judges on the right to strike.

Whatever the status of the 'right to strike', what are its practical scope and limits? According to ex-Prime Minister Tony Blair, UK laws are among 'the most restrictive on trade unions in the Western world'.[255] Importantly what is called 'secondary action' is prohibited under TULRCA 1992, section 224.[256] This means when workers strike against someone who 'is not the employer party to the dispute'.[257] Who counts as the 'employer'? In *Dimbleby and Sons Ltd v NUJ*, the House of Lords held that the National Union of Journalists was not allowed to strike at Dimbleby and Sons Ltd, to prevent it supplying newspapers for printing to TBF (Printers) Ltd, because it was in a dispute with another company in its group – T. Bailey Forman Ltd – after it dismissed twenty-eight NUJ journalists. The problem with this view is that corporate groups invariably function as single social units. They transfer profits between one another, the same shareholders benefit from the revenues of companies in the group and they often share a co-ordinated management or business strategy. It remains unclear, therefore, why the word 'employer' should not be construed to disregard the legal form of organisation, in the same way that competition law, tax law or accounting law does.

The apparent ban on secondary action also precludes general strikes, like that in the UK in 1926, to protest against wage cuts for miners. In *National Sailors' and Firemen's Union v Reed*, Astbury J said the general strike was

253 [1977] ICR 686. But see also, *Mercury Communications Ltd v Scott-Garner* [1984] ICR 74 (injunction against workers striking against newly licensed, privatised Mercury Ltd in connecting telecoms networks).

254 [1983] 1 AC 366, 392.

255 Tony Blair, 'We Won't Look Back to the 1970s', *The Times* (31 March 1997). To Blair, this seemed a strength.

256 TULRCA 1992, s. 220 enables peaceful picketing, but not when the picket engages in secondary action. A code of practice suggests that six people should be the maximum on a picket, a seemingly unjustified restriction on people's freedom of assembly.

257 *RMT v United Kingdom* [2014] ECHR 366 declined to find TULRCA 1992, s. 224 violated art. 11, where the railway union wished to take strike action against all members of a group, but did not decide the issue finally.

'illegal',[258] although the reality was that the court's judgment was irrelevant and the strike continued.

A lawful strike requires complex balloting rules to be followed. Under TULRCA 1992, section 226, industrial action has to have the majority support of a ballot, among all those entitled to vote (that is, everyone who is a member of the union in the workplace where the strike takes place). Under a new section 226(2C)–(2E) in health services, schools of children under age 17, fire, transport, nuclear work and border security, at least 40 per cent of eligible members must vote in favour.[259] This means that the union has to have much higher turnouts for the vote. Under section 226A, notice of intention to hold a ballot must be given to the employer at least seven days before the ballot, and a sample ballot paper three days before. Under sections 231–231A a union must then inform their members and the employer of the numbers of people eligible to vote, votes cast, people answering 'yes' and 'no' or spoiling their papers and whether the majority and 40 per cent thresholds were reached. Under section 234A the ballot lasts for six months, and written notice of the action must be given to the employer fourteen days before it starts.

How strictly should these rules be applied? In *British Airways plc v Unite* the Court of Appeal held that a union did not lose its strike immunity under section 231 when it communicated the result of a ballot through texts, emails, websites and noticeboards, rather than informing workers individually. In fact, 80 per cent of the members had voted in favour of the strike, and Lord Judge CJ observed 'there is a certain irony that it is the employers . . . whose application is based on an asserted non-compliance by the Union . . . when the employers know perfectly well that an overwhelming majority of its members wish to take strike action'.[260] Similarly, in *P v NASUWT* the House of Lords held that the union's failure to notify two members who were entitled to vote about the ballot did not invalidate it. Everyone had the right to vote 'so far as reasonably practical'.[261] These cases, from higher courts, suggest that the rules are not to be applied so as to frustrate the right to strike.[262]

What if unions fail to follow the ballot or other rules? In theory employers may apply for an injunction or damages against a union undertaking a strike. An injunction is designed to stop a strike happening: a court orders a union not to undertake any strike action, or otherwise risk being in contempt of court. Damages for the employer's economic loss would be, for most unions, financially crippling. Under section 21, there may be no damages against a union if workers undertake a strike that is not authorised by the union, and the union repudiates such action publicly. Under section 22, damages are

[258] [1926] Ch 536, 539–49.

[259] Although it is beneficial that these rules do not apply to university staff, it is not clear why universities are not listed as an 'important public service'!

[260] [2010] EWCA Civ 669. [261] [2003] UKHL 8.

[262] Sadly, a host of High Court and differently constituted Courts of Appeal have done the opposite, e.g. *Metrobus Ltd v Unite* [2010] ICR 173.

capped at a range between £10,000 and £250,000 depending on the number of union members. In practice, matters never reach the award of injunctions or damages, because an 'interim injunction' is usually granted before any strike after an employer's complaint about a union's failure to follow rules. If it is acknowledged that there is a positive right to strike at common law or in equity, an employer should not be entitled to do this, and remedies for a union's failure to follow balloting rules should be available for union members only.

What protections exist for individual employees when they take part in a strike? Under TULRCA 1992, section 238A, every 'employee' has the right to not be unfairly dismissed for taking part in a strike. Dismissal is automatically unfair. This protection, however, only lasts for twelve weeks. This right is also limited to 'employees', and so it appears that 'non-employee workers' are not protected. On the other hand, any employer who begins dismissing striking workers is likely to face escalating protests and hostility, so despite the law on the books, it is not always prudent for an employer to try everything that they might legally get away with.

(4) Job Security

Rights to job security are essential parts of the human right to 'social security'.[263] These are human rights because they underpin democracy and freedom. 'People who are hungry and out of a job', said President Roosevelt in 1944, 'are the stuff of which dictatorships are made.'[264] There are three main job security rights: (a) everyone has the 'right to work',[265] which means government should have policies to maintain full employment at fair wages. People also have (b) the right to reasonable notice and protection from unfair dismissal,[266] a right ultimately to be treated, as Magna Carta said, according to the 'lawful judgment of [one's] Peers, or by the Law of the Land'.[267] Finally, if enterprises face restructuring or insolvency, there is (c) the right to protection against redundancy or changes of terms.

(a) Full Employment

The 'right to work' in the Universal Declaration was originally the same thing as a duty on government to create full employment, through fiscal and monetary policy.[268] Generally speaking, unemployment is caused by lack of investment to employ people, whether that investment is private, public or

[263] UDHR 1948, art. 22; ICESCR 1966, art. 9. Charter of Fundamental Rights of the EU 2000, arts. 30, 34.
[264] F. D. Roosevelt, 'Eleventh State of the Union Address' (1944).
[265] UDHR 1948, art. 23; ICESCR 1966, art. 6.
[266] Termination of Employment Convention 1982 (c. 158).
[267] Magna Carta 1297, cl. XXIX.
[268] See also Employment Policy Convention 1964 (c. 122).

international.[269] Given the gaps where people change jobs, 'full employment' was defined by Lord Beveridge to mean a rate of consistently under 3 per cent, where people are to have all hours they need 'at fair wages', and 'having always more vacant jobs than unemployed men, not slightly fewer jobs'.[270] After the cross-party White Paper on *Employment Policy* in 1944,[271] the UK government successfully held unemployment at around 2 per cent until economic theories arguing that unemployment was 'natural' took hold, and the OPEC oil shocks had the effect of raising all production costs and inflation (see Ch. 11). EU law currently recommends that employment policies focus on soft measures to encourage private investment,[272] yet the absence of confidence in the private sector to invest is the problem that a public guarantee of full employment was designed to remedy. The Work and Welfare Reform Act 2016, section 1 did create a short-lived duty on the government to report to Parliament 'annually on the progress which has been made towards full employment', but this was left to lapse in 2017, and failed to define full employment as including fair working time and wages. Instead, while unemployment rates before the Covid-19 pandemic had been consistently falling, underemployment has been soaring since 2010: far more people are in intermittent or unsecure jobs, and therefore coping with unstable incomes. As Figure 5.4 shows, through the period of 1944 to around 1970, nearly full employment was maintained with low inflation until the US–Vietnam War, the OPEC crisis and Margaret Thatcher.

There have been a growing number of proposals for a 'job guarantee' in addition to social security benefits such as unemployment insurance. However, the UK has not yet taken this step: to provide a job from government at a living wage – for instance, eight hours a week of work, which evidence suggests is the average optimal working time for good health.[273] Instead the Jobseeker's Act 1995 requires people to fill out endless job application forms through public Jobcentres, and suffer the indignity, humiliation and demoralisation of constant rejection,[274] even though enough jobs simply do not exist. The administrative costs of this are significant,[275] and greater, rather than providing a universal income, or a job at a living wage,[276] to everyone not registered through the tax and national insurance system as in employment. Particularly given the climate

[269] E. McGaughey, 'Will Robots Automate Your Job Away? Full Employment, Basic Income, and Economic Democracy' (2021) *Industrial LJ*, part 2(3).

[270] W. Beveridge, *Full Employment in a Free Society* (1944) 18.

[271] White Paper, *Employment Policy*, Cmd 6527 (1944).

[272] Economic Policies Recommendation (EU) 2015/1184 and Employment Decision (EU) 2020/1512.

[273] D. Kamerāde, S. Wang, B. Burchell, S. U. Balderson and A. Coutts, 'A Shorter Working Week for Everyone: How Much Paid Work Is Needed for Mental Health and Well-Being?' (2019) 241 *Social Science & Medicine* 112353.

[274] Jobseekers Act 1995, ss. 1–6J, with 'work-related' and 'preparation requirements' or sanctions of benefit cuts.

[275] Welfare Reform Act 2012, ss. 1–17, on so-called 'universal' credit, and similar conditions.

[276] Cf. *R (Reilly) v Secretary of State for Work and Pensions* [2013] UKSC 68, where people were forced to work without wages for benefits for private companies who profited from free forced

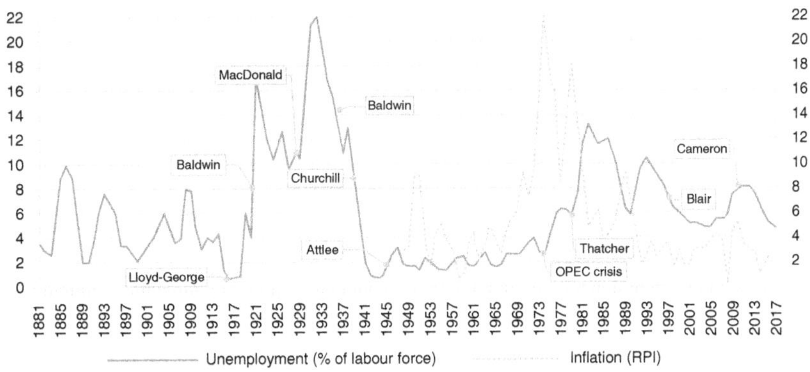

Figure 5.4 UK unemployment 1881–2017 and inflation, 1948–2016
Sources: J. Denman and P. McDonald, 'Unemployment Statistics from 1881 to the Present Day' (1996) 104 *Labour Market Trends* 5; ONS, Unemployment Rate, MGSX (1995–2017); ONS, RPI All Items: Percentage Change over 12 Months, CZBH (2017)

emergency, and the need to build new energy infrastructure, reforest land, insulate homes and install road chargers (see Chs. 12–15), and the growing needs of old age and early childhood care, there are considerable benefits in a job guarantee and universal income insurance. On top of public employment agencies, there are also private employment agencies. These are regulated to prohibit fees being charged to people for finding work.[277] Agencies in agriculture, shellfish or packing must be licensed, a rule reintroduced after dozens of cockle-picker deaths in Morecambe Bay in 2005.[278] It would appear that to uphold employment rights of every agency worker,[279] and to ensure that people find direct, permanent employment with a minimum cost, a general system of licensing and control of unreasonable and extortionate agency fees is desirable.[280]

(b) Notice and Fair Dismissal

The easier it is for employers to make people unemployed, the more unemployment there will probably be. The contrary theory is that if the law raises the costs of firing someone, employers will be deterred from hiring. However, there is no credible evidential support for this theory. The evidence suggests that job

labour. Further, A. Paz-Fuchs and A. Eleveld, 'Workfare Revisited' (2016) 45(1) *Industrial LJ* 29.

277 Employment Agencies Act 1973, s. 6. 278 Gangmasters Licensing Act 2004, ss. 4–13.

279 Conduct of Employment Agencies and Employment Businesses Regulations 2003/3319 contains more standards, e.g. no detriment for workers taking other jobs, no ads for non-existent jobs or strike-breaking.

280 Cf. *Stevens v Northolt High School, Teach 24 Ltd* (15 July 2014) Unreported, Westlaw 10246849, where an agency, Teach 24, got paid £228 a day for the work of a teacher, Miss Stevens, and Miss Stevens got £155 a day.

security rights are closely correlated with lower unemployment,[281] and also with greater innovation measured by numbers of patent filings.[282] The crucial issue is who decides hiring and firing policy in an enterprise, given the multiple conflicts of interest involved. First, a supervisor may have *personal* conflicts of interest, for instance if a dispute should actually result in the supervisor being removed, not the worker. Second, there are *stakeholder* conflicts – for instance, if directors want to reduce labour costs to augment their bonuses or salaries, or shareholders pressure directors to redistribute wealth to them, despite the damage to long-term sustainable enterprise. Third, there are *social* conflicts, where if all enterprises dismiss workers to externalise the costs they face (particularly in an economic crisis) there will be a reduction of overall incomes, depressing aggregate demand for business products, leading to more job cuts, and so deepening a spiral of depression. Clearly employees will usually want to retain their jobs, but co-workers will also have an interest in efficient enterprise if they share in the benefits. The main types of job security law are for reasonable notice before a fair dismissal with fair reasons and a redundancy payment if workers' positions are no longer there (see Ch. 5(4)(b)).

First, the Employment Rights Act 1996, section 86 requires employees receive at least one week's notice after one month's work, two weeks after two years, three weeks after three years and so on up to twelve weeks. A contract can improve upon this (very low) statutory minimum.[283] Common law may do so as well, since this requires that notice is 'reasonable',[284] unless there is a major breach of contract by an employee that justifies immediate dismissal.[285] A contract cannot otherwise be unilaterally terminated. Unless there are justifications for immediate dismissal, an indefinite contract operates according to its terms until both parties agree to end it.[286]

Second, there must be a fair dismissal procedure. Any express dismissal procedure in a contract of employment must be followed, and any worker may apply for an injunction to secure that the contractual procedure is followed.[287] There is further 'an implied contractual right to a fair process',[288] and

[281] Adams et al., 'The Economic Significance of Laws Relating to Employment Protection and Different Forms of Employment'.

[282] V. V. Acharya, R. P. Baghai and K. V. Subramanian, 'Labor Laws and Innovation' (2013) 56(4) *JL & Economics* 997.

[283] Cf. Germany's Civil Code, §622, 4 weeks for all workers, and then 2 months for workers over 5 years, 3 months for 8 years, 4 months for 10 years, 5 months for 12 years, 6 months for 15 years, 7 months for 20 years.

[284] *Creen v Wright* (1875–6) LR 1 CPD 591 (a month's notice reasonable for indefinite hiring of a clerk).

[285] ERA 1996, s. 86(6); *Atkin v Acton* (1830) 172 ER 67 (sexual assault of another employee).

[286] *Société Générale, London Branch v Geys* [2012] UKSC 63 (a clause stating the employer could terminate 'with immediate effect' irrelevant; it continued in a notice period, so entitling the employee to a bonus).

[287] *Edwards v Chesterfield Royal Hospital NHS Foundation Trust* [2011] UKSC 58.

[288] *West London Mental Health NHS Trust v Chhabra* [2013] UKSC 80, [37].

indicative guidance is elaborated by the ACAS Code of Practice.[289] If there is failure to comply with this, a court may raise an award of compensation for unfair dismissal by up to 25 per cent.[290] In conducting a dismissal procedure, employers should always first give warnings (again, unless there is action justifying summary dismissal), be prompt and consistent, investigate any allegations, inform employees and allow them to put their case, allow employees to be accompanied, and allow the employee to appeal any formal decision. The main institution which is often lacking, however, in most UK workplaces is an elected work council to determine these issues. By contrast, the University of Oxford gives its staff congregation the right to determine dismissals, and German law empowers an elected work council to veto dismissals based on conduct or capability. Particularly in larger organisations, elected members of the workforce, who are independent from the dispute, are likely to have the fewest conflicts of interest. In cases where conduct or capability is at issue, the tendency for management and 'HR' staff to line up with supervisors who are personally involved is a common detriment to sustainable enterprise.

Third, there must be fair reasons before any dismissal. At common law,[291] and in equity,[292] there has long been a requirement for fairness, albeit haphazardly enforced.[293] At common law, the right to fair reasons before dismissal covers at least those cases where an employer breaches the 'duty of mutual respect'.[294] In addition, the Employment Rights Act 1996, section 94 partially codifies 'the right not to be unfairly dismissed by his employer'. However, the statutory right, unlike common law and equity, is currently subject to a two-year qualification period, which has ping-ponged up and down through changes in Conservative and Labour governments.[295] Under section 98, an employer has a duty to show that a dismissal is 'fair' in the sense that 'the employer acted reasonably' and had a reason related to 'capability or qualifications', conduct, redundancy or a legal obligation.[296] Sadly, the courts have chosen to interpret 'acted reasonably' to allow a 'reasonable range of responses' test. This does not mean 'Wednesbury unreasonableness' or 'perversity', but

[289] *ACAS Code of Practice 1: Disciplinary and Grievance Procedures* (2015).

[290] TULRCA 1992, s. 207A.

[291] *R v Richardson* (1758) 97 ER 426, per Lord Mansfield (removal of a portman only for good cause). Also, *Johnson v Unisys Ltd* [2001] UKHL 13, [44], Lord Hoffmann remarking he would 'be able to' find the power to award a remedy for unjust dismissal at common law, if this was consistent with statute.

[292] *Dean v Bennett* (1870) LR 6 Ch 489 (removal of minister had to be according to 'ordinary principles of justice').

[293] Cf. *Ridge v Baldwin* [1964] AC 40, per Lord Reid doubting *obiter* the extent of common law rights.

[294] *Wilson v Racher* [1974] ICR 428 (landowner treated gardener arrogantly, justifying the gardener treating himself as constructively dismissed, before notice period for a statutory claim). *Chhabra* [2013] UKSC 80 approved.

[295] ERA 1996, s. 108; E. McGaughey, 'Unfair Dismissal Reform: Political Ping-Pong with Equality?' [2012] *Equal Opportunities Rev*, issue 226.

[296] ERA 1996, s. 98.

appears to deny that a Tribunal court has power to substitute its judgment for the judgement of an employer. This appears to be precisely what the Act was intended to achieve. The result is uneven application of the requirement for fairness in dismissal, depending on the judge and the case. For example, in *Bowater* the Court of Appeal upheld a Tribunal decision that a National Health Service trust unfairly dismissed a senior staff nurse, who had to restrain a naked patient and joked that 'It's been a few months since I have been in this position with a man underneath me.'[297] While it may not have been the wisest remark, the notion that someone should lose their job over it was one that the Tribunal and Court of Appeal rightly rejected. On the other hand, in *Turner*, Elias LJ held that it was within the reasonable range of responses for a train company to dismiss a senior train conductor after they found that an abnormal number of 'automatic non-issued tickets' were issued by her from her 'Avantix' machine.[298] Although the employer investigated, and found no evidence of wrongdoing, the Tribunal held she could legitimately be found to have engaged in 'spasmodic pilfering'. The chances of someone litigating this case to the Court of Appeal, to defend her reputation of honesty, without actually being honest, are vanishingly small; the real explanation was that the 'Avantix' machine was difficult to use, and someone within the employing entity made a decision to dismiss and then stuck to it with pig-headed malice. The better approach would be to recognise that an employer must act reasonably or proportionately in pursuit of a legitimate aim, and taking action as suitable, necessary and in a balanced fashion. An alternative, which would relieve the courts of second-guessing employer choices in most cases, would be to defer to an enterprise dismissal decision only if an elected work council, which is independent, has determined that a dismissal is just. The remedy for unfair dismissal is usually damages, consisting of a 'basic' award for the fact of dismissal, and a 'compensatory' award that includes economic losses and injury to feelings as is 'just and equitable', but currently capped at fifty-two weeks' pay.[299] Damages at common law should generally be consistent with the statutory scheme.[300] Courts may award reinstatement, although this is rare after a dismissal.[301] This underlines the importance of injuncting and preventing unjust dismissals through workplace machinery before the fact.

(c) Redundancy and Transfers

There are additional rights relating to economic dismissals, which arise due to restructuring or insolvency. 'Redundancy' means that someone's job is no

[297] *Bowater v Northwest London Hospitals NHS Trust* [2011] EWCA Civ 63.
[298] *Turner v East Midlands Trains Ltd* [2012] EWCA Civ 1470.
[299] ERA 1996, ss. 119, 123 and 124. [300] *Johnson v Unisys Ltd* [2001] UKHL 13.
[301] ERA 1996, ss. 114–17; *Port of London Authority v Payne* [1993] EWCA Civ 26.

longer viewed as necessary in an enterprise because of 'diminished' demand,[302] or more simply dismissals that are 'not related to the individual'.[303] There are three main rights. First, there is a duty to consult any individual, follow at least five steps of warning, secure a result 'with as little hardship to the employees as possible', set and follow selection criteria and seek to offer alternative employment.[304] Otherwise any dismissal will be unfair. A controversial reference to dismissals for 'some other substantial reason' in unfair dismissal rules has been interpreted by Lady Hale in the Supreme Court to mean 'not contractual misconduct',[305] but in the past has been (it appears erroneously) interpreted to allow dismissals when employees do not accept wage cuts.[306]

Second, for any proposal of twenty or more redundancies within ninety days there is a duty to consult employee representatives, meaning a trade union, to avoid, reduce and mitigate the consequences of dismissal.[307] Failure to do this will result in a 'protective award' of up to ninety days' pay from the date the unlawful dismissals were made.[308] The consultation should begin before a decision is made, and 'in good time', including any controlling undertaking.[309] The same duties are triggered if there is to be a transfer of an 'undertaking'[310] – that is, an 'organised grouping of resources'. Employees of a transferred undertaking have the right to the same terms before and after the transfer. In practice, redundancies are both widespread and routine in the UK, since they are used as a supposed signal to the stock market that an enterprise is making 'tough decisions' in the interests of shareholders:[311] a petty habit that damages enterprise sustainability, and signals total failure of those managers.

Third, wherever redundancies do eventuate, employees have a right to redundancy pay, usually a week's pay per year worked, and one and a half week's pay for people aged 41 or more.[312] If an enterprise is also insolvent, there is limited protection of wages through priority rules and the National Insurance fund (see Ch. 7(1)(a)(iv) and 7(1)(c)). If the rules' goal is to internalise the social costs of job losses, it does not yet appear that the duties and remedies are sufficient.

302 ERA 1996, s. 139. 303 TULRCA 1992, s. 195.

304 *Williams v Compair Maxam Ltd* [1982] ICR 156 (EAT).

305 *Reilly v Sandwell Metropolitan Borough Council* [2018] UKSC 16, [32].

306 *Hollister v National Farmers' Union* [1979] ICR 542.

307 TULRCA 1992, s. 188; Collective Redundancies Directive 98/59/EC.

308 TULRCA 1992, s. 189.

309 *AEK ry v Fujitsu Siemens Computers Oy* (2009) C-44/08; *United States v Nolan* [2015] UKSC 63.

310 Transfer of Undertakings Directive 2001/23/EC, art. 7.

311 E.g. J. Eley, 'M&S Warns of Tough Decisions Ahead on Job Cuts and Store Closures', *Financial Times* (10 July 2018).

312 ERA 1996, ss. 135, 141 and 162.

(5) Conclusion

Labour is the heart of enterprise, and yet in three major respects the law falls short of both standards in international human rights and the principle of enterprise that governance power should mirror people's contributions. First, although the UK has a workable system of minimum standards for labour rights, these are deeply precarious – for example, in failing to ensure universal coverage, in allowing low pay and long hours, and failing to guarantee adequate job security. This failure to uphold universal standards harms productivity and innovation, yet virtually all limits of the law could be rectified through existing powers to enact secondary legislation.[313] The same limits exist in the minimum standards set by EU law. Second, the right to voice at work, to ensure that people share fairly in the prosperity of enterprise, is a systematic failure. The regression away from sectoral collective bargaining and agreements, and the paucity in protecting the right to vote at work – board representation and elected work councils with binding rights in management – result in an absence of fair wage scales and the fostering of unfair competition across industry. Although highly imperfect, the exceptions in the UK are universities where (for all the faults) those in London, Scotland, Cambridge and Oxford guarantee votes of staff for governing councils, ensure that elected bodies determine important issues such as job tenure, and there is a system of national pay bargaining and sectoral collective agreement. This could be altered at any point through several measures such as updating the Model Articles for companies and the UK Corporate Governance Code.[314] The third limit, in common with the problems in Chapter 4, is that workers do not yet have adequate control over their capital in pension funds: this can be amended at any point by increasing the proportion of member nominated trustees.[315] Increasing the responsiveness of enterprise to people who contribute to it would also mark great strides towards fairer competition, the focus of Chapter 6.

[313] McGaughey, 'A Social Recovery, Workplace Democracy and Security', explaining the ERA 1999, s. 23 (extending scope); ERA 1996, s. 209 (eliminating qualification periods); Welfare Reform and Work Act 2016, s. 1 (exemplifying how government could resume action for full employment); and Work and Families Act 2006, s. 13 (power to raise holidays).

[314] CA 2006, s. 19 (power to issue new Model Articles).

[315] Pensions Act 2004, s. 243 (power to raise pension fund democracy).

6

Competition and Consumers

Contents

The central justification for private enterprises, where investors may profit from production, is that competition ensures they serve the public interest. The father of economics, Adam Smith, believed that, with corporations banned, a world of competitive partnerships would 'make nearly the same distribution' as if 'the earth [were] divided into equal portions', like they were 'led by an invisible hand'.[1] Even the pursuit of a cardinal sin like greed would, with competition, paradoxically advance the public interest. 'It is not from the benevolence of the butcher, the brewer, or the baker, that we expect our dinner', wrote Smith, 'but from their regard to their own interest.'[2] An enemy of monopoly, Smith also saw that when competitors speak it often ends in a 'conspiracy against the public'.[3] For this reason, rules against restraint of trade and unlawful combinations developed into modern competition law. First, the law prohibits 'abuse of a dominant position' by large enterprises. Second, it prevents mergers that create dominant positions that impede competition. Third, it bans collusion between enterprises that restrict competition. The problem is, there is no consensus in law or economics about what 'fair competition' means, either in the scope of regulated 'undertakings', the extent of legitimate corporate power, or the role of public enterprise.

[1] A. Smith, *The Theory of Moral Sentiments* (1759) Part IV, ch. 1, §10.

[2] A. Smith, *An Inquiry into the Nature and Causes of the Wealth of Nations* (1776) Book I, ch. 2, §2 and ch. 7, 'A competition will begin among them . . . .'

[3] Smith, *The Wealth of Nations*, Book I, ch. 10.

Competition law engages at least two fundamental rights: the 'freedom to conduct a business', and 'a high level of consumer protection'.[4] These connect with US President Roosevelt's address in 1944, that argued for a right to 'freedom from unfair competition and domination by monopolies at home or abroad'.[5] Most of the time, competition law's goal is 'consumer welfare'. Yet this is just a part of the law's aim to prevent 'competition from being distorted to the detriment of the public interest'.[6] By contrast, Chicago School (see Ch. 2(1)(b)) lawyers argue the single goal of competition law (or 'antitrust') should be consumer welfare.[7] The same school argues that most competition laws do not maximise consumer welfare, and even that 'monopoly power, and the concomitant charging of monopoly prices ... is an important element of the free-market system'.[8] But in most democratic countries, a reductive consumer welfare standard is rejected, and broad competition law rules are better enforced. Where the so-called 'consumer welfare' standard is applied the most, namely in the USA, the outcomes are the worst, from higher food prices to tech monopolies exploiting user data (see Ch. 6(2)(c)(i)). This chapter outlines (1) the framework of fair competition; (2) dominance, abuse and merger control; (3) cartels and collusion; and (4) state involvement and aid.

(1) Framework of Fair Competition

As Chapter 1 explained, the basic shape of modern competition law crystallised over the twentieth century, to focus on the abuse of power by big business. Crucially this meant separating labour, internal firm governance and social services from most prohibitions on monopoly and cartel behaviour. The framework of fair competition that has emerged involves (a) a basic set of minimum consumer rights, (b) the application of competition law to 'undertakings' for fair standards beyond these minimum rights and (c) enforcement through judicial remedies and government regulators. In addition, this section discusses (d) value added tax, and other duties, that raise revenue from consumption.

[4] CFREU 2000, arts. 16 and 38. Cf. ICESCR 1966, art. 6 ('right to work'); art. 11 ('improvement of living').

[5] F. D. Roosevelt, 'Eleventh State of the Union Address' (1944).

[6] E.g. *Konkurrensverket v TeliaSonera Sverige* (2011) C-52/09, [22]. See also, *British Airways plc v Commission* (2007) C-95/04, [106] law not only about 'prejudice to consumers directly' but 'an effective competition structure'.

[7] E.g. R. Bork, *The Antitrust Paradox: A Policy at War with Itself* (1978) 426–9, arguing for 'consumer welfare' not 'a multi-goal jurisprudence', to make 'us as wealthy as possible', but 'distribution of that wealth' is for 'other laws'. But how does wealth reach consumers absent distribution? Bork's thesis is a paradox, at war with itself.

[8] *Verizon Communications Inc. v Trinko*, 540 US 398 (2004) per Scalia J.

(a) Consumer Rights

The foundations of fair competition are a minimum set of consumer rights: a floor of rights through which nobody should fall. Unlike a system of so-called 'freedom of contract',[9] rights in statute, at common law and in equity mitigate consumers' unequal bargaining power, flowing from the unequal distribution of property (see Ch. 2(2)(f)). A marginal group of consumers may shift markets, by switching where they buy, and so impelling producers to alter their production to avoid loss.[10] But consumers evidently cannot have such an effect if they are given take-it-or-leave-it deals on standard-form contracts where 'all competitors use the same clauses'.[11] There is no credible empirical evidence to support an unqualified claim that 'firms cannot have a significant impact on the prevailing conditions of sale, such as prices, if its customers are in a position to switch easily'.[12] Instead, there is overwhelming evidence that competition does not alter basic imbalances of 'bargaining power', including a consumer's 'level of knowledge' or asymmetries of information (see Ch. 2(2)(d)).[13] Further, businesses routinely take advantage of the very human and irrational choices and errors we persistently make (see Ch. 2(2)(g)).[14] In law, the main definition of a consumer is 'an individual acting for purposes that are wholly or mainly outside that individual's trade, business, craft or profession'.[15] Thus, transactions for the purpose of consumption, not production, are the core concern, and set the scope, of modern consumer rights.

In 1962, US President John F. Kennedy gave a landmark speech on the need to advance consumer rights, identifying four types that remain a good

[9] 'A fearsome weapon in the fist of the strong, a blunted tool in the clutch of the weak . . . .': O. Gierke, 'The Social Role of Private Law' (1889) trans. E. McGaughey (2018) 19(4) *German LJ* 1017.

[10] D. Cayne and M. J. Trebilcock, 'Market Considerations in the Formulation of Consumer Protection Policy' (1973) 23(4) *U Toronto LJ* 396.

[11] F. Kessler, 'Contracts of Adhesion – Some thoughts about Freedom of Contract' (1943) 43 *Columbia L Rev* 629, 631–2; M. Jensen and W. Meckling, 'Theory of the Firm: Managerial Behavior, Agency Costs and Ownership Structure' (1976) 3 *J Financial Economics* 305, 330. On empirical work, see E. Warren, 'Product Safety Regulation as a Model for Financial Services Regulation' (2008) 43(2) *J Consumer Affairs* 452.

[12] EU Commission, *Notice on the Definition of the Relevant Market for the Purposes of Community Competition Law* [1997] OJ C372/5, [13]. This notice is not law, but reflects the evidence-free views of Commission staff in 1997. A rather different view was taken in *easyJet Airline Co. Ltd v Commission* (2006) T-177/04, [99], the Court stating 'demand substitution constitutes the most immediate and effective disciplinary force on the suppliers of a given product'. This does not mean switching is always effective, as the Commission mistakenly implies.

[13] A consistent view in EU law, e.g. in *Aziz v Caixa d'Estalvis de Catalunya* (2013) C-415/11, [44]–[45].

[14] See H. Collins, 'Book Review' (2014) 77(6) *MLR* 1030; O. Bar-Gill, *Seduction by Contract: Law, Economics, and Psychology in Consumer Markets* (2012).

[15] Consumer Rights Act (CRA) 2015, s. 2. Cf. Unfair Terms in Consumer Contracts Directive (UTCCD) 1993 (93/13/EEC) art. 2 referring to a 'natural person'. The previous UK definition included small businesses, even if incorporated: *R&B Customs Brokers Ltd v United Dominions Trust Ltd* [1988] 1 WLR 321 and Unfair Contract Terms Act 1977, s. 12(1)(a). The UK reference to an 'individual', arguably, could still encompass legal individuals.

framework today.[16] First, there is the right 'to safety', and to this can be added the long-standing duty to provide goods of 'quality' – that is, at least satisfactory – and no unfair terms.[17] In the UK, the Consumer Protection Act 1987, after the Product Liability Directive 1985, aims to prevent defective products that 'may distort competition', and seeks to achieve 'a fair apportionment of the risks inherent in modern technological production'.[18] All producers are jointly and strictly liable for any product 'defect' that causes death, injury or property damage and, if producers are insolvent, suppliers and retailers are liable.[19] The producer may only defend itself by arguing that the state of science meant they could not know of the danger.[20]

Related to this, the Consumer Rights Act 2015 says goods must be of 'satisfactory quality'[21] and be repaired or replaced if defective.[22] Services must be performed with reasonable care and skill.[23] The problem is, a right to goods of 'satisfactory' quality still lets companies sell products that are not 'built to last', or 'made to break'. Consumers constantly buying cheap things is good for business sales figures. Yet the material, resource and environmental costs of excess production and waste are massive and disproportionate.[24]

Surrounding these rights of 'safety' and 'quality', the Consumer Rights Act 2015 enshrines a general control of 'unfair terms', following the Unfair Terms in Consumer Contracts Directive 1993. First, a term is in the scope of regulation if it is not part of the 'price payable', or does not specify the 'main subject matter of the contract'.[25] The meaning of price-payable or main-subject-matter terms must be construed restrictively,[26] and a term is excluded from regulation 'only if it is transparent and prominent'.[27] Second, a term will be unfair if 'contrary to the requirement of good faith, it causes a significant imbalance in the parties' rights' to the consumer's detriment.[28] An unfair term

[16] See also UN Conference on Trade and Development, *UN Guidelines for Consumer Protection* (2016).

[17] J. F. Kennedy, 'Special Message to the Congress on Protecting the Consumer Interest' (15 March 1962). Kennedy put the issue of 'quality' together with the right to choose, though it makes sense to treat this with safety now.

[18] Product Liability Directive (PLD) 85/374/EEC, recitals 1 and 2.

[19] Consumer Protection Act (CPA) 1987, ss. 1–3 and 5; PLD 1985, arts. 1, 3, 5–6 and 9.

[20] CPA 1987, s. 4; PLD 1985, art. 7. This exception is construed extremely tightly.

[21] CRA 2015, s. 9, and also 'fit for purpose' in s. 10.

[22] CRA 2015, ss. 19 and 23; s. 31 (a contract term cannot 'exclude or restrict the trader's liability' for these rights).

[23] CRA 2015, s. 49 and generally among business, Supply of Goods and Services Act 1982, s. 13.

[24] E.g. J. Hickel, *Less Is More* (2020) ch. 5, and washing machines' average lifespan dropping under 7 years.

[25] CRA 2015, s. 64(1); UTCCD 1993, art. 4.

[26] *Kásler v OTP Jelzálogbank Zrt* (2014) C-26/13, [54]–[58]. This approach was not adequately adopted in *OFT v Abbey National plc* [2009] UKSC 6, saying unplanned overdraft fees were in a 'package' of bank account prices. Cf. *Director General of Fair Trading v First National Bank plc* [2001] UKHL 52, [12] per Lord Bingham.

[27] CRA 2015, s. 64(2).

[28] CRA 2015, s. 62(4). UTCCD 1993, art. 3. The better view is that 'significant imbalance' is part of good faith, not a separate and additional requirement to prove.

is severed from the contract and not binding on the consumer.[29] The aim of unfair term control is 'based on the idea that the consumer is in a weak position vis-à-vis the seller or supplier, as regards both his bargaining power and his level of knowledge', and so the aim is that the law 're-establishes equality' between the parties that primitive contract law lacks.[30]

Schedule 2 of the Act and the Directive's Annex lists examples of unfair terms. This includes any term binding a consumer to an arbitration claim, or hindering a right of access to courts.[31] It includes binding consumers to terms that a business purports to unilaterally alter, without a valid reason, or terms limiting liability for death or personal injury.[32] As consumer contracts are often a gateway to other human rights, consumer law must be construed to give effect to those other rights. For example, in *Kušionová v SMART Capital a.s.* the Court of Justice held a bank security contract term, which allowed enforcement against the debtor's home without any review in court, was ineffective. This was necessary as 'the loss of a home is one of the most serious breaches of the right to respect for the home' and so review in court must be possible (see Ch. 14).[33] Consumers, along with any 'person', also have a fundamental right to equal treatment in access to 'services', regardless of their gender, sexual orientation, race, disability or belief, under the Equality Act 2010.[34]

The second main right, according to JFK, was the right 'to be informed'. As well as rights against misrepresentations of fact or law,[35] consumers have a right that products match samples, descriptions or models.[36] Advertising is regulated to prohibit misleading information, including a prohibition on subliminal persuasion techniques (see Ch. 17(4)(b)). Various unfair, misleading and aggressive marketing practices are also prohibited.[37] Labelling is regulated, particularly for food ingredients, warnings for safety and to show the jurisdiction where a production was made (see Ch. 13(4)(b)). However, a major problem is that information is usually not clearly presented to enable full comparative choices. For example, although nutritional information is there, food does not have quick, easy-to-read traffic-light labelling (e.g. green = healthy; amber = less so; red = unhealthy). Nor is there a requirement yet for products to display the

[29] CRA 2015, ss. 62(1)–(2) and 67; UTCCD 1993, art. 6.

[30] *Aziz v Caixa d'Estalvis de Catalunya* (2013) C-415/11, [44]–[45].

[31] CRA 2015, Sch. 2, para. 20. *Asturcom Telecomunicaciones SL v Nogueira* (2010) C-40/08. Cf. *AT&T Mobility LLC v Concepcion*, 563 US 333 (2011) 5:4 opinion, holding arbitration clauses must be given effect.

[32] CRA 2015, Sch. 2, paras. 1 and 11; UTCCD 1993 Annex.

[33] *Kušionová v SMART Capital a.s.* (2014) C-34/13, [64]–[65].

[34] Equality Act 2010, ss. 28–9; see both *Constantine v Imperial Hotels* [1944] KB 693 and *Kruse v Johnson* [1898] 2 QB 91 for anti-discrimination rights at common law. These go beyond rights codified in statute. Cf. *Bull v Hall* [2013] UKSC 73 (successful claim against hotel for refusing access on grounds of sexual orientation); and *Lee v Ashers Baking Co. Ltd* [2018] UKSC 49 (unsuccessful action against cake shop refusing to write 'support gay marriage' on a cake's icing).

[35] Misrepresentation Act 1967, s. 3 from the Unfair Contract Terms Act 1977, s. 8.

[36] CRA 2015, ss. 11, 13–14.

[37] Unfair Commercial Practices Directive 2005/29/EC, arts. 6–9.

carbon intensity of production and distribution, even if consumers want to stop climate damage. Even when there is full information, this is not enough by itself for consumers to be informed. Information must be quick and easy to process, as we often think fast, not slow (see Ch. 2(2)(g)). There must also be a way for consumers to get fair terms beyond the minimums.

(b) Scope of Competition Law

A third right, according to JFK, was the 'right to choose' from 'a variety of products and services at competitive prices'. But where 'competition is not workable and Government regulation is substituted', there would be 'an assurance of satisfactory quality and service at fair prices'.[38] This recognised competition may lead to a 'just price',[39] but if conditions for workable markets are absent, 'reasonable terms' should be guaranteed in law.[40] In Chapter 2(2)(h) it was argued that one essential condition for private competitive enterprise is wide distribution of the material assets and finance for production. This condition is often not met. As Chapters 8–19 explain, price regulation is the norm for the most important things in economic life, namely in education, health, finance, energy, transport, food, water, housing, communication and media. Though 'price regulation' is sometimes seen as 'the antithesis of the free market',[41] few would argue that prices controlled by corporate power are 'free' or somehow 'unregulated'. Markets are built by laws of contract, property, corporations and other rights, and these all regulate prices with foreseeable results. The common law, the Sale of Goods Acts and every system of civil law have long implied terms that a reasonable price (if not specified in a contract) must be paid,[42] as does consumer law.[43] But otherwise, the law uses the concept of an 'undertaking' to set the limits of competition law.[44]

38 Kennedy, 'Special Message to the Congress'.

39 *Corpus Juris Civilis* (*c.* 534) Codex, Book IV, Title XLIV, §2, had a rule known as *laesio enormis*, enabling unjust transactions to be unwound. Common law, equity and statute long had substantive and procedural limits on prices, e.g. *Vernon v Bethell* (1762) 28 ER 838. See also, W. Boyd, 'Just Price, Public Utility and the Long History of Economic Regulation in America' (2018) 35 *Yale J Regulation* 721.

40 Cf. *Allnutt v Inglis* (1810) 12 East 527, 537, per Lord Ellenborough: 'the general principle is favored, both in law and justice, that every man may fix what price he pleases upon his own property, or the use of it; but if . . . the public have a right to resort to his premises and make use of them, and he have a monopoly in them for that purpose . . . he must, as an equivalent, perform the duty attached to it on reasonable terms . . . .' This concerned a London Dock Company's warehouses. See also, *Munn v Illinois*, 94 US 113 (1876).

41 A. Jones and C. Townley, 'Competition Law' in C. Barnard (ed.), *European Union Law* (2nd ed. 2017) 536.

42 Sale of Goods Act 1979, s. 8(2): 'Where the price is not determined [by contract] the buyer must pay a reasonable price.'

43 CRA 2015, s. 51.

44 'Undertaking' is a literal translation of the German *Unternehmen*, which in German law discourse is often used in the same way as 'enterprise'. However, the EU law meaning of 'undertaking' is narrower than the term 'enterprise' as used in this book.

An 'undertaking' in the Treaty on the Functioning of the European Union (TFEU), and the Competition Act 1998,[45] is subject to the prohibitions on abuse of dominance (article 102) and unjustified collusion (article 101). But its meaning is not yet codified. The Court of Justice has consistently stated the law's purpose is 'to prevent competition from being distorted to the detriment of the public interest, individual undertakings and consumers'.[46] Unlike Chicago theory, the text of TFEU, article 102 shows that 'prejudice of consumers' is a subcategory of harm, such as 'unfair trading conditions'.[47] The idea that 'consumer welfare' is European Union (EU) law's goal, or even a primary goal, is mistaken, and would in any case be deeply undesirable. For example, under a limited consumer welfare view, competition law might not endorse agreements by business to phase out energy wasting or environmentally damaging products,[48] nor might it break up monopolies that threaten democratic stability (see Ch. 17). Protecting the environment and democracy, or upholding competition, benefits consumers indirectly,[49] but there is no sound legal or empirical reason to limit the law to one goal of consumer welfare (see Ch. 2(1)(b)). Slogans, like competition law, '[exist] to protect consumers, not competitors',[50] are historically false, legally dubious[51] and in the US have been deployed to endorse mass-concentration of industry. They forget that in private enterprise, 'wherever competition is not, monopoly is; and that monopoly, in all its forms, is the taxation of the industrious for the support of indolence, if not of plunder'.[52] Competition law is ultimately about power and the public interest,[53] and this purpose is essential to interpret what is an 'undertaking'.

[45] Competition Act 1998, ss. 1 and 2. Note that s. 60 requires that UK law is interpreted to be 'consistent with the treatment of corresponding questions arising in EU law'.

[46] *Konkurrensverket v TeliaSonera Sverige* (2011) C-52/09, [22]; *GlaxoSmithKline Services Unltd v Commission* (2009) C-513/06, [63]; *British Airways plc v Commission* (2007) C-95/04, [106]. Also the TEU, art. 3(3) embeds competition in the broad goals: 'on balanced economic growth and price stability, a highly competitive social market economy, aiming at full employment and social progress, and a high level of protection and improvement of the quality of the environment'.

[47] TFEU, art. 102(b) mentions 'prejudice to consumers', while other forms of abuse do not. As a matter of literal interpretation alone, EU law cannot be constrained to consumer welfare: *Europemballage Corp. and Continental Can Co. Inc. v Commission* (1973) Case 6-72, [26].

[48] E.g. *CECED* [2000] OJ L187/47, on washing machines, holding there was no elimination of competition as business could compete on price, image and technical performance.

[49] Cf. *Post Danmark v Konkurrencerådet* (2012) C-209/10, [20], referring to 'practices that cause consumers harm through their impact on competition'.

[50] R. H. Bork and J. G. Sidak, 'What Does the Chicago School Teach about Internet Search and the Antitrust Treatment of Google?' (2012) 8(4) *J Competition L & Economics* 663.

[51] *Brown Shoe Co. v United States*, 370 US 294, 320 (1962) per Warren CJ, that legislative history of antitrust shows 'concern with the protection of competition, not competitors'. This is a good policy: in particular, a dominant competitor should not be protected. Cf. *Reiter v Sonotone Corp.*, 442 US 330 (1979) endorsing Bork's stance.

[52] J. S. Mill, *Principles of Political Economy* (1848) Book IV, ch. 7, §7.

[53] L. Khan and S. Vaheesan, 'Market Power and Inequality: The Antitrust Counterrevolution and Its Discontents' (2017) 11 *Harvard L & Policy Rev* 235.

So, what is an 'undertaking' according to the Court of Justice? It 'encompasses every entity engaged in an economic activity, regardless of the legal status of the entity or the way in which it is financed'.[54] But what is an 'economic' activity? The Court of Justice's main answer has been that this means *not* organisations based on 'solidarity' that pursue a 'social purpose'. These are not undertakings.[55] But then, which entities are 'social' or characterised by 'solidarity'? There is no clear answer, but it seems to depend mostly on case-by-case identification. Like the meaning of 'employee' or 'worker' it must be guided by a purpose. That said, the absence of 'bright-line rules' could come from the court's reluctance to 'limit their jurisdiction', and a desire for 'preserving the ambit of their own power'.[56] Nevertheless, five exemptions are clear: for labour, legal entities, corporate groups, social insurance or care, and sovereign acts.[57]

First, since the US Clayton Act of 1914 and the founding of the International Labour Organization in 1919, it has been settled that 'labour is not a commodity' and should never be a target of competition law.[58] 'Competition on the merits',[59] on quality and efficiency in making products or services, is damaged if businesses may profit in a competition to cut wages. Even if prices fall, total social welfare is harmed as workers earn less income to consume. People who unionise must never be treated as a cartel, and unions that cover sectors must never be treated as monopolies, because the very purpose of unions, collective bargaining and action is to eliminate practices that will undermine fair competition 'on the merits'.[60] The clear position of UK law is that no person who works personally can be subjected to competition law or any other type of tort,[61] and in international law 'everyone' including the self-employed may organise or take collective action.[62] In EU law, the position is the same. As 'workers' in the Treaties,[63] employees are not undertakings, but part of the

54 *Höfner and Elser v Macrotron GmbH* (1991) C-41/90, [21], holding that a public employment agency is an 'undertaking'. It was further held under art. 106 (now) that failing to satisfy demand would be an abuse.

55 *Federación Española de Empresas de Tecnología Sanitaria v Commission* (2003) T-319/99.

56 N. Dunne, 'Knowing When to See It: State Activities, Economic Activities, and the Concept of Undertaking' (2010) 16 *Columbia J Eur L* 427, 457–8.

57 NB: In the CJEU case law, the rationale of 'solidarity' may not have been made explicit for corporate groups but, as explained below, this may be the preferable way to rationalise the law.

58 Clayton Act of 1914, §6, 15 USC, §17. This was adopted by the ILO. Cf. *In re Debs*, 64 Fed 724 (1894), 158 US 564 (1895); *Loewe v Lawlor*, 208 US 274 (1908) reversed by the National Labor Relations Act of 1935.

59 *Intel v Commission* (2017) C-413/14 P, [133]–[134].

60 See also *Albany International BV v Stichting Bedrijfspensioenfonds Textielindustrie* (1999) C-67/96, [59]: 'certain restrictions of competition are inherent in collective agreements between organisations representing employers and workers. However, the social policy objectives pursued by such agreements would be seriously undermined if management and labour were subject to' the competition laws applicable to business.

61 Trade Union and Labour Relations (Consolidation) Act 1992, s. 296, leading to protection under s. 219.

62 UDHR 1948, art. 23; ICESCR 1966, art. 8.

63 TFEU, art. 45.

undertaking they work for, like all other agents.[64] Furthermore, self-employed people are not undertakings, since TFEU, article 49 states that the right of establishment 'shall include the right to take up and pursue activities as *self-employed* persons *and* to set up and manage *undertakings*' (emphasis added).[65] It follows that 'self-employed' persons are distinct from 'undertakings'. Self-employed persons may become undertakings – for instance, by incorporating a company with others or by creating a partnership or another entity. But as sole-traders they begin as non-undertaking service providers. The scant case law to the contrary, particularly *Pavlov v Stichting Pensioenfonds Medische Specialisten*,[66] is regrettable in that it did not pay sufficient regard to the text of the Treaties, or appear to have any understanding of the history of international human rights. It also failed to ensure consistency with the transfers of undertakings case law, and now Directive, which defines an 'undertaking' as an 'entity', and an 'entity' in turn as an 'organised grouping of resources', not a human being that is self-employed (see Ch. 5(4)(c)). In any event, *Pavlov* should now be considered wrong, because the Charter of Fundamental Rights of the EU (CFREU), ratified afterwards, affirmed the right for all 'Workers and employers' (that is, including the self-employed) 'to negotiate and conclude collective agreements' and 'to take collective action to defend their interests, including strike action'.[67]

Thus, on their plain meaning, the Treaties foresee a threefold division:

Undertakings (arts. 101–7)	**Self-employed** (art. 49)	Workers (*Albany*)

The spectrum of EU legal status among persons performing work

However, in *FNV Kunsten Informatie en Media v Nederlanden*, Dutch orchestra staff were given contracts stating they were self-employed, and were then pursued by the Dutch Competition Authorities for organising a union. The Court of Justice held they were outside the scope of competition law, if they were 'false self-employed' (see also Ch. 4(1)(b)).[68] However, in an unhelpful *obiter dicta*, the court said if they were genuinely self-employed, the workers could be 'undertakings',[69] and therefore subject to the same suppression tactics that scarred late-nineteenth-century US labour law. This opinion was mistaken; it failed to refer to TFEU, article 49, and it has been subject to withering

64 *Suiker Unie v Commission* (1975) C-40/73, [539]; *Criminal Proceedings Against Becu* (1999) C-22/98, [99].

65 TFEU, art. 49.

66 *Pavlov v Stichting Pensioenfonds Medische Specialisten* (2000) C-180/98, [74]–[77] on whether a compulsory pension fund for self-employed medical specialists contravened competition law. It did not.

67 CFREU 2000, art. 28.

68 *FNV Kunsten Informatie en Media v Staat der Nederlanden* (2014) C-413/13, [38]–[41].

69 *FNV Kunsten Informatie en Media v Staat der Nederlanden*, [28].

criticism.[70] It is flatly incompatible with international human rights law, and the express terms of the EU Treaties. For example, self-employed advocates, cab drivers or book sellers who are sole traders may always organise a union, bargain, protest or strike – in precisely the same way that they may organise partnerships and companies, but not be separately subjected to competition law.[71] This is the core human right to freedom of association.[72]

Second, like people in unions, individuals who combine as partners, in corporations or other legal entities are not treated as separate undertakings. The partnerships or corporations are undertakings. If they are not in the same economic group (see below) and they collude, they will violate competition law. In one sense, a corporation is a cartel of capital, because the same effects as a cartel can be achieved if different people merge their businesses, instead of remaining separate and colluding (see Ch. 6(3)). The rationale for exempting firms from competition law was never entirely clear as a matter of history,[73] but the best justification today may be that internal corporate governance could be regulated to follow democratic principles,[74] and 'could become a vehicle for rationalized wealth distribution'.[75] By contrast, contractual networks are not subject to a code like companies.

Third, corporate groups are exempt if they are a 'single economic unit'.[76] In *Viho Europe BV v Commission*, the Court of Justice held that Parker Pen making an agreement with its wholly owned subsidiary could not be found to have violated article 101 (banning collusion), because the corporate group acted as a 'single economic unit within which the subsidiaries do not enjoy real autonomy'.[77] If one company has 'decisive influence' over another, either through a majority shareholding, special rights or jointly held control rights, that economic unit will be exempt.[78] The group will also be jointly responsible

70 Cf. V. de Stefano and A. Aloisi, 'Fundamental Labour Rights, Platform Work and Human-Rights Protection of Non-Standard Workers' in J. R. Bellace and B. Haar (eds.), *Labour, Business and Human Rights Law* (2018); Bocconi LSR Paper No. 3125866.

71 An obvious limit could be that a partnership or company could not collude with one or more other such entities. There are also good policy arguments for enabling small businesses to organise under art. 101(3).

72 ECHR 1950, art. 11; CFREU 2000, art. 12(1).

73 Cf. S. Paul, 'The Firm Exemption and the Hierarchy of Finance in the Gig Economy' (2019) 16(1) *U St Thomas LJ* 44.

74 Some entities are more democratic than others, depending on jurisdiction. Unions have the most democratic governance: Ch. 5(1)(d). Companies follow some principles of accountability, depending on their recognition of investor and employee votes: Chs. 3(2)(a), 4(1)(c), 5(3)(a).

75 A. A. Berle, 'Property, Production and Revolution' (1965) 65(1) *Columbia L Rev* 1, 17.

76 In the USA, see *Copperweld Corp. v Independence Tube Corp.*, 467 US 752 (1984) on a parent and subsidiary, and *Sunkist Growers Inc. v Winckler & Smith Citrus Products Co.*, 370 US 19 (1962) on co-operatives.

77 *Viho Europe BV v Commission* (1996) C-73/95, [16].

78 E.g. *Akzo Nobel NV v Commission* (2009) C-97/08, *Fuji Electric System Co. Ltd v Commission* (2011) T-132/07 and *Shell Petroleum NV v Commission* (2013) C-585/12 P.

for violations of other members of the group,[79] even if an entity transfers activities to another legal form.[80]

Fourth, insurance, health or care services are exempt if they are 'social'. In *FENIN v Commission*, a group of medical goods and equipment sellers (FENIN) sued the Spanish national health system group (*Sistema Nacional de Salud*) for paying debts late, alleging it was an 'undertaking' and that late payments were an abuse.[81] The CJEU Grand Chamber held that, as the Court of First Instance had said, the national health system was not an undertaking because it acted 'according to the principle of solidarity in that it is funded from social security contributions and other State funding and in that it provides services free of charge to its members on the basis of universal cover'.[82] So, whenever services involve cross-subsidies, and socialised risk-sharing, they will not be undertakings.[83] Curiously, the UK government decided to subject the National Health Service (NHS) to competition law in 2012, despite the NHS's obvious basis in solidarity (see Ch. 9).[84] Notably, the same reasoning has not been applied to collectively bargained pension schemes: these are undertakings.[85] This contrasts to US antitrust law which exempts any state action or government corporations, such as the US Postal Service offering savings accounts.[86] It is a general principle of EU law that the 'Treaties shall in no way prejudice the rules in Member States governing the system of property ownership',[87] so EU law cannot require privatisation of any sector. However, in the EU market, publicly owned enterprises may sell services (such as electricity, trains, buses or telecoms) to people in other member states that may have no influence through the vote over that public service. This fact may be argued to warrant some accountability in competition law, when citizens in another member state lack the vote.[88]

Fifth, public authorities that carry out administrative acts are not undertakings. For instance, the European Organisation for the Safety of Air Navigation (Eurocontrol) did not count as an undertaking even though it collected route charges, set by its member states.[89] Similarly, the national port authority in

79 *Akzo-Nobel v Commission* (2009) C-97/08, [58]–[59].

80 *Parker-Hanifin v Commission* (2014) C-434/13, [41].

81 *Federación Española de Empresas de Tecnología Sanitaria (FENIN) v Commission* (2006) C-205/03.

82 (2003) T-319/99, [39]. Also *AOK Bundesverband v Ichthyol-Gesellschaft Cordes* (2004) C-264/01 (German social health insurance fund).

83 Also *Cisal di Battistello Venanzio & C Sas v INAIL* (2002) C-218/00, holding Italian workplace national insurance for accidents and disability to not be an undertaking.

84 Health and Social Care Act 2012, s. 72.

85 *Albany International BV v Stichting Bedrijfspensioenfonds Textielindustrie* (1999) C-67/96.

86 E.g. *US Postal Service v Flamingo Industries*, 540 US 736 (2004). Also *Southern Motor Carriers Rate Conference Inc. v United States*, 471 US 48, 64 (1985) on trucking rates; *Parker v Brown*, 317 US 341, 352 (1943) on raisin crop marketing.

87 TFEU, art. 345.

88 An interesting question is how social accountability and public funding could operate between countries.

89 *SAT Fluggesellschaft mbH v Eurocontrol* (1994) C-364/92.

Genoa delegated its power to charge port users to a private company, but this was still not an undertaking.[90] While it is easy to state a distinction between administrative and economic services, it is not entirely clear what the difference is. What is the point of principle between entities selling air or port services (which are not undertakings), and entities selling train or postal services (which are undertakings)? A better approach to courts defining 'undertakings' would be to write legislation exempting all public services that are accountable through the vote to the customers they serve, in whatever member state.

(c) Enforcement

The fourth main consumer right suggested by JFK was the right 'to be heard', meaning both consideration in formulating government policy and a fair hearing in court. First, as Chapters 8–19 show, there are many enterprises in which consumers and the public have real rights to be heard through the vote or (and often much more loosely) through administrative systems of voice such as consultation. But in purely private enterprises, where competition is thought to work, consumers do not usually have a vote.[91] 'Voting with your feet', or the threat, by choosing another competitor, is often a good way to be heard.

Second, there is always a private right of litigation for consumer or competition violations, even if it may cost time and money. In EU law there must be adequate and effective sanctions for breaches and the right to bring representative actions, where consumer groups have a 'legitimate interest', and joint actions against all those in supply chains.[92] In UK law, small claims can be made relatively easily through www.moneyclaim.gov.uk and courts should consider if contract terms are unfair even if this is not specifically claimed.[93] Yet the incentives to spend money and time to go to court, a daunting prospect, mean many consumers will not litigate even where they would win. For competition law, any business that can prove harm from an abuse of dominant position, or from unlawful collusion, has a claim for 'full compensation' and defendants face penalties for failing to disclose relevant evidence.[94] For example, in *Courage Ltd v Crehan*, the Court of Justice held that a pub subject to an unlawful vertical restraint (a contract tying it to buy beer exclusively from a brewery) would be entitled to damages for losses after

[90] *Diego Cali e Figli Srl v SPEC* (1997) C-343/95. Also *Compass-Datenbank GmbH v Austria* (2012) C-138/11, [42] (data collection authority not an undertaking despite charging fees).

[91] A contrary proposal was made by R. Nader, J. Seligman and M. Green, *Taming the Corporate Giant* (1976) 124–5 to require corporate boards have consumer directors, though the authors mainly had in mind quasi-public, and highly regulated, enterprises, such as the automotive industry. It is not clear why this is needed, say, in a very competitive butcher, baker or brewer company.

[92] UTCCD 1993, art. 7. [93] CRA, 2015, s. 71.

[94] Competition Damages Directive 2014/104/EU, arts. 3–8.

its business failed. Although the pub was party to the unlawful collusion (see Ch. 6(3)(c)), it was not the pub's fault, because the beer tie was imposed by the brewery: a national court had to take into account 'the respective bargaining power and conduct of the two parties to the contract'.[95] This illustrates that, like consumer rights, competition law too is ultimately concerned with abuse of bargaining power.

Third, there is public regulation. In the UK, the Competition and Markets Authority (CMA) considers consumer complaints, can require information from firms, injunct unfair terms or settle deals with firms.[96] However there is a clear lack of activism by government regulators. The CMA seems to have fought one significant case since 2014, against a care home,[97] and its predecessor, the Office of Fair Trading, fought just two successful cases from 2003 to 2013.[98] This is abysmal complacency, and shows a lack of incentives to do the job. Competition law enforcement is led by the Commission in the EU, with the ability to impose fines up to 10 per cent of world turnover and behavioural or structural remedies (see Ch. 6(2)(d)).[99] But in general, competition regulators have failed to combat monopolies,[100] and in the worst cases (such as *FNV*, see Ch. 6(1)(b)) have targeted vulnerable workers, presumably because attacking the poor is easier than doing their job. Fines make competition authorities look good as they generate money, but structural remedies that return far more in value to the public are lacking.

(d) Value Added Tax and Other Duties

Value Added Tax (VAT) is a major charge on consumption and revenue source, deriving from the VAT Directive 2006, and predecessors dating back to 1973 for the UK. The rate of VAT has gone from 8% in 1974, to 15% in 1979, 17.5% in 1991 (apart from two years over the financial crisis) and now 20% from 2011,[101] even though the minimum EU rate is 15%.[102] Under the Value Added Tax Act 1994, section 1(1) VAT is charged 'on the supply of goods or services' in the UK or imports into the UK.[103] Under sections 3–5, however, it must be a 'taxable supply ... other than an exempt supply' and done for consideration, by a taxable person, as part of the economic activities of that person. Schedule 8 sets out seventeen groups of supplies that have zero rates of VAT, including non-catered and generally healthy food (group 1); domestic

95 *Courage Ltd v Crehan* (2001) C-453/99, [32]. Lack of power means a claimant has 'clean hands' in UK law.

96 CRA 2015, Sch. 3, paras. 2–7 and Sch. 5, para. 14. E.g. *OFT v Foxtons Ltd* [2009] EWCA Civ 288.

97 *CMA v Care UK Health and Social Care Holdings Ltd* [2019] EWHC 2828 (Ch).

98 *OFT v Ashbourne Management Services Ltd* [2011] EWHC 1237; *Foxtons* above.

99 Implementation Regulation (IR) (EC) No. 1/2003, arts. 1–5 and 23.

100 Cf. *Guidance on the Commission's Enforcement Priorities in Applying Article 82* [2009] OJ C45/7, paras. 16–31.

101 Finance (No. 2) Act 2010, s. 3(1); VAT Act 1994, s. 2.

102 VAT Directive 2006/112/EC, art. 97.

103 VAT Act 1994, s. 1(1).

sewage and water (2); books and talking books for the blind (3–4); home building, 'substantially reconstructing a protected building', houseboats and caravans (5–6 and 9); transport (8); bank notes (11); medicines (12); charities (15); children's clothes (16); and women's sanitary products (19). These exemptions reflect the desire to not raise the cost of socially desirable goods and services, while zero rates for international services (7), gold (10), imports and exports (13) and European research (18) appear calculated to 'keep British goods and services as competitive as possible' internationally.[104] There are additional taxes on undesirable or harmful products, particularly tobacco, alcohol and petrol, diesel and other fossil fuels. Although in EU law there is a principle of 'fiscal neutrality' and a desire that sales taxes do not distort competition,[105] the UK's approach to VAT rightly prioritises social goals in its application. Since VAT is regressive, it appears undesirable for it to be so high, but it also appears not yet to take account of crucial matters such as the carbon footprint of products.

(2) Dominance, Abuse and Merger Control

Probably the most important function of competition law is to prevent private monopolies. Monopolies have long been seen as the 'great enemy to good management',[106] and, where not run by the public, they are 'the taxation of the industrious for the support of indolence, if not of plunder'.[107] It is also clear that 'monopoly is itself likely to be a product of complete *laissez-faire*'.[108] The law today aims to halt undertakings that 'abuse . . . a dominant position',[109] and the acquisition by merger of any dominant position. 'Competition on the merits' is condoned by the law,[110] and in rare cases this may lead to businesses becoming dominant through better products and efficiency. But the law is very sceptical that 'merit' involves mergers, takeovers or certainly restraint of trade, as a way to become dominant.

This view of the law was attacked in 2004 by a US Supreme Court judge, who asserted that 'monopoly power, and the concomitant charging of monopoly prices . . . is an important element of the free-market system'. Supposedly the 'opportunity to charge monopoly prices . . . is what attracts

[104] G. Morse and S. Eden, *Davies: Principles of Tax Law* (9th ed. 2020) 473; VAT Act 1994, Sch. 8.
[105] *Rank Group Ltd v Revenue and Customs Commissioners* (2012) C-259/10.
[106] Smith, *Wealth of Nations*, Book I, ch. 11.
[107] Mill, *Principles of Political Economy*, Book IV, ch. 7, §7.
[108] A. A. Berle, 'Modern Functions of the Corporate System' (1962) 62(3) *Columbia L Rev* 433, 436, noting the corporation at best 'fits awkwardly' in that frame. Indeed, Smith and Mill opposed corporations: Ch. 2(1).
[109] TFEU, art. 102; Competition Act 1998, s. 18(1). Schedule 3 lists major exceptions as planning obligations; anything involving 'services of a general economic interest'; compliance with law; international obligations; 'exceptional and compelling reasons of public policy' as designated by the Secretary of State; and coal, steel or agriculture agreements.
[110] *Intel v Commission* (2017) C-413/14 P, [133]–[134].

"business acumen" . . . [and] produces innovation and economic growth'.[111] This is an empirical assertion, and it is contradicted by all evidence.[112] The strangling of US antitrust, the aim to ensure that it is 'dead',[113] has meant that monopolies have become entrenched, especially in the digital economy, developing mass networks around core products and monetising personal data. Google, Facebook, Microsoft, Amazon and Uber are leading examples. Instead of innovating themselves, they copied others' innovations,[114] and took over other companies that innovated, and then limited that innovation. It was said by an early Facebook and PayPal investor that 'competition is for losers'.[115] But the evidence suggests that monopolies and dominance are what makes society lose, through higher prices, lower output and lower innovation.[116] This section discusses (a) dominance, (b) the categories of illegal abuse, (c) remedies and (d) merger control.

(a) Dominance

The acquisition of a dominant position, by competition 'on the merits', is not itself unlawful. However, as we see below, dominance does create 'special responsibility' and means conduct that might not otherwise be unlawful will count as an illegal 'abuse'.

111 *Verizon Communications Inc. v Law Offices of Curtis V. Trinko*, 540 US 398 (2004) per Scalia J. Stevens J, Souter J and Thomas J concurred in the result, rather than reasoning.

112 E.g. J. F. Reinganum, 'Uncertain Innovation and the Persistence of Monopoly' (1983) 73(4) *Am Economic Rev* 741.

113 See Judge Richard Posner (2017) YouTube at 5:04: 'antitrust is dead, isn't it? That was my impression . . . Amazon, Microsoft and Google [are] the three best companies in the world, so who's concerned whether they have monopolies, right? . . . I don't have any problem with prices, quality of the products . . . and neither does my cat who is an avid consumer of extremely expensive cat food, right? So we're happy.'

114 For example, Microsoft Windows (after 'DOS') replicated the Apple operating system; Zuckerberg's Facebook copied a network idea developed by the Winklevoss twins; Amazon is an online marketplace that originally sold other people's books and has since used data to copy others' products; Uber is a simplistic piece of software coupled with tax and rights evasion; Google came up with a better algorithm than rival search engines, but with this advantage soon captured a dominant position as a web portal, and aggressively took over other businesses. For an example of how founders do not see their riches as based on luck, see B. Gates, *The Road Ahead* (1996) 19, 'luck has played a role, but I think the most important element was our original vision'. See further, P. Piff, 'Does Money Make You Mean?' (2013) www.ted.com/talks/paul_piff_does_money_make_you_mean?language=en, showing that rigged Monopoly game players who got twice the money, more for passing Go, and double dice rolls, viewed their (inevitable) victory as deserved, despite knowing the game was rigged in their favour.

115 Whether or not this is true, monopoly is for fascists. Cf. P. Thiel, 'Competition Is for Losers', *Wall Street Journal* (12 September 2014). This second meaning of this quip, made a few years before Thiel spoke at Trump rallies, suggests that investors should try to identify market middle-man positions to exploit and monopolise. See Ch. 18.

116 E.g. J. Furman and P. Orszag, 'A Firm-Level Perspective on the Role of Rents in the Rise in Inequality', Presentation at 'A Just Society' Centennial Event in Honor of Joseph Stiglitz, Columbia University (16 October 2015).

The first step to defining dominance is usually the definition of a relevant market.[117] The basic test is to ask if goods or services are 'reasonably interchangeable by consumers', as explained in *United Brands Co. v Commission.*[118] Here, United Brands Co. (UBC – formerly United Fruit, now Chiquita Bananas) was exposed in 1975 by the US Securities and Exchange Commission (SEC) for bribing Honduran President Arellano to reduce export taxes (see also Ch. 13(1)). The European Commission then claimed that UBC had abused a dominant position by pricing its bananas excessively (see Ch. 6(2)(b)(i)). The Court of Justice held that to establish this, both the product and geographic markets were relevant. The 'banana is a privileged fruit', because it was not easily substituted with apples or oranges, for instance by 'the very young, the old and the sick'.[119] The relevant geographic market was Germany, Denmark, Ireland, the Netherlands, Belgium and Luxembourg (but not France, Italy and the UK) because of UBC's import practices. UBC's relevant European Community market share was 40–45 per cent (its world market share 35 per cent),[120] and the Court held this was enough to be dominant given the 'barriers to competitors entering the market'. These barriers were 'exceptionally large capital investments' needed to start and run banana plantations, the need for alternative sources from bad weather, a 'system of logistics', 'economies of scale' that newcomers cannot match and the 'mounting of very large-scale advertising campaigns'.[121] However, the Court concluded there was no abuse, and the Commission had not sufficiently proven prices were unfair, 'especially as for nearly 20 years banana prices, in real terms, have not risen on the relevant market'. Moreover the 7 per cent price difference with competitors 'cannot automatically be regarded as excessive'.[122]

Since *United Brands*, a mathematical rule of thumb is often used to define a market, known as the 'Small but Significant Non-transitory Increase in Price' test (or 'ssnip').[123] Although this is not binding, the European Commission's approach is to ask whether a permanent 5–10 per cent price rise would lead consumers to 'readily' switch to other products or services (e.g. apples to pears).[124] The more broadly a market is defined, the bigger it is and the less likely an undertaking will be found dominant.

117 *Volkswagen AG v Commission* (2000) T-62/98, [230]: a finding of dominance 'presupposes that such a market has already been defined'.

118 *United Brands Co. v Commission* (1978) Case 27/76, [12].

119 *United Brands Co. v Commission*, [25]–[31].

120 *United Brands Co. v Commission*, [36]–[57], [97] and [108].

121 *United Brands Co. v Commission*, [122] and [123]: competitors face 'almost insuperable practical and financial obstacles'.

122 *United Brands Co. v Commission*, [265]–[266].

123 J. E. Fortenberry, 'Definition of Markets in Merger Cases: Developments since the 1968 Department of Justice Merger Guidelines' (1982) 25 *Howard LJ* 595, on its introduction by the US DoJ in 1982.

124 European Commission, *Notice on the Definition of the Relevant Market for the Purposes of Community Competition Law* [1997] OJ C372/5, [17].

What is the lowest market share in which an undertaking may be dominant? So far, the lowest was in *British Airways plc v Commission*, where British Airways (BA) had a share of 39.7 per cent in the air travel agency services market. Despite BA losing some market share in recent years, it was dominant as it had global reach, and its nearest competitor had 5.5 per cent.[125] The Court concluded that BA had abused its dominant position by giving travel agents rewards for recommending it over other airlines, as it had 'no interest in applying its reward schemes other than ousting rival airlines' (see Ch. 6(2)(b)(iii)).[126] If there is a market share over 50 per cent then this will be, 'save in exceptional circumstances, evidence of the existence of a dominant position'.[127] A minority viewpoint argues that 'barriers to entry' rarely exist,[128] and that therefore almost every market is competitive. However, in many cases size itself can be enough.[129]

The 'market' is a contested concept, although it may not be necessary under EU law.[130] The plain wording of article 102 prohibits *any* 'abuse by one or more undertakings of a dominant position within the internal market'. This should merely require dominance over property, not a 'market'. It must simply be 'within' the EU's internal market or a 'substantial part' of it.[131] For example, undertakings may dominate people by taking their data. However, in 2014, the EU Commission cleared a merger between Facebook and WhatsApp for $19 billion, when WhatsApp had 600 million users. It said that WhatsApp 'is not active in online advertising', and 'regardless of whether Facebook' would 'start collecting WhatsApp user data' for use on its own ads, this would raise no competition concern in the online market for ads.[132] After this, and the disasters of Brexit and Trump (see Ch. 17(3)(b)(ii)), in 2017, the Commission fined Facebook €110 million for misrepresenting that it could not do 'reliable automated matching between Facebook … and WhatsApp users' accounts', which it immediately did. 'Facebook staff were aware of the

125 *British Airways plc v Commission* (2003) T-219/99, [211], [224]–[225].

126 (2003) T-219/99, [288].

127 *AKZO Chemie BV v Commission* (1991) C-62/86, [60]. Cf. *Hoffmann-La Roche & Co. AG v Commission* (1979) Case 85/76, [41]: 'very large shares are in themselves … evidence of … a dominant position'.

128 Bork, *The Antitrust Paradox*, ch. 16, 311, arguing size usually indicates 'forms of superior efficiency'.

129 J. S. Bain, 'Economies of Scale, Concentration, and the Condition of Entry in Twenty Manufacturing Industries' (1954) 44 *Am Economic Rev* 15. Cf. A. Jones, B. Sufrin and N. Dunne, *EU Competition Law: Text, Cases and Materials* (2019) 126, where it is said that 'a firm can exercise market power for a significant time only if barriers to entry exist' and, at 128–34, goes on to list dozens of potential barriers to entry, based on costs, structure and behaviour.

130 This differs from the Competition Act 1998, s. 18(1): 'abuse of a dominant position in a market is prohibited'.

131 A member state is substantial, e.g. Belgium, *General Motors Continental NV v Commission* (1975) Case 26/75.

132 Case M.7217 – Facebook/WhatsApp, C(2014) 7239 final. Press Release (3 October 2014) IP/14/1088.

user matching possibility.'[133] While there is an active market for data, and a market in adverts, the true concern is a dominant position over data to which consumers have personal rights. This is a competition concern, since the dominant data holder may sell or use data, replacing the consumer's ability to act as his or her own data-seller: the presence of rights does not change the factual possession of data, and the possibility that data spreads uncontrollably to third parties, including hostile foreign governments. By contrast, the Commission considered that 'privacy-related concerns' from 'data within the control of Facebook . . . do not fall within the scope of the EU competition law rules'.[134] It is wholly unclear what justified this. Arguably dominance of any kind – over a market or not – is a competition issue over which the Commission has jurisdiction.

Another question concerns the conditions in which 'one *or more* undertakings . . . of a dominant position' may commit an abuse. The clear wording of the law suggests that not only a monopoly, but a duopoly or oligopoly can dominate and abuse. This requires no collusion or concerted practices as are found in article 101 (see Ch. 6(3)). In *Società Italiana Vetro SpA v Commission*, it was suggested that if 'undertakings jointly have, through agreements or licences, a technological lead', this could be collective dominance. It also spoke cryptically of 'economic links' as a possible requirement.[135] The Court of Justice later added in similar cryptic fashion that an 'agreement' or 'links in law' are not needed, and there could be 'other connecting factors' depending on 'an economic assessment' or 'the structure of the market'.[136] The better view is there must simply be 'market concentration, transparency, and product homogeneity', meaning the parties can 'anticipate one another's behaviour and are therefore strongly encouraged to align their conduct'.[137] It would follow that if a group of independent undertakings with a dominant market share (e.g. 15%, 20% and 25%) engage in the same abusive practices, this is prohibited, without need for proof of any further condition. The same abuse could include high prices, patent hoarding, discrimination, exclusive dealing or anything else listed in the text and case law of article 102.

133 Knowing one fact and representing another is prima facie fraud, especially since staff knowledge is attributable to a company, but the Commission seemed unable to draw that conclusion: (18 May 2017) IP/17/1369.

134 C(2014) 7239 final, para. 164.

135 *Società Italiana Vetro SpA v Commission* (1992) T-68/89, [358].

136 *Compagnie Maritime Belge Transports SA v Commission* (2000) C-395/96, [41]–[45]. Cf. *Laurent Piau v Commission* (2005) T-193/02, saying three hypothetical conditions are (1) the oligopolists can know and monitor others' behaviour; (2) there must be no incentive to depart from a common policy; and (3) foreseeable reactions of competitors or consumers must not jeopardise this. These hurdles are not in the Treaties.

137 *Gencor Ltd v Commission* (1999) T-102/96, [276].

(b) Abuse

The categories of 'abuse' of a dominant position are unlimited in law, but contested in economic theory. In particular, it has been claimed that unfair prices,[138] exclusive dealing, predatory pricing, or price discrimination,[139] are not problems for efficiency, and may even be 'pro-competitive' by increasing output. These arguments, made without evidence, stand in stark contrast to the express terms of the law. Giving four main examples, article 102, like the Competition Act 1998, section 18, says:

abuse may, in particular, consist in:

(a) directly or indirectly imposing unfair purchase or selling prices or other unfair trading conditions;
(b) limiting production, markets or technical development to the prejudice of consumers;
(c) applying dissimilar conditions to equivalent transactions with other trading parties, thereby placing them at a competitive disadvantage;
(d) making the conclusion of contracts subject to acceptance by the other parties of supplementary obligations which, by their nature or according to commercial usage, have no connection with the subject of such contracts.

While these are general examples, and can only be a starting point for interpretation, they are also concrete types of abuse that have no further qualifications in law. To be within EU jurisdiction, the abuse must potentially 'affect trade between Member States'.[140] This phrase has been interpreted broadly,[141] meaning most cases create concurrent jurisdiction, and so often require co-operation of competition authorities in the EU or even globally (see Ch. 6(1)(c)). The categories of abuse are not closed, as the four groups above are 'not an exhaustive enumeration'.[142] However, the problem has often been an unduly narrow interpretation of, and enforcement against, even the abuses that the law names.

(i) Unfair Prices and Conditions

The first category of abuse involves (a) 'prices' or 'trading conditions' that are 'unfair'. This covers what are commonly referred to as price exploitation,

[138] E.g. R. H. Coase, 'The Problem of Social Cost' (1961) 3 *JL & Economics* 1 asserting distribution and efficiency are separate.

[139] E.g. Bork, *The Antitrust Paradox*, chs. 15, 18 and 20 respectively.

[140] TFEU, art. 102. Competition Act 1998, s. 18(1): similarly if abuse 'may affect trade within the United Kingdom'.

[141] *Société Technique Minière v Maschinenbau Ulm GmbH* (1966) Case 56/65, [249] (if an effect can be foreseen that is at least potential or indirect); *Javico International and Javico AG v Yves Saint Laurent Parfums SA* (1998) C-306/96.

[142] *Europemballage Corp. and Continental Can Co. Inc. v Commission* (1973) Case 6/72, [26].

predatory pricing and margin squeezing.[143] First, on unfair prices, there are four options for how prices could be set. These are (1) by a public body that is democratically accountable, (2) by firms in a competitive market where none have influence, (3) by a public body subject to weak or non-existent democratic accountability or (4) by firms that exercise highly unequal bargaining power against their customers, either individually or collectively. In the first two cases, a reasonable return above costs may be expected from its pricing structure (since the public bodies or competitive firms are accountable), while the latter two cases are a cause for concern. As we saw above, in *United Brands* the Court of Justice in 1978 rejected the allegation that bananas had been priced excessively, when they cost 7 per cent more than competing bananas. In its view an excessive price 'has no reasonable relation to the economic value of the product supplied', and this involves asking if 'the difference between the costs actually incurred and the price actually charged is excessive' – that is, either 'unfair in itself' or 'compared to competing products'.[144] The EU Commission later stated it 'is not and does not wish to act as a price regulator'.[145] By contrast, the Treaty expressly requires that 'any abuse' is prohibited.

If banana prices in *United Brands* were fair enough, what is an 'unfair' price? In 2001, in a *Deutsche Post* decision by the Commission, a price 25 per cent higher than the company's estimated costs was found to be unfair.[146] In 2018, in a *Gazprom* decision, the Commission found that prices 170 per cent higher than costs in gas imports to Bulgaria, Estonia, Latvia, Lithuania and Poland were (unsurprisingly) unfair.[147] In this way comparisons to competitor prices may not be as useful as cost estimates,[148] and while the figure of 25 per cent above costs may be regarded as abusive, a figure lower than this may be also. Of course, monopolies are likely to inflate their 'costs' – for instance, if their executives overpay themselves, create excessive managerial hierarchy, spend wantonly on fancy 'business' excursions or buy lavish and unnecessary buildings. A court should be mindful to estimate what a reasonable pay and expense structure ought to be.[149] If a standard rate of dividends is 8 per cent in a competitive market, a reasonable return for a dominant private enterprise should

[143] UTCCD 1993, Annex. Examples of unfair terms could also be relevant to interpreting any 'trading conditions' (see Ch. 6(1)(a)).

[144] *United Brands Co. v Commission* (1978) Case 27/76, [250]–[252].

[145] E.g. European Commission, *XXVIIth Report on Competition Policy* (1997) 29.

[146] COMP/C-1/36.915, *Deutsche Post AG – Interception of cross-border mail* (25 July 2001) para. 166.

[147] Case AT.39816, *Upstream Gas Supplies in Central and Eastern Europe* (24 May 2018) paras. 69–79.

[148] Cf. *AKKA/LAA v Konkurences padome* (2017) C-177/16, [58]–[60] on a copyright royalty distribution agency, the Court of Justice advised a Latvian court that comparison to other member states could be useful, but suggested a 20:80 cost-distribution ratio was not unreasonable.

[149] Cf. *United States v E.I. du Pont*, 351 US 377 (1956) finding a low market share, but assuming a dominant price was fine.

be construed restrictively, and probably be lower: for instance, a 7.5 per cent excess in prices (i.e. 0.5 per cent over the *United Brands* level) over reasonable costs may be a presumptive limit to what is appropriate. The key point is that the current state of the law lacks *any* standard.[150] To combat monopoly, a choice must be made.

Second, imposing unfair prices includes cutting pricing to force out competitors, a practice known as 'predatory pricing'. Before its landmark US antitrust case, J. D. Rockefeller's 'Standard Oil routinely slashed prices in order to drive rivals from the market', to then charge 'monopoly prices in markets where it faced no competitors'.[151] It has been asserted by Chicago School economists (the University of Chicago was founded by J. D. Rockefeller) that predatory pricing is 'a phenomenon that probably does not exist'.[152] Yet under European law it does exist in many successful cases. For example, in *AKZO Chemie BV v Commission*, a company called Engineering and Chemical Supplies Ltd in the benzonyl peroxide market (used for bleaching flour and plastic) complained to the Commission that AKZO BV had threatened to sell its chemicals at lower prices to ECS Ltd's flour customers if ECS Ltd entered into the plastic market. Internal documents showed AKZO BV did intend to undercut its competitors. The Court of Justice held that AKZO BV had abused its dominant position. 'Prices below average variable costs . . . those which vary depending on the quantities produced', said the court, 'must be regarded as abusive. A dominant undertaking has no interest in applying such prices except that of eliminating competitors' to later raise prices through 'its monopolistic position'. If prices are above average variable costs, but 'under average total costs', then it is abuse if a plan to eliminate a competitor is shown.[153]

Both EU and UK law have rejected the idea that a 'predatory pricing' strategy must be shown to be likely to recoup its up-front losses.[154] This was, however, held to be the law in the USA, a stance calculated to eliminate any finding of predatory pricing, as the future is somewhat difficult to prove.[155] A central business strategy to achieve growth in many online or app-based firms – such as YouTube (now Google), Facebook, Uber, Amazon and Deliveroo – is

150 Cf. C. Townley, E. Morrison and K. Yeung, 'Big Data and Personalized Price Discrimination in EU Competition Law' (2017) 36 *YB Eur L* 683.

151 L. Khan, 'Amazon's Antitrust Paradox' (2017) 126 *Yale LJ* 710, 723; I. Tarbell, *A History of the Standard Oil Company* (1904) 188.

152 Bork, *The Antitrust Paradox*, 154.

153 (1991) C-62/86, [71]–[72]. Cf. *Post Danmark v Konkurrencerådet* (2012) C-209/10, holding that selective discounts were not abusive where they were higher than average incremental costs.

154 *Tetra Pak International SA v Commission* (1996) C-333/94 P, [44] (where Tetra Pak held 90–95% of the market); *France Télécom SA v Commission* (2009) C-202/07, [110]–[113] (where France Télécom's subsidiary Wanadoo unlawfully undercut competitors).

155 *Brooke Group Ltd v Brown & Williamson Tobacco Corp.*, 509 US 209, 226 (1993). See also, *Matsushita Electric Industrial Co. v Zenith Radio Corp.*, 475 US 574, 589–94 (1986) 5–4, stating that Bork's evidence-free view that predatory pricing was impossible had become 'consensus'.

predatory pricing.[156] They all began by offering products for 'free', and consistently made losses, but built up large networks, with funding from eager investors. Once dominance was established, they raised prices (or increased the ads). An extra dimension is the exploitation of customer personal data (in the cases of YouTube, Google and Facebook, whose monopolies are substantially secure) and the exploitation of labour by denial of rights (in the cases of Uber, Amazon and Deliveroo, whose monopolies are still being consolidated). Once prices are raised (e.g. by growing the number and length of ads, or taking larger cuts from suppliers, drivers or riders), competitors find it impossible to break back in because the networks have become ubiquitous.

Third, there are cases where a dominant undertaking has infrastructure for (or is a supplier to) a market where it also competes with firms relying on its infrastructure. If it raises prices, it can 'squeeze the margins' of profit made by its competitor, and force them out. In *Deutsche Telekom AG v Commission*, the Commission found Deutsche Telekom AG overcharged retail market competitors to access the circuits connecting telephones to distribution frames (the 'local loop'). It charged its own retail customers less. These charges were in fact approved by the German telecoms regulator. The Court of Justice agreed with the Commission it was an abuse for Deutsche Telekom to 'squeeze the margins' of competitors. If 'it has an exclusionary effect on competitors who are at least as efficient as the dominant undertaking', it will be an abuse.[157] Similarly, in *Konkurrensverket v TeliaSonera AB*, on a preliminary reference after the Swedish competition authority found TeliaSonera squeezed its broadband competitor margins, the Court of Justice repeated that if an 'as efficient competitor' would likely be excluded, there will be an abuse. But it does not matter if 'the desired result, namely the exclusion of those competitors, is not ultimately achieved'. Margin-squeezing conduct will be an abuse all the same.[158]

(ii) Limiting Production and Technical Development

The second category of abuse in article 102 is (b) 'limiting production, markets or technical development to the prejudice of consumers'. Unlike other categories of abuse, this expressly requires that prejudice to consumers is shown, although there is no requirement for the prejudice to be direct. An example of limiting production, which created the broad definition of 'undertaking' (see Ch. 6(1)(b)), is *Höfner v Macrotron GmbH*. Here, an executive recruitment agency claimed that the German public employment agency (*Bundesanstalt für*

[156] E.g. Khan, 'Amazon's Antitrust Paradox', 746–68 (on Amazon's method).

[157] (2010) C-280/08, [253].

[158] (2011) C-52/09, [65]. See also *Telefónica SA v Commission* (2014) C-295/12 (Spain's privatised telecom operator fined €151.875m for squeezing margins in broadband market); *Slovak Telekom a.s. v Commission* (2018) T-851/14, [265] (General Court reduced a fine after Commission finding of abuse, as no exclusionary effect, requiring that practice was 'likely to make it at least more difficult for the operators concerned').

Arbeit) abused a dominant position by holding a monopoly on recruitment services and being 'manifestly incapable of satisfying demand' in the executive recruitment market.[159] All enterprises may limit production out of laziness, as in *Höfner*, but private enterprises in a dominant position will especially aim to limit production out of desire to raise prices and profits.[160]

Another obvious kind of limit on production or technical development is patent hoarding, or simply not developing a technology held under patent despite a clear social need.[161] Currently the leading case related to patents is *AstraZeneca plc v Commission*. For a stomach ulcer drug, omeprazole, branded as Losec, AstraZeneca plc misrepresented the dates of invention to national patent offices and courts, and deregistered a capsule version, to obtain longer patent protection (so limiting public use). The Court of Justice upheld a fine of €60 million by the Commission for depriving generic drug manufacturers of the ability to produce the drug, based on 'highly misleading representations with the aim of leading public authorities into error'. The fact that AstraZeneca could otherwise withdraw Losec capsules (under registration procedures) did not mean it was not an abuse to do so under article 102.[162] Similarly, in *Tetra Pak Rausing SA v Commission*, acquiring an exclusive patent licence (for ultraviolet light milk packaging) that would shut out competitors, when a company already had 90 per cent market share, was an abuse even though the same conduct would not be an abuse for other companies.[163] In *Google Android*, the Commission also fined Google €4.34 billion for, among other things, 'obstruction of development and distribution of competing Android operating systems' by paying manufacturers not to install any version other than its own (see Ch. 16(3)(c)(i)).

A notorious example of patent hoarding, but one on which competition authorities are yet to take action, concerns electric vehicles. From 1990, automakers developed a viable electric car, but then buried the technology, conspiring with oil companies and the George W. Bush government to do so.[164] Similar limits on production of clean transport, with the same specious arguments (e.g. 'there is not enough consumer demand'), are currently being practised by all European auto-makers (see Ch. 15(2)(a)). Because of the terminal threat to the environment as we know it, this action is clearly against the public interest, including the consumer interest.

159 (1991) C-41/90, [31]–[34].

160 E.g. Commission Decision, *German Electricity Balancing Markets (E.ON)* (26 November 2008) COMP/39/388, accepting commitments from E.ON after it was accused of limiting electricity production to raise prices.

161 Note also the human right to the benefits of science: UDHR 1948, art. 27(1) and ICESCR 1966, art. 15(1)(b).

162 (2012) C-457/10 P, [98] and [132].

163 *Tetra Pak Rausing SA v Commission* (1990) T-51/89.

164 See the documentary films, *Who Killed the Electric Car?* (2006) and *Revenge of the Electric Car* (2011).

Limits on production and innovation are not exceptional, but systemic and familiar for most of the enterprises discussed in this book. This is particularly true for private, competitive enterprise, not just dominant ones, and is why there is a universal human right to the benefits of science.[165] Private education excludes students on the basis of their (parents') wealth (see Ch. 8). Private health firms in the USA refuse to insure people in need (Ch. 9). Banks fail to lend, particularly in crises when lending is most needed (Ch. 10). Electricity companies fail to build rural infrastructure (Ch. 12). Water companies fail to build pipes and sewers (Ch. 13). Builders fail to build enough houses (Ch. 14). Bus and train companies fail to run enough services (Ch. 15). Communication companies do not connect rural residents to the post, phones or the Internet (Ch. 16). Private media companies often do not provide quality viewing, but instead churn other people's content, or make cheap reality TV (Ch. 17). In many sectors, private enterprises, precisely when they are competitive, have an inherent incentive to restrict output, raise prices and reduce quality whenever they can. They need not be dominant. But stopping this abuse is even more important when they are.[166]

(iii) Price and Term Discrimination

The third main category of abuse is (c) 'applying dissimilar conditions to equivalent transactions with other trading parties' placing them 'at a competitive disadvantage'. This means discrimination, and it necessarily follows – as with equality rights at work, or in housing – that there is no such thing as an absolute right of a business (particularly a dominant undertaking) to deal or not deal with whoever they wish. First, a major group of cases concern price discrimination that affects 'other trading parties'. The right to run a business carries responsibilities to use those powers in the public interest.[167] In *British Airways plc v Commission*, it was held that BA abused its dominant position (with a 39.5 per cent market share) by giving some travel agents extra commissions when they promoted BA tickets over competitor tickets. With respect to the element of 'competitive disadvantage', the Court of Justice held that the practice must at least be capable of (1) 'making market entry very difficult' and (2) 'making it more difficult' for the dominant undertaking's 'co-contractors to choose between various sources of supply or commercial partners'.[168] The Court went on to explain that, because 'of its significantly higher market share', BA 'generally constitutes an unavoidable business partner in the market', and competitors lacked 'a sufficiently broad financial base to allow them effectively

[165] UDHR 1948 art. 27(1); ICESCR 1966, art. 15(1).

[166] See also A. A. Berle, 'A New Look at Management Responsibility' (1962) 2 *Human Resource Management* 3, who suggested that, with regard to maintaining full employment, companies 'ought not to hoard when expenditure is needed' and they might need 'to slow down under some conditions'.

[167] Cf. CFREU 2000, arts. 16 and 38.

[168] *British Airways plc v Commission* (2007) C-95/04, [68].

to establish a reward scheme' on the same scale. It is open to a dominant undertaking to objectively justify such discrimination, on the basis that it does in fact benefit consumers, but its conduct must not go 'beyond what is necessary'.[169]

A second group of cases concerns 'refusal to supply' another undertaking that is a competitor. In *Commercial Solvents Corp. v Commission*, the subsidiary of a US company, Commercial Solvents Corp. (CSC), stopped selling an ingredient for a drug used against tuberculosis (aminobutanol) to the Giorgio Zoja pharmacy lab in Milan. CSC stopped selling to Zoja because it made the drugs itself. The Court of Justice held that if 'an undertaking . . . has a dominant position in the market in raw materials' it commits abuse if it 'refuses to supply a customer, which is itself a manufacturer . . . and therefore risks eliminating all competition on the part of this customer'.[170] Similarly, the Court suggested it would be an abuse for a car-maker, such as Volvo, to refuse to supply spare parts to repairers, charge unfair prices for them or no longer produce spare parts for models in circulation.[171] It was held to be an abuse where Irish TV companies refused to give programme information to a TV guide publisher even though it was under copyright.[172] It was also an abuse for drug companies that developed a computer grid to determine where drugs were demanded, which had become an 'industry standard', to deny licences to competitors for access.[173] In cases of electricity (see Ch. 12), rail (Ch. 15)[174] and telecoms infrastructure (Ch. 16),[175] there are also specific legislative requirements for access that automatically require fair terms.

These 'refusal to supply' cases have been framed by the EU Commission as falling under category article 102(b) – of limiting production to the prejudice of consumers – reasoning that refusal to supply does not mean a competitor is 'made subject to conditions', but is rather 'not offered at all'.[176] However, the better view is that when an undertaking makes the identity of the contracting party an essential condition (as in all other types of discrimination) this is the very core of category (c).[177] It is an extreme form of charging higher prices to

169 *British Airways plc v Commission*, [75]–[86]. This is the same conceptual structure as justification in equality cases: Ch. 5(2)(d).

170 *Istituto Chemioterapico Italiano SpA and Commercial Solvents Corp. v Commission* (1974) Cases 6–7/73, [25].

171 *AB Volvo v Erik Veng (UK) Ltd* (1988) Case 238/87, [9].

172 *Radio Telefis Eireann and Independent Television Publications Ltd v Commission* (1995) C-241/91 P (the Magill guide).

173 *IMS Health GmbH & Co. OHG v NDC Health GmbH & Co. KG* (2004) C-418/01, [12].

174 Cf. Commission Decision, *Baltic Rail* (2 October 2017) where the Lithuanian railway undertaking physically removed rail track to prevent its use by an oil refining company with which it had a dispute.

175 *Slovak Telekom v Commission* (2018) T-851/14, [121].

176 *Oscar Bronner GmbH & Co. KG v Mediaprint Zeitungs- und Zeitschriftenverlag GmbH & Co. KG* (1998) C-7/97, [30].

177 Indeed, in many member states, the essential conditions of any contract, or *essentialia negotii*, are often thought to include the price, subject matter and the parties' identity. This distinction is therefore bizarre.

others than to a related party.[178] One reason why this matters is that category (c) does not require 'prejudice of consumers' is shown, but category (b) does.

Otherwise, it was held in *Oscar Bronner GmbH v Mediaprint GmbH* that a dominant undertaking will not be held to unlawfully refuse to supply a competitor unless (1) the refusal would likely eliminate all competition, (2) there is no objective justification and (3) there is no potential substitute, which makes that good or service 'indispensable'.[179] This is too strict a view of the law, since article 102(c) merely requires that competitors are put at a 'disadvantage', not eliminated.[180] Even under article 102(b) there is no need for 'elimination' of a competitor for there to be abuse.

In the largest case, *Microsoft Inc. v Commission*, Microsoft had refused to give server companies such as Sun Microsystems Inc. information necessary to enable it to build servers that operated with Microsoft Windows, which held 90 per cent of the operating system (OS) market, after Microsoft itself entered the server market. (Operating systems such as Windows, iOS or Android function as networks – platforms on which other software must operate – and so have an inherent tendency towards monopoly, because it is cheaper to have one OS, not develop apps for many.) After five years, the Commission fined Microsoft €497,196,304, and directed Microsoft to make server connectivity information available in 120 days. The General Court upheld the decision.[181] Notably, it rejected Microsoft's assertion that this ruling would deter 'incentives to invest' in technology as 'vague and theoretical arguments'.[182]

While article 102(c) concerns 'trading parties', it is worth asking here, could discrimination against consumers be an abuse under article 102(a)? Price discrimination is pervasive, from supermarkets charging different prices for the same food in different locations, to train fares rising or falling based on the time (and often need) of purchase, to internet sites extracting more or less data, showing more or fewer ads and showing different prices, depending on the person. It has been argued that price discrimination should be no concern where it increases output.[183] This argument endorses private enterprises redistributing wealth between groups of consumers, based on often arbitrary criteria that suit the firm: it may use its bargaining power to extract the greatest

[178] See also *Google Shopping*, Case 39740 (27 June 2017) (Ch. 18(3)(b)(ii)).

[179] (1998) C-7/97, [40] and [46], holding that a newspaper company with a 3.6% market share did not have a right from a newspaper company with a 46.8% market share to deliver its papers through its home delivery service.

[180] Cf. *Post Danmark v Konkurrencerådet* (2012) C-209/10, [30], suggesting price discrimination is not abuse without the effect of exclusion. If so, this must be regarded as an unwarranted addition to art. 102(c). If this group of cases is classified under art. 102(b) this is still an unjustified and restrictive addition to the text.

[181] NB: It categorised Microsoft's abuse as art. 102(b), of limiting production to the prejudice of consumers.

[182] *Microsoft Corp. v Commission* (2007) T-201/04, [698].

[183] E.g. R. Schmalensee, 'Output and Welfare Implications of Third Degree Price Discrimination' (1981) 71 *Am Economic Rev* 242.

sum based on a consumer's need. There seems to be no reason why this could not be unfair under article 102(a).

(iv) Tying, Bundling, Exclusive Dealing and Supplementary Obligations

The fourth express category of abuse is (d) requiring 'supplementary obligations' in contracts that 'by their nature or ... commercial usage, have no connection with the subject of such contracts'. The two main groups of case concern tying or bundling products or services and exclusive dealing. First, 'tying' is said to be requiring someone to buy a second product as a condition of buying the first (e.g. requiring retail stores to buy your unpatented nails, when they buy your patented nail guns[184]), while 'bundling' is said to be selling two products together (e.g. giving Coca-Cola retailers discounts only if they buy Coca-Cola's non-coke products, or giving rebates to reserve shelf space[185]). Not much of substance turns on this distinction. But more importantly, without any evidence, it has been argued by Chicago School lawyers that tying or bundling is not a problem, because a monopolist or dominant company can only ultimately charge a consumer one monopoly price (which, conveniently, it is said should not be regulated anyway) and so tying or bundling is therefore not a separate problem.[186] By contrast, the majority view is that a dominant undertaking may use tying/bundling to project its dominance from one market to another, thus colonising and monopolising an ever-increasing number of products or services.

The leading EU case so far on tying or bundling is *Microsoft Corp. v Commission*, where Microsoft Windows held 90 per cent of the computer OS market, and pre-installed its Windows Media Player: the OS and the media player were one 'bundle'. In 2004, the Commission found this abused a dominant position, as bundling software with the OS, 'in a market characterised by network effects', gave it 'a decisive momentum' over other competitors.[187] It fined Microsoft €497,196,304 for abuse, and required it to sell retailers both a Windows OS without the media player, and one with it. Predictably, perhaps, no retailer took up the option without the media player. Still, in 2007, the General Court upheld the Commission, approving the idea that media-player competitors must deploy major resources to 'overcome end users' inertia and persuade

184 *Hilti AG v Commission* (1994) C-53/92, upholding the Commission's finding of abuse by 'reinforcing its dominance on the Hilti-compatible nail market (where it is potentially more vulnerable to new competition)'.

185 *Coca-Cola Italia Undertaking* (1989) explained in European Commission, *XIXth Report on Competition Policy* (1989) [50] and *Coca-Cola Undertaking* [2005] OJ L253/21.

186 See the evidence-free assertions in *Schor v Abbott Laboratories*, 457 F 3d 608 (7th Cir 2006) per Easterbrook J, 'If the monopolist gets control of another component as well and tries to jack up the price of that item, the effect is the same as setting an excessive price for the monopolized component. The monopolist can take its profit just once; an effort to do more makes it worse off and is self-deterring.' This fails to see that monopoly prices can take more or less, by taking a greater share of supplier profits or consumer surplus.

187 Commission Decision, *Microsoft* (2004) COMP/37.792, [980].

them to ignore the pre-installation' of media player.[188] It was enough that Microsoft's action was 'liable to foreclose competition', or was 'capable of restricting competition'.[189] (A main competitor, RealPlayer, was in fact crushed.) It was also irrelevant that the Commission's remedy proved ineffective.

Having learned its lesson, and now with a precedent, in 2011 the Commission required Microsoft to make a commitment to provide a 'Choice Screen' for web browsers instead of having Internet Explorer as the default at download. In 2013, it then fined Microsoft €561 million for failing to comply with this commitment, affecting 15 million Windows customers in the EU.[190] Even more dramatically, in July 2018, the Commission imposed a €4.34 billion fine on Google for (among other things) bundling its Android app with its Chrome browser, Search app and Play Store: if manufacturers wanted to pre-install *one*, Google told them to pre-install *all* others. As in Microsoft's media-player case, the Commission said '[p]re-installation can create a *status quo* bias' and deters innovation and investment in development of other apps.[191] (See also Ch. 16(3)(e).) Of course, the issues overshadowing these cases are why there is not a choice of OS at the point of every computer purchase, and why there are so few competitors: Windows dominates the desktop market, Android dominates mobile while Apple has maintained a vertically integrated niche market that (in itself) is equally anti-competitive. The simple answer is that each OS is a natural, network monopoly, requiring not merely behavioural, but structural change.

A second main group of cases concerns 'exclusive dealing'. This is a requirement imposed by a dominant firm to mostly buy from (or sell to) the dominant firm. Logically, this is a 'supplementary obligation' that has 'no connection with the subject of such contracts' under article 102(d), as it simply serves to augment dependence on the dominant firm. For instance, in *Hoffmann-La Roche v Commission*, Hoffmann-La Roche dominated the vitamin market and told retailers they had to buy all their vitamin pills from it to get rebates. The Court of Justice agreed this was an abuse, namely in requiring a 'promise on [the retailers'] part to obtain all or most of their requirements exclusively from the said undertaking', whether done through a simple clause or 'discounts conditional on the customer's obtaining all or most of its requirements . . . from the dominant undertaking'. This was 'designed to deprive the purchaser of or restrict his possible choice of sources of supply and to deny other producers access to the market'.[192]

188 *Microsoft Corp. v Commission* (2007) T-201/04, [1052].

189 *Microsoft Corp. v Commission*, [857] and [864].

190 *Antitrust: Commission Fines Microsoft for Non-compliance With Browser Choice Commitments* (6 March 2013) IP/13/196.

191 *Antitrust: Commission Fines Google €4.34 Billion for Illegal Practices Regarding Android Mobile Devices to Strengthen Dominance of Google's Search Engine* (18 July 2018) IP/18/4581.

192 *Hoffmann-La Roche v Commission* (1979) Case 85/76, [89]–[90]. Curiously the court also suggested that 'the effect of fidelity rebates is to apply dissimilar conditions to equivalent transactions with other trading parties' so placing exclusive dealing under art. 102(c). But this

Similarly in *Intel v Commission*, the Commission fined Intel €1.06 billion for abuse, by giving rebates on x86 computer processing units if makers, such as Dell, bought 80–100 per cent of their chips from Intel. The General Court held 'exclusivity rebates granted by an undertaking in a dominant position are by their very nature capable of restricting competition' and the 'capability of tying customers to the undertaking in a dominant position is inherent in exclusivity rebates'.[193] However, on appeal the Court of Justice set aside the General Court's judgment on a narrow ground (and not quashing the fine) that it had failed to address Intel's arguments about whether an 'as efficient competitor' could have been excluded by the rebate system.[194] The case was reheard by the General Court in March 2020.

(v) Categories not Closed

The Court of Justice has continually stressed that the categories of abuse are not limited to the four listed in article 102.[195] The court often emphasises this when confronted with cases where a type of conduct seems to cross between more than one category and if there is an (admittedly barren) debate about which category fits. The bigger question is the principle that unifies the concept of 'abuse'. This must turn on broader theories of fair competition, economics and human rights, and should be driven by evidence and international law.

(c) Mergers or Takeovers

'Competition on the merits' is endorsed by the law,[196] and occasionally some firms may become dominant by merit. Unfortunately, the more common routes to dominance are takeovers, including mergers,[197] often coupled with the luck of finding a new network monopoly (e.g. Microsoft, Google, Facebook). As we saw in Chapters 4(3) and 5(4), the reasons for takeovers often involve governance failures. The history of major takeovers is laden with disaster: CEOs seek to build empires, to aggrandise their self-perception with firm size and to redistribute wealth from investors, employees or consumers to themselves (and also shareholders) by breaking implicit understandings and

cannot be correct: there are the same 'conditions' for retailers who take the rebates or not (i.e. if you deal with us, you get a rebate). Instead, the better view is this is an additional or supplementary obligation (i.e. as well as buying from us, only buy from us). By contrast, the rebate (the tool here used to achieve exclusivity) if applied differently can be unfair pricing: art. 102(a). The rebate itself also may properly be classed as discrimination under art. 102(c) if people refuse.

193 *Intel v Commission* (2014) T-286/09, [85]–[86]. The tying reference agrees with an art. 102(d) category.

194 *Intel v Commission* (2017) C-413/14, [144]–[147].

195 E.g. *Europemballage Corp. and Continental Can Co. Inc. v Commission* (1973) Case 6-72, [26].

196 *Intel v Commission* (2017) C-413/14 P, [133]–[134].

197 NB: As explained in Ch. 4(3), a merger is one form of 'takeover', e.g. where shares of two companies are placed under control of (i.e. taken over by) a new 'merged' entity.

consolidating power. The distributive impact of takeovers depends on governance power within the firm. Yet it is also true that some takeovers enable more efficient production with economies of scale: combined production may be more efficient, and mean less waste, than competition. Here, then, is a central, unspoken difficulty for competition law: competition itself may be inherently wasteful and inefficient, but a privatised, monopolised enterprise could be worse. This section summarises the extent to which takeovers and mergers are regulated.

(i) The Concentration of Modern Enterprise

Both European and American markets are concentrating. In Europe, the 10 per cent largest companies increased their market shares by 2 to 3 per cent from 2001 to 2012,[198] and a similar or more extreme trend is evident in the USA.[199] From 2002 to 2018 there was an average of 316 mergers notified to the EU every year, and the Commission prohibited around 7 per cent of these. Compared to the USA, where no significant mergers have been prevented recently, this is positive. Yet it suggests that the EU and nation states are enabling monopolisation to continue: notable recent examples are the takeover of WhatsApp by Facebook (see Ch. 16), of Fitbit by Google, of investments in Deliveroo by Amazon (Ch. 18), of BG Group by Royal Dutch Shell (Chs. 11 and 12), of Innogy by E.On (Ch. 12), of Cadbury by Kraft and of Kraft by Heinz (food), of Monsanto by Bayer (Ch. 13) and of Grupo Modelo and SAB Miller by Anheuser-Busch InBev (beer and drinks).[200] A central argument has been that any merger in supply chains (vertical) or in different sectors (conglomerate) should be deemed 'pro-competitive', as opposed to mergers between competitors (horizontal).[201] This argument is based on baseless theory, and is driven with business funding,[202] and meanwhile global corporations have relentlessly focused on establishing infrastructural monopolies. Consumers have seen consistently rising prices, the ever-greater extraction of revenue,

198 M. Bajgar, G. Berlingieri, S. Calligaris, C. Criscuolo and J. Timmis, 'Industry Concentration in Europe and North America', OECD Productivity Working Paper No. 18 (January 2019) 2.

199 Furman and Orszag, 'A Firm-Level Perspective on the Role of Rents in the Rise in Inequality', 11, showing % change in revenue share of the 50 largest firms: increasing by 12% for transport and warehousing, 7.6% for retail trade, 7.4% for finance and insurance, 6.6% for real estate, 5.6% for utilities and 4.6% for wholesale trade. Concentration only dropped in services, arts and healthcare.

200 See the useful page on Wikipedia: List of largest mergers and acquisitions.

201 E.g. S. Bishop and M. Walker, *The Economics of EC Competition Law: Concepts, Application and Measurement* (2009); S. Bishop, A. Lofaro and F. Rosati, 'Turning the Tables: Why Vertical and Conglomerate Mergers are Different' [2006] *ECLR* 403 (also in (March 2006) RBB Brief, 2), not accepting that horizontal mergers may lead to price rises. Simon Bishop is a co-founder of RBB Economics, a profit-making consulting and lobby group, which according to its website, has been paid by companies including Google, Wal-Mart, Ryanair, Heinz, Coca-Cola, BP, BHP Billiton, Anglo-American, BA, etc. For reality see Furman and Orszag, 'A Firm-Level Perspective on the Role of Rents in the Rise in Inequality'.

202 Cf. Khan, 'Amazon's Antitrust Paradox', 731ff.

especially across the Internet with increasing length of ads, and a consequent growth in inequality.[203] Much of this appears to be driven by asset managers and banks, who have an incentive to foster 'softer' competition or mergers with shareholder votes.[204]

(ii) Concentrations, Decisive Influence and Notification

The Merger Regulation 2004, article 1 applies to 'concentrations', and will probably catch any activity by a company in the global top 500, or most FTSE 100 companies, if it has a 'community dimension'. For example, it will catch a merger of companies with at least €100 million in turnover in the EU, crossing three member states (unless two-thirds of that revenue is from just one state), and over €2.5 billion worldwide.[205] A 'concentration' means a 'merger' or 'acquisition' of undertakings 'whether by purchase of securities or assets, by contract or by any other means, of direct or indirect control' in any undertakings. In turn control means 'decisive influence' (by ownership, rights or contract) over assets, voting or decision-making.[206] In other words, a merger or takeover is regulated whatever the nature of its legal form (by property, contract or corporate entity). Within the UK, the Enterprise Act 2002 gives jurisdiction to the Competition and Markets Authority (CMA).[207]

To ensure that business can carry out beneficial merger and takeover activity, the EU has a swift notification and approval procedure. Under article 4, an undertaking may inform the Commission ahead of a deal. Under article 10, it should receive a decision within twenty-five working days of notification, after preliminary investigations and a possible declaration of compatibility.[208] However, concentrations are suspended before they are declared compatible, and may be declared incompatible or subjected to a longer investigation.[209] If a concentration takes place without authority, the Commission may 'require the undertakings concerned to dissolve the concentration', by selling shares or assets.[210] Fines up to 1 per cent of aggregate turnover of the undertakings can be imposed for giving misleading information, such as incomplete accounts and questions in interviews, and up to 10 per cent of aggregate turnover for failing to notify a concentration, carrying one through in breach of the law or

[203] Furman and Orszag, 'A Firm-Level Perspective on the Role of Rents in the Rise in Inequality'.

[204] E. A Posner, F. S. Morton and E. G. Weyl, 'A Proposal to Limit the Anti-Competitive Power of Institutional Investors' (2017) 81 *Antitrust LJ* 669.

[205] Merger Regulation (EC) No. 139/2004, art. 1(2) applies to a proposed merged entity with (a) worldwide turnover of €5bn, and (b) EU turnover of two undertakings over €250m, unless each undertaking has over two-thirds of that within one member state. Concentrations are also caught under art. 1(3) with (a) a worldwide turnover over €2.5bn, (b) combined turnover over €100m in three member states, (c) turnover over €25m in each and (d) aggregate EU turnover over €100m.

[206] Merger Regulation 2004, art. 3. [207] Enterprise Act 2002, ss. 22ff.

[208] Merger Regulation 2004, arts. 6 and 8(1)–(2).

[209] Merger Regulation 2004, arts. 8(3), 11 and 13. [210] Merger Regulation 2004, art. 8(4).

not following a condition or obligation imposed by the Commission.[211] These remedies are directed against mergers or takeovers that 'significantly impede effective competition'.

(iii) Significantly Impeding Competition

What kind of mergers are prohibited? Article 2(3) prohibits any 'concentration which would significantly impede effective competition', including (but not only) by 'the creation or strengthening of a dominant position'.[212] In other words, *any* merger or takeover that creates or strengthens a dominant position is illegal, and is automatically deemed to significantly impede competition. Recital 23 makes clear that, as for all competition law, merger control by the Commission 'must' follow the objectives in the Treaty on European Union (TEU), article 3, including 'full employment and social progress', the environment as well as competition: in short the public interest.[213] This means that a firm dominant in one market (e.g. Amazon in online sales) could be prohibited from further acquisitions in other markets (e.g. Deliveroo in food delivery) where there would be no dominant position – for instance, out of a concern for protecting jobs and working conditions, the environment, or preventing 'conglomerate' or infrastructural dominance.[214] As in abuse cases, the market must be defined (see Ch. 6(2)(a)) to assess whether a merger would 'significantly impede effective competition'.[215] Different approaches are taken depending on whether a merger is horizontal or vertical or builds a conglomerate.

(iv) Horizontal Mergers and Collective Dominance

The least controversial kind of merger – in the sense that most competition lawyers think it should be scrutinised – is between competitors (horizontal). For example, in *Ryanair plc v Commission*, it had been found in 2007 and again in 2013 that the proposed takeover by Ryanair of Aer Lingus would mean that by 2012 a new entity would have a monopoly on twenty-eight air routes, and over a 60 per cent market share on eighteen routes. The General Court, upholding the Commission's first decision to block the takeover, rejected Ryanair's arguments that it served different markets, based on consumer price sensitivity.[216] This would impede competition, although it also held the Commission had no ground to make Ryanair (as Aer Lingus argued) divest its 29.3 per cent shareholding in Aer Lingus.[217] This was not enough to have

[211] Merger Regulation 2004, art. 14. [212] Merger Regulation 2004, art. 2(3).
[213] Merger Regulation 2004, recital 23; TEU, art. 3(3), formerly art. 2.
[214] However, see 'UK U-turn Allows Amazon to Invest in Deliveroo', BBC News (24 June 2020), the CMA authorising a 16% share purchase in Deliveroo, because Covid-19 might have meant sales drop. They rose.
[215] *France v Commission* (1998) C-68/94, [143].
[216] *Ryanair Holdings plc v Commission* (2010) T-342/07, [212] and [216].
[217] *Aer Lingus Group plc v Commission* (2010) T-411/07.

'control' or 'decisive influence', and so fell outside the scope of the Merger Regulation 2004,[218] even though Ryanair had attempted to reduce competition through its shareholding by threatening to sue management for breaches of duty, acquiring strategic information and blocking resolutions. In the Court's view these were merely 'commercial disputes between them and their shareholders or to remove all uncertainty', outside the Merger Regulation's scope.[219]

If merging companies would create an oligopoly, not just a monopoly, and could 'collectively dominate' a market, this could also be prohibited.[220] According to the Commission's *Guidelines on the Assessment of Horizontal Mergers*, competition could be impeded either by creating or strengthening a dominant position (as Ryanair wanted) or simply by reducing the number of competitors so that firms 'are now significantly more likely to coordinate and raise prices'. That is, there could be an oligopoly where the different firms might engage in 'keeping prices above the competitive level ... limiting production or the amount of new capacity brought to the market', all without any collusion within the meaning of article 101.[221] However, the Commission's practice also states that this risk of tacit co-ordination could be eliminated if new market entrants are 'likely, timely and sufficient'.[222] This is not binding, and appears an undesirable hypothesis to follow.

In the most significant case to date, *Gencor Ltd v Commission*, the General Court upheld the Commission blocking the joint purchase by Gencor Ltd (in South Africa) and Lonrho plc (a UK company) of Impala Platinum Holding Ltd (SA), even though the South African Competition Board had cleared the transaction. This would have created a collectively dominant position (a duopoly with Anglo American plc) on the world platinum and rhodium markets. Crucially, it explained that the only 'economic links' needed are 'market concentration, transparency, and product homogeneity', meaning the parties can 'anticipate one another's behaviour and are therefore strongly encouraged to align their conduct'.[223] By contrast, in *Bertelsmann AG and Sony Corp. of America v Impala*, the Commission endorsed a joint venture of Bertelsmann AG and Sony Corp. (creating a firm called Sony BMG), even though it reduced the firms in the recorded industry market from five to four.[224] The Court of Justice upheld this, and overturned the General Court which annulled the Commission decision allowing the merged entity. (In fact,

218 Merger Regulation 2004, art. 8(4). 219 (2010) T-411/07, [46] and [68]–[71].

220 E.g. *France v Commission* (1998) C-68/94, [171] (holding this was possible in principle).

221 *Guidelines on the Assessment of Horizontal Mergers* [2004] OJ C31/5, [22] and [40].

222 [2004] OJ C31/5, [68] and see also [76]–[88], stating a defence may be brought that an oligopoly will create efficient benefiting consumers, or at [90] that concentrating the markets is necessary to prevent a firm failing.

223 *Gencor Ltd v Commission* (1999) T-102/96, [276].

224 *Bertelsmann AG and Sony Corp. of America v Impala* (2008) C-413/06, recapping the criteria in *Airtours plc v Commission* (2002) T-342/99, [62] where the takeover of First Choice plc by Airtours plc was approved, even though the number of players in the package holiday market was reduced from four to three.

the joint venture ended three months after the judgment.) In its reasoning, the Court of Justice emphasised that three criteria were (1) 'sufficient market transparency' enabling co-ordination, (2) 'some form of credible deterrent mechanism' to prevent breaking co-ordination and (3) 'current or future competitors, and also the reactions of customers' should not 'jeopardise' the expected results. But these criteria should not be applied with a 'mechanical approach involving the separate verification of each'. Instead, a court should hypothesise whether tacit co-ordination could work.[225] The problem of this test is the lack of a simple presumption about how few is too few, like the presumption of dominance at 50 per cent market share. To copy each other's conduct, five may be quite alive, and three is not a crowd.

(v) Vertical and Conglomerate Mergers

Vertical and conglomerate mergers are more controversial, since they do not eliminate direct competitors.[226] Yet it seems clear that power over a supplier to competitors, or swarming competitors with polycentric takeovers, is a strategy constantly pursued. Just as a player in the Monopoly board game could buy up blue, brown, red, green or station properties as they go, so can a corporation buy up firms at multiple levels in a market based on securing key positions in the economy as a whole.

However, this is not the current view of the courts. In *Honeywell International Inc. v Commission*, the Commission blocked the merger of Honeywell Inc. and General Electric Co., two giant American industrial and production corporations, worth $42 billion.[227] It argued the merged entity would (1) strengthen its dominant position in the commercial jet engine market (horizontally) and (2) be able to project power in the corporate jet markets, with predatory price cuts, to drive out competitors and become dominant. This prompted an unhappy response of various American authors. One official at the US Department of Justice, which approved the merger under George W. Bush, lamented that he had 'more confidence in the self-correcting nature of the markets' and that 'strong empirical proof' should be needed before rejecting any merger.[228]

Ultimately the General Court upheld the Commission's block, but only on the grounds that there was a strengthened dominant position (horizontally) for commercial jets. As for the Commission's claim that the new GE/ Honeywell might cut prices and drive out competitors, it was suggested that

225 (2008) C-413/06, [123]–[126].

226 Cf. *Guidelines on the Assessment of Non-horizontal Mergers* [2008] OJ C265/7, [12]–[14] starts with this presumption, but suggests there could be effects of tacit co-ordination, foreclosure or limiting rivals' access to supplies.

227 *Honeywell International Inc. v Commission* (2005) T-209/01; Commission Decision in GE/ Honeywell (3 July 2001) M.2220.

228 W. J. Kolasky, 'Conglomerate Mergers and Range Effects: It's a Long Way from Chicago to Brussels', George Mason University Symposium (9 November 2001).

'convincing evidence' was needed 'that it would have been likely to engage in those practices' to become dominant.[229] In *Tetra Laval BV v Commission*, the General Court further asserted that 'the effects of a conglomerate-type merger are generally considered to be neutral, or even beneficial'.[230] This view has led, for example, to the approval of the Microsoft/Skype takeover[231] and then the Microsoft/LinkedIn takeover,[232] and the Google/DoubleClick takeover[233] and then the Google/DeepMind takeovers. As the strategy of infrastructure monopolisation has become ever more obvious, a Commission report has acknowledged that '[b]uying up promising start-ups' for 'early elimination of potential competition threats' should be scrutinised more, 'to inject some "horizontal" elements into the conglomerate theories of harm'.[234] The better, simpler view might be that 'merging' and 'competing' are fundamentally opposite things and that, if dominant firms are so good, they should compete on the merits.

The 'strong empirical proof' suggests that in fact US markets have acquired a serious, systemic monopoly problem,[235] and that in this respect 'the self-correcting nature of the markets' is an ideologically driven fantasy. As this became more evident, in 2017 the US Department of Justice filed its first action to block a vertical merger against AT&T and Time Warner. Yet, in 2018 the District Court of the DC Circuit (which is largely packed with extremist Republican party judges) overturned the Department of Justice and allowed the merger as there was (ostensibly) no probable harm to consumers.[236] In lieu of court-led reform, a different political consensus has been emerging, and it suggests that to deal with mass economic concentration, the presumption should be that mergers are blocked or unwound.[237]

(d) Remedies

The right to fair competition ultimately depends on the remedies. National competition authorities and the EU Commission can impose 'behavioural or structural remedies' under the Implementation Regulation 2003, article 7.[238] Under article 9, the Commission may also accept binding commitments to

[229] (2005) T-209/01, [405]. The quoted text applied to the commercial jets, but appears to be the reasons used.

[230] *Tetra Laval BV v Commission* (2002) T-5/02, [155], rejecting the block of Tetra Pak buying Sidel SA, a stretch blow moulding and PET maker.

[231] *Microsoft/Skype* (7 October 2011) M.6281.

[232] *Microsoft/LinkedIn* (20 January 2017) M.8124.

[233] *Google/DoubleClick* (2008) M.4371.

[234] J. Crémer, Y. A. de Montjoye and H. Schweitzer, *Competition Policy for the Digital Era* (2019) 11.

[235] E.g. J. Mauldin, 'America Has a Monopoly Problem', *Forbes* (11 April 2019).

[236] Upheld on appeal in *United States v AT&T Inc.*, 310 F Supp 3d 161 (DC Circ 2019).

[237] E.g. Bernie Sanders, *Corporate Accountability and Democracy* (2019); Elizabeth Warren, *Promoting Competitive Markets* (2019) and *How We Can Break Up Big Tech* (2019).

[238] IR 2003, art. 7.

settle cases.[239] These will be 'an indication, if not prima facie evidence' of breaches,[240] that can be relied on in private damages claims.

Behavioural remedies (e.g. pay a fine, stop abuse, disclose information) dominate current practice. Structural remedies are not defined in article 7, but include breaking enterprises up into distinct entities, requiring divestment and requiring 'access to key infrastructure or inputs on non-discriminatory terms'.[241] This list is not closed. Behavioural remedies have included a duty in *Commercial Solvents* to supply materials to the claimant;[242] in *Microsoft*, to supply interoperability information for its software free of charge;[243] and, in *Alrosa*, there was a commitment to limit exclusive sales of diamonds to De Beers.[244] To use a structural remedy there must be 'no equally effective behavioural remedy'.[245] The EU has been reluctant to use this power. It has accepted structural commitments,[246] but the Commission has not yet imposed structural remedies. In 2014, the EU Parliament voted to break up Google, though only the Commission has power to carry this through.[247] By 2020, despite record fines for abuse by Google, and its enabling of far-right hate through YouTube (see Ch. 18), Competition Commissioner Vestager repeated that she thought it would 'never come to' a break-up.[248] This is all the more remarkable since the case of Facebook's takeover of WhatsApp, and its deceitful claim that it could not merge user data.

It is unclear that behavioural remedies restore fair competition if the sector involves network monopolies, especially those controlling vast databases. In the mid-twentieth century, Joe Bain argued that a market's structure produces foreseeable conduct, which in turn affects that market's performance: 'structure ⟶ conduct ⟶ performance'.[249] If firms have power, it must be presumed they will use it. Undertakings could be broken up to prevent abuse, such as where an enterprise owns a platform and is also a competitor on it, like

239 IR 2003, art. 7. In *Microsoft* (2013) Case AT.39530, Microsoft received a €561m fine for breaking its commitment to have a browser choice screen. The fine was set at 1.02% of world turnover, which was €55bn in June 2012.

240 *Gasorba SL v Repsol Comercial de Productos Petrolíferos* (2017) C-547/16, [29].

241 Commission Notice on Remedies Acceptable [2008] OJ C267/1, paras. 10 and 17.

242 *Commercial Solvents Corp. v Commission* (1974) Cases 6 and 7/73.

243 *Microsoft v Commission* (2007) T-201/04, [142].

244 *Commission v Alrosa* (2010) C-441/07, [41], the Court of Justice restoring the commitment decision, which does not need to be the least onerous option, unlike a remedy imposed under art. 7.

245 IR 2003, art. 7(1) and recital 12 suggests structural remedies for a 'risk of a lasting or repeated infringement'.

246 E.g. *Bulgarian Energy Holding* (2015) COMP/39.767 (the Bulgarian state energy company committed to transfer its power exchange operations to the Bulgarian Finance Ministry to set up an independent entity).

247 S. McGrath, 'European Parliament Votes to Break Up Google', *MicroScope* (27 November 2014).

248 E.g. 'EU Antitrust Chief Does Not See Breakup of Tech Giants: Paper', *Reuters* (1 November 2020).

249 J. S. Bain, 'The Impact on Industrial Organization' (1964) 54(3) *Am Economic Rev* 28, 29, crediting this to E. H. Chamberlin, *Theory of Monopolistic Competition: A Re-orientation of the Theory of Value* (1932); but see J. S. Bain, *Industrial Organization* (2nd ed. 1968) chs. 10–11.

Amazon's marketplace for its booksellers, or Google Shopping and rival sellers. It could also be done if undertakings accumulate a monopoly network. However, simply breaking firms up may not be sufficient. If assets or shares are sold to another competing shareholder, a new large player may follow the same practices. If a company is split into two or more new companies, shares may over time be traded so the shareholders are no longer the same. The theory goes that, as the share owners become different, the companies will compete, or act as arm's-length businesses. This is dubious: when there is common ownership, there will be common goals and, if shareholders change, they may maintain the same preferences contrary to the public interest. Firms aim to remerge when a new government comes into power, committed to less oversight. In the USA, this was true for Standard Oil, which was broken into thirty-four companies in 1911,[250] but which are now largely run by ExxonMobil, BP, Chevron and Marathon on a global scale far more vast than before (see Ch. 11). This is also true for AT&T, broken into nine new telecoms companies in a 1982 settlement, which are now mostly held again by AT&T and Verizon (see Ch. 16).[251]

Another structural option is to take enterprises into public ownership, the most common structural response to competition failures among EU or Commonwealth members (Chs. 8–19). There is no express power for this in EU law yet. However, structural remedies can include granting voting rights to other stakeholders within the enterprise, if a change in voting structure – to rebalance power, if not ownership – is deemed necessary to combat abuse. This could include limiting voting rights of major shareholders and granting voting rights to employees, or to consumers or traders that suffer from abuse of a dominant position, when having voice appears suitable, necessary and reasonable to prevent abuse in future.[252] This will be particularly true when conditions for markets are not met (Ch. 2(2)(h)).

Fines are charged by an undertaking's 'total turnover' – that is, worldwide with 'no territorial limit'.[253] The Commission can impose a 1% fine for providing misleading information or not co-operating with investigations (e.g. Facebook, €110 million), a 5% a day fine for ongoing infringements (e.g. Microsoft, €1.2 billion) and a 10% fine for substantive infringements of abuse or collusion (e.g. Google, €2.42 billion).[254] Insolvency is not a reason to not impose a fine, but the Commission will in exceptional cases take account of the 'social and economic context'[255] – for instance, loss of jobs. The central issue is often the directors or shareholders in control and removing them to free the workforce or consumers from abuse.

[250] *Standard Oil Co. of New Jersey v United States*, 221 US 1 (1911).

[251] *United States v AT&T* (1982) (settled out of court as AT&T feared it was to lose).

[252] See the powers in TFEU, arts. 50 (shareholders), 153(1)(f) (employees) and 169 (consumers).

[253] *Cimenteries CBR SA v Commission* (2000) T-25/95, [5022]. [254] IR 2003, arts. 23–4.

[255] *Guidelines on the Method of Setting Fines Imposed Pursuant to Article 23(2)(A) of Regulation No. 1/2003* [2006] OJ C210/2, para. 35.

Fines are stated to be 'not of a criminal law nature', but national laws do criminalise competition violations, to some degree. The Enterprise Act 2002, sections 188–188B contain a 'cartel offence' – for instance, by agreeing to fix prices or rig bids.[256] There is not yet any statutory codification of a crime for abuse of dominant position, though monopolisation may be a common law offence where restraint of trade involves an 'aggravating feature' such as 'misrepresentation, compulsion, intimidation' or other established criminal wrong (several examples come to mind).[257] All directors must be disqualified for up to fifteen years if they engage in 'a breach of competition law', contributed to it or should have known.[258] But despite the apparent stringency of this rule – it means, any abuse by a UK company should lead its CEOs and chairs to be disqualified – it is not used that often.[259]

Individual criminal liability and disqualification should concentrate the mind, and makes it clear that abuse and price fixing is theft from the consumers, traders, employees or other stakeholders that suffer. In *Norris v Government of United States*, Mr Ian Norris participated in a cartel to fix automotive and aerospace parts (see Ch. 15) from 1989 and 1998, but the UK's 'cartel office' was only enacted in 2002. The US statutory crime did not require proof of dishonesty, and it was held that a US conviction was not enough for Norris to be extradited: an offence at common law required aggravating factors such as dishonesty.[260] Norris was, however, then extradited for the crime of obstructing justice.[261]

(3) Cartels and Collusion

Monopolisation is the greatest threat to the economy and society, but competition law's other main role is banning unjustified collusion. 'Freedom of association' is a human right, not a business right, and in any case it is limited as 'necessary in a democratic society' for the 'rights and freedoms of others'.[262] Most people agree, a price-fixing cartel among business competitors must be unlawful, and is a 'conspiracy against the public'.[263] This is the core target of the TFEU, article 101, and the Competition Act 1998, section 2, but other types of collusion that (a) restrict competition are banned as well. Yet for beneficial

[256] Enterprise Act 2002, ss. 188–188B.

[257] *Norris v Government of the United States of America* [2008] UKHL 16, [13].

[258] Company Directors Disqualification Act (CDDA) 1986, ss. 9A–E; see also Ch. 7(4)(c).

[259] CDDA 1986, s. 24 limits the extent to directors (or shadow directors) in England, Wales and Scotland.

[260] [2008] UKHL 16, [59]–[62].

[261] *Norris v Government of the United States of America (No. 2)* [2010] UKSC 9.

[262] ECHR 1950, art. 11.

[263] Smith, *The Wealth of Nations*, Book I, ch. 10. But contrast the House of Lords in *Mogul Steamship Co. Ltd v McGregor, Gow & Co.* [1892] AC 25 (approving ship traffic limits and rebates for exclusive dealing with a shipowner association) shortly after the US Sherman Act of 1890 was passed.

kinds of co-operation, the law (b) exempts undertakings that can objectively justify co-operation. The most contentious questions turn on (c) vertical restraints, where power is unfairly projected without a 'dominant position'. This section treats each in turn.

(a) Restricting Competition

The central prohibition in the TFEU, article 101(1) – mirrored in the Competition Act 1998, section 2(1) – is on (i) collusive practices, that (ii) affect trade and (iii) 'have as their object or effect the prevention, restriction or distortion of competition'.[264] In principle, this creates a duty on undertakings to act independently on the market. Those who wish to merge are subject to merger control, but otherwise undertakings are meant to compete. The law targets 'all agreements between undertakings, decisions by associations of undertakings and concerted practices', but the 'only essential thing is the distinction between independent conduct, which is allowed, and collusion, which is not'.[265] The case law therefore must define the limit of what counts as collusion, not unilateral action, and what unjustifiably restricts competition or not. Like article 102, article 101 gives examples of unlawful conduct as follows:

(a) directly or indirectly fix purchase or selling prices or any other trading conditions;
(b) limit or control production, markets, technical development, or investment;
(c) share markets or sources of supply;
(d) apply dissimilar conditions to equivalent transactions with other trading parties, thereby placing them at a competitive disadvantage;
(e) make the conclusion of contracts subject to acceptance by the other parties of supplementary obligations which, by their nature or according to commercial usage, have no connection with the subject of such contracts.

These examples are the same as the types of abuse listed above, with the addition of (c) sharing markets or sources of supply,[266] and the subtraction

264 TFEU, art. 101; Competition Act 1998, s. 2. The effect on trade, and the unlawful restriction of competition, is 'between member states' and 'within the internal market' or 'within the UK' respectively.

265 *Commission v Anic Partecipazioni SpA* (1999) C-49/92, [108], upholding a €750,000 fine (then 'ecu's) on Anic SpA for being in a cartel limiting output and targeting prices for polypropylene. It was unnecessary to distinguish agreements, decisions or concerted practices.

266 E.g. *Consten SaRL and Grundig GmbH v Commission* (1966) Cases 54/64 and 58/64, [8], holding that a (vertical) agreement by a German company to appoint a French company as an exclusive distributor was unlawful, as it 'might tend to restore the national divisions in trade between Member States and might be such as to frustrate the most fundamental objectives of the Community'.

in (b) of any requirement for 'prejudice of consumers' to be shown if there are limits on production or investment.

In the simplest kind of case, competitors meet and make a deal to fix prices. For example, in *Parker ITR Srl v Commission*, eleven corporations that made marine hoses to carry oil from offshore rigs (see Ch. 11) were fined €131 million by the Commission for fixing prices, rigging bids and sharing markets from 1986 to 2007. For contract bids, the group would designate a 'bid champion' who would win after others put in fake bids designed to lose. The corporations had many meetings to set up the system, until the last one in Houston. A Japanese cartel member reported it to the authorities, and the meeting was raided by US agents, co-operating with the EU, UK and Japanese competition authorities. The fine was imposed jointly and severally, bound successor companies and resulted in criminal actions and jail time for the managers.[267] A cartel that fixes prices above the competitive level is regarded by many as morally equivalent to theft. The consensus stands in stark contrast to the treatment of price exploitation by monopolies, which has been legitimised by pro-corporate apologists such as Posner or Scalia (see Ch. 6(2)).[268]

What if there is no direct evidence of an agreement or exchange? In *ICI Ltd v Commission*, a group of ten chemical dye producers had been observed to raise prices three times within days of each other, and the Commission imposed a fine for collusion. There was no direct evidence of a cartel, but no other plausible explanation for the price rises. The court agreed that their parallel conduct was 'strong evidence' of a concerted practice if it departs from 'the normal conditions of the market' regarding 'the nature of the products, the size and number of the undertakings and the volume of the said market'.[269] However, in *A. Ahlström Osakeyhtiö v Commission*, the Court of Justice held that the Commission could not establish that forty wood pulp producers, who allegedly fixed prices from 1975 to 1981, were engaging in unlawful collusion because there were other explanations for their behaviour. Among other things, the market was highly transparent, there were relatively few buyers, and there were 'rapid means of communication, such as the telephone and telex'. This meant competitors could plausibly align their prices independently.[270] If telex was rapid then, the use of lightning algorithms to

[267] *Commission v Parker Hannifin Manufacturing Srl and Parker-Hannifin Corp.* (2014) C-434/13 P (upholding the Commission fine). For background, see Jones and Townley, 'Competition Law', 567–8.

[268] E.g. R. H. Lande, 'A Traditional and Textual Analysis of the Goals of Antitrust: Efficiency, Preventing Theft from Consumers and Consumer Choice' (2013) 81(5) *Fordham L Rev* 2349; and see Senator Lane (1914) 51 *Congressional Record* 13223, referring to 'the fraud and the theft which is being practiced upon the people of this country', and that people are 'being compelled to pay arbitrarily fixed and unjustly high prices for what they consume, they are being robbed'. Unless the law acted, they 'shall continue to be robbed as they are now being robbed, and by the same set of criminals'.

[269] *ICI Ltd v Commission* (1972) Cases 48–57/69, [66].

[270] *A. Ahlström Osakeyhtiö v Commission* (1993) C-89/85, [83]–[88].

monitor competitors and set prices now has become a massive problem. According to the EU Commissioner for Competition, Margrethe Vestager, competition law 'enforcers need to be suspicious of everyone who uses an automated system for pricing' and whether automated or not 'will be held responsible for what it does'.[271]

(b) Exemptions

Though competition may be beneficial some of the time, the law recognises exceptions to the prohibition on collusion: in effect it becomes lawful co-operation. As Chapter 6(1)(b) explained, many entities are completely outside the scope of regulated undertakings, namely democratic labour organisations, firms, social or public services, and state action. In addition, article 101(3) says the ban does not apply to any agreement, decision or practice which:

> contributes to improving the production or distribution of goods or to promoting technical or economic progress, while allowing consumers a fair share of the resulting benefit, and which does not:
>
> (a) impose on the undertakings concerned restrictions which are not indispensable to the attainment of these objectives;
> (b) afford such undertakings the possibility of eliminating competition in respect of a substantial part of the products in question.

So, improving distribution or promoting progress, while benefiting consumers and restricting competition no more than is necessary for those aims, means 'collusion' becomes lawful co-operation. The burden of proof is on the undertakings. Three main exceptions follow.

First, the Commission says that agreements do not appreciably restrict competition if they do not restrict competition by 'object', and competitors' market shares do not exceed 10 per cent, or non-competitors' market shares exceed 15 per cent.[272] However, a restriction by 'object', such as the examples listed in article 101(1)(a)–(e), will automatically be caught no matter how small.[273] It is completely unclear that this is an appropriate policy when large numbers of small businesses must often bargain with giant monopolies. For example, thousands of restaurants are dictated terms by Deliveroo or Google

[271] M. Vestager, *Algorithms and Competition*, Bundeskartellamt 18th Conference on Competition (16 March 2017).

[272] European Commission, *Notice on Agreements of Minor Importance which Do Not Appreciably Restrict Competition under Article 101(1)* [2014] C-291/1.

[273] *Expedia Inc. v Authorité de la concurrence* (2012) C-226/11, [38], suggesting national authorities are not precluded from taking action against small undertakings because of the Commission's Notice. It does not endorse them doing so: targeting the vulnerable is cheap, easy and lazy. Focus on corporate power is plainly more difficult.

Maps.[274] Thousands of booksellers are forced to accept escalating cuts from their sales taken by Amazon or eBay. Thousands of farmers are told by supermarkets to accept cuts in the price of milk or vegetables, impoverishing rural incomes.[275] A preferable policy is to (1) break up monopolies and make networks accountable; (2) empower small business to co-operate, including to bargain over prices with dominant firms; if (3) the co-operatives' constitutions are made transparent and follow democratic principles. An absolutist approach to banning small business co-operation, and kid-gloves for monopolies, suggests an inversion of the law's true purposes.[276]

Second, certain types of co-operation are exempt, particularly to promote environmental sustainability, supporting local jobs and industry, and research and development. For instance, in a decision on the *Conseil Européen de la Construction d'Appareils Domestiques*, the Commission held that an agreement among washing-machine makers to phase out low-energy efficiency machines was exempt. There was no elimination of competition as the makers could still compete on price and quality, it would lead 'to reduced pollution from electricity generation' – 3.5 million fewer tonnes of carbon dioxide, 17,000 fewer tonnes of sulphur dioxide and 6,000 fewer tonnes of nitrous oxide – and this (with some understatement) was 'likely to deliver both individual and collective benefits for users and consumers'.[277] The Commission has also held that relieving unemployment or building up domestic industry are beneficial grounds for co-operation and exempt from competition law.[278] The problem is that the Commission no longer makes such exemptions: it is now left to courts, who lack a bright-line rule. In the case of environmental regulation particularly, it is completely unacceptable that *all* forms of co-operation to stop greenhouse gas emissions and pollution are not already clearly exempt, given the scale of climate crisis. A model could be the Research and Development Regulation 2010, which grants a block exemption to 'horizontal' agreements that generally keep the benefits of innovation open, up to a time limit of seven years.[279]

[274] E.g. R. Murray, 'Two Bristol Restaurants Stop Using Deliveroo as Service Takes "Whopping Cut"', *Bristol Post* (9 April 2020), reporting charges of 35% of food cost, as well as charges for delivery to customers.

[275] E.g. A Renton, 'British Farmers Forced to Pay the Cost of Supermarket Price Wars', *The Guardian* (2 July 2011); 'Farmers in Fresh Protests over Supermarket Milk Prices', BBC News (4 August 2015); 'Farmers Raise Concern as Tesco Demands Supplier Price Cuts', *Farming UK* (8 July 2020).

[276] Contrast, previously, *Völk v Vervaecke* (1969) Case 5/69: 'an exclusive dealing agreement, even with absolute territorial protection, may, having regard to the weak position of the persons concerned on the market in the products in question in the area covered by the absolute protection, escape the prohibition' in article 101.

[277] *CECED* [2000] OJ L187/47, [48]–[51]. See also *Philips/Osram* [1994] OJ L378/37.

[278] E.g. *Stichting Baksteen* [1994] OJ L131/15 (unemployment); *Optical Fibres* [1986] OJ L236/30 (domestic industry).

[279] Research and Development Regulation (EU) No. 1217/2010, arts. 2–4, expiry by 2023. See also the Specialisation Regulation (EU) No. 1218/2010.

In stark contrast, the Vertical Block Exemption Regulation 2010 gives broad exemptions for agreements among buyers or sellers with under 30 per cent market share, that do not involve (a) price fixing, (b) sharing of territory or restrictions on (c) reselling, (d) cross-supplies or (e) spare parts.[280] Thus, undertakings that exercise huge bargaining power over suppliers or buyers, with up to 29.99 per cent market share, are free to impose exclusivity deals in a way that restrains trade. This has been legitimised by a narrative that vertical restraint largely does not matter.

(c) Vertical Restraints

Unlike collusion among competitors (horizontal), vertical restraints typically aim to induce reliance, projecting power and taking revenue by contract, without responsibility or risk. Typical examples are (i) duties to deal mainly or exclusively with a supplier, (ii) bans on reselling products and (iii) rebates and pricing to induce loyalty. It has been argued that vertical restraints, among suppliers or buyers at different market levels, should be unregulated. Robert Bork stated in 1978 that 'all vertical restraints are beneficial to consumers and should for that reason be completely lawful', adding 'vertical control never creates . . . restriction of output'.[281] Thus, as well as asserting that monopolies were mostly beneficial, this view argued anything that is not a monopoly (and EU case law's lowest market share has been 39.75 per cent) should be able to dominate other suppliers or buyers through contractual power.[282]

The argument by Bork and others to allow vertical restraints is so extreme ('all' benefit consumers and it 'never' reduces output) that, as an empirical assertion, any single instance to the contrary proves it wrong. To give one example, when the UK Parliament prohibited breweries from tying pubs to exclusively buy all beer from them, the UK underwent a rapid, dramatic and unprecedented revolution in beer innovation, quality and price. In the 2000s, a typical pub might sell a bitter, a couple of lagers like Carling and Foster's, and perhaps an 'exotic' beer like Peroni – brands owned by one multinational, such as SAB Miller (taken over by AB InBev in 2015). Other pubs would sell other beers tied to one brewery. Thus, even if a pub had space in its fridges or on its taps, even if customers wanted choices, even if the drinks on offer were tasteless, mass-produced swill, the pub was restrained from trade. Tying happened because to buy a pub building, publicans would take loans from pub companies and, in return, publicans bought beer exclusively from that company. Once tied, beer prices could increase and, by 2014, one survey found that 80 per cent of publicans earned below £15,000, many below minimum

280 Vertical Block Exemption Regulation (EC) No. 330/2010, arts. 3–4.

281 E.g. Bork, *The Antitrust Paradox*, 297–8.

282 Bork and Posner's evidence-free views were manifested in *Continental TV v GTE Sylvania*, 433 US 36 (1977) per Powell J abolishing a bright-line rule against vertical restraints. Marshall J and Brennan J dissented.

wage for a full-time job.[283] After years of court indecision on whether these practices were anticompetitive,[284] the Small Business, Enterprise and Employment Act 2015, section 42 created a 'Pubs Code', and required that publicans have the freedom to not buy beer exclusively from the owner, and instead be given a 'market rent only' option.[285] It also limited price rises at tied pubs to 3 per cent per year.[286] This has prevented the expansion of brewery power, a clear success, witnessed in huge innovation. Yet many pubs have stayed tied in effect due to lack of information and enforcement.[287]

The core fact, recognised in *Courage Ltd v Crehan*, is that vertical restraints exploit the 'markedly weaker position [of] the other party, such as seriously to compromise or even eliminate his freedom to negotiate the terms of the contract'.[288] This restraint of trade, through vastly unequal bargaining power, has long been recognised.[289] Yet EU and UK courts have still been uncertain about classifying agreements as unlawful if a trading partner lacks bargaining power and is being dictated terms. In *Ford of Europe Inc. v Commission*, the Court of Justice held that Ford's decision to stop giving right-hand drive cars to UK distributors (to limit parallel imports) was an agreement, and unlawful even though the distributors had little say.[290] This catches undertakings that may not be dominant under article 102 case law, but who still exercise immense power. However, in *Commission v Bayer AG*, Bayer reduced supply of a heart drug, Adalat, to Spanish and French wholesalers, to stop parallel imports to the UK where the drug cost more. The Court of Justice held it was not collusion. Though the wholesalers and Bayer AG were contracting for fewer drugs, this was 'only the expression of a unilateral policy' by Bayer.[291] The Court of Justice then seemed to change its mind once more in *GlaxoSmithKline Services Unltd v Commission*, holding that a contract term between GlaxoSmithKline and Spanish wholesalers that obliged them to not resell drugs to the UK was unlawful collusion.[292] The truth is, the wholesalers in *Bayer* or *GlaxoSmithKline* take whatever terms they are given, because they

283 NB: As it became clear that the 2015 Act would pass, 'Pub Shares Slide after Vote to Break Beer "Tie"', *BBC News* (19 November 2014).

284 E.g. *Delimitis v Henniger Bräu AG* (1991) C-234/89, suggesting beer ties could have anti-competitive impact through cumulative effect but were not a restriction of competition in isolation. *Courage Ltd v Crehan* (2001) C-453/99, enabling a damages claim for late payment for supplies of beer by the brewery to a tied pub.

285 Small Business, Enterprise and Employment Act 2015, ss. 42–4, 68.

286 Pubs Code, etc. Regulations 2016, reg. 3.

287 E.g. E. Hardy, 'How Pub Companies Are Still Pricing Publicans Out of Business', *ThisIsMoney* (8 August 2019).

288 *Courage Ltd v Crehan* (2001) C-453/99, [33].

289 E.g. in the German Empire Court (29 May 1906) 63 RFZ 333, exclusive beer purchasing contracts for pubs were characterised as a *Knebelungsvertrag* (or throttling contract) that unlawfully limited economic freedom.

290 *Ford of Europe v Commission* (1985) Case 25/84.

291 *Bundesverband der Arzneimittel-Importeure eV and Commission v Bayer AG* (2004) C-2/01, [101] and see [70].

292 *GlaxoSmithKline Services Unlimited v Commission* (2009) C-513/06, [58].

have no bargaining power, and there is no distinction between reducing sales or a term requiring fewer resales. The wholesalers are not to blame, but the dominant business that dictates unfair terms is. This either suggests the interpretation of a dominant position is unrealistically high or that all contractual dealings (including non-supply) should be caught and remedies apportioned by fault.

(4) State Involvement and Aid

The final element of competition law is its application to state enterprises, or private enterprises that are given special rights by law. This includes (a) the principle of ownership neutrality, (b) application of competition law to public enterprises and those with special rights and (c) the principle that state aid must not act as 'corporate welfare'.

(a) Principle of Ownership Neutrality

A fundamental principle of the TFEU in article 345 is that the 'Treaties shall in no way prejudice the rules in Member States governing the system of property ownership.'[293] There can be no restriction on member states either privatising, socialising or nationalising any enterprise, or in the regulation of private or public property rights. Beyond the minimum standard required in human rights law,[294] this should leave economic management open to experiment, an approach that is justified where there is rational disagreement about the economic constitution's content.[295]

Despite article 345, the Commission and the European Central Bank, with the International Monetary Fund, have used their powers of contract against indebted states to demand privatisation in the Eurozone banking and sovereign debt crisis. In 2015, Greece was directed to privatise large swathes of its petroleum, electricity, gas, water, housing, roads, rail, air ports, sea ports, post and telecoms,[296] largely to satisfy debts owed to British, German and French

[293] TFEU, art. 345, while art. 346 makes clear that member states can take any security measures they want, including in 'production of or trade in arms, munitions and war material'.

[294] Cf. ECHR 1950, Prot. 1, art. 1, under which case law sets standards for compensation for nationalisation of enterprises. See discussion in *James v United Kingdom* [1986] ECHR 2, [64]–[68]. The court has not yet intervened to set standards when a government privatises an industry without guaranteeing equivalent compensation to the public, e.g. by ensuring a stock market float is at a true market price (not a discount), and compensating members of the public individually for loss of control.

[295] Contrast the famous dissent in *Lochner v New York*, 198 US 45 (1905) per Holmes J: 'a constitution is not intended to embody a particular economic theory . . . It is made for people of fundamentally differing views.' Holmes J's view appears to contrast 'theory' with evidence and (today) data.

[296] Hellenic Republic Asset Development Fund, *Asset Development Plan* (30 July 2015); for background see J. Rankin and H. Smith, 'The Great Greece Fire Sale', *The Guardian* (24 July 2015).

banks (see Ch. 10). Thus, actions that are plainly ultra vires for any EU legislation or case law were carried out through contracts, directed by EU bureaucracy. This went unchallenged as Greece accepted the terms and lawyers did not fight the case in court. Arguably doing by contract that which cannot be done by legislation may not be *intra vires* the European Commission or Central Bank, whatever the legal form.[297]

(b) Competition Law and Public Service Delivery

Although the Treaties are technically neutral between the poles of total capitalism and full communism,[298] legislation does require transparency of public ownership, requiring member states to disclose their holdings in enterprises.[299] Further, article 106(1) says member states may not 'maintain in force any measure' violating competition law for any undertakings that are 'public',[300] or with 'special or exclusive rights'. However, article 106(2) says rules on competition do not apply if they 'obstruct the performance in law or in fact, of the particular tasks assigned to' undertakings 'entrusted with the operation of services of general economic interest or having the character of a revenue-producing monopoly'.[301]

So, as we saw in *Höfner v Macrotron GmbH*, while Germany could create a monopoly for its public employment agency in recruitment services, it was an abuse if it failed to fulfil demand for executive recruitment.[302] By contrast, in *Procureur du Roi v Corbeau*, the Belgian Royal Mail held a monopoly over postal services and it did fulfil demand. The Court of Justice held the monopoly was justified, particularly to prevent the 'cream-skimming' practices that would take place if private companies could have competed. This is where private operators often serve the cheap and most profitable mail routes in cities

[297] The basic principle is an executive's powers are bound by the entity's constitution and can be restrained by an internal claim, although third parties may rely on conduct with apparent authority. Cf. *Hazell v Hammersmith LBC* [1992] 2 AC 1 and CA 2006, s. 171, discussed in Ch. 3(1)(c). See also TFEU, art. 245: 'Members of the Commission shall refrain from any action incompatible with their duties'; TEU, art. 13(2): 'Each institution shall act within the limits of the powers conferred on it in the Treaties'; TEU, art. 17(1): the Commission 'shall ensure the application of the Treaties'.

[298] These poles are, admittedly, fictitious, since full communism (i.e. complete common ownership, even of your socks, toothbrush or you) cannot seriously be contemplated and existed never. It is 'no place'; cf. T. More, *Utopia* (1516) Book II (ironically describing this). Total capitalism, where everything is private, also cannot be contemplated, because there must be common rules to establish private property. Rules mean an enforcement mechanism and this means common property in a state. Again, this exists in 'no place', despite some true believers who fail to grasp irony; cf. R. Nozick, *Anarchy, State and Utopia* (1974). All societies mix ownership.

[299] Financial Transparency Directive 2006/111/EC, arts. 1–2.

[300] *Commission v France, Italy and UK* (1982) C-188/80, [25] ('public' undertaking is where 'public authorities may exercise directly or indirectly a dominant influence' in the enterprise through capital, votes or other rights).

[301] TFEU, art. 106.

[302] *Höfner and Elser v Macrotron GmbH* (1991) C-41/90.

but, for example, fail to serve more costly rural routes. The Court of Justice agreed that a public monopoly can be justified by the member state for such social reasons, to deliver the public service under 'economically acceptable conditions'.[303]

Thus, the Treaties give broad discretion to the member state to democratically determine its priorities. This is reaffirmed both in the TFEU, article 14, and the CFREU, article 36.[304] The meaning of 'services of a general economic interest' includes examples like electricity, water and telecommunications.[305] There are, however, principles to ensure that the same public enterprise does not act as a referee and a player at the same time. For instance, in *Elliniki Radiophonia Tiléorassi AE v Pliroforissis*, the Court of Justice held that a Greek public broadcaster, which transmitted its own programmes, could not also have the exclusive right to retransmit other programmes because this would inevitably mean it 'favours its own programmes', an abuse of a dominant position.[306] Similarly, in *Régie des télégraphes et des téléphones v GB-Inno-BM SA*, the Court of Justice held that the Belgian public telephone company could not also have an exclusive right to grant approval of telephones when it sold telephones itself.[307]

The result is that a public enterprise and a regulator of others should be separate bodies, to remove any conflict of interest. Both can be publicly owned, and a member state has complete freedom to require that all enterprises in a sector are publicly owned if it chose (even for making telephones, though it is doubtful that many would still regard this as wise). For example, in *Netherlands v Essent NV*, the Court of Justice held that a Dutch law requiring all electricity and gas distributors to be publicly owned was protected by TFEU, article 345 (see Ch. 12(3)(c)).[308] Thus, the EU legislature has pursued a policy of 'liberalisation' under TFEU, article 106(3) to implement these basic principles against abuse and to remove conflicts of interest. They have often been seen as back-door privatisation, or a prelude to it, and indeed some may have this goal. But this is not the law. The Directives passed structurally separate public undertakings from regulators, and require different entities to run grids or operations, to ensure transparency and non-conflicted governance.[309] Again, it is a fundamental principle that member states can maintain public

303 *Procureur du Roi v Corbeau* (1993) C-320/91, [54].

304 TFEU, art. 14: services of general economic interest must 'operate on the basis of principles and conditions, particularly economic and financial conditions, which enable them to fulfil their missions'. CFREU, art. 36: the EU 'respects access to services of general economic interest as provided for in national laws and practices'.

305 Lisbon Treaty, Prot. 26, art. 1.

306 *Elliniki Radiophonia Tiléorassi AE v Pliroforissis* (1991) C-260/89, [37].

307 *Régie des télégraphes et des téléphones v GB-Inno-BM SA* (1991) C-18/88.

308 *Netherlands v Essent NV* (2013) C-105/12, [4].

309 See Chapters 12(3)(a)(iii) on electricity, 15(3)(b) on railways, 16(3)(d) on telecoms and 16(3)(f) on post.

ownership of enterprise, or private ownership, based on what is democratically determined.

A real, and underexplored, danger arises with the granting of special rights to private enterprises, especially those obscured by the passage of time, which entrenches unaccountable corporate or financial power. To give just one example, a German company law gives banks the right to vote on other people's shares, so long as it casts votes in their 'best interests'. The banks define what these are, because there is no representative voting mechanism. This rule was originally codified into the Public Companies Act 1937 by the Hitler regime[310] and survives in the Public Companies Act 1965, §135.[311] It wrote into law a cartel agreement among banks from 1929,[312] where the banks agreed with one another – and then announced to the public – that they would take company voting rights from shareholders, who had to deposit their share certificates in banks for safekeeping. Ever since, banks have used these voting rights on other people's money, posing a major conflict of interest. Banks not only sell financial products to companies (such as retail banking, or insurance through connected enterprises) but cast shareholder votes in them. Three banks control around 60 per cent of all votes on shares in German companies.[313] On orthodox analysis, this violates EU law by (1) granting special rights under article 106(1), (2) writing into law a cartel agreement in violation of article 101(1)(a) and (e), and (3) abusing a dominant position under article 102(a) and (d). This would justify enforcement action by the Commission to prohibit banks, when they perform shareholding depositary services, from voting on client's money (an unfair condition, or tying in an unjustified supplementary obligation).

(c) State Aid

A final element of competition in EU law is the regulation of state aid. The goal is often said to be to stop 'corporate welfare', where money is given to profit-making companies that fail to innovate or compete.[314] Article 107(1) says that 'any aid' from a member state in any form that may 'distort competition by favouring certain undertakings or the production of certain goods', and affects

[310] *Aktiengesetz* 1937, §114. [311] *Aktiengesetz* 1965, §135.

[312] Centralverband des deutschen Bank- und Bankiergewerbes (1930) BankA 1930–1, 116, Beschluß 'daß die Mitglieder unseres Verbandes einander gegenüber die Verpflichtung übernehmen, an die Besitzer bein ihnen hinterlegter Aktien eine ausdrückliche Anfrage über die Art der Ausübung des Stimmrechts zu richten, wenn ihnen von einem anderen Verbandsmitglied zwei Wochen vor der Generalversammlung die Absicht einer Opposition bekanntgegeben worden war'. That is, a decision that the members of the bank cartel assume the duty among one another to expressly consult the owners of shares if contentious issues arise on votes, and otherwise vote as they pleased. For background, see E. McGaughey, *Participation in Corporate Governance* (2014) ch. 6(2).

[313] Deutsche Bundesbank, *Statistische Sonderveröffentlichung 9* (2005) 32 and (1998) 32.

[314] E.g. *DaimlerChrysler Corp. v Cuno*, 547 US 332 (2006); and see D. Schenck, 'The Cuno Case: A Comparison of US Subsidies and European State Aid' (2006) 5(1) *Eur State Aid LQ* 3.

trade, is unlawful.[315] However, aid is also often an important part of policy on development and innovation, and so article 107(2) makes clear that aid is lawful if it (a) has 'a social character, granted to individual consumers … without discrimination' or (b) is for 'natural disasters or exceptional occurrences'.[316] Article 107(3) goes on to say aid may be lawful for (a) 'economic development of areas where the standard of living is abnormally low' or for 'serious underemployment', (b) for important projects of common European interest or to remedy serious economic disturbance,[317] (c) to develop certain economic 'activities' or 'areas',[318] (d) to 'promote culture and heritage conservation' or (e) other categories decided by the Council on a Commission proposal. Thus, the law distinguishes bad and good aid, depending on its purpose. There is very wide scope for state aid, although there are also large differences between countries' spending: by 2017 Germany's state aid had been around 1.3 per cent of its Gross Domestic Product, while the UK spent just 0.5 per cent.[319] Curiously, the issue has become a significant one in the UK government's negotiation of a UK–EU trade agreement, possibly as UK politicians fail to grasp how broad the rules are, and how abysmally low its failure had been to invest in public infrastructure and regional development.[320]

What exactly counts as state aid? What if money is given to private enterprises to provide public services? In *Altmark Trans GmbH v Nahverkehrsgesellschaft Altmark GmbH*, a competitor claimed that aid given to another transport company in Magdeburg was unlawful. The Court of Justice set out four conditions for the money to fall outside of the category of state aid altogether, namely if (i) the undertaking has a public service obligation, (ii) there are objective and transparent criteria for receipt of money, (iii) the compensation is enough to cover costs with 'a reasonable profit' and (iv) the aid is calculated based on costs of a typical undertaking.[321] For example, a half privately owned Dutch gas company that gave low gas prices to a private gas company was held to have given state aid.[322] However, the German government setting minimum prices to be paid by private electricity companies to consumers and small electricity generators that produced solar and clean energy did not count as state aid (see Ch. 12(2)(c)).[323] The most important set of exemptions are in the General Block Exemption Regulation 2014,

[315] TFEU, art. 107(1).
[316] TFEU, art. 107(2)(c) added a temporary exception for German reunification.
[317] E.g. *ABN Amro Group NV v Commission* (2014) T-319/11, allowing aid to banks in a global banking crisis.
[318] E.g. *Kahla/Thüringen Porzellan GmbH v Commission* (2008) T-20/03, allowing aid to porcelain-makers in Thuringia that faced insolvency, but eventually went through a successful restructure.
[319] European Commission, *State Aid Scoreboard 2017* (29 November 2017) COMP.A3, Annex 2.
[320] See P. Foster and C. Giles, 'Lawyers Offer Johnson Help to Break State Aid Impasse in EU Talks', *Financial Times* (21 September 2020).
[321] *Altmark Trans GmbH v Nahverkehrsgesellschaft Altmark GmbH* (2003) C-280/00, [89]–[93].
[322] *Kwekerij Gebroeders Van der Kooy BV v Commission* (1988) Case 67/85.
[323] *PreussenElektra AG v Schleswag AG* (2001) C-379/98, [62].

which endorses aid for twelve categories, starting with regional development, to small and medium enterprises, for environmental protection and for innovation.[324] Contrary to some perceptions, this would allow, for example, unlimited spending to ensure swift transition to renewable energy, by individual grants to homeowners, or small and medium businesses if each project is under €7.5 million (e.g. solar panels, turbines, trees, electric vehicles, plugs and batteries).[325] Again, there are no limits on the creation of public enterprises, of any scale, that are given public money for public projects.[326]

(5) Conclusion

The central concerns of competition law are to create a plural, accountable economy which works in the public interest. Its prohibitions on abuse by monopolies, oligopolies, anti-competitive takeovers and unjustified collusion are powerful weapons but they have not been used to the fullest, and do not yet cohere with structural remedies. Competition regulators are now increasingly focused on multinational monopolies as their patterns of abuse, if not outright crime, have escalated to the point that democracy has been imperilled, while their controllers back authoritarians in politics. The key measures of fair competition are fair prices for consumers, in balance with a reasonable return for traders and investors, fair wages and conditions for workers, and a clean environment. This notion of the public interest, and regard to multiple stakeholders, may appear more complex, at least superficially, than evidence-free hypotheses about consumer welfare. But the reality is that reductive standards serve more to protect corporate monopolies than any other group. In many cases it is true that competition systematically fails, despite the best efforts of competition regulators to create and enforce behavioural remedies. Where structure is at issue, the more competition fails, the more consumers and the public need governance voice.

324 General Block Exemption Regulation (GBER) 2014 (EU) No. 651/2014, art. 1.

325 GBER 2014, arts. 1(c), 4(1)(c) and 36–49 on other environmental exemptions.

326 See further A. Biondi, P. Eeckhout and J. Flynn, *The Law of State Aid in the European Union* (2004).

7

Insolvency and Creditors

Contents

As Chapter 6 explored, competition is meant to benefit consumers and the public, because people exercise choice and influence over what is produced. Enterprises producing what people want often get more business. But competitions also have 'losers',[1] and all too much, losing means insolvency. 'Enterprises live (and sometimes die) by credit', and corporate insolvency, like individuals' bankruptcy, is an inability to pay debts.[2] Enterprises may avoid insolvency by diversifying production as losses mount.[3] But for many businesses – especially small ones – this is not always possible. Competition and insolvency inherently cause waste and loss; and so, within this frame, the law's goal is to fairly distribute the losses.[4] First, it may place risks on those best able to bear them. While limited liability shields investors from full responsibility (see Ch. 3(1)(b)), insolvency law allocates losses among creditors. Second, the law may require businesses are rescued, not liquidated, in administration procedures that aim for the best possible outcome. Third, the law may deter irresponsible trading or lending.

The dominant view in the UK is that insolvency law's goal is to promote a 'rescue' and 'enterprise' culture.[5] Protecting creditors is a goal equal with

[1] E.g. Peter Thiel, founder of PayPal. Cf. 'Competition Is for Losers', *Wall Street Journal* (12 September 2014).
[2] E. McKendrick, *Goode on Commercial Law* (2010) ch. 22, 619; Insolvency Act (IA) 1986, s. 123.
[3] Cf. A. O. Hirschman, *Exit, Loyalty and Voice* (1970) 24, suggesting a slow landing, rather than a crash, is better.
[4] E. Warren, 'Bankruptcy Policy' (1987) 54 *U Chicago L Rev* 775, 777.
[5] K. Cork, *Report of the Review Committee on Insolvency Law and Practice*, Cmnd 8558 (1982); cf. Cmnd 9175 (1984), before the IA 1986. HM Treasury, *Enterprise Britain: A Modern Approach to*

'other interests of society'.[6] However, many law and economics scholars have argued insolvency law's only legitimate goal is maximising creditor wealth, and secured creditors (usually a bank) should always come first to encourage lending.[7] They also suggest secured creditors should dominate insolvency procedures.[8] Unlimited rights for secured creditors benefit everyone, it is said, because without lending there would be no business. These theories lack empirical evidence.[9] Banks do not restrict lending if the law restrains them from sweeping up all assets and dominating procedures in insolvency. Bank lending is primarily driven by monetary and fiscal policy (see Ch. 10). The better view is that creditors' interests are best served by companies being rescued, not split up for the benefit of banks. Secured creditors' interests often conflict with other creditors, and it is difficult to defend any system where the gains for a bank in insolvency are smaller than the overall social cost to small business, taxpayers, employees, tort victims or communities. This chapter concentrates on corporate insolvency, as opposed to individual bankruptcy, how it sets priorities, how it is governed and who may be accountable after.

(1) Priority, Security and Insurance

Insolvency means that people cannot pay their debts as they fall due, and that there is not enough money left to repay everyone, particularly bank loans, trade partners, tax bills, worker wages, consumers or tort victims. When there is not enough money, insolvency law must decide rules to ensure these losses are fairly distributed.[10] But what counts as 'fair' depends on our view of insolvency's causes. First, some insolvencies are inevitable in a system of competition and private property. Like Mr Salomon, who lost a major order to supply British army boots, some companies go insolvent through no fault of their own: sharp technology change, lucky competitors or a crash.[11] Second, the immediate trigger for many companies going insolvent is late payments from other businesses,[12] potentially causing a ripple effect throughout the economy. Third, companies may be mismanaged. Like the Barings Bank directors who

Meeting the Enterprise Challenge (2002) Foreword, saying the aim is to 'widen and deepen the enterprise culture' in the Enterprise Act 2002 (c. 40).

6 Cork Report, §192.

7 E.g. T. H. Jackson, 'Bankruptcy, Nonbankruptcy and the Creditors' Bargain' (1982) 91 *Yale LJ* 857.

8 D. G. Baird and T. H. Jackson, 'Corporate Reorganizations and the Treatment of Diverse Ownership Interests: A Comment on Adequate Protection of Secured Creditors in Bankruptcy' (1984) 51(1) *U Chicago L Rev* 97.

9 E.g. R. Goode, *Principles of Corporate Insolvency Law* (2011) ch. 2; J. Franks and O. Sussman, 'The Cycle of Corporate Distress, Rescue and Dissolution: A Study of Small and Medium Size UK Companies', IFA Working Paper No. 306 (2000).

10 Warren, 'Bankruptcy Policy', 777.

11 See Ch. 3(1)(b) and *A. Salomon & Co. Ltd v Salomon* [1896] UKHL 1.

12 R. B. Callander, 'Late Payments Put a Quarter of Small Firms at Risk of Insolvency', *Daily Telegraph* (8 August 2015).

failed to stop Nick Leeson's speculation at the Singapore futures trading, directors may be negligent.[13] Like Robert Maxwell, who stole his employees' pensions,[14] or BCCI's criminal and terrorist funding,[15] some directors may be fraudulent. In the UK, unpaid creditors are mostly left to fend for themselves, though there is residual insurance particularly for employees, pensions and tort victims. This section examines (a) the priority system – which creditors get paid first, (b) fixed and floating charges and (c) social insurance.

(a) Priority in Case Law and Statute

(i) The Basic Rule of *Pari Passu*

When companies go insolvent the six main parties who usually have unpaid debts are banks, trade creditors, tax authorities, employees, consumers and tort victims. The basic rule (which virtually never operates alone) in the Insolvency Act 1986, section 107 is that a company's property should be sold and used 'in satisfaction of the company's liabilities *pari passu*', with any remainder given to members according to their rights under the constitution. *Pari passu* means proportional. Imagine a company has three creditors: a bank owed £500, Her Majesty's Revenue and Customs owed £400 and an employee owed £100. But the company only has £500 left over. If the law worked on a purely *pari passu* system, the bank gets £250, HMRC £200 and the employee £50. This system of 'rate and rate like' dates to Henry VIII.[16] It is simple. But few societies have recognised it as just.[17] The difficulty is, UK law displays no coherent alternative policy: we have a system of priorities that is clearly influenced by a desire to protect vulnerable creditors. But the law also allows security interests to be created that potentially elevate powerful claimants above all unsecured claims.

(ii) Security Interests

If the example above were in real life, the bank would usually have contracted for a security interest over the company's property. A historic assumption of the law is that property rights (i.e. legal or beneficial ownership) rank above personal obligations (i.e. rights in contract, tort or unjust enrichment). If someone owns property that a company still possesses, they may physically take that property if a company goes insolvent, ahead of claims by a contractual or tort creditor.[18] But also, the law recognises rights to security interests. For

[13] See Ch. 3(4)(c) and *Re Barings plc (No. 5)* [2000] 1 BCLC 523.

[14] See Ch. 3(4)(a) and *Bishopsgate Investment Management Ltd v Homan* [1994] EWCA Civ 33.

[15] See Ch. 5(1)(c) and *Mahmud and Malik v BCCI SA* [1999] UHKL 23.

[16] Statute of Bankrupts Act 1542 (34 & 35 Hen. VIII, c. 4) put it into statute.

[17] E.g. the Talmud (*c.* 200 AD) in Kethuboth, x. 4, 93a required that each creditor shared equally in what was left, up to the value of their debts. In the example above, this would mean the employee gets £100, HMRC £200 and the bank £200. L. Levinthal, 'The Early History of Bankruptcy Law' (1918) 66(5) *U Penn L Rev* 223.

[18] E.g. *Re David Lloyd & Co.* (1877) 6 Ch D 339, 344–5, per James LJ.

instance, if a bank gives a company a loan, the bank may agree that in the event of the company going insolvent, it may take the company's building, its van, the goods in its warehouse or collect unpaid debts on the company's account books. With registration (see Ch. 7(1)(b)(iii)) this will become a secured property right, though ironically this 'property' right starts as a contract. In fact, the bank has no desire to take the building, the van, goods or book debts. It wants interest repaid on its loan. Yet the law allows the bank to agree that, if insolvency comes, the bank may take the secured property ahead of contractual creditors. In the Renaissance, security interests were sometimes thought to be fraudulent, because the debtor holds and trades with the property as if it were their own.[19] But by the late nineteenth century the law accepted corporate security interests of two main types.[20] 'Fixed' charges apply to things typically kept by the company on a lasting basis (e.g. the building and van). 'Floating' charges apply to things that the company buys and sells in the course of trade (e.g. the goods and book debts: Ch. 7(1)(b)) but these are demoted behind preferential claims.

(iii) Preferential Claims

It is often argued that security interests are necessary to establish business confidence, and therefore encourage lending, particularly in the credit and banking system. However, since the late nineteenth century it was recognised that security may unjustly negate the rights of vulnerable creditors. In 1883 employees acquired the right to be paid in preference to other *unsecured* claims,[21] and in 1888 tax revenue was given the same statutory preference.[22] But they were still behind any holder of a fixed or floating charge. As we saw in Chapter 3(1)(b), in *Salomon v A. Salomon & Co. Ltd*, Mr Salomon had elevated his own claims to debt repayment over his company's creditors by contracting for a floating charge over the company's assets. (This is unusual: it is usually banks contracting for floating charges today.) Lord Macnaghten called the law which allows secured creditors to 'step in and sweep off everything' a 'great scandal', advocating legislation to enable small trade creditors to get statutory priority.[23] In the event, in 1897, employee and tax revenue claims were given

19 *Twyne's case* (1601) 3 Co Rep 80b, 76 ER 809. A farmer called Pierce 'sold' sheep to a debtor, Twyne, but continued marking and shearing them. When another creditor, owed money by Pierce, sent the Sheriff of Southampton to collect the sheep, the sale was held to be void because, among other reasons, Pierce 'traded and trafficked with others, and defrauded and deceived them'.

20 IA 1986, s. 248 says '"security" means . . . any mortgage, charge, lien or other security'. A 'lien' involves someone holding onto property in their possession until a debt is satisfied. Under 'other security' is also a pledge, where you hand over property in return for money, as at a pawnbroker. Charges are the most important. For a definition of sorts see *National Provincial Bank v Charnley* [1924] 1 KB 431, 449, per Atkin LJ.

21 Companies Act 1883 (c. 28), ss. 4–6.

22 Preferential Payments in Bankruptcy Act 1888 (c. 62), s. 1.

23 [1896] UKHL 1, [1897] AC 22.

a preference above the claims of a floating-charge holder.[24] In 1906, a minority of the Loreburn Report advocated complete abolition of the floating charge,[25] but despite continued calls this has not happened yet.[26] Instead the statutory preference for tax was removed in 2002, and unsecured creditors were given a limited priority over floating-charge holders, known as a 'ring-fenced fund'.[27]

(iv) The Priority List

The result is that UK law has a mish-mash system of priority, summarised in *Re Nortel GmbH*.[28] The 'effect of insolvency legislation', said Lord Neuberger. 'as interpreted and extended by the courts' is a priority system as follows:

(1) Fixed charge creditors;
(2) Expenses of the insolvency proceedings;
(3) Preferential creditors;
(4) Floating charge creditors;
(5) Unsecured provable debts;
(6) Statutory interest;
(7) Non-provable liabilities; and
(8) Shareholders.

First, 'fixed charge creditors' are paid, usually in full, because they are empowered to take the secured assets and sell them. This is a result, though by no means a necessary one, of uncodified common law assumptions on the hierarchy of property over obligations. No percentage has to be given to unsecured creditors under statute, yet. The fixed-charge holder is usually a bank (like HSBC, Barclays, RBS or Lloyds) with a registered charge or mortgage.

Second, the 'expenses of insolvency proceedings' mean the practitioners who are appointed as an administrator, liquidator or receiver. This is in statute.[29] The practitioners will often be four major accountancy firms: Deloitte, PwC, KPMG or EY. It is usually said that guaranteeing insolvency

24 Preferential Payments in Bankruptcy Amendment Act 1897, s. 2. See Mr George Kemp, HC Debs. (10 February 1897) vol. 46, cols. 70–87, pointing out the injustice to workers of banks taking assets when 'raw material had been benefited by the work of the workpeople to the extent of the time for which their wages were in arrear'.

25 Loreburn Report, Report of the Company Law Amendment Committee, Cd 3052 (1906) 28, per Gore-Brown, Faber and Holland: a company 'ought to be rendered incapable of charging after acquired chattels, or future book debts, or other property not in existence at the time of the creation of the charge'.

26 See R. Goode, 'The Case for the Abolition of the Floating Charge' in J. Getzler and J. Payne (eds.), *Company Charges: Spectrum and Beyond* (2006).

27 Changes in the Enterprise Act 2002, ss. 251–2.

28 *Re Nortel GmbH* [2013] UKSC 52, [39], holding a financial support direction of the Pensions Regulator is not administration expenses, but provable debts, and so rank as unsecured, below floating-charge holder claims.

29 IA 1986, ss. 115 and 176ZA.

practitioner pay is necessary to ensure they take insolvency work, but it also reduces discipline on escalating practitioners' fees, a phenomenon exacerbated where creditors do not exercise effective, collective control.[30] So, the reality of most insolvencies is that eight banks and accountant firms claim most assets first.[31]

Third, employees and their pension funds have a limited preference, created by statute.[32] The amount of wages is capped at £800, plus outstanding holiday pay. The legislature has failed to update this figure since 1986,[33] and so it has dwindled arbitrarily with inflation. Contributions to pensions have similar arbitrary limits.[34] Behind these preferential creditors,[35] but also in the 'preferential' category, is a 'ring-fenced fund' for unsecured creditors.[36] This comes out of the money that is otherwise subject to a floating charge. It is 50 per cent of the property up to £10,000, and 20 per cent of property up to £600,000.[37] In other words, in any major insolvency, £120,000 is available for unsecured creditors: small businesses, money owed in taxes or workers' wages over £800. Small creditors may also lose their claims if the costs of administering them outweigh the benefits.[38] Before the ring-fenced fund was introduced, a study in 2000 found that banks recovered on average 77 per cent of their claims, preferential creditors got 27 per cent and unsecured creditors got virtually nothing.[39] It is not clear that the position is much better now.

Fourth, insolvency practitioners, employees, pensions and the ring-fenced fund are paid in preference to floating-charge holders. The floating-charge holder is usually a bank which has loaned the company money, contracted for fixed charges over everything that is legally permissible (see Ch. 7(1)(b)), 'and a floating charge over the remaining assets'.[40]

Fifth, unsecured creditors' remaining debts are paid after the floating-charge holder. In most cases under the current law, they will get nothing. Sixth,

[30] E. Kempson, *Review of Insolvency Practitioner Fees: Report to the Insolvency Service* (July 2013).

[31] The big four banks have 75% of the current account market. The big four accountants have 97% of auditing.

[32] IA 1986, ss. 40, 175, 386 and Sch. 6, paras. 9–16.

[33] Insolvency Proceedings (Monetary Limits) Order 1986, SI 1986/1996, art. 4.

[34] IA 1986, Sch. 6, para. 8 points to the Pension Schemes Act 1993, Sch. 4, paras. 1–2, stating the last 4 months of employee contributions and 12 months of employer contributions are due. It is unclear why the full amount is not due. Similarly, *Re Nortel GmbH* [2013] UKSC 52, held that where a final-salary pension is underfunded, a 'financial support direction' to pay up the deficit by the Pension Regulator ranks merely as an unsecured provable debt, rather than an expense of administration (which would give it fuller priority).

[35] NB: Lord Neuberger's list should probably have had an extra entry for the ring-fenced fund; cf. S. Worthington, *Sealy & Worthington's Text, Cases, & Materials in Company Law* (2016) ch. 12.

[36] IA 1986, s. 176A. [37] IA 1986 (Prescribed Part) Order 2003 (SI 2003/2097) regs. 2–3.

[38] E.g. *Re Hydroserve Ltd* [2007] EWHC 3026 (Ch), [2008] BCC 175, per Rimer J.

[39] Insolvency Service, *A Review of Company Rescue and Business Reconstruction Mechanisms, Report by the Review Group* (2000) para. 57.

[40] Cf. *Re Atlantic Computer Systems plc* [1992] Ch 505, per Nicholls LJ: 'Typically, when lending money to a company, a bank will take as security a charge over all or most of the assets of the company, present and future, the charge being a fixed charge on land and certain other assets, and a floating charge over the remaining assets.'

interest is paid to creditors.[41] Seventh, non-provable liabilities as opposed to debts are paid. Eighth, members of the company are paid. Lord Neuberger's seemingly unconscious assumption that 'shareholders' are usually the members is often accurate in practice, but not in law (e.g. members may be guarantors, see Ch. 3(1)(e)). Money is paid according to the company's constitution, which may specify priority between preferential or ordinary members.[42]

Paradoxically, although security interests are created by contract, it has been firmly held that the priority system should not be circumvented by non-proprietary contracts. In *British Eagle Ltd v Air France*, the liquidator of British Eagle claimed that a debt-clearing system used among it and other airlines was unlawful.[43] Many airlines, including Air France, were members of the International Air Transport Association (IATA). To avoid thousands of bilateral payments, airlines settled their debts through IATA every month. When it went insolvent, British Eagle owed money to IATA, but Air France owed money to British Eagle. The liquidator wanted that money. Air France argued it should not be made to pay money to British Eagle's liquidator (rather than the IATA clearing system) because its debt should be reduced by the amount of British Eagle Ltd's debts to IATA first. The House of Lords held this scheme was void under the priority rules: it would be contracting out. Lord Cross urged that 'documents were not drawn so as to create charges but simply so as to set up by simple contract a method of settling each other's mutual indebtedness at monthly intervals'.[44] In other words, their Lordships were perfectly aware that Air France could have achieved priority through a system of proprietary charges. A dissenting minority would have held the system valid.[45] None of their Lordships explained why either a contract or a property-based system should be able to advance claims over unsecured creditors, such as the 2,500 employees who had outstanding wages, or the holiday-goers who lost their flights.

A variation of the same idea is called the 'anti-deprivation' principle. This says any contractual provision that deprives a company of assets at or just before the point of insolvency is invalid.[46] Again, it is strictly enforced, but in the grand scheme of things appears insignificant when security interests are so easily created.

41 IA 1986, s. 189.

42 Also IA 1986, ss. 735 (money due under share redemption) and 74(2)(f) (debts due to members).

43 *British Eagle International Air Lines Ltd v Compagnie Nationale Air France* [1975] 1 WLR 758.

44 See also *Re Jeavons, ex parte Mackay* (1873) LR 8 Ch App 643, holding that an agreement that a creditor could keep royalties on an armour-plate patent could not be effective against other creditors (it was not property).

45 [1975] 1 WLR 758, Lord Morris and Lord Simon dissented.

46 *Belmont Park Pty Ltd v BNY Corporate Trustees Ltd* [2011] UKSC 38, [74]–[78], Lord Collins emphasising that good faith, fair transactions will not fall within this rule.

(b) Fixed and Floating Charges

This next section sets out (i) why security interests are seen as important and the debate about their limits; (ii) how fixed charges are distinguished from floating charges; (iii) how they are registered; and (iv) the problems of quasi-security interests that fall outside registration rules.

(i) Importance of Security and Its Limits

Secured credit is a fundamental component of modern finance. It is the basis for most loans made by banks (see Ch. 10), and commonly argued to be necessary not only for banks to lend, but also for the development of a modern economy.[47] Empirical literature does not produce final views on what is the optimal legal regime. But it seems obvious that stable, fair credit is needed for capital formation, business development and to avoid financial crisis. This requires that banks or other lenders can take security to some extent: mortgages to take buildings upon non-payment ('safe as houses'), fixed charges on company property, floating charges over assets that are traded or 'quasi-security' interests over materials or money used in the course of trade. As Chapter 3(1)(b) noted, banks often also seek personal guarantees from the real people who operate a company.

It is also obvious that creditors are not all the same. Some have more bargaining power. The big four UK banks (HSBC, Barclays, RBS and Lloyds) can offer credit to all but the largest companies on a take-it-or-leave-it basis. They are in a position both to become over-secured, and to abuse their bargaining position. While security interests are contracts between a creditor and debtor, in insolvency they have a negative impact on parties external to the contract,[48] like any externality (see Ch. 2(2)(c)). Those third parties give no consent to a security interest. If they cannot adjust their risk exposure as easily as the secured creditor (i.e. they lack bargaining power), then the secured creditor is effectively conducting a forced transfer of wealth without the unsecured creditor's consent. If secured creditors know their security is absolute, they may also fail to lend as responsibly as possible, a phenomenon on graphic display in the global financial crisis of 2007–8.[49] This amounts to

[47] U. Lilienfeld-Toal, D. Mookherjee and S. Visaria, 'The Distributive Impact of Reforms in Credit Enforcement: Evidence from Indian Debt Recovery Tribunals' (2012) 80(2) *Econometrica* 497; and cf. S. Djankov, C. McLiesh and A. Shleifer, 'Private Credit in 129 Countries' (2007) 2(84) *J Financial Economics* 299.

[48] L. A. Bebchuk and J. M. Freid, 'The Uneasy Case for the Priority of Secured Claims in Bankruptcy' (1996) 105 *Yale LJ* 857.

[49] E.g. J. Coffee, 'What Went Wrong? An Initial Inquiry into the Causes of the 2008 Financial Crisis' (2009) 9(1) *J Corporate L Studies* 1, documenting both (1) irresponsible lending by mortgage houses to homeowners, on extortionate terms, and (2) irresponsible trading by banks of collateralised debt obligations, and related derivatives, supposedly secure in the knowledge that everything was safe as houses.

a misallocation of resources that damages enterprise. It is possible so long as fixed charges remain sacrosanct.

(ii) Distinguishing Fixed and Floating Charges

A 'fixed charge', as we saw at Chapter 7(1)(a)(iv), is subjected to no preferential claims yet. A 'floating charge' is, so the law must police this fixed/floating distinction. The floating charge was invented by lawyers in the late nineteenth century to cover, not just specific, identifiable property, but also goods that one could not pin down at any moment because they were being traded. Soon after *Salomon*, and the statutory extension of preferential creditors, *Re Yorkshire Woolcombers Association* held the defining features of a floating charge are that (1) it charges 'assets of a company present and future', (2) those assets are 'changing from time to time in the ordinary course of business' and (3) 'the company can trade in the normal way' (unless, for instance, the company goes insolvent).[50] This meant the Association was not allowed to create a floating charge over its book debts.

Plainly, if the courts were bound by the contracting parties' words (rather than economic reality) any contract could be written in terms that defeat the law's purpose: to protect creditors who cannot bargain for security. Unfortunately, in 1978 a High Court judge held that a charge, labelled in a contract as a 'fixed charge' over book debts, was just that: not floating, and so not subject to statutory preferences. This position lasted until *Re Spectrum Plus Ltd* in 2005.[51] Here, the Inland Revenue (now HMRC) argued that Spectrum Plus Ltd had merely given a floating charge over its assets to NatWest plc, its bank, even though its security contract read it was granting a fixed or 'specific charge [of] all book debts and other debts . . . now and from time to time due or owing to' Spectrum Ltd.[52] Following the Enterprise Act 2002, it was even more important for the tax authorities to stop misrepresented floating charges sweeping up assets because they lost their preferential status.[53] The House of Lords held that it could not be a floating charge, despite being labelled as a 'specific charge', because the company could continue to use that money once it came in. Recognising that it is a floating charge when one 'is left free to use the charged asset', said Lord Scott, 'reflects the mischief that the statutory intervention . . . was intended to meet and should ensure that preferential creditors continue to enjoy the priority that section 175 of the 1986 Act and its statutory predecessors intended them to have'.[54]

Since *Spectrum*, many reforms to the law have been suggested. First, it has been argued by John Armour that companies could still use other legal forms

[50] *Re Yorkshire Woolcombers Association* [1904] AC 355, approving the decision of Romer LJ at [1903] 2 Ch 284. The Earl of Halsbury LC and Lord MacNaghten, who decided *Salomon*, featured in the same case.

[51] [2005] UKHL 41. [52] [2005] UKHL 41, [78]. [53] Enterprise Act 2002, s. 251.

[54] [2005] UKHL 41, [111].

to circumvent the *Spectrum* case and its aim to protect creditors, pointing to 'invoice discounting' and 'factoring'.[55] He concludes that we should abolish all preferential status because it is pointless. Second, Roy Goode and others have called instead for abolishing the floating charge.[56] This would restrict contractual freedom to create property rights, but it is argued there are twin-gains that (1) all left-over, non-fixed assets could fulfil claims by unsecured creditors, and (2) though banks would get less, they would be saved paperwork, and could concentrate on other profitable activities. Third, an additional alternative is to not only abolish the floating charge, but also require preferential status or a ring-fenced fund (or both) for vulnerable creditors over fixed-charge holders. This is the logic of acknowledging, as Lucian Bebchuk and Jesse Fried have stated, that a security interest creates a negative externality for non-adjusting creditors.[57] While acknowledging that rights of property are important, this would recognise that they should not entirely defeat other universal human rights such as fair pay, social security and pensions, health and the environment.[58]

(iii) Registration and the Limits of Transparency

All company charges require registration, to create transparency and let creditors check a company's assets before deciding to lend. The word 'debenture' in law means any loan,[59] though in business it usually refers to a secured loan. Only a loan with security – a 'charge' upon a company's property – must be registered.[60] Under the Companies Act 2006, section 859A, this must be done within twenty-one days of its creation. If it is not registered, the security interest (though not the loan itself) is void under section 859H. This system means there is a twenty-one-day 'invisibility' period, because the charge does not lose validity until twenty-one days expire. The alternative, used in the USA, would be to acquire validity when the charge is filed.[61]

While registration is about transparency, some creditors will still be unable to bargain for security, no matter how transparent charges are. Equity has long recognised this problem. In 1765, *Vernon v Bethell* held that a debtor must

[55] J. Armour, 'Should We Redistribute in Insolvency?' in J. Getzler and J. Payne (eds.), *Company Charges: Spectrum Plus and Beyond* (2006). Cf. *Twyne's case* (1601) 3 Co Rep 80b, 76 ER 809.

[56] Goode, 'The Case for the Abolition of the Floating Charge'.

[57] Bebchuk and Fried, 'The Uneasy Case for the Priority of Secured Claims in Bankruptcy'. Cf. *FHR European Ventures LLP v Cedar Capital Partners LLC* [2014] UKSC 45, [42], on recognising 'wider policy considerations' in a case on constructive trusts over bribes, so having priority.

[58] UDHR 1948, arts. 17, 22–5 and 27.

[59] CA 2006, s. 738. The word debenture can be relevant for tax statutes, e.g. *British India Steam Navigation Co. v IRC* (1881) 7 *QBD* 165 (applying stamp duty to debentures).

[60] CA 2006, ss. 859A–Q.

[61] US Uniform Commercial Code, art. 9, an approach recommended by the Law Commission, *Company Security Interests* (August 2005). The changes in the Companies Act 2006 (Amendment of Part 25) Regulations 2013 (SI 2013/600) were a missed opportunity to update this system.

always be free to pay off a debt and recover secured property. Any contract term that prevents a debtor getting back the property is void.[62] This led to the phrase that there must be 'no clog on the equity of redemption',[63] or 'once a mortgage, always a mortgage' (not a sale). The reason, said Lord Henley LC, is that 'necessitous men are not, truly speaking, free men, but, to answer a present exigency, will submit to any terms that the crafty may impose upon them', a phrase immortalised by Roosevelt's speech on the Second Bill of Rights in 1944 (see Ch. 1(4)). Unfortunately, while the rule survives in general, this protection for small companies was removed from 1907, to enable 'perpetual debentures'.[64] Other than an outdated taste for 'freedom of contract', it is not clear what justified this.

(iv) Quasi-security Interests

Two further kinds of quasi-security interests create problems in the law because they are currently not registrable. First, there are so-called *Romalpa* clauses, where a person seeks to retain the title of goods that he sells until he receives payment. In *Aluminium Industrie Vaassen BV v Romalpa Aluminium Ltd*, the Court of Appeal held a Dutch supplier of industrial aluminium foil could retain title to the raw materials, up to the point that Romalpa Ltd had changed them into something else.[65] This meant that when Romalpa Ltd went insolvent, the floating charge of its bank did not cover the unused foils.

Second, there are *Quistclose* trusts, where a person seeks to ensure they are the beneficiaries of a trust of money which they lend until the point that the purpose of the loan succeeds. In *Barclays Bank Ltd v Quistclose Investments Ltd* the House of Lords held that this form of security was lawful.[66] Rolls Razor Ltd, already in debt, wanted to pay a dividend to its shareholders. Quistclose Ltd lent it money to pay the dividend, and paid this into Rolls Razor Ltd's account with Barclays Ltd on the condition it would be used only for the dividend. When Rolls Razor Ltd went insolvent, Quistclose Ltd successfully argued it could get the money back, ahead of Barclays Ltd's right to set off its debts. This case has (to the joy of trusts students) been criticised as being a trust for a purpose without clear beneficiaries (and so supposedly violating one of the 'three certainties' to form a trust).[67] But the main policy problem is that *Romalpa* clauses and *Quistclose* trusts are not yet registrable, and so transparent or in the same priority system, as are all other proprietary claims.

[62] *Vernon v Bethell* (1762) 28 ER 838.

[63] See also *Howard v Harris* (1681) 1 Vern 33; *Toomes v Conset* (1745) 26 ER 952.

[64] CA 2006, s. 739. This was introduced in the Companies Act 1907, s. 14.

[65] [1976] 1 WLR 676. [66] [1968] UKHL 4.

[67] While Lord Wilberforce framed the trust as being for a purpose, the analysis recognised in *Twinsectra Ltd v Yardley* [2002] UKHL 12, [13] per Lord Hoffmann, is that Q is the settlor, R is the trustee and Q is also the beneficiary, but R also has a power to apply the money for a purpose: there is no trust for a purpose.

(c) Social Insurance

While the scope of preferential status is very limited, the law does create social insurance for three important groups of people. First, both European Union (EU) and UK law require that unpaid wages are reimbursed.[68] The National Insurance fund pays an amount equal to any redundancy payment due to employees who have lost their jobs,[69] and also up to eight weeks' worth of wages up to £538 a week,[70] compensation for failure to give notice, holiday pay and the basic award for compensation for unfair dismissal.[71] Employees are entitled to select which are the most favourable eight weeks' worth of wages.[72] Second, for pensions, the Pension Protection Fund places a levy on all funds which is used to reimburse 90 per cent of a pension if an employer is insolvent.[73] Third, in practice tort victims that could be owed money have their medical costs (if not full compensation) covered by the National Health Service (NHS) (see Ch. 9), unlike in other countries such as the USA. While social insurance is essential for people's welfare, this shifts costs onto tax payers, while secured creditors, mainly banks, are typically paid in full.

(2) Governance of Insolvency Procedures

If the law worked optimally, questions of priority among creditors' claims would arise more rarely because companies would be rescued, not liquidated. Today, there are four main kinds of insolvency procedure: administration, administrative receivership, liquidation and voluntary arrangements. The first, administration, is the most important because an administrator has a duty in the Insolvency Act 1986, Schedule B1, paragraph 3(1) of (a) 'rescuing the company as a going concern' or, if not, (b) achieving a better result than liquidating, usually through selling the business or, if not, (c) 'realising property' to pay 'one or more secured or preferential creditors'. This means the administrator can try to rescue a company, but, if not, sell the business (hopefully as a going concern) and liquidate the assets to pay the creditors. There is no need to appoint a separate liquidator.

Before the Enterprise Act 2002 introduced administration, floating-charge holders could appoint an 'administrative receiver', who would 'receive' money

[68] Insolvency Protection Directive 2008/94/EC, arts. 3–4, and note the famous *Francovich v Italy* (1991) C-6/90 case, concerning damages against a member state for failure to implement the original Directive 80/987.

[69] Employment Rights Act (ERA) 1996, ss. 166–70.

[70] Employment Rights (Increase of Limits) Order 2020 (SI 2020/205) Schedule.

[71] ERA 1996, ss. 182–90.

[72] E.g. *Mann v Secretary of State for Employment* [1999] UKHL 29, where a shipbuilder went insolvent, and 408 people dismissed, without any consultation with the union.

[73] Pensions Act 2004, ss. 173–4 and 177(3) require that levies should 'result in at least 80% of the amount raised by the levies for that year being raised by the risk-based pension protection levy'. Cf. *Robins v Secretary of State for Work and Pensions* (2007) C-278/05, holding that the UK's original protections were inadequate.

only to pay that secured creditor. Without facing any consequence from other creditors, receivers ran up excessive costs.[74] The administrative receiver process remains, however, for six enterprises in the public and regulated sectors.[75] The difference, on paper, is that the administrator must, under paragraph 3(2), act 'in the interests of the company's creditors as a whole'. But despite this stakeholder-oriented text (and just as directors usually follow shareholder interests because shareholders have the vote[76]), secured creditor interests dominate, because this is the group with voting power. This section discusses (a) the reality of administrator appointment and removal; (b) the duties that operate otherwise, and their enforcement; and (c) the other procedures of liquidation, receivership and voluntary arrangements.

(a) Appointment of Administrators

(i) Rights of Appointment

While administrators superficially owe duties to 'creditors as a whole',[77] in practice they are likely to respond to the interests of the creditors who vote them in. It was said, when introduced, that 'rescue is at the heart' of administration.[78] This is questionable. Schedule B1, paragraph 12 states the company (by a majority of members), its directors, any creditor or magistrate may apply for a court to order that a company enters administration.[79] But if they do, the applicant must notify the holder of a 'qualifying floating charge', which is one that 'relates to the whole or substantially the whole of the company's property'.[80] This is usually a bank which has given the biggest loan to a company. Notification gives it the opportunity under paragraph 36 to intervene 'to have a specified person appointed as administrator'. A court 'shall' appoint the bank's choice 'unless the court thinks it right to refuse the application because of the particular circumstances of the case'. Banks usually maintain a list of favourable insolvency practitioners that they will wish to appoint.[81]

[74] R. J. Mokal, *Corporate Insolvency Law: Theory and Application* (2005) ch. 6(6).

[75] IA 1986, s. 72A, floating-charge holders cannot appoint administrative receivers, except in cases of: ss. 72B capital market arrangements, 72C public–private partnerships with step-in rights (see Chs. 8–9, 14–15), 72DA urban regeneration projects, 72E project finance over £50m (Ch. 10), 72F financial markets (Ch. 10), 72G social landlords, 72GA water companies (Ch. 13), protected railway companies (Ch. 14), licensed airlines.

[76] Cf. CA 2006, s. 172; and see Ch. 3(4)(b). [77] IA 1986, Sch. B1, para. 3(1).

[78] Lord McIntosh, Hansard HL Debs. (29 July 2002) col. 766: 'Company rescue is at the heart of the revised administration procedure. We want to make sure that viable companies do not go to the wall unnecessarily.'

[79] IA 1986, Sch. B1, para. 12.

[80] IA 1986, Sch. B1, paras. 12 and 14. This also refers to parties who can appoint an administrative receiver (s. 29(2)), who is also someone with a 'qualifying floating charge'.

[81] See Goode, *Principles of Corporate Insolvency Law*, 389 and 418.

The company or its directors may also appoint an administrator without applying to court.[82] Again, they must give the qualifying floating-charge holder five days' notice,[83] so it can intervene under paragraph 36. The qualifying floating-charge holder can itself appoint an administrator out of court, if the floating charge's terms allow it.[84] The result is that, with the agreement of three parties – the board, bank and accountant – an administration could potentially begin without the consent of any other creditor or prior court approval. In effect the bank, as a qualifying floating-charge holder, monopolises the vote on administrators.

(ii) Conditions for Appointment

If the court hearing goes ahead, to decide whether to appoint an administrator (as opposed to a liquidator to wind up immediately), the court must ask, under paragraph 11, if the company 'is or is likely to become unable to pay its debts' (i.e. because it is insolvent) and whether 'the administration order is reasonably likely to achieve the purpose of administration'. That means rescuing the company, the business or paying some creditors under paragraph 3(1). For example, in *Re Harris Simons Construction Ltd*, a building company applied to the court for administration after it fell out with a contracting partner, worth £27 million in turnover.[85] Hoffmann J granted the order on the ground that this major creditor would grant funding to continue a final four building contracts. He said the statutory test requires only that there is a 'good arguable case' for realising a goal of administration. This is easier than the 'balance of probabilities' or 'beyond reasonable doubt'. The courts want to avoid immediate winding up, so they exercise their discretion liberally.[86] In practice, the goal of 'realising property' to pay 'one or more secured or preferential creditors' (i.e. at worst to pay one secured creditor) is not hard.

(iii) Rescue or Pre-packs

At least on paper, once the administrator is in place, it should propose a plan to achieve its objectives and circulate the plan within ten weeks to the registrar and unsecured creditors. The creditors should then have a meeting to approve the plan by a simple majority vote.[87] Voting rights are apportioned according to the creditors' provable debts. If there is no vote, a court can order as it thinks fit.[88] This takes time, but the administrator under paragraph 59 is empowered to do 'anything necessary or expedient for the management of the affairs,

[82] IA 1986, Sch. B1, paras. 22. [83] IA 1986, Sch. B1, paras. 25.
[84] IA 1986, Sch. B1, paras. 14. [85] *Re Harris Simons Construction Ltd* [1989] 1 WLR 368.
[86] Cf. *Re AA Mutual International Insurance Co. Ltd* [2004] EWHC 2430, per Lewison J, clarifying that the test for being unable to pay debts in para. 11(a) is itself 'more probable than not'.
[87] IA 1986, Sch. B1, paras. 49, 51 and 53. [88] IA 1986, Sch. B1, para. 55.

business and property of the company'.[89] In practice this enables the sale of the business by the administrator to a willing buyer before any creditor meeting takes place (option (b) under paragraph 3(1)). The only way to challenge such a decision would be to show the sale was beyond the administrator's powers, that it breached the duty of care, or acted upon the possibility of a conflict of interest (below). This means litigation after the fact, unless other creditors move swiftly to get an injunction.

Since the Enterprise Act 2002 there have been more and more 'pre-packaged' administrations. This phenomenon is not expressly foreseen in the law,[90] but the practice was well-developed in the USA under the Bankruptcy Act of 1978.[91] The typical pattern is that, as a company's directors realise they will be unable to pay off a large number of debts, they approach their bank (usually the qualifying floating-charge holder). They both agree that the business could survive, and maybe prosper, if they could only not pay debts to various trade creditors, tax collectors and perhaps employees, consumers or tort victims. They agree on who a good choice of administrator will be, usually from the bank's list. The plan will be that a company enters administration out of court, and immediately its assets and business (as a going concern) will be sold – perhaps to the directors of the failed company itself – and the bank is paid its debts. But none of the other creditors are paid: they only have claims against a remaining shell company, while a fresh, new debt-free business has emerged, maybe with the same management. The administrator, as it was chosen between the bank and the existing management, is unlikely to pursue claims against the former-directors. For this reason, pre-pack administrations have been described as 'shadowy bargains'.[92]

Are pre-pack administrations inherently corrupt? In their favour, people paid by the industry usually argue that a quick sale, which involves no litigation, no court and a ready-to-go plan, benefits employees in keeping their jobs.[93] It is true that avoiding unemployment is one of the most important social policies in a democratic society. Yet credible empirical evidence, which is not conflicted by industry-funding, does not exist to support the claim of any 'job-preserving effect'.[94] To back such a claim it would be necessary to

[89] IA 1986, Sch. B1, paras. 60–6 and Sch. 1 list further powers, including replacing directors, calling creditors' meetings, applying to court for directions, controlling company officers or distributing assets to creditors.

[90] Institute of Chartered Accountants, *Statement of Insolvency Practice 16* or 'SIP 16', para. 1 sets out a definition.

[91] Bankruptcy Act of 1978, 11 USC ch. 11. See L. M. Lopucki, E. Warren and R. M. Lawless, *Secured Transactions: A Systems Approach* (2019).

[92] V. Finch, 'Pre-packaged Administrations: Bargaining in the Shadows of Insolvency or Shadowy Bargains?' [2006] *J Business L* 568, 569.

[93] S. Frisby, 'A Preliminary Analysis of Pre-packaged Administrations', Report to R3 – The Association of Business Recovery Professionals (2007). R3 is the Association of Business Recovery Professionals (standing for Rescue, Recovery, Renewal) or the insolvency practitioner group.

[94] Cf. K. Creighton-Salvey, 'Pre-packed Administrations: An Empirical Social Rights Analysis' (2013) 42(2) *Industrial LJ* 85.

enumerate the jobs that are preserved, not just immediately after a business sale in one company, but job retention in six or twelve months, plus the net job-effect among unpaid creditors who may cut jobs, or indeed the government which loses tax revenue. Even going by the information of the insolvency industry, in 88% of pre-pack insolvencies unsecured creditors are paid nothing, and only in 3% of cases are unsecured creditors paid more than 25% of their debts.[95] It is also clear that creditor control on insolvency practitioner fees, which rank second only to secured creditors,[96] are weak.[97] In 2010 the Office of Fair Trading (OFT) found that when banks control the insolvency, fees rise by 9 per cent.[98] It is difficult to argue that this is what was intended for the administration procedure.[99]

If pre-pack administrations (at the least) raise questions about conflicts of interest, what oversight should the courts exert? In *Re Kayley Vending Ltd*, a cigarette-machine company faced insolvency after smoking in pubs and restaurants was banned, owing 'some £79,000' in debts to HMRC – a sum of money that might, for example, pay for two extra teachers or nurses for a year. Upon HMRC's petition for winding-up in court under paragraph 12, the directors proposed a business sale to competitors (i.e. not an inherently conflicted sale to themselves). HH Judge David Cooke held that despite the 'cynical concerns of those outside the process', it would usually be enough to 'provide creditors with information on the basis of which they may ask questions and, possibly, seek redress after the fact'.[100] In that case itself, it was said that the deal was at arm's length, and raised no actual conflict. Another view could be that a competitor-buyer has no interest in paying more money for the business to repay unsecured creditors, and the director-appointed administrator simply wants a deal. It is not 'cynical' to acknowledge that all parties have interests that conflict with the public interest in companies paying their fair share of taxes.

These 'cynical concerns', as HH Judge David Cooke chose to put it, arise because creditors are deprived of a chance to ensure that administrators are in fact appointed to represent the 'creditors as a whole'. Even if there is a meeting, a conflicted administrator may attempt to suppress creditors' voting rights. In *Revenue and Customs Commissioners v Maxwell*, the Revenue claimed that the administrators, appointed out of court, had failed to properly record its votes

95 Frisby, '*A Preliminary Analysis of Pre-packaged Administrations*', 57–8.

96 IA 1986, s. 176ZA; see Ch. 7(1)(a)(iv).

97 Insolvency Rules 1986, rule 2.106–109D (after SI 2015/443) required up-front estimation of fees, but see now Insolvency (England and Wales) Rules 2016.

98 OFT, *The Market for Corporate Insolvency Practitioners: A Market Study*, OFT1245 (June 2010) 30 and 57.

99 Cf. *In Re Transbus International Ltd* [2004] EWHC 932, [9], per Lawrence Collins J, referring to the judgment of Neuberger J in *Re T&D Industries plc* [2000] BCC 956, that administration was meant to be 'a more flexible, cheaper and comparatively informal alternative to liquidation' and 'the fewer applications which need to be made to the court the better'.

100 *Re Kayley Vending Ltd* [2009] EWHC 904 (Ch) [10]–[12].

in the creditors' meeting.[101] The company had proposed a management buy-out. But in counting votes, the Revenue had found that extra tax debts were due, as managers claimed tax deductions, unlawfully, for money transferred into trust funds and put into loans to directors themselves. The Court of Appeal had no difficulty in substituting its judgment for the administrator. Such cases, however, appear rare.

(iv) Moratorium

Formally, the administrator replaces the directors in the capacity to manage the company (although directors may appoint it).[102] On appointment, formally, a statutory moratorium prevents any creditor from taking or selling assets without a court's permission.[103] The moratorium is meant to provide a 'breathing space' for restructuring to take place (if that is actually to happen). It lasts for one year, but can be extended on application to court.[104] In *Re Atlantic Computer Systems plc (No. 1)* the claimant banks wished to repossess computers that the insolvent company had sublet. Nicholls LJ held that the banks would have permission because the benefits to the company were smaller than the cost to the banks, and repossession would not unduly impede the purpose of administration.[105] The moratorium also extends to criminal proceedings. For example, in *Environmental Agency v Clark*, the Court of Appeal was asked to approve the prosecution of Rhondda Waste Disposal Ltd for pollution of a landfill site in Wales. Leave was granted, because the breaches were long-standing and serious, and the 'polluter pays' principle should not therefore be overridden by the interests of creditors.[106] This suggests that, just as UK company law prioritises the public interest over shareholders, UK insolvency law prioritises the public interest over creditors.

(b) Duties of Administrators

The duties of an administrator, like a company director, necessarily take the form of minimum standards of conduct. Whatever they may say, it is more likely that the party who appoints will drive the administrator's behaviour. Like any fiduciary, an administrator's central duties are threefold: (1) to act according to the terms of one's office, similar to sections 171–3 for company directors; (2) to take care, like section 174; and (3) to avoid any possibility of a conflict of interest, like sections 175–7.[107] These duties must logically be

[101] [2010] EWCA Civ 1379. [102] IA 1986, Sch. B1, para. 67.
[103] IA 1986, Sch. B1, paras. 40–4. [104] IA 1986, Sch. B1, para. 76.
[105] [1992] Ch 505, 539–40. [106] [2001] Ch 57.
[107] Cf. *AIB Group (UK) plc v Mark Redler & Co. Solicitors* [2014] UKSC 58, per Lord Toulson [51], formulating these as '(1) a custodial stewardship duty, that is, a duty to preserve the assets of the trust except insofar as the terms of the trust permit the trustee to do otherwise; (2) a management stewardship duty, that is, a duty to manage the trust property with proper care; (3) a duty of undivided loyalty, which prohibits the trustee from taking any advantage from his position without the fully informed consent of the beneficiary or beneficiaries'.

enforced by creditors or parties to whom the law gives standing. Schedule B1 does not express these duties in a clearly structured manner, as found in the Companies Act 2006. But paragraph 74 does create a general duty, under which these categories fall, to not 'unfairly harm' the interests of creditors. Like 'unfair prejudice' in company law,[108] this enables an action against administrators for any breach of common law or equitable duty.

First, the terms of an administrator's office are set by paragraph 3: to rescue the company, rescue the business or pay secured or preferential creditors. An administrator must also, like directors in section 171, act for a proper purpose. The old cases on administrative receivers (see below) have the same standards. For example, in *Downsview Nominees Ltd v First City Corp. Ltd* a creditor, First City Corp. Ltd, sued the administrative receiver of Downsview Ltd, Mr Russell, for failing to accept an offer to discharge all of the money owed to the creditor that appointed him.[109] Downsview Ltd, a New Zealand company, had created two floating charges, first in favour of Westpac Bank, and second in favour of First City Corp. Ltd. Upon its insolvency, the directors convinced Westpac to assign its floating charge to Mr Russell, a friend, who promptly ran up further losses of $500,000. As this was happening and because he was their friend, Mr Russell refused First City Corp. Ltd's offer to repay all the money owed under the first floating charge. The Privy Council advised that Mr Russell acted out of an improper purpose and was bound to make good the losses. Furthermore, like directions under section 172, an administrator is meant to act in the interests of creditors as a whole, but may do so in the way 'he thinks' is most appropriate. But this subjective formulation makes it hard to challenge the administrator's discretion.

Second, an administrator must exercise due care and skill. Specifically, it breaches a duty under paragraph 74 if it is not performing its 'functions as quickly or as efficiently as is reasonably practicable'. As with company directors, administrators' behaviour is not to be viewed as negligent purely because a good-faith decision proved to be unfavourable, when reasonable people could have disagreed about an appropriate course of action. For example, in *Re Charnley Davies Ltd (No. 2)* creditors claimed that the administrator sold the insolvent company's business at an unduly low price. This was said to be 'unfair harm'.[110] Millett J held there was no breach of the duty of care: the duty, as in professional negligence, should be that of an 'ordinary, skilled practitioner'. But the administrator 'is not made liable because his perception is wrong, unless it is unreasonable'. This said, if there is a gross disparity in prices before and after a sale, the courts are willing to declare that a duty of care is breached.[111]

[108] See Ch. 3(4)(e) and CA 2006, ss. 994–6. NB: IA 1986, s. 27 previously used the term 'prejudice'.
[109] [1993] AC 295. [110] [1990] BCLC 760.
[111] E.g. *R (Glatt) v Sinclair* [2011] EWCA Civ 1317, where the receiver sold a house, which was immediately sold again by the estate agent at a 38% higher price.

By contrast, *Medforth v Blake* illustrates the breach of the duty of care in the case of an administrative receiver.[112] Mr Medforth, a pig farmer, claimed the receivers (Mr Blake and Mr Jones appointed by Midland Bank plc) had breached a duty of care because they failed to make use of discounts for pig food, worth 'about £1,000 a week'. The bank had taken control of the company, but despite Medforth's repeatedly urging them to get the discounts, the receivers did not: this ran up greater debt, prolonging the time before Mr Medforth could take back his business. The Court of Appeal held this breached a duty of due diligence. Sir Richard Scott VC framed this as an 'equitable duty', although it is generally accepted since then that the same duty is owed as a matter of common law.[113]

Third, there is a duty to avoid any possibility of a conflict of interest. The difficulty is that the appointment process for administrators is itself inherently exposed to conflicts, and there are few, if any, cases on conflicts of interest of administrators. Although it is regarded as one on 'proper purposes', *Downsview* was fundamentally also a case of conflict of interest, since the receiver failed to take payment to preserve his friend's business. But while the law fails to grapple with conflicts in appointment, it is doubtful other duties of loyalty will be enforced in practice.

How do creditors bring a claim? Under paragraph 74, creditors 'whether alone or in common' may apply to the court alleging unfair harm has taken place, or is proposed. The court may grant relief, dismiss, adjourn, give an interim order or any other appropriate order, including instructing the administrator how to behave. Creditors, therefore, have a simple procedural remedy as of right under statute. There are not, however, separate rights in the tort of negligence. For example, in *Oldham v Kyrris* a former Burger King franchise employee alleged he had not been paid £270,000 in wages, and that he either had an equitable charge against the company, or the administrator owed him a duty of care to pay.[114] The Court of Appeal held that no charge could be established, and that duties were owed to the company (and so must now be litigated under the statute) not to individual creditors.[115]

(c) Liquidation, Receivership and Voluntary Arrangements

Liquidation, receivership or administrative receivership, and voluntary arrangements have now become subsidiary procedures in insolvency for different reasons. First, 'liquidation' means the selling of assets (i.e. turning assets into liquidity or money) to pay creditors, rather than attempting any further rescue. However the appointment of a liquidator is less likely than an

112 *Medforth v Blake* [1999] EWCA Civ 1482.
113 E.g. *Bristol and West Building Society v Mothew* [1996] EWCA Civ 533.
114 *Oldham v Kyrris* [2003] EWCA Civ 1506.
115 Also *Hague v Nam Tai Electronics* [2008] UKPC 13. Cf. *Peskin v Anderson* [2000] EWCA Civ 326 in company law.

administrator since an administrator is empowered to do exactly the same work, realising assets for creditors.[116] Otherwise a liquidator may be court-appointed when nominated by a majority of creditors.[117] Liquidators similarly owe their duties to the company,[118] but are liable for failing to distribute assets to creditors correctly[119] or for negligence such as settling a non-existent claim.[120] It is not clear what purpose there is in duplicated, parallel rules.

Second, there is 'receivership', which refers to the appointment of someone to 'receive' (but rather, really 'take') assets to pay debts. At common law, the receiver would owe a duty to creditors. The main creditor to a company would be the holder of a floating charge, who could appoint a 'receiver and manager' to run the company while collecting debts. The 1986 Act codified and raised standards with the aim of reducing wasteful conduct, under the new name of 'administrative receiver', since it was appreciated that a debt collector with obligations only to one creditor tended to waste the business to the detriment of other creditors with no voice. In the Enterprise Act 2002, the administrator became the dominant form of insolvency practitioner with the existing receiver duties, plus those above (see Ch. 7(2)(b)). However, it was decided that enterprises connected to the public interest, or often those indebted to government, and (with infinitely less justification) major project finance, should still have administrative receivership, as follows:[121]

- capital market investments over £50 million
- public–private partnerships with step-in rights (see Chs. 8–9 or 15–16, potentially)
- utility projects (Chs. 12–13)
- urban regeneration projects (Ch. 14)
- project finance with step-in rights
- financial market, system and collateral security charges
- registered social landlords (Ch. 14)
- water, rail and air traffic companies (Chs. 13 and 15).

It seems clear that greater control to maintain continuity of public services justifies exceptions, but the rationale for capital market, project finance or financial market cases appears more as a gift to investment banks (see Ch. 10).

[116] IA 1986, Sch. B1, paras. 83–4.

[117] Three alternatives are in IA 1986, ss. 84, 89 and 91 (solvent, voluntary winding up, where companies appoint on special resolution, after director solvency declaration), 90, 96 and 100 (insolvent voluntary winding up, where creditors appoint if company cannot be declared solvent) and 124 and 139 (compulsory winding up on application of directors, shareholders or creditors, where court appoints). See also *Mann v Goldstein* [1968] 1 WLR 1091, on the need for debts to actually be due, rather than contested, to make a petition.

[118] *Knowles v Scott* [1891] 1 Ch 717, Romer J.

[119] *Re Home and Colonial Insurance Co. Ltd* [1930] 1 Ch 102; *Pulsford v Devenish* [1903] 2 Ch 625, Farwell J.

[120] *Re Windsor Steam Coal Co. (1901) Ltd* [1928] Ch 609.

[121] IA 1986, ss. 72B–GA.

The third subsidiary procedure involves 'voluntary arrangements'. If three-quarters of creditors approve, then creditors may collectively accept a debt reduction on the promise that this is better than the business closing and everyone getting little or nothing.[122] However this company voluntary arrangement cannot bind secured and preferential creditors, and therefore has limited use. There are also 'schemes of arrangement' that can bind all creditors but must be approved in court.[123]

(3) Creditor Liability and Voidable Transactions

If a company is not rescued by an administrator, and the business is to be sold or liquidated, creditors may aim to recover more assets from other parties who have dealt with a company. Normally, the law says that a contract only needs sufficient, not adequate, consideration,[124] including for a security interest.[125] However in insolvency, this laissez-faire ideal begins to look very unfair on the people who are not paid, if others got a company's assets near insolvency on the cheap. For this reason, the law enables five main groups of transaction to be avoided: those that (a) are made after a winding-up order, (b) are made at an undervalue, (c) create an unlawful preference, (d) create floating charges where no new money is given or (e) are made fraudulently. A sixth category is that if a security interest is not registered the security is void, leaving that creditor unsecured.[126] This array of rules has seemingly minor and seemingly arbitrary differences. Arguably the law would be simplified, and better served, with a general norm that unfair contracts may be vitiated if they are not duly made in good faith for a fair price, and the contract took place within an (extendable) two years of insolvency.

(a) Dispositions after Winding Up, Section 127

The Insolvency Act 1986, section 127(1) says that 'any disposition of a company's property ... after commencement of the winding up is, unless the court otherwise orders, void'.[127] The date of commencement is actually deemed to begin with a winding-up petition, if successful. Lord Cairns LC

[122] Insolvency Rules 1986, rule 1.19 and Insolvency (England and Wales) Rules 2016, rule 2.36.

[123] CA 2006, ss. 895–901.

[124] *Chappell & Co. Ltd v Nestle Co. Ltd* [1960] AC 87, per Lord Somervell: a 'peppercorn does not cease to be good consideration' even if 'the promisee does not like pepper and will throw away the corn'. Cf. Cork Report, para. 1209, viewing voidable transactions as necessary to preserve *pari passu*.

[125] *National Provincial Bank v Charnley* [1924] 1 KB 431, per Atkin LJ: 'no doubt' that if 'in a transaction for value both parties evince an intention that property ... shall be made available as security for the payment of a debt ... there is a charge'.

[126] CA 2006, ss. 860–74.

[127] IA 1986, s. 127. Section 436 defines 'property' in an all-encompassing fashion to include 'also obligations ... arising out of, or incidental to, property'.

described this as 'a wholesome and necessary provision, to prevent, during the period which must elapse before a petition can be heard, the improper alienation and dissipation of the property of a company *in extremis*'.[128] If a company has already been subject to a winding-up petition, contracts made after by the directors or managers may be suspicious, and not in creditors' interests. It follows that courts may validate post-petition transactions as they choose, but the starting point is that everything comes to a halt.

How do courts exercise their discretion? In *Re Gray's Inn Construction Co. Ltd*, a liquidator applied to invalidate transactions of the company, most unprofitable, out of its NatWest account after a creditor presented a winding-up petition.[129] Buckley LJ held that all transactions in and out of the bank account were 'dispositions' and the key principle for whether to validate transactions was 'to ensure that the interests of unsecured creditors will not be prejudiced'. Specifically, a 'disposition carried out in good faith in the ordinary course of business at a time when the parties are unaware that a petition has been presented' would 'normally be validated by the court', unless there is reason to think it was 'an attempt to prefer the disponee'. While this appeared to suggest that the default was that transactions would be validated, another Court of Appeal decision in *Express Electrical Distributors Ltd v Beavis* affirmed there is no right that such a disposition should be validated.[130]

Does a bank have secondary liability if a company's money is unlawfully paid from its account? In *Hollicourt (Contracts) Ltd v Bank of Ireland* the Court of Appeal held that only the final recipients of money, not a bank, were liable to repay, as the bank's transactions 'are merely part of the process by which dispositions of the company's property are made'. This would, said Mummery LJ, be 'unwelcome' for liquidators as banks are a 'readily identifiable target to proceed against'.[131] The position would seem to differ, however, if banks do or should know of a winding-up petition, particularly since banks profit from their customers' accounts and transactions.

(b) Transactions at an Undervalue, Section 238

What about transactions before the presentation of a winding-up petition? Creditors, directors and shareholders can all bring petitions, and each may have advance or 'insider' knowledge of a likely insolvency. The Insolvency Act 1986, section 238 enables a liquidator or administrator to claim that the value a company received in a transaction was 'significantly less than the value' that was fair, if it was made within two years.[132] The company must also have been

[128] *In re Wiltshire Iron Co.* (1868) LR 3 Ch App 443, 446. [129] [1980] 1 WLR 711.

[130] [2016] EWCA Civ 765, per Sales LJ.

[131] *Hollicourt Ltd v Bank of Ireland* [2000] EWCA Civ 263, [2001] Ch 555.

[132] IA 1986, s. 238(2) refers to the 'relevant time' defined in s. 240(1) as two years (whether connected or not).

insolvent when the transaction was made, but this is presumed to be the case if the transacting party was 'connected' – namely a director, shadow director, a husband, wife, partner, other relative, an employee, an employer and a parent or a subsidiary company.[133] The company may raise a defence of 'good faith' if the transaction was done in 'carrying on its business' and it would be reasonable to think it would 'benefit' the company.[134]

How should the 'value' of a transaction be interpreted? In *Phillips v Brewin Dolphin & Co. Ltd* the liquidator of an insolvent stockbroking firm, A. J. Bekhor & Co., claimed that it had transferred shares in another company for an undervalue. It 'sold' its stockbroking business to a subsidiary, Bekhor Securities Ltd, for £1. Then, Brewin Dolphin & Co. Ltd bought the subsidiary's shares. In 'return', the parent of Brewin Dolphin & Co. Ltd made a contract with A. J. Bekhor & Co. to pay it four sums of £312,500 and (ostensibly) get the right to sublease computer equipment (that was owned by another two companies). But then A. J. Bekhor & Co. went insolvent, payments for leasing the computers were not made and the subleases necessarily cancelled. Hence, none of the £312,500 payments were made, but Brewin Dolphin & Co. Ltd still had the stockbroking business. The House of Lords held that there was a transaction at an undervalue, and the whole chain of transactions could be taken into account. Although it was argued that the computer lease agreement was the same value at the time as the sale of the stockbroking business, Lord Scott said that for the 'valuation of the consideration for which a company has entered into a transaction, reality should . . . be given precedence over speculation'. Because it was speculative that payment for the computer leases would ever be made, it could not count towards objective value.[135]

What counts as a 'transaction' at an undervalue? In *Re MC Bacon Ltd* a liquidator argued that a bank overdraft, secured with a debenture, was a transaction at an undervalue. The pork business run by two directors had lost a major gammon and bacon supplier; it was forced to make redundancies and so it applied to NatWest for a loan in May 1986. It would have been insolvent without the loan to keep going, but in August 1987, owing £33,000 to creditors it was forced into liquidation anyway. Millett J held that the secured overdraft was not a 'transaction' at an undervalue because the 'creation of a security over a company's assets does not deplete them and does not come within' section 238. By creating the security 'the company parted with nothing of value'.[136] It could, however, be an unlawful preference, but the time limits to claim are less favourable and a 'desire' to prefer is required.

[133] IA 1986, ss. 249 and 435. [134] IA 1986, s. 238(5). [135] [2001] UKHL 2.
[136] [1990] BCLC 324.

(c) Unlawful Preferences, Section 239

Section 239 applies if a company has 'given a preference to any person', and that preference was 'influenced' by a 'desire' to put that person in a 'better' position (but for the preference).[137] A preference includes any kind of security interest without a 'transaction' in the sense of assets moving. There are, however, two main limits. First, there are different time limits from section 238. The preference is open to challenge within two years, but only with 'connected persons'. If not with a connected person, a preference can only be challenged within the last six months.[138] On the other hand, there is a presumption that there is a desire to prefer someone if they are connected.[139]

Second, the requirement of being influenced by a 'desire' to prefer someone was held in *Re MC Bacon Ltd* to require an evaluation of the reasons for the preference, not the fact that it was given, and 'desire is subjective'. Millett J held that it only needed to be 'one of the factors which operated on the minds' of those in the company, and evidence of a desire could be 'inferred from the circumstances'. But on the facts, the directors were held not to have been influenced by a desire to prefer NatWest when it gave them security for an overdraft: they just gave security to get a loan because they had to. A person 'can choose the lesser of two evils without desiring either'.[140] By contrast, paying off a loan to a company, when a major shareholder has guaranteed that loan's repayment (to try and extinguish the shareholder's guarantee), shortly ahead of insolvency will be an unlawful preference.[141]

(d) Voidable Floating Charges, Section 245

Another kind of preference could be the creation of a floating charge, but since 1907 this has been regulated on its own. The Loreburn Report, instead of abolishing the floating charge, said that a floating charge should only be valid to the extent of new value given.[142] So, today according to section 245, a floating charge is invalid 'except to the extent of ... money paid', credit given or debts discharged 'at the same time as, or after, the creation of the charge'.[143] Charges can be attacked going back two years for connected persons, but twelve months for others (in contrast to the six months for preferences and two years for undervalue transactions).[144] If successful, the action only invalidates the floating charge, not the whole contract: debts still need to be paid, but they become unsecured.[145]

137 IA 1986, s. 239(2) and (5).

138 IA 1986, s. 240(1)(b). Also s. 240(2) requires the company to be insolvent at the time.

139 IA 1986, s. 239(6). 140 [1990] BCLC 324.

141 *Re Agriplant Services Ltd* [1997] 2 BCLC 598. See further *National Westminster Bank plc v Jones* [2001] EWCA Civ 1541 and *Re Sonatacus Ltd* [2007] EWCA Civ 31.

142 *Report of the Company Law Amendment Committee*, Cd 3052 (1906) §41.

143 IA 1986, s. 245(2). 144 IA 1986, s. 245(3).

145 E.g. *Re Parkes Garage Ltd* [1929] 1 Ch 139, Eve J held that a motor dealer who gave Mr Ling a floating charge still had to repay the debt (so reducing the amount available to another unsecured creditor, Midland Bank).

Two further issues are what counts as new value, and what counts as 'at the same time' or after a charge. First, the extension of credit through the use of a bank account will fulfil the requirements of section 245, even though no new money may be advanced.[146] Second, the context matters for determining whether new value is given at the same time: if credit is advanced weeks before, and a floating charge is created later, this will not be counted as 'the same time' and the charge will be void.[147]

(e) Transactions Defrauding Creditors, Section 423

'All acts to defraud creditors or to defraud the public law of the land . . . are absolutely void.'[148] This principle, which dates back at least to the Fraudulent Conveyances Act 1571,[149] is now found in the Insolvency Act 1986, section 423. A transaction at an undervalue that 'was entered into by [a company] for the purpose . . . (b) of otherwise prejudicing the interests' of creditors will be void. For example, in *Arbuthnot Leasing International Ltd v Havelet Leasing Ltd (No. 2)*, Scott J held that section 423 applied when Havelet Ltd transferred all of its business, assets and agreements to a related company to avoid a receiver appointed by Arbuthnot Ltd to enforce a judgment. It was fraudulent, simply because its purpose was to put the assets out of reach. This was true whatever the motive in making the transaction, and even if lawyers had advised (wrongly) that the scheme was lawful.[150]

(4) Director Liability and Unlawful Trading

After creditors, another potentially solvent defendant could be the company directors. While the law generally shields directors behind the 'corporate veil', and the directors' actions are attributed to the company,[151] the law makes exceptions. There may be (a) liability for breach of directors' duties, and wrongfully or fraudulently trading while insolvent, which (b) may be enforced by the administrator or liquidator, or perhaps by an assigned claims company and (c) there is a risk that directors are disqualified if they are found unfit.

These norms cover directors who are really appointed to the board (*de jure*), but also directors who undertake 'functions in relation to the company which could properly be discharged only by a [real] director', without being formally

[146] *Re Yeovil Glove Co. Ltd* [1965] Ch 148.
[147] *Re Shoe Lace Ltd or Power v Sharp Investments Ltd* [1994] 1 BCLC 111.
[148] *Alderson v Temple* (1768) 96 ER 384, per Lord Mansfield. A fraudulent preference is also caught.
[149] Fraudulent Conveyances Act 1571 (13 Eliz. I, c. 5), against actions that would 'overthrow of all true and plain dealing, bargaining and chevisance between man and man, without the which no commonwealth or civil society can be maintained or continued'.
[150] [1990] BCC 36.
[151] *Williams v Natural Life Health Foods Ltd* [1998] UKHL 17; but see *Rainham Chemical Works Limited v Belvedere Fish Guano Co. Limited* [1921] 2 AC 465.

appointed (de facto),[152] and shadow directors, who in practice conduct company affairs. For instance, a shadow director could be a major shareholder or the director of a parent company, 'in accordance with whose directions or instructions the [real] directors of the company are accustomed to act'.[153] It is not enough to be someone who merely gives advice, particularly a lawyer giving advice about duties under an enactment, or a government minister giving guidance in their capacity as a Minister of the Crown.[154]

(a) Unlawful Trading

There are three main post-insolvency claims for unlawful trading. First, under the Insolvency Act 1986, section 212 an administrator or liquidator may seek a 'summary remedy against delinquent directors' for 'misfeasance or breach of any fiduciary or other duty in relation to the company'. The court may on application of the official receiver, liquidator 'or of any creditor or contributory' examine 'the conduct' of the director and 'compel him' to 'repay, restore or account for the money or property' or 'contribute such sum' for 'breach of fiduciary or other duty as the court thinks just'.[155] This could be a claim for breach of any director's duty, such as the duty to act within powers, care and skill, or the duty to avoid conflicts of interest. However, if one creditor brings and funds a claim, the recovered assets or money will be available to all creditors, because the directors' duties are owed, and misfeasance claims belong, to the (insolvent) company.[156]

Second, under section 213, directors are liable if 'any business of the company has been carried on with intent to defraud creditors', including 'any persons who were knowingly parties' to the fraud.[157] This requires proof of dishonesty, where the standard is whether the person would objectively be considered to be dishonest, not that they subjectively believed they were.[158] The remedy available, however, is open to some debate as it was suggested that the only amount recoverable is compensatory, without any punitive element.[159] The alternative, and better view, is that the ordinary law enables exemplary damages where a statutory tort is calculated to make a profit, and the appropriate award should be at least sufficient to deter such

[152] *Re Hydrodam (Corby) Ltd* [1994] 2 BCLC 180, per Millett J.

[153] CA 2006, s. 251. There must be control over the whole board: *Re Lo-Line Electric Motors* [1988] Ch 477.

[154] CA 2006, s. 251(2), e.g. *Secretary of State for Trade & Industry v Deverell* [2000] 2 BCLC 133.

[155] IA 1986, s. 212, and also against liquidators or administrative receivers, like IA 1986, Sch. B1, para. 75.

[156] E.g. *Re Anglo-Austrian Printing & Publishing Union* [1895] 2 Ch 891.

[157] IA 1986, s. 213.

[158] *Ivey v Genting Casinos (UK) Ltd* [2017] UKSC 67. Contrast the older position in *Re Patrick and Lyon Ltd* [1933] Ch 786, and the dicta of Hoffmann J in *Re Augustus Barnett & Son Ltd* [1986] BCLC 170.

[159] *Morphitis v Bernasconi* [2003] EWCA Civ 289, per Chadwick LJ, in *obiter dicta*.

conduct.[160] This approach recognises the greater gravity in fraudulent conduct, which is 'a thing apart'.[161]

Third, under section 214, directors can be liable for 'wrongful trading' or trading where they 'knew or ought to have concluded that there was no reasonable prospect that the company would avoid going into insolvent liquidation'.[162] This is an objective standard, the same as negligence for directors in section 174,[163] and there is only a defence if the director 'took every step with a view to minimising the potential loss to the company's creditors'.[164] For example, in *Re Produce Marketing Consortium Ltd (No. 2)*, the insolvent company's liquidator brought a claim against the two ex-directors, Eric and Ronald, after their lemon, grapefruit and orange importing company ran up debts.[165] They lost the business of a large Spanish supplier, and made losses of £14,000, £25,000 and £21,000 in 1981, 1982 and 1983. They did manage to scrape a profit of £43 in 1984 while the bank overdraft went up to £91,000. But then the accounts were produced late for 1985 and 1986, and they continued to trade with losses until a creditor voluntary liquidation commenced in October 1987 with debts of £317,694. Half was owed to one Cypriot fruit-shipping firm. They told the liquidator they knew insolvency was inevitable in February, and were sued to contribute £107,946 each, plus costs. Knox J held that they were jointly liable for a total of £75,000, reflecting losses run up since July 1986, when they should have known there was no reasonable prospect of avoiding insolvency. It was also relevant that Ronald had experience as a bookkeeper and should have managed the accounts better. A wrongful trading order may be made in addition to a misfeasance and breach of directors' duty order, and the awards may accumulate.[166] A court may also take account of difficult circumstances facing directors, even including bad weather.[167] In the Covid-19 pandemic, wide exceptions were made from wrongful trading rules for directors, along with many others, temporarily.[168]

(b) Litigation

The largest practical limitation on enforcement of director responsibility after insolvency is who can sue. An administrator, liquidator or other practitioner

[160] *Rookes v Barnard* [1964] UKHL 1, per Lord Devlin. In *Re William C. Leitch Ltd* [1932] 2 Ch 71, Maugham J had said that there was a punitive element.

[161] *HIH Casualty and General Insurance Limited v Chase Manhattan Bank* [2003] UKHL 6, [15] per Lord Bingham.

[162] IA 1986, s. 214(2).

[163] See Ch. 3(4)(c) where s. 174 followed the wrongful trading after *Re D'Jan of London Ltd* [1994] 1 BCLC 561.

[164] IA 1986, s. 214(3). [165] *Re Produce Marketing Consortium Ltd (No. 2)* [1989] BCLC 520.

[166] *Re Purpoint Ltd* [1991] BCLC 491.

[167] *Re Brian D Pierson (Contractors) Ltd* [2001] 1 BCLC 275.

[168] Corporate Insolvency and Governance Act 2020, ss. 12–13.

may assign a claim for breach of director's duty under section 212 to a specialist claims company, because the claim is treated as an asset belonging to the company.[169] This is positive because insolvency practitioners, many in the accountancy profession, may not have legal resources to run litigation: their line of business is mainly restructuring, not fighting in court. Assignment of claims, if done for money, could also offer a swift way to increase the assets for creditors, while the law firm can take the risk of failure but also the profits. Unfortunately, in *Re Oasis Merchandising Services Ltd* it was held that claims under section 214 cannot be assigned because ostensibly they are conferred solely on the liquidator.[170] This judgment, which harked back to ancient rules on champerty and vexatious litigation, seems inappropriate, and has the practical effect of unduly limiting enforcement.

(c) Director Disqualifications

As well as liability for breaches of duty, the Company Directors Disqualification Act 1986 means anybody may be disqualified from being a director, as well as an administrator or other insolvency practitioner. Disqualifications are made for indictable offences concerning formation, running or liquidation of companies; for three or more breaches of companies legislation (such as accounts or capital regulations: see Ch. 4(2)); for any fraud or summary convictions relating to companies at home or abroad;[171] and for participation in wrongful trading. Most generally, under section 6, directors must be disqualified if their company is in administration or liquidation and they are found to be 'unfit to be concerned in the management of a company'. In Schedule 1, 'unfitness' is determined by whether directors have breached directors' duties (see Ch. 3(4)), engaged in voidable transactions (Ch. 7(4)), and particularly have failed to keep proper records or accounts.[172] Disqualifications must also be made if a director is found unfit and has committed 'a breach of competition law' whether or not the company is insolvent (see Ch. 6(2)(d)). Disqualifications are usually made for a minimum of two years and up to fifteen years.[173] While the disqualification system should mean that directors' duties, and following the law, are 'inescapable personal responsibilities',[174] the general lack of enforcement makes this less true.

169 See *Re Anglo-Austrian Printing and Publishing Union* [1895] 2 Ch 891.

170 *Re Oasis Merchandising Services Ltd* [1995] 2 BCLC 493. Cf. R. Mokal, 'Agency Costs and Wrongful Trading' (2000) 59 *Cambridge LJ* 335.

171 Company Directors Disqualification Act (CDDA) 1986, ss. 2–5A and 10.

172 CDDA 1986, s. 6 and Sch. 1.

173 CDDA 1986, s. 6(4) but contrast ss. 2(3)(a), 3(5) and 5(5), maximum of 5 years. It is not clear why this changed.

174 *Re Westmid Packing Service Ltd* [1998] 2 BCLC 646, per Lord Woolf MR.

(5) Shareholder Liability and the Corporate Veil

A final group of potentially solvent defendants are corporate shareholders. While limited liability for shareholders is often seen as a basic feature of corporate law (see Ch. 3(1)(b)), it can always be contracted around through security interests. The law also makes exceptions, generally speaking, for parties unable to contract for security. The 'non-adjusting creditor' has increasingly won cases despite the so-called 'corporate veil'. This is particularly true for tort victims who never have the opportunity to contract for security, or employees who lack bargaining power, and the same logic could extend to consumers. This section covers (a) the standard rule that creditors cannot claim debts from shareholders, but that 'fraud unravels everything'; (b) the responsibility in corporate groups between parents and subsidiaries in competition, accounting, tax and increasingly tort law; and (c) the potential liability of other shareholders, outside a corporate group.

(a) Separate Personality and Fraud

The starting point of *Salomon*'s case is shareholders are not liable for insolvent company debt. It 'may be that after incorporation the business is precisely the same as it was before', said Lord Macnaghten, 'and the same persons are managers, and the same hands receive the profits, [but] the company is not in law the agent of the subscribers or trustee from them'.[175] Creditors may contract around limited liability. A bank can require a personal guarantee, or security interest, from a shareholder personally before giving a loan. But under the Insolvency Act 1986, section 74(2)(d) those who do not cannot make claims against the assets of a shareholder of a limited liability company.

This statutory rule gives way to the principle that 'fraud unravels everything'.[176] The legal meaning of fraud is setting up or using a company to avoid a legal duty.[177] Accordingly, the law on 'piercing the corporate veil' aims to 'prevent the misuse of the privileges of legal personality, as in certain cases or fraud or malfeasance, to protect third persons ... or to prevent the evasion of legal requirements'.[178] This can work in two directions. First, a shareholder could be liable for the debts of a company, if they are responsible for fraud that a company commits. In *Standard Chartered Bank v Pakistan National Shipping Corp. (Nos. 2 and 4)* the House of Lords held that a company and its main shareholder and director of a bitumen shipping company, Mr Mehra, were liable for damages after they fraudulently changed dates on bills of

[175] *Salomon v A. Salomon & Co. Ltd* [1897] AC 22, per Lord Macnaghten.

[176] *Lazarus Estates Ltd v Beasley* [1956] 1 QB 702, 712, per Denning LJ.

[177] E.g. *Jones v Lipman* [1962] 1 WLR 832, where Lipman sold a house, but then changed his mind, set up a company and transferred a house to it, to avoid a specific performance order. Russell J 'pierced the veil'.

[178] *Barcelona Traction, Light, and Power Company, Ltd* [1970] ICJ 3.

lading.[179] Thus, the shareholder is made jointly liable for the company's debts. Second, a company can be liable for debts of a shareholder. In *Prest v Petrodel Resources Ltd*, the Supreme Court held that the companies in possession properties, including a £4 million home at 16 Warwick Avenue, London, were held on resulting trust for the shareholder, Michael Prest, because he had transferred them to avoid a divorce settlement with his ex-wife.[180] As Lord Walker noted, rules where the corporate veil is 'pierced' really come down to the result of a 'statutory provision, or from joint liability in tort, or from the law of unjust enrichment, or from principles of equity and the law of trusts'.[181]

(b) Corporate Groups

A second set of cases is where a group of companies, though legally separate, operate as a single economic unit. Here, the traditional justifications for limited liability, to shield real investors from personal ruin and bankruptcy, tend to end, because the shareholder of a subsidiary is simply another parent company. The real business, the underlying enterprise, is different from the legal forms.[182] As we have seen, responsibility of corporate groups is a fundamental part of accounting law,[183] competition law[184] and also group relief on tax.[185] The separate identity of corporate groups may also be ignored for the purpose of labour rights.[186] In tort law, the matter has been more contested. For example, in a 1925 US railway case involving injured cattle, Brandeis J held that if a 'company actually controls another and operates both as a single system, the dominant company will be liable for injuries due to the negligence of the subsidiary company'.[187] Yet through the next century, corporate law cases in the US frequently held that tort victims of subsidiary companies could not sue parent companies,[188] a lesson that was implicitly followed in the thinking of corporate lawyers in many other jurisdictions. This was not always true; for example, after the disaster of the *Amico Cadiz* tanker's oil spill in 1978, an Illinois court held that an 'integrated multinational

[179] *Standard Chartered Bank v Pakistan National Shipping Corp. (Nos. 2 and 4)* [2002] UKHL 43, [38]. Lord Rodger said the action does not depend on the defendant being a shareholder or director, but simply engaging in fraud.

[180] *Prest v Petrodel Resources Ltd* [2013] UKSC 34.

[181] *Prest v Petrodel Resources Ltd*, [106].

[182] A. A. Berle, 'The Theory of Enterprise Entity' (1947) 47(3) *Columbia L Rev* 343.

[183] E.g. Companies Act 2006, ss. 393–407; and see Ch. 4(2)(b).

[184] E.g. *Viho Europe BV v Commission* (1996) C-73/95, [16]; and see Ch. 6(1)(b).

[185] E.g. Corporation Tax Act 2010, ss. 93 and 152 defining subsidiaries with 51% or 75% ownership, depending.

[186] E.g. *RMT v United Kingdom* [2014] ECHR 366, but cf. Trade Union and Labour Relations (Consolidation) Act 1992, s. 244.

[187] *Davis v Alexander*, 269 US 114 (1925).

[188] E.g. *Berkey v Third Avenue Railway Co.*, 244 NY 602 (1927), Cardozo J holding a parent tram company was not liable for its subsidiary's debts for personal injury, ostensibly to be consistent with statute; *Walkovszky v Carlton*, 223 NE 2d 6 (1966), also in NY law, holding the parent of a taxi subsidiary group not liable for personal injury of a pedestrian, Keating J dissenting.

corporation which is engaged through a system of subsidiaries' in oil business 'is responsible for the tortious acts of its wholly owned subsidiaries and instrumentalities'.[189] But in the USA, because of its failure to create free universal healthcare (see Ch. 9), claims of tort victims have been very expensive, and the courts' reaction has seemed to be to defend corporations, not claimants. By contrast, UK law saw almost zero cases,[190] probably because the NHS meant any medical bills for personal injury were covered. In only one case the Court of Appeal doubted in *obiter dicta* that a UK parent company could be liable for the asbestos injuries caused by a US subsidiary,[191] but the House of Lords,[192] and the Supreme Court,[193] have rejected this notion.

In the leading case, *Chandler v Cape plc*, Mr Chandler, an employee of Cape Building Products Ltd, claimed damages for asbestosis from the parent company, Cape plc, because the subsidiary was insolvent. Instead of asking for the 'corporate veil' to be 'pierced', he argued that a duty of care was owed by the parent company to him in tort. Among other things, the parent had a group health and safety policy. Arden LJ held that if 'the parent has a practice of intervening in the trading operations of the subsidiary' for any issue (and not necessarily health or safety), if the business is 'in a relevant respect the same', if the parent does or should have superior safety knowledge and foresee lack of safety, then there will be an 'attachment' of responsibility.[194]

Despite inconsistent decisions by other courts,[195] in *Lungowe v Vedanta Resources plc* the Supreme Court approved *Chandler*. It held that a group of citizens who suffered damage from toxic discharge of the Nchanga Copper Mine in Zambia had a good arguable case in tort against a UK parent company.[196] The pollution was directly caused by Vedanta plc's subsidiary, Konkola Copper Mines plc. To bring a claim in the UK, it had to be shown that the UK courts have 'jurisdiction', and it was then assumed that the appropriate choice of law was Zambian tort law. It was held that access to justice was limited in Zambia because, despite the independence of the judiciary, there was an absence of legal aid and conditional fee arrangements for the claimants.

189 *In re Oil Spill by the Amoco Cadiz off the Coast of France on March 16, 1978*, 1984 AMC 2123 (ND Ill 1984) per McGarr J, at 2191.

190 C. Mitchell, 'Lifting the Corporate Veil in the English Courts: An Empirical Study' [1999] *Company, Financial and Insolvency L Rev* 15, finding just one personal injury case.

191 *Adams v Cape Industries plc* [1990] Ch 433.

192 *Lubbe v Cape plc* [2000] UKHL 41, [20] per Lord Bingham.

193 *VTB Capital plc v Nutritek International Corp.* [2013] UKSC 5, [127] per Lord Neuberger. *Adams* and other cases 'include *obiter* observations and are anyway not binding in this court'.

194 *Chandler v Cape plc* [2012] EWCA Civ 525, [64] and [80]. This follows the principle of liability for third-party actions in *Smith v Littlewoods Organisation Ltd* [1987] UKHL 18 and the tests in *Caparo Industries plc v Dickman* [1990] 2 AC 605.

195 E.g. *Thompson v Renwick Group plc* [2014] EWCA Civ 365; *Okpabi v Royal Dutch Shell plc* [2018] EWCA Civ 191; but cf. *AAA v Unilever plc* [2018] EWCA Civ 1532, where Sales LJ held that Unilever plc was not liable for a (supposed) wrong of the subsidiary in Kenya failing to protect workers from inter-tribal violence in the 2007 presidential election. Unlike *Thompson* or *Okpabi*, it seemed much less likely there was an arguable case.

196 [2019] UKSC 20.

Further, there was a real triable issue in tort that the parent company could owe the victims of environmental damage a duty of care. Although Zambian, not English, law was to be applied, it was arguable that 'Zambian common law [was] in accordance with those' principles 'established in England'.[197] This case means UK multinationals can be held accountable for torts anywhere in the world, if the criteria in *Chandler* are made out and if access to justice may be limited abroad. A narrow view may fear that this places UK corporations at a competitive disadvantage, that they might be sued more than US, French, German or Chinese multinationals. The better view is that *Chandler* and *Lungowe* have triggered a fundamental debate in jurisdictions worldwide, and that UK companies will be improved by being held responsible for any wrongs. It will mean UK companies do not get regulatory subsidies for externalities and harm to others, and so become more efficient by producing and competing on the merits.

(c) Other Shareholders

A final question is whether shareholders outside a corporate group may be held liable for debts of an insolvent company. In *Chandler*, Arden LJ pointed out that 'at no relevant point in time did Cape cease to be an operating company itself or merely hold the shares in its subsidiaries as if it were an investment holding company'.[198] Implicitly, this suggests the courts may be more doubtful about claims against shareholders who are personal investors, as opposed to corporate shareholders. This said, it is clear that any shareholder can be forced to give up 'property obtained through unlawful conduct', including giving back dividends.[199] It has also been forcefully argued that shareholders should have unlimited liability for torts of companies they invest in, because tort victims never have the ability to contract for protection, but that to prevent undue burdens there should be liability only on a proportionate basis (i.e. not joint and several liability, if some shareholders are insolvent).[200] Ultimately the issue comes down to the moral justifications for imposing any tort liability at all, and the incentives the law wishes to set for productive enterprise.[201]

[197] [2019] UKSC 20, [56]. [198] *Chandler v Cape plc* [2012] EWCA Civ 525, [8] per Arden LJ.

[199] Proceeds of Crime Act 2002, ss. 241–3.

[200] H. Hansmann and R. Kraakman, 'Towards Unlimited Liability for Corporate Torts' (1991) 100 *Yale LJ* 1879. In *Barker v Corus (UK) plc* [2006] UKHL 20, Lord Hoffmann suggested proportionate liability was appropriate in asbestos cases, involving other defendants that are insolvent, but Parliament disagreed, and restored joint and several liability in the Compensation Act 2006.

[201] The same issues may be raised for companies that control supply chains, not through shares, but by contract. See further E. McGaughey, '*Donoghue v Salomon* in the High Court' (2011) 4 *J Personal Injury L* 249.

(6) Conclusion

Insolvency law is an attempt to limit and reverse the inherent waste in competitive enterprise but it cannot be said, in the UK, to achieve this goal efficiently yet. This is inseparable from corporate and labour laws, since many insolvencies would be reduced if there was greater responsiveness to alter business models before crises erupted through broader involvement of those with most at stake: the true investors and the workforce. First, it is too easy for secured creditors, mainly banks, to externalise the costs of their poor or profligate lending decisions onto unsecured or even preferential creditors. A fair system of priority for debts would elevate non-adjusting creditors, particularly workers and pensions, consumers, tort victims or those claiming environmental harm, above a portion of secured debt: this will ensure secured creditors take greater care in lending. Second, the multiplicity of governance procedures should be merged, through administration, but with suitable exceptions only where a public body is concerned. Third, it should be easier for insolvency practitioners to bring claims against errant creditors, directors or shareholders to recover costs. There is, in particular, no justification for limited liability of shareholders in relation to anybody that lacks bargaining power to get security interests.

Part III
Specific Enterprise Law

8

Education

Contents

Education is probably the most important enterprise for a country's future because it influences people's capabilities in almost all of life's endeavours. At the very centre of a just society is the 'essential importance of human development in its richest diversity'.[1] 'Everyone has the right to education' in international law. Elementary education 'shall be free', and higher education must be 'equally accessible to all on the basis of merit' and 'in particular by the progressive introduction of free education'.[2] Despite this, there is still fierce conflict over whether private finance is legitimate, who should have access and who should govern. In fact, the UK used to go far beyond these international human rights. Everyone used to have the right to access free and grant-funded education,[3] including at university. But from 1997 grants were abolished and tuition fees were introduced.[4] The surviving model of fee-paying schools, which had expanded since 1979,[5] was rolled out to universities. Higher tuition fees were imposed, governance was not reformed, staff have been treated as 'service providers' and students have been labelled as 'consumers', but without any real votes or other rights.

Partly because of the English language, partly its unique traditions, UK educational institutions are often seen as among the best, if not the best, in

[1] Cf. W. Humboldt, *Sphere and Duties of Government* (1854) ch. 6.

[2] UDHR 1948, art. 26; ICESCR 1966, art. 13. Cf. ECHR 1950, Prot. 1, art. 2; *Belgian Linguistic case (No. 2)* (1968) 1 EHRR 252 (no meaningful standards). CFREU 2000, art. 14 (right to education, no reference to merit).

[3] See the Robbins Report, Cmnd 2154 (1963) and the Education Act 1962.

[4] Dearing Report, 'Higher Education in the Learning Society', Report of the National Committee of Inquiry into Higher Education (1997).

[5] P. Bolton, 'Education: Historical Statistics', SN/SG/4252 (27 November 2012) 9.

the world. That reputation is sustained more by popular fiction novels than the current law.[6] The UK school and university system is chaotic: there are at least five kinds of school, three conflicting finance methods, no coherent pattern of governance, no clear standards of rights and not yet a National Education Service. Underlying this fact is ideological disagreement about the proper way to organise education. Defenders of private finance assert that it raises investment, improves outcomes and protects parents' right to choose their children's education. Against these arguments is the evidence that systems that segregate children, by wealth, class or gender, tend to have inferior outcomes.[7] Tuition fees deter poorer students from entering university, and lack of money, with the associated stress, hinders the ability to concentrate on learning once there.[8] Still, students from free public schools perform relatively better at university than those from fee-paying schools,[9] suggesting that segregation and discrimination restrict potential, and that fee-paying schools overcharge parents for education that does not last. Institutions that see students and staff as members, not revenue sources or interchangeable commodities, also tend to promote participation in governance and basic rights.

(1) Historical Background

Education is as old as humanity, but organised and universal education was a nineteenth-century invention. In Ancient Athens, a systematic body of teaching began with the Sophists, followed by Socrates, who was put to death for 'corrupting the youth' – he questioned God's nature, and those in authority. Socrates's trial and death for teaching were immortalised by his students, Xenophon and Plato, and it remains one of the great defences of freedom of ideas and the social contract.[10] Plato founded an 'Academy',[11] and his student Aristotle taught in the temple called the 'Lyceum'. In Ancient Greece, collective education of children was expected; however, it remained confined to

6 E.g. J. K. Rowling, *Harry Potter and the Philosopher's Stone* (1997). 'Hogwarts' is a no-fee selective school.

7 L. Crehan, *Cleverlands: The Secrets Behind the Success of the World's Education Superpowers* (2016); OECD, *Programme for International School Assessment: 2018 Results* (2019) vol I.

8 E.g. M. Hübner, 'Do Tuition Fees Affect Enrollment Behavior? Evidence from a "Natural Experiment" in Germany' (2012) 31(6) *Economics of Education Rev* 949. C. Callender and J. Jackson, 'Does the Fear of Debt Deter Students from Higher Education?' (2005) 34(4) *J Social Policy* 509.

9 HEFCE, 'Differences in Degree Outcomes: Key Findings', March 2014/03 (2014) 4, 38. These are averages.

10 Xenophon, *Apology of Socrates to the Jury* (*c.* 350 BC); Plato, *Apology* (350 BC) and *Crito* (*c.* 350 BC) trans. B. Jowett (1892); J. S. Mill, *On Liberty* (1857) ch 1.

11 Plato, *Laws* (*c.* 350 BC) Book VII, suggests that a child should be treated as 'a slave' and that if passers-by see a teacher and student uncontrolled, they have a duty to 'inflict upon [both] the punishment which he deserves'. Bizarrely, Book XII says a higher education curriculum is 'incapable of being stated beforehand'.

nobility.[12] In Rome, students were to learn grammar and rhetoric, which was meant to include virtue and skill in negotiating public life.[13] Perhaps the first law, the *Codex Theodosianus* in 374 AD required grammarians and rhetors to be established 'throughout each diocese in the most populated cities', mostly benefiting Gaul.[14] When Rome fell to invasions, the centres of learning moved to Egypt, and then the Islamic world. The Quran exalted 'My Lord, increase my knowledge',[15] while China had long established a Confucian system of education. As Xunzi, said, 'I hear and I forget. I see and I recall. Involve me and I learn.'[16]

The world's oldest schools, which have been running continuously, were established in Britain in the 'Dark Ages', starting with the King's School, Canterbury, after St Augustine's arrival in 597. The first universities were originally established by executive order, by statute, or by a 'Papal Bull' (a decree of the pope). If their origins were uncertain, they were later recognised as common law corporations.[17] The first teaching began after the Justinian Code was rediscovered and the University of Bologna was established in 1088. The University of Paris was created in 1090, and Oxford around 1096, expanding considerably in 1167 as King Henry II (in his attempts to conquer France) banned English students attending Paris.[18] In turn, Cambridge was established in 1209 when masters left Oxford in protest at scholars being hanged without consultation of the ecclesiastical courts.[19] Oxford and Cambridge were recognised in case law,[20] and by the pope,[21] and were officially (re-)incorporated by statute in 1571.[22] Meanwhile, St Andrew's University was inaugurated by Papal Bull in 1413, Glasgow in 1451, Aberdeen in 1495 and Edinburgh received

[12] Aristotle, *Politics* (*c.* 320 BC) Book 7, chs. XIV–XVII and Book 8, starts by distinguishing 'those who govern and of those who are governed' and 'the mode of education should be adapted to this distinction'.

[13] E.g. Cicero, *On Oratory* (55 BC) trans. J. S. Watson (1860).

[14] *Codex Theodosianus* (376 AD) 13.3.11. [15] Quran (632) 20:114.

[16] Xunzi, 8 Confucianism, 23 or 荀子 8, 儒效 23 (*c.* 250 BC). The quote in the text is a modern shortening of the following: 不聞不若聞之, 聞之不若見之, 見之不若知之, 知之不若行之. This appears to be remarkably accurate, as J. B. Biggs, *Teaching for Quality Learning at University: What the Student Does* (1999) 63, citing American psychologist William Glasser, suggests people on average remember 10% of what they have been reading, 20% hearing, 30% seeing, 50% seeing and hearing, 70% discussing, 80% using, and 95% of what they have taught others.

[17] D. Farrington and D. Palfreyman, *The Law of Higher Education* (2nd ed. 2012) 13–14. Also H. de Ridder-Symoens (ed.), *A History of the University in Europe*, vol. I: *Universities in the Middle Ages* (1992).

[18] A. B. Cobban, *The Medieval English Universities: Oxford and Cambridge to c. 1500* (1988).

[19] P. Zutshi, 'The Dispersal of Scholars from Oxford and the Beginnings of a University at Cambridge: A Study of the Sources' (2012) 127(528) *English Historical Rev* 1041.

[20] E.g. *Redvers v Bardolf* [1292] YB 20 Edw I, 296 (Rolls Series), the earliest recording of a Chancellor.

[21] E.g. Cambridge was recognised as a *studium generale* by Pope John XXII in 1318; see A. B. Cobban, 'Edward II, Pope John XXII and the University of Cambridge' (1964) 47(1) *Bulletin of the John Rylands Library* 49.

[22] Universities of Oxford and Cambridge Act 1571.

a royal charter in 1583. After this, there were no new universities until teaching opened in London to non-Anglicans at University College in 1826, and at King's College in 1829. Both formed the University of London under a royal charter in 1836.[23] Durham received a royal charter in 1832. In 1895, the London School of Economics was established, and for the first time as a company limited by guarantee.

From the seventeenth century, Scottish education became among the world's best, and significantly ahead of English education, as it had required publicly funded, church-supervised schools in every parish.[24] John Locke's ideas about education were spreading, that the mind was ready to be channelled 'as water it self', and to be filled through experience (including, it was thought, strict discipline).[25] With the era of political and industrial revolution, Wilhelm von Humboldt argued that education like 'truth and virtue' had to spread as part of the 'the ultimate task of our existence . . . to give the fullest possible content to the concept of humanity'.[26] But the reality was far more grim in England: the schools that existed were limited, mostly institutions funded by endowments, with grants of land,[27] or involved menial and punishing 'education' supplied under the poor laws.[28] The real change came with expansion of the vote, as following the Second Reform Act 1867, Members of Parliament sought to 'educate our masters'.[29] The so-called Public Schools Act 1868 (for private, fee-paying) and Endowed Schools Act 1869 (for selective 'grammar') brought new oversight, and then the Elementary Education Act 1870 required an elementary school in every district, under the supervision of the Education Department.[30] The age of universal literacy began (see Figure 8.1).

Meanwhile, until the twentieth century, universities were funded through grants from the church or government, and maintained through aristocratic patronage. Otherwise-forgettable figures, like John de Balliol or Charles Viner, often managed to attach their names to a college, a professorship or a building in return for money.[31] Endowments would be invested and held on trust, and

[23] N. B. Harte, *The University of London, 1836–1986: An Illustrated History* (1986).

[24] School Establishment Act 1616, Education Act 1633 and then Acts of 1646 and 1696.

[25] J. Locke, *Some Thoughts Concerning Education* (1693) 2; *An Essay Concerning Human Understanding* (1690).

[26] W. Humboldt, *Theory of Human Education* (1793).

[27] School Sites Act 1841 enabled grants of land for schools for 'poor persons'. Cf. *Fraser v Canterbury Diocesan Board of Finance* [2005] UKHL 65 (return of land after school closure claimed).

[28] Poor Law Amendment Act 1834. Cf. C. Dickens, *Oliver Twist* (1838).

[29] Mr Robert Lowe, Hansard HC Debs. (15 July 1867) vol. 188, col. 1549; A. J. Marcham, 'Educating Our Masters: Political Parties and Elementary Education 1867 to 1870' (1973) 21(2) *Brit J Educational Studies* 180.

[30] Elementary Education Act 1870 (c. 75), preceded by the Education Department Act 1856 (c. 116).

[31] This phenomenon has not changed with the passage of time. Contemporary examples will be left unnamed.

Figure 8.1 Literacy in the UK, France and the world, 1500–2020

Sources: R. C. Allen, 'Progress and Poverty in Early Modern Europe' (2003) 56 *Economic History Rev* 403, 415; L. Stone, 'Literacy and Education in England 1640–1900' (1969) 42 *Past & Present* 69, 120; Our World in Data, 'Literate and Illiterate World Population'; World Bank, 'Literacy Rate' (2020)

would, with good fortune (or legal requirements to maintain estates), enable the future funding of teaching.[32] Students would also be charged fees upon admission, completion of the degree, or by the year: a haphazard, grossly corrupt system, that could be 'differentiated according to the rank of the entrant'. This meant nobles at Cambridge, for example, at three times the price might be 'awarded a degree without taking an exam'.[33]

Each university had a different governance structure, according to the terms of the charter, bull, statute or articles. However, coinciding with the European Revolutions of 1848, and widespread dissatisfaction among staff, Parliament appointed an Oxford University Commission in 1852, which aimed to reverse 'successive interventions by which the government of the University was reduced to a narrow oligarchy'.[34] Though Oxford's statutes were in disarray, the Commission said the university appeared 'to have been at the first an association of teachers united only by mutual interest'.[35] On the Report's recommendations, the Oxford University Act 1854, sections 16 and 21 set out the composition and a new right of election of 'fellow' employees to the Hebdomadal Council, the governing body. Similarly, the Cambridge

[32] E.g. *Earl of Oxford's case* (1615) 21 ER 48, where the master of Magdalene College, Cambridge, sold land in London to the queen, and then on to a merchant, Spinola, apparently contrary to 13 Eliz. c. 10, which made any conveyance over 21 years void. Coke CJ held the transfer was indeed void, since the statute was meant to maintain funds for education. Lord Ellesmere LC held that in equity the transfer was valid. This landmark constitutional case also established that equity prevails over the law (and, in effect, the king over the courts).

[33] R. Nield, *The Financial History of Cambridge University* (2012) 4–5.

[34] Oxford University Commission, 'Report of Her Majesty's Commissioners Appointed to Inquire into State, Discipline, Studies and Revenues of University and Colleges of Oxford' (1852) 8. See also P. Searby, *A History of the University of Cambridge*, vol. III: *1750–1870* (1997) 518–23 and 530–3 on the parallel report aiming to end the 'contradictory elements of democracy, anarchy, and oligarchic centralism'.

[35] Oxford University Commission (1852) 7.

University Act 1856, sections 5 and 12 required 'electors' to have votes in 'graces' (referendums to bind management) and to elect the University Council.[36] The University of Wales was founded in 1893, with colleges in Cardiff, Bangor and Aberystwyth.[37] The London School of Economics was founded in 1895 and incorporated by 1901.[38] From 1900 to 1909, Birmingham, Manchester, Liverpool, Leeds, Sheffield, Belfast and Bristol were founded. Over the twentieth century, staff and student voice gradually, but unevenly spread.

From 1889, government began providing grants to universities out of concern to widen access.[39] Though student fees were still charged, grants were gradually increased, particularly from the creation of a University Grants Committee in 1918.[40] A small number of students could win scholarships, bursaries or grants from universities or local authorities. Those without faced direct wealth discrimination: they could either afford the fees or not. In the post-war period, free public schools were reorganised by the Education Act 1944 to be under the supervision of Local Education Authorities, who could also provide meals, milk, clothing and transport for pupils, as well as fund universities and students. Fees were prohibited, but private fee-paying or 'independent' schools remained, and so did grammar schools that segregated children after primary school based on that year's tests. Post-war universities were established in Nottingham, Southampton, Hull, Exeter, Leicester and then a further wave through the 1960s.[41] In 1961, the European Social Charter, article 10(4) called for 'reducing or abolishing any fees or charges',[42] and the Education Act 1962 finally ensured government paid all tuition fees, and gave students maintenance grants at university. In an important statement of policy, the Robbins Report 1963 said the goal of expanding university places was 'to produce not mere specialists but rather cultivated men and women' and 'common standards of citizenship'.[43] After this the International Covenant on Economic, Social and Cultural Rights 1966 required the 'progressive introduction of free' higher education, ratified by the UK.[44] Maintenance grants fluctuated, and there were fewer places than today. The Further and Higher Education Act 1992 gave polytechnic institutions, which had focused on

[36] Oxford University Act 1854, ss. 16 and 21; Cambridge University Act 1856, ss. 5–51.

[37] J. G. Williams, *The University of Wales 1893–1939: A History of the University of Wales* (1997).

[38] R. Dahrendorf, *LSE: A History of the London School of Economics and Political Science, 1895–1995* (1995) and see the original Memorandum of Association (1901).

[39] R. Anderson, 'University Fees in Historical Perspective', History & Policy (8 February 2016) www.historyandpolicy.org/policy-papers/papers/university-fees-in-historical-perspective.

[40] EA 1918, s. 44. Anderson, University Fees in Historical Perspective', notes that Cambridge and Oxford accounted for 'about 40% of all English students' in 1910, but they took no state aid.

[41] 1961–9: Keele, East Anglia, York, Newcastle, Lancaster, Strathclyde, Kent, Essex, Warwick, Loughborough, Aston, Brunel, Surrey, Bath, Bradford, City, Heriot-Watt, Salford, Dundee, Stirling and the Open University.

[42] European Social Charter 1961, art. 10(4) also calls for 'reducing or abolishing any fees or charges'.

[43] Robbins Report, Cmnd 2154 (1963) §§26–8.

[44] ICESCR 1966, art. 13.

technical training, the right to recast their status as universities, and forty-three did. University was free at the point of use, and formally accessible according to merit to the extent that the school system allowed, from 1962 to 1998.

However, following the Dearing Report set up under Prime Minister John Major, the Blair administration introduced £1,000 tuition fees, and a system of student loans for home students. These were raised to £3,000 in 2004, and £9,000 in 2011, now set at £9,250. Universities tend to charge whatever they can to international or postgraduate students, and at the time of writing as much as £103,400 for an MBA.

(2) Finance

The legitimate sources of education finance have been among the most fiercely contested issues in modern politics. Historically, there have been three main options for (a) universities: (i) funding from general taxation; (ii) funding from private donors, often ex-students, or other benefactors; and (iii) fees taken from students or parents. For (b) schools, funding is primarily either from (i) government grants or (ii) fees taken from parents.

(a) Universities

(i) Public Funding

In 2017, around 24 per cent of university funding remained public, deriving from the Treasury (and Parliament levying taxation) and the European Union (EU) (3.5% of the 24% – see Figure 8.2). Since 2017, a body called UK Research and Innovation (UKRI) has become largely responsible for this funding.[45] UKRI's functions are to 'facilitate, encourage and support' (i.e. fund) 'research into science, technology, humanities and new ideas' (i.e. universities).[46] UKRI has nine subcouncils (e.g. the Economic and Social Research Council),[47] which distribute special grants through peer review when academics or students apply for research funding. One of these, called 'Innovate UK', has the special 'purpose of increasing economic growth' in the UK.[48] Under Schedule 9, UKRI has a twelve- to fifteen-member board, including a chair, chief executive and chief financial officer. All are appointed by the Secretary of State,[49] after

[45] Higher Education and Research Act (HERA) 2017, s. 91. From 1992 to 2017 this was the Higher Education Funding Council for England, with counterparts in Wales and Scotland: Further and Higher Education Act 1992, ss. 62–9, 81 and 89 (funding councils). From 1988 to 1992 there was a 'University Funding Council'. A 'University Grants Committee' lasted from 1919 to 1988.

[46] HERA 2017, ss. 93–4.

[47] HERA 2017, s. 92(1) naming the Arts and Humanities Research Council, Biotechnology and Biological Sciences Research Council, Economic and Social Research Council, Engineering and Physical Sciences Research Council, Medical Research Council, Natural Environment Research Council, the Science and Technology Facilities Council, Innovate UK, and Research England. Amendable by the Secretary of State.

[48] HERA 2017, s. 96(1). [49] HERA 2017, Sch. 9, para. 2.

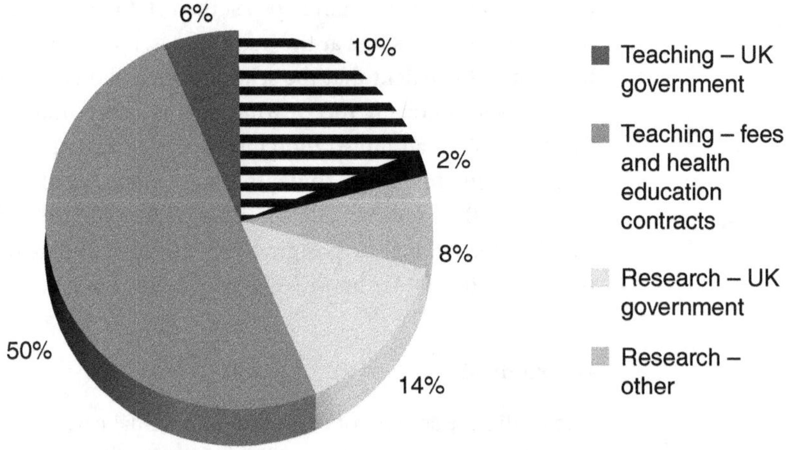

Figure 8.2 UK higher education funding sources, 2017, total £35.7bn
Source: Universities UK, *Patterns and Trends in UK Higher Education 2018* (2018) 31

consulting the existing UKRI chair and paying regard to the candidate's 'experience' of research and development in science, technology and humanities, and 'industrial, commercial and financial matters', charities or professional practice. The Secretary of State must consider representing Wales, Scotland and Northern Ireland.[50] Academic staff have no right to vote for members.

The amount of overall funding that UKRI distributes is determined in the budget year to year, 'as the Secretary of State considers appropriate'.[51] The Secretary of State may also 'give UKRI directions about the allocation or expenditure by UKRI of grants'.[52] This discretion is bound by 'the principle that decisions on individual research proposals are best taken following an evaluation of the quality and likely impact of the proposals', as was advocated by former Lord Chancellor Haldane.[53] However there is no legal guarantee that university funding from government will remain adequate or fairly distributed, without university staff or students asserting effective social and political pressure.

(ii) Private Endowments and Finance

While small in overall terms, private financing of older universities is substantial, and enabled the creation of large endowment trust funds. For instance, by 2020 the five largest combined endowments were held at the University of Cambridge with over £7.1 billion; Oxford with £6.3 billion; Edinburgh with £487 million; King's College, London with £252 million; and Manchester with £220 million. These funds are still small compared to North American universities: Harvard presides over a $40 billion endowment, and Yale $31 billion.

[50] HERA 2017, Sch. 9, para. 2(4)–(6). [51] HERA 2017, s. 101. [52] HERA 2017, s. 102.
[53] HERA 2017, s. 103; Ministry of Reconstruction, *Report of Machinery of Government Committee*, Cd 9230 (December 1918) 30–5.

Each accumulation of capital is invested in the standard way (see Ch. 4) – namely, company shares, bonds, in property or other financial products. The annual income could be used to fund teaching and research, though this depends on a university's governance.

Endowment funds can be beneficial, but also create legal and social problems. They are held on trust for the university (or college) which as a legal entity will be controlled by its governing body. As Chapter 8(2) explains, control may be removed from staff and students, and in practice rest in the hands of an insulated management. Trust money must, of course, be used according to the trust terms, and otherwise in the interests of the ultimate beneficiaries, which may differ from pure financial interests.[54] For example, a growing number of students and staff have campaigned for divestment from fossil fuels, both on the basis that fossil-fuel polluters have and can be expected to perform poorly and that it is morally wrong to damage the climate even if it were profitable.[55] The issue is arguably more acute at educational institutions, which are grounded in a long-term view of human welfare and in scientific understanding of the world. When there are divergent views, trustees must not blindly maximise financial returns[56] but follow the interests of the beneficiaries, and this may require actually asking what beneficiaries want.[57] But in practice the use of endowment funds may be closely guarded, with opaque, unaccountable university managers.

Academics in natural science and social science departments have increasingly been encouraged to seek private funding for research, both from business and from charities. The same practice is growing in law and humanities. In many cases, academic appointments are made contingent upon seeking research funding, whether it is a public or private source. This creates substantial conflicts of interest: formally research money may be given (e.g. by GlaxoSmithKline, Google or Garfield Weston) without any strings attached. But in practice, academics will not find much funding for projects that criticise those enterprises, or their business practices, or a charity's agenda (which may be also be privately funded). While such income is under 8 per cent of total funding, examples of conflicted 'research' findings are legion.[58]

[54] Trustee Act 2000, ss. 3 and 6.

[55] E.g. A. Mooney, 'Cambridge to Defy Students and Academics on Shunning Fossil Fuels', *Financial Times* (4 March 2018).

[56] See *Harries v Church Commissioners for England* [1992] 1 WLR 1241, per Sir Donald Nicholls VC: 'Trustees may, if they wish, accommodate the views of those who consider that on moral grounds a particular investment would be in conflict with the objects of the charity, so long as the trustees are satisfied that course would not involve a risk of significant financial detriment.' Cf. P. Smith, 'Church of England Becomes Top World Performer', *Financial Times* (21 May 2017): 'The Church's ethical investment policy dictates that all investments should be compatible with Christian values'; A. Mooney, 'UK Churches Divest from Fossil Fuel Companies', *Financial Times* (3 August 2018).

[57] Law Commission, *Fiduciary Duties of Investment Intermediaries*, LC No. 350 (2014) ch. 6.

[58] E.g. T. Berger, C. Benedikt Frey, G. Levin and S. Rao Danda, 'Uber Happy? Work and Well-Being in the "Gig Economy"' (2019) 34(99) Economic Policy 429, claiming Uber drivers are

(iii) Student Fees

Probably the most controversial source of funding in recent history has been the extraction of fees from students. In 1997, the Dearing Report, commissioned by the John Major government, recommended that grants be ended and that students or their parents pay fees for university. Its justification was that graduates (on average) had 'improved employment prospects and pay'.[59] Despite a new Labour government's election that year, the Teaching and Higher Education Act 1998 enabled universities to charge student fees of up to £1,000.[60] The Higher Education Act 2004 enabled £3,000 fees.[61] In 2010, despite one of the coalition partners in the new government promising their abolition, tuition fees were raised to £9,000 a year.[62] This was coupled with a goal of eliminating government funding for teaching.[63] Mass student and staff protest met each rise, arguing it would make university harder for poorer students, inducing worry about money, not study and potentially leading to a start in life with more debt than any generation before.[64] Government ministers argued in response that fees were necessary to secure investment, and that those who did not go to university should not have to pay for those who did (even though progressive income tax meant, on average, they would not). It is notable that the leading political supporters of fees all attended fee-paying secondary schools.[65] In 2017, one of the drafters of the £3,000 fee rise decided that he had been wrong, and that fees should now be 'scrapped'.[66] By contrast, in Scotland the governing Labour Party, like the Scottish National Party, refused to introduce tuition fees in 1998. Study remains free, but only for residents in Scotland before university.[67]

In 2018 tuition fees in England, Wales and Northern Ireland were capped at £9,250.[68] Technically, any university may charge less, but few universities have taken that option. This may suggest that any market 'equilibrium' price is higher than the cap; however, the better view is that prices are determined by the bargaining power of universities, and the unbounded future income

'happy', where two co-authors are Uber employees, while the other two have done many projects with corporate money. Uber systematically denies its drivers employment rights: Ch. 5(2).

59 Dearing Report, para. 18.24.

60 Teaching and Higher Education Act 1998, ss. 22–8.

61 Higher Education Act 2004, ss. 23–4; Student Fees (Approved Plans) Regulations 2004.

62 Higher Education (Higher Amount) Regulations 2010, reg. 4.

63 See the Browne Review, Independent Review of Higher Education Funding and Student Finance (12 October 2010) chaired by the former CEO of BP plc.

64 E.g. R. Adams, 'Poorest Students Will Finish University with £57,000 Debt, Says IFS', *The Guardian* (5 July 2017).

65 E.g. Tony Blair (Fettes), Margaret Hodge (Oxford High School), Andrew Adonis (Kingham Hill School), Nick Clegg (Westminster) and David Cameron (Eton).

66 A. Adonis, 'I Put Up Tuition Fees. It's Now Clear They Have to Be Scrapped', *The Guardian* (7 July 2017).

67 Scotland Act 1998, ss. 28–9, Schs. 5–6, devolve higher education fees to the Scottish Parliament (i.e. not a 'reserved' matter).

68 Higher Education (Higher Amount) (England) Regulations 2016, reg. 6.

students may sacrifice to secure a good job. Highly sought-after universities or professors have a 'natural monopoly' on their skills (see Ch. 2(2)(f)), and rather than an equilibrium, they may take an ever-growing proportion of students' future pay. Home student fees are set by the Secretary of State, which may be charged up to the 'higher amount'.[69] Under EU law, students must be treated equally compared to other students in the same member state. There can be no discrimination in entry requirements[70] or in fees. But this does not affect 'internal' arrangements. So, before Brexit, non-UK EU students also paid £9,250 in England, but they paid £0 in Scotland like Scottish students. However, if students from the rest of the UK registered for study in Scotland, Scottish universities still charge students £9,250 in fees. The economic logic appeared to be to prevent English or Welsh students flooding Scotland – a possibility, albeit one that has not transpired with students from the Republic of Ireland.[71] By contrast, the obvious effect of the policy is to segregate English and Scottish education, a phenomenon that does not seem conducive to holding the UK together. The logic of EU law, which refrains from prohibiting this direct discrimination, was that because discrimination is within the UK, it is an 'internal' matter beyond EU law's scope.[72] Such anomalies may be regarded as an inevitable result of fees and EU law's failure to create standards for public services.

Universities have a statutory duty to draft an 'access and participation plan' which is meant to include the 'promotion of equality of opportunity'.[73] These are submitted to the new 'Office for Students' (OfStu), which like UKRI has a ten- to fifteen-member board appointed by the Secretary of State.[74] 'OfStu' is meant to promote 'quality, and greater choice and opportunities for students', 'competition' among universities, 'value for money' and 'equality of opportunity'.[75] Its statutory remit does not appear to be concerned with enlightenment of the human condition or the pursuit of knowledge. Its 'access and participation' plans also do not seem to affect the direct wealth discrimination inherent in fees themselves.

So far as fees go for non-EU international students, there is no cap. In 2017, around 23 per cent of total teaching income was extracted from non-EU international students. Informally, many universities have appeared to adopt

69 HERA 2017, Sch. 2, para. 2, formerly Higher Education Act 2004, ss. 23–4.

70 *Commission v Austria* (2005) C-147/03 (higher requirements for non-Austrians (mainly Germans) held invalid despite the alleged 'structural, staffing and financial problems'). *Commission v Belgium* (2004) C-65/03 struck down a Belgian university limit on foreign (mainly French) students.

71 E.g. Trinity College Dublin, Undergraduate EU Fee Schedule 2018/19 (2018) charged €5,681 a year for a law degree (around £5,000). There is no mass exodus of rationally calculating students from Ireland to Scotland, or from the UK to Ireland. Contrast the sensationally entitled article by S. Johnson, 'Hundreds of Northern Irish Students Exploit Free Scottish Degree Passport Loophole', *Daily Telegraph* (1 June 2012).

72 Cf. *Brown v Secretary of State for Scotland* (1988) Case 197/86.

73 HERA 2017, ss. 29–32: OfStu power to approve an 'access and participation plan'.

74 HERA 2017, Sch. 1, para. 2. 75 HERA 2017, s. 2.

a policy of internal quotas (e.g. one-third UK, one-third other EU, one-third international students) in order to raise fees, abandoning admission policy on the basis of merit and therefore inviting discrimination claims.[76] In this 'global market for higher education', international fees may be double or more those of home and EU student fees. For instance, a UCL website in 2018, after saying '[w]e know that money can be a worrying topic for most students', listed fees at £20,040 for law and £33,650 for medicine every year. There is some variation between different universities' fees,[77] which could suggest either that the market ensures that fees reflect the marginal cost of production, or simply that universities are collectively extracting as much money as possible. The historical rise in international fees suggests the latter. There appears to be no correlation between rising fees and improvement in teaching – for instance, by reducing class sizes or raising academic staff pay. Instead, the evidence suggests fees are used by university managements to construct new buildings or increase management bureaucracy and pay.[78]

To pay fees and living costs, a system of student loans is available for UK students through local authorities and the government-owned Student Loans Company. Passed under the Teaching and Higher Education Act 1998,[79] the Education (Student Support) Regulations 2011 set out the requirements.[80] Means-tested grants used to be available, but were mostly abolished for students starting university after August 2016. While EU students qualified for the same fees as UK students before it ceased EU membership, they only qualified for loans (or previously grants) if they had been resident for three years in the UK. This rule was accepted in *R (Bidar) v London Borough of Ealing*, where a French national, Danny Bidar, claimed the right to a loan.[81] The local authority, Ealing, required that he had lived in the UK for three years before beginning university (reading economics at UCL). It also required that Bidar held 'settled status' – for instance, by having 'indefinite leave to remain' under the Immigration Act 1971. The Grand Chamber held that while a three-year residence requirement was legitimate for acquiring the right to a student loan, the need for settled status was unjustified, and constituted indirect nationality discrimination under the Treaty on the Functioning of the European Union, articles 18–21.

[76] See below Ch. 8(3)(ii).
[77] E.g. for 2019 entry to law degrees, KCL is £23,490, LSE is £19,920, Cambridge is £20,157.
[78] 'Where Do Student Fees Really Go? Following the Pound', HEPI Report 113 (2018), summarised by R. Adams, '"Less than Half" of Tuition Fees Spent on Teaching at English Universities', *The Guardian* (22 November 2018).
[79] Teaching and Higher Education Act 1998, ss. 22 and 42.
[80] Education (Student Support) Regulations 2011, which have been heavily amended.
[81] Cf. *R (Bidar) v London Borough of Ealing* (2005) C-209/03.

(b) Schools

School funding, unlike the more unified university system, depends mostly on whether a school is a free public school, or a fee-charging private school. Out of a total education budget of £103 billion for 2019–20, 13.7 per cent of the total (see Ch. 20), the budget for schools was £43.84 billion through the 'Dedicated Schools Grant',[82] on top of which is the pupil premium allocation, and the Teachers' Pay Grant. By contrast, fee-charging schools are funded primarily by escalating tuition fees imposed upon parents, and by tax subsidies.

(i) Free Public Schools

The two main types of free public schools are local authority 'maintained' schools (there are five subgroups of these) and academies (including 'free schools'). Under the Education Act 1996, section 11 the Secretary of State exercises 'powers in respect of those bodies in the receipt of public funds' that provide 'primary, secondary or further education'.[83] Further, the Secretary of State may, in accordance with regulations, pay grants 'to persons other than local authorities'.[84] School funding was cut by 8 per cent in real terms from 2010 to 2019.[85] Local authorities set financial budgets for all maintained schools, subject to minimum school budgets set by the Secretary of State, in consultation with schools.[86] The Secretary of State also has power to give financial assistance for a wide range of education activities, such as teacher training grants.[87] However, it is the Prime Minister who determines teachers' pay and conditions of service by statute through a review body, and by collective agreement.[88] Academies may also seek private donations and, unfortunately, this has come to interfere with those schools' governance.[89]

(ii) Fee-Charging Private Schools

Fee-charging schools account for around 6.5 per cent of UK school students. They are misleadingly referred to in statute as both 'public' schools (when they

[82] Education & Skills Funding Agency, Dedicated Schools Grant (DSG): 2018–19 Financial Year Allocations (July 2019).

[83] EA 1996, s. 11(1).

[84] EA 1996, s. 485, while s. 484 states the National Assembly of Wales can pay education standards grants.

[85] H. Stewart and R. Adams, *The Guardian* (31 August 2019), but noting a government commitment to increase funding by 4.5% in the following three years.

[86] School Standards and Framework Act 1998, ss. 45–7A.

[87] EA 2002, s. 14. Further, the Apprenticeships, Skills, Children and Learning Act 2009, s. 10, grants to the Skills Funding Agency, which funds adult learning, and the Education Funding Agency.

[88] EA 2002, ss. 119–29.

[89] C. Sambrook and W. Mansell, 'The Brexit-Backing Businessmen Taking Control of England's Schools', *openDemocracy* (11 December 2019).

are private[90]) or 'independent' (when they depend upon charging fees[91]). These schools are predominantly funded by charging fees to parents, and they therefore discriminate among children in access to education based upon parental wealth. Although it is a universal right for parents 'to choose the kind of education that shall be given to their children',[92] this does not mean a right to discriminate against others,[93] and a major consequence for parents is that fees have continually escalated. From 1991 to 2016, private school fees rose 250 per cent beyond inflation.[94] They increased again by over 10 per cent from 2016 to 2019.[95] This is evidence of multiple market failures. Furthermore, in 2005, the predecessor to the Competition and Markets Authority found that fifty fee-charging schools violated the Competition Act 1998 prohibition on cartels after illegally exchanging information about their proposed fees.[96]

Around half the UK's fee-charging schools are also funded through tax subsidies that derive from their ostensibly 'charitable' status. Under the Charities Act 2011, sections 2–4, a charity is something that is for 'the advancement of education' or other purposes, and is 'for the public benefit'.[97] Past governments have accepted that conduct such as giving a small number of places to non-fee paying students, giving money to nearby schools or opening their facilities is enough to make the whole operation a charity.[98] The better view is that a closed, fee-charging system, which makes donations, is not a charity, but an occasional, self-interested donor. However, once classified as 'charities', they are exempted from paying business rates, estimated in 2017 to cost the public (and provide a tax-funded subsidy of) around £522 million a year.[99]

[90] Public Schools Act 1868, using the word 'public' in the same way as a 'public house' where you also pay to access services. It followed the Clarendon Commission, bringing Harrow, Eton, Winchester, Charterhouse, Rugby, Shrewsbury and Westminster under government supervision, and setting governance standards.

[91] Cf. EA 1996, s. 463, which defines 'independent' within the meaning of the Act as 'not a school maintained by a local authority'.

[92] UDHR 1948, art. 26(3).

[93] UDHR 1948, art. 2, 'Everyone is entitled to all the rights and freedoms set forth in this Declaration, without distinction of any kind, such as race, colour, sex, language, religion, political or other opinion, national or social origin, property, birth or other status.' Also ICESCR 1966, arts. 13 and 2(2).

[94] B. Chu, 'The Charts that Show How Private School Fees Have Exploded over the Past 25 Years', *The Independent* (11 May 2016).

[95] T. Hale, 'Why Are Private School Fees so High?', *Financial Times* (26 September 2019).

[96] OFT (November 2005); 'Private Schools Fee-Fixing Ruling', *BBC News* (9 December 2005).

[97] Charities Act 2011, ss. 2–4.

[98] R. Long, 'Independent Schools (England)', Briefing Paper No. 07972 (28 June 2019).

[99] H. Osborne, 'Private Schools to Save £522m in Tax Thanks to Charitable Status', *The Guardian* (11 June 2017).

(3) Governance

The governance of education has four main levels of (a) the Department for Education and devolved authorities; (b) universities governed by their own constitutions, or statute; (c) schools, governed in multiple ways; and (d) at international level, the United Nations Educational, Scientific and Cultural Organization (UNESCO).

(a) Department for Education

The Department for Education is led by the Secretary of State, who has a duty to 'promote the education of the people of England and Wales',[100] while education is devolved in Scotland and led by the Learning and Advanced Learning and Science Directorates. As well as its funding roles and appointing the OfStu, the Secretary of State can determine disputes between local authorities.[101] It may prevent unreasonable exercise of functions, and may give directions, enforceable by mandatory order, to a local authority or governing body that fails to discharge its duty.[102] However, it must be satisfied that a local authority has acted in error of law, or otherwise show that its decision was so unreasonable that no reasonable authority could do the same.[103] The Secretary of State often, unfortunately, has had no teaching experience,[104] and in practice decisions are delegated to and taken by the School Commissioner Group. This includes the National Schools Commissioner and eight Regional Schools Commissioners (RSCs). Each RSC is advised in turn by a Head Teacher Board that includes four to eight members from the local area, usually heads, former heads, trustees and business people. The RSCs' functions include monitoring school performance, making recommendations about free-school applications and encouraging conversion to academies.[105] There is not yet a requirement for teacher or parent representation in RSCs.

(b) Universities

The governance of universities, despite its lack of codification, is one of the sector's most important achievements. Among all UK enterprises, universities do the most to promote the right to vote for staff and for students, in selecting representatives on governing bodies. The slow, evolutionary trend has been from one of authority to democratisation, though the process of development is still far from finished.[106] Although the Dearing Report recommended

[100] EA 1996, s. 10. [101] EA 1996, s. 495. [102] EA 1996, ss. 496–7B.

[103] *Education Secretary v Tameside Council* [1977] AC 1014.

[104] The exception has been Estelle Morris, who had a teaching career, and was in post from 2001–2. Ed Balls also had a brief stint as a teaching fellow, and was in post from 2007–10. Prime ministers who were teachers include Gordon Brown and Clement Attlee.

[105] 'The Role of Regional Schools Commissioners', First Report of Session 2015–16, HC 401 (2016).

[106] See also Farrington and Palfreyman, *The Law of Higher Education*, ch. 5.

statutory minimum standards for staff and student representation in university governance in 1997,[107] outside Scotland there has been no such law, yet.

Today, each university has rules for appointment, removal and accountability of its governing body, and may have multiple organs. Four main groups can be identified. First, if a university is not created by royal charter, statute or the Companies Acts, the Education Reform Act 1988 sets the rules. These are generally newer universities, and there are forty-six currently.[108] Draft university charters are approved by the Privy Council, and laid before both Houses of Parliament or the Scottish Parliament.[109] The Privy Council then prescribes an order, which outside Scotland must comply with the minimum rules in Schedule 7A. The 'articles of government' should determine the powers of a 'board of governors' and an 'academic board'. University governing bodies should have between twelve and twenty-four members. There should be up to thirteen lay members appointed by the board itself, up to two teachers nominated by the academic board, up to two students nominated by students, and one to nine members co-opted by the board.[110] Even though these requirements for staff and student representation are inflexibly low, in 2011 the government proposed their abolition. This attempt was defeated by trade union opposition.[111]

Second, fifty-two English universities are incorporated by a royal charter or statute, or perhaps both. These universities generally appear to have higher proportions of staff and student voice in governance.[112] For example, Cambridge University's governance documents give the 'Council' day-to-day management power.[113] The Council is a twenty-five-person executive body and is elected by (1) staff, with sixteen seats, weighted according to seniority; (2) students, with three seats but not necessarily by direct election; and (3) existing management, with six seats, including the Vice-Chancellor and Chancellor. The Vice-Chancellor, who is effectively the CEO and chair of the Council (a practice at odds with the UK Corporate Governance Code), is appointed by the 'Regent House', but on the Council's nomination. The Chancellor is elected by the 'Senate', which includes the Regent House and

107 Dearing Report, para. 377.

108 E.g. Anglia Ruskin, Birmingham City, Brighton, East London, Kingston, Lincoln, Manchester Metropolitan, Nottingham Trent, Oxford Brookes and Portsmouth.

109 College Charter Act 1871, s. 2.

110 Education Reform Act 1988, s. 124A and Sch. 7A, para. 3, inserted by Further and Higher Education Act 1992, s. 71(4) and Sch. 6. Note also s. 128 (power to dissolve higher education corporations after consulting the funding council), Sch. 7 (one to three initial appointments are made by the local authority).

111 'Government Withdraws College Governance Reforms', *University and College Union* (3 November 2011).

112 E.g. Bath, Birmingham, Birkbeck, Bristol, Brunel, City, East Anglia, Essex, Exeter, Kent, Lancaster, Leeds, Leicester, Liverpool, Manchester, Newcastle, Nottingham, the Open University, SOAS, Queen Mary, Reading, Sheffield, Sussex, UCL, Warwick and York. See Farrington and Palfreyman, *The Law of Higher Education*, ch. 5, 161–3.

113 University of Cambridge, Statute A.IV.1.

graduates.[114] The Regent House is the 3,800 members of staff, from 'fellows' upwards in the academic hierarchy.[115] Crucially, the Regent House can also pass 'graces' that function as referendums to bind management. These can be powerful. For example, in 2016 an anti-fossil-fuel student group campaigned for staff to vote for their university endowments to divest, or engage fossil-fuel corporations to meet climate targets. The university management, fearing a grace, promised to meet the body's concerns.[116] In this way, Cambridge is possibly the most 'democratic' of universities, a fact which may not be entirely unrelated to its success. Oxford University is probably the second most democratic, as it requires eleven out of twenty-five members of the University Council to be elected by the Congregation, and a further four to be appointed subject to Congregation's approval, while three students may attend but without voting rights.[117] Staff voice is important, illustrated in the 2018 pension strike, where academics threatened to sack the Vice-Chancellor if she did not change her stance on cutting staff pensions.[118] Other universities typically fix certain proportions of staff and student representation, but this will usually be a minority, and may lack rights to bind management by proposals.[119]

At least one strange anomaly is the King's College London Act 1997. Under section 15, King's is required to have a thirty-eight-member Council, which serves as the university's governing body. There should be five members appointed by virtue of their management office, twenty appointed lay persons, eight elected by academics, three elected by students and two by non-academic staff members. This means that roughly one-third of the governing body should be elected by staff and students. However, although section 15 was put into effect, most elected members were unilaterally abolished in 2009.[120] Meanwhile, under the current King's College, London Charter and Statutes, article 1 states that the Council shall be a twenty-one-member board, with twelve lay members, eight staff and one student, but all but three staff are appointed by the existing board, not elected.

114 University of Cambridge, Statute A.I.7.

115 University of Cambridge, Statute A.III.10(d) and A.IV.2 exclude part-time or fixed-term teaching staff from voting rights: they are not 'fellows', even if they do the same work. Could this violate the Part-time Workers Regulations 2000 or the Fixed-Term Employees Regulations 2002?

116 'University Plans to Cut Greenhouse Gas Emissions to Zero by 2038', *The Guardian* (1 October 2020); M. Taylor, 'Cambridge University to Divest from Fossil Fuels by 2030', *The Guardian* (1 October 2020).

117 Oxford University, Statute VI, arts. 4 and 13; Council Regulation 13 of 2002, regs. 4–10.

118 R. Adams, 'Oxford University Backs Down in Pensions Dispute', *The Guardian* (7 March 2018).

119 See Ch. 3(2)(b) on the right of company members to make proposals in the Companies Act (CA) 2006, s. 292.

120 King's College London Act 1997, s. 3.

Third, twenty-five universities are companies limited by guarantee.[121] For example, the London School of Economics has a memorandum that was signed by Sidney Webb, George Bernard Shaw and other Fabian socialists when it was formed in 1895. Its articles have been continually updated, but article 10.5 requires a seventeen-member 'Council' to have two students, three staff representatives and the remainder lay representatives.[122] In 2014, the composition was altered, primarily to reduce the numbers, to be set 'by the Court' of the university. This is a large, mostly self-perpetuating body of lay members.

Fourth, in Scotland minimum standards of governance are codified in law. Following the Von Prondzynski Report in 2012,[123] the Higher Education Governance (Scotland) Act 2016 required basic rights of staff and students in all universities.[124] Under section 10, a governing body must have at least two persons elected by staff, one appointed by an academic-staff trade union,[125] one by a support-staff trade union, two appointed by students and one senior lay person elected by all staff, students and governing members. The Universities (Scotland) Act 1966 requires that a Rector and a Vice-Chair are elected by students (but in Edinburgh, staff also vote). This means seven persons are accountable to staff and students.[126] However, limits in the total numbers of the governing body are not clearly established. For example, in Edinburgh, the 'Court' which is the governing body has twenty-three members. Better governance practice tends to involve fewer members on boards, because they are ideally a place to get work done, rather than a place for senior figures to acquire decorative titles. In this respect, universities have not kept up with best practices in modern enterprise governance.

(c) School Governance

Among schools, governance is even more disunited than universities, and lacking in principles. The three main groups of school are local authority-maintained schools, academies and free schools that receive more funding directly from government, and fee-charging schools. In the first group, local authority-maintained schools, there are five main types.[127] First, 'community

[121] E.g. Chichester, Derby, Greenwich, London Metropolitan, London South Bank, Roehampton and Westminster.

[122] Memorandum and Articles of Association of the London School of Economics and Political Science, art. 10.5.

[123] F. von Prondzynski, Report of the Review of Higher Education Governance in Scotland (16 January 2012).

[124] Further and Higher Education (Scotland) Act 2005, Sch. 2 lists these, following the Higher Education Governance (Scotland) Act (HEGSA) 2016, s. 18.

[125] An independent trade union: Trade Union and Labour Relations (Consolidation) Act 1992, s. 178(3).

[126] HEGSA 2016, ss. 1–10 and 15 (composition of the academic board).

[127] School Standards and Framework Act 1998, s. 20(1).

schools' are wholly maintained by a local council, which employs staff, owns land and buildings and determines admissions.[128] Second, 'foundation schools' are maintained by the local authority but staff are employed by the governing body, and other parties may hold the land on trust for the school – for instance, because of a charitable donation.[129] Third, 'voluntary schools' are of two types and both local authority funded, namely 'controlled schools' where a foundation or trust is a religious body often making up a quarter of the governing body, and 'aided schools', which are mainly religious or faith schools. Fourth, there are community special schools, for children with special needs. Fifth, there are foundation special schools, with charitable history similar to other foundation schools.[130]

Each local authority school has an 'instrument of government' as its constitution. This records the name, category and founding date, and is approved by the local authority. Governing bodies should be between nine and twenty members, but for those constituted after 2012 the minimum was reduced to seven.[131] The Education Act 2002, section 19 requires that governing bodies include parents, the head, staff, local authorities and foundation or partnership governors (if a foundation school). However, in 2011 the number of required staff and local authority representatives was reduced to one in England, but not Wales.[132] It is very unclear why this overcomplicated and restricted approach is desirable, as opposed to requiring at least one-third staff, one-third parents and any others as the school community decides (such as staff, alumni, community representatives or other people with expertise).

The duties of local authorities are considerable for maintained schools.[133] They include a general duty to organise education in partnership with the Secretary of State,[134] promoting high standards and fair access to education, providing 'sufficient schools' for demand in their area[135] and maintaining those schools.[136] They act as the admissions authority into schools and have powers to require that a particular child is admitted to a school.[137] Local authorities should train and support governors, decide school terms and

[128] EA 2002, s. 35.

[129] EA 2002, s. 36, staff employed by governing body unless the delegated budget is suspended under Sch. 2.

[130] EA 1996, ss. 324–9 (parents can request their child is assessed for special needs). Children and Families Act 2014, ss. 22–4 (duty to identify children with special needs or disability). Under s. 49, a special needs child has a personal budget, and under s. 63 this may include pay for a fee-charging school.

[131] School Standards and Framework Act 1998, s. 19(3); School Governance (Constitution) (England) Regulations 2007; and School Governance (Constitution) (England) Regulations 2012/1034, no maximum.

[132] EA 2002, s. 19(1A) inserted by EA 2011, s. 38; s. 19(2) amended to apply to Wales only, and adding requirement for community governors (unless a voluntary aided school).

[133] EA 2002, s. 21(3) enables regulations to define local authority, governor and head roles.

[134] EA 2002, s. 1. [135] EA 2002, ss. 13A–14.

[136] School Standards and Framework Act 1998, s. 22.

[137] School Standards and Framework Act 1998, ss. 85A–96.

holidays, deal with student exclusions, set the curriculum, and may arrange nursery education and services to safeguard pupil welfare.[138] In this way, local authorities, numbering in the hundreds, have long performed wide-ranging co-ordination functions.

However, second, dissatisfaction with certain local authorities and examples of 'failing' schools led government to enable the establishment of 'academies' outside local authority co-ordination. While existing since the Learning and Skills Act 2000, the Academies Act 2010 recast the rules and drove the mass conversion of maintained schools, so that by 2018, 72 per cent of secondary schools and 27 per cent of primary schools had converted, or 7,472 of the 21,538 total number of schools. Funded directly by the Department for Education, rather than through the local authority, academies must have open admissions, no fees and a 'balanced and broad based' curriculum that will prepare students for later life.[139] Academies are incorporated under the Companies Act 2006, and so their directors must fulfil duties and standards within it. A funding agreement with government is the primary tool of oversight, and these follow the template Master Agreement but can be varied for each academy.[140] Most old selective grammar schools have converted into academies. Many academies are run as chains, in a multi-academy trust. In a number of situations, the transparency and governance of the academies have led to serious problems in debt and quality of education.[141]

Third, fee-charging schools are governed by the constitution of each. The Public Schools Act 1868 identifies the governing bodies of seven older fee-charging schools and codified some of the powers of their governing bodies, including to alter their own regulations. The Independent Schools Inspectorate, guided by the Department for Education, exercises some oversight.[142]

(d) UNESCO

UNESCO was established in 1945, recalling that 'since wars begin in the minds of men, it is in the minds of men that the defences of peace must be constructed', and that 'the education of humanity for justice and liberty and peace are indispensable to the dignity of [humankind] and constitute a sacred duty which all the nations must fulfil'.[143] Its purpose is 'promoting collaboration among nations through education, science and culture' to uphold justice, the rule of law and human rights. To this end, it will recommend international

[138] EA 2002, ss. 22, 32, 52, 79, 153 and 175 respectively. [139] Academies Act 2010, ss. 1–1A.

[140] See Department for Education, 'Academy and Free School Funding Agreements' (2020); 'Academy and Free School Model Funding Agreement: Single Academy Trust' (April 2016).

[141] E.g. L. Lightfoot, 'Nepotism, Fraud, Waste and Cheating . . . Welcome to England's School System', *The Guardian* (8 September 2020).

[142] Education (Independent School Standards) Regulations 2014.

[143] Constitution of UNESCO 1945, Preamble.

agreements that 'promote the free flow of ideas by word and image'; give 'fresh impulse to popular education and to the spread of culture'; develop education activities with members; uphold equal opportunity without discrimination; and maintain, increase and diffuse knowledge through books, art and exchange programmes.[144] Its membership is each member of the United Nations (UN). However, its budget, for global education, is very small at just $1.3 billion in 2020–1. It has not yet become a forum to co-ordinate the free exchange of students or teachers, for instance, by settling the balance of funds between systems that provide free public education that is funded through tax. Instead, its activities have been primarily focused upon technical assistance and advice to developing countries.

(4) Students' Rights

Aside from the rights of students (or parents) to choose between education institutions and the right to participate in governance, common law and statute recognise an array of other rights that can ultimately be enforced in court. These rights correlate with the duties owed by the education institution, and are fulfilled by governing body members or staff. While litigation will rarely, if ever, be a satisfactory mechanism to settle disagreements in education, the lack of a codified list of student rights may frustrate their fulfilment.

(a) University Student Rights

Although there is no codified list of rights,[145] conceptually the rights of students are similar to those of company members in claiming for breach of directors' duties, or members of the public in judicial review of public authorities.[146] Whether an organisation is a company, a public body or any other association, the same principles of accountability will inevitably arise. The differences among the rules increasingly seem more cosmetic than real, and this is particularly true for universities as they cross between the imagined public–private law divide. It is also apparent that wherever staff may claim under judicial review or contractual principles, analogous rights are likely to be available for students.

There are many different ways to categorise rights and duties in organisations, but four categories are useful in practice. First, there are rights to ensure that the rules of a university are followed, and discretion used in a justifiable

[144] Constitution of UNESCO 1945, art. I.

[145] Some attempts have been made – for instance, by the European Students' Union's Students' Rights Charter.

[146] It is notable that two leading decisions in company law and public law were decided by the same judge in a short space of time, namely Lord Greene MR in *Re Smith and Fawcett Ltd* [1942] Ch 304 and *Associated Provincial Picture Houses Ltd v Wednesbury Corporation* [1948] 1 KB 223.

manner. This matters most in cases concerning the award of degrees. Second, there are rights to equal treatment, flowing from the Equality Act 2010 and other basic rights. Third, there is a requirement on education institutions to act with reasonable care, and proportionately within legitimate fields of discretion. The quality of teaching is a basic concern for students. Fourth, educational institutions should not allow conflicts of interest to affect any decision.

(i) Right to Have Rules and Law Followed

First, every student has the right to see that the rules of a university are followed, and that discretion is used in a legally justified manner. In administrative law, a public body's exercise of power may not be ultra vires; powers must be exercised for a proper purpose; and they must act reasonably, take into account relevant factors and fulfil legitimate expectations. In company law, a constitution or articles must be followed and powers used for a proper purpose, with independent judgment.[147] In contract law, the terms of a contract with a university and reasonable expectations[148] amount to the same thing. Where there is nothing in a statute, a constitution or a contract, the law implies basic rights. For example, in *R (Bentley) v Cambridge University*, in 1723, a student whose degree was removed after he allegedly spoke 'contemptuous words' had the right to a fair hearing. As Fortescue J said, 'even God himself did not pass sentence upon Adam before he was called upon to make his defence'.[149]

In more modern examples, in *Clark v University of Lincolnshire and Humberside* a student claimed that the award of a third-class degree was a breach of contract, because (among other things) its own regulations enabled a mark better than a third class in a resit.[150] Ms Clark had been a humanities undergraduate and said her computer crashed just before she submitted her final paper on 'A Streetcar Named Desire'.[151] She was then only able to submit some brief notes from a Meuthen commentary, which the university board decided was plagiarism, and she was graded with zero. After appealing, she was given a resit, but was only allowed a third-class degree. Regulation 6.5.4 said a resit 'shall not normally' result in a higher grade, but expressly left open the possibility that it could. Ms Clark claimed this was a breach of contract. The university argued any claim in contract was an abuse of process, because the limit for judicial review is three months and for contract is six years. The Court of Appeal rejected the university's attempt to strike out the claim. The court said it 'will not involve itself with issues that involve making academic judgments' but would require adherence to its own rules. The university was 'a statutory body with public functions', but also with a 'fee-paying student' there

[147] CA 2006, ss. 171–3. [148] E.g. *Equitable Life Assurance Society v Hyman* [2000] UKHL 39.
[149] (1723) 93 ER 698.
[150] *Clark v University of Lincolnshire and Humberside* [2000] EWCA Civ 129.
[151] T. Williams, 'A Streetcar Named Desire' (1947).

is a contract.[152] However, as Sedley LJ said, the 'single important difference between judicial review and civil suit' was 'the differing time limits' and to allow 'a public law challenge to be brought as of right up to six years later if the relationship happens also to be contractual will in many cases circumvent' the three-month limit in judicial review.[153] On the facts, it was just to extend the time limit, and not 'to stifle on procedural grounds'.[154] Time limits aside, *Clark* shows how 'public' law and 'private' contract claims serve identical functions and should be construed as a consistent whole.

Similarly, in *R (Persaud) v University of Cambridge*, an astronomy Ph.D. student claimed judicial review after her graduate status was ended.[155] The university's General Regulation 10 conferred a power on the Board of Graduate Studies to withdraw graduate status if not working satisfactorily or not complying with conditions. As Persaud's progress apparently stalled, conditions were imposed and then her status was withdrawn, but she contended that she had been given no chance to make representations and the Board failed to read material she submitted. Overturning the High Court's refusal,[156] Chadwick LJ held the board acted unfairly and quashed the decision because fairness required a hearing and a response to the allegation that materials had not been read. Echoing similar statements in *Clark*, it was emphasised that 'this case is not . . . a challenge to academic judgment; it is a challenge to the process by which it was determined that she should not be reinstated'.[157] It follows that procedures requiring academic judgment are not second guessed, but process will be.[158]

Because court is likely to be time-consuming, and unsatisfactory in practice, each university should also follow a statutory complaints mechanism. Before 2004, a 'visitor' delegated by the Privy Council could adjudicate disputes in universities not only for students but also staff, with decisions counting as a judicial act (albeit subject to review).[159] This was abolished,[160] and now the Office of the Independent Adjudicator (OIA) can receive complaints about

[152] [2000] EWCA Civ 129, [12] and [14].

[153] [2000] EWCA Civ 129, [17]. See now Civil Procedure Rules 1998, Part 24 and, at the time, RSC Order 53, rule 4(1).

[154] [2000] EWCA Civ 129, [18]. Ward LJ and Lord Woolf MR agreed.

[155] *R (Persaud) v University of Cambridge* [2001] EWCA Civ 534.

[156] The refusal was made by Maurice Kay J.

[157] [2001] EWCA Civ 534, [41]. May LJ and Schiemann LJ agreed.

[158] E.g. *Gajree v Open University* [2006] EWCA Civ 831, rejecting an M.Sc. student's challenge to a 38% mark because they were 'essentially complaints about academic matters . . . not a proper basis for judicial review'. The student in fact arrived late to the Court of Appeal hearing, interrupting the judgment of Rix LJ.

[159] Most cases concerned staff, e.g. *R (Page) v Lord President of the Privy Council* [1993] AC 682, on a lecturer's challenge to being dismissed not for 'good cause', as university statutes said, but redundancy, but limiting judicial review to the visitor acting outside power; *Hines v Birkbeck College* [1986] Ch 524, per Hoffmann J, on an economics professor claiming about dismissal; *Philips v Bury* (1694) 90 ER 198, on a rector's ejection from Exeter College, Oxford.

[160] Higher Education Act 2004, s. 20.

a university, but not if 'it relates to matters of academic judgment'.[161] The OIA requires that universities have a first-instance complaint procedure, and if this does not solve the issues, the student can complain to the OIA, which writes a report each year.[162] Like any other public body, challenging the OIA's decisions in judicial review requires showing decisions are irrational.[163] Complaints have been rising alongside rising tuition fees, and law, business and international students appear most likely to lodge grievances.[164] It is unclear whether consumer rights are useful to improve student standards, compared to finance and governance reform.

(ii) Equal Treatment

The second main right is to be treated equally. This is implicit in judicial review as a rational part of the exercise of discretion.[165] The history of access to education has been founded upon religious,[166] sex,[167] race[168] and wealth discrimination, but the law today has established some basic rights. The Equality Act 2010, sections 91–4 require equality in access and treatment at any university based on the six standard protected characteristics,[169] while marriage and civil partnership are excluded to enable extra benefits to be given to such students, for instance childcare.[170] This prohibits direct discrimination and indirect discrimination (see Ch. 5(2)(d)). Indirect discrimination is likely to be more prevalent, where neutral rules put some groups at a particular disadvantage. Schedule 12 lists exceptions, including single-sex institutions if 'numbers are comparatively small', essentially to allow three surviving all-women colleges in Cambridge to continue.[171] It also allows institutions 'with a religious ethos' to discriminate, presumably for people who may actually work in the church.[172] As exceptions to the general rule of equal access, they should be construed narrowly. Universities also have a duty, important in practice, to ensure that reasonable adjustments are made for any student with a recognised disability.[173]

[161] Higher Education Act 2004, ss. 12 (qualifying complaints), 13 (Secretary of State designates complaint body).

[162] Higher Education Act 2004, s. 14 and Sch. 3, para. 6.

[163] E.g. *R (Thilakawardhana) v Office of the Independent Adjudicator for Higher Education* [2018] EWCA Civ 13, which upheld the OIA's decision to affirm a medical student's exclusion, after he posted a Facebook meme saying 'I will find you. And I will kill you' towards another student, who circulated explicit pictures of the claimant's friend.

[164] OIA, *Annual Report 2017* (April 2018) 14.

[165] See *Matadeen v Pointu* [1998] UKPC 9, per Lord Hoffmann.

[166] E.g. before the University Tests Act 1871 religious discrimination had been allowed.

[167] E.g. the first university to award degrees to women was the University of London in 1869.

[168] E.g. *Brown v Board of Education of Topeka*, 347 US 483 (1954).

[169] Equality Act 2010, ss. 5–12: age, disability, race, belief, sex (and gender reassignment) and sexual orientation.

[170] Equality Act 2010, s. 90 and Sch. 12, paras. 6 and 7.

[171] These are Lucy Cavendish, Murray Edwards and Newnham College.

[172] Equality Act 2010, Sch. 12, para. 5. This excludes 'a course of vocational training'.

[173] Equality Act 2010, ss. 6, 15, 20–2 and Sch. 13.

The major limit to equal treatment is that the current structure of UK universities, and their reliance on fees, entails direct wealth discrimination. For example, Oxford records that over 40 per cent of home students attended private schools, compared to 6 per cent of the UK school population.[174] It fails to record the school background of non-UK students, over 20 per cent of entrants. Ex-state school students outperform ex-private school students in university by a statistically significant margin of 4 per cent,[175] despite the financial privileges, housing luxury and reduced financial stress that wealthier students will have during their studies. Tuition fees also deter poorer students from applying to university,[176] and compound stress and disadvantage throughout study. This may produce indirect discrimination for other protected characteristics – a statistical disparity in students entering university. Few if any cases have yet been brought, as many universities aim to address disparities in race, gender and religion. There appears to be less positive action, however, on the basis of wealth. This means that where wealth and race, gender or religion intersect, the roots of inequality are ignored.

While international human rights instruments contain the right to access university education on the basis of 'merit', there is no such legal guarantee in UK statute. On the other hand, although untested, the European Convention on Human Rights (ECHR), Protocol 1, article 1, says 'No person shall be denied the right to education', while ECHR, article 14 says there is a further right to suffer no discrimination 'on any ground' or 'status' including 'property'. Could this enable a human-rights-based challenge to tuition fees, on the ground that fees discriminate against people based on class, wealth and income? This could be possible, although it has to be said that the European Court of Human Rights has exercised extreme caution, and may be less likely than Parliament to act fast, even though it could.

(iii) Quality and Competence

An obvious right of students is not merely to receive 'education of [no] particular type or at [no] particular level',[177] but of quality, competence and ideally of a kind that enlightens the human condition. One cannot, of course, expect every teacher to be a Blackstone, Einstein or Wittgenstein, and by all accounts the research geniuses just listed were somewhat erratic as teachers. These are standards analogous to the general duty of care and skill, or at least to refrain from negligence, found in common law and equity.

[174] University of Oxford, *Annual Admissions Statistical Report* (May 2018) 16. F. Green and D. Kynaston, *Engines of Privilege: Britain's Private School Problem* (2019).

[175] Higher Education Funding Council for England, *Differences in Degree Outcome: Key Findings* (2014); and see J. Grove, 'State Pupils on Same Grades as Private Counterparts "Get Better Degrees"', *The Times* (28 March 2014).

[176] E.g. Callender and Jackson, 'Does the Fear of Debt Deter Students from Higher Education?'; Hübner, 'Do Tuition Fees Affect Enrollment Behavior?'

[177] *Belgian Linguistic case (No. 2)* (1968) 1 EHRR 252, [3].

The best assurances of quality are unlikely to be litigation, but instead a culture of care and attention, as well as sufficient resources. There appear to be few, if any, reported cases on lack of care in universities. However, *The Times* in 2002 reported that one Mr Austen succeeded in settling for £30,000 a claim that, when he arrived to study law at the University of Wolverhampton, modules were unavailable, classes overcrowded, lecturers did not turn up, the library was understocked and the university failed to take complaints seriously.[178] By contrast, in *Abramova v Oxford Institute of Legal Practice* the High Court rejected the claim of a Legal Practice Course student that guidance on taking exams, or giving feedback, fell below a reasonable standard. According to Burnett J, the claimant was 'ready to blame anyone but herself for her misfortunes'.[179]

In another, perhaps optimistic judgment, *Siddiqui v University of Oxford*, while ultimately rejecting a student's claim for negligent teaching, Foskett J noted that 'when students are incurring substantial debts to pursue their university education, the quality of the education delivered will undoubtedly come under even greater scrutiny than it did in the past'.[180] The case concerned a modern history student who graduated with a low 2:1 in 2000. Siddiqui alleged that he would have received a high 2:1 or first-class degree, and would have had a better chance of getting into Harvard, Yale or another US law school, had he received adequate teaching and had his college tutor shown more concern about his insomnia, depression and anxiety. The claim failed because it was not established that teaching was inadequate, and his applications to US law schools would have been rejected for reasons additional to Siddiqui's grades. 'Litigation is costly', remarked Foskett J in conclusion, and there 'must be a better way of dealing with this kind of issue'.[181]

(iv) No Conflicts of Interest

While most university life is free from conflicts of interest, there may be some. In contrast to conflicts of interest claims in company law,[182] and other fields of judicial review,[183] there are few, if any, cases on successful claims of bias of staff towards students in examinations.[184] Most institutions have in place systems

[178] *The Times* (1 February 2002). After changing to Bristol, he tried to sue Wolverhampton for defamation, breach of confidence and privacy, but the claims failed: *Austen v University of Wolverhampton* [2005] EWHC 1635 (QB).

[179] *Abramova v Oxford Institute of Legal Practice* [2011] EWHC 613 (QB), [52].

[180] *Siddiqui v University of Oxford* [2018] EWHC 184 (QB), [244], on 'gobbet'. Papers at Brasenose, Oxford.

[181] *Siddiqui v University of Oxford*, [244]. [182] CA 2006, s. 175; see Ch. 3(4)(d).

[183] E.g. *Dimes v Grand Junction Canal* (1852) 3 HLC 759 (a judge that was a shareholder in a company had to decline to hear a case); *R (Pinochet Urgarte) v Bow Street Stipendiary Magistrate (No. 2)* [2000] 1 AC 119 (a judgment to extradite the Chilean dictator had to be reheard as Lord Hoffmann was involved in Amnesty International).

[184] Cf. *R v Leeds Metropolitan University ex p Manders* [1998] ELR 502, a claim of bias failing on procedural grounds.

to pre-empt any appearance of bias or unconscious bias. These include anonymous marking, second marking and a third opinion for borderline exams. Most teachers encounter the fact that they may guess from style, substance or perhaps handwriting which students have written what in small groups, but this becomes difficult or impossible in large lectures. Invariably teachers doing marking have neither the desire nor the time to guess, let alone prejudge a candidate. Thus, it may be argued that the best safeguard against bias is an institutional culture that promotes fair judgement, and a desire to ensure that every student succeeds well before exams or assessments take place.

On the other hand, UK universities have generally held onto written exams unlike, for example, American universities where typed exams are standard.[185] Moreover, unconscious bias is a systemic problem that may also manifest itself in classroom discussion and result in an atmosphere of exclusion if certain voices are allowed to dominate, or if topics for discussion are framed with stereotypical assumptions about gender, race, religion, disability, sexual orientation or class. This issue, of course, is also a problem among student bodies, which systematically rate non-male, non-white lecturers lower than others.[186] By contrast, when lecturers rate themselves, a notorious US study in 1977 found, 94 per cent believed themselves to be above average.[187] Different countries will differ, and can improve over time if proactive steps are taken. For such systemic problems, a solution likely involves workplace equality law (Ch. 5(2)(d)), and the portrayal of people in the media (Ch. 17(4)), while abandoning the use of personal rankings and reducing hierarchy.

In the case of Ph.D. examination, where the viva is face to face, students and supervisors will usually suggest examiners that are likely to be experts in the field – this is a chance to not propose examiners that may be unsympathetic to the thesis. But in order to pre-empt favouritism, universities will then review the proposed examiners and exclude those with links to the Ph.D. candidate or supervisors, such as jointly written publications or extended research co-operation.

Among staff members, a promotion decision will have to be reheard if a hostile colleague takes part in a review.[188] Educational institutions themselves may also complain of bias, for instance where the panel giving a rating for funding could have 'unintentional bias' through its composition. Even if there is no free-standing duty to give reasons for decisions, a public body must 'account intelligibly for their decisions by explaining not simply how but why

[185] Cf. Equality Act 2010, ss. 20–1, which requires reasonable adjustments for students with disabilities, which may include personalised exam arrangements, such as typing.

[186] K. M. W. Mitchell and J. Martin, 'Gender Bias in Student Evaluations' (2018) 51(3) *Political Science & Politics* 648, a study in the US; Y. Fan et al., 'Gender and Cultural Bias in Student Evaluations: Why Representation Matters' (2019) 14(2) *Plos One* 1, a study in Australia.

[187] K. P. Cross, 'Not Can, But Will College Teaching Be Improved?' (1977) 17 *New Directions for Higher Education* 1, 10. Some 68% also ranked themselves as being in the top quarter.

[188] *R (Evans) v University of Cambridge* [1998] Ed CR 151, [1998] ELR 515 (a promotion to readership in history).

they have reached them'.[189] The reality of funding decisions and panels, of course, is that monetary allocations involve intense lobbying and ongoing attempts to get staff from institutions into the right places. Bar some unexpected change, this results in a roughly identical perpetuation in the existing distribution of funding. Structural bias may be unavoidable to the extent that a university finance system is dependent on expert research evaluation, rather than one determined by objective priorities or educational need.

(b) School Student Rights

As with university students, there is not yet a codified charter of school student rights; rather, there is a large mass of sometimes weak standards. As in universities and judicial review generally, there is a basic right to have the rules and law followed, although the House of Lords has emphasised that, while decision-makers must take rights into account, they cannot always 'be expected to make such decisions with textbooks on human rights law at their elbows'.[190] Stepping back, the most important rights for the quality of education are (i) class sizes, (ii) admissions and equal treatment and (iii) standards of teaching. There are also multiple individual rights such as free school meals[191] and medical services,[192] or in the fair handling of disputes that arise from time to time.[193]

(i) Class Sizes

Class sizes and the attention that teachers can devote to each individual school student are crucial for education. Although there have been multiple attempts to argue it does not matter at all, largely motivated by money, modern empirical evidence shows that smaller class sizes have a significant positive impact on learning outcomes, which range from small to large depending on the study.[194] However (and if this was not already obvious to students and teachers involved), the positive impacts of outcomes with smaller groups increase the more complex a subject becomes. Additional benefits of smaller groups include the ease for teachers to maintain a harmonious learning environment, and the psychological well-being of both staff and students. In

189 *R (Institute for Dental Surgery) v Universities Funding Council* [1994] 1 WLR 242.

190 *R (Begum) v Governors of Denbigh High School* [2006] UKHL 15.

191 School Standards and Framework Act 1998, s. 114; Requirements for School Food Regulations 2014; and dating back to Education (Provision of Meals) Act 1906.

192 Education (Administrative Provisions) Act 1907, introduced medical services.

193 *Board of Education v Rice* [1911] AC 179 (the Board had to give a fair hearing, and an opportunity to the parties to correct or contradict any relevant statement that prejudiced them).

194 E.g. J. Francis and W. S. Barnett, 'Relating Preschool Class Size to Classroom Quality and Student Achievement' (2019) 49 *Early Childhood Research Q* 49; N. Koc and B. Celik, 'The Impact of Number of Students per Teacher on Student Achievement' (2015) 177 *Procedia – Social and Behavioral Sciences* 65.

2018, the UK had among the worst averages in the Organisation for Economic Co-operation and Development (OECD), with a ratio of 23 students per teacher in early childhood education, 19.9 per teacher in primary, and 17.1 per teacher in secondary schools,[195] although these statistics appear to include teachers who are not teaching. According to the Department for Education, the average size for early and primary classes is 27.1, and for secondary school it is 21.7.[196] The only legal requirement is for children aged 5 to 7 ('infants') to have a class size limit of thirty,[197] a standard that has not changed for around a century.

(ii) Admissions and Equal Treatment

A second key right is to be admitted to a school, and to equal treatment throughout. Local authorities have a duty to respect parental preferences on where their child goes to school,[198] but it ultimately decides, and schools themselves put up considerable barriers. As noted above, the UK has a substantial fee-charging school sector, which directly discriminates against children on the basis of parental wealth. By contrast, the most successful school systems tend to have large, well-funded public systems, and do not segregate children on the basis of parental wealth.[199] UK schools also widely segregate based on gender, and to a more limited extent based on religion. The Equality Act 2010 prohibits discrimination based on the protected characteristics of race and makes exemptions for single-sex schools, religious schools and disability for the purpose of selection.[200] It also fails to cover wealth discrimination. In other words, discrimination and segregation is a rampant, inherent feature of UK schools, which in the end holds back the potential of every child.

UK school admissions policy still allows for 'grammar' schools to maintain a practice of 'selective admission' for only those children who pass a test.[201] While the thinking has historically been that children will perform better if placed in groups at their same level, this has been problematic for four reasons. First, children change and develop at different speeds. Test performance at age 11 may say very little about that child's potential relative to others by age 14 or 17. Second, children may test well in one subject, such as maths, but less well in others, such as English, but selective schools segregate across the board. Third, a negative stigma results from school segregation. Fourth, the best systems of education do not segregate schools, but provide smaller class sizes for personalised advancement at every stage. It is possible to have different groupings

[195] OECD Data, 'Students per Teaching Staff' (2020).
[196] Department for Education, 'Schools, Pupils and Their Characteristics: January 2019' (27 June 2019).
[197] School Standards and Framework Act 1998, ss. 1–4.
[198] School Standards and Framework Act 1998, s. 86. [199] Crehan, *Cleverlands*.
[200] Equality Act 2010, ss. 84–5 and Sch. 11.
[201] School Standards and Framework Act 1998, s. 104, designation of grammar schools with 'selective admission'.

within schools (for instance, standard, middle and advanced maths groups) without the stigma, to be sensitive to subject and flexibly accommodate students' changing progress. While selection based upon merit becomes a basic part of applying for jobs or universities as an adult, schools are there to develop merit, not select it. Segregation brings everyone down.[202]

(iii) Standards of Teaching

A third key right is to a high standard of education. This should accommodate 'the general principle that pupils are to be educated in accordance with the wishes of their parents', and this may ring particularly importantly for spiritual or religious teaching.[203] The school should take account of, but is not obliged to give effect to, parents' wishes.[204] Ultimately, parental voice within the governance structure is the most important way to give effect to this right. Generally, the National Curriculum is set and revised by the Secretary of State (again depending on networks of teaching commissioners) as is thought to be expedient.[205] The curriculum in the UK currently has five 'key stages' from 5 to 18 years old, which require English, maths and science up to final year; history, geography, language, design, art, music and sport up to the ninth year; and computing, 'citizenship' and 'careers' in later years. In the final year of school, A-Levels enable an inordinate degree of specialisation, with as few as three subjects, in contrast to broader systems of the International Baccalaureate (IB). This has caused more UK schools to shift to the IB.

Probably the most important mechanism to ensure higher standards of teaching is to pay teachers more money, invest in their education, and reduce working hours and reduce needless administrative tasks that are often used for monitoring school performance or league tables. Under the Education Act 2002, the Secretary of State can prescribe certain levels of staffing for schools and qualifications for teachers,[206] yet there is scant attention to raising pay, reducing working time and eliminating barriers to teaching. The Secretary of State may require local authorities to appraise teacher performance.[207] In addition, the Office for Standards in Education, Children's Services and Skills or 'Ofsted' undertakes regular inspections of schools, and has powers to intervene and ultimately recommend 'special measures' or closure of schools that are 'failing'.[208] The problem is that this focuses unnecessary attention on motivation through punitive measures, which work less well

[202] Cf. *Griggs v Duke Power Co.*, 401 US 424 (1971) showing data for North Carolina's segregated school system, and achievement levels there for both black and white people being vastly lower than non-segregated states.

[203] EA 1996, s. 9. [204] *Watt v Kesteven CC* [1955] 1 QB 408. [205] EA 2002, s. 87(1).

[206] EA 2002, ss. 132–5. [207] EA 2002, s. 131.

[208] Education and Inspections Act 2006, ss. 17, 61–9, 112–36. Also Academies Act 2010, s. 4(A1) (school needing significant improvement or special measures).

than investing money to ensure people want to become and stay working as a teacher.

(5) Conclusion

The most salient feature of education is the gap between the rights enshrined in international law, and the practice in the UK, a gap seen in many other countries. First, to uphold international law, there is a need to progressively eliminate fees for education, particularly at universities, to relieve students who start careers with mountains of debt. An integrated system of lifelong adult education is also needed, so that people who do not – or may not want to – go to university after school have the option later in life. Second, to ensure the most innovative, efficient and productive use of resources, it is necessary to reform governance, especially since the most successful universities are the most democratic. Third, and more generally, there is a serious problem with enabling any educational institution, but particularly schools where children have no choice, to continue discriminatory admission practices, on the basis of either wealth, gender or religion. The right of parents 'to choose the kind of education that shall be given to their children' can be accommodated within a non-discriminatory system,[209] and the evidence shows this improves outcomes. The problem of cross-border flows of international students need not be coupled to forced-fee access. A system of international treaties could enable reciprocal access for study, with a commitment of countries to share and settle the costs of funding on an annual basis.

[209] UDHR 1948, art. 26(1).

9

Health and Care

Contents

'Restoration of a sick person to health', wrote Lord Beveridge in 1942, 'is a duty of the State and the sick person, prior to any other consideration.'[1] When the Minister for Health, Nye Bevan, introduced the National Health Service Act 1946, he said it was 'repugnant to a civilised community for hospitals to have to rely upon private charity', and that 'money ought not to be permitted to stand in the way of obtaining an efficient health service'.[2] Today, most countries have universal healthcare (large exceptions are the USA, Nigeria and Indonesia). Most countries fulfil the universal human right to 'health and well-being' including 'medical care and necessary social services'.[3] But beyond these minimums, the UK also provides healthcare freely, without buying an insurance policy, and funds it with progressive tax. The main alternative to the UK's 'Beveridge' model is the 'Bismarck' model of insurance for health. Health insurance typically is acquired through work, family members or the state, if people cannot afford private or other insurance. However, insurance usually requires paying extra money for medicine, hospital or GP visits. The UK had an insurance system from 1911 to 1946,[4] but abandoned it for the National Health Service (NHS). The evidence shows that UK health, despite cuts and privatisation, has better outcomes in life-expectancy for less money (see Figure 9.1).

1 W. Beveridge, *Social Insurance and Allied Services*, Cmd 6404 (1942) Part VI, §427.

2 Mr Aneurin Bevan, National Health Service Bill, Hansard HC Debs. (30 April 1946) col. 43.

3 UDHR 1948, art. 25; ICESCR 1966, art. 12(2)(d); European Social Charter 1961, art. 13; CFREU 2000, art. 35; ECHR 1950, arts. 2, 3 and 8 (right to life, no torture, private and family life) recognise minimal standards.

4 National Insurance Act 1911, ss. 1–80.

The NHS is seen as one of the most important parts of the UK constitution,[5] yet the nature of the right to health is contested. Since 1982, the NHS has undergone continual restructuring.[6] From 2012 private finance accelerated, and governance was restructured, diminishing staff and patient voice. Ideological conflict remains over whether private provision in a health service is good, and what should be its extent (if any). Should private companies or insurers run any hospitals? Should social care be brought onto the NHS? Should charges for prescription medicine rise or go? NHS finances are decisively influenced by government public health policy – to promote a healthy environment, diet or lifestyle (Chs. 11–13 and 17–18) and accident prevention (Chs. 5 and 15) – and a population's age. The Covid-19 pandemic has magnified this fact, as the UK saw appalling death rates, due to a slow, confused, cynical government that prioritised the economy over health, and lost both.[7] Day-to-day use of resources will be affected by who has governance power beneath the Department of Health. The NHS does not have a settled governance structure, and it was only recently that an NHS 'constitution' and patient 'rights' were codified. The UK's comparative experience should be influential for the United Nations (UN) goal of 'universal health coverage' by 2030,[8] though the goals, like human rights, take no position on what healthcare systems may be better. The evidence, however, is ever more clear. Public health makes people well.

(1) Historical Background

Before the twentieth century, medical care was as limited as our understanding of human anatomy, disease and cure. The oldest written records discussing health were from ancient Egypt, the Kahun Papyrus, analysing women's health and problems in conception, and the Edwin Smith Papyrus discussing cures, ailments and anatomy.[9] In ancient Athens, the Hippocratic Corpus, composed by the physician Hippocrates and his students, collected sixty medical works from the time, categorising various illnesses.[10] The famous Hippocratic oath, usually attached to the corpus, exhorted physicians to hold teachers in esteem, teach without fees, help the sick and do no harm.[11]

[5] ICM, 'State of the Nation 2006' (October 2006) (88% said prompt NHS treatment should be in a Bill of Rights).

[6] C. Newdick, *Who Should We Treat?* (2005) 67 ('organisational upheaval' almost yearly).

[7] Cf. R. Shrimsley, 'For Boris Johnson, Covid-19 Is Now an Economic not a Health Crisis', *Financial Times* (1 June 2020).

[8] 2030 Agenda for Sustainable Development (2015) Goal 3.8.

[9] P. W. Brandt-Rauf and S. I. Brandt-Rauf, 'History of Occupational Medicine: Relevance of Imhotep and the Edwin Smith Papyrus' (1987) 44 *Brit J Industrial Medicine* 68.

[10] E.g. Hippocrates, *On Ancient Medicine* (380 BC) trans. F. Adams.

[11] Hippocrates, *The Oath* (380 BC): 'to teach [others] this art, if they want to learn it, without fee or indenture … I will use treatment to help the sick according to my ability and judgment, but never with a view to injury and wrong-doing. Neither will I administer a poison to anybody when asked to do so … I will enter to help the sick … .'

Building on the Greeks, a Roman physician named Galen produced what became the most important work until the Middle Ages, *On the Natural Faculties* (*c.* 200 AD).[12] The Greeks and Romans theorised that the body's four 'humours' had to be in balance for each person: red blood, yellow bile, black bile and phlegm. Supposedly, imbalance caused illness, and the humours were like the four 'elements' of wind, fire, earth and water. It was only in 1543 that Andrea Vesalius, working in Padua, showed how Galen's work was filled with at least 200 faults, and that the body was an interdependent system of organs.[13]

Without any serious medicine or care, recurrent pandemics were a fact of life. The Black Death of 1347–51 killed a third of Europe and half of London.[14] By 1600, with London's population around 200,000, there were just 500 medical practitioners, and all had to be paid for.[15] There were probably 800 physicians in the whole country.[16] Bills of Mortality showed 15,003 died from plague in 1593, 33,347 in 1603, 41,313 in 1625 and over 14,000 between 1640 and 1647. Average life expectancy was 30–40 years. Common methods of 'treatment' for all things were to bleed a patient, make them vomit or sweat, or administer whacky pills, powders or ointments – most of which were useless or damaging. The Great Plague of London starting in 1665 killed a quarter of its population (around 100,000), and people still believed that herbs or posies might ward off disease.[17] The City and government had no legislative measures to care for people or control the plague, except draconian quarantines: people had to get a certificate of good health from the Lord Mayor to escape.[18] According to Samuel Pepys' diary, 'in Westminster, there is never a physician and but one apothecary left, all being dead'.[19] It was the last major plague, but after it the Great Fire of 1666 burnt much of the City to the ground. London was rebuilt, with effort in Sir Christopher Wren's designs to promote wider avenues and public amenities,[20] although most of the street planning failed to pass, with property

12 C. Galenus, *On the Natural Faculties* (1523) trans. A. J. Brock.

13 A. Vesalius, *De Humani Corporis Fabrica* (1543).

14 The bubonic plague killed unknown millions of people across Asia, and came to Europe through a Mongol army invading Crimea and catapulting infected bodies over city walls in 1347. (The first Mongol invasion of Europe had previously halted unexpectedly with the death of Ogedei Khan in 1241.) Escaping Genoese traders brought the plague into Western Europe and it spread through fleas, sometimes on rats.

15 C. Webster, 'Medical Practitioners' in *Health, Medicine, and Mortality in the Sixteenth Century* (1979) 183.

16 J. Lane, *A Social History of Medicine: Health, Healing and Disease, 1750–1950* (2001) 3–4.

17 'Ring-a-ring o' roses, A pocket full of posies, Atishoo, Atishoo, We all fall down.' This famous nursery rhyme was said in the 1940s to have come from the plague. This is thought to be false, although it is true that smells and miasmas were believed to keep the plague away. For this reason, people burned fires and smoked more.

18 J. Leasor, *The Plague and the Fire* (2005) ch. 3, 58.

19 S. Pepys, *Diary* (16 October 1665). Also D. Defoe, *Journal of the Plague Year* (1722) fictionalising the plague.

20 Rebuilding of London Act 1666.

owners' refusal to shift. Everyone, including royalty, continued to be at the mercy of what is now curable disease.[21]

Hospitals had been built since 936,[22] particularly to contain leprosy and syphilis. But there was no real healthcare, as opposed to the barest bones of charitable institutions, which were often preoccupied more with legal disputes than care.[23] The Hospitals for the Poor Acts enabled buildings, but what happened in these buildings was another matter.[24] The Act for the Relief of the Poor 1601 was supposed to give 'necessary relief of the lame, impotent, old, blind and such other among them being poor and not able to work'.[25] But little if anything was done for sickness. When the Poor Law Commission of 1834 reviewed the law, there was no reference to health because 'treatment of sick persons was … hardly recognised as important, either from a curative or a preventative standpoint'.[26] After the Poor Law Amendment Act 1834, workhouses ran medical 'relief' in a room dedicated to inmates who fell ill (usually because of overwork). It was supervised by a local doctor contracted by a Board of Guardians. The Boards could give a Medical Order to an ill person and provide relief through money or food, but would typically do so on loan, and would threaten to recover costs.[27] This made people indebted, which often led to debtors' prison (Ch. 1(2)).

Nevertheless, the creation of standing institutions may have affected the development of modern medicine. The London Dispensary in 1696 gave medicine to poor, sick people, and the great hospitals such as St Mary's Bethlehem, St Thomas's, Guy's and St George's in the seventeenth and eighteenth centuries.[28] Their work was limited to those who could pay or find charity, but medical advances included finding causes or cures discovered for scurvy in 1752, smallpox in 1796 and cholera in 1854.[29] Modern methods for

[21] E.g. in 1502 Henry VII's son, Prince Arthur, died of sweating sickness. In 1612, James I's son died of typhus. In 1694, Queen Mary died of smallpox.

[22] E.g. Hospital of St Peter and St Leonard in York (est. 936); St Mary Magdalene, Ripon (est. 1139); Christ's hospital, Durham (est. 1181); Burton Lazars, Leicestershire (est. 1138–62).

[23] E.g. *Case of Sutton's Hospital* (1612) 77 Eng Rep 960, where heirs to a charitable donor, who set up a hospital and school at Charterhouse, unsuccessfully argued the entity had no legal personality and the transfer was void.

[24] E.g. Hospitals for the Poor Act 1572, Hospitals for the Poor Act 1597 and Hospitals Act 1623.

[25] Act for the Relief of the Poor 1601 (43 Eliz., c. 2).

[26] S. Webb and B. Webb, *The Break-up of the Poor Law* (1909) ch. 5, 212–13.

[27] Webb and Webb, *The Break-up of the Poor Law*, 213.

[28] St Mary's of Bethlehem (est. 1247), St Thomas's (rebuilt 1693–1709), Guy's (est. 1721–4), St George's (est. 1733), London (est. 1740) and Middlesex (est. 1745). Note that Thomas Guy took his wealth from the slave-trading South Sea Company. At the time of writing there is a movement to rename the hospital, and relocate Guy's statue to a suitable museum where the crime against humanity can be understood in context.

[29] John Lind's identification of scurvy led the Royal Navy to bring fruit on long voyages. Edward Jenner found that cowpox protected humans from smallpox. John Snow found cholera was caused by filthy water from the pump on Broad Street, Soho.

surgery were developed from 1739,[30] and nursing by Mary Seacole and Florence Nightingale at St Thomas's from 1860.[31] Life expectancy, however, remained flat until the first Public Health Act 1848 authorised local health boards to be established with powers to secure adequate water supply, if a new General Health Board recommended and 10 per cent of ratepayers petitioned.[32] After legislative efforts to limit profits of water companies failed (see Ch. 13(1)), the Public Health Act 1875 created a duty on local authorities to supply adequate running water and drainage, have a medical officer and sanitary inspector, pave streets and prohibit poor house building.[33] The Public Health Act 1904 required filthy housing be shut, and imposed liability on landlords for tenant health.[34] This coincided with improvements in infant mortality. Still people lacked care, and were victims of quack medicine like the infamous Carbolic Smoke Ball for flu outbreak.[35] Changes in life expectancy and infant mortality needed both public health and adequate healthcare (see Figure 9.1).[36]

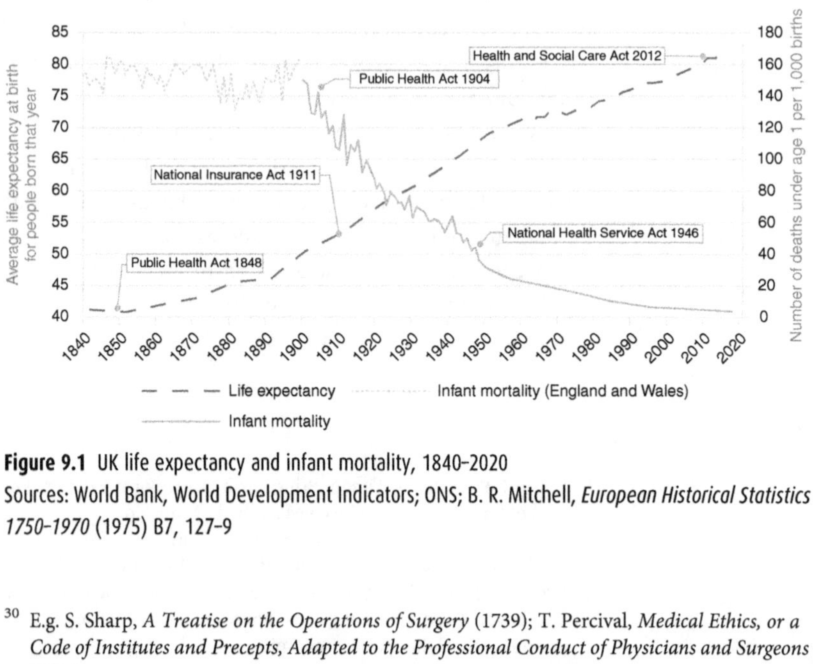

Figure 9.1 UK life expectancy and infant mortality, 1840–2020
Sources: World Bank, World Development Indicators; ONS; B. R. Mitchell, *European Historical Statistics 1750–1970* (1975) B7, 127–9

30 E.g. S. Sharp, *A Treatise on the Operations of Surgery* (1739); T. Percival, *Medical Ethics, or a Code of Institutes and Precepts, Adapted to the Professional Conduct of Physicians and Surgeons* (1803).

31 See also M. Seacole, *Wonderful Adventures of Mrs. Seacole in Many Lands* (1857) chs. 8ff, on the Crimean War.

32 Public Health Act 1848, 11 & 12 Vict., c. 63; Public Health Act 1866.

33 E.g. Public Health Act 1875, ss. 13 and 35 (no building without toilets). Also Public Health (London) Act 1891.

34 Also the Public Health Act 1936, s. 14 (general duty on local authorities for sewerage).

35 *Carlill v Carbolic Smoke Ball Co.* [1892] EWCA Civ 1, [1893] 1 QB 256. Also noteworthy is that the most famous tort case *Donoghue v Stevenson* [1931] UKHL 3, [1932] AC 562 was a health case in failed consumer law.

36 See also, https://ourworldindata.org/life-expectancy and https://ourworldindata.org/child-mortality.

The National Insurance Act 1911 was the first healthcare system. This was similar to Bismarck's state insurance system in Germany from 1883, which had aimed to ward off social democracy.[37] By 1911, UK residents had been sold 40 million private insurance policies, often just covering funeral fees, for horrendous rates of industrial injury, disease, dangerous products and accelerating road accidents. Four major insurers – Prudential, Royal Liver, Liverpool Victoria and Pearl – had, in David Lloyd George's words, 'an army numbering scores, if not hundreds of thousands, of agents and collectors who make a living out of collecting a few pence a week from millions of households'. Up to 50 per cent of receipts were used to administer insurance and 'poor widows and children [were] by this extravagant system robbed of one half of the benefits'.[38] The National Insurance Act 1911 originally proposed health insurance to be democratically administered by membership-led friendly societies.[39] But because of their lobbying, health came to be provided through insurance companies. This was progress: social security was entirely crushed in the USA until 1935, and excluded health even then.[40] The Ministry of Health Act 1919, section 2 also empowered ministers to take 'measures conducive to the health of the people', including preventing and curing disease, 'treatment of physical and mental defects, the treatment and care of the blind' and research. But national health insurance only covered a third of people to begin with, and half by 1945. This gap impelled cross-party proposals for an NHS.[41]

The NHS Act 1946 replaced private insurance and hospitals with publicly funded hospitals and care. Doctors in general practice remained independent contractors with the NHS, but to win their acquiescence the Minister for Health, Nye Bevan, said he had 'stuffed their mouths with gold'.[42] For those who complained about the NHS being too big, Bevan's answer was he was not 'a devotee of bigness for bigness sake' but he 'would rather be kept alive in the

[37] Sickness insurance in 1883 (Gesetz betreffend die Krankenversicherung der Arbeiter vom 15. Juni 1883), accident insurance in 1884, old age and disability insurance in 1889. See E. McGaughey, 'The Codetermination Bargains: The History of German Corporate and Labour Law' (2016) 23(1) *Columbia J Eur L* 135, 151.

[38] B. B. Gilbert, 'The British National Insurance Act of 1911 and the Commercial Insurance Lobby' (1965) 4(2) *J Brit Studies* 127, 134, quoting the Cricceth Memorandum (17 August 1910).

[39] Cf. National Insurance Act 1911, ss. 23–9; and cf. Gilbert, 'The British National Insurance Act of 1911'.

[40] E. Sydenstricker, 'Public Health Provisions of the Social Security Act' (1936) 3(2) *L & Contemporary Problems* 263, saying that healthcare was not included to leave 'the medical profession to study the matter'.

[41] W. Beveridge, *Social Insurance and Allied Services*, Cmd 6404 (1942) and *A National Health Service*, Cmd 6502 (1944) 47, proposed three freedoms of (1) the doctor and patient to use or not use the public service, (2) patient choice of doctor and doctor's ability to refuse patients and (3) doctor's pursuit of own professional methods. Today these freedoms appear subject to the need to provide healthcare.

[42] B. Abel-Smith, *The Hospitals in England and Wales: 1800–1948* (1964) 480, appears to be the first attribution. Bevan is reported to have said this at a Manchester hospital on the NHS's first day in 1948, referring to the British Medical Association of that era.

efficient if cold altruism of a large hospital than expire in a gush of warm sympathy in a small one'.[43] Bevan said the system of young people getting 'a load of debt around [their necks] in order to practise is an altogether evil one'.[44] (See Ch. 8(2)(a)(iii).) He said doctors should have 'full participation in the administration of their own profession' and wanted to ensure that 'communal interests' would 'be safeguarded'. The NHS Act 1946 created fourteen Regional Hospital Boards that paid for staff, buildings and equipment at hospitals. Each had a chair and members appointed by the minister 'as he thinks fit', but consulting the board and with two members experienced in mental health.[45] It gave grants to local councils to run health centres, overseen by Executive Councils for General Medical Services.[46] Thus, health followed the Morrisonian model of governance (see Ch. 1(3)), pledging staff and patient 'involvement' but leaving key appointments dominated by the Health Minister or Whitehall. Despite his success, and the model of free public health followed the world over, Bevan resigned in 1951 in protest over the cabinet's decision to bring back prescription charges for dental and optical health.[47]

In the post-war era, the first NHS's first major change was the NHS Reorganisation Act 1973. This renamed regional hospital boards as Regional Health Authorities, while 90 Area Health Authorities and 205 District Health Authorities took over from local health authorities. Labour continued this system but also in 1974 commissioned a report on Democracy in the NHS. The 'separation of functions' between management, staff and patients, it said, should not be allowed to 'challenge in a fundamental way the essence of democratic control'. It said 'real devolution to those operating the service' was needed.[48] The result, however, rather than giving staff or patient groups votes was to increase local government representation in the 90 Area Health Authorities to one third.[49] In 1982, Area Health Authorities were subsumed into District Health Authorities, but the Thatcher government did not attempt to privatise the NHS as it had most other sectors (see Ch. 1(3)). This was probably because, as Thatcher's Treasurer, Norman Lamont, complained, the NHS is 'the closest thing the English people have now to a religion'.[50]

Although not privatised, the National Health Service Community and Care Act 1990 required an 'internal market' to be created in the NHS, so that different bodies had to price and account for all transactions, and it allowed the creation of NHS Trusts to run hospitals and borrow privately.[51] From the Blair government in 1997, these basic structures were extended using private

[43] Mr Aneurin Bevan, National Health Service Bill, Hansard HC Debs. (30 April 1946) col. 43.
[44] Bevan, National Health Service Bill, col. 55. [45] NHS Act 1946, ss. 11, 53 and Sch. 3.
[46] NHS Act 1946, ss. 19, 52 and Schs. 4–5.
[47] Cf. Bevan, HC Debs. (30 April 1946) col. 43: 'The condition of the teeth of the people of Britain is a national reproach.'
[48] 'Democracy in the National Health Service', C(74)49 (21 May 1974).
[49] NHS Act 1977, Sch. 5, para. 2.
[50] N. Lawson, *The View from No. 11: Memoirs of a Tory Radical* (1992) 613.
[51] National Health Service Community and Care Act 1990 (c. 19) s. 9 and Sch. 3.

finance, and allowing an 'open market' so that private companies could bid to perform work.[52] Labour changed health authorities into Primary Care Trusts (PCTs), and required more staff and patient representation, albeit not in a systematic way (cf. Ch. 9(3)(c)). The major reform, however, came with the Conservative and Liberal Democrat government in the Health and Social Care Act (HSCA) 2012. While private work had been held below 2 per cent of total work, this opened private provision of UK health up to a 49 per cent limit.[53] This Act, which intended to have no cap at all, was met with enormous staff and political protest. Since 2010, and with limited investment, NHS costs rose and outcomes worsened. Since 2012, life expectancy has stagnated in the UK (see Figure 9.1). The contributions to this multi-causal phenomenon probably include the legislative changes to health, as well as the 'austerity' programme of cuts to welfare, diesel fraud (see Ch. 15(2)(a)) or other air pollution. Meanwhile, political figures still argue for NHS privatisation to closed business groups, but publicly deny it.[54]

(2) Finance

Financing of the NHS is probably the most contentious issue in modern politics. The key topics are (a) the extent of public health funding, in light of international comparisons; (b) the privatisation of service provision; (c) exceptional charges, including for foreign patients who fall ill whilst in the UK; (d) intellectual property policy; and (e) public health policy.

(a) Public Funding, Outcomes and International Comparison

Since its foundation, the NHS has been funded directly by the UK Treasury from general taxation, mostly from the Consolidated Fund, and partly the National Insurance fund (see Ch. 20). The NHS requires nobody to buy insurance, and the general principle is that nobody must pay up-front costs. This was not written into an Act, but after a proposal in 2008,[55] a new NHS Constitution for England stated in article 1(2) that access 'to NHS services is based on clinical need, not an individual's ability to pay'.[56]

The main chain of money starts with the Treasury allocating funds to the Department of Health. In 2019–2020 there was £166 billion in total spending, or 22 per cent of the government budget. In England, the Department gives

[52] J. Meek, 'It's Already Happened' (2011) 33(18) *London Rev Books* 3.

[53] Health and Social Care Act (HSCA) 2012, ss. 164–5, inserting NHS Act 2006, s. 43(2A); see Ch. 9(2)(b).

[54] E.g. R. Mason, 'Film Shows Nigel Farage Calling for Move Away from State-Funded NHS', *The Guardian* (12 November 2014), referring to a 2012 speech. A spokesperson for Forage said, 'That was then and this is now. It doesn't stand up to say that's still his view.'

[55] Department of Health, A Consultation on the NHS Constitution (2008).

[56] Department of Health, NHS Constitution for England (27 July 2015) art. 1(2).

funds to NHS England,[57] as well as the various supervisory bodies: National Institute for Health and Care Excellence (NICE), NHS Improvement, the CQC and Healthwatch (Ch. 9(3)(d)). Crucially, NHS England then distributes money to around 8,000 general practices and specialist doctors, and 106 Clinical Commissioning Groups (CCGs), companies organised mostly by GPs. At the time of writing, the Health and Care Bill 2021 proposed to replace CCGs with an expected forty-four 'Integrated Care Boards' (ICBs). Either ICBs or CCGs give money to 151 NHS Foundation Trusts in return for services that the trusts provide to people through their hospitals. The ICBs or CCGs buy or 'commission' services.[58] For instance, the 'Guy's and St Thomas's NHS Foundation Trust' runs Guy's Hospital near London Bridge, St Thomas's Hospital near Westminster Bridge and Evelina London Children's Hospital close by. In 2021, these got most funds from the NHS Lambeth CCG and NHS Southwark CCG.[59] They take patients who are referred from GPs in those areas, but may also have patients referred from GPs elsewhere if those patients choose. These look set to be replaced by forty-four ICBs. So, the standard chain of funding is as set out as follows:

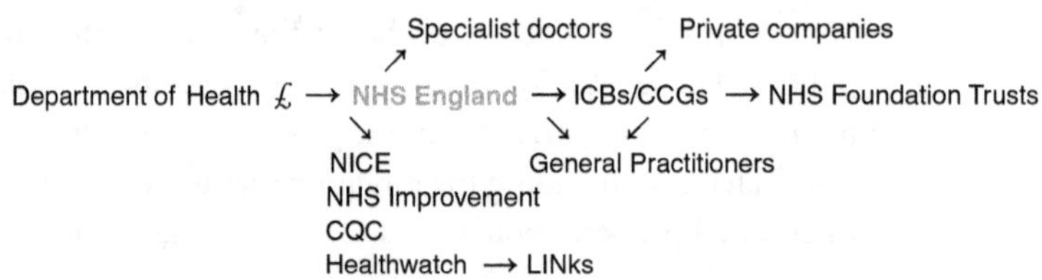

As a proportion of gross domestic product, UK spending on health has risen from 4% in 1970 to 6% in 2000, 8% by 2010,[60] and 9.6% in 2018. Factors leading to rising expenses are often said to include (i) rising life-spans, meaning more elderly people need more care, (ii) scientific progress making more treatments available, (iii) higher expectations of patients, (iv) increased private profit and (v) an increase in clinical negligence litigation driven by courts and the legal profession.[61] Private profit and litigation aside (see Ch. 9 (2)(b) and (4)), higher health spending should not be framed so much as a cost as an outcome that every society should be glad to fund, because it means people can live longer, happier lives. It must also be remembered that higher life expectancy alone is not enough: in the UK, for example, the average life expectancy in 2017–19 of women is 83.4 years, but 19.9 years are spent in 'not good' health, and for men 79.8 years, but 16.6 years 'not good'.[62]

[57] NHS Act 2006, s. 1H, referring to the NHS Commissioning Board: it adopted the brand name of NHS England.
[58] NHS Act 2006, s. 3. [59] See the list of CCGs at www.england.nhs.uk/ccg-details/.
[60] The rise from 7.3% in 2007 to 8.5% in 2010 was primarily due to the global financial crisis cutting GDP.
[61] Cf. E. Jackson, *Medical Law: Text, Cases and Materials* (2016) 38–9.
[62] V. Raleigh, 'What's Happening to Life Expectancy in England', King's Fund (2021).

UK health spending (9.6% of Gross Domestic Product (GDP)) is considerably lower than in the USA (16.9% in 2018) or Germany (11.2%), yet it has better life expectancy outcomes than both. As a matter of comparative law, countries with a 'Beveridge' model of health appear to have superior healthcare outcomes on average for money spent compared to those with insurance or 'Bismarck' systems of health. Table 9.1 categorises countries by system, but excludes outlier countries: the USA, Japan, Chile and new EU member states in Central and Eastern Europe.

Figure 9.2 shows 2011 statistics on life expectancy plotted against total spending in US$ for Organisation for Economic Co-operation and Development (OECD) countries with the same exclusions.

In 2011, the UK spent significantly less money than countries like Ireland, Germany, the Netherlands and Denmark, but had similar or better life expectancy. What explains the differences among spending and outcome? Factors may include climate, culture, type of work, quality of life, public health policy but also health governance. Following the US Social Security Administration classifications,[63] countries with triangles have primarily public health paid through tax and provided primarily by government. Diamond countries have public insurance systems, paid for through a public insurance company. Square countries have private health insurance systems, typically provided

Table 9.1 Health systems by type

Public health	Public insurance	Private or public insurance	Private insurance
Australia	Belgium	Austria	Netherlands
Canada	Czech Republic	Chile	Switzerland
Denmark	Estonia	Germany	
Finland	France	Israel	
Greece	Hungary	Turkey	
Iceland	Japan		
Ireland	Latvia		
Italy	Lithuania		
NZ	Luxembourg		
Norway	Poland		
Portugal	Romania		
Sweden	Slovakia		
Spain	Slovenia		
UK	South Korea		

[63] US Social Security Administration, *Social Security Programs throughout the World* (2018). These classifications are a useful general guide, but are no more than a generalisation. A full guide would include multiple indicators for the extent of private involvement, public subsidies and patient or resident voting rights.

Figure 9.2 Health spending in US$ and life expectancy, 2011
Sources: OECD Statistics, https://stats.oecd.org/index.aspx?DataSetCode=HEALTH_STAT#; US Social Security Administration, *Social Security Programs throughout the World: Europe and Asia* (2018)

through an employer, but if people cannot pay, they can fall back on a social or government insurer, and they may choose the government insurer. Circles have systems of private insurance, with subsidies for people who cannot afford it. On average, public health systems produce longer lives at a lower overall cost. But these categories are not clear.[64] Australia, Canada, Denmark and the UK have expanded private health provision, and in 2015 Ireland had 40 per cent private insurance. This appears to worsen the position.

When all OECD countries are plotted for 2015–16 (Figure 9.3), a dynamic picture emerges, and it is clear that the USA is in a category of its own. During the New Deal, President Roosevelt failed to include healthcare in the Social Security Act of 1935. The Social Security Amendments of 1965 created Medicare which guarantees free hospital insurance to people at retirement age.[65] It also created Medicaid which gives money to states to provide care for people who do not have insurance through work or cannot afford private insurance,[66] but it does not give people insurance. By 2010, 40 million people were uninsured, and among insured people the leading cause of bankruptcy was medical bills. Hospitals are fierce in pursuing debt. Insurance policies require charges for medicines and doctor visits ('copayments'), and require up-front fees before insurance covers an excess ('deductibles'). The Patient Protection and Affordable Care Act of 2010 tried to increase coverage by requiring people to pay a fine if they did not buy insurance

[64] Cf. P. L. Ferreira, A. I. Tavares, C. Quintal and P. Santana, 'EU Health Systems Classification: A New Proposal from Euro-Healthy' (2018) 18 *BMC Health Services Research* 511, Table 1, showing different systems.

[65] Social Security Act of 1935, title XVIII.

[66] Social Security Act of 1935, title XIX.

Figure 9.3 Health spending US$ and life expectancy, 2015–16
Sources: OECD Statistics, https://stats.oecd.org/index.aspx?DataSetCode=HEALTH_STAT#; US Social Security Administration, *Social Security Programs throughout the World: Europe and Asia* (2018)

(repealed in 2017[67]), prohibiting insurers from denying coverage if someone had a pre-existing illness, providing more subsidies, requiring that essential benefits could be covered and attempting to improve transparency in an online 'marketplace' for healthcare insurers at healthcare.gov. Still, a 2019 study found medical costs contributed to 66.5 per cent of bankruptcies.[68] There are limited controls on prices for prescription drugs, or hospital treatments: these are primarily market-driven. The USA is the world's most expensive health system, has the worst outcomes in the industrial world for life expectancy and money, and is the most unequal. Japan is one of the best, and is thought to be influenced by healthy diet, good technology and policies that aim for equality in outcome.[69] Depending what one values, Spain may also be the best.

Between 2011 and 2015 a striking fact is that the UK's average life expectancy fell significantly behind New Zealand, but spending became significantly higher, now closer to Denmark or Ireland. This coincided with the increase in privatisation.

(b) Privatisation

Private money enters the UK health system in three main ways: (i) by private entity services being bought (or 'commissioned') by NHS institutions which

[67] Tax Cuts and Jobs Act of 2017. The Affordable Care Act and this aspect in particular was previously held 'constitutional' in *National Federation of Independent Business v Sebelius*, 567 US 519 (2012).

[68] D. U. Himmelstein et al., 'Medical Bankruptcy: Still Common Despite the Affordable Care Act' (2019) 109(3) *Am J Public Health* 431.

[69] N. Ikeda et al., 'What Has Made the Population of Japan Healthy?' (2011) 378 *Lancet* 1094.

have a duty to guarantee open competition, (ii) through the 'private finance initiative' (PFI) where private contractors run NHS health facilities and (iii) through the sale of private insurance, which may work within or outside the NHS system.

(i) Private Provision and Competition

First, since amendments by the HSCA 2012, sections 164 and 165, the National Health Service Act 2006, section 43(2A) says the 'greater' part of the 'total income' of an NHS foundation trust must be 'for the purposes of the health service in England, rather than 'any other purposes' (i.e. profit). This opaque formulation is commonly said to mean that up to '49 per cent' (or accurately 49.999 … per cent) of NHS foundation trust work since 2012 could be private and profit-making work. Before this, section 44 had limited 'private health care' to around 2 per cent, which was the amount prevailing in the 2002–3 financial year.[70] This limit was removed, and section 44(6) allows an NHS foundation trust to provide 'accommodation or further services' if patients 'pay any charges imposed'.

At the time of writing, the Health and Care Bill 2021 was set to reverse the position from the HSCA 2012 that the NHS was subjected to competition law on use of a dominant position and co-operation (see Ch. 6(1)(b)).[71] However it is not clear that the most damaging norm, under HSCA 2012, section 75, will be repealed. This enables the Secretary of State to write regulations to ensure NHS England and Clinical Commissioning Groups 'promote the right of patients to make choices' (which sounds fine) but also 'do not engage in anti-competitive behaviour'. What does that mean? The NHS (Procurement, Patient Choice and Competition) (No. 2) Regulations 2013 state that NHS England and CCGs (which may be updated to ICBs) must 'treat providers equally and in a non-discriminatory way … in particular on the basis of ownership'. Thus, private corporations have a right against direct discrimination when they tender to provide health services to CCGs, at the time of writing. Presumably this cannot preclude indirect discrimination if private healthcare is persistently inferior.[72] NHS England (and CCGs) must seek 'best value for money' and 'must not award a contract' where 'potential conflicts' of interest 'affect, or appear to affect, the integrity of the award of that contract'.[73] NHS Improvement (called 'Monitor' before) polices competition violations and investigates conflicts.[74]

[70] NHS Act 2006, s. 44(1)–(3) as originally formulated.

[71] HSCA 2012, s. 72 to be omitted under the Health and Care Bill 2021, cl. 72.

[72] See Ch. 5(2)(d) for a description of direct and indirect discrimination in employment rights.

[73] NHS (Procurement, Patient Choice and Competition) (No. 2) Regulations 2013 (no. 500) regs. 3–6.

[74] NHS (Procurement, Patient Choice and Competition) (No. 2) Regulations 2013 (no. 500) reg. 13.

The 2012 Act led to a steady increase in private work done by NHS foundations. From 2006 to 2014 the proportion of NHS patients treated by non-NHS providers rose from 0.5% to 2.6% for inpatients (who stay overnight in hospitals), and 0.2% to 5.5% for outpatients (who are referred to specialists).[75] But more recent statistics are obscured: one study based on Freedom of Information requests in 2018 to 153 acute hospital trusts had 114 responses, and of these 73 were unable or unwilling to report expenses in treating private patients.[76]

Experience with private health institutions is largely negative. For example, from 2006 to 2011 the Runcorn Independent Sector Treatment Centre, near Liverpool, gave a five-year contract to Interhealth Canada to perform hip and other joint replacements. Its contract was ended, as its costs proved to be 25 per cent higher than the rate at which NHS providers did operations.[77] Another example starting in 2011 is that the coalition government decided to award Circle Healthcare Ltd, a subsidiary of Circle Holdings plc, a ten-year contract to run Hinchingbrooke Hospital near Cambridge.[78] The business was started by an ex-surgeon and an ex-Goldman Sachs banker; it gave employees shares and it attracted international investment. Its share price reached £2. The management cut hospital staff, and left wards empty to generate money. In 2015, its share price dropped to 22 pence as Circle said it would terminate its contract ahead of a Care Quality Commission (CQC) report finding it was inadequate, and recommending the hospital be put into special measures. In 2016, after coming back under NHS management Hinchingbrooke hospital was once again rated as 'good'.

While private companies appear unable to compete, without government forcing it, a possible future source of privatisation could be 'market access' provisions in future international trade agreements. Under EU law, there can be no direct or indirect discrimination of goods or services based upon the national origin of the products or services.[79] This cannot, however, extend to a positive duty to open markets to private corporations, because the Treaty on the Functioning of the European Union (TFEU) article 345 requires that the Treaties must 'in no way prejudice the rules in Member States governing the system of property ownership'.[80] By contrast, free trade agreements in the framework of World Trade Organization (WTO) rules may seek greater 'market access', and therefore create pressure on the government to award more contracts (whatever the evidence) to private companies to run NHS services. In leaked discussions from March 2018 from the UK–US Trade & Investment

[75] J. Appleby, 'Paid for by the NHS, Treated Privately', *British Medical Journal* (13 June 2015) 16.
[76] S. Walpole and CHPI, 'NHS Treatment of Private Patients: The Impact on NHS Finances and NHS Patient Care', CHPI Report (March 2018).
[77] J. Meek, 'It's Already Happened' (2011) 33(18) *London Rev Books* 3.
[78] G. Plimmer, 'Private Company in NHS Hospital Takeover', *Financial Times* (10 November 2011).
[79] TFEU, arts. 34–7 and 56. [80] TFEU, art. 345.

Working Group, it was made clear that US trade negotiators 'wanted total market access to be the baseline' in any trade negotiation that might follow 'Brexit'.[81] Despite UK government denials, US officials have consistently and publicly made it clear that health market access should be part of trade talks. The UK's bargaining ability to say otherwise is not clear,[82] but it is clear that this should be regarded as fundamentally wrong.

(ii) Private Finance Initiative

The NHS (Private Finance) Act 1997, section 1 enables the Secretary of State to certify 'externally financed development agreements'. While the practice of private finance had existed before, there was a significant expansion after 1997. Typically, a health authority contracts with a private company to build hospitals, and the hospitals are leased back to the NHS with a contract to supply health services lasting twenty-five or thirty years. Major contractors include Telereal Trillium Ltd, Innisfree Ltd or HSBC Infrastructure Co. Ltd. An accounting 'benefit' was that future contract payments would not appear as public borrowing, although it was economically identical.[83] The cost was that PFI buildings were frequently much more expensive than public provision: expected to be £80 billion by the time contracts end.[84]

(iii) Private Insurance Policies

There are a growing number of private health insurance companies in the UK, the largest being Vitality, Bupa, Aviva and AXA. Around 10 per cent of the UK population has some form of policy, often provided by an employer as an extra workplace benefit. This cover is often irrelevant given that everyone has the right to treatment on the NHS, but it may cover dental or optical treatment, or specialist visits that are not covered by the NHS. Insurance policies also typically offer gym membership, and increasingly novel items like an Apple watch. Insurers have invested in data collection on customers, so that their personal health information can be used to target users with further sales in future.[85]

[81] Department for Trade, UK–US Trade & Investment Working Group (21–22 March 2018) 42.

[82] E.g. H. Stewart, 'Theresa May Refuses to Exclude NHS Contracts from US Trade Deals', *The Guardian* (7 February 2018); J. Elgot, 'US Wants Access to NHS in Post-Brexit Deal, Says Trump Ally', *The Guardian* (2 June 2019).

[83] E.g. H. Mance and G. Parker, 'UK Finance Watchdog Exposes Lost PFI Billions', *Financial Times* (18 January 2018).

[84] D. Campbell, 'NHS Hospital Trusts to Pay Out Further £55bn under PFI Scheme', *The Guardian* (12 September 2019).

[85] E.g. J. McAlevey, *The Nation* (12 March 2018), on West Virginia teachers required to wear FitBit surveillance devices, or pay higher health insurance costs as part of their employment contracts. Strikes ended this.

(c) Exceptional Charging and Foreign Patients

Originally, the NHS was designed to be free from charges. According to Aneurin Bevan, 'money ought not to be permitted to stand in the way of obtaining an efficient health service' and free health was a 'triumphant example of the superiority of collective action and public initiative'.[86] But under fiscal pressure, in 1951 the NHS introduced prescription charges for dental care and for glasses, and Bevan resigned. Jokes about British people's teeth have remained common, but reflect the very serious legal fact that dental services must be invariably paid for even when available on the NHS.[87] The same is true for optical care.[88] In England, there are also prescription charges for 'drugs, medicines or appliance, or pharmaceutical services', unless people qualify for reimbursement.[89] In Wales, Northern Ireland and Scotland prescription charges were scrapped between 2007 and 2011.

Charges cannot be made to people while they are in hospital, but if people are 'not ordinarily resident in Great Britain' then under section 175, the Secretary of State can make regulations for charging.[90] Most health services and hospitals found it illogical to charge patients even where they could because of the expense and time in administration, and out of compassion for human suffering. But in 2015, the government placed a duty on hospitals and health services to charge overseas visitors.[91] Students have also been forced to pay an annual charge, despite being generally healthy and resident. Charging appears to be strongly supported in newspapers that are owned by billionaires, printing stories demonising 'health tourists'.[92] However, the evidence suggests that the costs of administering the system significantly outweigh receipts, and not treating migrants costs more if it leads to more infectious disease.[93]

(d) Intellectual Monopoly Rights and Medical Patents

Intellectual monopoly rights, typically but somewhat mistakenly called 'intellectual property', are both a major source of finance for pharmaceutical corporations, and a cost to health services for medicines or equipment.

86 Mr Aneurin Bevan, National Health Service Bill, Hansard HC Debs. (30 April 1946) col. 43. N. Bevan, *In Place of Fear* (1952) 109.

87 NHS Act 2006, ss. 176–7. 88 NHS Act 2006, ss. 179–181. 89 NHS Act 2006, ss. 172–4.

90 NHS Act 2006, s. 175.

91 National Health Service (Charges to Overseas Visitors) Regulations 2015, regs. 3–9 (charges cannot be made for emergency treatment).

92 E.g. L. Donnelly, '"Health Tourists" to Be Charged Up-Front for NHS Care', *Daily Telegraph* (20 October 2017); N. McDermott, 'Health Tourists Are Costing Britain £10 Million as Foreign Mums Rip Off the NHS to Get Free Treatment', *The Sun* (2 January 2018); J. T. M. Thomas, 'It's Not Racist to Charge Health Tourists. It's the Only Way Our NHS Can Survive', *Daily Mail* (27 June 2019).

93 See J. M. K. Reynolds and C. Mitchell, '"Inglan Is a Bitch": Hostile NHS Charging Regulations Contravene the Ethical Principles of the Medical Profession' (2019) 45 *J Medical Ethics* 497.

Under the original Statute of Monopolies 1624, section 6 exempted 'any letters patent and grants of privilege for the term of fourteen years' for 'the true and first inventor and inventors' for the 'sole working or making of any manner of new manufactures'.[94] Monopolies over information on how to make a new invention ('inventive step, capable of industrial application')[95] – that is, a patent – differ from rights of property, because the peaceful enjoyment of one's possessions (such as a chair) is not inconsistent with other people owning or making other chairs. By contrast, a monopoly over an invention, enforceable today in the Patents Act 1977, section 25 and in WTO law for twenty years from the date of filing,[96] prevents other people from making the same.[97] This may enable the holder of a patent for a particular Covid-19 vaccine, a treatment for asthma or medicine for a headache. The profits from patents primarily benefit the global pharmaceutical companies (see Table 9.2).

The top ten companies hold a global market share of just over 40 per cent, yet this seemingly competitive market derives profits from multiple intellectual monopolies. The central argument in favour of patent monopolies is that these are what 'the public owe to the inventor, in order to compensate and reward [them] for the service'. Without an exception of 'temporary duration' from the

Table 9.2 Top 10 companies by global market share of prescription drugs, 2019[i]

	Company	Market %	Revenue	HQ
1	Roche	5.5%	$60.18bn	Switzerland
2	Novartis	5.3%	$47.45bn	Switzerland
3	Pfizer	5%	$51.75bn	USA
4	Merck & Co	4.7%	$46.84bn	USA
5	Johnson & Johnson	4.6%	$82.06bn	USA
6	Sanofi	4%	$39.28bn	France
7	AbbVie	3.7%	$33.27bn	USA
8	GlaxoSmithKline	3.6%	$43.92bn	UK
9	Bristol-Myers-Squibb	2.9%	$26.15bn	USA
10	AstraZeneca	2.7%	$24.38bn	UK, Sweden

[i] M. Mikulic, 'Top 20 Pharmaceutical Companies Worldwide Based on Prescription Drug Market Share in 2019', *Statista* (July 2020).

[94] Also *Liardet v Johnson* (1778) 62 Eng Rep 1000, per Lord Mansfield (need for instruction on making invention).

[95] Patents Act 1977, s. 1.

[96] WTO, Agreement on Trade-Related Aspects of Intellectual Property Rights 1995, art. 33; European Patent Convention 2000, art. 63.

[97] Cf. E. W. Kitch, 'Patents: Monopolies or Property Rights?' (1986) 8 *Research in L & Economics* 31, who suggests that close substitutes often are developed, that it may take time to make monopoly profits and the patent runs out. These arguments have no evidential basis and are mostly irrelevant to legal classification.

ban on monopolies, 'nobody except very opulent and very public-spirited persons, or the state' would undertake the work of inventing.[98] For these reasons, patents have often been defended, including for life-saving medicines.[99]

There are, however, three difficulties with patents over medical inventions. First, corporations, who are not the true inventors, usually take the rewards today. Inventing done in the course of employment (including for patents, copyrights or trademarks) is often appropriated by the employer as an implied contract term.[100] Thus, there is often no relationship between invention and reward, because most employees will be on fixed salaries, not remunerated after they depart, and have no legal guarantee of reward except whatever is found in their contracts. Moreover, for many drugs, hundreds of people often contribute to invention. For example, in 2018, the expiry of a drug patent held by AbbVie, called Adalimumab, used to treat arthritis, saved the NHS an estimated £150 million every year.[101] This was developed, with funding from the UK's public Medical Research Council and three university academics, involving the 'expertise of many hundreds of professionals'.[102] The drug was then further developed and manufactured by BASF and Abbott Laboratories. Later, the companies were reorganised as AbbVie. The belief that patents are either encouragement or compensation for inventiveness is incompatible with modern enterprise.

Second, most medical developments are funded directly by universities and public research grants, and carried out by staff who have invariably had publicly funded education (see Ch. 8(2)). Among the most popular Covid-19 vaccines, the Moderna vaccine required £1.9 billion in funding, which almost entirely came from the US government. The Pfizer/BioNTech vaccine was invented in Germany, and developed with $320 billion investments from Pfizer and Chinese company Fosun, and $564 billion from the EU and German governments. The Oxford/AstraZeneca vaccine was developed by an academic research team at the University of Oxford, who, after making a partnership agreement with AstraZeneca, received a UK government grant of £68 million and a US government grant of £1.2 billion in return for securing of doses. While final and reliable calculations are not available at the time of writing, it appears clear that most major vaccines received substantial or complete public

98 J. S. Mill, *Principles of Political Economy* (1871 ed.) Book V, ch. 10, §4, 551–2, and to abolish patents would be to 'enthrone free stealing under the prostituted name of free trade, and make the men of brains, still more than at present, the needy retainers and dependents of the men of money-bags'.

99 See also F. Machlup and E. Penrose, 'The Patent Controversy in the Nineteenth Century' (1950) 10 *J Economic History* 1.

100 *Stevenson, Jordan & Harrison Ltd v MacDonald & Evans* [1952] 1 TLR 101.

101 E. Dent, 'Most Expensive NHS Drug Comes Off Patent' (2018) 301 *Pharmaceutical Journal*: 'Humira'.

102 This is called Cambridge Antibody Technology plc; and see J. McCafferty, 'The Long and Winding Road to Antibody Therapeutics' (2010) 2(5) *mAbs* 459.

funding.[103] By contrast, drug companies have continually reduced their investments in research and development, while increasing dividends and share buybacks.[104] There is little reason to give a corporation monopoly rights on medicines beyond the price they can secure in a competitive, productive market for manufacture. Whatever research they do with monopoly profits will be less efficient than that which is university and publicly funded.

Third, wherever patents limit the right to health, it is difficult to assert that they should not give way. It certainly seems true that neither the rights of inventors (who again, typically receive fixed salaries), nor the supposed incentive function of patents for research can justify patents, and in particular 'patents in developing countries interfere with access to medicines without a justification'.[105] This is particularly important in cases such as the AIDS epidemic in South Africa, where President Mandela signed the Medicines and Related Substances Control Amendment Act, 1997 enabling generic drugs to be produced regardless of patents over anti-retroviral drugs. This was met by massive lobbying and litigation from US and European drug corporations to prevent this,[106] in the very middle of an epidemic that dropped the average life-expectancy of all South Africans by ten years. The better view is that it should be 'up to the democratic process in industrialized countries to preserve the industry's incentive for research',[107] rather than blanket monopolies that undermine health.

(e) Public Health

Healthcare finance is strongly influenced by public health policy outside the NHS through environmental law,[108] health and safety at work,[109] consumer rights and food standards.[110] Public health is a human right,[111] and saves

[103] L. Hooker and D. Palumbo, 'Covid Vaccines: Will Drug Companies Make Bumper Profits?', *BBC News* (18 December 2020).

[104] W. Lazonick and Ö. Tulum, 'US Biopharmaceutical Finance and the Sustainability of the Biotech Business Model' (2011) 40 *Research Policy J* 1170; and M. Mazzucato, *The Entrepreneurial State: Debunking Public vs Private Sector Myths* (2018) 32 and 75.

[105] H. P. Hestermeyer, *Human Rights and the WTO: The Case of Patents and Access to Medicines* (2007) ch. 4.

[106] Hestermeyer, *Human Rights and the WTO*, ch. 2, Part IV.

[107] Hestermeyer, *Human Rights and the WTO*, ch. 2, 165–6.

[108] E.g. Environment Act 1995, s. 80 (requiring a National Air Quality Strategy); Clean Air Act 1993, ss. 1–6 (banning or restricting smoke and furnaces) and 30 (power to regulate motor fuels). See Ch. 15.

[109] Health and Safety at Work Act 1974, s. 2 (duty of employers to have systems of work without risks); Employment Rights Act 1996, s. 44 (right to no detriment for refusing to work in a dangerous workplace).

[110] Food Safety Act 1980, s. 7; Food Safety Regulation (EC) No. 178/2002, art. 14.

[111] European Social Charter 1961, art. 11, saying member states should 'remove as far as possible the causes of ill-health', provide advice and education to promote health and 'prevent as far as possible' epidemics, diseases and accidents. CFREU 2000, art. 31: 'Every worker has the right to working conditions which respect his or her health, safety and dignity'; art. 35: 'Everyone has the right of access to preventive health care.'

money. The leading causes of death in the UK are lung and heart failures,[112] primarily due to pollution, poor food, drink and smoke, and unsafe or stressful workplaces. Corporations often argue that people should have 'personal freedom' to buy motors that give school children asthma, or make teenagers addicted to sugar, fat and smoke, when often their real goal is to protect corporate freedom to profit from people's death. A rational government would eliminate public health risks to reduce costs to the NHS. The Secretary of State has a duty to protect public health through measures like 'advancing knowledge and understanding', 'training' or 'information', while each local authority should take similar 'steps'.[113]

Before 2021, a body called Public Health England co-ordinated strategy, but at the time of writing this was being replaced by the UK Health Security Agency and the Office of Health Promotion, under powers of the Secretary of State.[114] These powers also enable the Secretary of State to confer public health functions on NHS England, a step that would enable the NHS (which bears the cost of threats to health) to tackle the costs. But what is needed most of all is for other Secretaries of State to use other more direct powers, such as to end 'motor fuel' from oil and shift to only clean electric fuel,[115] to ban unhealthy food, to create traffic light labelling for nutrition (red for poor, green for good) and label the air pollution that products create.[116] This approach would radically alter the current business model of firms such as Shell, Esso, Texaco, McDonalds or KFC, and shift supermarkets to becoming responsible partners in promoting people's health.

The Covid-19 pandemic illustrated for us all the imperative nature of a public health policy for the NHS. The Johnson government has led at the time of writing to the world's worst death rate, or close to it,[117] worse than Trump's America or Bolsonaro's Brazil. This was not bad luck, or the fault of the NHS, but the fault and calculated result of the use of powers under the Public Health (Control of Disease) Act 1984. This includes (1) decisions to delay any lockdown or travel restrictions even while the virus spread through Europe

[112] Office for National Statistics, 'Leading Causes of Death, UK: 2001 to 2018' (20 March 2020) 3.

[113] NHS Act 2006, ss. 2A–B; Public Health Act 1961 (buildings, streets and trade effluent). See also Public Health (Minimum Price for Alcohol) (Wales) Act 2018; Public Health (Wales) Act 2017 (obesity, tobacco, toilets, intimate piercings); Public Health, etc. (Scotland) Act 2008.

[114] NHS Act 2006, s. 7A. Cf. Public Health England, Strategic plan for the next four years: better outcomes by 2020 (April 2016) with 7 priorities of tackling obesity, reducing smoking, reducing harmful drinking, ensuring that every child has the best start in life, reducing dementia risk, tackling antimicrobial resistance and reducing tuberculosis.

[115] Clean Air Act 1993, s. 30 (power to regulate motor fuels). See Ch. 15.

[116] Food Safety Act 1980, s. 7 (offence to render food 'injurious to health'); Food Act 1984, ss. 6–7 (labelling).

[117] Two types of statistics are (1) deaths as officially recorded as Covid-19 related, in which the UK is currently third behind Belgium, (2) excess deaths over previous years, where the UK is either first or just behind Spain. E.g. C. Giles, 'UK Excess Deaths since Start of Pandemic Surpass 100,000, Data Suggest', *Financial Times* (19 January 2021).

in February and March;[118] (2) after the virus's suppression by summer 2020, instructing universities to teach face to face, to secure student rental income to landlords, leading a million students and parents to travel across the UK and surging death rates in September and October; and (3) in this infected state, allowing mass Christmas shopping and gatherings.[119] Once the virus was endemic – a result avoided by competent governments of New Zealand, Australian states, Norway and Denmark – the decision to try and 'balance' the interests of the economy with health meant the UK government lost both.[120] Particularly to blame is Johnson's recklessness;[121] and that of the education, health and other ministers. They are primarily responsible for over 150,000 dead people, over double the civilian deaths from bombing of Britain in World War Two.[122]

(3) Governance

NHS governance cannot be said to have a settled, or principled, system, despite major recent changes. Scotland, Wales, Northern Ireland and England organised its systems in line with the Beveridge Report of 1942,[123] but each has evolved separate structures.[124] Within each entity in the NHS there has been a clear shift towards greater voice for staff and patients or members of the public. The NHS Constitution now states staff and patients should be 'involved' and 'engaged' in decision-making,[125] but actual rights to vote are not yet made clear. The key actors are (a) the Department of Health and NHS England; (b) Clinical Commissioning Groups; (c) NHS foundation trusts, GPs and specialists; and (d) the various supervisory bodies, namely NICE, NHS Improvement, the CQC and Healthwatch.

[118] Public Health (Control of Disease) Act 1984, s. 45B (power to make regulations restricting travel).

[119] Public Health (Control of Disease) Act 1984, ss. 45C–F (enabling regulations to protect against spread of infection, where proportionate, and ability to confer functions on local authorities, or impose penalties). Under s. 1, local authorities also administer the Act. See then the Public Health (Coronavirus, Restrictions) Regulations 2020.

[120] Cf. R Shrimsley, 'For Boris Johnson, Covid-19 is now an economic not a health crisis', *Financial Times* (1 June 2020).

[121] E.g. R. Mason, 'Boris Johnson Boasted of Shaking Hands on Day Sage Warned Not To', *The Guardian* (5 May 2020).

[122] In the Blitz and Battle of Britain, there were 67,200 civilian deaths. Cf. Boris Johnson, *The Guardian* (17 March 2020): 'we announced the steps yesterday that we did – advising against all unnecessary contact – that are unprecedented since World War Two'.

[123] *Social Insurance and Allied Services*, Cmd 6404 (1942) ch. 1, 11: 'Medical treatment covering all requirements will be provided for all citizens by a national health service organised under the health departments … .'

[124] E.g. Scotland Act 1998, s. 28, powers over matters not reserved in Sch. 5.

[125] NHS Constitution for England (2015) arts. 3a (on patient rights and involvement) and 4a (on staff rights and engagement).

(a) Department of Health and Social Care and NHS England

The Department of Health and Social Care, since the establishment of its predecessor in 1919,[126] has become one of the most important offices of state, run by the Secretary of State for Health. Sadly, the Health Minister often has zero understanding of health, but their work is scrutinised by Parliament and three main supervisory committees. The Health Committee oversees Department expenditure, administration and policy. The Public Accounts Committee oversees finances. The Public Administration Committee oversees health service Commissioner reports. They may summon the Secretary of State, other ministers, or health officials to give evidence, and they frequently recommend changes to Parliament. The Secretary of State has a duty under the NHS Act 2006, section 1 to 'continue the promotion in England of a comprehensive health service' that improves the 'physical and mental health of the people' and the 'prevention, diagnosis and treatment of physical and mental illness'. The Secretary is meant to continually improve the service, pay regard to the NHS Constitution and reduce health inequalities.[127] Like other aspirational duties,[128] how these are fulfilled depends on political goals and power. It may be unlikely (however desirable) in judicial review to find breach,[129] without evidence of bad faith, neglect or conflicting interest.

NHS England is the brand name for the 'NHS Commissioning Board', as it is called in statute. Since 2012 it receives and distributes money to doctors, specialists and Clinical Commissioning Groups.[130] Its chair, and at least five other members, are appointed by the Secretary of State. Non-executive directors are required to outnumber executive directors,[131] similar to the UK Corporate Governance Code requiring a majority of independent non-executive directors, except there is no need for NHS England directors to be 'independent'. There is not yet any right of staff in the NHS or patients and residents to vote for executives, which could be more useful than non-executive directors who are appointed by the Secretary of State in the same way as executives. In 2022, NHS England had twelve members: a chair and five other non-executives, plus six further executive directors.

126 Ministry of Health Act 1919. Since 2018, it has been called the Department of Health and Social Care.

127 NHS Act 2006, ss. 1A–C.

128 Recall the Companies Act 2006, s. 172 (see Ch. 3(4)(b)) or the Insolvency Act 1986, Sch. B1, para. 3 (see Ch. 7(2)(b)).

129 Cf. J. Herring, *Medical Law* (2017) 55, 'The wording of these duties is so vague that it is hard to imagine a legal action being successfully brought for a breach of them.'

130 NHS Act 2006, s. 1H and Sch. A1. Between 1995 and 2006, an 'NHS Executive' managed the NHS in England, but was then subsumed by the Department of Health. It oversaw the 10 Strategic Health Authorities (previously 28) and the 101 Primary Care Trusts (previously 303).

131 NHS Act 2006, Sch. A1, para. 2.

(b) Integrated Care Boards

At the time of writing, a new system of ICBs was proposed under a Health and Social Care Bill 2021, to replace 'Clinical Commissioning Groups', which in turn replaced 'Primary Care Trusts'. The function, number and governance of each of these intermediary fund-funnelling bodies has been significant and unsettled. First, the function of each is to distribute money to hospitals and doctors, and so determine spending: who certain services and equipment are bought from ('commissioned') and who they are sold to within the NHS ('provided'). Resource-allocation choices affect personal and regional disparities in health, and the level (if any) of privatisation. Second, the number of ICBs is proposed to be 44, while there were originally 205 CCGs but these merged down to 106, and before 2012 there were 101 PCTs. The more bodies there are, the more duplication there is likely to be, the lower the level of co-ordination, and the lower the bargaining power that any purchasing body has against any private drug or equipment seller. It is not clear why there are not large, organised regional health boards.

Third, the governance of ICBs, set out in the draft Bill, to be the NHS Act 2006, Schedule 1B, states that the constitution of boards includes a chair and a chief executive appointed by NHS England with the Secretary of State's approval, and three ordinary members, approved by the chair, but nominated by the NHS trusts and foundation trusts in the area, by persons who 'provide medical services' of a prescribed description, and by the local authorities.[132] However, as well as concentrating power in the hands of the minister, this does not appear to include members of staff having the right to vote. Worse, it was being reported that 'private health providers like Virgin Care could be given seats on the boards' and 'be involved in deciding who gets what contracts'.[133] Giving private corporations or their delegates seats in governance would present a mortal conflict of interest to the NHS, a hostile act of privatisation. This alone is probably worse than the deeply flawed governance of CCGs. Supposed to be a 'liberating force',[134] the short-lived experiments of CCGs had five members consisting of a nurse, secondary care specialist, a financially qualified person and two lay people.[135] They were meant to 'promote the involvement of patients, and their carers and representatives', but no patients or staff had actual voting rights in choosing the CCG members.[136] The PCTs

[132] NHS Act 2006, Sch. 2, paras. 3–7.

[133] D. Campbell and A. Allegretti, 'Johnson to Announce Controversial Plans for Greater NHS Control', *The Guardian* (4 July 2021), quoting Dr David Wrigley, the British Medical Association's deputy chair of council.

[134] Department of Health, *Equity and Excellence: Liberating the NHS*, Cm 7811 (2010).

[135] National Health Service Reform and Health Care Professions Act 2002, s. 15; and see the National Health Service (Clinical Commissioning Groups) Regulations 2012, regs. 11–12.

[136] NHS Act 2006, ss. 14U and 14Z2. Also Sch. 1A, paras. 10 and 13(1) provided that CCG members paid themselves. CCGs had duties under competition law to not co-operate (although some did: https://nhsfunding.info/), to get 'value for money' and avoid conflicts of interest, even though this was systemic in GPs selling services.

that preceded CCGs had boards all appointed by the Secretary of State, and had patients' forums but without any votes.[137]

The NHS is tired of constant restructure. No government has appeared capable of making the least intrusive changes possible, with the greatest positive impact. A far better system would be to retain the ICBs (although recognising that a smaller number is better) and to give NHS staff and GPs of the area votes for the trust and provider seats, and require that local authorities appoint members based on recommendations of a local patients' forum. Alternatively, elected staff and local representation could be added to existing members, so long as no corporate representative is allowed.

(c) NHS Foundation Trusts, GPs and Specialists

After 2003, NHS foundation trusts were created, and took over hospitals and other trusts that used to be managed by the Department of Health and health authorities. There are 151 in England. With 'foundation trust' status, originally acquired through good management, the trust can merge with others, borrow money without Department of Health approval,[138] and therefore more easily go insolvent. As Chapter 9(2)(b) explained, NHS foundation trusts must make a majority of its income from health, and not for-profit work.

Each NHS foundation trust has the same basic governance requirements. It must have a Council of Governors, and between three and one-half must be elected by the trust's employees, one by the local authorities and one by a university (if there is one in the area).[139] An inspiration for foundation trusts was Spanish hospitals, where governance included trade unions, patient representatives and community groups.[140] There is no requirement, however, for unions, patients or local residents to have a vote, albeit that the NHS foundation trust could allow this. Perhaps even less responsive, at least on paper, are NHS trusts without 'foundation' status. These are bodies corporate with a chair appointed by the Secretary of State, executives who are employees and non-executives who are outside, but generally they are appointed under the authority of the Secretary of State by Order.[141]

The other significant bodies are General Practices and specialist doctors. When most people are ill, but it is not an emergency, a GP is the first port of call. The GP is typically an independent corporate or partnership entity that makes contracts with NHS England, and is paid for the different types of work it performs. A model General Medical Services Contract sets the basic terms for most GPs, but is in reality less of a contract as it takes the form of

[137] National Health Service Reform and Health Care Professions Act 2002, s. 15 (repealed).

[138] NHS Act 2006, ss. 40–2. [139] NHS Act 2006, Sch. 7, paras. 3 and 9.

[140] J. Carvel and G. Tremlett, 'Milburn Seeks Hospital Role Model in Spain', *The Guardian* (6 November 2001).

[141] NHS Act 2006, s. 4 and Sch. 4, paras. 3–5.

Regulations.[142] Each GP must have a 'patient participation group' where it consults patients,[143] but as in other NHS institutions, without any right to vote patients can be ignored. Specialist doctors function in a similar way. Because of the bargaining power that NHS England has when compared to 8,000 GPs, the public is able to moderate doctor salaries to a fairer level.

(d) Supervisory Bodies

There are four main supervisory bodies in the UK health service. First, NICE approves technology, medicine and clinical practices.[144] Second, NHS Improvement monitors competition law and conflicts.[145] Third, the CQC inspects and reports on hospitals.[146] Fourth, Healthwatch is a CQC committee and is meant to 'give advice, information or other assistance' to NHS bodies and local patient or resident groups called 'Local Involvement Networks' (LINks).[147] It would appear that a preferable approach, however, would be for those taking part in LINks to be directly involved in foundation trusts, or other governing bodies.

(e) Social Care and Homes

While not yet part of the NHS, social care is closely linked with health since it is often people with persistent health conditions that require assistance or housing. Since 1948, local authorities have had duties to provide accommodation and services for adults that were unable to always care for themselves, but enabled certain charges.[148] Under the Chronically Sick and Disabled Persons Act 1970, there are duties to 'meet the needs' of a person including assistance at home, recreation, changes to the home for safety or comfort, meals and communications.[149] Local authorities should assess the needs of disabled people who need care, and respond to their requests.[150] The disabled person has a right to be involved in any assessment.[151] However, when providing accommodation, support at home, counselling, goods and facilities, or other advice or information, the local authority can impose charges. There was supposed to involve a cap, initially reported to be a mere £72,000 a year, but the plans for such a cap were scrapped as they would involve very high

142 National Health Service (General Medical Services Contracts) Regulations 2015.
143 National Health Service (General Medical Services Contracts) Regulations 2015, reg. 26.
144 HSCA 2012, s. 232 and Sch. 16. 145 HSCA 2012, ss. 61–71. 146 HSCA 2008, Sch. 1.
147 HSCA 2012, ss. 181 and 184, amending HSCA 2008, s. 45A and Sch. 1, para. 6 and Local Government and Public Involvement in Health Act 2007, s. 223.
148 National Assistance Act 1948, ss. 21–9.
149 Chronically Sick and Disabled Persons Act 1970, ss. 1–2.
150 Disabled Persons (Services Consultation and Representation) Act 1986, ss. 4–16; NHS and Community Care Act 1990, s. 47.
151 *R v Mayor and Burgesses of the LB of Merton ex p Wiggins* [1996] ELR 332.

administration costs.[152] Most of the important care service functions have been outsourced to profit-making companies, that repeatedly have been found to be neglectful. Despite poor performance, and being outsourced public functions, it was held in *YL v Birmingham CC* that Southern Cross Healthcare plc was not a public body under the Human Rights Act 1998, section 6, and owed no duties under the European Convention on Human Rights, article 8 when it ejected an elderly resident with just twenty-eight days' notice.[153] According to Lord Scott it was 'carrying on a socially useful business for profit' and 'operating in a commercial market with commercial competitors'. Four years after the judgment, Southern Cross plc went into administration, and among many incidents one home was found in 2013 to have been 'mismanaged and understaffed', with treatment of the elderly amounting to 'institutional abuse'.[154] Care homes, including for children, disabled adults or the elderly, are subject to regulatory oversight. However, it would appear that the cost to families, the service received, and the pay of carers would all be far improved if care was placed within the NHS.[155]

(f) World Health Organization

The global governance of healthcare is overseen by the World Health Organization (WHO), whose objective is 'attainment by all peoples of the highest possible level of health'. The WHO's role is to co-ordinate health work, assist governments, provide technical assistance, promote co-operation in research and practice, and take 'all necessary action to attain the objective of the Organization'.[156] This has been particularly important in the Covid-19 and other pandemics, yet the WHO is entirely constrained by the resources available to it. Each UN member has one vote and provides finance. Its two-year budget for 2020 and 2021 was $4.84 billion. While UN member states have a fundamental duty for the healthcare of their citizens, there has been increasing movement of people between countries. The WHO has not yet been used to co-ordinate the pooling of funds to ensure free health coverage, and most countries outside the EU have instead relied upon costly systems of bilateral treaties.

(4) Patients' Rights

While patients and residents do not have clear voting rights in NHS England, in ICBs or in NHS foundation trusts, certain rights for patients are enforceable in court. The central rights are (a) to treatment, albeit limited by the good faith judgement of health and care services, (b) to be treated equally, (c) to be treated

[152] Care Act 2014, ss. 8–20. [153] *YL v Birmingham CC* [2007] UKHL 27.
[154] 'Orchid View Inquest: Home Riddled by "Institutional Abuse"', *BBC News* (18 October 2013).
[155] Care Standards Act 2000, ss. 1–11. [156] Constitution of the WHO 1946, arts. 1–2.

competently and (d) for there to be no bias or conflicts of interest. It is unclear, however, that litigation advances the universal right to healthcare.[157] Litigation may unduly deplete resources, since the legal profession probably has interests in litigating that are at odds with doctors, patients and the public.

(a) Right to Treatment

The human right to health finds an expression in UK law through the Secretary of State's duty in the NHS Act 2006, section 1 to promote and improve 'the prevention, diagnosis and treatment of physical and mental illness'. The Secretary of State must also try to continually improve the service and pay regard to the NHS Constitution. Though formulated more loosely than a 'right to healthcare', in this public duty is an implicit right of members of the public.[158] What is questionable is the extent to which litigation, as opposed to governance, is the best way to uphold this right to health. Legal systems with high levels of litigation, particularly the USA, are evidently worse at providing health.[159]

The NHS is designed to provide universal healthcare for everyone, but its resources are limited by political spending decisions (see Ch. 20). More money spent in one area could mean less in another. A growing number of challenges have been brought over the NHS's refusal to provide treatment, often in very difficult cases. In *R (B) v Cambridge Health Authority* the parents of a 10-year-old girl applied for judicial review of the health authority after she was refused a second bone marrow transplant. They hoped that this might stop acute myeloid leukaemia. Consultants at Addenbrooke's Hospital in Cambridge and the Royal Marsden Hospital in London agreed the procedure would not succeed, would cause unnecessary suffering and was therefore inappropriate to fund. In the USA, the treatment could have been paid for, and a consultant in Hammersmith said he would treat her for £75,000. *The Sun* said she was 'Condemned by Bank Balance' and the *Daily Mail* led a campaign for the child to get treatment, saying she was 'Sentenced to Death' by the NHS. Laws J held that the health authority's decision to refuse treatment was unlawful, because they should 'explain the priorities that have led them to decline to fund the treatment' and 'do more than toll the bell of tight resources'. The Court of Appeal overturned this, restoring the health authority's refusal. Sir Thomas

[157] UDHR 1948, art. 25; ICESCR 1966, art. 12(2)(d): 'conditions which would assure to all medical service and medical attention in the event of sickness'; European Social Charter 1961, art. 13: 'any person who is without adequate resources' should have 'the care necessitated by his condition'; CFREU 2000, art. 35: 'right to benefit from medical treatment' under national law and a 'high level of human health protection'; ECHR 1950, arts. 2, 3 and 8 (right to life, no torture, private and family life) indirectly recognise minimal standards in case law.

[158] Cf. *Stovin v Wise* [1996] UKHL 15 (see Ch. 15(3)(a)(ii)).

[159] See also O. Ferraz, 'The Right Health in the Courts of Brazil: Worsening Health Inequities?' (2009) 11(2) *Health and Human Rights* 33, suggesting that judicialisation of rights in Brazil has limited health provision.

Bingham MR held the health authority acted rationally and fairly. 'Difficult and agonising judgments have to be made as to how a limited budget is best allocated to the maximum advantage of the maximum number of patients. That is not a judgment', he said, 'which the court can make.'[160] After the litigation, an anonymous private donor came forward to pay for the procedure. The consultant in Hammersmith then ended up performing, not a second bone marrow transplant, but an experimental procedure named donor lymphocyte infusion. The girl died a few months after this, her suffering intensified and prolonged as a result.[161]

The matter differs, however, when treatment or care has been promised or assured. In *R (Coughlan) v North and East Devon HA* Mrs Coughlan claimed she should be able to stay at the Mardon House care home near Exeter, Devon. She had suffered a road traffic accident in 1971, become tetraplegic and needed constant care. She had been assured by senior officers of the previous Exeter Health Authority that she and other residents had a 'home for life'. But in 1996 it was decided that the home had ostensibly become 'a prohibitively expensive white elephant' leaving 'fewer resources available for other services'. The Court of Appeal held that it would violate Mrs Coughlan's legitimate expectations to withdraw the home. Lord Woolf MR said that frustrating this expectation 'will amount to an abuse of power', and this was 'equivalent to a breach of contract in private law'.[162] The Secretary of State's general duty to promote a comprehensive, free health service 'may never, for human, financial and other resource reasons, be achievable',[163] but this did not justify having immunity for breaking specific promises.

A common reason given by NHS bodies for refusing treatment had previously been to say there were general policies about what could be funded and that, although exceptions could be made depending on need, individual cases were not exceptional. This was challenged in *R (Ann Marie Rogers) v Swindon Primary Care Trust*, where Ms Rogers claimed she should receive Herceptin treatment for HER2 breast cancer, despite this not yet being authorised by NICE. She argued her right to life was engaged under the European Convention, article 2, and that the policy to refuse treatment was irrational. Her consultant, Dr Cole, requested the treatment but was refused by Swindon PCT because her case was not 'exceptional' as all women with stage 1 breast cancer were in her position. However, the PCT's policy did allow funding for Herceptin, where it was prescribed by a clinician, and if it was decided that there were exceptional circumstances. Ms Rogers could only herself afford two

160 [1995] EWCA Civ 43. See also *R (Rose) v Thanet Clinical Commissioning Group* [2014] EWHC 1182 (Admin) (refusal by NICE to fund oocyte preservation for a woman with Crohn's disease undergoing treatment that would leave her infertile).

161 See P. Toynbee, 'Jaymee and Final Choices: The Story Behind the Story', *The Independent* (22 May 1996).

162 *R (Coughlan) v North and East Devon HA* [1999] EWCA Civ 1871, [57] and [86].

163 [1999] EWCA Civ 1871, [25].

doses. The Court of Appeal held the decision was irrational, because simply saying a case was not 'exceptional' was not enough. Sir Anthony Clarke MR held that 'once the PCT decided … it would fund Herceptin for some patients and that cost was irrelevant' it should focus on a patient's clinical needs and fund patients 'who were properly prescribed Herceptin by their physician'.[164] As a decision was reached at common law, it was not necessary to consider the engagement of the right to life under article 2.

What if there are long waiting lists for the NHS in the UK, and someone goes abroad to get treatment in an EU member state, and they pay for treatment? From 2013 to 2020, before Parliament drove through 'Brexit' and rights were scrapped, UK residents had a statutory right to go to other member states for treatment, and be reimbursed, if waiting times were unreasonably long – an assessment that had to be based on objective criteria.[165] This right flowed from the right to receive services under the TFEU, article 56 and the Patients' Rights Directive 2011.[166] The leading case is *R (Watts) v Bedford Primary Care Trust*, where in 2003 Mrs Watts travelled to France, paid £3,900 for a hip replacement operation and claimed she should be reimbursed. At the time, NHS waiting lists were four to six months. The Court of Justice's Grand Chamber held that healthcare did count as a 'service' under the Treaty. High demand could justify waiting lists in a national health system, but individual circumstances of the patient had to be assessed. This right to move for healthcare still applies among EU member states, but the Johnson government removed these rights for UK citizens as it halted EU membership.[167]

The duty in the NHS Act 2006, section 1 refers to the Secretary of State's duty to the people 'of England', and the duty under section 175 to make services available only to those 'ordinarily resident' in the UK. This raises the issue of charging foreign patients (see above Ch. 9(2)(c)), but what if someone is resident yet faces deportation to a country without adequate health facilities? This has become a human rights issue. In *N v United Kingdom*, a Ugandan citizen with HIV/AIDS claimed that she should not be deported, and it would amount to inhuman and degrading treatment under the ECHR, article 3, because, without treatment, she would be unlikely to live longer than two years in Uganda. The House of Lords and the European Court of Human Rights both held that there was no duty on the UK 'through provision of free and unlimited health care to all aliens without a right to stay within its jurisdiction. A finding to the contrary', it said, 'would place too great a burden on the Contracting States.'[168] On the other hand, if someone's death would be

[164] *R (Ann Marie Rogers) v Swindon Primary Care Trust* [2006] EWCA Civ 392, [81].

[165] NHS Act 2006, s. 6BB. NHS Constitution for England (27 July 2015) art. 3a(iv) states there is a right 'in certain circumstances, to go to other European Economic Area countries or Switzerland' for services that are also available on the NHS.

[166] TFEU, art. 57; the Patients' Rights Directive 2011/24/EU.

[167] (2006) C-372/04. See the National Health Service (Cross-Border Healthcare and Miscellaneous Amendments, etc.) (EU Exit) Regulations 2019/777, reg. 3.

[168] *N v United Kingdom* [2008] ECHR 453.

imminent the European Court of Human Rights has held that a decision to remove would violate article 3.[169] It is deeply regrettable that the UK chooses only to adopt the minimum standards of the Convention, rather than developing a more humane policy that prioritises life, wherever people are from. The question is not whether the UK has 'responsibility for the inadequacy of the healthcare system in the country of return',[170] but whether the UK values human life.

(b) Equal Treatment

The second main right is to be treated equally. According to the NHS Act 2006, section 1C, 'the Secretary of State must have regard to the need to reduce inequalities between the people of England with respect to the benefits that they can obtain from the health service'. The NHS Constitution further states there is a 'wider social duty to promote equality through the services it provides'.[171] As in education, the right to equal treatment is implicit in judicial review, so that where 'the clinical needs are equal, and resources are not an issue, discrimination between patients in the same eligible group cannot be justified on the basis of personal characteristics not based on healthcare'.[172] This is reaffirmed in the Equality Act 2010, section 29 where any 'service-provider' including for health or care may not discriminate against any person in the terms, or in the terminating, of provision or by any other detriment.[173]

(c) Medical Negligence

A third main right is for medical treatments to be performed competently. The ability to sue the NHS or doctors in the tort of negligence at all is controversial, given the waste inherent in the tort system.[174] In New Zealand, tort litigation was largely replaced by the Accident Compensation Corporation. Because of the cost of lawyers, and to people's lives in fighting, tort is uniquely poor at distributing money efficiently, or in ensuring that people have closure. For example, in 2020 it was reported that there were 11,682 clinical negligence claims against the NHS, and it paid out almost £2.324 billion in damages and legal fees.[175] Lawyers certainly profit, and it is entirely unclear that injured

[169] *D v United Kingdom* (1997) 24 EHRR 423 (deportation delayed, so the claimant could die in the UK).

[170] *GS (India) v Secretary of State for the Home Department* [2015] EWCA Civ 40, per Underhill LJ.

[171] NHS Constitution for England (27 July 2015) art. 1.

[172] *R (Ann Marie Rogers) v Swindon Primary Care Trust* [2006] EWCA Civ 392, [79].

[173] Equality Act 2010, s. 29 and Sch. 3, paras. 13–15 for limited exceptions of blood donations, for health of pregnant women or for care within the family.

[174] See generally J. Goudkamp and P. Cane, *Atiyah's Accidents, Compensation and the Law* (2018).

[175] NHS Resolution, *Annual Report and Accounts 2019–20* (2020). 'Lawyers Who Target the NHS Banned from Advertising or Setting Up Shop in Hospitals', *NHS News* (29 January 2018): 'The

patients, or the relatives of a deceased loved one who are dragged through the recurrent pain of litigation, gain as much.

However, regardless of the mechanism, there is a strong case for legally enforceable standards. Without standards of competence, there may be defective incentives for health managers to have systems that prevent accidents, or improve medical or nursing practices. For any wrong, the relevant NHS or other employer will be vicariously liable for any harm.[176] The duty will also be whether competence in performing a task fell below a standard of reasonable care, rather than achieving success in an operation. For example, in *Thake v Maurice*, the Court of Appeal held that two new parents could not sue Mr Maurice, who performed a vasectomy operation on Mr Thake, when the operation was unsuccessful and a new baby girl called Samantha was later born.[177] On the other hand, there was a breach of duty in tort for failing to warn of the small risk that the operation may not succeed. As the Supreme Court has said, an 'adult person of sound mind is entitled to decide which, if any, of the available forms of treatment to undergo, and [their] consent must be obtained before treatment interfering with [their] bodily integrity is undertaken'.[178]

(d) Conflicts of Interest

A fourth main right is for there to be no bias or conflicts of interest in medical decisions. This is implicit in judicial review. However, it can quickly be seen that every element of money in healthcare provision raises the prospect that health professionals may over-prescribe drugs or treatments when it is not in their patients' objective interests. This is primarily a structural problem which leaves individuals in an unfortunate position, since 'bias operates in such an insidious manner that the person alleged to be biased may be quite unconscious of its effect'.[179] The abolition of CCGs removed the conflict of interest in GPs being on GP boards, but at the time of writing an even worse proposal is to allow private corporation representatives to sit on ICBs.[180] General Medical Council Guidance further says that those with a financial or commercial interest in an organisation to which patients are referred must be told, and it must not influence decisions to refer.[181] However, the basic conflict comes

NHS spent £1.7 billion on clinical negligence claims in 2016/17, with legal costs accounting for 36 per cent of the total bill.'

176 *Majrowski v Guy's and St Thomas's NHS Trust* [2006] UKHL 34.

177 *Thake v Maurice* [1986] QB 644 (this was a question of breach of contract, although the same standards may be applied in judicial review).

178 See also *Montgomery v Lanarkshire Health Board* [2015] UKSC 11, [85]–[87].

179 *R v Gough* [1993] AC 646, 672, per Lord Woolf.

180 C. Newdick, 'From Hippocrates to Commodities: Three Models of NHS Governance' (2014) 22(2) *Medical L Rev* 162, 176. Cf. NHS Act 2006, s. 140(4) and HSCA 2012, s. 25.

181 General Medical Council, Good Medical Practice (2019) paras. 78–9.

from any measure of profit motive, or private corporations, interfering with decisions about people's lives and health.

(5) Conclusion

The UK's NHS goes far beyond the minimum health standards in international human rights law and, like other public systems, it is better. Despite many problems, the UK has longer life expectancy at lower cost because healthcare is social. The NHS is politically 'untouchable' because it works.[182] Its performance was, however, weakened by the HSCA 2012, which over mass protest diverted NHS resources to private profit, mainly through a conflicted and fractured system of CCGs. The failure to integrate social care and public health policy into the NHS has further costs, particularly since local authorities lack the size and powers necessary to combat leading causes of ill health, such as air pollution, the marketing of unhealthy food and excessive alcohol or use of tobacco. It is not merely that it is morally repugnant to make money out of sick people. Financing of the right to health is less efficient where it is more private, and private companies have an inherent incentive to sell unhealthy products whatever the cost to health. While public ownership of the NHS is better, its governance does not yet adequately represent staff, or patients and the public, through the vote. The rights to adequate, equal, competent and impartial treatment are closely upheld by the courts, but best resolved through open, accountable and democratic governance.

[182] P. Armstrong, 'Socialized Healthcare: The "Untouchable" of UK Politics', *CNN* (5 May 2010). British Future, *State of the Nation* (2013) 16–18 and 26, polling 2,515 people in 2012. 'Public Satisfaction with the NHS' (2016) www.kingsfund.org.uk.

10

Banking

Contents

Whether or not 'the love of money is the root of all evil',[1] access to money is the root of much enterprise. Ideally, banks should channel savings into investment.[2] Banks make loans, and so have huge influence on economic activity. If banks give more credit, people spend more money. If everyone spends money wisely, if more people are productively employed and the supply of goods and services expands proportionally, this creates beneficial economic development. But if more people spend (without improving productivity) and the supply of goods and services does not expand, the increased competition for limited resources will result in inflation: price rises, relative to people's income or wealth. History is littered with hyperinflation, asset price bubbles, crashes, savings lost and unemployment. Banking law therefore engages many human rights. Banks are at the heart of the system of private property,[3] even though depositors are told they have no property in their accounts, only a contract. Banks affect the prices of goods and services, including the human rights to 'food, clothing, housing', or any other right

[1] 1 Timothy 6:10: *radix malorum est cupiditas*. G. Chaucer, 'The Pardoner's Tale' in The Canterbury Tales (1389).

[2] Similar definitions appear in the Credit Requirements Regulation (EU) No. 575/2013, art. 4(1), as one that acts to 'take deposits or other repayable funds from the public and to grant credits for its own account'. In the USA, see the Bank Holding Company Act of 1956, 12 USC ch. 17, §1841(a).

[3] Cf. ECHR 1950, Prot. 1, art. 1 (peaceful enjoyment of possessions); UDHR 1948, art. 17 (right to own property).

sold on markets. Banks also influence the 'right to work' and 'just and favourable remuneration', because credit influences employment.[4]

Today, banking law appears to accept a theory that there should be some degree of competition, but banks should be left to maximise profit, while central banks or regulators merely administer a framework of rules for minimal prudence and competence.[5] Private bank competition is limited. In UK retail banking, there are four big firms managing 75 per cent of current and 85 per cent of business accounts: HSBC, Barclays, RBS and Lloyds. In investment banking, the global market is dominated by US firms: J. P. Morgan, Goldman Sachs, Bank of America/Merrill Lynch and Citi. Banks have few incentives to lend money to new competitors to start up. Also, if banks' main customers are employers, it will be profitable to restrict the supply of credit, to maintain enough unemployment to keep wages down and capital returns up. Meanwhile banks' global growth has shifted the balance of power away from the public. Central banks, like the Bank of England, European Central Bank (ECB) and the US Federal Reserve mainly influence inflation and employment by changing the interest rates they charge to private banks in their jurisdictions, or by using the state's tax-backed power to buy or sell enough securities to influence the total money supply. But if global private banks can finance themselves, if their profession controls central bank practices, or if their staff run Treasuries, monetary policy starts pursuing conflicted goals. At the moment, central bank action does not directly help consumers, workers or business: it is filtered through private banks. This raises the simple question of why the public cannot access central bank credit on the same terms as private banks, or why public banks could not do the same.

(1) Historical Background

The history of banking law is one of periodic ruin, exploitation, prejudice and greed, and yet it shows that sound finance is essential for human development. Banks have existed for thousands of years, from the ancient civilisations who first created debt and interest,[6] to Christian crusaders who financed war through the Knights Templar, learning the arts of lending from the Muslims they fought.[7] The word 'bank' developed in medieval Italy from the benches, or banca, where money lenders used to sit. Christianity originally taught that money-lending for interest was usury and evil,[8] so popes and kings had relied

[4] UDHR 1948, arts. 23 and 25; ICESCR 1966, arts. 6–7 and 11.

[5] Cf. E. P. Ellinger, E. Lomnicka and C. V. M. Hare, *Ellinger's Modern Law of Banking* (2011) chs. 1–2 and 5.

[6] D. Graeber, *Debt: The First 5,000 Years* (2011) chs. 8–9, and 261, noting in ancient Mesopotamia that by the time of King Enmetena of Lagash, around 2400 BC, 'Usury – in the sense of interest-bearing consumer loans – was also well established.'

[7] Graeber, *Debt*, ch. 10, 291. The Knights Templar were tortured and killed by King Philip IV, in debt to them.

[8] T. Aquinas, *Summa Theologica* (1274) II-II, Q. 77.

on Jewish communities for banking services. At the same time, Jewish people were stigmatised, confined to ghettos, persecuted or expelled throughout history.[9] However, Christian theories against usury were relaxed after the Black Death as trade resurrected. Starting in Florence, networks of banks were established that, in effect, loaned money for profit through bills of exchange in different currencies.[10] Gradually, the most significant bank came to be that of Giovanni di Bicci de' Medici, the banker to the papacy when his friend was elected as Pope John XIII in 1410. The Medici family's wealth was then rapidly translated into power. Giovanni's son Cosimo first ruled over Florence from 1434 and, under Cosimo, a Medici bank branch opened in London, with the other Italian banks populating Lombard Street in the City.[11] Cosimo's grandson became Pope Leo X in 1513, and started selling 'indulgences', supposedly passports into heaven for the rich, to finance lavish rebuilding of St Peter's Cathedral in Rome. This led Martin Luther to nail his ninety-five theses to the door of the church in Wittenberg (now in Germany) and triggered the Protestant Reformation. Despite the disastrous start to this bank-led takeover of Christianity, quite distant now from rules against usury, the Medici descendants controlled the papacy until 1605, and inhabited the French Crown until 1630.

The myth and hypocrisy of Christian purity and Jewish usury continued in fiction,[12] while charging interest on money continued in fact, and new banks were incorporated around Europe.[13] The Bank of England was established as a joint-stock corporation in 1694,[14] originally to raise money for the Nine Years' War with Louis XIV of France. Known by its headquarters from 1734 as 'the Old Lady of Threadneedle Street', the Bank of England used capital from investors to lend money to the Crown. It also gave loans to people in Flanders to wage war, started accounts for other bankers and goldsmiths, issued notes

[9] E.g. in England, *Statuta de Judaismo* 1218, 1222, 1253 and 1275 (preventing Jews owning property, employing Christian servants or even eating with Christians); Edict of Expulsion 1290. B. L. Abrahams, 'Expulsion of the Jews from England in 1290' (1894) 7(1) *Jewish Q Rev* 75. This lasted until 1655.

[10] R. A. Goldthwaite, 'The Medici Bank and the World of Florentine Capitalism' (1987) 114 *Past & Present* 3, 7. To evade usury laws, instead of simply lending money at a certain interest rate, merchants in Florence would be given, say, 100 florins in return for a cheque, and they would repay 500 livre (which was worth more than 100 florins on international exchange rates) in Lyon 90 days later, after selling goods and making a profit: D. DeMatos, 'The Medici Bank and Letters of Credit', Tontine-Coffee House Blog (21 January 2019).

[11] NB: At the same time Italian bankers had invented the lotho, lotteries used to raise finances, and these spread as a mechanism of fiscal policy (see Ch. 20). They were used to finance the colony of Virginia, Harvard and Yale, and the 'Million Adventure' lottery of 1694 raised £1m (5 & 6 Will. & Mar., c. 7) alongside the Bank of England. R. D. Richards, 'The Lottery in the History of English Government Finance' (1934) 44 (Supp) *Economic J* 57.

[12] E.g. W. Shakespeare, 'The Merchant of Venice' (1605) where Shylock the Jewish money-lender gives the merchant, Antonio, a loan on the promise of a pound of flesh if the loan is not repaid. At the climax, Shylock's contract is construed *contra proferentem* by the Venetian court, so only flesh not blood may be taken for non-payment.

[13] E.g. Bank of Amsterdam in 1609, Bank of Hamburg in 1619 and Bank of Sweden in 1656.

[14] Bank of England Act 1694 (5 & 6 Will. & Mar., c. 20). £500 of stock bought one vote.

and grew as a 'clearing' house for people to settle debts.[15] The Bank, of course, differed from the Mint, which by royal proclamation had long had a monopoly on the coins that people used.[16] Isaac Newton, appointed Master of the Mint from 1696 to 1727, was probably more famous then for his prolific work in putting people to death for breaking the laws of 'treason' (i.e. for coin clipping or counterfeiting) than for his laws of physics.[17] In this time, there was still no real understanding or public policy on how much credit (from bank lending) should be created, but there was increasing confidence in the creation of a national debt, to be repaid periodically to the Bank (and its shareholders) by government through tax.

By the Acts of Union 1707, the new government of Great Britain had accumulated heavy debt to many creditors. As a rival to the Bank of England (which was backed by the Whig faction in Parliament), the South Sea Company was established by royal charter in 1711. It was to engage in the British-sponsored slave trade in the seas around South America, and at the same time consolidate the national debt, by letting people swap government bonds for South Sea Company shares.[18] After Britain's victory in the War of Spanish Succession and the Treaty of Utrecht 1713, it acquired the right to supply Spain's genocidal colonies with people forcibly abducted from Africa and enslaved.[19] At the end of 1719, it was agreed that the South Sea Company should assume even more of the national debt and, to encourage business, its directors started spreading rumours about all the lucrative 'opportunities' in the New World.[20] As more people wanted in, the share price rose, and as the share price rose, more wanted in. The price soared from around £100 to nearly £1,000 a share.[21] In June 1720, the Bubble Act was passed incorporating two insurance companies and banning any other corporation that did not have an Act of Parliament or a royal charter, leading to another boost in South Sea Company stock.[22] Everyone was in: dukes, bishops, ministers, royalty, poets, even physicists. But then by August 1720, people realised the company's prospects were not so brilliant, and the stock bubble burst, ruining thousands. Newton is reputed to have said he 'could calculate the motions of the heavenly

[15] J. Clapham, *The Bank of England: A History* (1944) chs. 1–2.

[16] E.g. Coin Act 1696, and Acts of 1351, 1402, 1523, 1662, 1666, 1672, 1685, 1694, 1695, 1696, 1697, etc.

[17] R. S. Westfall, *Never at Rest: A Biography of Isaac Newton* (1991) ch. 12.

[18] J. Carswell, *The South Sea Bubble* (1960); J. Hoppit, 'The Myths of the South Sea Bubble' (2012) 12 *Transactions of the Royal Historical Society* 141, 142–3, explaining how debt owed by the UK government was primarily to (1) the South Sea Company, (2) the Bank of England and (3) the East India Company.

[19] Real Asiento de Inglaterra 1713.

[20] R. Dale, *The First Crash: Lessons from the South Sea Bubble* (2004) ch. 3.

[21] Hoppit, 'The Myths of the South Sea Bubble'.

[22] Royal Exchange and London Assurance Corporation Act 1719 (6 Geo. I, c. 18) ss. XVII–XXIV. Note, the old system of dating referred to the Bill's introduction in Parliament, not its Royal Assent.

stars, but not the madness of people'.[23] Crucially, the South Sea Company collapse solidified the Bank of England as the primary lender to the British government, and bank of banks.[24]

Over the 1700s and 1800s, the Bank of England remained a private institution, but with a steadily increasing number of statutory rights recognising and solidifying its power.[25] Other savings banks were set up, but from 1817 they were required to invest in government bonds, or put deposits with the Bank of England.[26] While other banks had issued their own notes before, the Bank Charter Act 1844 gave the Bank of England the sole right to issue notes and coins. It adopted an explicit 'gold standard', requiring new notes to be backed by gold reserves, and fixing a rate by law for exchanging gold for bank notes.[27] The idea of this 'bullionism', propounded by the mildly cult-like 'metallists',[28] was to fix currency in the British Empire to something (supposedly) stable, and fix the exchange rate of any other currency that adopted this gold standard too.[29] This rejected the idea that people could rely on money's value through trust and confidence in the state's sound economic management, and indeed there was precious little of that. In periodic slumps, the Bank acted as an emergency lender to prop up other banks that faced collapse.[30] In practice, because other banks had deposits with it, the Bank could influence interest rates across the economy by altering its interest rate on other banks' bank accounts. With cheaper credit, it could drive a boom and, with dearer credit, it could dampen all lending and economic activity. Paying out steady dividends to shareholders,[31] the Bank of England began and remained until 1947 a private institution, yet one that financed the state and was intimately involved in political power.

23 Westfall *Never at Rest*, ch. 15.

24 E. P. Ellinger, E. Lomnicka and C. V. M. Hare, *Ellinger's Modern Banking Law* (5th ed. 2011) ch. 2, 30.

25 E.g. Bank of England Act 1716 had widened its borrowing powers after a shortage of funds crisis. Bank Restriction Act 1797 removed the requirement to convert notes to gold on demand.

26 Savings Bank (England) Act 1817. Also Savings Banks Act 1828 and Savings Banks Acts Amendment Act 1863. Savings Bank Act 1891 limited assets. Savings Banks Act 1904 enabled purchase of land and buildings.

27 See generally I. Frame, 'Between the "Bank Screw" and "Affording Assistance". Rules, Standards, and the Bank Charter Act of 1844' (2019) 83(1) *MLR* 64. Bank Charter Act 1844, ss. II and IV (set at £3 17s 9d per ounce).

28 Graeber, *Debt*, ch. 9, on metallism.

29 See later Coinage Act 1870 (defined sovereign as 123.27447 grains troy of standard gold), Currency and Bank Notes Act 1914 (abandoned), Gold Standard Act 1925 (resumed), Gold Standard (Amendment) Act 1931 (abandoned). Cf. *Norman v Baltimore and Ohio Railroad Company*, 294 US 240 (1935) after the USA declared contracts linking payment to gold against public policy after the USA came off the gold standard in 1933; and cf. *Feist v Société Intercommunale Belge d'Électricité* [1934] AC 161; *R v International Trustees for the Protection of Bondholders* [1937] 2 All ER 164; O. Kahn-Freund (1937) 1(2) *MLR* 158.

30 W. Bagehot, *Lombard Street: A Description of the Money Market* (1873) discussing Overend, Gurney and Co.

31 J. Clapham, *The Bank of England: A History* (1944) vol. II, Appendix A.

Meanwhile, since US independence, Americans had been intensely opposed to bank and corporate power, and the early national banks were scuppered. Alexander Hamilton, the first Secretary of the Treasury, established the first national Bank of the USA in 1791, with 20 per cent of stock held by the federal government, but its charter was time-limited. Hamilton was keen to emphasise that large shareholder voting power was capped,[32] because allowing one vote per share would be 'extreme' and enable 'a few principal stockholders, to monopolize the power and benefits of the bank'.[33] Even then, with opposition from farming interests and suspicious states, who preferred their own smaller banks, the bank charter was left to expire in 1811. The War of 1812, in which British troops set fire to the White House, exposed the inability of state banks to raise war finance.[34] A second Bank of the USA was chartered from 1816 to 1836, but again lapsed with President Andrew Jackson's opposition.[35] In the Civil War, with southern opponents absent from Congress, the National Banking Act of 1863 enabled federal chartering of state banks. Yet there were many panics and slumps among the thousands of state and federal banks.[36] Eventually, this led to the Federal Reserve Act of 1913. It created an association of District Federal Reserve banks, regulated by a new US Federal Reserve Board of Governors, appointed by the president. All national chartered banks had to be members, and state banks could choose to be. Members would then have to hold 6 per cent of their capital in District Bank stock, would maintain reserves that they did not lend out and could buy and sell government bonds. This cultivated reliance and, like the Bank of England, gave the 'Fed' influence over credit and interest levels in other banks.

The US Federal Reserve system did nothing to stop an irrational boom and then the Wall Street Crash of 1929. Republican presidents from 1918 to 1932 seemed more concerned with stoking a 'red scare' after the Russian Revolution led to Lenin's bank nationalisations.[37] The crash affected everyone, because the size of the American economy after World War One had led to huge US investment in the UK, Germany and the world over. When markets crashed in the USA, investment withdrew, exacerbated by the Hoover policy of putting up

[32] National Bank Act of 1791 §7, 1 Stat 191, 193.

[33] Alexander Hamilton, Report on a National Bank, Communicated to the House of Representatives (14 December 1790); H. C. Lodge, *The Works of Alexander Hamilton* (1904) 388, 423.

[34] W. A. Lovett, *Banking and Financial Institutions Law* (7th ed. 2009) ch. 1, 9.

[35] Lovett, *Banking and Financial Institutions Law*, 10–11.

[36] Cf. L. Brandeis, *Other People's Money and How the Bankers Use It* (1914) ch. 1.

[37] V. I. Lenin, 'Nationalisation of the Banks' in *The Impending Catastrophe and How to Combat It* (1917), where Lenin set out his policies to nationalise banks by swapping shares for debt, though the reality was that banks were taken by force without compensation: J. N. Westwood, *Endurance and Endeavour* (2002) ch. 11, 275–7. Cf. *Russian Commercial and Industrial Bank v Comptoir d'Estcompte de Mulhouse* [1923] 2 KB 630, Atkin LJ dissenting (upheld in [1925] AC 112), said that it was 'assumed too readily that nationalization involves extinction . . . a business may be nationalized or amalgamated without the persons who owned the business being extinguished'.

tariffs to supposedly protect domestic trade.[38] The crash occurred because without modern securities law to give investors information, there was wild speculation on shares (see Ch. 4(2)(b)) and because, without public pensions, millions of Americans saved in the stock market for retirement (see Ch. 5(2)(b)).[39] Furthermore, many commercial banks had engaged in investment banking, underwriting stock and bond issues. When the stock crash bankrupted investment banks, millions of small savers' bank accounts were lost too.

To rescue America from depression, the new Roosevelt government started by passing the Banking Act of 1933. This separated commercial banking from investment banks, and created the Federal Deposit Insurance Corporation, to guarantee people's deposits and so prevent bank runs.[40] The disaster of 24 per cent unemployment also led to changes in all priorities of government. Roosevelt's 'New Deal' included massive programmes of public works such as the Works Progress Administration to re-employ people,[41] and the Federal Reserve's priorities, with a new Federal Open Market Committee, were changed to include achieving 'maximum' employment by 1946.[42] Back over the Atlantic, in the UK, the response to depression in the Macmillan Report of 1931 (much of it written by John Maynard Keynes[43]) recommended nationalisation of the Bank of England, government regulation of international trade and a minority advocated a wide programme of public works.[44] It did not succeed at the time, but would after World War Two, as the Bank of England Act 1946 finally ended its private ownership, with the power of the Treasury to give directions to the Bank on monetary policy 'in the public interest'.[45] This complemented the commitment of the UK government to achieve full employment, by fiscal spending, by changing monetary policy and by the regulation of trade.[46]

The Wall Street Crash, Great Depression and global collapse were major causes of a psychopath with a silly moustache, who blamed communists and Jews for all his problems, coming to power in Germany.[47] As President Roosevelt put it towards the end of the war, 'People who are hungry and out of a job are the stuff of which dictatorships are made.'[48] And so for after the

[38] Smoot-Hawley Tariff Act of 1930.

[39] *Buckstegge v Arizona*, 158 Pac 837 (1916) struck down an attempt to create a state pension.

[40] Banking Act of 1933. [41] Emergency Relief Appropriation Act of 1935.

[42] Employment Act of 1946, 15 USC, §1021.

[43] See also J. M. Keynes, *The General Theory of Employment, Interest and Money* (1936).

[44] H. P. Macmillan, *Committee on Finance and Industry*, Cmd 3897 (1931).

[45] Bank of England Act 1946, s. 4. Cf. *Commonwealth of Australia v Bank of New South Wales* [1950] AC 235, (1949) 79 CLR 497 (Privy Council advised the Banking Act 1947 violated the Australian Constitution, s. 92).

[46] White Paper, *Employment Policy*, Cmd 6527 (1944).

[47] E.g. A. Hitler, *Mein Kampf* (1924) 254, says the 'sole task' of the 'lying Marxist press' is to 'break the national backbone of the people, thus preparing the nation to become the slaves of international finance and its masters, the Jews'. I do not really recommend reading it, but a glance at this book shows Hitler was nasty nuts.

[48] F. D. Roosevelt, 'Eleventh State of the Union Address' (1944).

war, a new international financial system was seen as essential for geopolitical stability. In 1944, the Bretton-Woods conference was held among allied nations.[49] First, it decided there should be a new World Bank with power to give money for international reconstruction and development. Second, an International Monetary Fund (IMF) would have power to lend. A central goal of the IMF was stability in currency exchange rates: countries could restrict the free movement of capital, but currencies were pegged to the US dollar, and in turn the USA pledged to back its currency with gold reserves. This was meant to limit currency speculation for stable trade, but it broke down in 1971 after Germany left the Bretton-Woods system, and Nixon's US government unilaterally ended its commitment to give other countries gold for their dollar reserves. Since then, most currencies came to float, with exchange rates valued largely by the confidence (or approval) of financial institutions in the credibility of their governments to maintain the currency as a store of value (i.e. if you think pounds will not buy you much, especially if the UK produces little, you will hold fewer pounds). A third pillar, an International Trade Organisation to promote free trade and redistribute large trade surpluses, as proposed by Keynes, was vetoed by the USA because it benefited too much from its trade surplus. Instead, there was the looser General Agreement on Tariffs and Trade 1947, expanded into the World Trade Organization in 1994. It only had mandates for reducing tariffs or 'regulatory barriers', but not raising standards for financial prudence, development, the environment or labour rights, or anything to truly mitigate imbalance of trade.[50]

After 1979, there were three major shifts in banking law. First, both the Thatcher and Reagan governments adopted theories of 'monetarism', largely associated with Milton Friedman and Friedrich von Hayek,[51] that fiscal spending for full employment was no longer desirable, and that all economies needed was steady expansion of the money supply (i.e. banks lending on credit) to achieve growth. Too much credit would be inflationary, and higher wages were also inflationary. As soon as these theories were tested, they spelt disaster. Coupled with the OPEC hikes in oil prices (see Ch. 11(1)), spending cuts by government and high interest rates from the central bank made unemployment soar in the 1980s. Yet the theories remained. When the Blair/Brown government passed the Bank of England Act 1998, designed to create arm's-length 'independence' from the Treasury,[52] it seemed to prioritise price

49 UN Monetary and Financial Conference (July 1944).

50 Cf. Singapore Ministerial Conference 1996, declining to integrate labour standards and B. Hepple, *Labour Laws and Global Trade* (2005) predicting the multiplication of bilateral treaties given the global failure.

51 E. McGaughey, 'Will Robots Automate Your Job Away? Full Employment, Basic Income and Economic Democracy' (2021) *Industrial LJ*, explains these evidence-free theories and the alternatives.

52 This idea was modelled on the Accord of the US Federal Reserve and US Treasury of 4 March 1951.

stability,[53] with less regard to full employment, fair wages or regional development. When the European Union (EU) created the Euro in 2002, the ECB's mandate appeared similar.

Second, there was a general pattern of deregulation, expanding the number of institutions that could perform banking services, and enabling mutuals and building societies to convert into profit-making companies.[54] In the USA, deregulation led to the Savings and Loans Crisis from 1986.[55] The Gramm–Leach–Bliley Financial Services Modernization Act of the 1999 Republican-led Congress, not vetoed by Bill Clinton, removed the ban on commercial and investment bank mergers that had existed since the Glass–Steagall Act of 1932. Under George W. Bush, the federal government encouraged home loans with few conditions, but allowed extortionate variable interest rates to be hidden in the small print. It also halted any real oversight of derivatives markets, which traded sub-prime mortgage debt.[56] This culminated in the global financial crisis, when Bear Stearns, and the Lehman Brothers, then everyone, realised that people were going bankrupt and not able to repay their mortgages. This made the billions of dollars of derivatives on sub-prime mortgage debt worthless, leaving losses on bank balance sheets and sending them insolvent. The US government gave its banks money under its 'Troubled Asset Relief Program'. By contrast, the UK government nationalised its insolvent banks, but failed to prosecute or disqualify directors that caused the losses. From 2010, a Cameron-led coalition decided to launch an 'age of austerity' which led to the longest wage fall in modern history, blaming errant public-sector spending for the crash, rather than the banks that caused it.

Third, public international institutions, including the IMF and World Bank, began to couple loans to 'structural adjustment' requirements, namely privatisation and deregulation. The same logic was taken up by the ECB after the global financial crisis, as speculators began to bet on the weaknesses of members of the Euro. Greece, in particular, had less stable finances and was hit harder by the contraction of international investment in the global financial crisis. This was nothing, however, compared to the hit when international bond markets raised interest rates for Greek government borrowing to impossible levels. This caused more speculation about 'sovereign bankruptcy'. Though precluded by the Treaties from lending directly, the ECB bought Greek government debt on the secondary market, averting collapse. Yet it

53 Bank of England Act 1998, s. 11.

54 Banking Act 1979, s. 1; Building Societies Act 1986; Banking Act 1987, s. 1(1) (duty of supervision); Trustee Savings Banks Act 1981; Trustee Savings Banks Act 1985; *Vincent v Trustee Savings Banks Central Board* [1986] 1 WLR 1077 (a depositor in TSB Scotland had property in its assets, and no right to compensation).

55 Depository Institutions Deregulation and Monetary Control Act of 1980; Garn St Germain Depository Institutions Act of 1982.

56 J. C. Coffee, 'What Went Wrong? An Inquiry into the Causes of the 2008 Financial Crisis' (2009) 9(1) *J Corporate L Studies* 1; E. Warren, 'Product Safety Regulation as a Model for Financial Services Regulation' (2008) 43(2) *J Consumer Affairs* 452.

decided that in return for these loans, it would demand with the Commission and the IMF (the 'troika') an austerity programme, as it would also do for Spain and Ireland. This turned a debt crisis into a humanitarian disaster, with 1930s levels of unemployment, and social breakdown. Policies of monetarism, deregulation and austerity have, to some extent, been abandoned since the disasters of Trump, Brexit and the rise of the far-right in Europe. But the theories still hold much sway.

(2) Finance of Finance and Public Banks

The state ultimately backs the financial system by raising revenue from tax (see Ch. 20) but, like anyone else, it may also borrow and lend money. Though less reliant today, private banks draw financial support from central banks, invariably owned by governments. This section explains (a) central banks, (b) how monetary policy works, (c) the role of the World Bank and IMF, and (d) the limited existence of public option banks. Before this, some basic facts on the flow of funds, UK bank size, international banks and currencies need to be set out.

Outside crises, banks do not usually receive money from the state or central banks, but they do enjoy three main financial and legal subsidies. First, by monetary policy, private banks typically get lower interest rates in borrowing from the central bank than they charge on loans to their borrowers (see Ch. 10(2)(b)). Second, the solvency of private banks is usually guaranteed implicitly by law, and may lead to a direct 'bailout' (see Ch. 10(3)(d)). Third, deposits of bank customers are guaranteed by the state, eliminating a bank's own insurance costs (see Ch. 10(4)(b)). These regulatory subsidies mean bank profits would not exist without state support. Thus, the tacit flow of funds is as follows:

Account holders
↗
HM Treasury £ → Bank of England → HSBC, Lloyds, Barclays, RBS, etc → Homebuyers
↘
Businesses

The concentration of banks' market share in the UK, and across the world, is a remarkable feature of modern economies. Among the seven largest banks, six held 94% of the market share for current accounts in 2014,[57] 67.6% of the market share for mortgages in 2019[58] and over 90% of small business current accounts in 2015 (see Table 10.1).[59]

[57] Competition and. Markets Authority (CMA), *Personal Current Accounts: Market Study Update* (18 July 2014) 26 (note Lloyds then sold TSB).

[58] I. Tew, 'Mortgage Market Dominated by "Big Six"', *FT Advisor* (31 July 2019).

[59] CMA, *Retail Banking Market Investigation: Final Report* (9 August 2016) 222, Table 7.3, but this fails to give an accurate picture, rather than ranges (e.g. 20–30%). The statistics above therefore give the mean of each.

Table 10.1 Top UK banks

FTSE	Name	Current accounts	Mortgages	Small business
2	HSBC Holdings	12%	8%	15%
14	Lloyds Banking Group	31%	15.8%	25%
18	Royal Bank of Scotland (+ NatWest)	17%	11.4%	25%
20	Barclays	17%	8.6%	25%
28	Standard Chartered	-	-	-
-	Santander Group SA	10%	10.5%	7.5%
-	Nationwide	7%	13.3%	-

Big business banking statistics are harder to find. This mainly means investment banking – that is: (i) finance for major projects (e.g. a wind farm or bridge); (ii) guaranteeing (or 'underwriting') that shares will be sold in a public offer, as the promoter, or by promising to buy any unsold surplus (see Ch. 4(2)); or (iii) giving credit and advice in a takeover (see Ch. 4(3)).

The UK's largest banks also have a major presence abroad. Standard Chartered is entirely abroad for retail accounts and mortgages, but also offers business loans in the UK. Retail banking differs from investment banking, where global revenue is largely dominated by five US firms: J. P. Morgan, Goldman Sachs, Bank of America/Merrill Lynch, Morgan Stanley and Citi.[60] However, revenue (from takeovers, equity, bonds and loans) is just one guide, and differs from assets. In 2019, the world's largest banks by assets were as set out in Table 10.2.[61]

All these banks fall under the jurisdiction of a central bank: the People's Bank of China, the Bank of Japan, the US Federal Reserve, the Bank of England and the ECB for eurozone countries like France, Germany, Spain. International payments between businesses are financed through currency holdings of each bank, and regularly settled. In turn, the quantity of transactions done in each currency affects the foreign exchange rate.[62] If a currency's exchange rate is high, this makes buying goods and services relatively more expensive for foreign investors. If costs are unduly high, it inhibits trade. If an exchange rate appears low, this may attract investment, but if a currency is unduly low, a country's assets may often be sold to foreign owners, and citizens share less in the proceeds of growth and economic production. As well as operating monetary policy to influence prices and employment (see Ch. 10(2)(b)), central banks

60 'League Tables: % of Fees Collected by Product First 3 Quarters 2020', *Financial Times* (28 September 2020).

61 S. Garido and S. Chaudhry, 'The World's 100 Largest Banks', *S&P Global* (5 April 2019).

62 E.g. if Marks & Spencer, a UK company, wants to open business in China, it must buy buildings and pay staff in renminbi, purchased from the Bank of China with pounds. Many transactions like this will drive up demand for the renminbi. More investment in a country strengthens its currency relative to others, and vice versa. Cf. T. Hancock, 'Marks and Spencer Retreats from Mainland China', *Financial Times* (1 April 2017).

Table 10.2 Top world banks

	Name	Country	US$ bn assets
1	Industrial and Commercial Bank of China	China	4027.44
2	China Construction Bank Corporation	China	3376.52
3	Agricultural Bank of China	China	3287.36
4	Bank of China	China	3092.21
5	Mitsubishi UFJ Financial Group	Japan	2812.88
6	JPMorgan Chase & Co.	USA	2622.53
7	HSBC Holdings plc	UK	2558.12
8	Bank of America	USA	2354.51
9	BNP Paribas	France	2336.66
10	Credit Agricole	France	2123.61
11	Citigroup Inc.	USA	1917.38
12	Japan Post Bank	Japan	1911.48
13	Wells Fargo & Co.	USA	1895.88
14	Sumitomo Mitsui Financial Group	Japan	1848.2
15	Mizuho Financial Group	Japan	1837.8
16	Santander Group SA	Spain	1670.79
17	Deutsche Bank	Germany	1543.55
18	Société Générale	France	1485.31
19	Groupe BPCE	France	1462.7
20	Barclays plc	UK	1444.39
24	Lloyds Banking Group plc	UK	1016.55
36	Royal Bank of Scotland	UK	884.82
44	Standard Chartered	UK	688.76
84	Nationwide	UK	306.01

may buy and sell their own and other currencies to inflate or deflate demand, depending on the desired trade outcomes. All of these decisions have profound distributional implications, and this makes each central bank's governance structure a crucial social question.

(a) Central Bank Governance

As we have seen, in the UK the Bank of England became the dominant financial institution after the South Sea Bubble, and over the nineteenth century. Public money paid to the Exchequer through tax goes to the 'Consolidated Fund' and the Treasury's account is kept at the Bank of England.[63] The Bank of England is the main issuer of notes, while coin

[63] Exchequer and Audit Departments Act 1866, ss. 10–11 (consolidated fund at Bank of England) and 18–19 (choice of banks and separate accounts at the Bank).

production is entrusted to the Mint.[64] If the Bank makes a profit from issuing notes (known as 'seigniorage'), this must be paid to the Treasury.[65] As a rule, the Bank should never issue new notes, or the Mint issue coins, that do not reflect tax or bond receipts, or which are not paid for by other banks: if it just 'prints money' out of the blue, and gives this to itself, this devalues the currency because everyone can see (or will notice) what is happening.[66] Today, with increasing card and phone payments (which require a bank account), it seems likely that notes and coins may become rare, but it may also be an important social right, and a question of privacy, to buy goods and services without a bank account. While there is both a 'Bank of Scotland' and a 'Royal Bank of Scotland', which can also issue banknotes, these are private companies that do not have the Bank of England's constitutional functions.

The Bank of England Act 1998, section 1 states the Bank of England's 'court of directors' is 'appointed by Her Majesty' – that is, the Prime Minister on the royal prerogative. The government's original intent was for the court of directors to be 'able to take account of the full range of industrial and business views' and 'be fully representative of the whole of the United Kingdom'.[67] But nothing was made explicit in law. There simply needs to be a governing director, four deputy directors (for financial stability, markets and banking, monetary policy, and prudential regulation) and up to nine non-executives (up to fourteen in total). In 2021, there were twelve directors, including five women. One, Frances O'Grady, is also the head of the Trades Union Congress, while all others had careers in finance or management, including two with past jobs at Goldman Sachs, one at McKinsey, one in oil and two in private equity.[68] The Treasury may change the number of deputy directors after consulting the Bank's governor.[69] There are no formal requirements for regional or stakeholder representation.

The 'independence' of the Bank is partly meant to be seen in the appointment and removal of directors. The Bank's governor is appointed for eight years, and deputy governors for up to two five-year terms.[70] But a director can only be removed by the court with the Chancellor of the Exchequer's consent if they become a minister, get a job at a government department or the Bank itself, are absent for over three months, become bankrupt or are 'unable or

[64] Bank Charter Act 1844, ss. 10–11 (prohibition on issuing bank notes except for those banks issuing notes at the time); Currency and Bank Notes Act 1954, s. 1 (legal tender). The Royal Mint Ltd is a company wholly owned by the Treasury.

[65] Currency and Banknotes Act 1928, s. 6.

[66] This is how hyperinflation occurred in Germany: it was said that to pay punitive reparations under the Versailles Treaty 1919, Part VIII, Germany should simply print more notes. Printing excessive money is a stupid policy, or as put more diplomatically by R. Cranston, *Principles of Banking Law* (2nd ed. 2002) ch. 4, 111, 'a currency is a potent symbol of a polity's unity, integrity and perhaps strength. Governments interfere with it at their peril.'

[67] Mr Gordon Brown, Hansard HC Debs. (20 May 1997) col. 509.

[68] See www.bankofengland.co.uk/about/people/court-of-directors.

[69] Bank of England Act (BEA) 1998, s. 1A(1).

[70] BEA 1998, Sch. 1, paras. 1–2.

unfit to discharge [their] functions'.[71] The Bank is also 'independent' in what it pays: a subcommittee of three or more non-executive directors sets pay for the governor and deputies, while non-executives are paid whatever the Bank sets with the Chancellor of the Exchequer's approval.[72] In 2017 the governor, Mark Carney, was paid £880,042, while a deputy director received £357,402. That same year, the Bank's maintenance and security staff were forced to go on strike for a 1 per cent pay rise from wages under £20,000 a year.[73]

The relatively closed and unaccountable structure of the Bank of England contrasts with the USA. The Federal Reserve Act of 1913, §241 enables the president to appoint the Board of Governors, with the advice and consent of the Senate, but they 'shall have due regard to a fair representation of the financial, agricultural, industrial and commercial interests, and geographical divisions of the country'.[74] The Federal Reserve system has a group of twelve constituent banks. On the board of directors of each of these, three are chosen to represent stock-holding banks, and six to represent the public with regard to the interests of 'agriculture, commerce, industry, services, labor, and consumers', but three of those by the (central) Federal Reserve board.[75] The chair of the Fed was paid $203,500 in 2019, and other Fed governors $183,100. The Federal Reserve is therefore closer to a model of stakeholder-based accountability, but in practice it follows the political priorities of the president. As in the UK, there are no rights for stakeholder or regional representation.

For the nineteen Eurozone countries, the ECB, based in Frankfurt, controls monetary policy. Each country still also has a central bank (the Bundesbank, Banque de France, Banco de España and so on). But their roles have become subsidiary, and they have a duty to act compatibly with ECB policy.[76] The ECB has an executive board with a president, vice president and four other members, all appointed by the European Council by qualified majority, after consulting the European Parliament, and the Governing Council of the ECB.[77] This Governing Council is the existing ECB executive board as well as the governors of the central banks of the member states that use the euro.[78] The ECB members have eight-year, non-renewable terms. They can only be removed for gross misconduct, open to review by the Court of Justice of the EU (CJEU).[79] In 2019, there was one woman, four men and one vacancy on the board. In 2018, the president received a salary of €401,400. In all cases the central bank's most important function is setting monetary policy.

[71] BEA 1998, Sch. 1, paras. 5, 7–8. [72] BEA 1998, Sch. 1, paras. 14–15.
[73] See City & Finance Reporter, *This Is Money* (6 July 2017). [74] 12 USC, §241.
[75] 12 USC, §302. [76] TFEU, art. 131. [77] TFEU, art. 283(2). [78] ECB Statute, art. 10.
[79] ECB Statute, art 11.

(b) Monetary Policy

Monetary policy tries to steer inflation and employment across the economy, by influencing private banks. At the Bank of England, this is determined by the Monetary Policy Committee, which includes the governor, two deputies, two other Bank officials, and four more members appointed by the Chancellor of the Exchequer. They meet once a month, act by majority and carry out operations.[80] The ECB does not have a special committee, while the US Federal Reserve has the Federal Open Market Committee. There is fierce disagreement over the proper approach of monetary policy, because it has a powerful impact on income and wealth distribution. This section explains (i) some basic macroeconomic logic, (ii) the different goals of monetary policy in law and (iii) what the Bank of England and other central banks do, and can do, to achieve their goals.

(i) Macroeconomic Logic

Suppose that HSBC, Lloyds, Barclays, RBS and other private banks all put their interest rates up (i.e. the price of borrowing money) for people wanting personal loans, mortgages on homes or business credit. Fewer will borrow. Businesses will invest less, hire fewer people and spend less money. If fewer people are spending money and competing to buy goods and services then (other things being equal) prices in competitive markets are likely to fall. This might be good if inflation is rising too quickly and is reducing the worth of people's money. But it might be bad for regions that are depressed and need investment. If there are falling asset prices and wages – a sustained drop in 'effective aggregate demand' – it is a depression.[81] Extreme inequality in income and wealth also has a depressive effect, because poorer people have a higher 'propensity to consume' all their income.[82] Wealthier entities cannot consume everything, and instead invest in the financial system with transaction costs, or may save or hoard capital,[83] withdrawing it from productive use.

On the other hand, if all private banks put their interest rates down for loans, more people and businesses will borrow. More will be invested, more people will be hired, more money will be spent and the 'velocity of money' flowing through the economy will be higher, with higher aggregate demand.[84] If people spend more, and productive output is rising proportionally to meet demand, almost everyone will be better off. This balanced expansion of money and

[80] BEA 1998, s. 13 and Sch. 3, paras. 10–13.

[81] Keynes, *The General Theory of Employment, Interest and Money*, chs. 3 and 9.

[82] Keynes, *The General Theory of Employment, Interest and Money*, ch. 22, noting society might have 'social practices and . . . a distribution of wealth which result in a propensity to consume which is unduly low'.

[83] M. S. Eccles, *Beckoning Frontiers: Public and Personal Recollections* (1951) 75–7.

[84] Keynes, *The General Theory of Employment, Interest and Money*, chs. 15 and 21.

growth is ideal to raise everyone's real wages and living standards, if it is environmentally sustainable (see Chs. 11–15).

But if the output or supply of goods and services is not expanding to meet the rising demand (because the extra credit is not used productively), prices are likely to rise. That means inflation. If there are general price rises, but not corresponding wage rises, people who work for a living are becoming poorer in real terms. An insidious fact of inflation, as opposed to general pay cuts, is that people seem to notice it less.[85]

The first important distributional conflict in monetary policy concerns wages and employment. Suppose there is inflation for all prices and wages at 2% a year: this means everything is staying the same. But if prices rise at 4% a year, and wages rise at 2% a year, real wages are falling at −2% a year. Working people are getting poorer, but this may enrich business or asset owners who make income from capital or sell goods, not from work. Conversely, if wages are rising by 4% a year, and prices at 2% a year, working people are 2% better off a year. Asset owners may be better off as well, but if wealth also buys corporate power (see Ch. 3(2)), and increases bargaining power (Ch. 5(3)), business owners may object.[86]

The second important distributional conflict concerns regional development. In a competitive market, there are likely to be very similar interest rates across the country as a whole (and central banks set one rate). A higher interest rate could cool overspending or inflation in London, the Loire or Los Angeles, yet starve the necessary investment from a depressed Lancashire, Latvia or Louisiana. A lower interest rate faces the opposite problem, but it is likely to be resolved according to the political influence of the different regions. Normally, a country could overcome this and use fiscal policy (see Ch. 20) to invest directly in depressed areas, if monetary policy does not stimulate the private sector to help. Tax and spending provoke intense political conflict, but it can happen in the UK, USA or elsewhere. However, in the EU there is a prohibition on lending money by EU institutions to member states.[87] This prohibition responded to the political objection to richer member states having to unduly subsidise poorer member states, but it led to the Eurozone crisis (see Ch. 10(2)(b)(iii)).

(ii) Goals of Monetary Policy

Three very different approaches to the goals of monetary policy are seen between the UK, the Eurozone and the USA. First, the Bank of England Act 1998, section 11 states that the objectives of monetary policy are to (a) 'maintain price stability, and (b) subject to that, to support the economic policy of Her Majesty's Government, including its objectives for growth and

[85] Keynes, *The General Theory of Employment, Interest and Money*, ch. 19, point (6).
[86] M. Kalecki, 'Political Aspects of Full Employment' (1943) 14(4) *Political Q* 347, 352.
[87] TFEU, art. 123(1).

employment'. Thus 'price stability' appears more important than 'growth and employment', but there is no further definition of what 'price stability' means. Instead, under section 12, each year the Treasury gives its interpretation of 'price stability' and 'economic policy', and an inflation target. This gives great discretion to the executive.

How could 'price stability' be interpreted? First, it could mean stability in the prices of goods and services, typically measured by the Consumer Price Index (CPI). Second, it could also include stability in house or rent prices, which together with other goods and services are measured by the Retail Price Index (RPI).[88] The USA uses the CPI, while the UK government has used the RPI, but has been under pressure to switch. The Bank of England did switch to using the CPI in 2003 for its inflation targeting.[89] Thus, it has ignored escalating house and rent prices, which may profit banks that give mortgages, and homeowners, but disadvantage people who are indebted or renting their homes. Third, price stability could be taken to include wages, so that if there are real wage rises (particularly with full employment) central bankers may think it appropriate (but few would say it[90]) to suppress lending and cool wage growth. There seems to be less concern among central banks about escalating CEO pay, and income inequality.

A second model is the ECB, where the 'primary objective ... shall be to maintain price stability. Without prejudice to that objective, it shall support the general economic policies in the Union.'[91] However, unlike in the UK, interpretation of price stability is left to the ECB itself, where members are mainly drawn from the banking profession. This is reflective of the German Bundesbank's historic concern with price stability since the politically induced hyperinflation of the 1920s.[92]

But although the specific rules on the ECB prioritise maintaining price stability and leave its interpretation to the Bank, it has been convincingly argued that this cannot conflict with the general rules of the Treaties.[93] The Treaty on European Union (TEU), article 3(3) states the EU's aims to include

[88] Office for National Statistics, *Consumer Price Indices: A Brief Guide* (2013) 5 and 20.

[89] HM Treasury, 'Annex: The New Inflation Target' (December 2003): 'Following his announcement on 9 June 2003, the Chancellor has confirmed that the new inflation target will be based on the harmonised index of consumer prices.' Then it predicted 'house price inflation at these rates [seen since 1997] is unlikely to continue'. This was wrong, and it was worse until the global banking crash: see Ch 14(4)(a)(i).

[90] Cf. Pandora's Box, Episode 3: The League of Gentlemen, BBC 2 (Thursday, 18 June 1992): A. Budd speaking of his 'nightmare' that while he was working at the Treasury on monetary policy, people working with him could have thought the policy of raising interest rates 'would be a very, very good way to raise unemployment, and raising unemployment was an extremely desirable way of, of reducing the strength of the working classes'.

[91] TFEU, art. 282.

[92] Cf. B. Hayo, 'Inflation Culture, Central Bank Independence and Price Stability' (1998) 14 *Eur J Political Economy* 241.

[93] See M. Roth, 'Employment as a Goal of Monetary Policy of the European Central Bank' (2015) https://papers.ssrn.com/sol3/papers.cfm?abstract_id=2656646.

'balanced economic growth and price stability, a highly competitive social market economy, aiming at full employment and social progress, and a high level of protection and improvement of the quality of the environment'.[94] Stable prices have no social value if there is mass unemployment or poverty. But the reality is the ECB currently reserves to itself a broad margin of discretion, largely unchallenged. From 2011–14, it contributed to catastrophic rates of unemployment and inflation in the Mediterranean, while inequality has spiralled across Europe (below).

A third model is the US Federal Reserve Act of 1913, which requires that the Fed maintains the 'long run growth of the monetary and credit aggregates commensurate with the economy's long run potential to increase production, so as to promote effectively the goals of maximum employment, stable prices, and moderate long-term interest rates'.[95] These goals, which prioritise full employment, seemingly ahead of stable prices and moderate interest rates, were enacted in the post-war period,[96] follow the philosophy of the Universal Declaration of Human Rights, that embodies the 'right to work' with 'just and favourable remuneration'.[97] The goal of full employment was generally seen as paramount in the post-war period, because 'people who are hungry and out of a job are the stuff of which dictatorships are made'.[98] But despite these legal goals, the reality is that monetary policy practice follows the priorities of those in the central bank, appointed by the US president. Like all countries, the keys to uphold the human rights of full employment, fair wages, clothing, food or housing, are pocketed in central bank governance (see Ch. 10(2)(a)).

(iii) Monetary Policy Powers

There are four main types of policy powers to influence inflation or employment, which have been used to a greater or lesser extent by different central banks.[99] Though there are different limits to each across jurisdictions, in principle a central bank could (1) fix private banks' lending rules or interest rates; (2) fix private banks' reserve requirements; (3) lend money to banks, known as 'discount operations'; or (4) subsidise private banks through cheap government debt, known as 'open market operations' (OMOs). In a field that delights in impenetrable jargon, to evade accountability, OMOs are favoured by the banking industry.

First, a central bank could direct private banks to adopt specific deposit or loan policies – for instance, at a certain interest rate or requiring a minimum down-payment. The Bank of England Act 1946, section 4(3) says that the Bank,

[94] TEU, art. 3(3). Also TFEU, art. 9 refers to a 'high level of employment'.

[95] Federal Reserve Act of 1913, 12 USC, §225a.

[96] Employment Act of 1946 and the Humphrey-Hawkins Full Employment Act of 1978. See K. V. W. Stone, 'A Right to Work in the United States' in V. Mantouvalou (ed.), *The Right to Work* (2015) ch. 15.

[97] UDHR 1948, art. 23. [98] Roosevelt, 'Eleventh State of the Union Address'.

[99] Cranston, *Principles of Banking Law*, 121–2.

if 'necessary in the public interest ... may, if so authorised by the Treasury, issue directions to any banker for the purpose of securing that effect is given to any such request or recommendation'.[100] No order has ever been issued, and a general view among bankers, as Professor Cranston has put it, is that it would be 'transparent and quickly effective, although it will soon lead to distortions'.[101] There appears, however, to be no credible empirical evidence (as opposed to economic theory) to support the claim that setting sensible minimum standards would create 'distortions', particularly when confronted with a financial crisis that itself is a market failure. In turn, the Treasury may give directions to the Bank,[102] but if concerned with monetary policy, only 'if they are satisfied that the directions are required by the public interest and by extreme economic circumstances'.[103] The Treasury may not give directions concerning the Bank's role as the Prudential Regulation Authority (PRA), a fact which creates an odd asymmetry in the structure of democratic accountability.[104] The Federal Reserve used to have such powers, but these were removed.[105] The ECB does not have any such powers.[106] On the other hand, consumer protection laws are probably among the strongest 'prudential regulations' – for instance, by limiting exploitative interest rates (see Ch. 10(4)(c)).[107] The problem is, if a public option bank does not exist to provide competition at reasonable cost (below), it is likely that banks will collectively raise fees and restrict the supply of capital. It is in their collective interest to do so, and it is difficult to see what difference competition can make to such a unity of interest.

Second, the central bank may direct private banks to set aside higher or lower reserves, proportionate to their lending. The Bank of England Act 1946, section 4(3) empowers the Bank to impose reserve requirements by order, but again it has never done so because banks typically respond to requests.[108] If banks have to hold more money in reserves (e.g. 10 per cent) for the amount that they lend (e.g. £1 billion = £100 million) then they are likely to lend less than if they were required to have no reserves. The ECB[109] and the US Federal

[100] BEA 1946, s. 4(3) provided that it is general and not about 'the affairs of any particular customer of a banker', and the Bank must allow a bank to make representations on the issue.

[101] Cranston, *Principles of Banking Law*, 121, but see also the new, third edition (2018) edited by R. Cranston, E. Avgouleas, K. van Zwieten, C. Hare and T. van Sante.

[102] BEA 1946, s. 4(1). [103] BEA 1946, s. 19.

[104] BEA 1946, s. 4(1)(b). Why should the Treasury be able to direct monetary policy, but not bank authorisation?

[105] B. Jacobsen, 'The Law of Monetary Policy' (2008) SSRN, 19: 'the Federal Reserve no longer has the statutory authority to impose credit controls or deposit-rate ceilings'. The authority was originally provided by Executive Order No. 8843 (August 9, 1941) and subsequently the Defense Production Act of 1950, §601. See now 50 USC, §4531.

[106] ECB Statute, Prot. 4, arts. 18–19 enumerate powers.

[107] E.g. Consumer Credit Act 1974, s. 140A; see *Kerrigan v Elevate Credit International Ltd* [2020] EWHC 2169 (Comm) on payday lending. Power to regulate 'high cost short term credit' in the Financial Services and Markets Act (FSMA) 2000, ss. 137C–D.

[108] BEA 1946, s. 4(3). [109] ECB Statute, art. 19.

Reserve[110] have similar reserve requirements. Since the global financial crisis of 2007, the Basel Committee on Banking Supervision (composed of twenty-eight central bank members) has strongly advocated this. First, it is said that if regulators raise reserve duties on riskier lending practices, those practices will be discouraged because they become costly. Second, reserves are argued to provide a cushion of capital, so if the bank goes insolvent, creditors draw on this and taxpayers need not bail banks out. The first argument assumes regulators actually identify risky practice. The second argument is the same as the that for minimum capital requirements in companies, which has largely been rejected on the ground that it does not work, or there are better ways to achieve the desired result (see Ch. 4(2)(b)). One certainty is that reserves freeze vast quantities of capital, which are not productively utilised.

Third, the central bank may lend money to private banks, and if those private banks are sufficiently dependent, the central bank's change of interest rates may affect the private banks' own interest rates. This is the relevance of the Bank of England 'base rate', the ECB interest rates and the US Federal Reserve 'federal funds rate', and goes together with (unhelpfully named) 'discount operations'.[111] The Bank of England does this through contract,[112] the ECB has a general power[113] and they are itemised specifically in the US Federal Reserve's powers.[114] First, there is 'discounting', which means that the central bank lends money to a bank in respect of particular loans that bank has made.[115] The bank effectively transfers loans to the central bank in return for money. Second, there are 'advances', where the central bank lends ('advances') money to private banks at a given rate of interest.[116] The Bank of England, due to its historical dominance, has also served as a bank for other UK banks to settle their accounts among one another. By changing the rate of interest on these accounts, the Bank of England 'influences the general level of interest rates throughout the financial system',[117] and change of the Bank's base rate 'will typically, in turn, produce a change in the base rates of the banks'.[118]

The problem is, 'typically' having 'influence' is not the same as directly having effect. As the Chancellor of the Exchequer reported in 1980, 'it is not feasible for the authorities to exercise an exact control over bank lending

110 Federal Reserve Act of 1913, 12 USC, §461. These are tapered, so banks over $43.9m must have 10% in reserve, banks with $9.3–43.9m must have 3% and banks under $9.3m have 0%. The justification is to not place smaller banks at a competitive disadvantage.

111 The term 'discount rate' is synonymous with 'interest rate', because according to the jargon, if you owe me £100, but we agree that you do not pay me today, and instead give me £1 to hold onto the money each month, you are getting a 'discount'. Of course, you are really being charged 12% interest per annum.

112 See 'Bank of England Market Operations Guide: Our Tools' (2019), www.bankofengland.co.uk/markets/bank-of-england-market-operations-guide/our-tools: 'Participating in our operations is generally voluntary, and eligible firms can choose which operations they sign up to.'

113 ECB Statute, art. 18.1 ('credit operations').

114 Federal Reserve Act of 1913, 12 USC, §§343–347c.

115 12 USC, §343.

116 12 USC, §347c.

117 Ellinger et al., *Ellinger's Modern Banking Law*, ch. 1, 19.

118 Cranston, *Principles of Banking Law*, 121.

through interest rates in the short run'.[119] It also now appears doubtful in the long run. Banks may simply not change their interest rates for customers – even if the central bank rate is at 0 per cent: hence enjoying massive subsidies – because collectively they do not want to, because they make profit, regardless of the social cost. By contrast, since 2014, the ECB introduced 'negative interest rates' (i.e. an account charge) for banks that put money with it to settle interbank transactions overnight. The ECB is able to require banks hold and use its accounts, and by 2019 it had been paid €21.4 billion.[120] This policy, essentially taxing idle capital, appears to have resulted in improved lending.[121] US banks are less reliant on the Federal Reserve: it uses the next tool.

Fourth, a central bank may buy or sell vast numbers of government bonds, or other securities, in an attempt to move the interest rates at which banks lend. These are called 'open market operations' (or 'money market transactions'). Again, the Bank of England's power to do this comes from contract, while the powers are expressed for the ECB[122] and the Fed.[123] The central bank buys government bonds (or other securities), or sells them, or buys them back again (a 'repo' transaction) at rates aiming to reach its inflation target. If the central bank buys new government bonds, and then sells them on to other parties (e.g. a bank or pension fund) at lower prices, then it puts more money into the financial system. Ideally, more money should reduce interest rates, and raise lending, except that often it merely acts as a subsidy to banks. A government bond (in the UK, a 'gilt') will promise to pay the holder interest over the future (e.g. for twenty years, yielding a variable interest rate). Most central banks sell government bonds through 'primary dealers', a list of favoured private banks.[124] The bank may then resell the bonds to the public, usually at a higher rate to make a profit. This is often said 'to inject more liquidity into the banking system',[125] a euphemism for bribing banks to lend. After the financial crisis, and banks refusing to lend much more despite a nearly 0% interest rate, 'quantitative easing' referred to central banks buying massive quantities of bank securities and loans, with the ostensible intention of 'easing' the banks to lend more by increasing the 'quantities' of assets (and therefore risks) on the central

[119] *Monetary Control*, Cmnd 7858 (1980) para. 1.7.

[120] E. Smith, 'European Banks Have Paid over 20 Billion Euros to the ECB since Negative Interest Rates', *CNBC* (10 June 2019).

[121] S. Demiralp, J. Eisenschmidt and T. Vlassopoulos, 'Negative Interest Rates, Excess Liquidity and Retail Deposits: Banks' Reaction to Unconventional Monetary Policy in the Euro Area', Working Paper No. 2283 (May 2019): 'banks highly exposed to the policy tend to grant more loans'.

[122] ECB Statute, art. 18.1: 'operate in the financial markets by buying and selling'.

[123] 12 USC, §§353, 356 and 359.

[124] Primary Dealers Act of 1988 in the US regulates this explicitly. In the UK, the equivalent term is 'Gilt-edged Market Makers'. The ECB has no primary dealers.

[125] E.g. J. Marte, 'New York Fed Offers to Inject More Liquidity into the Banking System', *Reuters* (24 October 2019).

bank's reserves.[126] An advantage of open market operations is claimed to be that 'smaller, incremental impacts can be achieved in outstanding bank reserves'.[127] For example, the US Federal Reserve's assets from its 'QE1' programme in 2008 to 'QE3' increased from $870 billion to $4.5 trillion. Over the Covid-19 pandemic it chose to increase its purchases again to $7.78 trillion in 2021.[128] This may also have no positive impact, and detrimental distributional impact, on the real economy, because money goes to corporations and banks, not people who need it.

An illustration of open market operations was seen during the Eurozone crisis of 2013–14, to avoid the bankruptcy of Greece, but indirectly to preserve the solvency of private banks to which Greece owed money.[129] In *Gauweiler v Deutsche Bundestag*, a right-wing German politician claimed that the ECB had overstepped its legal competence in its 'outright monetary transactions' programme. The Treaty on the Functioning of the European Union, article 123 prohibits the ECB from lending money directly to governments – for instance, by buying their debt directly on the international bond market.[130] However, when Greece found itself unable to borrow except on exorbitant rates, and speculators were betting on its insolvency, the ECB chair Mario Draghi promised to do 'whatever it takes' to stop the Eurozone crisis,[131] promising to purchase bonds on the secondary market (i.e. not buying a bond from Greece, but from someone who had bought a bond from Greece). Almost immediately, the ECB solved the crisis, because this guaranteed the solvency of the Greek state: speculation on its insolvency was pointless. The German Constitutional Court made a reference to the CJEU, accompanied by a highly sceptical judgment suggesting that the ECB had taken an 'economic policy' decision (which it cannot) instead of a 'monetary policy' decision (which it can).[132] However, the CJEU held that the use of outright monetary transactions to buy Greek government debt on secondary markets was lawful: indirectly it might have achieved the same result but the fact that Greece was

[126] R.A., 'What Is Quantitative Easing? And How Does It Work?' *The Economist* (9 March 2015): 'To carry out QE central banks create money by buying securities, such as government bonds, from banks, with electronic cash that did not exist before. The new money swells the size of bank reserves in the economy by the quantity of assets purchased – hence "quantitative" easing. Like lowering interest rates, QE is supposed to stimulate the economy by encouraging banks to make more loans. The idea is that banks take the new money and buy assets to replace the ones they have sold to the central bank. That raises stock prices and lowers interest rates, which in turn boosts investment.' The last part is, however, what is hoped for, not always what happens.

[127] Lovett, *Banking and Financial Institutions Law*, 111.

[128] See www.federalreserve.gov/monetarypolicy/bst_recenttrends.htm.

[129] R. Janssen, 'Greece and the IMF: Who Exactly Is Being Saved?', Center for Economic and Policy Research (2010).

[130] TFEU, art. 123(1), prohibiting 'the purchase directly from them by the European Central Bank or national central banks of debt instruments'.

[131] (2015) C-62/14. See D. McCrum, 'Mario Draghi's "Whatever It Takes" Outcome in 3 Charts', *Financial Times* (25 July 2017).

[132] *Outright Monetary Transactions case* (14 January 2014) BVerfG, 2 BvR 2728/13; TFEU, art. 123(1).

subject to conditions put it in the legitimate realm of monetary, rather than economic, policy.[133] This was an entirely necessary decision to end the crisis, but one that highlights the defective design of the Treaties.

(c) International Monetary Fund and World Bank

Globally, the two primary financial institutions are the IMF and World Bank. Both depend on the United Nations (UN) member states for funding and governance. The IMF's purposes include promoting 'international monetary cooperation', 'balanced growth of international trade', 'high levels of employment and real income' and 'development of the productive resources', avoiding 'competitive exchange depreciation', assisting multilateral current and foreign exchange transactions and restricting imbalances of payments.[134] The members are those in the UN, but the voting rights of each member to select the executive board are weighted based on the 'special drawing rights' that reflect the money put into the fund.[135]

Similarly, the World Bank's Board of Governors is elected by votes of members, according to basic votes and share votes, weighted according to the member state's investment.[136] Its purposes are to assist in rebuilding after war; to promote private foreign investment with guarantees or loans where private investment is lacking; to promote growth in trade and equilibrium in balance of payments; and to build a 'peacetime economy'.[137] Because they have more money, the USA and EU have historically dominated the IMF and World Bank, with each head being from either jurisdiction. The control over international monetary policy, and the loan and structural adjustment programmes of the IMF and World Bank, led to the criticism that its policies are calculated to augment US and European economic power, and use the influence of loans to privatise assets that Western banks and companies buy up.

(d) Public Option and Mutual Banks

A fourth, but in the UK largely missing, feature of banking are public or socially owned banks. In 1968, the Girobank run by the Post Office was established, but privatised and sold in 1989 to Alliance & Leicester (now owned by Santander). Similarly, many of the mutual banks and building societies owned by their customers were 'demutualised' in the 1980s, and transformed into shareholder-dominated limited companies. As opposed to retail banking and mortgage services, there have been many proposals for – but there is not yet – a significant investment bank in the UK. A 'British Business

[133] *Gauweiler v Deutscher Bundestag* (16 June 2015) C-62/14, [103]–[105].
[134] Articles of Agreement of the IMF (2012) art. I.
[135] Articles of Agreement of the IMF (2012) arts. II–III and XII, section 5.
[136] IBRD: Articles of Agreement (2012) art. II, section 1 and art. V, sections 2–3.
[137] IBRD: Articles of Agreement (2012) art. I.

Bank' was established in 2014, but in 2019 was lending around £9 billion annually targeted at small and medium enterprises. By contrast, the German investment bank KfW (Kreditanstalt für Wiederaufbau) had a total business volume of €77.3 billion, or around £67 billion annually. It appears that given the scale of investment needed to replace coal, oil and gas with wind, solar and battery power (see Chs. 11–12), upgrade agriculture (Ch. 13), decarbonise buildings (Ch. 14) and electrify transport (Ch. 15), the expansion of public investment is desirable.

(3) Private Bank Governance

In the absence of effective public option or mutual banks, the governance of private banks is relatively uniform in the UK. This involves (a) the model of shareholder dominance, invariably controlled by asset managers, subject to (b) standards set in licences from the PRA and Financial Conduct Authority (FCA), (c) capital requirements, particularly influenced by the Basel Committee and (d) a different insolvency regime since the financial crisis.

(a) Standard Governance Model

Beyond the central bank, the standard governance model of private banks is profit-making corporations, without meaningful representation for customers, despite the systemic market failure of banking enterprises. The largest UK banks are HSBC, Barclays, the Royal Bank of Scotland and Lloyds, each incorporated under the Companies Acts, and as listed companies following the UK Corporate Governance Code. A board nomination committee of existing directors typically appoints future directors.[138] They remain for whatever term of office the constitution sets, unless company members (invariably shareholders) remove them by majority vote.[139] A remuneration committee will typically set pay, since most companies follow the Model Articles that say directors receive 'such remuneration as the directors shall determine'.[140] Bank directors pay themselves. Bank pay structures, particularly with high variable components compared to fixed salaries, were seen after the financial crisis to exacerbate risk-taking behaviour: people act to inflate bonuses, even to the point of outright cheating and fraud.[141] However there has been little effective regulation except for banks that received government support.[142] There is a requirement in EU law for a worker representative to sit on bank

[138] Companies (Model Articles) Regulations (CMAR) 2008, Sch. 3, para. 20; UK Corporate Governance Code 2018, 3.17.

[139] Companies Act (CA) 2006, ss. 168–9.

[140] CMAR 2008, Sch. 3, para. 23; UK Corporate Governance Code 2018, 5.32.

[141] D. Ariely, *The Upside of Irrationality* (2010) ch. 1 (on psychological tendency to commit crime with higher incentives); J Cassidy, 'The Men Who Earn Too Much', *G2* (25 November 2009) 4–7, extracts from J. Cassidy, *How Markets Fail: The Logic of Economic Calamities* (2009).

[142] Credit Institutions Directive 2013/36/EU, art. 93 (limiting variable pay unless justified).

remuneration committees, but only if member state law requires worker representation (see Ch. 6(3)).[143] There should be a policy on board diversity to ensure gender and ethnic balance.[144] Directors are meant to 'engage' with shareholders,[145] but most shareholders are asset managers, managing other people's money, also based in the City of London. There is virtually no channel to represent the ultimate investors.[146] Asset managers rarely if ever sue for breach of directors' duties (for negligence or conflicts of interest), through derivative claims.[147] This makes the 'stewardship' functions that they perform highly questionable.

(b) Licensing Oversight

The primary mechanism of public oversight for banks is meant to be the licensing or 'authorisation' system.[148] This is carried out by the UK's twin regulators. First, there is the PRA, a limited company and subsidiary of the Bank of England.[149] Second, there is the FCA. The Financial Services and Markets Act 2000, section 19 contains the 'general prohibition' on performing a 'regulated activity', including accepting deposits from the public, without authority.[150] The Credit Institutions Directive 2013 requires a similar set of authorisation and prudence provisions in all EU member states.[151] Within the EU, once a bank has been authorised in one member state, it is entitled to a 'passport' to operate in any member state, as part of freedom of establishment.

(c) Capital Requirements

One of the major results of the global financial crisis was a revised system aimed to prevent bank insolvencies. In the 'Basel III' programme, created by an international banker group, banks are required to hold more money in reserves (i.e. not lent out) based on the risk-profile that a country's regulator suggests. If banks hold more speculative assets, their reserve requirements should rise, so raising their costs, and discouraging risk. The EU Capital Requirements Regulation 2013 codified these measures, for example mandating that proportionally less in reserves is needed if more government debt is held, but more if mortgage-backed securities are held.[152]

[143] Credit Institutions Directive, art. 95: 'If employee representation . . . is provided for by national law, the remuneration committee shall include one or more employee representatives.'
[144] Credit Institutions Directive 2013/36/EU, art. 89(10).
[145] UK Corporate Governance Code 2018, 1.3.
[146] E. McGaughey, 'Does Corporate Governance Exclude the Ultimate Investor?' (2016) 16(1) *J Corporate L Studies* 221.
[147] CA 2006, ss. 170–7 and 260–3. [148] FSMA 2000, ss. 19–23 and 418–19.
[149] FSMA 2000, s. 2A. [150] FSMA 2000, s. 19.
[151] Credit Institutions Directive 2013/36/EU, arts. 8–14.
[152] Capital Requirement Regulation (EU) No. 575/2013, arts. 114–34.

(d) Bank Insolvency

Ultimately the government guarantees the banking system and, as repeated crashes and crises have shown, governments cause widespread economic ruin if they let a financial crisis reach the economy. It has long been accepted that the Bank of England has a general responsibility for exercising oversight of the banking system. In *Three Rivers DC v Governor of the Bank of England*, the House of Lords held that a claim against the Bank for misfeasance, in failing to prevent the collapse of BCCI SA, would not be struck out and could proceed to trial.[153] Here, depositors claimed damages for loss from the Bank failing to exercise sufficient oversight and spot the fraud of its executives. As Lord Steyn said, it was 'indisputably the case that the Bank knew from April 1990 onwards that BCCI was in imminent danger of collapse with inevitable loss to depositors unless there was a real prospect of an effective rescue package'.[154] Yet it is not clear that potential liability from tort or judicial review does much.[155]

By 2009, the UK had nationalised Northern Rock, Bradford & Bingley, the Royal Bank of Scotland and part of HBOS-Lloyds TSB. As 'bailing out the banks' was met with widespread disapproval, the Banking Act 2009 introduced a new insolvency system. If there is a 'serious threat to the stability of the financial systems of the United Kingdom', the Bank of England, together with the Treasury and Financial Conduct Authority, may pursue one of three 'stabilisation options'.[156] First, the Bank of England will try to sell the failed bank to another private-sector purchaser.[157] Second, it may set up a subsidiary company to run the failing bank's assets, known as a 'bridge-bank'.[158] Third, the last option is for the UK Treasury to take shares in 'temporary public ownership'.[159] Doing so will eliminate shareholder investments, but keep creditors' claims intact, and therefore limit the spreading of losses. The problem is, this system added nothing about the accountability of executives.

(4) Customers' Rights

While governance rights are scant, the rights of bank customers to minimum standards of service and protection have become standard in many countries. The three main elements are (a) the common law starting point that bank depositors have no property, only contract rights, in their deposits, and (b) statutory deposit protection to roll back this basic position, plus (c) consumer protection against unfair banking terms.

153 *Three Rivers DC v Governor of the Bank of England* [2001] UKHL 16.

154 [2001] UKHL 16, [6].

155 On judicial review of the FCA and predecessors, see *R (Davies) v Financial Services Authority* [2003] EWCA Civ 1128 and *R (C) v FSA* [2013] EWCA Civ 677.

156 Banking Act 2009, ss. 1, 7–13.

157 Banking Act 2009, s. 11.

158 Banking Act 2009, s. 12.

159 Banking Act 2009, ss. 9 and 13.

(a) Contract and Property Rights

In 1848, the House of Lords held in *Foley v Hill* that bank customers who deposit money in an account do not retain any proprietary interest. They merely have contractual claims in debt for their money to be repaid.[160] The practical significance is that if a bank goes insolvent, customers cannot argue they have any priority to certain assets, or any particular proportion of assets, nor can they apply for proprietary remedies of following or tracing against third parties. They are unsecured creditors and will probably receive nothing. In 1986, the Court of Appeal restated this position in *Vincent v Trustee Savings Banks Central Board*, even though the very name of the bank ('Trustee') suggested a proprietary trust–beneficiary relationship.[161] The same type of rule has spread through almost every country in the world, although around the financial crisis there was some clamour for change. In a proposed Safety Deposit Current Accounts Bill 2008, clauses 1–2 state that banks may offer customers the option of a proprietary saving account (which of course they can do anyway) but even this did not pass. In 2018, a Swiss people's initiative proposed that banks have to have full reserves for all money (*Vollgeld*), but this was defeated by a large margin.

(b) Deposit Protection

Given that banks do not protect people's deposits in insolvency, since the Great Depression governments have been forced to. The US government model of the Federal Deposit Insurance Corporation has been successful in preventing bank runs since 1933,[162] and the same practice is followed worldwide. The UK guaranteed deposits up to £85,000,[163] which was meant to reflect an EU-wide minimum guarantee of €100,000 (although exchange rates have not been favourable).[164] Given that government ultimately backs the deposits of all bank accounts, it is strange that a stronger public option bank has not been created.

(c) Consumer Protection

Bank consumers are protected in the same way as other consumers, for instance in the Consumer Rights Act 2015, sections 62–5, prohibiting the use of unfair terms (see Ch. 6(1)(a)). The two leading cases, however, have not seen

[160] (1848) 2 HLC 28.

[161] *Vincent v Trustee Savings Banks Central Board* [1986] 1 WLR 1077, denying that the Trustee Savings Bank customers were, despite the name of the bank, in any trustee–beneficiary relation, either at common law or under statute. The customers, apparently, only had contractual rights.

[162] Banking Act of 1933, 12 USC, §§1811ff.

[163] FSMA 2000, ss. 214–15. SI 2013/598 gave the PRA and FCA rulemaking power.

[164] Deposit Guarantee Directive 2014/49/EU, art. 6.

much success. In *Director General of Fair Trading v First National Bank plc*, the House of Lords held that it was not unfair for a bank to substitute a market rate of interest for a statutory rate set after a court judgment, designed to help an indebted customer repay a loan.[165] Similarly in *Office of Fair Trading v Abbey National plc*, the Supreme Court rejected that banks charging very high unplanned overdraft fees was even capable of being reviewed, on the (dubious) ground that overdraft fees were part of a package of charges, and the 'price' of the account.[166] It seems clear that this approach was wrong under EU law,[167] though banks did begin to make charges more transparent.

However, particularly important are the Consumer Credit Act 1974 provisions which also prohibit unfair credit relationships, and extortionate interest rates. Under section 140A a court may order that any terms or the way rights are enforced are unfair, and under section 140B(9) the burden of proof is on the creditor to prove the relationship is fair. This gives the court wide discretion to decide what is fair or not and make orders accordingly.[168] It replaced an earlier higher standard of only cancelling 'extortionate' credit bargains.

(5) Conclusion

Given the centrality of banking law to human rights, it may seem surprising that duties on banks for financial prudence, objectives of full employment, raising living standards and environmental improvement are not also found in international law, and are not more central to bank law itself. While banking often seems opaque, the consequences for rights are profound, given the repeated disasters from the Wall Street Crash to the 2007–8 crash, to the daily pressure faced by people in debt. Three main reforms could prevent this. First, the option of public retail and investment banks could provide at-cost lending and interest, inject a greater element of competition and be a direct mechanism to inject investment into the economy, without excessive private bank costs. Private enterprise would be encouraged to compete on the merits, rather than through hidden fees or high rates. Second, the right of bank staff to be elected to bank boards, as found in most Organisation for Economic Co-operation and Development countries, could be complemented with representation for depositors or business borrowers who have accounts lasting more than a short period of time. Third, whatever the theories of property or contract adopted in the nineteenth century, customers of any insolvent bank should rank in priority over others, in order to ensure that those best able to bear the risks of enterprise do so.

165 [2001] UKHL 52. 166 [2009] UKSC 6.

167 E.g. *Kušionová v SMART Capital a.s.* (2014) C-34/13 and *Aziz v Caixa d'Estalvis de Catalunya* (2013) C-415/11, recognising that exceptions to the general rule of review must be narrowly construed.

168 See E. Lomnicka, 'Credit and Security' in H. Beale (ed.), *Chitty on Contracts* (33rd ed. 2018) ch. 39, 220.

11

Natural Resources

Contents

When God says 'Let there be light', the Old Testament refers to one of Earth's greatest natural resources,[1] but also the hope of human enlightenment itself. Light and heat come to Earth from our Sun. Heat differences create air pressure. Air pressure creates wind. And both light and wind can power the modern world a thousand times. With water, light gives life to plants, trees, algae, plankton and creatures including ourselves. Plants photosynthesise light, they live, they are eaten, they die, and over millions of years they become fossilised. Coal comes from ancient forests, which were buried and compressed before they decayed. Oil comes from ancient sea life, settling layer after layer on the beds of seas where oxygen was low. Fossil or 'natural' gas is trapped beneath pockets of rock, and given off from oil deposits, coal seams or shale. 'The world's fossil fuels were formed out of 500 million years of buried sunshine',[2] but since the Industrial Revolution humanity has been releasing all that light and heat in just 250 years. For all of human history to 1775, atmospheric concentration of carbon dioxide (the molecule that plants breathe in, and we let out when we burn coal, oil and gas) was around 280 parts per million (ppm) in the air. By 2015 it rose to 400 ppm. In 2021 it is 415 ppm. At 430 ppm global average temperatures rise by 1.5°C, and at 450 ppm by 2°C. This is not climate 'change'. It is massive climate damage, caused mainly by those who profit. International law protects 'the inherent right of all peoples to enjoy and utilize fully and freely their natural wealth and resources'.[3] And

[1] Gen. 1:3. On the universe's origins, S. Hawking, *A Brief History of Time* (1988) chs. 1–3.
[2] T. Mitchell, *Carbon Democracy: Political Power in the Age of Oil* (2013) 260.
[3] ICCPR 1966, arts. 47 and 1(2); ICESCR 1966, arts. 25 and 1(2).

burning fossil fuels, not using sun and wind, destroys everyone's most vital natural resource: a living planet. Decisive action will save it.

The right to natural resources is indivisible from the 'right to life', and the right to 'the benefits of scientific progress'.[4] This means there is a universal human right to clean technology. Historically, humanity was powered by water mills or burning timber. The industrial revolution was powered by coal. The corporate revolution was powered by oil and gas. The next revolution is being powered by sunshine and wind, but 'the benefits of scientific progress' do not spread themselves.[5] The world's top companies are deeply involved in fossil-fuel extraction, finance, transportation or burning, and they stick to the status quo (see Ch. 2(2)(g)). The end of fossil fuels is an economic revolution because sun and wind are not stuck to land, like coal, oil or gas, and cannot be easily enclosed or monopolised. The desperation of fossil-fuel firms and states to keep their pollution privileges has geopolitical results. It results in outright denial of climate damage; intense lobbying to lie that coal, oil or gas can be a 'transitional' part of the 'energy mix'; the promotion of baseless beliefs in 'clean coal' or 'decarbonised gas';[6] or waging war. But time is ticking, so this chapter discusses how coal, oil and gas can be shut down as fast as scientifically and technologically possible, so that our true natural resources can survive.

(1) Historical Background

Since the start of human existence, fire and stone have been part of our lives. Our Sun was created 4.57 billion years ago, and our Earth around 10 million years later. Our ancestors probably began to regularly use fire by 400,000 years ago,[7] and for most of human history timber was the main source of heat. But coal burns hotter, and the first evidence of its use appears in China around 3490 BC,[8] while in Ancient Greece the first records of coal use in metalwork appeared around 300 BC.[9] The use of oil, for heating, in lamps, in bitumen for roads or buildings, or in weapons for war, is recorded throughout ancient and medieval times.[10] In England, Magna Carta 1215, the Charter of the Forest 1217, and the 'forest law' that developed under it, gave people the right to collect wood (estover) and peat (turbury) from common land, and gave traders

4 UDHR 1948, arts. 3 and 27(1). ECHR 1950, art. 2; ICCPR 1966, art. 6(1); ICESCR 1966, art. 15.

5 L. Shaver, 'The Right to Science and Culture' [2010] *Wisconsin L Rev* 121, 143 and 138–9.

6 E.g. www.worldcoal.org says 'Coal is likely to remain the most affordable fuel for power generation in many developing and industrialised countries for decades.' This is false. It is the most costly power source.

7 W. Roebroeks and P. Villa, 'On the Earliest Evidence for Habitual Use of Fire in Europe' (2011) 108(13) *PNAS* 5209, but noting potential fire use as far back as 1.6m years.

8 J. Dodson, X. Li, N. Sun, P. Atahun, X. Zhou, H. Liu, K. Zhao, S. Hu and Z. Yang, 'Use of Coal in the Bronze Age in China' (2014) 24(5) *The Holocene* 525.

9 Theophrastus, *On Stones* (c. 300 BC), trans. E. R. Caley and J. F. C. Richards (1956) 48.

10 E.g. Herodotus, *Histories* (430 BC) Book I, Clio, trans. W. Beloe (1830) 134.

in wood and coal the right to move freely.[11] Meanwhile, increased burning of coal in London created so much toxic smoke that a royal proclamation of 1306 required a return to timber and charcoal.[12] By the 1500s, the forests of England had been cut down so fast that people had to move back to coal,[13] and the first mine opened in 1575 in Culross, Scotland. Elizabeth I asserted that 'by the law all mines of gold and silver . . . belong to the Queen by prerogative',[14] whether found in another mine or not. Parliament reacted after the Civil War and Revolution, the Royal Mines Act 1688 stating that 'Noe Mine of Copper Tin Iron or Lead shall hereafter be adjudged reputed or taken to be a Royall Mine.'[15] Yet the really valuable good would not be the stones that glistened, but the ones that burned. Everything changed when, in 1775, James Watt patented the steam engine, driven by water, heated from burning coal.[16] (See Table 11.1.)

The Industrial Revolution marked humanity's liberation from scarcity because, for the first time, people had machines, and 'machines that make machines', with power far beyond any living thing.[17] It also marked the start of our ecosphere's destruction, a mass extinction like a slow and silent version of the meteor that killed the dinosaurs (see Table 11.1). At the Industrial Revolution's centre in London, every few decades it had become so cold that the Thames froze over, leading people to hold 'frost fairs', with markets, ice skating, dancing and football on the ice. The last fair was in 1814, and as the coal burned, engines steamed, chimneys smoked and the planet heated, imperceptibly at first. The Thames never froze solid again.[18]

The use of coal in Britain, and the spread of railways, meant that by 'the 1840s, coal was providing energy that in timber would have required forests covering twice the country's area, double that area by the 1860s, and double again by the 1890s'.[19] In 1865, Stanley Jevons predicted that coal would run

[11] Magna Carta 1215, cll. 31 and 47–8; Charter of the Forest 1217, cll. 9–12; G. Standing, *Plunder of the Commons* (2019) ch. 1, 3–9.

[12] R. L. Galloway, *A History of Coal Mining in Great Britain* (1882) ch. 1, 10.

[13] J. O. Kaplan, K. M. Krumhardt and N. Zimmerman, 'The Prehistoric and Preindustrial Deforestation of Europe' (2009) 28 *Quaternary Science Rev* 3016, 3023. 20.1% of England and Wales could be forested, 72.9% of Scotland. Now 10% England, 15% Wales, 19% Scotland: Forest Research, *Woodland Statistics* (2020) 5.

[14] *R v Earl of Northumberland or Case of Mines* (1568) 1 Plowd 210.

[15] Royal Mines Act 1688, s. III, while ss. I–II repealed the Act Against Multipliers 1404 (5 Hen. IV, c. 4) that had made it a felony to create gold and silver by alchemy. Isaac Newton claimed in a letter to John Locke that this was procured by the chemist, Robert Boyle, who perhaps thought he might succeed in performing alchemy.

[16] This followed and vastly improved the Thomas Newcomen engine in 1712.

[17] G. Orwell, *The Road to Wigan Pier* (1937) ch. 2: 'Our civilisation, pace Chesterton, is founded on coal, more completely than one realizes until one stops to think about it. The machines that keep us alive, and the machines that make machines, are all directly or indirectly dependent upon coal.'

[18] In 1832, London Bridge was rebuilt and its arches were widened leading to stronger river flow, but the fact was that it just never became cold enough again, despite one hopeful prediction in 1881. The Thames did freeze at Windsor in 1863. Cf. M. Lockwood et al., 'Frost Fairs, Sunspots and the Little Ice Age' (2017) 58(2) *Astronomy & Geophysics* 2.17.

[19] Mitchell, *Carbon Democracy*, 15.

Table 11.1 Major environment events

Years ago	*Event*
13.8bn	Universe starts with big bang, we think
4.57bn	Sun + Earth form in molecular cloud
4–3bn	First single-cell organisms
609m	Multi-cell organisms
530m	Fish
385m	Trees
300m	Coal formations
252m	Permian-Triassic extinction event
201m	Triassic-Jurassic extinction event
66m	Gulf of Mexico impact, dinosaurs die
3.4m	Stone Age begins
400,000	Humans habitually using fire
12,000	Farming
2560 BC	Pyramid at Giza completed
1775 AD	Holocene mass extinction begins

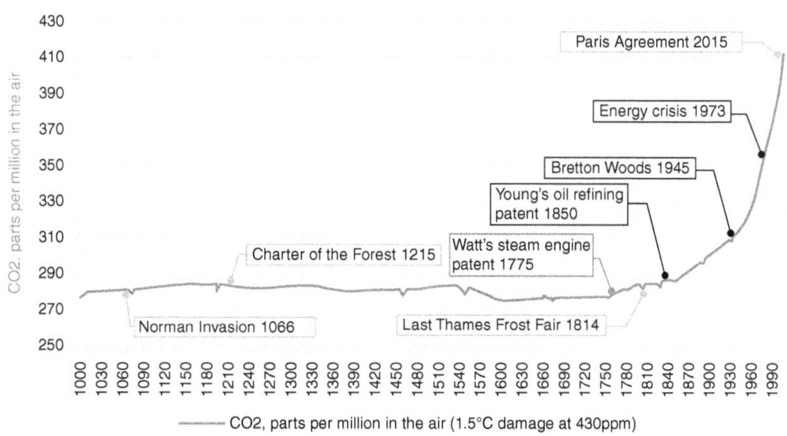

Figure 11.1 Carbon dioxide concentrations, 1000 AD–2020
Sources: US EPA, 'Atmospheric Concentrations of Greenhouse Gases'; www.co2.earth/daily-co2

out, and noted that 'the sun annually showers down upon us about a thousand times as much heat-power as is contained in all the coal'.[20]

While Jevons was right about the sun, scarcity has tragically not proven to be coal's problem, rather than its pollution and the human exploitation in its mines. Britain became the workshop of the world, and its coal mines shaped and scarred generations of the working classes, including children, who lived

[20] W. S. Jevons, *The Coal Question* (1865) 122–5.

and died down the pit.[21] But coal meant the labour movement also had power, to sit down and just say 'no'.[22] People could exert pressure, and slowly won freedom to organise, the vote in Parliament and labour rights for fair pay.[23] Believing that public ownership under a worker government would revolutionise people's lives, the new Labour Party pushed for public ownership of coal,[24] with other key industries. Failure to get agreement, and malicious cuts to miners' pay from £6 to £3 18s since the end of World War One, led to the General Strike of 1926.[25] Nearly the whole of Britain was shut down, as transport and other industry workers struck in solidarity. Armed with the law,[26] but more importantly with force and hunger, Home Secretary Winston Churchill broke the strike. Yet in its wake a minority Labour government came to power in 1929, and coal reserves (if not yet mines) were put in public ownership in 1938 with £66 million in compensation.[27] In 1945, the great reforming Labour government of Clement Attlee won a majority, turfing Churchill out. The Coal Industry Nationalisation Act 1946 put the industry in the National Coal Board's hands, with reserve powers of direction for the government.[28] Undoubtedly people's lives were improved, but since power still rested with Whitehall and the minister, with no votes for the workforce, the Board was not what was expected. The Board, its predecessors, and its successor, the British Coal Corporation, have been responsible for 1.13 per cent of the whole world's greenhouse gas emissions from 1751 to 2016 (see Figure 11.2).[29]

21 E.g. Children's Employment Commission, First Report of the Commissioners. Mines (1842) Appendix, Part II, 293, Derbyshire, No. 110: Richard Clarke: 'Is 12 years old. Has worked in a pit five years; drives the ass and wears the belt . . . Goes down at five to eight, for a whole day . . . never receives any rewards and is punished by sticks or anything the loader or corporal lays his hands on . . . had beaten him with a piece of wood . . . until his back and head were all over with bruises.'

22 Mitchell, *Carbon Democracy*, ch. 1, 21: 'Strikes became effective, not because of mining's isolation, but on the contrary because of the flows of carbon that connected chambers beneath the ground to every factory, office, home or means of transportation that depended on steam or electric power.'

23 Second Reform Act 1867 and Trade Union Act 1871. Trade Disputes Act 1906 and Representation of the People Act 1918. Representation of the People (Equal Franchise) Act 1928.

24 Coal Industry Commission Act 1919 set up a Commission whose members included R. H. Tawney, Sidney Webb and Sir Leo Chiozza Money, who advocated nationalisation of the mines. The majority opposed.

25 Cf. Samuel Commission (10 March 1926) recommending further cuts.

26 Cf. *National Sailors' and Firemen's Union v Reed* [1926] Ch 536, 539–49, Astbury J asserting pathetically, 'The so-called general strike called by the Trades Union Congress Council is illegal . . . .'

27 Coal Act 1938, s. 1 created the Coal Commission and vested coal reserves in the Coal Corporation. This followed the Coal (Registration of Ownership) Act 1937.

28 Coal Industry Nationalisation Act 1946, ss. 1 and 3; and see *Scottish Insurance Corp. Ltd v Wilsons & Clyde Coal Co. Ltd* [1949] AC 462 (preference shareholders had no special right to extra compensation upon nationalisation); *Re Chatterly-Whitfield Collieries Ltd* [1948] 2 All ER 593 (reduction of capital by paying off preference shareholders, after nationalisation, held fair and lawful).

29 Climate Accountability Institute, 'Summary of CO_2 & Methane Emissions from Identified Fossil Fuel & Cement Production' (2020) 4.

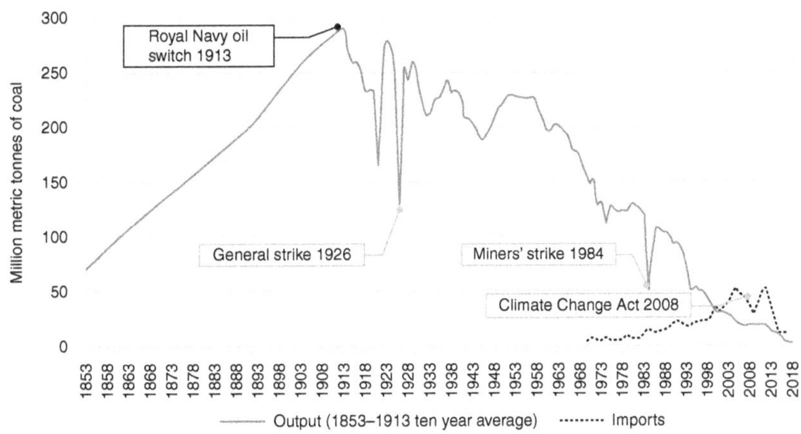

Figure 11.2 UK coal production and imports, 1853–2018
Source: DBEIS, 'Historical Coal Data: Coal Production, Availability and Consumption 1853–2018'

By the early twentieth century, British coal was already being eclipsed. If coal powered the nineteenth century of the British Empire, oil powered the twentieth century of the Empire State. In 1850, James Young registered the first patent to refine a new, thicker oil in Britain. But the world's first commercial oil well was opened in Ontario in 1858, then in Pennsylvania, then Ohio, and demand soared with the internal combustion engine (see Ch. 15). Oil production was rapidly monopolised by the Standard Oil Corp., founded in Ohio by major shareholder John D. Rockefeller, and controlled by a voting trust of close associates. Despite the Sherman Act of 1890 being passed to prevent 'restraint of trade', by 1899 Standard Oil owned 82 per cent of refining capacity.[30] Abroad, Standard Oil bought up assets, and one 'of our greatest helpers', said Rockefeller, 'has been the State Department' which 'aided us to push our way into new markets to the utmost corners of the world'.[31] Only in 1911 was it broken up at the suit of President Theodore Roosevelt, continued by President Taft.[32] However its successor corporations slowly remerged, its assets mostly held today by Chevron (3.13% of all global emissions), ExxonMobil (2.98%), Shell (2.18%) and BP (2.29%).[33]

British Petroleum began life as the Rangoon Oil Company to develop oil fields on the Indian subcontinent. This became Burmah Oil,[34] and in 1909 the

[30] E. Shaffer, *The United States and Control of World Oil* (1983) 23: Rockefeller's tactics were 'manipulation of freight rates, industrial espionage and the threats against distributors who bought from his competitors'.

[31] Shaffer, *The United States and Control of World Oil*, 33.

[32] *Standard Oil of New Jersey v United States*, 221 US 1 (1911).

[33] Climate Accountability Institute, 'Summary of CO_2 & Methane Emissions', 4.

[34] NB: *Burmah Oil Co. (Burma Trading) Ltd v Lord Advocate* [1965] AC 75 held that compensation was payable for destruction of Burmah Oil assets in World War Two to prevent them falling into the hands of the advancing Japanese army, but swiftly reversed by the War Damage Act 1965, s. 1: 'No person shall be entitled at common law to receive from the Crown

Anglo-Persian Oil Company was incorporated as its subsidiary to control and exploit the massive new reserves in Iraq, Iran and the wider Middle East. In 1913, to secure navy and military supplies, Winston Churchill as First Lord of the Admiralty made a deal to buy a 50.0025% stake in the Anglo-Persian Oil Co., for £2.2 million.[35] During World War One, the Defence of the Realm Act 1914 enabled the government to enter land to search for and acquire petroleum, and the Petroleum (Production) Act 1918 effectively took over all oil supplies by prohibiting any searching or drilling for oil or gas without a licence. Whether powering planes, tanks or destroyers, oil was essential for war.

In the 'past 35 years', said a US State Department bulletin in 1945, 'petroleum has historically played a larger part in the external relations of the USA than any other commodity'.[36] Something similar might be said of UK foreign policy,[37] and indeed for much geopolitics both during and long after World War Two. Japan attacked Pearl Harbor in 1941 to prevent US warships interfering in oil movements in its conquest of Indonesia. The bloodbath of Stalingrad was fought by Hitler, not just over a name, but to secure control of access to oil in the Caucasus, and to cut supplies to the USSR from Persia.[38] 'It was the ... Nazi's lack of gasoline, not the loss of plane production, that gave [the Allies] air superiority.'[39] After the war, and with the US dollar convertible into gold under the Bretton Woods system (see Ch. 10), dollars flooded the world markets as oil was the biggest traded commodity. The most oil-rich regions, one by one, became the most authoritarian as US and UK interests sought friendly regimes to secure supply whatever the human rights cost.[40] This included the backing of the House of Saud in the Arabian Peninsula, the Emirates of Dubai, the Shah in Iran[41] and Saddam Hussein in Iraq.

compensation in respect of damage to, or destruction of, property caused ... [in] a war in which the Sovereign was, or is, engaged.'

35 Anglo-Persian Oil Company (Acquisition of Capital) Act 1914 and extended in 1919 by £2.05m. G. Jones, *The State and the Emergence of the British Oil Industry* (1981) 120–1 notes this effectively nationalised Shell's subsidiary in Egypt.

36 J. Loftus, US State Department, 'Petroleum in International Relations', US Department of State Bulletin, vol. XIII (5 August 1945), 173–5.

37 Cf. Testimony of US State Department's WWII Petroleum Attaché in the Near East in R. Engler, *The Politics of Oil* (1961) 199: 'The [UK] government, wherever it has a shadow of influence, uses its power by fair means or underhand to secure markets or concessions for its British-owned companies. Every conceivable subterfuge, use of assumed authority over mandates, threat, intimidation, distortion of the laws or bribery, is used to aid their companies in securing oil concessions in weak countries and holding their market against all comers, even British companies that are foreign-owned.'

38 T. Wheelwright, *Oil and World Politics* (1991) 8–9.

39 US Strategic Bombing Survey (1945) quoted in E. B. Crossman, *The Air Battle of Ploesti* (1949) B-6.

40 L. Wenar, *Blood Oil: Tyrants, Violence and Rules that Run the World* (2017).

41 Wheelwright, *Oil and World Politics*, 12: 'The overthrow of Mossadeq by the Shah, engineered by the CIA, paved the way for the displacement of the British. The State Department made no attempt to get the seized properties of Anglo Iranian returned to Britain, and vetoed a British attempt to take military action against Iran.'

The cost of the oil economy is incalculable, both for economic and climatic stability. In 1952, the US Federal Trade Commission (FTC) determined that it would take no serious action against the 'Seven Sisters' cartel (now BP, Shell, Chevron and ExxonMobil) that shared and dominated global oil.[42] As a balance, the Organization of Petroleum Exporting Countries (OPEC) formed in 1960, and in 1973 it cut supply and raised prices in retaliation for US and UK support of Israel in the Yom Kippur War. This drove more rapid exploitation of North Sea oil, discovered in 1965, with 'Brent Crude' becoming a standard index.[43] That same year, in 1965 President Johnson was informed that carbon emissions would produce 'marked changes in climate' that may be 'deleterious from the point of view of human beings'.[44] But nothing was done. The UK set up a public British National Oil Corp. in 1975[45] but, when Margaret Thatcher took power, this was privatised, along with the sale of the long-standing government stake in British Petroleum.[46] After the miners' strike was defeated in 1986, the coal industry was wound down and then privatised.[47]

But even though school children were taught about global warming in the 1990s, and anyone could see it was wrong, the Iraq war was launched by George W. Bush (himself an ex-oil executive) to invade and seize Iraqi oil, after Saddam Hussein had fallen out of favour. Britain, out of naivety or Tony Blair's messianism or both, decided to follow. This $3 trillion war, which killed millions,[48] and which led to a so-called 'Islamic' state death cult, ironically came just as oil was destined to be worthless. The UK passed a Climate Change Act 2008, which now targets zero or negative emissions, although in 2015 it undermined itself by legislating to 'maximise the economic recovery of oil'.[49] Coal, oil and gas have been the worst performing investments every year since 2017, damaging everyone's pensions.[50] Air pollution still kills 40,000 people

[42] *Oil Cartel* case (1952) following the FTC, *The International Petroleum Cartel*, the DoJ initiated a suit against the 'seven sisters', on worldwide sharing arrangements. The State Department was simultaneously negotiating treaties to give them more control. But then DOJ advised the agreement did not violate antitrust laws, if each US company surrendered a 1% share to US independent companies. The Antitrust Division dismissed all charges. See also J. M. Blair, *The Control of Oil* (1976).

[43] Petroleum (Production) Regulations 1966. See also K. W. Dam, 'The Pricing of North Sea Gas in Britain' (1970) 13 *JL & Economics* 11; R. H. Coase, 'The Auction System and North Sea Gas: A Comment' (1970) 13(1) *JL & Economics* 45.

[44] R. Revelle, W. Broeker, H. Craig, C. D. Keeling and J. Smagorinsky, 'Atmospheric Carbon Dioxide' in Restoring the Quality of Our Environment: Report of the Environmental Pollution Panel, White House, President's Scientific Advisory Committee (November 1965). See now US EPA, *Climate Change Indicators* (2019).

[45] Petroleum and Submarine Pipe-lines Act 1975. The UK also passed the Oil Taxation Act (OTA) 1975.

[46] Also, Petroleum Revenue Tax Act 1980 reducing taxes. [47] Coal Industry Act 1994.

[48] J. Stiglitz and L. Bilmes, *The Three Trillion Dollar War: The True Cost of the Iraq Conflict* (2009).

[49] Infrastructure Act 2015, s. 41 inserting Petroleum Act (PA) 1998, s. 9A.

[50] B. Nauman, 'Sharp Rise in Number of Investors Dumping Fossil Fuel Stocks', *Financial Times* (9 September 2019); '2019 Stock Index Results Show Fossil Companies as Worst-Performing Segment', *Energy Mix* (14 January 2020).

a year in the UK, costing the NHS at least £6 billion a year.[51] The imperative today has become ending it all: every drop of oil, each lump of coal and the last puff of smoke. This mainly means change in electricity, energy (see Ch. 12) and transport (Ch. 15). Coal, oil and gas companies believe they can instead lobby for 'net zero' carbon emissions with false promises of offsets, instead of closing. They need to go, so that the true natural resources of sun, wind and clean materials can replace them.

(2) Finance

The finance of fossil-fuel enterprises, at first, appears to be equity and debt through ordinary company law, because major companies are no longer publicly owned. BP plc, Royal Dutch Shell plc and BHP Billiton plc are listed on the London Stock Exchange, the New York Stock Exchange and others around the world, raising equity through shareholders,[52] or debt capital from banks (see Ch. 10) or internal reserves. The official government stance is the 'UK does not have fossil fuel subsidies', a stance based on the International Energy Agency definition of 'subsidy' as any 'measure or programme' that reduces fossil-fuel costs 'below world market prices'.[53] Yet despite this façade, there are three giant regulatory subsidies – namely: (a) the failure of international targets to deal with the mass damage caused by fossil fuels, (b) subsidies from cheap resource extraction licences and non-enforcement of competition law and (c) the failure of tort or criminal law, so far, to stop the damage or internalise the costs of pollution. These regulatory subsidies make the 'world market price' of coal, oil or gas a chimera, because externalities, and cut-price land or sea, rig the markets.[54]

(a) Climate Damage Science and International Targets

The science of climate damage is well established, despite the denial of fossil-fuel companies, states or fanatics. After the 1965 report to Lyndon B. Johnson (above),[55] in 1977, Exxon Corp. conducted internal research saying that 'mankind is influencing the global climate through carbon dioxide release from the burning of fossil fuels', and in 1978 it said there was a 'time window of five to ten years before the need for hard decisions regarding changes in energy strategies might become critical'. But instead, it chose to promote doubt

[51] Royal College of Physicians and Royal College of Paediatrics and Child Health, 'Every Breath We Take: The Lifelong Impact of Air Pollution', Report of a Working Party (February 2016) xliii; A. Hunt and C. Brand, 'Health Damage from Cars and Vans Costs £6 Billion Annually to NHS and Society' (6 June 2018).

[52] See the constitutions of BP plc, Royal Dutch Shell plc and BHP Billiton plc.

[53] See UK government Response to Petition (4 November 2019).

[54] Cf. D. Coady, I. Parry, L. Sears and B. Shang, 'How Large Are Global Energy Subsidies?', IMF Working Paper No. 15/105 (2015) 10, defining a subsidy to include internalising externalities.

[55] Revelle et al., 'Atmospheric Carbon Dioxide'.

about science,[56] a practice systematically used by Putin, Bolsonaro, Trump and Abbott – even as wildfires burnt the Arctic, Amazon, Alaska and Australia. Companies who no longer feel able to defraud the public about the obvious, instead shift to arguing for longer transitions, and use the language of 'mitigation', 'adaptation' and 'limits' to the planet burning. The term 'climate change' is not neutral, but is actively preferred by Republican strategists over 'global warming' whose connotations are too negative.[57] 'Change' sounds good. In law, knowledge of climate damage by Exxon employees, or any others, from 1977 is attributable to the company (see Ch. 5(1)(a)).

The process of climate damage is that burning coal, oil and gas releases carbon dioxide, methane, nitrous oxide and other poisons into the atmosphere. Our air is made up of 78% Nitrogen (N_2), 20.9% oxygen (O_2), 0.934% argon (Ar), 0.0415% carbon dioxide (CO_2) and then neon, helium, methane (CH_4), krypton, nitrous oxide (N_2O) and many other gases. Carbon dioxide, with methane or nitrous oxide, has the effect of trapping heat in the Earth's atmosphere as it radiates from the sun (nitrous oxide also damages human health: see Ch. 15). The right balance of this 'greenhouse effect' is essential for life as we know it. With too little, we enter into an ice age. With too much, we become an uninhabitable furnace. In 1780, carbon dioxide was 0.0280% or 280 ppm, 315 ppm in 1950, 363ppm in 1997 as the Kyoto Protocol to the UN Framework Convention on Climate Change was signed, and 415ppm in 2021.[58]

The Kyoto Protocol's model was that countries set emission reduction targets,[59] without explicitly stating the need for fossil-fuel corporations to be shut down and replaced. This as well as the Copenhagen Accord and the Paris Agreement fail to even name the problem as 'coal', 'oil' and 'gas', and fail to attribute blame, a product of the corruption of the process by fossil-fuel interests. In the Copenhagen Accord of 2009 major countries acknowledged 'the scientific view that the increase in global temperature should be below 2 degrees'.[60] But this is not a scientific view, because science only explains what will happen, not what should. Any credible view suggests there should be 0 degrees warming, and accountability for those who cause harm. In the Paris Agreement of 2015, a further 'ambition' of limiting temperature rises to 1.5 degrees centigrade was agreed.[61] But already by

56 N. Banerjee, L. Song and D. Hasemyer, 'Exxon's Own Research Confirmed Fossil Fuels' Role in Global Warming Decades Ago', *Inside Climate News* (16 September 2016).

57 O. Burkeman, 'Memo Exposes Bush's New Green Strategy', *The Guardian* (4 March 2003).

58 The Kyoto Protocol committed countries to reduce six greenhouse gases in Annex A, namely carbon dioxide (CO_2), methane (CH_4), nitrous oxide (N_2O), hydrofluorocarbons (HFCs), perfluorocarbons (PFCs) and sulphur hexafluoride (SF_6).

59 Kyoto Protocol of 1997, Annex B lists reductions compared to a base year, usually 1990. The UK was 92%.

60 The Copenhagen Accord (18 December 2009) is not a legally binding agreement, but a statement of intent.

61 This is a legally binding agreement in international law. Enforcement turns on domestic courts and pressure.

2012, it was estimated that just 565 more gigatons of carbon dioxide could be released into the atmosphere to stay below 2 degrees warming; 31 gigatons was released in 2011, and the limit was predicted to be reached in 2028. By 2012, fossil-fuel companies had 2,795 gigatons of carbon in proven coal, oil and gas reserves, which would result in a 6–8 degrees rise.[62] In 2017, Donald Trump, with a former Exxon-Mobil CEO as Secretary of State, denounced the Paris Agreement, just as Putin wanted.

While the scale of environmental damage is immense, surprisingly few people are responsible for it. In some loose, abstract and diversionary sense 'we are all responsible', since consumers drive petrol cars, use gas stoves or buy plastic-wrapped goods. But individuals cannot 'shop around' for the energy system. Profit creates responsibility. Out of all historical greenhouse gas emissions, 63% are from just ninety companies[63] and 35% are from twenty companies since 1965.[64] Today, the board of directors of each major fossil-fuel company has nine to thirteen members,[65] but power is truly concentrated among three to five CEOs, chairs and executive officers. This means on a planet of 7.7 billion, just one or two hundred people in these and other corporate bodies are ultimately responsible for continuing climate damage today.

The top historical emitters are mainly located among the permanent members of the UN Security Council (see Table 11.2). Not in this list of historic emitters – but among the biggest entities today – are China's Sinopec and Russia's Rosneft and Lukoil, each generating tremendous revenue.[66] Over $3 trillion was generated in revenue in 2018 by the top twenty-five emitters alone, including $730 billion from just three UK companies,[67] close to the whole UK budget (see Ch. 20). These resources can be used to switch to clean energy and reverse climate damage, now.

Who uses fossil fuels? As Figures 11.3 and 11.4 show,[68] petrol is almost half of fuel, which can be replaced by electric transport, also saving total energy consumption because electric vehicles use less energy than the equivalent in petrol (see Ch. 15). Natural gas is mostly for heating buildings, which can become electric (see Ch. 14). Electricity still partly comes from coal, oil and gas, but can be replaced by wind turbines, solar panels and batteries (see Ch. 12). From 2015 to 2018, energy consumption (measured in 'million tonnes of oil equivalent' (mtoe)) went up from 145.7 to 151.3 mtoes.[69] There was also no meaningful change in energy use.

62 B. McKibben, 'Global Warming's Terrifying New Math', *Rolling Stone* (19 July 2012).

63 R. Heede, 'Tracing Anthropogenic Carbon Dioxide and Methane Emissions to Fossil Fuel and Cement Producers, 1854–2010' (2014) 122 *Climatic Change* 229.

64 R. Heede, 'Carbon Majors: Update of Top Twenty Companies 1965–2017', Climate Accountability Institute (2019).

65 See boards of ExxonMobil (10), Chevron (10), Gazprom (11), BP (12), Shell (13), Peabody (9) and BHP (10).

66 Sinopec $426bn, Rosneft $133.7bn and Lukoil $115.2bn.

67 2018 data is taken from company annual reports. Revenue sources in italics are from 2017.

68 DBEIS, *Digest of UK Energy Statistics* (2016) ch. 1.

69 DBEIS, *Digest of UK Energy Statistics* (2019) 15–16.

Table 11.2 Top 25 historical carbon emitters

	Name or country	All emissions	CO_2+CH_4 Mte	Revenue 2018 ($bn)	Fossil fuel
1	China (coal and cement)	13.73%	240,406	-	Coal
2	Former Soviet Union	7.70%	134,720	-	Coal, oil, gas
3	Saudi Aramco	3.40%	59,530	355.9	Oil, gas
4	Chevron, USA	3.13%	54,796	158.9	Oil, gas
5	ExxonMobil, USA	2.98%	52,237	290.2	Oil, gas, coal
6	Gazprom, Russia	2.47%	43,230	118.83	Gas
7	BP, UK	2.29%	40,039	298.75	Oil, gas
8	Shell, UK and Netherlands	2.18%	38,154	388.37	Oil, gas
9	National Iranian Oil Co.	2.13%	37,294	110	Oil
10	Poland	1.55%	27,096	-	Coal, oil, gas
11	Pemex, Mexico	1.35%	23,692	85	Oil
12	Coal India	1.32%	23,126	2.4	Coal
13	British Coal Corp.	1.13%	19,746	-	Coal
14	ConocoPhillips, USA	1.08%	18,846	111.46	Oil
15	Russia	1.06%	18,562	-	Coal, oil, gas
16	Peabody Energy, USA	0.92%	16,148	5.58	Coal
17	Peroleos de Venezuela	0.91%	15,980	-	Oil
18	PetroChina	0.89%	15,632	-	Oil
19	Total, France	0.83%	14,554	209.36	Oil, gas, coal
20	Abu Dhabi, UAE	0.79%	13,845	-	Oil
21	Kuwait Petroleum Corp.	0.79%	13,774	251.94	Oil
22	Iraq National Oil Co.	0.72%	12,675	-	Oil
23	Sonatrach, Algeria	0.71%	12,351	39	Oil
24	BHP Billiton, UK and Australia	0.57%	9,894	43.63	Coal
25	CONSOL Energy, USA	0.56%	9,877	1.5	Coal

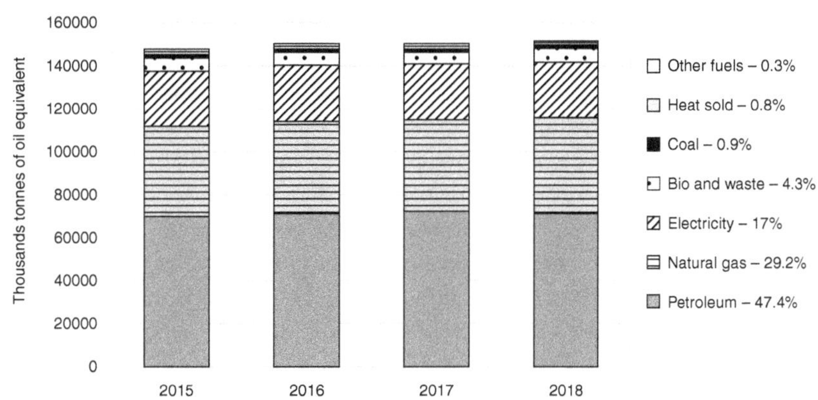

Figure 11.3 UK final energy consumption, 2015–18
Source: Digest of UK Energy Statistics (25 July 2019) Dataset, Tables 1.1–1.3

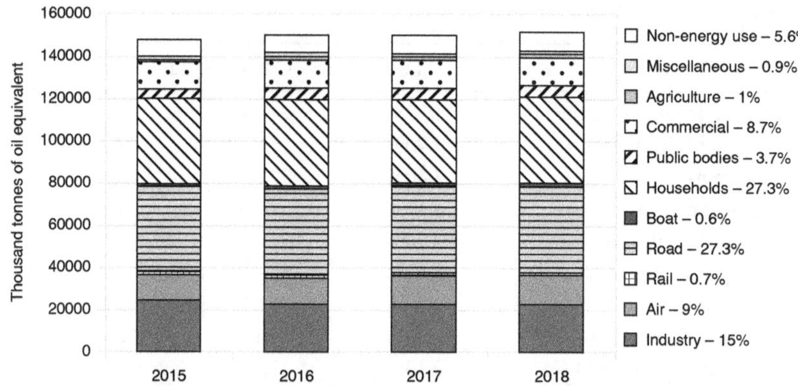

Figure 11.4 UK final energy consumption by user, 2015–18
Source: Digest of UK Energy Statistics (25 July 2019) Database, Tables 1.1–1.3

In the absence of duties to cease fossil-fuel production, what are the targets for emission reduction? The UK's Climate Change Act 2008 has a target in 'the net UK carbon account for the year 2050' that is '100% lower than the 1990 baseline'.[70] This means that the UK by 2050 should have a zero-carbon or carbon-neutral economy. In setting the target the Secretary of State must take account of advice from the non-departmental public body, the Committee on Climate Change.[71] This is regularly proclaimed as one of the 'most ambitious' targets in the world, but there are at least three problems with this approach.

First, the measure of the 'UK carbon account' focuses on domestic production, and ignores the volume of carbon intensive products that are imported into the UK. For instance, emissions are not counted from petrol refining abroad but sold in the UK (only when it is burned), nor is manufacture of steel abroad, or coal generation of electricity used in any imported product (such as the electric lights in a clothing factory or the coal burned on ship containers). Thus, the UK 'exports' pollution without legal provision for oversight.

Second, the measure does not take into account the unique damage caused by major UK companies that operate globally. This includes BP, Shell and BHP Billiton, but also UK-headquartered banks, such as HSBC, Standard Chartered, Barclays, Lloyds and RBS that fund fossil-fuel projects or underwrite global polluters. Further, it fails to take account of the investments from UK pension and savings assets in corporations worldwide, including fossil-fuel production. Because it does not mandate divestment, the Climate Change Act 2008 turns a blind eye to UK profits from climate damage abroad. This is senseless, because we are on the same planet.

Third, action to stop the planet burning is needed now, not by 2050. The language of 'net zero' by 2050 is a licence to pollute till 2050, at horrible cost.

70 Climate Change Act 2008, s. 1. This was amended up from 80% by the Climate Change Act 2008 (2050 Target Amendment) Order 2019 SI 2019/1056, reg. 2.

71 Climate Change Act 2008, ss. 3(1) and 32, establishing the Committee on Climate Change.

The mechanism in the 2008 Act for the interim is that the Secretary of State sets decreasing 'carbon budgets' for each five-year period, and currently we are in the third carbon budget for the 2018–22 period,[72] which has been met,[73] although by the fourth (to 2027), fifth (to 2032) and sixth budget (to 2037) there would need to be a 78 per cent reduction in emissions, including new cars, vans and replacement boilers, to be zero carbon by its start.[74] It is completely unclear that this is adequate since every new fossil-fuel vehicle or machine is causing harm. Under the Energy Act 2013, the Secretary of State has power to set a binding 'decarbonisation target range' by order, and the 'earliest year in relation to which a decarbonisation target range may be set is 2030',[75] after the fifth budget. This approach fails to give investors a clear, certain message for when fossil fuels will cease and enables the fossil-fuel industry to continue damage to the climate, or relocate to unregulated jurisdictions. Thus, international co-operation is necessary.

In European Union (EU) law, the Renewable Energy Directive (RED) 2009 also has a system of targets. The EU's overall target for 2020 was to have 20% renewable energy.[76] Each member state also has targets, and for the UK this was merely 15% by 2020, for Germany 18%, France 23% and Sweden 49%.[77] These targets reflected the progress member states were already making. Individual countries can go further. The targets reveal a low ambition and a lack of urgency compared to the scale of the crisis. Coal production remains a major industry in Germany. A huge gas pipeline from Russia, Nordstream 2, was close to completion in 2019. Vehicle producers in Germany, France, Italy, the UK and elsewhere have no binding duties to cease petrol- and petrol-burning cars, vans or trucks (see Ch. 15). What explains the complacency of UK and EU leaders? It is hard to resist the conclusion that meaningful action is not taken because most policy-makers will be dead before climate damage hurts them, and they just do not care enough. If they did, coal, oil and gas would end now.

(b) Ownership of Resources

The second major source of finance for fossil-fuel enterprise is cheap licensing of resources. English law had long viewed minerals and mines as belonging to the Crown by default[78] and, although actual ownership of resources was left

[72] Climate Change Act 2008, s. 4.

[73] 'UK Projected Emissions Set to Breach 4th and 5th Carbon Budgets', *Environment Analyst* (18 April 2019).

[74] S. George, 'Sixth Carbon Budget: UK Will Need to Cut Emissions by 78% by 2035 to Meet Net-Zero', *edie* (9 December 2020).

[75] Energy Act 2013, s. 1. [76] RED 2009/28/EC, art. 3. [77] RED 2009/28/EC, Annex I.

[78] *R v Earl of Northumberland or Case of Mines* (1568) 1 Plowd 210: 'that by the law all mines of gold and silver within the realm . . . belong to the Queen by prerogative'. But the Royal Mines Act 1688 made exceptions for 'tin, copper, iron, or lead'.

undefined,[79] it is unlawful to extract coal, oil or gas without a licence from the Crown.[80] Coal is primarily found on land, and there may be either deep mines or open-cast mines. Oil may be found on land, but the biggest reserves are North Sea oil, requiring drilling below the sea, through offshore oil platforms. Gas is also found at sea, but much is under land, and can be extracted by 'hydraulic fracturing' or fracking. This involves pumping chemicals and steam through bore holes to fracture rocks beneath the ground, to release gas. A landowner, though they may have the freehold to a property, does not have the right to oil or gas beneath the surface: they must have a licence to extract it.[81]

The oil, gas and other resources at sea are usually found on the continental shelf, the area extending out from land beneath the sea before the slope off into deep ocean. In the last Ice Age (ending around 10,000 BC), much of the continental shelf would have been land as well, but the sea has risen since. The Convention on the Continental Shelf 1958 designated the zone around a country's territory into the sea, to a depth of 200 metres, as belonging to that country.[82] Other states need permission to explore or drill, as it is considered a sovereign right, but a country's own rigs or platforms should not affect recognised shipping lanes, or unjustifiably interfere with fishing, conservation of living resources or open scientific work.[83] Where two countries' coastlines meet, the International Court of Justice held in the *North Sea Continental Shelf Case* that agreement should be reached about boundaries on the sea bed, but based on the natural prolongation of territory, using principles of proportion and equity.[84] This meant that when North Sea oil was discovered, lines were drawn between the UK, Norway and the Netherlands, to designate each country's rights, which could be licensed out.

What if a company with a licence diagonally drills for oil or gas, or digs for coal, and 'accidentally' encroaches on land beneath another person's property? In *Bocardo SA v Star Energy UK Onshore Ltd*, a landowner in Surrey, Bocardo SA, claimed damages for trespass after Star Energy Ltd drilled beneath its property for petroleum. Star Energy held a licence originally issued to Conoco (UK) Ltd in 1980,[85] and had three diagonal wells to between 250 and 950 metres below Bocardo's land. Bocardo claimed damages for a share of the oil that was extracted, winning £621,180 plus interest at first instance, calculated

[79] Cf. Continental Shelf Act 1964, s. 1(1): 'rights . . . to the sea bed and subsoil and their natural resources . . . are hereby vested in Her Majesty'. Coal was vested in the Coal Commission and successors: Coal Act 1938, s. 3.

[80] For oil and gas, see the Petroleum (Production) Act (PPA) 1918; PPA 1934, s. 1; Continental Shelf Act 1964, s. 1(1); and now the PA 1998, s. 2. For coal, see Coal Industry Act 1994, s. 1. For gas storage rights in the UK continental shelf, see Energy Act 2008, s. 1.

[81] PA 1998, s. 2.

[82] Convention on the Continental Shelf 1958, art. 1, following the Truman Proclamation 2667 (28 September 1945) 327 Department of State Bulletin 485, 10 Fed Reg. 12,305, Executive Order 9633.

[83] Convention on the Continental Shelf 1958, arts. 2 and 5.

[84] *North Sea Continental Shelf Case* [1969] ICJ Reports 3 and also *Tunisia/Libya Continental Shelf Case* [1982] ICJ Reports 3.

[85] Issued under PPA 1934, s. 2. Now PA 1998, s. 2.

at 9 per cent of the oil extracted between 2000 and 2007. However, the Supreme Court by a majority of three to two held that only nominal damages for trespass were available. Although having a petroleum licence was no defence to trespass, it seemed the majority was most concerned about stopping the 'powerful bargaining position of a landowner able to control access to a valuable oil field partially sited beneath their land'.[86] The result of this decision is that oil and gas companies were able to act with impunity, and pay off landowners easily, a precedent that is highly unfortunate.[87] However, the government went further in the Infrastructure Act 2015, section 39, which enables use of land over 300 metres below the surface for 'exploiting petroleum or deep geo-thermal energy' without securing an owner's consent.[88]

(c) The Failure of Tort and Criminal Law?

The most striking feature of the law on climate damage is the paucity of provisions in tort and criminal law to make negligent perpetrators compensate and to punish those who recklessly or intentionally cause damage. It is a scientific consensus that burning coal, oil and gas causes global warming: the companies that extract fossil fuels and sell them cause it. However, both the common law of tort and crime have an exceptionally poor historical record in holding environmental polluters to account. For instance, oil spills into Sydney Harbour and a subsequent explosion was damage that was too 'remote' in *The Wagon Mound (No. 2)*.[89] Chemical spills polluting Cambridge groundwater were also too 'remote' a consequence to have to compensate in *Cambridge Water*.[90] The common law attitude differed when it came to strict liability for dangerous escapes from a reservoir flooding a coal mine in *Rylands v Fletcher*.[91] Today, the main paradigm for tort is negligence[92] but, according to Professor Maria Lee, 'any action against emitters will face profound and extensive doctrinal challenges, at every step of the process'.[93] Thus, it is necessary to identify the appropriate questions 'at every step of the process'.

86 *Bocardo SA v Star Energy UK Onshore Ltd* [2010] UKSC 35, [63], per Lord Brown, raising the issue rhetorically. Lord Hope and Lord Clarke dissented.

87 Previously *BP Petroleum Developments Ltd v Ryder* [1987] 2 EGLR 233 had held that statutory provisions did not enable compensation by reference to the value of oil deposits.

88 Infrastructure Act 2015, ss. 43–8, and allowing the Secretary of State to make regulations to give landowners notice and make payments.

89 *The Wagon Mound (No. 2)* [1961] UKPC 2.

90 *Cambridge Water Co. Ltd v Eastern Counties Leather plc* [1993] UKHL 12; cf. the Environment Act 1995, ss. 5–6.

91 *Rylands v Fletcher* [1868] UKHL 1.

92 Strict liability, however, probably covers more accidents, because it is the norm for workplaces, products and in road accidents (see Ch. 15) where there is no remoteness principle at play, and an insurance system.

93 M. Lee, 'Climate Change Tort' (2015) https://papers.ssrn.com/sol3/papers.cfm?abstract_id=2695107, disapproving of overcoming the problem 'creatively'.

(i) Tort Law

In the tort of negligence there are five main questions for actions against polluters: (i) is there damage; (ii) is there a duty of care; (iii) is there a breach of that duty; (iv) is there causation; (v) and is the cause too remote? First, there are a growing number of climate-damage events, ever more extreme: flooding in the UK, bushfires in Australia, hurricanes in America. This results in damage to property, personal injury and death. Second, is there a duty of care? In the established categories of damage to property and person,[94] this depends on whether harm is reasonably foreseeable; whether there is proximity; and whether it is fair, just and reasonable to impose a duty.[95] As we have seen, climate damage was foreseen already in 1965, and fossil-fuel companies like Exxon were doing extensive research on the issue from 1977. Third, is there a breach of a duty of care? If the reasonable person should know their action could cause harm, but acts anyway, there is a breach of duty.[96]

Fourth, does a fossil-fuel company's actions cause climate damage? Here it is clear that multiple parties pollute the atmosphere in different quantities, but as we have seen only ninety companies are responsible for 63 per cent of all historic emissions.[97] There is scientific uncertainty about the link between any given source of emissions and the resulting damage, because emissions in one place lead to uneven global patterns of warming. But, in the face of such uncertainty, it was established in *Fairchild v Glenhaven Funeral Services Ltd* that a tortfeasor is responsible for the material increase in risk that they cause.[98] The preferable principle appears to be that tortfeasors are jointly and severally liable, although an alternative theory is that they may have proportionate liability, a rule that matters where some companies have gone insolvent.[99] The regularity and severity of these events is increasing, which means that a percentage likelihood that any event is caused by climate damage rises. The fifth question is whether the causal chain is too 'remote', to which the answer must be 'no', as climate damage from fossil fuels is expected and well understood.

94 Cf. *Robinson v Chief Constable of West Yorkshire Police* [2018] UKSC 4

95 *Caparo Industries plc v Dickman* [1990] UKHL 2, adopting the reasoning of Bingham LJ [1989] QB 653.

96 *Donoghue v Stevenson* [1931] UKHL 3, per Lord Atkin.

97 Heede, 'Tracing Anthropogenic Carbon Dioxide and Methane Emissions to Fossil Fuel and Cement Producers'.

98 *Fairchild v Glenhaven Funeral Services Ltd* [2002] UKHL 22; *McGhee v National Coal Board* [1972] UKHL 7. In the USA, see *Sindell v Abbott Laboratories*, 26 Cal 3d 588 (1980).

99 *Barker v Corus (UK) plc* [2006] UKHL 20, which appears to follow the reasoning in H. Hansmann and R. Kraakman, 'Toward Unlimited Shareholder Liability for Corporate Torts' (1991) 100 *Yale LJ* 1879, but see the Compensation Act 2006, where Parliament disapproved of this limitation. It may be prudent to distinguish joint liability of individuals (an original concern of Hansmann and Kraakman) from corporate entities, though *Barker* was in principle approved again in *International Energy v Zurich* [2015] UKSC 33.

The most likely step on which fossil-fuel defendants will place their weight of argument will be causation. In the German state court for Essen, an ongoing case named *Lliuya v RWE AG* admitted that a major energy company, RWE AG could be liable in principle for damage to a glacier in Peru. Mr Lliuya's village, Huaraz, was near a melting mountain glacier, increasing the size of lake Palcacocha, and requiring flood defences. It was submitted that RWE had contributed to 0.47 per cent of global carbon emissions, and should therefore be liable for 0.47 per cent of the cost of flood protection. While the State Court dismissed the claim, arguing there was no 'linear casual chain', in November 2017 the Upper State Court admitted the claim to move to the evidential phase on the threat of mudslides, and RWE's exact contribution, to be assessed by experts.[100] Plainly, if one case establishes liability for one company for climate damage, every company under Germany's jurisdiction could be sued for their contribution: this would probably make fossil-fuel companies insolvent. A simple application of first principles in English law compels the same result.

A sixth issue can be added: should judges decide profoundly political issues? War and nuclear holocaust aside, no issue is as important as climate damage: it determines the future of life on Earth. This raises the question of 'justiciability'. In negligence, it arises under whether it is 'fair, just and reasonable' to impose a duty of care for climate damage.[101] It could be argued that the Paris Agreement 2015, or the Climate Change Act 2008, should displace tort law in application to greenhouse gas emissions. In the USA, a similar argument found success. In 2007, the US Supreme Court held by a five to four decision that its Environmental Protection Agency (EPA) had a duty to regulate greenhouse gas emissions under the Clean Air Act of 1963.[102] This apparent victory was short-lived, as *American Electric Power Co. v Connecticut* held by eight to zero that given the EPA's jurisdiction, federal tort law and public nuisance[103] was pre-empted.[104] For the US Supreme Court, the fact that statute 'speak[s] directly to [the] question' displaced the claim against the five largest power companies, emitting 650 million tonnes of CO_2 a year, for contributing to global warming.[105] This uniquely broad approach to pre-emption ignored the objective of the Clean Air Act, which, like all environmental law, sets minimum standards for 'clean air' or 'air pollution prevention'. It does not set

[100] (2015) Case No. 2 O 285/15 Essen Oberlandesgericht.

[101] *Marcic v Thames Water plc* [2003] UKHL 66; and see Ch. 13(4).

[102] *Massachusetts v Environmental Protection Agency*, 549 US 497 (2007), under 42 USC, §7521(a)(1).

[103] While public nuisance was pleaded under US law, it would appear that negligence is the more appropriate tort in English law.

[104] *American Electric Power Co. v Connecticut*, 564 US 410 (2011).

[105] 564 US 410 (2011) per Ginsburg J. See also *Native Village of Kivalina v ExxonMobil Corp.*, 696 F 3d 849 (2012) certiorari (i.e. appeal) denied by Supreme Court (2013) (claimed damages for sea level rise and future floods).

a fixed standard and a fixed licence to pollute.[106] English law should not replicate this reasoning: in environmental matters there should be no pre-emption of tort at any level, without explicit words in statute.[107] The US Supreme Court majority did suggest that state tort law might not be pre-empted,[108] but in subsequent cases courts may conclude that, as the issue crosses state boundaries, state law is pre-empted as well.[109] Executive action therefore is currently needed in the US to control federal pollution, a position that is incompatible with an effective system of justice.[110]

It is increasingly accepted that common law and equity must be interpreted in light of human rights, particularly under the European Convention on Human Rights (ECHR),[111] and in international law,[112] as in the International Covenant on Economic, Social and Cultural Rights (ICESCR). For this reason, the Dutch Supreme Court's decision in *Urgenda v State of Netherlands* could be influential. It held the Dutch government had to reduce greenhouse gas emissions by 25 per cent before 2020, a standard taken from the UN Framework Convention on Climate Change, Annex I, and a report of the Intergovernmental Panel on Climate Change (IPCC) in 2007. This lists developed countries which must reduce emissions between 25 and 40 per cent by the end of 2020 to stay below 2 degrees of climate damage.[113] The Dutch Supreme Court held failure to meet even the lower end of this target violated both the right to life in ECHR, article 2 and the right to private and family life in ECHR, article 8.[114] In a similar *Klimaschutz* or *Climate Change* case in 2021, the German Constitutional Court held that the government had a duty to speed up its climate protection measures, as part of its constitutional duty to protect the rights to life and the environment under the Grundgesetz 1949, articles 2 and 20a.[115] The significance of decisions on these grounds is that, if followed by other courts around Europe, UK courts have strong grounds to

[106] Cf. 42 USC, §7401(a)(3) referring to the 'primary responsibility of States and local programs', with (4) federal assistance. This does not refer to 'exclusive responsibility'.

[107] Even if there are express words displacing tort claims, this may be incompatible with human rights, as below.

[108] 564 US 410 (2011) Ginsburg J, leaving 'the matter open for consideration on remand'.

[109] Cf. *City of New York v BP plc* (2nd Cir 2021) dismissing an action.

[110] Cf. E. McGaughey, 'Fascism-Lite in America (or the Social Ideal of Donald Trump)' (2018) 7(2) *Brit J Am L Studies* 291, on the breakdown of democracy and justice, due to the US Supreme Court.

[111] Human Rights Act 1998, s. 6; *R (Unison) v Lord Chancellor* [2017] UKSC 51, [89], per Lord Reed: ECHR case law is 'relevant to the development of the common law'.

[112] *Saad v Secretary of State for the Home Department* [2001] EWCA Civ 2008, [15], per Lord Phillips MR; cf. *R (SG) v Secretary of State for Work and Pensions* [2015] UKSC 16, [247]–[257], per Lord Kerr (dissenting).

[113] UN Framework Convention on Climate Change 1992, Annex I; recommendation from the IPCC Working Group III, Climate Change 2007: Mitigation of Climate Change (2007) Contribution to the Fourth Assessment Report, ch. 13, 776, Box 13.7. Note that the RED 2009/28/EC, Annex I target for the Netherlands was just 14%.

[114] Judgment (20 December 2019) 19/00135, text in Dutch but best translated through deepl.com.

[115] *Klimaschutz* or *Climate Change* (24 March 2021) 1 BvR 2656/18.

interpret common law norms, including the tort of negligence, so as to be compatible with protection of the right to life and privacy.

It is likely that the same issues come before the UK courts, as they already have to the courts in New Zealand, and again in the Netherlands.[116] There is then a choice to make about whether tort law plays a positive role: either it helps end the ecosphere, or it helps to end fossil-fuel damage. In *Smith v Fonterra Co-Operative Group Ltd*, the New Zealand Court of Appeal refused a claim of Mr Smith over damage to coastal property. He argued the damage was contributed to by a subsidiary of Bathurst Resources Group (the largest coal miner in New Zealand), an oil refinery (owned mainly by ExxonMobil, BP and Z Energy), a power station owned by Genesis Energy LP (in turn held mainly by US asset managers such as Invesco, ALPS Advisors, J. P. Morgan and Chickasaw[117]) and other emitters. Mr Smith did not attempt to bring evidence of these entities' contribution to climate damage, or set about detailed quantification of loss to him. In the High Court, Wylie J held that climate damage would occur anyway, that the 'defendants' collective emissions are minuscule' (without evidence of what they were), and that 'reasonable persons in the shoes of the defendants could not have foreseen the damage'. Such damage was (apparently) 'an unlikely or distant result of the defendants' emissions'.[118] This exceptionally callous reasoning is false, since one of the defendants, ExxonMobil, actually did foresee climate damage in 1977.[119] On the contrary, if companies know of, or turn a blind eye to, damage, in *Rookes v Barnard*, the House of Lords established that exemplary damages are available where conduct is 'calculated to make a profit'. 'Where a Defendant with a cynical disregard for a Plaintiff's rights', said Lord Devlin, 'has calculated that the money to be made out of his wrong-doing will probably exceed the damages at risk, it is necessary for the law to show that it cannot be broken with impunity.'[120] However the Court of Appeal upheld the decision. French J reasoned that although 'reasonable foreseeability of harm is arguably a trial issue and not of itself a ground for striking out' in this case, there was no 'proximity'. By this it asserted, bizarrely, that there was no 'physical or temporal proximity', as if the case law and limits on psychiatric harm could be likened to the scientifically undoubted connections between fossil fuels and climate damage. Furthermore, it rejected there was an adequate causation connection in law, because not every potential plaintiff was before the court: it asserted, quite wrongly, that in cases on material increase in risk, 'one or more of [the defendants] was responsible for all the harm suffered'. This is false: an essential point of the material increase of risk test is that there may be liability when potential

[116] *Smith v Fonterra Co-Operative Group Ltd* [2020] NZHC 419.

[117] See CNN Business, 'Top 10 Owners of Genesis Energy LP', https://money.cnn.com/quote/shareholders/shareholders.html?symb=GEL&subView=institutional.

[118] [2020] NZHC 419, [82].

[119] [2020] NZHC 419, [89]–[96] also rejecting a relationship of proximity.

[120] [1964] UKHL 1.

co-defendants are insolvent. Then, instead of serious engagement with the issues, the Court of Appeal retreated into floodgates platitudes, that defendants were 'virtually limitless', that being unable to find every one was 'an insuperable problem' and they were unprepared to 'abolish the [so-called] relational underpinnings that are fundamental to tort law'.[121]

Where the New Zealand courts invented 'insuperable' problems, Dutch courts have surmounted them. In *Friends of the Earth v Royal Dutch Shell plc*, the Hague District Court held that under the Dutch Civil Code, Book 6, section 162(2), failure to abide by the Paris Agreement 2015, article 2(1) would be tortious: that is 'what according to unwritten law has to be regarded as proper social conduct'. In interpreting this general tort law duty (which appears identical to open-textured norms, such as the 'neighbour' principle in common law), the Court took into account ECHR, articles 2 and 8 on the rights to life and a private, family and home life, and the parallel provisions in the ICCPR, articles 6 and 17. It noted that the 'serious and irreversible consequences of dangerous climate change in the Netherlands . . . pose a threat to the human rights of Dutch residents'. It followed that Shell had a duty to cut its emissions in accordance with the Paris Agreement duties by 45 per cent by 2030, whether those were generated directly by its corporate group (scope 1), indirectly from its purchases (scope 2) or indirectly from its value chain or the purchase and use of its products (scope 3). Moreover, Shell was required to take action immediately and not wait for any appeal process.[122] Following the case, Shell plc deleted 'Royal Dutch' from its name and announced a relocation of its headquarters to London, presumably in the hope that it can escape judgment, although predictably its PR operations denied this. Enforcement and legal reasoning in English courts should follow the Dutch model, not the New Zealand model. Indeed, it is difficult to see why the New Zealand courts failed to have the presence of mind to reason in a similar way to the Dutch court, or perhaps they just do not care about the international human rights treaties that New Zealand has signed and ratified: an unforgivable frivolity and failure of legal reasoning, worthy of the utmost condemnation.

(ii) Directors' Duties

A related aspect of negligence liability is the duty of directors under the Companies Act 2006, section 174. While tort claims focus on damage to third-party victims of a company's conduct, company members (and arguably other stakeholders such as bondholders, employees and the ultimate investors) may also bring derivative claims against directors for negligent loss to the company. This raises two main types of claim. First, a director who fails to take action to cease carbon emissions, and subsequently faces tort claims, could be liable to

[121] [2021] NZCA 552, [96]–[113].

[122] (26 May 2021) C/09/571932/HA ZA 19-379, especially paras. 4.4.9 and 4.4.10.

compensate the company. Premiums for 'Director and Officer' insurance are likely to be affected also if the likely cost of defending claims were to rise.

Second, directors could also be liable for negligently failing to eliminate fossil-fuel energy simply on the ground that it costs more money. This flows from the general duty of care imposed upon anybody in a fiduciary position, including insolvency practitioners or trustees, and this explicitly applies to directors in their fulfilment of duties.[123] For example, in *Medforth v Blake* the Court of Appeal held that a receiver and manager was liable to the owner of an insolvent farming business after he failed – despite being told by the owner – to get £1,000 per week in discounts for pig food. This resulted in excessive costs being run up, and therefore breached a general duty of 'good faith' and within that 'a duty to manage the property with due diligence', including 'reasonable steps to be taken in order to try to do so profitably'.[124] It follows that where directors could save money – for instance, by (1) buying electric vehicles, with lower total costs than fossil-fuel vehicles,[125] (2) installing solar panels or building wind turbines to buy energy more cheaply than from the grid[126] or (3) insulating buildings to reduce energy bills – and they fail to take such simple steps, they must be regarded as liable for negligence under section 174 for the extra costs to the company.

(iii) Criminal Law

In addition to civil law liability, the Criminal Damage Act 1971, section 1(1) states:

> A person who without lawful excuse destroys or damages any property belonging to another intending to destroy or damage any such property or being reckless as to whether any such property would be destroyed or damaged shall be guilty of an offence.

It would appear that a fossil-fuel executive is, at the very least, 'reckless as to whether ... property would be destroyed' by carbon emissions.[127] Under section 1(2) it would also appear that fossil-fuel executives are reckless as to

[123] Companies Act 2006, s. 170(4): 'The general duties shall be interpreted and applied in the same way as common law rules or equitable principles, and regard shall be had to the corresponding common law rules and equitable principles in interpreting and applying the general duties.'

[124] *Medforth v Blake* [1999] EWCA Civ 1482, per Sir Richard Scott VC.

[125] Cf. K. Palmer, J. E. Tait, Z. Wadud and J. Nellthorp, 'Total Cost of Ownership and Market Share for Hybrid and Electric Vehicles in the UK, US and Japan' (2018) 209 *Applied Energy* 108.

[126] E.g. I. Johnston, 'Tesco to Switch to 100% Renewable Electricity this Year in UK and by 2030 Worldwide', *The Independent* (16 May 2017); 'Volvo Cars unveils first solar energy installation at Ghent car factory', *Automotive World* (4 October 2018); E. Logiudice, 'Solar Power Is Saving this Farmer Money', *Yale Climate Connections* (2 October 2018).

[127] *R v G* [2003] UKHL 50, [41], quoting the Draft Criminal Code Bill, cl. 18(c) that a person acts recklessly with respect to '(i) a circumstance when he is aware of a risk that it exists or will exist; (ii) a result when he is aware of a risk that it will occur; and it is, in the circumstances known to him, unreasonable to take the risk'.

the endangering of life, which constitutes 'aggravated' criminal damage.[128] They are reckless because they know what climate damage is, and they know that coal, oil and gas cause it. If anything, knowing what you are doing and doing it is intentional. The direct motive of fossil-fuel companies may not be to destroy the ecosphere, because their direct motive is profit. But motive is irrelevant to the existence of a crime in English law.[129] Under section 5, the only relevant, available 'lawful excuse' is that someone consented to the damage, and this is not likely. Displaying concern for the issue with investments in advertising for going 'Beyond Petroleum' or public relations to greenwash a corporate image also does not mitigate the bases for criminal liability. As damage grows worse, it seems likely that criminal laws will, and should, be enforced.

(3) Governance of Private Corporations

Despite the unique damage they cause to local communities and the global environment, the governance of coal, oil and gas corporations in the UK follows the standard pattern of the Companies Act 2006 and Insolvency Act 1986. Directors of BP plc, Royal Dutch Shell plc, BHP Billiton plc and others generally appoint themselves, with oversight by asset managers that control shares.[130] However, additional rules come from (a) two sector regulators, the Oil and Gas Authority (OGA) and the Coal Authority, which issue licences; (b) procedural requirements to secure a licence and planning or other permission; and (c) rules upon insolvency to secure that installed facilities are properly decommissioned. Lacking is a duty to wind up coal, oil and gas companies, whether operating at home or abroad.

(a) Oil and Gas Authority and Coal Authority

There are two main UK regulators for the fossil-fuel industry. First, since the Energy Act 2016, section 1, there has been a new Oil and Gas Authority, headquartered in Aberdeen and with an office in Bloomsbury, London. Following the government's request to the Wood Review in 2013,[131] and its introduction in 2015, the Petroleum Act (PA) 1998, section 9A makes the 'principal objective' of the OGA 'maximising the economic recovery of UK petroleum'. This is to be done with the 'equipment used in the petroleum industry', and collaborating with petroleum licence holders, operators and

[128] Criminal Damage Act 1971, s. 1. [129] E.g. *R v Hales* [2005] EWCA Crim 1118.

[130] See Ch. 4(1)(b), and constitutions of BP plc, Royal Dutch Shell plc or BHP Group plc at Companies House.

[131] Sir Ian Wood, 'UKCS Maximising Recovery Review: Final Report' (2014) for Ed Davey, Liberal Democrat Secretary of State for Energy and Climate Change.

infrastructure owners.[132] This conflicts with the goal of eliminating emissions in the Climate Change Act 2008, section 1.

The OGA is appointed by the Secretary of State, and currently has eight directors. Its main function is to issue licences to 'search and bore for and get' petroleum within Great Britain, territorial waters and the continental shelf, on any terms it thinks fit.[133] The OGA sets the price, or 'such consideration', as it 'with the consent of the Treasury may determine'.[134] The OGA may also charge fees on licence applicants and holders.[135] The Secretary of State may give directions to the OGA as 'necessary in the interests of national security', or 'otherwise in the public interest' if the 'circumstances are exceptional'.[136] 'Petroleum' is defined to include 'any mineral oil or relative hydrocarbon and natural gas',[137] and so its two primary competences are offshore oil rigs and onshore 'fracking' (see Ch. 11(3)(b)(ii)). The OGA must have regard to the 'need to minimise public expenditure' in future (although catastrophic climate damage is being routinely ignored), having a 'secure supply of energy', 'storage of carbon dioxide', collaborating with other agencies, innovating and regulating predictably.[138]

The legislation's salient feature is that the OGA's 'principal objective' contradicts the goal to stop climate damage under the Climate Change Act 2008, section 1. It also conflicts with the clear duty in section 8 to 'minimise public expenditure' in future. The proper way to reconcile this is that the duty of 'maximising production' ought to be read to mean 'maximising production consistently with the duty to prevent climate damage and minimise future expenditure'. It is therefore arguable that the OGA's principal objective should be read to phase out all fossil-fuel production as soon as possible, and the OGA should, under the PA 1998, section 9A(2), issue a strategy to do so.[139]

A similar system exists for coal, though it is almost finished. The Coal Industry Act 1994, section 1 established the Coal Authority, which succeeded the Coal Corporation that owned Her Majesty's coal.[140] Its functions are to hold interests and rights in 'unworked coal', 'licensing of coal-mining operations', manage subsidence or matters in opencast mining and provide information as necessary under the Act. Between two and eight people are appointed by the Secretary of State.[141] Section 2 requires it to act to ensure there is 'an economically viable coal-mining industry' and a range of other duties.[142] But in practice, coal mining is not economic for electricity because

[132] Infrastructure Act 2015, s. 41 introduced this.

[133] PA 1998, ss. 2–3, referring further to the Continental Shelf Act 1968, s. 1.

[134] PA 1998, s. 3(3).

[135] Energy Act 2016, ss. 12–13, referring to OTA 1975, Sch. 1; Energy Act 1976, s. 12A; PA 1998, ss. 3 and 15–17; PPA 1934, s. 2; and Energy Act 2008, ss. 4 and 18.

[136] PA 1998, s. 9. [137] PA 1998, s. 1. [138] PA 1998, s. 8.

[139] PA 1998, s. 9A(2). The OGA has to produce strategies to meet the objective.

[140] Coal Act 1938, s. 3 vested coal reserves in the Coal Corporation.

[141] Coal Industry Act 1994, s. 1(2) and Sch. 1. [142] Coal Industry Act 1994, ss. 2–3.

wind energy is now far cheaper.[143] It is argued that coking coal is needed for the hot temperatures in blast furnaces for steel production, but in late 2019 a technological breakthrough enabled steel to be produced by 2026 with hydrogen-based heat,[144] a date which could presumably be brought forward with proper investment. Arguably all production should be shut by the Coal Authority, because an 'economically viable coal-mining industry' under section 2 can no longer exist, let alone when the cost of climate damage is taken (as it must be) into account.

(b) Licensing and Planning Permission

Licences to extract oil and gas offshore, frack onshore and dig coal are mainly contractual: the state agrees to let companies extract on terms it sees as fit, subject to statutory requirements. The Crown retains property. Companies have contracts. Local authorities may give planning permission, if extraction is in their region, on terms they choose. This system is open to the inherent danger that regulators and authorities are lobbied, or charmed, or individuals working there are lured with future job prospects to grow comfortably close to the industry. The same is true of a governing political party which could be captured by fossil-fuel interests. Alternatives are not without problems. State ownership of natural monopolies may also be misused or squandered if a corrupt political party holds power.[145]

(i) Oil and Gas Offshore

How does a company practically acquire a licence to drill for oil or gas offshore? Now under the control of OGA, there have been thirty-two offshore licensing rounds, and recently one each year, where companies submit bids for different blocks in the sea.[146] The first seventeen rounds, with the associated statutory instruments, are mapped out in Figure 11.5.

First, a company needs a Petroleum Exploration and Development Licence from the OGA.[147] In law the OGA must consider an environmental statement

[143] E.g. E. Crooks, 'New Wind and Solar Generation Costs Fall Below Existing Coal Plants', *Financial Times* (8 November 2018). The same is predicted for gas by 2022: S. Evans, 'Analysis: Record-Low Price for UK Offshore Wind Cheaper than Existing Gas Plants by 2023', *Carbon Brief* (20 September 2019).

[144] See 'SSAB: Pioneer in Fossil-Free Steel', IG News 24 (27 December 2019); B. Lewis, 'Arcelormittal Aims for 30% Cut in Emissions in Europe by 2030', *Reuters* (13 December 2019).

[145] NB: Annual Financial Statements Directive 2013/34/EU, arts. 42–3 require disclosure of all payments to governments anywhere in the world over €100,000 for oil, gas, mining and logging industries. The Bribery Act 2010, ss. 1–9 further discourages corrupt payments, but hardly with complete success.

[146] OGA, 'Offer of Awards for the UK's 32nd Offshore Licensing Round', Press Release (3 September 2020). A thirty-third round is 'paused'.

[147] PA 1998, s. 3.

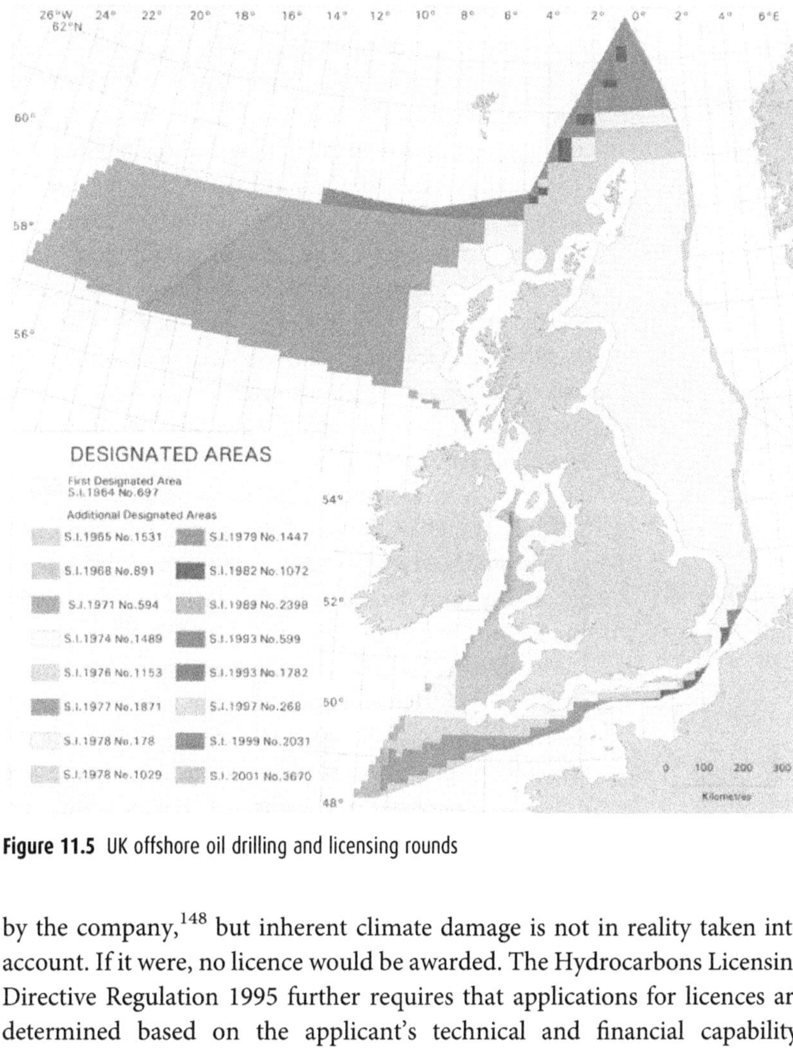

Figure 11.5 UK offshore oil drilling and licensing rounds

by the company,[148] but inherent climate damage is not in reality taken into account. If it were, no licence would be awarded. The Hydrocarbons Licensing Directive Regulation 1995 further requires that applications for licences are determined based on the applicant's technical and financial capability, methods, price and previous conduct. Applicants must be treated equally by objective and non-discriminatory criteria, and advertisements for tenders must be public.[149] Second, an operator must submit a 'design notification' for oil-rig installations, technology or pipelines to the Health and Safety Executive to be accepted.[150] Third, there must be an environmental impact assessment for production over 500 tonnes of oil a day, 500,000 cubic metres of gas a day, deep drilling or drilling of an area over half a hectare.[151] Because

[148] Offshore Petroleum Production and Pipe-lines (Assessment of Environmental Effects) Regulations 1999, SI 1999/360, para. 5.

[149] Hydrocarbons Licensing Directive Regulations 1995, SI 1995/1434, regs. 3–5, following the Hydrocarbons Directive 1994/22/EC, arts. 2–4.

[150] Offshore Installations (Safety Case) Regulations 2005, SI 2005/3117, para. 6.

[151] SI 2017/571, Sch. 1, para. 14 and Sch. 3. SSI 2011/139 for Scotland.

there are no property rights or councils to deal with at sea, the system is far more simple than onshore gas or oil.

To avoid complex contractual relations with companies, there is a statutory model contract set out in legislation, automatically incorporated into petroleum licences, subject to the minister's discretion to modify.[152] The Petroleum Licensing (Production) (Seaward Areas) Regulations 2008, Schedule 1 has the list of model clauses for offshore drilling.[153] Clause 2 concerns the grant of a licence for payment. The OGA has discretion over the licence term, the licensee's obligation to submit its work programme, revoking a licence due to breach, arbitration for disputes, and health and environmental safety.[154] Usually a licence will hold two four-year exploration terms, when areas where nothing is found are given back, followed by an eighteen-year production period if there are areas, which can be revoked if progress is poor. No licence holder can sell or transfer the licence without permission,[155] underlining that the oil is not the company's property. Given that rights are purely personal, the OGA could cancel all contracts, and no specific performance award could be given.[156] Arguably, the appropriate level of damages for breach of contract must deduct future public cost of climate damage, and will therefore be zero or negative.

Alongside the licence conditions, there is a right for companies that do not own pipelines to interconnect and use infrastructure if a company has spare capacity.[157] This is not, however, used in practice, and companies will prefer to negotiate albeit in the shadow of the law. Alternatively, the Oil and Gas Authority may require the owner of a pipeline to give another company access, should companies not use the rights themselves for fear of damage to their commercial reputation.[158]

(ii) Fracking

In November 2019, in the run-up to the UK general election, the Conservative-led government announced a moratorium on fracking, in line with calls long made by the opposition Labour Party,[159] although the industry has lobbied for a reversal.[160] Scotland had already banned fracking, as had France and a number of German states, given the widespread opposition to the pollution and earthquakes that it causes.[161] Between 2008 and 2014, over 300 exploration

152 PA 1998, s. 4(1)(e).
153 Petroleum Licensing (Production) (Seaward Areas) Regulations 2008, SI 2008/225, Sch. 1.
154 SI 2008/225, cll. 2, 4–7, 16–17, 41–2, 43 and 23 or 45. 155 SI 2008/225, cl. 40.
156 Cf. *Southern Foundries (1926) Ltd v Shirlaw* [1940] AC 701 – see Ch. 3(3)(a).
157 PA 1998, ss. 17–17H. 158 Energy Act 2011, ss. 82–3.
159 'Labour Vows Fracking Ban if It Wins General Election', *BBC* (26 September 2016).
160 N. Thomas, 'Cuadrilla Lobbies Regulators for Progress on UK Fracking', *Financial Times* (24 December 2019).
161 E.g. W. L. Ellsworth, 'Injection-Induced Earthquakes' (2013) 341(6142) *Science*.

and development licences were granted,[162] and it was said to be 'irresponsible of government not to do everything' to get more domestic shale gas, instead of importing it. The need to phase gas out has been ignored.[163] Imports come through the Langeled pipeline from Norway, Interconnector from Belgium, BBL from the Netherlands and further supplies extend back to the Nordstream 1 and 2 from Russia.[164] In 2019, 39.4 per cent of the European Union's gas and 26.8 per cent of its oil were from Russia.[165] The procedure to get a licence to frack may now be moot, but it could return, and it builds on offshore oil or gas.[166]

First, any onshore drilling requires land, either through purchase, consent or negotiation with the landowner.[167] If coal seams are nearby, the Coal Authority must give permission and, if there are any naturally occurring radioactive materials, the Environment Agency also.[168] Second, the Mineral Planning Authority must approve exploratory wells. Third, planning permission from the local council is needed to develop the land.[169] This gives the opportunity for the local council to just say no, but also for fracking companies to pay off cash-strapped councils with sums that may seem large (even if small relative to profit). For instance, the UK Onshore Operators Group wrote a community charter in 2013 pledging a £100,000 'donation' to communities for each well, and 1 per cent of proceeds from production.[170] Councils are also entitled to retain all business rates, as opposed to the normal 50 per cent.[171] Fourth, the fracking company will need permission for waste disposal.[172] Fifth, it will need permission for abnormal water use.[173] Sixth, it will need consent from OGA in consultation with the Environment Agency, the Health and Safety Executive and the Health Protection Agency.[174] Seventh, if a borehole is

[162] L. Brinded, 'UK Energy Minister Michael Fallon: Whitehall to Accelerate Shale Gas Development', *IB Times* (1 July 2014). Fallon was later sacked for multiple instances of sexual harassment.

[163] HM Treasury, 'Harnessing the Potential of the UK's Natural Resources: A Fiscal Regime for Shale Gas', Consultation Outcome (2013) para. 0.2.

[164] Gazprom, Uniper, Wintershall, OMV, Engie and Royal Dutch Shell are responsible for Nordstream 2.

[165] 'EU Imports of Energy Products – Recent Developments', *Eurostat* (November 2019) 4–5.

[166] E. Albrecht and D. Schneemann, 'Fracking in the United Kingdom: Regulatory Challenges between Resource Mobilisation and Environmental Protection' [2014] *Carbon & Climate L Rev* 238, has a good summary.

[167] Infrastructure Act 2015, ss. 43–8 gave a new statutory right to use deep-level land for petroleum and geothermal development, subject to a modest payment for the landowner.

[168] Radioactive Substances Act 1993, ss. 1B–D define radioactive materials.

[169] Town and Country Planning Act (TCPA) 1990, s. 57.

[170] E.g. 'First Community Payment under UKOOG Shale Community Engagement Charter' (2017) www.ukoog.org.uk/about-ukoog/press-releases/206-first-community-payment-under-ukoog-shale-community-engagement-charter.

[171] M. M. Roggenkamp, C. Redgwell, A. Rønne and I. Guayo (eds.), *Energy Law in Europe: National, EU and International Regulation* (2016) 64.

[172] Environmental Permitting (England and Wales) Regulations 2010.

[173] Water Resources Act 1991, s. 24A.

[174] Albrecht and Schneemann, 'Fracking in the United Kingdom'.

sunk more than 100 feet deep, the British Geological Survey should be notified, which has the right to access a site at all reasonable times.[175]

Within these steps there is room for procedural challenge, but it has often failed. For example, in *R (Frack Free Balcombe Residents Association) v West Sussex CC*, the Balcombe resident group brought an action for judicial review of West Sussex County Council giving planning permission to Cuadrilla Balcombe Ltd to explore the fracking potential. This involved driving boring holes into the ground to see if there was gas, before actual fracking took place. The group claimed the council's planning officer had wrongly advised the council's committee that issues of pollution control, emissions and the well's integrity were to be left to the Environment Agency and the Health and Safety Executive; that Cuadrilla's history of breaching planning conditions was irrelevant; and that the number of objections by members of the public was irrelevant. Gilbart J dismissed the claim that the council made any error of law or that it disregarded relevant considerations. He even suggested the council would have acted unlawfully if it had taken the mass protests against fracking into account.[176] Similar challenges have also failed,[177] but it would seem that the proper view is that a planning authority may always legitimately consider public opinion as relevant on an issue of public importance, as opposed to tabloid opinion on an issue of individual rights.[178]

(iii) Coal Extraction

Despite the closure of most coal plants, and the refusal of permission for an opencast mine in Northumbria in 2016,[179] a new deep coal mine was approved in Cumbria in November 2019.[180] The courts have not been helpful in this regard, apparently construing the law so as to encourage decisions to allow mining. In *H. J. Banks & Co. Ltd v Secretary of State for Housing*, Ouseley J granted an application for judicial review of the Secretary of State's initial refusal to grant permission for the opencast mine in Northumbria. According to Ouseley J, the Secretary had failed to set out the reasoning for refusal in the proper two stages required. Ostensibly, the Secretary failed to give adequate reasons for how renewable energy could fill the gap by not producing coal. Unfortunately, Ouseley J's reasoning and the legal grounds for his decision are (in his own words) 'wholly unclear and inadequate on a critical issue' of why

175 Mining Industry Act 1926, s. 23.

176 *R (Frack Free Balcombe Residents Association) v West Sussex CC* [2014] EWHC 4108 (Admin), [128].

177 E.g. *R (Friends of the Earth Ltd) v North Yorkshire CC* [2016] EWHC 3303 (Admin), refusing judicial review over whether a financial bond for (unknowable) long-term financial impacts should be required.

178 Cf. *R v Home Secretary ex p Venables and Thompson* [1997] UKHL 25.

179 'Opencast Coal Mine Application "Called In" over Climate Change Concerns', *The Guardian* (9 September 2016).

180 H. Pidd, 'Government under Fire for Approval of New Coalmine in Cumbria', *The Guardian* (3 November 2019).

that needs to be spelled out,[181] when there is overwhelming evidence that renewable energy can and must replace coal.

Similar to fracking, a company that wants to dig coal must first have land. Second, they must secure planning permission from the local council.[182] As with fracking, the lure of 'jobs' (typically fewer than renewable energy)[183] and payments are likely to be appealing for councils starved of revenue from central government. Third, the Coal Authority must grant a licence.[184] Fourth, if the mine is open cast, there is a mandatory environmental impact assessment. Fifth, there must be a licence for water abstraction.[185] Sixth, there must be notification to UK Research and Innovation for any boreholes deeper than 30.48 metres, and officers appointed have inspection rights for research.[186] Upon leaving a coal mine, there is an obligation to restore the land to the state that it was in.[187] Unlike one of the notorious US cases on contract law,[188] this statutory duty is binding also on liquidators of insolvent companies, which may not abandon land.[189]

(c) Decommissioning and Insolvency

To ensure that companies building major infrastructure in oil and gas do not simply go insolvent leaving piles of junk, there are a set of duties on decommissioning. Under the PA 1998, section 28A it is an offence to abandon 'an offshore installation or submarine pipeline'. The Secretary of State may give written notice to require that an abandonment programme is prepared.[190] A notice can be served on an installation operator, licensee, a joint operating agreement participant or (and crucially) anyone owning an interest or an associated company. The Secretary of State can also write an abandonment programme, revise or impose it and serve a default notice for any non-compliance.[191] This system goes far to preventing use of the corporate form to hide behind subsidiary companies or the corporate veil.

The difficulty is that the costs of decommissioning are very high, and environmental benefits are not clear. The famous Brent Spar oil rig was occupied by Greenpeace in 1995, gathering worldwide media attention, after it was proposed by Shell to release the installation out to sea. The original rules

[181] [2018] EWHC 3141 (Admin), [102] and [110], not following the cases he cites with any real 'particularity'.
[182] TCPA 1990, s. 57.
[183] 'Whitehaven Coal Mine: Government Refuses to Call in Plans', *BBC News* (6 January 2021).
[184] Coal Industry Act 1994, s. 26. [185] Water Industry Act 1991, s. 24A.
[186] Mines Industry Act 1926, s. 23. [187] Coal Industry Act 1994, s. 54.
[188] *Peevyhouse v Garland Coal & Mining Co.*, 382 P2d 109 (1962). The Supreme Court of Oklahoma held a coal company that failed to restore land only had to pay damages for the land's difference in financial value: apparently the land was so worthless that only $300 was due, not the $25,000 cost of the work.
[189] *Re Scottish Environmental Protection Agency* [2013] CSIH 108. [190] PA 1998, s. 29.
[191] PA 1998, ss. 33–7.

were written in response, following a 1998 Convention signed by the UK.[192] There are around 470 platforms and 5,000 wells, but it has since been argued that leaving installations (so long as oil is removed) may be less harmful to the environment, given that sea life attaches itself to the rigs over the years they operate, and tearing them up further disturbs the marine environment.[193] The oil industry and government have shared an estimate of it costing £16.9 billion in ten years, and between £75 billion and £100 billion in total to decommission the UK's offshore platforms.[194] This work, of course, is done by oil companies that have a very strong incentive to overestimate the true cost of their work. Indeed, the industry body OGUK writes that, in the next ten years, £15.2 billion will be spent on decommissioning on the UK shelf, and 'the emerging global market is worth a massive $85 billion (£67 billion)'.[195] Why does it seem so enthusiastic? In 2012, the UK government resolved to set off all work on decommissioning from petroleum tax. In essence, the UK government has since been paying billions to fossil-fuel companies for work of questionable utility, which could be used for building renewable energy instead.

(4) Public Rights

Given the incalculable damage that fossil-fuel extraction causes to the environment, and humanity's future, the idea of public rights in fossil-fuel extraction is mildly ridiculous. However, it can sensibly be said that (a) there is a right to end coal, oil and gas and to clean energy, and (b) there are three main types of taxes that could fund other rights.

(a) The Right to Clean Energy

As we have noted, both of the International Covenants of 1966 protect 'the inherent right of all peoples to enjoy and utilize fully and freely their natural wealth and resources'.[196] This may have previously referred to a right to exploit coal, oil or gas, or to mine other minerals before, but now it is clear that it conflicts with everyone's right to the 'natural wealth and resources' of a living planet: that is, clean air, a stable climate and seas that do not rise. There is also the right in 'the benefits of scientific progress' in article 27 of the UDHR and article 15 of the ICESCR.[197] According to the United Nations Educational,

[192] Convention for the Protection of the Marine Environment of the North-East Atlantic 1998, known as the OSPAR Convention.

[193] Cf. KIMO, 'Should Shell Be Allowed to Leave Decommissioned Oil Rigs in the North Sea?' (4 September 2019).

[194] 'Taxpayers May Be Liable for North Sea Decommissioning Bill, Says Study', *BBC News* (21 November 2016).

[195] OGUK, 'Decommissioning Insight' (2019) 1.

[196] ICCPR 1966, arts. 47 and 1(2); ICESCR 1966, arts. 25 and 1(2).

[197] UDHR 1948, arts. 3 and 27(1); ECHR 1950, art. 2; ICCPR 1966, art. 6(1); ICESCR 1966, art. 15.

Scientific and Cultural Organization (UNESCO) expert group, 'this right is inextricably linked ... to other rights, such as to a clean environment [and] sustainable development'. States have positive obligations to 'adopt a legal and policy framework to establish institutions to promote the development and diffusion of science and technology'.[198] This came from experience in electrifying rural America in the New Deal and distributing a polio vaccine.[199] Very simply, it means that in international law, the UK and all countries should be using every executive, legislative and judicial means to realise this right as fast as possible, not set distant targets.

(b) Taxation or Subsidies

While coal, oil and gas need to be shut down, not used for money, taxes may accelerate this process. There are three main types but, unfortunately, they have become subsidies. First, a 'petroleum revenue tax' was introduced by the Oil Taxation Act, section 1. This was originally 45%, then 60% in 1979, 60% in 1980, 75% in 1983, but reduced to 50% in 1993, and all new fields were exempt.[200] In 2016 the petroleum revenue tax was cut to 0%.[201] Further, in 1987, it was held that an oil company is entitled to tax relief for expenditure on building an oil platform,[202] meaning that company activity is financed by other taxpayers. Second, there is a 'ring-fenced corporation tax' on individual fields, where profits are separated (or 'ring-fenced') from a company's other activities. The Corporation Tax Act 2010 sets this at 30% for larger and 19% for smaller fields.[203] Third, an additional 'supplementary charge' of 10% of profits was introduced in 2002 as it was assessed that oil companies were generating excessive profits. It was increased in 2006 to 20%.[204] It was again reduced to 10% in the Finance Act 2016. This charge does not, however, allow costs to be deducted, unlike the ring-fenced corporation tax. Finally, it was normal for oil companies to make royalty payments of 12.5% of the market value of produce, but this was mostly cut in 1982, and ceased entirely in 2003 because of ostensible 'concerns that royalty had an inhibiting effect upon exploration and development'.[205]

While the industry group OGUK claims that it has contributed '£334 billion in direct production tax payments since the early 1970s',[206] the true position today is that the direct financial benefit to the UK public from the fossil-fuel industry is close to zero, and taking climate damage into account,

198 UNESCO, Venice Statement on the Right to Enjoy the Benefits of Scientific Progress and its Applications (2009) §§12(d) and 16.

199 Shaver, 'The Right to Science and Culture', 143 and 138–9.

200 Finance Act 1993, s. 185(4)(a).

201 Finance Act 2016, s. 140(1).

202 *Inland Revenue Commissioners v Mobil North Sea Ltd* [1987] 1 WLR 1065.

203 Corporation Tax Act 2010, s. 279A.

204 Finance Act 2006, s. 152; Corporation Tax Act 2010, s. 330(1).

205 G. Gordon, J. Paterson and E. Usenmez, *Oil and Gas Law* (2011) 83.

206 OGUK, Decommissioning Insight (2019) 3.

overwhelmingly negative. Indeed, all tax revenue that was received, meagre as it was compared to astonishing profits, was squandered through the current accounts of governments in the 1980s and 1990s. By contrast, when North Sea oil was discovered, Norway put proceeds in a national fund. This is now worth $1 trillion, or £753 billion. The UK's production was slightly higher than Norway's[207] and, if the same measures had been taken, the fund would be worth £11,409 for every person in the UK. Instead, there is nothing.

(5) Conclusion

The problem of natural resources is that we can continue to have fossil fuels, or we can have a living planet, but we cannot have both. First, the greatest natural resources are sunshine and wind, and now that technological alternatives to coal, oil and gas are there, they should be used (see Chs. 12–15). Second, the revenue absorbed by the fossil-fuel economy should be redeployed, if necessary by emergency legislation,[208] to build clean infrastructure. This needs to be done immediately, while coal, oil and gas corporations are put into insolvency, and wound up in the public interest.[209] Clean energy also involves retooling factories that make cars, motors, or gas heaters and accelerating production of wind turbines and solar systems with even greater urgency than the Covid-19 vaccines or protective equipment.[210] Third, this should be done in a way that is co-ordinated across all public bodies, and all private corporations, following the example of the proposed Green Recovery Act 2020.[211] Because coal, oil and gas are inherently monopolistic, the economic benefits will cascade across banking, transport and energy systems, and improve the wealth of all enterprise.

207 The UK had produced 42.8bn barrels of oil equivalent, and Norway around 40bn, by 2014.

208 Civil Contingencies Act 2004, s. 22(1)–(2)(a), (c) and (j): 'Emergency regulations may make any provision . . . appropriate for the purpose of – (a) protecting human life, health or safety, . . . (c) protecting or restoring property, . . . (j) preventing, reducing or mitigating the effects of disruption or destruction of plant life or animal life . . . .'

209 Companies Act 1985, Part XIV (investigation) and Insolvency Act 1986, s. 124A (winding up).

210 In the US, the Defense Production Act of 1950, 50 USC, §§1ff enables this.

211 Green Recovery Act 2020, ss. 20–2 with an introduction from Mat Lawrence and Common Wealth (2020).

12

Electricity and Energy

Contents

For life to improve on Earth, energy will be clean. Electricity will come from wind, solar, hydro or geothermal sources, with battery or pump storage, and not from coal, oil or gas. Today we use electricity for light, computers, anything that plugs in. It is used for heating and transport (Chs. 14 and 15), though gas and oil remain. To electrify transport, generation must expand by 10–50 per cent,[1] and electric heating requires more electricity again. But electricity is more efficient than fossil fuels: it consumes only a quarter of equivalent energy used in oil, and the benefits of renewable electricity go far beyond stopping climate damage.[2] First, it improves health. Renewable electricity does not pollute our air (Ch. 15(2)(a)) and it changes dangerous fossil-fuel jobs into safer jobs in wind, solar or battery manufacture. Second, it makes us richer. Wind and solar costs are falling continually, while coal, oil and gas are the worst performing assets and more expensive even without climate damage factored into their price.[3] Third, clean energy enhances freedom because corporations monopolise the land or sea to extract fossil fuels, but nobody can monopolise the wind or the sun. The raw materials for turbines, panels and batteries are

[1] S. Evans, 'Factcheck: How Much Power Will UK Electric Vehicles Need?', *Carbon Brief* (13 July 2017).

[2] Other clean energy sources such as hydrogen, or perhaps nuclear fusion, might also be developed at scale.

[3] B. Nauman, 'Sharp Rise in Number of Investors Dumping Fossil Fuel Stocks', *Financial Times* (9 September 2019); '2019 Stock Index Results Show Fossil Companies as Worst-Performing Segment', *Energy Mix* (14 January 2020).

abundant,[4] and their manufacture can be dispersed and competitive. This reduces our dependence on a handful of global energy firms.

The transition to clean energy is a human right, because everyone has the right to 'the benefits of scientific progress',[5] as well as rights to life, health and housing.[6] The right does not, however, solve the political problem. Fossil-fuel companies invest money to persuade public opinion that coal can be 'clean', that gas is a 'transition' fuel or that wood should be burned in ex-coal plants instead. Similarly, and despite meltdowns at Chernobyl and Fukushima, nuclear lobbyists say their industry is necessary, and now safe, because lessons were learned. The main arguments, summed up by the International Energy Agency lobby, are that 'energy demand' is expanding[7] and fossil fuels or nuclear are needed when the wind does not blow or the sun does not shine. Even aside from the unthinkable costs of climate damage, and the security risks, these assertions are false. Clean energy is cheaper. Batteries work. And life must improve. The bigger picture is who leads the energy transition. First, governments could leave it mostly to existing energy companies, but they will act too slowly to halt climate damage even with subsidies. Second, governments could directly finance infrastructure, whether publicly or privately owned. Third, government could enhance diversified and community ownership. The choices in transition all have implications for the cost of energy, for democracy and for the quality of service.

(1) Historical Background

For most of human history, fire and wood provided light and heat, but with the invention of the wheel ancient civilisations began to use the power of water. Vast hydraulic-powered cities were created, with water wheels using 22 per cent of energy in a stream, often for milling.[8] Technology perhaps remained primitive, however, given the abundance of slave labour;[9] it was not until the Middle Ages that inventors added gears and cranks for sawing, grinding or furnace blowing. In 1086, Domesday Book recorded one mill for every fifty households; by 1700 there were up to five water mills for every mile

[4] E.g. for turbines, steel, iron, copper and aluminium; for solar panels, also quartz; for batteries, cobalt and lithium.

[5] ICESCR 1966, art. 15; UDHR 1948, art. 27.

[6] ICESCR 1966, art. 11; also CFREU 2000, art. 34(3).

[7] E.g. IEA, *World Energy Outlook 2019* (2019). The IEA governing board is ministers from OECD member countries, with votes weighted to economic size: Agreement on an International Energy Programme 1974, arts. 61–2. Its affiliated groups are dominated by coal, oil and gas corporations.

[8] J. Getzler, *A History of Water Rights at Common Law* (2004) ch. 1, 13–26. This is by far the topic's best history.

[9] M. Bloch, *Feudal Society* (1965) and 'The Advent and Triumph of the Watermill' in *Land and Work in Mediaeval Europe* (1935): 'an invention rarely spreads until it is strongly felt to be a social necessity'.

of usable stream, and water continued to provide most power until the 1830s in Britain.[10] Meanwhile, electricity had long been observed, from lightning in the sky, to electric fish on the Nile. But not until 1600 did a scientist from Colchester named William Gilbert distinguish the electric force created by rubbing amber from the seemingly similar force of magnetism in a lodestone.[11] In 1745 a Dutch scientist called Pieter von Musschenbroek made a jar that could hold an electric charge between foil and a chain, with sparks jumping out of a metal thread at the top, known as the Leyden jar. In 1751 Benjamin Franklin, determined to show that lightning was like the electricity in the jar, attached a metal key to a damp kite string and flew it in a storm, observing sparks jumping from the key to his hand.[12] Then, in 1791 an Italian physicist Luigi Galvani explained that neurons passed signals to muscles in the body through electricity.[13]

As coal use had grown by the 1700s (see Ch. 11(1)), people noticed a flammable gas came from coal seams, and when coal was heated for purity ('coked') in iron and steel smelting, coal gas could be stored as a by-product. In 1792, William Murdoch, an employee of the steam engine firm, Boulton & Watt (see Ch. 15(1)), used coal gas to light his house in Cornwall, and in 1806 he installed gas lighting at cotton mills in Manchester. This meant gas was ahead of electricity for light. Alessandro Volta invented the electric battery in 1800,[14] Michael Faraday the first electric motor in 1821,[15] Georg Ohm the electrical circuit in 1827[16] and James Clerk Maxwell explained the relations of electricity, magnetism and light in 1861.[17] These people gave their names to our energy units (see Table 12.1), but electric lighting was not invented till 1857, and the light bulb not till 1878, to really bring electricity into people's homes.

So, despite electricity's discovery, the first networked energy companies were gas. The Gas Light and Coke Company was established by royal charter in 1812. The South Metropolitan Gas Company was formed in 1829. Like many other companies they began installing street lighting in cities and

[10] Getzler, *A History of Water Rights at Common Law*, ch. 1, 18 and 22; A. E. Musson, *The Growth of British Industry* (1978) 142.

[11] W. Gilbert, *De Magnete, Magneticisque Corporibus, et de Magno Magnete Tellure* (1600) or *On the Magnet, Magnetic Bodies, and on that Great Magnet the Earth.* Gilbert's term *electricus* or 'like amber' was turned into 'electricity' by Sir Thomas Browne in 1646.

[12] B. Franklin, *Experiments and Observations on Electricity* (1751) and 'The Kite Experiment', *Pennsylvania Gazette* (19 October 1752). Franklin later co-authored the US Declaration of Independence 1776, Treaty of Paris 1783 and US Constitution 1787. He was the Postmaster General for British America (1753–74) and for the USA after independence (1775–6).

[13] L. Galvini, *De viribus electricitatis* (1791).

[14] A. Volta, 'On the Electricity Excited by the Mere Contact of Conducting Substances of Different Kinds' (1800) 90 *Philosophical Transactions of the Royal Society of London* 403.

[15] M. Faraday, *Experimental Researches in Electricity* (1844), recounting earlier experiments.

[16] G. Ohm, *Die galvanische Kette: mathematisch bearbeitet* (1827) or *The Galvanic Circuit Investigated Mathematically.*

[17] J. C. Maxwell, 'On Physical Lines of Force' (1861) 21 *Philosophical Magazine* 281 (part II).

Table 12.1 Units of electrical measurement and meaning

Unit	Meaning
Joule, J	Energy (work) on object from a 1 metre distance with a 1 Newton force.
Watt, W	Rate of energy transfer. 1 joule per second. 1,000 W = kW x 1,000 = MW x 1,000 = GW.
Coulomb, C	Quantity of electricity carried in 1 second by a current of 1 amp.
Amp, A	A unit of electricity charge or current. 1 A = 1 C/s.
Volt, V	Electric potential between two points in a wire with 1 amp current with 1 watt of power.
Ohm, Ω	Unit of electrical resistance in a conductor with potential difference 1 volt at 1 amp current.

towns.[18] The Lighting and Watching Act 1833 gave local authorities powers to employ 'inspectors' to light the streets with gas and oil lamps,[19] although companies would carry out most work. Concern over companies' monopoly positions led to controls on prices and dividends in their constitutions.[20] The Gasworks Clauses Act 1847 limited dividends to 10 per cent, or any other prescribed rate, while also enabling companies to break up streets and open drains to lay pipes, setting standard company powers and penalties for pollution.[21] Standard units of measurement for gas were fixed to protect consumers in 1859.[22] However, for London, where there were thirteen gas companies, the Metropolis Gas Act 1860 enabled separate districts to be administered by each.[23] Prices rose, while prices elsewhere fell,[24] and attempts were soon made to require companies' accounts to be public.[25] Dividend ceilings were reduced to 7 per cent and then 4 per cent, but companies initially evaded them by converting loan capital to share capital (to spread profits over a nominally bigger share-capital base) or with new stock issues at par value, before requirements to publicly auction stock.[26] Ratepayers were hardly

18 J. Foreman-Peck and R. Millward, *Public and Private Ownership of British Industry 1820–1990* (1994) 30–7.

19 Lighting and Watching Act 1833 (c. 90) s. XLV. Under s. XIV to vote for inspectors, ratepayers had to have paid rates for at least one year. This followed the Lighting of Towns (Ireland) Act 1828 (c. 82) s. XLV.

20 Foreman-Peck and Millward, *Public and Private Ownership of British Industry 1820–1990*, 32, referring to price and dividend controls for Nottingham, Oxford, Worcester and Bristol.

21 Gasworks Clauses Act 1847, ss. XXIX, V, XII–XVI and XX respectively.

22 Sale of Gas Act 1859, s. II: 'the only legal Standard or Unit of Measure' was 'the Cubic Foot containing 62.321 Pounds Avoirdupois weight of distilled or Bain Water weighed in Air' measured at 62 degrees Fahrenheit.

23 Metropolis Gas Act 1860, s. V. Under s. XII companies were subject to orders of the Secretary of State.

24 Cf. D. Matthews, 'Rogues, Speculators and Competing Monopolies: Early London Gas Companies, 1812–1860' (1985) 2 *London Journal* 39.

25 City of London Gas Act 1868.

26 Foreman-Peck and Millward, *Public and Private Ownership of British Industry 1820–1990*, 45–6.

empowered. Nor were workers, who could only strike against low wages. The 1890s saw mass strikes and, in response, the South Metropolitan Gas Company Act 1896 gave workers a right to elect one to three directors to its board,[27] but only if workers collectively bought £40,000 in shares. It was not much, and yet an advance.

Then, in 1878, Joseph Swan demonstrated his new light-bulb invention to the Newcastle Chemical Society. He settled a dispute with American inventor Thomas Edison, to enable a patent in 1879, and co-founded the Edison and Swan United Electric Light Co. While the intense beams of arc lamps had been used for lighthouses and in football stadiums before,[28] the softer light of the light bulb's carbon filament caused shareholder panic at the London Gas Company. In 1881, the House of Commons was given electric light, as were the Savoy Theatre, Mansion House, the British Museum and Royal Academy, and in 1884 Lord Kelvin even got electric lamps installed at Peterhouse College, Cambridge.[29] As with gas, the Electric Lighting Act 1882 enabled local authorities to break up streets for wires, though most development happened through companies outside the Act, putting copper wires overhead. At the insistence of the Liberal MP Joseph Chamberlain, the Act also set maximum prices, forbade price discrimination between customers and enabled local authorities to purchase electric companies after twenty-one years.[30] This was later delayed to forty-two years in 1888,[31] on the spurious ground that these rights were limiting innovation.[32] The reality was electricity companies were developing fast, and if not faster then probably because UK gas companies were more efficient than abroad. Gas remained cheaper than electricity till 1900.[33]

Over the early twentieth century, the central task of energy policy was to spread the benefits to as many people as possible. This occurred through the patchwork of municipal and local companies,[34] until the Electricity (Supply) Act 1926 established the Central Electricity Board (CEB). The CEB was appointed by the minister, with goals to merge small suppliers or compulsorily

[27] South Metropolitan Gas Act 1896, s. 19. The Commercial Gas Co. and the South Sub-urban Gas Co. started similar schemes. See S. Webb and B. Webb, 'Cooperative Production and Profit Sharing', *New Statesman* (Special Supplements 1914–15). E. McGaughey, 'Votes at Work in Britain: Shareholder Monopolisation and the "Single Channel"' (2018) 47(1) *Industrial LJ* 76.

[28] L. Hannah, *Electricity before Nationalisation* (1979) ch. 1, 3, and a tragically bright dinner party for Lord Salisbury.

[29] Hannah, *Electricity before Nationalisation*, 4.

[30] Electric Lighting Act 1882, ss. 19–20.

[31] Electric Lighting Act 1888. See also Electric Lighting (Clauses) Act 1899.

[32] Hannah, *Electricity before Nationalisation*, 5–6.

[33] Hannah, *Electricity before Nationalisation*, 9.

[34] The statutes were regularly tinkered with: the Electric Lighting (Clauses) Act 1899 set standard powers and duties; the Electricity (Supply) Act (ESA) 1919 created an Electricity Commission to oversee reorganisation of the electricity industry; ESA 1922 added more piecemeal fixes. See also the Gas and Water Works Facilities Act 1870, Amendment Act 1873 and the Gasworks Clauses Act 1871, on duties for supply, for testing gas and illuminating standards. After, Gas Regulation Act 1920 and Gas Undertakings Acts 1929, 1932 and 1934.

purchase, connect a national grid and regulate prices.[35] This was very far from the goals of the Labour Party for public ownership, though it favoured mergers because this would make future public ownership more efficient.[36] Still, at least one knight of the realm screamed that the Act 'out-Herods Herod in its Socialism' with 'nationalisation of a very bad kind, and . . . spoliation also'.[37] An element of truth was that the CEB's price-fixing powers could easily favour the largest companies, ensuring smaller entities with higher costs could not compete. But by 1938 the CEB had created the national grid. Dissatisfaction with high prices and disorganised operation remained.

Meanwhile, in the USA, with a vaster geography, and its socialist movement suppressed by the Supreme Court,[38] states had developed utility and price regulation,[39] starting with Wisconsin in 1907.[40] By 1917, seventeen states had enacted public utility laws, and by 1930 every state except Delaware had regulators for water, gas and electricity, but private companies were simply not providing electricity and other services to rural America.[41] When the Rural Electrification Act of 1936 was passed, just 3 per cent of farm homes had electricity. Federal loans were distributed, and electrician teams were empowered to install wires and circuits everywhere.[42] By 1959, electrification had risen to over 90 per cent, when private companies had claimed only 10 per cent of rural homes were 'economic' to serve.[43] The experience of rural electrification, the refusal of private enterprise to connect people and the recognition of need for positive government action, led directly to the right to 'the benefits of scientific progress' being put into the Universal Declaration of Human Rights 1948.[44]

After World War Two, the Labour government nationalised energy in the Electricity Act 1947 and the Gas Act 1948.[45] Over 600 municipal and corporate electricity suppliers were brought into a system of fifteen Area Electricity

35 ESA 1926, ss. 7–13 on price and term regulation.

36 Hannah, *Electricity before Nationalisation*, ch. 10, 330–1.

37 Sir Charles Wilson, HC Debs. (29 March 1926) vol. 193, col. 1734. Sir Charles's main complaint appeared to be: 'Why should the reasonable profits of the municipalities and the power companies be taken away?' The Electricity Commissioners were apparently 'armed with powers as dictators—such powers as have never been given to any body of people in this country before'.

38 See Ch. 1(4)(b) on the imprisonment of Eugene Debs and the Lochner era.

39 This was enabled by *Munn v Illinois*, 94 US 113 (1877) holding that property 'affected with a public interest' could be regulated, unlike (ostensibly) private property: *Civil Rights Cases*, 109 US 3 (1883).

40 Written by John R. Commons, see W. L. Crow, 'Legislative Control of Public Utilities in Wisconsin' (1934) 18(2) *Marquette L Rev* 80.

41 W. Boyd, 'Public Utility and the Low-Carbon Future' (2014) 61 *UCLA L Rev* 1614, 1640–1.

42 Rural Electrification Act of 1936, 7 USC ch. 31; in 1949 telephones were added, in 2008 broadband.

43 A. H. Chayes, 'Restrictions on Rural Electrification Cooperatives' (1951) 60(8) *Yale LJ* 1434, 1435.

44 UDHR 1948, art. 27; ICESCR 1966, art. 15. See L. Shaver, 'The Right to Science and Culture' [2010] *Wisconsin L Rev* 121, 143 and 138–9.

45 See *The Gas Industry, Report of the Committee of Enquiry*, Cmd 6699 (1945).

Boards, under the British Electricity Authority, renamed the Central Electricity Generating Board (CEGB) in 1957.[46] They were bound to break even, not profit, and avoid 'undue preferences' in supply and pricing.[47] Similarly, the Gas Council was established, and in place of 1,064 private and municipal companies, there were twelve new regional gas boards.[48] Under both Acts, the minister appointed all the board of directors for electricity and gas, with non-binding assurances that labour and consumer interests would be represented.[49] Each Act established 'Consultative Councils' with twenty to thirty members from among local authorities and consumer groups, but again appointed by the minister.[50] These councils were widely seen as 'important',[51] but despite their statutory complexity they were mostly powerless. There were also statutory duties for directors to consult trade unions.[52] But the model of governance, as urged by Herbert Morrison, and carried out by Hugh Gaitskell as Minister for Fuel and Power, retrenched all worker-elected directors in gas companies, their roles denigrated.[53] As North Sea oil and gas was discovered, the government led an expensive but swift switch from coal gas ovens and heaters to natural gas in eight years from 1968, converting 40 million appliances, including cookers and heaters, in 14 million homes.[54] The Gas Act 1972 recast the standard model, as it merged area boards into one British Gas Corporation. Directors were appointed by ministers, and subject to their directions.[55] British Gas had a duty to supply reasonable demand, ensure revenues were 'not less than sufficient' to meet outgoings, and make accounts public.[56] But there were no actual voting rights for ratepayers and workers, on this model of public ownership.

Thatcher's Gas Act 1986 and Electricity Act 1989 broke up and sold off the boards to shareholders. 'Competition forces the economy to respond to the needs of the consumer', argued the 1987 Manifesto, so long as the sectors were 'subject to proper regulation'.[57] Instead of energy directors chosen by ministers,

[46] Electricity Act 1957, s. 2. See *Report of the Committee of Inquiry into the Electricity Supply Industry*, Cmd 9672 (1956).

[47] Electricity Act 1947, ss. 1–3 and 36–7(8). [48] Gas Act 1948, ss. 1–7.

[49] Electricity Act 1947, s. 3; Gas Act 1948, s. 5. [50] Electricity Act 1947, s. 7; Gas Act 1948, s. 9.

[51] See J. W. Grove, 'The Consumer Councils for Gas and Electricity' (1950) 28(3) *Public Administration* 221. See later the Gas Act 1972, ss. 9–13.

[52] Electricity Act 1947, s. 53. Gas Act 1948, s. 57.

[53] Mr Hugh Gaitskell, Second Reading, Hansard HC Debs. (10 February 1948) vol. 447, cols. 233–4. On Herbert Morrison's theories, see Ch. 15(1).

[54] C. Elliot, *The History of Natural Gas Conversion in Great Britain* (1980) 1. Rapid Transition Alliance, 'The Great Switch – Lessons from When 14 Million Homes and Businesses Changed Fuel in Less than a Decade' (26 February 2020), quoting Sir Denis Rooke: 'perhaps the greatest peacetime operation in the nation's history'. C. Hanmer and S. Abram, 'Actors, Networks, and Translation Hubs: Gas Central Heating as a Rapid Socio-technical Transition in the United Kingdom' (2017) 34 *Energy Research & Social Science* 176. Also (2013) 52 *Energy Policy* 25, 40. The transition also reduced suicide, as coal gas had been more toxic and accessible.

[55] Gas Act 1972, ss. 1 and 4. [56] Gas Act 1972, ss. 2, 14 and 23.

[57] Conservative Party General Election Manifesto: The Next Moves Forward (1987) Privatisation. Competition.

Table 12.2 Big Five UK energy companies

	Brand	Owners in 2020	2005 market % gas – electricity	2020 market % gas – electricity
1	British Gas Ltd	Centrica plc (shareholders)	55% – 24%	28% – 19%
2	SSE plc	(shareholders)	9% – 14%	10% – 13%
3	EdF SA	84.5% French government	5% – 14%	8% – 11%
4	Scottish Power Ltd	Iberdrola SA (shareholders)	9% – 11%	10% – 9%
5	E.ON SE	(shareholders)	12% – 21%	10% – 12%
6	npower	E.ON SE (shareholders)	10% – 15%	7% – 8%
			100% – 99%	**73% – 71%**

directors were chosen by directors, removable by City shareholders as in standard corporate law (see Chs. 3 and 4). The transmission operations of the CEGB were not broken up, but passed to a new National Grid plc, which listed shares in 1995. Yet companies had a new regulator: the Director of Gas Supply, and the Director General of Electricity Supply, whose offices were merged into Ofgem in 2000.[58] These regulators acquired some previous powers, to limit prices and try to raise standards, against the constant profit motive of companies to do the opposite.[59] In effect, the system came to look again more like that operating in the USA,[60] albeit with fewer of the Enron-type blackouts and bankruptcies.[61] A series of mergers took place from 1980s to today which left a rather less than vibrant competitive market. In 2020, the 'Big Five' (down from six in 2019 when E.ON bought npower) controlled over 70 per cent of the market (see Table 12.2).

Particularly since 2013 and smaller competitors acquiring rights to access infrastructure, the Big Five market share has declined from nearly 100 per cent of households to 71–3 per cent.[62] This points to the possibilities with decentralised electricity generation, even if 'transmission and distribution remain natural monopolies'.[63] Yet the greater issue has become transition to clean energy, and reducing our total consumption. A combination of statutory renewable obligations and feed-in tariffs did push electricity generation sharply away from coal, but gas for heating remains prevalent. Compared to the necessity of ending all coal, oil and gas as fast as technically possible, a feat

58 Gas Act 1986, s. 1; Electricity Act 1989, s. 1; Utilities Act 2000.

59 *Foster v British Gas plc* (1990) C-188/89, [1991] 2 AC 306 (on nature of a public service).

60 NB: The Public Utility Regulatory Policy Act of 1978, §§111–12 required utility companies to substitute discounts for larger customers with rates to incentivise energy conservation, §§202–4 set standards on interconnection and §210 required utilities to buy power at 'avoided cost' from small generators and qualifying facilities.

61 L. Khan and S. Vaheesan, 'Market Power and Inequality: The Antitrust Counterrevolution and Its Discontents' (2017) 11 *Harvard L & Policy Rev* 235, 263–5.

62 Electricity and Gas (Ownership Unbundling) Regulations 2014/3333; Electricity Act 1989, s. 10F; Gas Act 1986, s. 8H; Electricity Directive 2019/944, arts. 3 and 6. See J. Warner, 'Are the Big Six Suppliers Losing Their Grip on the UK Energy Market?', *IG* (12 March 2018).

63 Khan and Vaheesan, 'Market Power and Inequality', 263.

Table 12.3 Examples of energy use or generation

Appliance	Energy
Light bulb	15 W (using 15 Wh over an hour)
Average laptop	10 W if idle, or 180 W if running full power
Fridge	150–500 W
Kettle	3,000 W (3 kW)
Power shower	8.5 kW
UK household electricity a year	3,000 kWh
London Array windfarm	630 MW
Apple	230 kJ (equivalent to 64 Wh)
Person	9,000 kJ a day (equivalent to 100 Wh)

well within our present technology, our current pace of decarbonisation looks asphyxiated. There are also no inherent incentives for energy companies to reduce consumption (see Table 12.3), or if they do, reduce prices.

(2) Finance

Like fossil-fuel enterprises, electricity and gas companies seem to rely on ordinary corporate finance, but are really financed mainly by not paying for climate damage. Ratepayers over-subsidise energy companies wherever competition fails due to natural monopolies in energy and an oligopolistic market. This section covers (a) polluters not being held responsible or taxed for climate damage, (b) subsidies to expand renewable energy in the Contracts for Difference scheme, (c) the feed-in tariff for smaller and renewable producers and (d) natural monopoly, particularly in distribution and transmission.

(a) Climate Damage and Carbon Taxes

The first main subsidy is that energy producers do not pay for climate damage. The goal of energy regulation must be to end coal, oil and gas as fast as technically possible, but the law is not there yet. This requires analysing three issues: (i) the total energy consumption and its composition, (ii) methods to decarbonise all consumption and (iii) taxation.

(i) Total Energy Consumption

The UK's total energy consumption in 2019 was the equivalent of 142 million tonnes of oil each year, or 1,651 terawatt hours a year. Of this, 18% is electricity (25.7 'million tonnes of oil equivalent' (mtoes) or 290 TWh), 44% is petroleum

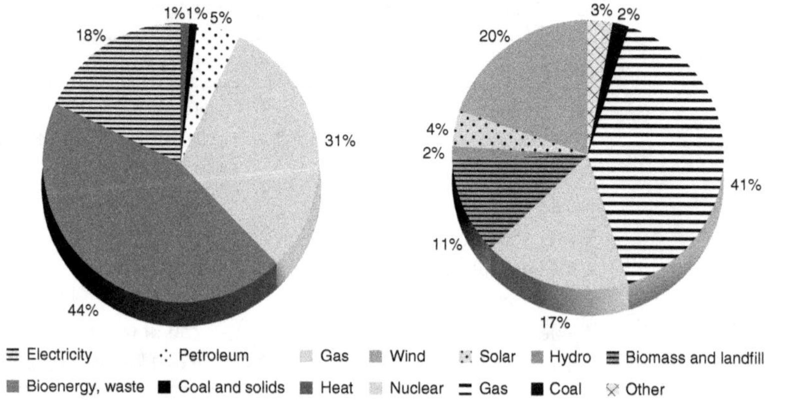

Figure 12.1 UK energy and electricity composition, 2019
Sources: Digest of UK Energy Statistics (2019) Table 1.1.5 and (2020) Charts 5.6 and 6.4

(mostly transport), 30% is natural gas (mostly heating) and 1% is the remaining coal (see Figure 12.1).[64]

It is estimated that just 10–50 per cent more electricity is needed to electrify all land transport,[65] and this indicates the inherent waste of fossil fuels. In 2018, electricity itself was 33 per cent from 'renewable' sources, but 'renewable' sources included 'plant biomass' which emits greenhouse gases when burned. Under the Renewable Energy Directive (RED) 2009,[66] biomass and biofuel can count towards renewable energy statistics on the theory that unlike coal, oil or gas, plants absorb greenhouse gases when they grow. It enables ex-coal power stations to be refitted to burn biomass. This is bad policy because biomass burning releases more greenhouse gases than coal, and smoke from bio-burning still damages people's health.[67]

(ii) Methods to Decarbonise Consumption

The Climate Change Act 2008, section 1 creates a 'duty of the Secretary of State to ensure' that the level of carbon dioxide and other greenhouse gases 'for the year 2050 is at least 100% lower than the 1990 baseline'.[68] The percentage was amended in 2019, up from 80 per cent, but the dangerously distant target year has not yet been changed.[69] The Act also fails to count emissions produced by UK companies abroad, or in products and services imported to the UK. The Secretary of State must set carbon budgets for each five years to

64 DUKES (2019) Table 1.1.5.

65 S. Evans, 'Factcheck: How Much Power Will UK Electric Vehicles Need?', *Carbon Brief* (13 July 2017).

66 RED 2009, art. 17 and Annex V.

67 M. Le Page, 'The Great Carbon Scam', *New Scientist* (21 September 2016) 20–1, also explaining that before changes in the law, old growth forests were originally being felled.

68 Climate Change Act 2008, s. 1.

69 Climate Change Act 2008, s. 2(2) according to 'scientific knowledge'.

reach the target. The third budget of 2018–22 requires reduction from 2.78 billion to 2.5 billion tonnes of CO_2 equivalent, with a projection of reducing to 1.95 billion tonnes by 2027 and 1.72 billion by 2032,[70] when the political careers of the drafters will be long gone. The Energy Act 2013, section 1 replicated this ineffectual model for a 'decarbonisation target range' in electricity generation, but then said the 'earliest year' for setting that range 'is 2030'.[71] It failed to say that oil for transport and gas for heating must be electrified. Section 131 said the Secretary of State should publish an annual 'Strategy and Policy Statement' for how any targets will be achieved.[72] But the essential policy goal, to ban coal, oil and gas corporations, including those abroad, is not yet written into law.

The same model of enabling emissions up to 2050 is used in the RED 2009.[73] Article 3 set a target for gross final energy consumption to be 15 per cent renewable, but by 2019 the UK had only achieved 12.3 per cent.[74] The Paris Agreement 2015 makes reference to holding 'the increase in the global average temperature to well below 2°C above pre-industrial levels and to pursue efforts to limit the temperature increase to 1.5°C'.[75] It fails to mention the words coal, oil, or gas once, and fails to say they must be eliminated (subject to strict exceptions). This is an infinite subsidy for dirty energy corporations, which do not pay for the infinite social costs.

(iii) Taxation

Tax, in economic theory, is an ideal method to internalise 'externalities' like pollution (see Ch. 2(2)(c)) even though bans in tort and criminal law work better, including politically.[76] In the UK, the Finance Act 2000 introduced a 'climate change levy', which rose with inflation from 2006.[77] However the rates have been low. In 2020, the rates were 0.811 p/kWh for electricity, 0.406 p/kWh for gas, 2.175 p/kg of petrol (about 1.68p per litre) and 2.653 p/kWh for any other taxable commodity.[78] If the goal is to eliminate the use of fossil fuels, it seems obvious that measures at these levels are an ineffective distraction.

Originally, renewable energy sources were exempt from the climate change levy, but in 2015 the exemption was removed, on the pretext that direct subsidies in the Contracts for Difference scheme (below) would be more

70 Final Statement for the Second Carbon Budget (May 2019) 3, made under Climate Change Act 2008, s. 18.

71 Energy Act 2013, ss. 1–4. 72 Energy Act 2013, ss. 131–8.

73 RED 2009, art. 3 and Annex I.

74 See EU Commission, 'Europe 2020 Targets: Statistics and Indicators for the United Kingdom' (2021) under 'Share of Renewable Energy'.

75 Paris Agreement 2015, art. 2. The Agreement limits greenhouse gases, but not the gas industry as such.

76 F. Green, 'Anti-fossil Fuel Norms' (2018) 150 *Climatic Change* 103 on the importance, and success, of bans, using the examples of ending slavery, aggressive war and nuclear testing.

77 Finance Act 2000, s. 30 and Sch. 6.

78 See www.gov.uk/guidance/climate-change-levy-rates and Finance Act 2000, Sch. 6, para. 42.

effective. The exemption's removal was challenged unsuccessfully in *Infinis Energy Holdings Ltd v HM Treasury*, as allegedly violating the company's legitimate expectations, the European Union (EU) law principles of foreseeability and certainty, and being disproportionate.[79] Sir Terence Etherton MR held that to have a legitimate expectation there must be 'a precise, unconditional and unambiguous assurance, whether by words or conduct' on how the government would behave in future. There were none, because neither HM Treasury nor HMRC had assured there would be an indefinite exemption, and the change 'is the kind of assessment which, in a democratic society, is primarily for the Government and Parliament to make'.[80] The result is that all electricity generators pay the climate change levy whether they cause climate damage or not. This may make sense as a tool to raise revenue, but not to eliminate environmental harm, and ensure clean energy.

(b) Contracts for Difference and Renewable Obligations

The second main source of finance for energy companies is the Contracts for Difference scheme. Entering its fourth allocation round in 2020, companies can bid to build renewable infrastructure, such as wind farms or solar installations. Since the Energy Act 2013, companies make contracts to build with the government procurement body, Low Carbon Contracts Company Ltd (LCCC), designated as the 'CFD counterparty'.[81] The LCCC and a developer agree contracts typically lasting fifteen years, and the company is paid the difference between the future market price of electricity (the 'reference' price) and a price set by the LCCC that is predicted to give enough money to invest extra renewables (a 'strike' price). As the contract continues, the LCCC pays the developer daily instalments, but if market (reference) prices rise sharply and go above the strike price then the developer pays the LCCC the difference. This is a speculative contract (if prices go too high, the developer pays the LCCC, but if prices are low the LCCC is subsidising the developer) but is seen as a way of protecting consumers against the risks of high market prices.[82] But the system is simply procurement with long-winded auction contracts and, because the electricity decarbonisation targets are not to be implemented till 2030,[83] there are few incentives to replace existing fossil-fuel generation with clean energy and batteries.

79 [2016] EWCA Civ 1030, [7]–[22] give an excellent summary of statutory clean energy initiatives.

80 [2016] EWCA Civ 1030, [45] and [96], Lloyd Jones LJ and Sales LJ joining.

81 Energy Act 2013, s. 7. See www.lowcarboncontracts.uk.

82 LCCC, 'Contracts for Difference: Generator Guide' (12 February 2019) 32–5; DECC, 'FiT Contracts for Difference: Standard Terms and Conditions' (1 May 2019) version 3; DECC, *Planning our Electric Future: A White Paper for Secure, Affordable and Low-Carbon Electricity*, Cm. 8099 (2011) 148–50.

83 Energy Act 2013, s. 1; see Ch. 12(2)(a)(ii).

Until 2013, generating companies had a duty to buy increasing numbers of 'Renewable Obligation Certificates' (ROCs) from clean generators, or generate it themselves.[84] Clean generation would be accredited by Ofgem.[85] The cost of buying ROCs or investing clean generation would, depending on the state of competition and like Contracts for Difference, be reflected in prices for consumers. The key was that funding went directly from large energy companies to clean energy generators. It was closed in 2013 for new installations over 5 MW in capacity, and all installations in 2017,[86] though accredited generation typically receives support for twenty years, meaning existing ROCs last up to 2037. The closure led to several legal challenges. In *Solar Century Holdings Ltd v Secretary of State for Energy and Climate Change*, a group of solar companies applied for judicial review arguing a policy document gave them a legitimate expectation that government would be 'maintaining support levels'.[87] The Court of Appeal rejected the claim, because there was no promise the scheme would continue.[88] The government could change its policy if there were rational grounds, so long as there was no abuse of power.[89]

(c) Feed-In Tariffs

A third main source of finance is the feed-in tariff under the Energy Act 2008, section 41.[90] This began as another programme to increase renewable infrastructure. The Secretary of State was empowered to amend electricity supply licences under the Electricity Act 1989, section 6 (below) to require energy companies to distribute and pay for 'electricity generated by small-scale low-carbon generation'.[91] Developed in Germany, this policy gave money to homes or businesses installing solar panels on roofs or in fields, or to landowners installing wind turbines. The maximum capacity was 5 MW, which, for example, led the Westmill Solar Farm in Oxfordshire to install around 21,000 solar panels on a 30-acre site, at a cost of £12 million, powering 1,500 homes.[92] From April 2010 to 2011, the feed-in tariff, required to be paid by energy companies, was set at 48.29 p/kWh, for new solar photovoltaic installations up to 4 kWh, and 39.28 p/kWh for 100 kW to 5 MW installations. However, this was reduced by 3.87 p/kWh by 2019,[93] even though electricity

[84] Electricity Act 1989, ss. 32–32M, from Energy Act 2008, ss. 37–40. See also the Utilities Act 2000, ss. 62–7. An equivalent is known as a 'renewable portfolio standard' in the USA.

[85] *GEMA v Infinis plc* [2013] EWCA Civ 70: successful claim that generating stations from landfill should be accredited for ROCs; violation of the right to property under ECHR, Prot. 1, art. 1.

[86] Renewables Obligation Closure Order 2014 (SI 2014/2388) and Renewables Obligation Closure (Amendment) Order 2015 (SI 2015/1947), art. 2, made under Electricity Act 1989, ss. 32K–L.

[87] [2016] EWCA Civ 117, [9]. [88] [2016] EWCA Civ 117, [49]–[60].

[89] [2016] EWCA Civ 117, [50]. [90] Energy Act 2008, ss. 41–3.

[91] Energy Act 2008, s. 41(2)(b); see the Feed-in Tariffs Order 2012 (SI 2012/2782).

[92] This is roughly 12 ha, or about 300 m x 400 m. The cost is around £8,000 per home, and lasts for 25 years, or £320 a year, considerably cheaper than most energy bills.

[93] See www.ofgem.gov.uk/environmental-programmes/fit/fit-tariff-rates.

prices that energy companies charge their customers were typically 13–16 p/kWh. The government's intention was then to allow the market to determine what people got paid by energy companies for exporting energy (which would otherwise be wasted). Predictably it has remained low: a typical offer of 5.5 p/kWh.[94] In effect, the current operation of the feed-in tariff has been reversed, so that instead of large companies subsidising the small-scale building of renewable power, small producers are now subsidising major energy companies.

Unlike challenges to renewable obligations, reductions in the feed-in tariff were successfully challenged on two occasions in the Court of Appeal. First, it was held that, once set for a particular year, the Secretary of State had no power to retroactively reduce a rate under section 41.[95] Second, it was held that businesses were entitled to compensation for losses from abandoning existing contracts when the unlawful retroactive rate reduction was announced, because such a reduction interfered with the right to property.[96]

By contrast, a challenge to the introduction of a feed-in tariff scheme as unlawful state aid was unsuccessful when it was first launched in Germany. In *PreussenElektra AG v Schleswag AG*, a major energy company, now owned by E.ON, claimed the feed-in tariff should be classed as state aid under the Treaty on the Functioning of the European Union (TFEU) article 107, and therefore have to apply for an exemption. It protested that, although the state was not actually giving money to small businesses or households producing energy, the effect was the same as taxing companies and consumers, and giving small producers grants. Advocate General Jacobs pointed out in his opinion that if this argument were accepted 'then all sums which one person owes another by virtue of a given law would have to be considered to be State resources', a notion that was 'impossibly wide'. The Court of Justice agreed, and rejected that the feed-in tariff could be classed as state aid. Even though it had 'negative repercussions' for big energy companies, it 'cannot be regarded' as giving to small producers 'a particular advantage at the expense of the state'.[97] Of course, the Advocate General and the companies were right about the economic equivalent effects of the feed-in tariff and direct loans, even if the legal distinction should be defended. There are good reasons to control governments giving money to corporations in that form (see Ch. 6(4)), but the case highlights how regulation may enable undue profit, and this itself is like a tax.

94 E.g. Octopus Energy (2020).

95 *Secretary of State for Energy and Climate Change v Friends of the Earth* [2012] EWCA Civ 28.

96 *Breyer Group plc v Department of Energy and Climate Change* [2015] EWCA Civ 408, based on ECHR, Prot. 1, art 1. Future lost income streams could not be recovered as they were not a possession: *R (Countryside Alliance) v Attorney General* [2007] UKHL 52.

97 (2001) C-379/98, [62].

(d) Natural Monopoly

A fourth source of finance to energy companies is their exploitation of natural monopolies. Generation can now be more competitive if barriers to entry from building panels or turbines are reduced, but 'transmission and distribution remain natural monopolies'.[98] It is costly to duplicate grid infrastructure, cables or pipes. They only need one owner. Vast offshore wind farms or solar arrays realise major economies of scale, but the essential ability of people to go off the grid, generate their own power and not rely on others' facilities, creates an effective check on prices. So how have prices changed? (See Figure 12.2.)

UK electricity prices fell steadily from 1992 to 2002, but from 2003 to 2019 the price of electricity has risen by 84 per cent in real terms.[99] Similarly, UK gas prices were stable or fell from 1992 to 2001, and then rose from 2001 to 2019 by 90 per cent in real terms.[100] What do the extra bills pay for? Energy companies argue that the wholesale costs of generating electricity or distributing gas are rising with world market prices for coal, oil or gas, or that the costs of renewable energy investment are rising, and they have no choice but to pass costs on.[101] The more credible explanation is that rising prices reflect the inefficiency of an anti-competitive industry in transmission and distribution,

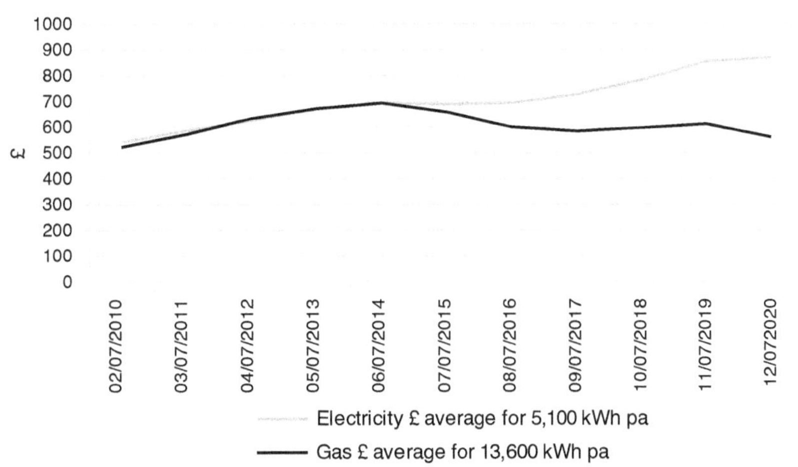

Figure 12.2 UK nominal electricity and gas average prices, 2010–20
Source: DBEIS, 'Domestic Energy Price Statistics', Tables 2.2.1 and 2.3.1

[98] Khan and Vaheesan, 'Market Power and Inequality', 263.

[99] Department for Business, Energy & Industrial Strategy (DBEIS), 'Average Annual Domestic Electricity Bills by Home and Non-home Supplier' (2019) Table 2.2.1 (St) 3,800 kWh, looking at the annual bill of the typical home that consumes 3,800 kWh of electricity; the bill in 2003 would have been £330 in today's prices, and is £608 a year today.

[100] DBEIS, Table 2.3.1: 15,000 kWh, from £298 a year to £566.

[101] Cf. S. Pfeifer, 'Burning Up Cash: Are UK Energy Suppliers Ripping Us Off?', *Financial Times* (25 October 2013).

enabling excessive dividends[102] or management salaries,[103] or both. There would also be no concern with world energy prices if all generation were domestic and renewable. Thus, the governance of energy enterprise matters.

(3) Governance

Since privatisation under the Gas Act 1986 and the Electricity Act 1989, the basic model of the energy company has become like other companies, but operating under licences from Ofgem. This section considers (a) licensing and planning requirements, which could be used to exert significant influence, but realistically speaking are not; (b) planning rules for building infrastructure; (c) the voice of stakeholders, or its absence, in the UK compared to other countries; and (d) special rules for insolvency.

(a) Ofgem, Licensing and Competition

The main features of the UK's licensing system, also reflected in the Electricity Directive 2019 and the Gas Directive 2009,[104] are (i) the constitution of the regulator, Ofgem; (ii) its licencing, duties and powers; and (iii) the competition requirements for separation in transmission from distribution and generation.

(i) Constitution of GEMA and Ofgem

Under the Utilities Act 2000, section 1, the UK regulator is the 'Gas and Electricity Markets Authority' (GEMA),[105] but it still operates with the older brand name of Ofgem (Office of Gas and Electricity Markets). GEMA is regarded as the governing body for Ofgem, and it has a minimum of three but currently ten directors (or 'members') all appointed by the Secretary of State, with tenure of five to seven years.[106] They are exhorted to not 'seek or take any instructions' or 'have any financial or other interest' that could potentially 'compromise, that person's impartiality'.[107] Nevertheless, the minister can give general directions on what they should have regard to in making decisions and what their priorities are.[108] Unlike the energy companies they

[102] E.g. V. Moss, *Daily Mirror* (15 July 2012), the Big Six combined paid £7bn to shareholders in dividends.

[103] E.g. J. Bloodworth, *Left Foot Forward* (29 October 2013), summarising executive pay and bonuses.

[104] See the Electricity Directive 2019/944 and the Gas Directive 2009/73/EC.

[105] Utilities Act 2000, s. 1.

[106] Utilities Act 2000, Sch. 1, paras. 1 and 3. See Ofgem, 'Members of GEMA'. The chair, Prof. Martin Cave, co-authors a leading text: R. Baldwin, M. Cave and M. Lodge, *Understanding Regulation: Theory, Strategy, and Practice* (2011).

[107] Utilities Act 2000, Sch. 1, para. 2A.

[108] Electricity Act 1989, s. 47(2) and Gas Act 1986, s. 34(3).

regulate, GEMA members cannot determine their own salaries: these are set by the Secretary of State.[109]

(ii) Licences, Duties and Powers

The basic norm of energy regulation is that no electricity or gas business can be run without a licence.[110] This enables Ofgem to exercise broad control over energy companies on the threat of withdrawing a licence, if it ever sought to do so. Licences are contracts, and therefore can be terminated for the breach of a major term (a condition) or according to the licence's terms.[111] The Secretary of State can also make exemptions from the need to get a licence. The main exemptions are electricity generators that at any time provide under 10 MW in power, or stations that provide under 50 MW and have a 'declared net capacity of less than 100 MW' (i.e. solar panels and wind turbines whose generation fluctuates), with a deduction for power supplied to the persons generating 'on the same site'.[112] There are also exemptions for minor gas transporters, suppliers or shippers, for instance transporting bottles of gas under 47 kg.[113]

The duties of Ofgem in the Electricity Act 1989, section 3A are to 'protect the interests of existing and future consumers' including their interests in 'reduction of electricity-supply emissions of targeted greenhouse gases', securing supply and the pro-competition objectives of the EU internal market for electricity.[114] Ofgem should also ensure reasonable demand is met, that licence holders fulfil obligations of service and that there is sustainable development, paying regard to people who are sick, elderly, lower-income and in rural areas.[115] The Secretary of State must issue guidance to Ofgem on 'any social or environmental policies' it sets, after consulting it, Citizens Advice, licence holders or anyone else it wants, and putting guidance before Parliament.[116] There are analogous duties for gas,[117] creating the obvious contradiction between these environmental duties and the reality that natural gas causes climate damage. It does not yet acknowledge that gas must be shut down.

The conditions of licences can be set by Ofgem under section 7 as it thinks 'requisite or expedient having regard to the duties' it has, and requiring

109 Utilities Act 2000, Sch. 1, para. 4.

110 Electricity Act 1989, s. 4. (offence for electricity generation, transmission, distribution or supply without licence) and Gas Act 1986, s. 5 (offence for conveying gas through pipes, operating a gas interconnector, a gas transporter, or a smart meter without a licence); Electricity Directive 2019/944, art. 8 and the Gas Directive 2009/73/EC, art. 4.

111 Litigation could follow but damages (if any), rather than an injunction, are the appropriate outcome: *Cooperative Insurance Ltd v Argyll Ltd* [1997] UKHL 17.

112 Electricity Act 1989, s. 5, enabling the Secretary of State to pass the Electricity (Class Exemptions from the Requirement for a Licence) Order 2001 (SI 2001/3270) Sch. 2. Schs. 3–4 also have exemptions for distribution and supply on site.

113 Gas Act 1986, s. 6A and Gas (Exemptions) Order 2011 (SI 2011/232), art. 16.

114 Electricity Act 1989, s. 3A. It is not clear how long the EU internal market duty will operate.

115 Electricity Act 1989, s. 3A(2)–(3).

116 Electricity Act 1989, s. 3B.

117 Gas Act 1986, ss. 4AA (general duties) and 4AB (social and environmental matters).

payment of any fee 'as may be determined by or under the licence'.[118] Licences can also require the holder to follow any directions given by Ofgem or the Secretary of State.[119] For example, the Standard Electricity Supply Licence indicates which contractual terms are most prevalent for the Big Six, although they could be modified for each case.[120] These terms contain crucial electricity consumer rights, including price, supply continuity, tariff calculations, feed-in tariffs and renewable energy. But they could be far more ambitious in adding duties to decarbonise, to encourage small-scale generation and in becoming more efficient than they presently are. Ofgem may modify licences with twenty-eight days' notice, giving reasons,[121] although the Secretary of State could exercise a veto.[122]

Similar provisions apply to nuclear power,[123] but the case for licensing any new nukes is non-existent with the development of safe battery technology in cases where wind or solar supplies drop. There are eight remaining UK nuclear plants: four due to close between 2023 and 2024, and four between 2028 and 2035, all run by the French state-owned EDF Energy. Yet Hinkley Point C nuclear power station is being built for £20.3 billion by 2025, to be paid over a thirty-five-year period. Two firms promised to build wind turbines for £57.50/MWh for 2022–23, while Hinkley's costs mean £92.50/MWh.[124] This makes no sense.

(iii) Competition and Separation

During privatisation, it was believed that competition could be created by separating transmission of electricity and gas from supply to consumers.[125] This idea of legal (but not ownership) separation was put into the Electricity and Gas Directives,[126] and is now formally written into UK statute. Electricity transmission must be independent, and certified as such, by meeting the 'ownership unbundling requirement'.[127] This means that the transmission company does not control 'a relevant producer or supplier', have 'a majority

[118] Electricity Act 1989, s. 7(1). A transmission or distribution licence can require interconnections and agreements with others and restrict other activities. Gas Act 1986, ss. 7ZA and 7A.

[119] Electricity Act 1989, s. 7(3) followed by a host of other conditions that might be set, but all well within s. 7(1)(a).

[120] Standard Conditions of Electricity Supply Licence (2020) and Standard Conditions of Gas Supply Licence (2019).

[121] Cf. *R (Scottish Power) v Director General of Electricity Supply* [1997] CLY 4949, on the discretion of Ofgem's predecessor in modification, and treating companies in similar situations equally.

[122] Electricity Act 1989, ss. 11A–B; Gas Act 1986, s. 23A; Utilities Act 2000, s. 68.

[123] Nuclear Installations Act 1965, ss. 1, 65–87 (nuclear licensing).

[124] See H. Watt, *The Guardian* (21 December 2017). See also R. Harrabin, 'Offshore Wind Power Cheaper than New Nuclear', *BBC News* (11 September 2017).

[125] E.g. in 1997, British Gas plc demerged into Centrica plc which did gas sales, trading and retail, plus North Sea production, and BG plc that held oil and gas reserves in 25 countries.

[126] Electricity Directive 2019/944, art. 35 and the Gas Directive 2009/73/EC, art. 9.

[127] Electricity Act 1989, ss. 10A–E.

shareholding' or exercise other 'shareholder rights', and that its 'senior officers' do not either, or vice versa.[128]

In the UK, National Grid plc owns both the NG Electricity Transmission plc and NG Gas plc.[129] There are fourteen further regional electricity distribution networks and eight gas networks. The licence terms of each transmission and distribution company require separate accounts. They must enable access to networks to ensure co-operation.[130] The operators are under a series of duties to not give any undue preference or to discriminate.[131] But since the grid is a monopoly, and prices are fixed, all shareholder profit is effectively a tax on the public paid to City and Wall Street investors. This makes a bad example of private enterprise.

(b) Planning Permission

As well as securing a licence, under the Electricity Act 1989, section 36 energy generators over 50 MW require planning permission by the 'appropriate authority', namely the Scottish Minister, Welsh Minister or the Secretary of State.[132] This consent displaces the ordinary requirement for local authority planning permission.[133] Between 2016 and 2020, in a bid to placate people who did not like how wind turbines looked (but seem to have not objected to ubiquitous electricity pylons), the government returned power to block wind turbines to English and Welsh councils.[134] But it announced it would allow onshore wind again in 2020.[135] Before, one Secretary of State had been active in blocking wind farm applications, and courts gave these decisions deference even when the Secretary had been biased by lobbying against them.[136] The judicial review time limit is three months, and without undue delay.[137]

A spurious challenge to offshore wind development was also made by Donald Trump against turbines near his Aberdeenshire golf course in *Trump International Golf Club Scotland Ltd v The Scottish Ministers*. Although he subsequently took the electoral college and US presidency

[128] Electricity Act 1989, s. 10F.

[129] In north Scotland, SSE owns Scottish Hydro-Electric Transmission Ltd, and Scottish Power owns Scottish Power Transmission Ltd.

[130] Electricity Act 1989, s. 7(3C) and Gas Act 1986, ss. 10–11 and 19; Electricity Directive 2019/944, arts. 3(4) and 6.

[131] Electricity Act 1989, s. 10F(9A) and Gas Act 1986, s. 9(2).

[132] Electricity Act 1989, ss. 36(1) and 36(10). 50 MW is around 20 wind turbines.

[133] Planning Act 2008, s. 33 and see the Town and Country Planning Act 1990, ss. 55–7 and 70 for the need for permission and 'local plans'.

[134] Electricity Act 1989, s. 36(1D) and see TCP (General Permitted Development) (England) Order 2015 (wind turbines that do not require permission).

[135] R. Harrabin, 'Onshore Wind "to Make Comeback in UK"', *BBC News* (2 March 2020).

[136] E.g. *Broadview Energy Developments Ltd v Secretary of State for Communities and Local Government* [2016] EWCA Civ 562 (a Minister's decision to block a wind farm could not be challenged for bias even though he lobbied against it, as lobbying was realistically part of an MP's job, and the relevant procedures were otherwise followed).

[137] See *Finn-Kelcey v Milton Keynes BC* [2008] EWCA Civ 1067 on the meaning of undue delay.

(see Ch. 17(1)), Trump lost in the UK Supreme Court. He argued it was necessarily implied in section 36 that the Scottish ministers were only entitled to grant planning to exempt or existing licence holders.[138] The case is relatively simple, since Trump was looking for any argument possible against the turbines, regardless of merit.[139] He subsequently lied that turbines create a 'bird graveyard', and create 'tremendous fumes', while announcing his 'favorite color, orange'.[140] In *Sustainable Shetland v Scottish Ministers*, the Supreme Court also rejected that planning permission could be challenged based on the duty to protect birds under the Birds Directive 2009.[141] The estimates were that an average of 3.7 whimbrel died, while flying to the Shetlands, compared to 72–108 annual deaths from other causes:[142] the most significant cause of bird deaths appears to be skyscrapers,[143] such as Trump Tower.

Similar planning challenges are common against solar panel installations. For example in *R (Gerber) v Wiltshire Council*, Mr Gerber argued the construction of a 22 hectare solar farm near his grade II listed home Gifford Hall, near Bath, violated his legitimate expectations.[144] Gerber had failed to notice the plan until construction began. He wrote to the Council arguing it would have a 'detrimental impact' on the 'setting' and then, when the Council rejected his complaint, he argued the Council's 'Statement of Community Involvement' should have meant he was individually notified. Overturning a quashing order from the High Court, Sales LJ rejected that this contained any promise, and therefore legitimate expectation, that a neighbour of new construction should be individually notified. Dismantling the farm would have cost £1.5 million, and the balance of factors affecting good administration, the importance of renewable energy, and certainty and finality all meant the quashing order was set aside.[145]

(c) Stakeholder Governance

While the UK regulatory system enables considerable control over energy companies, there are few specific rules on internal governance and stakeholder rights yet. As we saw, the history of energy company governance involved many experiments in local ratepayer involvement, and worker representation on company boards (see Ch. 12(1)). This dissipated under the Morrisonian

[138] [2015] UKSC 74.

[139] See also L. Fisher, 'Law and Energy Transitions: Wind Turbines and Planning Law in the UK' (2018) 38(3) *Oxford JL Studies* 528.

[140] E.g. R. Luscombe, '"I Never Understood Wind": Trump Goes on Bizarre Tirade against Wind Turbines', *The Guardian* (24 December 2019).

[141] Birds Directive 2009/147/EC, arts. 2 and 4.

[142] [2015] UKSC 4, [10].

[143] L. Aratani, 'Buildings Are Killing up to 1bn Birds a Year in US, Scientists Estimate', *The Guardian* (7 April 2019).

[144] See Mr Gerber's home at https://historicengland.org.uk/.

[145] [2016] EWCA Civ 84, [66].

model of nationalisation: experts were appointed by the minister to run electricity and gas enterprises, and under the Thatcher model of privatisation, shareholders monopolised governance. The remnants of customer voice were expressed after 1947 in the Consultative Councils, but these and their successors had no voting rights: they were more a place where complaints went to die. After being rebranded and merged several times – as the Gas and Electricity Consumer Council (Energywatch), the National Consumer Council (Consumer Direct), Consumer Focus and Consumer Futures[146] – in 2014 the government gave up the charade and merged its functions into the Citizens Advice Bureau.[147]

Voting rights to elect directors for energy customers or workers can be enacted with or without public ownership, though the two often coincide. For example, like many German states, North Rhine-Westphalia requires that where an energy company is majority publicly owned, there should be between one- and two-thirds worker representatives elected to the board, extendable to one-half, and representatives for councillors including the mayor.[148] Among many potential models, there are always fundamentally three stakeholders: the investor of capital, the workers and those who finance through their custom. It would seem that voting rights for each of these three groups is becoming best practice. In a 2019 report, the public ownership advocacy group 'We Own It' proposed a model of board representation for public companies to include four local councillors from the region, two customers, two worker representatives and four other government appointees.[149]

In Britain, a handful of public energy companies were created though there has not yet been proper experiment to empower workers or customers to improve accountability. In 2015, Nottingham City Council incorporated Robin Hood Energy Ltd, which bought 95 per cent of its energy from renewable sources. It made an operating profit in 2018, but made losses again in 2019 and went insolvent. Its directors were solely appointed by the City Council. Despite its failure, it inspired similar companies to be established, such as Bristol Energy from 2015, and London Power in 2020, which commits to buy

[146] Utilities Act 2000, s. 2, replaced by the Consumers, Estate Agents and Redress Act (CEARA) 2007, ss. 1 and 4 (also concerning post office 'consumers').

[147] CEARA 2007, s. 1, as amended under SI 2014/631, with the Public Bodies Act 2011, s. 1, 'bonfire' powers.

[148] Community Ordinance North Rhine Westphalia or Gemeindeordnung Nordrhein-Westfalen 1994, §§107–14.

[149] We Own It, *When We Own It: A Model of Public Ownership in the 21st Century* (2019) 36. This model was complicated by an additional proposal to create a 'supervisory board' structure separate from the executive board. This mirrors Germany, where supervisory boards were originally introduced so the Prussian military regime could have state oversight of business, and were made unavoidable by Hitler's regime in 1937. Although they may function today, they are an unnecessary governance complication and reduce accountability of directors on the management board to stakeholders: E. McGaughey, *Participation in Corporate Governance* (2014) ch. 4(2).

only renewable electricity.[150] These remain 'virtual' companies as they rely on other generators, but they could start their own generation, or procure feed-in business from local residents. They enable combined customer bargaining power. There is also local council ownership of UK energy generation from abroad. For example, the Munich Council runs Stadtwerke München (Munich City Utilities) and supplies electricity, gas, water and telecoms to its residents. It has invested 30 per cent of the capital in the Gwynt y Môr wind farm in North Wales.[151] With huge success, Stadtwerke München has a governance structure including worker and public representatives,[152] although not yet direct voting rights for residents.

According to Professor Massimo Florio there is 'clear evidence' that 'consumers pay lower electricity net-of-tax prices in countries where there are still incumbents owned by national governments'.[153] But is public ownership compatible with EU law? Yes. In *Netherlands v Essent NV*, a major Dutch energy company (now owned by E.ON) tried to argue that a Dutch law violated EU law principles of unbundling and free movement of capital.[154] The Dutch Act required all electricity and gas distributors to be publicly owned, that system operators could not be connected by ownership to generators and limited the level of debt.[155] The Dutch government argued they were protected by the TFEU, article 345, that the 'Treaties shall in no way prejudice the rules in Member States governing the system of property ownership.' The Court of Justice's Grand Chamber held there was no violation of the Directive, nor free movement of capital, because although it interacted with those rules it was justified by 'overriding reasons in the public interest', 'to protect consumers' and for the 'security of energy supply'.[156] It further pointed to the foundational case of *Costa v ENEL*, where the Court held in 1964 that the Treaties do 'not prohibit the creation of any state monopolies' so long as they do not operate commercially and discriminate.[157] The approach of EU law is that even where energy companies are privatised, they still are subject to the same rules as the state on direct effect, because it remains that they are 'providing a public service'.[158] The concept of 'public service' in EU law does not depend on member states' privatisations.

[150] See www.bristol-energy.co.uk and https://mylondonpower.com/. See A. Vaughan, 'Publicly Owned Energy Minnows Take on Big Six in Troubled UK Market', *The Guardian* (27 October 2017).

[151] The wind farm is also 50% owned by RWE, 10% by Siemens and 10% by the UK Green Investment Bank. The latter used to be owned by the UK government, but was privatised in 2017.

[152] Gesellschaftsvertrag der Stadtwerke München GmbH, §7.

[153] M. Florio, 'The Return of Public Enterprise', Working Paper No. 01/2014 (2014) 7–8. Also R. Brau, R. Doronzo, C. Fiorio and M. Florio, 'EU Gas Industry Reforms and Consumers' Prices' (2010) 31(4) *Energy J* 163.

[154] TFEU, art. 63. [155] *Netherlands v Essent NV* (2013) C-105/12, [4].

[156] *Netherlands v Essent NV*, [66]. [157] *Costa v ENEL* (1964) Case 6-64.

[158] *Foster v British Gas plc* (1990) C-188/89, [22] and [1991] 2 AC 306, 316. BG plc 'provided a public service, the supply of gas, to citizens of the state generally under the control of the state

(d) Insolvency

Also in recognition of energy networks' public importance, since the Enterprise Act 2002 a special insolvency procedure has been codified. Energy companies are likely to owe most debts to government – for instance, by non-payment of tax, the climate change levy or renewable obligation certificates. Insolvencies are also increasingly likely as more small competitors enter the market.[159] Under the Insolvency Act 1986, section 72D, electricity and gas companies are exempt from the prohibition on administrative receivership when a project includes step-in rights.[160] Moreover, the Energy Act 2011 created a special 'Energy Supply Company Administration Order'. A court may appoint an administrator to keep a supplier trading 'at the lowest cost' if there is no willing buyer, with government financial assistance.[161] Under the Standard Electricity Supply Licence, Ofgem can impose a duty on energy companies to be a supplier of last resort,[162] but ultimately the government runs energy when enterprises fail.

(4) Customers' Rights

The absence of voting rights for customers on energy company boards and the limits of competition make it unlikely that the customers' interest guides energy enterprise. There are, however, three main groups of minimum rights, including (a) to switch suppliers, in the hope this might improve competition; (b) to limited prices, so long as the government thinks it necessary; and (c) to be supplied and not unfairly disconnected.

(a) Vote with Feet?

It has accurately been stated that the 'right to change supplier is perhaps the strongest tool available to the consumer' of energy,[163] and unfortunately this highlights how weak customer rights are. The 'right' to switch is not in legislation but in the electricity licences negotiated by Ofgem. The standard licence requires that no termination fee is payable, and no notice, but this does not enable the customer to end a fixed-term contract before its deadline.[164]

which could dictate its policies and retains its revenue'. This was a claim by Mrs Foster for sex discrimination, being made to retire earlier than her male colleagues. The Court held that she had a direct claim under the Treaties. See Ch. 5(2)(d).

[159] See N. Thomas, 'Energy Suppliers Face New Audit Rules in Ofgem Crackdown', *Financial Times* (22 October 2019).

[160] Insolvency Act 1986, s. 72D and Sch. 2A, para. 10(1)(c)–(d).

[161] Energy Act 2011, ss. 94–102.

[162] Ofgem, 'Supplier of Last Resort: Revised Guidance' (2008) and Standard Conditions of Electricity Supply Licence (2020) condition 8.

[163] M. M. Roggenkamp, C. Redgwell, A. Rønne and I. Guayo (eds.), *Energy Law in Europe: national, EU and International Regulation* (2016) 1109.

[164] Standard Conditions of Electricity Supply Licence (2020) condition 24.8.

The reality, however, is that a right to switch to other companies offering similar terms has no inherent value. Behavioural evidence further suggests that while people could have significant savings, people systematically fail to switch,[165] and this is the reason that supplier licences may be modified to reduce the number of confusing tariffs.[166] 'Voting with one's feet' is ineffective.

(b) Price Regulation

Price regulation has become increasingly important because it is clear that prices have risen without constraint. Price controls for domestic consumers were in place until April 2002, and then removed.[167] As we have seen, this coincides with the consistent rise in energy prices. The original plan was that regulators could 'wither away' as competition replaced state control, and that in the transition period prices could be capped by an RPI – X formula: that is, prices could only be raised by the retail price index, minus an amount reflecting efficiency savings, or adding an amount for investment.[168] In this respect, the duty of Ofgem for 'promoting effective competition' has entirely failed.[169]

Under the Electricity Act 1989, section 44, Ofgem can direct 'the maximum prices at which electricity supplied by authorised suppliers may be resold'.[170] Further, after consistent public outrage, the Domestic Gas Electricity (Tariff Cap) Act 2018 was passed, enabling Ofgem to set a price cap, with regard to the apparent needs 'to create incentives' to improve efficiency; 'compete effectively'; give 'incentives for domestic customers to switch'; and secure finance.[171] One view is that the reintroduction of price regulation 'wrongly prioritises equality of outcome rather than equality of opportunity in the market', and the law should only regulate prices for the most vulnerable.[172] There are extra rules to subsidise families living in fuel poverty,[173] but these do not help the vast majority of people who may be able to afford bills, but struggle to do so.

[165] B. Richards, 'Should Switch, Don't Switch: Overcoming Consumer Inertia', *Social Market Foundation* (October 2015).

[166] Energy Act 2013, s. 139. [167] Roggenkamp et al. (eds.), *Energy Law in Europe*, 1090.

[168] J. Meek, 'How We Happened to Sell Off Our Electricity' (2012) 34(17) *London Review of Books* 3.

[169] Utilities Act 2000, ss. 9 and 13, revising Electricity Act 1989, s. 3A and Gas Act 1986, s. 4AA.

[170] Electricity Act 1989, s. 44.

[171] Domestic Gas and Electricity (Tariff Cap) Act 2018, ss. 1–3. See *Federutility et al. v Autorità per l'energia elettrica e il gas* (2010) C-265/08, on price caps being clearly compatible with EU law. Also *ENEL Produzione SpA v Autorità per l'energia elettrica e il gas* (2011) C-242/10, [42].

[172] M. Ioannidou and D. Mantzari, 'The UK Domestic Gas Electricity (Tariff Cap) Act: Re-regulating the Retail Energy Market' (2019) 82(3) *MLR* 488, citing extensively N. Reich, 'Vulnerable Consumers in EU Law' in D. Leczykiewicz and S. Weatherill (eds.), *The Images of the Consumer in EU Law: Legislation, Free Movement and Competition Law* (2016). The authors' preference for not allowing price regulation unless there were 'exceptional circumstances' failed, quite rightly, to make it into the revised Electricity Directive 2019.

[173] Warm Homes and Energy Conservation Act 2000, ss. 1–3, covering those 'on a lower income in a home which cannot be kept warm at reasonable cost'. Initiatives include the Cold Weather Payments, Winter Fuel Payments and Warm Home Discount scheme.

The more credible view is that energy distribution markets systematically fail, and that energy companies extract ever-greater slices of people's income while paying dividends and bonuses indiscriminately. The true debate is about the extent to which any energy companies should stay in private ownership.

(c) Supply and Disconnections

While there is no right to energy, without paying the regulated price, there are duties in licences against disconnection. In a standard licence, a company cannot disconnect a customer unless it 'has first taken all reasonable steps to recover those charges' including installing a pay-as-you-go meter, and people of pensionable age cannot be disconnected at all in winter.[174] Even so, there were 43,900 extra deaths, for example, in the winter in 2015, and it was estimated 9,000 of those deaths were from fuel poverty.[175] The introduction of pay-as-you-go meters, recommended by the standard licence, also remains a convenient way of letting customers disconnect themselves (by not paying to top up) instead of the energy company disconnecting them. The moral responsibility remains the same.

(5) Conclusion

Clean electricity and energy are essential to end climate damage, to shift as fast as possible to 100 per cent clean sources, and increase capacity to cover all electric transport demand. The UN Sustainable Development Goal 7 is to ensure 'access to affordable, reliable, sustainable and modern energy for all' by 2030,[176] but this lacks any real ambition, and for the UK would be possible only with complacency of the highest order. The abundance of wind ensures that clean electricity is the cheapest electricity,[177] while the plummeting cost of solar panels already outprices the grid over the medium term for homes and businesses. First, Ofgem should have a principal duty to eliminate fossil fuels in energy generation as fast as technology allows. Second, all licence holders should have a duty to eliminate emissions in five years. Third, there should be restoration of the feed-in tariff to 90 per cent of market prices. Fourth, the ownership of the grid, distribution companies and generation companies should be made public wherever existing companies do not eliminate emissions at an adequate pace. As more clean energy develops, the economy will become more decentralised, fluid and mobile, like a breath of fresh air.

[174] Standard Conditions of Electricity Supply Licence (2020) condition 27.9.

[175] 'Cold Homes Caused 9,000 Deaths Last Winter, Study Suggests', *BBC News* (21 March 2016); Office for National Statistics, 'Excess Winter Mortality in England and Wales: 2016 to 2017 (provisional) and 2015 to 2016 (final)' (22 December 2017).

[176] Sustainable Development Goals (2015). Goal 7.2 also aims to 'increase substantially the share of renewable energy in the global energy mix'. This does not mean anything.

[177] Conservative Party Manifesto (2019) promised just 40 GW of wind by 2030, unambitiously low.

13

Food, Forests and Water

Contents

'Of all the occupations', wrote Cicero in 44 BC, 'none is better than agriculture, none more profitable, none more delightful, none more becoming to a free man.'[1] Growing a garden, the countryside, the shade of trees, the sound of running water, have long been things of romance. But unlike for Roman nobility, over most of human history people's toil for food and water was a matter of survival. The Industrial Revolution enabled society to live beyond subsistence, sustaining modern towns and cities, and crucially shifting work away from the farm. In the nineteenth and twentieth centuries, social change (though painfully slow) was able to limit water pollution and recurrent famines from the maldistribution of food. Food and water came to be seen as public responsibilities. Food was subsidised and water socially owned or controlled. But worldwide, the problems persist. In 2017, out of 7.5 billion, 3 billion people still went hungry, lacked water, toilets or hand-washing facilities.[2] The United Nations (UN) Sustainable Development Goals 2015 aim to 'end hunger', 'promote sustainable agriculture' and ensure 'availability and sustainable management of water and sanitation for all' by 2030.[3] But these very *goals* underline that the universal human *rights* are not yet real: these are to 'a standard of living adequate for the health and well-being' of everyone, including the rights to 'food' and water.[4]

[1] Cicero, *De Officiis* (44 BC) Book 1, §151. For this chapter, I am grateful to Oğuzhan Sarıca and Tim Ashton.

[2] WHO, *Progress on Household Drinking Water, Sanitation and Hygiene* (2019) 7–9; J. Hickel, *The Divide* (2017) ch. 2, 44–7.

[3] UN Sustainable Development Goals 2015, Goals 2 and 6.

[4] UDHR 1948, art. 25(1); ICESCR 1966, art. 11(1); UN Committee on Economic, Social and Cultural Rights (2002) General Comment No. 15, water implicit in right to food.

Three main obstacles stand in the way of rights to food and water. First, subsidies to private agricultural land in Europe, America and elsewhere have historically aimed to uphold the right to a living income for farming communities and support the countryside. Subsidies could also be a vital instrument to end climate damage. But with tariffs, the system depresses incomes in already low-income countries. It sustains hunger and poverty. Since 2008 the UK has created thousands of food banks because despite subsidies people *still* cannot afford to eat.[5] Second, people struggle to pay water bills. In England and Wales this is partly because water is privatised. Scottish Water is public, quality is better and bills are 10 per cent lower.[6] The evidence is not unclear: water privatisation was an error. Yet privatisation and deregulation policies were absorbed by the World Bank and International Monetary Fund (IMF), which have demanded water sell-offs, and even bread loaf cuts, in 'structural adjustment' programmes worldwide.[7] Third, outdated agricultural practice damages the climate, causing food and water insecurity. At home, fossil-fuel burning machinery, over-tilling the soil, livestock methane and lack of trees increase greenhouse gases. From abroad, the choice to import unsustainable meat or crops drives deforestation and more climate damage. Each of these problems is soluble, and discussed through the finance and governance of, and rights in, agriculture and water enterprises.

(1) Historical Development

For most of human history we were a wandering species. The oldest evidence of Stone Age tools dates to around 3.3 million years ago, in today's Kenya,[8] and we may have begun cooking food with fire around 1.9 million years ago.[9] We followed the seasons, the flocks of birds or animals we hunted, or the fresh water sources we found. People began to settle around the end of the last ice age, near 10,000 BC. When we did, crops and livestock could generate a surplus, and so 'farming was the precondition for the development of the first great urban civilizations', in the Middle East, Egypt, India, China, the Americas and Africa.[10] The first irrigation probably began in the Indus Valley, today's

[5] P. Alston, 'Extreme Poverty and Human Rights' (26 September 2018), Report of the Special Rapporteur on extreme poverty and human rights, cites 2,000 food banks, up from 29 in 2008.

[6] E.g. Scottish Water, 'Your Charges 2018–2019' (2019): average Scottish bill, £363; England and Wales, £405.

[7] E.g. IMF, Egypt, 1991, EBS/91/213, 'Reduce the size of the "popular" bread loaf by 15 grams to reduce subsidies by LE 150 million in 1991/92'. S. Grusky, 'IMF and World Bank Push Water Privatization' (2001) 23.

[8] S. Harmand et al., '3.3-Million-Year-Old Stone Tools from Lomekwi 3, West Turkana, Kenya' (2015) 521(7552) *Nature* 310.

[9] R. W. Wrangham, 'The Raw and the Stolen' (1999) 40(5) *Current Anthropology* 567; but P. Karnakas, 'Evidence for the Habitual Use of Fire at the End of the Lower Paleolithic' (2007) 53 *J Human Evolution* 197 says the first archaeological evidence of controlled fire use is 400,000 BC. See further J. K. Balch et al., 'Fire in the Earth System' (2009) 324(5926) *Science* 481.

[10] G. Barker, *The Agricultural Revolution in Prehistory: Why Did Foragers Become Farmers?* (2006) 1–2.

Pakistan, around 4500 BC. As irrigation spread it was regulated: compensation for water damage was written into the *Codex Hammurabi* of 1750 BC.[11] In Europe, the civilisations of classical antiquity developed later. Around 800 BC Homer wrote the *Iliad* and the *Odyssey*, where after Odysseus fights the war in Troy, he longs to return home to his wife, children and his father's farm.[12] In 44 BC, when Cicero in Ancient Rome wrote that agriculture was noble, he expressed the prejudice of the 'civilised'. Rome's agriculture, irrigation, aqueducts, water wheels and mills, like those found from Petra to Hampi,[13] were thought to be the sources of the empire's greatness.[14]

Ancient civilisations grew vast hydraulic-powered cities,[15] yet 80–90% of Europe's population remained agricultural labourers until the Middle Ages;[16] in 1300, England was estimated to have been 76.4% agricultural workers, while 19.2% lived rurally and 4.4% lived in towns or cities – similarly across Europe.[17] After the First Barons' War, Magna Carta 1215 and the Charter of the Forest 1217 required that the land King John had enclosed (the 'forests') must 'be disafforested' and made common.[18] On land still owned by the king since Henry II, people were guaranteed the right to forage for plants or herbs. On common land there was the right to graze animals. On private freehold land people had the right to farm, fish and mill, if 'no injury is thereby given to any neighbour'.[19] But the vast majority of people were landless, having no private property of their own. When the Black Death struck, the lords and king imposed wage-suppression laws and a poll tax,[20] eventually leading to the Peasants' Revolt of 1381. Its leaders demanded that 'everything be common . . . that we may be all united together, and that the lords be no greater masters

[11] Codex Hammurabi (1750 BC) arts. 55–6 (negligence liability for crops, strict liability for works).

[12] Homer, *The Odyssey* (*c.* 700 BC) Book I.

[13] Cf. Pliny, *Natural History* (77 AD) trans. H, Rackham (1986) 36.24, claiming of 'the abundant supplies of water' there was never 'anything more remarkable in the whole world'. Remarkable yes, but far from unique.

[14] See also Cato, *On Agriculture* (160 BC) 1:4; Vitruvius, *De Architectura* (25 BC) on aqueducts. This idea of 'civilisation' and the source of wealth plainly ignores that slavery was the dominant source of wealth – it is no coincidence that Cicero thought labouring for others was ignoble. See A. Launaro, *Peasants and Slaves: The Rural Population of Roman Italy (200 BC to AD 100)* (2011) 60, Table 3.2. Rome's population was 20–40% slaves.

[15] J. Getzler, *A History of Water Rights at Common Law* (2004) ch. 1, 13–26. This is by far the topic's best history.

[16] P. Erdkamp, 'Agriculture, Underemployment, and the Cost of Rural Labour in the Roman World' (1999) 49(2) *Classical Q* 556.

[17] R. C. Allen, 'Economic Structure and Agricultural Productivity in Europe, 1300–1800' (2000) 3 *Eur Rev Economic History* 1, 8, Table 2.

[18] Magna Carta 1215, cl. 47 (disafforesting common land) and cl. 48 (abolishing 'evil customs' banning land use).

[19] Charter of the Forest 1217, cl. 1 (right of herbage in forests, gathering plants), cl. 9 (agistment and pannage, right of grazing including pigs) and cl. 10 (right to farm).

[20] Ordinance of Labourers 1347, Statute of Labourers 1351 and a Poll Tax of 1377, then 1379 and 1381; see C. C. Fenwick, *The English Poll Taxes of 1377, 1379 and 1381: A Critical Examination of the Returns* (1983).

than we be'.[21] They lost,[22] yet a system of common law and rights lasted until the Tudor kings. Then, lords began accelerating enclosures for sheep farming to make more money,[23] and around 1600 Sir Edward Coke discredited and dismantled the forest jurisprudence.[24] The idea of common land was replaced by the 'improvement' movement, where people who had lived on the lords' land were made to pay ever higher rents, were evicted if they could not afford them and were replaced with other desperate people.[25] Through cruelty, dispossession and poverty, land was 'improved', productivity rose and the agricultural workforce shrank.

As land became monetised, famine became rife. Political economy theories were written to justify this as part of a logical order.[26] In 1729, Jonathan Swift satirised these arguments in *A Modest Proposal*, suggesting famines in Ireland could be resolved if people sold their children as food. This would relieve the 'constant breeders' from 'the charge of maintaining' children.[27] The problem, of course, was not that food did not exist, but that it was hoarded. From the Importation Act 1773,[28] known as the 'corn laws', tariffs were set on food imports to raise incomes of farm owners. Thomas Malthus, a landowner, argued famine was natural: 'no possible form of society could prevent the almost constant action of misery upon a great part of mankind'.[29] Indeed for Maltus, the corn laws were not enough: all poor-law payments should be given to farm owners, as 'premiums ... for turning up fresh land'.[30] By contrast, Adam Smith argued that free trade would benefit everyone, as if helped by 'an invisible hand', and it was corn merchants not landowners that truly benefited from trade tariffs.[31] The corn laws were renewed again in 1815 and, as the Tambora volcano erupted in Indonesia a month later and crops suffered, there was another disastrous famine.[32] In 1817, David Ricardo argued that, by a theory of comparative advantage, even if English farming was less efficient, taking away important restrictions would leave everyone better off as people

21 J. Froissart, *The Chronicles of Froissart* (1385) trans. G. C. Macaulay (1895) 251, quoting John Ball.

22 Cf. G. Chaucer, *The Canterbury Tales: General Prologue* (1400). It is said of the ploughman, who represented most people, 'God loved he the beste.' But the brutal suppression of the peasantry showed the king did not.

23 T. More, *Utopia* (1516) Book 1, and translated best by P. Turner (Penguin ed. 2004).

24 See E. Coke, *The Fourth Part of the Institutes of the Laws of England: Concerning the Courts* (1644) ch. 73.

25 Hickel, *The Divide*, 77–83.

26 E.g. B. Mandeville, *The Fable of the Bees* (1714).

27 J. Swift, *A Modest Proposal For preventing the Children of Poor People from Being a Burthen to Their Parents or Country, and for Making Them Beneficial to the Publick* (1729).

28 An act to regulate the importation and exportation of corn 1773 (13 Geo. III, c. 43) repealing controls on grain speculation since Elizabeth I.

29 T. Malthus, *An Essay on the Principle of Population* (1798) ch. 2.

30 Malthus, *An Essay on the Principle of Population,* ch. 5, and on the recurrent theme of 'misery and vice' see chs. 1, 3, 5–7 and 10.

31 A. Smith, *An Inquiry into the Nature and Causes of the Wealth of Nations* (1776) Book IV, ch. 2.

32 Importation Act 1815 (c. 26) and Importation Act 1822.

naturally specialised in the produce they were best at.[33] These arguments did not succeed and the corn laws continued.

The turning point was the Great Famine of Ireland, which began in 1845. After years of enclosure, Irish peasants had been forced into ever smaller plots of land, where only potatoes yielded enough calories to survive. When a potato blight struck it wiped out crops, killing a million people and forcing 2 million to migrate. During this time Ireland exported thirty to fifty shiploads of food to England and Scotland each day, because that made more money than feeding the starving poor.[34] Finally, the Importation Act 1846 repealed the corn laws, a decision backed by the conservative Robert Peel, the price he had to pay to remain Prime Minister. Yet tariffs and famines continued throughout the British Empire. In India, famines had begun the moment the East India Company took control of tax, tariffs and therefore the land and grain trade: 10 million starved in Bengal in 1770.[35] Millions more continued to die in drought and famine, through years of enclosure.[36] In 1877 and 1878, 5.5 million people starved even as 6.4 million tonnes of wheat was exported to Britain.[37] The last famine was in 1943, again in Bengal with 3 million dead through deliberate Keynesian strategy of profit inflation, before the British Empire was finally forced to quit India.[38] As all the tragedies of loss of life unfolded, there was relentless deforestation, from 15% forests in England in 1086 to a low of 5.2% in 1905, and 4.7% for the UK. The Forestry Act 1919 established the Forestry Commission, and this has overseen a rise to 10.1% forest coverage in England, and 13.2% for the UK as a whole. Worldwide, forests used to cover 55% of the Earth's habitable land, and this is now just 38%, an unimaginable ecocide.

Meanwhile, nineteenth-century urbanisation meant more sewage and toxic water. Water services were 'treated as ordinary commodities which could be readily provided by private enterprise'.[39] Companies were created that established local monopolies. After an 1821 Select Committee found prices were extortionate,[40] all future Acts incorporating water companies contained

[33] D. Ricardo, *Essay on the Influence of a Low Price of Corn on the Profits of Stock* (1815) and *On the Principles of Political Economy and Taxation* (1817) ch. 7, but note that cut-throat competition limits developed.

[34] Hickel, *The Divide*, 84.

[35] W. Dalrymple, 'The East India Company: The Original Corporate Raiders', *The Guardian* (4 March 2015).

[36] E.g. Indian Forest Acts of 1865 and 1878.

[37] Hickel, *The Divide*, 88. At 92, it is pointed out that China underwent famine as it lost grain market control following the post-Opium war imposition of free trade.

[38] A. Sen, 'Indian Development: Lessons and Non-Lessons' (1989) 118(4) *Daedalus* 369; U. Patnaik, 'Profit Inflation, Keynes and the Holocaust in Bengal, 1943–44' (2018) LIII(42) *Economic & Political Weekly* 33.

[39] J. Foreman-Peck and R. Millward, *Public and Private Ownership of British Industry 1820–1990* (1994) 29–30. Also Getzler, *A History of Water Rights at Common Law*, 328–52.

[40] *Select Committee on Supply of Water to the Metropolis* (1821).

clauses to limit price rises.[41] Yet many people had no water or sewers at all. Cholera swept the world regularly: in 1817, in 1830, and a third pandemic struck England in 1848. The Public Health Act 1848 banned new housing without drains, and let Local Boards of Health be created if ratepayers petitioned, with powers over sewers and to provide 'sufficient' water supplies.[42] It was believed that 'miasma' or bad air caused disease, but in 1854, with an outbreak in Broad Street, Soho, Dr John Snow showed cholera was caused by sewage polluting drinking water. At this time, flushing toilets, like those made by Thomas Crapper, had grown wildly in popularity, and in London the drains went into the Thames. So much sewage flowed that in 1858, a 'Great Stink' occurred. Parliament temporarily relocated, and commissioned Joseph Bazalgette to build the London sewers.[43] It was not until the Public Health Act 1875 that local authorities, *if* they built waterworks, had a duty to provide 'pure and wholesome water' in return for rates.[44]

By 1944, there were over 1,000 water entities in England and Wales, but just 26 supplied half the volume, 97 another quarter,[45] and 1,400 entities provided sewage services.[46] Despite all these companies, 20 per cent of rural households lacked piped water.[47] The Water Act 1945 brought water under the supervision of a national planning committee, and encouraged local authority companies to merge and create joint water boards. This disjointed system was replaced when the Water Act 1973 organised ten regional water authorities reflecting river basins, with local and central government directors, but it left statutory water companies in place, including those privately owned, but subject to dividend and interest payment controls.[48] Scottish water became public under regional councils in 1980,[49] but for England the Water Act 1983 eliminated local council representation on water authorities. The Water Act 1989 privatised them, selling the authorities for £4.9 billion, but writing off £4.9 billion in debt, and giving the companies £1.5 billion in cash to invest in environmental repairs, more than 'eliminating any proceeds to the taxpayer from privatisation'.[50] This counts among the most costly acts in the UK

41 Waterworks Clauses Act 1847 (c. 17) codified the standard provisions, followed by Acts in 1852 and 1863. Statutory water companies were mainly created in the mid-nineteenth century following these model clauses.

42 Public Health Act 1848, ss. XII, XLIII, XLIX and LXXV.

43 Metropolis Management Act 1855, s. XLIII had set up the Metropolitan Board of Works. Bazalgette was chief engineer.

44 Public Health Act 1875, ss. 55–6. Public Health Act 1936, Part IV recast sewer regulation. See before, the Public Health Act 1866.

45 E. Porter, *Water Management in England and Wales* (1978) 29.

46 Ofwat and Defra, *The Development of the Water Industry in England and Wales* (2006) 1.

47 Rural Water Supplies and Sewerage Act 1944 was passed to extend piped water. See D. Kinnersley, *Troubled Water: Rivers, Politics and Pollution* (1988).

48 Water Act 1973, s. 12 (supply by authorities through statutory water companies).

49 Water (Scotland) Act 1980 (c. 45).

50 Ofwat and Defra, *The Development of the Water Industry*, 38–40. This also points out provision for £7.7bn in capital tax allowances was made, ostensibly to prevent any 'disadvantage

government's recent history. A regulator, now called Ofwat, would supervise controls on prices and terms.[51] Scottish Water remained public after fierce protests, and has kept prices around 10 per cent lower than in England and Wales.[52]

In agriculture, the mid-twentieth century witnessed a 'Green Revolution' (see Figure 13.1 in respect of the UK). Crop yields dramatically improved from the 1930s, because of two main factors. First, Nikolai Vavilov, a Soviet geneticist, explained seed genes. Growing up with tsarist famines, and the Russian Revolution where Lenin promised 'peace, bread and land',[53] Vavilov worked through Stalin's famines of 1922 and 1932 caused by forced collectivisation of land.[54] Driven by ending hunger, he collected millions of seeds from around the world to understand which could be used together to breed the most resilient plants.[55] Vavilov was imprisoned by Stalin in 1941 and murdered in 1943, though his work would feed and save the lives of billions of people.

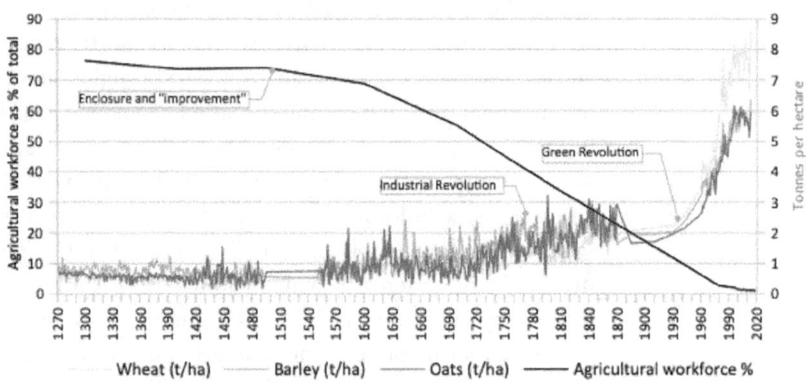

Figure 13.1 UK agricultural workforce and wheat, barley and oats output, 1270–2014
Sources: H. Ritchie and M. Roser, *Our World in Data, Long Term Crop Yields in UK* (2017); R. C. Allen, 'Economic Structure and Agricultural Productivity in Europe, 1300–1800' (2000) 3 *Eur Rev Economic History* 1, 8 (England); World Bank, 'Employment in Agriculture' (UK) https://data.worldbank.org/indicator/SL.AGR.EMPL.ZS

compared with other companies who had not built up capital allowances over time'. This was just another gift.

51 Water Act 1989, ss. 4, 83–5 were the initial privatisation provisions. See C. Harlow and R. Rawlings, *Law and Administration* (3rd ed. 2009) ch. 7, 293–5.

52 Scottish Water, 'Your Charges 2018–2019' (2019) (average Scottish bill £363, England and Wales, £405).

53 V. I. Lenin, *On The Agrarian Question* (June 1920) 'The proletarian state must effect the transition to collective farming with extreme caution and only very gradually, by the force of example, without any coercion of the middle peasant.' This is the very opposite of what the Soviet Union did.

54 The Holodomor in Ukraine starved up to 12m: T. Snyder, *Bloodlands: Europe between Hitler and Stalin* (2011).

55 N. Vavilov, *The Origin, Variation, Immunity and Breeding of Cultivated Plants*, trans. K. S. Chester (1951).

Second, in the Great Depression, the US Agricultural Adjustment Act of 1933 fostered new land management. The USA had suffered problems of overproduction. Soil had eroded, creating the 'dust bowl' storms of the early 1930s.[56] Excessive crop supplies also depressed prices, making farm incomes unpredictable and entrenching rural poverty. The 1933 Act was declared 'unconstitutional'[57] but fresh laws were passed, paying farmers to reduce production and protect soil,[58] and providing support for cotton, corn, wheat and a host of other crops, as well as insurance for failure.[59] These were the supports for what President Roosevelt called the 'right of every farmer to raise and sell his products at a return which will give him and his family a decent living'.[60] As federal government now subsidised and managed production, it was interested in driving efficiency. Increasingly, farms used higher-yield cereals, hybrid seeds, expanded irrigation, better management, fertilisers and pesticides. Through USAID, the practices were also exported, starting in Mexico. Altogether this became the Green Revolution.[61]

The need for the Green Revolution was especially pressing after World War Two. The 'Third World' (not aligned to either the USA or USSR) desperately needed an end to hunger, a task to which the new UN Food and Agriculture Organization was devoted. Europe too was starving, and so the US Marshall Plan paid for European managers, technicians and unionists to go to the USA on 'productivity missions',[62] and it sent Europeans money to buy food.[63] Four-fifths of all wheat in Europe from 1949 to 1951 came from US dollars.[64] Meanwhile, in Central America, the US government launched violent interventions to stop democratic land reform. In 1954, under President Eisenhower, the Secretary of State, John Dulles, was an ex-lawyer for the United Fruit Company (UFC), and the CIA Director, his brother Allen Dulles, was on the UFC board. President Árbenz of Guatemala, democratically elected in 1950, passed Decree 900 in 1952 compulsorily purchasing unused land over 224 acres in size, and transferring it to poor peasants. This affected around 85 per cent of UFC land, and so in 1954 the CIA backed a military coup to oust Árbenz, giving way to a series of incompetent, murderous puppets and decades of civil war.[65]

56 The setting to J. Steinbeck, *The Grapes of Wrath* (1939). On itinerant farm labour also *Of Mice and Men* (1937).

57 *United States v Butler*, 297 US 1 (1936).

58 Soil Conservation and Domestic Allotment Act of 1936.

59 Agricultural Adjustment Act of 1938, 7 USC, §§1281ff.

60 F. D. Roosevelt, 'Eleventh State of the Union Address' (1944).

61 N. Borlaug, 'The Green Revolution, Peace, and Humanity', Nobel Lecture (11 December 1970).

62 In the UK, the Agriculture Act 1947 (c. 48) copied a US model of guaranteeing food prices on conditions.

63 G. Marshall, 'Speech to Harvard Graduates' (5 June 1947).

64 T. Judt, *Postwar* (2005) 95–6.

65 Cf. M. Kettle and J. Lennard, 'Clinton Apology to Guatemala', *The Guardian* (12 March 1999): 'support for military forces and intelligence units which engaged in violence and widespread repression was wrong, and the United States must not repeat that mistake'. Over 36 years, 200,000 people died.

The European Economic Community – now the European Union (EU) – was formed in the Treaty of Rome 1957 and, largely due to France's insistence, began a Common Agricultural Policy (CAP).[66] Agricultural security was a massive issue because a third of EEC employment, and a fifth of Gross Domestic Product (GDP), was in agriculture in 1960.[67] From 1962, the CAP aimed to secure fair farm living standards and affordable food by buying surplus production. By 1988, the CAP was two-thirds of the European Community budget and so, to end the 'wine lakes' and 'butter mountains', the McSharry Reforms of 1992 shifted from market price fixing to direct payments to farmers. With the customs union that raised tariffs on food imports, like the USA, it kept prices high even as the farm workforce plummeted, and productivity soared. Inevitably, this excluded the rest of the world. Though food productivity has also soared, the poorest countries have not been able to maintain competing systems of supports. This inequality was only worsened by IMF and World Bank 'structural adjustment' programmes, which told countries to privatise water or cut regulations and subsidies – even for the size of bread loaves – if they asked for loans.[68] The unequal system was further entrenched in the World Trade Organization (WTO), as the Agreement on Agriculture of 1995 negotiated some tariff reductions but enabled subsidies to continue: rich countries kept protection, poor countries got 'free trade'.[69] Thus, what began as efforts to stop farm poverty in America and Europe had come to entrench farm poverty abroad. There was an absence of agreement on preserving forests and stopping fossil fuels in agriculture or the rest of the economy. Today climate damage is the biggest threat to food, forests and water.

(2) Finance

The finance of food, forests and water is predominantly public, even though much of each enterprise is held privately in the UK.[70] Food and water are distinct enterprises, with distinct ownership structures but neither they, nor human beings, can do with one and not have the other. Land, lakes and rivers, forests, farming and irrigation are all part of one ecosystem. The three common sources of finance, beyond standard corporate equity or debt, are (a) subsidies from government, particularly the EU CAP; (b) the natural

66 Treaty establishing the European Economic Community 1957, arts. 38–47.

67 J. C. Bureau and A. Matthews, 'EU Agricultural Policy: What Developing Countries Need to Know', IIS Discussion Paper No. 91 (2005) 3.

68 E.g. IMF, Egypt, 1991, EBS/91/213, 'Reduce the size of the "popular" bread loaf by 15 grams to reduce subsidies by LE 150 million in 1991/92'. S Grusky, 'IMF and World Bank Push Water Privatization' (2001) 23.

69 WTO Agreement on Agriculture 1995, art. 4 (market access). See M. J. Trebilcock and R. Howse, *The Regulation of International Trade* (2012) ch. 12.

70 For excellent works on water law, see S. Hendry, *Frameworks for Water Law Reform* (2014) ch. 5, 86; and Harlow and Rawlings, *Law and Administration*, ch. 7, 292–304.

monopolies that land and water systems occupy; and (c) the subsidies in not paying for pollution.

(a) Common Agricultural Policy and Water Subsidies

The first and main type of finance for agriculture and water is direct government subsidy.

(i) UK Agriculture Act 2020

In the UK, the Agriculture Act 2020 will be the structure to administer subsidies after an eventual withdrawal by the UK from the EU's CAP. At the time of writing, it is not clear what exactly that will mean, or what level of subsidies there will be. The Act gives the Secretary of State the power to give financial assistance, to make regulations on conditions and to monitor what is done by farmers in return for subsidies.[71] This gives enormous discretion to the Department for Environment, Food and Rural Affairs in administering payments. In 2018, the UK's share of the EU CAP was £3.5 billion,[72] from a total of €58.8 billion across the EU (over a third of the EU's €160.1 billion budget).[73] Experience of the CAP will likely inform the UK's choices, and its sheer size and global impact means the CAP should be understood for its own sake.

(ii) EU Common Agricultural Policy

The CAP is made up of three main programmes. First, the European Agricultural Guarantee Fund (EAGF) manages 'direct payments'.[74] These are 70.9 per cent of the CAP budget. Under the Direct Payments Regulation 2013, payments are available to any 'active farmer' that carries out a minimum of agricultural activity, grazing or cultivation; does not operate airports, rail, waterworks, real estate, sport or recreation grounds; and has the land at their disposal.[75] To get subsidies, under the Directive the farm must have at least 1 hectare and receive over €100, but member states can set higher thresholds: the UK set a threshold of 5 hectares and €200.[76] A hectare is 10,000 square metres (100 m x 100 m) or 2.47 acres. Payments are made for each hectare, but when payments reach over €150,000 there is a 5 per cent reduction for each hectare.[77] This 'degressive' scheme may appear to favour smaller farms, but in the UK the

71 Agriculture Act 2020, ss. 1–6.

72 D. Rhodes and H. Barbieux, 'Brexit: EU Subsidy Loss "Could Wipe Out Farms"', *BBC News* (9 July 2019).

73 See 'The Common Agricultural Policy at a Glance' (2018) https://ec.europa.eu/info/food-farming-fisheries/key-policies/common-agricultural-policy/cap-glance_en.

74 Management and Financing Regulation (EU) No. 1306/2013, art. 4.

75 Direct Payments Regulation (DPR) (EU) No. 1307/2013, arts. 9 and 33.

76 DPR, art. 10 and Annex IV. 77 DPR, arts. 10–11 and 32.

largest 1 per cent of farms (typically profitable commercial operations) receive 15.6 per cent of all subsidies, ranging from £180,000 to over £6 million a year.[78]

Agriculture payments are subject to conditions, so that farms may be required to comply with standards for the environment, to limit climate damage, keep land in good condition, and for public, animal and plant health.[79] But although conditions are provided for by law, these have not yet been used in a systematic and meaningful way to require the elimination of carbon, rather than incremental steps. To diversify crop ecology (and reduce risk of failure), farmers must have over two crops if they have 10 hectares, keep at least 5 per cent as an 'ecological focus area' (that is, not farmed intensively) over 15 hectares and have three crops over 30 hectares.[80] Environmentally sensitive grasslands, as designated by the Habitats Directive 1992 and the Wild Birds Directive 2009, should not be turned into more than 5 per cent agricultural area.[81]

The second main programme, also carried out by the EAGF, is 'market measures'. Under the Agricultural Products Regulation 2013, certain crops and meat are eligible for purchase by member state authorities, to be 'stored by them until disposed of', with extra aid for storage.[82] The goal of this is to restrict supply and therefore raise prices, particularly in response to unexpected drops in demand, a health scare or international market volatility. In 2018, this was 4.59 per cent of the CAP budget.

The third main programme, administered by a different European Agricultural Fund for Rural Development, is 'rural development' payments. These are 24.4 per cent of the CAP budget.[83] Following the 'Europe 2020 Strategy by promoting sustainable rural development',[84] payments are made for knowledge transfer, advice, asset investment and business development aid.[85] Priorities may include improving water and energy use.[86]

(iii) US Farm Bills

The other major influence on global food is subsidies administered by the US Department of Agriculture through 'Farm Bills'. In 2019 these were \$22.42 billion (€19.5 billion).[87] Since the New Deal, the US Congress has

[78] See CAP Payments Search at https://cap-payments. defra.gov.uk/. The highest UK recipients are public or charitable bodies: Natural England, the Rural Payments Agency, the National Trust, the Welsh Assembly Government and RSPB.

[79] Management and Financing Regulation (EU) No. 1306/2013, arts. 91–101.

[80] DPR 2013, arts. 44 and 46.

[81] DPR 2013, art. 45; Habitats Directive 92/43/EEC; Wild Birds Directive 2009/147/EC.

[82] Agricultural Products Regulation (EU) No. 1308/2013, art. 8.

[83] Management and Financing Regulation (EU) No. 1306/2013, arts. 4–5.

[84] Rural Development Regulation (EU) No. 1305/2013, art. 3.

[85] Rural Development Regulation, arts. 7–9, 17 and 19.

[86] Rural Development Regulation, art. 5.

[87] D. Charles, 'Farmers Got Billions from Taxpayers in 2019, and Hardly Anyone Objected', *NPR* (2019).

renewed and amended agricultural programmes found in the US Code Title VII, and other parts, roughly each five years. The largest element of this, but only since 2017, has become spending by the Commodity Credit Corporation,[88] with $14.3 billion in 2019, but authorised to spend up to $30 billion a year.[89] These payments are intended to be used to compensate for fluctuations in trade, and their acceleration began with the US 'trade war' on China and Europe. The second largest component of Farm Bill payments, around $8 billion a year, is the Federal Crop Insurance Corporation.[90] This subsidises insurance to farms with shortfalls in revenue or crop yields. In fact, farmers receive more in claims than they pay in premiums,[91] so while it is insurance in form, it is a subsidy in substance. There are at least seven other programmes, including Agricultural Risk Coverage, Price Loss Coverage, conservation aid, marketing loans, disaster aid, export promotion and research funding.[92]

In contrast to the EU, (non-trade related) direct payments to US farms were cancelled in 2014, though the Commodity Credit Corporation payments perform an equivalent function without the need for transparency. Insurance subsidies come with similar, and limited, conditions on environmental management.[93] The distribution of this money is highly skewed towards large agri-business: in 2009, 62% of all subsidies went to commercial farms with over $250,000 in gross annual sales.[94] While EU markets tend to remain more segregated by geography, four supermarkets make up over 50% of the total US sales: Walmart, Kroger, Costco and Safeway, up from 17% for the top four in 1994.[95] Four food processors (Cargill, Tyson, JBS and NBPC) control 80% of beef, 60% of pork and 50% of poultry. This concentration extends globally in grain and seeds. Four grain producers (Cargill, ADM, Bunge and Dreyfus) control up to 90% of global grain trade.[96] Four seed companies, though now just one US-based, control 63% of the global seed market (DuPont, Bayer, BASF and ChemChina).[97] Thus, while US subsidies are smaller than in the EU, the global market power of its agricultural businesses tends to be greater.

[88] 31 USC, §§9101–10, originally created by Executive Order 6340 (16 October 1933).
[89] 15 USC, §714b(i). [90] 7 USC, §1508(k).
[91] Congressional Budget Office, 'Options to Reduce the Budgetary Costs of the Federal Crop Insurance Program' (2017) 2–5.
[92] 7 USC, §§5801 and 5939, on the Sustainable Agriculture Research and Education, and Foundation for Food and Agricultural Research.
[93] PL No. 113-79, §2611 and §11014(a).
[94] J. Stiglitz, *The Price of Inequality* (2012) 320, fn. 54.
[95] L. Khan and S. Vaheesan, 'Market Power and Inequality: The Antitrust Counterrevolution and Its Discontents' (2017) 11 *Harvard L & Policy Rev* 235, 254–5.
[96] S. Murphy, D. Burch and J. Clapp, *Cereal Secrets* (2012) 3.
[97] Khan and Vaheesan (2017) 11 *Harvard L & Policy Rev* 235, 255. Since 2017, Bayer took over Monsanto, DuPont merged with Dow Chemical, while ChemChina took over the Swiss company Syngenta.

(iv) The True Destination of Subsidies

While £3.5 billion is paid to UK farms, €58 billion EU wide, and $22 billion in the USA, who is really being subsidised? First, little money reaches farm workers. The rationale for farm subsidies in the 1930s was to ensure the 'right of every farmer to raise and sell his products at a return which will give him and his family a decent living', and also to feed a starving Europe post-war (see Ch. 13(1)). But today, many farms are corporations or businesses where workers do not own the farm, or profit from their work. In Europe, most farm workers are paid minimal wages and live in precarious conditions.[98] In the USA, agricultural workers are excluded from basic labour rights and migrant workers face systematic exploitation.[99] In England, an Agricultural Wages Board, which required fair wage scales above the minimum, was abolished in 2013, though equivalent boards still operate in Scotland and Wales.[100] Many farms do pay fair wages, but there are no conditions to do so, despite receipt of public funds.

Second, even farm owners often do not benefit from subsidies to a full extent. Farms sell their crops and meat to agents or manufacturers, who in turn mostly sell to supermarkets. In the UK, five supermarkets hold 73.9 per cent of the market (see Ch. 18(2)(d)). In the USA, four supermarkets dominate over 50 per cent of the market and, with greater geographical distribution, 'food deserts' are common. Against thousands of farmers, supermarkets or distributors have the bargaining power to lower the prices they pay, and so appropriate farm subsidies. These concerns motivated an Agricultural Unfair Trading Practices Directive 2019.[101] It prohibits practices such as late payments by buyers to suppliers, cancellations at short notice, unilateral alteration of terms, threats of commercial retaliation and payments by suppliers to the buyers (i.e. from farmers *to supermarkets*) for stocking, adverts, marketing or staff.[102] These prohibitions limit supermarkets' abuse of a dominant position. But they do not change that position or ensure subsidies reach farm communities.

Third, farm subsidies do not benefit consumers to a full extent for the same reasons. Because supermarket markets are highly concentrated, consumers lack meaningful power. Shoppers might choose between Tesco, Sainsbury or Asda, but each supermarket has similarly high profits and similar shareholders

[98] E.g. P. Lord, 'Valuing Labour: The Interaction of Law and Informal Norms in UK Agriculture' (2019) 1 *J Oxford Centre of Socio-legal Studies* 22–38.

[99] E.g. M. Dias-Abey, 'Justice on Our Fields: Can Alt-Labor Organizations Improve Migrant Farm Workers' Conditions?' (2018) 53 *Harvard Civil Rights-Civil Liberties L Rev* 167.

[100] Agricultural Wages (Scotland) Act 1949, s. 1 and *Re Agricultural Sector (Wales) Bill* [2014] UKSC 43, after the repeal of the Agricultural Wages Act 1948, s. 1 by the Enterprise and Regulatory Reform Act 2013, s. 72.

[101] For background, see E. Livingstone, 'Europe Rips Up Free-Market Rules to Help Farmers', *Politico* (11 July 2017). The eventual Directive did far less than empowering more farm co-operatives to raise bargaining power.

[102] Agricultural Unfair Trading Practices Directive 2019/633, art. 3.

(see Ch. 18(3)(a)). Shopping around among similar prices and products does little to change the imbalance of power. Despite massive food waste, there has also been an explosion of food banks since 2008. Many people cannot afford food. The fact that food prices are higher than people's incomes is also closely connected to the cost of housing (see Ch. 14(4)(b)), labour rights and social security (see Ch. 5).

Fourth, while EU farming communities and shoppers are barely helped by subsidies, a higher cost hits farming communities worldwide. With subsidies, the EU raises import tariffs on food from abroad.[103] The WTO Agreement on Agriculture 1995 enables this, as a deviation from the standard prohibitions on barriers to trade. While this lowered many tariffs, it enabled others to be maintained.[104] The aim of tariffs is that EU crops and meat are not outcompeted, as workers abroad are paid even less than EU workers. A cut-throat competition, or 'shipping jobs overseas', it might be argued, would benefit nobody except the profits of global agri-business. Yet the EU has failed so far to negotiate trade treaties that improve labour rights to stop such a 'race to the bottom' problem. By maintaining tariffs, farmers abroad are unable to sell on equal terms into the giant EU market. For example, Indian tomato sellers, instead of receiving a market price from UK supermarkets, receive that price minus a tariff levied by the EU. This restricts development in the global farming community and entrenches poverty. It is the very opposite outcome from the agricultural system's goals in the New Deal or Marshall Plan.

(v) Subsidies from and to Water

Water is both a subsidy to agriculture and itself subsidised by government. As a subsidy, since privatisation water companies have charged different prices for water, so that the higher the volume of water used by the business, the less they pay.[105] This enables cheap water for livestock or irrigation where water is not directly abstracted, compared to higher prices per unit paid by households. Again, the actual benefits of cheap water may flow to supermarkets, rather than farms, depending on the relative bargaining power of the parties.

As a subsidised enterprise, the main subsidy to water companies occurred during privatisation in 1989, when the nine new water companies in England and Wales were collectively relieved of £4.9 billion in debt, and given

[103] WTO, 'Trade Policy Review', WT/TPR/S/395 (2019) 63, Table 3.4, showing simple average import tariffs of animal products 19%; dairy 32.3%; fruit and veg 13%; coffee, tea and cocoa 11.5%; cereals 17.2%; sugar 27%; beverages, spirits and tobacco 12.9%; and cotton 0%.

[104] WTO Agreement on Agriculture 1995, art. 3.

[105] Water Industry Act (WIA) 1991, s. 11 gives Ofwat power to impose conditions, but this has not been done. Ofwat, 'Wholesale Charging Rules Issued by the Water Services Regulation Authority under Sections 66E and 117I of the Water Industry Act 1991' (20 December 2018) rule 15 requires only that charging 'structures must reflect the long-run costs associated with providing the relevant service'. I am grateful to Natalie da Costa for this.

£1.5 billion in public funds. This was worth £12 billion in 2017 prices,[106] or around £400 million a year since privatisation, in addition to the guaranteed revenue stream from having a monopoly (below). A further kind of subsidy to water companies is non-payment of tax. To give just one example, from 2011 to 2015 Thames Water plc in London paid no corporation tax, yet it paid dividends to its shareholders throughout that period: from 2006 to 2015 its dividends totalled £1.16 billion.[107] This non-enforcement of tax duties, compared to other companies, is therefore a major subsidy.

(b) Natural Monopoly and Patents

A second main type of finance is the ability of companies to hold a natural monopoly over land or water infrastructure. First, it was argued by Winston Churchill that land 'differs from all other forms of property' because it 'is a necessity of human existence ... strictly limited in extent' and 'fixed in geographical position', making it 'by far the greatest of monopolies'.[108] It is true that in England and Wales, around 36,000 landowners own half the rural land,[109] and in Scotland, just 432 people own over half the private land, while 10 per cent of land is in public ownership.[110] But it seems obviously wrong to still say land remains 'the greatest' monopoly, given obvious examples like Google (see Chs. 16–18), and were it a monopoly it would not need subsidies. What changed since the nineteenth century is the Green Revolution, making agricultural productivity infinitely greater compared to our needs. That said, if large landowners do grab enough, they could corner production. From 2007 to 2011, with the onset of the global financial crisis, food prices started fluctuating wildly, partly driven by commodity futures traded by global banks. This proved an opportunity for investors to buy up large tracts of land around the world. Estimates range from 80 million to 220 million hectares,[111] the latter an area the size of Western Europe. As land's supply is fixed, and much will die because of climate damage, an ongoing concentration of land would enable price control.

106 G. Plimmer, 'Privatised Water Costs Consumers £2.3bn More a Year, Study Says', *Financial Times* (6 June 2017), summarising a report by K. Bayliss and D. Hall, 'Bringing Water into Public Ownership: Costs and Benefits' (May 2017).

107 G. Plimmer and J. Espinoza, 'Thames Water: The Murky Structure of a Utility Company', *Financial Times* (4 May 2017); and see the Annual Report, *Investing in Our Future* (2014) stating £231.4m in 2012/13 and £208.5m in 2013/14.

108 W. S. Churchill, 'Speech Delivered at King's Theatre in Edinburgh' (17 July 1909).

109 G. Shrubsole, *Who Owns England?* (2019) 21. Statistics are unclear as land is not all registered or transparent.

110 J. Hunter, P. Peacock, A. Wightman and M. Foxley, '432:50 – Towards a Comprehensive Land Reform Agenda for Scotland', A Briefing Paper for the House of Commons Scottish Affairs Committee (2014).

111 Oxfam, 'Land and Power', Briefing Paper No. 151 (2011); F. Pearce, *The Landgrabbers* (2013) ix.

Second, the ability to control patents enables monopolies. In the Biotechnology Directive 1998, article 4(1) 'plant and animal varieties' and 'essentially biological processes for the production of plants or animals' cannot be patented, but a 'microbiological or other technical process' or a product can be.[112] This largely reflects the European Patent Convention 1973, where article 53(b) also excluded patents on plant varieties, including genetically modified plants (e.g. making a plant resistant to herbicide).[113] However, invention of methods to genetically modify more than one plant (e.g. how to make many plants resistant to a fungus) can be patented.[114] These standards are generally reflected in the WTO Agreement on Trade-Related Aspects of Intellectual Property Rights (TRIPS).[115] However, countries with less bargaining power in trade, such as Tanzania and Mozambique, have been pressured into enabling corporate patents on plant seeds themselves, or even to stop the distribution of 'free and unimproved seeds'.[116] Such rules offend economic freedom and underline the threat of corporate power.

Third, water resources and networks are a classic natural monopoly, where the average cost in providing water to an extra user tends to decline. There are, of course, a limited number of reservoirs, lakes and rivers that may provide drinking water, but also it makes no sense to have competing water pipes, or sewers running under cities or towns. England and Wales are exceptional worldwide in that no other country has completely privatised its water systems. The facts speak for themselves: people in England and Wales pay on average 10 per cent more than in Scotland where water was not privatised, a gap that has been rising.[117] Under the Water Industry Act 1991, section 11, the Water Services Regulation Authority, known as Ofwat, can set any conditions it thinks 'requisite or expedient', including prices, while section 12 enables Ofwat to have the power to direct water companies.[118] Thus, water companies can only logically generate maximum returns for shareholders by pressing their prices to the limit enabled by Ofwat's price cap, or by lobbying for Ofwat to allow profitable price caps. There is no constraint from competition. The evidence (which is not complicated) suggests public ownership is cheaper and more efficient. Investors that have a conflict of interest with the public will continue to claim the opposite no matter how dry their arguments run.[119]

[112] Biotechnology Directive 98/44/EC, art. 4.

[113] European Patent Convention 1973, art. 53(b).

[114] *Novartis/Transgenic plant G01/98* [2000] EPOR 303.

[115] See further T. Aplin and J. Davis, *Intellectual Property Law: Text, Cases, and Materials* (3rd ed. 2016) ch. 11.

[116] Hickel, *The Divide*, 237.

[117] E.g. Scottish Water, 'Your Charges 2018–2019' (2019) (average Scottish bill £363, England and Wales £405).

[118] WIA 1991, ss. 11–12.

[119] E.g. G. Plimmer, 'Privatised Water Costs Consumers £2.3bn More a Year, Study Says', *Financial Times* (6 June 2017). The chief executive of a lobby group, Water UK, was quoted saying a report, that said privatised water costs £2.3bn more a year, was 'flawed [and] does not

It does not follow, however, that public ownership is the only thing that matters: public-sector governance can be better or worse (see Ch. 13(3)).

(c) Climate Damage and Pollution

A third source of subsidies is non-liability of agricultural enterprise and water companies for climate damage or pollution.

(i) Agriculture

In the case of agriculture, the sector, as a whole, accounts for around 9 per cent of the UK's total greenhouse gas emissions, and emissions have remained fairly constant since 1990.[120] There are four main sources of agricultural pollutants. First, there is the management of the soil. Ploughing or tilling has been thought to be good to loosen soil before planting crops, but modern practice suggests this is detrimental: it may kill some weeds, but also destroys worm populations, and releases nitrous oxide (N_2O) which, like carbon dioxide (CO_2), contributes to climate damage. While there may be lower crop yields from not tilling in the first or second year, yields are back to normal or higher in the third, without the expense of doing the tilling, retaining N_2O, and increasing the worm and therefore bird populations.[121]

Second, there is the use of heavy fossil-fuel-burning machinery. Ploughing machines, which are extremely costly, can be abandoned if there is no tilling: farmers may receive angry correspondence from manufacturers, but save tens or hundreds of thousands of pounds. Large herbicide crop-spraying machines can also now be abandoned, as small, cheap, electric robots have been developed that map crops, and squirt weedkiller on individual weeds, also saving around 95 per cent of herbicide cost.[122] Combine harvesters remain necessary, but could be powered by electric motors like road vehicles (see Ch. 15).

Third, there is climate damage from livestock. Forests are cleared for livestock to graze, and no information is required to be given to consumers about this when they buy products. Methane is around 16 per cent of global greenhouse gas emissions,[123] and cows alone 'emit' 37 per cent of this. A greater plant-based diet would improve public health, and the replacement of meat with plants would solve these problems. But without everyone becoming vegetarian, feeding cows seaweed decreases cow methane 'emissions' by

do justice to the achievements of the water industry since privatisation'. The reason he failed to explain why the report was flawed, of course, was because it was not.

120 See Figure 15.3.

121 I am very grateful to Tim Ashton for first-hand experience of how this works. See further D. R. Montgomery, *Growing a Revolution: Bringing Our Soil Back to Life* (2017).

122 E.g. C. M. Scolaro, 'This Weed-Killing AI Robot Can Tell Crops Apart', *NBC* (4 June 2018).

123 EPA, 'Climate Change Indicators: Atmospheric Concentrations of Greenhouse Gases', Figure 2, Methane.

50 per cent.[124] Grazing fields can be replanted with at least some trees, known as 'silvopasture', and this also improves the land.[125] Conditions such as these could accompany agricultural subsidies.

Fourth, pesticide sprays and machinery have been drastically overused, driven by pesticide companies, and insecticides in particular could also be reduced by 60 per cent with no change in yields, or more yields.[126] The EU's regulations on pesticides were updated in 2018 to prohibit three neonicotinoids, a group of nicotine-based nerve agents.[127] These were responsible for reducing insect populations by 76 per cent since 1989 (and probably more from before), including the mass killing of bees.[128] The two largest manufacturers are Syngenta (now owned by ChemChina) and Bayer, and they still sell their toxic products in the USA.[129]

(ii) Water

Water companies contribute to climate damage through overly energy-intensive waste-water treatment, but the most immediate source of pollution is the mismanagement of sewage. Often water company polluters do not pay. Pollution was never taken seriously by the common law, as in most of tort law's famous cases, such as the *Wagon Mound*[130] or *Cambridge Water Co. Ltd v Eastern Counties Leather plc*,[131] the House of Lords declined to hold people responsible for the damage they caused, by inventing theories of 'remoteness'.[132] When a water company (or electricity or gas company) carries

124 G. Volpicelli, 'The Strange War against Cow Farts', *Wired* (1 December 2018).

125 P. Hawken (ed.), *Drawdown: The Most Comprehensive Plan Ever Proposed to Reverse Global Warming* (2018).

126 M. Lechenet, 'Reducing Pesticide Use While Preserving Crop Productivity and Profitability on Arable Farms' (2017) 3(17008) *Nature Plants* 1.

127 Plant Protection Products Regulation (EC) No. 1107/2009, sets out the framework, and the Active Substances Regulation (EU) No. 540/2011 lists the permitted substances, amended by Regulations 2018/783, 784 and 785 to prohibit imidacloprid, clothianidin and thiamethoxam. Others may still do damage.

128 C. A. Hallmann et al., 'More than 75 Percent Decline over 27 Years in Total Flying Insect Biomass in Protected Areas' (2017) 12(10) *Plos One*.

129 L. Fang, 'The Playbook for Poisoning the Earth', *Intercept* (18 January 2020). The companies astroturfed 'research', pretending billions would be lost if the EU ban came into force: e.g. S. Noleppa and T. Hahn, 'The Value of Neonicotinoid Seed Treatment in the European Union', HFFA Working Paper No. 01/2013 (2013).

130 *Wagon Mound (No. 1)* [1961] UKPC 2, holding that oil pollution of Sydney Harbour, and then an explosion, resulted in no liability because apparently the explosion was not 'foreseeable'. This is a morally empty position: whether the defendant or claimant could have foreseen it, did the defendant not harm the claimant? The *Wagon Mound (No. 2)* [1966] UKPC 10 held the test for negligence depends on what a reasonable person would have done. Does a reasonable person not make up for harm they cause whether they foresaw it or not?

131 *Cambridge Water Co. Ltd v Eastern Counties Leather plc* [1993] UKHL 12 (a tanner business not responsible for polluting Cambridge's water supply).

132 The moral rule of directness was used among landowners: *Rylands v Fletcher* [1868] UKHL 1. Because large landowners or company owners are more likely to cause harm than be harmed, the remoteness rule in effect creates a subsidy for big business: it is one rule for the powerful, another for the weak, and is thus indefensible.

out street works that damage property (by leaks, explosions, etc.), they must compensate regardless of negligence.[133] However a more general regime covers water companies where they operate a 'regulated facility', including water discharge or groundwater activity.[134] Under the Integrated Pollution Control Directive 2010, and the implementing regulations, a water company must apply for a permit to run a regulated facility[135] and, if it contravenes the permit's conditions (e.g. by polluting), it commits an offence.[136] The penalties are up to £50,000, the polluter commits an offence, and there are unlimited fines that can run into millions.[137]

Yet these statutory systems have in at least one case been interpreted to pre-empt tort law, such as negligence or nuisance, where damages could be greater. In *Marcic v Thames Water plc*, the House of Lords held that Thames Water plc was not liable in nuisance, or for breach of a homeowner's right to property, when sewage repeatedly overflowed into residents' gardens. Lord Hoffmann affirmed that the owners had to use statutory mechanisms to secure accountability, not sue in tort.[138] There is no real reason why this should be the case, however, since environmental protection statutes are invariably made to create minimum standards: there should be no encouragement to pollute. In another unfortunate case, *Manchester Ship Canal Co. Ltd v United Utilities Water plc*, the Supreme Court held that United Utilities was not responsible in trespass for polluting canal ways with surface water and treated effluent, from outfall pipes existing at the time of the privatisation statute in 1991. It had been implicit in sewage statutes since 1875 that a ban on untreated sewage discharge meant treated sewage could be discharged.[139] But when privatisation transferred 'all property, rights and liabilities' this did not enable new outfalls to be created. The effect is that there is immunity for discharge from old pipes unless this causes 'damage' when doing works (and does not include simple pollution), but not from pipes after 1991.[140] These cases are inconsistent with the principle that polluters should pay and the scheme of the Water Framework Directive 2000 to ensure proper enforcement of clean water standards.[141] The limited liability for harm is therefore another significant subsidy.

133 New Roads and Street Works Act 1991, s. 82 and, on predecessor statute, *Department of Transport v North West Water Authority* [1984] AC 336.

134 Environmental Permitting (England and Wales) Regulations (EPR) 2010, reg. 8.

135 Integrated Pollution Control Directive 2010/75/EU, art. 4; EPR 2010, reg. 12.

136 EPR 2010, reg. 38.

137 *R v Anglian Water Services Ltd* [2003] EWCA Crim 2243. The Court of Appeal held that fines for pollution should always be set to ensure sufficient deterrence, but reduced a fine from £200,000 to £60,000. Cf. S. Laville, 'Southern Water Fined Record £90m for Deliberately Pouring Sewage into Sea', *The Guardian* (9 July 2021).

138 [2003] UKHL 66.

139 Public Health Act 1875, s. 17 (banning sewage and filthy water); *Durrant v Branksome UDC* [1897] 2 Ch 291.

140 [2014] UKSC 40, [19]–[21]; WIA 1991, s. 116 and Sch. 12, para. 6.

141 Water Framework Directive 2000/60/EC, recital 53; and see E. Fisher, B. Lange and E. Scotford, *Environmental Law Text, Cases, and Materials* (2013) ch. 14.

(3) Governance

The governance of food, forests and water encompasses a vast diversity of ownership and power models, a fact that suggests the deeply unsettled, and unprincipled, state of the law. In agriculture (a) the most important part of governance is the administration of subsidies food by agencies. Without this, the structure of private land-ownership would be very different. Public or quasi-public ownership of land is minor by comparison, owned largely through the Forestry Commission, the Ministry of Defence, the National Trust, the Crown Estate and others. In the case of water (b) English water companies have shareholders and are regulated. Welsh Water is a company limited by guarantee and non-profit. Scottish Water remained public. Alongside national or EU governance, (c) the UN and WTO have specialist agencies and rules devoted to food and water. Their progress in upholding human rights has been too slow, but this probably reflects less on international agencies, and more on our nations' own complacency about global hunger and clean water.

(a) Agriculture

Agricultural land governance, while ostensibly based upon private property and corporate management, cannot be understood without subsidies. In the UK, there has been some recent increase in public land, but artificially supported private ownership remains the norm.

(i) Administration of Subsidies

As Chapter 13(2)(a) explained above, since World War Two agricultural land has been financially sustained by subsidies. The Management and Financing Regulation 2013 creates the two EU agencies that distribute funds: the EAGF and the European Agricultural Fund for Rural Development (EAFRD). Both are 'implemented in shared management between the Member States and the Union'.[142] This means that member states designate 'paying agencies' that control spending delegated by the EAGF and EAFRD, ensuring proper internal control and accounting. The Commission accredits these to ensure proper governance.[143] Payments are made monthly, but member states – not the funds – bear costs of administration.[144]

In the UK, the paying agencies had been the Department for Environment, Food and Rural Affairs; the Scottish Government; the Welsh Government; and the Northern Ireland administration. With the end of EU membership, the government said it would maintain funding for the same level for direct

[142] Management and Financing Regulation (EU) No. 1306/2013, arts. 3–5.
[143] Management and Financing Regulation, arts. 7–8.
[144] Management and Financing Regulation, arts. 18–19.

payments, while rural development funding continues until 2023 under the terms of the Withdrawal Agreement.[145] Under the new Agriculture Act 2020 the Secretary of State will determine what payments and conditions are given in future.[146]

(ii) Private Land-Ownership

The second tier of governance in agricultural land is private ownership. According to the best estimates, land in England is owned at least 30% by the aristocracy, 18% by corporate bodies, 17% by newer private owners, 8.5% by the public sector and 17.6% unknown (see Table 13.1).[147]

The reason so much is unknown is that the Land Registry does not yet have the power to require that land is registered unless there is a transfer: 15 per cent remains unregistered because much land stays in old families without ever having been transferred. Even if land is registered, the register is not public, and can only be looked up with a payment of £6 a plot. Among the largest corporate owners are privatised water companies (United Utilities, Welsh Water and Yorkshire Water are the top three) who are restricted from selling the land.[148]

Aside from lack of registration, there are three other main differences between agricultural land and the land of most homeowners (with 5 per cent; see Ch. 14).

First, there are subsidies, as explained above. A business managing land for agriculture may not be economically viable for many firms without subsidies. Imagining that trade tariffs and subsidies ended, it is generally thought that most farms would cease production in favour of cheaper imports, leaving the

Table 13.1 Who owns England and Wales?

Landowner	% of England and Wales	Acres	Sq. km
Aristocracy	30%		
Companies and LLPs	18%		
'New money'	17%		
Public sector	8.5%		
Homeowners	5%		
Conservation charities	2%		
Crown	1.4%		
Church	0.5%		
Total of England and Wales	*82.4% known*	*37.3m*	*150,947*

[145] Withdrawal Agreement 2019, art. 132(2)(c). [146] Agriculture Act 2020, s. 1.
[147] Shrubsole, *Who Owns England?*, 267.
[148] Shrubsole, *Who Owns England?*, 299, respectively holding 140,124 acres, 77,975 acres and 68,927 acres. These are followed by two mining companies and then Severn Trent Water.

countryside to be used for recreation, or to grow over. This may not, however, be the reality as in 1986 New Zealand ceased to pay subsidies, and farming has fully survived and is thought to be more efficient.[149] But whatever one might predict, the management of private property on land has long since been driven, not by economic uncertainties of supply and demand, but by conscious political choice.

Second, owners of agricultural and forestry land are not required to get planning permission before developing land,[150] a fact that probably reflected political expediency more than principle. To some extent it is limited by the possibility to impose conditions in return for subsidies, though as we have seen these have not yet been meaningfully used.

Third, if people rent agricultural land, their tenancies have marginally greater rights than people in homes. The minimal notice period for a notice to quit is twelve months (not twenty-eight days), even if the contract states a shorter period.[151] If granted before 1995, agricultural tenants also have the right to not be evicted without a Tribunal's approval, where the landlord must show it is necessary for a list of reasons surrounding good land management.[152] The tenant may also pass the land to a successor.[153] There is a default right to a statutory rent review for farm business tenancies, but this can be excluded by contract,[154] making it somewhat pointless. A tenant also has a right to be compensated on termination for improvements to agricultural land made with the landlord's written consent.[155]

(iii) Public Land-Ownership

At least 9.9 per cent of UK land is known to be held publicly, by public-sector bodies and the Crown. Much of this land is leased or licensed out as farming land, although statistics are not transparent on how much. Another 2.5 per cent is held by the Church of England, the National Trust, the Royal Society for the Protection of Birds (RSPB) and Woodland Trust. These bodies, while private, tend to function less as privately interested groups because as charities they are bound by law to advance a 'public benefit'.[156]

The largest landholding public-sector body is the Forestry Commission, which holds 2,064,598 acres in the UK.[157] The Forestry Act 1967 requires that

149 E.g. D. N. Harris and A. N. Rae, 'Agricultural Policy Reform and Industry Adjustment in Australia and New Zealand', Paper Presented to International Agricultural Trade Research Consortium, 'Adjusting to Domestic and International Agricultural Policy Reform in Industrial Countries', Philadelphia (6–7 June 2004).

150 Town and Country Planning Act 1990, s. 55(2)(e) (next to exemptions for changes to building interiors, ones that do not materially affect exteriors, road works, sewer, pipe or cable works or Secretary of State orders).

151 Agricultural Holdings Act (AHA) 1986, s. 25 and Agricultural Tenancies Act (ATA) 1995, s. 6.

152 AHA 1986, s. 27. 153 AHA 1986, s. 34. 154 ATA 1995, s. 9.

155 ATA 1995, ss. 15–27.

156 Charities Act 2011, ss. 1–4. The Church Commissioners are registered as a charity.

157 Shrubsole, *Who Owns England?*, 297.

a chair and up to ten members govern the Commission, all appointed by Her Majesty, but having special knowledge in forestry, science and the timber trade.[158] Its 'general duty' is 'promoting the interests of forestry, the development of afforestation and the production and supply of timber and other forest products', with 'adequate reserves of growing trees'. This role is reminiscent of its establishment in 1919 to provide timber after shortages in World War One to prop up trenches. But it should also balance 'conservation and enhancement of natural beauty and the conservation of flora, fauna and geological or physiographical features of special interest'.[159] The Commission's role in stopping climate damage is not explicit, though it had been given a power to promote renewable electricity – that is, not from fossil fuels.[160] The Commission must 'have regard to the national interest in maintaining and expanding the forestry resources',[161] and that means buying and growing more trees. Anyone leased land by the Forestry Commission needs a licence to fell trees, and the Commission may both buy and sell land, and the Ministry may use compulsory-purchase powers except in relation to ancient monuments, parks, local councils, statutory undertakings (e.g. water), the post or National Trusts.[162] Aside from the Forestry Commission, the other largest public bodies are the Ministry of Defence (see Ch. 19), Highways England, Network Rail (Ch. 16), Cambridge and Oxford Colleges (Ch. 8), local councils and other central departments.

The Crown as a whole holds 532,568 acres of land and 545,378 on riverbeds and foreshores, much of which is becoming leased for windfarms (see Ch. 12). However, the Crown is composed of several entities. The Crown Estate Act 1961 determines use of the 'Crown Estate', a body that has up to eight commissioners appointed by Her Majesty (i.e. the Prime Minister).[163] It holds 330,000 acres. It is operated by the government, but is partly used to fund the monarchy.[164] Also belonging to the Crown, though notionally to the monarch personally (an uncomfortable position given its seizure by the king from 1066 onwards), are the estates of the Duchy of Cornwall, the Duchy of Lancaster and the Sandringham Estate. All, and especially the Crown Estate, are managed largely like commercial operations.[165]

Last, accounting for 1,010,812 acres, are three main conservation charities. The National Trust holds 614,000 acres. The RSPB holds 332,812 acres. The Woodland Trust holds 64,000 acres.[166]

[158] Forestry Act 1967, s. 2. [159] Forestry Act 1967, s. 1(2) and (3A).

[160] Forestry Act 1967, s. 7AA(3). Fossil fuels means coal, lignite, peat, natural gas, crude liquid petroleum, petroleum products, or any derived substance. This power referred to s. 1(2A), now repealed; but as it merely clarified what could be done in relation to the general duty, the Commission may plainly still promote renewables.

[161] Forestry Act 1967, s. 8A, inserted by the Forestry Act 1981, s. 4.

[162] Forestry Act 1967, ss. 39–41. [163] Crown Estate Act 1961, Sch. 1.

[164] Sovereign Grant Act 2011, ss. 1–6 (25% of revenue, raised from 15% by SI 2017/438, art. 2).

[165] Shrubsole, *Who Owns England?*, ch. 3. [166] Shrubsole, *Who Owns England?*, ch. 10.

(b) Water

Water governance differs between Scotland, Northern Ireland, Wales and England.

(i) Scotland, Northern Ireland and Wales

The Water Industry (Scotland) Act 2002 now constitutes the publicly owned Scottish Water. It has an eight- to thirteen-member board appointed by the Scottish ministers.[167] It is overseen by the Water Industry Commission for Scotland, whose function is 'promoting the interest of persons' who 'are connected to the public water supply system' or might be connected.[168] Although it is rightly said that the 'proper representation of the customer interest is a vital part of good governance', there is no right to vote for water-bill payers, but just a 'Customer Forum' that can make representations. This forum can also be ignored.[169]

Scottish Water holds water and sewer infrastructure, employs all its staff and has powers to do anything not inconsistent with its water and sewage management functions.[170] These are 'to promote the conservation and effective use of the water resources' and 'provide a supply of wholesome water' at 'a reasonable cost' throughout Scotland.[171] They are also 'to provide such public sewers' for 'effectually draining' all 'sewage, surface water and trade effluent' and providing treatment as necessary for 'dealing with the contents of its sewers', including building sewers, treatment or other work, but not anything 'which is not practicable at a reasonable cost'.[172]

In Northern Ireland, water has also remained public and is governed through the Water and Sewerage Services (Northern Ireland) Order 2006, itself passed through the devolution legislation as power sharing has stalled.[173] In Wales, Welsh Water (Dŵr Cymru) is a not-for-profit company limited by guarantee. After a privatised company, Hyder, faced insolvency, its assets were sold to Western Power Distribution, an electricity company, and again in 2001 to a group of people organised by its first chair, Lord Burns, who believed it should not be state-owned or private.

[167] Water Industry (Scotland) Act 2002, s. 20 and Sch. 3.

[168] Water Industry (Scotland) Act 2002, s. 1.

[169] Hendry, *Frameworks for Water Law Reform*, 104–5, and contrast 95, fn. 282.

[170] Water Industry (Scotland) Act 2002, ss. 21–5 and 70(2), referring to the Water (Scotland) Act 1980 and Sewerage (Scotland) Act 1968.

[171] Water (Scotland) Act 1980, ss. 1–4.

[172] Sewerage (Scotland) Act 1968, s. 1, and reasonable cost is determined by Scottish ministers by regulation.

[173] Northern Ireland Act 2000, Sch., para. 1. The Water Supplies and Sewerage Act (Northern Ireland) 1945, s. 4 still requires no new houses without proposals for 'supply of wholesome water'.

(ii) England

In England, the water industry was fully privatised following the Water Act 1989. Ten companies took over the assets from ten water authorities, and therefore held regional monopolies. It is unclear what credible justification there was for making water ownership private, where there is and can be no competition. Each company board is appointed by itself, with oversight from shareholders under the Companies Act 2006. Predictably, water companies seek to maximise dividends (see Table 13.2) and management pay at the expense of homeowners who drink and wash, farms that irrigate and businesses that use water. There is a Consumer Council for Water, appointed by the Secretary of State and the Welsh Assembly with powers to acquire and review information, publish it and investigate.[174] It does nothing to ensure

Table 13.2 Water companies, dividends and major shareholders, 2018

Company	Acres[i]	Yearly dividends, average 2007–16[ii]	Major shareholders in 2018[iii]
United Utilities	140,124	£266.3m	Lazard (8%), BlackRock (5%), Norges (3%), JK (2%), Vanguard (1%), Norway (1%), L&G (1%)
Yorkshire Water	68,927	£217.9m	Singapore (34%), Corsair (30%), Deutsche Bank (23%), NSW superannuation (13%)
Severn Trent	51,668	£244.2m	BlackRock (7%), Lazard (5%), L&G (4%), Vanguard (3%), Standard Life (3%) etc
Northumbrian	21,032	£180.8m	CK Hutchison (80%), Li Ka Shing (20%)
Anglian Water	17,607	£370.9m	Canadian Pension (33%), IFM investors (32%), Commonwealth Bank (20%)
Thames Water	15,987	£253.1m	OMERS (27%), USS (11%), UAE (10%), Kuwait (9%), BCIMC (9%), Hermes (9%), China (9%)
South West	15,816	£101.4m	Lazard (10%), Banque Pictet (6%), BlackRock (5%), Ameriprise (5%), AXA (5%)
Wessex Water	6,862	£111.8m	YTL Corp. (100%)
Southern Water	5,506	£66.7m	J. P. Morgan (40%), UBS (22%), Hermes (21%), MTAA (8%), CK Hutchison (5%)
Welsh Water	77,975	*None*	*None*
Scottish Water		*None*	*None*
Northern Ireland		*None*	*None*
Totals		**£1.8129bn**	CK Hutchison (7%), OMERS (6%), YTL (5%), Canada Pension (4%), Commonwealth Bank (4%)

[i] Shrubsole, *Who Owns England?*, 299–305, Table 4.
[ii] D. Hall and K. Bayliss, 'Bringing Water into Public Ownership: Costs and Benefits' (May 2017) 14, Table G.2.
[iii] 'Who Owns Your Water and How They'll Try to Keep It', *Corporate Watch* (18 December 2018).

[174] Water Industry Act 1998, ss. 27A–K and Sch. 3.

customers have voting rights in the council, let alone water companies. Despite being private, the law still recognises water companies as having a 'public' character, for instance under discrimination law or for public access to environmental information.[175]

Water companies are constrained by the rules set by the Water Services Regulation Authority, known as Ofwat. Ofwat has at least three members appointed by the Secretary of State.[176] It must co-operate with other government bodies.[177] Ofwat has a duty to 'protect the interests of consumers' but it is meant to fulfil this 'wherever appropriate by promoting effective competition'. It is also meant to ensure companies have 'reasonable returns on their capital'.[178] This underlines that water companies (as opposed to Ofwat) have no duty to protect their customers' interests, and that Ofwat's goals are the opposite of Scottish Water's duty to provide water at a reasonable cost.

One might argue that competition could arise in the process of licensing: Ofwat licenses water 'undertakers' to operate water and sewer services by contracts known as 'instruments of appointment' with any conditions it sees fit.[179] Licences may last twenty-five years, though they can be terminated upon ten years' notice. But plainly any competition is fictitious because once the water company has a licence, it will try everything it can to make money short of having its licence revoked. If it goes insolvent, Ofwat is left with the cost. The Water Act 2014 attempted to manufacture more 'competition' by requiring suppliers to access and pump water through other companies' pipes at a reasonable cost, hoping that then customers could 'choose' their company.[180] This followed growing public outrage at rising water bills.[181] In Scotland, it had been decided that enabling pipe access could pose a public health risk.[182] Of course, it has not worked. Unlike other markets, where there can be some product differentiation, or different ways of supplying goods and services, there is only one type of clean water, and one set of pipes. The idea of competition is, at best, a sodden dream of economic ideology.

Internationally, the water governance structure in England and Wales is unique in its degree of private capture. Of course, the fact that Ofwat exists shows there cannot be a functioning market, so why bother with privatisation when the outcomes are so poor? One of the better, more recent models abroad

[175] See *Griffin v South West Water Services* [1995] IRLR 15; *Fish Legal v Information Commissioner, United Utilities, Yorkshire Water and Southern Water* (2014) C-279/12.

[176] WIA 1991, s. 1A and Sch. 1A, para. 1. This was amended by the Water Act 2003.

[177] Water Act 2003, s. 52, referring to the Secretary of State, the National Assembly for Wales, the Environment Agency and the Natural Resources Body for Wales.

[178] WIA 1991, s. 2. [179] WIA 1991, s. 11.

[180] WIA 1991, ss. 66A–L. Slightly different, ss. 105A–C enable transfer of lateral drains and private sewers to water companies where they were draining to a public mains sewer and treatment works, to avoid deterioration. Water Industry (Schemes for Adoption of Private Sewers) Regulations SI 2011/1566.

[181] E.g. R. Graham, 'Water in the UK – Public Versus Private', *openDemocracy* (19 December 2014).

[182] Hendry, *Frameworks for Water Law Reform*, ch. 5, 81.

is that, since 2009, a new public water company for the city of Paris, *Eau de Paris*, has been set up. Unlike Scottish Water's appointments by ministers, this has a board of directors representing councillors, staff, customers and other experts appointed by the city.[183]

(c) International Agencies

In international law there are three main specialist agencies devoted to food, forestry and water. First, the UN Food and Agriculture Organization (FAO), established in 1945 and headquartered in Rome, along with the World Food Programme (WFP) established in 1961 after an FAO conference and a UN General Assembly resolution. The FAO's constitution confers the functions of research and data collection, recommending policy and co-ordination and giving governments technical assistance, in pursuit of its goals of 'raising the levels of nutrition and standards of living', improving 'distribution of all food and agricultural products' and 'freedom from hunger'.[184] The WFP has a budget for emergency food relief and, partly because of its work in Yemen against the Saudi dictator's policy of mass starvation, it was awarded the Nobel Peace Prize in 2020. Second, the International Fund for Agricultural Development, established in 1976 and also located in Rome, has a small fund that aims to improve agricultural production and nutrition.[185] This is, in essence, a micro-version of the CAP, but at nowhere near an adequate scale. Third, UN Water was established in 2003 in Geneva, again to do research and co-ordinate policies. However, these agencies have very limited resources, and negligible power compared to the vast leverage exercised by the World Bank and the IMF, both in lending money and imposing 'structural adjustment' conditions that affect the finance and governance of agriculture and water.

(4) Human Rights

Food and water are human rights, enshrined in international law[186] and in many countries' constitutions. These rights have been the topic of some of the most controversial litigation on social and economic rights,[187] though little has entered into UK or European law because food and water are not yet specified

[183] See 'Liberté, Égalité, and a Glass of Fizzy Water?', *WeOwnIt Blog* (31 August 2018).

[184] UN Food and Agriculture Organization Constitution (1945) Preamble and art. 1.

[185] Agreement Establishing the International Fund for Agricultural Development (1976) Preamble and art. 2.

[186] UDHR 1948, art. 25(1); ICESCR 1966, art. 11(1). The UN Committee on Economic, Social and Cultural Rights (2002) General Comment No. 15 says the right to water is implicit in the right to food. M. Ssenyonjo, *Economic, Social and Cultural Rights in International Law* (2016) 481–9.

[187] E.g. Constitution of the Republic of South Africa 1996, s. 27(1)(b); *Mazibuko v City of Johannesburg* [2009] ZACC 28.

in the European Convention or Charters.[188] They are guaranteed by statutory duties and institutions. Of course, food and water are essential for the right to life, but this right is invariably framed to stop people being 'intentionally' or 'arbitrarily deprived' of life.[189] Rights to food and water have not yet broken from the status of economic commodities: in national laws they are reduced to 'customer rights' because people have to pay for them, or rely on charity since government infrastructure is so threadbare. Three main rights can be grouped, as we see regulation for (a) fair prices, (b) good quality and (c) the right to be supplied with water, or at least not disconnected.

(a) Fair Food and Water Prices?

Despite agricultural subsidies and tariffs in agriculture, there is no statutory right to food, or to fair food prices. As Chapter 13(2) explained, subsidies benefit neither worker nor customer, rather the supermarkets with greater bargaining power. Food being too expensive is a relative problem: prices are higher than people can afford due to tariffs, and people's incomes are too low due to growing inequality, the lack of voice at work and cuts in social security (see Ch. 5).[190] From 2009 to 2018 the number of charitable food banks in the UK rose from 29 to over 2,000.[191] A single charity, the Trussell Trust, operates 1,200 of these, and while they may be essential if there is nothing else, their aims are not to eliminate themselves, but expand.[192] Charities may feel they provide people with redemption and even be hostile to social security as a rival system,[193] but consistent research shows 'the damage to people's dignity that using food banks causes'.[194] Food-bank funding comes mostly from voluntary donors, yet local councils (i.e. taxpayers) spent at least £3 million on food banks in 2014.[195] Supermarkets donate and profit most: simultaneously claiming they are reducing food waste, and giving to charity to improve their image, while maintaining unfair prices.[196] Food banks risk being a contractual arm of supermarket profit, as they extol their 'significant on-going relationships with

188 CFREU 2000, art. 36 'recognises and respects access to services of general economic interest' which, at the least, means network utilities including water.

189 ECHR 1950, art. 2; ICCPR 1966, art. 6; UDHR 1948, art. 3; CFREU 2000, art. 2.

190 E.g. Welfare Reform Act 2012.

191 S. Duffy and C. Gillberg, *Extreme Poverty in a Time of Austerity* (2018) 11–12.

192 Trussell Trust, *Report of the Trustees and Financial Statements* (2015) 5, with the aim to 'help the Christian faith community to take a more active, practical and effective role in social action' 7, refers to hunger later on.

193 'Funding for Food Banks' (15 April 2014) Public Sector Executive, quoting a Trussell Trust manager voicing hostility to working closely with councils lest they become a 'contractual arm of the welfare state', www.publicsectorexecutive.com/News/funding-for-food-banks/74961.

194 K. Garthwaite, 'It's Not the Hungry Who Gain Most from Food Banks – It's Big Business', *The Guardian* (25 March 2019).

195 'Councils Spending £3m on Food Poverty and Food Banks', *BBC News* (3 March 2014).

196 Garthwaite, 'It's Not the Hungry Who Gain Most from Food Banks'.

Tesco, Waitrose', Asda and others.[197] In 2017, it was estimated that replacing food banks and catering to a doubling of demand would cost just £68.7 million a year, removing all food insecurity would cost £4 billion a year and a full community food programme (of public canteens and food boxes of all basics to everyone) would cost £21.2 billion.[198] While price controls and food rationing were part of post-war policy, a full community food programme would be the opposite and shift food markets to luxury food and drink.

Water prices are limited by law, but not in a consistent or principled way. In Scotland, water services must be provided at a 'reasonable cost',[199] which is determined in regulations by Scottish ministers,[200] and this publicly determined price has kept costs 10 per cent lower than in England. By contrast, since the Water Act 1989, water bills have increased by 40 per cent in real terms, mostly in the years immediately after privatisation (see Figure 13.2).[201]

According to the more elaborate Water Industry Act 1991, Ofwat may set prices and supply conditions in the Instruments of Appointment, including

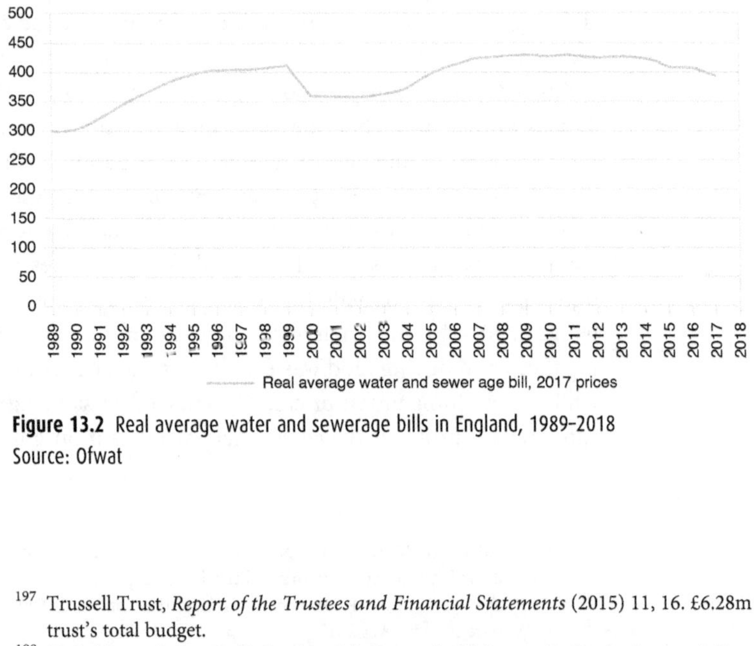

Figure 13.2 Real average water and sewerage bills in England, 1989–2018
Source: Ofwat

[197] Trussell Trust, *Report of the Trustees and Financial Statements* (2015) 11, 16. £6.28m was the trust's total budget.

[198] H. L. Moore, J. Portes, H. Reed and A. Percy, *Social Prosperity for the Future: A Proposal for Universal Basic Services* (2017) 44–5. The authors acknowledge that these estimates were extremely generous: it is possible that, when taking into account savings from altering farm subsidies, and production chains, the true sums may be far lower.

[199] Water (Scotland) Act 1980, s. 6(1); Sewerage (Scotland) Act 1968, s. 1(2).

[200] Provision of Water and Sewerage Services (Reasonable Cost) (Scotland) Regulations 2015/79, regs. 3–5 limit rises according to a statutory formula. Previously the Provision of Water and Sewerage Services (Reasonable Cost) (Scotland) Regulations 2006, regs. 4–5 limited rises to 3.75% each year.

[201] Ofwat and Defra (2006) 24, Figure 3.3.1b show average household water and sewer age bills rising from around £27 to £84 in 1974 prices, a 210% price increase.

prices for water.[202] These conditions can be modified by agreement, and Ofwat may request an investigation by the Competition and Markets Authority (CMA) that could also lead to recommendations for a change in conditions.[203] Ofwat and the CMA exercise concurrent competition law powers, to prevent collusion or abuse of a dominant position, and there is a duty to review any mergers over £10 million in turnover.[204] But given that competition is fictitious anyway, what really matters are price limits. Water companies are meant to produce a 'charging scheme' for the next year, but it does 'not take effect unless it has been approved by' Ofwat.[205] This will be affected by Ofwat's plan for upgrading waterworks and sewers, which it must report to the Secretary of State, along with detailed information on appointments and licences.[206] The theory was that prices would follow an increase formula of the Retail Price Index, minus efficiency savings, plus necessary capital costs ($RPI - X + K$).[207] If this equation were taken seriously, it would suggest the industry has become radically more inefficient. The reality is the regulator has mainly been concerned with maintaining a reasonable return for water companies, not fair prices. After all, this is what the law says: that the Secretary has a duty to 'secure that companies ... as relevant undertakers are able (in particular, by securing reasonable returns on their capital) to finance the proper carrying out of those functions'.[208] The priority of profits over service to people does not make sense.

(b) Quality of Food and Water

While fair price regulation may not exist, quality is more comprehensively regulated. Under the Food Standards Act 1999, the Food Standards Agency is appointed to 'protect public health' from risks in 'consumption of food' and 'protect the interests of consumers in relation to food'. It has eight to twelve members appointed by the Secretary of State and devolved administrations, who can also make requests that must be complied with as far as reasonably practicable.[209] It provides information and monitors enforcement which is carried out by local authorities, and (oddly) the appropriate Treasurer for the Inner and Middle Temple.[210] It is an offence to render any food 'injurious to health' with 'intent that it shall be sold for human consumption'.[211] It is also an offence to sell any food unfit for human consumption, and local authorities may ultimately close premises, where offences are committed, that are unsanitary.[212] Food labelling must be accurate, and ministers can make regulations for food labelling, marking or advertising, such as the ingredients

[202] WIA 1991, ss. 11–12. These are typically set for 5 years. [203] WIA 1991, ss. 13–17.
[204] WIA 1991, ss. 31–5. [205] WIA 1991, s. 143(6). [206] WIA 1991, ss. 192A–B, 201–2.
[207] Cf. J. Stern, 'What the Littlechild Report Actually Said', Regulation Initiative Working Paper No. 55 (2003).
[208] WIA 1991, s. 2(2A)(c). [209] Food Standards Act 1999, ss. 1-2.
[210] Food Safety Act 1980, s. 5.
[211] Food Safety Act 1980, s. 7; Food Safety Regulation (EC) No. 178/2002, art. 14.
[212] Food Act 1984, ss. 8 and 21.

list.[213] This has not yet been used to label the greenhouse gas emissions used in making products, or labour standards.

The duty to provide 'pure and wholesome' water was first created in 1875,[214] and the same language of 'wholesome' water remains today,[215] and is reflected in the Drinking Water Quality Directive 1998 which refers to water that is 'wholesome and clean'.[216] The Secretary of State has power to make regulations on what counts as wholesome or not,[217] while a court held that it means at least 'pleasant and fit to drink'.[218] If water company standards drop, then Ofwat must issue enforcement orders to uphold standards.[219] It may not merely accept undertakings.[220] There is also a Drinking Water Inspectorate which has powers to investigate water quality.[221] While drinking water is generally thought to be good, this has not kept up with the huge growth in microplastics now found to be in almost all drinking water. There are also standards for quality of bathing waters, enforced in a similar way.[222]

(c) Water Supply and Disconnections

As explained above, there is not yet a right to food or water. However, in the case of water there is a duty on water companies to provide connections to 'persons who demand' supply,[223] and to provide 'effectual drainage',[224] although in both cases water companies may require that connections are made at the customer's expense.[225] There is also a right to not be disconnected in cases of non-payment for anyone in a 'private dwelling-house', caravan or house boat, and a prohibition on water companies installing limiting devices.[226] This right was created in 1999, after privatisation (as water bills rose by 35 per cent) and experience of water companies shutting people off.[227] Instead, people who cannot pay and are classed as 'vulnerable' (e.g. on welfare,

213 Food Act 1984, ss. 6–7. 214 Public Health Act 1875, s. 55.

215 Water (Scotland) Act 1980, s. 6; WIA 1991, s. 68.

216 Drinking Water Quality Directive 98/83/EC, art. 4 defines this as free from micro-organisms and parasites dangerous to health, and compliant with chemical and biological standards in Annex I. See the Water Supply (Water Quality) Regulations 1989, SI 1989/1147.

217 WIA 1991, s. 67.

218 *McColl v Strathclyde RC* 1983 SC 225, successfully challenging water fluoridation.

219 WIA 1991, s. 18.

220 *Commission v United Kingdom* (1992) C-337/89, holding the UK system under WIA 1991, s. 19 of accepting undertakings from water companies (instead of s. 18 enforcement orders) inadequate to comply with EU law.

221 WIA 1991, s. 86.

222 Bathing Waters Directive 2006/7/EC. See *Commission v Spain* (2003) C-278/01 confirming fines of €624,150 a year and per 1% of bathing areas in Spanish inshore waters which were found unclean.

223 WIA 1991, s. 37. 224 WIA 1991, s. 94. 225 WIA 1991, ss. 45 and 99.

226 WIA 1991, s. 61(1A) and Sch. 4A, and s. 63A (limiting devices) from WIA 1999, ss. 1–2.

227 *R (Oldham MBC) v Director General of Water Services* (1998) 31 HLR 224 held automatic disconnection from water through a prepayment meter did not comply with the law. *R (Lancashire CC) v Director of Water Services* [1999] EnvLR 114 stopped disconnections or limiting devices.

with large families or medical conditions) may apply to be put on a different charging scheme based on the water company's average charges to other households.[228] This is far from real help, as companies can still get court judgments and send debt collectors. Inevitably, many companies simply accumulate bad debts and pass these costs onto other customers, damaging their credit rating. Finally, water companies are required to meet maximum response time for letters and phone calls, keep up adequate water pressure, restore supply of water in emergencies and prevent sewer flooding or provide compensation of up to £1,000.[229] On the whole people's satisfaction with water companies is not outstanding, and consistently among the top five in 2017 and 2018 is the non-profit Welsh Water.[230]

(5) Conclusion

Although food and water are essential for life, their finance and governance are very different. It has generally been accepted that full public ownership of land and farming is not desirable, although the model of subsidies has shifted dramatically since the post-war period. While farm subsidies used to guarantee a living wage for a vastly greater agricultural workforce, they have become unconnected in Europe and North America to this goal, and have the effect of entrenching rural poverty in developing countries. At the same time, there is no adequate coupling of subsidies to climate security and environmental goals. Water differs entirely, reflecting the natural monopoly of river and reservoir resources. Just 10 per cent of water companies around the world are privatised,[231] and these tend to be less efficient and more expensive,[232] and England and Wales are included in this. Privatisation has coincided with higher household bills, but increasing subsidies to business, as well as the disappearance of public water services, such as drinking fountains and toilets. Three options would be to link agricultural subsidies to the achievement of social and environmental goals, to de-privatise water and to give residents voice in the governance of their land and services.

[228] Water Industry (Charges) (Vulnerable Groups) (Consolidation) Regulations 2015, reg. 3.

[229] Water Supply and Sewerage Services (Customer Service Standards) Regulations 2008 (SI 2008/594), regs. 6–12.

[230] Consumer Council for Water, 'Satisfaction by Company' (2018).

[231] Hendry, *Frameworks for Water Law Reform*, ch. 5, 78, quoting P. Marin, *Public Private Partnerships for Urban Water Utilities: A Review of Experiences in Developing Countries* (2009), finding 7% of companies were privatised and suggesting even if this is too low, 15% would be a 'generous estimate'.

[232] D. Hall, E. Lobina and P. Terhorst, 'Re-municipalisation in the Early Twenty-First Century: Water in France and Energy in Germany' (2013) 27(2) *Int'l Rev Applied Economics* 193; J. Meek, 'Not a Drop to Drink' in *Private Island: Why Britain Belongs to Someone Else* (2014).

14

Housing and Construction

Contents

The idea that a person's home is their castle, that 'its roof may shake ... the storm may enter – the rain may enter – but the King of England cannot enter', has been in law for 500 years.[1] Yet for many, rights at home – and to a home – are insecure. Many cannot afford to buy homes. Of those who can, many spend their lives in debt to banks, paying off a mortgage. More and more people rent. Rents rise faster than wages, and house prices rise faster than people can save. Since 2010, more people in the UK live in temporary accommodation and more are homeless, on the streets, without shelter or anyone but charities to care. The UK population, like the world's, has steadily risen, and it is often said that neither the private nor public sector has supplied enough homes to keep pace. But the link between house prices and supply or demand is tenuous at best, as houses and flats are built but kept vacant. Vacant land is also held within property portfolios, without any construction, because land is a major target for speculative investment, epitomised by the bank crisis of 2007–8. Everyone has the human right to 'housing' and to 'respect for [their] private and family life, [and their] home'.[2] But the monetisation of housing, through rent, mortgages and financial asset trading, increases the insecurity that people face at home, in childhood, in adulthood and in old age.

[1] Chief Justice John Fineux, 'a man's house is his castle': 21 Hen. 7, YB fol. 39, case 50; *Semayne's case* (1604) 77 ER 194, per Sir Edward Coke; F. Thackeray, *A History of the Right Honorable William Pitt* (1827) vol. II, 29; *Southam v Smout* [1963] 1 QB 308, 320, per Lord Denning MR.

[2] UDHR 1948, art. 25; ICESCR 1966, art. 11 (housing); ECHR 1950, art. 8 (private life and home) and Prot. 1, art. 1 (property). Also CFREU 2000, arts. 7 and 34(3) ('the right to social and housing assistance').

There are at least two main, and irreconcilable, views of housing and construction. The first is that buildings, and the land underneath, should be treated like other assets. Land's supply may be fixed, but because we can build upwards, the market can expand. Supply and demand determine prices, and freedom from regulation, tenant rights, price standards or planning laws boosts investment.[3] The second view is that land is the original and natural monopoly,[4] and that the possession of property creates unequal bargaining power. Unequal power gives property owners the means to raise prices and hoard land or housing. This explains why 1 per cent of the population owns half of England, and all the homeowners hold just 5 per cent of the total country.[5] Rent and mortgages take a growing slice of people's income, benefiting banks, landlords and few (if any) other people. Rent-seeking subtracts investment in productive assets. Globally, 24 per cent of people live in slums.[6] The UN Sustainable Development Goals include 'access for all to adequate, safe and affordable housing'. But 'access' is not the universal 'right'. Buildings are also a major source of climate damage, through concrete and energy use, a problem markets have not solved. This makes the finance of building, how housing is run and the rights people have at home essential to understand.

(1) Historical Background

The development of urban life, the primary centres for housing and construction, began in ancient societies, just as the merits of 'property' were first discussed. In *The Republic*, Plato argued that the philosopher kings who ruled should not 'have a private house or store closed against any one', but that others might.[7] By contrast, Aristotle thought that it 'is clearly better that property should be private, but the use of it common', because he thought if 'everyone has a distinct interest, men will not complain of one another, and they will make more progress', while the role of legislation 'is to create in men [a] benevolent disposition' of pooling their property for common use.[8] Public buildings and spaces were always seen as an important part of planning. In ancient Rome, Vitruvius Pollio wrote that the power of Augustus's state was reflected 'with distinguished authority in its public buildings' and elaborated principles of architecture, street and town planning and the construction of everything from theatres to aqueducts and sundials.[9] This vast, planned

[3] E.g. R. A. Epstein, 'Rent Control and the Theory of Efficient Regulation' (1988) 54 *Brooklyn L Rev* 741; J. Burton, *Retail Rents, Fair and Free Market* (1992) 82–3, of the 'Adam Smith Research Trust', using Smith's name somewhat in vain.

[4] A. Smith, *An Inquiry into the Nature and Causes of the Wealth of Nations* (1776) Book I, chs. 6 and 11.

[5] G. Shrubsole, *Who Owns England?* (2019) ch. 10.

[6] UN Sustainable Development Goals 2015, Goal 11.

[7] Plato, *The Republic* (*c.* 350 BC) Book III, trans. D. Lee.

[8] Aristotle, *The Politics* (*c.* 300 BC) Book II, Part V.

[9] Vitruvius Pollio, *De architectura* (*c.* 10 BC) trans. M. H. Morgan (1914) Book V.

structure supported a population in the city of Rome probably numbering around 450,000, and up to a million people in the surrounding region.[10] Few ancient or medieval cities are thought to have reached this size or more, but they included Xi'an, Baghdad, Cairo and Constantinople. It was only in the Industrial Revolution that London reached well over 1 million souls, and then 2, and 4, and 6 and 7.4 million people by 1914. Then New York City reached 10 million in 1936, and Tokyo reached 20 million in 1975.[11] By 2007, over half the world's population had come to live in urban environments, with ever denser housing, and more rent.

The long prelude to London's urban and industrial revolution was the 'improvement' movement in agriculture (see Ch. 13(1)), where landlords disowned duties to tenants, and turfed out villages, mainly for sheep, sending a desperate populus searching for work in towns. An attempt was made after the Great Fire of 1666 to rebuild and plan London afresh.[12] Sir Christopher Wren rebuilt St Paul's and many of the church spires, but his plans for broad avenues and boulevards were largely left in suspense, and the winding streets in place, as they could not displace the twists and warrens of landowner property rights. Aside from the lucky few who had freehold land, most people rented. Adam Smith's *Wealth of Nations* explicitly targeted their exploitation, where labourers had to 'give up to the landlord a portion of what his labour either collects or produces'.[13] Rent of the land 'is naturally a monopoly price', and 'not at all proportioned to what the landlord may have laid out upon the improvement of the land, or to what he can afford to take; but to what the farmer [or dweller] can afford to give'.[14] This approach to rent, that landlords 'grow richer, as it were in their sleep, without working, risking, or economizing',[15] was largely followed in political economy, but precious few reforms followed soon. There was no right to rent housing that was even of habitable quality until 1885.[16] There was no restriction on building and invasive construction from neighbours,[17] except the barest threads of nuisance law.[18] By around 1870, England and Wales had become mostly urban, and the

[10] G. R. Storey, 'The Population of Ancient Rome' (1997) 1 *Antiquity* 966, 976.

[11] T. Chandler, *Four Thousand Years of Urban Growth: An Historical Census* (1987).

[12] Rebuilding of London Act 1666 and Rebuilding of London Act 1670. S. Pepys, *Diary* (6 September 1666).

[13] Smith, *The Wealth of Nations*, Book I, ch. 6.

[14] Smith, *The Wealth of Nations*, Book I, ch. 11. Similarly, see K. Marx, *Capital* (1894) vol. III, chs. 37–47. H. George, *Progress and Poverty* (1879).

[15] J. S. Mill, *Principles of Political Economy* (1848) Book V, ch. 2: 'What claim have they, on the general principle of social justice, to this accession of riches?'

[16] *Hart v Windsor* (1844) 152 ER 1114 (denied a right to habitable accommodation). Housing of the Working Classes Act 1885, s. 12 (implied condition of being fit for human habitation for working classes).

[17] *Tapling v Jones* (1865) 11 HLC 290 (complaints about factory next door overlooking a property), per Lord Cranworth: 'Every man . . . a right to use his own land by building on it as he thinks most to his interest.'

[18] *Sturges v Bridgman* (1879) LR 11 Ch D 852 (finding a nuisance from a sweet-maker disturbing a doctor).

Building Societies Act 1874 encouraged more mutually owned societies, allowing them to make loans via mortgage. But through the nineteenth century, 'almost all working-class housing was privately rented' and rents rose steadily, so that the average working-class family paid 16 per cent of income in rent, while the middle classes just 8–9 per cent of theirs.[19] Today, and for many, this may even appear low, although it was also a time when there were higher prices for food, and virtually no pensions, public education, healthcare or the basics of social welfare.

The late Victorian views of housing developed a kind of social conscience, but one deeply offensive to the people involved, and exculpating the landlords responsible. In 1885, in the Royal Commission on slums, it was asked, 'Is it the pig that makes the stye or the style that makes the pig?'[20] Even Octavia Hill, a pioneer of low-return housing who invented the 'Green Belt' concept and helped found the National Trust, argued that the so-called 'destructive classes' needed strong 'paternal supervision' as tenants.[21] Though she and others opposed municipal socialism and housing subsidies 'bitterly',[22] it was understood by Parliament in the Housing of the Working Classes Act 1890 that councils needed powers to build, and yet the compromise to the moralisers was that housing had to be sold within ten years. Only 20,000 homes were built, and yet this led public bodies to become 'the main suppliers of housing for the needy and largely usurped the role of charities and self-help organisations'.[23] In the Housing, Town Planning, etc. Act 1909, councils acquired powers to develop planning schemes, particularly targeting sanitary conditions, and in section 17 empowering inspectors to close down housing unfit for human habitation.[24] A trickle of public housing was not enough, however, to ensure prices were stable, instead of taking a larger portion of people's income. During World War One, the first controls were introduced to halt unfair increases of rent, for homes with rateable values under £35 in London, £30 in Scotland and £26 elsewhere,[25] followed by a long line of further measures.[26] At the war's end, David Lloyd George promised the returning veterans, and the people who had sacrificed so much, to 'make Britain a fit country for heroes to live in'. The 'homes fit for heroes' campaign was begun with the Housing, Town Planning, &c. Act 1919, enabling subsidies for house building, and leading to 213,800 homes being built.

[19] P. Balchin and M. Rhoden, *Housing Policy: An Introduction* (4th ed. 2002) 122; E. Gauldie, *Cruel Habitations: A History of Working-Class Housing 1780–1918* (1974).

[20] *Royal Commission on the Housing of the Working Classes* (1885) 14.

[21] *Royal Commission on the Housing of the Working Classes* (1885) paras. 9122–4.

[22] A. S. Wohl, 'Octavia Hill and the Homes of the London Poor' (1971) 10(2) *J Brit Studies* 105.

[23] Balchin and Rhoden, *Housing Policy*, 230.

[24] *Local Government Board v Arlidge* [1915] 1 AC 120. Viscount Haldane LC held the Local Government Board, to which a closure order was appealed, acted judicially, allowed a fair hearing and did not breach natural justice.

[25] Increase of Rent and Mortgage Interest (War Restrictions) Act 1915.

[26] Increase of Rent and Mortgage Interest (Restrictions) Act 1920.

While Parliament's support for fair rent regulation went back and forth,[27] a succession of further housing Acts meant that by 1939, the number of homes had risen from 8 million to 11.3 million.[28] As the space for housing expanded, to ensure that people also had access to nature, the Green Belt (London and Home Counties) Act 1938 legislated for designations of green space.

With the end of World War Two, and with much of London, Berlin, Moscow, Tokyo, Europe and Asia in ruins, the Universal Declaration of Human Rights 1948 enshrined the right to a 'standard of living adequate for ... housing' for everyone.[29] Through the New Towns Act 1946, and the Housing Act 1949, the post-war Labour government built 1 million homes, and this continued under the Conservative governments at a pace that 'crowded in' investment by private developers.[30] As this happened, fair rent regulation was restored up to the Rent Act 1977, which also protected the security that people had in their homes, not being evicted without reason, but calibrated to allow rent increases with housing repairs.[31] Without controls, rents rose, a fact that could hardly be explained by excesses of demand over supply, as the rate of *house* completions consistently outpaced population (see Figure 14.1).

Nevertheless, upon Margaret Thatcher's election, housing law became swiftly and almost entirely emptied of rights. First, the Housing Act 1980 aimed to eliminate most council homes by spreading the 'right to buy' at a cut price, while the Local Government, Planning and Land Act 1980 eliminated any duty on councils to build homes. Home ownership grew from 55% of the population in 1980 to 73.3% in 2008 but, as more people were wedded instead to mortgages, as rents and house prices escalated, home ownership fell back to 65% in 2019. Second, fair rent regulation was eliminated on most new homes with a new 'shorthold' status being introduced. Instead of focusing on a fair balance between rent prices and investment in improving housing, it appeared that the main focus became for landlords 'to secure a reasonable rate of return on their

[27] Increase of Rent and Mortgage Interest (Restrictions) Act 1923, Rent and Mortgage Interest Restrictions (Amendment) Act 1933, Increase of Rent and Mortgage Interest (Restrictions) Act 1938, reducing controls, so that from 1923, 4.5m dwellings were decontrolled, leaving 4m still controlled: Balchin and Rhoden, *Housing Policy*, 128. The Rent Act 1939 controlled rents below £100 in London, £90 in Scotland and £75 elsewhere.

[28] E.g. Housing (Financial Provisions) Act 1924, Housing Act (HA) 1930, HA 1935, HA 1936, etc.

[29] UDHR 1948, art. 25; ICESCR 1966, art. 11 (housing).

[30] E.g. Housing (Temporary Accommodation) Act 1944; New Towns Act 1946, ss. 1 and 8 (designating sites and housing plans); HA 1949 (raising grants for individuals and subsidies to councils); Housing Repairs and Rent Act 1954 (extending assistance, and grants to 50% of repair cost, allowing rent rises after repair); HA 1957; House Purchase and Housing Act 1959; Housing Subsidies Act 1967; HA 1969; HA 1971; and Housing Finance Act 1972.

[31] E.g. Rent Act 1957 (reducing controls to release 5m properties to the market, and rising problem of landlords harassing tenants to leave), Rent Act 1965 (increasing regulation, rent officer decides 'fair rent'), Rent (Control of Increases) Act 1969 (rent officer has powers to increase rent monitoring), and Furnished Lettings (Rent Allowances) Act 1973.

Figure 14.1 Population growth and cumulative house completions, 1949–2019
Source: ONS, Population Statistics and House Building Completions

investment',[32] even though there were increasingly few duties on landlords to invest. This contrasted with other countries where fair rent regulation continued and worked.[33] Third, with the rise of 'shorthold' status, few could be assured of security of tenure aside from their contracts, which could often last as little as six months, before the threat of eviction and rent rises. Growing numbers of homeless people or people in precarious, overpriced accommodation meant that, by 2016, people in London spent nearly 50 per cent of their income on rent, and 27 per cent of their income across the UK.[34]

(2) Finance

The finance of housing and construction is a volatile market, as it monetises a basic social right. The three main kinds of finance are for (a) building, (b) renting and (c) buying. The law has not yet created a right to a freehold home, funded by tax.[35] In the 2018 autumn budget, £32 billion was allocated to 'housing and the environment', and most of this was housing benefit (around £22 billion) that goes mainly to landlords.

[32] Department of the Environment, 'Finance for Housing Associations: The Government's Proposals', Paper Reference DEP 3206 (1987) para. 3.16.

[33] H. Lind, 'Rent Regulation: A Conceptual and Comparative Analysis' (2001) 1(1) *Int'l J Housing Policy* 41; R. Arnott, 'Time for Revisionism on Rent Control?' (1995) 9(1) *J Economic Perspectives* 99.

[34] K. Peachey and D. Palumbo, 'How Much of Your Salary Is Spent on Rent?', *BBC News* (1 December 2017).

[35] Historically, colonisation in the USA, Australia or South Africa, did this, promising supposedly 'vacant' land that was forcibly taken by murder and genocide of the indigenous population. In Australia, see K. Grenville, *The Secret River* (2005) for a fictionalised history.

(a) Building, Construction and Developers

The house building and construction sectors have historically been carried out, if not entirely financed, by private enterprise. In the UK, house builders tend to be specialised, and general construction companies build commercial space, offices, schools, hospitals or other infrastructure. They are financed by the expected profits on rents or sales, often protected in contracts procured from government. Tables 14.1 and 14.2 list the top ten house and construction firms.

The top builders are constituted under the Companies Act 2006, and almost all are subject to the UK Corporate Governance Code. This means directors generally appoint themselves (see Ch. 3), and asset managers who dominate shareholder rights may dismiss directors (Ch. 4). The resulting culture favours maximising 'shareholder value', except as constrained by contract, planning or environmental laws. For example, one of the largest construction companies, Carillion plc, collapsed into liquidation in 2018, leaving unfinished schools, hospitals, roads, defence housing and major pension liabilities. A Select Committee reported Carillion was driven by a 'relentless dash for cash', and it 'presented accounts that misrepresented the reality of the business, and

Table 14.1 House builders, by number of houses sold

	Company	House sales	Average price	Revenue 2019
1	Barratt Developments plc	17,500	£288,000	£4,763m
2	Persimmon plc	16,400	£215,000	£3,649m
3	Taylor Wimpey plc	14,900	£263,000	£4,341m
4	Bellway plc	10,300	£284,000	£3,213m
5	Redrow plc	5,718	£332,000	£2,112m
6	Countryside plc	4,295	£252,000	£1,237m
7	Galliford Try plc	4,193	£235,000	£2,713m
8	Vistry plc (before: Bovis)	3,759	£273,000	£1,130m
9	Berkeley Group plc	3,678	£725,000	£2,957m
10	Crest Nicholson plc	3,020	£393,000	£1,086m

Table 14.2 Construction companies, by revenue

	Company	Revenue 2018		Company	Revenue 2018
1	Balfour Beatty plc	£8,234m	6	Amey UK plc	£2,581m
2	Kier Group plc	£4,282m	7	Keller Group plc	£2,070m
3	Interserve plc	£3,250m	8	Mace Ltd	£2,036m
4	Galliford Try plc	£2,820m	9	Laing O'Rourke plc	£2,034m
5	Morgan Sindall plc	£2,793m	10	Skanska plc	£1,802m

increased its dividend every year, come what may'.[36] Though concentrated at the top, the construction industry is also 'disorganised' and dispersed across thousands of medium and small businesses, with a highly casualised workforce.

After World War Two, house building was carried out for the benefit of both the private and the public housing sectors, and in particular homes were built that continued in council ownership and management. However, from 1979, the Thatcher, Major, Blair, Cameron and other governments brought new public housing mostly to an end.

As Figure 14.2 shows, the number of houses built each year has roughly halved since councils were stopped from building. However, the private sector and housing associations, which are loosely non-profit, still receive at least five types of finance from government.

First, as well as raising investment from equity or debt markets, house building and construction companies benefit from government and local council contracts. For example, in the 2018 autumn budget, of the £32 billion (3.8 per cent) allocated for the following year in housing spending, £1.215 billion was in affordable housing, £1.165 billion in a 'Housing Infrastructure Fund' and £1.235 billion from removing a cap on local authority borrowing to build. The government's aim was to reach 300,000 houses built a year by 2022.[37] Homes England, first established in 2008, has a statutory object to 'improve the supply and quality of housing in England', regenerating land and communities sustainably.[38] The Secretary of State also has broad

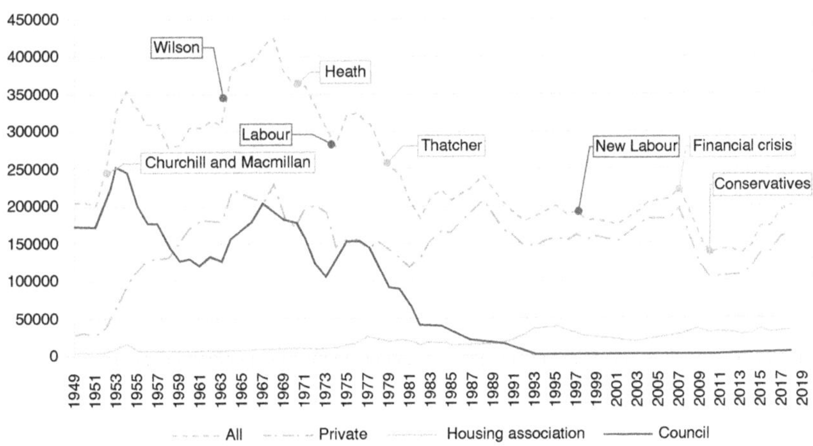

Figure 14.2 House building in the UK, 1949–2019
Source: ONS, UK House Building: Permanent Dwellings Completed by Sector, Table 3a

[36] HC DBEIS and DWP Committee, *Carillion*, HC 769 (16 May 2018) 3.

[37] HM Treasury, *Autumn Budget* (2018) 4, 37 (but cap at £385m in 2019, £850–5m in 2020–1), 54, 62–4.

[38] Housing and Regeneration Act 2008, ss. 1–2, before the Homes and Communities Agency and Housing Corp.

power to 'give financial assistance for regeneration and development', by building, 'providing employment for local people' or creating 'educational facilities or health services'.[39] Like the private finance initiative in health,[40] central government or councils contract with private developers for building.

Second, though numbers have been low, and borrowing powers were constrained, since 2008 councils may build social housing without the previous duty they had: to show it is better to keep property public than be in the private sector.[41] For example, Southwark Borough Council in London stated in 2015 that it planned to build 11,000 new council homes by 2043 (that is, 290 homes a year). An indication of the gap between practice and need is that in 2020 Southwark had 10,000 people on a council house waiting list, and 2,000 lived in temporary housing.[42]

Third, housing and construction companies receive financial benefits by being given planning permission from councils or government, because changes in permitted land use can raise land's sale price. Such profits are also a way for councils to raise revenue: it was estimated in 2008 that councils raised £4.9 billion from planning commitments.[43] Under the Town and Country Planning Act 1990, section 106, councils can give planning permission to private developers on conditions, 'either indefinitely or for such a period as may be specified'.[44] This may also include commitments that houses rented, sold or resold remain 'affordable'. There is no legal meaning of what is 'affordable', which leads to widely varying definitions, as well as bargaining by developers to drop affordability commitments (e.g. to sell homes at 80 per cent of market price) when they encounter overruns in the cost of building.[45] The obvious solution is not to base affordability on market prices, as these have an arbitrary relation to what people can afford. A test of 'affordable' could be that rent or mortgage payments are 25 per cent of people's income. Less is affordable for more people if inequality grows.

Fourth, building could be financed by compulsory purchase of land at a fair value. By the Acquisition of Land Act 1981, section 2, a government minister may compulsorily purchase land by order, after drafting the map and publishing the notice of the order in a local newspaper.[46] The amount of

[39] Housing Grants, Construction and Regeneration Act 1996, s. 126.

[40] NHS (Private Finance) Act 1997, s. 1 enabled trusts 'to enter into externally financed development agreements', certified by the Secretary of State.

[41] Cf. Local Government and Housing Act 1989, s. 80B. Councils could build new social homes 'only where [the council] offers better value for money than other options'. Repealed in Housing (Wales) Act 2014, s. 131.

[42] *Southwark Housing Strategy 2020 Consultation draft* (2020) 2.

[43] Department for Communities and Local Government, *Section 106 Planning Obligations in England, 2011–12* (May 2014) 1.

[44] Town and Country Planning Act (TCPA) 1990, s. 106.

[45] W. Wilson and C. Barton, 'What Is Affordable Housing?', HC Briefing Paper No. 07747 (23 December 2019).

[46] Acquisition of Land Act 1981, s. 2 and Sch. 1. Also Compulsory Purchase Act 2004, s. 44 for national infrastructure projects.

compensation should be 'the amount which the land if sold in the open market by a willing seller might be expected to realise', disregarding any rise in land value from the scheme the authority will later carry out. This wide definition is generous to landowners, as the idea of an 'open market' is more theoretical than real, and the unequal bargaining power of landowners (flowing from their very possession of property) artificially raises prices beyond a fair value based on the land's use.[47] Under the Land Compensation Act 1961, if compensation is disputed, it is set by the Upper Tribunal.[48] If someone refuses to convey the land, the acquiring authority pays money into court, the land 'shall vest absolutely' and the authority is 'entitled to immediate possession'.[49] Though a minister can carry out compulsory purchases, local authorities can only do so if 'authorised ... by the Secretary of State', and must show the power is needed for 'economic', 'social' or 'environmental well-being of their area'.[50] Where compulsory purchase powers are used to buy land, only to be then given to private developers, the Supreme Court has emphasised that a 'stricter approach is ... called for' than where the land will be held publicly. The rationale for compulsory purchase is to advance the public interest. So, if land is to be transferred to a private company, but a council claims this will improve the community, then as Lord Walker put it, a 'real, rather than a fanciful or remote, connection' must be shown 'between the off-site benefits and the proposed redevelopment'.[51]

Fifth, as buildings release greenhouse gases, the construction companies that make and profit from buildings receive a regulatory subsidy, as they do not pay for climate damage. In particular, buildings made with gas boilers, or inadequate insulation that leads to excessive energy use (assuming the electricity grid still runs from fossil fuels), or the use of concrete that relies on fossil fuels, all mean that the building industry is being subsidised by the future costs of the ecosphere's degradation. Building standards are discussed below at Ch. 14(3)(a).

(b) Renting and Housing Benefits

Once houses or other buildings have been built, they can either be rented out or sold. At both stages there are further subsidies that finance housing enterprises. These tend to benefit landlords and banks, not home dwellers. First, renting businesses get tax exemptions if financed through 'Real Estate Investment Trusts' (REITs). Following models in the USA, the Corporation

[47] Cf, ECHR 1950, Prot. 1, art. 1, where case law reads into compulsory purchase as requiring compensation at a fair value.

[48] Land Compensation Act 1961, ss. 1, 5(2) and 6A. [49] Compulsory Purchase Act 1965, s. 9.

[50] TCPA 1990, s. 226. Local Government Act 1972, ss. 120–1, councils need minister approval for compulsory purchase.

[51] *R (Sainsbury's Supermarkets Ltd) v Wolverhampton CC* [2010] UKSC 20, [84], Sainsbury's objecting to land compulsorily acquired to be developed by Tesco.

Tax Act 2010 states that a 'property rental business' with 'at least 3 properties' where 'no single property represents more than 40% of the total value' can be a REIT, typically organised as an open-ended investment company, or run by an institutional investor.[52] REITs are exempt from paying corporation tax and capital gains tax.[53] The justification for this is to create more investment in housing. Evidence to support this justification does not exist. REITs do however enable tax-free speculation on home dwellers paying income. When the UK introduced REITs in 2006, the German government decided not to follow, as it thought REITs would lead to house price inflation.[54] UK REITs have made especially high profits from student housing.[55]

Second, landlords who rent out property are financed by the inherent inequality of bargaining power against their tenants. Because tenants need homes more than landlords need tenants, prices will often be raised to the limits, because (in absence of a tax) landlords can choose to keep properties vacant. Since 1996, UK banks offered 'buy to let' mortgages, available to people who already owned homes, but wished to buy more houses purely to rent out and earn more income from tenants. In this way, the rent a tenant pays discharges the landlord's mortgage, while the tenant gains no equitable proprietary interest in their home. The main difference between the landlord and the tenant is that the landlord is already wealthy enough to be given a loan by a bank. This can enable highly profitable business. For example, one 'buy to let' business claimed it made 1,200 per cent returns between 1996 and 2014.[56] In 2012, Camden Borough Council began charging 50 per cent additional council tax for homes left empty for two years, leading to a 40 per cent drop in vacant homes by 2015.[57] In 2016, an additional 3 per cent stamp duty land tax surcharge was introduced for the transaction when buying an additional property. These measures, however, do little to outweigh the tax subsidies that finance REITs or the general profitability of a rental market without fair price regulation (see Ch. 14(4)(a)(i)).

Third, tenants who rent mainly pay through the income they have from work, and, if their incomes rise, landlords have a bargaining position to take a growing share. In 2018, private renters spent an average of 32.9% of income on rent, social tenants spent 28% and most mortgagees spent 10–20% or less.[58]

52 Corporation Tax Act 2010, ss. 528–9. Otherwise, under the Trustee Act 2000, s. 8, trustees can invest in real estate.

53 Corporation Tax Act 2010, ss. 518 and 534–5.

54 A. O'Sullivan, 'Residential Shut Out Fears for UK Reits Played Down after German Move', *CityWire* (2006).

55 E.g. P. Collinson, 'Investors' Huge Profits on Student Housing Are an Academic Failure', *The Guardian* (4 September 2019).

56 E. Dunkley, 'Buy-to-Let Market in UK Is No Easy Street', *Financial Times* (29 April 2014).

57 'Council Tax on Second and Empty Homes in Camden to Rise', *BBC News* (7 December 2012). E. Cumming, '"It's Like a Ghost Town": Lights Go Out as Foreign Owners Desert London Homes', *The Guardian* (2015).

58 MHCLG, *English Housing Survey, Social Rented Sector 2017–18* (July 2019) Tables 2.14 and 2.15; *Home Ownership* (2019) Table 2.1.

Landlords often demand that tenants provide pay slips, not only to ascertain ability to pay rent, but also to know if they can demand that a tenant pays more.[59] For people who are unemployed, or low paid, the Social Security Contributions and Benefits Act 1992, section 130 makes 'housing benefit' available. This is for people with 'no income' or insufficient income, but is capped at an 'appropriate maximum' determined by a 'rent officer'.[60] Rent officers have broad discretion to determine whether rents are 'significantly higher than the rent which the landlord might reasonably have been expected to obtain', yet this operates as a restriction on the tenant's right to a home, not the landlord's taking income.[61] Local authorities also have power to pay assistance to people on housing benefit at their discretion.[62] The guiding theory of housing benefits has been less to ensure that people can afford a home, but rather to enable landlords – in the UK government's words in 1987 – 'to secure a reasonable rate of return on their investment'.[63] Spending on housing benefits rose from £3.8 billion in 1986/7 to £11.7 billion in 1999/2000, and to £22 billion in 2018/19.[64] Without fair rent regulation, the primary function of housing benefit is to finance super-inflationary landlord profit.[65]

(c) Buying and Mortgage Finance

If people who hold houses do not rent, or keep property vacant, they may sell. As a share price classically follows predictions of dividends that can be declared, house prices follow predictions of the rents that could be demanded. If rents can escalate, house prices will escalate. People will need to pay more, or borrow more from a bank, to afford a home.

Three main types of finance are available to buy homes. First, the law has created different forms of the 'right to buy' houses from landlords. At one time, the Leasehold Reform Act 1967 created a limited right to buy rented property from a private landlord, if in the tenancy for over two years.[66] However, this general right to buy was abolished, and from 1980 there was, in effect, only a right to buy from public landlords, particularly council homes that had been designed to keep affordable homes available, and keep homes outside the markets that are shaped by private landlord power. Under the Housing Act

59 Cf. R. Clancy, *PropertyWire* (19 September 2017).
60 Social Security Contributions and Benefits Act 1992, ss. 130–130A.
61 Rent Officers (Housing Benefit Functions) Order 1997/1984, art. 3, Sch. I, para. 1. Cf. *R (Heffernan) v The Rent Service* [2008] UKHL 58 (holding the whole of Sheffield could not be a locality, reversed by SI 2008/3156).
62 Discretionary Financial Assistance Regulations 2001/1167.
63 Department of the Environment, 'Finance for Housing Associations', para. 3.16.
64 Cf. Balchin and Rhoden, *Housing Policy*, 100.
65 Cf. P. Johnson, 'Doubling of the Housing Benefit Bill Is Sign of Something deeply Wrong', *IFS* (4 March 2019).
66 Leasehold Reform Act 1967, ss. 1–3; and see *James v United Kingdom* (1986) 8 EHRR 123, holding this right to buy from private landlords did not breach the right to property in ECHR, Prot. 1, art. 1. More recently, *Sequent Nominees Ltd v Hautford Ltd* [2019] UKSC 47.

1985, section 126 a qualifying tenant is entitled to buy the freehold or have a long lease at a discount. The discount – which reflects that the tenant has paid rent for a number of years – goes up to 60 per cent for houses and 70 per cent for flats. But if the new homeowner sells the house on within five years, they must repay the discount.[67] A qualifying tenant is a 'secure tenant',[68] and it only applies to public, not private landlords (see Ch. 14(4)(a)(ii)). The right to buy policy has privatised 2.4 million homes (see Figure 14.3).

Second, people can finance purchases by applying to a bank for a mortgage. In 2020, banks generally lend people four to five times their income, although these borrowing margins have changed: before the global financial crisis mortgages at ten times salaries were offered.[69] A mortgage begins as a contract that entitles the lender, typically a bank or building society, to enter a charge on the property register and take possession of the secured property if the contract terms are not fulfilled, typically by failing to repay debts.[70] This property right – the charge by way of legal mortgage – grants the lender priority over the borrower or his or her creditors in insolvency. It is created through a deed and registration.[71] The reason that contractual debts

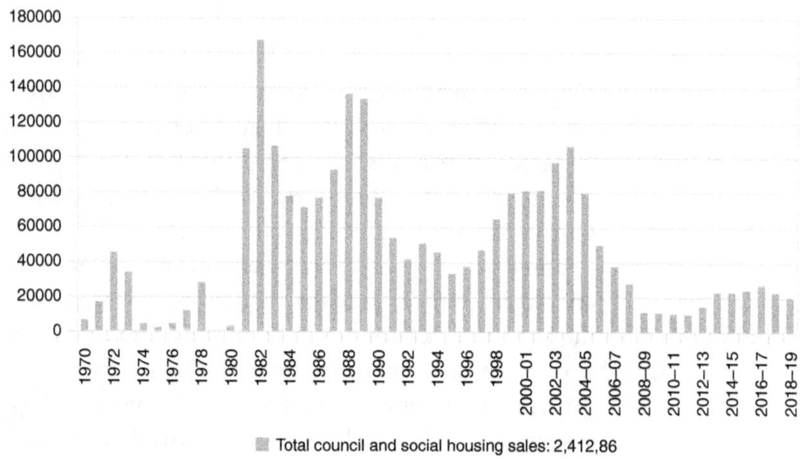

Figure 14.3 Council and social housing sales in Great Britain, 1970–2019
Sources: P. Balchin and M. Rhoden, *Housing Policy: An Introduction* (4th ed. 2002) Tables 8.1 and 8.5 (1970–98); ONS, Table 678: 'Annual Social Housing Sales by Scheme for England'; Scottish Government, Housing Statistics: 'Sales of Social Sector Housing' (1999–2019)

[67] HA 1985, ss. 126, 129 and 155(2). [68] HA 1985, ss. 118–19.
[69] E.g. C. Francis, 'Borrowers Offered 10 Times Salary', *The Times* (15 April 2007).
[70] Administration of Justice Act 1970, s. 36: a court can stop possession proceedings if the 'mortgagor is likely to be able within a reasonable period to pay any sums due under the mortgage'.
[71] Law of Property Act 1925, s. 85 (mortgage needs a deed); Law of Property (Miscellaneous Provisions) Act 1989, s. 1 (deed); Land Registration Act 2002, ss. 23–7 (charge effective with notice at Land Registry).

for home loans are usually secured is that lenders have the bargaining power to demand absolute priority, or they will not advance credit. As rents, and then housing prices, escalate, so too do the size of bank loans, and the total number of years of interest rate payments that banks receive. Far from a 'property-owning democracy', the monetisation of homes means the UK is 'a real-property-mortgaged-to-a-building-society-[or-bank]-owning, democracy';[72] a country of renters and rentiers. While mortgages seem to be a source of finance to buy homes, they also operate as a source of finance to banks from homebuyers (see further, Ch. 10(2)).

A third source of finance to buy homes can be subsidies or tax exemptions. From 1983 to 2000, mortgage interest tax relief was given to homebuyers, and disproportionately benefited the wealthiest home owners rather than those on lower incomes.[73] Landlords were also able to deduct interest payments from their tax bill as an expense of business, meaning that their loans were effectively free, enabling greater accumulation of property. This was not available for people who simply used a home to live: for example, there is no right to deduct rent and housing costs from income tax. For first-time buyers, a considerably less generous 'help to buy' scheme gives a loan of up to 20 per cent of a house price, or 40 per cent in London for homes costing up to £600,000.[74] Again, without rent regulation, and due to inequality of bargaining power, help-to-buy assistance partly finances homebuyers, but many of the benefits will end up flowing to house traders and banks.

(3) Governance

The governance of housing and construction differs between (a) builders and developers, (b) the landlord relation and rented market and (c) home ownership. The governance relations, which fix decision power over real property, usually emerge through a web of contracts and regulatory standards.

(a) Builders and Developers

As noted at Chapter 14(2)(a), house builders and general construction companies are formed under company law, and typically seek to maximise shareholder value. There are no specific regulations for building companies as such; however, their governance is shaped in the public interest in two main ways: by planning law and building or environment standards.

First, the Town and Country Planning Act 1990, section 58 hands the default power to grant or refuse planning permission to local authorities, the Secretary of State, or other statutory developing agencies. In section 55,

[72] *Pettitt v Pettitt* [1970] AC 777, 829, per Lord Diplock.

[73] Balchin and Rhoden, *Housing Policy*, 100.

[74] See www.helptobuy.gov.uk/equity-loan/equity-loans/.

'development' means 'building, engineering, mining or other operations in, on, over or under land' or making 'any material change in the use of any buildings', such as demolition or structural alterations.[75] Existing land uses are divided into classes, where material changes are taken to mean changing use of land from one class to another.[76] Exempt changes include those that 'affect only the interior of the building' or 'do not materially affect the external appearance'; work for roads and water; or 'the use of any land for . . . agriculture or forestry'.[77] There are also block exemptions.[78] Without an exemption, 'planning permission is required for . . . any development of land'.[79] Through the planning system, it is therefore established that democratic decision-making supersedes purely private decisions, without regard to the interests of the local community. Beyond individual planning decisions, the New Towns Act 1981 enables the Secretary of State in consultation with local authorities to designate areas for new towns and designate a 'development corporation' for this. It must aim for 'sustainable development', 'good design' and 'provide water, electricity, gas, sewerage and other services'.[80] For all planning, local authorities should have and comply with a 'statement of community involvement' for planning decisions,[81] but the main form of involvement is ultimately voting in elections.

Second, the Building Act 1984, section 1 enables the Secretary of State to make regulations including for conserving fuel or power; stopping waste; or enhancing the environment on 'the design and construction of buildings', demolition or 'services, fittings and equipment'.[82] Following this, the Building Regulations 2010 crucially require energy performance ratings for buildings. Where 'a new building is erected it must be a nearly-zero energy building' with energy 'to a very significant extent by energy from renewable sources' including 'produced on-site or nearby'.[83] While the Secretary of State approves the 'methodology' to decide what this means,[84] it does not yet list obvious requirements to stop greenhouse gas emissions: full insulation, electric (and no gas) heating, solar panels, batteries, bicycle facilities, electric vehicle charging points in any parking spaces and minimising concrete or unsustainable building materials. This said, local councils can generally refuse any planning permission wherever buildings are not made to the standards it wants, whether that is zero emissions, negative emissions or 'every building a power station'.[85] It is also possible for the Secretary of State to write regulations on the energy performance of privately rented properties, refuse to allow lettings until obligations are complied with[86] and create rights for tenants to

[75] TCPA 1990, s. 55(1)–(1A). [76] Town and Country Planning (Use Classes) Order 1987.
[77] TCPA 1990, s. 55(2).
[78] Town and Country Planning (General Permitted Development) Order 1995.
[79] TCPA 1990, s. 57. [80] New Towns Act 1981, ss. 1 and 4.
[81] Planning and Compulsory Purchase Act 2004, s. 18. [82] Building Act 1984, s. 1(1)–(1A).
[83] Building Regulations 2010 (SI 2020/2214) regs. 22, 24, 25B and 35 and Sch. 1, para. 1, Part L.
[84] Cf. Energy Performance of Buildings Directive 2010/31/EU, arts. 4–11.
[85] A. Pettifor, *The Case for a Green New Deal* (2019). [86] Energy Act 2011, ss. 42–6.

improvements. No widespread use of these powers has yet been undertaken and, given their complexity and precariousness in tenants' rights, they lack enforcement.[87]

(b) Landlords, Estate Agents and Tenants

The governance of the landlord-and-tenant relationship, often through estate agents, is based on a mixture of contract and weak property or other rights (below Ch. 14(4)). The types of landlords are many, disorganised and follow few standards compared to more successful housing systems. In 2018, there were around 2 million private landlords in the UK, with 4.7 million properties. Around 20 per cent of the UK population rented, compared to 12 per cent in 2007.[88] There are also public and social landlords who have extra duties, where tenants have some extra rights (see Ch. 14(4)(a)) and without estate agents as intermediaries. This is preferable from the tenants' viewpoint, although the lack of autonomy over property improvement may be inhibiting.

As explained in Chapter 14(2)(b), more and more private landlords are organised around REITs, as they are exempt from capital gains or corporation tax. REITs are typically organised as open-ended investment companies and have an ordinary board and shareholder structure. Otherwise, landlord businesses often operate as companies limited by shares. For example, the Grosvenor Group Ltd runs the properties in much of Mayfair and Belgravia. Shares are owned by the Grosvenor family which has inherited land in central London since it was seized after the Norman invasion of 1066. Most landlords, however, are individuals that subcontract estate agents to manage and extract rent from tenants.

Estate agents often operate through limited companies, and are regulated loosely under the Estate Agents Act 1979. They do not need licences, but can be prohibited by a 'lead enforcement authority', such as the National Trading Standards Estate, or a council,[89] for fraud, dishonesty, violence, discrimination or other offences and undesirable conduct designated by the Secretary of State.[90] Estate agents conduct the marketing operations for selling houses and, for renting, often perform both marketing and management functions. They typically charge percentage fees for rent and housing, meaning the business is driven by high-powered personal incentives to raise prices as much as possible.

Since its founding in 2008, practically the world's biggest estate agent has become AirBnB, a California-based corporation. Although it claims it is merely

[87] See the Energy Efficiency (Private Rented Property) (England and Wales) Regulations 2015.

[88] E. Harvey, 'Proportion of UK Renters Has Doubled in 20 Years – and Here's Why', *BuyAssociation* (13 July 2018), based on the English Housing Survey.

[89] E.g. *Littlewood v Powys County Council* [2018] CTLC 293, one of relatively few cases.

[90] Estate Agents Act 1979, ss. 3 and 24A.

an app, and an information society service under European Union (EU) law,[91] AirBnB takes fees from customers for short-to-long stays in apartments or houses through its web platform. Because AirBnB takes percentage fees, it is indistinguishable from a landlord, jointly with the homeowner. This is similar to an employment agency, which is best understood as a joint employer with an end-user (see Ch. 5(4)(a)). It encourages higher prices, and it has been found that it contributes to raising overall rents and house prices in large cities.[92] In short stays for holidays, AirBnB customers will typically only have a 'licence' rather than a lease, although AirBnB functions identically to an estate agent where people use its platform to access a main home.

(c) Home Ownership

The third main 'governance' structure is home ownership, primarily through freehold. The individual nature of property means there is not so much organisation that is 'governed' but homeowners will be subject to planning law determined by the council, and if they mortgage their homes, they are subject to the terms of a contract with a bank. With mortgages, 'ownership' becomes something less than absolute. The number of owners rose primarily through the 'right to buy' sales, but has fallen as housing has reconcentrated (see Figure 14.4)

There are around 25 million homes in the UK, and a population of around 67 million, suggesting there is one home for each 2.68 people. There are also

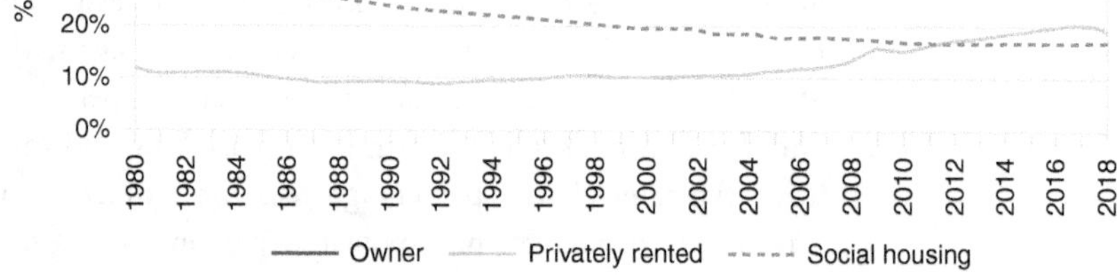

Figure 14.4 UK housing ownership and rent, 1980–2018
Sources: English Housing Survey

[91] *Re AirBnB Ireland UC* (2019) C-390/18, where the Court of Justice of the EU held AirBnB is an information society service.

[92] E.g. B. Benítez-Auriolesa and I. Tussyadiah, 'What Airbnb Does to the Housing Market', *Annals of Tourism Research* (2020).

10.94 million mortgages, and people had an average mortgage debt in 2020 of £137,934.[93]

(4) Home-Dweller Rights

Compared to the universal human right to 'housing', and the right to 'respect for . . . private and family life' and 'home',[94] statutory housing rights in the UK fall far short. In England in 2018, around 9.5 million households were rented (36%), 7 million households had mortgages (30%) and 7.8 million were owned outright (34%).[95] So three groups of rights are those of (a) tenants against landlords, (b) mortgagors against banks and (c) homeowners.

(a) Tenant Rights against Landlords

The three most common cases litigated in housing law practice today are actions for possession, cases on repair and applications to be housed. There is also the right to equal treatment. Yet overshadowing all of these areas is the lack of affordable or guaranteed housing, with fair rent regulation. This section begins with (i) rent regulation, and then discusses the minimal rights of UK tenants to (ii) security of tenure (iii) rights to repair and habitability, (iv) the right to be housed and (v) the right to equal treatment.

Before looking at rights themselves, it is necessary to understand the scope of rights. UK law has traditionally distinguished people who hold a 'lease' (and have more rights from statute or common law) and people who only have a contractual 'licence'. For example, no legal system gives tenant rights to people who stay in hotels: thus, a line must be drawn somewhere. This is the same problem as the distinction between the 'employee' and 'self-employed', as businesses or sympathetic judges argue the relations created in contract towards tenants do not involve rights. In a case from 1985, *Street v Mountford*, the House of Lords held that a right of 'exclusive possession' was the hallmark of a lease, and even stated that the statutory rights in play were 'irrelevant to the problem of determining the legal effect of the rights granted by the [rental] agreement'.[96] This reasoning was plainly defective in protecting rights, as an unscrupulous landlord could simply state in a contract that it has a right to enter, or possess the property in an attempt to evade any rights. Since then, another leading case, expressly approved by the Supreme Court in *Autoclenz* (see Ch. 5(1)), is *Bankway Properties Ltd v Penfold-*

[93] M. Boyle, 'Mortgage Statistics: The Average UK Mortgage Size, Payments and Debt', *Finder* (23 March 2021).

[94] UDHR 1948, art. 25; ICESCR 1966, art. 11 (housing); ECHR 1950, art. 8 (private life and home) and Prot. 1, art. 1 (property). Also CFREU 2000, arts. 7 and 34(3) ('the right to social and housing assistance').

[95] MHCLG, *English Housing Survey: Home Ownership, 2017–18* (July 2019) 3; and *Private Rented Sector, 2017–18* (July 2019) 3.

[96] *Street v Mountford* [1985] AC 809.

Dunsford. Here, Arden LJ approved a test that a contract term can be a sham if it is 'intended to evade the operation of a statute out of which the parties cannot contract',[97] there being no requirement for a 'common intention' (as landlords and tenants have opposing interests). Arden LJ further stated that:

> Where an Act of Parliament, like the [Housing] Act of 1988, confers protection on a person whose bargaining position may be disadvantaged when compared with that of the counterparty, it may be the duty of the Court in certain circumstances to scrutinise critically a transaction which is onerous, like the one in this case, to see if it constitutes a sham.

Although Arden LJ had 'no view' to express on this, as the point was not argued, the importance of bargaining power was the essence of the Supreme Court's judgment in *Autoclenz.* This appears to be the proper basis for social rights, including for agricultural or business tenants.[98] While multiple factors (such as exclusive possession) may be considered when distinguishing a lease from a licence, 'the relevant bargaining power of the parties must be taken into account',[99] because the purpose of rights is to protect those who are unlikely to be able to contract for protection in markets by themselves.

(i) Rent Regulation

Until 1981, and 1987 in London, there was comprehensive fair rent regulation, limiting how much landlords could charge tenants. The Housing Act 1980 began to end this system, by giving power to the Secretary of State to abolish any requirement of a landlord to get a 'certificate of fair rent' for new 'shorthold' tenancies.[100] This meant private landlords could opt out of rent regulation. Most did as soon as they could. The Housing Act 1985, section 24 made explicit that local authorities could charge 'such reasonable charges as they may determine'.[101] The Housing Act 1988, section 22 for new tenancies gives tenants the 'right' to apply to a Rent Assessment Committee for a rent review in the first six months, but the Committee cannot change rents unless 'the rent payable under the assured shorthold tenancy in question is significantly higher than the rent which the landlord might reasonably be expected to obtain'.[102] Since these changes, rent levels, and with them house prices, have increased exponentially, only halted by financial crashes (see Figure 14.5).

97 *Bankway Properties Ltd v Penfold-Dunsford* [2001] EWCA Civ 528, [42]–[44].

98 *Johnson v Moreton* [1980] AC 37, per Lord Simon: 'palpably lacking the prerequisites for the beneficent operation of *laisser-faire* [. . . is the relation . . .] of landlord and tenant . . . the constriction of the market and the inequality of bargaining power enabled the landlord to dictate contractual terms which did not necessarily operate to the general benefit of society'.

99 *Autoclenz Ltd v Belcher* [2011] UKSC 41, [35].

100 HA 1980, s. 52(1)(c) and (4), triggered in Protected Shorthold Tenancies (Rent Registration) Order 1981.

101 HA 1985, s. 24.

102 HA 1988, s. 22. The word 'significantly', if argued to mean 'statistical significance', could be used to limit price increases beyond the local area prices by more than, say, 2–3%. This has not been done yet.

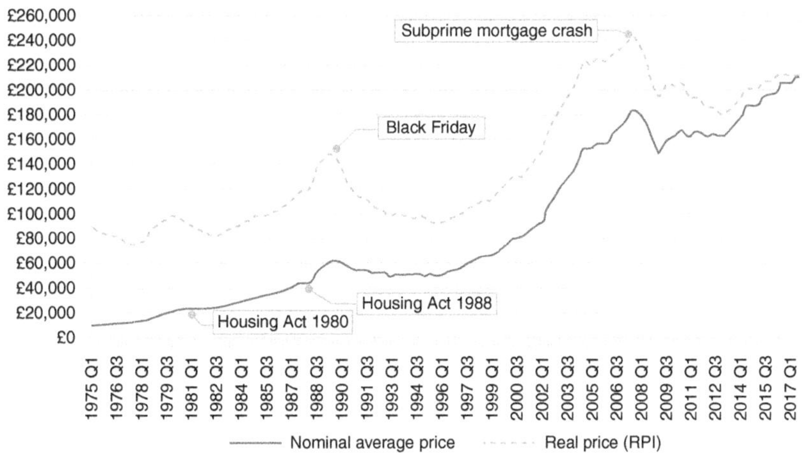

Figure 14.5 UK house prices, nominal and real, 1975–2017
Sources: ONS, All UK Properties; www.nationwide.co.uk/house-price-index/

A small number of houses owned by local councils and housing associations still have rents regulated under the Rent Act 1977, if created before 1988. The formula for rent increases is determined by the Rent Acts (Maximum Fair Rent) Order 1999, where the 'maximum fair rent' is calculated as:

$$LR\ (1 - xy/y - P)$$

In this formula (which is not immediately intuitive) LR is the existing registered rent; x is the price in the 'fair rent' index under the Act; y is the index for the month when the rent was registered; and P is 0.075 for the first rent registration application, and 0.05 for each subsequent application. In the private sector, however, by 2018 only 0.9 per cent of private tenants had regulated rents.[103]

Otherwise, tenants are protected against deposit theft by landlords. This is a widespread practice of dishonest landlords, particularly among companies, refusing to return some or all of a tenant's deposit based on fictitious or exaggerated claims of housing being 'damaged' or needing 'repair'. The Housing Act 2004, sections 213–15 requires deposits to be held under an authorised scheme, and information given to the tenant within thirty days, or the landlord must pay a penalty of three times the deposit value.[104] Furthermore, the landlord cannot seek possession in retaliation for complaints about deposit misuse, or until the deposit scheme is complied with.[105] Finally, since the Tenant Fees Act 2019, estate agents and landlords are prohibited from charging tenants fees outside the rent that is due,[106] an important law that

[103] MHCLG, *English Housing Survey: Private Rented Sector 2017–18* (July 2019).

[104] HA 2004, ss. 213–15; cf. *Tiensia v Universal Estates* [2010] EWCA Civ 1224. In a judgment plainly calculated to destroy this system, Rimer LJ said that the landlord could comply with the scheme later to not be penalised (Sedley LJ dissented, but Thorpe LJ agreed). Reversed by Localism Act 2011, s. 184.

[105] See *Charalambous v Ng* [2014] EWCA Civ 1604.

[106] Tenant Fees Act 2019, ss. 1–5.

ensures landlords with greater bargaining power are not blind to the arbitrary fees that tenants are usually unable to resist.

The UK's approach to rents is extreme compared to other countries. Without credible evidence, it has been argued that fair rent regulation decreases investment in housing, reduces services, increases harassment, inflates demand, discourages labour mobility and encourages evasion of rights.[107] Yet experience shows these assertions are false. For example, the German Civil Code, §§557 and 558 gives a tenant the right to not have rents increased beyond what is 'customary in the locality' (known as the *Mietspiegel* or rent mirror), and in no case more than 20 per cent over three years. In states and cities, stronger protections favouring the tenant may be passed. For instance, a Berlin law in 2020 froze rents, and requires that after 2022 rises can be a maximum of 1.3 per cent, with exceptions for new buildings.[108] Combined with tenant rights to security, full repairs, a reduction in rents for defects, and higher building standards, German rent regulation has increased, not decreased, investment. UK homes are the smallest compared to EU member states on average.[109] In 2018, 5.4 per cent of UK home dwellers were unable 'to keep home adequately warm' compared to 2.3 per cent in Germany.[110] This means there was less investment in UK housing, as landlords concentrated on profiteering, not investing. Fair rent regulation has also consistently been held to be compatible with the right to 'peaceful enjoyment of . . . possessions' for the landlord in the European Convention on Human Rights,[111] so long as corresponding repair duties leave room to cover costs.[112] As most policy-makers follow reality, not evidence-free theory, fair rent regulation is widespread across countries and cities around the world.[113]

107 S. Bright, *Landlord and Tenant Law in Context* (2007) 454–5 gives a good summary of these arguments, citing among other things F. A. Hayek et al., *Verdict on Rent Control*, Institute of Economic Affairs (1972). Cf. Arnott, 'Time for Revisionism on Rent Control?': 93.5% of economists surveyed agreed with a statement that 'A ceiling on rents reduces the quantity and quality of housing available.' Arnott points out that new types of rent regulation differ, and 'the case against second-generation rent controls is . . . weak'.

108 B. Knight, 'Berlin's New Rent Freeze: How It Compares Globally', *Deutsche Welle* (23 October 2019).

109 M. Morgan and H. Cruickshank, 'Quantifying the Extent of Space Shortages: English Dwellings' (2014) 42(6) *Building Research & Information* 710, Table 1. Average floor space in UK new builds, 76 m^2; Germany, 109.2 m^2. Average floor space in all buildings is 85 m^2 (ahead of Finland, Portugal and Greece) reflecting that older buildings – constructed in periods of rent regulation, higher standards or more rights – are larger.

110 Eurostat, 'Inability to Keep Home Adequately Warm – EU-SILC Survey' (2020) https://appsso.eurostat.ec.europa.eu/nui/show.do?dataset=ilc_mdes01&lang=en.

111 E.g. *Mellacher v Austria* (1990) 12 EHRR 391. Also, *Yee v City of Escondido, California*, 503 US 519 (1992).

112 *Hutten-Czapska v Poland* [2005] ECHR 119, [186] where statutory duties for maintenance cost 40% beyond the lawful rents. Also *Bittó v Slovakia* (2014) 30255/09. The outcome may differ if the aim is to stop climate damage, and up-front repair costs are high, yet past landlord profits have been high.

113 E.g. M. Haffner, M. Elsinga and J. Hoekstra, 'Rent Regulation: The Balance between Private Landlords and Tenants in Six European Countries' (2008) 8(2) *Int'l J Housing Policy* 217. Lind, 'Rent Regulation: A Conceptual and Comparative Analysis'.

(ii) Security of Tenure

The second main right, but almost wholly lacking in the UK, is to security of tenure. Business tenancies in the Landlord and Tenant Act 1954 have a unified standard for security of tenure. Under sections 25 and 26, a notice can be given by the landlord to terminate the tenancy, and the tenant can give notice requesting a new tenancy.[114] The landlord may only oppose a new tenancy on the grounds of section 30. These include breach of repair duties, 'persistent delay in paying rent', other substantial breaches of contract, 'the provision of alternative accommodation' that is 'suitable for the tenant's requirements' or plans for reconstruction or self-occupation.[115] This amounts to a general right to renew a business tenancy at a market rent. This right promotes business stability and ensures more continuity for service provision to consumers.[116] But while businesses have protection, people in their homes generally do not, and people with farming tenancies also do not.[117]

For people renting their homes, the bare system of rights begins with the Protection from Eviction Act 1977, section 5. No landlord can evict any tenant with 'less than 4 weeks' notice', a period that was briefly extended to three months during the Covid-19 pandemic, but then lapsed.[118] It is an offence for landlords to harass tenants or enter the premises except by court order.[119] However, beyond these minimal rights, most landlords apparently need to give no good reasons for eviction, once the contract term is finished. Five main types of tenancy are called 'shorthold' (unsecure),[120] 'assured' (secure and private sector), 'introductory' or 'demoted' (a probationary tenancy in public or social sector), 'flexible' (two-year fixed term, unsecure and in the public or social sector) and 'secure' (secure and public sector).

Around 94.7% of private renting tenants have shorthold tenancies,[121] or have less security because they have a resident landlord or are students, while 4.5% have assured tenancies and 0.9% have tenancies still regulated under the Rent Act 1977. Shorthold tenancies last a minimum of six months, and tenants may be evicted with two months' written notice under the Housing Act 1988, section 21.[122] Any contract can last longer – for one, two or three years, or may require a landlord only evicts a tenant for good reasons. But this depends on negotiation between landlord and tenant. Landlords have no interest in giving tenants rights in their contracts, have the bargaining power to impose their will

[114] Landlord and Tenant Act 1954, ss. 25–6. [115] Landlord and Tenant Act 1954, s. 30.

[116] But note that 'market' rents for business can be as arbitrary as in the case of homes, and is frequently the cause of closing independent shops, restaurants, pubs and other businesses, loved by the community.

[117] Contrast the former Rent (Agricultural) Act 1976.

[118] Protection from Eviction Act 1977, s. 5 and Coronavirus Act 2020, Sch. 29, para. 2.

[119] Protection from Eviction Act 1977, ss. 1–2.

[120] The full name, confusingly and misleadingly, is 'assured shorthold tenancy'. 'Shorthold' will be used here.

[121] MHCLG, *English Housing Survey: Private Rented Sector 2017–18* (July 2019).

[122] HA 1988, s. 21.

and give no security in practice. In April 2019 the government announced it would consult on ending evictions without a reason, but by 2020 this had still not happened.[123]

In the public or social sector – in council homes, or a housing action trust that is often subcontracted by councils – tenants may have 'introductory' terms of one year. This means they can be evicted at the end for any reason.[124] However, if the landlord is satisfied, the tenant may become a 'secure' tenant of a council, or an 'assured' tenant of a housing association. Nevertheless, for anti-social behaviour, the tenant may lose secure or assured status and become a 'demoted' tenant.[125] Since 2011, councils and housing associations can create 'flexible' tenancies, meaning that a tenant has the 'flexibility' of being evicted after two years.[126] Otherwise, councils can offer a 'secure' tenancy immediately.

The meanings of 'secure' and 'assured' tenancy, while differing between public and private sector, come down to the need to give reasons before eviction. In the vast majority of cases, non-payment of rent is the reason for eviction: one study from 2003 found this for 92.5 per cent of cases, whereas anti-social behaviour was 6.2 per cent of cases.[127] This means the very people who are most vulnerable, and need housing most, are the people evicted: those who cannot afford to pay. The main reasons a secure tenant can be evicted are for unreasonable rent arrears (usually two months), breach of contract, nuisance or violence, or damage to premises or furniture.[128] The main reasons an assured tenant can be evicted are the same, but also include mandatory grounds such as whenever a landlord who lives in the property wants to evict, or a mortgagee (usually a bank) enforcing security.[129] In *Kay v Lambeth LBC*, the House of Lords held that the right to a private and family life and home under the European Convention on Human Rights (ECHR), article 8 did not enable any challenge against landlords seeking possession, because ostensibly the legislative frame means 'the court will in effect have undertaken the very assessment which article 8(2) requires'.[130] Their Lordships did not attempt to justify the position in shortholds, but in *McDonald v McDonald*, the Supreme Court held that where a bank had stepped into the shoes of a landlord, it could gain possession under section 21 even though the tenant was disabled and the evidence showed eviction

[123] J. Elgot, 'Short-Notice Evictions Face Axe in Tenant Rights Victory', *The Guardian* (15 April 2019).

[124] HA 1985, Sch. 1, para. 1A; HA 1996, ss. 124–5.

[125] HA 1985, s. 82A and Sch. 1, para. 1B; HA 1988, s. 6A, inserted by the Anti-social Behaviour Act 2003, s. 14 and Sch. 1, para. 2.

[126] HA 1985, s. 107A, from Localism Act 2011, s. 154. In classic doublethink, the section reads 'a flexible tenancy is a secure tenancy'.

[127] H. Pawson et al., 'The Use of Possession Actions and Evictions by Social Landlords', ODPM (June 2005) Table 3.3, cited in Bright, *Landlord and Tenant Law in Context*, 604.

[128] HA 1985, Sch. 2. On redevelopment, see below.

[129] HA 1988, Sch. 2.

[130] *Kay v Lambeth LBC* [2006] UKHL 10.

would be detrimental to her health. Still, the Supreme Court held that there was no incompatibility with ECHR, article 8, and that an 'order mandated by the contractual relationship' could not be shifted where 'there are legislative provisions which the democratically elected legislature has decided properly balance the competing interests of private sector landlords and residential tenants'.[131]

The rules on security of tenure have arbitrary distinctions between private, social and public sectors. In 2006, the Law Commission recognised this when suggesting the creation of just two tenures: secured and standard tenancies.[132] However, it appears pointless to allow landlords to opt out of secured tenancies, because virtually all will. The alternative approach is that every tenant should be able to expect fair reasons before losing their home,[133] and that not having enough money is not *in itself* a good reason for eviction. When someone loses their job and income, the personal crisis can only be worsened if they also lose their home: contrast this to the landlord (or the bank that funds them) that may lose a few months of profit that they do not work for. Many evictions for non-payment of rent happen because housing benefit is paid late, a problem that could be easily solved with more security. The ending of a shorthold tenancy is the main cause of homelessness, in around 25–30 per cent of all cases,[134] while in the typical experience of 4.9 million private renters, and many in public or social sectors, periodic threat of eviction creates constant anxiety. By contrast, in an economic crisis, more security of tenure has a stabilising effect. The Coronavirus Act 2020 recognised this in part by extending notice periods to three months.

(iii) Right to Repair and Habitability

As noted earlier, new UK housing is physically smaller than in any EU country, while heating and repair problems are disproportionately high. In 2017, 24.5% of private rented houses in England were rated as 'non-decent', 19% were in 'serious disrepair' and 7.2% were damp. There were better, yet still poor, levels among councils and housing associations.[135] It was estimated in 2003 that it would cost just £14 billion to ensure all homes were 'decent',[136] and this has

131 *McDonald v McDonald* [2016] UKSC 28, [40] and at [41] rejecting making the ECHR enforceable 'as between private citizens', apparently on a presumption that rights do not do this all the time, e.g. in ECHR, art. 11.

132 Law Commission, *Renting Homes: The Final Report*, Law Com. No. 297 (2006) paras. 1.4–1.5. The Law Commission's reference to extend 'consumer protection principles of fairness', yet create no rights, was absurd: a home dweller is not a 'consumer'.

133 E.g. German Civil Code, §573.

134 See MHCLG, *Statutory Homelessness Live Tables*, Table A2.

135 MHCLG, *English Housing Survey: Private Rented Sector 2017–18* (July 2019) Figure 4.1. Councils had rates of 14.8%, 14.4% and 6.2%; housing associations 11.3%, 8.3% and 5.2%; and owned homes 18.7%, 11.1% and 2.2%.

136 ODPM, 'English House Condition Survey 2002: Annual Report' (March 2006) Tables 2.4 and 2.5.

become an ever-larger issue as the imperative of insulation and reduced energy use to halt climate damage grows. Low UK housing standards reflect the minimal rights of repair. The Landlord and Tenant Act 1985, section 9A requires that a dwelling in England 'is fit for human habitation at the time the lease is granted' and 'will remain' so.[137] Under section 10, 'regard shall be had' to 'repair, stability, freedom from damp, internal arrangement, natural lighting, ventilation, water supply, drainage and sanitary conveniences, facilities for preparation and cooking of food and for the disposal of waste water' or 'any prescribed hazard'.[138]

Under section 11 there is a further right, enforceable with damages or injunctions (but not rent reduction),[139] to repair (but not improvements) to 'the structure and exterior of the dwelling house', to keep working all 'water, gas and electricity' and installations for 'space heating and heating water'.[140] The reference to 'gas' appears outdated, given the need to end use of fossil fuels for clean electric heating or cooking. The courts have interpreted these repair duties to include, for example, wall plaster, windows, partition walls and access paths, but not garden paving.[141] A landlord also has a duty to ensure that premises are not defective so as to cause any personal injury or damage to property.[142] The House of Lords has been proactive in ensuring a tenant could enforce repair duties against a landlord, even though a landlord could not technically grant a lease out of its estate.[143]

Overall, however, repair duties have been minimally interpreted, without taking into account standards of international law for decent housing. In *Southwark LBC v Tanner*, the House of Lords refused to include a duty to provide adequate noise insulation. In the view of Lord Hoffmann this was 'very much a matter for the allocation of resources in accordance with democratically determined priorities . . . the common law should not get out of step with legislative policy'.[144] However this view rests on the false assumption that the common law default of 'no standards' does not allocate resources – redistribute wealth – from the tenant (who lives in squalor and noise) to a landlord (that often lives off the tenant).[145] Similarly it was held that a mouldy flat was not a violation of the right to have property in repair.[146] The better approach is to construct the common law, like statute, in a way that upholds rights to a decent

[137] Cf. Homes (Fitness for Human Habitation) Act 2018, after standards lapsed by rental value since 1985. This has eclipsed the HA 2004, s. 3 duty for councils to review housing conditions to keep them fit, but which was not enforceable against councils. It has also made irrelevant the absurd debate on whether nuisance law could ensure a tenant got a sink in the lavatory: *Birmingham CC v Oakley* [2001] 1 AC 617.

[138] Landlord and Tenant Act 1985, ss. 9A and 10.

[139] Landlord and Tenant Act 1985, s. 17.

[140] Landlord and Tenant Act 1985, s. 11.

[141] *Hussein v Mehlman* [1992] 2 EGLR 87, *Boswell v Crucible Steel of America* [1925] 1 KB 119, *Green v Eales* (1841) 2 QB 225, *Hopswood v Cannock Chase DC* [1975] 1 WLR 373.

[142] Defective Premises Act 1972, s. 4.

[143] *Bruton v London & Quadrant Housing Trust* [1999] UKHL 26.

[144] *Southwark LBC v Tanner* [2001] 1 AC 1, 9.

[145] Cf. *Shelley v Kraemer*, 334 US 1 (1948).

[146] *Lee v Leeds City Council* [2002] EWCA Civ 06.

home consistent with international law. This is all the more important as international human rights law includes a right to the benefits of science.[147] This includes technology such as solar panels, batteries, electric charging points or even the replacement of gas boilers and insulation that can reduce energy and stop climate damage. Simply saying it is not the court's problem, when courts enforce property rights that create the problem, suggests an ideologically driven blind spot.

(iv) Right to Be Housed

The basic right in international law is the right to housing. This is realised defectively in two ways in the UK. First, the Homelessness Act 2002, sections 1–3 places duties on councils to provide a review and strategy to prevent homelessness, and enough accommodation.[148] However, the law demotes the claims of the 'intentionally' homeless, where it 'would have been reasonable ... to continue to occupy' accommodation.[149] In *Samuels v Birmingham CC*, the Supreme Court interpreted this phrase to not include failing to pay rent, as the claimant's income was too low.[150] The court pointed out that Parliament's original concern was people who left homes to jump ahead on the housing queue, but if this is 'intentionally' homeless it would appear that the undersupply of housing is the true problem caused by government policy, not the homeless person.[151]

Second, a local authority has a duty to house anyone in priority need (whether 'intentionally' homeless or not), meaning people who are pregnant; with children; on account of their age, an illness or a disability; or facing emergency.[152] For people who are 'unintentionally' homeless there is a duty to secure accommodation and, for others without housing, the local authority merely has a power and discretion to house.[153] However, a local authority can argue an applicant has no local connection and should go to another authority where he or she was ordinarily resident.[154] There is also no duty to house migrants subject to immigration control.[155] In 2018, it was estimated that 4,677 people in the UK were sleeping rough on a given night, a problem requiring just modest investment to solve.[156] Temporary housing shelters often charge for each night, costing up to £35 a week, requiring people to beg (at a time when more people use cards and have no spare change). The current policies, simply put, do not stop homelessness, and appear to be 'intentionally' designed that way.

[147] UDHR 1948, art. 27(1) and art. 15(2). [148] Homelessness Act 2002, ss. 1–3.

[149] HA 1996, s. 191. [150] [2019] UKSC 28.

[151] Cf. Homes (Fitness for Human Habitation) Act 2018.

[152] HA 1996, ss. 189–90. For 'intentionally' homeless the duty only lasts 28 days.

[153] HA 1996, ss. 192–3. [154] HA 1996, ss. 198–201. [155] HA 1996, s. 185.

[156] Public Health England, 'Health Matters: Rough Sleeping', Guidance (11 February 2020); Shelter, '280,000 People in England Are Homeless, with Thousands More at Risk' (18 December 2019) refers to temporary accommodation.

Third, local authorities must have a scheme to allocate housing, and follow the scheme's priorities in doing so.[157] People can also be excluded from the right to housing due to anti-social behaviour,[158] a fact often tied to mental and physical disabilities of the most vulnerable groups (see below). A 'reasonable preference' has to be given to people who are homeless, live in unsatisfactory housing, have medical or welfare needs to move or who may suffer hardship.[159] To the extent that there is not a shortage, the council should follow 'choice-based letting', and applicants are to be given a copy of the council's policy on choice.[160] Again, if housing becomes available, it can be lost through 'unacceptable behaviour serious enough to make [the person] unsuitable to be a tenant'.[161] Of the 2 million social renters for under ten years, 912,000 waited under three months to be housed, 363,000 waited three to six months, 303,000 waited six months to a year and 505,000 waited one to five years.[162] The undersupply of public housing at fair rents inflates unregulated private housing prices, though some parts of the UK have an oversupply. Private investment tends to concentrate, particularly around cities like London, Edinburgh, Manchester or Cardiff, and it drains away from regions. This problem is solvable with active investment policy in jobs, education and infrastructure that is deliberately spread across regions (see Chs. 5(4)(a) and 20).

(v) Equal Treatment

As in employment and access to all services available to the public,[163] the Equality Act 2010 creates rights to equal treatment in access to 'accommodation' on the protected grounds of gender, race, sexual orientation, religion or belief and disability.[164] However, it excludes grounds of age and marriage and civil partnership from the scope of its remedies. Also it does not yet codify the protection against actions 'unequal in their operation as between different classes',[165] nor protection against unequal treatment based on income, wealth, property or 'other status' as the European Convention, Universal Declaration and International Covenants do.[166] This means the most obvious and directly unequal kind of discrimination – denying people housing, or evicting them, when they cannot afford to pay rent – lacks protection in UK statute, as in EU legislation. On the other hand, direct wealth discrimination (i.e. no home if one cannot pay) produces systemic or indirect discrimination (see Ch. 5(2)(d))

157 HA 1996, s. 167. 158 HA 1996, s. 167(2C). 159 HA 1996, ss. 167–9.

160 HA 1996, s. 193(2). 161 HA 1996, s. 160A(7).

162 MHCLG, *English Housing Survey 2017–18* (July 2019) Table 3.12.

163 Equality Act 2010, ss. 28–9 and 39–41. 164 Equality Act 2010, ss. 32, 6–7 and 9–12.

165 *Kruse v Johnson* [1898] 2 QB 91, per Lord Russell CJ, on a bylaw against singing a hymn near dwelling houses.

166 ECHR 1950, art. 14 (equality based on property or other status in ECHR rights); UDHR 1948, art. 7 (equal protection before law); ICESCR 1966, art. 3 (equal treatment in Covenant rights); ICCPR 1966, art. 3.

on other grounds, such as gender or race, because property and wealth are unequally distributed. The lack of codification in the Equality Act 2010 does not preclude case law construction that upholds international law standards. Any action must be based on common law rights of equality,[167] and rational treatment.[168]

The Equality Act 2010, sections 33–5 require equal treatment in any 'disposal' or 'management' of premises, while section 36 creates a 'duty to make reasonable adjustments' to 'a controller of let premises', a commonhold association, or a person responsible for common parts.[169] The duty to make adjustments especially applies in favour of disabled people, and yet Schedule 4, para. 2(8) excludes any duty on a landlord that would 'involve the removal or alteration of a physical feature', as opposed to providing an 'auxiliary aid'.[170] This contrasts with work or service provision where there are such duties. It is completely unclear why no duty is codified for any landlord, whatever their size or profits. Schedule 5 adds in more exemptions, limiting protection in disposals only 'as they relate to race', and depriving protection against someone who gives permission to make disposals on grounds of 'religion or belief' or 'sexual orientation'. These codified equality rights (but, again, common law may go further) and remedies under the Act thus seem comfortable with arbitrary refusal to sell a home to anyone who is gay, heterosexual, Catholic, Muslim, atheist, male, female, young, or old. This falls short of international treaties ratified by the UK. A landlord who rents out premises that are 'the only or main home' of the landlord seems exempt from any duty.[171] These limited equal rights are reflected in the non-codification of housing equality, aside from race, in EU law.[172]

A related problem is that many evictions, including for anti-social behaviour, relate to either mental or physical disability – 27 per cent in one study.[173] Recognising these difficult cases, and the need to protect potentially difficult but also vulnerable people, in *Manchester CC v Romano* the Court of Appeal suggested that a landlord must only pursue eviction if necessary to protect the health or 'complete physical, mental and social well-being' of others. This was

[167] E.g. *Constantine v Imperial Hotels Ltd* [1944] KB 693, Birkett J finding that a West Indies cricket player had a right in tort to damages for exclusion from a hotel, where racist southern US soldiers objected and the hotel owner denied Mr Constantine, instead of kicking out the racist soldiers: L. Constantine, *Colour Bar* (1954). Given the Equality Act 2010, s. 32(3) exclusion for 'short stays', non-discrimination in hotels is covered by s. 29.

[168] As in *Kruse v Johnson* [1898] 2 QB 91, Lord Russell CJ suggested a stricter standard for private enterprise, those with a 'public representative character entrusted by Parliament with delegated authority . . . or other like companies, which carry on their business for their own profit'.

[169] Equality Act 2010, ss. 33–6.

[170] Equality Act 2010, Sch. 4, para. 1.

[171] Equality Act 2010, Sch. 4, para. 2(1) using the concept of a 'controller'.

[172] Race Equality Directive 2000/43/EC, art. 3(h). See further H. Silver and L. Danielowski, 'Fighting Housing Discrimination in Europe' (2019) 29(5) *Housing Policy Debate* 714.

[173] Cf. C. Hunter, J. Nixon and S. Shayer, *Neighbour Nuisance, Social Landlords and the Law* (2000) 18–19, found 18% of anti-social behaviour cases in their sample related to mental disability, and 9% to physical disability; cited in Bright (2007) 620, fn. 122.

a result compelled by the duty to interpret domestic law compatibly with the European Convention, and in particular articles 8 and 14, though equally neighbours' rights must be taken into account.[174] In such cases, it seems doubtful that landlords have rights under the European Convention that must be balanced with, or may limit, a home dweller or seeker's right to equality, because the 'right to property' in Protocol 1, article 1 is a right to 'peaceful enjoyment' of 'possessions'. In the case of a home a tenant has exclusive possession.

(b) Mortgagor Rights against Banks

Most people who can afford it purchase homes through a bank loan, and remain indebted through a legal mortgage against a bank. So long as the mortgagor (the borrower) may repay, the mortgagee (the bank or building society) is prohibited in equity from converting the loan into a sale. This is because, as Lord Henley LC put it in 1762, 'necessitous men are not, truly speaking, free men, but, to answer a present exigency, will submit to any terms that the crafty may impose upon them'.[175] This right, the 'equity of redemption', is to keep property if debts are paid. If debts are not paid, a mortgaged homeowner risks losing the property and being evicted, and a sale of land according to a court procedure.[176] If children will be affected, the court must take their welfare into account.[177] Under the Consumer Rights Act 2015, sections 62–4, interpreted in light of the human right to a home and family life under the ECHR, mortgage contract terms may be declared void if they create a significant imbalance, or are against the requirement of good faith. This has been used both to protect the right to review in court[178] and to allow a remedy that enables people to keep their home (not just receive damages).[179] The Financial Conduct Authority Handbook also requires that everything is done to ensure that arrears are paid, rather than seeking an order for possession.[180] However the basic features of mortgage law – that people can be made homeless, even where any private gain to the bank is outweighed by the social costs – remain.

(c) Homeowner Rights

The final rights of homeowners are primarily those against the state. A freeholder of property in English law has rights to the extent that they are

[174] *Manchester CC v Romano* [2004] EWCA Civ 834, [69]–[70], adopting the WHO definition.
[175] *Vernon v Bethell* (1762) 28 ER 838.
[176] Trusts of Land and Appointment of Trustees Act 1996, s. 14.
[177] Insolvency Act 1986, s. 335A(2)(b)(iii).
[178] *Kušionová v SMART Capital a.s.* (2014) C-34/13, [25]–[30] and [46]–[68].
[179] *Morcillo and García v Banco Bilbao Vizcaya Argentaria SA* (2014) C-169/14.
[180] FCA Handbook, *Arrears and Repossessions: Regulated Mortgage Contracts and Home Purchase Plans* (MCOB 13).

consistent with equal rights of people they neighbour and in their local community. According to the Latin maxim, *sic utere tuo ut alienum non laedas*, or use of property should not harm others. This means property carries responsibility, and its private use is always bound by the public good. This is seen in the tort of nuisance, so that landowners must not harm their neighbours or interfere in their peaceful enjoyment of property.[181] As well as planning determining the extent to which construction can be performed, the grant of planning permission is relevant to decide whether certain conduct is a nuisance or not.[182]

(5) Conclusion

The changes in housing law mean that today fewer people are able to afford homes, and more remain mired in bank debt for longer parts of their lives. The UK has a poor track record of housing quality and suffers from underinvestment, including for zero-energy and energy-producing housing infrastructure. As well as failing to ensure everyone has an adequate standard of living for housing, this fails to uphold the right to the benefits of science. However, three main reforms could reverse this trend. First, the duty to build homes could be restored, particularly focusing on underutilised or vacant land in towns and cities, coupled with investment in green space and local services. Second, there is a strong need for fair rent regulation, and investment duties on landlords to be restored, coupled with a code of tenants' rights to security, habitability and energy efficiency. Third, the subsidies to private landlords in the housing benefit system should be changed to ensure that the expenditure is returned to the public, either by increased house building, by fair rental prices or by requiring conditions to invest in upgrading homes. Greater stability and security at home is the basis for people to live freely, and to play a full part in other enterprises beyond one's home.

[181] E.g. *Vaughan v Menlove* (1837) 132 ER 490; *Hunter v Canary Wharf Ltd* [1997] UKHL 14.
[182] *Wheeler v J. J. Saunders Ltd* [1994] EWCA Civ 32.

15

Road and Rail Transport

Contents

'Dear Tony, I see the Russians have put a space vehicle on the moon', wrote a voter to their MP in 1959. 'Is there any chance of a better bus service in Bristol?'[1] Transport is a wonder of technology, giving us space travel, and sometimes even buses, but its use for good or ill depends on our law. An electric revolution is under way, yet the last shift took fifty years, for petrol motors to replace horses, and today we are out of time. Transport expels 27 per cent of UK greenhouse gas emissions, mainly by road and rail, and 24 per cent of global emissions.[2] Buses, taxis and delivery vehicles alone account for 56 per cent of exhausts.[3] Of all the people who die worldwide each year, 20 per cent die from air pollution.[4] In the UK, at least 40,000 people a year die from toxic air, and Covid-19 killed far more people in polluted areas than clean ones.[5] The scale of death is even more obscene after the 'Dieselgate'

[1] T. Benn, *Letters to my Grandchildren: Thoughts on the Future* (2010) 5, Letter 2.

[2] DfT, *Transport Statistics for Great Britain 2017* (November 2017) 81, Table TSGB0306. H. Ritchie, 'Cars, Planes, Trains: Where Do CO2 Emissions from Transport Come From?' (6 October 2020) https://ourworldindata.org/co2-emissions-from-transport. On shipping and air transport, E. McGaughey, 'Liability for Climate Damage and Shipping' (2021) https://papers.ssrn.com/sol3/papers.cfm?abstract_id=3783111; M. Bobek and J. Prassl, *Air Passenger Rights: Ten Years On* (2016).

[3] Defra and DfT, *UK Plan for Tackling Roadside Nitrogen Dioxide Concentrations* (July 2017) 7.

[4] K. Vohra et al., 'Global Mortality from Outdoor Fine Particle Pollution Generated by Fossil Fuel Combustion: Results from GEOS-Chem' (2021) 195 *Environmental Research*.

[5] Royal College of Physicians and Royal College of Paediatrics and Child Health, 'Every Breath We Take: The Lifelong Impact of Air Pollution', Report of a Working Party (February 2016) xliii; M. Travaglio, 'Links between Air Pollution and COVID-19 in England' (2021) 268 *Environmental Pollution*.

fraud from 2015, where auto-makers deliberately sold toxic motors. All road and rail can be electric, and since 2020 the total cost of ownership of electric cars is cheaper than petrol, even without including subsidies.[6] The up-front cost of an electric car is still £5,000 more, and this points again to auto-makers' role. There is a universal 'right of everyone' to 'enjoy the benefits of scientific progress' and this includes a clean environment, and clean transport.[7]

There are three main possibilities to get clean transport. First, we could allow clean technology to be rolled out entirely by existing private enterprises. These are auto-makers and bus, taxi and train corporations, which generally rely on public subsidies of road and rail building for profit. This is unlikely to work because it has failed already. Auto-maker, bus, taxis and train companies are routinely subsidised or bailed out. They profit from pollution, and this conflicts with our environmental needs. Second, we could couple more legal duties with higher subsidies; for instance, linking clean air targets to state aid. The problem here is that it rewards those responsible for harm, and leaves the risk of lobbying by corporations leading to diluting targets or just no action at all. Third, we can reverse the irrational bans on rail and buses being in public ownership by UK (but not other) governments,[8] and run cleaner enterprises, like road- and rail-track building. We can restore public voice in auto-makers, taxi or delivery companies until transport is clean. Consumer preferences are harder to shift, so the fastest gains will come with focus on the largest, regulated entities, tackling the problem at its roots.

(1) Historical Development

Horses, camels or elephants were the main vehicles for transport for most of our history. The word 'road' came from the Anglo-Saxon *ridan*, to ride,[9] and without either roads or vehicles, overland travel was inevitably slow. Until the Industrial Revolution, the largest, lasting empires were held together by maritime trade. The Roman Empire had the Mediterranean at its centre, and its domination of land worked because the Romans pioneered straight roads across the European continent, leaving us Oxford Street and Park Lane, stretching from Colchester to Exeter, and Dover to Shropshire. Roman roads' primary purpose had been 'military rather than commercial' and they were built 'to enable the legions to march quickly'.[10] But even then, the speed of crossing was a major hindrance against land-based expansion: beyond

6 'Electric Dreams: Green Vehicles Cheaper Than Petrol', *Direct Line Group* (29 June 2020).

7 ICESCR 1966, art. 15; UDHR 1948, art. 27; see Ch. 11. Also, CFREU 2000, art. 36 ('services of general economic interest'), art. 37 ('improvement of the quality of the environment') and ECHR 1950, art. 2 (life).

8 Railways Act 1993, s. 25; Bus Services Act 2017, s. 22, bans public ownership, but not for foreign governments.

9 See Wiktionary entry for 'road' under 'Etymology'.

10 S. Webb and B. Webb, *English Local Government*, vol. V: *The Story of the King's Highway* (1913) ch. 1, 4.

Hadrian's Wall in Britain, beyond the Danube in Germany, or deeper into Africa or Asia. This may also be one reason why, although the Khans' horse-led armies swept throughout Asia and Europe in a matter of decades, from 1279 the far-flung Mongol Empire quickly distanced itself into separate blocs, and could not hold together (see Ch. 19(1)).

In medieval England, highways were maintained through parish labour. The Saxon kings made road upkeep part of the *trinoda necessitas*, the three basic duties of landowners to contribute to maintain roads and bridges, fortifications and arms. The Lord of the Manor would usually throw these duties onto his tenants. For instance, the Statute of Winchester 1285 required 'that highways leading from one town to another shall be enlarged . . . so that there be neither dyke nor bush whereby a man may lurk to do hurt'. This did not work well: road quality was rarely good enough for wheeled traffic, and almost everyone travelled on horseback.[11] After the Black Death the laborious practice of maintaining roads had languished even further, leading to less trade and fewer market fairs. So the first Statute of Highways 1555 required that each year 'two honest persons' would be elected in each parish to be the surveyor of highways, while taxes and labour were levied against local householders to do the work for four days a year.[12] A new system of turnpike trusts was established from 1706 after the proposal of Sir Edward Littleton that every person 'ought to contribute to the repair of roads in proportion to the use they make' of them.[13] Hundreds of Acts of Parliaments empowered trustees to construct and maintain roads, levying tolls, usually for limits of ten or twenty-one years.[14] The Highways Act 1835 abolished forced labour to work on roads, with a new system of surveyors paid through rates levied by a new Highways Board. In the Local Government Act 1888, section 11 gave county councils a duty of maintaining roads.[15] The last traces of parish control over highways disappeared by 1894.

In the Industrial Revolution, coal and rail reshaped Britain. From 1759, canals spread across the country to transport coal from mines to cities,[16] and the first efficient steam engine was patented in 1775 by James Watt, mainly to lift the coal. The partnership of Boulton & Watt set about selling the engines to mines and ironworks, for lifting coal, pumping water or other heavy work. In 1814, George Stephenson perfected a 'locomotive', used again first at a coal mine, but finally in 1825 the Stockton & Darlington Railway started to carry

[11] E.g. G. Chaucer, *The Canterbury Tales* (*c.* 1400). Webb and Webb, *English Local Government*, vol. V, ch. 1, 8.

[12] Highways Act 1555 (2 & 3 Ph. & Mary, c. 8) extended by the Highways Act 1562 (5 Eliz. 1, c. 13).

[13] Webb and Webb, *English Local Government*, V, ch. 7, 114.

[14] E.g. Turnpike Roads Acts 1766, 1773, 1774, 1776, 1778, 1781, 1815, 1817, 1822, 1823, 1824, 1827, 1828, 1831, 1832, 1835, etc., as well as numerous Acts concerning roads, highways and tolls.

[15] Local Government Act 1888, s. 11.

[16] Canal Enabling Act 1759 sparked a canal boom, after the Sankey Brook Canal Act 1755 led to its opening in 1757.

coal and people. The Liverpool & Manchester Railway followed in 1830.[17] Rail speculation was set alight, despite the farmers protesting rail sparks setting their haystacks actually alight.[18] Railways boomed, authorised by around 900 private Acts that granted planning permission, compulsory purchase and immunity from the environmental destruction and personal injuries they caused.[19] Parliament quickly saw the advantages and the problems. Duties were placed on railways to transport mail and then troops at special rates.[20] From 1840, no railway was to be opened without notice to the Board of Trade, companies had to provide adequate financial accounts, inspectors were appointed and company bylaws had to be approved by the Board.[21]

There was deep scepticism that this could ever be a competitive private enterprise. William Gladstone's Railway Regulation Act 1844 originally proposed nationalisation, but Parliament settled on a five-person panel to judge railway proposals, which it was said 'knew of no instance of public benefit from direct competition between railway lines'.[22] Crucially, it created a power for government to buy out private companies after twenty-five years (1869), and it also required that at least one train each way down a line charged fares no higher than 1d per mile,[23] known as the 'Parliamentary train', so that workers could afford to travel. From 1845, railway companies would follow model clauses, including a requirement for equal treatment of customers.[24] Railway gauges were standardised to ensure trains could operate together.[25] Overturning a case allowing exemption clauses for injured horses,[26] the Rail and Canal Traffic Act 1854 put duties on railway companies to provide facilities and deliver passengers and goods without delay or partiality, and any exemption clause had to be in writing and 'just and reasonable'.[27] In 1863, the first London Underground line opened between Paddington and Farringdon. By the 1869 expiry, the building of railway networks was largely complete, and the Regulation of the Forces Act 1871 (perhaps with an eye to Bismarck's now-unified Germany) empowered government to take control of railways.[28] This was not used, however, until World War One.

[17] London and Manchester Railway Act 1826.

[18] E.g. R. Coase, 'The Problem of Social Cost' (1960) 3 *JL & Economics* 1, on spark problems.

[19] G. A. Bonner, *British Transport Law by Road and Rail* (1974) ch. 19, 284–5.

[20] Railways (Conveyance of Mails) Act 1838; Railway Regulation Act 1844, s. XI.

[21] Railway Regulation Act 1840, ss. II–VIII. Also Railway Regulation Act 1842.

[22] J. Foreman-Peck and R. Millward, *Public and Private Ownership of British Industry 1820–1990* (1994) 16–19.

[23] Railway Regulation Act 1844, ss. 2 and 6.

[24] Railways Clauses Consolidation Act 1845, s. XC.

[25] Regulating the Gauge of Railways Act 1846, legislating Brunel's defeat to Stephenson.

[26] *Carr v Lancashire and Yorkshire Railway* (1854) 14 Eng L & Eq R 340. Parke B held an exclusion clause for injured horses from negligent train shunting was effective.

[27] Rail and Canal Traffic Act 1854, ss. II and VII, a dozen decades ahead of the Unfair Contract Terms Act 1977. Also no unreasonable preference could be given to any particular customer or class of goods.

[28] Regulation of the Forces Act 1871, s. 16: if 'an emergency has arisen in which it is expedient for the public service that Her Majesty's Government should have control over the railroads'.

The question of the age, with the growth and power of rail corporations, was 'whether the state shall manage the railways or whether the railways shall manage the state'.[29] It was clear to many that 'competition must fail to do for railways what it does for ordinary trade',[30] especially since 'ordinary trade' relied very much on having a transport network. Rail was also vital to military power and communication, and this (not public service) was the main reason why tracks were built across the Indian subcontinent and the empire. But the solution of public ownership, obvious to Gladstone or the people who worked on the rail,[31] was not taken up. Instead from 1873, there was a new Railway Commission to regulate rates, which gradually became a Transport Tribunal,[32] and charges were bound more by law.[33] During World War One, essential workers stayed on the tracks that fed the troops to the front, filling trenches with souls, as they were emptied of life.[34] Government took control of rail but, after the war, public ownership was rejected. The government also proposed worker representation on company boards, but management opposition halted this.[35] The Railways Act 1921 merged the different companies into four big entities: Great Western; London, Midland & Scottish; London and North Eastern; and Southern Railway. Rates were put under the Railway Rates Tribunal, with three permanent members, appointed on recommendation of the government, and revenue was meant to stay as it was in 1913.[36]

While the canals and then railways had stretched across the landscape, there was still a need for point-to-point transport. Horse-drawn vehicles on muddy roads remained the main form of traffic until the first cars were invented.[37] Wealthier people could take individual 'Hackney carriages', which were first recorded as 'plying for hire' in 1634.[38] The Town Police Clauses Act 1847 and Metropolitan Public Carriage Act 1869 regulated taxis outside and in the capital. Omnibuses (carriages drawn by horses) also operated, and the

[29] Sir Henry Tyler, Board of Trade (Conservative), Evidence before the Parliament Joint Select Committee, *Report on Railway Amalgamation* (1872) BPP xxxviii.

[30] Sir Henry Tyler, xxxviii, xviii: 'Committees and commissions have for the last thirty years clung to one form of competition or another yet it has become more and more evident that … competition must fail to do for railways what it does for ordinary trade.'

[31] Cf. US Strike Commission, *Report of the Chicago Strike of June–July 1894* (1895) 163, Eugene Debs: 'Government ownership of the railroads is decidedly better for the people than railroad ownership of the Government … if the people owned and operated the railroads in the interest of the people instead of for private gain and profit, that the service would be greatly improved, the condition of men infinitely better, and another strike would never come.'

[32] In 1888 it became the Railway and Canal Commission. Bonner, British Transport Law by Road and Rail, 288.

[33] E.g. Cheap Trains Act 1883 and Railway and Canal Traffic Act 1894 prevented charge inflation going beyond 1893.

[34] See generally A. J. P. Taylor, *The First World War: An Illustrated History* (1974).

[35] *Outline of Proposals as to the Future Organisation of Transport Undertakings in Great Britain and their Relation to the State*, Cmd 787 (1920) suggested worker participation on rail boards; proposed five English groups and a Scottish group.

[36] Railways Act 1921 (c. 21), ss. 1, 20 and 58.

[37] See Bonner, *British Transport Law by Road and Rail*, ch. 19, 282.

[38] Bonner, *British Transport Law by Road and Rail*, ch. 22, 349.

Licensing of Stage Coaches Act 1826 enabled the first service from Paddington to Bank. Then 'steam coaches' used as buses began, all under strict control. The Locomotive Act 1865 set the maximum speed at 2 mph in cities, and 4 mph in the country, and required a man waving a red flag to walk in front of it as a warning. This was still a time where roads were filled with commerce, not just transport, and children played, but this was not to last much longer. In 1885, Gottlieb Daimler patented an internal combustion engine for a motorbike, and a few months later Karl Benz patented the first motor car, both in Germany. The Locomotives on Highways Act 1896 freed petrol vehicles from the red flag rules, and raised the speed limit to 12 mph. It was raised again to 20 mph in 1903.[39]

From this point, and when mass motor production began in 1908 at the Model T Ford factory in the USA, 'the horse was doomed'.[40] Some would not accept this fate. In 1908, one Mr H. B. Brown wrote that soon cars would 'cease to be a fashionable fad [and] the public will probably return to carriage and horses'.[41] Cars, said Brown, were 'attended by a cloud of dust and smoke' and 'the emission of a noisome odor'. The 'automobile lacks one of the most attractive concomitants of pleasure driving in the companionship of the horse'.[42] But despite Brown's nostalgia, history stomped on the horse. In the USA, the horse population fell from 26 million in 1915 to 3 million by 1960, as motor vehicle sales soared (see Figure 15.1).[43] Yet this was a trot not a gallop: left to the market, even though they were 'technologically' obsolete, it took around half a century for horses to be abandoned. This fact is relevant for transition to electric vehicles today.

While successive highway and road Acts maintained duties of public authorities for roads,[44] the development of public transport on roads was slow. In 1855, the private London General Omnibus Company (LGOC) was founded, strangely in Paris, and ran horse-drawn services. With motorisation, the London Road Car Company was founded, and competed with the LGOC, often duplicating routes. According to Herbert Morrison, the Minister for Transport from 1929 to 1931 and leader of the London County Council from 1934, this was 'unnecessary competition' and 'led to the racing and "nursing" of rival buses, the duplication

[39] Motor Car Act 1903.

[40] Bonner, *British Transport Law by Road and Rail*, ch. 19, 283: 'From 1903 onwards the horse was doomed. After 1914 the horse-drawn omnibus was seen no more in London . . . .' Cf. G. H. H. Oliphant, *The Law of Horses, Including the Law of Innkeepers, Veterinary Surgeons, etc* (6th ed. 1908).

[41] H. B. Brown, 'The Status of the Automobile' (1908) 17(4) *Yale LJ* 223, 227.

[42] Brown, 'The Status of the Automobile', 225–7. The 'cold and heartless mechanism of the automobile' was a 'veritable terror'.

[43] E. R. Kilby, 'The Demographics of the U.S. Equine Population' in D. J. Salem and A. N. Rowan (eds.), *The State of America's Animals IV* (2007) ch. 10, 176, drawing data from E. M. Ensminger, *Horses and Horsemanship* (1969).

[44] E.g. Special Roads Act 1949 (building motorways), Highways Act 1959 and today the Highways Act 1980.

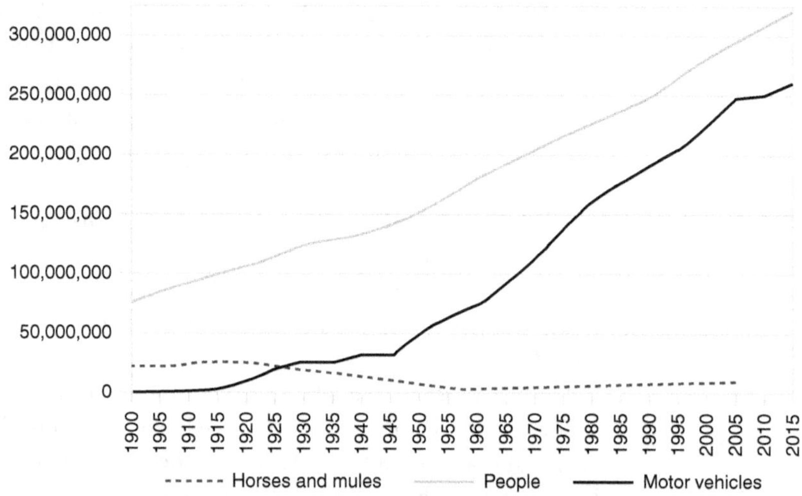

Figure 15.1 US horse, motor and people populations, 1900–2015
Sources: E. R. Kilby, 'The Demographics of the U.S. Equine Population' in D. J. Salem and A. N. Rowan (eds.), *The State of America's Animals IV* (2007); Department of Transport; Census

of routes and many collisions'.[45] Though Morrison lost his seat as an MP, his London Passenger Transport Act 1933 subsequently passed, enabling London to take buses and rail into public ownership. Morrison staunchly rejected that anyone but 'experts' (as chosen by the biggest 'experts', like Minister Morrison) should be placed on the boards of public corporations. Apparently, passenger representation risked including 'the various employers' organisations', and apparently if workers were allowed to have votes for the board, 'it would be difficult to resist a similar claim from the users of transport'.[46] In other words, passenger voice would hinder worker voice, but worker voice would encourage passenger voice, so best to give nobody any voice at all. Instead, the public corporation, said Morrison, should 'have a social conscience, a corporate spirit and a public purpose; the legitimate rights of the consumer [would] be safeguarded; so also those of labour in the industry'. It was just that the 'consumer' and labour – over the compelling objections of many in the labour movement[47] – could not have any role in that safeguarding themselves.

After World War Two, with the four big railways bankrupt, the Transport Act 1947 nationalised rail, road haulage and some buses. This was managed by the British Transport Commission (BTC) and a series of transport executives.

[45] H. Morrison, *Socialisation and Transport: Organisation of Socialised Industries with the Particular Reference to the London Passenger Transport Bill* (1933) ch. 1, 16.

[46] Morrison, *Socialisation and Transport*, ch. 11, 197.

[47] Morrison, *Socialisation and Transport*, ch. 11, 199–203. To Morrison's credit, he extracts a speech to Labour Party Conference by Harold Clay, from the TGWU and later President of the Workers' Educational Association, putting forward a compelling case for worker representation. Today it appears that Clay was right.

Like Morrison's model, the BTC was to 'be appointed by the Minister from among persons appearing to him to be persons who have wide experience', without worker or passenger voting rights.[48] This was, however, designed to be a 'properly integrated system of public inland transport'.[49] The BTC did not complete public ownership of all buses, and when Labour lost the 1951 election the Conservatives reprivatised most trucking. Nationalised industry was bound by ordinary rules of law[50] and, from experience, the government made efforts to ensure it ran like a financially responsible business – for instance, by introducing performance targets.[51] The Transport Act 1962 replaced the BTC with a new British Railways Board (BRB) and the Transport Holding Company for buses.[52]

But as car ownership soared the tragic Beeching Report of 1963 led to the axing of 2,363 stations, 266 routes and over 4,000 miles of track (see Figure 15.2).[53] Most buses were finally made public with the Transport Act 1968 under a National Bus Company.[54]

All the progress was ended by Thatcher's privatisations. The Transport Act 1985 sold off buses and gave employees shares (without any real voice) to try and divide workforce opposition (a strategy later used in post-Soviet Russia).

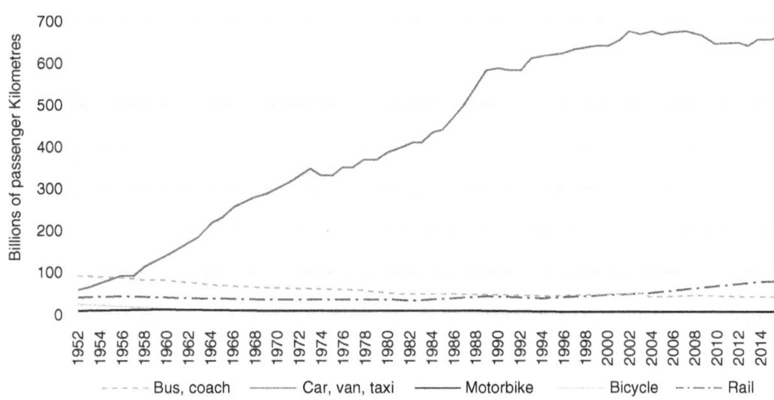

Figure 15.2 UK passenger transport mode, 1952–2017
Source: Dept for Transport, Table TSGB0101: 'Passenger Transport: By Mode, Annual from 1952'

48 Transport Act 1947, ss. 1(2), 5 and Sch. 2.

49 Transport Act 1947, s. 3.

50 E.g. *Tamlin v Hannaford* [1950] 1 KB 18, holding that the BTC could not rely on Crown immunity when ejecting a tenant, and was bound to normal obligations.

51 White Paper, *The Economic and Financial Obligations of the Nationalised Industries*, Cmnd 1337 (1961).

52 O. Kahn-Freund, 'Transport Act, 1962' (1963) 26(2) *MLR* 174. By enabling exemption clauses 'the Act [went] much further in giving effect to laissez-faire in the law of transport than English law has ever done at any time since the seventeenth century'. Also s. 3(1) created a duty of BRB to provide rail 'in Great Britain' with regard to 'efficiency, economy and safety of operation'.

53 R. Beeching, *The Reshaping of British Railways* (1963).

54 After the report, *Public Transport and Traffic*, Cmnd 3481 (1967).

Only in London did buses survive under public regulation, but not public ownership,[55] and democratic oversight itself was abolished as the Greater London Council was closed. Ironically, the government showed that, with some competence and care, British Rail efficiency could be improved.[56] But then the Major government sold off rail as well.[57] What Thatcher said was a 'privatisation too far' (as if the buses or petroleum were okay), was left to John MacGregor MP, the new Minister for Transport, and also an accomplished magician. But the magic did not work for rail. The Railways Act 1993 sold the tracks to one monopoly private company (Railtrack) and section 25 said that no UK public body could own the new privatised rail franchise contracts to operate trains. Yet foreign governments could bid for UK railways, leading to the incomprehensible situation that we still have today, where the only governments in the world that cannot own UK railways are our own. Worse, the same idea has persisted for buses, now in the Bus Services Act 2017, section 22.[58] The Labour Party was forced to bring the tracks back into public ownership after multiple mass deaths from crashes on unsafe tracks. Train operating companies also kept going insolvent, particularly on the East Coast main line, and yet the government kept privatising it even though public ownership plainly worked better. Scotland reacquired the power to run railways in 2016, and the Williams Review from 2019 has mooted merging the multiple franchisees, like going back to the big four. But at the time of writing, in the Covid-19 pandemic, the UK government has in effect nationalised rail again.[59] Meanwhile, electrification of rail lags far behind other countries, currently around 42 per cent compared to 100 per cent in Switzerland. The absence of proper buses outside London means that cars and toxic fumes are still a deadly part of life.

(2) Finance

The five main types of enterprise for inland transport are auto-makers, bus companies, taxi companies, general businesses and train companies, and each receives large subsidies. The UK government budget for transport was £37 billion in 2019–20, and this includes road and rail-track work. Altogether, (a) auto-makers profit from free roads for vehicles, non-payment

[55] London Regional Transport Act 1984 (c. 32).

[56] T. R. Gourvish, 'British Rail's "Business-Led" Organization, 1977–1990: Government-Industry Relations in Britain's Public Sector' (1990) 64(1) *Business History Rev* 109, 149, suggesting that by 1989, British Rail was 40% more efficient than 8 comparable European rail systems, while in 1979 it had been 14% more efficient.

[57] DfT, *New Opportunities for the Railways: The Privatisation of British Rail*, Cm 2012 (1992) [3], itself bizarrely pointing out the very productivity of British Rail as the highest in Europe.

[58] Bus Services Act 2017, s. 22.

[59] T. Powley, 'ONS Recognises Full Nationalisation of the UK Railways', *Financial Times* (31 July 2020).

for accidents, climate damage and pollution and state aid; (b) buses receive the same subsidies and state aid; (c) traditional taxis mostly have sound finance, but Uber and other private hire firms are currently benefiting from tax evasion and non-enforcement of rights; (d) business vehicles generally benefit from tax deductions; and (e) train companies benefit from cheap rail tracks, their natural monopoly position and state aid.

(a) Auto-makers

While auto-makers are some of the largest, most profitable corporations in the world, they would not exist in their current form without express and implicit subsidies. Table 15.1 shows the top twenty auto-makers for 2016, including for cars, vans and trucks, and lists the commitments they had made so far for electrification.[60]

(i) Public Roads and Space

The first main subsidy for auto-makers is public roads and space, funded by tax. Roads are for driving, but also simply parking: the average car spends 96 per cent of its life parked.[61] Most residential roads are taken up with parked cars, instead of street life and gardens, and were so monopolised by motors that they long ago became dangerous for children to play in.[62] As well as this, there are 50,000 acres (200 km^2) of actual car parks in the UK.[63] This is as if London's zone 2, or from Richmond to Greenwich, and Stratford to Wembley, was just a concrete and tarmac lot. Obviously, roads also benefit consumers and businesses who buy and drive motor vehicles, but auto-makers are the parties that profit most. In the UK there are around 31 million personal vehicles, but just 6.8 million buses, taxis and delivery vehicles. The latter group accounts for 56 per cent of exhaust emissions.[64]

[60] E.g. T. Dixon, 'Changan Automobile Aims to End Sales of Traditional Fuel Vehicles by 2025 and Invest 100 Billion Yuan (15 Billion USD) into Electrification' *EVObsession* (26 October 2017); 'Chinese Auto Giant BAIC Going 100% Electric by 2025', *CleanTechnica* (18 December 2017); 'Geely Holding Group Celebrates World Earth Day by Banning all Single Use Plastics from Geely Facilities', *Automotive World* (22 April 2020).

[61] J. Bates and D. Leibling, *Spaced Out: Perspectives on Parking Policy* (2012) vi, 80% at home, 16% elsewhere.

[62] C. Ward, *The Child in the City* (1979) 73: 'One should be able to play everywhere, easily, loosely, and not forced into a "playground" or "park". The failure of an urban environment can be measured in direct proportion to the number of "playgrounds".'

[63] 'Government Owned Car Parks Could Hold the Key to 110,000 New Homes', *Knight Frank* (15 July 2020).

[64] See Defra and DfT, *UK Plan for Tackling Roadside Nitrogen Dioxide Concentrations* (July 2017) 7, Figure 3. For NOx emissions, vans and HGVs are 40%, buses 16%, taxis 2%, cars 43% and other vehicles 1%. This assumes similar exhaust-pipe emission breakdowns for carbon dioxide and other gases.

Table 15.1 Top 20 auto-makers, 2016

	Name	Vehicles 2016	Electric commitments	HQ
1	Toyota	10,213,486	2025, all electric or hybrid	Japan
2	Volkswagen	10,126,281	2028, 70% electric, 2025, 50%[i]	Germany
3	Hyundai and Kia	7,889,538	-	S. Korea
4	GM and Chevrolet	7,793,066	2035, 100% electric[ii]	USA
5	Ford	6,429,485	2026, electric or hybrid option[iii]	USA
6	Nissan	5,556,241	2022, 40% electric or hybrid	Japan
7	Honda	4,999,266	2025, all electric option	Japan
8	Fiat Chrysler	4,681,457	2022, 60% models hybrid[iv]	Italy
9	Renault	3,373,278	-	France
10	Groupe PSA (Peugeot, Vauxhall)	3,152,787	2025, all hybrids	France
11	Suzuki	2,945,793	-	Japan
12	SAIC (MG)	2,526,450	-	China
13	Daimler (Mercedes)	2,359,756	2025, 25% models electric	Germany
14	BMW	1,715,871	2025, 15–25% electric[v]	Germany
15	Changan	1,586,013	2025, 100% electric	China
16	Mazda		2030, all electric or hybrid	Japan
17	BAIC	1,391,643	2025, 100% electric	China
18	Dongfeng Motor	1,315,490	-	China
19	Geely (Volvo, LT London)	1,266,456	2025, 50% electric	China
20	Great Wall	1,094,360	2025, 33% electric	China

i P. Campbell, 'Volkswagen Sets Bold Targets as It Steps Up Electric Ambitions', *Financial Times* (12 March 2019).

ii 'General Motors Announces Plan for all-Electric Lineup by 2035', *The Guardian* (28 January 2021); California indicates it will ban sales in 2035, i.e. doing nothing for 14 years.

iii P. Campbell, *Financial Times* (17 February 2021).

iv J. Dow, 'Fiat, Formerly Headed by an EV Detractor, Says 60% of Models Will Be "Electrified" in 2021', *Electrek* (1 December 2020).

v C. Hetzner, 'BMW Re-Affirms Position against Electric-Only Platform', *Automotive News* (4 February 2020).

(ii) Road Deaths and Casualties

Second, auto-maker enterprises do not pay for the cost of accidents that their products inevitably create. We are accustomed to blame drivers for accidents,[65] and yet road transport is notoriously unsafe.[66] In 2015 the deaths from *avoidable* traffic collisions totalled 84,589 in Europe, 34,064 in the USA, 238,562 in India, 261,367 in China and 1.25 million worldwide.[67] Roads have become safer, but in the UK in 2017 alone, 1,793 people were killed, and 24,831

65 Cf. P. Cane and J. Goudkamp, *Atiyah's Accidents, Compensation and the Law* (2018) ch. 1, 7–8 for discussion.

66 E.g. R. Nader, *Unsafe at any Speed: The Designed-In Dangers of the American Automobile* (1965).

67 WHO, *Global Status Report on Road Safety 2015* (2015) Table A2.

were seriously injured.[68] Every death is an unimaginable loss to people's families and friends. There is also an enormous financial cost, for healthcare and economic loss. The Department for Transport estimated for 2011 that each death costs an average of £1.69 million, and the cost of a serious casualty was £189,519.[69] With the 2017 accident statistics, this amounts to £7.73 billion every year, compared to the £145 billion health budget, over 5 per cent of total health spending. It is possible that driverless technology (should it transpire) could help. Yet the raw fact is that 365,000 people have been killed on UK roads since World War Two, and 4.2 million people have been seriously injured.[70] Almost everyone knows someone who has been killed or seriously injured on the road. Auto-maker enterprises have been able to externalise these costs entirely.

(iii) Climate Damage and Toxic Air

Third, road transport enterprises receive a direct subsidy to the extent that they are not held responsible for toxic emissions which their vehicles are designed to burn. The majority of emissions come from 'working' vehicles. As we have seen, compared to the 31 million cars, the 6.8 million buses, taxis and delivery vehicles are alone responsible for 56 per cent of exhaust emissions.

Four main types of emissions are (1) carbon dioxide, CO_2; (2) carbon monoxide, CO; (3) nitrogen oxides, NOx (a group of different gases including nitrous oxide, N_2O); and (4) particulate matter, PM. As Chapter 11 explained, carbon dioxide is one of the primary causes of climate damage, but in transport it is still not directly regulated. The Renewable Energy Directive (RED) 2009, article 3(4) required that member states ensured at least 10 per cent of transport was fuelled from renewable energy by 2020, and the RED 2018, article 25 required that final energy consumption in transport is 'at least 14%' renewable.[71] This unambitious figure falls within the 'mandatory national targets for the overall share of energy from renewable sources in gross final consumption of energy', 15 per cent by 2020 and now 32 per cent by 2030.[72] These targets are too low and not working. The UK missed its 10 per cent target for 2020.[73] The problem is the auto-makers, who are not yet under a duty to electrify everything as fast as technologically possible. This is why transport emissions stay stagnant.

[68] DfT, *Reported Road Casualties in Great Britain: 2017 Annual Report* (2018) down from 6,352 deaths in 1979.

[69] See Making the Link which refers to DfT, *Reported Road Casualties Great Britain: Annual Report 2011* (2012).

[70] In World War Two itself, for the UK, there were 383,700 military deaths, 450,900 total deaths and 376,239 military wounded.

[71] RED 2018/2001, arts. 25 and 27 (on calculations).

[72] RED 2009/28/EC, arts. 1, 3(4), 21–3.

[73] In 2016, the UK share of renewable energy in transport fell to 4.23%. The Renewable Transport Obligations Order 2007 (SI 2007/3072) suggested increasing the number of biofuels (including rapeseed, sugar beet and cane oil) which are blended with ordinary fuels, and result in decreased emissions.

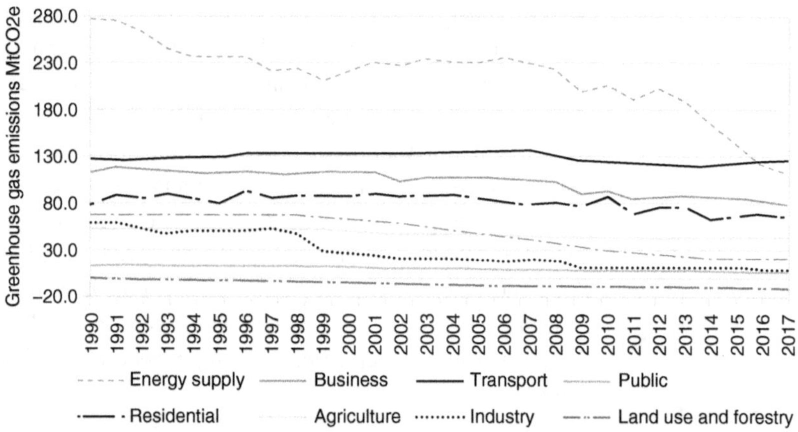

Figure 15.3 UK greenhouse gas emissions, 1990–2017
Source: DBEIS, 2017 UK Greenhouse Gas Emissions: Final Figures – Data Tables (2019) Table 3

The UK has been particularly poor in reducing transport CO_2 emissions (see Figure 15.3), but the European Union (EU) also lacks any hard rules. The Emission Performance Regulation 2019 suggests manufacturers of passenger cars should not allow emissions to exceed 120 grams of CO_2 per kilometre and, after 2020, no more than 95 grams.[74] Manufacturers can agree to pool their production quotas, so as to meet their targets on average,[75] but there is no legal sanction for failure to meet the target. Member states are simply required to record the relevant success or failure, and manufacturers' performance is published.[76] This is abysmal compared to Chinese auto-makers, such as Changan and BAIC, pledging to produce 100 per cent electric vehicles by 2025, while Geely has a 50 per cent pledge. China has heavily subsidised clean-vehicle purchases.[77]

Transport emissions other than CO_2 are regulated because of the damage to health. Carbon monoxide, nitrous oxide and particulate matter cause respiratory illness. These (and ozone) are estimated to cause around 400,000 premature deaths in the EU, and 40,000 early deaths in the UK each year. This costs the NHS an estimated £6 billion a year: again, a subsidy to road transport enterprise.[78] It follows that nearly 10 per cent of the total NHS budget is spent because of road accidents and emissions. The Vehicles Emissions Regulation 2007, as amended in 2012,[79] sets standards in maximum emissions that car manufacturers can have. Since 1992, and the introduction of the 'Euro 1'

[74] Emission Performance Regulation 2019 (EU) 2019/631, arts. 1–2.
[75] Emission Performance Regulation, art. 6.
[76] Emission Performance Regulation, arts. 7–10. Also art. 11 derogations.
[77] E.g. C. Clover, 'Subsidies Help China Sell the Most Electric Cars', *Financial Times* (24 October 2017).
[78] C. Brand and D. Hunt, *The Health Costs of Air Pollution from Cars and Vans* (2018).
[79] Vehicle Emissions Regulation (EU) 459/2012, Annex, setting out the Euro 6 limits.

standard, each four to five years standards have become more stringent. Article 2 defines the categories of vehicle to which the limits apply, up to those under 2,610 kg, while a 2019 regulation applies to heavier vehicles and has loose limits for CO_2.[80] Article 4 states manufacturers must 'demonstrate that all new vehicles sold, registered or put into service in the Community are type approved in accordance with this Regulation'. Article 6 requires manufacturers to 'provide unrestricted and standardised access to vehicle repair and maintenance information' should there be any non-compliance. Article 13 requires penalties imposed by member states for breach are 'effective, proportionate and dissuasive', and breaches include any 'false declarations' as well as 'use of defeat devices'. Table 15.2 sets out the emission limits. It is unclear why they differ for petrol and diesel.[81]

Table 15.2 Toxic vehicle emissions and Euro 1–6 limits

Light vehicle emission limits							
		CD		NOx		FM	
	Date	Petrol	Diesel	Petrol	Diesel	Petrol	Diesel
Euro 0	Oct. 1991	-	-	1	1.6	-	-
Euro 1	Jul. 1992	2.72	2.72	0.49	0.78	-	0.14
Euro 2	Jan. 1996	2.2	1	0.25	0.73	-	0.1
Euro 3	Jan. 2000	2.3	0.6	0.15	0.5	-	0.05
Euro 4	Jan. 2005	1	0.5	0.08	0.25	-	0.025
Euro 5	Sep. 2009	1	0.5	0.06	0.18	0.005	0.005
Euro 6	Sep. 2014	1	0.5	0.06	0.08	0.005	0.005
Heavy vehicle emission limits							
		CO		NOx		FM	
	Date	Petrol	Diesel	Petrol	Diesel	Petrol	Diesel
Euro 1	Jan. 1992	2.72	3.16	-	-	-	0.14
Euro 2	Jan. 1996	2.2	1	-	0.55	-	0.08
Euro 3	Jan. 2000	2.3	0.64	0.15	0.5	-	0.05
Euro 4	Jan. 2005	1	0.5	0.08	0.25	-	-
Euro 5	Sep. 2009	1	0.5	0.06	0.18	0.005	0.005
Euro 6	Aug. 2014	1	0.5	0.06	0.08	0.005	0.005

80 Heavy Vehicle Emission Regulation (EU) 2019/1242, arts. 4–5, the Commission determining limits ad hoc, and a zero-emission vehicle counting as two. This appears to be propelling research into better technology.

81 See 'EU: Light-Duty: Emissions', www.transportpolicy.net/standard/eu-light-duty-emissions/, and 'EU: Heavy-Duty: Emissions', www.transportpolicy.net/standard/eu-heavy-duty-emissions/ (2021).

These standards do not encompass CO_2, but in practice they push to all electric vehicles. Following the trend, a 'Euro 7' standard should simply eliminate fossil fuels and eliminate the toxic combustion engine. But by 2021, the EU Commission had still failed to make a decision,[82] and is still consulting on what an alternative should be. Given the scale of climate damage, and that the total cost of electric vehicles is already cheaper once lifetime fuel is included, failing to end fossil fuels is a massive, daily economic cost.

As well as having low standards, emissions enforcement has failed. In 2015, the US Environmental Protection Agency issued a Clean Air Act of 1963 violation notice against Volkswagen (VW), for both VW and Audi vehicles. A report commissioned by the California Air Resources Board in May 2014 claimed that VW was cheating in emissions testing. In 2007, Martin Winterkorn became VW CEO, and embarked upon 'Strategy 2018' to become the world's largest car manufacturer. In fact, in May 2018, this 'strategy' resulted in Winterkorn being indicted for criminal fraud and conspiracy. VW had decided that building more diesel cars could prove popular, because diesel fuel can provide more power. Diesel fuel also emits less CO_2 but emits far more carbon monoxide, nitrous oxides and particulate matter. A simple exhaust filter can stop this, but filters also reduce a car's performance. Therefore, VW started using 'defeat devices' in its exhausts that could detect when the car was undergoing a regulatory test (because the car's wheels are not on the ground, as it is suspended in a laboratory). During a test the car's computer would put the filter on. On the road, the filter would be off. The California Air Resources Board correctly alleged that cars were emitting around forty times the nitrous oxide when they were on the road. After this VW issued vehement denials of their fraud. When this was no longer credible, they hired a law firm called Jones Day to conduct an 'internal investigation' which promptly blamed 'rogue engineers'. This was also a lie. Between 2009 and 2016, it is estimated that VW vehicle sales alone resulted in an additional 2,200 deaths worldwide,[83] including roughly 240 additional deaths in the UK. In 2016, VW did indeed become the biggest car company in the world.

It was not just Volkswagen. In April 2016, a UK Department for Transport study of thirty-seven diesel engines from BMW, Ford, Honda, Hyundai, Jaguar, Kia, Mazda, Mercedes, Mini, Peugeot, Renault, Skoda, Toyota, Vauxhall and VW showed exhaust emissions were twelve times higher than the EU maximum when tested on the road. Every vehicle exceeded legal NOx emissions, even though they were said to have complied with the Euro 5 limits in laboratory testing.[84] But even though this wanton pattern of fraud was

[82] 'EU to Tighten Euro 7 Emissions Standard for All Tests', *Electrive* (16 November 2020).

[83] J. Armour, 'Volkswagen's Emissions Scandal: Lessons for Corporate Governance?' (parts 1 and 2) (2016) Oxford Business Law Blog.

[84] E.g. P. McGee, 'EU Finds Evidence Carmakers Are Manipulating Results', *Financial Times* (24 July 2018); D. Keating, 'Carmakers Are Cheating Again – But This Time They're Inflating Their Emissions', *Forbes* (26 July 2018).

exposed, enforcement action and the process of bringing corporate criminals to justice has been unforgivably flawed. For example, VW paid $15.3 billion in the USA to settle civil enforcement claims in June 2016. In Germany, it took until June 2018 before VW was fined €1 billion by prosecutors. At the time of writing Winterkorn has been indicted, but is not yet in jail; he may keep his millions and his lawyer is pleading that he is in poor health. Nothing has been done to vindicate the thousands of deaths caused by toxic air. In the UK, despite a select committee report, group litigation at the time of writing has been launched but no results have yet materialised.[85] Perhaps the most meaningful result has been a push, albeit weak, to turn production towards electric vehicles. For instance, VW states that by 2025, it aims for 25 per cent of the vehicles it sells to be electric.[86] This is completely inadequate: cars should be electric, and all people involved should be punished for the mass deaths from which they profited.

(iv) State Aid for Manufacturing

As well as implicit regulatory subsidies, auto-makers receive explicit state aid. National governments granting aid to private business has been important partly because competition is international: most countries with successful sectors have attempted to create 'national champions' as a way to maintain highly paid jobs and profits within their country. Across the EU, the automotive sector employs 12.9 million people, while in the UK in 2016 there were 186,000 people employed directly in manufacturing, and 856,000 people employed in the automotive industry generally.[87] In the EU as a whole, between 2007 and 2014 €341 million in aid was given to manufacturers.[88] In the USA, vast sums of money were spent in the global financial crisis to bail out General Motors, Ford, Chrysler and more.[89]

Since 1979, the UK largely abandoned this approach and currently spends just 0.5 per cent of its annual Gross Domestic Product (GDP) on state aid, compared to Germany with 1.3 per cent of GDP.[90] Closing the gap would easily be enough to make transport and energy clean.[91] As explained in Chapter 6(4)(c), subsidies can be used pro-competitively to buy electric

85 See www.vwemissionsaction.com/legal-case.

86 E.g. P. McGee, 'Volkswagen's Plan to Kill Off Tesla', *Financial Times* (30 January 2019).

87 Society of Motor Manufacturers and Traders, *Motor Industry Facts* (2018) 6.

88 'State Aid in the Automotive Sector: An Overview', Occasional Discussion Papers by the Competition Directorate-General of the European Commission (2014).

89 Emergency Economic Stabilization Act of 2008 enabling loans and grants of $80.3bn for GM and Chrysler.

90 'State Aid Scoreboard 2017', European Commission Competition DG, Policy and Strategy State Aid Policy and Strategy, COMP. A3 (29 November 2017) 31.

91 E. McGaughey, 'EU Law Empowers a Big Green New Deal and State Aid Rules Stop Corporate Welfare', *LSE British Politics and Policy* (12 December 2018).

cars – for instance, by the UK's plug-in car and van grants.[92] EU law also exempts aid for 'environmental protection', including infrastructure, tax incentives and education.[93] But although some motor production remains in the UK, all major UK brands have become foreign-owned: Rolls Royce and Mini are owned by the German company BMW, Jaguar and Land Rover are owned by the Indian Tata family, Bentley is owned by Volkswagen, MG is owned by the Chinese company SAIC and the London Electric Vehicle Company that makes the new black cabs in Coventry is owned by the Chinese company Geely. While jobs may persist in UK factories for the time being, dividends are not being spent or reinvested in UK social development. This may not be negative for overall global development in itself. If more people have improved livelihoods in India and China as a result, and if those countries effectively tax profits and use them for social development, this may result in overall higher levels of human development across the globe. Yet the UK is forced to offer incentives for production to stay, and keeps no profits.

(b) Buses

Bus companies benefit from similar subsidies to auto-makers. Details of the top ten bus companies are set out in Table 15.3. In particular, they use public roads, and buses account for around 16 per cent of emissions. The major bus companies are owned by other governments, or by shareholders, while just thirty-three councils in the UK have maintained municipal bus networks.[94]

In addition, when these companies buy a business vehicle, they are entitled to reduce the profits they report by the vehicle's cost, whether that vehicle is clean or not.[95]

(c) Taxis and Private Hire Vehicles

Taxis and 'private hire vehicles' are licensed by local authorities, and account for 2 per cent of emissions. In law, a 'taxi' is a Hackney carriage or a 'black cab' that can pick people up on the streets, while a private hire vehicle must arrange pickup in advance, and this includes Uber. Traditional taxi enterprises are regulated self-employed people. They benefit from public roads, but given their expertise like bus drivers they have exceptionally low rates of accidents, and in London since 2019 all new black cabs have to be electric.[96] There are around 21,000 black cabs, but a 9,000 'zero emissions capable' target for the

[92] In 2021, for electric cars priced up to £35,000, a grant of up to £2,500 was available, £3,000 for up to 2.5 tonne vans, and £6,000 up to 3.5 tonne vans.

[93] State Aid Block Exemption Regulation 2014 (EU) No. 651/2014, arts. 1(c) and 36–49.

[94] These include Suffolk, Nottingham, Blackpool, Guisborough, Skipton, Cardiff, Newport, Ipswich, Edinburgh, Dumfries and Galloway, Moray, and Northern Ireland.

[95] Capital Allowances Act 2001, s. 104AA(4).

[96] G. Topham, 'First 100% Electric Black Cab for 120 Years Launches in London', *The Guardian* (23 October 2019).

Table 15.3 Top 10 bus companies in London and UK

	Bus company brands	Owner	London Routes
1	Abellio London	Nederlandse Spoorwegen	3, 24, 27, 45, 49, 68, etc.
2	Arriva London	Deutsche Bahn	2, 19, 29, 34, 38, 41, 175, etc.
3	Quality Line, etc	RATP (French govt)	9, 18, 404, 413, etc.
4	Go-Ahead London plc	London Stock Exchange listed	1, 11, 15, 171, 175, 176, etc.
5	Metroline	ComfortDelGro (Singapore listed)	4, 6, 7, 16, 17, 98, etc.
6	Stagecoach London	Brian Souter (Scottish billionaire)	8, 25, 47, etc.
7	Sullivan Buses	Dean Sullivan, former LU manager	217
8	Tower Transit	Australian family business	13, 23, 218, etc.
9	HCT Group	Hackney Community Transport	20, 26, 309, 385, 388, etc.
10	Uno	University of Hertfordshire	383, 692

end of 2020 was sidelined.[97] There are currently around 4,000 electric black cabs.

By contrast, the major private hire vehicle corporation, Uber, systematically evades tax, and the rights of its drivers. It misrepresents that its drivers are self-employed, arguably amounting to fraud, to evade paying income tax or National Insurance, or the cost of dismissal, childcare or other rights.[98] It argues that its passengers are not consumers, to evade paying Value Added Tax, and now faces a £1.5 billion bill for years of breaking the law.[99] Uber even argued it was not a transport company, to evade licensing requirements. It has a pathetic pledge to have zero emissions in its global fleet 'by 2040', 'by 2030 in US, Canadian and European cities' and 'by 2025' in London,[100] dressing up its delay in ending the mass toxification of air as something socially responsible. Despite all these subsidies, it has consistently failed to make a profit, suggesting its goal is predatory pricing to maintain a monopoly network, until it can introduce driverless vehicles.

(d) Business Vehicles

Business vehicles, such as for deliveries, are subsidised by tax deductions, and account for around 40 per cent of roadside emissions. Because of tax deductions,[101] and the fact that total cost of vehicle ownership is lower for

[97] P. Richardson, 'The 9,000 Zero-Emission Capable Taxi Target Is "No Longer Relevant" Says London Mayor', *TaxiPoint* (26 February 2020).

[98] E. McGaughey, 'Uber, the Taylor Review, Mutuality, and the Duty to Not Misrepresent Employment Status' (2019) 48(2) *Industrial Law Journal* 180.

[99] 'Good Law Project Forces HMRC to Collect £1.5bn in VAT from Uber', *Good Law Project* (23 October 2020).

[100] 'Uber Pledges All-Electric Fleet by 2040', *BBC News* (8 September 2020).

[101] Capital Allowances Act 2001, s. 104AA(4).

electric,[102] our current tax system encourages business to both lose money and pollute. This makes no sense.

(e) Train Companies to Great British Railways?

Train companies, at the time of writing, were subsidised by cheap access to tracks by the publicly owned Network Rail Ltd, and insolvent without government support due to collapse in travel with Covid-19. Train companies were still franchised by the government, but in 2021 these franchises were proposed to be replaced, along with Network Rail, with a new 'Great British Railways' (GBR), running five regions. New 'Passenger Service Contracts' would set timetables and fares, which GBR would collect. By contrast, the current franchising model allows train companies to set timetables and fares, and so predict improvements when bidding for contracts, but deliver much less in practice as they extracted maximum profit from their regional monopoly.[103] The new GBR is envisaged to be run 'in the public interest'.[104]

While the details and legislative changes are not yet released, Great British Railways would be a significant improvement. In 2018–19 train companies took £7.1 billion a year in subsidies,[105] and yet paid around £400 million a year in profit to shareholders.[106] The gap between subsidies and performance, however, is stark. On 15,811 km of track, only 42 per cent of UK rail lines are electrified,[107] among the worst records in Europe.[108] If we take an estimated cost to electrify a 'single track kilometre' as £1 million, this means full electrification will cost around £9 billion, or twenty-two years of train company profits.[109] Because of a statutory ban on public ownership, only the Scottish government in the UK can own British railways since 2016.[110] Yet the nationalised French, German and Dutch train companies (SNCF, Deutsche Bahn, Nederlandse Spoorwegen) own our train companies,[111] as well as shareholders. This means that subsidies to UK rail are no different from

[102] K. Palmer, J. E. Tait, Z. Wadud and J. Nellthorp, 'Total Cost of Ownership and Market Share for Hybrid and Electric Vehicles in the UK, US and Japan' (2018) 209 *Applied Energy* 108, finding lower costs after 16,000 miles for hybrid vehicles and, that with government subsidies at the time of writing, electric cars were cheaper overall.

[103] DfT, *Great British Railways*, CP 423 (May 2021) 54–5.

[104] DfT, *Great British Railways*, 11 and 30.

[105] ORR, 'Rail Finance: 2018–19 Annual Statistical Release' (14 November 2019).

[106] E.g. N. Sommerlad, 'All on Board the Gravy Train – Rail Firms' £3.5billion Profit Despite Passengers' Fury at Dire Service', *Daily Mirror* (2 January 2017).

[107] 'Will the UK Ever Get Electrification Back on Track?', *Railway Technology* (13 June 2018): 'a paltry 42%'.

[108] 'Electrified Railway Lines' (2016) ec.europa.eu. Switzerland has 100% electrified rail.

[109] K. Barrow, 'British Electrification Costs Could Be Cut by 50%, Says Report', *International Railway Journal* (14 March 2019), explaining costs may range from £750,000 to £1.5m for complex projects, with savings.

[110] Scotland Act 2016, s. 57.

[111] Railways Act 1993, s. 25; D. Keating, 'Almost All British Train Lines Are Now Owned by Other EU Countries', *Forbes* (15 August 2019).

sending the French, German and Dutch governments a big annual cheque. This makes no sense, and the rule should also be abandoned in a future GBR system.

(3) Governance

Transport governance since privatisation has remained unprincipled and chaotic. Like private persons need to have a driving licence to go on the roads,[112] there are patchy systems of licensing for enterprises themselves. The six main enterprise governance structures are (a) public infrastructure, headed by the Office of Rail and Road; (b) auto-makers, mostly private corporations, but with a history of 'golden shares' and public ownership; (c) licensed bus companies; (d) licensed taxis and private hire vehicles; (e) business vehicles, particularly those owned by other large enterprises; and (f) train companies.

(a) Public Infrastructure

The three main public infrastructure bodies are (i) the Office of Rail and Road, (ii) the various Highway authorities and (iii) Network Rail Ltd.

(i) Office of Rail and Road

Since 2015, the Office of Rail and Road (ORR) has been a combined regulator for railways and highways.[113] The chair and four other members are appointed by the Secretary of State for terms of up to five years, and can be dismissed for a good reason.[114] At the time of writing, the government had just proposed a new system of central timetabling and fare control, akin to London buses, under a new body called 'Great British Railways'.[115] However, at present, although it exercises no direct control, under the Railways Act 1993, section 4 the ORR has a long list of duties that do not touch these central problems. They include duties to improve railway service performance in the interest of passengers; promote usage, 'competition', interconnection and safety; but also to enable railway companies 'to plan the future of their businesses with a reasonable degree of assurance'.[116] Section 67 requires it to exercise competition functions with the Competition and Market Authority, even though there is essentially no competition.[117] Section 4(3) requires it to consider 'the

[112] Road Traffic Act 1988, ss. 87–8, and 110–12; Driving Licences Directive 2006/126/EC.

[113] Railways and Transport Safety Act 2003, ss. 15–16. The Infrastructure Act 2015, s. 10(9) and SI 2015/1682 renamed this as the ORR from 'Ofrail', which had existed since 2003, and in turn replaced the Rail Regulator.

[114] Railways and Transport Safety Act 2003, Sch. 1, para. 2: dismissal possible for absence from meetings for 3 months, financial or personal interest, 'has misbehaved' or 'is unable, unfit or unwilling to perform his functions as a member'.

[115] DfT, *Great British Railways*. [116] Railways Act 1993, s. 4.

[117] T. Prosser, 'Economic Regulation in a Plural Public Sector: The Office of Rail and Road and Network Rail' [2020] *Public Law* 116.

need to protect all persons from dangers' and 'the effect on the environment' from rail, but there is not yet a duty and a timescale to electrify the rail tracks.

Under the Infrastructure Act 2015, the ORR 'must also carry out activities to monitor how a strategic highways company', particularly Highways England, exercises its function, including investigating and reporting on goals under a Road Investment Strategy, and 'have regard to ... safety of users of highways' and 'environmental impact'.[118] But again, there are not yet duties to eliminate fossil fuels on roads, by decarbonising traffic and installing electric charging: on the contrary the same 2015 Act required 'maximising economic recovery of UK petroleum' in the oil industry (see Ch. 11),[119] a singularly toxic goal.

(ii) Highways, Charging and Pricing

Since the Highways Act 1835, the responsibility for building roads has generally been assumed to be a public service, funded through general and local taxation. Today's Highways Act 1980 distinguishes between 'trunk roads' (motorways, as in 'M' roads, or large 'A' roads),[120] ordinary roads, bridleways (for walking, horse-riding or 'a right to drive animals' but not vehicles) and footpaths.[121] Under section 36, highways are 'maintainable at the public expense' if they have been historically designated as highways,[122] or are newly built by highways authorities, by councils under the Housing Act 1985 or are designated as trunk roads.[123] The expense falls upon the relevant 'highway authority' set out in section 1. First, the Minister for Transport is the highway authority for a trunk road or anything made by the minister's order. Second, a 'strategic highways company', namely Highways England Ltd, in practice performs the building and maintenance of the trunk (i.e. 'strategic') road network: its board is wholly appointed by the minister. When constructing new highways, it must give notice and receive representations from every council the road passes through.[124] Third, outside London the authorities are the County Council or Metropolitan District Council. Fourth, in London, the authority is Transport for London (TfL) for Greater London Authority (GLA)

118 Infrastructure Act 2015, ss. 10–12.
119 Infrastructure Act 2015, s. 41 and Petroleum Act 1998, s. 9A.
120 Like a tree, the Trunk Roads Act 1936 first differentiated major 'trunk' roads from other 'branches' of the network.
121 Highways Act 1980, ss. 42(2) on council responsibility and 329 on interpretation.
122 Highways Act 1980, s. 36, referring to what were highways under the previous Highways Act 1957.
123 Highways Act 1980, s. 36 also refers to footpaths created under the Town and Country Planning Act 1990, ss. 247 and 257; the Harbours Act 1964, ss. 14 and 16; and the Transport Works Act 1992, ss. 1 and 3.
124 Highways Act 1980, s. 24.

roads,[125] and the borough or common council for their roads.[126] Scotland and Northern Ireland have separate statutory systems.[127]

All authorities have a duty to pay regard to 'needs of agriculture and forestry', and conserving 'flora, fauna and geological and physiographical features'. They must also conduct environmental impact assessments when the road affects a 'sensitive area' such as a National Park or area of outstanding beauty.[128] Authorities have powers of compulsory purchase to create roads and paths, but must pay compensation for 'the amount of the depreciation or damage'.[129] If voicing concerns during public consultation fails, challenge to the construction of highways takes place through judicial review. For instance, in *Bushell v Environment Secretary*, the Secretary of State published two draft documents on building motorways and connected roads on the green belt, south of Birmingham.[130] Mr Bushell, who lived a previously peaceful life at Alvechurch, Worcestershire, objected to the new M42 through his farm. He argued that the public local inquiry, which the Secretary of State had set up voluntarily, illegitimately denied him the opportunity to cross-examine Department witnesses on traffic predictions. High traffic predictions, and therefore high utility, were seen as key for the road being approved. While the Court of Appeal held that this amounted to a breach of natural justice,[131] the House of Lords held that ultimately a right to cross-examine witnesses was not required by its (more minimal) view of procedural fairness.

Importantly, under section 41 authorities 'are under a duty . . . to maintain the highway' whenever they are responsible for it,[132] as well as having a general power for highway improvement.[133] This general duty owed to the public does not, however, automatically create a duty of care in tort owed to private individuals. For instance, in *Stovin v Wise*, Mr Stovin crashed his motorbike into Ms Wise's car, in part, because an earthen bank at an intersection in Wymondham obscured her view as she turned right.[134] The High Court held

[125] *Southwark LBC v Transport for London* [2018] UKSC 63, [6] on no single meaning of 'highway'. TfL took over.

[126] Highways Act 1989, s. 1, also making clear in (3A) that in Wales the authority is the borough or county council.

[127] Transport (Scotland) Act 2001, ss. 3–48 and Transport Act (Northern Ireland) 2011, ss. 4ff.

[128] Highways Act 1980, s. 105A, referring to the Countryside Act 1949 and the Countryside and Rights of Way Act 2000, s. 82. See also the Wildlife and Countryside Act 1981 (site of scientific interest); the Norfolk and Suffolk Broads Act 1988; the UNESCO Convention 1972, art. 11(2); the Ancient Monuments and Archaeological Areas Act 1979; and the Conservation of Habitats and Species Regulations 2017, reg. 8. See also the Environmental Impact Assessment Directive 2011/92/EU.

[129] Highways Act 1980, ss. 26–8 and 239–50, where s. 250(4) points to the Compulsory Purchase Act 1965.

[130] *Bushell v Environment Secretary* [1981] AC 75.

[131] (1980) 39 P&CR 341, Lord Denning MR and Shaw LJ quashed the schemes, Templeman LJ dissented.

[132] Highways Act 1980, s. 38, highway authorities may also make agreements to undertake maintenance.

[133] Highways Act 1980, s. 62.

[134] *Stovin v Wise* [1996] UKHL 15.

that Ms Wise was 70 per cent responsible for the accident, and also held Norfolk County Council 30 per cent responsible for omitting to remove the bank. The House of Lords overturned this, holding that the failure to exercise its power as a highway authority, for irrationality or other grounds, would unduly 'expose the authority's budgetary decisions to judicial inquiry', and potentially force councils to 'spend less on education or social services'. Those spending priorities had to be left to elected officials, not courts. Similarly, in *Gorringe v Calderdale MBC*, the House of Lords held that the council's failure to ensure there was a sign warning drivers about danger before a hill was not a breach of duty. The word 'slow' had been painted on the road before but had worn away when Mr Gorringe collided with a bus coming over the hill. According to Lord Hoffmann, it was 'difficult to imagine a case in which a common law duty can be founded simply upon the failure (however irrational) to provide some benefit which a public authority has power (or a public law duty) to provide'.[135]

Increasingly, private parties have become involved in providing works, and under the Highways Act 1980, section 38 an authority may adopt the road as a public highway. Further, under section 38(6) the authorities can make any agreement they 'think fit' for 'the bearing of the expenses of the construction, maintenance or improvement'. The problem is, private companies seek to minimise expenses they have committed to driven by shareholders. For instance, in *R (Redrow Homes Ltd) v Knowsley MBC*, a developer built 525 houses and roads between them, and the council adopted the roads.[136] Planning permission for the development was only granted on the basis that Redrow Homes Ltd paid £39,000 for the cost of future street lighting maintenance. After the project was done, Redrow Homes Ltd tried to argue that section 38's purpose was to enable highway authorities to fully adopt roads, including their cost, and so any agreement under section 38(6) to require private parties to pay for costs must be void. Like the High Court, the Court of Appeal threw this out: the council and a private party could agree to whatever future arrangement it wanted.

Similarly, in *Amey Birmingham Highways Ltd v Birmingham CC*, a company engaged through a private finance initiative contract for twenty-five years to update and maintain Birmingham roads tried to argue that it only had to do work on the road which was originally included in a computer database.[137] This database was in fact incomplete: it left out certain roads and footpaths, which the company neglected to repair. The Court of Appeal, unsurprisingly, held the company's duty was to maintain the roads and footpaths as they existed in real life, not on the database, and this extended to the whole road network. *Redrow* and *Amey* illustrate that the public cost of private finance is

[135] *Gorringe v Calderdale MBC* [2004] UKHL 15, [32]. See also *Sumner v Colborne* [2018] EWCA Civ 1006 (no duty to cut back vegetation obscuring view of a cyclist).

[136] *R (Redrow Homes Ltd) v Knowsley MBC* [2014] EWCA Civ 1433.

[137] *Amey Birmingham Highways Ltd v Birmingham CC* [2018] EWCA Civ 264.

not limited to the tender that a bidder submits: likely costs of future litigation, companies trying to shirk their undertakings, and publicly funded court time should also be factored in.

As road vehicles electrify, electric charging points are joining highway infrastructure. Under the London Local Authorities and Transport for London Act (LLATLA) 2013, both TfL and borough councils were empowered to 'provide and operate charging apparatus for electrically powered motor vehicles', either in public car parks or on highways they were responsible for.[138] The spread of charging points which have sufficient voltage to fill a battery at speed has been relatively slow,[139] a fact which can in turn hold back the willingness of people to buy electric vehicles. Private petrol stations had committed to opening but a handful of charging points, so to hasten their spread, the Automated and Electric Vehicles Act 2018, section 11 empowers the Secretary of State to write regulations that 'impose requirements on … large fuel retailers' or 'service area operators' to provide public charging points.[140] The meaning of 'service area operator' is to be defined by (as yet unwritten) regulations. It seems logical to build charging points at car parks and workplaces, to minimise the need for multiple stops.

While roads have generally been seen as a public service, since 2003 road pricing has returned to London to reduce congestion, improve air quality and raise revenue. The Greater London Authority Act (GLAA) 1999 empowered TfL to 'establish and operate schemes for imposing charges' for 'keeping or use of motor vehicles on roads in its area'.[141] After Ken Livingstone won the 2000 mayoral election on a promise to introduce the charge, the Conservative-run Westminster Council argued the scheme should be quashed for failing to undertake an environmental impact assessment or sufficiently consult, and because residents' property values might diminish and this would violate their human right to a fair trial in determination of their civil rights. All these arguments were rightly rejected.[142] The congestion charge, originally £5 and by 2021 upto £15 per day, was from 2019 joined by a 'toxicity charge', £12.50 in 2021, that applies to vehicles that do not meet the 'Euro 5' or 'Euro 6' standards for emissions: older, dirtier vehicles. From October 2021, the 'Ultra Low Emissions Zone' for this charge extends to the north and south circular roads, an area similar to the Underground zone 3. The problem with charges, not bans, is that governments have an incentive to maximise revenue, setting

138 LLATLA 2013, s. 16, after under ss. 17–18 publishing a notice, consulting and getting planning consent.

139 On locations, see e.g. www.zap-map.com: the yellow chargers are 3 kW, blue 7 kW, green 43 kW, pink 50 kW.

140 Automated and Electric Vehicles Act 2018, s. 11.

141 GLAA 1999, s. 295, with details in Sch. 23. Under s. 141, the Mayor of London is to 'develop and implement policies for the promotion and encouragement of safe, integrated, efficient and economic transport facilities and services to, from and within Greater London'. See also Transport for London Act 2008, ss. 4–8.

142 *R (Westminster CC) v Mayor of London* [2002] EWHC 2440 (Admin).

charges high enough to allow polluters to just be able to pay and drive, instead of minimising pollution.

Outside London, the Transport Act 2000 enables road charging, but local councils have not yet done anything.[143] Schemes in Cambridge, Edinburgh and Manchester were aborted.[144] Towns and cities have become increasingly filthy and congested because bus services have become so degraded (see Ch. 15(3)(c)). People have few alternatives but to drive. This makes road charging politically more difficult. There is, however, a levy administered by the Secretary of State on heavy goods vehicles since 2013. Vehicles over 12 tonnes (i.e. a small truck) have to pay varying amounts, depending on vehicle weight and emissions, starting at £900 a year.[145] It does not appear that these charges create any significant incentive for businesses to shift their vehicle fleets to low-carbon or zero-carbon models.

(iii) Network Rail Ltd to Great British Railways?

Network Rail Ltd is the public infrastructure body for rail tracks, but at the time of writing it has been proposed that it will be replaced by 'Great British Railways', a public body that would co-ordinate regional railway companies with regulated timetables and fares.[146] Since 2002 Network Rail Ltd has been a public body,[147] although this has only been officially recognised in official statistics since 2014.[148] Tracks were originally privatised and held by Railtrack plc. Contrary to any sense, this was meant to be a privately owned and regulated monopoly holding railway tracks, signalling, tunnels, bridges and level crossings, on the theory that private ownership is inherently better than public ownership, even without any semblance of competition. However, after the Hatfield train crash in 2000, which killed four people and injured seventy, and the Potters Bar crash in 2001, which killed seven and injured seventy-six, Railtrack plc asked the government for a subsidy, but this was wisely refused; it was forced into insolvent administration and government placed the assets in Network Rail Ltd.[149] In *Weir v Secretary of State for Transport* a group of

[143] Transport Act 2000, ss. 163–177A.

[144] L. Butcher, 'Local Road Charges', HC Briefing Paper No. SN 01171 (14 March 2018) 15–17.

[145] HGV Road User Levy Act 2013, ss. 1–4 and Sch. 1. [146] DfT, *Great British Railways*.

[147] L. Whitehouse, '"Railtrack Is Dead – Long Live Network Rail?" Nationalisation under the Third Way' (2003) 30 *JL & Society* 217; *The Future of Rail: White Paper*, Cm. 6233 (July 2004). Cf. R. Jupe, 'Public (Interest) or Private (Gain)? The Curious Case of Network Rail's Status' (2007) 34 *JL & Society* 24, 252, noting that former Prime Minister Tony Blair disparaged, 'the sterile debate between wholesale privatisation and old-style state control'.

[148] Prosser, 'Economic Regulation in a Plural Public Sector', giving a summary at 122–3.

[149] See P. Ireland, 'Limited Liability, Shareholder Rights and the Problem of Corporate Irresponsibility' (2010) 34 *Cambridge J Economics* 837, 845–6: 'Just one week before the court handed down its decision, Network Rail (the company that replaced Railtrack) and the engineering firm Balfour Beatty had been fined £13.5 million for their part in the Hatfield rail disaster of 2000, where four people died, seventy injured. Hatfield was one of a long series of fatal rail accidents in which Railtrack's working practices and safety record was implicated (Wolmar, 2001). On this issue the shareholders were silent. At no point had they spoken up, let alone campaigned, about the company's safety record. They did not, apparently, feel in any

48,000 shareholders challenged the minister's decision to force an insolvency procedure, arguing their property was being illegally taken and the minister was guilty of misfeasance in public office, but these arguments were completely rejected.[150]

Whereas Network Rail Ltd originally had over 100 members reflecting rail stakeholders, now the Secretary of State is the sole member. This has not led to an ideal situation of accountability, and executive pay may be unreasonably high.[151] The separation of infrastructure like tracks from train-operating companies reflects the EU requirement for functional distinction to prevent conflicts of interest in excluding other operators.[152] Each must have separate accounts and member states are obliged to run railways 'at the lowest possible cost for the quality of service required'.[153] But unlike electricity or telecoms, the separation of tracks from railway companies is fairly pointless in the UK, given that 'less than 1% of passenger miles' are 'open access', with multiple companies competing on the same line.[154] There would appear to be little point in functional separation (as opposed to transparent accounting and governance) where a rail system is publicly owned.

New rail infrastructure projects require planning permission and environmental impact consultation. One of the most controversial is the High Speed Rail 2 (HS2) project from London to Birmingham, and then on to Manchester and Leeds by 2035. In *R (HS2 Action Alliance Ltd) v Secretary of State for Transport*, a group of people opposed to HS2 claimed that it failed the consultation standards in the Environmental Impact Assessment Directive 2011, because there was a party whipped vote in Parliament for its approval. The Supreme Court rejected the claim, because in its view the political organisation of member voting by whips did not stop proper consultation and debate taking place. It further held that requirements for environmental impact assessment could not be interpreted to interfere with the Bill of Rights 1689, article 9, on the courts not reviewing Parliamentary proceedings.[155]

way responsible for the behaviour of the company from which they had been drawing dividends and whose management was legally bound to act in their interests. The cases are illustrative of the tendency of shareholders to schizophrenically identify themselves very closely with the companies in which they hold shares for some purposes, while seeing themselves as completely separate from them for others.'

150 [2005] EWHC 2192 (Ch) per Lindsay J.

151 TUC, *Rebuilding Rail* (2012), pointing out high CEO pay at Network Rail.

152 Single European Railway Directive 2012/34/EU, arts. 4 and 7. This followed the First Railway Directive 91/440/EC.

153 Single European Railway Directive 2012/34/EU, arts. 5–6.

154 Prosser, 'Economic Regulation in a Plural Public Sector', 120–1.

155 [2014] UKSC 3, [207]–[209] suggesting that there are constitutional statutes that cannot be overridden.

(b) Auto-makers

As we have seen, most UK auto-makers are now foreign owned, but each entity will be incorporated under the Companies Act 2006, or international equivalents. Governance is usually dominated by the asset managers or banks that take over shareholder voting rights (see Chs. 3–4). This is true in Germany, France, Italy, the USA, Japan and South Korea where most top-twenty vehicle manufacturers are headquartered, but not in China, where vehicle manufacturers (with the exception of Geely) are state-owned enterprises. It is significant that Chinese auto-makers lead electric production, and seem to be outcompeting their rivals.

In Europe, asset managers and banks do not and did not always dominate manufacturer governance. First, both Germany and France (with a majority of EU member states) have laws that guarantee the right of staff to elect minority representation on company boards. This applies to companies with over 5,000 staff in France, and delivers two representatives.[156] In companies with over 2,000 staff in Germany, workers elect just under half the supervisory board, which in turn elects the management board, where the CEO and executive directors carry out day-to-day management of the company.[157] In the USA, similar reforms have been supported since 2018 by Barack Obama, Elizabeth Warren, Bernie Sanders, Kamala Harris and others.[158]

Second, many European manufacturers, particularly in sectors which had previously been publicly owned, used to have governments' 'golden shares' in company constitutions. These could, for instance, enable a government body to veto company policies. However, beginning in 2006, the Court of Justice of the European Union (CJEU) began to develop a new theory that golden shares violated the right of free movement of capital. In October 2007, this idea was applied to Volkswagen in *Commission v Germany*.[159] The EU Commission had claimed that the Volkswagen Act 1959, §2(1) violated the Treaty on the Functioning of the European Union (TFEU), article 63, by limiting the voting rights of any individual shareholder to 20 per cent of the company. Also, §4(3) enabled 20 per cent of shareholders to block any decisions, and those shares were held by the government of the German state of Lower Saxony. The Court of Justice agreed, holding that freedom of movement of capital was unjustifiably restricted by the Volkswagen Act 1959. Although the German government could justify restrictions based on an overriding public interest, it only

[156] Code de Commerce, art. L225-27-1. [157] Mitbestimmungsgesetz 1976, §§1–9.

[158] See the proposed Reward Work Act, Accountable Capitalism Act, and *Corporate Accountability and Democracy* (2019) https://berniesanders.com/issues/corporate-accountability-and-democracy/. Further *Letter to Jay Clayton* (15 October 2018) noting 'Congress has proposed several pieces of legislation to promote worker engagement with corporate management and in the selection of directors.' B. Obama, 'Remarks at the University of Illinois', *The Atlantic* (7 September 2018): 'Democrats aren't just running on good old ideas like a higher minimum wage, they're running on good new ideas, like Medicare for All, giving workers seats on corporate boards . . . .'

[159] *Commission v Germany* (2007) C-112/05, released 23 October 2007.

argued the measures were to protect workers. The Court said it failed to show this to be 'appropriate and necessary for the Federal and State authorities to maintain a strengthened and irremovable position in the capital of that company'.[160] However, any government may have golden shares in a company, so long as this is a proportionate way to achieve a legitimate aim. Protecting the environment and instructing a board to reduce emissions would be one.

The consequences were that in lieu of Lower Saxony's influence, the Porsche family dominated Volkswagen shares.[161] The new CEO, Martin Winterkorn, acquired his position in 2007, as the CJEU litigation was under way. Winterkorn then announced the intention in 'Strategie 2018' to become the world's largest auto-manufacturer, ahead of Toyota and General Motors, and as explained above in Chapter 15(2)(a)(iii) diesel was the preferred engine, and cheat devices to conceal the toxic levels of emissions were used. In 2014, the year that VW fraud was first alleged, Winterkorn was paid €18 million, of which €16 million was 'performance based' variable pay.[162] There can be little doubt that such strong incentives to 'perform' lead to more cheating. Today the share price of Tesla and other heavily electric vehicles indicates that companies with the greatest zero-carbon commitments will succeed,[163] but this has only come after big shifts in regulation, and the results of the 2020 US presidential election. The absence of stakeholder voice in car companies therefore appears to be a central cause of corporations' sociopathic conduct.

(c) Buses

The governance of buses, outside London and towns where services remain municipally owned, has not been a success. In 1955 the number of people catching buses was roughly equal to those driving cars, vans or taxis. By 2005, outside London, the proportion of passenger miles on bus journeys was dwarfed by individual transport. Less public transport generally leads to more congestion, pollution, poorer health, road rage and stress. However, at the time of writing, and similar to trains, a 'Bus Back Better' strategy was released that would see existing transport authorities acquire timetable and fare-setting powers, known as 'Enhanced Partnerships', expected to operate from April 2022.[164]

[160] *Commission v Germany* (2007) C-112/05, [74].

[161] The Volkswagen supervisory board had 21 members: 5 appointed by the Porsche family, the controlling shareholder; 2 by Qatar Sovereign wealth fund (17% shares); and 2 by Lower Saxony (20% shares). Under the Codetermination Act 1976, 10 were appointed by employees, unions and middle management.

[162] Armour, 'Volkswagen's Emissions Scandal: Lessons for Corporate Governance?' (parts 1 and 2).

[163] Cf. Tesla Inc., Form 10-K (2016) Item 1A Risk Factors.

[164] DfT, *Bus Back Better: National Bus Strategy for England* (2021).

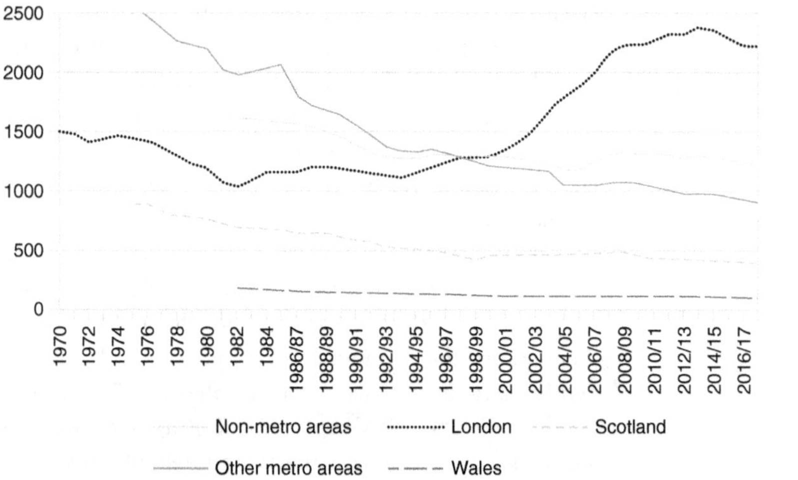

Figure 15.4 Bus passenger journeys, 1970–2017
Source: Dept for Transport, Annual Bus Statistics, Year Ending: March 2018, Tables BUS0103 and BUS0108

There are two main and separate statutory frameworks, inside and outside London. Within London, the use of buses has increased significantly compared to 1970, when official statistics became available by region, and particularly after the Greater London Assembly formed (see Figure 15.4).[165] London government plans fares and timetables, and can take buses into public ownership. Outside London, deregulation of fares and timetables has meant a steady level of cuts by local councils. Like the Railways Act 1993, section 25, the Bus Services Act 2017, section 22 says that a relevant authority 'may not, in exercise of any of its powers, form a company for the purpose of providing a local service'.[166] This means the only governments in the world that are not able to set up new companies to own UK buses are UK governments. The 2021 *Bus Back Better* strategy said that this was 'ripe for review',[167] a polite way of saying that this was a terrible policy (as it is in rail) and should never have happened. It appears a local authority may, however, use an existing company to provide services, as Transport for Greater Manchester has done since March 2021, ending the franchise with Stagecoach. But even though this is a big exception, section 22 makes no sense.

Under the GLAA 1999, the Mayor of London has a duty to develop 'safe, integrated, efficient and economic transport facilities', and publish a transport strategy with his or her proposals.[168] The Mayor delegates these functions to TfL, a 'body corporate' with eight to seventeen members appointed by the Mayor, and subject to the Mayor's directions.[169] TfL is empowered to 'form,

165 Office for National Statistics, 'Annual Bus Statistics, Year Ending: March 2018 tables' (2019) Bus0103 and Bus0108.

166 Bus Services Act 2017, s. 22(1): 'A relevant authority may not, in exercise of any of its powers, form a company for the purpose of providing a local service.'

167 *Bus Back Better*, 50. 168 GLAA 1999, ss. 141–2. 169 GLAA 1999, ss. 154–5 and Sch. 10.

promote and assist, or join with any other person . . . a company' for 'carrying on any activities which Transport for London has power to carry on'. This means that London is able to have a fully publicly owned bus network. From 1999 to 2009 there was one such company, East Thames Buses, which took over from 'Harris Bus' after it was placed in insolvent administration and no private buyers were immediately forthcoming. Following Boris Johnson's election in 2008, the decision was made to reprivatise the routes ostensibly for 'value for money'.[170]

TfL is empowered to make provision for control over fares and the structure of routes in its tender agreements.[171] Moreover, no bus can operate as a 'London local service' except under conditions set by TfL.[172] This means that TfL is able to limit what it considers to be unnecessary profit, and may threaten taking a company back into public ownership. It remains unclear why London does not run its bus services directly: the argument that private companies are superior to the public sector is untenable, as so many London buses are owned by the Dutch, French and German governments (see Table 15.3).

Outside London, the Transport Act 1968, with the Transport Act 2000, creates 'Integrated Transport Authorities' and 'Passenger Transport Executives' to run transport services. Geographically, these map onto the 'metropolitan counties' in England and Wales, and then Scotland.[173] Each local authority, or an Integrated Transport Authority where those exist, must develop a 'local transport plan' for 'safe, integrated, efficient and economic transport' for the people living and working there.[174] This ostensible goal is severely limited by the fact that the Bus Services Act 2017, section 22 says local authorities may not 'form a company for the purpose of providing a local service'. This prohibition does not apply to the GLA, the Scottish Parliament or the Welsh Assembly, or the government of any other country. It also has no application to companies that already exist, but rather ones newly formed. Again, buses would be better if section 22 were gone.

Under whatever plan is developed, local authorities license buses to run. The Public Passenger Vehicles Act 1981 states that a 'public service vehicle' (PSV) is any motor vehicle other than a tram that is adapted to carry more than eight passengers 'for hire or reward', or one that is not adapted but is still used for hire and reward.[175] Under section 12, a public service vehicle may not operate 'except under a public service vehicle operator's licence' which is issued by

[170] TfL, 'TfL to Consider whether East Thames Buses Could Offer Better Value' (10 December 2008). The reasoning for this decision appears unclear. The company was passed to Go-Ahead Group.

[171] GLAA 1999, ss. 174–5. [172] GLAA 1999, ss. 180–8.

[173] Transport Act 1968, ss. 9–9A and Public Passenger Vehicles Act 1981, s. 3 listing Great Britain traffic areas as 'the Metropolitan, Northern, Yorkshire, North-Western, West Midland, East Midland, Eastern, South Wales, Western, South-Eastern and Scottish Traffic Areas'.

[174] Transport Act 2000, s. 108. [175] Public Passenger Vehicles Act 1981, s. 1.

Traffic Commissioners appointed by the Secretary of State for Transport.[176] Once a licence is issued by (centrally appointed) Traffic Commissioners, any business must simply register to provide 'local services' under the Transport Act 1985, section 6. Further, local authorities can enter 'quality partnership schemes', jointly with others if they wish, to deliver their local transport policies, after giving notice in at least one newspaper.[177]

A Traffic Commissioner may find that an operator fails to operate a service in the way that they have proposed.[178] For instance, in *Jones (t/a Shamrock Coaches) v Department of Transport Welsh Traffic Office*, a bus company was given a financial penalty[179] for failure to run a quarter of its timetabled buses. When buses did run, 13 per cent were not on time. The company argued that the Traffic Commissioner had exercised his discretion too broadly, and erred in quantifying financial penalties. A Transport Tribunal upheld this, and remitted the issue to the same Commissioner who imposed re-quantified penalties once more. On another complaint, the Court of Appeal held the Commissioner was not bound to recuse himself: it was not shown that he was in any way biased.[180] Otherwise, powers of fixing fares and timetables are absent. From 2008 to 2018, the dividends paid out to the largest five companies who run diminishing bus services (Arriva, FirstGroup, Go-Ahead, National Express and Stagecoach) totalled £1.5 billion, while fares had risen an average of 55 per cent, and passenger numbers have atrophied.[181]

(d) Taxis and Private Hire Vehicles

If people do not have access to bus routes, it is often possible to pay for taxis or 'private hire vehicles' at a considerably higher cost. The poorest 20 per cent of UK residents take more taxi journeys a year than any other income group,[182] a fact that reflects the disintegration of buses outside London, and the high cost of a car. The law distinguishes two main kinds of service: an ordinary 'private hire vehicle', and a 'hackney carriage' taxi which can 'ply for hire' (picking people up from the street) and drive in bus lanes. As with buses, different statutory systems operate for London and for the rest of the country.

In London, the Private Hire Vehicles (London) Act 1998, section 1 defines a 'private hire vehicle' as one 'adapted to seat fewer than nine passengers other than a taxi or public service vehicle' and that is hired. In other words, with nine or more seats it is a bus, and in the language of the statute, a 'taxi' is a hackney carriage (below). TfL has the exclusive right to license private hire vehicles on

[176] Public Passenger Vehicles Act 1981, ss. 4–4A, and Sch. 2. Also ss. 12A–B enable PSVs to be detained or stopped if a licence is contravened.

[177] Transport Act 2000, ss. 114–15.

[178] Transport Act 1985, ss. 6 and 26.

[179] Transport Act 1985, s. 111.

[180] [2005] EWCA Civ 58.

[181] E.g. M. Ellis, 'Bus Firms Pay Fat Cats £1.5 Billion', *Daily Mirror* (5 November 2018).

[182] Institute for Public Policy Research, 'Greasing the Wheels: Supporting and Improving Britain's Rail and Bus Services', Report (2014) 29–30.

any conditions it thinks fit.[183] No vehicles can be operated without a licence;[184] they must be booked in advance and have a 'listening' service where a passenger has 'voice contact'.[185] Very similar and equivalent rules operate outside London for licensing, the need for advance booking and oversight by traffic commissioners.[186]

Private hire vehicle business has been considerably 'disrupted' by the multinational app-based corporation, Uber. Uber claims to have around 40,000 drivers in London, and with over a million drivers worldwide it has become one of the world's largest employers.[187] However, Uber has developed a reputation for suing public authorities around the world when it faces rules it does not like. For example, Uber argued the requirement to have voice contact infringed its right to freedom of establishment in EU law.[188] In *R (Uber London Ltd) v Transport for London* the Court of Appeal rejected all of Uber's arguments, given that TfL had a legitimate interest in securing high levels of public safety and consumer protection, and because there was no evidence that Uber's costs in providing voice contact were disproportionate.[189] In other cases, Uber has sued over English-language tests for drivers,[190] it has litigated to avoid the minimum wage and paid holidays for its drivers,[191] and in the Court of Justice Uber has even argued it is not a 'transport service', but rather an 'information society service' that has the freedom to be regulated by the lowest standards of any member state.[192] Most of these challenges have failed. Because of Uber's refusal to deal promptly with cases of sexual assault in its vehicles, TfL revoked its licence in September 2017. A judge quashed the revocation, leading TfL to grant a fifteen-month probationary licence in June 2018. It then transpired that the judge's husband, Lord Arbuthnot, worked for a consulting firm that Uber has paid for advice.[193] In September 2020, the High Court held that Uber was by then fit to hold a licence, but awarded costs to TfL in the case.[194] It has been prohibited from a large number of other countries where it refused to comply with the law.[195]

183 Private Hire Vehicles (London) Act 1998, s. 3.
184 Private Hire Vehicles (London) Act 1998, ss. 2, 6 and 12–13.
185 Private Hire Vehicles (London) (Operators' Licences) Regulations 2000, reg. 9(11).
186 Local Government (Miscellaneous Provisions) Act 1976, s. 48.
187 See McGaughey, 'Uber, the Taylor Review, Mutuality, and the Duty to Not Misrepresent Employment Status'.
188 TFEU, arts. 49 and 54. 189 [2018] EWCA Civ 1213, per Gloster LJ.
190 *R (Uber London Ltd) v Transport for London* [2017] EWHC 435.
191 *Uber BV v Aslam* [2018] EWCA Civ 2748, Sir Terence Etherton MR and Bean LJ, Underhill LJ dissenting.
192 *Asociación Profesional Élite Taxi v Uber Systems Spain SL* (2017) C-434/15.
193 J. Doward, 'Judge in Uber's London Legal Battle Steps Aside over Husband's Links to Firm', *The Guardian* (18 August 2018).
194 *Uber London Ltd v Transport for London* [2020] EWHC 00 (Admin) on Private Hire Vehicle (London) Act 1998, ss. 3 and 25.
195 McGaughey, 'Uber, the Taylor Review, Mutuality, and the Duty to Not Misrepresent Employment Status'.

The more familiar London taxis, known as 'Hackney carriages', are regulated primarily by the Metropolitan Public Carriage Act 1869. This extends to the 'metropolitan police district, and the city of London' (today synonymous with the GLA area). TfL grants licences to operate, lasting for a year at a time, for a fee.[196] Two central differences are that only these taxis may 'ply for hire' to pick up passengers in a public street, and that they may use bus lanes, whereas private hire vehicles cannot. A private hire vehicle or 'minicab' company attempted to challenge their prohibition on using bus lanes in *R (Eventech Ltd) v Parking Adjudicator*, after it got two fines. It came up with the novel argument that the right of hackney carriages to use bus lanes was state aid under TFEU, article 107.[197] On a reference from the Court of Appeal, the Second Chamber of the Court of Justice unsurprisingly held that it was not. Enabling the use of bus lanes was not committing state resources, and the legal status of taxis and minicabs was sufficiently distinct that there could be no selective economic advantage. TfL may also regulate the furnishing and fittings of hackney carriages, their rates and fares based on time and distance, and make these publicly available.[198] Similar and equivalent rules apply outside London for licensing and regulation of hackney carriages under the Town Police Clauses Act 1847.[199]

(e) Business Vehicles

Although road haulage was nationalised under the Transport Act 1947, and the National Freight Corporation (NFC) operated until the Transport Act 1980,[200] delivery vehicles today are subject to few special rules. The HGV Road User Levy Act 2013 imposes a duty of excise for heavy goods vehicles using the roads, which means 12 tonnes or more. The charges range from £85 to £1,000 a year.[201] The impact of heavy goods on communities can be significant, not only in the cost of repairing roads, but also for emissions. For instance, in *Schmidberger v Austria*, a large number of protestors blocked the Brenner Motorway through the Austrian alps, to try to stop the volumes of traffic from Germany to Italy that had ballooned after Austria's accession to the EU. The trucking company claimed Austria's failure to ban the protest amounted to an infringement of its rights of free movement of goods. The Court of Justice disagreed, holding that because protest is part of the fundamental rights of freedom of expression and assembly, any interference with the right to movement of goods would be justified.[202] Extra rights do apply in favour of delivery vehicle drivers under the Road Transport Regulation 2006. This limits daily

[196] Metropolitan Public Carriage Act 1869, s. 6. [197] (2015) C-518/13.
[198] Metropolitan Public Carriage Act 1869, s. 9.
[199] Town Police Clauses Act 1847, ss. 1, 37–54.
[200] Transport Act 1980, ss. 45–51, transferring the NFC to a successor company that was privatised in 1982.
[201] HGV Road User Levy Act 2013, Sch. 1. [202] *Schmidberger v Austria* (2003) C-112/00.

driving time to nine hours a day, a maximum of fifty-six hours a week, and requires at least a forty-five-minute break after four and a half hours. Drivers may also not be paid according to distance travelled if this would endanger road safety.[203]

(f) Trains

As stated at Chapter 15(2)(e), at the time of writing, it is proposed that a new 'Great British Railways' body will transform the existing train franchising structure, so that companies with 'Passenger Service Contracts' are subject to planned fares and timetables nationwide. However, until this system is implemented (possibly in 2023), to run a train company the Railways Act 1993, section 8 currently requires that companies apply to the Office of Rail and Road for a licence, and pay Network Rail an access charge. As in EU law, access to track must be 'equitable, non-discriminatory and transparent',[204] but charging practices can be set according to the regulator's view of what is fair. In *Great North Eastern Railway Ltd v Office of Rail Regulation*, GNER sued the ORR because it was charged a fixed rate for track access, and other operators were not: others paid rates varying with the number of passengers. GNER argued this was unlawful discrimination and state aid, but Sullivan J held the ORR had a broad discretion to set prices in the passengers' interest, and should be slow to challenge the expert regulator's decisions on technical pricing issues.[205] GNER subsequently lost its franchise of the East Coast Main Line, after widespread public dissatisfaction, to a temporary public operator called East Coast.

The most controversial, incomprehensible, part of the law is the Railways Act 1993, section 25, prohibiting any government body or government-appointed corporation from becoming a rail franchise in England and Wales.[206] The government-owned rail operators of France, the Netherlands and Germany all run trains in the UK. But the UK government, and English and Welsh governments, are the only ones in the world prohibited from running UK trains. In 2016, Scotland was empowered to make Scottish trains public again.[207] Public ownership is supported by a large majority.[208] In buses, an equivalent provision was said to be 'ripe for review', and so it follows that section 25 should also be put under 'review', or candidly scrapped.

203 Road Transport Regulation (EC) No. 561/2006, arts. 6 and 10.

204 Single European Railway Directive 2012/34/EU, art. 10: Conditions of access to railway infrastructure (1) 'Railway undertakings shall be granted, under equitable, non-discriminatory and transparent conditions, the right to access to the railway infrastructure in all Member States for the purpose of operating all types of rail freight services.'

205 [2006] EWHC 1942 (Admin). 206 Railways Act 1993, s. 25.

207 Scotland Act 2016, s. 57, amending Railways Act 1993, s. 25.

208 E.g. 'Jeremy Corbyn's Nationalisation Plans Are Music to Ears of Public', *The Guardian* (1 October 2017): 76% support rail nationalisation, Yougov (6 August 2015) finding 58% support and 17% oppose.

Different rules apply in London, where the most controversial policies have been the cost of Public Private Partnerships (PPPs).[209] The GLAA 1999 transferred responsibility for TfL back to an elected Mayor,[210] but also required that the Mayor follow public–private partnership agreements in rebuilding the London Underground and train network.[211] The elected Mayor, Ken Livingstone, had been elected on a platform opposing privatisation, and he argued the law put him in an 'impossible position'. But despite a challenge in the High Court, it was ruled that statute bound him to PPPs.[212] In 2008, one of the two main companies responsible for tube upgrades, Metronet, went into administration with an estimated cost of £410 million.[213] It had repeatedly paid excessive dividends to its shareholders, at a cost to the public.[214]

Among the franchised train companies and London Underground, there is not yet adequate public voice or passenger voting rights for their transport. Train passengers are represented in a 'Passengers' Council', with a chair appointed by the Secretary of State. Other members represent regional governments and passenger groups.[215] But the Passenger Council has no binding rights against train companies. They may merely investigate issues and make representations.[216] Voting representation remains underdeveloped around Europe but there are an increasing number of experiments.[217]

If train-operating companies go insolvent, a special 'railway administration order' may be made, giving the government, rather than banks and creditors, control over administration.[218] The Office of Rail and Road and a minister still retain powers to make directions against a train-operating company in administration.[219] In practice, train companies cannot go insolvent: like the

209 See C. Wolmar, *Down the Tube: The Battle for London's Underground* (2002) noting that PPP contracts were 28,000 pages long or 2m words.

210 The London Regional Transport Act 1984 had abolished the Greater London Council and established London Underground Ltd, controlled by central government.

211 GLAA 1999, ss. 41 and 141 (Mayor duties for transport) and ss. 210–30 (PPP agreements).

212 *R (Transport for London) v London Regional Transport* [2001] EWHC Admin 637, per Sullivan J: 'Entering into agreements may be wise, as asserted by the Government, LUL and LRT, or it may be foolish, as claimed by the Mayor and . . . TfL . . . judgments about the merits, as opposed to the legality of entering into the proposed PPP agreements, must be made by elected politicians and not by judges.'

213 C. Millett, 'Metronet Failure Cost Taxpayer up to £410m', *Contract Journal* (5 June 2009). See also *Re Metronet Rail BCV Ltd* [2007] EWHC 2697 (Ch).

214 House of Commons, Transport Committee (January 2008): 'The return anticipated by Metronet's shareholders appears to have been out of all proportion to the level of risk associated with the contract . . . In terms of borrowing, the Metronet contract did nothing more than secure loans, 95% of which were in any case underwritten by the public purse, at an inflated cost . . . Metronet's inability to operate efficiently or economically proves that the private sector can fail to deliver on a spectacular scale.'

215 Railways Act 2005, ss. 19–21 and Schs. 5–6. 216 Railways Act 1993, ss. 76–8.

217 See H. L. Dienel and M. Schiefelbusch, *Public Transport and its Users: The Passenger's Perspective in Planning and Customer Care* (2009).

218 Railways Act 1993, ss. 59–65 and Sch. 6.

219 *Winsor v Special Railway Administrators of Railtrack plc* [2002] EWCA Civ 955.

East Coast mainline, they are simply nationalised. Given that government always bails out train companies, it would seem better to be in public ownership with representation for staff and passengers on its board.

(4) Passenger Rights

International law creates a right to the benefits of science, and EU law 'recognises and respects access to services of general economic interest',[220] but detailed rights of national legislation often go far further than human rights norms.[221] There is not yet a universal right to free, clean transport but there is (a) free travel for elderly and children, (b) regulation of fares and (c) rights to compensation against delays and various others.

(a) Free Travel and Service

The most important right in practice since 2008[222] is that residents who reach the women's state pension age, or are disabled, are entitled to free bus travel anywhere in England.[223] In Scotland and Wales the relevant age is 60, and in London the 'freedom pass' also entitles elderly residents to free travel on the Underground.[224] Bus operators claim the money back from local authorities.[225] A system of concessions that local authorities are required to give also operates for other groups, including school children. Proposals have also been made to raise the age for free bus travel to 25.[226] For large parts of the population, this would effectively make bus travel a free public service. There is, however, no automatic right to transport as such. In *R (Save Our Railways) v Director of Passenger Rail Franchising*, a passenger group argued that the Regulator unlawfully allowed a reduction in services in rural areas in its franchises. The Court of Appeal accepted that the group had a right to bring judicial review, but referred the question back to the Regulator for reconsideration.[227]

(b) Fare Regulation

While free travel is not available on trains, the Office of Rail and Road can set any conditions in licences, including 'the fares to be charged for travel'.[228]

220 CFREU 2000, art. 36.

221 Cf. Italian Constitution 1947, art. 16: 'All citizens may travel or sojourn freely in any part of the national territory, except for general limitations which the law establishes for reasons of health and safety.'

222 Concessionary Bus Travel Act 2007.

223 Transport Act 2000, s. 145A.

224 GLAA 1999, ss. 240–3.

225 Transport Act 2000, s. 149.

226 S. Morrison, 'Jeremy Corbyn Pledges Free Bus Travel for Those under 25', *Evening Standard* (11 April 2018).

227 [1996] CLC 596.

228 Railways Act 1993, s. 28(1): 'A franchise agreement may include provision with respect to the fares to be charged for travel by means of the franchised services.' Also, s. 29(5): 'subject to any

Nevertheless, UK train prices have risen consistently every year since privatisation, usually beyond inflation.[229] There is no statutory control over bus fares, outside London. In London the Mayor has control over fares.[230] Fares have been consistently low when Labour mayors have been elected, and consistently rose when Boris Johnson, a Conservative mayor, was elected.[231] This suggests that there is a basic problem with transport fare regulation even by an elected public body: certain political parties or individuals may act against the public or passenger interest. This suggests that public ownership should always be coupled with votes for the stakeholders.

(c) Delays and Other Rights

Delays are regulated by EU law and its UK derivatives. When buses are delayed in journeys over 250 km, the Bus Passenger Rights Regulation 2011 entitles passengers to compensation.[232] Under article 19, a delay over two hours must result in compensation of 50 per cent of the ticket price, as well as rerouting and reimbursement. Article 6 says 'Carriers may offer contract conditions that are more favourable for the passenger', although it is not clear many take up this option. The Rail Passenger Rights Regulation 2007 similarly states in article 17 that 25 per cent of the ticket price should be refunded for a one-hour delay, and 50 per cent over two hours, with a threshold of €4 to claim. There are also miscellaneous other rights, including passengers having a right to take bicycles on trains if not too crowded, proper information on tickets and rights to make reservations.[233]

(5) Conclusion

Because transport makes up such a large share of emissions, its finance and governance are key to stopping climate damage. In World War Two, the US government told auto-companies they needed to retool all production to make planes for the war. The companies said this was impossible, and only

[statutory] requirements a franchise agreement may contain any such provisions as the Franchising Director thinks fit'.

229 E.g. DataBlog, 'Rail Fares Rise: All the Available Data on British Rail Revenues', *The Guardian* (17 August 2011), fares rising 8% and ticket holders' prices rising 13%. T. de Castella, 'Have Train Fares Gone Up or Down since British Rail?', *BBC News* (22 January 2013).

230 GLAA 1999, s. 174. However, courts have attempted to intervene in the past: *Bromley LBC v Greater London Council* [1981] UKHL 7 (no deficit spending for fare reductions).

231 See R. Holdsworth, 'London Transport Fares 2000–2016', *Londonist* (2016), showing a 56% increase in zones 1–4 tube fares (with Oyster cards from 2004) under Boris Johnson, while fares were held constant under Ken Livingstone and Sadiq Khan.

232 Bus Passenger Rights Regulation 2011 (EU) No. 181/2011, art. 2. Article 7 says member states cannot set maximum compensation for death or injury lower than €220,000 per passenger or €1200 per item of luggage.

233 Passenger Rights Regulation 2007 (EC) No. 1371/2007, arts. 3 (bikes) and 8–9 (information and tickets).

10–15 per cent was possible a year. But then it was done, at incredible speed.[234] If needed with emergency legislation, the same effort should be made for clean transport today.[235] First, there should be a duty on the ORR, as well as all other public and private bodies, to decarbonise all transport as fast as scientifically possible. Each rail, bus or transport company should be bound, with subsidies where necessary. Second, banks and asset managers should no longer dominate governance of corporations that led to the Dieselgate scandal, crashing and bankrupt trains or the unaffordable bus fares and falling service. Auto-maker corporations will be better managed, without fraud, with golden shares restored and probably with public representatives as well as staff on board. Train and bus routes should be run publicly wherever private enterprise fails to provide solvent service: before and during the Covid-19 pandemic, that is often. However, the old Morrisonian model of top-down selection of public corporations would be best avoided, by ensuring that passengers have voting rights, not just toothless consultation. Third, with public transport restored, total vehicle ownership will reduce, and highway authorities could bring the roads and streets back to life, not as car parks but real parks. We might even want transport less.

[234] J. Zeitlin, 'Flexibility and Mass Production at War: Aircraft Manufacture in Britain, the United States, and Germany, 1939–1945' (1995) 36(1) *Technology and Culture* 46, 52, Table 1 and 56.

[235] E.g. Civil Contingencies Act 2004, s. 22.

16

Communications

Contents

'The power of communication of thoughts and opinions is the gift of God,' said Lord Eyre CJ in 1794, 'and the freedom of it is the source of all science, the first fruits and the ultimate happiness of society.'[1] For those with slow Wi-Fi, a 'gift of God' might seem a stretch, but there is no doubt that modern communication is both a source, and a wonder, of science. Historically, most of us communicated in person, or not at all. A post open to everyone and mass literacy only developed in the nineteenth century. Then came telegraph, telephone and now the Internet. The Internet works with devices (like a phone) sending data over the radio spectrum to receivers (like a Wi-Fi box). Cables (fast fibre or slow copper) then connect buildings to base stations. Base stations send data via cables on land or ocean floors, or up to satellites. Email, web search, directories, voice calls and video calls are eclipsing traditional post, phone book or telephone services. This expands our freedom of expression, 'to seek, receive and impart information and ideas of all kinds, regardless of frontiers',[2] yet privacy problems are worse. Letters can be tampered with or phones can be tapped, and data can be intercepted at connection points and in software. There is a human right against 'arbitrary or unlawful interference with [our] privacy, family, home or correspondence'.[3] Yet, as well as government, corporate surveillance is the business model of Google,

[1] *Hardy's Case* (1794) 24 How St Tr 20, per Lord Eyre CJ.

[2] ICCPR 1966, art. 19(2). See also UDHR 1948, arts. 18–19; ECHR 1950, arts. 9–10; and CFREU 2000, arts. 10–11. It goes without saying that if we lose privacy, we express ourselves and even think less freely: art. 19(1).

[3] ICCPR 1966, art. 17; UDHR 1948, art. 12(1); ECHR 1950, art. 8(1); CFREU 2000, art. 7.

Facebook, Amazon and others.[4] They target ads to predict and influence what consumers want. The power of communication is basic for work, business and education, but also essential for autonomy over our own lives.

Two main problems in communication systems are (1) ensuring infrastructure is technologically optimal for reasonable costs, and (2) defending the right to privacy, against authoritarian power. First, communication infrastructure is a natural monopoly,[5] and was among the first industries to be publicly owned in the UK. Selling telephones is sometimes thought to be a privatisation success. To evaluate this claim, the amazing technology since the 1980s must be separated from the less amazing innovations in the governance and finance of communications. The fastest Internet is usually public. Second, privacy issues are not solved by ownership. Privacy can be destroyed by corporations using our data as their commodities, by states politically exploiting people's intimate lives, or both. If ownership rules do not automatically solve these issues, privacy depends on who has votes in enterprise governance, and what rights consumers can enforce. The Internet, and the idea of an 'information society service', was designed to protect private communication so that email servers, for instance, would not check or be responsible for mail passing through. The risk today is companies using this very concept to evade rights. This chapter examines the cables, radio spectrum, calls, data, email and post, and Chapter 17 looks at web media.

(1) Historical Development

The post was the first distance communication, but closed to most until the nineteenth century. In 500 BC, Herodotus's *Histories* recorded that for the ancient Persian mounted postal carriers, on the Royal Road: 'Neither snow nor rain nor heat nor gloom of night stays these couriers from the swift completion of their appointed rounds.'[6] But most could not afford the post, or indeed read it.[7] The mechanical printing press was invented in 1439 by Johannes Gutenberg; in 1491 the Holy Roman Emperor Maximilian I started a royal mail route between Brussels, Innsbruck and Italy;[8] and in 1516 Henry VIII established the Royal Mail. In 1591, Elizabeth I gave it a postal monopoly for mail abroad, and in 1609 James I extended the monopoly in the kingdom,

[4] S. Zuboff, *The Age of Surveillance Capitalism* (2019) chs. 3–5; S. Zuboff, 'It's Not that We've Failed to Rein In Facebook and Google. We've Not Even Tried', *The Guardian* (2 July 2019).

[5] E.g. J. Rohlfs, 'A Theory of Interdependent Demand for a Telecommunications Service' (1974) 5(1) *Bell J Economics* 16, 25 (assuming a regulated monopoly).

[6] Herodotus, *Histories* (*c.* 440 BC) trans. A. D. Godley (1924) Book VIII, §98. This was inscribed into the US Post Office building in New York City.

[7] See https://ourworldindata.org/literacy. In 1550, UK (or English) literacy was 16%, 53% by 1820, 76% by 1870.

[8] Franz and Janetto von Taxis were employed and held a monopoly. They were made princes, and their ancestors today are the wealthy Thurn and Taxis family.

but also licenced private operators to raise Crown revenue.[9] The General Post Office was created in 1660.[10] This monopoly licensing was approved by Adam Smith, as it worked.[11] A government-run postal service (though not a monopoly) was written into the US constitution.[12] As the Industrial Revolution increased the speed of transport, a reformer named Rowland Hill proposed a simplified rate structure for the Royal Mail, and in 1837 he persuaded Parliament to start an affordable, uniform penny post. Hill was driven by ideals, hoping 'the religious, moral and intellectual progress of the people would be accelerated by the unobstructed circulation of letters and of the many cheap and excellent publications of the present day', the post 'a powerful engine of civilisation'.[13]

By 1835, the discovery of electricity (see Ch. 12(1)) had led to the invention of the electrical relay, swiftly used to make telegraphs.[14] A first UK patent was granted in 1837 to William Cooke and Charles Wheatstone, and a patent in the USA was granted in 1840 to Samuel Morse. Through switches triggering electrical pulses down a copper wire, text messages (for instance by 'Morse code') could be sent as far as the telegraph lines could stretch. Telegraph companies built lines across the country, and in 1858 the first message was sent through a new transatlantic telegraph. In the Austro-Hungarian Empire, the emperor forbade private messages, suppression lasting until after the revolutions of 1848.[15] Telegraphs were important for the military. The UK Railway Regulation Act 1844 that required rail companies carried military forces, also allowed telegraph lines to run alongside rail tracks. And, telegraphs built by private companies had to be 'open for the sending and receiving of Messages by all Persons alike, without Favour or Preference'.[16] Recognising the monopoly of telegraph lines, and their strategic, military importance, the Telegraph Act 1868 gave the Postmaster General power to buy telegraph companies.[17] The Act also codified an offence for any post officer to 'intercept

[9] Also R. Wilberforce, *The Law of Restrictive Practices and Monopolies* (1966) ch. 1, 18. In 1654 Mr John Manley was recorded as paying £10,000 p.a. for a tender on the 'postage of letters both inland and foreign.'

[10] A. Clinton, *Post Office Workers: A Trade Union and Social History* (1984) 20–2. In 1710 the Master of the Posts was renamed Postmaster General.

[11] A. Smith, *An Inquiry into the Nature and Causes of the Wealth of Nations* (1776) Book V, ch. 2, §6: 'the only mercantile project which has been successfully managed by, I believe, every sort of government. The capital to be advanced is not very considerable. There is no mystery in the business. The returns are not only certain, but immediate.'

[12] Constitution of the United States of America 1789, art. I, section 8, cl. 7.

[13] R. Hill, *Post Office Reform: Its Importance and Practicability* (1837) 8.

[14] J. Foreman-Peck and R. Millward, *Public and Private Ownership of British Industry 1820–1990* (1994) 48–58; J. J. Fahie, *A History of the Electric Telegraph to the Year 1837* (1984).

[15] Foreman-Peck and Millward, *Public and Private Ownership of British Industry 1820–1990,* 58.

[16] Railway Regulation Act 1844, s. XIII. Also Railway Regulation Act 1842, s. XX (military conveyance).

[17] Telegraph Act 1868, s. 4. The Telegraph Act 1869, s. 8 gave the Post Master General the right to buy companies.

the Contents or any Part of the Contents of any Telegraphic Messages'.[18] The Telegraph Act 1869 gave the Postmaster General an exclusive right to send messages, and a monopoly on telegraph business.[19] As the economist Stanley Jevons said, in telegraphs 'we have neither the advantages of monopoly nor those of free competition' and he 'would rather see that monopoly in the hand of Government than that of a private company'.[20]

Telegraphs could only send pulses down wires, but in 1865 physicist James Clerk Maxwell argued that an electromagnetic spectrum existed in the air, and developed four equations for the behaviour of waves through it, including light.[21] Building on this in 1888, German physicist Heinrich Hertz showed Maxwell was right, and measured electromagnetic waves in the air.[22] Reputedly Hertz thought it was 'of no use whatsoever'. The utilisation of the spectrum would wait, but in 1876 Alexander Graham Bell patented a telephone in the USA that carried a voice through its electric signals,[23] and founded the Bell Telephone Company in 1877 under Massachusetts law. The Bell Telephone Co. created the American Telephone & Telegraph Co. (AT&T) as a New York subsidiary in 1885, and AT&T took over its parent in 1899 to avoid the Massachusetts corporate law limit of $10 million in market capitalisation.[24] AT&T was becoming a monopoly, and its president, Theodore Vail, declared in 1907 that it wanted to be so, because monopoly was better. Instead of competing companies that did not connect together, he wanted 'one policy, one system, universal service'.[25] Federal lawmakers disagreed, but before the Clayton Antitrust Act of 1914 was passed, AT&T promised to request approval from the Interstate Commerce Commission (ICC) before buying any more

[18] Telegraph Act 1868, s. 20. Also Telegraph Act 1863, s. 45: offence if any company officer 'improperly divulges to any Person the Purport of any Message'. The 1863 Act gave powers similar to gas and electricity firms for building infrastructure: see Ch. 12(1).

[19] Telegraph Act 1869, ss. 4–5 (with exceptions). Sch. 1 lists the companies that were bought out: the Electric and International Telegraph Co. (£2,938,826); the British and Irish Magnetic Telegraph Co. Ltd (£1,243,536); Reuter's Telegram Co. Ltd (£726,000); the United Kingdom Electric Telegraph Co. Ltd (£562,264); the Universal Private Telegraph Co. (£184,421); and the London and Provincial Telegraph Co. Ltd (£60,000).

[20] Clinton, *Post Office Workers*, 33. Also W. S. Jevons, 'On the Analogy between the Post Office, Telegraphs and other Systems of Conveyance of the United Kingdom as regards Government Control', read at the Manchester Statistical Society (10 April 1867) 91–104. Jevons later decided that too much 'traffic on the Government wires consists of complimentary messages, or other trifling matters, which we can know of no sufficient motive for promoting', and 'press telegrams' should not be subsidised 'on principle': W. S. Jevons, *Methods of Social Reform and Other Papers* (1883).

[21] J. C. Maxwell, 'A Dynamical Theory of the Electromagnetic Field' (1865) 155 *Philosophical Transactions of the Royal Society of London* 459.

[22] See H. Hertz, 'Ueber die Ausbreitungsgeschwindigkeit der electrodynamischen Wirkungen' (1888) 270(7) *Annalen der Physik* 551. This means 'On the Propagation Speed of Electrodynamic Effects'.

[23] See *The Telephone Cases*, 126 US 1 (1888). The Western Union Telegraph Co. lost its challenge to Bell's patent.

[24] J. Brooks, *Telephone: The First Hundred Years* (1970) ch. 5, 107.

[25] E.g. the AT&T advertisement found in (18 December 1909) 101(25) *Scientific American* 474.

independent phone companies,[26] and divest a recently purchased interest in Western Union.[27] In the New Deal, the Communications Act of 1934 created the Federal Communications Commission, with jurisdiction over all electronic communication: telegraph, phone, radio and broadcast, with powers to regulate prices and standards.[28]

Meanwhile in the UK, the formation of the new telephone company of Thomas Edison led to the remarkable case of *Attorney General v Edison Telephone Company of London Ltd*.[29] The Attorney General claimed the company, formed in 1879 to make telephones by two patents, would breach the Postmaster General's monopoly on the telegraph, and the Queen's Bench agreed because it held the company failed to prove the telegraph and telephone were technically different: a telephone was a 'telegraph' under the Telegraph Act 1869. Stephen J said 'absurd consequences would follow' if the post office's monopoly was 'dependent upon the means employed for the purpose of giving the information'.[30] Thus, a court nationalised telephones, though the Postmaster General and economist, Henry Fawcett, declared 'it would not be in the interest of the public to create a monopoly'.[31] Instead the Post Office used its monopoly to give out telephone licences. Predictably, one business, the National Telephone Company (NTC), expanded and took over competing regional telephone companies one by one. The Telegraph Act 1899 (note the name) gave municipalities power to establish their own local telephone companies (one still today is Hull City Council's Kingston Communications, serving around 190,000 homes). But otherwise mergers continued, and the idea of leaving communications to private parties grew unpopular. Economist Alfred Marshall said that while he opposed a total monopoly, a public post office with a 'virtual monopoly' was an 'absolute necessity', and privatising the post 'would not be the act of a sane man'.[32] In 1892, the government decided to take over the trunk line system connecting telephone switchboards (as opposed to the 'local loop' from switchboards to homes) and bought the NTC's main lines in 1896.[33] Finally, in the Telephone Transfer Act 1911, the NTC's assets were nationalised and the company was liquidated.[34]

26 The Mann-Elkins Act of 1910 gave the ICC power to regulate telecommunications, extended from its original jurisdiction over railroads in the Interstate Commerce Act of 1887. See P. M. Nichols, 'Redefining "Common Carrier": The FCC's Attempt at Deregulation by Redefinition' [1987] *Duke LJ* 501.

27 Known as the Kingsbury Commitment (19 December 1913) after a letter of the AT&T vice president.

28 Communications Act of 1934, 47 USC, §§151ff.

29 (1880) 6 QBD 244.

30 (1880) 6 QBD 255.

31 On 17 July 1882. Cited in I. Walden, *Telecommunications Law and Regulation* (3rd ed. 2009) 124.

32 A. Marshall, 'The Post Office and Private Enterprise', *The Times* (6 April 1891), sent on 31 March 1891, Letter 353 in J. T. Whitaker (ed.), *The Correspondence of Alfred Marshall Economist* (1996) vol. II, 22.

33 Telegraph Act 1892, s. 1 and Telegraph (Money) Act 1896, s. 1.

34 Telephone Transfer Act 1911, s. 8 and Telephone Transfer Amendment Act 1911. In 1905, agreement was already reached on transfer on the NTC's licence expiry, and in *Postmaster*

From then, the Postmaster General ran the post, telegraph and telephone and, although it could grant licences, the main telecoms company, Cable & Wireless became fully public after 1946.[35] After the radio was invented ('radio' using the electromagnetic spectrum from 30 Hz to 300 GHz), and the first broadcasts took place in 1920, followed by television in 1936 (see Ch. 17(1)), the Wireless Telegraphy Act 1949 recast the Postmaster General's monopoly and its power to license the radio spectrum.[36] It also prohibited unauthorised interceptions.[37] These functions were altered in form in the Post Office Act 1969, replacing the Postmaster General with the Minister of Posts and Telecommunications, and establishing the Post Office as a statutory corporation, with a chair and twelve others appointed by the minister.[38] Like other nationalised companies, it had 'Users' Councils' without power,[39] and without voting rights for consumers. On the other hand, in the Post Office Act 1977, the board of directors was enlarged from thirteen to nineteen directors, and the government included seven trade union representatives.[40] But these were soon to be retrenched.

Without warning the electorate in the 1979 Manifesto,[41] Thatcher's government passed the British Telecommunications Act 1981. It separated BT from the Post Office and enabled competing operators to be licensed. This experiment, alongside privatisation of military production and oil (see Chs. 19 and 11), started by selling Cable & Wireless in 1981 (a private company until 1947) to Barclays Bank and British Petroleum, trading as Mercury Communications Ltd. Its business focused on creaming off low-cost, high-profit customers such as users in the City, without providing service to most other people. The 1983 Manifesto promised to sell 51 per cent of BT, and the Telecommunications Act 1984 created a Director General of Telecommunications as a licensing body (running 'Oftel').[42] It and the Secretary of State had duties to provide universal services unless 'impracticable' and to promote 'the interests of consumers' primarily through 'effective competition'.[43]

The regulator, Oftel, was predicted by an economist adviser, Stephen Littlechild, to eventually wither away.[44] In reality, it was BT's main competitor,

General v National Telephone Co. Ltd [1909] AC 269, the scope of the exception for private communications from the monopoly was litigated, a prelude to negotiating NTC's compensation.

35 Cable and Wireless Act 1946, s. 1 (transfer of shares to person Treasury nominated).

36 Wireless Telegraphy Act (WTA) 1949, ss. 1–3 (licence, fees, frequency allocation).

37 WTA 1949, s. 5.

38 Post Office Act 1969, ss. 1–7. The minister could control and direct the Post Office under ss. 11–12.

39 Post Office Act 1969, ss. 14–15. Also British Telecommunications Act 1981, s. 9.

40 Post Office Act 1977, s. 1. Lord Winterbottom, Second Reading, Hansard HL Debs. (14 July 1977) vol. 385, cols. 981–97.

41 Conservative Party Manifesto (1979).

42 Telecommunications Act (TA) 1984, ss. 5–27.

43 TA 1984, ss. 1–3.

44 S. Littlechild, *Regulation of British Telecommunications Profitability: Report to the Secretary of State* (1983).

Mercury Ltd, that withered: its assets were sold by 2000, as competition for land telephone lines was always impracticable. The system simply looked much more like the one in the USA, where the major telecommunications corporation, AT&T, had assumed a monopoly position. AT&T had been broken up in 1982 by the Department of Justice. Regional monopolies succeeded, but these simply remerged over the coming years, leading to AT&T and Verizon being dominant today.[45] However, the invention of mobile phones, which could operate across the far more divisible radio spectrum, did enable more competitors. In 2002 Ofcom replaced Oftel, and the Communications Act 2003 gave it powers for radio and TV licensing, across the radio spectrum, as it was seen that the era of 'spectrum scarcity [was] drawing to a close'.[46] The regulator's most lucrative role was auctioning off the spectrum as technology advanced. On brick-like mobile phones, '1G' was sold in the 1980s, 2G was sold in 1993, 3G in 2000, 4G in 2013,[47] and 5G in 2021.

Meanwhile, the technology to eclipse them all was the Internet, 'a telecomms system for computer networks'.[48] In 1957, the Soviet launch of the Sputnik satellite into space alarmed US President Eisenhower enough to create the Advanced Research Projects Agency (ARPA), funded by the Department of Defence. ARPA wanted a communication system that could withstand nuclear attack. Telephones used single lines, a 'circuit switching' network, but it was theorised that messages could instead be broken into 'packets' of data, so that if one line was broken (or nuked), the packets could go down alternative routes until all arrived.[49] An 'Arpanet' was built with packet switching between computers at Californian and Utah universities by 1969, using existing AT&T systems.[50] In parallel, the University of Hawaii developed a wireless radio network called 'Alohanet', where any impeded messages would keep being resent until complete. The US researchers also teamed up with the UK and Norway to create a satellite network, Satnet. In 1972 Arpanet, Alohanet and Satnet together formed the 'Internetworking Architecture Layer'. The four protocols to communicate between each network were that (1) each network stood on its own, (2) packets would be resubmitted until they arrived, (3) routers connecting networks would retain no information about packet flows and (4) there would be no global control at the operations level.[51] Just as the post carried packets without knowing what was in them, so the Transmission

45 L. Khan and S. Vaheesan, 'Market Power and Inequality: The Antitrust Counterrevolution and Its Discontents' (2017) 11 *Harvard L & Policy Rev* 235, 256–60.

46 DCMS, *Regulating Communications: The Way Ahead*, Cm. 5010 (2000) §5.2.4.

47 Walden, *Telecommunications Law and Regulation* (4th ed. 2012) 110–15.

48 See A. Murray, *Information Technology Law: The Law and Society* (3rd ed. 2016) 16–27, for an excellent, detailed history. Also Internet Society, *Brief History of the Internet* (1997).

49 L. Kleinrock, 'Information Flow in Large Communication Nets', RLE Quarterly Progress Report (July 1961).

50 Murray, *Information Technology Law*, 18–19.

51 V. G. Cerf and B. E. Kahn, 'A Protocol for Packet Network Intercommunication', IEEE Trans on Comms, Vol Com-22, No. 5 (May 1974).

Table 16.1 Frequency and wavelength uses[i]

	Designation	Frequency	Wavelengths	Uses
ELF, SLF, ULF	Extremely, Super and Ultra Low Frequency	3 Hz–30 Hz 30 Hz–300 Hz 300 Hz–3 kHz	10,000,000 km–100 km	Submarine communication, mines
VLF	Very Low Frequency	3 kHz–30 kHz	100 km–10 km	Submarine, avalanche beacons, wireless heart monitors, geophysics
LF	Low Frequency	30 kHz–300 kHz	10 km–1 km	AM radio broadcast, navigation, time signals
MF	Medium	300 kHz–3 MHz	1 km–100 m	AM broadcast (medium wave)
HF	High	3 MHz–30 MHz	100 m–10 m	Shortwave broadcast, amateur radio, military communication
VHF	Very High	30 MHz–300 MHz	10 m–1 m	FM broadcast, TV, ground-to-air, air-to-air communication
UHF	Ultra High	300 MHz–3 GHz	1 m–10 cm	TV, mobile phones (1G–3G), Wi-Fi, Bluetooth, micro-wave ovens
SHF	Super High	3 GHz–30 GHz	10 cm–1 cm	Wi-Fi, radar, 4G and 5G mobile
EHF	Extremely High	30 GHz–300 GHz	1 cm–1 mm	5G mobile, radio astronomy, high-speed microwave radio

[i] Walden, *Telecommunications Law and Regulation* (4th ed. 2012) ch. 7, 363, Table 7.1 ITU Radio frequency designations.

Control Protocols would send 'datagrams' without looking inside.[52] Out of this developed email, file transfer protocol and hypertext transfer protocol. 'Http' was the idea of Tim Berners-Lee, a contractor at the European Organization for Nuclear Research, who in 1990 proposed that pages with text and embedded links (hypertext) could be the basis for a worldwide web.[53] Just after the first fibre-optic cable was put across the Atlantic in 1988, for faster transfer than copper, the first-ever website, explaining the web, was published in December 1990.[54]

The early experience of the Internet was much more like a library or a café on a computer than what it has become today: it was quieter and more freely expressive at once. Users originally had a preferred (but often clunky) search engine among many, chose from many different email accounts, saw relatively

[52] Murray, *Information Technology Law*, 20–2.

[53] T. Berners-Lee and R. Cailliau, 'WorldWideWeb: Proposal for a HyperText Project' (12 November 1990).

[54] See a picture of the webpage at https://home.cern/science/computing/birth-web.

simple websites with text and pictures, knew nothing of 'cookies' and tried to avoid the few websites with annoying, flashy pop-up ads. Friends were people you knew and really liked. The legal discussion in the 1990s was dominated by litigation against Microsoft's abusive monopoly practices, by tying the Windows operating system to its web browser in the USA,[55] and to its media player in the European Union (EU).[56] As this was happening, online business was growing. A business called Amazon began selling books in 1994. A business called Google developed a new search engine algorithm in 1998, and it was so much better that everyone was using it by 2003. A phone book with pictures, and the ability to post notices, called 'The Facebook', was launched in 2004 to university campuses, and it grew exponentially. These sites grew because most were free from ads, until Google launched Gmail in 2004, with a new business plan: to trawl people's emails to generate small, text-based targeted ads.[57] A video-streaming service called YouTube launched in 2005, only to be bought by Google in 2006. Facebook started ads in 2007. A mobile message application called WhatsApp was created in 2009, but it was bought by Facebook in 2014. So was Instagram (created 2010, bought 2012). The basis of each company's monopolising advantage – Amazon, Google and Facebook – quickly became the masses of data harvested from its own users, usable for predicting what products they might like and for advertising. Websites' use of tracking files (thoroughly misrepresented by the cute label of 'cookies'), saved into web browsers, became ever more prevalent as they were sold opportunities by Google, Facebook and Amazon to advertise. A requirement from EU law in 2009 was introduced to get user 'consent' to cookies on every webpage.[58] These pop up like the annoying pop-up ads once did, almost everywhere. As it has been enclosed, the Internet has eclipsed all forms of traditional communication (see Table 16.2).

Just as the Internet, made out of publicly funded infrastructure, was being enclosed, the UK's Royal Mail with its old privacy guarantees was sold on the stock market after 2011.[59]

(2) Finance

If privatised, communication companies, for landline, mobile, broadband and online services, seem financed by equity or debt (Chs. 4 and 7), but there are at least three further explicit and regulatory subsidies. These are (a) government

[55] *United States v Microsoft Corporation*, 253 F 3d 34 (DC Cir 2001) overturning an order to break up Microsoft.

[56] *Microsoft Corp. v Commission* (2007) T-201/04, issuing a €497m fine.

[57] Zuboff, *The Age of Surveillance Capitalism*, chs. 3–5.

[58] Privacy and Electronic Communications Directive 2002/58/EC, art. 5(3), inserted by 2009/136/EC; Privacy and Electronic Communications (EC Directive) Regulations 2003, reg. 6; and see further *Lloyd v Google LLC* [2019] EWCA Civ 1599, allowing an action for non-consented use of tracking files.

[59] Postal Services Act (PSA) 2011, ss. 1–3.

Table 16.2 The Internet's eclipse of everything

Traditional	Online	Brands and market share %	Owners
Post	Email	Gmail (~65%), Outlook (~17%)[i]	Google, Microsoft
Phone or text	Web call, messenger	WhatsApp, Messenger, Skype, Zoom	Facebook, Microsoft
Phone directory	Search	Google (~93%)[ii]	Google
Phone book	Social media	Facebook, Instagram	Facebook
Shopfront	Website	-	-
Advertisements	Ad-boxes	Google Ads, FB Ads, Amazon Ads	Google, FB, Amazon
Warehouse	Data storage, clouds	AWS, Google Cloud, MS Azure	Amazon, Google, Microsoft
Radio (see Ch. 17)	Web radio, podcasts	-	-
TV (see Ch. 17)	Streaming	YouTube, Prime, Netflix, Hulu	Google, AZ, Netflix, Disney

[i] N. Gilbert, 'Number of Email Users Worldwide 2020', www.FinancesOnline.com. These are estimations, as there is no clear statistical information on the number of total email accounts. Email client market share statistics are not relevant, because this refers to the application rather than the information stored: Apple takes a large share.

[ii] M. Capala, 'Global Search Engine Market Share in the Top 15 GDP Nations', *Alphametic* (19 March 2020).

subsidies through infrastructure and tax, (b) the implicit subsidy from consumers by virtue of holding a natural monopoly and (c) data harvesting for the purpose of targeted advertisements.

(a) Government Subsidies

The first major source of finance is state aid to telecoms companies, which in turn benefits web companies. As state aid is legitimate for infrastructure investment, in 2013 the EU Commission issued guidelines on state aid rules for deploying fast broadband,[60] with a goal of ensuring by 2020 that all Europeans have access to speeds of 30 megabits per second (Mbps), and 50 per cent to 100 Mbps, needing €330 billion in investment.[61] (This target failed.[62]) It noted the four most common kinds of state aid are (1) direct monetary grants to communication companies; (2) support in kind, such as civil engineering work enabling cables to be installed in ducts; (3) giving access to a publicly owned network; and (4) licensing use of a public network through competitive tender.[63] There are also significant subsidies in all forms of research and development, which included developing the Internet.[64]

60 TFEU, art. 107(3)(a)–(c); see Ch. 6(4)(c).

61 EU Commission, *EU Guidelines for the Application of State Aid Rules in Relation to the Rapid Deployment of Broadband Networks* [2013] OJ C25, paras. 1–2.

62 See the European Court of Auditors, 'Broadband in the EU Member States', Special Report No. 12 (2018).

63 *EU Guidelines* (2013) Annex I.

64 E.g. the publicly funded JANET. See further M. Mazzucato, *The Entrepreneurial State: Debunking Public vs Private Sector Myths* (2013) ch. 3.

In the UK, in 2012 the government had allocated an estimated £1.5 billion under its Broadband Delivery UK scheme, to ensure everyone had internet speeds of at least 2 Mbps.[65] In the Budget 2020, the government promised a further £5 billion would be spent on 'gigabit-capable broadband', and £510 million to give 4G mobile-phone reception to 95 per cent of the UK under a 'Shared Rural Network agreement', to be 'more than matched by industry'.[66] The lack of investment up to 2020 meant that just 10 per cent or 3 million UK properties had access to fibre-optic internet.[67] Without any subsidies, it seems unlikely private companies would have paid for even this.[68] Subsidies therefore enable the profits of all broadband or mobile providers.[69] All online companies further benefit from this infrastructure, including search, email, web calls or streaming (see Ch. 17) and online marketplaces (Ch. 18). Just as real highways subsidise auto companies (Ch. 15), the 'information superhighway' subsidises companies that sell services online. Notably, YouTube or Google, Netflix and Facebook were reported to account for at least 38.96 per cent of global data traffic in 2020, but had not paid for infrastructure.[70]

The second major subsidy is the non-enforcement of tax against big-tech companies, since the law enables transfer pricing, or reporting of profits in other jurisdictions, despite generation of enormous revenues within the UK (see Table 16.3).[71]

Under EU law, non-payment of tax can count as state aid if the tax is applied selectively, under TFEU, article 107. In 2016, the Commission claimed Ireland unlawfully allowed Apple Inc. to report all its EU sale profits there, and then pay no tax on profits, and required it to collect €13 billion in tax,[72] but this decision was annulled by the General Court in 2020.[73] In 2019, the EU Commission began investigating Google's affairs.[74] The basic point is that filthy rich corporations are still paying lower rates of tax than even the lowest-paid workers.

65 *Broadband Delivery UK* (2012) C(2012) 8223 final, finding the UK plan compliant with state aid rules.

66 *Budget 2020* (March 2020) para. 1.134–1.136.

67 'Full-Fibre Broadband in the UK', Briefing Paper No. CBP8392, HC Library (2020) 3. Some 95% of UK premises had access to 24 Mbps speeds which the government called 'superfast'.

68 As Ch. 2(2)(b) explains, the Internet is not formally a 'public good', as people are excludable through Wi-Fi passwords, etc. But they need not be. With more infrastructure, there is no need for goods to be rivalrous.

69 Frontier Economics, *Future Telecoms Infrastructure Review: Annex A. A Report for DCMS* (13 July 2018) 11, Figure 2, suggested that 100% full fibre coverage would cost £20.3bn if there was a national monopoly provider, instead of £32.3bn under 'enhanced competition'.

70 Sandvine, *The Global Internet Phenomena Report: COVID-19 Spotlight* (May 2020) 7: YouTube 15.94%, Google 2.91%, Netflix 11.42%, Facebook 5.97% and Instagram 2.72%. This may not include WhatsApp or others.

71 In 2017, Google paid $46.6m tax on £1.27bn revenue, or 3.6%. Facebook paid £15.8m tax on £1.3bn revenue, or 1.2%.

72 EU Commission, 'State Aid: Irish Tax Treatment of Apple Is Illegal', Press Release (30 August 2016).

73 *Apple Sales International v Commission* (2020) T-778/16, currently on appeal to the CJEU.

74 M. Sheehan, 'Google's Irish Taxes Come under Closer EU Scrutiny', *Independent.ie* (14 April 2019).

Table 16.3 Big-tech tax and revenues in the UK, 2018

Company	2018 tax	2018 revenue	% tax on revenue
Google	£65.3m	£1,410m	4.6%
Facebook	£28m	£1,600m	1.7%
Amazon	£220m	£10,900m	2%
Microsoft	£28.2m	£2,100m	1.3%

(b) Network Monopoly

The second main source of finance is natural and network monopoly. First, there are cables, base stations and satellites, which do not need duplication, particularly if there are safety concerns.[75] By contrast, markets for Wi-Fi boxes, telephone or mobiles can plainly be competitive. But why do we need dozens of competing signals in every city or town, all closed off by passwords, instead of one good source? Broadband and line-rental price movements appear to cluster around regulatory caps, or the market leader. In the case of UK landline prices, until 2014, the public UK Post Office followed wholesale price movements, below the 'market rate' set by BT and others. When it was privatised in 2011, prices went up (see Figure 16.1).[76] This suggests BT and others charge consumers far above costs, like a monopoly would.

Second, it has long been recognised that a single network is more valuable the more people join it, a 'positive externality'.[77] This is true of telephone connections, as marketed by the AT&T president for 'universal service' in 1907 (see Ch. 16(1)). It is also true of online networks, such as Facebook, Instagram or Twitter. For example, when Google+ was launched to compete with Facebook, it failed dramatically and was shut down after a few years: the world's biggest tech company could not displace Facebook.[78] The same appears to be true of communication apps that refuse to allow interoperability, such as WhatsApp, Skype, Teams or Zoom. Unlike email or telephone, a WhatsApp caller cannot reach a Skype receiver. This makes markets concentrate, limited by the many similar apps people want to tolerate.

Third, accumulated data is becoming an important source of natural monopoly. Google's search engine and Amazon's marketplace have developed such extensive databases on people's preferences that it may have become impossible to compete. This is because the companies' algorithms predict which search results or products we want, based on masses of information from prior

75 *Ofcom v Information Commissioner* [2010] UKSC 3, (2011) C-71/10 (base-station locations had to be disclosed).

76 Ofcom, 'Landline Prices Review to Protect Elderly and Vulnerable' (1 December 2016); 'Ofcom to Investigate Rising Landline Prices Amid Concern for Elderly', *The Guardian* (1 December 2016).

77 E.g. Rohlfs, 'A Theory of Interdependent Demand for a Telecommunications Service'.

78 C. Fox, 'Google Shuts Failed Social Network Google+', *BBC News* (2 April 2019).

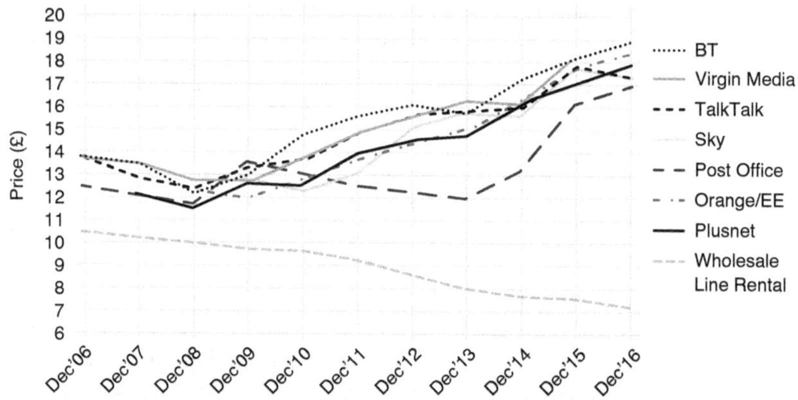

Figure 16.1 Ofcom wholesale and retail line-rental price movements, 2006–16 £/month in December 2016 prices

searches. In 2013, Microsoft, wishing to challenge Google, launched a 'Bing it on' challenge website, designed to compare its own search engine, similar to blind tests between Coke and Pepsi. People would choose which search results they preferred, without seeing which company generated them. Users preferred Google, leading Microsoft to shut down its site.[79] It makes sense to concentrate data into one repository, and that web search or marketplaces may be best performed by one entity. That explains why Google's market share in search is 91%, Facebook's share in social networks is 51% and Amazon's share of e-commerce is 44%. These are all dominant positions. In telecoms, BT is dominant in infrastructure and landline markets (see Ch. 16(3)(d)).

(c) Data and Ads

A third main source of finance is data enabling exploitation of privacy, not just as monopoly. While the right to privacy and data protection is in law a human right,[80] in business it has become a source of value, and enables a new type of production based on extraction of our personal information.[81] Everything from your messages, locations, preferences to search histories is aggregated and used for targeted ads. Though search engines, email, social networks or data storage appear to require no payment, the price is monetisation of

[79] W. Oremus, 'A Professor Fact-Checked the "Bing It On Challenge". Bing Lost', *Slate* (2 October 2013).

[80] Below at Ch. 16(4)(a); and see CFREU, art. 8(1): 'Everyone has the right to the protection of personal data concerning him or her'; art. 8(2): 'Such data must be processed fairly for specified purposes and on the basis of the consent of the person concerned or some other legitimate basis laid down by law. Everyone has the right of access to data which has been collected concerning him or her, and the right to have it rectified.'

[81] Zuboff, *The Age of Surveillance Capitalism*, ch. 3.

Table 16.4 Worldwide net ad revenues, 2019[i]

	Company	Worldwide revenue %	Net digital ad revenue
1	Google	31.1%	$103.73 billion
2	Facebook	20.2%	$67.37 billion
3	Alibaba	8.75%	$29.20 billion
4	Amazon	4.2 %	$14.03 billion
			$333.53 billion total

[i] J. Enberg, 'Global Digital Ad Spending', eMarketer (28 March 2019).

people's private lives. Though known for their online software, Google and Facebook are ad firms. By 2020, Amazon was catching up (see Table 16.4).

As well as dominating communication markets, big tech also monopolises ads: in 2019, Google, Facebook and Amazon captured nearly 70 per cent of global online ad spending.[82] Online ads are 66.4 per cent of total ad spending in the UK. The dominance in ads, mostly paid for by smaller and medium businesses, is also a form of exploitation of small and medium-sized enterprises (SMEs) by big-ad companies.

(3) Governance

Governance of communications is incoherent and the law is unwieldy. Three main levels of communication production are (1) cables, receivers and infrastructure; (2) retail broadband or mobile contracts; and (3) software services online, such as email, calls, search, social media, websites and data storage. At the moment these are governed by (a) the public regulators, namely Ofcom, the Information Commissioner, the International Telecommunication Union (ITU) and Internet Corporation for Assigned Names and Numbers (ICANN) to assign web addresses; (b) telecoms companies; (c) web companies, particularly Google, Facebook, Microsoft and Amazon; and (d) the Royal Mail and competing postal companies.

(a) Public Regulators: Ofcom, Information Commissioner, ITU and ICANN

(i) Ofcom

The Office of Communications (Ofcom) was designed to be the 'super regulator' for the communication industry, superseding six entities,[83] though it has failed to keep pace with changes in internet and data management. The Office of Communications Act (OCA) 2002, section 1 requires it to have a board of

[82] G. Sterling, 'Almost 70% of Digital Ad Spending Going to Google, Facebook, Amazon, Says Analyst Firm', *Marketing Land* (17 June 2019).

[83] These were the DGT and Oftel, ITC, BSC, Radio Authority and Radiocommunications Agency.

three to twelve directors, including a chair appointed by the Secretary of State, a director appointed by the Scottish minister and a director appointed by the Welsh minister.[84] There is also provision for Ofcom directors to be appointed 'from amongst their employees'. But in 2020, on the nine-person board, there did not seem to be elected workforce representation. There is no provision for consumer representation. Board members had experience in finance, media company management, and at least three had worked for BT,[85] while others were also on boards at a university, a bank, a health board and an environmental regulator.[86] No board member appeared to have expertise in engineering, data, web communications or web media.[87] One appeared to have some legal training. Ofcom is subject to directions by the Secretary of State regarding networks and the radio spectrum.[88]

Ofcom's principal duty in the Communication Act 2003, section 3 is to 'further the interests of citizens' and 'consumers in relevant markets, where appropriate by promoting competition'. The duties include securing 'optimal use for wireless telegraphy of the electro-magnetic spectrum', and making electronic communications available 'throughout' the UK.[89] Ofcom should have regard to 'promoting competition', 'effective forms of self-regulation', 'encouraging investment and innovation', 'availability and use of high speed data transfer' and different people's 'needs and interests' in spectrum use, and 'choice, price, quality of service and value for money' for consumers.[90] Under sections 2A–C, Ofcom has to follow a 'Statement of Strategic Priorities' set by the government.[91] In 2019, this was written to aim for 'nationwide deployment of gigabit-capable broadband at pace', mobile coverage reaching 95 per cent of the country by 2022, and a 5G network for a 'majority' of the country by 2027.[92] It reasserts that the government regards 'competition where possible as a key driver of network roll-out'.[93] However, UK internet speeds remain low compared to prices.

With separation and consumer rights powers (see Ch. 16(4)), Ofcom fulfils its duties by licensing. There is no need for a licence to start an electronic

[84] OCA 2002, s. 1 confusingly terms these directors as the Ofcom 'members'. Ofcom itself refers to directors.

[85] See www.ofcom.org.uk/about-ofcom/how-ofcom-is-run/ofcom-board. Three members worked for BT.

[86] This may be a problem because collecting prestigious directorships, like stamps, probably does not enable adequate attention to a job at Ofcom, or thought about new problems.

[87] This may explain Ofcom's non-regulation of those fields despite its powers: see also Ch. 17(3)(a).

[88] Communications Act (CA) 2003, s. 5(2).

[89] CA 2003, s. 3(2). Cf. Electronic Communications Code Directive 2018/1972, arts. 5–11. CA 2003, s. 4 requires Ofcom to comply with EU competition law, develop the internal market and comply with international standards.

[90] CA 2003, s. 3(4)–(5).

[91] CA 2003, ss. 2A–C, laid before Parliament. Added by the Digital Economy Act 2017, s. 98.

[92] DCMS, *Statement of Strategic Priorities* (October 2019) 3.

[93] DCMS, *Statement of Strategic Priorities*, 8.

communications company[94] or a postal company,[95] but there is for using the radio spectrum or the 'airwaves', affecting mobile telephones contracts and data. The Wireless Telegraphy Act 2006, section 8 makes it unlawful to establish a wireless telegraphy station or use apparatus, unless exempt, without a licence,[96] punishable by up to two years in prison and a fine.[97] Section 2 requires Ofcom publishes a UK Frequency Authorisation Plan, with allocation criteria that are non-discriminatory, proportionate and transparent.[98] Under section 5, the Secretary of State can give Ofcom directions about the use of the spectrum.[99] Ofcom can set any licence terms it thinks fit, set charges and make regulations about bidding for licences.[100] The power to license, or withdraw licences for breach, enables Ofcom to set any terms or any rights for consumers it wants. The Wireless Telegraphy (Exemption) Regulations 2003 exempt limited frequency bands from licensing and devices that are available for public use.[101]

Ofcom's licensing powers are the basis for the periodic licensing rounds: 4G auctions in 2013 made £2.3 billion (the forecast was £3.5 billion) and the first 5G auctions in 2018 made £1.4 billion.[102] In *EE Ltd v Ofcom*, the Secretary of State was unhappy about the licence fees that were set and gave an order under section 5 to revise fees to reflect 'full market value'. On a judicial review application by EE Ltd, the Court of Appeal held that the Secretary of State's Order could not deprive Ofcom of its own independent duty to set fees according to the legislation.[103]

Ofcom's blind spot is the Internet, even though it can set 'general conditions', conditions for provision of universal service, conditions for access or conditions for companies with significant market power.[104] This applies to anyone providing 'an electronic communications network' or service,[105] which means any 'transmission system' for conveying electric or magnetic signals; any 'apparatus', 'software and stored data' and 'other resources'; but not

94 CA 2003, s. 147, repealing licensing for telecommunication systems defined in the former TA 1984, s. 4.

95 PSA 2011, s. 28(1).

96 WTA 2006, s. 8; Electronic Communications Code Directive 2018/1972, art. 46.

97 WTA 2006, s. 35.

98 WTA 2006, s. 2.

99 WTA 2006, s. 5.

100 WTA 2006, ss. 9 and 12–14.

101 WTA 2006, s. 8(3) enables the Secretary of State to issue the Wireless Telegraphy (Exemption) Regulations 2003; reg. 4 exempts several bands and devices listed in Schs. 3–9. Amended in 2006, 2011 and SI 2016/486.

102 'Ofcom raises £2.34bn in 4G Auction, Less than Forecast', *BBC News* (20 February 2013); M. Sweney, 'UK Mobile Operators Pay Close to £1.4bn for 5G Spectrum', *The Guardian* (5 April 2018).

103 *EE Ltd v Office of Communications* [2017] EWCA Civ 1873, an order under WTA 2006, s. 5 and CA 2003, s. 4(2) on six requirements; and cf. Electronic Communications Code Directive 2018/1972, arts. 5–6.

104 CA 2003, s. 45(2). For general conditions, ss. 51and 52–5. For universal service, ss. 65–72B. On significant market power, ss. 78–93. Also access, ss. 73–6A.

105 CA 2003, s. 46(2).

a 'content service' (i.e. media with or without editorial control).[106] Under the Communications Act 2003, section 55 Ofcom can enforce general conditions against 'public electronic communication services',[107] to secure 'necessary protection for [its] customers'.[108] It can regulate email, web call, search and data storage companies, but has failed to do so. At the time of writing, an *Online Harms White Paper* proposed designating Ofcom as regulator for internet communication, and to establish a 'duty of care' to limit harassment, abuse and misinformation, though this mainly involves public media (see Ch. 17(3)(a)) and there remains a deafening silence when it comes to privacy in communications.[109]

(ii) Information Commissioner

A second main regulator, the Information Commissioner, was re-established by the Data Protection Act 2018.[110] The Information Commissioner is 'appointed by Her Majesty' (i.e. the Prime Minister) by Letters Patent for one seven-year term, and cannot be removed except by an Address from both Houses of Parliament.[111] The Commissioner may appoint an office and staff to form the Information Commissioner's Office (ICO), and its functions are listed in the Data Protection Act 2018, which implements the General Data Protection Regulation (GDPR) 2016.[112] Its powers are broadly to uphold data protection rights,[113] by investigations, by enforcing effective penalties or by changes in contracts and 'binding corporate rules'.[114] Power over contracts and corporate rules aims to ensure global reach. This is crucial for privacy rights (see Ch. 16(4)(a)).

(iii) International Telecommunications Union

A third main regulator, and world's oldest international organisation, is the ITU, now a specialist body of the United Nations (UN), established in 1865.[115] Its purposes include to 'extend international cooperation' for member states in

[106] CA 2003, s. 32(1)–(2) and (7). On powers over media, see Ch. 17(3)(a).
[107] CA 2003, s. 151, defining this as someone who makes services 'available to members of the public'.
[108] CA 2003, s. 55(1).
[109] HM Government, *Online Harms White Paper*, CP 57 (April 2019); DCMS and Home Office, *Online Harms White Paper – Initial Consultation Response* (12 February 2020).
[110] Data Protection Act (DPA) 2018, ss. 114–41 and Sch. 12. The predecessors were the Data Protection Commissioner in the DPA 1998, s. 6 and Sch. 5, and the Data Protection Registrar in the DPA 1984. The ICO is the relevant regulator for the General Data Protection Regulation (GDPR) (EU) 2016/679, art. 51.
[111] DPA 2018, Sch. 12, paras. 2–3.
[112] DPA 2018, s. 115 and GDPR 2016, arts. 57–8 and European Union (Withdrawal) Act 2018, s. 3.
[113] GDPR 2016, art. 58(1) on investigations and (2) warnings, reprimands and orders.
[114] GDPR 2016, arts. 58(3)(h) and (j), and arts. 46–7.
[115] International Telegraph Convention 1865. The ITU merged with the International Radiotelegraph Union (est. 1906) in 1932, and was renamed. In 1947, it became part of the UN.

'rational use of telecommunications', 'foster fruitful cooperation', extend 'the benefits of ... technologies to all the world's inhabitants' and promote 'peaceful relations'.[116] Ofcom has a duty to co-ordinate with European and international counterparts, including the ITU.[117] The ITU co-ordinates radio-spectrum use, ensures satellite orbits do not clash, suggests standardisation in telecoms, gives technical assistance and conducts and publishes research.[118] Ofcom is the national notifying authority to the ITU, to co-ordinate satellite networks.[119] For example, in *R (ICO Satellite Ltd) v Ofcom* the Court of Appeal held that Ofcom had lawfully cancelled a satellite and frequency assignment, by notifying the ITU, because the company delayed launching the satellite.[120] There are currently around 2000 satellites orbiting Earth, mainly for communication or observation.[121]

(iv) Internet Corporation for Assigned Names and Numbers

A fourth regulator, albeit not private, is ICANN, responsible for allocating website domain names, such as .com, .net, or .org. ICANN was incorporated in 1998 under the California Nonprofit Public Benefit Corporation Law.[122] Its articles can be amended by a two-third majority vote of the directors. The sixteen directors are appointed by an 'Empowered Community', made up of representatives from registries, commercial stakeholders, intellectual property experts, internet service providers (ISPs) and other internet users who work their way through a maze of self-perpetuating appointments.[123] It assigns domain names, by subcontracting with a range of profit-making companies to become accredited registrars with ICANN. As well as issuing domain names, ICANN adjudicates disputes over intellectual property infringement or if domain names are registered in bad faith.[124] Although its governance structure is obscure,[125] it nevertheless exemplifies how a global system of communication regulation is possible.[126]

116 Constitution and Convention of the International Telecommunication Union (2019), art. 1(2).
117 CA 2003, s. 4(9)–(10) including the European Committee for Standardization, ECES and ETSI.
118 Constitution of the ITU, art. 1(2). 119 CA 2003, s. 22.
120 *R (ICO Satellite Ltd) v Office of Communications* [2011] EWCA Civ 1121, Pill LJ rejecting there was any duty to consider financial loss to ICO Ltd, that Ofcom considered irrelevant factors or acted disproportionately.
121 T. Ryan-Moseley, E. Winick and K. Kakaes, 'The Number of Satellites Orbiting Earth Could Quintuple in the Next Decade', *MIT Technology Review* (26 June 2019).
122 See the Articles of Incorporation (1998). It is a charity under the Internal Revenue Code of 1986, §501(c)(3).
123 ICANN Bylaws (1998) section 7.2 and 6.1.
124 See G. Robertson and A. Nicol, *Media Law* (2008) 814, giving an example of www.billyconnolly.com being won back by the comedian, after ICANN rejected the purchaser's claim – that it was for their dog – for bad faith.
125 Cf. J. Weinberg, 'ICANN and the Problem of Legitimacy' (2002) 50 *Duke LJ* 187; A. M. Froomkin, 'Wrong Turn in Cyberspace: Using ICANN to Route around the APA and the Constitution' (2002) 50 *Duke LJ* 17.
126 See also the structure of Wikipedia in Ch. 17(3)(b)(i).

(b) Telecoms Companies

Telecoms companies provide mobile and broadband contracts, and run or access infrastructure. Since privatisation, despite rules on separation and access, BT still dominates (see Table 16.5).

First, it would appear that as an alternative to a single, privatised monopoly, ensuring there are competitors must be desirable. But, second, competition brings costs of duplication, and competition is largely fictitious where there are seven players, where they have similar or identical shareholders, where contracts are regulated and all seem to 'follow the leader' on price and terms (see Ch. 16(2)(b)). So why not, third, take the dominant broadband and mobile company (that is, BT and EE) into public ownership, while allowing others to compete where they can? This is the model in most countries with the fastest internet (see Table 16.6).[127]

Romania is interesting, because it has the world's fourth-fastest broadband speeds, and it developed neighbourhood-owned internet, before larger companies built any infrastructure.[128] Under the Communications Act 2003, section 148 expressly empowers local authorities to borrow money for 'providing a public electronic communications network' or service, and can also extend these outside their area.[129] This means that any London Borough Council, a city or county council could begin a free public Wi-Fi service, a broadband service or telephone lines, with any governance arrangements

Table 16.5 Broadband, mobile and landline market shares, 2019[i]

Name	Broadband %	Mobile %	Landline %	Ownership	Profit
BT and EE	31%[ii]	28%	60.1%	BT Group plc	£2.15bn
Virgin Media	18%	4%	7%	Liberty Global Inc.	£5.16bn
Vodafone	2%	21%	-	Vodafone plc	£697m
Three	1%	12%	-	CK Hutchison Ltd	£1.5bn
Sky Broadband	24%	1%	-	Comcast Inc.	£2.23bn
O2	1%	26%	-	Telefónica SA	£1.6bn
TalkTalk	12%	1%	-	TalkTalk plc	£47m

[i] Ofcom, *Telecommunications Market Data Update* (2019) Q1 2019 for landline; Ofcom, *The Communications Market* (2016) 154, Figure 4.2.1; Ofcom, *Communications Market Report* (2017) 147, Figure 4.15.

[ii] BT and EE broadband are separate, but the same company. EE was formed as a joint venture of the French state-owned company, Orange, and the German T-Mobile in 2010. This was acquired by BT in 2016.

[127] J. M. Alonso, 'The Race for International Markets: Were Privatized Telecommunications Incumbents More Successful than Their Public Counterparts?' (2013) 27(2) *Int'l Rev Applied Economics* 215.

[128] See K. Rogers, 'Why Romania's Internet Is So Much Faster Than America's', *Vice* (2 February 2015).

[129] CA 2003, s. 148.

Table 16.6 Internet speeds and government ownership by country, March 2021[i]

	Country	Broadband Mbps	Mobile Mbps	Major co(s)	Govt stake %
1	Singapore	247.54	66.44	Singtel (Temasek)	51.2%
2	Hong Kong	229.45	70.13	China Mobile HK	100%
3	Thailand	220.59	50	TOT	100%
4	Romania	198.01	47.69	Locally owned	100%
5	Denmark	190.32	73.91	Telenor (Norway)	54%
6	France	188.03	59.39	France Telecom	26.97%
7	Monaco	187.88	-	Monaco Telecom	45%
8	Switzerland	187.08	89.38	Swisscom	51%
9	Spain	186.06	46.16	Movistar (Telefónica)	0%
10	Hungary	185.92	46.62	Magyar Telecom (Deutsche)	59% (31.98%)
12	US	179.06	69.23	AT&T, Verizon	0%
13	South Korea	174.66	171.26	KT (National Pension)	12.19%
16	Chile	171.02	18.4	VTR, Movistar	0%
17	Sweden	165.97	74.29	TeliaSonera	50% (+ Finl.)
18	China	162.12	149.68	Telecom, Mobile, Unicom	70–100%
20	Norway	153.20	107.83	Telenor	54%
26	Japan	138.30	41.25	NTT	33.33%
34	Germany	113.55	60.79	Deutsche Telekom	31.98%
47	UK	82.36	53.69	BT	0%
59	Italy	79.62	42.57	Gruppo TIM	0%
61	Australia	58.25	104.16	Telstra	0%

[i] See www.speedtest.net/global-index. These are calculated very differently by other bodies depending on method (e.g. time or place of testing for the 'average' speed). Also, Organisation for Economic Co-operation and Development, *Communications Outlook* (2013).

that the local authority thought best for its residents.[130] However Hull's KCom remains the sole example of any scale.

Without public ownership, separation for 'competition' comes in two types. First, competitors are separated 'horizontally' on the market, on the theory that they should compete. Second, they are separated vertically, on the theory that costs will be charged fairly. The Competition and Markets Authority (CMA) can make a reference to its chair where it believes 'features of a market' distort 'competition in connection with the supply or acquisition' of 'communication products'.[131] Until 2013, this power was held by Ofcom, and in 2005 Ofcom considered its use against BT Group plc, given its ownership of physical infrastructure, and its participation in the retail market (selling customers

[130] Cf. D. Jefferies, 'Should Councils Be Investing in Free Public Wi-Fi Networks?', *The Guardian* (5 December 2011).

[131] Enterprise Act 2002, s. 131, as amended by the Enterprise and Regulatory Reform Act 2013, Sch. 5.

landline, broadband and mobile services). Before any referral, BT undertook to Ofcom to operationally separate physical infrastructure, setting up Openreach.[132] It was required to treat all customers on a non-discriminatory basis. In 2017, it made another undertaking to legally separate Openreach Ltd, but this remains a wholly owned subsidiary of the BT Group plc.[133] The purpose of separation is to be able 'to identify all elements of cost and revenue, with the basis of their calculation and the detailed attribution methods used'.[134] The goal is that with accounting knowledge, a regulator should be able to fix prices accurately for access to the network monopoly owner's services.

Access conditions may also be imposed by Ofcom, requiring undertakings to use networks of an owner on a negotiated contractual basis.[135] For example, although Vodafone or TalkTalk may have no infrastructure, they have a right to access Openreach infrastructure on a negotiated and non-discriminatory basis. For companies with 'significant market power' or 'dominance of the market'[136] (which Openreach has), Ofcom can impose conditions for the 'relevant network or relevant facilities'.[137] This includes access to the network, its use and availability. It can also include 'such price controls as Ofcom may direct' for network access. Ofcom must first do a 'market analysis' showing a 'risk of adverse effects arising from price distortion' and that price controls are 'appropriate' to promote 'efficiency', 'sustainable competition' (even though it does not exist), and to confer 'the greatest possible benefits on end-users'.[138] Companies can appeal Ofcom decisions to the CMA.[139]

(c) Web Communication Companies

The greatest monopolies exist online: Google, Facebook, Microsoft and Amazon, but this is not inevitable. Emails are not natural monopolies, because they are interoperable (one email address can email any other). Messenger and web-call apps are network monopolies, but only because they are not interoperable (e.g. WhatsApp and Skype refuse to connect). The social networks of Facebook and Instagram are network monopolies because they also do not connect, and, like a phone book, the value of the service grows with the number on it. Google's search engine has become a natural monopoly because it has

[132] Enterprise Act 2002, s. 154 (power to accept undertaking); Ofcom, *Final Statement on the Strategic Review of Telecommunications, and Undertakings in Lieu of a Reference under the Enterprise Act 2002: Statement* (22 September 2005) 57.

[133] Ofcom, 'BT Agrees to Legal Separation of Openreach' (10 March 2017).

[134] Electronic Communications Code Directive 2018/1972, arts. 17, 71 and 77–9 on accounting and functional separation.

[135] CA 2003, ss. 73–6; Electronic Communications Code Directive 2018/1972, arts. 61–2; and see formerly Access Directive 2002/19/EC, arts. 3–6 and Annex I.

[136] CA 2003, s. 78. Under s. 79 Ofcom should identify the relevant market following EU law.

[137] CA 2003, s. 87. [138] CA 2003, ss. 87(3) and (9) and 88.

[139] CA 2003, ss. 192–3. The CMA's decision is subject to judicial review on normal grounds.

accumulated so much data, which it does not share, that its search results are likely superior.[140] Because they still mostly regulate themselves, it is necessary to understand who governs each company.

(i) Google and Gmail

Google, Gmail and all of Google's services are, since 2015, owned by Alphabet Inc., incorporated in Delaware.[141] Google, of course, is the world's leading search engine. Gmail is the leading email service. Hangouts is its web-call app. It also runs YouTube (see Ch. 17(3)(c)(iii)), Google shopping (Ch. 18(3)), Google Maps, the Chrome browser, the Android mobile operating system and an ecosystem of other functions. Alphabet's main source of revenue is advertising: the largest advertising firm in human history, its 2019 revenue was $161.8 billion, 83% from advertising, 5.5% from 'Cloud' storage and 10.5% from YouTube media sales.[142]

Alphabet Inc. has 3 billion shares split into Class A, Class B and Class C stock, and 100 million shares of Preferred stock.[143] Class B stock carries ten votes per share. Class C stock, is given to employees and it carries no votes. The founders of Google, Larry Page and Sergey Brin, control Class B stock, giving them total control over the company. Multiple or non-voting shares are rare outside the USA,[144] historically discouraged in UK regulation, prohibited in most EU member states and opposed by most US pension funds.[145] They were discouraged in the USA from the 1920s, but standards were dismantled in the 1980s.[146] In Delaware law, the majority of shareholders can remove directors from the board 'for cause', and the board may amend the bylaws of the corporation with majority approval of shareholders.[147] For example, in 2017 they used their power to vote down proposals from other shareholders to shift to 'one share, one vote', to reduce the gender pay gap and to study the societal impact of hate-speech and fake news on Google's platforms.[148] This ability to have multiple voting shares, or non-voting shares, enables an unaccountable concentration of power despite the contributions of public investors, and despite the considerable importance of Google's staff to its

[140] E.g. T. Bishop, 'Study Says Google Wins "Bing it On" Challenge; Microsoft Calls Findings "Unfair"', *Greek Wire* (3 October 2013).

[141] Alphabet Inc., Certificate of Incorporation (2015) and Bylaws (2 October 2015).

[142] *Alphabet Announces Fourth Quarter and Fiscal Year 2019 Results* (2020) 5, https://abc.xyz/investor/static/pdf/2020Q4_alphabet_earnings_release.pdf?cache=9e991fd.

[143] Alphabet Inc., Certificate of Incorporation (2015) art. IV.

[144] ISS, Shearman & Sterling and ECGI, *Report on the Proportionality Principle in the European Union*, Ref. Ares (2016) 140624 – 11/01/2016 (12 June 2007) 81.

[145] E. McGaughey, *Participation in Corporate Governance* (2014) ch. 5(1).

[146] McGaughey, *Participation in Corporate Governance*, ch. 5(3).

[147] Delaware General Corporation Law, §242(b)(1), also requiring shareholders in an affected class to approve.

[148] T. Townsend, 'Alphabet Shareholders Want More Voting Rights but Larry and Sergey Don't Want It that Way', *Recode* (13 June 2017). Asset managers also opposed the gender pay, hate-speech and fake news proposals.

business. There is no voting power for Alphabet's customers in its governance, despite its monopoly.

The EU Commission has commenced two actions relating to Google's search and advertising businesses (and a third on Google Shopping: Ch. 18(3)). First, in July 2018, in *Google Android*, the Commission fined Alphabet Inc. €4.34 billion (4.5 per cent of worldwide turnover) for paying large manufacturers to exclusively pre-install Google search and Chrome apps as a condition for licensing Google Play, the app marketplace. Although Android is open source, if manufacturers wanted Google apps they were required to use Google's version of Android.[149] The Commission stated Google was dominant in the web search, smartphone OS and app store markets, and it abused its dominance by (1) tying its search app and Chrome to phones, (2) making payments to manufacturers that competitors could not afford to match and (3) obstructing competing Android operating systems.[150] While appealing the fine, Alphabet said it would give buyers an option of search and browser apps when they bought their phone, not require installation of Google apps to use Google Play and enable manufacturers to market devices using other Android versions in the EU.[151]

Second, in March 2019, in *Google AdSense*, the Commission fined Alphabet Inc. €1.49 billion (1.29 per cent of world turnover) for stopping third-party websites displaying ads in embedded search widgets.[152] Google provides search widgets on many webpages, like newspapers, to search their own sites, and at the top of results appear Google ads. These excluded rival ads, such as those from Microsoft or Yahoo. The Commission found Google was dominant in the market for search advert intermediation since at least 2006, and abused its dominance by excluding competitors from its results. Google had already stopped its practice in 2016 when the Commission first issued a statement of objections. Its profits were not dented and, by the time the law was enforced, competitors were already eliminated.[153]

(ii) Facebook, Instagram, WhatsApp

Meta Platforms Inc., the owner of Facebook, Messenger, Instagram and WhatsApp, was incorporated as Facebook Inc. in Delaware in 2004, and renamed under a new holding company, Meta Platforms Inc., in 2021.[154] Its

[149] In 2005, Google had bought the original Android developer. By 2018, 80% of mobile devices in the EU and globally used Android.

[150] *Google Android* (18 July 2018) Case 40099.

[151] 'Google to Charge Smartphone Makers for Google Play in Europe', *Reuters* (18 October 2018); 'Google to Prompt Android Users to Choose Preferred Browsers to Allay EU Concerns', *Reuters* (19 March 2019).

[152] *Google AdSense* (20 March 2019) Case 39740.

[153] J. Espinoza, 'Vestager Warns Big Tech She Will Move Beyond Competition Fines', *Financial Times* (8 October 2019).

[154] See Meta Platforms Inc., Amended and Restated Certificate of Incorporation (28 October 2021) and cf. Facebook Inc., Amended and Restated Bylaws (21 April 2012).

certificate of incorporation, when it made its 'initial public offering' (IPO),[155] created three classes of share: 5 billion shares of Class A Common stock, 4.141 billion shares of Class B Common stock and 100 million shares of Preferred stock.[156] Mark Zuckerberg and a close group of insiders holds the Class B shares, amounting to 16 per cent of shares. But these also carry ten votes per share, leading Zuckerberg to hold around 60 per cent of voting rights.[157] Zuckerberg can act without accountability, despite the company's funding from public investment. Facebook made $70.7 billion in revenue in 2019, 98.5 per cent from advertising. It has been argued that because of these problems, Facebook should be put into public ownership,[158] though proposals of how (if at all) are another issue.

Before its IPO in 2012, Facebook had a remarkable, if minimal, system of user participation. Facebook's contract terms, its *Statement of Rights and Responsibilities* and its *Data Use Policy*, enabled users to block changes if enough comments were made on a proposal and a majority voted against those changes.[159] But when Facebook made its IPO, it sought to scrap this. Facebook users could object, so in order to get the result it wanted, Facebook required that turnout exceeded '30 percent of all active registered users' to stop the change, an entirely unrealistic feat to accomplish. Facebook argued the previous 'system incentivize[d] a high quantity of comments over quality feedback'.[160] It then proceeded to change the terms of privacy and data use to eliminate most rights, including merging data from Facebook and Instagram users. When Facebook bought WhatsApp in 2014, it also merged user data despite promising regulators that it would not.[161] The current statements of user terms are unilaterally altered by Facebook at will.[162]

In the run-up to Facebook's IPO, the US Federal Trade Commission (FTC, the equivalent of the UK's Competition and Markets Authority) had threatened to prosecute Facebook for misuse of users' data without their consent. In 2011, in an 'Agreement Containing Consent Order' to settle the case, the FTC procured Facebook's agreement to not misrepresent 'the extent to which it maintains the privacy or security' of information on users, the extent to which

155 Facebook's IPO share price was $38. This rose to over $200 in 2018, but fell to $162 by March 2019.

156 Facebook Inc., *Restated Certificate of Incorporation* (22 May 2012) art. IV.

157 See 'Facebook and the Meaning of Share Ownership', *The Economist* (30 September 2017); D. Crichton, 'Congress Should Demand Zuckerberg Move to "One Share, One Vote"', *TechCrunch* (9 April 2018).

158 N. Srnicek, *Platform Capitalism* (2017) ch. 3.

159 P. Sloan, 'Commenters Push Facebook Policy Changes to Public Vote', *Cnet* (27 November 2012).

160 J. Constine, 'Facebook Asks Users if It Can Abolish Their Right to Vote on Future Site Governance Changes', *TechCrunch* (21 November 2012).

161 'EU Fines Facebook Over "Misleading" WhatsApp Data Claim', *BBC News* (18 May 2017). The fine was €110m.

162 Facebook, 'Statement of Rights and Responsibilities' (19 April 2018) and for Germans (2 February 2016).

a 'consumer can control the privacy' of their data or the extent to which it made that 'information accessible to third parties'.[163] This agreement lasts for twenty years, till 2031. However, following the Brexit poll in June 2016, and Donald Trump's success in November 2016, it transpired that Facebook had enabled massive harvesting of user data without their consent. Facebook enabled third-party app developers to access user data to run 'services' on their platform. One app, made by a psychologist called Aleksandr Kogan,[164] and his company 'Global Science Research', sold user data (on what people like, or their psychological profiles) to a New York corporation called Cambridge Analytica LLC, owned by American billionaire Robert Mercer and Strategic Communications Group Ltd.[165] Cambridge Analytica sold the data to a Canadian corporation, Aggregate IQ Ltd.[166] The chair of 'Vote Leave' then hired Aggregate IQ to target UK voters using psychologically profiled ads to procure Brexit. After this, Cambridge Analytica worked for the Ted Cruz campaign for president, and then the Donald Trump campaign. The UK Information Commissioner found that people's data was taken without their consent,[167] and imposed a £500,000 penalty on Facebook.[168] Under the GDPR 2016 today, a fine amounting to billions could be imposed. In February 2019, it was reported that the FTC was negotiating a 'multibillion-dollar fine' with Facebook's lawyers for enabling improper access to 87 million Facebook users.[169] Any such fines are unable to undo the damage to politics.

(iii) Microsoft, Outlook, Skype, LinkedIn

Microsoft Corp. is most famous for Windows, Office, Explorer and Xbox, but is also a major communication company with Outlook, Skype, its more recent 'Teams' web-call app, Bing search, the professional network LinkedIn and a cloud service called Azure. Founded in 1981 in Washington, it incorporated

163 FTC, 'Agreement Containing Consent Order' (2011).

164 Information Commissioner, 'Investigation into the Use of Data Analytics in Political Campaigns' (11 July 2018) 8.

165 See the House of Commons Select Committee on Fake News Hearing (27 March 2018) on YouTube, especially at 1:29:38.

166 See the Collected Documents for the Fake News hearing (27 March 2018) especially from p. 10.

167 Information Commissioner (2018) 21, Kogan's app users did not give 'sufficiently informed consent'. At 32, 'We also have evidence that some data brokers had failed to obtain lawful consent.'

168 Data Protection Act 1998, s. 55 made it a criminal offence 'to knowingly or recklessly without the consent of the data controller obtain, disclose or procure the disclosure of information in personal data'. See now the Data Protection Act 2018, s. 170, introduced since the GDPR (EU) 2016/679. Cf. S. Ghosh, 'It Would Take Facebook Just 18 Minutes to Pay Off Its £500,000 Fine for the Cambridge Analytica Scandal', *Business Insider* (11 July 2018); N. Bernal, 'Facebook Fined £500,000 by UK Watchdog for Cambridge Analytica Scandal', *Daily Telegraph* (25 October 2018).

169 'Facebook May Face Multibillion-Dollar US Fine over Privacy Lapses – Report', *The Guardian* (15 February 2019).

in Delaware from 1986 to 1993, but returned to Washington state. It follows a 'one share, one vote' rule on its common stock, and does not have any weighted or non-voting shares like Google or Facebook.[170] Its co-founder and director, Bill Gates, became the largest shareholder during the 1980s and 1990s, but retired as CEO in 2000 and has sold or donated all but 1.3 per cent of its shares. Microsoft's 2019 revenue was $125.8 billion, with $7.63 billion from advertising. Its main profit base has remained its software and hardware sales.[171]

(iv) Amazon and Data Storage

Amazon.com Inc. is the dominant online marketplace (see Ch. 18) but is also a communication giant through its developing services in Prime Video, advertising and its cloud storage, Amazon Web Services. Amazon's constitution, like Microsoft, follows a 'one share, one vote' structure.[172] The largest shareholder and – until 2021 – the CEO, Jeff Bezos, holds 11 per cent of Amazon shares (and also has bought the Washington Post) and has become the world's richest person through this. Amazon's 2019 revenue was $280 billion, with $14.1 billion from advertising.

(d) Royal Mail and Post Office

Though dwarfed by the global web communication companies now, Royal Mail plc and the Post Office Ltd still provide much the same services, albeit slower. Under the Postal Services Act 2011, the Royal Mail was opened for 90 per cent of its shares to be privatised, and in 2013 it was sold off mainly to US and UK asset managers, with 10 per cent for employees.[173] Despite this, employees have no representation on the company board, and there is no representation for customers. The Post Office Ltd, which runs the network of post offices, was separated and is wholly owned by UK Government Investments, but could be transferred to become a 'mutual' owned by employees or 'other persons engaged in the provision of its post offices'.[174] The Post Office had engaged in the broadband market, offering far cheaper prices until the Royal Mail was privatised, but it still offers these services today.

Nobody needs a licence to provide postal services,[175] but Ofcom has a duty to ensure that universal service is provided in the UK.[176] There is also a requirement to notify Ofcom if a company acts as a postal operator, and Ofcom can impose 'essential conditions' for purposes of 'confidentiality' of letters or information conveyed, security and ensuring packets reach their

[170] Articles of Incorporation (2009) art. 4.1. See also Bylaws (2008).
[171] Microsoft, *Annual Report* (2019). [172] Articles of Incorporation (2019) and Bylaws (2019).
[173] PSA 2011, ss. 1 and 3. [174] PSA 2011, ss. 4–7. [175] PSA 2011, s. 28(1).
[176] PSA 2011, ss. 29–30.

addresses, or any 'consumer protection condition' that Ofcom thinks 'necessary to secure effective protection'.[177] The international courier DHL, for example, tried to argue it was not a postal operator,[178] but the High Court held it was because it performed the 'service of conveying postal packets' or 'services of receiving, collecting, sorting and delivering postal packets'.[179] There is also a special administration system if a company goes insolvent that ensures the government maintains universal service.[180]

(4) Consumer Rights

There are not yet any clear rights for consumers to vote in communication companies, underlined by the fact that Ofcom merely has a duty to appoint a 'Consumer Panel', with the Secretary of State's approval, that advises on services for different groups, rural, urban, small business, low income and elderly people.[181] Instead, four main groups of consumer right involve (a) privacy, including the concept of an information society service; (b) free expression, fair prices and roaming; (c) standards of service, including 'net neutrality'; and (d) the right to switch providers without detriment, including porting phone numbers and data.

(a) Privacy

Privacy was historically central to post, telegraph and telephone legislation, and after World War Two it became a universal human right.[182] In this time, the Internet's architects ensured data packets were transmissible without intermediaries ever having to 'open' them. Privacy justified the norm in the US Telecommunications Act of 1996, §230(c) that 'No provider or user of an interactive computer service shall be treated as the publisher or speaker of any information provided by another information content provider.'[183] This was mainly intended to cover ISPs, or servers hosting emails and websites,[184] ensuring they had no duty to monitor and therefore violate customer privacy.

A similar concept of the 'information society service' was first put into the Information Society Directive 1998, though its recital noted it would 'be

[177] PSA 2011, ss. 48–9 and 51–2. Ofcom can also require general access conditions to give operators or users access to infrastructure within the universal service scope.

[178] *R (DHL International (UK) Ltd) v Ofcom* [2016] EWHC 938 (Admin).

[179] PSA 2011, s. 27. [180] PSA 2011, ss. 68–88. [181] CA 2003, ss. 16–17.

[182] UDHR 1948, art. 12(1); ECHR 1950, art. 8(1); ICCPR 1966, art. 17; CFREU 2000, art. 7.

[183] 47 USC, §230(c) and (f)(2) defines 'interactive computer service' as 'any information service, system, or access software provider that provides or enables computer access by multiple users to a computer server, including specifically a service or system that provides access to the Internet and such systems operated or services offered by libraries or educational institutions'.

[184] Cf. *Carafano v Metrosplash.com*, 339 F 3d 1119 (9th Cir 2003) (immunity for dating website in defamation suit).

premature to coordinate national rules' entirely because 'enough is not yet known about the form the new services will take or their nature'.[185] After this, the Electronic Commerce Directive 2000 aimed to ensure free movement of information society services (ISSs).[186] Though the starting point is that member states should allow services to move in freely from other member states, the services can be restricted if the restriction is proportionate to achieve a public policy, prevent crime, fight incitement to hatred, protect individual dignity, protect health or protect consumers or investors.[187] These exceptions are wide. For instance, 'protection of consumers' includes anti-discrimination law, good faith and fair dealing, as routinely found in consumer law.[188] But under articles 12, 13 and 14, an information society service that operates as a 'mere conduit' for information, or does 'caching' or 'hosting', has limited liability for information it receives and sends. In particular, for hosting, the ISS is 'not liable for information stored', if the 'provider does not have actual knowledge of illegal activity' and 'is not aware of facts or circumstances from which the illegal activity or information is apparent'.[189] However, the 'provider, upon obtaining such knowledge or awareness' must act 'expeditiously to remove or disable access' to the unlawful information. Article 15 states that member states should 'not impose a general obligation on providers ... to monitor the information which they transmit or store' nor 'seek facts' on illegality.[190]

How far does the concept of an information society service extend?[191] First, an ISP is an ISS. In *Cartier International AG v BT plc*, the UK Supreme Court held that BT and the four other largest ISPs were ISSs, and 'mere conduits' within article 12. Although the ISPs had a duty to remove access to websites infringing the trademarks of Cartier and other luxury goods designers, they could recover costs for doing so under English law.[192] This did not mean, however, that the same considerations would necessarily 'apply to intermediaries engaging in caching or hosting ... because these operations involve a greater degree of participation in the infringement'.[193] The same is true for a Wi-Fi host.[194] Second, in the Electronic Commerce Directive 2000, recital 11 states email services, search engines, data storage and streaming are ISSs,

185 Information Society Directive 98/48/EC, recital 11, and art. 1(2) amending Directive 98/34/EC, art. 1(2).

186 TFEU, arts. 56–7 and 52 (restrictions).

187 Electronic Commerce Directive 2000/31/EC, arts. 1 and 3. Under art. 3(4)–(5) if the ISS is based abroad, the member state must ask the host member state to regulate, and inform the Commission if measures are inadequate and that it will take its own measures. Member states can derogate if the case is urgent.

188 E.g. Equality Act 2010, s. 29 and Consumer Rights Act 2015, s. 62.

189 Electronic Commerce Directive 2000/31/EC, art. 14.

190 Electronic Commerce Directive 2000, art. 15.

191 Information Society Directive 2015/1535 Annex I lists those that are not, e.g. TV and radio.

192 [2018] UKSC 28, [21] per Lord Sumption.

193 [2018] UKSC 28, [37].

194 *McFadden v Sony Music Entertainment Germany GmbH* (2016) C-484/14.

although an individual email is not. Third, a series of cases have stated that an ISS includes the online marketplace eBay,[195] Facebook[196] and Airbnb,[197] but Uber is not included.[198] But this status establishes merely that companies are not responsible for monitoring information, not that they cannot.

The most serious invasions of privacy take place through standard contract terms, enabling targeted ads. The strategy is used by Facebook, Google, Microsoft and a host of other software, continually raising privacy concerns: the latest is the web-call app, Zoom.[199] In 2017, Gmail announced it would no longer scan emails for targeted ads, but it quickly transpired that Google still allowed app developers to utilise people's private emails for money.[200] This problem is serious for email because, even if consumers leave Gmail themselves, many of the people they write to will still be at Gmail addresses, meaning their communications are read by Google without consent.

What substantive rights to privacy are there? Three main rights found in the GDPR 2016 are for people (or 'data subjects') to have data about them processed only on the basis of 'consent' or other justifiable grounds; to be informed about identifiable data being kept on them;[201] and a 'right to be forgotten' or the data deleted.[202] Among these, the first point is the most crucial. Do the standard-form contracts of Google, Facebook, Amazon or Microsoft count as 'consent'? Consumers have no bargaining power and are given 'contracts of adhesion' on a 'take it or leave it' basis.[203] There are often few alternative services that have become essential for communication – particularly web calls or social networks – if they refuse to accept the terms. The GDPR recitals state the aspiration that 'processing of personal data should be designed to serve mankind', before stating that consent means 'separate consent' for 'different personal data processing operations'. In article 4(11) consent is defined as 'freely given, specific, informed and unambiguous indication of the data subject's wishes by which he or she, by a statement or by a clear affirmative action, signifies agreement to the processing of personal data'. It seems unrealistic to say that consent is 'freely given' in a standard-form contract. It has already been held that consent is not given if

195 *L'Oréal SA v eBay International AG* (2011) C-324/09.

196 *Glawischnig-Piesczek v Facebook Ireland Ltd* (2019) C-18/18; see Ch. 17(4)(a).

197 *Airbnb Ireland UC* (2019) C-390/18; see Ch. 14(3)(b).

198 *Asociación profesional Élite Taxi v Uber Systems Spain* (2017) C-434/15, see Ch. 15(3)(d).

199 Doc Searls Weblog, 'Zoom Needs to Clean Up Its Privacy Act', *blogs.harvard.edu* (27 March 2020).

200 E.g. J. Roettgers, 'Google Will Keep Reading Your Emails, Just Not for Ads', *Variety* (23 July 2017); and D. Macmillan, 'Tech's "Dirty Secret": The App Developers Sifting Through Your Gmail', *Wall Street Journal* (2 July 2018).

201 GDPR 2016, arts. 12–16, including a right to have mistaken data rectified.

202 GDPR 2016, art. 17, where data is no longer necessary for legitimate purposes, or consent is withdrawn.

203 On this phenomenon, see F. Kessler, 'Contracts of Adhesion – Some Thoughts about Freedom of Contract' (1943) 43(5) *Columbia L Rev* 629.

there is 'a pre-checked checkbox which the user must deselect to refuse'.[204] If a case decides that standard-form contracts are not true consent, it will further undermine the business model of big-tech advertisers, and therefore be bitterly contested. But if a case decides that standard-form contracts do amount to 'consent', the human right to communication privacy online is more fictitious than real.

The weakness of protection was affirmed in *Lloyd v Google LLC*. Lloyd (also a director of consumer group, Which?) claimed Google unlawfully gathered iPhone user data, bypassing privacy settings, and tracked people online in the Safari web browser. Google used the information in its DoubleClick ad service, to specifically target people such as 'football lovers' or by race, sexual orientation, politics and class. The claim was made that this amounted to £750 for each of 4.4 million iPhone users, totalling £3.3 billion. Although Warby J held that there was no proof that iPhone users suffered any 'damage', and refused permission for the claim to be served on Google in Delaware, the Court of Appeal allowed the case to proceed.[205] However, the Supreme Court reversed this, ruling that under the Data Protection Act 1998, section 13 damage from any unlawful processing had to be proven, and how that caused individual loss. There could not, in effect, be a group claim, like a US class action based on a hypothetical £750 loss per person. This decision clearly points to a gap in the law and the failure to make privacy rights effective. Whatever the purpose of the Act as originally written, without adequate enforcement, rights are simply ineffective.

(b) Free Expression, Fair Prices and Roaming

Freedom of expression in practice requires technology to communicate, 'to seek, receive and impart information and ideas of all kinds, regardless of frontiers'.[206] Logically this depends on public service provision, or at least fair prices. Today, a mobile phone and the Internet are almost essential to find good jobs, claim welfare and receive education, so the cost of communication matters. If customers have variable bills (e.g. pay as you go) they have the right to agree a mobile-phone bill limit (e.g. each month).[207] But this involves no actual cap. Ofcom's general licensing powers influence prices, but it also has specific price powers.

Ofcom can set price conditions if a provider has 'significant market power' at any level of the market.[208] To establish there is market power, Ofcom must

[204] *Bundesverband der Verbraucherzentralen v Planet49 GmbH* (2019) C-673/17.

[205] *Lloyd v Google LLC* [2021] UKSC 50, [125]; [2019] EWCA Civ 1599.

[206] ICCPR, art. 19(2). As was pointed out at the beginning of this chapter, if we lose privacy, we express and even think less freely: art. 19(1). See also UDHR 1948, arts. 18–19; ECHR 1950, arts. 9–10; CFREU 2000, arts. 10–11.

[207] CA 2003, ss. 124S–T, inserted by the Digital Economy Act 2017, s. 102.

[208] CA 2003, ss. 87(1) and (9), 91 (end-users) and 93 (apparatus); Electronic Communications Code Directive 2018/1972, arts. 3(2)(d), 69(2) and 74.

do a market study. Between this study and making a determination of market power, Ofcom must be assured there is no material change.[209] It must also conduct market analysis so that, if it 'appears to' Ofcom that there is a risk that a company 'prices at an excessively high level' or squeezes competitor margins, then controls must be 'appropriate' for 'promoting efficiency', 'sustainable competition' and conferring the 'greatest possible benefits on the end-users'.[210] The law therefore gives Ofcom broad discretion. However, in *Telefónica O2 UK Ltd v British Telecommunications plc* the Supreme Court held that Ofcom's decision to restrict new charges by BT had been unlawful. BT had introduced variable fees for connecting other networks ('termination charges') when consumers called 08 numbers. Before, BT had charged standard fees when O2 consumers called 08 numbers. But from 2009, if callers paid more, BT's termination charges would go up. Lord Sumption held that Ofcom's decision, that these new charges were unlawful, was wrong. In his view, Ofcom did not sufficiently specify the benefits to consumers (i.e. 'end-users'), rather than just suggesting there might be benefits.[211] The difficulty with this decision is that Ofcom's discretion is phrased in terms of what price control 'appears to them' to be needed.[212] There was no limiting language in the Directive.[213]

Ofcom's price controls can be appealed to the CMA,[214] and the Competition Appeal Tribunal (CAT) is required to follow the CMA's determination unless it is legally wrong.[215] All decisions are subject to judicial review. For example, in *Vodafone Ltd v British Telecommunications plc*, BT complained that four-year price caps set by Ofcom on Vodafone and others for connecting mobile-phone callers to receivers on other networks (the 'wholesale service of mobile call termination') were too high. The CAT agreed and directed Ofcom to reset the prices. The Court of Appeal held there was no power to retrospectively adjust price controls decided by Ofcom. Instead, Ofcom's decision, if void, would have to be made again.[216] If there are disputes between telecom companies about access to networks and charges, they may ask Ofcom to adjudicate the dispute.[217]

[209] CA 2003, ss. 79 and 86(1)(b). E.g. *TalkTalk Telecom Group plc v Ofcom* [2013] EWCA Civ 1318 held that Ofcom's price controls on BT for access to its broadband network did not need to be reviewed, despite a 7 month delay between a market power and charge control determinations. BT was dominant before and after, and TalkTalk's hope of having price controls reopened and reduced was thwarted.

[210] CA 2003, s. 88.

[211] [2014] UKSC 42, [43]. Lord Sumption somewhat obliquely refers to, without quoting, the Electronic Communications Directive 2002/21/EC, art. 8(2).

[212] Cf. *Everything Everywhere Ltd v Competition Commission* [2013] EWCA Civ 154, holding that Ofcom did not need to produce a detailed customer survey before imposing price controls based on EE's long-run incremental costs in mobile call termination charges.

[213] See now Electronic Communications Code Directive 2018/1972, arts. 68 and 74.

[214] CA 2003, ss. 192–5. [215] CA 2003, s. 193(6)–(7). [216] [2010] EWCA Civ 391.

[217] CA 2003, ss. 185–91. E.g. *British Telecommunications plc v Office of Communications* [2012] EWCA Civ 1051. BT, represented by Prof. Andrew Burrows QC, argued that a four-month

Particularly important to reduce trade barriers, the Roaming Regulation 2012 reduced and then eliminated charges for phone calls and text messages when travelling abroad, or 'roaming'. By July 2017, roaming charges imposed by mobile-phone carriers for voice or data services had to be eliminated.[218] Wholesale charges are also regulated.[219] In *R (Vodafone Ltd) v Secretary of State for Business, Enterprise and Regulatory Reform*, Vodafone attempted to argue the Regulation was unlawful, and disproportionate to the EU's legislative power under the Treaties. The Court of Justice's Grand Chamber held that these price controls were necessary for competitive markets to function, and 'only the regulation of retail charges could improve the situation of consumers directly'.[220] There are also cases on margin squeezing and access costs,[221] and on predatory pricing (see Ch. 6(2)(b)(i)).[222]

(c) Service and Speed

The third set of rights concern service and speed of communication, particularly universal service and net neutrality. In telecoms,[223] and in the post,[224] there are public duties of 'universal service'. Universal service obligations receive much attention, but they are less helpful in practice than they sound for two reasons. First, universal service duties were introduced more as a prelude to privatisation[225] than to improve service. As we saw in Chapter 16(1) 'universal service' was originally a marketing slogan of the AT&T president to get a monopoly in 1907, though the language was written into US law in 1996[226] and EU law in 1997.[227] Second, universal service

time limit in s. 186(6) applied to a dispute on BT overcharging others to hire network connecting main cables to customers ('partial private circuits'). It held that this limit did not apply to disputes in general.

218 Roaming Regulation (EU) No. 531/2012, art. 7 (previously Regulation 717/2007).

219 Roaming Regulation 2012, art. 9.

220 (2010) C-58/08, [66]. Contrast the sentiments of Lord Sumption in *Telefónica* above.

221 E.g. *Deutsche Telekom AG v Commission* (2010) C-280/08, [253]; *Telefónica SA v Commission* (2014) C-295/12 (Spain's privatised telecom operator fined €151.875m for squeezing margins in broadband market).

222 E.g. *France Télécom SA v Commission* (2009) C-202/07 (FT's subsidiary Wanadoo unlawfully undercut competitors; no need to show power to recoup if prices are below average variable cost).

223 CA 2003, ss. 45–8. Ofcom sets conditions on universal service. See also Electronic Communications Code Directive 2018/1972, art. 84.

224 PSA 2011, ss. 29–30 (duty on Ofcom to ensure universal service).

225 E.g. Department of Trade and Industry, *Green Paper on Postal Reform* (1994) and see Hansard HC Debs. (19 May 1994) cols. 952–74.

226 Telecommunications Act of 1996, 47 USC, §254, expressing vague and largely unenforceable standards.

227 Postal Services Directive 1997/67/EC, art. 1, followed by the PSA 2000, s. 4. The Universal Service Directive 2002/22/EC, arts. 3–4 and 9–13 did the same for telecoms; see now Electronic Communications Code Directive 2018/1972, art. 84. Also Electricity Market Directive 2003/54/EC, now the Electricity Market Directive 2019/944, art. 27.

standards are so vague as to be unenforceable[228] or, if not, so minimal as to function more like non-regression duties than duties to improve. Ofcom designates universal service providers, and these are predictably the privatised BT and Royal Mail.[229] For broadband, the universal service must be at least 10 Mbps but, if any connection costs over £3,400, the end-user pays.[230] This is 100 times slower than the government's aspiration for 1 gigabit broadband, illustrating the gap between the political language of 'universal service' and the reality of the law. For the post, the universal service is at least one delivery of letters every Monday to Saturday to everyone's home, *or* to identifiable delivery points that Ofcom approves, and collection from 'every access point'.[231] A preferable, alternative model, would be to progressively raise service standards.

Net neutrality is possibly the most important norm affecting service levels online. Originating in US law,[232] net neutrality requires that ISPs do not discriminate in the speeds at which their customers connect to different websites. For instance, Sky broadband cannot be allowed to connect you more quickly to Sky TV than to YouTube or BBC iPlayer. This has a dual effect of ensuring that internet users can access any website on equal terms, and also that different websites do not face unfair competition by ISPs making deals with larger websites for privileged exposure to internet users. The Net Neutrality Regulation 2015, article 3(3) states: 'Providers of internet access services shall treat all traffic equally' but this shall not prevent 'reasonable traffic management measures'.[233] In the USA, unfortunately, the net neutrality protection was repealed by a new Trump administration chair of the Federal Communications Commission, who had formerly been an employee of Verizon Inc., the second largest ISP after AT&T.

(d) Switching, Telephone Numbers and Data Portability

In a competitive market, an important right is to vote with your feet, and shop elsewhere. Because telecoms and the Internet systematically fail as competitive markets, rights of switching without detriment have been required by law. First, since 2017 there has been an explicit power for Ofcom to set conditions on electronic communication providers to 'enable an end-user to change

[228] See the relevant US and EU rules above.

[229] CA 2003, s. 66 and PSA 2011, s. 35. In Hull, KCOM is also the universal service provider, changing nothing.

[230] CA 2003, s. 65(2B)(b); SI 2018/445, Sch. 1, para. 2. Download limit may be 100 GB a month.

[231] PSA 2011, ss. 31–2, also requiring affordable prices, a uniform tariff, registered, insured and blind services. On Monday to Friday there must be a delivery and collection of postal packets up to 20 kg.

[232] Communications Act of 1934, Title II, common carrier, and 29 FCC Rcd 5561(7) (2014).

[233] Net Neutrality Regulation 2015/2120, art. 3. See also WTA 2006, s. 5. The Secretary of State should also consider desirability of technological and infrastructure service neutrality.

communications provider on request'.[234] As explained at Chapter 16(3)(a) Ofcom could apply conditions both to telecoms providers, and to any online communication service if it chose. The GDPR 2016, article 20 also gives a data subject the right to receive their data 'in a structured, commonly used and machine-readable format and have the right to transmit those data to another controller without hindrance'.[235] It may seem unlikely that mass transportation of users from one platform to another will happen,[236] though there are precedents.[237] For landline and mobile phones, a practical hindrance to switching providers would be the prospect of having to lose a phone number, so Ofcom gives people the right to keep numbers if they switch.[238] Finally, Ofcom has used its condition-setting powers to limit the length of contracts to which mobile phone and broadband customers may be bound – last in 2011 to set the maximum contract length at two years and requiring that one-year contracts are available.[239]

(5) Conclusion

The Covid-19 pandemic of 2020–1 illustrated how vital communication networks are for work, business, education and life. Increasingly, the right to free expression entails proactive state policy to ensure people are connected to the Internet, and that companies uphold the right to privacy. But there are three main limits to communication policy now. First, it would seem that duplication of signals and infrastructure serves no real purpose, and that countries performing better at lower cost have publicly owned networks with a high degree of customer voice. Second, the Internet, and the major tech corporations that have colonised it, need to be regulated equally. The powers Ofcom assert are, as the *Edison* case once said, 'absurd'.[240] What does it regulate? Mail yes, email no. Phone calls yes, web calls no. Phonebook yes, Facebook no. Directories yes, search engines no. In most of these, the key issue is privacy, and the vast quantities of stored private data, harvested for online targeted advertising and product prediction. Third, infrastructure should be interoperable. Web calls, search engines and social networks refuse to connect their networks, in order to maintain dominance. There has been little or no innovation in WhatsApp or Facebook, when set against the extraordinary revenue extracted from, and privacy intrusions against, their users. But given their stupendous profits, there is ample room for raising standards of public accountability.

[234] CA 2003, s. 51(2)(i). [235] GDPR, art. 20.

[236] Cf. EU Commission, *A European Strategy for Data* (2020) COM(2020) 66 final.

[237] E.g. Wikitravel was created by users, but owned by a company that ran ads. Disgruntled, the editors asked the non-profit Wikimedia foundation (see Ch. 17(3)(c)) to create Wikivoyage, and moved content there.

[238] CA 2003, ss. 58(1)(e) and 59 on Ofcom's powers. Also Universal Service Directive 2002/22/EC, art. 30.

[239] M. King, 'Ofcom Bans Three-Year Broadband and Phone Contracts', *The Guardian* (26 May 2011).

[240] *Attorney General v Edison Telephone Company of London Ltd* (1880) 6 QBD 244.

17

Web and Broadcast Media

Contents

'Nothing travels faster than the speed of light', wrote the author Douglas Adams, 'with the possible exception of bad news.'[1] Just like our personal communications, the Internet has revolutionised our media, both in speed and nature. With ever-faster technology, public news and entertainment has shifted from print, to radio, to television and now to the web. Each new development widened the audience, and created greater psychological intimacy. Politicians and other performers entered the living room, as personal as a coffee house, a debating club in a pub,[2] or a theatre.[3] Where print, radio and TV were one-way, the web made media 'social' again. We interact, we broadcast ourselves, yet even the keenest YouTuber relies on networks. 'Press barons' and governments maintained a proprietary grip on media sources in the twentieth century,[4] but today's sheer volume of information alters that task. Platforms and algorithms, not outlets, influence the media people see ever more. There is a universal 'right to take part in the government', and in a deliberative democracy this is built upon freedom of opinion and expression, to 'receive and impart information and ideas through any media and regardless

[1] D. Adams, *Hitch Hiker's Guide to the Galaxy* (1992) Book 5, 'Mostly Harmless', ch. 1.

[2] The world's oldest debating or 'free speech society' is 'Cogers', meeting since 1755 on Fleet Street, London.

[3] E.g. Sophocles, *Antigone*, *Oedipus the King* and *Oedipus at Colonus* (*c.* 400 BC) where theatre was political critique.

[4] J. Curran and J. Seaton, *Power without Responsibility: The Press, Broadcasting and New Media in Britain* (8th ed. 2018) ch. 1, 5.

of frontiers'.[5] Freedom of expression foresees that states require 'the licensing of broadcasting, television or cinema enterprises'.[6] But just as an undemocratic state threatens free expression and privacy,[7] unbalanced media ownership, with the likes of Facebook, Google or Murdoch, threatens deliberative democracy.

The Internet was supposed to bring the world together, and strengthen the free, accountable media that is essential for democracy and human rights. Instead, internet penetration has correlated with a growth in neo-fascist politics and authoritarian influence on power, including Putin, Le Pen, the AfD, Lega Nord, Xi Jinping, Modi, Bolsonaro, the Brexit Party, and all epitomised by Trump's attack on the US Capitol. The Internet has even made people believe in 'flat Earth' nonsense again.[8] Lies are not free expression, because people who follow lies are imprisoned by the liar, not free. True information is a 'public good' (see Ch. 2(2)) that can spread at low cost. Unless you are Schrödinger's cat, there is only one set of facts, so information networks tend towards monopoly, because a network's value increases with each producer and consumer. But investment in local, investigative and courageous journalism is often restricted by opposing private interests. Authoritarians favour suppression of local news that helps solve people's real problems, and want national news to become entertainment.[9] They do not want plural, open debate. Today, most print, radio and TV appears online, so this chapter focuses on the web. The law is completely undeveloped, and highly likely to change.

(1) Historical Development

Before the twentieth century, media law reflected the disempowerment of humankind. Freedom of thought in the Middle Ages was violently suppressed. In England, from the development of the printing press in 1439[10] until 1695, news was controlled by the Star Chamber, and simple print required government licence.[11] The 'Stamp Act 1712' imposed a duty of one penny per newspaper, and one shilling per advertisement within it.[12] This caused publications with poorer readers to cease business, an obvious result of raising

[5] UDHR 1948, art. 21 and ICCPR 1966, art. 25 (government). UDHR 1948, art. 19 and ICCPR 1966, art. 19 (expression).

[6] ECHR 1950, art. 10(2); CFREU 2000, art. 11: 'The freedom and pluralism of the media shall be respected.'

[7] *Entick v Carrington* [1765] EWHC KB J98; UDHR 1948, art. 12; ECHR 1950, art. 8; CFREU 2000, art. 7.

[8] E.g. I. Sample, 'Study Blames YouTube for Rise in Number of Flat Earthers', *The Guardian* (17 February 2019); R Lewis, 'Alternative Influence', *Data & Society* (2018).

[9] T. Snyder, *The Road to Unfreedom: Russia, Europe, America* (2018) ch. 5, 'Truth or Lies (2015)'.

[10] Johannes Gutenberg printed the Bible in 1455. William Caxton printed *The Canterbury Tales* in 1477.

[11] E.g. Licensing of the Press Act 1662, lapsing in 1695.

[12] This was actually the Taxation Act 1711 (10 Anne, c. 18), before short agreed names of Acts became standard.

prices. Radical publications became a constitutional battleground in *Entick v Carrington*, in 1762. A writer named John Entick had his house ransacked by the King's Chief Messenger, looking for 'very seditious papers' which simply criticised the government. Lord Camden CJ held that there was no legal basis for Entick to be searched, and the 'great end, for which men entered into society, was to secure their property',[13] which he understood to include liberty of expression and privacy.[14] However, government suppression continued as the Stamp Act 1765 imposed the same penny duty 'upon every news paper, containing publick news, intelligence, or occurrences' in the American colonies. It was met with mob revolt.[15] Parliament repealed this the following year, but its attempt to restore other taxes,[16] and eventually just a symbolic tax on tea,[17] resulted in the rebellions that in 1776 led to the US Declaration of Independence. Back in the UK, the 'tax on knowledge' remained and, alongside waves of political repression during the French Revolution and Napoleonic wars,[18] from 1789 to the Stamp Act 1815, it was raised by 266 per cent.[19] The tax continued until its abolition in 1854.[20] While formally freed from constraint, the 'radical papers had limited money at their disposal for editorial development'. Liberal politicians thought funding through ads enabled 'a cheap press in the hands of men of good moral character, of respectability, and of capital'.[21] Yet ads made news dependent.

As print media settled,[22] telegraph was invented in 1837, photographs in 1839, telephone in 1876, phonograph recordings from 1877[23] and from 1893 the Edison Manufacturing Co. was showing films. Cinema boomed in Hollywood during World War One,[24] and in 1920 the Marconi electronics company sent out a public radio broadcast from its Chelmsford factory. It was promptly prohibited by the General Post Office (GPO), asserting its monopoly on communications (see Ch. 16(1)). In 1922 the GPO decided to license a new consortium called the British Broadcasting Company Ltd, and from Marconi

[13] *Entick v Carrington* [1765] EWHC KB J98.

[14] Lord Camden CJ was quoting J. Locke, *Two Treatises of Government* (1689) chs. 9, §123 and 11, §§134–5, defining 'property' as 'lives, liberties, and estates'.

[15] This was supported in the UK Parliament. See Pitt the Elder, *Speech against the Stamp Act* (14 January 1766).

[16] See the Townshend Acts 1767 and 1768 (7 Geo. 3, c. 55, 56, 59 and 8 Geo. 3, c. 19 and 22).

[17] Tea Act 1773 (13 Geo. 3, c. 44).

[18] E.g. Unlawful Oaths Act 1797, Unlawful Societies Act 1799, Combination Act 1799 and Combination Act 1800.

[19] Curran and Seaton, *Power without Responsibility*, 6.

[20] E.g. Stamp Tax Act 1819, and subsequent Acts, all repealed by Stamp Act 1854, s. 1.

[21] Curran and Seaton, *Power without Responsibility*, chs. 2–3, 11 and 20, quoting Thomas Milner-Gibson MP, President of the Association for the Promotion of the Repeal of the Taxes on Knowledge.

[22] The oldest newspapers are *The Times* (est. 1785), *The Guardian* (1821), *Daily Telegraph* (1855), *Financial Times* (1888) and *Daily Mirror* (1903). Many people also consider the *Daily Mail* (1896) to contain news.

[23] Cf. 'The voice of William Ewart Gladstone' (1888) recorded by Thomas Edison.

[24] E.g. Charlie Chaplin, *Laughing Gas* (1914) and *The Tramp* (1915).

House on Aldwych in London, the first licensed public radio broadcasts were made from its station '2LO'. The BBCo was led by John Reith, whose stated mission was to 'inform, educate and entertain'.[25] In 1923, as the company fell into financial distress, the Sykes Committee recommended the introduction of a licence fee levied on signal receiving equipment, splitting revenue with the GPO.[26] In 1927, after the recommendations of the Crawford Committee,[27] a new British Broadcasting Corporation, the BBC, received a royal charter. Reith advocated for the licence fee to avoid the advertisements proliferating on American radios. After the growth of cinema, the first television broadcasts were made from Alexandra Palace in 1936. But meanwhile, in Germany, radio, film and TV were fuelling fascist propaganda. The 'mass psychology of fascism',[28] fetishising the sound and image of a supposedly pure Aryan race (ironically led by two decidedly inadequate men[29]) was spread into every German home and theatre.[30] In Britain, TV was suspended over World War Two, leaving the public huddled around the wireless for the BBC each evening, like Roosevelt's 'fireside chats' in America. Media was ever more intimate, in the dark or the light.

Under the first post-war Conservative government,[31] the Television Act 1954 opened up the BBC's monopoly by creating an Independent Television Authority.[32] The Authority had a board of seven to ten people selected by the Postmaster General.[33] It received a portion of licence fee revenue and franchised programming from contractors, which could have advertisements.[34] This became ITV. BBC2 was created in 1964,[35] and the Broadcasting Act 1980 enabled Channel 4,[36] running from 1982. The Broadcasting Act 1990 allowed creation of Channel 5, renamed the regulators as the Independent Television Commission and Radio Authority and wrote into law the requirement of 'due impartiality' and accuracy in reporting. This mirrored the practice under the

[25] Curran and Seaton *Power without Responsibility*, ch. 11, 'Reith and the Denial of Politics'.

[26] Sir Frederick Sykes, *Report of the Broadcasting Committee*, Cmnd 1951 (1923).

[27] Earl of Crawford, *Report of the Committee on Broadcasting*, Cmnd 2599 (1925).

[28] W. Reich, *The Mass Psychology of Fascism*, trans. T. P. Wolfe (1933).

[29] Joseph Goebbels suffered an inferiority complex due to his crippled leg, while Adolf Hitler had failed at everything in life, except making people angry, like being rejected from art school in Vienna. Cf. R. Greenslade, 'Don't Damn the Daily Mail for Its Fascist Flirtation 80 Years Ago', *The Guardian* (6 December 2011), on the less organised UK equivalents.

[30] E.g. *German Youth Parade* (1937). Contrast the American counter-propaganda film, *Here Is Germany* (1940).

[31] See also White Paper, *Broadcasting Policy*, Cmd 6852 (1946).

[32] Afterwards the Sound Broadcasting Act 1972 renamed it the Independent Broadcasting Authority.

[33] Television Act 1954, s. 1: 'persons appearing to him to be qualified for the office'. Also s. 17 required wages and conditions to be no less favourable for staff and contractors as for those of government departments.

[34] Television Act 1954, s. 4. The first advertisement to air on UK TV was for toothpaste. On dental coverage and the NHS, see Ch. 9(1).

[35] See Sir Harry Pilkington, *Report of the Committee on Broadcasting*, Cmnd 1753 (1962).

[36] Broadcasting Act 1980, ss. 2–6.

US 'fairness doctrine' that had just been abandoned in 1987 by the Reagan administration. That had required since 1929 that the 'public interest requires ample play for the free and fair competition of opposing views',[37] accurate reporting and giving people who are personally attacked a right of reply.[38] The US abolition of the fairness doctrine swiftly led to Murdoch's 'Fox News' propaganda with its dystopian slogan through the 1990s that it was 'fair and balanced', dropped in 2016 with the election of Trump. Back in the UK, the fact that only five channels were available reflected the scarcity of spectrum in analogue broadcasting. With the development of digital television (not to mention the Internet) it was recognised that this scarcity would end.[39] The new regulator, the Office of Communications, or Ofcom, was established in 2002.[40] It had powers to regulate all broadcasting on electronic communications under the Communications Act 2003.[41]

After 2002 while dozens of 'Freeview' channels opened, drenched in ads, the Internet began to eclipse everything, but Ofcom failed to regulate it. Quickly, portals to the web developed, starting with search engines to catalogue millions of new websites. The first search engines were poor, and had annoying, flashing ads. In 1998, Google was launched by two Stanford Ph.D. students with a better algorithm and plain text ads. People flocked to it. In 2004, 'thefacebook' was launched by a university dropout, and it spread around universities in the USA, then the UK, before opening to the world, all without ads, but these were accelerated as it did its initial public offering in 2011. In 2005, YouTube was launched independently, again without ads, but it was bought in 2006 by Google. In 2006, Twitter was launched, and it refused to sell to Facebook twice, and did its 'initial public offering' in 2013. In 2009, WhatsApp launched, and was bought by Facebook in 2016, mainly to monetise people's data for ads. In 2010, Instagram launched, and was bought by Facebook in 2012. Only Wikipedia did not sell itself to a monopolising network, or to advertisers. Wikipedia launched in 2001, and became part of the Wikimedia Foundation Inc., a charitable company, in 2003. These four corporations – Google, Facebook, Twitter and Wikimedia – are the most important web media today. They still essentially regulate their own content.

[37] Radio Act of 1927, §4, established the Federal Radio Commission (FRC), which gave this opinion in *Great Lakes Broadcasting Co.*, 3 FRC Ann Rep 32, 33 (1929) and made licences conditional upon conveying opposing views. The Communications Act of 1934 replaced the FRC with the Federal Communications Commission.

[38] *Red Lion Broadcasting Co. Inc. v Federal Communications Commission*, 395 US 367 (1969) following the *Report on Editorializing by Broadcast Licensees*, 13 FCC 1246 (1949).

[39] DCMS, *Regulating Communications: The Way Ahead*, Cm. 5010 (2000) 5.2.4.

[40] Office of Communications Act 2002, s. 1.

[41] E.g. Communications Act (CA) 2003, s. 319 refers to 'television and radio', while the concept of 'broadcasting' on any 'electronic communications network' applies to various other rules, such as the prohibition on broadcasting originating 'from a place outside' the UK: Representation of the People Act 1983, s. 92 and the European Union Referendum (Conduct) Regulations 2016, SI 2016/219, Sch. 1, para. 21.

The Internet connected most of the world, but has faced three main limits. First, the web and its major portal sites is segregated in China and Russia, as well as other authoritarian regimes. As a mechanism to ensure control, China's major companies replicate sites in the open world: Baidu and Sohu compare to Google; QQ compares to WhatsApp or Facebook; Weibo compares to Twitter; Tmall, Taobao and JD compare to Amazon. In Russia, Yandex compares to Google, and VKontakte compares to Facebook.[42] This ensures that the Communist Party and Putin's Kremlin do not lose grip on the dominant media channels. Like multiple sites in Russia,[43] Wikipedia has been completely blocked in China since 2019, because it is a largely trustworthy and accurate source of information.[44] Second, mass media has enabled mass surveillance, exposed in 2013 when a former contractor for the US National Security Agency (NSA), Edward Snowden, revealed his role in mass data collection.[45] Code-named PRISM, the NSA secured the secret co-operation of Google, Facebook, Microsoft, Yahoo!, Skype, Apple and AOL to send it personal data. The original pretext was fighting George W. Bush's so-called 'war on terror', but mass data collection went further. Third, the monopolisation of the web by advertising companies means that media has been driven by money, regardless of how damaging the content. This has led to the proliferation of far-right and extremist content;[46] the streaming of gun massacres, public executions and torture[47] and genocide in Myanmar;[48] and the regular glorification of hate-speech and discrimination. This enabled both the Brexit and Trump campaign victories in 2016, through the extraction of personal data from Facebook to be used in targeted political ads without people's consent,[49] as well as 'sweeping and systematic' cyber-war by the Kremlin against voters in the USA and Europe.[50] In the home of Facebook, YouTube and Twitter, this culminated in 2021 with Trump inciting a national terrorist mob to attack the US Capitol.

[42] E.g. J. Edwards, 'Putin Has Taken Control of Russian Facebook', *Business Insider* (22 April 2014), reporting that the founder sold his stake to 'two investors allied with Putin'.

[43] E.g. *Flavus and Kasparov v Russia* [2020] ECHR 463 (blocking of a website criticising government violated art. 10).

[44] 'Wikipedia Blocked in China in All Languages', *BBC News* (14 May 2019).

[45] This programme began under George W. Bush's administration and ostensibly the FISA Amendments Act of 2008, §702.

[46] T. Snyder, 'Fascism Is Back. Blame the Internet', *Washington Post* (21 May 2018); see further his book *The Road to Unfreedom: Russia, Europe, America* (2018).

[47] See countless videos on YouTube, such as Saddam Hussein's execution, Colonel Gaddafi's pre-death torture, and see 'Facebook, YouTube Sued over Christchurch Shootings Video', *BBC News* (26 March 2019).

[48] 'A Genocide Incited on Facebook, with Posts from Myanmar's Military', *New York Times* (6 November 2018).

[49] E. McGaughey, 'Fascism-lite in America (or the Social Ideal of Donald Trump)' (2018) 7(2) *Brit J Am L Studies* 291 and 'Could Brexit Be Void?' (2018) 29(3) *King's LJ* 331.

[50] R. Mueller, *Report on the Investigation into Russian Interference in the 2016 Presidential Election* (March 2019) 1.

(2) Finance

'Comment is free', as the saying goes, 'but facts are sacred.'[51] Facts, and their distribution, also cost more money to investigate and establish than comment or opinions, just as creating quality entertainment often costs more than reality TV or user-generated social media. Where media corporations aim to make profit, journalists are notoriously underpaid, and revenues simply from sales or subscriptions often are not enough to earn investors and staff a return for their enterprise. The three other main sources of finance are (a) advertising and data; (b) owners willing to make losses, or distribute anything, to have anti-democratic influence; and (c) for public broadcasters, grants, voluntary subscriptions and licence fees.

(a) Advertising and Data

While ads in the media are often understood as funding services for users, another way to see the issue is that users fund services for advertisers. Especially where you do not pay for the product, the product is you.[52] For example, if you rely on entertainment or are addicted to social media, a platform's advertisers are securing you as a revenue stream, under the illusion of giving you 'what you want'. The most striking fact is how much money is made from media networks that invest little or nothing in content. In 2018, Alphabet's revenue was $136 billion, Facebook $55.8 billion and Twitter $2.1 billion, whereas without advertising Wikipedia (the world's fifth-largest site) had expenses of just $81.4 *million*.[53] Google, Facebook and Twitter servers host more content, and so have some higher costs, but even so Wikipedia ran a bigger service with twenty-five times less money than Twitter, and 1,670 times less than Google. These revenues show the scale of excessive monetisation of our media (see Table 17.1).

The scale of the largest web media outlets and their advertising revenues is made possible by the network monopoly logic (see Ch. 16(2)(b)). YouTube quickly eclipsed rival video sites, like Vimeo. Facebook grew far beyond MySpace, and even Google+ could not compete. Wikipedia overtook non-user generated models, like Britannica and Encarta, in scope and quality early on. Each owes its size to network monopoly, and each happened without ads.

The monetisation of web media networks, which followed their free development in all cases except Wikimedia, is accelerated by data in three main ways. First, data on 'users' (a term also used for addicts) can be harvested for targeted advertising on-site. For example, in 2013 a group of psychology scholars explained that simply by analysing people's often publicly available

[51] C. P. Scott, 'A Hundred Years', *The Guardian* (May 1921).

[52] J. Lanchester, 'You Are the Product' (2017) 39(16) *London Review of Books* 3.

[53] Wikimedia Foundation Inc., 'Financial Statements' (30 June 2018); S. Loeb, 'How Does Wikipedia Make Money?', *Vator* (13 November 2015).

Table 17.1 Largest websites, 2019, and monetisation, 2018[i]

UK	World	Alexa ranking	Owner	Global revenue 2018
1	1	google.com	Alphabet	$136,000m
2	2	youtube.com	Alphabet	..
3	3	facebook.com	Facebook	$55,800m
4	..	google.co.uk	Alphabet	..
5	..	bbc.co.uk	UK	$5,530m
6	10	amazon.co.uk	Amazon	$232,890m
7	5	wikipedia.org	Wikimedia	$81m
8	..	ebay.co.uk	eBay	$10,700m
9	11	twitter.com	Twitter	$2,100m
10	21	reddit.com	Advance Publications	$100m

[i] See *Top Sites in United Kingdom* (2019) and *The Top 500 Sites on the Web* (2019).

information on Facebook, of which pages people 'liked', detailed probabilities could be assembled on what personality types people have, and therefore which kinds of ads they would be most susceptible to. For instance, people who 'like' curly fries tend to have high intelligence, and people who 'like' Hello Kitty tend to be highly open personalities but low on emotional stability.[54] Facebook began to enable ever-closer targeting of people with advertisements, based on geography, gender, age, but also on psychological data. This was one of the key functions that made it, or Google ads, attractive.

Second, data can be accumulated on one platform, and used across others. For example, Google's search or Gmail, is notionally 'free' but accumulates data from people's private messages for use in advertising on YouTube and across the web through Google Adsense (see Ch. 18). When Facebook took over WhatsApp, it merged user data despite promising EU regulators that it would not (see Ch. 6(2)(a)). People's data can also simply be accumulated and then sold to third parties.[55] This appropriation of data, typically disregarding their true choices or desire for privacy, finances the largest internet companies. Thus, failure to protect the right to personal data operates as a large legal subsidy.[56]

Third, data can be taken for purposes that media companies may not want, but from which they still profit. In the Brexit referendum, the organisers of Vote Leave boasted they had targeted 'roughly 7 million people, who saw

[54] M. Kosinski, D. Stillwell and T. Graepel, 'Private Traits and Attributes Are Predictable from Digital Records of Human Behavior' (2013) 110 *Proceedings of the National Academy of Sciences* 5802. It is important to point out that this data suggests average tendencies and individuals may be the opposite.

[55] Such a practice would violate the Consumer Rights Act 2015, ss. 62–4 and Sch. 2, para. 19, among other things.

[56] Cf. CFREU 2000, art. 8: 'data must be processed fairly for specified purposes and on the basis of the consent of the person concerned or some other legitimate basis laid down by law.'

something like one and a half billion ads',[57] with messages tailored to what could make those people vote or discourage them from voting. The data on users was accumulated through a company named Cambridge Analytica, which composed profiles on voters on Facebook. This was done without people's consent.[58] After procuring Brexit, the same technology was used by the Ted Cruz campaign and then the Donald Trump campaign for US President. The Information Commissioner imposed what was the maximum fine on Facebook at the time, £500,000, for failing to prevent customers' data being taken without their informed consent.[59] Under the new General Data Protection Regulation 2016 fines can amount to up to 4% of annual turnover, or €20 million, whichever is higher.[60]

On traditional television broadcasting, data cannot be used in the same way, as ads are general, not targeted (yet). Since the Television Act 1954 the independent station (now ITV), as well as Channel 4, Channel 5, Freeview and others have been entitled to run ads. The Communications Act 2003, section 321 empowers Ofcom to set standards for advertising and programme sponsorship, including prohibitions. Political advertising (which is 'wholly or mainly political', or directed at a 'political end') is prohibited, except in prescribed slots during election campaigns.[61] This has apparently not affected use of the Internet for political campaigning, and the weaponisation of social media to that end through dark spending, for instance through bots that spread propaganda. Under section 322, Ofcom can give any directions to TV stations on maximum advert time, minimum slots between periods or the exclusion of certain kinds of adverts,[62] taking into account international obligations. Misleading ads are controlled by Ofcom,[63] as well as the non-statutory Advertising Standards Authority funded and controlled by the industry group, the Advertising Association.[64] Despite this regulation, the quantity of ads has been increasing. Even if lower than the USA, Australia and Germany, the average person saw between thirty-nine and forty-seven ads on TV every day from 2005 to 2018, but this is dwarfed by around 5,000 ads we may see in total from all sources, particularly online.[65]

57 McGaughey, 'Could Brexit Be Void?', 332, quoting Dominic Cummings, recorded in R. Darbyshire, '"We Dumped Our Entire Budget in the Last 10 Days": Inside the Behavioural Science Strategy of Vote Leave', *The Drum* (13 June 2017).

58 C. Wylie, *Mindf*ck* (2020).

59 ICO, 'Investigation into the Use of Data Analytics in Political Campaigns: Investigation Update' (11 July 2018) 13, referring to the Data Protection Act 1998, s. 55.

60 General Data Protection Regulation (EU) 2016/679, art. 83(5).

61 Representation of the People Act 1983, s. 75; Companies Act 2006, ss. 362–79.

62 CA 2003, s. 368F further prohibits on-demand services advertising cigarettes, prescription-only medicine, alcohol to under-18s or which encourages immoderate drinking, and anything discriminatory, prejudicial to health, the environment, parents and teachers.

63 Consumer Protection from Unfair Trading Regulations 2008, reg. 5 and CA 2003, ss. 319 and 321.

64 ASA, *UK Code of Non-broadcast Advertising, Sales Promotion and Direct Marketing* (2010).

65 Statista (2021); L. Story, 'Anywhere the Eye Can See, It's Likely to See an Ad', *New York Times* (15 January 2007).

(b) Democracy and Political 'Externalities'

A second main source of finance for media enterprises is from an owner that wants political influence, and will bear losses, or will aim to profit no matter what happens to the news through sensationalism, smut, hate or lies. In 2017, among the UK's best-selling newspapers in print were those owned by the Australian white supremacist, Rupert Murdoch (*The Sun* and *The Times*),[66] by Viscount Rothermere (*Daily Mail*), by the Barclay Brothers (*Daily Telegraph*) and by Russian oligarch Evgeny Lebedev *(The Independent* and *Evening Standard*).[67] Each of these also has successful websites, and Murdoch until 2018 owned a substantial part of the TV company Sky, until losing a bidding war to the American firm, Comcast.[68] Murdoch's media empire also extends, among many papers and TV stations, to Fox News in the USA, a leading promoter of hate and conspiracy theories.[69] Prominent examples of wealthy individuals purchasing media groups include Jeff Bezos (*Washington Post*), Gina Rinehart (Ten TV and Fairfax Media in Australia) and Silvio Berlusconi (Mediaset SpA in Italy). Media buys influence. Mark Zuckerberg was widely observed to be preparing for a presidential campaign in 2017,[70] although the consequences of the Facebook data thefts, Brexit and Trump, and the widespread ridicule at such a notion, gave that one a thumbs down.

To address these issues, the law restricts the monopolisation of media ownership. First, it was recognised by the European Court of Human Rights that, in response to Austria's legal requirement of a public monopoly in television, 'public monopoly ... imposes the greatest restriction on the freedom of expression' and 'can only be justified where they correspond to a pressing need'.[71] The same goes for private enterprise, as a Council of Europe Recommendation in 2007 says that states should consider adopting 'rules aimed at limiting the influence which a single person, company or group may have in one or more media sectors'.[72] Second, the Communications Act 2003, section 3 requires Ofcom to maintain 'sufficient plurality of providers of different television and radio services'. On the web the words 'television' and 'radio' may or may not apply, depending on whether one construes this

[66] E.g. J. Pilger, 'How the Murdoch Press Keeps Australia's Dirty Secret', *New Statesman* (12 May 2011).

[67] *The Sun*, *The Times* (and equivalent Sunday papers) are owned by Rupert Murdoch through News Corp. UK & Ireland Ltd. The *Daily Mail* is owned by Viscount Rothermere through DMG Media Ltd. The *Daily Mirror* and *Daily Star* are owned by Reach plc.

[68] J. Waterson, 'Rupert Murdoch's Sky Reign to End as Fox Sells All Shares to Comcast', *The Guardian* (26 Sept 2018).

[69] E.g. M. Pengelly, 'Fox News Host Tucker Carlson Calls QAnon Followers "Gentle' Patriots"', *The Guardian* (6 March 2021).

[70] A. Ohlheiser, 'A Year Ago, You Probably Thought Mark Zuckerberg Was Running for President', *Washington Post* (10 April 2018).

[71] *Informationsverein Lentia v Austria* [1993] ECHR 57, [39].

[72] Council of Europe, 'Recommendation of the Committee of Ministers to Member States on Media Pluralism and Diversity of Media Content', CM/Rec(2007)2.

purposively. After all, videos and sound on YouTube, Facebook or Twitter are functionally identical and direct competitors of TV and radio.[73] Under section 391, Ofcom must regularly review media ownership and report to the Secretary of State, with a focus on ensuring that control of share capital does not concentrate.[74] Third, there is an express prohibition on owning over 20 per cent of a national newspaper, over a six-month period, and at the same time holding a licence for Channel 3 (ITV).[75] It is questionable, however, whether these rules are enough, especially given the mass monopolisation of the web. Moreover, media plurality, where most owners are rich or following advertiser interests, still leads to media being run contrary to the interests of the public. Whoever the owner, the major element lacking is the ability of journalists, staff and the audience to elect editors and media boards.

(c) Public Grants, Voluntary Subscriptions and Licence Fee

A third source of finance can be public spending, voluntary subscriptions, or the 'licence fee' model that underpins the BBC. In UK television, in 2017–18, £655 million was spent by the Department for Work and Pensions (DWP) to fund the BBC, mainly for people over 75 to have TV licences, while £3.17 billion was raised through the TV licence fee.[76] For comparison, direct public grants fully fund the Australian Broadcasting Corporation, but it is much less well funded than the BBC, and politically more vulnerable.[77] In the USA, the Public Broadcasting Service and National Public Radio rely upon voluntary contributions, as well as very limited public grants.[78] Wikipedia's finance comes entirely from voluntary contributions, as well as relying on a larger volunteer network of editors and administrators. The drawback of public grants is their vulnerability to swings in government ideology, and the drawback of voluntary contributions is the limited amount, though Wikimedia's vast network solves this.

Most money for the BBC comes from the licence fee. In 2019, under the Communications (Television Licensing) Regulations 2004, written by the BBC in negotiation with government, the fee amounted to £150.50 a year for a full colour TV licence.[79] Concession rates – which are essentially free – are

[73] An analogous, purposive interpretation was given to the legislation on telegraphs, and applied to telephones after they were invented, in *Attorney General v Edison Telephone Company of London Ltd* (1880) 6 QBD 244, 255 (see Ch. 16(1)).

[74] CA 2003, ss. 349–57(2) state Ofcom can determine a person owning under 50% of share capital is in control. Enterprise Act 2002, s. 26(3) treats control as ability 'materially to influence the policy' of a company.

[75] CA 2003, Sch. 14, para. 1.

[76] BBC, *Annual Report 2017/2018* (2018) 172.

[77] E.g. A. Meade, 'ABC Loses $783m Funding since 2014 when Coalition Made Its First Cuts – Report', *The Guardian* (3 May 2020).

[78] Public Broadcasting Act of 1967, 47 USC, §396.

[79] Communications (Television Licensing) Regulations 2004, reg. 3 and Sch. 1, para. 2. A black and white TV licence costs around £50 a year.

available for people over age 75, for residential care homes and for blind people,[80] and the DWP commits to replacing the lost revenue with a direct grant to the BBC. Under the Communications Act 2003, section 363, use of a television receiver without a licence is an offence, which may result in a 'level 3' fine on the standard scale. This has drawbacks too. Because the fee is unrelated to income, it operates as a regressive or flat tax, taking up a higher proportion of poorer people's incomes and disproportionately hitting single parents or persons who do not share housing. The fee is highly enforced, as the task is outsourced to Capita plc. This profit-making corporation, acting under the Regulation of Investigatory Powers Act 2000, section 27A, carries out 'surveillance and covert human intelligence' for the 'detection of television receivers' by people who are not paying a licence fee.[81] It is estimated that it will receive £1.1 to £1.5 billion over its fifteen-year contract from 2012 to 2027. Prosecution rates are high: in 2012, fifty-one people were imprisoned for ultimately failing to pay fines, while proceedings were brought against 193,049 people. This is one in nine of all cases brought to magistrates' courts. Inevitably, those who do not pay are disproportionately among low-income groups, though 30 per cent of people prosecuted had a satellite or cable subscription. This raises the question why companies that collect subscriptions (such as Netflix, YouTube or Amazon Prime) are not required to help collect fees for the licence: this would be easier to enforce. Criminalisation of licence fee payers is a disproportionate cost to the public that could be eliminated.

(3) Governance

The governance of web and broadcast media is best seen in three main parts, namely with (a) Ofcom and its regulation of broadcasts; (b) web media companies, particularly Wikimedia, Facebook, YouTube and Twitter, which largely regulate themselves; and (c) the BBC.

(a) Ofcom and Broadcasters

Ofcom has the power to oversee the governance of media broadcasters. Ofcom's board is appointed by the Secretary of State, but does not yet represent media staff, viewers or listeners (see Ch. 16(3)(a)). Under the Communications Act 2003, section 3, its duties include promoting the interests of citizens and consumers (including 'where appropriate by promoting competition'), securing TV and radio with 'high quality' that appeals 'to a variety of tastes and interests', maintaining plurality, preventing 'inclusion of offensive and harmful material', and protecting the public from 'unfair treatment in programmes'

[80] Communications (Television Licensing) Regulations 2004, regs. 5–6.
[81] Regulation of Investigatory Powers (British Broadcasting Corporation) Order 2001, reg. 2.

or 'unwarranted infringements of privacy'.[82] Under the Broadcasting Act 1990, section 3 Ofcom can grant a licence for television broadcasting to people who are a 'fit and proper person to hold it'.[83] Section 4 gives Ofcom broad discretion to set licence conditions that 'appear to Ofcom to be appropriate', in fulfilment of its Communications Act 2003, section 3 duties. It can also require the payment of fees. Section 13 makes broadcasting a television service without a licence an offence.[84] This includes analogue, digital and satellite channels. Ofcom is empowered to regulate the BBC, based on the BBC Charter and Agreement.[85]

However, as already seen in Chapter 16(3)(a), Ofcom has not yet attempted to regulate pure web broadcasters, even though nearly all TV is now online. Under the Communications Act 2003, section 232(1)(b), the meaning of 'television licensable content service' includes 'the distribution of the service (whether by that person or by another) by any means involving the use of an electronic communications network'.[86] On a plain reading, that includes services over the Internet, particularly YouTube, Facebook and Twitter. Why has Ofcom failed to regulate pure web media, despite its powers? Could it simply seem too much effort? This is set to change with the proposal of legislation to tackle 'online harms', although the proposals at present focus on child sex abuse, terrorism, hate crime, harassment and cyberstalking, but not the broader issues of disinformation or discrimination. There would, however, be fines of up to 10 per cent of worldwide turnover imposed for violations, and the threat of further legislation to criminalise individual directors' conduct.[87]

Ofcom requires that all licensees comply with the 'Broadcasting Code'.[88] Under section 319(1) Ofcom has the duty 'from time to time to review and revise' the Code regarding 'standards for the content of programmes to be included in television and radio'.[89] Ofcom is empowered to give broadcasters directions to comply with any licence terms.[90] Fines up to 5 per cent of advertising revenue from the last accounting period can be issued, and Ofcom can also revoke licences if broadcasters fail to comply with

[82] CA 2003, s. 3(1)–(2). Ofcom must also have regard to a long list of other issues, such as child vulnerability; needs of the disabled, elderly or poor; preventing crime and disorder; ethnic communities, etc.

[83] Also CA 2003, ss. 214 and 235 (digital Channel 3 and 5 licences as Ofcom considers appropriate, fit and proper).

[84] CA 2003, s. 211 defines such TV services as those provided from the UK.

[85] CA 2003, s. 198.

[86] CA 2003, s. 32 defines an e-comms network as 'a transmission system for the conveyance, by the use of electrical, magnetic or electro-magnetic energy, of signals of any description' and any apparatus, software, data or other resources for conveying signals. Again, this includes the Internet.

[87] DCMS, *Online Harms White Paper* (15 December 2020) 2.2, Table 1; and contrast the private members' Online Harms Reduction Regulator (Report) Bill (2021) HL Bill 22, which covers discrimination.

[88] See *The Ofcom Broadcasting Code* (April 2017).

[89] CA 2003, s. 319(1).

[90] Broadcasting Act 1990, s. 40.

directions.[91] The Broadcasting Code is primarily focused on the control of content (see Ch. 17(3)). Ofcom also has power to regulate the governance of broadcasters through licence conditions – for instance, if this appeared to be an effective way 'to further the interests of citizens in relation to communications matters'.[92]

(b) Web Media Companies

Where Ofcom does not regulate, web media companies regulate themselves, limited only by their internal governance structures. From most to least democratic are (i) Wikimedia; a distant second, (ii) Facebook; (iii) YouTube and Google; and (iv) Twitter.

(i) Wikimedia

Wikipedia is the world's fifth largest website, and has a remarkable internal governance structure. The encyclopaedia site is generated by the readers, who themselves can contribute edits to each page. Despite its limits, and its constant revisions, experience has proven that it has equal or superior reliability compared to traditional encyclopaedias such as Britannica.[93] No source can compete in terms of sheer scope of topics, depth and ability to keep up to date. While its use is widely (and rightly) discouraged as a source in education,[94] Wikipedia has come to function as a portal to references contained within it. Structurally, the website is funded by the Wikimedia Foundation, a Florida corporation established in 2003,[95] which is also registered as a not-for-profit charitable organisation.[96] The Wikimedia Foundation also presides over sister Wikipedia projects, including the Wiktionary, Wikinews, Wikiquote, Wikivoyage (an online travel guide) and Wikimedia Commons (a database for images, video and sound) but Wikipedia remains its most successful project.

Florida's Incorporation Statutes enable a choice of rules on amending a corporate constitution, and appointment and removal of directors.

[91] Broadcasting Act 1990, ss. 41–2. [92] CA 2003, s. 3(1)(a).

[93] Unsurprisingly, Wikipedia also has an entry on the 'Reliability of Wikipedia'. One of the early articles to compare accuracy was J. Giles, 'Internet Encyclopaedias Go Head to Head: Jimmy Wales' Wikipedia Comes Close to Britannica in Terms of the Accuracy of Its Science Entries' (2005) 438(7070) *Nature* 900–1.

[94] Cf. J. Maehre, 'What It Means to Ban Wikipedia: An Exploration of the Pedagogical Principles at Stake' (2009) 57(4) *College Teaching* 229, arguing in favour of allowing Wikipedia to be cited. At least in law, the preferable view is that no secondary text (including a book or Wikipedia) should properly be used for citation of legal authority: legal writers and students must cite the relevant law. Textbooks should be cited, however, for opinions of the author. Since it is not meant to contain opinions, it would therefore be extremely rare for Wikipedia to be an appropriate source to cite in legal writing.

[95] See the Articles of Incorporation (2003).

[96] 26 USC, §501(c)(3) enables exemption from federal income tax.

Wikimedia's Articles of Incorporation leave these choices to the bylaws. These call the board of directors a 'board of trustees' (even though it is not technically a trust). Since 2008, there have been ten trustees who may exercise all corporate powers.[97] Three are elected by the 'community' of editors in Wikimedia projects. These elections do not appear that well publicised to encourage a large turnout. In 2017 elections, where any editor with a relatively active account could vote, the turnout was 5,581 people.[98] By contrast, in 2021 there were around 140,000 'active' editors defined as having made one edit in the past 30 days, and around 41.4 million registered user accounts.[99] Two trustees are selected by representatives of Wikimedia 'chapters', which are country- or regional-based groups to represent Wikimedia editors around the world. Four are selected by the existing board, and one seat is for Wikipedia's founder, Jimmy Wales.[100] All trustees have three-year terms, and a three-term limit, except for Wales who may be reappointed. Trustees can be removed by a majority vote of other trustees. The bylaws may be amended by the 'entire board' with 'at least ten days' written notice'.[101] Wikimedia's overall purpose is stated to be 'to empower and engage people around the world to collect and develop educational content under a free license or in the public domain' and to keep 'useful information' available 'on the Internet free of charge, in perpetuity'.[102]

Wikimedia's governance structure, in essence, ensures half of its board is directly elected by, or representative of, the editors who produce its content: its volunteer workers, and also those who use its content. Yet its participatory governance goes far beyond board representation. Policies to administer Wikipedia (and other projects) are built through consensus within its community of editors. Among the 270,000 or so active editors, a relatively smaller group of 'administrators' (1,106 in 2021) have special rights in relation to other users, and particularly dispute resolution. The Wikipedia:Administration page explains that administrators can protect and delete pages, and block other editors from editing.[103] The process to become an administrator is generally to demonstrate a keen interest in editing pages and then to be approved by gathering support, or a 'high level of trust' (nearing consensus), from other editors.[104] The disputes that may occur (usually hidden behind the 'Talk' tabs of Wikipedia entries) are typically over what should go in a given page, personality disputes and so on. If disputes extend over a long period of time, there are procedures for arbitration. Editors who are unable to resolve disagreements may request arbitration, whereupon a panel of administrators can

[97] Wikimedia Bylaws (2019) art. IV, §1.

[98] See https://meta.wikimedia.org/wiki/Wikimedia_Foundation_elections/2017/Results.

[99] See https://en.wikipedia.org/wiki/Wikipedia:Wikipedians.

[100] Wikimedia Bylaws (2019) art. IV, §3. [101] Florida Statutes, Title 32, ch. 617.0206.

[102] Wikimedia Bylaws (2019) art. II. [103] See Wikipedia:Administration.

[104] See Wikipedia:Requests for adminship.

volunteer and will reach a binding decision.[105] This may sometimes result in blocking users altogether.

Wikipedia has detailed policies on editor conduct, which evolved through discussion among active editors. First, Wikipedia editors may not set up automated 'bots' without special approval, and 'sock puppets' to 'mislead, deceive, vandalize or disrupt', or 'stir up controversy' are prohibited: the 'general rule is one editor, one account'.[106] Second, editors on Wikipedia are expected to edit and interact in 'good faith' and make 'no personal attacks'.[107] Any harassment, namely 'a pattern of repeated offensive behavior', is strictly prohibited and 'subject to blocking'.[108]

Third, editors are expected to always have a verifiable basis for what they write, and to present a 'neutral point of view' by explaining different sides where there are credible different views, and to do so 'fairly and without editorial bias'.[109] One result of these principles was that in 2017 the *Daily Mail* (which previously had the largest newspaper website after the BBC) was prohibited from being used as a source.[110] Reviewed again in 2019, Wikipedia stated: 'Consensus has determined that the *Daily Mail* . . . is generally unreliable, and its use as a reference is to be generally prohibited' due to its 'poor fact checking, sensationalism, and flat-out fabrication'.[111] It is significant that a major UK national newspaper has been largely banned from Wikipedia, as it demonstrates the power of a community-driven platform to regulate its own content. Readers of Wikipedia often notice that some pages have flags, usually placed by an editor in disagreement with one or more other editors, about the neutrality or factual accuracy of a page.[112] Other pages, which result in controversy, are stopped by administrators from being edited by people who have not registered an account, often to prevent vandalism. The remarkable features of these policies are how strict they are in upholding standards, and how effective they appear to be. Despite the many complications and difficulties surrounding Wikipedia governance, fake news, bots, harassment and other phenomena that poison Facebook, YouTube, Twitter and others, particularly since 2016, are swiftly and effectively contained.

(ii) Facebook

Facebook is the world's third-largest website, and reported $55 billion in advertising revenue in 2018.[113] In 2021 it was shifted underneath a new

[105] See Wikipedia:Arbitration. [106] See Wikipedia:Bots and Wikipedia:Sock puppetry.

[107] See Wikipedia:No personal attacks. [108] See Wikipedia:Harassment.

[109] See Wikipedia:Neutral point of view.

[110] J. Jackson, 'Wikipedia Bans Daily Mail as "Unreliable" Source', *The Guardian* (8 February 2017).

[111] See the 'Request for Comment' page on the *Daily Mail* Ban.

[112] A long-running page with such flags is the Israeli–Palestinian conflict. This is also a highly informed, well-referenced and sophisticated article.

[113] See 'Facebook Reports Fourth Quarter and Full Year 2018 Results', Facebook Press Release (30 January 2019).

holding company, Meta Platforms Inc., incorporated in Delaware (see Ch. 16(3)(c)(ii)). Facebook claims to have an average 2.3 billion users each month, and 1.5 billion users each day, rising to 2 billion each day when including Instagram, WhatsApp and Messenger. It is not clear, however, which of these people are real, because internal data is secret and not independently audited. It is reported that the UK has 40 million Facebook users, or 32.6 million 'regular' users, with 25–34-year-olds as the highest proportion of users.[114] Facebook, of course, has an inherent incentive to suggest that it has more users than in reality, because it profits from the quantity of ads sold. Ad buyers want to hear that more people are watching their ads. In May 2018, Facebook's public relations employees 'revealed' that it had 'shut down 583 million fake accounts' stating that it 'believes between 3 and 4 per cent [of] users were fake accounts'.[115] In November 2019, it was reported that Facebook had shut down '5.4 billion fake accounts',[116] something it did purely because of the political scandal and being publicly forced. Given these numbers, Facebook's user claims must be viewed as non-credible. This raises the question of whether Facebook's reporting of user data could amount to securities fraud towards investors.

Many fake accounts are astro-turfed by political actors, such as Kremlin intelligence. They have been found to have actively interfered in both US and UK politics. This included, for example, a Facebook group with hundreds of thousands of followers called 'the heart of Texas' advocating that Texas secede from the US. It was operated by Russian 'intelligence' services, the General Staff of Russian Armed Forces, and succeeded in organising actual rallies by Texans in Texas from computers in St Petersburg.[117] In July 2018, the House of Commons select committee on 'Disinformation and Fake News' called Kremlin activity 'unconventional warfare', after calling dozens of witnesses over data harvesting, offences in overspending and foreign interference.

In February 2019, the House of Commons' committee's final report on 'Disinformation and Fake News' recommended that the Communications Act 2003, section 319 standards be reflected in a 'compulsory Code of Ethics' for 'tech companies'.[118] These include that people under 18 are protected, no material encourages crime or disorder, news 'is presented with due impartiality' and 'due accuracy', that a 'proper degree of responsibility' is exercised in 'religious programmes', that ads which contravene political ad prohibitions are

114 M. Sweney, 'Is Facebook for Old People? Over-55s Flock In as the Young Leave', *The Guardian* (12 February 2018).

115 A. Griffin, 'Facebook Shuts Down 583 Million Fake Accounts as it Reveals It Is Packed with Abusive Content', *The Independent* (15 May 2018).

116 B. Fung and A. Garcia, 'Facebook Has Shut Down 5.4 Billion Fake Accounts this Year', *CNN* (13 November 2019).

117 C. Michel, 'How the Russians Pretended to Be Texans – and Texans Believed Them', *Washington Post* (17 October 2017).

118 House of Commons, Digital, Culture, Media and Sport Committee, *Disinformation and 'Fake News': Final Report* (14 February 2019) paras. 37–8.

not included and 'that there is no use of techniques' for 'influencing [people's] minds, without their being aware' of what has occurred. By contrast, Zuckerberg stated his view in July 2018 that Facebook users should have the right to publish Holocaust denial posts.[119] The problem with this stance is that, while free speech generally allows for any views to be expressed on a personal scale, for instance at Speaker's Corner,[120] there is no fundamental right to acquire the megaphone of an internet broadcaster. The rantings of madmen in a park are not the same as Facebook and YouTube broadcasters with thousands or millions of viewers. Moreover, there is no right for Facebook to profit from hate-speech and discrimination that undermines deliberative, democratic discourse. In this way Facebook, and its CEO, are far more dangerous than any individual racist on its platform. But instead of dealing with the problems it has generated, Facebook has focused its efforts on lobbying governments around the world to prevent any regulation.[121]

(iii) YouTube, Google and Alphabet

The governance of YouTube, the world's second largest website, and Google, the largest, is similar to Facebook, except that it never had any particular commitment to privacy or user participation. As Chapter 16(3)(c) explained, it is owned by Alphabet Inc. YouTube is Google's most important media organisation: it has millions of videos, which anyone with an account can put up. Below videos, extensive commenting and discussion takes place.

Like on Facebook, users of YouTube relate to the platform through standard-form contract terms, that incorporate YouTube's 'Terms of Service'. Varied unilaterally at the discretion of YouTube, like Google's privacy policy, these are framed largely in a 'take it or leave it' manner. 'By using or visiting the YouTube website . . . you signify your agreement' to its terms. These refer, for example, to YouTube's 'community guidelines' which say 'we don't support content that promotes or condones violence against individuals or groups based on race' and other protected characteristics. It follows that YouTube does not bind itself to regulate any content that does just this, and seemingly that it may or may not support violence against non-protected groups. It has no policies against discrimination that would violate the Equality Act 2010. Under its policy on 'harassment' it says 'users may be mildly annoying or petty and should be ignored'. This appears to demote serious instances of sexual, racial or other discrimination as merely 'annoying or petty', and carries no effective, pre-emptive enforcement mechanisms. This has led YouTube, like

119 K. Swisher, 'Full Transcript: Facebook CEO Mark Zuckerberg on Recode Decode', *Recode* (18 July 2018): 'I just don't think that it is the right thing to say, "We're going to take someone off the platform if they get things wrong, even multiple times."'

120 See J. S. Mill, *On Liberty* (1857).

121 C. Cadwalladr, 'Revealed: Facebook's Global Lobbying against Data Privacy Laws', *The Guardian* (2 March 2019).

Facebook, to become a haven for fascist and extremist broadcasters, as well as broadcasters backed by the Russian armed forces, to proliferate across people's screens. Only in August 2018, YouTube, Facebook, Apple and Spotify resolved to ban the extreme conspiracy theorist, Alex Jones, from their platforms, a man who, for example, stated that 'globalists' were 'putting chemicals in the water that turn the friggin' frogs gay'.[122] YouTube and Google, however, have escaped much of the scrutiny that Facebook has received. Like Facebook, YouTube profits from the volume of content and the ads on its service, and therefore has a direct financial interest in not preventing discrimination, hate-speech or fake news on its platforms.

(iv) Twitter

Though not as big as Wikimedia, Facebook or YouTube, Twitter has been uniquely influential and damaging given its role as the premier, public micro-blogging website. It is especially relevant for politicians, journalists, celebrities and all the media. Unlike Facebook and Google, its founder Jack Dorsey did not maintain control at its initial public offering in 2013, and is a minority shareholder: the largest shareholders are Vanguard, Morgan Stanley, BlackRock and State Street.[123]

Twitter's platform was particularly exploited by @realDonaldTrump, until his 'permanent suspension' after inciting the national terrorist attack on the US Capitol, 'due to the risk of further incitement of violence'.[124] Within Twitter's terms of service, Trump was able to spread hatred as a form of politics and conspiracy theories, and incite violence from well before his seizure of the electoral college to the riot against elected officials.[125] Of course, in *On Liberty*, John Stuart Mill wrote that the limit of free speech should be harm, and particularly any threat of violence. Yet the failure of Silicon Valley billionaires to appreciate a more modern concept of media regulation, a sense of history and a proper account of what 'harm' means, meant the USA had to stare fascism in the face for four years, saved only by the fact disarray of the attempts to storm the US Capitol, and refusal of officials to assist.[126]

(c) British Broadcasting Corporation

As explained at Chapter 17(1), the BBC was established as a legal entity under a royal charter, first issued in 1927, with an object to 'inform, educate and

[122] A. Hern, 'Facebook, Apple, YouTube and Spotify Ban Infowars' Alex Jones', *The Guardian* (6 August 2018). See also YouTube, recording Jones' frog theory in 2015.
[123] See Yahoo Finance (March 2021), with Vanguard at 10.41%, MS at 8.53%, BlackRock at 6.65% and SS at 4.48%.
[124] Permanent suspension of @realDonaldTrump (8 January 2021).
[125] Twitter, *Terms of Service, Rules, and Privacy Policy* (30 September 2016).
[126] McGaughey, 'Fascism-Lite in America'.

entertain'.[127] The BBC was set up by charter 'precisely for the reason that it was desired to avoid any suggestion that broadcasting in this country is an instrument of government'.[128] That 'suggestion', of course, does persist, but the BBC's charter has been continually renewed, and it emphasises 'independence' from government in its text. Article 3 stresses that the BBC 'must be independent in all matters concerning the fulfilment of its Mission and the promotion of the Public Purposes, particularly as regards editorial and creative decisions'. Article 5 states its 'Mission' is 'to act in the public interest', giving audiences 'impartial, high-quality and distinctive output and services which inform, educate and entertain'. Article 6 elaborates that this means 'impartial' news, supporting learning of all ages, the creative economy and reflecting UK culture and values to the world.[129] The BBC's activities, set out in article 7, are elaborated in the BBC Agreement. These activities include UK public service broadcasting, the World Service; 'non-service activities' which promote its public purpose; commercial activities aimed at 'generating a profit'; and trading activities that are not commercial, such as buying and selling assets or licensing content to provide its public service.[130]

However, beneath these high-sounding goals, the guarantee of BBC independence from government must be achieved through its governance structure. The BBC's board has a maximum of fourteen members. The chair and four national representatives are appointed by an Order in Council (i.e. the Prime Minister) but only after consulting the existing BBC board. The other nine directors, including the Director General, are appointed by the existing board.[131] The Secretary of State sets the terms of appointments, up to a four-year maximum, and sets pay. There is only express provision for terminating the executive and non-executive directors (not appointees of the Secretary of State). Non-executives can be terminated by an Order in Council, or if two-thirds of other non-executives vote that they are 'unfit or unwilling' to perform their role.[132] Executives can be terminated upon the chair's proposal with majority board support.[133] The terms of all other BBC employees will be set by the board.[134] In essence, like the Bank of England Act 1998, or the Morrisonian model of nationalised industry, government dominates appointment and removal and reserves for its ministers the dubious role of judging who has the most expertise in leading the BBC.

There are also important (if highly limited) provisions on the voice of viewers, listeners or readers, and of employees, in BBC governance. Article 10 of the charter requires 'engagement with the public' to 'carefully and

127 Royal Charter of the BBC, Cm. 9365 (2016) art. 5 still incorporates this.

128 *British Broadcasting Corporation v Johns* [1965] Ch 32, per Willmer J, holding that the BBC enjoyed no Crown immunity and was liable to pay tax.

129 Royal Charter of the BBC (2016) arts. 3–7.

130 BBC Agreement (December 2016) arts. 7, 16, 23, 31. A variety of (repetitive) reviews and competition tests are to be conducted for each of these.

131 Royal Charter of the BBC (2016) arts. 21–5.

132 Royal Charter of the BBC (2016) art. 28.

133 Royal Charter of the BBC (2016) art. 29.

134 Royal Charter of the BBC (2016) arts. 27–32.

appropriately assess the views and interests of the public and audiences, including licence fee payers' in the UK. There is, however, no right for viewers, listeners or readers to actually vote for representatives on the board whose salaries are funded by their licence fee. Article 35 requires 'communication with staff', meaning 'suitable arrangements' to 'consult BBC staff on all matters affecting the interests of those staff'. There is, however, not yet direct representation of staff on the board. Viewer, listener, reader and staff representation on the BBC board would probably be one of the best guarantees of true independence from governments. Since political parties may often be tempted to exercise undue influence on funding and governance, stakeholder representation is a surer mechanism to respond directly to the values of civil society.

(4) Viewer, Listener and Reader Rights

Viewer, listener or readers' rights in media enterprises are as disjointed as the governance. They range from Wikimedia's participatory democracy and its extensive, enforceable standards, to the threadbare, arbitrary norms and opaque, unaccountable complaint procedures on YouTube.[135] This may well change with new UK legislation against 'online harms', and with the EU Digital Services Act proposals.[136] But currently, the main rights are to (a) accurate and impartial media, though only so far in TV and radio; (b) equality and no offensive or harmful material, but highly limited online; and (c) privacy and data protection.

(a) Accuracy and Impartiality

Under Communications Act 2003, section 319(2)(d), Ofcom has a duty to ensure that the 'news included in television and radio services is reported with due accuracy'. This does not necessarily generate any private right, but it does enable complaints to be brought under the Ofcom Code. As already repeated, the main problem is that this is not extended to the web, where even flat Earth conspiracies are back.[137] Under section 319(2)(c) Ofcom also has a duty to ensure that news 'is presented with due impartiality' and this is further defined under section 320 as relating to 'industrial controversy' and 'matters relating to

[135] On complaints procedures for the BBC and others, see *The Ofcom Broadcasting Code* (April 2017).

[136] M. Khan, 'EU Draws Up Sweeping Rules to Curb Illegal Online Content', *Financial Times* (24 July 2019), writing of the new EU Digital Services Act: 'The new laws will mean social media giants will be subject to mandatory "notice and take down" orders forcing them to remove illegal content, including certain types of racism and xenophobia, from their sites, or face fines.'

[137] I. Sample, 'Study Blames YouTube for Rise in Number of Flat Earthers', *The Guardian* (17 February 2019).

current public policy'.[138] Section 333 requires Ofcom to specifically stop party political advertisements, except under fairly allocated time.[139]

While Ofcom receives many complaints, relatively few cases have reached the courts on the requirements of due impartiality. However, an extreme case, mixing several breaches, was *R (DM Digital Television Ltd) v Ofcom*. A claim in judicial review was brought against Ofcom for imposing financial sanctions against an Islamic 'scholar' who appeared on a small radio station called DM Digital. Ofcom concluded the 'scholar' had made remarks in his lecture that were likely to incite crime, including saying that all Muslims had a 'duty' to attack or kill apostates or anyone who insulted the Prophet Mohammed. He also praised the murder of the former Punjab governor, Salmaan Taseer, of the Pakistan People's Party who had opposed Pakistan's blasphemy laws. Ofcom held this breached the Broadcasting Code rules 3.1 against inciting crime, and rules 5.4 and 5.5, which reflect the duty of due impartiality in section 319(2)(c) and 320. Stuart-Smith J held that Ofcom was justified in imposing £85,000 and £20,000 fines under the Communications Act 2003, section 237. He rejected that Ofcom's process was tainted by bias, and rejected that the financial penalties were disproportionate. As he pointed out, Ofcom had not gone further, as it could have done, and revoked the broadcaster's licence.[140]

(b) Equality and Offensive or Harmful Material

The Communications Act 2003, section 319(2)(f) generally requires Ofcom to ensure that there is 'adequate protection' against 'offensive and harmful material'. Ofcom must also specifically ensure that people under 18 are protected, that no material encourages crime or disorder, that a 'proper degree of responsibility' is exercised in 'religious programmes' and 'that there is no use of techniques' for 'influencing [people's] minds, without their being aware' of what has occurred.[141]

These standards mirror the Audiovisual Media Services Directive 2010. In article 1, audiovisual media services mean those 'devoted to providing programmes, under the editorial responsibility of a media service provider, to the general public, in order to inform, entertain or educate, to the general public by electronic communications networks', either on TV or an 'on-demand' service.[142] An 'on-demand' service enables 'viewing of programmes at the moment chosen by the user and at his individual request on the basis of a catalogue of programmes selected by the media service provider'. This

[138] *Lynch v BBC* [1983] NILR 193, per Hutton J, originally held that the BBC's impartiality duties were not legally enforceable, rejecting a claim from a Worker's Party candidate against being excluded from BBC programmes before elections. This was changed by the Broadcasting Act 1990, and see now CA 2003, s. 319.

[139] Also the Political Parties, Elections and Referendums Act 2000, ss. 37 and 127.

[140] [2014] EWHC 961 (Admin). [141] CA 2003, s. 319(2)(a), (b), (e) and (l).

[142] Audiovisual Media Services Directive 2010/13/EU, art. 1(1)(a).

triggers, for example, the obligation under article 6 for member states to ensure audiovisual services 'do not contain any incitement to hatred' based on race, sex, religion, nationality or other protected characteristics.[143] Article 7 requires services are made 'more accessible to persons with disabilities'. Article 9 also prohibits programming that includes 'surreptitious' communication or 'subliminal' techniques; anything to 'prejudice respect for human dignity'; and anything that would 'promote any discrimination', prejudice health and safety or 'encourage behaviour grossly prejudicial to the protection of the environment'. The problem with the Directive's scope is that 'editorial responsibility' may be argued to exclude the responsibility of Facebook, Google or Twitter, even though their algorithms, from which they profit handsomely 'means the exercise of effective control' over programme selection and catalogues of available programmes.[144]

Most broadly, the meaning of what is 'offensive' turns on 'generally accepted standards'. In a tolerant society, this does not affect comedy, even the most profane, nail-biting comedy.[145] The greater problem is intentional harassment, discrimination and stereotyping. The leading case is *R (Gaunt) v Ofcom*. Here a right-wing commentator named Jon Gaunt stated on Talksport radio that a councillor appearing on his show was a 'health Nazi', an 'ignorant pig' and to 'shut up'. The councillor had proposed restricting smokers from fostering children, on the ground that smoking damages children's lungs. Talksport then summarily dismissed Gaunt; and Ofcom, after fifty-three complaints, issued a censure under the Broadcasting Code, rules 2.1 and 2.3, which reflect section 319(2)(f) against 'offensive and harmful material'. Talksport accepted that there was a breach, but Gaunt decided to bring a claim for judicial review that Ofcom's ruling disproportionately interfered with his human right under the European Convention on Human Rights (ECHR), article 10 to freedom of expression. Both the High Court and Court of Appeal found that Ofcom's ruling was justified. Lord Neuberger MR held there was no ground for finding that Gaunt's freedom of expression was interfered with. The interview, considered as a whole, was aggressive, constantly interrupting, ranting, insulting and had a lack of substantive content. Gaunt's only aim was 'to insult, belittle and berate' the councillor.[146] It would appear that such behaviour, however, is commonplace online.

If Ofcom chooses not to act, however, people who argue that the law or the Broadcasting Code is breached have limited recourse. In *Traveller Movement*

[143] Audiovisual Media Services Directive 2010/13/EU, art. 6.

[144] Audiovisual Media Services Directive 2010/13/EU, art. 1(1)(c): '"editorial responsibility" means the exercise of effective control both over the selection of the programmes and over their organisation either in a chronological schedule, in the case of television broadcasts, or in a catalogue, in the case of on-demand audiovisual media services'.

[145] Cf. A. Selby, 'Frankie Boyle Censored by BBC Bosses after He Makes String of Offensive Jokes about the Queen', *Daily Record* (14 May 2016). To be fair, these jokes were quite offensive, though it is not clear that matters.

[146] [2011] EWCA Civ 692. An appeal to ECHR was rejected.

v Ofcom, a group claimed that Ofcom had acted irrationally when declining to sanction Channel 4 for two programmes in 2012 entitled 'Big Fat Gypsy Weddings' and 'Thelma's Gypsy Girls'.[147] While Channel 4 described these as 'observational documentaries', the Traveller Movement claimed that the programmes negatively and racially stereotyped their community, and did so in a way that would likely result in further harm to their children. For instance, 'one 17 year old participant complained that she had been manipulated so as to portray her as a "freak", violent, tarty and stupid'. They also complained that the very use of the word 'gypsy' misleadingly ignored the distinctions among travellers (who are predominantly Irish) and Roma (who are largely from Eastern Europe), in favour of an offensive term 'gypsy'.[148] Ouseley J rejected all claims that Ofcom had acted irrationally – for instance, by failing to accept advice from the Equality and Human Rights Commission – stating there was no 'clear evidence' of harm that followed a line of causation from the programmes. This decision was wholly inadequate, although the claimants' grounds could have been better framed as Ofcom making an 'error of law'. The Equality Act 2010 prohibits racial harassment, although there is a specific exemption for TV, radio and online 'broadcasting'.[149] However, in interpreting what is 'offensive and harmful' in section 319(2)(f), general standards on equality and discrimination should have been taken into account: it is completely unclear what underlying principles guided Ouseley J's judgment. The programme racially stereotyped the communities involved. The programme's entire appeal for viewers was to disparage travellers who live in considerable deprivation, both in housing and income, and face systematic racial discrimination. While a duty to promote equality is not made explicit, at the very least the objective under section 319(2)(a) to protect persons under 18 should have been interpreted to include duties of equality. There was also a case to say that the programme violated the rights of privacy in ECHR, article 10 of those under 18 years, particularly read in conjunction with the duty of equality in human rights under article 14. None of these issues appear to have been given careful or concerned thought by Ouseley J.

(c) Privacy and Data

Privacy and the right to data protection are basic rights. But as explored in Chapter 16(4)(a) an enterprise that is classified as an 'information society service' has a 'safe harbour' against liability for content it hosts if it 'does not have actual knowledge of illegal activity or information'.[150] In *CG v Facebook*

[147] *Traveller Movement v Ofcom* [2015] EWHC 406 (Admin).

[148] Cf. Urban Dictionary, 'gypsy': 'While normally considered a racial slur, the word "gypsy" (in the US) refers to a person of Romani heritage. As with all cultures and groups, there are good and bad. They should not all be lumped into one group.'

[149] Equality Act 2010, ss. 9 and 29 (provision of services) and Sch. 3, para. 31 (exemption).

[150] Electronic Commerce Directive 2000/31/EC, art. 14(1)(a).

Ireland Ltd, the Northern Ireland Court of Appeal held that Facebook counted as an 'Information Society Service'. However, Morgan LCJ held that Facebook had breached a duty to promptly remove a page that was designed to persecute a former sex offender who had completed a prison sentence.[151] A group on Facebook named 'Keeping Our Kids Safe from Predators' posted the former sex offender's details, after he had served six years in prison. Comments on the page included saying that he should be burnt and driven out of his accommodation. Solicitors for the claimant wrote to Facebook on 15 November 2013. It was removed on 5 December, but no action was taken against the group (even though it was directly inciting criminal attacks). A picture was reposted on 23 December and not removed until 22 January 2014. The court accepted that while Facebook (ostensibly) was an information society service, there was still a breach of the Data Protection Act 1998, section 5, and the Electronic Commerce Directive 2000 did not provide any immunity. However, it also said that knowledge only arose when a solicitor wrote a letter to it highlighting the issues. It is not clear why Facebook, as well as YouTube or Twitter, should not simply be treated like any other TV enterprise, with the same responsibilities.

(5) Conclusion

Web and broadcast media law has had over two decades to engage with the Internet, but it was only with the disasters of Brexit, Trump and the rise of authoritarian politics that the law began to get serious. Ultimately, media matters for democracy; and so, with the massive influence the web may have, it should be regulated with standards as high as for TV, or higher. Fortunately, the most democratic web media sites, run by Wikimedia, show how user empowerment can drive better standards, and eliminate all the problems that Facebook, YouTube or Twitter have generated. The reluctance to adopt easy solutions to long-standing problems comes from the data- and ad-driven desire to extract profits from audiences, whatever the cost. Because these networks are global, public ownership is more complex than it has been for successful broadcasters like the BBC. However, there is no reason why, given the relatively low costs of servers, different countries could not fund independent, free server space to host international streaming and networks – ones that protect data, privacy and safety online, with few or no ads, and with viewer voice: in short, a truly social media.

[151] [2016] NICA 54.

18

Marketplaces

Contents

'If you seek economic growth, if you seek opportunity, if you seek social justice and human dignity', said George W. Bush as the economy collapsed in 2008, 'the free market system is the way to go.'[1] The problem is, the 'free market' is based (unlike its ideology) on binding public norms.[2] Markets result from many people interacting in the light of the law. Trust and good faith, for confidence in doing business, come from rule-based institutions, not some free-for-all.[3] One of these institutions is the physical and virtual space of a marketplace itself. Old markets for goods like Covent Garden, supermarkets like Tesco, and web markets like Amazon, eBay or Google Shopping, are all founded in law, if nothing other than property, contract and corporations. So are marketplaces for labour (an employment agency) or marketplaces for capital (e.g. London Stock Exchange). If there are more buyers and sellers, a marketplace's utility rises. A powerful middleman, it occupies the nexus of communication. Marketplace structure affects the 'right to work' and 'freedom to conduct a business', especially for small and medium enterprises, and it affects consumer protection.[4]

[1] G. W. Bush, White House Archive (13 November 2008).

[2] E. F. Cousins, *Pease and Chitty's Law of Markets and Fairs* (2012) 1, in law a 'free market' or 'franchise' means 'a market belonging entirely to the lord, free from the control of other persons'.

[3] H. Collins, *The Law of Contract* (2003) ch. 1, 13–14, 'there is no such thing as the market order . . . [but] considerable variety of regulatory strategies'. Also J. S. Mill, *Principles of Political Economy* (1848) Book V, ch. 11.

[4] UDHR 1948, art. 23 and ICESCR 1966, art. 6 (right to work); CFREU 2000, arts. 16 and 38 ('freedom to conduct a business' and 'consumer protection'). Further, Grundgesetz 1949, art. 12; ECHR, Prot. 1, art. 1.

The Internet created marketplaces of spectacular size and enrichment for their owners. Amazon, Google, eBay, LinkedIn, Tinder and iTunes are platforms to trade everything from clothes to second-hand goods, workers, sex, books and rock and roll. But there are three distinctive risks. First, the market owner may extract unfair charges for access, as it profits from a cut of each transaction, in money or data. Second, the market owner may also be a player which prefers itself. For instance, just as Tesco puts own-branded products on their shelves, Amazon takes data from successful traders, and releases identical products that it controls. Third, the marketplace may endorse reckless practices causing its own collapse, as well as exploiting traders and customers. A first option, preferred by Chicago theories of competition, is to say that the benefits of monopoly outweigh other costs.[5] This goes against experience that the accumulated power, and enrichment for one owner, is a threat to liberty itself. A second option is to replace all marketplaces with centrally planned direction of production. In Soviet Russia or Maoist China this was done, and it failed because the state was an unaccountable dictator, and without price signals it was harder to gauge what people wanted. It is true, however, that today's data can predict people's preferences more than ever before.[6] A third option is public regulation for certain marketplaces, including rights to access 'essential facilities', of fair and open dealing and strategic public ownership. This matters as more marketplaces gather data and shape preferences with algorithms and ads, profoundly affecting our economic autonomy.

(1) Historical Development

Marketplaces have been a foundation of enterprise, and a driving force of law, since recorded history began. In the Ancient Roman Republic, the first codified laws were the Twelve Tables, displayed in the marketplace (the 'forum') for everyone to follow.[7] The *Forum Magnum* was a public space, commissioned like other public works, and the Twelve Tables on display laid down rules on courts, theft, debt, family, property, enslavement, tort and public law. Many disputes were naturally created by virtue of the market itself.[8] Similarly, Plato's *Laws* recorded how wardens of the Athenian marketplace (the 'agora') would ensure 'the markets are orderly and that fair dealing is observed'.[9] Markets

[5] R. Posner (2017) YouTube at 5:04, 'who's concerned whether they have monopolies, right?' See Ch. 6(2)(a).

[6] C. Sunstein, *Choosing Not to Choose* (2015) and *Quain Lectures* (2014).

[7] Twelve Tables (*c.* 450 BC). The story is explained in Livy, *From the Founding of the City* (*c.* 20 BC) Book 3, §§34 and 57, trans. W. M. Roberts. M. Steinberg, 'The Twelve Tables and Their Origins: An Eighteenth-Century Debate' (1982) 43(3) *J History of Ideas* 379, on evolving understanding of its origins.

[8] Cf. Matt. 21:12–13, where Jesus turns traders out of the temple, accusing them of turning a 'house of prayer' into a 'den of thieves'.

[9] Plato, *The Laws* (*c.* 350 BC) Book VIII, trans. B. Jowett.

were places for business, trade and law but also a meeting point, and a centre for social life.

In medieval Europe, marketplaces were the centres that revived international trade by promoting 'the trust necessary for efficient exchange'.[10] The Five Fairs of Flanders and the Champagne fairs saw people come together for two or three weeks, usually six times a year, to trade exotic textiles, leathers, fur or spices that could not be grown or made at home.[11] Towns developed around these markets and fairs: simply having the right to hold a fair meant the possibility of real prosperity, and the opportunity for tax by the Crown. They were licensed by the monarchs. In England, King William I forbade markets and fairs except in cities, boroughs and castles, 'secure places where the customs of our kingdom and our common law and the dignities of our Crown ... cannot perish'.[12] The Stourbridge fair was granted a charter in 1199, becoming one of the largest in Europe, and a major reason for the dissidents from Oxford to set up a university at nearby Cambridge (see Ch. 8(1)). In the Great Fairs of England in the twelfth and thirteenth centuries, merchants traded from afar: for instance, a riot in Boston, Lincolnshire, in 1241 involved merchants from Winchester, York, London and Oxford.[13] Magna Carta itself said 'merchants shall have safe and secure exit from England, and entry to England, with the right to tarry there and to move about', and guaranteed the 'liberties of London' and other cities, boroughs and towns,[14] to regulate their trade. Many markets also sold people, especially farm labourers, hired in spring and autumn for the coming season. Marketplaces were therefore the objects of wage-fixing statutes.[15] Each market or fair had a 'court of piepowder',[16] which would swiftly deal with disputes, hand out fines or order people to be put in pillories. These only dealt with disputes, however, 'for matters of contracts, and for matters arising within the market and by the occasion of the market' – not, for example, general slander.[17]

[10] P. R. Milgrom, D. C. North and B. R. Weingast, 'The Role of Institutions in the Revival of Trade: The Law Merchant, Private Judges, and the Champagne Fairs' (1990) 2(1) *Economic and Politics* 1–23.

[11] H. Munro, 'The "New Institutional Economics" and the Changing Fortunes of Fairs in Medieval and Early Modern Europe: the Textile Trades, Warfare, and Transaction Costs' (2001) 88(1) *Vierteljahrschrift für Sozial- und Wirtschaftsgeschichte* 1, 5ff.

[12] B. Thorpe, *Ancient Laws and Institutes of England* (1840) 212, translated in Cousins, *Pease and Chitty's Law of Markets and Fairs*, 23.

[13] E. W. Moore, *The Fairs of Medieval England: An Introductory Study* (1985) 1.

[14] Magna Carta 1215, cll. 41 and 13, the latter still in force under Magna Carta 1297, cl. IX.

[15] Cf. Statute of Labourers 1351, referring to its wage suppression orders as applying 'within franchises as well as without', and the Statute of Artificers 1562 (5 Eliz. I, c. 4), stating it was lawful to continue labour markets or 'Petty-Sessions, otherwise called Statute-Sessions' where they had been held before.

[16] Piepowder, rather than market edibles, comes from the French *pieds poudrés* or 'dusty feet', referring either to travellers who might have dusty feet, or court members whose feet got muddy walking around the market.

[17] *Howel v Johns* (1599) Croke, Elizabeth 773, 78 ER 1004.

From the markets and fairs across Europe – the Hanseatic League and the Genoese and Venetians – developed the *lex mercatoria*, the common law of merchants. In 1765, Lord Mansfield declared that 'the law of merchants and the law of the land is the same',[18] and declared that 'by the law of merchants, all dealings must be fair and honest'.[19] While English case law on a requirement for fair prices is difficult to find,[20] price regulation was routinely written into statutes,[21] and in 1810 Lord Ellenborough declared that 'if for a particular purpose the public have a right to resort to [a person's] premises . . . and he have a monopoly . . . he must, as an equivalent, perform the duty attached to it on reasonable terms'.[22] There also developed the right to a business, that 'every person has of common right a liberty of coming into a publick market for the purpose of buying and selling', if they paid a toll to the market owner for a stall.[23] A standard incident of a market was monopoly, and preventing rival markets within 6⅔ miles,[24] but this was limited so that markets that did not take tolls could not be shut down.[25] Then again, setting up a stall even to sell biscuits and ginger beer could be stopped for obstructing a highway.[26] Modern human rights law similarly evolved, so as to recognise a right to trade, but under any conditions necessary for general welfare.[27] To authorise and delimit market monopolies, over the centuries dozens of Acts of Parliament established and regulated marketplaces, like the Smithfield meat market, the Borough Market in Southwark or the Sheffield

[18] *Pillans v Van Mierop* (1765) 3 Burr 1663, declaring that consideration was unnecessary, a decision sadly not followed. But also *Luke v Lyde* (1759) 97 Eng Rep 614, 618; (1759) 2 Burr 882, 887: law merchant 'is not the law of a particular country but the law of all nations'.

[19] *Pawson v Watson* (1778) 2 Cowp 786: 'as, by the law of merchants, all dealings must be fair and honest, fraud infects and vitiates every mercantile contract'. Also *Carter v Boehm* (1766) 3 Burr 1905, establishing good faith in insurance contracts. Also *Du Costa v Jones* (1778) 2 Cowp 729. Lord Mansfield aimed for this to be a general doctrine.

[20] C. Kennefick, 'The Contribution of Contemporary Mathematics to Contractual Fairness in Equity, 1751–1867' (2018) 39(3) *J L History* 307, 311 and contrast 314–16, also citing J. Gordley, *The Philosophical Origins of Modern Contract Doctrine* (1991) 150.

[21] Ordinance of the Staples 1353 (27 Edw. III, Stat. 2, c. 25), and Price of Victuals Act 1533 (25 Hen. VIII. c. 2): 'prices of such victuals [food] be many times enhanced and raised by the Greedy Covetousness and Appetites of the Owners . . . to the great damage and impoverishing of the King's subjects'.

[22] *Allnutt v Inglis* (1810) ER 359, 12 East 527, on use of a London Dock Company warehouse.

[23] *Mayor of Northampton v Ward* (1745) 2 Strange 1237, 93 ER 1155, per Lee CJ.

[24] Cousins, *Pease and Chitty's Law of Markets and Fairs*, 3.

[25] *R v Marsden* (1765) 3 Burr 1812. Sir Fletcher Norton objected to traders being in Wakefield every other Wednesday. Lord Mansfield held there were 'no marks of a fair or market; no toll claimed or taken by the lord of the soil'.

[26] *Simpson v Wells* (1872) LR 7 QB 214, per Blackburn J, rejecting a right by custom to continue a stall that had been there for over 50 years. Similarly, statute sessions were enabled by statute, not common law.

[27] In the USA, this results from the end of the *Lochner* era's protection of so-called 'freedom of contract' (see Ch. 1(4)), while human rights documents are typically qualified, e.g. CFREU, arts. 16 and 52(1). This important point was sadly overlooked in *Alemo-Herron v Parkwood Leisure Ltd* (2013) C-426/11.

market.[28] In the Markets and Fairs Clauses Act 1847, Parliament codified standard rules: setting the monopoly's geographical limit, primitive environmental regulations (i.e. no slaughter), payment of tolls only at the market's end and a power for the enforcement of bylaws.[29]

As well as small, physical marketplaces, the growth of corporate production created new markets of a different scale and nature, in goods, capital and labour. A Royal Exchange had been established by Queen Elizabeth I in 1571, though it initially only allowed trade in goods, such as alcohol or grain, not company shares, since stockbrokers were thought too rowdy.[30] So, the 'stock-jobbers' instead collected at Jonathan's Coffee House, on what is now Change Alley in the City, where brokers listed stocks and commodities for sale. This was where much of the trading that led to the South Sea Bubble took place, though after new companies were banned (see Ch. 1(2)), their work continued, and in 1773 they and 150 other brokers formed a 'Stock Exchange' with entrance fees for traders and a rule book. The essential problem of stock market bubbles was over-confidence in what was being done, leading to inflated prices, over-investment and then a bust. As the Industrial Revolution took off, the same patterns were evident across the whole economy. With the textile looms, the steam engine, the ever-quicker flow of information by telegraph and the expansion of production, early 'capitalism' repeatedly saw overproduction and investment, a glut of goods and capital, and then a bust as prices fell. Every four to twelve years, the annual rate of growth went negative,[31] until the post-World War Two shifts in economic theory. These shifts were compelled by the Wall Street Crash and Great Depression, which further led to creation of modern securities law, particularly for the New York Stock Exchange (see Ch. 4(2)). It had been believed that a 'business cycle',[32] and even a long term 'wave' of economic rise and decline,[33] was just a fact of life, like some mystic law, beyond the real laws that people create. Ignoring securities regulation, labour rights, banking law and investment policy, the cycles of recession and job destruction were 'market forces' for which nobody seemed responsible.[34]

The effect on labour was plainly severe, particularly as people in city factories or down in the mines were hired day to day, and discarded when not

[28] E.g. Smithfield Market, etc. Act 1708 (c. 6), Southwark Market Act 1755 (c. 9) and Sheffield Market Place Act 1784 (c. 5).

[29] Markets and Fair Clauses Act 1847, ss. 13 (offence for selling in market limits, unless a shop, or authorised by an Act), 18–19 (slaughter), 31 (tolls), 43 (bylaws).

[30] See generally A. Saunders, *Royal Exchange* (1997).

[31] Bank of England, 'The UK Recession in Context – What Do Three Centuries of Data Tell Us?' (2010) Data Annex.

[32] One of the last of these is A. F. Burns and W. C. Mitchell, *Measuring Business Cycles* (1946).

[33] N. Kondratiev, *The Major Economic Cycles* (1925) suggesting three main waves were 1790–1849 (peak in 1815), 1850–96 (peak in 1873) and 1896 to the time of his book. Kondratiev was murdered by Stalin in 1938.

[34] See also J. Schumpeter, *The Theory of Economic Development: An Inquiry into Profits, Capital, Credit, Interest, and the Business Cycle* (1934).

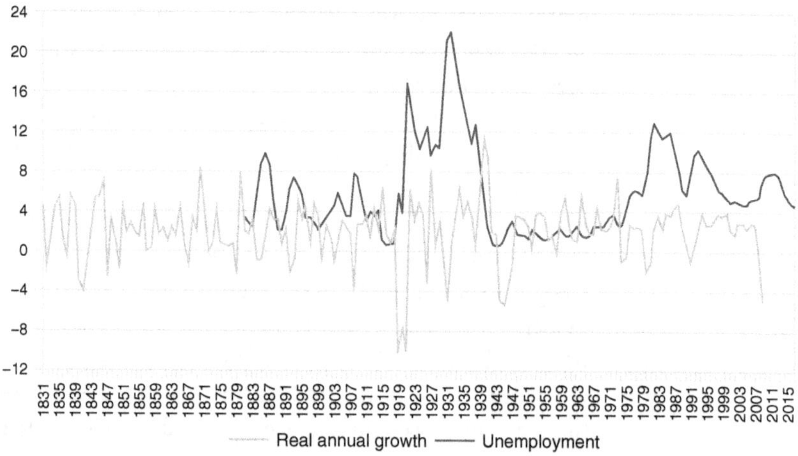

Figure 18.1 UK real annual growth and unemployment, 1831-2017
Sources: Bank of England and ONS

needed. Labour Exchanges developed to distribute work, and private employment agencies or gangmasters flourished, preying on the misery of the itinerant labourer. In the early twentieth century, the labour movement tried to ban private employment agencies,[35] and the first International Labour Organization (ILO) recommendation was for the replacement of these labour markets with public employment agencies,[36] arguing that 'labour is not a commodity' to be traded on a marketplace like any other. After the Russian Revolution, Lenin's Soviet Union went far further, attempting complete replacement of every market: for goods and capital, with labour becoming an obligation to society, not any employer. Lenin also banned free unions, subordinating them to the Communist Party.[37] In theory, the transition to communism was meant to lead to a 'withering away of the bourgeois form of law as such'.[38] The New Economic Policy, however, as Lenin passed on, acknowledged that some forms of property, contract and enterprise were still going to be necessary,[39] even as state control of society became ever more

[35] *Adams v Tanner*, 244 US 590 (1917) holding this was unconstitutional, Brandeis J dissenting.

[36] ILO Unemployment Recommendation 1919 (No. 1) art. 1 and Unemployment Convention 1919 (c. 2).

[37] V. I. Lenin, *The Role and Functions of the Trade Unions Under the New Economic Policy* (12 January 1922): 'it is absolutely essential that all authority in the factories should be concentrated in the hands of the management. The factory management . . . must have authority independently to fix and pay out wages . . . The trade unions must collaborate closely and constantly with the government, all the political and economic activities of which are guided by the class-conscious vanguard of the working class – the Communist Party.'

[38] Cf. E. Pashukanis, *The General Theory of Law and Marxism* (1924) 63; J. Hamilton and S. Deakin, 'Russia's Legal Transitions: Marxist Theory, Neoclassical Economics and the Rule of Law' (2015) 7 *Hague J Rule of Law* 283.

[39] Civil Code 1922, art. 4, protecting private rights and obligations 'for the purpose of the development of the productive forces of society'; and art. 5, citizens 'to choose any occupation

sinister and contradictory.[40] Stalin's central planning, administered by terrified bureaucrats, tried to project all needs and production for the year, but despite huge initial development, failed to give people incentives, except nationalism and terror, to work.

Back in the West, the growth of mass corporations led to mass consumption, and a new kind of consumer culture.[41] Department stores and supermarkets arose to replace the public spaces with every want under one roof, and one owner, and creating new riches for that person.[42] US competition law recognised the position of the consumer and their interest in fair treatment.[43] After World War Two, consumer culture became an accepted part of American and European life, and the competition among the supermarkets left a highly concentrated sector, with four or five corporations dominating in each country.[44] Meanwhile, the traditional marketplaces were struggling in competition but became remarkably innovative in their governance. For example, the Covent Garden Market Act 1961 required that the marketplace was run by an authority, whose management committee would be part elected by the embattled traders, and part by their suppliers.[45] On the other hand, as department stores grew, ever more pressure was put upon independent sellers.[46]

In the early twenty-first century, the Internet changed markets again, as more and more came online. The biggest driver was the American corporation, Amazon Inc., whose strategy was to monopolise all infrastructure of the modern economy.[47] It already held 46 per cent of e-commerce in the USA in 2017. In 2005 it also launched a labour exchange called Amazon Mechanical Turk, in 2017 it bought the Whole Foods supermarket, and in 2019 it bought a stake in Deliveroo, although despite its unparalleled global expansion only

and profession not prohibited by law, to acquire and alienate property within the limitations established by law, to enter into legal transactions and to incur obligations, and to organise industrial and commercial activities and protecting hired labour'.

40 J. Stalin, Speech to the Sixteenth Party Congress (1930): 'We are for the withering away of the state, and at the same time, we are for the strengthening of the dictatorship of the proletariat. . . .' Cf. Trotsky (1937) writing in exile, the state had not withered away but had 'grown into a hitherto unheard of apparatus of compulsion' (M. Head, *Evgeny Pashukanis: A Critical Reappraisal* (2008) 109).

41 T. Veblen, *The Theory of the Leisure Class* (1899).

42 E.g. Harry Gordon Selfridge establishing Selfridges in 1910 in London, and Kroger's and its employee Michael J. Cullen opening a supermarket in 1930 in Queen's, New York City.

43 Robinson-Patman Act of 1936, 15 USC, §13(f): it is unlawful 'in the course of such commerce, knowingly to induce or receive a discrimination in price which is prohibited by this section'.

44 In the UK, the big 4 are Tesco, Sainsbury, Asda (Walmart) and Morrisons. In the USA, Walmart, Kroger's, Safeway (Albertson's) and Ahold Delhaize. In Germany, Edeka, Aldi and Lidl.

45 Covent Garden Market Act 1961, ss. 1, 33 and Sch. 4.

46 In Sidi Bouzid, Tunisia, in 2010, the most extreme example was that a street vendor, Mohamed Bouazizi, had been for years harassed by local officials demanding permits for selling his goods, and arbitrarily confiscating his goods. Unable to keep going, he set himself on fire, an act which set off a chain of consequences leading to widespread protests of the 'Arab Spring' that brought down the Tunisian and other governments.

47 L. M. Khan, 'Amazon's Antitrust Paradox' (2017) 126 *Yale LJ* 710, 797.

Amazon Web Services had ever made a profit.[48] Faced with this predator, the High Street and independent traders have declined, and suffered a further massive blow from closures during Covid-19.

(2) Finance

Modern marketplaces, and particularly internet platforms, are mainly private enterprises, but it is highly doubtful that their dominance can be explained simply by being 'a lot more efficient', as distinct from economies of scale, at least with a straight face.[49] Four main sources of finance, other than equity and debt, are (a) occupying a network monopoly; (b) data exploitation, without true consent, from competitors or consumers; (c) not paying the cost of externalities, particularly waste; and (d) subsidies from government, such as web infrastructure, agricultural subsidies or non-enforcement of labour standards and tax.

(a) Network Monopoly

The first main finance source for marketplaces is occupying a network monopoly. Just as it made more sense for telecoms to use one network providing a universal service (see Ch. 16),[50] there is low incentive to have multiple marketplaces within the geographical limits that people are willing to travel, and the competitors that exist may focus on different income groups.[51] Online, there are no geographical limits.[52] If any marketplace has a good idea in bringing together buyers and sellers, competitors will usually adopt it rapidly. In web platforms, in the early stages of technical development, a competition takes place to be the market platform of choice, but then the winner takes nearly all. As it gets data on traders and consumers (below), the monopoly may forestall other market entrants.

48 Khan, 'Amazon's Antitrust Paradox', 748.

49 For a robust attempt at this, see D. S. Evans and R. Schmalensee, 'Network Effects: March to the Evidence, Not to the Slogans', *Antitrust Chronicle* (15 September 2017) 7, saying: 'The "winner" could just be a lot more efficient or innovative than other firms.' They then call for evidence that this is not the case (rather than giving evidence, other than 'winning', that 'winners' are efficient) and decline any discussion that web marketplaces habitually (1) make losses, (2) engage in predatory pricing, (3) exclude rivals and so on.

50 J. Rohlfs, 'A Theory of Interdependent Demand for a Telecommunications Service' (1974) 5(1) *Bell J Economics* 16: 'The utility that a subscriber derives from a communications service increases as others join the system. This is a classic case of external economies in consumption.'

51 E.g. J. Shannon, 'Beyond the Supermarket Solution: Linking Food Deserts, Neighborhood Context, and Everyday Mobility' (2016) 106 *Annals of the American Association of Geographers* 186; M. Ver Ploeg et al., 'Access to Affordable and Nutritious Food: Updated Estimates of Distance to Supermarkets Using 2010 Data', US Department of Agriculture Economic Research Report No. 143 (2012): 1.8% of people live further than 1 mile from a supermarket and have no vehicle, and 50% have fewer than 3 supermarkets within 2 miles.

52 In China, online web markets are, however, segregated. Alibaba, Tencent or Didi have dominated, due to the Chinese government policy favouring its own national champions.

Marketplaces could also become players in their own markets. Unlike Covent Garden, but like Tesco or Amazon, the marketplace could begin to sell its own products, or products it sources itself alongside others. 'Tesco finest' bread is sold next to Warburtons bread. Amazon Kindle is sold next to other e-book readers.[53] If the marketplace vertically integrates, it can project its monopoly into all production. It does not need to own the wheat farms or the e-book manufacturers as subsidiaries, or even stamp its brand, so long as it can extract the desired share of revenue through contract. Bargaining power determines the boundaries of the firm, but the boundaries of a firm do not limit the scope of control over other suppliers.[54] With a strong or dominant bargaining position, the marketplace-player can reduce the prices paid to anyone down the supply chain, like the wheat farmer. If it is a labour platform, it can reduce wages it pays to any worker, to increase its profit.

With the growth of the Internet, an economic theory of 'two-sided markets', as distinct from 'one-sided markets', developed.[55] On this view, a one-sided market can bring different groups together over a 'platform'. A newspaper, Facebook or Google search enables ads, but readers, users and searchers do not typically want to connect to advertisers. By contrast, in a two-sided market both sides want to connect: like the buyers and sellers in Covent Garden, on Amazon or Google Shopping. The platform reduces transaction costs.[56] In the theory of Rochet and Tirole, two-sided markets also risk being inefficient as the platform prevents buyers and sellers bargaining with one another in a way that could limit externalities, and the platform regulates prices or terms in a way that precludes efficient exchange. Other economists refuse to accept that even these problems exist.[57] The limit in this framework is that it does not recognise the full relevance of power.[58] Rochet and Tirole admit a firm (i.e. a company or an employment relation) is a two-sided market if labour and capital markets

[53] For fun, search 'ebook reader' on Amazon, but guess how many non-Amazon products you will find first.

[54] An alternative theory, without evidence, is that transaction costs exclusively determine the size of the firm: R. Coase, 'The Nature of the Firm' (1937) 4(16) *Economica* 386. Coase refused to recognise the role of bargaining power in affecting efficiency. The importance of transactions was first highlighted by J. R. Commons, 'Institutional Economics' (1931) 21 *Am Economic Rev* 648, who understood power.

[55] J. Rochet and J. Tirole, 'Two-Sided Markets: A Progress Report' (2006) 37(3) *RAND J Economics* 645 at part 3.2. See also an earlier version, 'Two-Sided Markets: An Overview', Working Paper (2004). I am very grateful to Savas Manoussakis for discussion of two-sided markets.

[56] NB: A platform could also be both one- and two-sided. For instance, YouTube is one-sided when it enables ads, but two-sided when it connects vloggers and viewers.

[57] E.g. D. S. Evans and R. Schmalensee, *Matchmakers, The New Economics of Multisided Platforms* (2016); D. S. Evans and R. Schmalensee, 'The Industrial Organisation of Markets with Two-Sided Platforms' (2007) 3(1) *Competition Policy Int'l* 151.

[58] See also S. Zuboff, *The Age of Surveillance Capitalism* (2019) ch. 2. Rochet and Tirole start with the 'Coase theorem'; see R. Coase, 'The Problem of Social Cost' (1960) 3 *JL & Economics* 1. As Ch. 2(2)(c) and (f) explain, Coase refused to recognise the relevance of bargaining power in undermining efficient exchange, even in his hypothetical transaction-cost-free world. For modern approaches, and acceptance of the relevance of bargaining power, see T. Piketty,

are not perfectly competitive,[59] but they assert these markets usually are competitive.[60] This cannot be accepted: labour and capital markets systematically fail without regulation for good faith, fairness and positive rights (see Chs. 3–5). Unequal bargaining power, from unequal property ownership, distorts the distribution of benefits in any exchange. Because fairness affects the motivation to work, power affects productive efficiency (see Ch. 2(2)(f)). It follows that marketplace power, and network monopoly in the extreme, becomes an inefficient finance source, from other people's money, labour and trade.

(b) Data and Information Asymmetry

Marketplaces also take other people's data, and its extraction is a second finance source. First, data can be used to understand and replicate rival products. For instance, a marketplace that sees successful sales in a brand of bread or e-book reader will naturally want to replicate that product. But unlike a normal competitor, the marketplace has asymmetric information and may take comprehensive data from the rival trader on sales volumes, prices or time of purchase, whenever it acts as the sales agent and handles payment.[61] It potentially knows more than the rival producers themselves. Brands that remain are typically capable of establishing an identity and consumer loyalty, despite the marketplace's efforts. This, however, may be increasingly difficult if the intermediary becomes an essential facility, to which buyers find no alternative. The information asymmetry also amplifies the marketplace's bargaining power in setting what margins it demands for resale: it knows the limits of what traders can afford.

Second, data may be extracted about consumer preferences for targeted advertising, discussed in Chapter 16, or in the 'recommended' products of online marketplaces. According to Shoshana Zuboff, this becomes the 'behavioural surplus' and 'vital raw materials derived from users' nonmarket online behavior'.[62] By analysing what other products customers buy, a marketplace can build consumer profiles for better targeting. For instance, it may know *Guardian* readers tend to buy muesli, and so it may put the two on close shelves.[63] Loyalty cards, bank card payments or online accounts ensure

Capital in the Twenty-First Century (2014) ch. 6, 212 (capital), ch. 9, 312 (labour) and 331 (executives).

59 E.g. like Covent Garden connects sellers to buyers, a firm connects workers' labour and capital to consumers.

60 Rochet and Tirole, 'Two-Sided Markets: A Progress Report', 656.

61 Khan, 'Amazon's Antitrust Paradox', 780–3, quoting G. Bensinger, 'Competing with Amazon on Amazon', *Wall Street Journal* (27 June 2012), writing of Amazon 'as a vast laboratory to spot new products to sell, test sales of potential new goods, and exert more control over pricing'.

62 Zuboff, *The Age of Surveillance Capitalism*, ch. 2.

63 I am grateful to a friend who worked at a supermarket in the loyalty card department for this anecdote.

individuals can be tracked even more. Online, searches can be logged, and so can movements of a mouse or cursor over a screen.[64] This data on consumer preferences becomes a powerful barrier to entry against rivals who cannot accumulate the same, and tends to entrench the network monopoly.[65] The data-driven acquisitions of big tech show the importance they place on it, such as Facebook's acquisition of WhatsApp (see Ch. 6(2)(a)). The race for data knows no limits, as 'Alexa', 'Siri' and 'Google Assistant' spy inside ever more homes, and Amazon's 'Ring' can even open the door.[66] Of course, consumer preference predictions are likely to work more for bread or other routine purchases than for books or other goods where preferences are changing.[67] But ads and product recommendations may sustain demand, against people's free will. For instance, a survey of American CEOs in the 1990s found that 85 per cent believed their ads persuaded people to buy things they did not need, and 51 per cent believed ads 'persuaded people to buy things *they didn't actually want*'.[68]

(c) Externalities and Waste

A third source of finance is not paying for externalities and, for marketplaces, that especially means the cost of waste. This includes the market crashes like the South Sea Bubble and Wall Street crash. In addition, UK supermarkets probably create most household waste, particularly plastic, although Covid-19 means e-commerce generates more, and Amazon alone is becoming the single biggest waster.[69] In 2018, the volume of UK plastic packaging rose to 903,000 tonnes, and an estimated two-thirds cannot be recycled.[70] Furthermore, supermarkets throw away thousands of tonnes of food, while households throw away 4.5 million tonnes of food,[71] encouraged by supermarkets who profit from over-purchasing or misleading 'best before' dates. Local authorities pay for recycling and waste disposal, and raise revenue from council tax or business

[64] E.g. *Letter from Facebook Inc. to the U.S. Senate Committee on the Judiciary* (8 June 2018) 86.

[65] M. Stucke and A. Grunes, *Big Data and Competition Policy* (2016) ch. 1, on Myths 4 and 5.

[66] D. Lynskey, '"Alexa, Are You Invading My Privacy?"', *The Guardian* (9 October 2019), in 1 in 5 US homes. C. Thorbecke, 'Senator Blasts Amazon's Ring Doorbell as an "Open Door for Privacy and Civil Liberty Violations"', *ABC News* (20 November 2019). The customer is said to control whether the door can be opened through an app, but obviously if this is possible through an app, an Amazon worker can do the same.

[67] Sunstein, *Choosing Not to Choose*, ch. 7, 182–3, on predictive shopping. This followed the Quain Lectures (2014) at UCL.

[68] Quoted in J. Hickel, *Less Is More* (2020) ch. 5.

[69] Oceana, 'Amazon's Plastic Problem Revealed', Report (15 December 2020) 13–14, states global e-commerce waste is 942,000 tonnes a year, and Amazon creates 210,000 tonnes. Amazon claimed it creates 60,000 tonnes: D. Vetter, *Forbes* (15 December 2020). Either way, Amazon is not paying for the waste and pollution it creates.

[70] Environmental Investigation Agency and Greenpeace, 'Checking Out on Plastics II: Breakthroughs and Backtracking from Supermarkets', Report (28 November 2019) 4.

[71] R. Smithers, 'UK Households Waste 4.5m Tonnes of Food Each Year', *The Guardian* (24 January 2020).

rates, without any extra charge on the marketplaces that create the waste. The marketing of 'recycling' itself also creates an illusion that product packaging will in fact be recycled, when it is not, a deliberate strategy of waste producers to place responsibility on someone else.[72] In 2009 UK local authorities spent an average of 26 per cent of their council tax revenue on waste disposal.[73] In 2014, total council waste spending was £2.3 billion.[74] This is therefore a subsidy to marketplaces that create waste.

Since 1996, there has been a landfill tax, but this is imposed on the 'landfill site operator', which in turn charges councils or businesses that directly send waste there.[75] It does not target businesses that create waste, and so it is ineffective in reducing waste. While households account for 87 per cent of municipal waste, and the recycling rate in 2019 was merely 45.5 per cent,[76] business rates of recycling tend to be even lower, suggesting this is not a problem of individual choices, but institutional decisions and regulation. Amazon is estimated to have shipped 5 billion parcels worldwide in 2018, while in the USA total parcels shipped were 165 billion, enough to cut down a billion trees.[77] When other people pay for marketplace waste, and without tax on waste creators, proportionate to the cost of recycling and disposal, marketplaces have no incentive to reduce waste.

(d) Government Subsidies

A fourth category of marketplace finance is fiscal subsidies from government. There are three main types. First, as Chapter 13(2) explained the EU Common Agricultural Policy or the UK Agriculture Act 2020 sustain farming incomes. However, because of their bargaining power, supermarkets, or online marketplaces selling food, appropriate a large share of these subsidies. Without subsidies, supermarkets would have to pay more to farmers. It follows that the economic effect of agricultural subsidies is partly or predominantly to fund supermarkets, depending on the relative bargaining power in each market.

Second, Chapter 16(2) explained how government funds internet infrastructure with taxes, and without this support telecommunication companies would not be profitable. The same holds true for internet marketplaces, like Amazon or Google Shopping. Without the government paying for the Internet, to get people online, their businesses would not exist.

72 See J. Oliver, 'Plastic', Last Week Tonight (21 March 2021) www.hbo.com/last-week-tonight-with-john-oliver/season-8/6-march-21-2021-plastics, showing an old recycling ad.

73 Data Blog, 'How Much Does Your Council Spend on Waste Disposal?', *The Guardian* (4 October 2009).

74 R. Nierynck, 'Council Waste Spending Topped £2.3 Billion in 2013/14', *LetsRecycle.com* (15 August 2016).

75 Finance Act 1996, s. 41(1) and Landfill Tax (Scotland) Act 2014, s. 16.

76 Defra, 'Statistics on Waste Managed by Local Authorities in England in 2019/20', ONS (3 March 2021).

77 A. Peters, 'Can Online Retail Solve Its Packaging Problem?', *Fast Company* (20 April 2018).

Table 18.1 UK supermarkets corporation tax, rates, profits and revenue, 2020; market share, 2018[i]

	Company	2020 tax, rates	2020 profit	2020 revenue	Tax as % of revenue	Market %
1	Tesco	£1,056m	£1,315m	£64,800m	1.6%	27.1%
2	Sainsbury	£553m	£586m	£32,394m	1.7%	14.5%
3	Asda	£435m	£800m	£23,000m	1.8%	13.7%
4	Morrisons	£361m	£408m	£17,500m	2.06%	9.8%

[i] The numbers in this table may vary in reality, given the differences or weaknesses of disclosure. Only corporation tax and business rates are included. For Asda, N. Craven, *ThisIsMoney* (3 October 2020). Business rates, J. Davey, *Reuters* (3 December 2020). Market share data, Environmental Investigation Agency and Greenpeace, 'Checking Out on Plastics II', 7. Further market share statistics are Aldi 8.7%, Lidl 5.6%, Co-op 5.3%, Waitrose 4.2%, M&S 3.3% and Iceland 2.2%.

Third, as Table 16.3 set out, it is clear that online marketplaces do not pay taxes in the UK proportionate to their revenue. This non-enforcement of taxes is therefore a third source of finance. In 2020, Amazon appears to have paid £14.46 million in corporation tax on £13,370 million UK revenue (or 0.001 per cent),[78] while supermarkets pay a relatively higher but absolutely low sum in business rates and tax (see Table 18.1).

The top four supermarkets in 2018 controlled 65.1 per cent of market share. The 2 per cent 'digital services tax' on UK revenues for a 'social media service, search engine or online marketplace' (i.e. Facebook, Google and Amazon, or any competitor should that ever transpire) would appear to make up some difference,[79] but still leave tax rates very low. Non-enforcement of privacy and labour rights may also be added to the list of government subsidies.

(3) Governance

Today's marketplace governance is mixed between the general rules of company and competition law, for general sales of goods and specific regulation for labour and capital. Beyond the remaining historical Acts for marketplaces, there is not yet specific regulation of (a) most markets and supermarkets or (b) internet marketplaces, despite their public functions and monopoly positions. In stark contrast, there is well-understood regulation of (c) employment agencies and (d) stock exchanges. Each is taken in turn.

[78] See the revenue figure from the AboutAmazon blog (8 September 2020), but also the corporation tax figure reported by S. Butler, 'Amazon UK Pays 3% More in Tax Despite 35% Rise in Profits', *The Guardian* (8 September 2020), since Amazon misleadingly counts its 'direct taxes' as including employer's NICs. These reflect employees' pay for their work.

[79] Finance Act 2020, ss. 43 and 47 (over £500m global, £25m UK sales). Cf. M. Marriage, *Financial Times* (30 October 2018).

(a) Markets and Supermarkets

As explained at Chapter 16(1) the most developed example of marketplace regulation, the Covent Garden Act 1961, enabled participation by traders in the marketplace's governance. An authority responsible for managing the marketplace was appointed by the Secretary of State. It was bound to consult with an elected management committee, which had seven members representing people with market stalls, and seven representing suppliers.[80] This supply-chain representation has not yet been extended to supermarkets or online marketplaces.

The constitutions of the four largest supermarkets (see Table 18.1) show considerable variety. The constitutions of Tesco plc, J. Sainsbury plc and Morrisons plc, are written in accordance with the Companies Act 2006. They are publicly traded companies, and their governance is monopolised by shareholders. Similar shareholders have major stakes in each.[81] Despite each relying on huge workforces, supermarket employees have no right to vote for representatives on their company boards (see Ch. 5(3)(a)). Two of the top five UK supermarkets are subsidiaries. Asda Stores Ltd is a wholly owned subsidiary of the US corporation Walmart Inc. One of the world's largest corporations by revenue, and number of employees, Walmart is incorporated in Delaware.[82] Although a publicly traded company, the Walton family collectively owns around 50 per cent of its shares;[83] however, in 2020 they sold Asda to EG Group. Aldi Stores Ltd is a wholly owned subsidiary of the Aldi group of companies, incorporated in Germany. Aldi's corporate structure was designed to evade co-determination duties, to extend both work councils and representation on boards for employees.[84] It is very unclear why there has not been better enforcement, either by government or unions.[85]

The only significant public regulation affecting supermarket governance is local planning law. Although it could impose conditions material to its development plan,[86] council planning permission has not yet set a goal of requiring community, customer, or employee voice within the supermarket. It focuses on the simple decision about whether supermarkets may be built or not. Often

80 Covent Garden Market Act 1961, ss. 1, 33 and Sch. 4.

81 Among major shareholders in 2020: (1) Tesco: BlackRock 6.6%, Schroders 4.9%, Norges 3.9%; (2) Sainsbury: Qatar Holdings LLC 21.9%, BlackRock 5%; (3) Morrisons: Silchester 12%, Schroders 9.6%, and various others before BlackRock 2.49%. Thus, BlackRock held stakes in all competitors.

82 See Walmart Inc., Form 10-K (2019).

83 N. L. Pesce, 'The Walton Family Gets $100 Million Richer Every Single Day', *MarketWatch* (17 August 2019).

84 M. Wortmann, 'Aldi and the German Model: Structural Change in German Grocery Retailing and the Success of Grocery Discounters' (2004) 8(4) *Competition and Change* 425, 435.

85 This may be changing, e.g. 'ver.di Demands Aldi North Stops Its Massive Campaign against Democratically Elected Work Councils', ver.di Press Release (20 September 2019).

86 Town and Country Planning Act (TCPA) 1990, ss. 70 and 106; Planning and Compulsory Purchase Act 2004, s. 38.

a supermarket's presence attracts further business and jobs,[87] although it may also damage the prosperity of a High Street and independent market traders. Local authorities typically require, in return for planning permission, that supermarkets give money to fund new infrastructure, such as roads.[88] This should be done considering the relevant development plan for the region, objectively interpreted.[89] Councillors can override planning officer recommendations, if fund offers are fairly related to the development.[90] This power generated £4 billion a year for local authorities in 2008.[91] Councils may also use compulsory purchase orders to enable the building of supermarkets,[92] like any other structure. If the beneficiary is a private corporation, the Supreme Court has warned that because this takes private property rights to 'produce large profits for powerful business interests', the 'courts rightly regard [such orders] as particularly sensitive'.[93] A 'real (rather than a fanciful or remote) connection must be shown between any off-site benefits' (such as funding a new road or hospital) 'and the proposed redevelopment'.[94] Planning powers could be used considerably more – for instance, to pay for waste or promote health.

(b) Internet Marketplaces

Internet marketplaces have even fewer legal duties than physical marketplaces, although this could change as (i) Amazon, (ii) Google Shopping and (iii) eBay attract ever more scandals.

(i) Amazon

Amazon is the dominant internet marketplace, and by 2017 it controlled over '46% of all e-commerce in the United States',[95] and over 30% of the UK e-commerce market.[96] As Chapter 16(3)(e) explained, its constitution is based on 'one share, one vote', yet it is dominated by the co-founder Jeff Bezos, who has become the world's most enriched man. Amazon failed to make a profit until 2016 as its cloud service, AWS, grew. Its goal was to favour

[87] See *Co-operative Insurance Society Ltd v Argyll Stores (Holdings) Ltd* [1997] UKHL 17, refusing an order for specific performance to keep a supermarket open within a department store.
[88] *Tesco Stores Ltd v Secretary of State for the Environment* [1995] UKHL 22.
[89] *Tesco Stores Ltd v Dundee City Council* [2012] UKSC 13.
[90] E.g. *R (Tesco Stores Ltd) v Forest of Dean DC* [2015] EWCA Civ 800 on TCPA 1990, s. 106 agreements.
[91] Department for Communities and Local Government, *Valuing Planning Obligations in England: Update Study for 2005–6* (2008) ch. 4, while the 2003/4 estimate was 'about £1.9 bn' (May 2006), ibid.
[92] TCPA 1990, s. 226.
[93] *R (Sainsbury's Supermarkets Ltd) v Wolverhampton CC* [2010] UKSC 20, [81].
[94] [2010] UKSC 20, [84]. [95] Khan, 'Amazon's Antitrust Paradox', 755.
[96] 'Amazon and eBay account for 40% of UK ecommerce', *Ecommerce News* (11 December 2019).

monopolisation (or 'market leadership') over profit.[97] It had built that growth through predatory pricing against competitors,[98] and by paying its workforce at or below minimum wage.[99] It had 500,000 workers in 2020 in the USA, and at least 798,000 worldwide.[100] Amazon is vertically integrated, so that as well as operating a website, it has thousands of warehouses and delivery centres. These have not yet attracted the attention of planning demands,[101] despite the well-documented abuse of labour rights and the depressing effect on regional wages that Amazon has: according to one study, Amazon cut local wages by 30 per - cent.[102] Amazon has also refused to recognise its responsibility for consumer rights, including product safety.[103] The consequences – first felt by local bookshops, and then whole High Streets that have struggled to survive – are aimed to be rolled out across the whole economy. Amazon's goal is to become the 'essential infrastructure across the internet economy'.[104]

As well as using predatory pricing to secure its network monopoly, Amazon has entrenched its dominance by taking information from other traders that use its online marketplace.[105] In 2018, the European Commission began investigating Amazon's use of data from other traders: the year before half the items sold on Amazon came from third-parties.[106] In July 2019, the European Commission formally announced an investigation against Amazon for abuse of a dominant position, and unlawful collusion. First, this concerned Amazon's collection of trader data and its use to benefit its retail business. Second, it was alleged that Amazon was unfairly advantaging chosen traders with the use of its 'Buy Box'.[107] The same month, an Amazon representative told the US House of Representatives: 'We do not use any seller data

[97] Khan, 'Amazon's Antitrust Paradox', 748–54.

[98] Khan, 'Amazon's Antitrust Paradox', 752: 'Amazon's strategy has enabled it to use predatory pricing tactics without triggering the scrutiny of predatory pricing laws' because, in US law, a claimant must prove that losses can be recouped, and this is nearly impossible.

[99] Cf. E. Ongweso, 'Why Amazon Is Flooding the Country with $15 Minimum Wage Ads', *Vice* (25 Feb 2021).

[100] AP, 'Amazon's U.S. Workforce Surpasses 500,000', *Los Angeles Times* (31 January 2020) and Statista (2020).

[101] Cf. *M7 Real Estate Investments Partners Vi Industrial Propco Ltd v Amazon UK Services Ltd* [2019] CSOH 73, enforcing a notice to quit by a landlord against Amazon on its warehouse in Gourock, Scotland. The landlord wanted more money: R. Steele, '400 Jobs Secured as Amazon Sign New Lease to Stay in Gourock', *Greenock Telegraph* (6 November 2019).

[102] 'What Amazon Does to Wages', *Economist* (20 January 2018). The building of an Amazon distribution centre led warehouse workers' annual earnings to fall from $47,000 to $32,000 in Lexington County, South Carolina.

[103] J. Espinoza, 'Amazon and eBay Should Be Liable for Faulty Goods, Says EU Group', *Financial Times* (5 May 2020), explaining a test of 250 products from Amazon, AliExpress, eBay and Wish showing two-thirds failed EU safety law. It would seem that Amazon or eBay are liable under the Product Liability Directive 85/374/EEC or the Consumer Protection Act 1987, which is strict and applies throughout the distribution chain.

[104] Khan, 'Amazon's Antitrust Paradox', 797. [105] Khan, 'Amazon's Antitrust Paradox', 755.

[106] R. Toplensky, 'EU Opens Probe into Amazon Use of Data about Merchants', *Financial Times* (19 September 2018).

[107] *Amazon Marketplace* (17 July 2019) Case 40462 (Press Release).

to compete with them' or 'use their individual data when we're making decisions to launch private brands'.[108] But in April 2020 Amazon's use of trader data was confirmed by press reports,[109] prompting the US House to threaten a subpoena against Bezos to testify.

(ii) Google Shopping

Although Amazon has dominated so far, Google Shopping has aimed to move into the same market. Chapter 16(3) explained that Google is owned by Alphabet Inc., and its constitution enables multiple voting shares. This means its governance is dominated by its two founders, Larry Page and Sergey Brin. In 2017, the EU Commission fined Google €2.4 billion for abuse of a dominant position. First, the Commission stated Google had given its own shopping comparison service an advantage over others in the results of Google search. The top result in Google search attracted 35 per cent of clicks, and the top ten got 95 per cent of clicks. This change led to a forty-five-fold increase in traffic for Google Shopping in the UK, thirty-five-fold in Germany and nineteen-fold in France.[110] It then transpired that Google was 'encouraging advertising agencies to create price comparison sites, which it presents in the Google Shopping box' to convey a fraudulent impression of more competition.[111] Unsurprisingly, in February 2020, Google appealed the fines.[112]

(iii) eBay

The third major online marketplace, largely known for second-hand auctions, is eBay. It held 9.8 per cent of the UK e-commerce market in 2019.[113] It is incorporated in Delaware,[114] and mainly owned and controlled by Pierre Omidyar. In 2011, the Court of Justice of the EU held that it was an information society service,[115] suggesting that Amazon and Google Shopping might similarly be regarded. It has not yet faced significant challenges for competition law violation.

[108] D. Lee, 'House Panel Calls Bezos to Testify on Amazon Data Use', *Financial Times* (1 May 2020).

[109] D. Mattioli, 'Amazon Scooped Up Data From Its Own Sellers to Launch Competing Products', *Wall Street Journal* (23 April 2020).

[110] *Google Shopping* (27 June 2017) Case 39740.

[111] R. Manthorpe, 'Google "Trying to Circumvent EU Ruling" with Price Comparison Sites Run by Ad Agencies', *Sky News* (8 October 2018).

[112] J. Espinoza, 'Google Stands Firm in Its Appeal against €2.4bn Shopping Fine', *Financial Times* (12 February 2020).

[113] 'Amazon and eBay Account for 40% of UK Ecommerce', *Ecommerce News* (11 December 2019).

[114] eBay Inc., Certificate of Incorporation (2012).

[115] *L'Oréal SA v eBay International AG* (2011) C-324/09.

(c) Employment Agencies

In contrast to supermarkets and internet markets for goods, labour marketplaces have long been regulated. From the start of the twentieth century it was understood that employment agencies, connecting workers to employers, threatened worker welfare, by charging desperate workers fees to find jobs, rotating workers so that more fees could be extracted and exacerbating unemployment.[116] In 1919, the first Recommendation of the International Labour Organization (ILO) was to prohibit any new profit-making employment agents, license and phase out existing ones, and the second ILO Convention required establishing public employment agencies in their place.[117] This was revised, so the ILO Private Employment Agencies Convention 1997 recognised that private agencies may exist alongside the public service, but they should be licensed, responsible for labour rights including workers' data protection and may not charge fees to workers.[118] The Employment Agencies Act 1973 requires licensing, but this was removed in 1994,[119] only to be reinstated for the agricultural, shellfish and packing industries in 2004[120] after twenty-three cockle-picking workers recruited through a criminal agency drowned. Agencies are generally prohibited from charging fees to workers,[121] and are recognised as an employer responsible for labour rights.[122] The Secretary of State can make prohibition orders against those who violate legal duties.[123]

While private agencies could be abolished, most countries have preferred to allow them, and have not held a total monopoly for public employment agencies.[124] These were developed from the early twentieth

[116] See *Adams v Tanner* 244 US 590 (1917) per Brandeis J; *Brazee v Michigan* 241 US 340 (1916), where mandatory licensing was held to be compliant with the fourteenth amendment, but McReynolds J said *obiter dicta* that regulation of fees would not be.

[117] Unemployment Recommendation 1919 (No. 1) art. 1 and Unemployment Convention 1919 (c. 2).

[118] Private Employment Agencies Convention 1997 (c. 171) arts. 3, 7, 11 and 12. Before this, at the Great Depression's height, the Fee-Charging Employment Agencies Convention, 1933 (c. 34) art. 2 called for abolition of agencies in 3 years, but the Fee-Charging Employment Agencies Convention 1949 (c. 96) recognised their persistence.

[119] Employment Agencies Act 1973 and Deregulation and Contracting Out Act 1994, s. 35 and Sch. 17.

[120] Gangmasters (Licensing) Act 2004, s. 7.

[121] Employment Agencies Act 1973, ss. 1 and 6, but note Conduct of Employment Agencies and Business Regulations 2003, reg. 26 and Sch. 3.

[122] This flows from the common law (see Ch. 5(1)(b)), and the requirement in the Temporary Agency Work Directive 2008/104/EC, art. 2, 'recognising temporary-work agencies as employers'.

[123] Employment Agencies Act 1973, s. 3A.

[124] See *Höfner and Elser v Macrotron GmbH* (1991) C-41/90, a leading case on the meaning of an 'undertaking'. It held the German government could maintain a public employment agency monopoly if it satisfied demand. *Job Centre Coop arl* (1997) C-55/96 stated a prohibition on private agencies was unlawful only if the public agency was 'manifestly unable to satisfy demand'.

century,[125] whereas before people had to rely on guilds and gangmasters to find work.[126] The modern public employment service is the Jobcentre,[127] although since 2012 it has outsourced many of its functions to private agencies.[128]

The growing online platforms have also entered into the job market, the two most notable being Amazon's Mechanical Turk and Microsoft's LinkedIn. First, Amazon 'MTurk' offers 'crowd workers' to anyone who wants to hire them, and enables the employer to set the fee. Marketing itself as selling 'humans as a service',[129] and ideal for 'simple and repetitive tasks',[130] this platform asserts that it is not an employer, while taking a 10 and then 20 per cent cut of wages on each transaction. This has around 2,000 workers working at any given time, and around 100,000 registered users. Amazon MTurk systematically violates labour rights: for instance, among a sample of US workers the median hourly wage was $2 an hour, while the minimum wage in a non-tipped industry is $7.25 an hour (itself inhumanly low).[131] The true position is that it is an employer, and an employment agency, because its functions include (among other things) controlling the workforce and benefiting from their labour.[132]

Second, LinkedIn was purchased by Microsoft Inc. in 2016, and has grown as a social network for professionals. By 2020, LinkedIn had 575 million registered users, and it had begun to aggressively expand its job-search services across the world. This currently functions as an advertising platform for jobs, but presumably as it captures a dominant share of the marketplace it could begin to monetise its position, for instance: (1) requiring fee payments are made through LinkedIn, (2) requiring wage payments are made through LinkedIn and, finally, (3) taking a percentage rather than a fixed fee for wages. Any of these steps would mean that LinkedIn would become an employment agency. It would therefore be responsible for employment rights, as well as the considerable personal data it holds.[133]

[125] Labour Bureaux (London) Act 1902 (for London Boroughs, funded by rates) and Labour Exchanges Act 1909. See further J. B. Seymour, *The British Employment Exchange* (1928) 8, 75% did not find work.

[126] M. Freedland, P. Craig, C. Jacqueson and N. Countouris, *Public Employment Services and European Law* (2007) 104–10.

[127] Jobseekers' Act 1995, ss. 1–6J, on the Jobseekers' Allowance.

[128] See P. Wintour, 'Unemployed to Be Forced to Use Government Job Website', *The Guardian* (20 December 2012), 'developed by the commercial job search firm Monster UK'.

[129] J. Prassl, *Humans as a Service: The Promises and Perils of Work in the Gig Economy* (2019) after the statement of Jeff Bezos, 'You've heard of software as a service. Well, this is basically humans as a service.'

[130] Amazon MTurk website (2020).

[131] K. Hara et al., 'A Data-Driven Analysis of Workers' Earnings on Amazon Mechanical Turk', CHI 2018, Paper No. 449 (2018), suggesting only 4% earned over $7.25 an hour.

[132] Prassl, *Humans as a Service*, ch. 3; A. Semuels, 'The Internet Is Enabling a New Kind of Poorly Paid Hell', *Atlantic* (23 January 2018), citing Prof. Miriam Cherry, suggesting any worker could file an ordinary lawsuit.

[133] Cf. *hiQ Labs Inc. v LinkedIn Corp.*, 938 F 3d 985 (9th Cir 2019) holding that LinkedIn could not injunct hiQ against mass collection of public profile data (web scraping) within LinkedIn.

(d) Stock Exchanges

Stock exchanges are the most important marketplaces for the trading of capital (see Table 18.2 for the top ten in 2019). Their activities have been comprehensively regulated since the Great Depression as a basic part of company and investment law, including standards of governance for companies that are allowed to list (see Ch. 3(2)(a) and (3)(b))[134] and requirements for disclosure when offering shares to the public, prospectuses or equal treatment in shareholder returns (Ch. 4(2)). These rights therefore primarily protect the integrity of the traders (that is, the listed companies who issue securities) on the platform and guard against the platform's collapse. Exchanges generally regulate their own membership.[135]

(4) Trader Rights

As the foregoing sections have already indicated, there are no codified rights for traders in relation to marketplaces, whether off- or online. It seems unlikely to remain this way. Growing monopolisation by online platforms has spurred political demands for greater duties, and competition law entails de facto duties, even if not codified. Of course, all labour (see Ch. 5) and consumer rights (Ch. 6(1)(a)) apply to marketplaces that carry out employer and service-provider functions, whatever their contracts say or deny. However, specifically in relation to traders, the human right to work and, within that, the freedom to conduct a business,[136] three main groups of emerging rights can be identified.

Table 18.2 Top 10 stock exchanges, 2019

	Stock exchange	Market cap US$
1	New York Stock Exchange	$22,923bn
2	Nasdaq	$10,857bn
3	Japan Exchange Group	$5,679bn
4	London Stock Exchange	$4,590bn
5	Shanghai Stock Exchange	$4,026bn
6	Hong Kong Stock Exchange	$3,936bn
7	Euronext	$3,927bn
8	Toronto Stock Exchange	$3,256bn
9	Shenzhen Stock Exchange	$2,504bn
10	Bombay Stock Exchange	$2,030bn

134 See also E. McGaughey, *Participation in Corporate Governance* (2014) ch. 4(3) on shareholder votes and the NYSE.

135 Cf. *Weinberger v Inglis (No. 2)* [1919] AC 606 (no right to claim unfair exclusion from LSE membership).

136 CFREU 2000, art. 16.

(a) Access to Marketplace

First, there is the trader's right of access to the marketplace. Any marketplace that is dominant has a special responsibility not to abuse its position. When a marketplace succeeds in becoming an essential facility for other traders to sell their products, a corresponding duty arises to access those facilities on fair terms.[137] These are analogous to 'common carrier' duties imposed at common law, which continue in the USA[138] and in UK law remain binding.[139] While it is sometimes argued that fair prices are difficult for a court to set, an appropriate test is what is the marginal unit cost of access for the marketplace, plus a reasonable charge. Price setting is routine in the Sale of Goods Act 1979,[140] or in any system of commercial law.

(b) Equal Treatment

Second, there is the trader's right to equal treatment among other traders. Price discrimination is an abuse of a dominant position, as is 'applying dissimilar conditions to equivalent transactions with other trading parties'.[141] This amounts, for example, to a de facto prohibition on Amazon, Google or Facebook preferring any of its own products, or anything that it profits from, on its platforms.[142]

(c) Right to Communication?

Third, a crucial right to limit the abuse of a marketplace monopoly is enabling communication between buyers and sellers, including their ability to make subsequent contracts off the marketplace. It is an abuse for a marketplace to make traders accept 'supplementary obligations which, by their nature or according to commercial usage, have no connection with the subject of such contracts'.[143] While a marketplace might protest that there is a 'connection' between preventing side-dealing among buyers and sellers, or restricting information, to the maintenance of its dominance, there seems no intrinsic

[137] See Ch. 6(2)(b)(iii); *Oscar Bronner GmbH & Co. KG v Mediaprint Zeitungs- und Zeitschriftenverlag GmbH & Co. KG* (1998) Case 7/97; *IMS Health GmbH & Co. OHG v NDC Health GmbH & Co. KG* (2001) C-418/01.

[138] Khan, 'Amazon's Antitrust Paradox', 797.

[139] *Allnutt v Inglis* (1810) ER 359, 12 East 527, 537, per Lord Ellenborough: 'There is no doubt that the general principle is favoured, both in law and justice, that every man may fix what price he pleases upon his own property, or the use of it; but if for a particular purpose the public have a right to resort to his premises and make use of them, and he have a monopoly in them for that purpose, if he will take the benefit of that monopoly, he must, as an equivalent, perform the duty attached to it on reasonable terms . . . .'

[140] Sale of Goods Act 1979, s. 8(2): 'Where the price is not determined . . . the buyer must pay a reasonable price.'

[141] TFEU, art 102(c). [142] Khan, 'Amazon's Antitrust Paradox', 797. [143] TFEU, art. 102(d).

connection to a contract itself. Whether any of these duties develop in the case law, or become codified, remains to be seen.

(5) Conclusion

Marketplaces lie at an essential nexus of communication between traders and consumers, but they have not yet become adequately conceptualised or regulated. Between the two poles of leaving marketplace monopolies as they are, or trying to replace markets entirely, there are a broad range of prudent regulatory alternatives. First, an option proposed by Nick Srnicek is 'to create public platforms', not owned by any state, but through some other form of financing, and made to 'enable democratic participation' that protects personal data.[144] The Wikimedia foundation could be one model (see Ch. 17(3)). Second, US Senator Elizabeth Warren has campaigned to 'break them up' – namely, Amazon, Google and Facebook – so that internet marketplaces cannot act both as a platform and sell on their platform. Warren would also 'unwind anti-competitive mergers', such as Amazon buying the supermarket Whole Foods[145] or shares in Deliveroo. There are signs that these calls have led to much more aggressive competition policy enforcement. A third option is to combine elements of these proposals, since social ownership may be better suited to platforms where there is less experimentation, and separating platforms from players may come at a cost to efficiency. But a crucial addition is to recognise the rights of the broader network of small and medium enterprises which have a stake in the marketplace, and guarantee their voice and rights.

144 N. Srnicek, *Platform Capitalism* (2017) ch. 3, 128.
145 E. Warren, 'Here's How We Can Break Up Big Tech', *Medium* (8 March 2019).

19

Military and Security

Contents

'If you want peace, prepare for war', wrote Vegetius in the fourth century.[1] Whether or not this was true in the twilight of Rome's military empire, it has little evidential basis today. 'Peace can be established', wrote the Versailles Treaty, 'only if it is based upon social justice.'[2] And as this wisdom went unheeded, as victors demanded reparations, World War Two engulfed the globe in flames again. Humanity's desire to end war was enshrined in the United Nations (UN) Charter, and the ideals of a just society in the Universal Declaration of Human Rights. The Preamble to the UN Educational, Scientific and Cultural Organization recalled that 'since wars begin in the minds of men, it is in the minds of men that the defences of peace must be constructed'.[3] Yet, despite a historical decline in violence,[4] the world remains gripped by horrific warfare and destruction. Armed conflict requires arms-makers, armed troops and it increasingly involves private military contractors. The reverse is also true: when driven by profit, arms-makers, armed troops and contractors require conflict. They are a permanent lobby for it. US President Eisenhower, European commander in World War Two, said that this 'military-industrial complex' could only be consistent with democracy with an

[1] Publius Flavius Vegetius Renatus, *Epitoma Rei Militaris* (c. 390 AD) Book III, *Si vis pacem, para bellum*.

[2] Versailles Treaty 1919, Part XIII.

[3] UN Educational, Scientific and Cultural Organization (UNESCO) Constitution, Preamble, adopted in London on 16 November 1945.

[4] R. Aguilera, *The Glass Half Empty: Our Delusion with Progress in the Twenty-First Century* (2020) ch. 7, on the complexities and realities of this. Cf. S. Pinker, *The Better Angels of Our Nature: Why Violence Has Declined* (2011).

'alert and knowledgeable citizenry . . . so that security and liberty may prosper together'.[5] 'Everyone has the right to life, liberty and the security of person.'[6] But to what extent are the enterprises of death and war truly needed for our security, liberty and life, or for how much longer?

Since World War Two, the need to eliminate the military has been stated, but is contested. A first view admits that diplomacy is the first tool of international relations, but a lethal military will always be necessary to 'negotiate from a position of strength'.[7] This view assumes a state of perpetual global fragmentation, when history witnesses an opposite trend. A second view is that we should unilaterally disarm, whether from nuclear weapons or conventional forces. There will be huge economic benefits, and it will limit climate damage because militaries are the leading users of fossil fuels. Yet unilateral disarmament involves risks in a world where aggressive war is still a reality, especially by the permanent members of the UN Security Council: the USA, UK, France, Russia and China. A third view is that disarmament must happen with trust and negotiation. 'Every gun that is made, every warship launched, every rocket fired', said Eisenhower, 'signifies, in the final sense, a theft from those who hunger and are not fed, those who are cold and are not clothed.'[8] Every country can pursue unilateral armament of human rights, and as humanity grows older and wiser, that is likely to happen faster. Social justice, and a living planet, are indivisible from peace. This chapter explores the military's finance, its governance and the human rights at stake.

(1) Historical Development

Warfare, like all forms of violence, has declined as humanity has developed from a primitive to a more intelligent and socially organised species. Possibly among humanity's first geopolitical actions was the genocide of our Neanderthal relatives, who disappeared around 35,000 BC, though it also appears that we co-existed for thousands of years.[9] In the Old Kingdom of Ancient Egypt, the pharaohs waged regular wars of extermination and enslavement of neighbouring people, relying on local governors to raise troops, and

5 D. D. Eisenhower, 'Farewell Address to the Nation' (17 January 1961).

6 UDHR 1948, art. 3; ICCPR 1966, arts. 6 and 9; ECHR 1950, arts. 2 and 5; CFREU 2000, arts. 2 and 6.

7 E.g. J. Mattis, *Summary of the 2018 National Defence Strategy of the United States of America* (2018) 1.

8 D. D. Eisenhower, *The Chance for Peace* (1953).

9 T. Higham et al., 'The Timing and Spatiotemporal Patterning of Neanderthal Disappearance' (2014) 512(7514) *Nature* 306 (estimating extinction 40,000 years ago, but 5,000 years co-existence); J. Zilhão et al., 'Precise Dating of the Middle-to-Upper Paleolithic Transition in Murcia (Spain) Supports Late Neanderthal Persistence in Iberia' (2017) 3(11) *Heliyon* e00435 (estimating 37,000 years ago); K. H. Ko, 'Hominin Interbreeding and the Evolution of Human Variation' (2016) 23 *J Biological Research-Thessaloniki* 17 (interbreeding); W. E. Banks et al., 'Neanderthal Extinction by Competitive Exclusion' (2008) 3(12) *PLoS One* e3972.

also 'caravans' as auxiliaries.[10] The Old Testament records enslavement, mutilation, genocide and disembowelling of pregnant women,[11] while the New Testament recorded habits of strict military command.[12] Yet the Bible also records concern even during war for the environment, the prophecy that people would 'beat their swords into ploughshares', and that 'nation shall not lift up sword against nation, neither shall they learn war any more'.[13]

But learn war we did. Around 500 BC in China, the first theory of military strategy, *The Art of War*, was written by Sun Tzu, a contemporary of Confucius. This explained the virtues of a commander as 'wisdom, sincerity, benevolence, courage and strictness'; it argued all 'warfare is based on deception' and 'supreme excellence consists in breaking the enemy's resistance without fighting'.[14] In Ancient Greece, while there were treaties among cities and leagues – a kind of embryonic international law – Thucydides recorded how the 'growth of the power of Athens' (not the details of disputes) 'made war inevitable' on the Spartans.[15] In an evocative dialogue on realism, he dramatises the Athenians telling the Melians, small allies of Sparta, that they must submit and pay tribute because 'right, as the world goes, is only in question between equals in power, while the strong do what they can and the weak suffer what they must'.[16] Later on, Vegetius composed the maxims of military practice from Rome's bloodthirsty history,[17] drawing on experience of the Punic Wars that eradicated Carthage (264–146 BC, up to 1.25 million dead), Caesar's campaigns to conquer Gaul and invade Britain (58–50 BC, up to 1 million dead), Augustus and Tiberius's occupation and campaigns in Judea and Palestine (the stage for Jesus's life) and Hadrian's ethnic cleansing and wall building (117–138 AD, up to 2 million dead), or Constantine's reconquest of the western Empire under the cross (312 AD). The scale of death was assured by Roman army training – for instance, to thrust not swipe swords – to kill. Romans, mostly peasantry, were Rome's main army though 'hired corps of foreigners' were used as auxiliaries 'from different parts of the Empire'.[18]

[10] 'The Inscription of Weni' (*c.* 2278 BC) the autobiography in the tomb of a thoroughly sycophantic, self-ingratiating and murderous adviser to the pharaoh Merenre Nemtyemsaf I (2287–2278 BC).

[11] Deut. 20:11 ('tributaries unto thee'); Judg. 1:6 (cutting off thumbs and toes); I Kgs 11:15 ('smitten every male in Edom'); II Kgs 8:12 and 15:16; Amos 1:13 ('rip up their women with child').

[12] Matt. 8:9, a Roman Centurion says to Jesus: 'I am a man under authority, having soldiers under me: and I say to this man, Go, and he goeth; and to another, Come, and he cometh . . . .'

[13] Isa. 2:4; Deut. 20:19, 'When thou shalt besiege a city . . . thou shalt not destroy the trees . . . for the tree . . . is man's life.'

[14] S. Tzu, *The Art of War* (*c.* 500 BC) I:9, 18. III:2.

[15] Thucydides, *The History of the Peloponnesian War* (*c.* 400 BC) Book I, §23.

[16] Thucydides, *The History of the Peloponnesian War*, Book V, §89: 'The Melians refuse to succumb, trying to persuade the Athenians based on their own interests, not justice. The Athenians lay siege, kill all men, and enslave the women and children.'

[17] Vegetius, *Epitoma Rei Militaris* (*c.* 390) Book I, 'only skill and discipline will insure' victory, not just courage.

[18] Vegetius, *Epitoma Rei Militaris*, Book II and see 'General Maxims'.

The sacking and fall of Rome by Goth and Barbarian invaders has been attributed to the growing softness, even Christianisation, of its society.[19] But as the invaders too became Christian, the wars of the medieval and pre-industrial periods stayed unimaginably brutal. This included the Norman Invasion of England (1066), the Crusades, where crusaders sacked Constantinople while they were meant to save it (1095–1291), or the Mongol conquests where mounted horse tactics annihilated Asia and Eastern Europe, reaching the gates of Vienna (1206–94).[20] Western Europe was only spared as Ögedei Khan (son of Genghis) died and his general, Subutai, returned to contest the throne (1242). A century later, the Black Death had spread from Asia along the Silk Road to Mongol armies who were besieging Caffa, Crimea. They catapulted infected bodies (early biological weapons) of their own dead over the city wall, and fleeing Genoese traders brought the plague to Italy. Plague killed up to half of Europe (1347–53). During and after, in the Hundred Years War between England (with Henry V[21]) and France (with Joan of Arc) 3 million more were killed (1337–1453).

A decisive turn in world history started in 1453, when the Ottomans took Constantinople, raising the cost and peril of European access to China down the Silk Road. Christopher Columbus, an Italian, also craved to fund a new crusade against Muslims through gold and spices 'to spend all the profits of this my enterprise on the conquest of Jerusalem'.[22] Queen Isabella I of Spain paid him to sail west to China. In 1492, he instead found the Americas. With the pope drawing a line between Spanish and Portuguese claims,[23] genocide and plague was released across the New World, as conquistadors used gun powder, steel and horses – but above all smallpox – against Central and South American peoples (estimates of deaths go over 100 million).[24] North Americans were similarly massacred by disease and French and British colonisers. Christianity and race were central justifications for colonisation and rampant murder,[25] as they were for the transatlantic slave trade, led in all its horror by the Royal African Company and the South Sea Company.

19 E. Gibbon, *The History of the Decline and Fall of the Roman Empire* (1789).

20 G. P. Carpini (1246) described the Mongol annihilation as follows: 'When we were journeying through that land we came across countless skulls and bones of dead men lying about on the ground. Kiev had been a very large and thickly populated town, but now it has been reduced almost to nothing, for there are at the present time scarce two hundred houses there and the inhabitants are kept in complete slavery.'

21 Sanitised and glorified, e.g. in Shakespeare, 'Henry V' (1599) Act IV, scene iii, on 'St Crispin's day'.

22 C. Delaney, 'Columbus's Ultimate Goal: Jerusalem' (2006) 48(2) *Comparative Studies in Society and History* 260, 261, quoting Columbus's diary.

23 Pope Alexander VI, *Inter Caetera* (4 May 1493) and a further Treaty of Tordesillas 1494 shifting the line west.

24 Aguilera, *The Glass Half Empty*, ch. 7; J. Hickel, *The Divide* (2017) ch. 3, 72.

25 E.g. Charter of Virginia (1606) the King conferring a monopoly 'in propagating of Christian Religion to such People . . . in Darkness and miserable Ignorance of the true Knowledge and Worship of God . . .'.

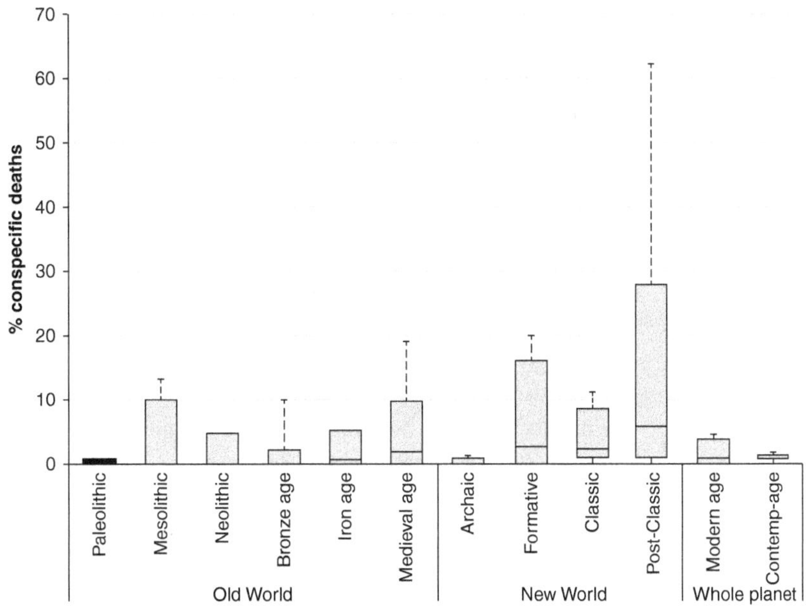

Figure 19.1 Most violent periods of human history

They transported 13 million people, and killed 3 million more. It was the most violent period in history (see Figure 19.1).[26]

Between the European invasion of the Americas and World War One, two major shifts in military relations were (1) from a world view of domination to a growing concept, if very limited, of peace based on sovereignty, and later on human rights, and (2) from private corporate armies to nationalised ones. The Thirty Years War, mainly among Spain, Holland, France, Sweden and the Holy Roman Empire in today's Germany (1618–48, 8 million dead) ended with the Peace and Treaties of Westphalia. This recognised sovereignty and non-interference in others' affairs (such as religion) as principles of international law.[27] It also cemented the end of the pope's authority in Protestant Europe. In England there was a civil war, the execution of King Charles I (1649), the monarchy's restoration (1660), the Glorious Revolution inviting William and Mary of Orange to the throne, and the Bill of Rights 1689 forbidding any standing army without Parliament's consent.[28] The 'Leviathan' who claimed sovereignty was not Thomas Hobbes's king, but the representative Parliament extolled by John Locke.[29]

[26] Aguilera, *The Glass Half Empty*, ch. 7, chart 7.1. World War Two was absolutely the most violent war. We have the capacity to do worse.

[27] E.g. Treaty of Westphalia (1648) XCII. H. Grotius, *De Jure Belli ac Pacis* (1625) proposed these concepts.

[28] Bill of Rights 1689, cl. 6.

[29] Cf. T. Hobbes, *Leviathan* (1651); J. Locke, *Second Treatise on Government* (1689) ch. 11.

Under Parliament, the union of England, Wales and Scotland followed, and a British empire began in earnest. The East India Company had been given a royal charter in 1600.[30] In this time, privateers were licensed by the Crown (like pirates with a royal seal) to raid ships or ports of other peoples, and this continued until the Crimean War.[31] The East India Company maintained its own standing army of private soldiers, weapons, ships and heavy guns. It colonised India by, first, establishing trading ports, like those in Mumbai, Kolkata or Chennai, by taking them from the Portuguese or coercing or buying them from local rulers. Second, it offered security services to Indian rulers, particularly the warring Mughal Empire, or else the company simply led its own wars against others, particularly under the company's 'unstable sociopath' and director Robert Clive.[32] Third, it offered the 'service' of administering finances for the Mughal emperors from 1765. The control of finance and security, the power to tax and enforce was the decisive point at which Company rule was cemented,[33] just as the power struggles leading to the English Civil War were about the right to tax, trade and military control.[34] After this, the Company led a series of wars against the Maratha Empire, taking control of the subcontinent by 1818, all still delegated, but not directly controlled, by the British government.[35] Profits from India went to the Company and the British state, not to mention the embezzling culture among its troops.[36] India's resources and its workforce directly funded Britain's industrialisation through India's impoverishment.

The British Empire's grip on North America was lost to the USA after the Declaration of Independence in 1776, a result of tax without voice for the North, and the judgment in *Somerset v Stewart* that slavery was unlawful at common law for the South.[37] In 1788, Britain instead sailed to colonise that great southern land, which it proclaimed was empty, and unleashed another

[30] The Spanish Armada's defeat in 1588 and then the Treaty of Utrecht periodically secured the seas.

[31] Paris Declaration Respecting Maritime Law (16 April 1856) (the UK, France and 53 others banned privateering).

[32] W. Dalrymple, 'The East India Company: The Original Corporate Raiders', *The Guardian* (4 March 2015).

[33] S. Tharoor, *Inglorious Empire: What the British Did to India* (2016) ch. 1, 4.

[34] *Five Knights' case* (1627) 3 How St Tr 1 (people forced to take loans from the King and, if they could not repay, imprisoned and not released) reversed by the Petition of Right 1628 (no tax without Parliament, arbitrary imprisonment, commissions of martial law). Also *R v Hampden* (1637) Salmon's State Trials, vol. 1, 698 and Ship Money Act 1640.

[35] East India Company Act 1772 (13 Geo. 3, c. 63), bailing out the company with a £1.5m loan in return for establishing judicial control over company territory, and East India Company Act 1784 (24 Geo. 3, c. 25), establishing a joint board of control by the company and the British government.

[36] Cf. S. H. Myerly, *British Military Spectacle: From the Napoleonic Wars through the Crimea* (1996) 1–9, explaining the poverty of British Army (as opposed to Company) soldiers, and the methods of spectacle in imperial power.

[37] *Somerset v Stewart* (1772) 98 ER 499.

century of plague and genocide on the first Australians.[38] Riven with contradictions, this was the formative era of human rights, as the revolutionary Thomas Paine wrote *Rights of Man*;[39] as the US Bill of Rights was added in Amendments to the Constitution of 1787; as the French Revolution proclaimed liberty, fraternity and equality in 1789; and as Mary Wollstonecraft in Britain extolled the Rights of Woman.[40] The declarations did not stop imperialism, slavery, the guillotines, the 5 million dead from the ensuing Napoleonic Wars nor the 'manifest destiny' of removing and murdering native Americans.[41] Yet these declarations were lasting ideas, as was a short tract by Immanuel Kant, *On Perpetual Peace* in 1795.[42] Kant argued that peace could last forever by (1) disposing of materials for war; (2) ending colonisation; (3) abolishing standing armies; (4) ending international debts; (5) prohibiting violent interference in other states' affairs; and (6) basic rules of war, such as prohibiting poisoners. Further, all states should (i) uphold freedom, the rule of law, and equal treatment of citizens; (ii) acknowledge the basis of international law as a 'federation of free states'; and (iii) guarantee universal rights of hospitality for all 'citizens of the world'.[43] This almost exactly summarises the post-World War Two system of the UN and the Universal Declaration,[44] except that the ending of war production, armies and debt – the most potent economic factors – still lacks clear standards in international law.[45]

After the Napoleonic Wars,[46] the nineteenth century's guiding theory was keeping a 'balance of power' – a kind of political realism, or *Realpolitik*.[47] The nineteenth century was superficially peaceful, with a so-called *Pax Britannica* under British imperial hegemony,[48] but one can make countless exceptions. The first horrors of trench warfare were in the Crimean War (1853–6, 400,000

[38] See the fictionalised account in K. Grenville, *The Secret River* (2005).

[39] T. Paine, *Rights of Man: Being an Answer to Mr Burke's Attack on the French Revolution* (1791).

[40] M. Wollstonecraft, *A Vindication of the Rights of Woman: with Strictures on Political and Moral Subjects* (1792).

[41] E.g. Indian Removal Act of 1830.

[42] I. Kant, *Zum Ewigen Frieden* (1795) (*Perpetual Peace*, trans. M. C. Smith (1903)).

[43] By this, Kant meant that visitors to another country were owed hospitality, but not necessarily more. A very different approach is now taken to refugees, seekers of asylum and both the desire and need for migrants.

[44] In turn, (2) ICCPR 1966, art. 1(1); (5) UN Charter 1945, art. 2(4); (6) Geneva Conventions 1864–1949, (i) UDHR 1948, arts. 2–3; (ii) UN Charter, art. 1; (iii) UDHR 1948, arts. 13–15.

[45] These factors are however seen in (1) non-proliferation of weapons treaties, (3) negotiations to decrease the military and (4) campaigns to cancel international debt, such as the Jubilee 2000 movement.

[46] This resulted in the Congress of Vienna 1815 and 'Concert of Europe' aiming to maintain a power 'balance'.

[47] L. Rochau, *Grundsätze der Realpolitik angewendet auf die staatlichen Zustände Deutschlands* (1853).

[48] E.g. M. Townsend, 'Will England Retain India?' (1888) 53 *Contemporary Rev* 795, 803 (a white supremacist tract, referring to the 'the Pax Britannica, the universal peace, beneath which India sleeps') or H. S. Perris, *Pax Britannica: A Study of the History of British Pacification* (1913) 252, on Anglo-American peace, because (after the British set fire to the White House in the War of 1812) 'Britain had enough on her shoulders, in India', etc.

dead). The Indian 'Mutiny' (1857, 1 million dead) was a liberation war against East India Company tyranny, and led to direct control by the British government over India.[49] The US Civil War (1861–5, 1 million dead) broke out after the 1860 election, the southern states declaring secession, as President Lincoln opposed slavery. It was the first to combine trench warfare with the invention of the automatic Gatling gun in 1862, ahead of the Maxim machine gun in 1884. The Franco-Prussian war was used by the Prussian Chancellor Otto von Bismarck to create political unity in a new German Empire (a supposedly 'second' *Reich*) by taking French land in Alsace-Lorraine in 1871. The nineteenth century also saw accelerated imperialism and murder as industrial economies, with industrial technology, seized the remaining surfaces of Earth.[50] According to one nasty poem in 1898: 'Whatever happens, we have got / The Maxim gun, and they have not.'[51] Many of these guns were made by private companies, but many others, like munitions or ships, were made in government factories and arsenals until World War One.[52] Relative peace in Europe meant unrestricted oppression globally, funnelling riches and resources into the pockets and palaces of London, Paris and Berlin, and an unending quest for more. The British Empire was supposed to be 'the Empire on which the sun never set',[53] but Germany's Kaiser Wilhelm too demanded 'a place in the sun'. If the balance were to break in Europe, the military tactician Alfred von Schlieffen said, Germany must first invade France, encircling Paris, before then taking out Russia. So, when an Austrian prince was shot in Serbia, the plans kicked in, like a script of a play that had to be read. Austria threatened Serbia. Russia mobilised against Austria and Germany. Germany invaded France. Britain and Russia declared war. World War One began because people believed in their own racial supremacy, they had boundless confidence in their own industrial technology and the international system legitimised aggressive, pre-emptive war.[54]

The era of total war, of the 'War to end all Wars' (1914–18, 30 million dead) and then again in World War Two (1939–45, 70 million dead), remains a living scar on our collective memory. In the mud of the Somme, the great lie came undone that 'dying for your country was sweet and dignified'.[55] But lasting

49 Queen Victoria became Empress Victoria from 1876.

50 E.g. Treaty of Berlin 1885, legitimising territorial division in the 'scramble for Africa'.

51 H. Belloc, *The Modern Traveller* (1898) 41. This man exemplifies imperialist and racist attitudes of the time.

52 E.g. B. G. Brunton, 'Institutional Origins of the Military-Industrial Complex' (1988) 22(2) *J Economic Issues* 599, 602 (in the USA, government arsenals made 68% of ships from 1866–83).

53 This was an old saying used many times before, for instance in Ancient Egypt. A typical retort was that if the sun never set on the British Empire, it was because God didn't trust the English in the dark.

54 Cf. A. J. P. Taylor, *The First World War: An Illustrated History* (1974) arguing rail and economics made it inevitable.

55 W. Owen, 'Dulce et decorum est' (1917), the poem taking its title from Horace, *Odes* (23 BC) Book III, *Dulce et decorum est pro patria mori.*

somewhat longer was Max Weber's lie in 1919 that states held a 'legitimate' monopoly on the means of violence. This was from start to finish an affront to the very core of universal human rights. The Russian Civil War (1917–22, 7 million dead) was fought after Lenin took power from the tsar in the Russian Revolution of 1917, believing murder was necessary just as in the French Revolution.[56] Power in turn was seized by a murderous bank robber, Stalin. Lenin wrote that imperialism and war result from capitalist systems being impelled to pursue profit, and so replace rival systems,[57] but had no trouble doing war within. He was himself sent by Germany to Moscow on a sealed train to destabilise the tsar, and in the Russian Civil War, thousands of British, American and other allied troops were sent to fight as, said Winston Churchill later, Bolshevism had to be 'strangled . . . in its cradle'.[58] The Versailles Treaty, at the end of World War One, demanded reparations against the defeated Germany, plunging it into a decade of poverty.[59] When the Wall Street Crash hit, and the Great Depression ensued, the crisis was Hitler's chance to seize political power, promising his big business and military-industrial backers that he would eradicate the Weimar Republic's social democracy, to ensure stable profits for capitalism.[60] Hitler rearmed, and launched another war to colonise and enslave the world.[61] The Holocaust, and *Generalplan Ost*, aimed to exterminate people across Eastern Europe, explicitly modelled on American, British and imperial power.[62] In Japan, the genocidal war waged by the imperial military was only ended after the US Air Force dropped two atomic bombs on Hiroshima and Nagasaki.

War like this is unimaginable and its lesson for those who saw it is that war must be made unthinkable. The ideals of the UN were for a world federative government, co-operation on all economic and social affairs and the fulfilment of the Universal Declaration of Human Rights. The absolute prohibition on aggressive war, without a resolution of the UN Security Council,[63] was meant to be the cornerstone of peace. But disarmament faltered with the division of Europe under Stalin, the lurch into the Korean War (1950–3, 4.5 million dead), the start of the Cold War, and the nuclear arms race. And economic integration faltered, as an International Trade Organisation to settle trade imbalances (and so limit debt) was never approved, leaving just the World Bank, the

[56] J. P. Westwood, *Endurance and Endeavour: Russian History 1812–2001* (2002) ch. 11.

[57] V. I. Lenin, *Imperialism, the Highest Stage of Capitalism* (1917). It appears Lenin viewed this as the only, or the primary, cause of imperialism. Cf. K. Marx, *Capital: A Critique of Political Economy* (1867) ch. 33.

[58] 'Remarks to the National Press Club, Washington' (28 June 1954).

[59] Versailles Treaty 1919, Part VIII. Results predicted in J. M. Keynes, *The Economic Consequences of the Peace* (1920).

[60] E. McGaughey, 'The Codetermination Bargains: The History of German Corporate and Labour Law' (2016) 23(1) *Columbia J Eur L* 135, part 3(3) on the 'second collective agreement'.

[61] F. L. Neumann, *Behemoth* (1944).

[62] T. Snyder, *Bloodlands: Europe between Hitler and Stalin* (2011).

[63] UN Charter 1945, art. 2(4).

International Monetary Fund (see Ch. 9), and a General Agreement on Tariffs and Trade (now the World Trade Organization). What became the European Union (EU) actively aimed to prevent war by socioeconomic integration, and despite Brexit this model of integration has worked.

Yet aggressive war has continued, in other forms, particularly led by permanent UN Security Council members. This included the French- and US-led war in Vietnam (1955–75, 3.8 million dead), or the US–UK invasion and occupation of Iraq (2003–11, 1 million dead) that contributed to the creation of a death-cult like 'Islamic' State, and the War in Syria (2011–today, 585,000 dead). The Soviet Union invaded Czechoslovakia, Hungary and Afghanistan, though under Brezhnev and Gorbachev it agreed with the USA to reduce nuclear weapons and stop nuclear weapon testing.[64] After the Soviet Union collapsed, and Putin seized power, Russia conducted the war in Chechnya, and invaded Georgia, Ukraine and Crimea. From 2015 it conducted a 'sweeping and systematic' cyber-attack on the USA and the West (which it delights in denying) by weaponising social media.[65] China has not launched an aggressive war, but claims Taiwan, and Indian territory, and has violated human rights *en masse* in Tibet, Xinjiang and Hong Kong. There were also countless other tragedies: the post-colonial wars on Indian partition; the Nigerian Civil War; Bangladeshi independence; the Rwandan genocide; the wars in Sierra Leone, the Congo, Sudan, Darfur; and in 2021 war continues in Afghanistan, Yemen, Syria and Iraq. Conflicts continue in Palestine and Israel, Somalia, Kashmir and Mexico. The more we fight, the less we have to develop (Figure 19.2). Peace is not yet won.

(2) Finance

The military and its 'industrial complex' currently depend on oil and nuclear energy (see Chs. 11–12), heavy machinery not dissimilar to transport manufacturing (Ch. 15) and control of information technology (Chs. 16–17). Having a production base for each enterprise cross-subsidises the military generally, just as some of the most important advances in those enterprises came from public military spending. For instance, the main tech components of an iPhone were researched and developed through military spending, including the Internet, GPS and LCD displays.[66] There are also four specific sources of finance. These are (a) taxes and government spending, mostly with legislative authority; (b) procurement contracts, particularly for arms manufacturing,

[64] Nuclear Non-Proliferation Treaty 1968 and Comprehensive Nuclear-Test-Ban Treaty 1996 (the latter followed a unilateral declaration in 1985 by Gorbachev to stop testing, reciprocated in 1986 by Reagan).

[65] R. Mueller, *Report on the Investigation into Russian Interference in the 2016 Presidential Election* (March 2019) 1.

[66] M. Mazzucato, *The Entrepreneurial State: Debunking Public vs Private Sector Myths* (2013) ch. 3. GPS is 'Global Positioning System' and LCD is 'Liquid-crystal display'.

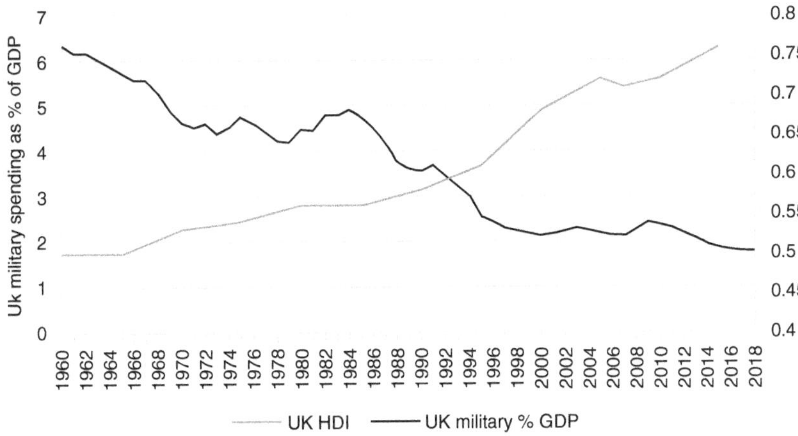

Figure 19.2 UK military spending and human development, 1960–2018
Sources: World Bank; L. P. de la Escosura, 'Historical Index of Human Development' (2018)

mercenary and cyberwarfare services; (c) subsidies by not paying for death or destruction; and (d) not paying for climate damage.

(a) Parliament Consent for Tax

The first source of military finance is tax. In 2019, the UK had the world's eighth-largest military budget, spending £38 billion or $48.7 billion (1.7 per cent of Gross Domestic Product (GDP)), while by far the largest spender was the USA with $732 billion (3.4 per cent of GDP). NATO recommends that its members spend 2 per cent of GDP on the military: an arbitrary figure whose sole, unprincipled justification seems to be to reverse 'declining defence budgets'.[67] The greater the proportion of a country's military spending over time, the lower its rate of human development and the higher the rate of poverty. As world GDP has grown, military spending has shrunk, yet world military spending is still a colossal US$1.9 trillion, or US$1,917,000,000,000, every year (see Figure 19.3).[68] That money could create clean energy, housing, health and education for all humanity.

The basis for UK military spending is the Bill of Rights 1689, clause 6, which says 'the raising or keeping of a standing army within the Kingdom in time of peace, unless it be with consent of Parliament, is against law'.[69] From the Mutiny Act 1689 on, a new Act was passed each year to authorise and maintain armed

[67] NATO, *Wales Summit Declaration* (2014). 20% should be R&D. In 1977, 3% was targeted: J. P. Dunne, 'The Changing Military Industrial Complex in the UK' (1993) 4(2) *Defence and Peace Economics* 91.

[68] N. Tian, A. Fleurant, A. Kuimova, P. D. Wezeman, T. Siemon, 'Trends in World Military Expenditure, 2019', Stockholm International Peace Research Institute (27 April 2020).

[69] Bill of Rights 1689, cl. 6.

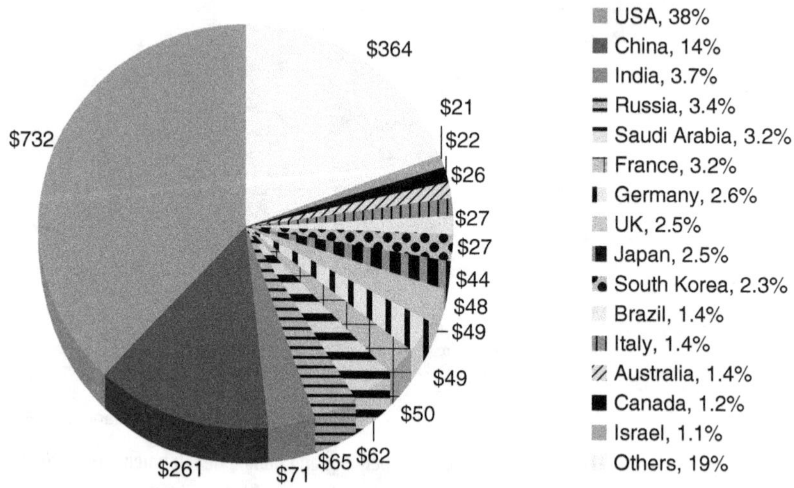

Figure 19.3 World military spending ($bn), 2019
Source: N. Tian, A. Marksteiner and D. Lopes da Silva, 'Trends in World Military Expenditure', SIPIRI Fact Sheet (April 2020) 2

forces, and also the air force from 1917.[70] Private companies, such as the East India Company, with a monopoly from Parliament operated their own private armies, but this effectively ended after the Government of India Act 1858 nationalised or 'imperialised' the company's operations.[71] The practice since 1955 became a simple annual resolution by both Houses of Parliament to renew military spending, with a fresh Act only each five years.[72] Even with a short renewal period, it has been argued that 'the British Army has been an "unlawful" body since [the Army Act] 1955 when Parliament stopped legalising its existence by passing annual Acts' and this is important as 'the army is increasingly being used in civil society – during strikes, and, potentially in public order situations'.[73]

In 2020, the British Army had 73,720 troops, the Navy and Marines had 29,043 and the Air Force had 29,688: a total of 132,451 service people.[74] By contrast, the Reserve Forces Act 1996, sections 1–3 give the power to maintain reserves, including the Royal Fleet Reserve, Army Reserve and Air Force Reserve up to a number authorised by Parliament. In 2020 there were 33,000

[70] Army and Air Force (Annual) Act 1917. The RAF was initially created under the Army Act 1881.

[71] Government of India Act 1858, ss. I and LVI.

[72] Armed Forces Act (AFA) 2006, s. 382(4) last amended by the AFA 2016 and AFA 2021.

[73] 'The British Army: 25 Years of Illegality' (1981) 4 *State Research* 149. Cf. J. Jaconelli, 'Do Constitutional Conventions Bind?' (2005) 64(1) *Cambridge LJ* 149.

[74] N. Dempsey, 'UK Defence Personnel Statistics', Briefing Paper No. CBP7930, HC Library (27 July 2020) 5.

reservists.[75] Reservists can be called up in time of national danger or emergency for a maximum of twelve months.[76] This was done for the illegal invasion of Iraq, as well as Afghanistan and the first Gulf War. Military recruitment tends to focus on small towns and regions, and avoids cities and urban areas.[77] In 2020, pay was £15,985 a year for a new recruit, £20,400 for a trained private and £27,326 a year for a lance corporal.[78]

(b) Private Procurement and Corruption

Much of the military budget is spent, not on direct army recruits, but private manufacturing companies, and 'Private Military Security Contractors' (PMSCs). First, the largest UK manufacturer is BAE Systems plc. Its predecessor was a nationalised and merged entity from 1977,[79] while the British Aerospace Act 1980 created a corporation and sold off shares from 1981 to 1986.[80] The Secretary of State guaranteed any liabilities of the company if it went insolvent,[81] and it transferred a few shares (quickly dissipated) to employees.[82] The government retains a 'golden share', enabling it to prevent foreign takeovers.[83] While its largest customer is the UK government, it also sells military hardware to the USA, Australia, India and Saudi Arabia. It was the world's fourth-largest arms dealer in 2018, but was seventh by 2020 as the USA began spending more and Chinese data became public (see Table 19.1).

BAE Systems' past practice exemplifies how the arms trade is financed by systemic corruption and bribery. In *R (Corner House Research) v Director of the Serious Fraud Office*, the Serious Fraud Office (SFO) had halted a criminal investigation into bribery by BAE Systems of Saudi officials to secure the 'Al-Yamamah' ('the dove') arms deal, dating back to 1985. The UK government originally exchanged fighter planes and arms for 600,000 barrels of crude oil a day, and BAE Systems officials persistently paid bribes to Saudis through shell companies, or 'marketing advisers'. This included a total of over £135 million from 2001 to maintain ongoing business.[84] In 2006, as the SFO investigated, the Saudi government threatened to cancel negotiations to buy

75 Dempsey, 'UK Defence Personnel Statistics', 11. 76 Reserve Forces Act 1996, ss. 52–5.

77 Dempsey, 'UK Defence Personnel Statistics', 19, see map. Cf. Vegetius, *Epitoma Rei Militaris*, Book I.

78 See https://apply.army.mod.uk/what-we-offer/army-life/benefits. This is similar in the Royal Navy, and the RAF pays £15,220–39,000, 'depending on the role', while housing is provided on training or in service.

79 Aircraft and Shipbuilding Industries Act 1977, s. 1, founded BAe from mergers of 11 other companies.

80 British Aerospace Act 1980 (Government Shareholding) Order 1981 SI 1981/622 and SI 1986/848.

81 British Aerospace Act 1980, ss. 1, 4 and 9.

82 Mr Adam Butler, Hansard HC Debs. (17 December 1980) vol. 996, cols. 178–80W.

83 M. Hillyard, 'The Golden Share' in *Select Committee on International Development Eighth Report*, HC Library (June 1998) Annex II.

84 US DoJ Press Release (1 March 2010).

Table 19.1 Top 20 arms dealers, 2020[i]

	Company	Country	Arms revenue	% arms
1	Lockheed Martin	USA	$56.5bn	95%
2	Boeing	USA	$34.3bn	45%
3	General Dynamics	USA	$29.5bn	75%
4	Northrop Grumman	USA	$28.6bn	85%
5	Raytheon	USA	$27.4bn	94%
6	Aviation Industry	China	$25bn	38%
7	BAE Systems	UK	$21bn	90%
8	China North Indust.	China	$14.7bn	22%
9	L3Harris Technol.	USA	$13.9bn	77%
10	United Tech Corp.	USA	$13bn	17%
11	China Aerospace S&I	China	$12bn	32%
12	Airbus	EU–UK	$11.2bn	14%
13	Leonardo	Italy	$11.1bn	72%
14	China Shipbuilding	China	$11bn	20%
15	China Electronics	China	$10.1bn	31%
16	Thales	France	$9.2bn	45%
17	Almaz-Antey	Russia	$9.1bn	95%
18	China South Ind.	China	$8.8bn	31%
19	Huntington Ingalls	USA	$8.1bn	91%
20	China Aerospace S&T	China	$7.7bn	21%
		Total:	$362.2bn	

[i] 'Top 100 for 2020', *Defense News* (2020). Cf. S. Stebbins and E. Comen, 'Military Spending: 20 Companies Profiting the Most from War', *USA Today* (21 February 2019) (showing no Chinese firms). The numbers of employees in the major companies are significant, e.g. Lockheed Martin, 105,000, Boeing 153,000, BAE Systems 83,200 and Airbus 133,671.

Typhoon aircraft, and cancel all counterterrorism and security co-operation. So, Prime Minister Blair pressured the SFO to drop the investigation.[85] It did. The Divisional Court held that the SFO violated the rule of law. But in the House of Lords, Lord Bingham held that the SFO 'Director was confronted by an ugly and obviously unwelcome threat' and his decision 'involve[d] no affront to the rule of law'.[86] Baroness Hale said the rule of law was connected

[85] *R (Corner House Research) v Director of the Serious Fraud Office* [2008] UKHL 60, [17].

[86] Cf. T. Bingham, *The Rule of Law* (2011) 8, where Lord Bingham uses the case as a starting point to develop his book. Note that any bribe paid to an army official can be recovered: *Reading v Attorney General* [1951] AC 507. Money paid out of the company in violation of CA 2006, s. 171 can be recovered from BAE Systems officials, or directors, personally in a derivative action by BAE Systems members: see Ch. 3(4). What is the point of the UK authorities, including courts, if not to enforce the law? The contrary argument suggests that corrupt international relations, bribes and immunity for them, is a reality, and therefore it ought to be a reality.

to 'the principle that no-one, including powerful British companies who do business for powerful foreign countries, is above the law', but ultimately held that the SFO decision was not irrational.[87]

With the UK investigation dropped, and the UK's highest court feeling this was acceptable, the US Department of Justice found BAE Systems guilty of bribery under its Foreign Corrupt Practices Act, found that officials had lied about it and fined BAE Systems $400 million, noting 'its appreciation of the significant assistance provided by the U.K.'s Serious Fraud Office'.[88] This humiliation forced the UK government to pass a new Bribery Act 2010, so as to give the appearance of a more serious approach to stopping corruption.[89] The importance of the absolute prohibition on bribery, and its full enforcement, was acknowledged in the Supreme Court in 2014.[90] Nevertheless, the systemic nature of the problem means that the profit and favours from bribing foreign officials must be seen as a natural part of doing business and a major source of arms finance.

The second type of private procurement, as well as arms-makers and dealers, is of private military and security contractors. These have taken a growing share of military operations abroad, particularly since the Iraq invasion. As these companies are largely secretive and unregulated (see Ch. 19(3)(b)), accurate public information is difficult to find. Table 19.2 lists what appear to be among the world's largest private military contractors, though their revenue, employees and weaponry are not disclosed in a comparable fashion.

Since the 2001 appointment of Donald Rumsfeld as US Defense Secretary, the US military has aimed to become a 'lighter fighting force', while most Western militaries had already attempted to outsource most services, except combat.[91] Two consequences are, first, that private military force deaths frequently occur, but are not reported as army deaths; and, second, that it could be claimed that 'US troops' left Iraq in 2011 while thousands of private contractors remained.[92] As well as these conventional forces, a growing ecosystem of private intelligence operative groups have developed: the most notorious of these was SCL Group, a military intelligence and psychological operations firm which sold 'consulting' services to produce propaganda that swayed elections. Its subsidiary, 'Cambridge Analytica', was used in the 2016 Brexit referendum by Vote Leave, as well as by the Ted Cruz and Donald Trump campaigns in the USA.[93] Thus

87 [2008] UKHL 60, [55]–[57]. 88 US DoJ Press Release (1 March 2010).

89 Bribery Act 2010, ss. 6 (bribery of foreign officials), 7 (failure of commercial organisations to prevent bribery), 12 (limited territorial and personal extent) and 16 (applies to Crown).

90 *FHR European Ventures LLP v Cedar Capital Partners LLC* [2014] UKSC 45, [42], per Lord Neuberger, referring to 'Wider policy considerations'.

91 R. Godfrey, J. Brewis, J. Grady, and C. Grocott, 'The Private Military Industry and Neoliberal Imperialism: Mapping the Terrain' (2014) 21(1) *Organization* 106.

92 C. Kinsey, *Corporate Soldiers and International Security: The Rise of Private Military Companies* (2006) ch. 5.

93 C. Wylie, *Mindf*ck* (2019) ch. 1; K. P. Vogel and T. Parti, 'Cruz Partners with Donor's "Psychographic" Firm', *Politico* (7 July 2015).

Table 19.2 Nine of the top private military contractors (apparently)[i]

	Company	Country
1	G4S	UK
2	Unity Resources	Australia
3	Erinys	British Virgin Isl.
4	Asia Security Group	USA
5	DynCorp	USA
6	Triple Canopy	USA
7	Aegis Defence Services	UK
8	Defion Internacional	Peru
9	Academi (Blackwater)	USA

[i] L. McKenna and R. Johnson, 'A Look at the Largest Private Armies in the World', *Business Insider* (3 June 2012) (note that this source is itself unsourced, and there is not clear, verifiable information as yet). See also A. Kemeroff, 'War for Money: Leading Private Military Companies of the World', *Medium* (2018), additionally listing FDG Corp., MPRI (USA) and Northbridge Services Group (Dominican Republic).

military enterprises may be financed, not just by governments, but by private groups that aim to take over governments.

In war or hostile zones, procurement contracts often hire private military groups for 'travel everywhere', and may engage in combat, yet governments attempt to deny responsibility for such groups: for example, in 2009, an employee of ArmourGroup (G4S) shot two people in a drunken brawl in Iraq, and it transpired that he was allowed to work despite being on probation for robbery and firearm offences in Manchester.[94] In another example, Blackwater employees in 2007 killed seventeen civilians, and injured twenty-four, in a firefight in Nisour Square, Baghdad, and were only sentenced to murder in 2014 and 2015.[95] The company itself had its US licence temporarily suspended and was then sold and renamed twice; it is now called 'Academi'. None of the company's executives were made to take responsibility for the mass killing. This lack of responsibility is heightened by the narrow state of international law: a 1977 protocol to the Geneva Conventions defines a 'mercenary' as someone recruited to fight in an armed conflict, for private gain, who is not a national and has not been sent by a state,[96] though this has not been adopted by most countries. In *Nicaragua v United States*, the

[94] M. Hastings, 'Soldiers of Fortune Cannot Remain Outside the Law', *Financial Times* (13 August 2009).

[95] N. Woolf, 'Former Blackwater Guards Sentenced for Massacre of Unarmed Iraqi Civilians', *The Guardian* (14 April 2015).

[96] Geneva Conventions, Additional Protocol I (1977), art. 47(2).

International Court of Justice held that the USA could only be liable for paramilitary groups, which it sent to overthrow the Nicaraguan government, if it had 'effective control of the operations in the course of which the alleged violations were committed'.[97] Similarly in *Ilascu v Moldova and Russia*, Russia provided political and military support to a Moldovan separatist group. The European Court of Human Rights held that Russia was liable, but only as the group was 'under the effective authority, or at the very least the decisive influence, of the Russian Federation'.[98] This equally narrow approach contrasts with the wide 'enterprise liability' standard in tort law,[99] and therefore enables both state and private military to operate without responsibility, and despite the damage they cause.

(c) Death and Destruction

A third source of finance is that military enterprises do not pay for the death and destruction that they cause. Damage is inherent in armed conflict. Yet the lessons of World War One, where Germany was forced to pay reparations and its economic collapse brought it to fascism, and World War Two, where the US Marshall Plan invested to rebuild Europe, were ignored. After the invasion of Iraq was launched by the USA and UK, the US Deputy Defense Secretary told Congress, Iraq is 'a country that can really finance its own reconstruction, and relatively soon', an assertion that appeared to be calculated upon restoring Iraqi oil flows, of which US and UK companies would take a large share.[100] The reality was around $12 billion in aid originally sent vanished in a sandstorm of theft.[101] Of the million dead, those displaced, or those whose homes were blown up or shot at, only a few received any compensation.[102]

The enterprises making weaponry also do not pay for, and are therefore subsidised by, the death and damage they cause. To export arms, the Export Control Act 2002 requires that a licence from the Secretary of State is secured.[103] BAE Systems sales mean, for example, that its weapons and planes have been used in the Saudi-led war against Houthi rebels in Yemen. The Saudi military is responsible for war crimes, including targeted civilian bombing and mass starvation. In *R (Campaign Against Arms Trade) v Secretary of State for*

[97] *Nicaragua v United States* [1986] ICJ Rep 14, [115]. [98] [2004] ECHR 318.

[99] *Catholic Child Welfare Society v Institute of the Brothers of the Christian Schools* [2012] UKSC 56.

[100] A. Fifield, 'Contractors Reap $138bn from Iraq War', *Financial Times* (18 March 2013). See further C. Kinsey, *Private Contractors and the Reconstruction of Iraq: Transforming Military Logistics* (2009). There was $94.09bn in foreign donations from 2003 to 2012, while the Iraqi population has grown from 25m in 2003 to 40m in 2020.

[101] D. Pallister, 'How the US Sent $12bn in Cash to Iraq. And Watched It Vanish', *The Guardian* (8 February 2007).

[102] E.g. M. Tran, 'US Compensation Payments to Iraqi Civilians Made Public', *The Guardian* (12 April 2007).

[103] Export Control Act 2002, s. 1 (controls for 'goods of any description') and Export Control Order 2008, SI 2008/3231.

International Trade, the Court of Appeal held that the UK government was required to review whether exports could be used in violation of international law, and that the Secretary of State had acted irrationally as it failed to ask 'whether there was an historic pattern of breaches' of international humanitarian law by 'Saudi Arabia in particular'.[104] Seventeen days after the judgment, the UK government announced its review conclusion, that any violations were 'isolated incidents', that it would renew arms sales and 'Saudi Arabia has a genuine intent and the capacity to comply with IHL' (i.e. international humanitarian law).[105] This came just nine months after the Saudi prince (an adolescent dictator) and his accomplices murdered, cut up and binned a *Washington Post* journalist, at its Istanbul consulate.[106] It is unclear what rational basis the UK government's conclusion has. It should be seen for what it is, a disregard for death because the Saudi neo-feudal regime pays money.

With civilians, the first victims of war are troops in combat. If veterans survive being blown up, shot, suffering disease or hypothermia, they often return with serious physical and mental trauma. For example, by 2012, 45 per cent of Iraq and Afghanistan US veterans had claimed disability compensation for psychiatric and non-psychiatric medical problems,[107] while rates of suicide doubled.[108] Families who share the horrors of war can be severely affected.[109] The UK Armed Forces Covenant, which is stated to be an 'enduring covenant' between the people of the UK and the armed forces, states 'the whole nation has a moral obligation to the members' of armed services and they 'deserve our respect and support, and fair treatment'.[110] However the Ministry of Defence has often argued to have no duty of care in tort to its own members. In 1996, in *Mulcahy v Ministry of Defence*, a soldier negligently firing a howitzer injured Mulcahy as he walked near the front of the gun. The Court of Appeal agreed that it was 'common sense and sound policy' that there was no liability for negligence during combat, and 'it could be highly detrimental to the conduct of military operations if each soldier had to be conscious that . . . he owed [a duty of care] to his comrade'.[111] This disingenuous justification ignores that the only purpose of a duty among soldiers is to impose vicarious liability on the employer (the Ministry) to secure full

104 [2019] EWCA Civ 1020, [138].

105 E. Truss, 'Trade Update: Written Statement', HCWS339 (7 July 2020).

106 E. Schmitt and N. Fandos, 'Saudi Prince "Complicit" in Khashoggi's Murder, Senators Say after C.I.A. Briefing', *New York Times* (4 December 2018).

107 R. J. McNally and B. C. Frueh, 'Why Are Iraq and Afghanistan War Veterans Seeking PTSD Disability Compensation at Unprecedented Rates?' (2013) 27 *J Anxiety Disorders* 520.

108 E.g. 'Veterans More Likely than Civilians to Die by Suicide, VA Study Finds', *NBC News* (18 June 2018). Disgracefully, UK statistics are kept of suicides while in the armed forces, but not among veterans where people become most vulnerable. See Ministry of Defence, 'Suicides in the UK Regular Armed Forces', ONS (December 2018). Cf. 'Is There a Suicide Crisis for British Veterans?', *BBC News* (16 February 2019).

109 In fictional accounts see *The Deer Hunter* (1978) on Vietnam, and P. Barker, *Regeneration* (1991) on World War One.

110 Armed Forces Covenant (2014).

111 [1996] QB 732.

compensation for injury at work,[112] and it would have no impact on the employee himself.

From 2008, it was first acknowledged that 'the soldier does not lose all protection simply because he is in hostile territory' and there could be human rights claims.[113] The Supreme Court tried to halt this development in 2010,[114] but recanted after an opinion of the European Court of Human Rights,[115] in 2013. In *Smith v Ministry of Defence*, Smith claimed the Ministry of Defence breached European Convention on Human Rights (ECHR), article 2 (the right to life) by failing to protect soldiers from foreseeable risks – for instance, against roadside bombs. The question was whether soldiers had any claim at all when they were in the field of combat, to fall within UK jurisdiction under ECHR, article 1. The Supreme Court agreed that jurisdiction extended wherever control and authority was exercised over a soldier, yet asserted that whether a duty exists still depends on the 'circumstances'.[116] While tort system has limited application, there is a less generous system in the Armed Forces and Reserve Forces (Compensation Scheme) Order 2011, and this has the major advantage of not requiring proof of fault. For example, damage to one tooth requiring 'a crown or root canal surgery' yields £3,090, 'burns affecting 70% or more of whole body' yields £298,700, and loss of both legs and arms yields £650,000.[117] How much money would you think was fair if it happened to you?

Because war and military expenditure is inherently destructive, it has been argued that it absorbs surplus capital and investment 'without increasing wages, and so maintains profits. Other forms of state expenditure do not do this.'[118] However, it is not clear that evidence supports this theory. It stands to reason that domestic military production may increase wages like any other production, provided it brings the economy closer to full employment (see Ch. 5(4)). Although the product of military equipment does not add to social wealth, the same is true for many kinds of socially useless work, such as pointless form filling, waiting on call or for instructions, and many other tasks that we often perform. But the impact on wages is a separate issue. The

[112] Cf. *Williams v Natural Life Health Foods Ltd* [1998] UKHL 17, per Lord Steyn suggesting an action against any employee personally would be precluded.

[113] *Smith v Assistant Deputy Coroner for Oxfordshire* [2008] EWHC (Admin) 694, per Collins J.

[114] *R (Smith) v Secretary of State for Defence* [2010] UKSC 29, denying ECHR, art. 2 applied in Iraq where soldier died of hyperthermia, as it was outside of the UK's control and the jurisdictional scope of the Human Rights Act 1998.

[115] *Al-Skeini v United Kingdom* (2011) 53 EHRR 18, holding that there is responsibility 'whenever the state through its agents exercises control and authority over an individual, and thus jurisdiction'.

[116] [2013] UKSC 41, [98].

[117] Armed Forces and Reserve Forces (Compensation Scheme) Order 2011 (SI 2011/517) regs. 7–12 and Sch. 3.

[118] Dunne, 'The Changing Military Industrial Complex in the UK', 93, summarising P. A. Baran and P. M. Sweezy, *Monopoly Capital: An Essay on the American Economist and Social Order* (1966).

true cost of the military arises whenever it is put into use. It is not only the destruction, but also the enormous diversion of opportunity for positive production that is inherent in military production. 'The cost of one modern heavy bomber is', said President Eisenhower, 'this: a modern brick school in more than 30 cities. It is two electric power plants, each serving a town of 60,000 population. It is two fine, fully equipped hospitals . . . This is not a way of life at all, in any true sense. Under the cloud of threatening war, it is humanity hanging from a cross of iron.'[119]

(d) Climate Damage

A fourth source of finance for the military is not paying for climate damage. The single largest user of fossil fuels is the US Department of Defense, responsible for an estimated average of 66 million tonnes of carbon dioxide (and equivalent greenhouse gas) emissions, equivalent to 14 million (American) cars every year.[120] This is because the movement of the military (even without a war) is still powered predominantly by oil and other fossil fuels. Paradoxically, the US Department of Defense has itself recognised that climate damage is the most 'urgent and growing threat to our national security, contributing to increased disasters, refugee flows, and conflicts over basic resources such as food and water . . . projected to increase over time'. [121] Further, the US government has recognised that switching military power sources to clean electricity was a security necessity – for instance, because oil tanks can ignite and explode during combat.[122] Electric power has fewer risks.

Climate damage also causes military conflict – and therefore propels spending – in two main ways. First, fossil-fuel states, particularly Russia, consistently support political parties and fanatics abroad – such as Trump, Farage, Le Pen, the 'Alternative für Deutschland', Lega Nord or Vox in Spain – that deny global warming is man-made, or are conspiracy theorists. Following her defeat in the 2016 presidential election, Hillary Clinton argued that the reason Putin attacked US democracy through cyber-war on social media platforms (see Ch. 17(3)(c)(ii)) was that Putin 'doesn't like democracy' and 'doesn't like us'.[123] While this may be true, the more complex and plausible motive, plus a financial incentive, is that stopping international co-operation to end climate damage enables the short-term survival of the Russian fossil-fuel economy.

[119] D. D. Eisenhower, 'The Chance for Peace' (16 April 1953). The cost of stealth bombers and drones is now more.

[120] N. C. Crawford, 'Pentagon Fuel Use, Climate Change, and the Costs of War', Brown University Working Paper (2019).

[121] Department of Defense, 'Congressional Report on National Implications of Climate Change' (23 July 2015) 3.

[122] E. Wolff, 'How the Department of Defense Could Help Win the War on Climate Change', *Politico* (4 January 2021).

[123] Hillary Clinton Interview, *Late Show with Stephen Colbert* (20 September 2017) YouTube at 5:10.

The same is true for climate damage deniers in other fossil-fuel states such as Australia, Canada or Saudi Arabia. The short-sightedness is that shutting down fossil fuels, and relying on clean natural resources, such as wind in Russia or Canada, and solar in Australia or Saudi Arabia, can boost the economy as all countries have vast deposits of metals needed for these and batteries.[124]

Second, there are direct conflicts over fossil-fuel resources. The US–UK invasion of Iraq from 2003 had multiple causes, both ideological and material[125] and, according to Tony Blair, it was 'absurd' to say it was driven by a desire to seize Iraqi oil because 'we could [have] probably cut a deal with Saddam tomorrow in relation to the oil'.[126] It was meant to have been about 'weapons of mass destruction', which intelligence and inspections before and after the invasion showed did not exist. Whatever was in the heads of the US and UK governments, an obvious conflict of interest comes from George W. Bush and his Vice, Dick Cheney, being heavily invested in oil businesses. What is 'absurd' is denying oil was a primary motivating factor for the Iraq war. As Trump put it, 'I always said: take the oil.'[127]

(3) Governance

The governance of the military can be analysed in two main parts: (a) the military command of the nation state and (b) the governance of military manufacturers or private contractors.

(a) Military Command

The defining feature of military governance is near absolute discretion through a chain of command, from Parliament down to the soldier. In Parliament, the Prime Minister is the person who can command a majority of the House of Commons, and at any moment, a majority of members may convene to replace any Prime Minister. Parliament can never be shut down by executive order.[128] The primacy of Parliament, with ultimate collective authority over the military, is essential for democracies to control the military.[129] The Prime Minister can

[124] See the 'Product export' charts at https://oec.world/ for Australia, Canada, Russia and Saudi Arabia.

[125] E.g. 'Tony Blair: "I Express More Sorrow, Regret and Apology than You Can Ever Believe"', *The Guardian* (6 July 2016).

[126] B. Gökay, 'Why You Can't Explain the Iraq War Without Mentioning Oil', *Conversation* (8 July 2016).

[127] B. Levin, 'Trump Twice Floated Plundering Iraq's Oil to Iraq's Prime Minister', *Vanity Fair* (26 November 2018).

[128] *R (Miller) v Prime Minister* [2019] UKSC 41 (on the illegality of Parliament's prorogation).

[129] R. H. Kohn, 'How Democracies Control the Military' (1997) 8(4) *J Democracy* 140 referring to (1) democracy and human rights; (2) making control of the military 'as an expression of the whole society's will . . . not simply [of] the incumbent president or prime minister'; (3) countervailing power, including dispersed centres of force (such as the police) and personal

replace any Secretary of State for Defence, and in turn this minister has 'general responsibility for defence', as well as holding title to Ministry of Defence rights and liabilities.[130] Together, a Defence Council has 'powers of command and administration over Her Majesty's armed forces, and of an Admiralty Board, an Army Board and an Air Force Board'.[131] The Defence Council includes the defence ministers, the Chief and Vice-Chief of the Defence Staff, and the chiefs of staff of the three services. Within the Cabinet, a Sub-Committee on Overseas and Defence is chaired by the Prime Minister, and may also be attended by the Chief of Defence Staff, heads of intelligence agencies or the chair of the Joint Intelligence Committee, and senior officials from the foreign, defence, home, international development and Cabinet offices and the Treasury. Within Parliament, three main committees, responsible for major inquiries scrutinising military activity, are the Committee on National Security, the Public Accounts Committee and the Defence Committee.[132]

There is a right to complain through the chain of command to a Services Complaints Ombudsman.[133] The rights of soldiers to talk to their Member of Parliament are also to be 'jealously safeguarded'.[134] Otherwise military command involves near total subordination. A member of the navy, military or air forces of the Crown has no statutory right to join a union,[135] though there is a positive right in international law, as in the common law of contract, to freely associate.[136] Strikes by armed force members are an offence,[137] though in reality, and despite law, military strikes have been essential for the preservation or restoration of democracy.[138] In times of genuine and historic crises of democracy, positive law bans are often beside the point. The maintenance of discipline is the primary goal of the Armed Forces Act 2006, with offences for disobedience to lawful commands, or for any conduct that is 'prejudicial to good order and service discipline'.[139]

For prosecution of offences in the military, there is a separate jurisdiction of court martial. Service members have a right to elect for this rather than having a commanding officer deal with a charge summarily.[140] Much of the Armed Forces

accountability for illegal acts; and (4) a culture of 'abstinence by the military from intervention in political life'.

130 Defence (Transfer of Functions) Act 1964, ss. 1(1)(a) and 2.

131 Defence (Transfer of Functions) Act 1964, s. 1(1)(b).

132 E.g. *Lessons of Iraq*, HC 57(2003–4), though this committee was denied orders issued by Chief of Defence Staff.

133 Armed Forces Act 2006, ss. 340A–O and 365B.

134 HC Debs. (9 May 1956) col. 1382.

135 Trade Union and Labour Relations (Consolidation) Act 1992, ss. 273–4.

136 E.g. *Matelly v France* [2014] ECHR 1017 (Defence Code blanket ban on joining union violated ECHR, art. 11).

137 Incitement to Disaffection Act 1934, s. 1 (seducing armed force member from duty). Cf. Police Act 1996, s. 91.

138 E.g. the English Revolution 1640, the Glorious Revolution 1688, the American Revolution 1776, the German Revolution 1918 or the fall of the Berlin Wall 1989. Many liberation and democratic movements have also been brutally suppressed, e.g. the Indian 'Mutiny' 1857.

139 AFA 2006, ss. 12 and 19. Cf. *R v Dodman* [1998] 2 Cr App R 338 on good order.

140 AFA 2006, ss. 50 and 129. Under s. 64, one cannot be tried for the same offence by a civil court.

Act 2006 rewrites powers of arresting, searching or detaining a suspect.[141] An Appeal Court from a summary conviction is a judge advocate and two officers, while a court martial is a judge and usually three to five lay members, but may have up to seven or no lay members.[142] There is a Court Martial Appeal court,[143] and then an appeal again to the Supreme Court. For example, in *R v Spear*, servicemen in the army and air force claimed their court martial lacked independence and was not a fair trial under ECHR, article 6, after being found guilty of assault and actual bodily harm. While the court martial had a permanent president, who may have acted for the Ministry of Defence, the House of Lords held there was no violation, and could be part of having 'disciplined forces' where 'lawful orders will be obeyed' and 'standards of self-control and conduct will be shown'.[144] Service law also applies to civilians outside the UK under officer command, or their family members.[145] In the case of NATO allies, the Visiting Forces Act 1952 excludes UK criminal court jurisdiction over visiting forces where the offence arises from military duty and is between the visiting force members.[146]

(b) Military-Industrial Complex

The governance of the 'military-industrial complex', since the retreat of state-owned enterprise, typically starts with the patterns set under the Companies Act 2006. As mentioned above, BAE Systems plc has an ordinary share structure since privatisation, but government retains a 'golden share', enabling it to prevent foreign takeovers.[147] This said, it is required to comply with licensing rules for the firearms it produces.[148] It must also generally secure a licence under the Export Control Act 2002 from the Secretary of State for arms exports.[149]

For domestic private military contractors, the Firearms Act 1968 requires that possession of firearms is licensed, that certain firearms such as automatic weapons and rocket launchers are banned altogether without authority[150] and that there are fees for acquiring and renewing licences updated by order of the Secretary of State.[151] There are special fees for PMSCs, as opposed to other

[141] AFA 2006, ss. 75–8, 83–93, 98–112. [142] AFA 2006, ss. 142 and 155.

[143] Courts-Martial (Appeals) Act 1968, s. 1(3).

[144] *R v Spear* or *Boyd v Army Prosecuting Authority* [2002] UKHL 31, [3].

[145] AFA 2006, Sch. 15. Cf. *Martin v United Kingdom* (2006) Application no. 40426/98 (composition of court martial raised legitimate fear that it lacked independence and impartiality under ECHR, art. 6).

[146] Visiting Forces Act 1952, s. 3. [147] Hillyard, 'The Golden Share'.

[148] Firearms Act 1968, s. 3 applies to manufacture of firearms.

[149] Export Control Act 2002, s. 1 (controls for 'goods of any description') and Export Control Order 2008, SI 2008/3231.

[150] Firearms Act 1968, ss. 1–6.

[151] Firearms Act 1968, ss. 32, 35 and 43; Firearms (Variation of Fees) Order 2015.

groups of firearms holders.[152] Furthermore, the Private Security Industry Act 2001 requires licences for any 'designated activities', such as 'manned guarding'.[153]

These Acts only extend to UK territory,[154] leaving out the vast private military industry, which has increased particularly since the invasion of Iraq. A Green Paper discussed regulation in 2002,[155] but the industry remains 'self-regulated'. In 2009, 500 private military companies had signed up to an 'International Code of Conduct for Private Security Providers' of 2010, 'around a third of them British',[156] but this does not create direct, domestic, binding rules. According to Professor Nigel White, there are at least four problems with self-regulation in this regard.[157] First, self-regulation is hardly regulation, as companies get to judge their own cause. Second, sanctions are limited or absent. Third, the application of standards in codes or elsewhere is open to lax interpretation. Fourth, the UK government itself seems to have 'limited willingness to engage with its positive responsibilities under human rights law to ensure that private actors' follow the law.[158] In this way, contractors such as G4S, Erynis or Aegis remain mainly driven by attaining more shareholder profit, an incentive that runs counter to the public interest in ending conflict.

(4) Human Rights

What is the purpose of the military? In general terms, most agree it is for upholding national security.[159] But what does that really mean? Is the military truly for self-defence? Or is it an instrument to subjugate people outside national borders, who have no say in its power, and who may threaten the economic assets of groups within a nation? The difficulty in this question from a lawyer's perspective is that force is the antithesis to law. As the Athenians told the Melians,[160] rights evaporate before power. Then, rights only exist to the extent that people take a critical, reflective attitude to moral wrongs.[161] This

[152] See www.gov.uk/guidance/firearms-licensing-police-guidance with total £616 fee for a 'PMSC first time' licence, £796 for a dealer and £569 for a 'carrier'.

[153] Private Security Industry Act 2001, ss. 1–3 and Sch. 2. Also Private Security Industry (Licence Fees) Order 2020 and Private Security Industry Act 2001 (Designated Activities) Order 2006.

[154] Firearms Act 1968, s. 60 (does not extend to N. Ireland). Private Security Industry Act 2001, s. 26(3) (UK).

[155] FCO, *Private Military Companies: Options for Regulation*, Green Paper, HC 577 (2001–2).

[156] Hansard (17 December 2012) col. 72WS.

[157] N. D. White, 'Regulation of the Private Military and Security Sector: Is the UK Fulfilling Its Human Rights Duties?' (2016) 16 *Human Rights L Rev* 585, 591–2 summarises these.

[158] White, 'Regulation of the Private Military and Security Sector', 592.

[159] E.g. T. Aquinas, *Summa Theologica* (1274) II, II, question 40, and he quotes Augustine: 'The passion for inflicting harm, the cruel thirst for vengeance, an unpacific and relentless spirit, the fever of revolt, the lust of power, and such like things, all these are rightly condemned in war.'

[160] Thucydides, *History of the Peloponnesian War* (*c.* 410 BC) Book V, §89, trans. M. I. Finley and R. Warner (1974).

[161] Cf. H. L. A. Hart, *The Concept of Law* (1961) ch. 4, 56–8.

becomes clear as two of the most important positive rights that relate to the military are not yet codified into statute, or made explicit in case law. These are (a) the right to security and (b) the right to life.

(a) Right to Security?

The right to 'security of person' is explicit in international law;[162] however, the nature of a corresponding duty is not. The UK Armed Forces Covenant says that the 'first duty of Government is the defence of the realm', an explicit commitment to national security and security of the person, which invites support for armed service members in return.[163] However, unless it is deemed a contract or a binding assurance, it is difficult to see what rights could flow from this covenant. Even a hypothetical statutory duty to provide 'security' would be problematic since the courts have held that public duties do not generate private rights.[164] If a foreign aggressor attacks the UK, the institutions of Parliament, the executive's departmental control and the ballot box are the means of accountability rather than litigation in court.[165] This is made more complex when conventional armed attacks are accompanied by hybrid and cyber warfare, used directly against citizens and voters on social media.[166] The state monopolises the meaning of national security and interests, so that protestors who argued nuclear weaponry threatened national security (somewhat predictably) lost their case when prosecuted for trespassing on an airfield.[167]

Outside UK borders, *China Navigation Co. Ltd v Attorney General* held there was no duty on the Crown to afford military protection. An English shipping company had requested armed guards on their ship to protect against pirates. They received armed guards by agreeing that they, the shipowners, should pay them, but then the shipowners claimed they need not pay. The

[162] UDHR 1948, art. 3: 'Everyone has the right to life, liberty and the security of person'; ICCPR 1966, art. 9; ECHR 1950, art. 5; CFREU 2000, art. 6.

[163] Armed Forces Covenant (2014).

[164] *Stovin v Wise* [1996] UKHL 15, per Lord Hoffmann.

[165] Cf. *Hill v Chief Constable of West Yorkshire* [1987] UKHL 12 (that the police had no duty of care to prevent the 'Yorkshire ripper' murders of his victims as he was 'never in the custody of the police force').

[166] See E. McGaughey, 'Could Brexit Be Void?' (2018) 29(3) *King's LJ* 331 (summarising House of Commons reports on Russian interference, in both the Scottish independence and Brexit referendums); Mueller Report, vol. I, Introduction. The principal beneficiaries of the 2016 polls contended there was no 'successful' interference by Russia (Johnson), and there was no 'collusion' (Trump). What is 'successful' differs from the appropriate test – namely, whether there was a material increase in risk. The US law definition of 'conspiracy' used by the Mueller Report accepted that ignorance of the law is a defence, relying on decisions of Kavanaugh J, who Trump appointed to the US Supreme Court. See Mueller Report, V.C.3.a. §185. Whether this system still functions is questionable.

[167] See *Chandler v DPP* [1964] AC 763, finding protestors at Wethersfield Airfield, occupied by the US Air Force and a 'prohibited place' under the Official Secrets Act 1911, guilty of espionage and not allowed to bring evidence of their genuine belief in what constituted the UK national security interest.

Court of Appeal held the Crown could agree to provide military protection on any terms it thought fit, including a requirement to pay costs.[168] It follows that even if the 'right to security' exists within the realm, it may not outside.

(b) Right to Life?

The right to 'life' is also explicit in international law,[169] but it is not clear what this means in relation to the military, either inside or outside borders. For people within the national borders, this is a core element of the right to security and, since the Crown Proceedings (Armed Forces) Act 1987, it is possible to bring a claim in tort against armed forces for any death (or personal injury or property damage). The Secretary of State may, however, revive immunity by order if there is 'imminent national danger or of any great emergency' or 'for the purposes of any warlike operations in any part of the world' outside the UK.[170] Compensation from the Crown is not as good, for most people, as the right to life, and so it is crucial that there will also be criminal liability for murder of a civilian, where armed forces are not acting in self-defence or by necessity. The days when soldiers shot people in the back while they ran away in Northern Ireland, and were acquitted, have changed with the quality of the judiciary,[171] and as both sides grew older. In *R v Clegg*, the House of Lords held that a soldier who shot a passenger in the back, as a car drove away, was guilty of murder.[172] If a soldier is following an order, the commanding officer giving the order is guilty of murder.[173]

Outside the UK, people are not afforded the same rights. In *R (Al-Skeini) v Secretary of State for Defence*, the House of Lords held that five claimants who were shot dead by British troops in Basra, Iraq, either in the streets or in their homes, were outside UK jurisdiction. A sixth, Baha Mousa, was tortured and beaten to death in a British military detention unit, and a majority (Lord Bingham dissenting) held that he was within UK jurisdiction for the purpose of the Human Rights Act 1998 and, consequently, subject to the right to life in ECHR, article 2, as well as the prohibition on torture in article 3. The Ministry of Defence later paid a total of £2.83 million to nine men, and to Mousa's family, admitting liability for killing and torture.[174] Yet only one soldier was

168 [1932] 2 KB 197.

169 UDHR 1948, art. 3: 'Everyone has the right to life, liberty and the security of person'; ICCPR 1966, arts. 6 and 9; ECHR 1950, art. 2; CFREU 2000, art. 2.

170 Crown Proceedings (Armed Forces) Act 1987, s. 2, referring to the previous immunity in Crown Proceedings Act 1947, s. 10.

171 Cf. *Attorney General for Northern Ireland Reference (No. 1 of 1975)* [1977] AC 105, where Lord Diplock held that thinking someone was a terrorist gave 'the accused [soldier] reasonable grounds for apprehension of imminent danger to himself and other members of the patrol if the deceased were allowed to get away'.

172 [1995] 1 AC 482.

173 Cf. *Keighley v Bell* (1866) 4 F&F 763, 790, per Willes J (if prosecution results from obedience to an order, a soldier is not liable unless the order was manifestly illegal).

174 'British Government Pays Compensation for Iraq "Torture"', *DW.com* (11 July 2008).

ultimately sentenced to just one year in jail for Mousa's murder, even though he was found guilty of a 'war crime' under the International Criminal Court Act 2002. So far as the other cases of wanton killing in Basra go, the European Court of Human Rights, in the appeal of the *Al-Skeini* case, made clear that the Convention applies 'whenever the state through its agents exercises control and authority over an individual, and thus jurisdiction', and 'when, as a consequence of lawful or unlawful military action, a Contracting State exercises effective control of an area outside that national territory'. It must secure 'the entire range of substantive rights set out in the Convention'.[175] Despite this, in *Ministry of Defence v Iraqi Civilians*, the Supreme Court held that tort claims by 600 Iraqis for unlawful detention and physical maltreatment between 2003 and 2009 were subject to a three-year time bar in Iraqi law, since the Foreign Limitation Periods Act 1984 required foreign time-limit laws to apply.[176] In Iraq itself, Coalition Provision Authority Order 17 gave coalition forces immunity from any legal process. While military objectives are said to include defence, and while 'life, liberty and security' may be human rights, the realisation of these rights in law is a different and unfulfilled matter.

(5) Conclusion

The biggest question overhanging the military is how can it be eliminated as fast and securely as possible? The rights to security, life and liberty, as well as a clean environment are paradoxically dependent on a military, but only so long as other hostile militaries remain. In other words, there is a human collective-action problem. Any business in the weapons trade is inherently likely to be riddled with corruption, because those who want arms to kill the most are likely to be terrible people. The top priority should be a negotiated diversion of military spending, by reciprocal commitment, to transfer finance from arms to productive assets. The second priority must be to drastically raise public oversight through the governance standards in any private military producers. If their affairs are transparent, it is likely that their business simply cannot continue in their current form. The third priority is to raise the costs of war, by increasing liability for death or destruction in civil law, and by making people pay for crimes. Ultimately, the incentives for war have to be eliminated, by ending the human struggle for resources, homes or a sense of superiority. Ending war means ending inequality and climate damage, and justice on a living planet means peace.

[175] *Al-Skeini v United Kingdom* [2011] ECHR 1093, [137]–[138]. [176] [2016] UKSC 25.

Part IV
Policy

20

Fiscal and Social Policy

Contents

'Don't you hate to pay taxes!' said a secretary once to Justice Oliver Wendell Holmes. 'No, young feller. I like to pay taxes. With them I buy civilization.'[1] Whether or not we really 'like' them, the old American judge had a point. The trouble is we do not yet have a consensus on our measure of 'civilization'. While most countries have pursued 'growth' in 'Gross Domestic Product' (GDP), this perversely counts all economic activity as positive, all contracts whatever the effect, even when they damage our health, well-being, environment or security. It 'counts air pollution and cigarette advertising, and ambulances to clear our highways of carnage … It counts napalm and counts nuclear warheads … It counts Whitman's rifle', said Robert F. Kennedy, before being shot in his 1968 US presidential run. It 'measures everything in short, except that which makes life worthwhile'.[2] More than this, and though material things can help prosperity, where acquisition is unceasing, it runs against our most basic human instincts for a fulfilled yet peaceful life. Fiscal and social policy, how we fund and define civilisation and how we make the really big choices ultimately determine whether our society is just. 'Everyone has duties to the community', says the last, great universal right, 'in which alone the free and full development of [their] personality is possible.'[3]

In our present chapter of civilisation, all governments choose how to arrange taxation and prices to achieve the goals they set. We must pay prices

[1] F. Frankenfurter, *Mr. Justice Holmes and the Supreme Court* (1938) 42–3. Cf. *Compania General De Tabacos De Filipinas v Collector of Internal Revenue*, 275 US 87 (1927), per Holmes J: 'Taxes are what we pay for civilized society.'

[2] R. F. Kennedy, 'Remarks at the University of Kansas' (18 March 1968).

[3] UDHR 1948, art. 29(1).

for property transfers, just as we must pay taxes for anything that we need, so the question is whether price- or tax-funded enterprises lead to better outcomes. But although we have long discussed 'principles of taxation', a unified discussion with 'principles of prices' has been neglected.[4] Each has profound distributional implications, and in turn affects people's motivation to work, invest and innovate. For example, low taxes may encourage top earners to profit from their office but not do good work, and employers taking an unfair share of gains are likely to dampen productivity.[5] Higher prices for labour promote higher capital investment, while taxes on idle land, capital or wealth may ensure they are utilised. The tax system also can be used, not just to raise revenue, but to 'correct' failures of enterprise, like inequality, pollution or hoarding of wealth. But this hardly tackles the problems' real source. Four main basic 'tax bases' have been land (see Chs. 13–14), labour (Ch. 5(2)(a)), capital or gains (Ch. 4(4)) and trade, goods and services (Ch. 6(1)(e)). The rules of each could change to ensure a better 'pre-distribution' rather than 'redistribution' after the fact. What we do with taxes also matters: investment in education, health, clean energy, transport, communication or infrastructure will affect the security and resources that people have to innovate. Thus, the grand shape of tax and spending decisions, budgets and public services is part of the whole economic constitution.

(1) The Goals of Government

Before deciding the details of taxes, prices, budgeting and public services, all governments should set goals. These should match the preferences of the people who lend them power. 'Everyone has the right to take part in the government of his country', says the Universal Declaration, 'directly or through freely chosen representatives.'[6] And just as some political governments are less (or not at all) representative of the people, enterprise governance may be too. This is partly a choice of our political institutions: to have an autocratic or democratic economy, or some unprincipled mix floating in between. A recurring theme in this book is that human rights are fundamental and yet incomplete, because declarations, covenants, conventions and charters do not explain to us the financial and governance structures to realise the rights: the laws to deliver rights and which social and economic choices we should make. But before we choose, we need a goal and, in political economy and law, three main goals have been argued for: (a) growth, (b) a steady state and (c) a dynamic goal of social justice.

[4] But see Ch. 2(2)(f) and Ch. 6(1)(b) on bargaining power, fair competition and just prices.

[5] A. A. Berle and G. C. Means, *The Modern Corporation and Private Property* (1932) Book I; A. Cohn, E. Fehr, B. Herrmann and F. Schneider, 'Social Comparison in the Workplace: Evidence from a Field Experiment' (2014) 12(4) *J Eur Economic Association* 877.

[6] UDHR 1948, art. 21(1); ICCPR 1966, art. 25.

(a) Growth

The basic idea of economic growth, since the Industrial Revolution, is that society will become more prosperous and free when we produce more things: more goods, more education, more health and life, more energy, more transport, more media, more money. For Jeremy Bentham, 'the greatest good for the greatest number' was an intuitively appealing goal for all society.[7] We should maximise our 'utility'. Utility (more pleasure, less pain) could mean fewer things or less money if 'too much' is making you unhappy.[8] But future writers often took the goal to mean 'more'. As economics became a profession, the idea of a 'production possibility frontier' developed, on the presumption that our goal should be to arrange resources to optimise production, to produce as much as our economic 'frontier' allowed.[9] This preceded modern understandings of environmental limits of climate damage, or behavioural psychology, and was conceived when even the richest countries were poor.

The measure of gross 'national income' was originally developed during the Great Depression[10] and explored in a 1934 report by Simon Kuznets for the US Senate. Kuznets devised a method to add up 'all commodities produced and all personal services rendered ... at their market value' subtracting 'the nation's stock of goods which was expended (both as raw materials and as capital equipment) in producing this total'. Thus gross 'national income' means contract prices, minus depleted stock, and these could be deduced from the accounts of firms. However, in doing this, Kuznets argued that it was necessary to exclude, for example, services in the home because there was 'no reliable basis ... for estimating their value', the services of durable goods such as a house (unless it is sold or rented) or the value of 'illegal pursuits' which should not be counted because of 'their disserviceability to society at large'. In fact, said Kuznets, it was 'dangerous' to 'simplify a complex situation' down to one metric and, though it might shed 'a good deal of light on the productivity of the nation', measuring national income was 'subject to this type of illusion and resulting abuse'. 'The welfare of a nation can, therefore, scarcely be inferred from a measurement of national income as defined above.'[11] 'National income' included income from nationals abroad, and subtracted income from foreigners within a country, while GDP calculated income within a country regardless of nationality. The UK tended to favour 'gross domestic product' over national income. It was clear in US politics, at least by Robert F. Kennedy's speech in

[7] J. Bentham, *An Introduction to the Principles of Morals and Legislation* (1789).

[8] Cf. B. Spinoza, *On the Improvement of the Understanding* (1662) pointing out that no object is inherently good or bad, but it depends on the relation you have to it.

[9] W. F. Stolper and P. A. Samuelson, 'Protection and Real Wages' (1941) 9(1) *Rev Economic Studies* 58, 67.

[10] Cf. W. Petty, *Verbum Sapienti* (1664) chs. 1–2: 'Containing several Computations of the Wealth of the Kingdom' and 'Of the Value of the People'.

[11] S. Kuznets, 'National Income, 1929–32: Letter from the Acting Secretary of Commerce Transmitting in Response to Senate Resolution No. 220 (72d Cong.) A Report on National Income, 1929–32' (4 January 1934) 1–7.

1968, that national income measures (like GDP) included harm to the environment, health and international security.[12] But instead of reform, the US simply shifted from national income to GDP calculations in 1991. China did so from 1993, abandoning, as Russia had done, the Soviet 'Material Product System' which focused on production of goods, not services or finance, and followed administered, not market prices.[13] Thus, by the 1990s, GDP had become the international standard measure of 'success'.

By contrast, Amartya Sen and others attempted to develop a more rounded metric, not just to focus on economic activity.[14] The 'human development index' added number of years in education and life expectancy to GDP. In 2011, each metric was also 'adjusted' for inequality, the 'IHDI', and is reported on by the United Nations (UN).[15] However, the basic perversity of GDP has remained. If you sell me an apple for £1, and then I sell it back to you for £1, GDP has gone up by £2, even though we are both in exactly the same position as before, and nothing has been achieved. However, GDP also measures damage, going up if:

(1) people pay more for private schools, or university tuition fees, even as class sizes grow and quality decreases, instead of receiving cheaper, tax-funded, tuition-free education
(2) people pay for health insurance, and live shorter lives, instead of organising cheaper, free public healthcare
(3) asset managers or banks constantly buy and sell assets, and charge people more in fees for doing it, as they deplete pensions and other retirement incomes
(4) people rent homes, instead of owning them, or are constantly buying and selling and moving, instead of leading a more settled existence
(5) coal, oil or gas is being mined, drilled and burned and this is destroying the ecosphere
(6) people are buying individual cars, instead of using healthier, efficient or public transport
(7) the media and the Internet are monetised with ads, rather than being ad-free and running at the cost of production through voluntary or public funding
(8) there is production of guns, tanks, bombs, bombers and nuclear, chemical and biological weapons that threaten and destroy life and property.

[12] Kennedy, 'Remarks at the University of Kansas', referring to 'Gross National Product', and on definitional changes see GDP Directive 89/130/EEC and GNI Regulation (EU) 2019/516.

[13] J. Heijster and D. DeRock, 'How GDP Spread to China: The Experimental Diffusion of Macroeconomic Measurement' (2020) *Rev Int'l Political Economy* 1, 4–5.

[14] A. Sen, 'A Decade of Human Development' (2000) 1(1) *J Human Development* 17, on the economist Mahbub ul Haq.

[15] E.g. UN Development Programme, *Human Development Report 2015: Work for Human Development* (2015) Table 3.

In these ways and many others, far from inferring the 'welfare of a nation', GDP can actually be a measure of poverty, ill-health and damage, so long as someone has a contract for it. To give just one example, in 2019 the US spending on privatised healthcare was $11,072 per capita each year, and people's average life expectancy was 78.7 years, while Spain's free public health system spent $3,616 per capita and had a life expectancy of 83.5 years.[16] Yet, this means that GDP is $7,456 'higher' per capita in the USA than in Spain, even though people were dying 4.8 years younger, under a system where health insurance companies profit from extorting money from the sick, the dying and their families.[17] Thus, it would be possible to raise GDP in the UK by privatising the National Health Service (NHS) and cutting lifespans, turning pensions into individual accounts and slashing retirement, increasing fees for education while raising class sizes, abolishing all buses and trains to put everyone in a cab, fracking the country or dumping sewage in a river and paying for clean-up again, or making bombs and blowing it all up. GDP growth makes no sense as a goal for the economy or society. It hurts us.

(b) Steady State

In contrast to the theories and measures of growth and GDP, a second main goal has been that we should pursue a 'steady state'. In 1848, when the prospect of ongoing economic expansion had become the reality, John Stuart Mill wrote that although growth of capital and wealth might be a 'necessary stage in the progress of civilization', a 'stationary state' would be better. As he wrote:

> I confess I am not charmed with the ideal of life held out by those who think that the normal state of human beings is that of struggling to get on; that the trampling, crushing, elbowing, and treading on each other's heels, which form the existing type of social life, are the most desirable lot of human kind, or anything but the disagreeable symptoms of one of the phases of industrial progress . . . It is only in the backward countries of the world that increased production is still an important object: in those most advanced, what is economically needed is a better distribution . . . Nor is there much satisfaction in contemplating the world with nothing left to the spontaneous activity of nature; with every rood of land brought into cultivation, which is capable of growing food for human beings; every flowery waste or natural pasture ploughed up, all quadrupeds or birds which are not domesticated for man's use exterminated as his rivals for food, every hedgerow or superfluous tree rooted out, and scarcely a

[16] OECD Data, *Life Expectancy at Birth* (2019) and *Health Spending* (2019).

[17] In 2019, US GDP was $65,240, and Spain $42,212. In addition to health, US spending per capita on the military was $2,223 and Spain $367, a $1,856 difference (data from SIPRI). These two counts alone reduce US 'real' wealth to $55,927, and further reductions would be likely regarding excessive costs of US education, financial services, its oversized rented sector, the effects of pollution and advertising.

place left where a wild shrub or flower could grow without being eradicated as a weed in the name of improved agriculture . . .[18]

By 1974, as the problems of environmental degradation were becoming more acute, Herman Daly argued that a 'steady-state economy' was necessary to keep our economy within the limits of our larger ecosystem. He defined a 'steady state' as involving (1) constant stocks of physical wealth, (2) a constant population and (3) low rates of throughput (e.g. low physical production) but of goods that are durable. To achieve this, he argued that society needed institutions to stabilise populations, to keep wealth within ecological limits and limiting the degree of inequality in distribution.[19]

Today we know that populations stabilise with better healthcare, particularly women's contraception and autonomy, and with welfare provision, particularly pensions. The adapted quip in development economics, that the 'rich get richer and the poor get children',[20] was historically accurate when children were like an insurance policy for old age care, and there is no welfare state. The 'fertility rates' (the number of children per woman) in Europe, North America, China and (increasingly) India are close to stable or declining, but not yet met by higher rates in Africa, and the poorer parts of Asia or the Americas where population is growing (see Table 20.1). China's 'one-child' policy, based on denying benefits, largely failed and was inhumane, so the solution is women's autonomy, public health, pensions and welfare.

The UN Population Division forecasts that our global population will stabilise at 11 billion people around 2100,[21] compared to a 2019 population

Table 20.1 Fertility rates among selected countries, 2018[i]

Rank	Country	Fertility	Rank	Country	Fertility
1	Niger	6.9	144	Brazil	1.7
8	Nigeria	5.4	145	USA	1.7
33	Ethiopia	4.2	151	China	1.7
52	Pakistan	3.5	152	UK	1.7
55	Egypt	3.3	165	Germany	1.6
87	South Africa	2.4	166	Russia	1.6
92	Indonesia	2.3	183	Japan	1.4
99	India	2.2	191	Italy	1.3
128	France	1.9	200	South Korea	1.0

[i] World Bank, 'Fertility Rate' (2018).

[18] J. S. Mill, *Principles of Political Economy* (1848) Book IV, ch. 6.

[19] H. E. Daly, 'The Economics of the Steady State' (1974) 64(2) *Am Economic Rev* 15, 19.

[20] S. F. Fitzgerald, *The Great Gatsby* (1925) ch. 5, preceding the US Social Security Act of 1935.

[21] UN Department of Economic and Social Affairs, 'Growing at a Slower Pace, World Population Is Expected to Reach 9.7 Billion in 2050 and Could Peak at Nearly 11 Billion Around 2100' (17 June 2019). In 2021, the global population is 7.86bn.

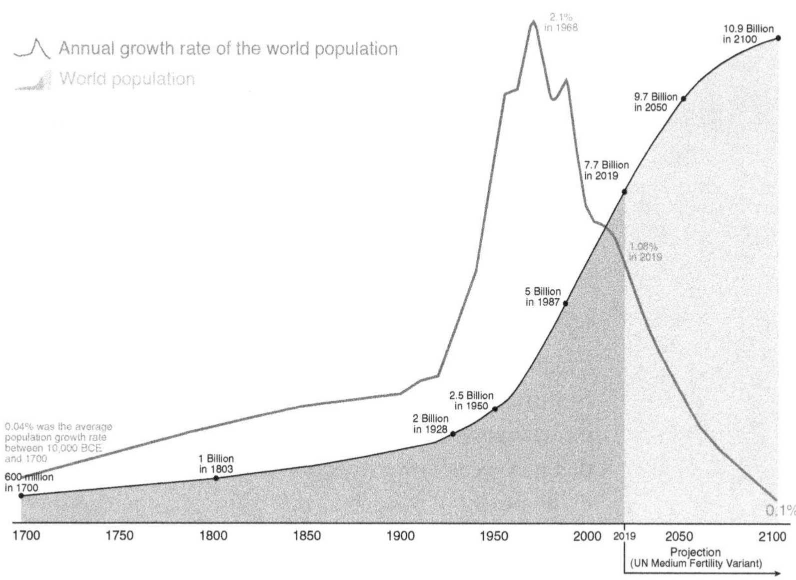

Figure 20.1 World population growth, 1700–2100
Source: Our World in Data

of 7.7 billion (see Figure 20.1). It is completely unclear that this forecast is right (given rapid recent slowing in the growth rate) let alone desirable. Stabilising populations is the same as realising universal human rights.

Stabilising populations through greater welfare is also likely to stabilise migration, particularly migration from economic necessity, and refugees from war. One perceived problem is often that if populations cease to grow, if they age or if they decline, there will not be enough young people to contribute to pensions with defined benefits for the retired. Benefits must be cut, contributions rise or both. This is untrue. Ample gains can be made by eliminating asset management fees, unnecessary churning of assets in financial services and raising taxes on the wealthy and corporations that benefit disproportionately from other people's labour.

How could stable 'stocks of physical wealth', and reduced 'throughput' be achieved? This would probably require a consumer right to products, not just of 'satisfactory quality', but of lasting and durable quality; full renewable energy; an end to waste, such as in packing food; higher-quality housing and buildings; a shift to sharing vehicles and public transport; and freeing our media and marketplaces from reliance on ads that impel us to buy things we do not need or want.[22] Since it leads us to insist on ever-increasing profits over human welfare, shareholding entities would have to be accountable to the real investors, any shareholder monopoly on enterprise governance would need to

[22] See also J. Hickel, *Less Is More* (2020) ch. 5, with five similar proposals.

end and GDP 'growth' would have to be replaced as a metric for fiscal policy of the government and monetary policy of the Bank of England (see Ch. 10). One option is to replace GDP with objective criteria of welfare (not including profits which are good or bad depending on the subject who profits) such as real wages and reductions of working time, while adding qualitative measures to life and education in the inequality-adjusted human development index.[23]

(c) Dynamic Justice

In contrast to 'growth' or a 'steady state', a third main goal of government is a dynamic vision of justice. As Chapter 2(4)(c) explained, the historical concept of justice that is 'social' (as opposed to corrective or distributive between individuals) matches the vision of the Universal Declaration in article 29 – that is, a society where people fulfil the duty to one another for the 'free and full development of the personality'. This is a concept similar to 'human development', as it recognises that nothing is stationary, but is not bound to a metric. Again, John Stuart Mill argued for this in his critique of growth. 'It is scarcely necessary', Mill went on:

> to remark that a stationary condition of capital and population implies no stationary state of human improvement. There would be as much scope as ever for all kinds of mental culture, and moral and social progress; as much room for improving the Art of Living, and much more likelihood of its being improved, when minds ceased to be engrossed by the art of getting on. Even the industrial arts might be as earnestly and as successfully cultivated, with this sole difference, that instead of serving no purpose but the increase of wealth, industrial improvements would produce their legitimate effect, that of abridging labour. Hitherto it is questionable if all the mechanical inventions yet made have lightened the day's toil of any human being. They have enabled a greater population to live the same life of drudgery and imprisonment, and an increased number of manufacturers and others to make fortunes. They have increased the comforts of the middle classes. But they have not yet begun to effect those great changes in human destiny, which it is in their nature and in their futurity to accomplish. Only when, in addition to just institutions, the increase of mankind shall be under the deliberate guidance of judicious foresight, can the conquests made from the powers of nature by the intellect and energy of scientific discoverers become the common property of the species, and the means of improving and elevating the universal lot.

It follows that, on this view, a dynamic goal of justice does not require stability in human development, or population, or economic production. In fact, there are many reasons why population or production could and should fall, or sometimes grow, and not be steady, wherever this is consistent with the goals of a just society as its people determine.

[23] See the draft Green Recovery Act 2020, s. 32, released by Common Wealth.

(2) Taxation and Prices

Once the goals of government are determined, a system of taxation and prices must fund their achievement. It was once said that 'in this world nothing can be said to be certain, except death and taxes',[24] although it would seem that throughout life the charging of prices may remain equally certain. Although a system might be imagined where resource allocations are determined without either prices or taxes, at present fulfilling goals of government requires us to establish (a) the proper principles of charging taxation and prices, (b) the mechanisms of raising tax and (c) the proper distribution of the taxation burden.

(a) Principles of Taxation and Prices

Possibly because tax laws are voluminous, and the myriad rules, exceptions and exceptions to exceptions may seem daunting, discussion of tax often begins with principles. Suggesting that there *are* principles may give a sense of legitimacy to the tax system,[25] or they may serve as a standard to measure reality against. In 1776, according to Adam Smith, four maxims of taxation should be equality, certainty, convenience of payment and economy in collection. These mean that:[26]

(1) people are taxed 'in proportion to their respective abilities' and 'in proportion to the revenue which they respectively enjoy under the protection of the state'
(2) taxes should be 'certain, and not arbitrary' with the time, manner, and quantity of payment being 'clear and plain to the contributor'
(3) taxes should be levied when 'most likely to be convenient for the contributor to pay it' – for instance, a tax on landlords to be paid when rents are paid
(4) tax collection costs should be minimised, by (i) reducing the number of 'officers, whose salaries may eat up the greater part', (ii) not levying taxes that would 'obstruct the industry of the people', (iii) not levying taxes in a way that encourages evasion, while ensuring that 'penalties of smuggling must rise in proportion to the temptation' to evade and (iv) not subjecting people unnecessarily to 'vexation' and to 'the odious examination of the tax-gatherers'.

[24] B. Franklin, *Letter to Jean-Baptiste Leroy* (13 November 1789) and D. Defoe, *The Political History of the Devil* (1726).

[25] A sense of legitimacy may be thought to encourage compliance, or as the finance minister to Louis XIV, Jean-Baptiste Colbert put it, somewhat cynically, 'the art of taxation consists in so plucking the goose as to procure the largest quantity of feathers with the least possible amount of hissing'. In W. S. McKechnie, *The State and the Individual* (1896) 77.

[26] A. Smith, *An Inquiry into the Nature and Causes of the Wealth of Nations* (1776) Book V, ch. 2, part II.

These basic principles have been seen as a starting point for any system, although their application is fiercely contested. For example, Smith envisaged that people who earn more pay more. 'It is not very unreasonable that the rich should contribute to the public expense', he went on, 'not only in proportion to their revenue, but something more than in that proportion.'[27] However Mill argued that although the second, third and fourth principles were right, and he was as 'desirous as any one ... to diminish [income] inequalities', taxing wealthier people at higher rates was 'to lay a tax on industry ... a penalty on people for having worked harder'. It was 'not the fortunes which are earned, but those which are unearned, that it is for the public good to place under limitation'.[28] The problem is that this argument has little application to today's systems of mass corporate production, and is why almost every system of tax accepts that it should be 'progressive', at least in part. Where higher earners are able to use unequal power within a corporate structure to distribute wealth to themselves, as directors, managers or shareholders, 'earned' and 'unearned' incomes cannot be separated. Power to take money comes from votes and influence in governance, and demand and supply merely set outer limits of constraint: the interplay of supply and demand rarely reflects a hypothetical 'marginal utility' added by labour, and it invariably reflects bargaining power. Mill did go on to say that any 'kind of income which constantly tends to increase, without any exertion or sacrifice' or 'complete passiveness', particularly rent, should be taxed more. This raises a further question of which enterprise structures enable an illegitimate 'pre-distribution' of wealth,[29] which it is right for tax to redistribute.

More recently, Joseph Stiglitz and Jay Rosengard have argued that 'five desirable characteristics of any tax system' are:

(1) economic efficiency: to 'not interfere with the efficient allocation of resources'
(2) administrative simplicity: 'easy and relatively inexpensive to administer'
(3) flexibility: 'respond easily, in some cases automatically, to changed economic circumstances'
(4) transparency: enough to enable political responsibility
(5) fairness: 'be fair in its relative treatment of different individuals'.[30]

First, efficiency raises detailed questions of the behavioural effects of a tax on individuals and enterprises: to what extent will corporate directors be deterred from hard work if they profit from other people's labour tax-free? To what extent do tax exceptions lead enterprises to adopt unduly complex structures

[27] Smith, *Wealth of Nations*, Book V, ch. 2, part II.
[28] Mill, *Principles of Political Economy*, Book V, ch. 2; and *The Collected Works of John Stuart Mill*, vol. V: *Essays on Economics and Society* (1861) calling income tax a 'graduated robbery'.
[29] J. S. Hacker, 'The Institutional Foundations of Middle-Class Democracy', *Policy Network* (6 May 2011).
[30] J. Stiglitz and J. K. Rosengard, *Economics of the Public Sector* (4th ed. 2015).

for avoidance? Where do taxes and exemptions subsidise, encourage or sustain pollution? These are questions that need evidence-based answers, combined with moral principles and a realistic appreciation that a greedy few will routinely aim to shift the burdens of paying for social institutions onto other people.[31]

Second, administration is generally agreed to be better when more simple. For example, the Organisation for Economic Co-operation and Development (OECD) found in 2010 that the UK spends around 1.1 pence on administration for each £1 in tax that is collected, while the US spends just over 0.5 cents for each $1.[32] However, from 2017, the OECD declined to publish 'cost of collection' ratios further, pointing out that lower costs could be a sign of efficiency, but also could be nothing to do with efficiency at all: for instance, a tax system could simply be failing to collect taxes.[33] Third, for flexibility Stiglitz and Rosengard give a main example that progressive taxes automatically stabilise the economy, because in a recession when incomes fall, everyone pays proportionally less, while, if incomes rise, so do taxes in a way that combats inflation. Thus 'flexibility' in the tax system is taken to mean responsiveness to achieve, not undermine, social policy goals.

Fourth, it appears clear enough that no country has a fully transparent system of taxes. In 2016, the 'Panama papers' from just one ex-medium law firm, Mossack Fonseca, exposed mass tax evasion from nearly every major country through offshore shell companies. While lip-service is routinely paid to the need to close 'loopholes', tax law is designed to be dodged, because countries recognise profit transfers to tax-haven trusts or companies as legitimate. To give just one example, the Recognition of Trusts Act 1987, which ratifies the Hague Trust Convention, requires reciprocal recognition of the parties to each other's trust laws, even where there is total secrecy and no accountability for tax fraud and evasion. Signatories include the UK, Australia, Canada, the Netherlands, Italy, Liechtenstein, Luxembourg and all the other notorious tax fraud havens like Bermuda, the Cayman Islands and the Isle of Man that form the UK's overseas territories and Crown dependencies. Where political transparency is lacking in tax, it seems so because political parties want none.

Fifth, Stiglitz and Rosengard argue that 'fairness' comprises both 'horizontal' equity to tax people in similar situations the same, and 'vertical equity' requiring that higher earners pay more: the progressive principle or the principle of equality. In contrast, there are those who advocate making all taxes 'flat', so that each person pays the same percentage rate, no matter what the scale of their income or whether the source is labour, capital, land or other

[31] Cf. O. W. Holmes, *The Common Law* (1881).

[32] OECD, *Tax Administration in OECD and Selected Non-OECD Countries: Comparative Information Series* (2010) Table 18.

[33] OECD, *Tax Administration 2019* (2019) 116–18.

wealth.[34] An even more extreme ideal is that all people pay, not the same percentage, but the same amount of tax: the 'poll tax' that caused riots and finished Margaret Thatcher's career was one of these. A final, perverse, but very real ideal is that the poor pay more tax either in percentage or absolute terms, and the rich pay less. In practice, UK tax law mixes all of these models in an entirely unprincipled manner.[35]

In contrast to these 'principles of taxation', there is little if any discussion about proper 'principles of prices'. Absent poll tax systems, nobody has to pay any taxes in order to live. It is just that if we work for someone else, buy and sell goods and services, invest money in companies or trade in land – in short when we at least benefit from the systems of contract, property and corporate law – the law usually requires that taxes are paid. As Mill put it, 'trade is a social act',[36] and it is always legitimate to tax to pay for the legal institutions that underpin trade, and the social and economic infrastructure from which people and enterprises benefit. Like a 'social contract',[37] with benefits come burdens. With rights come duties.

The same is true of prices: unless we are lucky enough to already have our own land (a right upheld by society), where we may grow enough food and drink from the rain, we must buy from others by paying prices. We must, for example, pay for the shopping, and for water, electricity, rent or internet bills. These prices are just as compulsory as taxes, so it might seem desirable that they are charged according to similar principles of equality, certainty, convenience and efficiency. However, prices usually do the very reverse. In particular, they are usually like 'flat' taxes at best, or at worst, the poor may pay more because when wealthier persons buy in bulk they get discount rates, such as for bank loans, water, electricity, rent or the Internet. Thus, wherever the price system is used it typically runs counter to one or more principles of taxation. It would seem that a coherent system of prices would always ensure that human rights are fulfilled.

(b) Raising Taxation

Once principles of taxation and prices are settled, governments must pass primary legislation to raise taxes. However, there is no duty to pass such laws to enable enterprises to charge prices: this is an inherent assumption (whatever its merit) of private property. By contrast, the Bill of Rights 1689, clause 4 states that 'Levying Money for or to the Use of the Crowne by pretence of Prerogative without Grant of Parlyament for longer time or in other manner then the same

[34] Cf. N. Brooks, *Flattening the Claims of the Flat Taxers* (1998).

[35] See also P. Johnson, 'Tax without Design: Recent Developments', IFS Working Paper No. 14/09 (2014) 1–2.

[36] J. S. Mill, *On Liberty* (1857) ch. 5.

[37] Cf. Plato, *Crito* (*c*. 350 BC) trans. B Jowett (1892), Socrates saying we have 'entered into an implied contract' to not break the law.

is or shall be granted is Illegall.'[38] Thus, an Act of Parliament is needed for new taxes. Taxes cannot be imposed by the executive, the Prime Minister, any other minister, or even a resolution of the House of Commons alone.[39] Any secondary legislation that imposes taxes and infringes the Bill of Rights will be void in court.[40] All money that has been paid pursuant to an illegal or ultra vires tax is recoverable by the taxpayer with compound interest.[41] It has also been accepted that the right to equal treatment, linked with the right to property, may be breached, for instance, where a bereavement tax allowance was available to widows but not widowers.[42] The European Court of Human Rights recognises 'a Contracting State's margin of appreciation in the tax field',[43] as often the very purpose of tax is to discriminate under some public policy. The government, under a Standing Order dating back to 1713, retains a monopoly on introducing legislation that would be charges on the public revenue,[44] meaning no Private Members' Bills can propose new taxes. In addition, the House of Lords has no power to delay Bills dealing with money.[45] All of this cements the position, since the Glorious Revolution, and the overcoming of the Stuart kings, that the elected government has the proper authority to tax.

Her Majesty's Revenue and Customs is in charge of administering taxes, and the Commissioners of HMRC are bound to 'comply with any directions of a general nature given to them by the Treasury'.[46] Under the Taxes Management Act 1970 the Commissioners are 'responsible for the collection and management of' income, corporation and capital gains tax[47] and, under an array of other laws, are also responsible for collecting National Insurance, Value Added Tax, duties, student loan receipts and various fines and penalties (e.g. under minimum wage laws). Any taxpayer can claim that they are incorrectly paying tax to the First-Tier Tribunal tax chamber, appealable to the Upper Tribunal and then the Court of Appeal. All money collected goes to the funds that government uses for its budgets.

(c) Tax Burden Distribution

The striking fact about the distribution of the tax burden is the absence of unified principles. Some taxes appear progressive, others are regressive, many force the poor to pay more. According to the 2019–20 budget, before the Covid-19 pandemic, first, 41.3 per cent of taxes came mostly (but not all) from labour, namely income tax and National Insurance. Second, 11.2 per cent came from corporation tax and business rates. Third, 25.3 per cent came from goods

[38] Bill of Rights 1689, cl. 4. [39] *Bowles v Bank of England* [1913] 1 Ch 57.

[40] *Commissioners of Customs and Excise v Cure and Deeley Ltd* [1962] 1 QB 340.

[41] *Woolwich BS v IRC (No. 2)* [1993] AC 70. [42] *R (Wilkinson) v IRC* [2005] UKHL 30.

[43] *National and Provincial BS v United Kingdom* (1997) 25 EHRR 127.

[44] Standing Order (1713). [45] Parliament Act 1911, s. 1.

[46] Commissioners for Revenue and Customs Act 2005, s. 11; *IRC v Nuttal* [1990] 1 WLR 631.

[47] Taxes Management Act 1970, s. 1.

and services trade – namely, VAT and excise duties. Fourth, 4.4 per cent came from Council tax, charged to people loosely based on the value of their property, but payable by residents not owners (see Figure 20.2 and Tables 20.2–20.9).

It appears impossible to defend the resulting distribution of taxes. The absence of any coherent approach predominantly benefits those with wealth. This is illustrated by the headline rates of tax set out in these tables.

Table 20.2 National insurance for employees and self-employed, 2021

Income	Employees	Self-employed	Name
£0–9,564	0%	0%	Lower earnings limit
£9,564–50,268	12%	9%	Primary threshold
Over £50,268	2%	2%	Secondary threshold
Over £8,844.12	*13.8%*	-	*Employer contributions*

Table 20.3 Income tax (employment, trade, dividends, etc.), 2021

Income	Rate	Name
£0–12,500	0%	Personal allowance
£12,501–50,000	20%	Basic rate
£50,001–150,000	40%	Higher rate
Over £150,000	45%	Additional rate

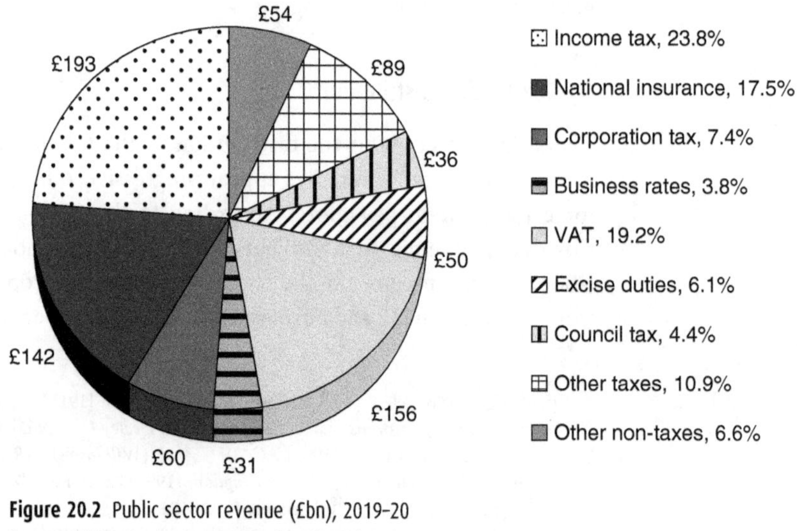

Figure 20.2 Public sector revenue (£bn), 2019–20
Source: HM Treasury, *Autumn Budget* (2018) 5

Table 20.4 Capital gains tax, 2021

Income	Rate	Name
Under £50,000	0%	Basic rate payer
Over £50,000	20%	Chargeable assets
Over £50,000	28%	Residential property

Table 20.5 Corporation tax, from 2023

Profits	Rate	Name
No 'profit' yet	0%	Expenses
Profits under £50,000	19%	Profits
Profits over £50,000	25%	Profits

Table 20.6 Business rates, 2021–2, based on 2015 valuation

Business rate	% of annual 'rated' rent
Small business	49.9%
Higher multiplier	51.2%

Table 20.7 VAT and excise duties, 2021

Items	Rate	Name
e.g. fresh food	0%	Zero rate
e.g. home energy	5%	Reduced rate
e.g. restaurants	20%	Standard rate
e.g. vodka, £11.50 per L	*Varies*	Alcohol tax
e.g. diesel, £0.57 per L	*Varies*	Oil tax

Table 20.8 Inheritance tax, 2021

Value of property, etc.	Rate
Below £325,000 or transfers to spouse or charity	0%
Home below £500,000 transferred to kids, grandkids	0%
Above £325,000, or home above	40%

If we compare the overall shape of these taxes to Smith's principles of (1) equality and progressive tax, (2) certainty, (3) convenience of payment and (4) economy in collection, meaning (i) reducing officers, (ii) not obstructing the

Table 20.9 Council tax bands in England, 2021, based on 1991 property values

Band	Value at 1 April 1991	Westminster	Oxford	Southwark
A	up to £40,000	£551.71	£1,446.16	£1,018.53
B	£40,001–52,000	£643.66	£1,687.18	£1,188.29
C	£52,001–68,000	£735.61	£1,928.20	£1,358.04
D	£68,001–88,000	£827.56	£2,169.23	£1,527.80
E	£88,001–120,000	£1,011.46	£2,651.28	£1,867.31
F	£120,001–160,000	£1,195.37	£3,133.33	£2,206.83
G	£160,001–320,000	£1,655.12	£3,615.39	£2,546.33
H	more than £320,000	£1,655.12	£4338.46	£3,055.60

industry of people, (iii) not encouraging evasion and (iv) reducing vexation, at least nine major problems can be identified.

First, taxation of income and National Insurance is separate,[48] even though each performs almost identical functions. For any employed or self-employed person, National Insurance is simply an addition to income tax, but both the lower earnings limit for employee and employer National Insurance Contributions (NICs) are below the tax-free personal allowance for income tax, and it fails to rise in a progressive manner above this. Since the money in both the Consolidated and National Insurance Funds is drawn upon by the Exchequer, an honest system would simply merge the two taxes into one figure: this would produce a transparent result that effectively people pay more than 32 per cent tax on income over £12,500, and 42 per cent tax on income over £50,268. That same rate should apply whether income is from employment or other sources. Similarly, since National Insurance comes from the employee's labour, and goes into the employee's pension, it would be more transparent to end the employer contributions as a separate category of NICs, and add it to accounts for employee's gross pay. For example, someone who currently has a '£30,000' income would see their gross pay accurately stated as £32,919.51 (with the employer contribution) and that the effective tax rate over £12,500 is 45.8 per cent, or 55.8 per cent over £50,268. These different figures also make calculating one's actual income less of a mystery, and enable greater political scrutiny. Transparency would also be less hampered if jobs were advertised at post-tax annual salaries or hourly wages (2).

Second, the fact that National Insurance of the employed, and self-employed, is charged at different rates (12 or 9 per cent),[49] creates a 3 per cent incentive for the worker to claim they are self-employed when they are not. Even more, an employer has an additional 13.8 per cent incentive to draft sham self-employment contracts, a fact that drives the contractual practices of Uber,

[48] Income Tax (Earnings and Pensions) Act 2003, ss. 3–8 and 62 (employment income); Income Tax (Trading and Other Income) Act 2005, s. 1 (self-employed, property, investment income).

[49] Social Security Contributions and Benefits Act 1992, ss. 1, 8–15 (NICs).

Deliveroo and many others (4)(iii). When this happens, the 'self-employed' become responsible for filing their own tax returns, a complex process creating problems for individuals and tax collectors, which would be done far more efficiently by a well-resourced corporation (4)(iv). It would be desirable to phase in reductions in the employee contributions down to 9 per cent (where they were in 1982).

Third, income tax also covers dividends from shares or income from property such as rent, but with a host of differing rules that are generally more favourable to people who make money from capital and assets, rather than by working. Dividends fall within the same income tax rules, while rental income is more favourable and capital gains tax rates are lower than the income tax rates.[50] Although statistics are not clear in the UK, for comparison in the USA where share ownership by individuals is far greater, 84 per cent of company shares are owned by the wealthiest 10 per cent of people, and half of Americans own no shares at all.[51] In the UK, only 2 million, or about 3 per cent of people, are landlords who take rent. This means that taxing rents, dividend income or capital gains tax at lower rates, or equal rates, is deeply contrary to the progressive tax principle (1) and it serves to accelerate and entrench inequality.

Fourth, corporation tax only takes effect on profits, unlike taxes on employment income which are charged according to a person's whole revenue (see Ch. 4(4)). This creates an inbuilt incentive for avoidance, and indeed most of the Corporation Tax Acts are preoccupied with defining profit and exceptions from paying tax. Fifth, corporation tax rates have been falling worldwide, and the largest corporations pay none. A preferable approach would be to tax revenue, and to significantly raise the rates of tax on profits for large companies, so that society shares equally in the prosperity that the economy generates.

Sixth, VAT is a regressive, not a progressive tax, and should be reduced as far as possible or eliminated. The various other specific taxes on consumption would be best codified, with statements of policy on whether the goal is to eliminate the use of the thing (as in the case of tobacco or petrol), or to have progressively higher tax on items that wealthier people may buy (such as stamp duty on houses). Seventh, there appears to be no good reason to have an inheritance tax rate set at 40 per cent,[52] which is lower than the top rate of tax on employment income, and certainly lower than the combined figure of employment income taxes and NICs. On the contrary, unearned inheritance should be taxed at a higher rate than the income that people work for. There also appears to be little reason not to generalise this to become a 'gift tax' at any point in life, subject to suitable exceptions for family homes.

50 Taxation of Chargeable Gains Act 1992 (asset rises).

51 E. Warren, 'Companies Shouldn't Be Accountable Only to Shareholders', *Wall Street Journal* (14 August 2018).

52 Inheritance Tax Act 1984, ss. 1–7 and Sch. 1.

Eighth, although there are Council taxes based on outdated property values,[53] there is no wealth tax, and given that most significant assets are fixed or registered, such as land or shares, it is the easiest to collect. For example, the draft US Ultra-Millionaire Tax Act of 2021 proposes taxing the net worth of any household or trust at 2 per cent per year of the net worth between $50 million and $1 billion, and 3 per cent a year over $1 billion.

Ninth, overall, the rich pay a lower proportion of their incomes, and sometimes less in absolute terms, than the poor. The poorest often cannot work because of disabilities and the absence of full employment. The middle earners pay a large part of their income in tax. But then the rich begin to earn money from capital – that is, other people's labour. The super-wealthy earn money by inheritance and hoarding assets. A preferable system would be to adjust the rates to ensure that people who have benefited from society the most, contribute more to ensure everyone has the opportunity to prosper as well.

(3) Budgeting and Public Services

Once taxes are collected, they can either be spent or saved and invested. Most governments have failed to save and invest, and have run up debts to banks that charge interest, instead of taxing and establishing sovereign wealth funds that could invest in enterprises.[54] There is nothing wrong with running a current account deficit (spending more than income in the odd year),[55] particularly in a crisis, or to invest money in infrastructure that will deliver a long-term return in prosperity. However, permanent debt means unnecessary interest payments become a lasting budget factor. Three relevant topics are (a) the legal structure of public debt and funds, (b) the annual budgets set by the Treasury and (c) deciding whether public services are universal or not.

(a) Public Debt and Public Funds

Government funds are the responsibility of the Treasury. Under the Budget Responsibility and National Audit Act 2011, section 1, the Treasury must produce a 'Charter of Budget Responsibility' for 'fiscal policy and policy for the management of the National Debt', and the Office for Budget Responsibility has to 'report on the sustainability of the public finances'.[56] There is, however, no mechanism required (i.e. taxes) for reduction of the national debt. In February 2021, the UK national debt stood at £2,131.2 billion or around 97.5% of GDP, though this compares favourably to Japan at 263%,

[53] Local Government Finance Act 1992, s. 1 (council tax).

[54] T. Piketty, *Capital in the Twenty-First Century* (2014).

[55] Cf. Fiscal Responsibility Act 2010, s. 1, which placed a duty on the Treasury to reduce 'public sector net borrowing' each year from 2011 to 2016 as a percentage of GDP. Repealed by the Budget Responsibility and National Audit Act 2011.

[56] Budget Responsibility and National Audit Act 2011, ss. 1–4.

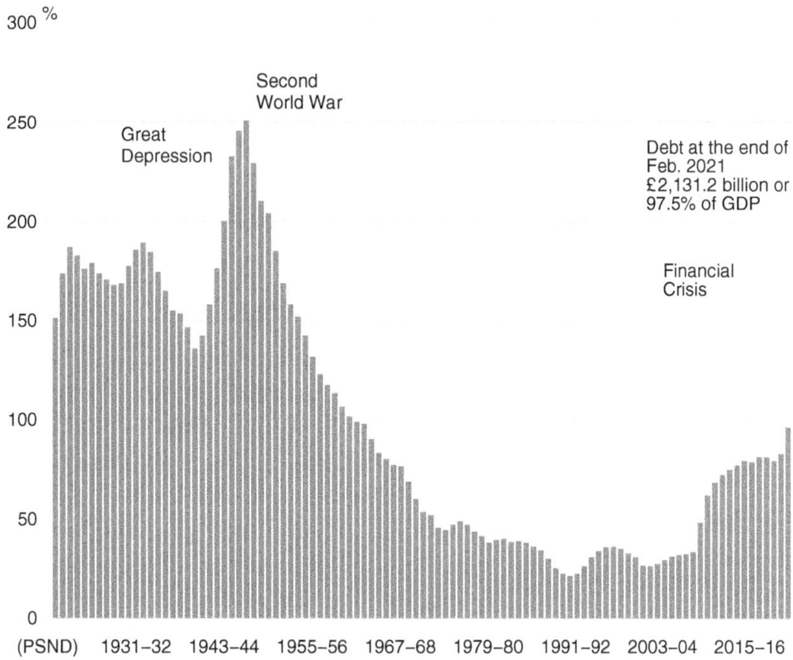

Figure 20.3 National debt as % of GDP, 1921-2021

Italy at 158% and the USA at 133%. The lowest point reached was 21.7%, and this went up slightly to 34% before increasing dramatically as a result of rescuing the insolvent banking system in 2007 (see Figure 20.3).

On the plus side, government has five main funds. First, the Consolidated Fund Act 1816 said that 'funds of Great Britain and Ireland, shall become one general consolidated fund'.[57] This is the main destination for 'public moneys payable to the Exchequer' as taxes.[58] Second, the Social Security Administration Act 1992, section 162 states that NICs are paid into the National Insurance Fund.[59] These first two are by far the largest government funds, and while legally separate, spending decisions are made drawing upon either. Like income tax and National Insurance, there would be no real difference if these were merged. Third, the civil contingencies fund is for emergencies,[60] and its limit was 2 per cent 'of the authorised supply expenditure for the year ending on the previous 31st March' (that is, the annual government budget).[61] But, for the Covid-19 pandemic, this was temporarily increased to 50 per cent – that is, government empowered itself to do emergency spending of half the whole annual

[57] Consolidated Fund Act 1816, s. 1. [58] Exchequer Audit Departments Act 1866, s. 10.
[59] Social Security Administration Act 1992, s. 162.
[60] Miscellaneous Financial Provisions Act 1946. [61] Contingencies Fund Act 1974, s. 1.

budget again to sustain jobs and the economy.[62] Fourth, the National Loans Fund is the main borrowing and lending account, established with the Bank of England, through which most domestic transactions pass and which is balanced daily.[63] Fifth, the Exchange Equalisation Account is a fund that holds UK reserves of foreign currency, gold and special drawing rights.[64] Further trading funds can be established by order.[65] These are separate from funds held by government departments. For these, the Treasury may direct accounts are done each year.[66]

(b) Annual Budgets

Money is typically spent following an annual budget, and is authorised annually by Parliament in the Appropriation Act. This 'appropriates' (takes property) money from the funds and disperses it according to whatever the Treasury says it wants to do.[67] Over time, there have been shifts, but slow ones, in the overall division of funds, as below.

In the budget for 2019–20, total projected spending was £841 billion, although this rose as the pandemic broke out and action was taken in March 2020.[68] The first and largest segment is spending on 'social protection' and 'care', which means pensions, unemployment and social care for the elderly or

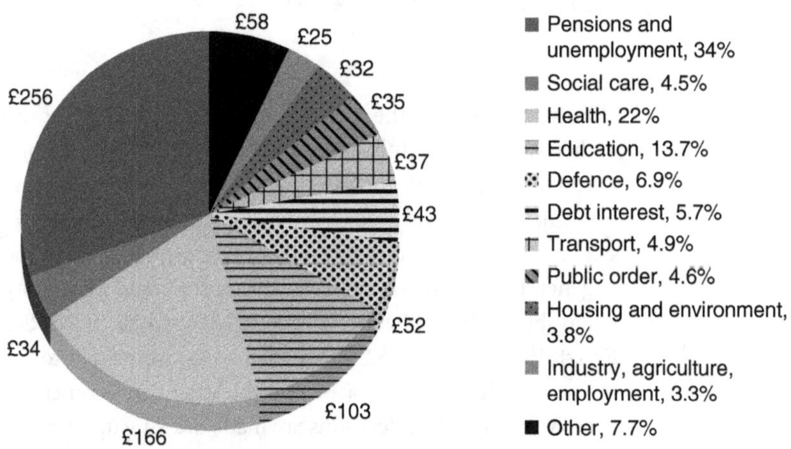

Figure 20.4 Public sector spending (£bn), 2019–20
Source: HM Treasury, *Autumn Budget* (2018) 4

62 Contingencies Fund Act 2020, s. 1. 63 National Loans Act 1968, s. 18.

64 Exchange Equalisation Account Act 1979, s. 1.

65 Government Trading Act 1990 and Government Trading Funds Act 1973, ss. 1–4A. By 2003, 19 funds were established, e.g. Land Registry Trading Fund from 1993.

66 Government Resources and Accounts Act 2000, ss. 5–9.

67 E.g. HM Treasury, *Autumn Budget* (November 2017) especially 5, 23–6, chs. 3–4 (31–57) and Annex C.

68 Budget 2021–2, £1,053bn spending, £820bn in income, a projected £233bn deficit.

vulnerable. The largest part of this is the state pension (see Ch. 5). Second, there is the National Health Service (Ch. 9). Third, there is education, predominantly schools and university research funding (see Ch. 8). Fourth, there is spending on the military (Ch. 19). Fifth, there are interest payments on the national debt, mainly funding banks after they crashed the economy from 2007 (Ch. 10). Sixth, there is transport, consisting mainly of road and rail subsidies (Ch. 15). Seventh, there is public order, particularly the police. Eighth, there is housing and the environment (Ch. 14). Ninth, there is industry, agriculture (Ch. 13) and employment. Implicit subsidies to coal, oil and gas companies (Ch. 12) and fossil-fuel energy generators (Ch. 13), which create immense future costs, through damage to the climate and public health, are not accounted for. Their economic effect is identical to borrowing money from people in future who will have to bear the tremendous harm they have caused. The absence of accounting for harm from fossil fuels in the government budget does not, therefore, make sense.

(c) Universal Services

The important question to ask is, what should the overall shape of public spending be? How should a society allocate its resources, and to what ends? In a 2017 report, Henrietta Moore, Jonathan Portes, Howard Reed and Andrew Percy advocated the production of 'universal basic services' – namely, public provision of universal education, health, legal services, shelter, food, transport, phones, the Internet and the BBC. In their view, the model of the NHS, free at the point of use, could and should be extended for university education and legal aid, and universally instituted for housing, removal of 'food insecurity' by providing 1.8 billion meals a year, free bus travel, and communications. In their calculations (which seem to *overprice* the cost of some services, particularly the Internet), the total extra cost of these universal basic services would be £42.16 billion a year, or around 5 per cent of the 2019 UK government budget. Adding a 'full community food programme' with free public canteens would total £59.36 billion, around 7 per cent of the budget.[69] Given that unnecessary debt interest is 5.7 per cent of the budget, and together with military spending this rises to 11.6 per cent, it would appear there are no real fiscal barriers to universal services. These investments would generate more income.

Added to this concept of universal public services (which span all of Chapters 8–9 and 13–17), the direct cost of creating a universal right to a simple bank account and full employment (Ch. 10) would appear to be minimal, and the indirect gains substantial. An online account can be administered cheaply, while the right to be guaranteed a job from government at a living wage appears to pay for itself and more. The evidence suggests that

[69] H. L. Moore, J. Portes, H. Reed and A. Percy, *Social Prosperity for the Future: A Proposal for Universal Basic Services* (2017).

around eight hours a week of work is optimal for people's mental health,[70] and so instead of young people, especially, receiving dole cheques and going through the indignity of filling out jobseeker forms for non-existent jobs, this could be the labour force needed to clean and rewild the country, deliver better social and childcare, and build our future infrastructure. We can see this works because from 1945 to 1979 government maintained full employment without running a current account deficit.[71] Guaranteeing to do whatever it takes was enough to give business confidence to hire and invest. It fell apart after the oil-shocks of the 1970s and the reversal of commitment to full employment by the Thatcher government.[72] It would also appear that clean energy investment (see Chs. 11–12), which is heavily publicly funded or subsidised, could enable basic energy services for household users, as could water services as well. Taking these services out of the world of contract and private enterprise in the UK or any country may, of course, reduce GDP, because lower bills and a more efficient service would mean less money changing hands. However, the benefits would be to spread prosperity to everyone, to be more economically efficient and raise the real wealth of nations.

(4) The Future of Democracy

The discussion of 'universal services' raises fundamental questions about the nature of democracy, and whether enterprises that are publicly funded must be centrally controlled. The old Morrisonian model of nationalisation, where the directors of public bodies were appointed by a minister alone, is in tension with a more educated population and a globalising economy. It is also in tension with the trends in education, health, utilities or websites for voting rights of the public. People expect less and less to simply be treated as 'consumers', and more as members with rights. Already in 1848, John Stuart Mill alluded to the problems of centralisation, when he remarked that government accountable to Parliament can become overcharged if it attempts to administer a state apparatus that extends across the whole economy.[73] This concern has proven somewhat overblown, since over the twentieth century governments developed more sophisticated civil services, and public-sector governance became more accountable. And yet centralising decision-making (in any enterprise,

[70] D. Kamerāde, S. Wang, B. Burchell, S. U. Balderson and A. Coutts, 'A Shorter Working Week for Everyone: How Much Paid Work Is Needed for Mental Health and Well-Being?' (2019) 241 *Social Science & Medicine* 112353.

[71] R. C. O. Matthews, 'Why Has Britain Had Full Employment Since the War?' (1968) 78(311) *Economic J* 555.

[72] E. McGaughey, 'Will Robots Automate Your Job Away? Full Employment, Basic Income, and Economic Democracy' (2021) *Industrial LJ*.

[73] J. S. Mill, *Principles of Political Economy* (1848) Book V, ch. 11, §4: 'Every additional function undertaken by the government, is a fresh occupation imposed upon a body already overcharged with duties.'

public or private) and particularly appointment powers, simply may not be a necessary or an optimal arrangement, where the people closest to a service are best placed to see its problems and take part in deciding its solutions. This is even more true as society becomes more educated than ever, and with more knowledge and data than ever before.

In the economic constitution a trend similar to the development of the political constitution has taken place. The long road to democracy within Britain passed through three main and overlapping phases – namely, the creation of:

(1) minimum standards, establishing principles such as the vote itself, and secret ballots
(2) institutional voice, gradually ensuring equal rights to vote in local government, and then gradually breaking down property or gender qualifications to vote for Parliament
(3) political democracy, by perfecting the systems of representative government, based on 'one person, one vote', and institutions, such as media, for deliberative discourse.

The economic constitution may be argued to have more moving parts than the political, given the multiple centres of authority, the absence (often) of a physical manifestation or location of enterprises (as opposed to the territory of a local or national government), and the differing inputs and stakeholder groups – namely, labour, capital investors and consumers or the public. Nevertheless, three similar transitions can be detected in:

(1) the codification of basic rights in international and domestic law, that articulate entitlements within the economic constitution
(2) the growing experience and understanding of the modern economic constitution, including increasing voice for workers and investors, as well as students, patients, residents, passengers, viewers, audiences and traders
(3) the growing availability of models and empirical evidence internationally of what appears to work in the finance of, governance of, and rights within enterprise.

A transition from minimum standards to institutional voice, to democracy, is emerging. There are questions both of moral values and what the most expedient institutional arrangements to reach those values should be. The decisive factors in the future of democracy ultimately are the understandings and the convictions of the people who constitute our economy and society.[74]

[74] E. McGaughey, 'The Future of Democracy and Work: The Vote in Our Economic Constitution', Sefton-Williams Lecture (2021).

Conclusion

The Future of Enterprise

In this book's introduction, the thesis was proposed that enterprise law can be regarded as a coherent subject. It is a preferable framework to understand the economic constitution and human rights, rather than systems which artificially segregate corporate, labour, competition or insolvency from one another, and each from public policy. On the contrary, the investor, worker, consumer, creditor and member of the public is often the same person. Dividing these actors against themselves is a diversion from unaccountable corporate power. In Chapter 2, after setting out the theories of enterprise law in political economy and human rights, ten principles were proposed, and are worth restating.

Principles of Enterprise Law

(1) The finance of enterprise should realise human rights as expediently as possible.
(2) Governance power should mirror people's investments of savings, labour and custom.
(3) Human rights should be made effective in legislation, courts and all social institutions.
(4) Private enterprise should follow broad distribution of productive property and finance.
(5) An enterprise state upholds social security, placing risks onto the broadest shoulders.
(6) An enterprise state educates, and distributes the benefits of science rapidly and equally.
(7) Environmental and human health should be improved, and no harm allowed.
(8) Communication privacy and deliberative media should strengthen democratic politics.
(9) Prices and taxes should be charged transparently, efficiently and by the ability to pay.
(10) Enterprise law should enable every member of society to realise their full potential.

Are these principles fulfilled in enterprise law today? The answer is only a partial 'yes'. First, it is plain that concerns over the modes of financing enterprise are central to virtually every sector, from education and health to transport and internet infrastructure. However, in each case the ideological and empirical debate is not settled, and this accounts for wide divergence between countries in the efficiency of delivering universal services for the lowest cost, particularly based on the decisions about the involvement of the private or public sector.

Second, it is true that the voice and voting rights of the real investors in capital, of workers, consumers and the wider public – students, patients, passengers or viewers – have been gradually, steadily spreading. Once people have voting rights, the cases where these are removed are rarer than cases where they are improved. However, a clear gulf of accountability through the vote, a separation of contribution and participation, is evident in the UK, the European Union and in countries worldwide.

Third, there is a growing body of jurisprudence and social practice that embeds human rights norms in legislation and case law, achieved foremost in the UK through the Human Rights Act 1998. However, the limit is that this falls far short of the standards in the Universal Declaration of Human Rights 1948. In any event what matters more is typically the use of detailed administrative powers or scattered statutory provisions which go beyond (and rightly so) the minimums that were set in international law in the mid-twentieth century.

Fourth, it is clear that private, competitive enterprise is not the norm in most sectors of enterprise, and this is particularly true in the focus of this book, in sectors where public regulation reshapes general laws of investment, competition or insolvency. It seems equally evident that there may be a beneficial role for private enterprises within many specific sectors in this book, including for banking (assuming a central bank's finance), solar or wind generation (with price and subsidy support), farming (usually with agricultural subsidies), homes (often after public building subsidies), taxis (with clean vehicle subsidies), communication devices, or media outlets (subject to ownership and editorial standards). In all these cases, there is broadly equal distribution of assets and finance – that is, the 'productive property' necessary for production. This enables private, competitive enterprise not just to work, but thrive and innovate. Yet these conditions are evidently unfulfilled in situations of very unequal bargaining power, particularly in enterprises that constitute natural or network monopolies. The law's recognition of 'principle 4' is partial, and central to the ongoing ideological clash of socialism and capitalism, and public or private ownership of the means of production. The better approach is to disaggregate and isolate functional questions of finance, governance and rights, rather than seeing the law of property as a unified monolith.

Fifth, the laws for social security, particularly in investment, labour and insolvency norms, are well developed, if uneven. Job security and full employment has not been a reality in the UK since the 1970s, and while people in most countries do not risk bankruptcy over healthcare today, many are at risk of losing their homes especially when their ability to earn an income is precarious.

Sixth, education and the benefits of science are often spread rapidly, and this is seen in the remarkable response in healthcare to the Covid-19 pandemic. However, there are severe limits in the normal operation of access to education – and, in many systems, healthcare – the moment that money operates as a barrier to either. The adoption of clean energy is catastrophically slow, since states have systematically failed, or outright refused, to confront the fossil-fuel lobby and shut them down in favour of the readily available technological replacements: wind, solar and battery energy; electric vehicles; clean agricultural equipment; and electric boilers and clean heating or insulation systems for buildings.

Seventh, it is clear that, while the right to safety at work is substantially protected, fossil fuels are the omnipresent spectre that haunts environmental and human health. Road transport safety has improved greatly, but a faster adoption of safe public transport would assist more.

Eighth, privacy on the Internet in particular has improved through recent data protection regulation, but it is far from clear that this is sufficient while the business models of email and social media rely on surveillance for advertising revenue. Similarly, while standards in television media are widespread, the vacuum online presents a stark difference.

Ninth, prices and taxes are often required by law to be transparent, and elements exhibit the progressive principle, but there is not a coherent structure to the system. On the contrary, consumption taxes are highly regressive, capital is taxed far less and work is taxed far more, while the shifting of enterprise into the privatised sphere normally creates price structures that require the poor to pay more.

Tenth, if the basic goals of enterprises are to fulfil human rights, as a whole enterprise law should aspire to a larger goal for human society: the right of every person to fulfil their potential to the utmost; to build the content of our character; to reach new levels of knowledge and common understanding; and to open a new chapter of human freedom, enlightenment and justice. The socioeconomic fundamentals that enterprise law creates – in education, health, material, energy and infrastructure security, at home or abroad and in our social discourse – should not be underestimated. The vast structure of twenty-first-century society– the sheer scale of our global civilisation, the life of our planet and the part we have in it – is as awesome as it is humbling, if it can be comprehended. Our society and our laws have not reached the point where every member of society can realise their full potential, and yet there are today the material resources and understanding to do just this.

So, the principles of enterprise law that this book has advanced are fulfilled only in part, but this in itself is an incredible feat. Of course, it could be argued that there should be no principles of enterprise law at all, or that these principles are defective and should be different. It could, for example, be contended that the finance of enterprises should be unconnected to human rights, or that business and human rights just do not mix. It could be said that governance power should be left with asset managers, banks or ministers that appoint 'experts' who are 'independent', and accountable to no member who invests in, works for or relies upon an enterprise for their livelihoods. In fact, human rights and democracy could be entirely eliminated from the law. Perhaps instead of determining the scope of private enterprise by a principle, it should simply be determined by a quantity: more or less, like the debates that consumed so much twentieth-century politics. Social security, the benefits of science, environmental and human health, privacy and a deliberative media, it could be said, should be subordinated to individual choices, or perhaps government discretion. Prices and taxes should be kept distinct, and there is no such thing as a social aspiration, or any concept of social justice, that could cover so many disparate fields of law. Perhaps enterprise law, it could be concluded, is just a random collection of subjects, and we are better off returning to a traditional legal text on property, corporations or public law.

There may be elements of truth in criticisms such as these, or others, but ultimately the test will be whether these or any other principles of enterprise law give a useful and workable account of what law does, consistent with evidence of what works. The future of enterprise, if humanity is to solve its greatest problems, will reverse escalating inequality; it will end the use of coal, oil and gas; and it will reduce to zero the finance and industries of war. It is not unreasonable to think that the easiest way to do this will be to ensure principled and progressive finance of enterprise, to disperse, not concentrate, governance voice through voting rights and to realise universal fair services for the fulfilment of human rights. How this is done depends on knowledge, reason and evidence, and ultimately what you do.

Afterword: Why I've Written a Book on 'Enterprise Law'

When I got my first full-time job as an academic, a professor that I admired very much took me for lunch, and I said I wanted to start a course on 'enterprise law'. I said it would be about the economic constitution, rights, corporations and public services. 'Oh, don't worry about that', said the professor. 'What you should really think about is who you want to be.' I went away and I thought about this carefully. I decided I wasn't so interested in 'being' anybody particular, if that just meant having a title or an office, but rather I wanted to 'do' something. A few days later, I went and explained this to the professor, and the next year I was allowed to start teaching 'enterprise governance', with a class of six masters students in 2016.

Perhaps the first time I thought about 'enterprise' was taking an introductory economics class at school. This was the late 1990s, and we were taught there were four factors of production: land, labour, capital and 'enterprise'.[1] I never quite knew what the 'enterprise' was. Was an 'entrepreneur' somehow different from 'labour', like brains from brawn?[2] The language of enterprise had been resurgent for some years, though little did I know at the time that its use was very different from before. As a younger child, I remembered watching on an old black-and-white TV as jubilant Berliners climbed atop the fallen Wall, and a year later we watched Margaret Thatcher, the ex-Prime Minister, being driven out of Downing Street. This second ignominious fall followed years of privatisation and conflict, where the supposed goal was for 'private enterprise to flourish'.[3] But the fall did not stop the ideas becoming the 'Washington Consensus'. From this, the post-Soviet-shock privatisations for Eastern Europe produced untold suffering, an unmitigated catastrophe for

[1] This view appears, for example, in F. A. Webster, 'Entrepreneurs and Ventures: An Attempt at Classification and Clarification' (1977) 2(1) *Academy of Management Rev* 54, 55, who attributes this idea of 'four factors' tenuously to R. Cantillon, *Essai sur la nature du commerce en général*, trans. H. Higgs (1755) 31.

[2] Contrast the views expressed by Andrew Carnegie, referring to a violent strike, where seven union members were murdered at his steel factory in 1892, to the US Commission on Industrial Relations, *Final Report and Testimony* (1915) vol. VIII, 8289: 'I told the great audience at Homestead upon my first visit after the strike, we shall one day all recognize capital, labor, and business ability as a three-legged stool, each necessary for the other, neither first, second, nor third in rank; but all equal.'

[3] M. Thatcher, 'Speech at Young Conservative Conference' (9 February 1975) two days before election as leader.

economic performance and human development, that ultimately gave us Russia's fossil-fuelled oligarchs of today. If that was meant to be it, then 'enterprise' wasn't working.

When I became an undergraduate law student, I was still interested in economics, so I chose land law, labour law and company law as second-year options. But there was no 'enterprise law' to learn. Instead, I took a course on 'legal and social change since 1750'. This was also the year when UK university tuition fees, imposed at £1,000 in 1998, were hiked again on the pretext of raising investment. By contrast, more money was also being promised for the National Health Service (NHS) from tax. And most vividly, American, British and Australian bombs began falling down on Baghdad, and young, brave men and women, people who were on the bus or down the pub before, started coming home in bags, their futures as stolen as the oil and the lives of countless Iraqis. Meanwhile in company law, my first week's reading included A. A. Berle and G. C. Means, *The Modern Corporation and Private Property.* For me, this brought corporations alive, showing how the thinking behind our modern law, quite separated from the seemingly neutral text of the Companies Act, was really forged in the Great Depression. The introduction also included Berle's article from 1965 on how the New Dealers saw an economic 'Second Bill of Rights' being built by legislation. In labour law, I learned about the ideas of work and capital being integrated in a more democratic economy, and one of my (best ever) teachers lent me an old blue copy of the *Bullock Report* on proposals for industrial democracy in the 1970s. In legal and social change since 1750, I wrote a paper on the history of property and the vote. Surrounded by the musty smells of nineteenth-century Hansard archives, I met Robert Lowe, the old MP for London University, who was the architect of modern company law and whose invectives in the Commons railed against democracy, and against empowering any member of the 'elite of the working classes' who were 'members of trade unions' founded on 'grinding tyranny'. We also had a module taught by another brilliant teacher attached to land law where we studied Richard Posner's *Economic Analysis of Law.* So clear in language, so opaque in reason, Posner's work drove me to read a lot more economics. I quickly realised that, as well as many famous economists having been lawyers, there was no consensus on how 'economics' works, particularly where theory is unconnected to empirical research. I also saw that economics, like sociology, or philosophy, was very concerned with how all kinds of enterprises worked in real life.

In a few years, before I became a Ph.D. student, I had the luck of being hired to teach 'commercial law' at the London School of Economics (LSE). It was actually a course on contract, company and insolvency law, offered to accounting, management, philosophy, economics, social policy or other non-law students. That was an ominous year to teach insolvency, because the global financial crisis was unfolding from its roots in the US housing collapse. You met bank employees wandering London with bleary eyes, expressing disbelief at what was happening. You saw economists trying to explain to the queen why 'nobody' could have foreseen the crash,[4] although many (including those whose articles we taught in insolvency law) had foreseen it, and had written about its very causes.[5] Among the students, from different majors, what always impressed me was how differently they tended to think depending on their discipline, and how differently other studies categorised the world. When I looked into the history, I found the course I was teaching used to be called 'Commercial and Industrial Law', and it was the oldest surviving course at the LSE. It was possibly the first subject where labour law was taught in the world, and its graduates appear to have included a younger Ronald Coase, who later moved to the University of Chicago and became a pioneer of the 'law and economics' movement with Richard Posner. A few years later, as I was pressing ahead in the Ph.D., I decided I would update the course name to 'Commercial and Enterprise Law', and include an element of labour rights, between company and insolvency law. But one big thing was missing. What about the governance of public services, or organisations that had shareholders but were regulated? In competition law, there was an extensive field of work involving sector-specific regulation, where often the premise was 'more competition is always good'.[6] I was never charmed by this ideal, and felt that the governance of public or regulated enterprises was a large, open space in our literature.

I was completely wrong about an 'open space'. When I landed a precious, full-time job, and began to prepare a broader course on enterprise law, I found nearly every conceivable book, on every conceivable topic. It just wasn't labelled 'enterprise law'. This was the year 2015, when Barack Obama's second term as US president was nearing an end, and only the first two years had seen any legislation: reform for slightly more healthcare, a post-crash stimulus and extensive but scattered financial law reform. Worse, Trump had launched his campaign for US president with the megaphones of Twitter, Facebook and YouTube, and fuelled by hate, conspiracy theories and lies, particularly that global warming is a 'hoax' that was 'created by and for the Chinese'. Then there was the campaign to break the UK's membership from the European Union (EU), which like the 2016 presidential election, we later learned, was backed through 'active measures' of Kremlin cyberwar.[7] The world was becoming a hotter, angrier, darker place, and the UK referendum and US election only made it worse.

[4] H. Stewart, 'This Is How We Let the Credit Crunch Happen, Ma'am . . .', *The Guardian* (26 July 2009).

[5] E.g. E. Warren, *The Two-Income Trap: Why Middle-Class Parents are Going Broke* (2004) and 'Bankruptcy Policy' (1987) 54(3) *U Chicago L Rev* 775.

[6] There is now a growing literature on this, including M. Meagher, *Competition Is Killing Us: How Big Business Is Harming Our Society and Planet – and What to Do about It* (2020) and M. E. Stucke and A. Ezrachi, *Competition Overdose: How Free Market Mythology Transformed Us from Citizen Kings to Market Servants* (2020).

[7] T. Snyder, *The Road to Unfreedom: Russia, Europe, America* (2018); US Senate, Report of the Select Committee on Intelligence: Russian Active Measures Campaigns and Interference in the 2016 US Election (2020) vol. V.

Yet in the splendid solace of the reading list for my students, I sifted through the chapters of each text that concerned finance, governance and rights in that enterprise. There was Dennis Farrington and David Palfreyman on universities;[8] Emily Jackson on the NHS;[9] E. P. Ellinger, Eva Lomnicka, C. V. M. Hare and Ross Cranston on banking;[10] Greg Gordon on oil and gas, and electricity and energy;[11] Sarah Hendry and Josh Getzler on water;[12] Carol Harlow and Richard Rawlings on railways;[13] John Armour on automakers;[14] Ian Walden on telecommunications and media;[15] Geoffrey Robertson and Andrew Nicol on media;[16] Ariel Ezrachi and Maurice Stucke and the work of my colleague Savas Manoussakis in the pioneering field of marketplaces;[17] and Anthony Bradley and Keith Ewing's writing on the military.[18] Added to this there was the wealth of literature on regulation, particularly by Tony Prosser,[19] Robert Baldwin, Martin Cave and Martin Lodge.[20] Then there were countless papers and books by company, labour, competition and insolvency law scholars that routinely focus on specific fields.[21] The great private lawyer of his time, Peter Birks, wrote that when the law lacks codification, textbooks are the codes.[22] What I found is that these texts were keeping our uncodified economic constitution alive. My goal was to bring the ideas together, with a unifying grammar of finance, governance and rights.

Now it's five years since I began teaching enterprise law, and as I write the world has become slightly calmer in the USA, UK and the EU. For better or worse (and let's face it, it's worse), Parliament after the 2019 general election resolved what a referendum never could, and the UK left EU membership.

[8] D. Farrington and D. Palfreyman, *The Law of Higher Education* (2nd ed. 2012) chs. 4, 5 and 12.

[9] E. Jackson, *Medical Law: Texts, Cases and Materials* (4th ed. 2016).

[10] E. P. Ellinger, E. Lomnicka and C. V. M. Hare, *Ellinger's Modern Banking Law* (5th ed. 2011) chs. 2 and 5; R. Cranston, *Principles of Banking Law* (2nd ed. 2002) chs. 3–5.

[11] M. M. Roggenkamp, C. Redgwell, A. Rønne and I. Guayo (eds.), *Energy Law in Europe: National, EU and International Regulation* (2016) ch. 14.

[12] S. Hendry, *Frameworks for Water Law Reform* (2014) ch. 5; J. Getzler, *A History of Water Rights at Common Law* (2004) especially 328–52.

[13] C. Harlow and R. Rawlings, *Law and Administration* (3rd ed. 2009) ch. 9.

[14] J. Armour, 'Volkswagen's Emissions Scandal: Lessons for Corporate Governance?' (parts 1 and 2) (2016) Oxford Business Law Blog.

[15] I. Walden, *Telecommunications Law and Regulation* (4th ed. 2012) chs. 3 and 7.

[16] G. Robertson and A. Nicol, *Media Law* (5th ed. 2008) ch. 16.

[17] A. Ezrachi and M. E. Stucke, 'Emerging Antitrust Threats and Enforcement Actions in the Online World' (December 2017).

[18] A. W. Bradley and K. D. Ewing, *Constitutional and Administrative Law* (2011) ch. 16.

[19] E.g. T. Prosser, 'Public Service Law: Privatization's Unexpected Offspring' (2000) 63(4) *L & Cont Probs* 63; T. Prosser, *The Economic Constitution* (2014).

[20] E.g. R. Baldwin, M. Cave and M. Lodge, *Understanding Regulation: Theory, Strategy, and Practice* (2013).

[21] E.g. P. Ireland, 'Shareholder Primacy and the Distribution of Wealth' (2005) 68(1) *MLR* 49; A. C. L. Davies, 'This Time, It's for Real: The Health and Social Care Act 2012' (2013) 76(3) *MLR* 564.

[22] P. Birks, *Introduction to the Law of Restitution* (1984).

Trump was ejected from the White House and Twitter. The Covid-19 pandemic has devastated society, and is still here, yet we are hoping for a swift vaccine rollout and a recovery of life. But the same underlying causes of the ruptures since 2015 remain unaddressed, and these are the same as the basic problems of twenty-first-century life: escalating inequality, climate damage and war. Covid-19 has shown everyone how rapid a social response to major issues can be, and also how broken and incompetent the systems of some country's governments, parties and ideologies are, and what effective responses look like, particularly in New Zealand, Denmark, Norway and Finland. Most of the problems can be explained by understanding our economic constitution, particularly where there are conflicting military, fossil-fuel, or financial interests, sitting at odds with the public good and universal human rights. A promising fact of today, and a major difference from twentieth-century political and economic discourse, is we can now simply access much more data and evidence. We know more history, what works and what fails. And it's no coincidence that, as it became clearer what works, as education has expanded, the political reaction to positive change turned to aggressive deceit, delay and violence. It's doubtful whether that will work, but people who believe in a just society have real work to do.

So you see, the reason I've written a book on enterprise law is that I believe we have a desperate need to understand our world's central problems, their causes and the options that our laws present to solve them. I believe from experience that many, if not most, of our problems revolve around our economic constitution and the unfulfilment of human rights. I only hope that this book will be valuable to people who are interested in understanding these problems and solutions. This book isn't for people who think that the law is neutral, and that it's possible to avoid real, hard politics. It's for people who understand that we have to be clear about the different points of view, explain openly what we have now, and do everything to find the best evidence of what works to achieve our social goals, even if those goals are themselves contested. This book is for everyone who teaches, studies and practises in company, labour, competition or insolvency law, as well as regulation, public law, administrative law, and law and economics. It starts with UK law and EU law, but it is global, and embedded in universal human rights.

As well as the authors above, many people have helped me in researching this book, and with advice, comments, discussion and debates while I have been writing, and in inspiration over many years. I would especially like to thank, and am deeply grateful to, Liv Jores, Declan Kuch, Danny Fairfax, Rodrigo Aguilera, Sam Jack, Pamela Cawthorne, Gavin Kitching, Joseph Le Jehan, Bronwen Morgan, Matt Dyson, Colm McGrath, David Caron, Satvinder Juss, Charles Mitchell, Vivien Prais, Eva Micheler, David Kershaw, Marc Moore, Paul Davies, Simon Deakin, Brian Cheffins, Peter Muchlinski, Hugh Collins, David Cabrelli, Bill Kovacic, Sandeep Vaheesan, Chris Townley, Alison Jones, Michelle Meagher, Riz Mokal, David Palfreyman, Lucy Crehan,

Emily Jackson, Octavio Ferraz, Eva Lomnicka, Timothy Mitchell, Greg Gordon, Leif Wenar, Tim Ashton, Sarah Hendry, Chris Howard, Carol Harlow, Ian Walden, David Stillwell, Savas Manoussakis, Keith Ewing, Jonathan Portes, Sean Hargreaves-Heap, Steve Daly, Thomas Piketty, Cat Hobbs, Mat Lawrence, Zoe Campbell, Maciej Kardas, Oğuzhan Sarıca, Neha Vasagiri, Leevi Lahtinen, Matthew Hartley and Thomas Raiser. I am also very grateful to the editors at Cambridge University Press, and particularly Caitlin Lisle and Jem Langworthy. Finally, all the students who have undertaken enterprise law so far have been tremendous: we have had constantly fascinating discussions; I am inspired and humbled by the creativity, rigour and breadth of their work; and I am continually amazed by their intelligence and enthusiasm.

London, Lockdown 3.0
February 2021

Postscript

Given enterprise law's dynamism, and the time to publish a book, many things changed since the Afterword. First, despite the cautious optimism of February 2021, Putin launched a full criminal war in Ukraine in February 2022, lost over 25 per cent of the Russian army's combat capability in two months, instructed massacres, mass rape, and countless war crimes. This is another fossil fuelled war (Ch. 19). Europe and Germany (with ex-Chancellor Gerhard Schröder as a Gazprom director) bankrolled Putin with imports for years. Now, the EU and UK have begun to eliminate Russian fossil fuels. As must be clear, the law should stop all fossil fuels. Swapping one dictator's oil or gas for another's will not reduce geopolitical risk, nor stop climate damage, nor deploy the clean, cheap technology already have.[1] Like in the 1970s OPEC crisis, fossil fuels are again driving mass inflation, as gas and oil price hikes cascade through the economy. The UK belatedly announced a windfall tax on excess oil and gas profits, and renationalisation of National Grid functions.[2] There is not yet a credible plan to move from 'blah blah blah', to 100 per cent wind, solar, and battery or hydro-storage, nor a credible monetary and fiscal policy for full clean energy (see Chs. 10–15). There is a plan to 'bet big on nuclear',[3] despite Chernobyl, Fukushima, and renewables or storage being cheaper. On the day of writing, Johnson is going through votes of no-confidence.

Second, Big Tech will see modest change in the EU and UK (Chs. 16-18). There will not yet be simple standards for good conduct on YouTube, Facebook, Instagram, or Twitter, like on TV, or vicarious liability for harm like in a workplace. Instead, under the EU Digital Services Act Regulation, liability for lies, conspiracies, or discrimination against users on platforms is exempt unless the platforms have failed to act with due diligence to stop certain illegal content, complying with transparent terms and algorithms. There may also be new codes of conduct. Fines for large platforms go up to 6 per cent of

1 See E McGaughey, 'How Can We Repower Europe? Ending Fossil Fuels and the Corporate Sustainability Due Diligence Directive' (10 May 2022) Oxford Business Law Blog. See further Green Recovery Act 2020 (CommonWealth) on a model UK law.

2 'Energy Profits Levy Factsheet' (26 May 2022) gov.uk; 'Government future proofs Britain's energy system with launch of new body to boost energy resilience' (6 April 2022) gov.uk

3 Nuclear Energy (Financing) Act 2022 (c 15). Cf. J Thornhill, 'It's time to bet big on fusion energy' *Financial Times* (18 November 2021).

annual turnover.[4] This is a far cry from empowering users. It does not deal with abusive bots or accounts. It does not change concentrated power over dominant platforms (at the time of writing Tesla executive Elon Musk was exploring buying Twitter). It is unclear that this will prevent fascism and extremism online. The Online Safety Bill similarly would require duties of care in content moderation, overseen by Ofcom, with fines up to 10 per cent of annual turnover.[5] The EU Digital Markets Act Regulation requires Big Tech platforms, particularly Google, Meta or Amazon, to not abuse their positions in relation to data, and against traders who conduct business through online marketplaces.[6] Again, this lacks genuine user-empowerment, and the balance was reached under a cloud of lobbying and threats.[7] Meanwhile, instead of improving public media, the UK proposed privatising Channel 4, and abolishing the BBC licence fee.

Third, in the general law of enterprise (Chs. 3-7), the UK Financial Conduct Authority decided to dilute its 'premium' listing rules to allow multiple voting shares in companies doing initial public offerings for five years.[8] This may allow useless executives to entrench themselves without accountability. While this is supposedly to attract innovation, the first beneficiary was Deliveroo, which had the worst IPO in London's history.[9] The EU has proposed new Collective Bargaining and Platform Work Directives, which would require Member States to increase collective agreement coverage, and uphold minimum wages, while also clamp down on companies like Deliveroo or Uber that evade worker rights, tax and social security by pretending their staff are self-employed. In the US, a new head of the Federal Trade Commission, Lina Khan, has signalled a shift to much more aggressive antitrust or competition enforcement, with a welcome focus on the consequences of monopoly for democracy (Chs. 7 and 18). Globally, a minimum corporate tax rate has been proposed, but it is still unclear what will come.

Fourth, within the UK, the Health and Care Act 2022 was passed to create new 'Integrated Care Boards', but fails to clearly ensure proper staff and patient representation, instead having largely self-selecting managers.[10] National Insurance was raised to pay for more social care (Ch. 18). Water companies continued to release shocking levels of sewage into rivers (Ch. 13), and as London and Southeastern Railway was renationalised, the private franchise

[4] EU Digital Services Act Regulation COM(2020) 825 final arts 3-7 (exemptions), 8-9 (illegal content and orders), 12-13 (terms and transparency) 35-36 (codes of conduct) and 59 (fines).

[5] Online Safety Bill, cls 6-9 (duties of care and illegal content), 37-47 (codes of practice) and Sch 12, para 4 (maximum penalties).

[6] EU Digital Markets Act Regulation COM(2020) 842 final.

[7] P. Davies, 'Meta warns it may shut Facebook in Europe but EU leaders say life would be 'very good' without it' *Euronews* (9 February 2022).

[8] FCA Handbook, Listing Rule 9.2.22A ff, but contrast the Companies Act 2006 s 168, which appears to be an effects-based rule.

[9] T. Bradshaw and A. Mooney, 'Disaster strikes as Deliveroo becomes 'worst IPO in London's history'' *Financial Times* (31 March 2021).

[10] Health and Care Act 2022 ss 21-25 and Sch 2.

system is ending. However there is still no coherent proposal for how a new publicly regulated or owned rail would work, particularly to coordinate both passenger and staff interests. ScotRail was brought into public ownership in April 2022, but on the old, top-down Morrisonian model, controlled by ministers (not giving votes to passengers and staff).[11] It seems to be producing similar results. The imperative of electrifying all transport was not yet in view, though a visible number of green rectangles on British vehicle number plates signified more all-electric vehicles (Ch. 15). Enterprise law is bound to undergo dramatic change, and so every year will throw up more issues that are central to politics, economics and law.

[11] This was triggered by the Railways Act 1993 s 30 (government operator of last resort, on not renewing franchise).

Appendix

There are at least ten further chapter topics that could have been included in this book, but in the interests of space they have not been in this edition. There is, however, a strong connection between many of these topics and human rights, and they are very interesting because they involve a wide variety of ownership structures. Simply for this reason they are worth noting:

(21) Sport clubs
(22) Religions
(23) Clothing
(24) Music, art and culture
(25) Public houses, breweries, restaurants and cafés
(26) Waste and recycling
(27) Social insurance
(28) Policing, fire and public safety
(29) Steel, iron and metals
(30) Law and accountancy

And of course, there can be a hundred more enterprises, with greater or more specialised focus that every reader can think of, research and write about. What is the most interesting enterprise to you?

Index

www.ingramcontent.com/pod-product-compliance
Lightning Source LLC
LaVergne TN
LVHW060007210926
848481LV00013B/3664
* 9 7 8 1 0 0 9 0 4 5 7 3 5 *